THE COLLECTED WORKS OF HAROLD CLURMAN

THE COLLECTED WORKS OF HAROLD CLURMAN

Six Decades of Commentary on Theatre, Dance, Music, Film, Arts and Letters

Edited by
MARJORIE LOGGIA and GLENN YOUNG

Introduction by
ROBERT WHITEHEAD

APPLAUSE BOOKS

AN APPLAUSE ORIGINAL

THE COLLECTED WORKS OF HAROLD CLURMAN
Six Decades of Commentary on Theatre, Dance, Music, Film, Arts, Letters and Politics

© COPYRIGHT 1994 Applause Theatre Books

Library of Congress Catalog-in-Publication Data

Clurman, Harold, 1901-
   [Selections]
   The collected works of Harold Clurman : six decades of commentary
on theatre, dance, music, film, arts, letters and politics / edited
by Marjorie Loggia and Glenn Young ; introduction by Robert
Whitehead.
      p.   cm.
   "An Applause original."
   Includes bibliographical references and index.
   ISBN 1-55783-132-7 : $49.95
   1. Performing arts—United States—Reviews.   I. Loggia, Marjorie.
II. Young, Glenn.   III. Title.
IN PROCESS   93-38691
791' .0973'0904—dc20   CIP

British Library Catalog-in-Publication Data

A catalogue record for this book is available from the British Library

APPLAUSE BOOKS
211 W. 71ST STREET
NEW YORK, NY 10023
PHONE: 212-595-4735
FAX: 212-721-2856

406 Vale Road
Tonbridge KENT TN9 1XR
PHONE: 0732 357755
FAX: 0732 770219

BOOK TEAM
EDITORIAL ASSISTANTS: Dana Pierce, Gareth Bannister
PRODUCTION COORDINATOR: Ian Hill
INTERIOR DESIGN: Leo Leung

FIRST APPLAUSE PRINTING: 1994

CONTENTS

THE COMPLETE CRITIC'S QUALIFICATIONS

Besides having cultivated taste, feeling and a talent for clear observation of people.

I. The critic should know the greater part of classic and contemporary drama as written and played. Added to this, he must be conversant with general literature: novels, poetry, essays of wide scope.

II. He should know the history of the theatre from its origins to the present.

III. He should have a long and broad playgoing experience–of native and foreign productions.

IV. He should possess an interest in and a familiarity with the arts: painting, music, architecture and the dance.

V. He should have worked in the theatre in some capacity (apart from criticism).

VI. He should know the history of his country and world history: the social thinking of past and present.

VII. He should have something like a philosophy, an attitude toward life.

VIII. He should write lucidly and, if possible, gracefully.

IX. He should respect his readers by upholding high standards and encourage his readers to cultivate the same.

X. He should be aware of his prejudices and blind spots.

XI. He should err on the side of generosity rather than an opposite zeal.

XII. He should seek to enlighten rather than carp or puff.

The best theatre critic in the English language since 1895 was George Bernard Shaw.

—Encore, Dec. 1964

FOREWORD

On February 2, 1920, Harold Clurman cut his afternoon classes at Columbia to attend the first performance, a matinee at the Morosco Theatre, of Eugene O'Neill's *Beyond The Horizon*. Already at the age of eighteen, when O'Neill himself was only thirty-one, and before the playwright had been recognized for any of his enduring plays, Clurman was *there*, propelled by his maturing faith in a truth that only a conspiracy of artists could create on stage. For the next sixty years, Clurman would conscientiously be there on the scene of our most resonant theatrical occasions.

Clurman was not truant that afternoon to take in a "Broadway show." He had merely chosen to attend another kind of university. For Clurman, all the most potent subjects discussed at Columbia and the forces behind them—history, psychology, philosophy, sociology and politics—converged, commingled and came to passionate life on the stage. Uptown there was a campus; downtown whole galaxies beckoned.

And as Clurman studied, he taught. Through his reviews, essays and manifestoes—over 2,000 of them—Clurman forged a new and vital syllabus for the American theatre. The following are nearly six hundred of Harold Clurman's weekly and monthly writings ranging from pieces in *The Nation* where for thirty years he served as its drama critic to his work first published in *Harper's*, *The New Republic* and *The New York Times*.

Those who heard him speak, may hear in his essays again, the urgent clamor, the fierce and playful vigor of his argument. As Irwin Shaw said, "his wild harangues on acting, politics, drama, sex, theatre, which he delivered wherever he happened to be— backstage, at Sardi's, in hotel rooms on the road, with a play in Boston or Washington, at the Russian Tea Room, on the movie sets in Hollywood—all came out in the same eloquent tumble of words and the same unflagging zest and wisdom."

A word about organization. It is chronological. No doubt the reader's life would have been made easier if we had batched together Clurman's observations on various discrete subjects and poured them into convenient chapters: Clurman on Chekhov, Clurman on Ibsen, Clurman on the Habima, etc. Our joy in reading Clurman's work in the heat of its own chronological moment was so profound that ultimately we could not deprive the reader of the immediacy of that discursive, dialectic pageant. With Clurman at its moving vortex, the chronological scheme offered the most vivid kind of historical scenography to a collection of his ideas. So, if we have not laid out Clurman's work in a neatly embalmed fashion, it is because we believe it possible to present him live, in situ, cigar in hand, embers burning bright.

It became clear that arranged in such a straightforward fashion, Clurman's work may well become one of the major chronicles of theatre in this century. Despite inevitable gaps left by engagements with Hollywood, World War II, the Group Theatre, directing, producing, lecturing, etc., Clurman's writings add up to a powerful history of our culture. The reader will not find many of our theatrical *scènes à faire* missing. With some notable exceptions, essays appear here in the order in which they were published rather than when the production to which it refers opened. Occasionally where the reader might expect to see a review of a significant new play, we have chosen Clurman's review of a revival which will appear later in the volume.

Social and political context was, after all, as vital to Clurman as sets and lights were to Robert Edmond Jones. No Clurman review was ever written in a vacuum. This appreciation of the social situation prompted Carey McWilliams, editor-in-chief of *The Nation,* to invite Clurman to write a new column for the magazine. "It goes without saying," McWilliams wrote "that I have long regarded you as this country's leading drama critic, but I also have the greatest regard for your astuteness as a political commentator. Again and again, I have told audiences out across the country that *The Fervent Years* is the best book yet written about the 1930's—not merely for what it says about the theatre but for what it says about the politics of the period."

Clurman was a critical humanist of wide-ranging

and cosmopolitan appetites. He was perhaps our least parochial critic. His beat was not configured by the grid of Manhattan streets. His most prized possession was the French Legion of Honor. He did not confine himself to theatre of any culture or period; nor did he confine himself to theatre. We have collected his encounters with Balanchine, Picasso, Chaplin, Stieglitz and Copland, from Tel-Aviv to Bucharest to Moscow.

Clurman objected to those who believed only in "genius," the great individual who made everything possible. He believed in the creation of an environment out of which a body of significant work might grow and in which "genius" would find its place and flourish. You will find in these reviews his sympathy with Whitman: "In order for there to be great poets there must first be poets." Clurman would frequently quote Brecht: "Young Alexander conquered India. He alone? Caesar beat the Gauls. Was there not even a cook in his army?" We have not edited too severely around the periphery of "genius." We have enlisted some cooks with the generals.

There are many nearly verbatim reiterations of Clurman's fundamental tenets throughout these thousand and some pages. Their function is similar to a reprise in a longer poetic work—accruing new and deeper significance with each repetition. Clurman was not short of imagination or vocabulary. We take these reiterations as the deliberate articulation of his philosophical litany, the unavoidable core of his integrity as a critic. In his own collections of his work, he ran a blue pencil through some of these seasonal arias. We have not been as modest on his behalf.

There are also repeated recitals of well-known plots by major dramatists such as Chekhov, Shakespeare, Williams, Euripides, etc. We have preserved these summaries for the fresh interpretive glimmers that even an ostensibly matter-of-fact retelling may reveal. Plot is, of course, rarely a matter of fact. It is more often a matter of one's own assumptions based on a critical interpretation of action.

In order to not merely represent his ideas but to reflect their remarkable prolificacy, we have occasionally included a second review of the same production written a week or two after the original. The reader might convincingly argue that one or the other review would have sufficed. For these and other editorial excesses, we ask the reader's forbearance.

We have in the main honored Clurman's selections of his work as they were established in his own collected editions, *Lies Like Truth*, *The Naked Image* and *The Divine Pastime*. Each successive volume contained many of the same essays as the volume before. Lest the reader feel he has all Clurman's collected works by virtue of owning those three volumes, may we advise that those essays comprise only about a quarter of the current volume.

It may not appear that we left very much out. In fact, these pages amount to about a third of his total output for twenty or so newspapers, journals, and magazines. We have not reprinted from his currently unavailable books *Ibsen* or *All People Are Famous* in order not to jeopardize their full re-publication later. And, of course, his available texts, *The Fervent Years* and *On Directing* speak for themselves.

Stella Adler who with Ellen Adler honored us with the commission to undertake this project, once said that to be free you must be either an aristocrat or an eccentric. Clurman was both.

We gratefully acknowledge the permission of all publications in whose pages Clurman's work first appeared.

—Glenn Young & Marjorie Loggia

"There is more of a nation's politics to be got out of poetry
than out of all the writers upon political affairs
and the constitution."
–Woodrow Wilson

INTRODUCTION
BY ROBERT WHITEHEAD

It was the summer of 1938 when I first connected with Harold Clurman. It was, however, not until ten years later when he first connected with me.

That summer I was working at the Barter Theatre in Virginia. I was acting. I was stage managing. I was building scenery and touring various productions. Yet I was haunted by the question of whether I had any talent for any aspect of the theatre—or was this a vagabond escape from responsible activities? That period of '38 was fraught with the increasing tension of Hitler's demand to annex Czechoslovakia—a step which he successfully executed unopposed and was accepted shamefully by Britain, France and even the United States. Being a twenty-one year old Canadian, I assumed that should Britain declare war, I would, of course, be involved. The hope and excitement of a life in the theatre began to seem unproductive, unimportant and selfish.

Then along came Harold Clurman. During that summer I read a piece by Harold whose powerful sentiments reverberate through this extraordinary collection of his work.

This is it—the first law of the theatre! It is a collaboration; it is a collective craft. "Though the play is indeed the thing, the play in the theatre is not only the text or the actor or the director, but the thing created when the spirit that moves the dramatist is given a concrete body by all the people in the theatre together. The spirit or idea of the play arises from the society of which the theatre people are part—from the audience which they aim to serve." The theatre is a very personal thing. As art out of life, our life, whether it is highly comic or tragic, must be a vital conversation with society; (i.e., the audience) and this conversation must make us see and understand ourselves—weep and laugh at ourselves—and the theatre must, through this exchange, enrich us all—and it would, according to Harold, ultimately create a better world. This, he made me realize, must be the reason and the force that compels the theatre and the people who work in it and it will sustain, even in our darkest hours, our excitement, hope and courage. (I say this knowing that Harold once said "There is nothing more despicable than 'official hope.'") This idea, in this simple abbreviated form was the belief and the basis from which Harold wrote, spoke, directed and lived.

His words in the summer of '38 lifted my spirit and gave me an understanding and an impetus that have informed my commitment ever since. Little did I know that in the years to come, Harold and I would do fourteen productions together.

The distinguished designer, Boris Aronson, with whom we worked many times, once said, "If Harold had not been in the theatre, he would have been Father Devine." Boris wasn't wrong. Harold's explosive passion created an important influence in the development of the theatre in New York and on the character and quality of acting in America. He was an extraordinary observer of people and life. He had an endless curiosity and a marvelous sense of the absurd. He possessed a lovely and penetrating understanding of human behavior, from its most degrading to its most courageous. He saw it all as it related to the theatre and to the world around us. To our lives and to our art—finally and totally art...for art as life is what forever obsessed him.

Harold was deeply and immensely sophisticated, but he was, also, a total innocent. He understood on every level the necessity, the problems and the pleasures of money and he sought it with vigorous idealism if it was to create or make possible a theatre or a production. But he never, even faintly, considered his own talents as a commodity through which he could make a lot of money. As a result, he never did make a lot of money. He simply made a living. This limitation, if you call it that, was at the heart of his immense talent.

He loved the sensuous aspects of life and he understood the complexities that went with them. He loved women and he understood the complexities that went with them. He loved one woman, Stella Adler, forever and ever. It was rooted in his teenage years seeing the Adler family during the great days of the Yiddish theatre on Second Avenue. Stella was part of it. She was a goddess. And though they both were involved with other affairs and marriages, and though their relationship tormented and bruised him, there was never a moment through all his years when he did not look upon its confused existence with pride. This love, this passion remained with Harold until the last moment of his life.

The last moments of Harold's life were filled with life. I know. I was there. Shortly before he died Harold made some sly comment about the theatre and the world that made me laugh. Even in his weakness, he reacted with amazingly spontaneous pleasure at the sight and feeling of my enthusiastic response.

I first met Harold in 1948. The miserable war years had come to an end. I had found spasmodic work acting or stage managing. Finally, out of frustration, I created my own work by producing a play, and much to my surprise it was successful. My second production was a dramatization of Dostoyevsky's *Crime and Punishment* (with John Gielgud and Lillian Gish) in which Sanford Meisner played Marmaladov. I talked to Meisner about my interest in doing Giraudoux's play *The Madwoman of Chaillot*, and he immediately arranged a meeting with Harold Clurman who was indeed enthusiastic about directing it. The conversations that ensued from that meeting were the first of many stunning experiences that invaded my life as I listened to and began understanding Harold's extraordinary mind.

However, through some unfortunate agency maneuvering, not unlike the author's intent in *The Madwoman of Chaillot*, I did not ultimately acquire the rights to that play. But more importantly I acquired Harold Clurman as a friend. When we did find a play we were prepared to do together, it was Carson McCuller's *The Member of the Wedding* with Ethel Waters, Julie Harris and seven-year-old Brandon de Wilde. The play was beautifully directed by Harold and became a prize-winning success. It was the first of those many productions we did together.

In the first three or four days of rehearsal, Harold and the company of actors would read the play two or three times. He would begin to discuss the life, the complexities and the purpose of the play and the journey each actor will take as he or she finds the way into the center of the play's world. As his own excitement generates in him more excitement—Harold, at this point, sets a blazing fire. The play's author could never have realized until then what a profound and extraordinary vision he and his play possessed. The actors feel they are embarking on a voyage of danger and magnificence that will bring them into a realm of acting they have never achieved before. I shared in the exhilaration many times in rehearsals with Harold.

Now—it has also been said that after those first incandescent days, rehearsal would subside and never again reach that illuminating fervor. Clifford Odets composed a particularly vehement appraisal of Harold's directing style during the Boston run of Odets' play *Night Music*: "Harold falls into certain doldrums of the senses...his inability to establish discipline for rehearsal and other purposes is shocking. This has one good effect; it relaxes the players so that their most creative feelings and ideas are permitted free play. He has been able to set a whole microcosm spinning, but is unable, after that, to control any of its actions. This flaw or split in Harold's personality seems to me explainable by the quality of his genius or talent, although genius is closer to the proper word. That quality is best explained by the phrase "The Russian temperament" as it was used in the old sense talking of Dostoyevsky characters. They are men of moods, not of action; they are deeply intuitive, 'irrational.' They bathe in their impressions, they stammer...are incoherent...and yet their inner climate is one of intense spirituality and truthfulness."

Though I disagree with much of Odets' view, there is a kind of almost humorous truth *about* it. First, one must remember that when Clifford Odets wrote this, he was 33 years old and Harold was in the process of directing a play of his. There is an obsessive impatience in a playwright. And though a director during the preparation and rehearsal period is his most valued and intimate relationship, he is also, in a way, his natural enemy. The playwright has created a very private and subjective world which has unfortunately to be invaded by the life and subjectivity of another person—the director. This marriage naturally, can generate a conflict and quite often does, particularly if the play is as personal and subjective as Odets' *Night Music*. And even more particularly, when (though it was filled with marvelous qualities) the play was not proving successful.

Harold had a way of grabbing an idea and then improvising on his own words till they built and built into a passion that was dazzling, frenzied and illuminating, and which finally seemed to exhaust him—and though he silently remained on a kind of high for a period of time—he then subsided into a pensiveness in which he very thoughtfully watched the results of the imagery he had set in motion. He was forming within himself an intention and design that could take the next step toward his ultimate vision.

His philosophic sense, comic and poetic, was greater than his visual sense; therefore, his staging and movement of a scene was not always as effective as his understanding of its content. Harold's belief in his own greatness was not in any way impeded by self-doubt. If you told him the physical composition of a scene was a mess, he accepted it

and discussed it openly and freely without any emotional insecurity. This was not only an enormous time saver, but was an unconscious and very big part of his brilliance and character as director—and as a person. The combination of it all—his civilizing force, his dynamic approach—had a profound effect on theatre in America and to certain extent in England. It is all powerfully present and evident in this remarkable book.

Throughout this century there have been many books, many essays and many interpretations, demonstrations, explanations, elucidations on the theatre and on the process of acting, directing, and production—and its application in creating a timely, modern expression of both classical and contemporary works. And, as this age of massive communication has become more and more intense so have the complexities, and the arguments involved at arriving at any one school of opinion. Harold Clurman's ideas and vision began forming in the Twenties became vigorously active in the Thirties and flowered in the Forties and Fifties—and on and on....Those ideas and visions have now found their way through the chaos to the center of the working theatre today. Whenever I encounter a strong, clear simple emotional line—and a kind of organic truth in the theatre (which is, and always was, very seldom) I think of our debt to Harold. This is Harold's message...this is his legacy.

ABBREVIATIONS

ATH	American Theatre
CTJ	N.Y. State Community Theatre Journal
DIM	Dimensions
DRA	The Drama
DW	The Daily Worker
ESQ	Esquire
FG	The Flying Grouse (Journal of Group Theatre)
FREE	The Freeman
GRIF	The Griffin
HARP	Harper's Magazine
JFK	JFK Center Program Notes
LAT	The Los Angeles Times
LO	London Observer
MUS	Music Man
NAT	The Nation
NEW	New Theatre Magazine
NR	The New Republic
NY	New York Magazine
NYT	The New York Times
NYTM	The New York Times Magazine
PDG	Philadelphia Drama Guild Program Notes
S.TRIB	The Sunday Tribune
SR	The Saturday Review of Literature
STGB	Stagebill
TA	Theatre Arts
TDR	Tulane Drama Review
TRW	Tomorrow
UNW	UN World
VAR	Variety
WEST	Westchester Magazine
WJT	World Journal Tribune
WOR	World Theatre (Paris)

THE
THIRTIES

CRITIQUE OF THE AMERICAN THEATRE

"What's wrong with the theatre?" is in our country a question of presumably perennial interest. Newspapers will print and benevolent souls will attend almost any kind of answer if it issues from a sufficiently imposing source. It seems never to have struck the participants of these discussions that nothing can be wrong with the theatre where no Theatre exists. And America has as yet no Theatre.

Such a statement may bewilder even those who regard themselves as the theatre's severest critics. For the outcry against our theatre is more often than not directed against the dearth of distinguished talent, the mercenary nature of the producers or the nefarious influence of the movie magnates. "We ought to have better playwrights; actors should be above personal vanity; managers should think less about making money and more about art; the price of tickets should be lower." No doubt! But the fact our devout sympathizers are apparently utterly unaware of is that if we were providentially blessed with a host of admirable plays and players, and an epidemic of virtue broke out over the entire theatre-world, we should still hardly have effected the establishment of any sort of Theatre. All the little strictures and animadversions of our friends constitute merely a welter of sentimental notions because they derive from no actual understanding, no basic conception of what the theatre really is.

Whatever justification there may be for our native distrust of "abstract ideas" or "theory," it must be evident that no clarity of judgment or soundness of craft can obtain in an art where all general principles, all sense of historical perspective, all background of thought have never even been considered the necessary foundation for a technique of criticism or creation. Some such definition of first principles, therefore, some elementary insight into the nature of the theatre, must be arrived at, not to remedy "what's wrong with the theatre," but simply to create the conditions outside of which no Theatre can possibly develop.

The first thing to recognize in considering the theatre, is that which gives it its special character among the arts, is the presence of the actor. The theatre begins with the actor and achieves expression through him; that is, he is its first and essential element. But he is not by himself the theatre, for the content of the theatrical performance generally arises from a group experience, which requires for its expression the group's united efforts. To achieve organic expression, therefore, it is absolutely necessary that all parts of the group be related to the central experience.

Imagine, to take a primitive instance, a group of savages in celebration. Their festivities include the representation of some major circumstance in their lives, such as the hunt. Only those who share the experience can become part of the play. They may share it in two ways: either they have actual knowledge of the hunt or they know it imaginatively—they have been made to feel all the emotions that hunting arouses. This group experience is the generating element of the play. But to transform this experience into art, a leader must emerge from amongst the actors.

This leader is what, nowadays, we would call the director and playwright in one. He is a sort of high priest of the play. He takes the material of the common experience and creates from it the scheme of a performance. If speech is inevitable to the dramatic content of the performance, words will come to the actors as spontaneously as do their gestures, though the leader, in designing the form of the performance, may give them words as he gives them actions to carry out. Or, there may be another actor in the group with a gift for speech who will suggest the words to be used. What constitutes the play, finally, is not that which may be written down as a text—these are only the words of the play—but the sum of the activities of the group under the leadership of one of its actors.

In this brief analysis, we have omitted what is perhaps the theatre's primary element. For the group of actors must of necessity spring from a larger group—the tribe. By the process of specialization that produced a leader from amongst the actors, the tribe develops a body of performing actors and another of passive actors or spectators. And the spectators are actors because they share in the experience of the others. They share the experience not only because they themselves may have known the joy and the terror of the hunt but because they are anxious for those who do participate in it, or because they know that its result may affect their own lives, or simply because they love the movement and struggle visioned in the performance. Should the same play be presented before the spectators of another tribe where conditions are so different that it could no longer be appreciated, you would no longer have the elements for a complete Theatre. In short, there can be a Theatre only where there is a community of desire, interest and understanding on all sides.

With the development of the theatre, the process of specialization continued beyond the breaking point. The play-leader first ceased to be an actor—although this does not prevent him from being one in spirit; the creator of the play-form and the writer of the play's words isolated their functions. And we have the stage director and the modern playwright. This was not necessarily a catastrophe as long as the latter remained a member of the theatre-unit. But the playwright began to dote on his words. He withdrew from the theatre; he became an independent literary artist. He no longer believed that his words were written for the theatre—it was the theatre which was made for his words. Literature, which had come into the theatre as an element of the play, began to dominate it. The theatre suffered from this, but it did not die. Only its energy is scattered; and complete chaos set in. The "serious public" was won over to the literary conception of the theatre, while the simpler, unlettered public remained faithful to a more complete theatre, which because of its audience, was devoted exclusively to the "lighter" aspects of life.

With this in mind, we are in a better position to judge our own theatre. If we examine the ordinary routine of American play production we immediately recognize a concrete example of the modern theatre's disintegration. A producer buys a play, that is, a script, a libretto with more or less valuable suggestions for theatre use. After the play is bought, the producer begins to think of a director, actors and a scene-designer. He collects these anywhere and everywhere—a director from Moscow, actors from the Middle-west, London and Times Square, a scene-designer from Vienna or Hoboken. When all these separate universes are collected and temporarily tricked into a sham harmony, they are placed before the public. The production is then hawked around like any other merchandise. This marketing of theatrical wares is rightly called show-business.

It may be objected that by generalizing in this fashion, account is taken only of the commercial stage which does not, after all, represent the worthiest and most encouraging aspect of our theatre. Approximately fifteen years ago there began in this country what might be termed a theatre reformation, a new movement that was then hailed, and to this day is considered something in the nature of a renaissance. But it is precisely this theatre of the new movement, with its sincerity and enthusiasm, that most strikingly reveals the defective structure of the American theatre in general.

Let us see what the new movement accomplished. It made a systematic attempt to produce good plays. That was its first noteworthy contribution. Its second was the recruiting of a public for such plays. Its third was the adoption of the permanent company idea. The movement introduced intelligence to the American theatre. It made taste a paying proposition. But the only fundamental difference between the new theatre and the old is that the former sells better stuff.

These are considerable gains, but hardly any of them go to the root of the matter. These theatres tried to institute effects before they created causes. A Theatre, we have seen, arises with a group of actors sharing a common experience and a common aim. These theatres always will begin with a play, and never with a group of actors that may be appropriately considered part of it. They will take a company of actors, usually trained in the petty realism of the average commercial play, and ask them to do French poetic-rhetorical drama, a modern German tragedy in the classic manner, or something equally foreign to them. Or, to take another instance, a few years ago a group of playwrights with radical economic ideas set out to establish a sort of workers' theatre. They hired young actors, whose chief ambition it was to become sufficiently well known to be engaged by Broadway (capitalistic!) managers, and set about producing their plays. There was no careful selection of the people who were to work with them, no preliminary attempt to weld them into a unified body. If these playwrights had understood the theatre, they would have known that the result of each production could not have been one play, but almost as many different plays as there were actors in the cast—many tunes and no music. And the engagement of permanent companies will not solve the problem. For unless there is unity of outlook in a company, this system only fosters permanent misunderstanding.

If this view shocks the habits of thought of the reader educated to the literary tradition of the theatre, to whom plays, in the old sense, are the beginning and the end of the art, let him reflect for a moment on the case of the Moscow Art Theatre universally accepted as the classic theatre of the twentieth century. It achieved its greatest success in the plays of Chekhov, but it did not originate with Chekhov. If it had merely produced Chekhov, as tomorrow the Shuberts may produce Shakespeare, it would hardly be any more important as a Theatre than had it produced the works of inferior authors. The group of actors of the Moscow Art Theatre had for a long time been trained under their two directors and were chosen by them not only for their ability, but because they all had a like feeling for their art and formed a more or less homogeneous unit. They were

prepared to express in terms of the theatre that experience of Russian life that had inspired Chekhov to write his plays. Had a lesser author brought them the same kind of material, it would still have been a great Theatre. Had it begun simply as a collection of talented actors and set about to do all the fine plays of the world, it would not only not have been a great Theatre but, in our sense, it would not have been a Theatre at all.

When sensitive or proud defenders of the American stage take it upon themselves to maintain our superiority or, at least, high excellence in this respect, they will name a series of outstanding artists or fine productions to prove their point. But this again betrays a misapprehension which must be repeatedly exposed. A production is a single piece of theatre-art: a Theatre is a cultural unit. The Theatre is not a picture-gallery in which each work of art preserves its value independent of the others or with little relation to the exhibition agent. The Theatre is a collaboration of artists to express a single vision. Unless that vision is common to all, there will be no complete expression. In such a collaboration the lone artists must wither from inanition. For the laws of the theatre are the laws of all art, and a theatre-work, though collective, must be judged as if it were the work of a single artist. We have, on the American stage, all the separate elements for a Theatre, but no Theatre. We have playwrights without their theatre-groups, directors without their actors, actors without plays or directors, scene-designers without anything. Our theatre is an anarchy of individual talents.

What our theatres lack is some integrating Idea. In the theatres of the day-before-yesterday (not to go back to the Greeks), in the theatre of Molière, of Shakespeare, of the Italian comedians, the Theatre as a cultural unit was almost an automatic fact. From the beginning, actors and playwrights were one with each other and with their public, and they could express all their experience of past and present in a common language. To have unity they did not need to come to the theatre with an idea; they were, so to speak, born with it.

But today, with our inheritance of many cultures, with the estrangement of all our artists, we need a conscious approach. The idea of a Theatre must act as its starting point, and form the basis of its unity.

For this we need leaders, men who are at once students, workers and craftsmen, men of ability and passion. They will not succeed if they attempt to force their Idea on unyielding material. They must gather together people predisposed to accept it: they must communicate its spirit to the humblest member of their group. The artistic will of one must become the artistic will of all. We shall not have a Theatre until this is realized.

—DRA, Apr. '31

THE GROUP THEATRE EXPLAINS

A news item can hardly be expected to convey the truth of any situation. When the closing of the Group Theatre was announced last week no light was shed on the reasons for this sudden decision. It must have been assumed that, discouraged by the failure of its latest production, it had decided to abandon its venture. This is quite false.

The actors and directors of the Group Theatre have never produced a play in anticipation of a "wow." The need for such anticipation is one of the good reasons why the establishment of any permanent theatrical organization with a coherent policy is rendered particularly difficult in our New York theatre.

When it is remembered that one of the finest plays of the English-speaking stage in recent years, Denis Johnston's *Moon in the Yellow River*, could achieve a six-week run only because of the Theatre Guild's subscription list, and was greeted by a singularly divided press, the basic fallacy of our theatrical system becomes evident.

But despite the realization that many of the Group Theatre plays were not destined to be box-office successes, its members were glad to undertake the production of plays which they believed pointed to a desirable goal in the theatre. The

actors had faced the inevitable difficulties in order to make possible the production of such plays as these and were prepared to face them again. Why, then, did the Group Theatre decide to close for the season?

This Theatre began its career during a period of severe economic depression, and, therefore, had to go about its work without the benefit of subsidy or patronage of any kind. This meant that it had to present its plays on practically the same basis as any other producer. But what the Group Theatre aimed to do was something fundamentally different from Broadway, and its position as a competing producing organization was entirely irrelevant and was even injurious to its aims.

Like every other producer, the Group Theatre has had to find individual backing for each of its plays; it has had to depend on the immediate reaction of the first-night audience and the reviewers' notices; it has had to compete with other managements in securing desirable scripts. None of these things are in themselves entirely reprehensible activities.

But when you choose your scripts, not as economic bait but for the pertinence of what they have to say; when you know beforehand that some of the scripts chosen are by no means perfect, the attempt of authors to say something that has not been said very frequently before; when you do not cast strictly according to the "type" system, which not only managers but many playwrights and even reviewers insist upon; when you have undertaken to sustain a permanent acting company which does not limit itself to the customary four-week rehearsal period; when, finally, the number of so-called good plays is alarmingly small in any event, persistence in pursuing the ordinary course of theatrical production becomes folly.

In other words, the Group Theatre might continue this season as it has for the past two years. But it refuses to strain itself along lines that do not advance or clarify its aims, but that, on the contrary, impede and falsify them.

The Group Theatre feels enthusiastic about what it has been able to accomplish under these conditions. But now that it has taken the first step and made known some of its aims in a concrete way, now particularly when money is scarce and available good scripts even scarcer, it has decided not to resume production unless it can create conditions for itself that will permit it to carry on freely to do what it really wants to do, and which its first two years of activity give only the first bare indications. The Group Theatre continues with the training of its actors, its quest of suitable plays, and is even now considering plans for a method of organization which will afford the most adequate conditions for the fulfillment of its purpose.

—NYT, 29 Jan. '33

WHEREIN JOY AND SADNESS PROVE SIMPLY EACH OTHER'S CONTRASTS

It is difficult to know about a play. When Clifford Odets brought the script of *Awake and Sing!* to me for a reading, my impression was of a bitter, almost suffocating realism, relieved only by passages of a sultry, sidewalk poetry. That was also the impression of my colleagues and friends.

I decided to show at least part of the play to an audience. During the summer the Group Theatre passed in the Adirondacks, the second act was presented on two occasions to some three or four hundred persons. To our surprise and delight, the audiences chuckled, guffawed and even roared nearly all the way through. This savage "slice-of-life" was a laugh show!

But as a comedy pure and simple there was something a bit unreal and shoddy about it. The presentation at camp, necessarily hasty, while sufficient to reveal the humorous aspects of the lines, robbed the play of much of its character.

When the play, after some drastic revisions, was about to be put into rehearsal for its present Group production, the director was advised by one person that the play was a tragedy and should be produced in that spirit, and by another he was assured that the play was essentially a comedy and ought to be staged for laughs.

Both statements seemed to be equally justified. For was the play not concerned with the heartaches, frustrations, struggles, even crimes which are the common experience of thousands of poor families? Yet this material, grave enough at its core, was presented in a language full of racy quips and phrases turned to surprise audiences into laughter.

The critical reception accorded the play showed the elements of the original paradox. Almost all the reviewers gave the play due credit for its sincerity, authenticity and underlying seriousness. But comparatively little emphasis was placed on the fact that the audience devoted much of the time to laughing.

The name of Chekhov has been brought up in connection with *Awake and Sing!* The reference is flattering of course, but perhaps a little misleading. For, while the American playwright does not especially cultivate his plot line, any more than the Russian, the whole quality of the former is active, impulsive and rather lusty, as compared to the thoughtful, delicately tempered and objective art of the man who wrote *The Cherry Orchard*.

If comparisons are at all helpful in defining the nature of a playwright's talent, perhaps the name of Sean O'Casey may fit better in this connection. Not only do we find in *Awake and Sing!* some of that special tenement tenderness that lends warmth to all the cold facts of O'Casey's Dublin dramas, but there is also a certain quality of improvisatory spontaneousness, a tendency to give to all the occurrences that are part of the character's lives the same importance and sympathy, whether they be intense suffering or workaday routine.

If we are disconcerted at first by such treatment, if it strikes us as too desultory or devil-may-care for good play-making, it is not only because we are used to more rigid patterns but because these playwrights are saying something through their plays that demands their special technique.

The lives of O'Casey's characters, like those in *Awake and Sing!,* move on a level where it is almost impossible to differentiate between "high" and "low," "important" and "trivial," "essential" and "incidental." Thus in *Juno and the Paycock* as much time is given to Boyle's "musicales" as to the more vital aspects of his life or to the many woes that surround him. (And, indeed, are not Boyle's "inconsequential" activities part of the tragedy that is his life?)

So, in *Awake and Sing!,* when the hapless son-in-law, whose wife has just told him that he is not the father of her child, says "Look, I'm so nervous! Twice I weighed myself on the subway," we have the same juxtaposition of the painful and the commonplace that calls forth deep laughter.

Poverty, or at least life-long economic pressure among city persons who still manage to get along "respectably," produces a certain lack of order, a confusion of physical details with spiritual crises which to the outside observer must appear just as laughable as it is saddening. Thus it is right in *Awake and Sing!* for Moe Axelrod to eat cake when he is told that he is losing the girl he loves, or to be angry because there are no oranges in the house while his heart is breaking.

The play is not "depressing," though some of its incidents are harshly "true to life"; nor is it farcical, though some of its lines cause as much hilarity as vaudeville "gags." The play is about real people struggling humbly with their everyday problems; it is tragic in the sense that we are led to see that these problems are almost life-or-death matters; it is comic in the sense that the manner in which these problems present themselves for the characters in the play (and for most of us in the audience) is so amazingly casual and haphazard in relation to their fundamental significance.

In the production we tried neither to achieve "depth" nor to "get laughs," but to show simple people living in a lower middle-class environment. That was the best way, we believed, to achieve both.

—*S.TRIB*, 10 Mar. '35

THE SOVIET DIARY
EDITED AND INTRODUCED BY JOAN UNGARO

*The Group Theatre was in its fifth year when it finally encountered box-office success in 1935 with three Clifford Odets plays—*Awake and Sing!,* *Waiting for Lefty *and* Till the Day I Die.* The windfall gave two of the Group's three directors enough time and money to travel to the U.S.S.R. for a look at Soviet Theatre. On April 26, 1935, Harold Clurman and Cheryl Crawford embarked on a five-week visit. (The year before, Sidney Kingsley's* Men in White *had helped fund a tantalizing two-week Soviet trip for Clurman, Lee Strasberg and Stella Adler.) In 35 days Clurman and Crawford saw 35 plays; as Clurman later noted, that amounted to not half of what was available. It would have taken six months to see everything! Neither American spoke Russian, which was of course the primary language employed on the Soviet stage, even for the numerous Shakespeare productions which enjoyed popularity at the time. French sufficed for their conversations with the leading figures of the Russian theatre: Stanislavsky and Meyerhold, Nemirovich-Dantchenko and Sergei Eisenstein, among others.*

The two Group directors were not the only visiting artists in Moscow at the time. Other outsiders were Bertolt Brecht, Gordon Craig, Edmund Wilson, Jay Leyda and Paul Strand (both long-standing Group friends) and Joseph Losey (as a reporter for the Moscow Daily News*). Clurman saw them all. During the trip he took notes in a leather-bound book given to him by his colleagues at the Group. He called the notes* Soviet Diary 1935. *What happened to the actual hand-written journal I do not know; someone typed it for him at some point, and he gave me a photocopy in the mid-70s. What follows in an excerpted version. He did not think of it as a book, so we have retained his shortened, diary-style phrasings.*

On his return, Clurman read these notes at two sessions with the Group; Crawford described outstanding productions in detail at a third. Group members—actors, playwrights and directors— were invited, as were friends of the Group and other artists.
—J. U., Nov. 1987

Moscow, April 29

In the evening went to see *King Lear* at the Jewish Kamerny Theatre. Hopes were high. First act seemed interesting and charming (almost piquant) due to a certain clarity in the business. The fluency of the play, the originality of the set: it was a miniature that had a kind of sharpness about it. A little grotesque like certain engravings I have seen that were "fantastic"—bizarre—yet clear. The second act began to lose its quality. I hesitate to condemn the whole thing, as these Russian productions have a way of growing on one. The American habit of judging a production as soon as one has seen it does not fit here. Yet, despite Gordon Craig's statement that this was the first production that made Lear clear to him, this was a strange interpretation that portrays Lear as a madman from the very beginning. (Mikhoels plays Lear without a beard; a small, skinny old man with an impish quality that changes at times to a crazy roaring that reminds me of a caricature I have seen somewhere of an old-time actor gone cuckoo.) I think, on further reflection, that what I liked best in this production was its wildness. Considering the sanguinary extravagance of most of Shakespeare's plays, nearly every American production I have ever seen has been as fitting as a Maxfield Parrish painting would be to illustrate the Book of Job.

April 30

At night saw *The Forest* at the Meyerhold Theatre. It began raggedly (the company was sort of a second company) and my hopes began to waver. But soon I found myself admiring it very much, and then knowing for a certainty that Meyerhold is a genius. Only two or three of the

performances were adequate. Yet the shape of the production—its form, its idea—are such that the *creation* that it is comes out clearly nonetheless. I have seen shows that I have enjoyed more (the raggedness and lack of distinction in many roles made complete enjoyment impossible), but very few that have impressed me more for sheer originality, inventiveness and a new kind of theatricality.

Meyerhold, I have discovered, is a kind of romantic (despite a certain coldness in his temperament), a romantic very much in love with the glamorous theatre, often even with the things that were colorful in the decayed societies of the past. But there is nothing decayed in this production: it is fresh and sound all through. What I learned might be summarized in one phrase: "Do anything you want in the theatre." This is a very dangerous maxim unless one also realizes that to do anything one wants in the theatre, study and work are necessary in order for you to do it so that other people want what you do.

After the show, Moscow, on the eve of May Day, was a blaze of glory. The whole town was aglow in red. Banners all over, slogans, portraits, electric lights proclaimed the holidays. When I look around and see how Moscow has grown in one year, and at the people who are building it with love and enthusiasm—rough people—it all seems like a miracle come true. It revives one's belief in man: in his ability to dream, to suffer, to fight, to sustain misfortune and still through great strength (which is fundamentally the *desire to live* and a love of life), to build and create.

May 2

In the afternoon, [the critic, editor and translator] Jay Leyda and I went to an exhibition of scenic design covering the past 17 years in the Soviet theatre. It was the most interesting exhibition of this sort I had ever seen. I do not speak of the quality of the design—though of course many of the models were amongst the best work in this field in the modern theatre—but of the variety, the individuality, the daring and, above all, the freedom. It is difficult to give any idea of how far a Soviet scene-designer can go when he wants to "experiment." He demands what would be technically and economically impossible in America. The stage-pictures of the Soviet theatre are therefore nearly always entertaining.

Of course this liberty has certain disadvantages. The settings can become a matter of display merely—and this may extend beyond the setting to the direction and even to the acting. A merely formalistic element enters into the theatre—the temptation simply to play with the medium—with a resulting emptiness. Even the subtlest effects in art—those wrought with the greatest technical and intellectual competence—can become dead and useless things if they have no roots in a sincere, humanly necessary desire to express a real experience. Naturally for us in America with our monotonous and technically inelastic theatre, the Soviet theatre is very stimulating and highly instructive, but our whole problem is to learn how to use the formal achievements of the Soviet theatre together with our own organic message (in which regard we have little to learn and much to give) in relation to our American audience.

Theatre-for-theatre's sake (and despite the revolutionary themes of the plays, I detect a good deal of this in the productions) is almost as bad as theatre-for-money's sake. And in no theatre—I can say this confidently now that I have really looked around—in no theatre today has the theoretical and practical basis been so established for this linking of theatre and life as in the Group. In other theatres, a clearer political line has been laid down, but this is rarely organic: It simply means that a director or board of directors has announced a political program affecting plays and the organization of audiences. It does not mean that the theatre expresses through its work—which includes the development of its directors, actors and audience—the very process of attaining political clarity the moving toward greater understanding of social issues through the medium of the theatre as an artform.

In the late afternoon Cheryl and I, accompanied by Jay Leyda, went to see Eisenstein. He lives in one room—this world-famous artist—surrounded by books of every description in an apartment that includes many other one-room apartments. If he were an American movie director, would he have a yacht, a mansion, a Hispano-Suiza and a well-publicized affair with a continental actress?

At night we went to see an act-and-a-half of a play called *The Prelude or Introduction* at the Meyerhold Theatre. We were told that only one act of this play was worth seeing, being the least successful of Meyerhold's productions, although by now I feel that one should see all of Meyerhold's work because technically he has most to teach in the theatre. The act we saw was not particularly distinguished.

This play, like *The Final Conflict*, seemed very bad. In fact, it was probably no play at all. But this may be partly due to Meyerhold's treatment of his scripts, which consists, it appears, of taking episodes and scenes from a play and presenting them as theatrical bits when he as a director can make them interesting and vivid. Thus, from a literary standpoint, and perhaps from a general artistic standpoint, havoc is wrought with character development or story development as we generally understand it. (I cannot be absolutely sure of this without knowing the lines.) I am afraid this might lead to a strengthening of theatrical craft but to a weakening of the playwright's technique as an artist. Certainly if any of us tried to do to our plays what Meyerhold and some of the other Soviet directors do to theirs, the playwrights would sue us and proclaim to the world that we were the enemies of art.

May 4

At 3 o'clock we have an appointment with Madame Toumansova, Stanislavsky's secretary. We find out first that Stanislavsky is in Moscow and that he works very hard. He is 72 and he is busy for seven or eight hours a day. He is directing Bulgakov's *Molière* as well as the opera studio and a school, and is finishing his book. He directs at home. The government, we are also informed, offered him a new, more spacious apartment where he would have greater facility for his rehearsals but he prefers to stay where he is. Another bit of information: when we remarked that the Moscow Art seemed the busiest theatre in Moscow, Madame Toumansova said, "Yes, we have 1,086 people employed in our theatre and 240 of them are actors. I suppose this is the largest dramatic company in the world." "What would the Group be like," Cheryl muses to me, "if it had 240 actors?"

Madame Toumansova arranged for all our tickets for the Moscow Art performances. So in the evening we see *Night Lodging* [Gorky's *The Lower Depths*] with Moskvin and Katchalov in their original parts. Moskvin is so relaxed, so simple, so real that he does not seem to be playing at all. But he is acting and his acting is an object lesson in concentration, listening, talking and true emotion borne without effort from these premises.

Here is an important difference between the Moscow Art Theatre today and the Meyerhold—at the Moscow Art it is the little things that are still good; at the Meyerhold the big things are good. In all such minor details as the actors really taking a new character in as he enters, really listening, watching, being at home in the environment of the play, the Moscow Art is still unmatched. Yet the whole performance (of this play at least) is very weak as a creation. Thus, we learn that a good technique, a repertory system, good actors and a very good play, all of them are not sufficient to make good theatre. What is needed in addition—and what is needed fundamentally—is a true production idea, a theatre idea, animated by the personal participation and effort of all the actors in the cast in bringing this idea to life within the scope of their part.

May 5

Last night's performance made my purpose in coming to the Soviet Union clearer than ever before. I have come to realize all the possibilities of the theatre—since all of them find an expression here. There are formal theatres, aesthetic theatres, naturalistic theatres, experimental theatres, fantas-

tic realistic theatres, revolutionary theatres and every sort of theatre—right and left. Out of all this I want to see what can be done with each of these methods so that we in the Group may learn to apply them if we wish to. The problem resolves itself to one of artistic choice, which is based, of course, on the exact content one wishes to express and the effect one wishes to make on the audience. This, in turn, depends on the sense of one's own role in the theatre and what one aspires to be and the function of our own theatre from a general point of view. Certainly, one should be capable at least of doing anything.

May 6

At night we saw the Moscow Art production of Gogol's *Dead Souls*, one of its more recent productions. There were excellent scenes in this and two or three superb characterizations in small parts. Nearly all of it had the usual Moscow Art maturity of acting which is very satisfying—almost like a lesson. Yet I did not feel that it was important: I shall not think of it as much as I have about some of Meyerhold's poor productions. One sees these Moscow Art productions as one picks up a well-bound classic sometimes: one reads a little, one says "this is first-class stuff" and stifles a yawn. There was no *drive* in this production, no creative fire. One did not feel as if all the actors were saying or the director had thought, "With this production I want to achieve something and say something that it is impossible to say in just this production alone, that it may take all our lives to say and to achieve." One does not sense some other world outside the frame of the production to which the actors belong and which they are making every effort to express.

One organizational element that interested me in the production of *Dead Souls*, however, was the fact that a good many important actors were playing bits in the large cast.

May 9

I saw the last two acts of *Carmen*—a new production and Stanislavsky's latest work. This interested me for two reasons. First, it proved once again that producing an opera as a real play is not only possible but actually desirable. Second, the staging of this opera with its action and speech necessarily slower than in a play gave me a good picture of Stanislavsky's new emphasis in his direction of acting. The acting in this opera—despite its passionate melodramatic story and the "big emotions" it requires—was as easy as A-B-C. This is instructive. For while Stanislavsky finds physical equivalents that are natural and sensible, which makes the acting a little too workaday; *the principle of the physical equivalent for each action carried out continuously and completely will give you a certain element of that external theatricality (without the loss of truth) which we in the Group are seeking.* What limits Stanislavsky, of course, is his realistic bias on the one hand, and a certain lack of truly general ideas on the other. (When more closely analyzed, these two faults will be seen to be almost inseparable and also to explain why in the realm of the deeper meaning of the conception implied in the term ensemble the Moscow Art Theatre is really not very strong.)

May 10

Got up early to meet [the photographer] Paul Strand. Saw him to the hotel and then had to rush off to a *biomechanics* class at the Meyerhold Theatre. I had seen funny pictures and had heard abstruse explanations of the theory of biomechanics, neither of which had interested me particularly. But this class, for which the teacher apologized continually, interested me greatly. To put it bluntly, this was the best body work for the actor I had ever seen. After seeing this (though other Soviet theatres do not use biomechanics exactly, they do use related systems of body training) I could understand why Russian actors are so fluent and graceful on the stage compared to our own Group actors, who as individuals have just as strong and muscular bodies.

The difference is in the *kind* of body training the Russians get. The biomechanics exercises are not only excellent in the purely physical elements

for training the muscles through tension and relaxation, movement and the stopping of movement, but remarkable for the dramatic elements (without any artiness), for each of these exercises is a kind of play, with two characters generally in conflict—so that the movement is always related to a partner and demands a constant adjustment of person to person—most often of a man to a woman. One can see at once that these exercises have been devised by a person with a profound sense of theatre. They demand agility and poise, feeling and physical freedom: they are actually a pleasure to see and they must be even a greater pleasure to perform.

Some of the things the students are able to do are extraordinary: a man jumps on another's chest while his partner stands erect; the first man slides off him, slowly, his feet never touching the ground till he gets down on the floor. Besides biomechanics—done three times a week—the Meyerhold actors also do acrobatics. Acrobatics, of course, are recommended by Stanislavsky as training for the actor.

At night I was supposed to see *Pickwick Club* at the Moscow Art but went instead to see Strand show his photographs to Eisenstein. Eisenstein was really impressed...I felt that this was a little victory for American art.

May 12

I went to see a matinee of *Cherry Orchard* rather reluctantly. I was beginning to be bored by the Moscow Art routine. But I was very glad later that I had gone—this was the best production of all those we saw at this theatre. In *The Cherry Orchard* the reality is personal, immediate, everyday, normal and, as Lee [Strasberg] once put it, "like bread." The main point is that in this production the realism is carried to perfection. This is the cream of the bourgeois art. It is not exalted or very intense but it has no vulgarity. It is decent, homely, tender and satisfying. The end of the play was the only time thus far in Moscow that tears came to my eyes at the end of a theatrical performance.

May 15

Got up early to visit a cigarette factory. It was not especially exciting although I find myself always fascinated when I go to a place where things are in the making. Work in the Group has had a subtle influence on me in this respect: Nowadays I am fascinated in the development of an object from the state of a plan to its conversion into materials that soon begins to function for an audience in an aesthetic way. Middle-class people and especially middle-class intellectuals have been spiritually impoverished by taking all the objects they use for granted. They have no sense of the rough material, the human labor, the energy and fatigue that go into the making of anything they use. Gorky has put this thought admirably: "The social and cultural development of people proceeds normally only when the hands teach the head and, having become wiser, the head in turn teaches the hands."

At night went to see *Love and Intrigue* by Schiller at the Vakhtangov Theatre. The chief charm of this production is visual—but it is not a matter of just pretty sets. These were by Akimov and they were amongst the most original, the most imaginative, the most beautiful I have ever seen. Yet despite great daring—they resembled nothing I knew from any stage—they were really quite simple. Certainly there was perfect coordination of the visual with the other elements. The actors had the proper "removal" for a romantic play, their background was rich and bright (the tinfoil took the light so that every scene had a different quality) and yet the eye was never distracted. The general characteristic of these settings was their freedom. The final moment, in idea, placement, lighting, etc., was a masterpiece—a *theatrical* creation.

I have always maintained, generally speaking, a play in the theatre was only what we see and hear on the stage and that therefore the essential artistic creation, while composed of the interrelation of all the elements, would sometimes rest predominantly on one of them. But I had never been able to think of an example of a set which made the art of a play (most sets are merely accessories, even when they

are good). Akimov's *Love and Intrigue* is such a set—though of course even this set could not function without the actors and other elements of the play. (In fact, without them the sets would not be comprehensible at all, since they don't look like anything.) Designers should be sent to the Soviet Union to see it. Also painters.

A curious thing at this performance was my increasing absorption with the *play* while the *plot* became increasingly unintelligible. But I had no desire to inform myself about it: I was enjoying it fully, simply by looking....Schiller's play was unimportant, some of the acting was mediocre and some of the casting as far as type was quite wrong and yet the *play I saw* (the play we *see*, I repeat, is the *only play* in the theatre) was magnificent.

There is a lesson—or rather symbolic value—in this. The lesson for designers, of course, is obvious. The lesson for theatre critics and theatricians is equally clear. The symbol for theatre people generally is this: A production of a play, if sufficiently thought out and creatively imagined, may become a true work of art—completely organic, completely integrated, and absolutely right from moment to moment (despite the literary limitations of the script and even the limitations of the actors) to the extent of seeming as *pure* an expression as a good piece of music or a fine bit of architecture.

I must confess that, allowing for the flaws noted, this evening at the Vakhtangov was the nearest thing to what might be described as an "art for art's sake" experience I have had in the Soviet theatre.

May 16

Went to see *Yegor Bulichev* again at the Vakhtangov Theatre. Last year I was impressed by the element of stylishness in this production, because it was much freer in its treatment of a realistic play than we are accustomed to in America. But this time I was impressed with the realness of the production: the observation, the concrete detail, the quiet truth. Everything is done lovingly, cleanly and clearly: nothing is missed, nothing is overstressed, nothing neglected. Shchukin as Bulichev is still superb. He dominates the play by his part and his personality (which is vigorous and young without a trace of coarseness or vulgarity) and yet he brings a perfect ensemble feeling to the stage. His spiritual attitude in the performance (and this counts a great deal in the first impression created by an actor on the audience) breathes dignity, simplicity and a masculine sweetness. He is universally loved by audiences and fellow actors. And because I know he is no miracle man but an honest theatre worker of talent who by force of a real desire to grow (he was an illiterate boy and is almost completely self-educated) has risen to the point of his present performance, I feel closer to him. I love him as an actor more than any I know. One does not sink to one's knees in admiring him, one feels like embracing him and working by his side.

There are great men in the theatre from whom we can learn little; from Shchukin and the Vakhtangov Theatre much can be learned: we are akin. The difference between us is not one of talent. It has to do with a certain kind of theatrical conscience or devotion, and a certain discipline.

May 17

I took the Metro—the new subway—which had just been opened to the public. I wonder what the opening of the subway in New York was like. This particular achievement really deserves the wonder and acclaim it is getting. When one buys one's ticket (50 kopeks) one has the feeling that one is buying opera seats. To see the workers who built this subway with their rough clothes, their still untamed bodies and their untutored earthy ways crowd into the decorative, modernistic halls of their creation is to realize once again the inspiring contradiction, the unparalleled and glorious paradox of the Soviet Union.

At night we went to see *Romeo and Juliet* at the Theatre of the Revolution. And indeed this production is brilliant. First of all, the sets have a sweep, a variety, a largeness, a colorfulness that are beyond anything I have ever seen in a classic

production in America. In fact, I explained to people during intermission that we were too poor in America to put on Shakespeare this way. The production cost for us would be over $100,000 surely—not to mention the fact that the production was rehearsed for over a year. The lavishness was overwhelming, as was the way the stage was used.

The first scene—the fight—was one of the most exciting theatrical moments you can imagine. Here the body training—the ease of movement, the ability to fence, to run, to jump—was used to the full with an effect that was Shakespearean in its energy, breadth, fluency and strength. What came through was not the romantic tragedy of love but the general colorfulness and splendor of the period: the physical dynamics. At last, a virile Shakespeare instead of the literary sissy, the drooping, swooning, lisping namby-pamby son of a professional bore that he is in every American production I have seen.

In the midst of all this we find very spirited and technically expert acting. But on the whole, it is characteristic of a general defect in production here that they treat the actors much too instrumentally. An actor directed externally only, howsoever brilliantly, remains slightly *untheatrical*. In other words, true theatricality does not reside only in business, in visually interesting or pictorially dramatic movement, in general stage colors, dances, leaps, etc.—it resides also and perhaps even to a greater extent in the inner life, in the emotion, in the spirit (to put it boldly) of the actor.

May 18

In the evening we saw *Revizor* (*Inspector General*) at the Meyerhold. A very brilliant production. It is harder, more complex, trickier and less revolutionary than *The Forest*. (Less revolutionary in the sense that it seems like an amazing picture of the past by someone who was very much part of it rather than the fresh breathing of new air that one gets from *The Forest*.) But it is full of a specifically theatrical genius: cultivated, inventive, incisive and profound in craftsmanship. A strange feeling comes from this production: It is very funny and it is tomblike. It has a definitely macabre quality—cold, beautiful, grimacing, distorted and graceful. The production ends with the actors running off stage laughing while on the stage we see their prototypes, who are puppets. Meyerhold's *Revizor* is a masterpiece, but somehow not a warming one: It leaves one slightly uncomfortable.

May 21

Quite suddenly came the announcement that Stanislavsky would see us. At 3:30 we were told we could visit him at 4:15. I brought him Stella Adler's gift and he shook my hand for it. And then I began asking questions—not too many, however.

"Miss Adler wants to know what you meant by inner clichés."

"Actors of experience often have certain emotional tricks by which they indicate sorrow, anger, etc. These are not pieces of business, physical things, but inner processes over which they have control and which they can use to indicate deep feeling. But they have little to do with life. They are born of the theatre. They do not derive from *action* but from representation (from performance). The way to overcome it is for the actor to say to himself or for the director to ask, 'What were you *doing* at that moment? Were you *doing* anything?' If the actor senses that he was only feeling (or trying to feel) but not doing (carrying out an action) he will be able to rid himself of the inner clichés."

Cheryl asked, "Do you set the problem for the actor or do you make him set it for himself?"

"I would like the actor to set the problem for himself. But the actor is lazy so I set the problem for him."

"Your actors are lazy!" I exclaimed in genuine astonishment.

"Oh, they know how to work," Stanislavsky replied, "but they don't unless you push them to it. They are willing to work as hard as you please on physical problems, position, etc., but on the other and more important things—yes, they are lazy."

He later spoke about body work. "Acrobatics

are very useful. But even more for the soul than for the body." We smiled at this paradox. "Yes, acrobatics train you not to be afraid in the big moments of your part. Because these moments—they may not be physical—are equivalent to a difficult jump. If you hesitate you are lost. Acrobatics prepare you for them."

The conversation turned to other aspects of the theatre. Stanislavsky tells us about his difficulties with a playwright. "We tell him a certain scene or speech has to be put into the play and he answers, 'The actor will do it.' And then the actor says, 'I can't do it. I need a speech. 'Finally, there is no acting and no speech."

Immediately after our Stanislavsky visit we had a date to see Meyerhold. He also received us in his apartment, composed of large pleasant rooms—by no means luxurious or ornate in any way. Meyerhold is utterly simple and direct in conversation. I found him sympathetic and charming. "Your productions," I began, "are built differently from anyone else's. Have you a special conception of dramaturgy?"

"Yes, I believe that plays should be written differently for the new theatre than they have been up to now. Because of this I have had constant conflicts with my playwrights. I have therefore become a director-author.

"I believe it would be useful to have a school for playwrights in the theatre. When I direct a play I can do nothing else, even write a letter. I think of nothing else, I see nothing else. And I can't work with assistants who might relieve me in my direction. Yes, the problem of the dramatist is now our most important problem. That and the problem of a new theatre architecture. The two problems are related."

"Do you work on your productions much before you go into rehearsal?"

"I thought about *Revizor* for 10 years before I produced it. I always knew I would do it. I always wanted to do it. But I was not ready and kept on thinking about it. There are plays about which I say to myself, 'This play I will do in three years or in five years.'"

"Do you write down your thoughts about your productions—your plans for the staging, etc.?"

"I used to when I was young, but now I am able to keep everything quite clearly in my head. Anyhow, I am likely to stage a scene one way and 10 days later come to rehearsal and change the staging completely. For me every rehearsal is a sketch. The actors do not write down that they must move here or there, because they know I am likely to change the staging at the very next rehearsal."

We then mentioned this biomechanic class we had seen and told him how much we liked it. "Yes," he said, "it is a theatrical method of body training for the actor. Each exercise is a melodrama. Each movement gives the actor a sense of performing on the stage."

"How long," Cheryl wanted to know, "would it take a person to learn it, so that he or she might teach it to American actors?"

"One winter," Meyerhold answered. "It is not very complicated. In fact, it is simple."

Cheryl and I both decided to try to find someone to learn it here in Moscow who would return and teach it to the Group.

May 22

In the evening we saw *The Magnificent Cuckold*, a typical Meyerhold production of the "wild," "constructivist," "modernistic" period (around 1924)—another Meyerhold masterpiece. I enjoyed it immensely and was deeply impressed with Meyerhold's extraordinary theatrical genius. Strangely enough, instead of finding this wild farce quite formalistic as a production, it seemed to me that this play could not and should not be done in any other way. I had seen it done realistically in 1921 in Paris, and while it was extravagant in idea, it was strained and repellent to see. There is no pathology in Meyerhold's production: all its extravagance and sickness is worked off in brilliant physical exercises that are made part of the play, in stage-business composed of amazing acrobatic hokum, in a theatrical freedom and imaginativeness that shows how strong stage illusion can be

with a minimum of means. But not only is the gymnastic splendor of the actors demonstrated here—all this ultrastylization expresses a real content, a content that one feels could not be communicated any other way.

And though this production of *The Magnificent Cuckold* is considered "experimental," to me it is no experiment at all. First, it is completely successful; second, it is truly creative in the sense that it embodies something quite personal to the author (Meyerhold himself) and third, it fits the spirit of the time for which it was made—a hungry, stark time when, despite physical deprivation and amidst all the grimness and hunger, people wanted to laugh and be boisterous. *The Magnificent Cuckold* to me is one of the big achievements of the modern theatre: and the fact that it depends on biomechanic expertness (without it the actors would break their necks) makes it keep its form better than Meyerhold's more recent productions such as *La Dame aux Camellias*.

The Forest, *Revizor* and this, together with the Habima *Dybbuk*—and, on quite another level, *Carmencita* and *The Soldier*—are the finest productions I have seen in the nonrealistic theatre. One should see these productions—or as many of them as possible—to be glad once again that we belong to this beautiful, lively art. Let no one speak lightly of Meyerhold: He is one of the really great men in the theatre of the world.

May 24

In the evening went to see the first performance in Moscow of the Vakhtangov Theatre's production of *The Aristocrats* directed by Zachava. After the first act I thought, "This is the nearest thing to an American production I have seen in Moscow." But Cheryl put it more precisely by saying, "This reminds me of a dress rehearsal back on 52nd Street." All in all, an undistinguished production.

Leningrad, May 26

At night (with the accidental aid of Edmund Wilson) we got to see *Pique Dame*, produced by

Meyerhold this year at the Little Opera Theatre, popularly known as the Michailowsky. I found the score very captivating in its romanticism, and the production itself, with a new specially written libretto, unusually good-looking, in Meyerhold's most tasteful and luxurious manner. The production has something of a nostalgia for grandiose, romantic gloom, a sense of mighty yet decorative oppression which fits this opera very well, and which is characteristic of one side of Meyerhold.

As I sat in the theatre I remembered Meyerhold's face as he sat laughing in his apartment and, in retrospect, I recognized in it the look of a very old, very cultured nobleman who was secretly sorcerer, part ballet master—an intellectual Dr. Caligari of the theatre.

May 27

During the last two days of our stay Cheryl and I began to talk about what we had learned from our trip. We were taking stock. An attitude of firmness and faith, coupled with the sentiment that the strong must use their strength to protect the weak so that the latter may also become strong, is the great human characteristic of the Soviet Union today. This attitude has infinite importance for us in America, particularly in organizations such as the Group. It must form the basis of the personal discipline we need. The theatrical discipline concerns the absolute necessity of every actor to do his utmost to correct every technical fault he may have, to work continually (apart from rehearsals as well as in rehearsal) to increase his professional proficiency and to complete himself as an artistic instrument.

Russian actors are not more talented or necessarily more intelligent than we are, but they are indisputably on a higher technical level—merely because of concentrated, systematic work. They make up better than we do, they have better voices, there are absolutely never any complaints of inaudibility (though almost all their theatres are larger), their bodies are freer. They do not neglect anything that has to do with their jobs as theatre workers. This is the most important part of their

lives. We shall never make great progress unless we begin at once to imitate them.

In this alone do we have to think of emulation. We must learn through ourselves by daring to work in our way. Nothing important can come from people who merely attempt to follow in the path of a master—however great. And last, we see the necessity of understanding our social-organizational-financial situation very realistically so that we never lose contact with all the facts of our immediate world—with the facts that we must forever cope with if we are to function successfully—which means continuously—as a collective group in the New York and the American theatre.

On the boat Cheryl and I confessed to one another how badly we needed the Group, how painfully we missed it and how damned anxious we were to be with it again.

—*ATH*, Mar. '88

SOVIET DIARY II

Saw *The Sorceress* at the Jewish Theatre. I wanted to see this production that was first presented in 1922 because it represents a certain extreme in stylization, which at a certain time in America was considered the norm. It also marks the first big production of Gronovski who in those days was a leading figure in the Soviet Theatre. What we see is a grotesque harlequinade—angular, distorted, abstract, garish, noisy. It is full of gestures, leaps, somersaults, nonsensical rhymes, bewildering props, heterogeneous songs, dances and a kind of crazy choral comment conveyed through strange sounds, stranger bits of mimicry and all sorts of corkscrew contortions.

It is a folk picture or ballet of the old Jewish Ghetto. But this Ghetto is crazy and fantastic because the Bolsheviks are going to clear it out, build anew so that it will become an unbelievable memory of the past, an impossible dream, half nightmare, half joke. The Jew of the new Socialist society is roaring his mockery of the cramped,

dislocated life of the old Ghetto. He is sweeping it away with energy and laughter. He buries it by making of it a topsy-turvy masque. And with the old Ghetto, the actors of the new Soviet Jewish Theatre were breaking the shackles of theatrical convention inherited from the old Jewish Theatre. At one moment a character cries out in a comic wail, "They are dead! They are dead! They are dead!" "Who is dead?" the chorus clamors. "The old Jewish theatres" is the reply. So the sentimental intonations of the provincial Jewish stage, the little comedy tricks, the fake pathos, the childish heroics, the professional Jewish theatre sweetness are all satirically exaggerated and caricatured.

This production was worked on for two years and is relatively short: two and one-half hours. Even the set which at first sight looks like a perfectly arbitrary arrangement of surfaces is based on the definite reality of a Russian Jewish village before the revolution with its poverty-stricken wooden materials, its ramshackle architecture, its cockeyed, helter-skelter, tattered effect. Though it is essentially a stage construction which permits the varied acrobatics of all the strange characters, the set gives the feeling of the kind of place the old Ghetto was.

Understood in this light the production is a real Bolshevik product. And the actors at the time—themselves liberated from diverse Russian, Polish and Roumanian Ghettos—must have felt it and acted it with all the enthusiasm of their young, vigorous bodies (no doubt the two years were used to train themselves to perform all the acrobatic stunts of the show), acted it with the joy of victory, with the hopefulness of pioneers amidst the ruins of an old world, with the iconoclasm of revolutionaries. And the audience likewise must have understood it quite clearly.

Today the actors play it coldly, without much inner urge, youthful plasticity or sense of fun. They have no emotion, and it is all a little like a bad reproduction of a bright painting. Gronovski never did work emotionally with his actors, but they had emotion at first that came from their personal relation to the period and to the situation.

Now only the form remains, but as an actor of the company explained, it remains technically accurate because Gronovski worked it out so that if the actor turned the wrong way he was likely to get a crack on the nose, or if he made a badly timed cross he might have one of his colleagues crash down on his head. "Gronovski did this on purpose," the actor said, "he wanted every movement to be as strictly coordinated as a machine." Indeed the production has something of the precise nature of a cuckoo clock.

After the performance I go backstage to talk with Goldblatt. He plays the leading part and he is at the same time the founder and chief director of the Gypsy Theatre. Our conversation leads to some interesting, though familiar facts. The company plays in Moscow till May 18th. Then it goes to Leningrad till the first of July and after that it tours the Union till September. Following this the actors take a six-week vacation. The regular Soviet vacation is four weeks but the actor is allowed these extra two weeks because as a worker he is supposed to be on the job only five days a week but since this is not always possible even with a large company playing repertory (there are forty-one in this group) the two weeks are added to compensate for the extra days he has worked during the season. Vacation in the Soviet Union is "with pay." Goldblatt informed me that a doctor had been to the theatre that very day to examine the actors and advise them where it would be best for them to spend this vacation. The mountains were recommended for some, the sea for others, etc.

"I wonder if you realize how lucky you are," I said. "The Jewish actors in New York are having a hard time and the American actors are no better off." Goldblatt answered "I do understand our good fortune. I was born in Romania and our only dramatic school was in Bucharest. If I wanted to study there I had to be baptized, as no Jew was permitted to enter. Second, the tuition was so high that I could not have afforded to pay even for one month. But now I teach in our own dramatic school. The students are young people from the

provinces, eighteen or nineteen years old. They are given free board and lodging in Moscow. During the day for about five hours they are instructed in all the branches of theatrical craft. At night as part of their training they are asked to see all the productions, and of course they do not pay for their tickets. Added to this they are given fifty or sixty roubles for pocket money. This goes on for four years and only then is it decided whether or not they may join the theatre. They imagine that life for the actor is this way everywhere."

In talking to Goldblatt about Gronovski who is now a successful and wealthy director of bourgeois films in Paris, I asked him why he had left the theatre. "Because he is an impressionable fool," was the answer.

When we came out of the dressing room onto the stage-landing I saw a big call-board all plastered with typewritten material. "What is that?" I inquired. "That is the theatre newspaper. It is used as a means of mutual criticism. Actors may write their criticisms of one another, of the director, the organization, anything they feel strongly or clearly about. The directors can do the same, as well as any member of the collective—including stage-hands." "What is the main paper now?" I asked pointing at the center of the board. "That is a comment by our electrician. He says that the criticisms directed against the theatre lighting are justified but for the lighting to be improved more time must be devoted to light rehearsals." I asked further, "Why don't the actors write letters to one another if they want to criticize each other. Why do they put the criticism on the board?" "That is the most impersonal and at the same time the friendliest way—this open criticism by means of the newspaper. The actors learn from one another, help one another this way. There is no desire to hurt or to find fault for its own sake. This system benefits everybody. All the actors learn and discipline themselves because of this, whereas personal discussions cause bad feelings and do great mischief." I go away quite impressed.

—*NEW*, Aug. '35

SOVIET DIARY III: CONVERSATIONS WITH TWO MASTERS

Stanislavsky lives in an old private house with a fair-sized courtyard. The rooms are large and there are probably a good number but there is something bare about the place that might horrify a director of Stanislavsky's position anywhere else. He looked much older than last year. At that time he had been on a long vacation and still seemed vigorous and unchanged. Now one could see the signs of his illness. Nevertheless he works all the time. He has not been out of his house since November. He conducts rehearsals at home; he has a school that trains professors in the 'system' (a six-year course!) and, as he expresses it, he directs his theatre by telephone.

He offered us tea, cake and jam. We began asking questions. The first was about tempo-rhythm, which he had mentioned in Paris last year but which I had not understood very well. He got up and showed me an electric gadget that had two discs on it, one red and one blue, and was attached to a metronome. He tried to untangle the wires but could not, so he did not demonstrate but explained. In certain scenes a definite rhythm is fixed (it was not entirely clear to me whether the rhythm was determined by him as regisseur or was based on the tempo that the actor himself established when he played the scene well, because Stanislavsky said, "When the actor feels the scene properly, his rhythm will be right"). This rhythm is fixed by number on the script and when the actor rehearses, if he imagines he is playing the scene properly but is not, the rhythm is given him for a few moments by the electric gadget. This engenders a more exact sense of the movement of the scene. Sometimes Stanislavsky gives the rhythm and tells the actor to improvise something to that particular rhythm.

"Have you used this method in any production?"

"No, only with students. Actors like to have

their parts explained to them, they like you to talk about the interpretation but they do not like to work on anything exact....The tempo-rhythm process is an exercise which of course gives results with rhythmic people. We have exercises for increasing people's sense of rhythm."

"I understand the importance of translating each psychological moment into a physical equivalent," I went on, "but it is often difficult to find the physical equivalents when the play does not require the actor to do anything overt and exact. How do you get the actor to understand these moments in other terms than those of thoughts and feelings?"

"Ask the actor what he would *do* in such and such a situation. He might say 'I will call my friend.' Good, make a note of this: it is already a physical impulse even if not performed. But what if the friend is not at home? 'I would send a wire home.' Make another note. This is another impulse. But this is also impossible because your folks are away. 'Then I will go to my neighbor next door and get help from him.' Good, do this—and you have the beginning of physical actions tied up with feeling and thought all the time."

We asked about voice exercises. He said that while on tour he had to rehearse all day, play at night, make speeches at parties, banquets, teas, and he realized that if he continued he would lose his voice and would not be able to play. So he began doing exercises, which he demonstrated a little, and did them every day. He did not lose his voice. "But one must have great patience," he added.

I told him about the Group Theatre and its new playwright, Clifford Odets: how he has been an actor in our theatre, how he has developed, his present success.

"Will he remain an actor or not?" Stanislavsky asked. But before I could reply, he said, "Tell Mr. Odets for me not to give up acting. It will always help him in his playwriting. When he needs time off to write a play, give him the time. But let him continue to act."

Immediately after our visit to Stanislavsky we had an engagement to see Meyerhold. He also received us in his apartment—large, pleasant rooms, by no means luxurious or ornate. His wife, the actress Zinaida Reich, opened the door to us, was introduced and disappeared, reappearing at the end of the interview to remind Meyerhold that he had not eaten yet and that he must go to the theatre.

"You didn't change *Camille* much," I noted, "Is that because you thought it was a well-constructed play for your purpose?"

"I changed *Camille*, although less noticeably than most. If you examine the French and Russian texts you will find minute changes which are very important. Also I took certain speeches from the novel and put them into the play."

"Why did you choose this play?"

"I am interested in showing the bad attitude of the bourgeoisie to women. Marguerite is treated like a slave or a servant. Men bargain over her, throw money in her face, insult her—all because they say they love her. I was interested to show this because we, too, in the Soviet Union, have had a wrong conception of love and of woman. Our attitude has been too biologic. This is all very well, but there is a deeper and loftier view of love. We build new streets, new houses, we try to improve our clothes and make our living more aesthetic. We must also have a more aesthetic relation to woman. This is a problem that the Communist Party [Meyerhold is one of the few important regisseurs in Moscow who are members] has begun to work on: the problem of changing the psychology of the people, to make it fit the new classless society we are building. There is a law (which will probably be changed soon) permitting any number of marriages and giving the utmost freedom in the matter of divorce. This freedom is good. But it is also bad. We must understand that the problem of man and woman is more complex than we used to think, and we must have a more delicate understanding and more cultured attitude than we have had. It used to be thought proletarian and communistic to be rude, but we are also changing this and teaching that good manners are indispensable to a sane humanity….The form of *Camille* is old, but the social motives are good."

"Shakespeare's *Hamlet* is still being discussed by critics, professors, theatre people. Was he mad or not? Why did he do this or that? Did Shakespeare contradict himself? Did Hamlet love his mother? Why are so many questions asked? Because Shakespeare put so much thought and feeling into his plays, because a whole life and a whole time are in them. Our modern plays are written lightmindedly. And I have enough technique to put them on without difficulty in six weeks. Not much thought has to be given them." I laughed.

"Yes," he finished. "I must confess to you quite frankly that we have as yet no Shakespeare in the Soviet Union."

"Did you yourself choose the admirable props and costumes of *Camille*?"

"Yes," Meyerhold replied, "I send assistants to various shops to make a choice of twenty objects. When they are found I go to the shop and choose one or two of the twenty—or something entirely different. Also we advertise in the papers: 'The Meyerhold Theatre wants furniture and costumes of such-and-such a period.' A man answers that he has a chair for us. I go to see it. Once an old actress—80 or more—wrote us that she had a trunkful of costumes from the year 1870. We took these costumes, remodeled them according to photographs from French newspapers of the period, corrected them by reference to Manet and Renoir, and our designer chose the color schemes."

—*TA*, Nov.'35

INTERPRETATION AND CHARACTERIZATION: A Theatre Workshop Discussion

When I returned from the Soviet Union last June, New York had a strange effect upon me. Nothing had changed in the eight weeks of my absence, yet everything had somehow altered its meaning. To sum up my impression: my whole environment—my good friends and intimates, the plays I saw, the books I read, the newspapers I scanned, the conversations I heard—all seemed a bit mad! People complained about woes that were mostly imaginary, overlooked conflicts that were immediate, belied their thoughts by their acts, explained their acts by ideas they professed to scorn. Many spoke of saving and spent beyond their means, others talked of sacrifice to ideals and wasted their time, still others clamored for things they had no real interest in, and waxed skeptical over struggles that were essential to their happiness.

When I came to direct Clifford Odets' new play *Paradise Lost*, the contradictions that are at the base of almost every scene became clear to me through my own experience of a few months back. This crazy world that Clifford Odets had wrought out of sheer artistic perversity, as some might believe, or out of a desire to emulate the great Chekhov, as many have said, or even out of a "Marxian prejudice" as the ignorant would have it—this crazy world was simply the world we live in—or to be more exact the middle-class world of our daily experience.

All the characters in *Paradise Lost*—excepting only Clara Gordon, the mother, and two of the workers from the shop delegation—are a trifle "touched." This does not make them "exceptional"—on the contrary, it makes them like us—but it was my job as the director to make the characters' madness clear not merely as "realism" but *as a comment*. Beyond this, there was the problem of making an audience feel what it was that all these characters were doing in their madness, what possibly caused the madness and how it was concerned with the life of the spectator. The main problem in the direction of *Paradise Lost*, in other words, was the problem of finding characterizations that were true to the individuals, yet part of an organic conception which made their world, despite particular differences, a common one.

Why are the characters—in *Paradise Lost* funny? Why are they bewildered, tragic, grotesque, violent as the case may be? They are all looking for reality in a world where nothing is altogether real, where there is something insubstantial and dreamlike in the most ordinary processes of behavior. The world of the ruling class is real in the sense that the rulers know where their interests lie, work hard and fight systematically to protect them against every possible enemy; the world of the working class is real because its struggle is so primitive and plain that there is no mistaking or avoiding it. But the middle class carries out the orders of the ruling class with the illusion of complete freedom, and it is sufficiently protected from the terror of material nakedness to believe in transcendental explanations of human woe that keep it "calm" without really satisfying it. There is no "enemy" in the middle-class world except an intangible "fate"; there is no fight except with one's own contradictions—and real life (the life that both the upper and lower classes know in their opposite ways) enters upon the scene like a fierce, unexplained intruder.

Though this interpretation may be regarded as "personal" it is the director's job to proceed from some such general conception to the minute details of the production. A more Chekhovian—that is, a less social—view might be taken of the play which would tend to make it "sadder," more fatalistic and generally "true to life" in the meaningless sense of the word! The "reading" I have given the script gives the play a definite *line* or what certain reviewers would call a propagandist slant. Also the comedy has been made organic with its tragedy, whereas in relation to the rest it might easily seem a forced whimsicality. Certain tragic characters like Leo have been treated more humorously than the text indicates; the musician Felix has been made less "sympathetic" than the author intended, the daughter of the house is taken a trifle less heroically in the production than in the script. In the following notes I sketch some of the character interpretations but a comparison of my statements with the published book will show throughout the addition of "business' and motivations that are distinct from, though compatible with, the play's lines. The text (the author's work) and the sub-text (the director's treatment) in these remarks are given as a unified whole.

Leo Gordon, the "hero" of *Paradise Lost*, is an unusual man only in the sense that few middle-class people are so aware of their own subtle misery or so fervent in their desire to cure it. He is always trying to remedy the suffering he sees about him, but being typically middle class he does not know how to do it. He would like to make war on injustice but does not know what weapon to use and any weapon more concrete than ideas frightens him.

How do we portray such a character in the theatre? We see his kindness not only in the actions given him by the author but in such a detail as his instinctive caress of the girl worker whom he wants to reassure. We visualize his confusion before simple objects and his inadequacy even in trivial situations. When the workers come to visit him, he is embarrassed and clumsy: He offers one of them a chair when there is none to sit on; at another time he serves brandy which he thinks is the same as wine; he dashes after his partner to convince him that wages in the shop must be raised, but he hesitates at the last moment, retreats to his own apartment, sits down, rises impetuously again, hammers his resolve on the table and then proceeds to get drunk! He traces imaginary figures in the air as he listens to memories of the past; he rarely completes any movement. As each act develops the character becomes soberer and more direct. Only in the end do we establish a stronger tone for him—something to suggest that now at last he may become an integrated person. Yet even his eccentricities in the first two acts are made to arise from a vital sensibility, a capacity for love.

Marcus Katz, Leo's partner, written "with a certain comic explosiveness" is given an even more tragic interpretation in the production. He wants to be loved but everyone hates him. Why? In order to exist as a small capitalist he is forced to do ugly, shameful things. Leo concerns himself only with the "artistic" side of the business, but Katz himself must do the dirty work, and for this he earns nothing but scorn or suspicion. He questions everybody. "Why are you better than I? I do the things I have to do in order to provide the where-withal which enables you to cultivate the airs of a fine gentleman. Why then am I the most despised of men?" The answer he gives himself is that because he does the terrible things that business demands he is actually better than anyone else. This is the source of his madness.

Gus Michaels, the family friend, fights imaginary battles and boxes with non-existent contestants, cries apropos of most of his grievances because he wants to assert his right to live even though he has never been able to earn a living. The man who fails in our middle class is generally looked down upon; unless he is strong he will always hanker for that degree of "respectability" which is denied him. So Gus vacillates between his true nature—an imaginative, sensitive one—and the stupidities of the bourgeois world he would like to feel part of. His greatest satisfactions are in his dreams and his memories of the past. I have tried to visualize all this in production by numerous small details which make clear both the positive and negative side of the character.

The equivocal Mr. May, the man who arranges fires so that troubled businessmen may collect insurance, is also a seeker after reality! He knows his little occupation is an illegal one, but if a fine "front" is put on it, if his vocabulary shows a degree of refinement and "ethics" what he is selling will find a buyer in the middle-class world. To sell at a profit is real—it is almost the only reality which is universally accepted in our society! So that the most "ordinary" character in the play, the one whose mental process is most "average" and most "normal"—the dull salesman of the play becomes in production the most insane, the most stylized figure of all. The details of dress, of make-up (the actor's hair does not naturally grow red), the conjurer's mannerisms, the sweetened speech is the director's way of making a theatrical comment on the scene, a means of

saying: "What the author has written here is the grotesque and tragic farce of our middle class life."

And in each character, whether "sympathetic" or not I have tried in a similar manner to create through special imagery the salient behavior or through special imagery the salient contradictions—the craziness!—of these middle-class types. Mrs. Katz knows the secret of her husband's tragedy, she protects him at all times, following him always, picking up the refuse he makes wherever he goes, always excusing herself for the trouble he causes. Foley, the local politician, is a good fellow, believing sincerely that Tammany is a kind of philanthropic society, but despite his hearty manner, we understand from the way he treats his henchman, from his reaction to the slightest word of criticism the brutality that goes with his "Democratic" kindness. Pearl, Leo's pianist daughter, is the type of romantic artist who from deep hurt tries to live in an ivory tower of "pure beauty": Her loneliness, her frustration, her almost comic adjustment to everyday life is embodied in slightly distorted physical mannerisms.

It is impossible in the space of a short article to point out all the ramifications of the director's problem, the pitfalls and obstacles that may attend its solution or the errors that may be committed in its name. Suffice it to say, that the scene (designed by Boris Aronson) though adequate to the naturalistic demands of the play is not quite in the tradition of the realistic box-set. It is abstracted to convey the sense of any middle-class room, to give some feeling of a "home" which is the actual milieu of the play without sacrificing the quality of a *stage* as a place where artists have a right to express something more than the "naked facts."

—*NEW*, Jan. '36

ALL IS GRIST

The debit and credit side of a Group season are not easy to figure. On the one hand, we may say that our season has not been a success. We did three new productions, but our longest run was only nine weeks. Against this, *Paradise Lost* was universally regarded by us as a consummation of our work on acting: Morris gave his best performance since *Connelly*, Sandy achieved his first authentic piece of acting, Gadget's characterization was rounded out in a way that made his work in *Lefty* seem a mere stroke of fortunate casting, Bud for the first time was a good actor rather than a capable performer, and many other things of a similar nature might be mentioned. And despite the abrupt and unnecessary closing of *Clyde Griffiths*, the universal recognition and praise of the Group's high level of excellence as a producing unit is certainly something that we may turn to good account.

It may be thought that taking heart in the fact that we understand our own mistakes is another form of Group rationalization. Is it not a little absurd to say that we have made progress simply because we acknowledge certain defects and defeats? No, our view is fundamentally correct, for only in a theatre with a conscious approach in matters of artistic and cultural growth, can failure become a step toward further advancement. In the ordinary production, failure only means economic distress; it reveals nothing since nothing is attempted beyond the job of making money. In our theatre (or any theatre like it) where we have a clear object in view for the individual as well as the collective, the realization of failure in relation to our conscious objectives can be a source of instruction, a stimulus to more considered craftsmanship. Rewards in a Group like ours do not come with the "initial investment"; they are long term affairs.

Organizationally, our season has taught us that our main problem is continuity of activity (42 to 46 weeks) at full salaries. This means closer attention to the problem of plays and some revision of our policy in choice of plays. Luther's argument for organizing the road gains weight from the fact that our double bill did keep us five weeks in Philadelphia alone, just as our successful return to New York in September in an "old bill" teaches us

to respect Group resourcefulness and to recognize the ability of Group actors to contribute valuably to Group business. Our fight for *Paradise Lost* was a vital step in the education of a theatre public, and Bill Challee's work in this connection and the cooperation of the actors deserves special commendation. Also Cliff's efforts and sacrifice (in a money way) for *Paradise Lost* (like Melvin's last year in behalf of *Gold Eagle*) must not pass unnoticed; they show how playwrights contribute to the Group in more than one way. (The closing of *Clyde Griffiths* in contrast to our work in behalf of plays like *Success Story*, *Paradise Lost* and *Gold Eagle* shows how much more the Group does for its plays than the ordinary producer). *Weep for the Virgins* was an interesting and worthwhile first play—a fact that no one ought to overlook despite the notices or one's own personal prejudices, and one of the things we may have learned from this failure is the necessity of working on certain script problems very early in the rehearsal period—if not sooner. The production committee, which should have a "literary department," can be useful in this. Indeed, as Stella points out, the production committee should be developed and given a more systematic function so that it can yield greater results.

In general, what stays with me most in relation to our last season is our need to keep up the spirit of constructive self-criticism, to bring ever new points of attack, new objectives into the consideration of our work. We should never lose a sense of our value, but we must also never lose sight of the fact that our value diminishes the moment we become easy with ourselves in relation to craftsmanship, or are reluctant to gather new force whenever and however it comes. The Group must always be inspired by inspiring itself—urging itself to greater efforts. This summer we ought to work hard on our voices, our speech and our bodies; there has been a definite falling off in some of these respects. There ought to be a greater precision in certain technical aspects of our staging and acting. We were not organized to live by a certain self-righteous standard of personal conduct, we are not here to prove to ourselves the private benefits of a collective theatre; we were formed to put on productions that would stir our audience and convince them through their excellence that our technique leads to the most satisfying entertainment. We used to say that only "good people" could bring forth good theatre; we must now reverse this and say we are "good people" only in so far as we bring forth good theatre. Our "morality" must consist in the most complete professionalism.

—*FG*, June '36

THE GROUP HALTS, BUT ONLY TO THINK IT OVER: Mr. Clurman, Proud of Its Past, Maps Out a Future That Will Be Fighting

One of the most pleasant experiences in the Group Theatre's existence occurred during the past week. The Group's publicity department had sent out a straightforward announcement stating that because of the need for further script revisions the production of Clifford Odets' play, *The Silent Partner*, was postponed until the fall and that, owing to lack of another immediate script, the Group Theatre had decided to discontinue its production activities till the new season. This was duly "interpreted" in some theatrical news columns as the "folding up" of the Group Theatre as such, or, to put it more bluntly, its finish. This "interpretation," more colorful than the actual facts, brought to the Group Theatre offices an avalanche of letters and phone calls in which playgoers and theatre workers outside the realm of our personal acquaintance assured us that it was the Group Theatre's duty to continue and that even a temporary lay-off was a serious loss to the American stage. Thus, despite the misinformation which under the best auspices travels fast on Broadway, the event became for us in the Group Theatre a very gratifying and encouraging sign.

Yet weren't the boys with the "inside story" right? When an individual manager calls quits for a season to make off to Paris, Palm Beach or the Coast, whether it be for reasons of success or failure or a surplus of profits, nothing in particular is predicted as to his future. When a theatre composed of a permanent company takes some similar step for any reason, it is considered safe to suggest that this theatre has no future at all. There is wisdom in this, since an individual producer represents no general responsibility, whereas a theatre by definition represents the idea of a certain continuity of activity and permanence.

The Group Theatre's decision to call off production activities for the remainder of the season has a meaning—we believe, in fact, an important meaning. But a very different meaning from that implied by the calamity criers and gossips.

The truth is that a makeshift plan or an emergency program (often resulting in a highly entertaining show) might have been devised for purposes of keeping the Group Theatre Acting Company together till the spring and upholding the policy of permanence. The Group Theatre did not choose to do this since it feels that it has arrived at a new stage of its development, the moment to progress toward a more stable achievement through a different approach to its work and to its public.

To make this clear, it is necessary to repeat the bare facts of the Group Theatre's history. In 1931, when the Group Theatre began its activities, it was not easy to raise money for the support of a new organization. The Group felt, however (and this was perhaps a little innocent of them), that if it could do at least one production of striking merit, it might persuade certain people that a theatre with a permanent company devoted to the perfecting of an ensemble technique for the intelligent production of valuable new plays was worthy of financial support. The critical reception accorded the first production of Paul Green's *The House of Connelly* exceeded all our expectations. The favorable comparison with the Moscow Art Theatre (not ours!) was to be read in many columns both in New York and elsewhere. Now we were set; we had proved something; a collective effort in the theatre, a company without "stars" working toward the best interpretations of the plays they believed in, could produce a result that was clearly outstanding, a contribution.

But we had not understood the deep-going nature of the depression. Patrons of the theatre approved our efforts but had no money "in those parlous times" for a non-commercial venture. Aided by the Theatre Guild, we tried again and produced the Siftons' *1931—*, the first play about the economic crisis to reach Broadway. Though it had a short run, it aroused great enthusiasm in an audience whose relationship to a growing theatre we had not yet learned to appreciate or use. Again, the production itself was highly praised and we were encouraged to proceed without subsidy or patronage of any kind.

We went on with our permanent company, which is absolutely essential to a theatre but a calamitous burden to an independent manager. We produced some fourteen plays, all but one by Americans, five of them first plays, one of them a Pulitzer Prize play and a box-office success, four others the work of a member of the Group's acting company, Clifford Odets. During this period in 1932, the Group was obliged to call a halt to its season in February. Respectful obituaries were written for it. Yet the two seasons after that were financially and artistically very successful. During this whole period the Group Theatre not only managed to retain its unity and the large majority of its personnel but to earn the respect of the audience and press alike in New York and in all the larger cities from here to Chicago.

All this might be set down as a sort of "success story," for, with all due modesty, it is not too much to say that the Group has made history in the American theatre. Yet during all this time the Group Theatre—its actors and directors—were conscious of a basic weakness. If the Group's activities had simply been the work of an individ-ual producer, its career might have proved not only honorable but lucrative. Its weakness derived, however, from the fact that while it planned to work as a theatre it operated under exactly the same conditions as the commercial producer. Its "backing" covered only single productions and most of its backers came in on its productions for the same reasons and with the same understanding that they might on shows produced by any manager.

This was perhaps fair enough, but the individual manager has no responsibility to a steadily growing public with certain fixed demands as to the quality and nature of the plays presented nor does the individual manager undertake to maintain and train a company or to produce at all except when he is satisfied that his "property" (the play) is a "good proposition." Thus the Group Theatre did all its work under the most adverse conditions, and though it succeeded in presenting a good number of well-liked productions, it never satisfied itself that it was fulfilling its whole function as a theatre.

What is the function of a theatre or, more properly, what are its needs? A theatre must guar-antee its company salaries at least for thirty-five weeks a year and it must be able to present enough plays each season to give its actors varied prob-lems and thus aid in their continuous training so that their work shall constantly show a strengthen-ing of their artistic powers and a broadening of their scope. A theatre, moreover, should find a permanent home, a playhouse which shall not only house its productions but which shall serve as a center for a school through which fresh talent may be brought into its ranks and where members of the company can pursue their "extracurricular" train-ing—in voice, in speech, in movement, in new types of acting or production. A theatre should have a fund to help toward the writing of new plays and to give financial assistance to promising playwrights. Theatre should even provide a train-ing ground through classes or discussion groups for younger writers. Much of this has already been done by the Group Theatre, but due to conditions stated none of it could be done completely so that the full value of these altogether practical steps might yield conclusive results.

For all this, of course, money is needed, some sort of subsidy. The word "subsidy" where the theatre is concerned is almost offensive to some ears. Yet a subsidy—whether in the form of a subscription audience, a board of "life members," individual patronage or government aid—has existed for every theatre the world over. The Moscow Art Theatre was subsidized for almost eight years before it became self-supporting. Copeau's famous Théâtre du Vieux Colombier (the only distinguished theatre effort in France since the war) was sustained by a body of "friends"; the Comédie Française is subsidized by the State, as are all the theatres of the Soviet Union. Many of these theatres actually made money (and this is quite feasible in the United States, too), but profitable or not the success of a theatre depends primarily on the kind of work done and the response of the audience. The Moscow Art Theatre was a success before it showed a profit because it was a real Theatre.

Just as the Group Theatre began its work non-professionally (though with professional actors) in 1928 in order to convince a number of people of the value of certain methods of work, and took a whole winter in 1930 to prepare for a group to begin regular work together, so now after the test and experience of the past six years the Group Theatre is going to devote approximately six months to the work of raising a subsidy for a theatre that is no longer a "theory" or an "ideal" but a fact, known and proved. Besides this most important work, the Group will devote much effort not merely to the reading of new plays but to an intensive collaboration with playwrights in the manner adopted with Paul Green, whose *Johnny Johnson* came out of the Group Theatre's suggestion, stimulation and actual assistance.

The Group Theatre's office during this period will be maintained and an executive staff will be in charge of the work that has become imperative for the Group Theatre to fulfill its ever more ambitious program. The enthusiasm which kindled the actors of the Group Theatre at its inception and which made it possible for the Group Theatre to survive success as well as failure has grown into a deep conviction and a firm belief in the kind of organization that for us represents the realest theatre. The actors and directors of the Group Theatre look toward a future of the most creative activity in which the struggle for a theatre shall be converted into a period of mature work in a theatre.

—*NYT*, 17 Jan. '37

FOUNDERS OF THE MODERN THEATRE

Two important books on the theatre have recently appeared. They are Nemirovitch-Dantchenko's *My Life in the Russian Theatre* and Konstantin Stanislavsky's *An Actor Prepares*. The former derives its value from the fact that it throws new light on various phases of the Moscow Art Theatre; the latter has absolute value; it must indeed be accounted one of the major classics of theatrical literature—as a book which presents the clearest and, to date, the most complete summary of the only organic technique of acting in the modern theatre.

Though these books differ in theme, form and purpose, it would be profitable to consider them together, not only because they happen to be the works of the two founders and directors of the Moscow Art Theatre, but because seen in relation to one another the two volumes constitute the most enlightening definition of the contribution made by that great institution, and clarify the central artistic problem of the modern theatre generally. For, ultimately, we shall see that all the developments in the modern theatre since 1898, both in Russia and outside, spring from seeds planted through the theory and example of these two masters, Nemirovitch-Dantchenko and Stanislavsky. In fact we believe it is historically correct to say that what we mean when we speak of "modern theatre" is the theatre that attempts to carry on the two-fold contribution of these men.

In a word, what Nemirovitch-Dantchenko brought to the theatre was a concern with a modern repertoire—plays that would not only serve as adequate vehicles for a company of virtuoso actors but plays with a living content, plays with the same artistic vitality that was to be found in the best novels of the period. At the end of the nineteenth century and during the beginning of the twentieth what interested the educated sensitive public most was character, individual psychology, a true picture of the tragedy of existence as seen through people who struggled with problems of real life. Thus Nemirovitch-Dantchenko brought to the theatre such writers as Chekhov, Tolstoy, Gorky and Andreyev. And though the worldview or fundamental spirit of each was somewhat different from the other, they all had this in common: they tried to give pictures of life mostly in terms of psychological portraits.

The theatre as Nemirovitch-Dantchenko conceived it did not necessarily distinguish between the "philosophies" of the authors they presented. Each author represented a certain truth and each was "objectively" presented. At a later period the Second Moscow Art Theatre (a studio derivative of the main institution) began to insist on the need for a *choice* of "philosophy"; each theatre, like each individual artist, must have a *leit-motif*, a main theme to be varied and developed through all its productions. "A theatre must have a meaning." In the Second Moscow Art Theatre the emphasis was *ethical*; it chose to show always that man was fundamentally good but was warped by various inner and outer circumstances. Thus this particular group chose to present a version of Dickens' *Cricket on the Hearth*, Berger's *Deluge*, Heijerman's *Good Hope*, etc., and gave their productions a corresponding interpretation. With the revolution, the idea of a particular "philosophy" being important to give meaning to the various productions in a theatre was sharpened by immediate social necessity. The revolution was to

be the meaning if not the actual social theme of all plays. This has developed with time to the present artistic goal of "socialist realism," a realism dynamically illuminated and directed by the socialist view of life. Each theatre in the Soviet Union today plays its own variation and gives its own version of the broad concept of "socialist realism."

But the point to be remembered is that while each period and each new theatre group modified or added to Dantchenko's particular esthetic, his basic emphasis on a repertoire important for its value in terms of life-significance, in terms of a communication between people who had something to tell one another (artist and public) has remained. So that, even in the choice of classics, when new plays were lacking or when new truths could be more satisfactorily expressed through old plays—the emphasis was always on the relevance of the play to its contemporary audience, not on the opportunity it might afford a favorite actor to appear in a famous role.

In short, the stress is not only on the *how* but on the *what*—the preoccupation with content (which in the theatre means primarily the nature of the plays chosen)—may be set down as the major contribution of Dantchenko to the modern theatre.

But all of this would have meant comparatively little as far as the *art of the theatre* goes if Dantchenko had not been conscious of the fact that for a play to *live* in the theatre, the matter of its presentation was not a subsidiary problem, but an organic one, or to put it differently, the content of a play in the theatre is inextricably bound up with the form of its presentation on the stage, and that to divorce one from the other is esthetic murder.

For the new plays that Dantchenko wished to present, there had to be a new kind of interpretation, that is, a new acting, a new type of stage setting, even, and not least important, a new kind of organization—in a word, a whole new theatre. The strangely severe (almost "religious") discipline, the abandonment of the "star system" and the whole new backstage code characteristic of the Moscow Art Theatre (especially in its early years) were not an "arty" pose, or even an expression of

"Russian temperament." (They were as new and startling to the Russian actors at that time as they would be to actors anywhere in the world.) They were simply the form that the new theatre had to take in order to express Chekhov and the other new playwrights as Dantchenko felt they should be expressed. After all, *The Seagull* had been performed with a fine company and it had failed miserably at its Petersburg premiere. It had failed because, as Dantchenko later learned, the old acting technique—even when good—did not convey Chekhov intelligibly in terms of the theatre. So for the new plays of Chekhov and the others, a new kind of theatre had to be established, a new technique of acting had to be evolved.

And it was Stanislavsky who through incessant effort, patient observation and constant searching slowly found the new technique. The so-called Stanislavsky system (or method) was not born with the first rehearsal of the Moscow Art Theatre. In fact, no such thing had ever been heard of—not even by Stanislavsky! What was present at the beginning was the aim that Stanislavsky shared with Dantchenko of expressing artistic truth instead of theatrical fiction, the stale bag-of-tricks of the old theatre. Stanislavsky, as we all know by now, did not appreciate Chekhov when he began directing *The Seagull*. Dantchenko interpreted it for him, and Stanislavsky tried to find an honest acting form for what he understood.

When the "system" became a conscious matter with Stanislavsky about a decade after the birth of the Moscow Art Theatre, it was Dantchenko who had to "sell" it to the actors. The actors were undoubtedly persuaded by Dantchenko's eloquence, but in practice resisted the system for a long time. Today Stanislavsky still insists that his best disciples were the younger people who came into the Moscow Art Theatre after the old actors had become famous, those younger actors who formed the studios that became independent theatres later on. It is worthwhile to recall these facts for the benefit of those who imagine that the Stanislavsky system was a "theoretic" concoction

for the benefit of a "theoretic" theatre run by a bunch of Russians who would naturally take to a "theory" of acting like a duck to water! No, the Stanislavsky system met with more scepticism and criticism amongst Russians than will ever greet it here, and with almost as much ignorance!

Stanislavsky had never written any extended work on his system until this book which now appears under the title *An Actor Prepares*. All his teaching was confined to work with student-actors and with players in production. Stanislavsky's previous attempts to set down an explanation of his system were failures, and his piece in the fourteenth edition of the Encyclopedia Britannica which purported to be a condensed exposition of his ideas is well nigh unintelligible even to a person well acquainted with them. We must also remember that the system is not static. While certain pupils were writing bumptious essays to contradict the master's words, the master himself had carried his ideas to a new stage, or had brought a new emphasis to correct an old error. When Michael Chekhov two years ago was asked to speak of the Stanislavsky system, he replied, "I can only tell you that I know of Stanislavsky up to 1926. He must have gone far since then!"

The system is not a "mystery." It is based on simple, understandable laws which merely represent a correct analysis of creative activity as it may be observed in fine artists generally, especially actors. Yet the system, because it is for actors and derives its ultimate validity only through results in acting, is not a matter to be "settled" or even discussed through literary debates or theoretical argument. Hence Stanislavsky's reluctance to write about it; and perhaps it is the great amount of nonsense that has been proffered in the way of explanation or objection that has stimulated him to the writing of the present volume which is comparatively easy, sometimes quaintly naïve, not at all theoretical.

There would be little point in an attempt to synopsize the book. Every word of it must be carefully read and reread (despite, or because of, its simplicity) and for full understanding, a competent teacher or a good director must be watched or worked with. (And every good director makes the system his own, thus transforming it somewhat; no one can direct by the book!) What would be useful however, in line with our main theme, would be to show how some of the leading elements of the system are *directly* connected with the problems of the modern theatre in general, and are not simply minor decisions of a particular "theory" of an individual Russian genius!

Many of the topics and sub-topics of the Stanislavsky book discuss technical matters that every thoughtful and experienced actor is acquainted with under other names. Thus "relaxation" as a prerequisite condition for creative freedom is accepted by almost any good actor; the same is true of "concentration" and the like. But, says Stanislavsky, all these are technical preparations, steps or means leading to the main purpose of the actor's art. And then he speaks of something which in the present translation is called the "super-objective!" The whole system exists for the "super-objective." The actor must find the motivating force—the fundamental wish or desire—that determines the character's actions all through the play. This, of course, must be closely related to the author's main purpose in writing the play or, to put it another way, the actor's super-objective is dependent on the fundamental action and conflict which the play is intended to represent.

For example, Hamlet's "super-objective," according to one director, is his search for the truth. Stanislavsky speaks of the struggle for self-perfection in Tolstoy, etc. The actor, to really create something that fulfills the demands of art, must seek for the "super-objective" of his character and of the play of which his character is a "part." What in plain critical terms does this mean? It means that the Stanislavsky system is primarily concerned with the interpretations of plays in the most literal sense of the word. It means that the whole of the actor's technique to Stanislavsky is mere virtuosity—like sword-swallowing, sleight-of-hand, ventriloquism, etc.—unless it relates to giving a living body, a human breath to the *meaning* of a play.

Think of the praise accorded to many of our stars. Some have "glamor," "vibrancy," "charm," "sex-appeal," "thrilling voices," "presence," "exquisite movement," "electricity," but of how many can you say, "Through this actor I understand this play. This actor conceives the part so and so?" Personally, the present writer acknowledges the natural endowment and attractiveness of many American players, but rarely does he see one whose performance represents a coherent interpretation. Most brilliant performances are nothing more than a series of disjointed impulses—more or less effective—transmitted through a more or less interesting "personality." But of interpretations that are organically continuous, related, purposeful—a significant series of actions which sum up a unified emotional meaning, an identifiable form that is composed like a recognizable and expressive portrait rather than a patchwork—there is very little even in some of our "ten best performances of the year."

We go further and say that though talent cannot be made through this or any other system (Stanislavsky repeats this truism all through his book) we have seen many very talented actors fail the purpose of the playwright or of any purpose, save that of exhibitionism, where less talented actors playing correctly (with a sound technique in the Stanislavsky or *interpretive* sense) have really created characters for us, and in a good ensemble really create a *play*. To sum up, the Stanislavsky system exists not for the purpose of "good acting" in the general sense that any actor who can make us laugh or cry is good, nor in the sense of making every actor "conscious" and "serious," but it exists so that plays can live in the theatre through the flesh and blood of the actor, through his breath, heart-beat, complexion, and mood, rather than simply through the learning and repetition of the authors' lines with the added decoration of the directors' business.

No discussion of the Stanislavsky system in America should be regarded as "safe" that does not sweep away certain abiding misconceptions. (1) The Stanislavsky system does not by itself produce "art"—it is merely a means. When an organization like the Group Theatre (which has been influenced by Stanislavsky among others) does a bad production, it is neither the fault of the system nor is it a question of the incompatibility of "Russian methods" with American temperament. (2) The system is not for Chekhov or tragic realism alone. Vakhtangov's stylized productions, including the gossamer-like fantasy of *Princess Turandot*, were brought into being with the aid of the system, and a gay and very good musical comedy could be produced by a Stanislavsky trained theatre. It is done in Moscow; it could be done in New York City. (3) The system is not for "art" plays only: the impact of a social play is not lessened by dramatic intelligence. (4) The system is not for "emotion," and for "depth of feeling" alone; even frivolity and lightness, melodrama and nonsense plays are dependent on the same technical requirements that are involved in all creative accomplishment.

The system is not only not "art" in itself; it is not even an esthetic. It is only a correct means to a desired end. Where the end is fundamentally different from that of the art of the theatre (as in many Broadway shows), there is no special need for its use; when the esthetic of the artists is radically different from that of Stanislavsky and the Moscow Art Theatre it will necessarily undergo a transformation. Where the artists of a theatre attempt to discard its law entirely there will be a noticeable lack in the results—as many an insurgent director in Russia has discovered. The individual actor can profit from the system in almost any theatre in any land, but the system in its deepest and broadest sense can be practiced only in permanent collectives or groups where the technique is shared in common and where the aims for which the technique is employed are common to all the members of the group.

The modern theatre, we repeat, stems from Dantchenko and Stanislavsky—and from their joint creation, the Moscow Art Theatre, because they represent interchangeably the ideals of content and form, plays and productions, regarded as a unity: social and human vision, made concrete and beautiful through their spontaneous organic embodiment in the complete medium of the theatre—of which the true focus is a group of actors. And for all of us the road to this achievement is paved by Stanislavsky's system and by the form of theatre organization first conceived and made to function in our day by Dantchenko.

—*TA*, Feb. '37

WHY EXPERIMENT? THE DIRECTOR OF THE GROUP THEATRE HERE SETS FORTH A MAJOR POLICY

The theatre, after all, is an art. It is true that conditions of modern life, particularly in America, have made it a business as well. There is no cause to be bitter on this account, but there is also little reason in accepting the fact to deny the theatre's true nature, to forget, in other words, that the theatre's development is not fostered by exclusively economic factors.

Perhaps the first characteristic of any art is that it does not emerge from and certainly cannot grow according to rules conveniently made to the measure of our bank accounts or of our workaday routine of living. There is at the source of all art something sportive, unpredictable, adventurous and forever new.

That is why the artistic innovation of today—provided it springs from spontaneous impulses—becomes the classic of tomorrow. The extravagance of a Beethoven, a Cézanne, a Whitman, a Debussy, an Ibsen become for our time the accepted vocabulary of culture. Each of these artists were, in different degrees, experimenters of their time. Shall there be no experiment in our American theatre because experiment is economically hazardous? To consider the limitations of Broadway commerce as final is to condemn our theatre to death—both as an art and ultimately even as a business.

Of course the word experiment in the theatre is rather forbidding. In the halcyon days before 1929 what used to be called an experimental play was often something noisy, disagreeable, pretentiously dolorous in thirty or forty half-lit scenes. Many a play by an impatient neophyte who had more eagerness than craft was tossed on the stage because money was easy and everything was fun. The results frequently revealed carelessness and impudence—rarely any art, business sense or even good hot showmanship.

Every theatrical production, of course, might be called an experiment. How many surefire "properties" have in performance turned out to be fateful errors. But when I speak of experimental work in the theatre I refer either to productions which are trying to extend the means and meanings of theatrical expression, plays, for example, like Pirandello's *Six Characters in Search of an Author*, Lawson's *Processional*, O'Neill's *The Great God Brown*, or plays that are sincere attempts to put down states of being—either light-hearted or tragic—that are special and limited in appeal, a sort of minority report of perhaps peculiar but none the less real emotions—plays like Susan Glaspell's *The Urge*, e. e. cummings' *him*, Gertrude Stein's *4 Saints in 3 Acts*. Some of these plays prove eventually to be major contributions to the theatre, some may always remain caviar to the general, but nearly all of them in one way or another suggest new modes of thought or new methods of expression.

The difficulty with most such plays, aside from the fact that they rarely "go" at the box office, is that they are decidedly difficult to produce in a manner adequate to their literary originality. It is probably much easier to do well by a play like *Craig's Wife* than by a play like O'Neill's *Lazarus Laughed*. The producer who undertakes a difficult experimental script must be far more severe with himself than the one who produces a more usual script, for the latter may give satisfaction even in a routine production due to its inherent accessibility while the experimental script requires the greatest care, forethought, consummate craftsmanship. (The first production of Chekhov's *Seagull*—a highly experimental script in its time—rendered it wholly unintelligible; it took the new technique of the Moscow Art Theatre to reveal its values.)

In a certain sense it may be said that the producer who undertakes to do an experimental play has no right to fail—artistically. Or, to put it another way, the experimental production to be justified must solve the problem presented by the author's script. To be good the experimental play must emerge in production as a good show.

The Group Theatre was an "experimental" organization from its very start mainly in one regard: that it tried to establish in New York what is one of the basic and most traditional attributes of any true theatre, namely, a permanent company. But from another angle the Group Theatre has always been—and I hope will continue to be—extremely conservative and against "experiment." The Group Theatre has always felt that its productions must attempt to be: (a) true to the spirit of the play's text; (b) intelligible to the audience it hopes to address; (c) technically as complete and as pleasing as possible, (d) and based on an idea or sentiment it considers vital, inspiriting, fresh and truly entertaining. The Group Theatre will always demand of itself that its productions appear not as so many laboratory efforts to improve either its actors or the minds of its audiences, but plays that through their poetry and reality can be sources of real enjoyment.

This is just as true of such plays as Saroyan's *My Heart's in the Highlands* or Irwin Shaw's *Quiet City*, which were frankly planned as "experiments," as of any of the regular productions. The only difference in our approach, let us say, to a play like Odets's *Rocket to the Moon* and to one like *My Heart's in the Highlands* is that in the latter instance we felt it wise to confess at the outset—through the method of presentation—that due to the naïveté or extreme simplicity of Saroyan's form, fewer people might be attracted to it than is usual with the more complex material of the Odets play.

Indeed, it was possible, we thought, that Saroyan's script was not a play at all, and that it would not come alive on the stage. In this sense *My Heart's in the Highlands* is an experiment, an experiment which has happily worked out successfully. In the case of Irwin Shaw's *Quiet City*, a far more ambitious and technically difficult script, we felt that the experiment of our collective work had not yet reached the point at which it was artistically proper to show it to a general audience. We agreed to allow that to be an experiment from which we had learned much but which was not at present complete enough to present as a successful solution of the theatrical problem the script had set for us.

Involved in this type of experimental work, of course, is the opportunity it gives our theatre to introduce new directing talent, a new scene designer, new actors or familiar actors in roles for which they might not ordinarily be cast but to which we believe they are eminently suited. Robert Lewis, a Group actor since our first production, has always had an inclination toward just such material as *Highlands*; Philip Loeb, always sympathetic to the Group's work, has rarely been regarded as a possible candidate for a "serious" part; and almost the whole ensemble of smaller parts in this production were chosen from among the young actors of the modest school the Group Theatre ran last year.

In all these ways the experimental production makes a positive contribution to the growing body of the living theatre.

—*NYT*, 7 May '37

THE
FORTIES

THE DIRECTOR OF 'NIGHT MUSIC' ON MR. ODETS AND THE REVIEWERS

Judgment of plays on Broadway is a very curious thing. It is curious because while there are many who will tell you that a play is "lousy," "swell," "great fun" or, in another tone, that a play "doesn't quite jell," has "good things in it," contains "a fine idea," or still again, that a play is marked by either "strong" or "sordid realism," is "too heavy" or "too slight," very few people will tell you what a play actually is, what they really see in it, what specifically it makes them experience.

When a very candid play like *My Heart's in the Highlands* is produced, we hear that it is terrible because it is meaningless or that it is wonderful because of its meaninglessness. One play is praised for its slick plot, another is damned for its lack of slick plot, and finally a discussion arises whether, after all, all plots aren't just an unnecessary evil. This is, of course, quite natural, but I submit that judgment of plays made in this spirit tells you no more about them than the exclamations "ouch" or "ah" tell you about the nature of the pain or pleasure that provokes them.

In the case of Clifford Odets' *Night Music* we have a play so simple, clear and direct in its form, theme and mood that we ought to assume that every one, save perhaps the professional reviewers, can easily appreciate it. It is possible, no doubt, that professional reviewers are not a race apart and that they represent a state of mind more general than we might suspect. If this is so—which it is difficult for me to believe because I have met very few people who think like professional reviewers outside the circle of those who are addicted to them—then *Night Music* may need a few words of explanation.

Whether or not *Night Music* is the best of the Odets plays I cannot say, but I am sure that among his longer plays it is the most integrated in its

feeling, the most completely conceived. The play stems from the basic sentiment that people nowadays are affected by a sense of insecurity; they are haunted by the fear of impermanence in all their relationships; they are fundamentally homeless, and whether or not they know it they are in search of a home, of something real, secure, dependable in a slippery, shadowy, noisy and nervous world. This search for a home—for security of a truly human sort—takes many forms, including the comic. On the whole, the play tends to present this deeply serious pursuit in a light vein—wistful, tender, pathetic and sometimes in a combination of the delicately charming and farcical.

Odets does not state this as his theme in so many words; he does not have to, since he has made it part of every character, of every scene, almost of every prop. It is not a thesis, it is the "melody" that permeates the play. The central character is made angry and adolescently belligerent by his inability to take hold in society: he carries a suitcase and refers to himself as Suitcase Steve, but his girl friend also carries her suitcase from the stage door of the theatre in which she is very briefly employed. The actress we first see leaving the theatre talks about "the little curtains" she likes to hang in her dressing-room—no doubt to give her momentary stay in the playhouse a semblance of homelikeness and permanence.

The brainless trollop at the Hotel Algiers wants to push her way into respectability; and the Little Man in the park wanders aimlessly, since he has to make a living from something he doesn't believe in, because he can put his dreams of solid dwellings only on paper while life is passing him by without his having left any mark on it. The sailor who is thrown out of the hotel is actually hurt because he is prevented from having the only bit of fun left to him, the man in the phone booth is drunkenly trying to contact someone because he probably is connected with no one; the girl's father is bewildered because he is dragged out of his routine world of accustomed fear into the world of the perpetual jitters where nothing is permanent enough to be taken too seriously. Besides the central character, who is young enough to want to fight this chaos which he does not understand, we see another young boy, who spends his winters getting shelter from the cold to the point where the army alone seems the only possible haven.

Steve's case is not individual, it is typical. "There are thousands of boys like me, tens of thousands," he says. Boys and girls. But it is not just a matter of the plight of youths who lack jobs that is in question. Steve talks of all the characters, including his girl's father, as "shivering in their boots," so that the people who manage to feel "secure" and "right" in this wilderness of uncertainty which is the modern world are graceless and funny people, like Eddie Belows, the girl's fiancé from Philly.

Why does Odets choose for the most part to be gentle and humorous in this portrayal of the world which is precisely the world in new terms of practically all his former plays? What, in short, is the source of Odets' new optimism? All of the Odets people are alive, they have strong desires, love, and above everything, aspiration. "They are not ripe, but they have a future"—because they are struggling, loving, aspiring. It is in this struggle itself—not to be won in a day or in the course of a play—in the acceptance of this struggle without bitterness, malice, or self-pity that Odets finds the possibility of growth, of a world wherein young people like Steve and Fay can make a home. Steve begins to learn this in this play through his girl, the most normal and healthy of all his characters, as Odets is learning it in his own development. And in this "lesson" which Odets appears to construe from the finest "relics of the old days," represented in the play by a man who is lonesome, on the verge of death, yet constantly seeking and thus hopeful, he (Odets) finds the keynote of his own lusty and devout Americanism.

Perhaps I will be accused of putting my own words into Mr. Odets' mouth, but it should be noted that these interpretations are merely all simple paraphrases of the scenes and speeches of the play. To understand this play and to enjoy it—

and I feel that one cannot but enjoy it if one understands it, although it may be enjoyed even without understanding—one has merely to listen to it, to watch it in the simple, direct fashion in which it was created. Then one will see that it is not a banal boy and girl story, the boy and girl here are the focus of a condition that is common to all the characters (there is hardly an "extra!"); it is not essentially a play about New York, but because Odets is mainly a New Yorker, Manhattan here represents the climactic background of Odets' America.

Then is this play I describe so glowingly the "perfect" play, the "great" play, the all-inspired play that every one feels the need to demand from Odets' thirty-three years? I do not know; I do not care now. I know that the play isn't just a haphazard assortment of fine phrases, of the kind of abstractly "brilliant dialogue" that Odets is supposed to write, of individually effective "scenes" or of generally "well-drawn characters," but a unified whole that has a meaning that touches me, delights me, and that even though this play is nearest among Odets' plays to our conception of "pure" entertainment, has real significance for me, a significance related to the whole of Odets' work, and which marks not only a variant on it but a progress. I know, above all, as a playgoer as well as a director, that I prefer many of Odets' faults to many another playwright's virtues, because even what Odets fails to accomplish is more vital than what the others already have accomplished.

When Odets first came upon the scene many people thought it appropriate to measure him favorably or unfavorably in terms of Chekhov (why not Lawson, O'Casey, Gorky or whoever?). Now we hear from some quarters talk of a Saroyan influence, although only yesterday some one was scolding Saroyan for imitating Odets, whose "loose structure" and odd little characters speaking apparent irrelevancies were only a day before yesterday supposed to betray Odets' imitation of Chekhov! Such comparisons serve only to confuse one's vision of what is directly in front of us. On the lowest level they are themselves irrelevant theatrical chit-chat; on another level they are academic twaddle, and, generally speaking, they are stuff and nonsense and of no value to the charming Saroyan, the maturing Odets, to the public health or to the American theatre.

—NYT, 3 Mar. '40

GROUP THEATRE'S FUTURE: THE DIRECTOR PUTS FORWARD A FEW THOUGHTS ON THE PROBLEM OF KEEPING A PERMANENT ORGANIZATION

I have been asked to write an explanation for "the first closing of the Group's offices in ten years." I did not do so, to begin with, because from the standpoint of the "street" the answer must be pretty obvious. And from another standpoint—my own and that of the people directly involved in the Group's work—I sometimes wonder whether we can make anybody really care.

For years I wrote "official" statements saying as clearly as possible that what the Group was attempting to do was being done under conditions which I considered entirely unfavorable, both artistically and economically. Despite the pride I took in what the Group was nevertheless able to achieve, and the remarkable reputation it made for itself, I never lost sight of the fact that all of this was not half of what might and should be done by a theatre with the aims the Group had in mind all the years it worked.

I ought to recall the fact that the Group gave up its headquarters in March, 1933, after the failure of *Big Night*. We had no funds at the time—I refer to most of the Group personnel as well as to the organization—and we couldn't have afforded anything as ambitious as an office! The Group's activities were concentrated in my apartment. I remember that the landlady objected to the frequency with which the elevator carried clusters of intense young people to the top floor where, no doubt, the characteristic shouting could be heard,

to the distress of our innocent neighbors.

I do not mention this for its color effect, but to point out that what is special about the closing of our offices in 1941 is not that it had never happened before, not that it proved the Group had a particular trying situation to face—as a matter of fact the Group people are better off and the general Group status is objectively much stronger than at many another time during the past ten years. What makes our present action significant is a different state of mind, a different attitude to the difficulties before us.

I do not know if I speak for everybody, but I can certainly say this for myself: that while on the one hand I still believe the Group type of organization the kind most conducive to solid, satisfying and truly representative work in the theatre, I also believe that to continue operating our Group on the old basis would be artistically misleading, financially disastrous, personally heart-breaking.

What was the old basis? It was the production of plays as separately backed shows. You had to find a new investor to make possible the preparation of each new package you wanted to put on sale. That may be acceptable enough for the producer who regards every play as "property"—something with which to make money. But though we hoped all our plays would please and thought some of them could make money, our approach was fundamentally different. We produced plays because we thought they were entertaining in the best sense—true expressions of valuable contemporary ideas and personalities. *Golden Boy* made more money than either *Awake and Sing!* or *Rocket to the Moon*, and all of these made more than the famous *Waiting for Lefty*.

But our approach in each case was precisely the same: an enthusiasm for the work of an important writer whose failures (even the artistic failures!) are as interesting and, in a sense, useful as the work of many another playmaker whose stuff might prove sounder as an investment. We put on Sidney Kingsley's *Men in White* because it was the best script available to us at the time; it happened to make money. We put on *My Heart's in the*

Highlands (with our own money taken from the profits of *Golden Boy*, because no one else would risk it on the then unpublicized Saroyan) and "lost" it, as we knew we must. We did not do one to be "practical" and the other to be "idealistic"; we did both because they seemed to fit the program of our organization. This is utterly sound from the standpoint of theatre; from the standpoint of show-business it is crazy.

The basic defect in our activity then was that while we tried to maintain a true theatre policy artistically, we proceeded economically on a show-business basis. Our means and our ends were in fundamental contradiction.

Two questions might be asked: Aside from the matter of the choice in play material, what difference does it make how such a theatre is financed? And if, as I always believed, it is completely wrong to run a theatre such as we wanted on the basis of separate backing for each show, why did we go on doing it? I will answer the second question first. When we began our career we knew it would be presumptuous to ask for any large sum of money for a new and untried organization. To make good our claim that we were an unusually valuable group of theatre people, we produced Paul Green's *House of Connelly*. The response was almost more encouraging than we had expected. But no financing for a theatre was forthcoming at the time. The depression, I was informed, made such hope utopian.

A little later, after we had done more plays, we were told that our hopes for a theatre subsidy were vain because we had had no real box-office success with our productions, though most of them had been admired. With *Men in White* we proved ourselves "commercial." Still, though we found people who were willing to back one or more of our shows, there was no person or group of permanent support. Hard times came again. There was a halt in our schedule. When we returned with *Golden Boy* all our efforts were bent on getting the money to put this one show on, which, despite the fact the play proved a "hit," was far from being an easy

task. The actors couldn't be kept waiting while money was raised for a large long-time project.

Nevertheless, with the great success of this play, both here and in London, we felt sure the time had arrived for us to launch our schedule of production on the secure foundation that it needed. Again people came forward to help. They asked us "What scripts have you?" *Rocket to the Moon* was too sad, *The Gentle People* was too slight, *Quiet City* was too experimental, *My Heart's in the Highlands* was too strange and too short. For none of these plays could we guarantee a picture sale! One man might be willing to gamble on this script, another chose a second, and the "experimental" plays were left to us to "squander" our money on.

Though I insisted that the block financing of a whole series of productions was sounder even from a business standpoint than the betting on single shows, none of these people could think in any such broad terms. You may say they were not real theatre people: they were just benevolent "angels" who suspected that the Group, despite its seriousness, might prove a good thing. But the longer I worked in the field the more I realized that the conception of the theatre as an institution devoted to a continuous activity of artistic endeavor has all but disappeared. It has disappeared not only from the thoughts of the business people who may never have had it, but in almost every other quarter—including a large part of the workers in the theatre, the critics, and in other people who presumably love the stage.

Practically speaking, a theatre does not merely put on shows; it develops playwrights. It does not simply engage actors, it trains them to interpret the work of the playwrights that make the theatre's program. It does not choose to revive a classic because some star thinks it might serve as an appropriate vehicle but because the theatre feels there is some special need or enthusiasm for it. A theatre does new things, like a Saroyan play even when that play is not "commercial," because that play is the first (sometimes perhaps the best) of its kind, and not to do it might mean killing the possibility of further work from a worthwhile talent.

A real theatre makes it its business to work with new people, perhaps encourage playwrights with laboratory productions, sustain them if need be with stipends; it should conduct a tuition-free school not only for actors but for writers, directors, designers. It should maintain the best of its people through their whole creative career—in the period of so-called failure as much as in their more flourishing days. It should work toward establishing a repertory of plays so that the more popular play might help the theatre find an audience for the more difficult one. Such a theatre is just as important when it fails with a *Johnny Johnson* or a *Success Story* as when it succeeds with a *Men in White*.

This is not "theory." Nor is it a plea for plays that don't please. We have it on the testimony of Nemirovitch-Danchenko that Chekhov was not a box-office success until his plays were repeated for years on the basis of the repertory system. We know further that the board of sponsors of the Moscow Art Theatre lost money on that institution for a long time. But it finally did click in the traditional sense—it became rich—and this in Russia before 1917! The kind of theatre I speak of was not exceptional in Germany before 1933, nor even in France. This kind of theatre has been financed in Europe by State and city governments, and also by groups of private individuals in days of prosperity, and even in hard times.

No one thinks of demanding that the Boston Symphony Orchestra, the Philharmonic (or a fine museum) be successful by enriching their various sponsors. Most of these highly popular institutions run at a deficit every year, and no one calls their activity a "flop." Beyond this, imagine what the situation in the musical field would be if no new piece of music could be given a hearing unless the conductor were assured as instantaneous a "hit" as Ravel's *Bolero*!

No doubt, in bringing up the example of these European theatres, or in citing the position of our symphony orchestras, I am going too far afield to make my point. I do not expect for my American theatre all the freedom enjoyed by these great institutions. But, to be completely frank, only such an approach to the theatre really interests me. The theatre as an art still is utterly fascinating, and despite all the other forms of present-day entertainment, I still believe in its capacity to amuse and excite vast audiences, but as a business I think it is pretty small potatoes!

To produce a swell show like *Life with Father* must be a highly pleasurable experience in every respect. To produce this "smash," to spend most of one's time exploiting all its money-drawing potentialities and then to wait a year, two or three, till some other equally bright prospect presents itself is to function correctly in the present set-up of the show business, but it has little to do, from my standpoint, with work in the theatre. You mention *Native Son* and *Watch on the Rhine* as two fine things on this season's stage. I do not doubt that they are. But Orson Welles is only a visitor in the theatre these days—he has found wider scope for his talents elsewhere—and what continuity of activity can he or any one else promise the actors of *Native Son* when it is presented not as part of a permanently functioning institution but as an individual venture in show business?

Herman Shumlin and Lillian Hellman are particularly fortunate (and deservedly), but the history of the profession teaches us that when the time comes for failures like Miss Hellman's *Days to Come* (which may prove no less meritorious than her more lucrative efforts), their work will be made as difficult for them then as it is gratifying today.

No, it is not enough to put on an occasional fine show. For the individual producer to do this may be admirable, even profitable. But for those who want to establish an institutional theatre, to conduct their work with the same skimpy resources as the one-show-at-a-time management, is to compromise in a way that in the end will betray their aims and bring them little gain. Exactly this compromise was forced on the Group for ten years. But it is a compromise that I no longer desire to make.

Is it all hopeless then? Not altogether. First I must assure you that whatever harsh things I say on my own account, I know there will be many willing or anxious to go on even with the kind of compromise of which I speak. And no doubt from such efforts a few victories are won, some good things will emerge from time to time, a bit of progress is always made. Each of these will be an achievement to be treasured, particularly by those who know all the hard work and sacrifice that they must entail.

For myself, I should want to continue in a theatre the stability of which was guaranteed for at least two seasons by some form of subsidy, whether it be public or private, individual or collective. Until a method of raising such a subsidy for our kind of theatre can be evolved, until a real working basis can be created, I would rather our offices remained closed. There can be no institutional product without an institutional foundation. Our past—that past which brought forth what I strongly believe was the most important theatrical accomplishment of the Thirties—has shown what we could do under the worst circumstances. We must now see if a means to work freely according to our own lights can be vouchsafed us.

—*NYT*, 18 May '41

THE PRINCIPLES OF INTERPRETATION

To put it as simply as possible, the function of the stage director is to translate a play text into stage terms: that is, to make the play as written, clear, interesting, enjoyable, by means of living actors, sounds, colors, movement.

Contrary to a widely held assumption, no dramatic text plays itself in the living theatre. The most clearly drawn character from the reader's standpoint may be immediately rendered false, even unintelligible, when improperly embodied by a wrongly directed or wrongly cast actor. The scene that strikes one as highly effective in the

book may become almost pointless if played with either a senseless motivation or in an inappropriate physical environment. In short, the function of the director is not merely "to edit" a theatrical performance, to see that it runs smoothly (in good tempo and with sufficient audibility), but actively to interpret the text in every way so that the play in the theatre is conveyed to the audience.

The job of the stage director is not primarily a technical one, in the sense of a neatly presented bundle that somehow contains the play's meaning, but a job of interpretation. The actors, the sets, the costumes, the music, and whatever else is used to make the production must in relation to one another, and as a whole, constitute the play's meaning. The degree of talent which individual actors may possess is not so vital from the standpoint of stage direction as the use to which these talents are put, the direction they are given, the interpretation, in a word, which their talents serve.

These are commonplaces, no doubt. Yet from reviews of plays it is clear that many theatrical commentators are under the impression that acting, stage setting, lighting, costuming, and stage direction are all separate elements of the theatre, to be considered departmentally, so to speak. The truth is that though the director does not act, he is or should be responsible for the kind of acting we see on the stage; though he does not usually design the sets, he is or should be responsible for the kind of impression the sets make, and this applies to everything else on the stage. The director coordinates the various elements of the production through his interpretation, which is the unifying principle of the whole. The director might be called the author of the stage production.

Let us illustrate this. In Clifford Odets' *Golden Boy,* the actor playing the protagonist, Joe Bonaparte, may either suggest a prizefighter who happens to be gifted with a feeling for music, or he may suggest an artist who happens to be muscular and agile enough to become a fighter. This is a problem of casting. The whole meaning of the play will change, according to the director's choice.

Granted that it will fall on an essentially sensitive boy for whom the fight business is an accident, another problem faces him. The actor may tend to see the boy as an artist. If the boy is interpreted as a conscious artist, a potential "big man," the play's story will become extremely difficult to believe, and less typical than it should be.

The point of the play can be made only if the boy is seen as a growing "kid," a sensitive but not too special youth, in whom, as in most of us, are various possibilities awaiting the social environment to act upon them. Further, the director must determine whether the boy's character is made entirely by the events of the play or by factors that preceded the play's specific action. All these questions must be answered by the director, not simply in statements to the actor, whose temperament will usually prove stronger than his conscious will, but by work with the actor. Without such work (and sometimes even with it, if the director fails renewedly to direct the actor's attention to the problem), the play's meaning may be altered, perhaps to the point of absurdity.

This holds true of every aspect of production. In Clifford Odets' *Paradise Lost,* we have a play that is both realistic and poetic. Almost naturalistic scenes are meant to convey an import and a feeling beyond the moment, and even beyond the concrete situation. It is necessary to make the audience sense this quality of the play almost immediately, for if it is missed, the play must produce a confused impression—the spectator does not know "how to take it." In this instance, the setting becomes a crucial matter. In the Group Theatre production the director failed to solve this problem. Note, I say the director failed, not the scene-designer. For it was not a matter of a "handsome set" or a realistically convincing one, or a plastically well-designed one, but a matter of style, of the feeling about the play as a whole which the set had to transmit to the audience with the rise of the curtain. The director had not been sufficiently aware of this problem when he undertook the production, and consequently had not stated it definitely enough to the scene-designer, so that it was never resolved for the audience.

Even a costume may have an interpretative significance for which the director, not the costume designer, must ultimately take the responsibility. In the Theatre Guild's production of Maxwell Anderson's *Mary of Scotland,* the costume worn by Elizabeth was far more ornate and splendid than anything worn by Mary. This was in direct contradiction to the intent of the play which was, in part, a contrast between Elizabeth's rigid, ascetic, "executive" nature, and the warm womanliness and estheticism of her rival, Mary. Be it noted again that the fact that the costume for Elizabeth was, abstractly speaking, beautiful, does not absolve the director from the blame of interpretative error or oversight.

We might go on to cite instances of excellent acting that was beside the point of a play, much applauded settings that damaged the effect of entire scenes played within them, direction that has been praised for painstaking care and precision which was actually symptomatic of the emptiness in the director's conception of a play. They would serve to re-emphasize our basic thesis that every attribute of a director's technique is not something added to the pleasure of a theatrical production ("good script, fine acting, lovely sets, *plus* expert direction") but an instrument to make every element of the theatre bring forth the play's essence, its reason for being, its fundamental value as a work of art.

With this approach in mind, we may proceed to a closer examination of the technique of interpretation seen from the stage director's standpoint. It goes without saying that no hard and fast rule can be set down for all directors. The director is not a mechanic but an artist, and there can be no binding rules for creative work. Every director is a new personality, and his emphasis will vary according to his nature. There are directors for whom the spoken word counts most, others are particularly visual-minded; some stress the acting in terms of character, others movement in terms of actors, and so on. But there are problems in stage direction that confront practically all who work at it, and though their solution will depend on the individual, a recognition and definition of these problems may prove valuable as a starting point.

The director reads the script. In fact, he reads it several times. Even in this first step there are different types of directors. Some find it virtually useless to go beyond this point without preparing in their minds, and even putting on paper, a kind of outline of their future work. Others rely more on their intuitive reaction to what happens at rehearsal, and in the course of rehearsal develop their ideas for the play, determine the particular direction they wish the scenes and characterizations to follow. Max Reinhardt has his famous *Regiebuch* (literally, direction book), in which his entire production—line for line, scene for scene, detail after detail—is worked out before the first rehearsal. But I have heard Stanislavsky say that such preliminary planning is characteristic of the young—the rather inexperienced—director! Be that as it may, it is more useful, for purposes of exposition, to say that the director does work out a general conception of the production in advance of rehearsal, whether he commits his thoughts to writing or not. Personally, the author of the present article never feels confident that he is really clear in his thought unless he has stated it for himself in written notes. Naturally, the most telling work will not be done till rehearsal, in which everything previously conceived is truly tested.

When the director has reread his script, he crystallizes in himself a general sense of the play. This first sense of the play may not take the form of "a production idea"—which is a specific scheme for the working out of the production. The sense of the play is not an intellectual perception of the play's theme—this is a critical function which every intelligent reader will arrive at for himself. It is a personal image or feeling peculiar to the director. My first reaction to Clifford Odets' *Awake and Sing!* was a sense of chaos. This chaos could be described in terms of conflicting colors laid on "cubistically" in uneven patches one over the other, or of incongruous combinations of objects, of voices in cacophonous counterpoint. While this chaos, like all disorder, had its comic side, it was, in this instance, essentially melancholy.

When the director arrives at his sense of the play, he will ask himself (a) "What features of the play have induced it?" (b) "What does it mean?" (c) "Why is it affecting or important?"

When he has answered some of these questions for himself, he will begin to note the methods the playwright has used to produce this effect on him. He will begin to examine the play's details; and he will decide which ought to be emphasized or minimized, according to a scale of values that he will evolve for himself.

From this point, he will begin to think of what *other elements,* besides those actually discovered in the playscript itself, *might be added* to heighten and vary his sense of the play. He begins, in other words, to think of the concrete means by which the play may be grasped by the audience. For example, in *Awake and Sing!,* the feeling of disorder and melancholy was heightened by making the settings, which originally called for a separate living room and a separate dining room, into one scene, so that we might see the whole apartment with its disparate and simultaneous activities at one time. What was typical of such households? For me, to mention one item, a large and prominently placed calendar always gave rise to a special feeling of almost comic gloominess; particularly when these calendars were decorated, as so often happens, with some picture of sentimental luxury.

None of these details were part of the original playscript. They suggested themselves, in reading, and when the playwright was told about them, he included them in the play, wrote new speeches around them, and added such other details as the alarm clock about which Bessie says "The clock goes; and Bessie goes, etc." Here we might make a digression to speak about the director's function relative to his possible contribution in the very making of the written play itself. But we cannot dwell on this here, since the director's direct collaboration in the dramatist's work is possible only in organizations that deal with new plays. Strictly speaking, moreover, the job of reworking or collaborating on a script is not the work of a stage-director, although it may be helpful to point out that here, too, the director worthy of the name may have a definite contribution to make.

The director works from the general sense of the play which, at first, may be as vague as you please, to specific details that will embody it in stage terms. So-called "pieces of business," bits of activity carried out by the players in connection with their lines or in silent moments, may come to mind. The introduction of certain types of sound—music or "natural" sounds like the animal noises in *Of Mice and Men;* physical, visual equivalents for the spirit of the whole play, like the bare platforms in *Golden Boy,* suggestive of the fight ring—all these accumulate in the director's consciousness.

All of this finally resolves itself into one question the director must ask himself: What is the *basic action of the play?* What is the play about from the standpoint of the characters' principal conflict? Every plot has a superficial resemblance to innumerable others. To give his play its specific meaning, the director must decide what fundamental desire does the plot of his play symbolize, what deep struggle gives it shape and direction. What is the play's *core?* For Gordon Craig, *Hamlet* is a story of a man's search for the truth. Saroyan's *My Heart's in the Highlands,* to its New York director, was the story of people eager to give things to one another—lovers all, in a sense. For me, Odets' *Night Music* had to do with the search for a home.

Whether these formulations are correct or not, the point is that the director's most important task at first is to find the basic line of the play. I call it *the spine* of the play because my first teacher in this field, Richard Boleslavsky, used the word. Stanislavsky calls it the *super problem.* The name does not matter, the exact phrasing may not be important, the definite intellectual consciousness

need not exist. But in one way or another, the director must be inspired in his actual stage "effects" by the "spine" which he has chosen for the play. It is the basis of the whole production.

When the director has become sufficiently familiar with the play to have found its main line (or "spine"), his next step, spontaneously, will be to find *the main line (or "spine") for each of the play's characters.* How do they relate to the play's main line? If the main line of *Night Music* is "the search for a home," what does the girl do about it? What's the detective in that play got to do with it? How do the minor characters typify the main line, in what way do they contribute? Do they make it develop, do they obscure it? Perhaps they are all connected with it, perhaps each is a subtle variation of the principal theme, and from the variations arise differences of mood, of color, of characterization. In any case, it is reasonable to suppose that no character of a play can be properly understood unless the play as a whole is understood. And we may presume that if the director wishes to help the actor to a proper interpretation of his role, he must have discovered the active center of the play as a whole, and the *exact position of the actor's part in relation to the whole.*

In other words, the director, at this point, must lay out his plan for the characters as he wishes the actors to convey them. His first job, as we shall see later, is not to say, this character stammers, that character is jumpy, the other character is soft-hearted, but to find the main line—"the spine"—the *basic motivation* which explains the entire behavior of each character throughout the play. Many characters will be angry, happy, hurt, jubilant, etc., in the course of the play. But what the director must find out, and make the actor understand, is how these moods are related to some permanent desire that possesses the character throughout the play and justifies his or her shifting moods and very often contradictory actions.

In *Awake and Sing!,* it is not very important for the director to inform the actress who is playing the mother, Mrs. Berger, that she is frequently strident (the actress can't miss it!); it is essential that she know that the character constantly wants "to take care of everything"—and that this desire is the source of all her qualities, positive and negative. The actor who plays her son Ralph in the same play need not concern himself with giving the effect of the "young idealist." He must *comprehend his basic action* in the play, which is "to get away from his environment." Since drama is action, it is best that these basic motivations or spines be stated in the form of a *verb: the desire is an action; the things it prompts the character to do are further actions.*

When the director is sure of the interpretation he wishes to give the play and the character line he wishes his actors to follow, he is almost ready to begin rehearsals. He may deem it advisable, indeed it is almost inevitable, to seek for the general scenic world in which he finds it fitting for the drama of his imagining to be played. If there is a great deal of time for the rehearsal period, the director may go ahead with the actors before he has the scenic scheme definitely worked out; and the scene-designer may well profit by attending the rehearsals to acquaint himself with the play as it actually lives in the movement of the actors. This privilege, however, is rarely granted the designer, who is often called upon to make his plans without much knowledge of the production as a whole.

The director's sense of the play will have dictated something of the general visual mood of the play. He will have at least an abstract picture of the kind of setting the action needs. I do not refer to the properties: furniture, objects to be handled, etc. (these are usually indicated by the playwright), but to the style of treatment required. For example, what shall the scale of the sets be? The scale is not determined primarily by the realistic imitation of actual places designated, but by the inherent nature of the play. In Paul Green's *Johnny Johnson,* for example, the places represented would, in life, be of imposing dimensions, but the play demands small sets for the quality of intimacy which is not only the play's style but even part of its meaning. Mechanical

considerations may also have artistic significance. A many-scened play like *My Heart's in the Highlands* would be utterly ruined if any attempt to make it naturalistically convincing or to change from one place to another by obvious technical means (like a revolving stage, etc.) were planned.

The director should ask himself, in this regard, what he wants to *see* on the stage to give the play its proper life. In Odets' *Rocket to the Moon,* the script calls for a dentist's waiting-room. Shall we therefore build a shabby little room like so many we have seen? Will such a room convey the loneliness, the feeling of a dark inner sanctum, that the play's spine—"the search for love"—requires? Will not the fussiness, the badly assorted detail common to such a place, actually take away from the nature of the play, which has very little to do with a dentist's work as such? There were, consequently, comparatively few properties on the stage for *Rocket to the Moon.* On the other hand, *Awake and Sing!,* where the discordant environment was part of the story, required a clutter of small properties.

One more word ought to be added here, not only for its own sake, but for the light it may throw on the director's relation to all his co-workers. The director does not usually design the scenery. But neither does the director leave this work entirely in the hands of the designer, as if it did not concern him. The scenic aspect of the production is as much the director's province as the acting. The director describes his requirements, he states the scenic problem of the play, he gives the designer an artistic, as well as a technical, objective to aim at. The designer does not take the director's guidance as a blueprint order, he does not simply comply to a demand from "above"; he makes the director's interpretation of his needs a creative springboard for himself, adding something to what the director has called for that only he, with his special gifts, can supply.

The first step, after these possibly theoretical needs are satisfied, is to cast the play. In the commercial theatre, casting is often done by a producer with little thought of the director. Often, too, a director begins his casting with very little of the preliminary thought suggested in the foregoing analysis. In either case, the results are likely to be far from satisfactory. For in casting a play the director makes the first moves toward concrete embodiment of his idea. Casting is a step in interpretation. It is silly, as frequently happens, to choose an actor, and then think of what the part ought to be. In casting for the non-professional theatre, the limitations of available material pose a special problem that has to be surmounted as well as possible.

The importance of casting is widely acknowledged, but as a subject for study it is most lamentably neglected. Casting should be done with an eye to ensemble; that is, with a feeling for the relation of one part to another. You cannot cast your "leading man," for example, without giving thought to who will be your "leading lady." Not only the physical type will count, but the quality of your actors' personality. The problem of casting in *Golden Boy* has already been cited. If Lorna Moon, the "leading lady" in that play, is just a tough girl, "a tramp from Newark," as she describes herself, her relation to the boy becomes meaningless. She is definitely a "spiritual" creature. If the boy is cast to convince the audience that he is a prizefighter, to make the girl see in him a person new to her environment is to belie her whole action. The matter of age, too, is relative. In the New York production of *Men in White,* the actor who played Dr. Hochberg, a man of sixty, did not strike the audience as a young man in make-up (which he was), because the entire cast was related to him by a properly balanced age-scale!

Yet casting for physical type is not entirely to be sneered at. In certain short parts where a quick impression is to be made, to have a convincing physical type—particularly if it is combined with a correspondingly apposite inner quality—is to make the director's task that much simpler, to say the least. Also, in certain plays—plays of actions, surface plays, melodramas, light comedies or farces—correct physical types are more important than in plays of deep feeling, or in plays in which

the moral nature of a whole milieu is delineated. If there is a general rule, I should say it is to cast for basic acting ability and the actor's capacity to capture the particular quality that is most essential to the character he is to portray, and to the play itself.

The director is ready for rehearsal. The thoroughness of the work done at rehearsal depends, to some extent, on the length of time available. In the Russian theatre today, the average rehearsal time extends over a period of three months. On Broadway three to four weeks is practically the limit. To my mind, four weeks means hurry. Wherever practical, more time should be taken. There are certain results that come only with time and care.

If the actors are not already familiar with the play, it should be read to them by whoever can read it most simply and smoothly. This is wiser than having the actors read the play for the first time with parts in hand, for the actor tends to concentrate immediately on his own part, and it is valuable for the actor first to seize the play as a whole. At the first few readings of the play by the actors, they ought to be warned not to try to give a performance—that is, a sense of a complete characterization. This is contrary to the routine of Broadway, where the actor most frequently fears that he will lose his job if he does not "give out" at first sight of his role. If the director presses the actor to an immediate "performance," the actor will of necessity employ the easiest indications associated with "the type of character" he is to play: growling for bad men, whinnying for age, breathiness for lovers, etc., etc. The actor is quick to form "habits" in his work, and a first reading that encourages a set way of playing a part is likely to keep the actor trapped in his first, and often conventional, pattern. The actors, to begin with, should be asked to *talk* their parts as themselves, simply—keeping the lines free of any big emotions or effects, using them as conversation between themselves and their partners.

First rehearsals are not so much for the director as for the actors themselves. At these first rehearsals the actors acquaint themselves with the play, its situations, style, and mood. Encouraged by the director's suggestions—which are best made after, not during, the readings—the actors will soon find themselves ready to begin acting in the accepted sense. For just as the director has had to prepare himself by studying the play, so the actor, if he is to be what he should be, will take inspiration from the play's text as he reads and rereads it with his fellow actors.

After a few such readings, the director will become aware of the paths the various actors are inclined to follow, sometimes unconsciously. He will notice that one actor overemphasizes the kindness that is in his role (perhaps he falls in love with this quality and exaggerates it), that another actor is unnecessarily timid and is repressing himself, that a third sees the most obvious side of his part and not the original quality it may have or may be given. From such observation, the director will learn what it is he must stress with each actor, for there is little point in the director's talking too much about qualities that come naturally and correctly to the actor.

After the early readings the director should pause to speak to the actors about the play. He might tell them something of his own feeling about it—if for no other reason than to fill them with enthusiasm. He might point out the theatrical possibilities that the actors may have overlooked, interpret the play in some striking vein, fire the actor with new ambition and love for the task he is called on to perform. A director should strive to make the production of a play a joyful experience for the actors engaged in it. There are many hardened showmen who will tell you that all this is sheer artiness, a waste of breath and time. There are directors—some of them extremely talented—who, having worked out all the movement of the play, will put the actors "through their paces" from the first day. No nonsense and abstract gab for them! Certainly there is something to be said for this method. But for any play beyond the run-of-the-mill, this purely technical approach usually results in acting that is lacking in spontaneity and real verve. A performance that is allowed to

develop normally, that is, without the push to results within five days (or five minutes!), tends to create a freedom for the actor that, if it does nothing else, eases audiences with a sense that they are watching a human being rather than a puppet. This ease—that the audience may not be sufficiently conscious of to mention—makes it more receptive to the play as an artistic reality rather than as a device.

After the director's talk the play may be read again, and the director now might interrupt more frequently, to point out specifically how his general remarks apply to this or that moment of the play. Again the director may profitably take time to stop and give an analysis of the acting parts, at least in their salient features. It is of immense value for an actor to know "the spine" of his part, its "through-line?" Much time is spent at rehearsals worrying the actor about this and that attribute, when an understanding of the character's essential *want* throughout the play would clarify much that puzzles the actor in the minor details.

At all times, in the first stages of rehearsal, the director should preserve a relaxed atmosphere. He must communicate a feeling of confidence that from the growing understanding between the company and himself, true characterizations will be born. The actor must not be put on trial. The director will do well to remember that what he is about to create are not characters wrought entirely out of his own imagination or probing of the author's text, but characters that have to include the actors themselves as integral parts of the whole creation. Only in this way can the actor fulfill his function in the theatre, which is not merely to illustrate a text, but to give it a living body, so that the dramatist's word becomes flesh in the actor's person.

In the procedure just described, there exists, no doubt, the danger of too much talk. When the director suspects that his discussions produce a kind of literary apathy or stimulate a debating-society atmosphere, he will ask the actor *to show* rather than to say. Characteristics that are only spoken about may be enacted. For example, the player in *Awake and Sing!* who was cast in the part of Jacob was asked to recount some memory from his boyhood days while he actually sewed a button on his coat. With this activity, a kind of homely repose came into the actor's demeanor. The director pointed out the relation of this mood to the character to be developed. Though there was no sewing called for by the text, and this was done as a kind of exercise to make clear in action what might have been vague in explanation, the sewing was later used as a piece of business in the production of the play.

After the reading, discussions, and general preparation by such small *character improvisations* as the one just described, the director will notice that the actors are impatient to move, to do, "to get on their feet," in a word, to act! The moment for the second stage of rehearsal has arrived.

In the early years of the Group Theatre's work, when circumstances were more favorable for longer rehearsal periods, a week or two was devoted to improvisations. The commercial theatre is unfamiliar with this method, and scornful of it.

What are these improvisations? There are two kinds that are most useful for production. The first is to *make the actors improvise situations similar but not identical to those to be found in the play.* For example, the character Feinschreiber in *Awake and Sing!* has a scene where he rushes to his "in-laws" to demand some explanation for his wife's violent behavior. He is desperately nervous. He is almost afraid to repeat what his wife has revealed to him. A scene may be improvised in which the actor playing Feinschreiber is asked to imagine that on some previous occasion Feinschreiber, exasperated with his wife, struck her, something he has never in his life done before; that his wife shut him out of the house, and that he goes to his mother-in-law for advice and help. Such a situation calls for the same fundamental actions as the scene in the play. But because the scene is improvised, the actor cannot simply repeat memorized lines; he is forced to visualize the antecedent circumstances

for himself, and he cannot anticipate the reactions of his partner (the actress playing his mother-in-law is not previously informed of the situation that Feinschreiber is going to play). He is compelled by the improvisation to watch, to listen, to react in character—and all the false steps in the logic of his thinking in the part are readily exposed. The same is true for his partner in the scene. There is no refuge in the playwright's written words behind which actors often mask their failure to grasp the true nature of their roles.

The second type of improvisation is based on the *doing of the actual scenes in the play with the actors using their own words*—substituting their own speech before they have committed the play's lines to memory. As such improvisations go on, the actor comes progressively closer to the play's text, till he is finally speaking the author's lines without ever having been aware of learning them at all. The advantage of this method, I repeat, is that it teaches the actor to listen to what is actually said instead of waiting mechanically for a cue, and, generally speaking, to involve him in the play as a living texture of action and reaction. In the ordinary routine of rehearsal, much time that could be devoted to working with the actor on his part is taken up by the sheer physical effort of learning lines and coordinating them with the movements. In improvisation the actor's movements spring organically from his impulses, and since the "room" he improvises in can correspond to the ground plan of the set to be used in the production of the play, the staging can be built up on the basis of natural reactions to the play's inner demands. It would be pointless at this time to argue that all this is "theory," and unpractical. This method was used in such widely admired productions as *The House of Connelly, Men in White,* and *Awake and Sing!*

Whether this or the more usual methods of staging are used, certain fundamental matters demand our attention. One of the greatest faults in the preparation of most productions is the time spent over minor details of readings, exits, entrances, for which the director feels called upon to interrupt the rehearsal so that they may be repeated till they are "right." In this process the sense of the whole may easily be lost, the actor may be left dangling over the sharp edge of innumerable small "points"; the sense of the part can be diluted by a confusion of tiny technical problems that impede the actor's spirit from reaching its main objective. Technical details, the accurate timing of crosses, the exact emphases and "build" in speeches, and so forth, should be left for the last, rather than struggled with at the beginning. Most vital is to give the individual actor and the company generally, a sense of the shape and form of each scene and each act. This can be done if the director will disclose the real actions of each scene: the *"beats"* of the play.

A play is not constructed on lines of dialogue. A play is fundamentally a series of actions. A character enters a room: what is essential to know is not what he says—"howdy" or "good morning"— but what he *wants,* what made him enter the room and what he intends to do to get what he wants. His want may be immediately satisfied, or a contrary (someone else's) want may balk him. In this case we have a small drama, a *scene. It* is imperative for the actor to know *what the character is trying to achieve at each moment of the play.* These are the basic actions of the play. As each of these actions is achieved or, owing to conflicting currents in the scene, is transformed into a new action, "the beat" changes for the actor. The line of these "beats"—their interconnection, logic, movement—shapes the actor's part: gives it a beginning, middle, and end; gives the part meaning, movement, climax.

For example, the opening lines of *Awake and Sing!* are:

> Ralph: Where's advancement down the place? Work like crazy! Think they see it? You'd drop dead first.
> Myron: Never mind, son, merit never goes unrewarded. Teddy Roosevelt used to say—

> Hennie: It rewarded you—thirty years a haberdashery clerk!
> Ralph: All I want's a chance to get to first base!
> Hennie: That's all?
> Ralph: Stuck down in that joint on Fourth Avenue—a stock clerk in a silk house! Just look at Eddie. I'm as good as he is—pulling in two-fifty a week for 48 minutes a day. A headliner, his name in all the papers.
> Jacob: That's what you want, Ralphie? Your name in the paper?
> Ralph: I wanna make up my own mind about things...be something! Didn't I want to take up tap dancing too?
> Bessie: So take lessons. Who stopped you, etc., etc.

During this conversation everyone is finishing dinner, but eating is only an incidental activity of the scene, not its main action. Ralph is calling attention to his problem; his action here is "to demand his due." This is directly related to the spine of his part which is "to get away" from his environment. Myron's action is "to quiet him," also closely related to the spine of his part which is "to make things good." Hennie's action here is "to provoke everybody," for she is in trouble herself and frustrated in her desire "to wrest joy from life," which is the spine of her part. Jacob's action is "to make Ralph understand something" for the spine of his part is "to find the path for himself and others." Finally, Bessie's action is "to stop the argument," for she has to deal practically with the whole complex of the household's problems. The actions come to a climax with Ralph's leaving the table. The "beat" for him is over. His next beat is probably "to brood about his problem"—it is a *silent beat:* he has no lines. For the others the beat changes too with Myron's line "This morning the sink was full of ants...."

The analysis of the play's beats, the characters' actions, can and should be made before the actual staging of the play is begun. The actors derive a basic direction from such an analysis and from the notation of the beats in their part-books, a guiding line that is the foundation for their entire work in the play. Without such groundwork, we may get a display of "general emotion" but not the meaning of the play. When the actors have understood their actions, it will be the director's job to help the actor play them truly, fully, interestingly. The actor's talent becomes evident in the manner in which he carries out these actions. But talent or not, they must be clearly presented for the play to become an intelligible, coherent whole.

It must be plain from everything that has already been said that, in our view, the function of the director is not merely to coordinate all the elements of the production so that the producer can "get the show on," but to work closely, that is, creatively, with all the people who make the production. This means, above all, the actors, whose work is the crux of the entire theatre phenomenon.

What are the laws, if any, about working with the actor? One cannot do justice to this subject without entering into a study of the technique of acting, something beyond our present scope. It is a subject, however, with which the director, to fulfill his function, must be intimately acquainted. From the directorial standpoint this subject may be approached as a matter of certain rehearsal problems. For example, the question is often asked "Should the director work by means of *explanation* or by *demonstration*? Should he tell the actor or should he show what he wants?" Another question that is frequently put is "At what moment should the business of the play be set?" Or again, "Is it necessary for the director to invent all the stage business? How much should be left to the actor?"

To begin with, it ought to be stated as a fact that very few directors are qualified by talent to demonstrate the acting of a scene to a *good* actor. Unfortunately, this is not known to many directors, who are either bad actors or not actors at all. Their demonstrations are rarely convincing to an actor, sometimes not even clear. Moreover, when a director is particularly graphic, as was the case with such directors as Reinhardt or Meyerhold, the brilliance of his demonstrations may paralyze the actor rather than help him, since he may feel that at best his repetition of the director's action will prove to be merely a pale copy. For the actor with temperament, moreover, it is far more exciting to create than to imitate.

The director, generally speaking, should strive to *stimulate the actor* to the desired type of action rather than perform for the actor's observation. The director should suggest, evoke, create an atmosphere around the actor that will draw out and inspire the sought-for result. By asking questions, by stirring the actor's imagination, by indicating the proper channels for the actor's thought, the director can induce a creative response. Above all, the director must not force emotion from the actor, he must not push the actor to an effort that the actor is not prepared in his thought or spirit to make. The director must even prevent the actor from giving too much before the actor has taken the necessary steps of listening, understanding, realizing the situations in which he finds himself.

When the director, despite all this, finds it most expedient to demonstrate his meaning directly, it is best for him to say "This is *the kind of thing* I mean," rather than "Do this." The good director does not feel that *he* is giving the performance which unfortunately has to be seen through the persons of a number of hired mummers. The director must know and make the actors feel that he is a medium through which the actors come to realize their own and the play's possibilities, so that they can enact it as no others could. The good director will remember that there comes a time in rehearsal when the actor will be closer to his part than anyone else, and that at that moment the actor must be the part's and his own master. If the director fails in this, no matter how hard he has worked, no matter how brilliantly he has done his job in a general sense, his production will be only half alive.

In any event, if demonstration is the only way in which a director seems to be able to communicate his meaning, he should see to it that the actor makes what has been demonstrated his own. If this does not happen, the director had better find another action more compatible with the actor's nature or abilities to convey the same idea. For "business" must not be imposed on an actor; it *must be made to come from the actor.* An actor carrying out a series of gestures and actions foreign to him will not only be "unhappy," but will remain emotionally static to the point where nothing he does can really stir the audience.

The business of the play is often invented by the director before rehearsals begin. As I have mentioned, some directors begin by giving all the business for the play from the first days of rehearsal. Undoubtedly good results have been known to come with such procedure—especially if the director knows his actors well, and the actors themselves are facile craftsmen; but on the whole, this is not to be recommended. Certain pieces of business are so integral to the director's vision of the play that they may be presented as much a part of the script as an entrance or a plot move. For example, in *Awake and Sing!* Jacob crawls under the table to pick up pieces of a broken plate while he speaks of the shattered state of the world. Other pieces of business may be introduced when the actor has become easy in his part, that is, when he understands its fundamentals. Example: In *Paradise Lost* the young musician Felix comes to visit his pianist fiancée, Pearl. He is wearing glasses. He waits for her to appear. She comes in, and seeing him, stops. He approaches her, removes his glasses. She removes hers. They kiss.

Other bits of business suggest themselves to the director as he watches rehearsals. Often these are the best, as they generally arise from the director's growing knowledge of his actors. The actors themselves ought to be watched for *impulses which arise spontaneously* within them; and these need the director's encouragement to develop them as regular pieces of business in the play's action. The action or *business that springs from the actor's work on the part*—through what is called "inspiration"—is perhaps the most useful of all, for it is generally the freshest, the most effortless. Directors will do well to avoid forcing business on an actor who finds difficulty in performing it. The director of the famous Vakhtangov Theatre in Moscow has written, "The most appalling of all faults in a director is the pedantic insistence upon a particular inflection and a particular movement in a particular part of a role." The present writer is wholly in accord with this view.

Where shall the actor be placed? How should he be moved on the stage? Certain directors are capable of working out exactly all the movements before the first rehearsal. This may have its advantages, but the ability to do this satisfactorily is no sign of genius in a director. Meyerhold, who is technically perhaps the most facile director in the world, changes his staging frequently before "setting it." Generally speaking, only the big moments, the dramatic high spots of each scene, have to be considered first. In the transitional moments, the actors may move where the logic of the scene and the drive of their impulses take them. Adjustments for the continuity and smoothness of the whole are not difficult to make.

Textbooks have been written to teach that certain sections of the stage are ideal for certain types of scenes. The important character must always occupy the *center of the stage,* for example; on the other hand, I know one director who has a phobia about stage center, and will strenuously prevent actors from using it, as he deems it too conventional to play scenes in that position! Love scenes must be placed right center, expository scenes left center, and so forth. All this, though based on "experience" and a certain amount of observation, is nonsense. Where scenes should be placed will depend on the type of setting, the furniture and other properties, and above all on the director's vision of the scene; that is, on his *interpretation of the effect* he wishes to produce, what he wants the audience to see, and in what manner. This must be judged by each director for himself. The center of the stage is determined not so much by geometrical measurements as by the *placement of objects or characters in relation to one another and to the audience.* The actor and the acting requirements of the scene usually may be taken as the best starting point for the judgment of proper placing of the actor on the stage.

What about such matters as tempo and rhythm? Critics are particularly aware of "direction" as it manifests itself in "pace." The director need give little thought to these matters independently of the whole context of a play. The reason critics rarely fail to mention "pace" when they discuss direction is that they know so little about the nature of direction, thinking of it mostly in terms of obvious mechanics. Though directors, under pressure, may have recourse to a forced speeding of pace, actually the correct pace for every play must depend on a correct playing of the scene, which is a question of a correct interpretation of the acting problem at each moment and the correct evaluation of each scene in its relation to the whole play.

Every scene has its own main point, its own climax. The relative importance of each scene will depend, naturally, on the line of the play as a whole. A feeling for variety of color, of sound, of movement, aside from the basic movement of the play itself, is to be taken for granted in even the least expert craftsman. There are directors known for the "speed" of their productions. Generally this is because their productions have little more to recommend them. Other directors are held to be "slow." This may mean only that problems, aside from "pace," have not been solved. Look to the heart of the matter, not to the clock!

There are times at rehearsal when director and actor seem about to reach an impasse with each other. The director is impatient with the actor, the actor "disagrees" with the director. This is not only a frequent occurrence; it is often held to be unavoidable, and there are some who even look forward to it, as if the theatre were a god-sent medium for hysteria and bad temper. I believe these unfortunate moments in rehearsal result largely from a misconception on the part of both directors and actors of their function in relation to one another, and therefore in relation to the whole production. Rehearsals are conceived as a kind of contest between director and actor. It is mostly in the hands of the director to show that he is there to help the actor. The actor is to some extent the director's instrument, but the director if he truly understands the theatre will realize that this instrument must itself be a creative person if the production is to come alive. If the director acts as a guide, an inspiration, and not as a self-sufficient entity, the actor will usually become his willing and eager follower. The actor's being must be respected for the director truly to triumph. It may be said to be a rule of the theatre that the actor will cling to anything or anyone who can help him. The director must be able to help.

When misunderstandings or disagreements do arise, the director will be wise to listen patiently, to seek out the cause of the actor's discomfort. Often the actor is right. Sometimes the actor is mistaken. If explanations will not do, the actor should be given the opportunity "to try" what he prefers to do. If the director is right, it will not be very difficult to convince the actor of this if the actor has had an opportunity "to do it his way." The director must be resourceful. It is dangerous for a director to win a forced battle. If he fails to convince an actor through one means, he must try to achieve his end not by a brutal reiteration of his point but by a fresh approach. He should find two or three different paths to the same point. If one piece of business will not do because of the actor's reluctance to perform it—for whatever reason!—the director should invent several new pieces of business of similar intention. A good maxim to remember is: the director is responsible for *the what,* the actor for *the how.*

If rehearsals are laboriously following one path—let us say the staging has occupied a good deal of the company's time—it is frequently useful to stop and return to a reading or to a "conference" around a table, to new discussion. *The actor's impulses must constantly be led with fresh nourish-*

ment. If there is time, it is even advisable for the director to revitalize himself by absenting himself from rehearsal for a day or two—or at least several hours! Or even by resting the entire company.

It is essential too that every act be run through a good many times without interruption from the director. Actors gain understanding and make progress very often by the sheer doing of their jobs. They themselves learn to feel when they are being true; they gradually sense the lack in their performance by becoming acquainted with the play through its repetition. The separate acts must be run through this way, and finally the play as a whole.

If possible, costume and make-up reviews should take place before any complete dress rehearsals are held. This is in line with another rule, that wherever possible, it would be wise to follow: *never begin two things at the same time.* For instance, if actors are learning lines, do not insist that they act their scenes fully; if they are being given positions, do not expect rounded characterizations at the same moment. When the sets are brought in, let the actors become acquainted with them—let them move about on them—before demanding a full performance.

Every rehearsal has its own purpose; don't expect or demand everything at once till the very last rehearsals. It is perfectly normal for "everything to go" when a new element is introduced. Directors are to be prepared for this, and to ask the actors to relax—not to worry—when they begin their first dress rehearsals. An actor, when he gets into costume and puts on his make-up for the first time, or when he first comes on the actual stage set under the new lights, generally feels thoroughly wretched. He swears that he has lost everything he has worked for. To clamor for a fluent performance under these circumstances is to increase the actor's sense of inadequacy. He should be made easy.

It is foolish to write about direction as if it took place in a void. The actual conditions of rehearsal are rarely the conditions that are implied

in a theatre manual or in a critic's essay. If possible, avoid having an "audience" of friends or colleagues at rehearsals. Sympathetic or not, they end by making the actor conscious of things he must not concern himself with till he is ready to open. Warn actors from taking the advice, however well meant, of observers, even intelligent observers. Prevent such advice from being given to the actors. Even the playwright, when he is present, should make his criticisms through the director. For the actor at rehearsal is not a "finished product." The process of creation is especially delicate for the actor, who is at once the maker and the thing created, and the advice of outsiders—and at a certain point even the playwright may be considered an outsider—is almost universally in terms of the criticism of complete and static works of art. Such criticism is not only rarely valuable to the actor—it is, more often than not, positively harmful. The motto for everyone concerned here is, "Do not disturb. Men working."

The director must view himself as the *leader* of a group. This is true in any type of theatrical production. The function of the leader is not to give commands, but to lead. He *must help the group realize its potentialities.* He must help each part to function at its best and in coordination with the demands of the whole. He must not sacrifice the individual to the ensemble, *he must see to it that the ensemble is served by the best efforts of each individual.* He must show the individual that he—the individual—achieves his truest stature by serving the ensemble.

—From *Producing the Play*
(1941) by John Gassner

NIGHTMARES FOR A PROSPEROUS PEOPLE

I might announce that the latest Lindsay-Crouse product *State of The Union* is the season's outstanding success—a fact that you were probably acquainted with even before its New York opening—but as a serious thinker on theatrical matters, you might expect me to state whether the play's success is merited. I submit that I cannot answer such a query. If I think about it for more than a minute, I begin not to understand it. It is like asking if a painting is worth the price asked for it. My answer can only be that if you pay the price, you have answered the question.

This is neither spoofing nor sophistry. It is on these simple issues that the whole matter of judgment in the arts rests. It is the failure to define these everyday terms of critical usage that has not only reduced the reviewing of our popular entertainments to the least rewarding kind of chitchat, but has ended by weakening and confusing many artists, while rendering the function of these entertainments ever more trivial.

When we speak of a work of art (or entertainment, if you will) we ought to make it real to ourselves to the extent of situating and defining it in some relation to our total personality—to our appetites, understanding, needs, social situation, education, moral conviction—of which we should make ourselves aware to some reasonable degree. The reviewer who does this becomes objective no matter how subjective he is—and I prefer him more rather than less subjective—since his definitions will give the reader some clear insight into what is being reviewed as well as into the reviewer himself.

An eminent European critic once remarked that all discussion of contemporary works of art was not criticism so much as conversation. What he meant, of course, was that the context within which we judge a new work is comparatively limited, since time and perspective have not yet provided sufficiently tested instruments by which to measure the more or less permanent values of the work in question. Yet despite our knowledge that works of art possess qualities which are rarely to be perceived on first contact, we ought to try to make sense of what we say even about the least important specimens in this much abused field of human activity.

Let us return to *State of The Union*. I do not conceive it to be my function to advise you to see it or to miss it. (If you are a habitual theatregoer you will undoubtedly see it, no matter what anybody says.) Nor do I have the impertinence to think my pleasure or pain at its performance should in any way serve as an indication of what you might feel when you see it. As a critic, I believe my private opinion ought to remain private!

What interests me here (a subject of no concern whatever to the play's backers or the ticket agents or the Variety box-score for critics) is its typicality as the successful propaganda play on Broadway. It ought to be noted to begin with that practically no one has called it a "propaganda play." A propaganda play is not a propaganda play, apparently, when people are pleased with it.

The effect of the play generally is equivalent to that of an evening's pleasant talk among agreeable people of good will, in which a number of bright things are said that make for a feeling of all around well-being. One approves of almost every sentiment expressed. But one is amazed to learn subsequently that what one has heard has not only been cheerful and clever, but actually "important," very nearly front-page material or the stuff out of which hot editorials are made.

What is actually dramatized in *State of The Union*?

> 1. The fact that the professional politician has very little faith in the people, and that he does not regard the broad masses as the sources of real power.
> 2. The fact that most candidates for high public office are forced by their political mentors to avoid issues instead of facing them, and...
> 3. That the old-guard leadership (Democrat and Republican) ought to be discarded.

Furthermore, the play suggests that it is wicked for politicians to divide the country through attacks on the unity of the United Nations or appeals to the prejudice of national minorities within the body politic. The play further indicates that the authors believe full-employment measures to be necessary, and that there are pernicious influences at work to turn our war veterans against organized labor.

Since no one can deny that these ideas represent some of the crucial concerns of our day, one would suppose they might cause a certain amount of disquiet beneath the laughter that greets the play's affability. Nothing of the sort. Everyone loves it. By what miracle has the contradiction between the play's controversial subject matter and the manner in which it is received to be explained? Humor, you may say, is the great solvent. Perhaps it is. But I wonder if all the useful things the play contains are at all controversial in the form they assume on the stage. Either we are a wholly unified people and the play's pleasant jokes are aimed at an enemy who is no enemy at all, or the play is so powerful a catalytic agent that within the space of an evening everybody in the audience is won over to its point of view and we need only wait for enough people to see it to solve all our major political troubles.

Perhaps it is truer to say the play exploits truisms, and never really gets to dealing with the ills it points to in any way that makes them hurt us in life. In other words, what is disturbing in the context of reality ceases to be controversial when it is transformed into a genial pleasantry that actually touches life in so general, oblique and abstract a level that it becomes an up-to-the-minute joke for readers of fashionable political periodicals and wisecracking digests of all descriptions. The subject matter has been rendered innocuous by taking from it all the poisonous but living ingredients that give it force in the world. A substance of life is cleverly indicated, but what is actually there is a prettily contrived dummy, just as the love motif of the play is nicely suggested without any relation to the palpable realities of love. A device and a substitution have craftily removed the very essence of the matter. As Louis Kronenberger recently wrote in another connection, "Broadway must somehow send its audiences home comforted even in the case of plays that are meant to disconcert. The result is that most people go out of the theatre, not with more sense of responsibility than they went with, but with less."

I do not ask that our political and social comedies have the bite and sting of Beaumarchais' *Mariage de Figaro* or Gogol's *Inspector General* (although, when you come to think of it, why not ask it?) but I believe we should make a distinction between the kinds of values that enter into the successful propaganda play on Broadway. That a popular comedy should speak of the things mentioned in *State of The Union* is all to the good. The level of Broadway production is thus raised nearer to that, let us say, of such a musical as *Of Thee I Sing*. But not to recognize at the same time exactly what that level is in relation to what our social situation demands—not to see that what we acquire this way is not far removed from the political wisdom that we might derive from the kidding around a poker game—is to do ourselves not only an artistic but a political disservice. For if we wonder how we can be so "progressive" even in our lighter entertainments and still remain so far from mature in our social life, we will detect that a complacency about such types of successful "propaganda" tends to make us forget the dense political inertia that still serves as the great impediment to the real progress still to be made in our country.

What I argue here, about an unpretentious comedy, might be argued with even more cogency in regard to plays with greater claims to social seriousness. It would be important to discuss them on more substantial artistic grounds than we generally do—not because art, as such, is of the greatest moment, but because only when art is interpreted in terms of real perception, closeness to life and relevance to human truth, does it perform its social function. To think that a successful propaganda melodrama—vociferously sincere—which does not deal with reality in its many-faceted complexity and its troublesome depths is truly useful socially, is ultimately to believe that well-delivered and high-minded Sunday-school talks are prime movers toward a good life. One cannot say that one is opposed to such talks. I will always champion a play, for example, that might influence only four people a night to a greater sympathy toward the dilemma of the Negro, but I still question the degree of efficacy of any superficial treatment of a deep-rooted social problem.

Perhaps I can make all this a bit clearer and more specific by saying that I found myself rather more concerned by the awkward and poorly projected dramatization of Lillian Smith's *Strange Fruit* than by the far more expert, sharper theatrics of *Deep Are The Roots*. The more fumbling effort had somewhat more scope, more extension and possibly more authenticity.

Finally I submit as a suggestive paradox that more might be learned about the South, let us say, from such relatively unpopular and conceivably "decadent" writers as William Faulkner, who does not particularly explain the South and who certainly is not concerned with reforming it, than from a few more generally accepted propagandists whose social viewpoint is probably closer to my own than Faulkner's.

It must be evident from the above that I hardly intend to review the theatre, painting, music and the rest in the accepted sense. I regard all these as forms of play which, not unlike dreams, very often reveal the truth about men even more deeply than their most conscious utterances. My interest in the reality of men spurs my interest in the manifestations of his play. For the sake of what might be called the semantics of criticism, it is essential that some such naïve introductory statement be made.

I hope to say something about the latest Dali work (now showing at the Bignou Galleries), the brilliance of which dazzled me and sent me home slightly ill over the accumulation of so much riches that added up to so great a poverty—for the decoration of wealthy interiors. I want to tell you some day soon why Hollywood pictures ought to stop making great progress and try to limit themselves to only very small gains such as the homely and grave quality of the *faces* in the Swiss film *The Last Chance*. I should like to point out at some future time why a shot of women's hips being given a mechanical massage in the latest March Of Time on *The American Beauty*—as cruel as any Grosz caricature and almost as freely "abstract" as many a modern painting—is a document of real significance.

In general this month—after two years away from New York—I received a distinct impression that much of our entertainment in various forms might be described as nightmares rendered into pretty ornaments for a prosperous people. Beautifully horrifying! Yet I received an impression of health, too, in such places as the orchestral concerts at the Civic Center, usually conducted by Leonard Bernstein—concerts not as good as many of those at Carnegie Hall, but in certain vital respects far better.

All these events of our night-life, I repeat, may be worth our consideration by daylight. The reason is that—believe it or not—they are ultimately connected with what goes on in your street—if not in your home.

—*TRW*, Feb. '46

THE REAL THING

Perhaps the adage about the leadership of the little child is nothing but an old wheeze. Still, when I heard that my daughter's playmates at college spent many idle hours listening to recordings of Darius Milhaud's music, I fancied I could detect a trend. The student intelligentsia of the late twenties was captivated by T. S. Eliot and Joyce, just as in the thirties the peculiar fascination of Proust held sway over the youth that was not dominated by writers of a leftward direction. Today, I hear, the same academic underground is devoted to Franz Kafka, while allowing room in their more frivolous moments for the prickle of Milhaud's music.

The news about the midnight Milhaud at school confirmed my sense of Milhaud as the musical man of the hour. This had occurred to me as I heard both his *Creation of the World* at the City Center (Leonard Bernstein conducting) and a piece for violin and orchestra, performed by the Philadelphia Orchestra under Ormandy, on the same day. A few weeks later I listened to a new *French Suite* and *Le Bal Martiniquais* played under the composer's guidance by the Philharmonic and a half-hour CBS *Invitation To Music* program—again under the composer's baton—only a few days apart. The audience in each instance—particularly the younger audience—was genuinely enthusiastic.

In the twenties, when "modernism" in music was more of a novelty than it is today, the only "best seller" in the French school of composers was Arthur Honegger. Milhaud was tolerated rather than appreciated. It is not only that time has served to get us accustomed to Milhaud's music, but our times have created in us a state of being which makes our reaction to him today spontaneous and real. We no longer hear his music as partisans of a special movement in the arts, but as people somehow sharing a common experience with the composer.

Our day is tragic, but, if we are honest, we are too confused to accept it tragically. We hesitate to be both serious and solemn. When an artist is solemn as well as serious in the vein, for example, of a Shostakovitch, we may be duly respectful, even impressed, but we are apt to become suspicious.

Milhaud is serious, yet playful—intelligent, yet light. His music is intelligent through its direct and realistic spirit. When it refers to local color—a Paris bar, Brazil, Marseilles—it may be jovial or somber, but it never becomes sticky, self-indulgent, touristic. The scenes described may remain the picturesque pleasure spots we expected them to be, but they are not pretty in post-card fashion; they disclose mysterious elements of ambiguity and contradiction. When Milhaud writes a funeral march, its introduction is rambunctious and gay before it grows ominous. We find ourselves becoming hushed and sober while we are still in the midst of a surprised laugh. For today we laugh, or try to, even at what should terrify or quiet us. Milhaud's new *Pearl Harbor Memorial* piece is not only musically paradoxical (and therefore attractive) because it sounds angry and indignant when we anticipated something respectfully mournful, but by being the kind of dirge it is, it becomes truly, realistically, ours.

The jazz we hear in *Creation of the World* may evoke acute nostalgia, but there is something brooding and nervous in it too. We are reminded of yesterday, but this yesterday is not as far removed from us as we had supposed. The jazz is not that of the luxurious, slick world which in Gershwin's music seems to be the permanent world, but a depressive jazz in a world without air, without real movement, despite all the outward tokens of twentieth-century speed. Factually, this was the music of the day after the first World War; in absolute terms, it is the music of a day without much hope.

Milhaud's music now, as exemplified in the jolly *French Suite*, is tart and fresh. His characteristic intelligence is here, lean, vigorous, always on the edge of a certain asperity. This is French music, not in a World's Fair sense, but in the sense that the modern Frenchman even at his gayest achieves unity through contradictory, almost warring elements—like a sweet syrup made out of pickles, olives and nuts! There are colors here that are suave and harsh at the same time—fibrous.

All this is not accidental, not simply a mode of art or a personal trait. It is intimately related to a certain uneasiness and strain that with a cultured Frenchman may mask itself in a cloak of elegant lightness—a lightness which nevertheless suggests that somehow, somewhere, there is division and dissonance. This style is the product of a nation that was shattered by a war and then lulled into a fitful simulacrum of peace, only to taste war and humiliation again. It is a real style because it was born of a people that dwelled within the orbit of fear, corruption and a diseased social system, while adhering for generations to classically restrained and tastefully modulated forms of expression.

In a sense, this style cannot be imported. When our composers attempt it, it often becomes silly, pink and precious. They do not possess the true acid, distilled by the special experience and background, which belongs to the French. For all our recent sophistication, we still owe too much to the benefits of Main Street, Coca-Cola, the ads in the *Saturday Evening Post* and an innocuous schooling that culminates on airy campuses in pretty country spots. Though it would be inaccurate and improper to speak of imitation, I am reminded that when Randall Thompson composes a light and very sympathetic *Second Symphony* (which Bernstein conducted early this season) it sounds like a valedictory speech at a university in Hawaii; and when Virgil Thomson composes a piece like the *Etudes* for piano (introduced by E. Robert Schmitz) it is largely a classroom joke.

The qualities that serve as a preservative agent in Milhaud's music are acidity and subtlety. These will keep its "simplicity" fresh for a long time. They spring from a realism that gives health to the whole of Milhaud's work. This realism is able to face the modern world with its fragmented tones of doubt and pain, its ambiguities of distress and disease, without itself becoming morbid, because it has frankness, understanding, even a certain relish—that is, a balanced acceptance of every part of the real world. This is the existent, it seems to say, and there can be no arguments about it.

Though this music, as I have pointed out, is not our own, it has become close to us. It speaks in accents which, perhaps unfortunately, we are ever more readily coming to understand. In this nervous, tough and basically hysterical period of ours—we hope we are going one way, we fear we are going another, and are uncertain whether we will get anywhere—we are unwilling to be amused

by pessimism in the fashion of the twenties, but we are even less able to be optimistic without the salt of some skepticism and shrewdness and even a measure of conflict. The optimism in Milhaud's recent works stands gracefully but unmistakably on a tragic foundation. There is occasionally a feeling of weight in this music which disturbs a little and makes its tread a bit heavier than is at first apparent in the general quality of lightness. It is significant of America today that it is the lightness which is being emphasized by the kids, the critics and the composer himself.

Leaving Milhaud, soon to return to his native land, we pay tribute to the work of the French film artists who carried on in their country during its occupation by the Nazis. *It Happened at the Inn* (*Goupi aux Mains Rouges*), the first importation of a French picture made under the conditions of cultural blackout, is now being shown with titles in English; but it is soon to be released with all its dialogue spoken in English. It is not only a picture that many will enjoy, but it may well stand as a sample of a tradition that is still deeply rooted and universally pertinent. Here again is a basically realistic spirit. This story of a clannish French peasant family spares nothing in its statement of their avarice, unimaginativeness, hard stubbornness. The picture has been called a French *Tobacco Road*. This may be commercially apt, but it is misleading. Despite the picture's wryness, there is never any attempt to make the Goupis into amusing ghouls. These peasants may be narrow, tough and even a little perverse, but they are presented as human beings far closer to the rest of humanity everywhere than we might care to admit. Beneath their special color, the Goupis are universal people, viewed without any sentimentality, but also without hatred or condescension. The makers of the film appear to be at once detached from and on most intimate terms with their characters.

Back of it all, in a word, is the antiseptic intelligence which is at the core of French classicism, a quality never wholly absent from any sound French creation, no matter of what school. There is a roundness, a perspective, a proportion that contains all.

In the end, the story, that appears at times to be wandering aimlessly as if it did not know its own goal (or as if it had none), resolves itself into a clear affirmation, affably and gently stated, that "money found is not money earned" and that for this reason there is evil in it. Was a social message intended here for a France so long corrupted by the middle-class dream of living its life on unearned income? It is difficult to be sure. We do come away from this picture thinking: No wonder these people endure, no wonder that even their vice of familial self-preservation, which stands fast even against the law (the *gendarmerie*) itself, ultimately becomes a virtue. Without our having been aware of it, an essence of profound secular wisdom has been suggested. Throughout we find an easy flow, quiet voices, subdued light, clarity, naturalness, a relaxed basic intelligence, a special kind of modesty, in photography, acting and language.

The ostensible lack of point in the French picture brings me to the consideration of a play now struggling in the Broadway cataract. I refer to the work of a new young playwright, Arthur Laurents, whose *Home of the Brave* recently opened and received what were definitely mixed notices.

There were those who held that the play made a point and named it; and those who explained why certain extraneous purposes hindered it from achieving its point. What struck me in the play was neither the point some people had named, nor what were described as the author's purposes—extraneous or otherwise.

The play relates a war episode, but it is not a war play. The play's central character is a Jew who is subjected to the raffish anti-Semitism of a comrade-in-arms, who is simply a callous, executive-type simpleton. Nevertheless, anti-Semitism isn't the play's theme. The play assumes that the audience is aware of the existence of anti-Semitism—in and out of the army—and in making this assumption the author has been both courageous—considering the backwardness of our theatre—and wise. The motif of anti-Semitism is used as an ingredient of the story; and it is really an impertinence, or a disguised form of either inferiority complex or social cowardice, to say that such a motif is not needed here, or that since he has introduced it, the author is obliged to declare himself on the subject. The author also assumes, with a liberal and decent forbearance, that the audience regards anti-Semitism as an evil and that its presence in the army is perhaps even more shameful than it is anywhere else. For this reason, and because it is not the crux of his play, the author does not feel called upon to "solve the problem."

At bottom, the boy in the play suffers from a sense of guilt because he experiences a feeling of relief when his pal, and not he, is killed on the battlefield. As this sense of guilt develops into a neurosis, he feels compelled—through the strange chemistry of his conscience—to prefer believing that the relief he experiences at his buddy's death derives from a desire for revenge (against the suspicion of an anti-Semitic infection in his friend) rather than a sheer physical joy at his own escape.

Through the psychologically complex, but fundamentally simple narrative of this play, the author leads us to his own conviction that the world must forever be faced without the fear of fear, since practically all people today, whoever and whatever they may be, carry within them some burden that may very well end by poisoning and paralyzing them. The name and source of the burden may differ, the suffering caused is the same. In this sense all people are equally burdened, no matter how different and special their burden may make them feel. Humanity, in this sense, shares an equality of suffering and is equally in need of a common deliverance.

The play arrives at its small but sufficient wisdom because its young author has turned his honest attention, and his capacity to reflect, on an incident from the recent war and its hospital aftermaths. The result has the virtue of a true experience both theatrically and humanly. The fusion of the play's motifs, which may make it baffling to an audience more eager to see what it expects than to

58

absorb what confronts it, creates a kind of complexity that contributes to sound values. Problems in life do not often manifest themselves in neat, airtight, clearly labeled compartments. This is something that both our pedagogues for playwrights and our professors of panaceas are ever prone to forget.

In the morass of professional fatuity which is the rule of the commercial theatre, I found this small play possessed of the integrity of a simple declarative sentence. Art or no, this afforded me more entertainment than the athletically articulated rendition of *Hamlet* by Maurice Evans. To generalize about *Hamlet* today is to indulge in abracadabra; to talk about it in relation to the particulars of its present performance would be to platitudinize over the value of having a more, rather than less, intelligible Shakespeare on a stage such as ours—as singularly lacking in any sense of the past as of adventure in the present.

As for *expression*, that is an emotionally significant and immediate play for residents of Manhattan in 1946, this *Hamlet* can best be described by a quote from its mangled text: "Words! Words! Words!"

I must return once more to the credo set forth last month. What I seek is not the prestige of "art form," the dignity of cultural aspirations, the renown and echo of aesthetic occasions. I think art important only as it reflects a truly festive spirit or a passion. All the rest is merely art commodity, art professionalism. That is why I am willing to emphasize what might be called the real thing in painting, drama or music. The real thing has to do with the human value in the animating spirit of the artist, the human impulse that moves him possibly before, but certainly simultaneously with, his so-called art impulse.

One of the devices of modern reviewing of such a play as *Home of the Brave*, let us say, is to point out that it cannot be considered a successful effort because it is not particularly well written. In my view, to say this is to say very little. Dreiser's novels are not well written, but they will endure beyond many that are. Literature does not begin or end with good writing, nor painting with either color or composition, nor music with melody, nor acting with elocution. All these categories, I repeat, are meaningful only as parts of a context. Only when the total work is understood through the focus of the real thing from which it emerges can any of the component parts be defined, not as additive elements, but as phases and attributes of the whole.

In this light it is difficult to discuss the Annual Exhibition of Contemporary American Painting at the Whitney Museum. Taken in one big department-store scoop, it shows an amazing progress in the competence of American painting. But ability by itself, as Tolstoy once said, is from the devil. At any rate, there would be little point in discussing the merits of single paintings by such established craftsmen as Sloan, Marin, Weber, or to judge more recent arrivals like Leon Kelly, Joseph Scharl, Everett Spruce, Gregorio Prestopino on the basis of isolated canvases.

What is to be noted about the show as a whole is that the prevailing mood is not a happy one. The subject matter generally expresses a pained melancholy. This made me ask myself not only "Why are we sad?" (as Anatole France once titled a review he wrote on a novel), but in what way are we sad. There was something quite conventional, limited, and unmoving in many of the pieces designed to achieve tragic statement. The world these past twenty-five years has certainly not been a joyous place, and the augury for the future is not altogether reassuring, yet the reflection of the world's doldrums in some quite expert canvases at the Whitney Museum failed to stir the slightest tremor in my soul. Much of the painting here was strident and terrible, but as a contemporary once said of Andreyev, "He tries to frighten me, but I am not afraid."

For all the devastation, loneliness and sorrow essayed, I felt very little terror, compassion or exaltation. Not even depression. We must some day stop to inquire why this should be so. For the moment, I can only indicate a line of thought. Very few of our painters have yet learned to use themselves; they fail therefore to arrive at an authentic personal vision. They deal too much in ambitious and detached generalities in a kind of bookish or editorial way. The hand is ahead of the heart; the brush is playing tricks that the soul does not follow. There is no human clarity, sincerity, no real simplicity. We have fabrication, not expression. The result is not only bad painting as such, but an emptiness very much like that produced by a political discussion in which the speaker says all the right things, while we have a distinct impression that he feels and knows nothing in particular. As a consequence, we judge that even his truth is misleading and dangerous.

—*TRW*, Apr. '46

THE FACE OF THE FORTIES

We are tired, it is true, and tiredness is a bad guide. But it may be well, for a time, to heed our tiredness. The world is not going to listen to even the faint suggestion of Isherwood's mystic cure, nor to any other great answer pronounced in terms of global generalities. We are afraid of the strenuous ultimates that puffed-up prophets in the arts, philosophy, or political lore might devise for us. We are not even to be terrified by the possibility of total annihilation through atomic power. We would sooner be destroyed altogether than run off half-cocked on the rainbow path of a final redemption through one word, one action, one epic yea!

This is a period of accommodation and in that, as we see on every hand, lurks the threat of something worse than cynicism. It is very frequently the road to complacency, to blindness, to fat. But with honest men it may be something more. With a quiet awareness, a caution that comes from discretion, not cowardice, a humility derived neither from cunning nor indifference, we may be led through some biologic sanity, some remainder of

spiritual wholeness, to a goal brighter than that furnished by years of grasping at phrases we zealously proclaimed to be the essence of scientific fact or religious illumination. For some time we shall have to content ourselves with the small truth.

There are two sides to this coin. Smallness is all too common. Truth is certainly rarer. Dali's paintings, for all their complex contrivance, are "small." True they are certainly not. They represent neither dream, desire, nor genuine imagination. Talent and technique they display to a remarkable degree, but they are basically decoration for an addled age, ornament and luxury for the ignorantly pretentious or the cultivatedly debased. It is the most brilliant modern academicism at the service of the wealthy wanton. There is a shriek of pain and protest in Picasso's *Guernica*; in Dali's most horrid imaginings there is something loathsomely seductive like the flirtation of an expensive siren with special equipment. Even the painting of a piece of bread is transformed into something unmuscularly fleshy that is worth its weight in gold. Perhaps gold is its final truth.

How shall we recognize truth? Not by definition. By the residue of health within us about which there is ultimately no mystery. The sick man knows himself; the empty man senses his emptiness; the healthy man experiences his health without examination. We hardly need an analyst to describe our delusions; and the greatest truth is always imminent in the smaller. But truth we must have and cling to, for without it there can be nothing but chaos.

The cult of smallness—or of the unpretentious—may often lead to falsehood. Consider the ideal of understatement. Hemingway helped foster it in recent American literature. It is often employed as a comedy device. The radio often resorts to it with a special elaborateness. Finally, understatement is confused with the real. The motion picture *A Walk in the Sun* depends almost entirely on the trick of terse, dry indirection that is supposed to be characteristic of GI thinking and speech. That is to say, the Harry Brown novel used this device, and the picture repeats it. The picture, however, has the advantage of a cleanly photographed landscape and honest American faces. They are the faces of young actors who were fed on something besides celluloid and grease paint. There is something warm and reassuring in them, and these give the picture a very special authenticity and charm.

Yet the effect of the whole does not seem to me to be inspiriting. The suppression of eloquence as a means of avoiding the falsely heroic extends beyond the speech. This suppression makes the very soul of the people inexpressive. There is such a thing as mute eloquence or the presentation of either wholly inarticulate or clumsy-speaking people—for instance in Flaubert's *Simple Heart* or in the peasant stories of Chekhov and Tolstoy— whereby depth of being is suggested without false rhetoric. In such things as *A Walk in the Sun*—and the same author's *Sound of Hunting*—the characters are finally so stripped of real as opposed to sentimental personality, they become such ciphers that one thinks perversely that if these are representative GIs, then our victory was possibly something to deplore.

Fortunately we do not believe our GIs are these paltry figures that the writer has given us under the delusion that they are honest-to-good-ness people because they speak trite irrelevancies and commonplace jargon. We do not believe they are GIs even if their talk is an exact recording of things overheard in the barracks and at the front, because they are not people at all. The lowest worm of a man who happens at the same time to be a deaf-mute has more stature—even in degrada-tion—than the dummies passed off as true-to-life in the fake simplicity of such writing.

Personally I am not very concerned with verisimilitude, but I suspect that the recording is that of radio literature. The adventitious use of Earl Robinson's chant and commentary in the film was perhaps the director's unconscious criticism of its lack of real pathos or content. Despite its several above-the-average merits—the director and cast have given it a value beyond its scenario. Actually this film is a work which in the end diminishes rather than deepens our sense of man. This is a biologic as well as an artistic sin.

The theatre was honored recently by the pres-ence of Martha Graham in a repertoire of new and old numbers. Miss Graham is not only a dancer of remarkable technical accomplishment, but also an artist. Simply stated this means she is a person who uses material—in this case the body—to communi-cate a sense of life.

What puzzles me about Miss Graham is that while her sense of life is concerned with the expression of primary human passions, the results assume forms of a singular deadness or inhuman-ity. I can see that Miss Graham is striving to speak about things like birth, death, man's relation to the earth—the stuff of the most fundamental human experiences—yet her symbols often strike me as cold as metal designs used for industrial advertis-ing. Miss Graham—in contrast and in reaction to the classic ballet—attempts to seize essential reality, yet her work very often appears more remote and even artificial to me than even some of the most meaningless of the traditional ballets. There is intensity in Miss Graham's work— certainly intensity of purpose which quite frequently gives her work an arresting quality of forceful dignity as of something not to be moved or altered—but the intensity does not preclude the feeling that her figures are spiritual automata— related on the one hand to the fanaticism of personal self-realization and on the other to the mechanism of robots performing mysterious and useless rites in a dance studio. At best, there is something here of the lithic cleanness of a grave-stone or the steadfastness of a fence permanently planted in some Midwestern plain or New England hill. There is very little sentimentality in her work, nor any coy pornography. But her expressions of sex—in both the male and female principle—are strictly non-generative. I almost suspect the marriage of a Puritan austerity with the arrogance of a German technology—both of which have a mysticism all their own.

—*TRW*, Apr. '46

THE ROUTINED AUDIENCE

Sometimes I feel we are all going down to damnation in a triumph of technique. Our chaos is composed of a multitude of precision instruments. We are dazzled, dizzied and exhausted by a deluge of simplifications, improvements and labor-saving devices. Our depravity is of a kind that admires skill and competence above everything else. We are dying of advancement.

Performances which are generally the easiest to watch and to be entertained by are becoming ever more wearisome to me. The smoother the technique, the harder I seem to work enjoying myself. During such performances everything clicks with a slot machine perfection, while I find my own organism growing increasingly jangled with every clever thrust of the manipulator's hand.

Let us start at the bottom. *Born Yesterday* is a play that Broadway correctly calls a piece of bright showmanship. It is cast, directed and mounted with crackerjack smartness. It is a kind of Kaufman-Hart show in terms of postwar New York. Its author-director, Garson Kanin, who grew up in the thirties, has acquired a feeling for social values in the Roosevelt-New Deal sense that was mostly an afterthought with such men as George Kaufman, whose work is essentially a product of the twenties. So *Born Yesterday*, though technically indebted to playwrights like Kaufman, has about it an air of social awareness, a feeling for the very plain people, a suggestion that even the lightest entertainment must in some way contribute to the progress of our democratic way of life. Without the background that produced the Group Theatre, The Theatre Union, The Federal Theatre Project, *Pins and Needles*, and other such lusty manifestations between 1935 and 1939, a play like *Born Yesterday* would hardly be thinkable.

As a result the play not only succeeds in lampooning with gay indulgence a selfish thug who wants to pervert the instruments of government to his own get-rich-quick ends, but also portrays with humorous raillery a temporarily ignorant young girl of the people on the way to maturity through sound instinct and the affectionate aid of her *New Republic*-educated lover. The scheme then is to broaden our sympathies for the common man, to chaff potentially fascist evil-doers, and generally to enhance our faith in the victory of the good fight—in the spirit of innocent, though up-to-date, fun.

All this is better than laudable. Yet the play—extremely successful in making its points for the greater part of two acts—troubled and discomfited me. The most palpable quality that emanates from it is a kind of shrewdness. This in turn may be defined as one part disguised condescension to the characters involved—the audience is made to feel that it is in every way superior to the characters it is observing—and another part the use of the audience's actual experience of life on a fairly mean level.

It is one thing to describe a chorus girl through the comic interplay of her feminine guile and her factual ignorance; it is quite another to make her the peg for a series of coyly dirty jokes or cartoon observations. (In Gorky's *Night Lodging* there is a prostitute who constantly tells of her adventures with a lover who is sometimes called Gaston, then Raoul, finally something else. The spectator never for a moment is made to feel above her.)

To illustrate the play's writing and directing method, consider the climax of the second act. The play's clownish villain slaps his chorus girl mistress twice across the face. She prepares to leave the room in order to think things over. "Will you please do something for me?" she asks her boy friend in a dryly sweet voice. "What?" he asks. "Drop dead," she replies with neatly unemphatic accuracy. Any suggestion of pain or venom is deftly avoided, for such a reaction would kill the point. The girl and her situation have been suppressed in favor of a trick. The audience roars, not at all aware that in doing so it has not only laughed at a gag as old as New York's Garment Center but has become party to a piece of brutality.

"People never get together through tact alone," I once heard an old man say. This remark came back to me as I reflected how the very shrewdness of this successful play and production militates against every unifying, human sentiment. The chief attribute of this shrewdness is to make the spectator applaud the adeptness with which author, producer and actors are putting things over. It is as if everyone were exchanging congratulatory winks as the shekels roll in with every guffaw.

This seemed to me particularly true in the gin-rummy scene of this play. In this scene, the play is really close to its audience—without sentimental or political pretense, without the snobism of the vulgar. The little chorus girl sits down and trims her callous boy friend with devastating dispatch. This is her small revenge, and the audience's delight. This is the actual level of the audience experience: it really knows and feels the exultation of beating a baboon at cards. The contact is complete.

In my opinion the author-director of this play writes and directs not so much as he feels but as he has learned. He has learned from the ablest showmen of our theatre. They in turn have learned from the audience. And the New York theatre audience today, with its inflationary mood and purse, is, by and large, a debased audience. I mean by that, it is a routined audience. Its thinking and feeling have been mechanized by the hotels it visits on the run, the ticket agencies that advise it what to see, the "rave" notices it reads quotes from, the whole psychology of transient heedlessness that marks the in-and-out-of-towner currently of better than average means. Its fools (the entertainers) learn to please it easily with an agile pickpocket touch. On both sides of the footlights everything exists only for the effective point and the function that produces a facile result—aimed not at winning the heart but at the capture of the dollar. For this reason, the feeling that finally takes possession of a play such as *Born Yesterday*, despite moments that contain the seeds of something finer, is truly ugly.

I have simplified the process. The entertainer (or artist) follows the routined audience and develops his technique through it because he knows a good part of his truth and salvation must ultimately stem from the audience. He is basically a good man and he trusts the audience. But to be anything but a prostitute the artist must also be a leader. He must be true to what is most eager, vital and boldest within himself. Only in this way can he serve his audience; only in this way can the audience gain something from him. By being awake himself, the artist must awaken the audience. This ultimately is what the audience also desires—to be awakened. Even this routined audience desires it. But it has been routined by the fruits of its own corruption; it has frightened its artists to think of it as nothing but a slumbering beast that must not be disturbed in its sleep. Consequently the Broadway theatre today is a vicious circle of artists making themselves technically proficient in the routine the audience imposes on them, while the audience becomes stultified by the adulterated pabulum it has made its artists provide for it.

Ascending the scale, there is the paradox of *Lute Song*. "Boring!" cry the customers for the usual entertainment. "Have you no feeling for Beauty?" reply the eaters of dreams. Since no terms are clarified, no one knows what the next fellow is talking about.

Lute Song is an adaptation of the classic fable of the faithful woman who bears every deprivation to remain true to her husband who has been taken from her by accident and mischance. What the original Chinese version of this story is like we cannot know—the prosaic text we listen to at the Plymouth Theatre is not a very fresh piece of writing—but no doubt it could serve as a scenario for a dignified, and even moving, spectacle—since the basic lines of the story as such are almost unshakably right.

However, the beauty that is advertised in relation to this show is probably not the beauty of its fundamental story but the beauty of the production. This beauty resembles the style of a genteel musical comedy or a kind of tasteful Macy's parade. If it deserves the designation at all, it should be qualified by the adjective inappropriate. Such a stoical and tender tale of primitive lineaments is not ennobled or made more universally relevant by Fifth Avenue antique-shop colors, expensive drapery, Valentina gowns and penny-sweet music lacking subtlety. On the contrary, such treatment empties the story of every living value. Beauty is not a pigment added to a surface; it is an essence that arises from a living context. The traits of the original story, the pedestrian adaptation, the collaboration of sundry well-meaning (even talented) but ill-assorted craftsmen cannot sum up to beauty of any kind, even visual.

And yet, some semblance of the thing may be hovering over Forty-fifth Street somehow. If so, it comes from the devious aspiration of many of those concerned in the production to escape mediocrity. If what they stammer remains only a false, esthetic gibberish, perhaps the effort is still worth something.

Further up—very much further—in the scale of values are the Edward Weston photographs recently seen in a retrospective show at the Museum of Modern Art. They represent a technical triumph. It is their virtue and their defect. They are amazingly clear and admirable in the statement of detail. Weston has a superb feeling for textures, particularly hard, bright, solid textures. Even a beard on a peasant's face is studied as if it were composed of brilliant steel points. Flesh becomes a kind of abstract surface made of a sensuous rubber material with mineral qualities and only incidental sexual potentialities.

All the substances in these photographs are transformed into one photographic substance—whether they be human, metal or vegetable. It is a kind of modern "composition" that is attractive, clear, strong and personal only as a modern bathroom appears personal. There is only a modicum of humanity here—the portraits have a certain forthrightness and decision—but the main emphasis falls on material studied with a devotion usually reserved for more animate life. This concentration on material which is mostly inorganic matter is real but somewhat disturbing. Man or woman as such seems to be absent. The limbs and roots of trees in the work of Paul Strand, for example, no matter how objectively viewed, take on an emotional connotation. Here they are as sensuous as the nudes, but the nudes, as noted, are sensuous only as material or fabric—even though they are usually shown to be the bodies of very handsome women.

The total impression (very American to my mind) is of some technological splendor. This is true even of the landscapes. The splendor may be in the object photographed or in the quality of the photography, which is astonishingly convincing, but there is very little sense of spiritual or human connection. Significant to me is the landscape which is actually a Hollywood set, and the dummy figures which have a hideous completeness, also Hollywood begotten.

The universe seems to have been translated into something luxurious as if it were some effulgent dead matter stiffly posing for the camera's admiration. I feel very little sorrow, joy, enthusiasm, very little pantheistic excitement, only a craftsman's pleasure and a precisionist's pride over a world very well laid out for his use.

The value of the current anti-Fascist Italian film *Open City* is the opposite of technical. In this respect it falters beneath—or never attempts—our American standards. Its story resembles what has already been spoiled for us in some of our own better-grade war films. But the homely truth of the details, the real faces, the shabby little sets, the unromanticized photography of actual streets, the general atmosphere of a bedraggled but sweet and sturdy humanity, above all, the endearing imperfections, the warm marks of care and suffering in the women's faces and figures, give the picture a proximity and consanguinity to an honest audience that our more mechanically expert product rarely achieves.

Nor is technique the outstanding attraction in the recent paintings of Marc Chagall. The technique indeed has become something of a possibly annoying mannerism. These are not major paintings in the usual sense; their real quality is something different from the startling fantasy associated with Chagall. They have a quiet warmth and a tenderness that were often missing in his more "amusing" vein.

Chagall is a sophisticate who remains essentially a folk poet. He has learned the trade of the big city but he has never forgotten his province. In Paris and New York he remembers the small Russian Jewish village from which he stems. This alone might make him only folksy and trivial. But in his little dream world he has caught the permanent and poignant truths that even the smallest community, when it is fundamentally sound, may contain. There is the moral law of his fathers and the glow of the ritual candles that represent them; there is simple music and the twisted but wryly honest little violinist who makes it; there is the naïve wedding that is taken at its full sacramental significance; and there is the penetrating and pure sensuality that gives the marriage its encompassing ardor. There is an intimacy with flowers and animals and a passion for sky, earth, water—bound together in the enchanting cosmos of a man who has remained humble even though his mind and hand have been informed with all manner of latter-day wit and calculation. In a profound sense, this comparatively recent example of the School of Paris in painting is quite old fashioned, but it is an old fashion well worth treasuring and preserving.

Old fashioned too is the ballet recently in New York (Ballet Russe de Monte Carlo at the City Center). Its fashion has much that is spurious and absurd about it. Its art is not only often poor because it belongs to a tradition that has ever weaker roots in the world around it, but because it has added airs to itself that are frequently puerile and false in its memory-of-Paris modernity. Frequently, too, the dancing is far from first rate.

Yet when all this is said, the fact remains, the ballet attracts. The pleasure that the audience generally derives from these performances is justified and even socially necessary. No argument or critical hair-splitting will do away with the fact that the ballet—even this old, silly, traditional ballet—satisfies an appetite that nothing else in our theatre or art world today quite fulfills. It is an appetite of youth even more than a dowager appetite. It is a classless appetite, for the poor and prosperous experience it alike. It is related not only to a need for the festive, the energetic, the graceful, but beyond everything to a desire for both form and freedom—a yearning for liberation through vigor, dream, ideality, a release of the body and the imagination, a physical soaring into a composed realm of the nonrational and the uncommon. It is this realm that everyone of us secretly realizes is our soul's proper habitat.

Musically the month of February belonged to the Hungarian composer Béla Bartók. I heard his *Concerto for Orchestra* conducted by Szell at the Philharmonic; the *Violin Concerto* played by Menuhin with the Philadelphia Orchestra; Szigeti's playing of the *Rhapsody No. 1* for violin and orchestra, and the *Portrait No. 1 in D* with Leonard Bernstein's New York City Symphony Orchestra. There were many other Bartók performances and concerts during the month—notably an all-Bartók program given under the auspices of the League of Composers.

Bartók was one of the finest craftsmen of contemporary music, but his real virtue lies in the fact that he was an extremely personal composer. His work—for all its folk-song and nationalistic bias—was the expression of intense inner emotion and conviction. Though his music, because of its arduousness, is often difficult to assimilate at first hearing, and his ultimate position may not be measured at present, it is always impressive. It is like the speech of a man bent on saying something that issues from the depths of his being. What is usually revealed is a man suffering the pressure of a terrible anxiety—an emotion crucial to our times.

Bartók was a sensitive artist and patriot living in a land dominated by a decadent aristocracy and an equally decadent imperialist foreign power. He lived through the years of fierce struggle for a new modern (post-Romantic) music; and he spent his maturity in a world rapidly allowing itself to disintigrate before the onslaught of the barbarians. The normal atmosphere in such a world is fear. It is the mark of Bartók's importance that the agony of this moral climate finds its echo throughout his work.

In his *Portrait in D* (composed around 1907) the voice that speaks is resigned, gentle and sorrowful. It is the voice of a man who speaks as if he expected to remain an unknown composer all his life. With the eminence his work has attained, we might say he was proved wrong. But he died in poverty last year in New York City. Perhaps in the deeper view, voices such as his—and what those voices have to say—are still unknown. That is possibly one reason why the *Portrait* was so genuinely affecting in Szigeti's compassionate reading.

—*TRW*, May '46

DANGEROUS THOUGHTS

In the spring of 1942 I was looking over a poll taken by the New York motion-picture reviewers who were deciding among themselves what pictures and players they considered the best of that period. On reading their observations I wrote the following comment in a private journal I was keeping at the time: "How we love to make lists of the 'best' in everything! Thus 'the best picture of the year' may be *Lady Eve* or *Citizen Kane* or *The Forgotten Village*. The 'best' director is John Ford, but it might be Preston Sturges, Orson Welles or Herbert Kline! By what standards are any of these the 'best'? There are no tests for these statements, because no standards have been defined by which any of them can be measured. To define standards one might have to refer to the needs of the day as well as to those of the person making the definition (a practice that might involve one in complex, even dangerous discussion) or one might have to

summon up the past which in these matters is quickly forgotten. All attention must be directed to the next moment in preparation for the next listing, while the old listing no longer has any interest since it wasn't meant to be taken seriously in the first place. It was just gossip, copy, advertisement. All this goes to make the environment in which artists are likely to live. It is futile to say that they ought to be indifferent to it. 'If you are in hell, you sweat.'"

As for the latest Academy winner, *The Lost Weekend*, it may very well have been more interesting than any of the rival pictures. In more general terms, however, it can only be deemed a masterpiece by contrast. This is a poor criterion by which to judge the quality of a given piece of work. *The Lost Weekend* strikes me as being distinguished chiefly by the daring of its subject matter. When we say "daring" here, we can speak of it only in relation to the restricted themes and treatment imposed by the Hays office. To introduce an "unpleasant" subject like alcoholism into any Hollywood-made film is naturally a mark of distinction. Subject matter in itself, however, tells us very little about the value of the result.

On this score there is much less to say. There is a certain modesty of setting in *The Lost Weekend*, an effort at plainness, that is to be commended. The performances are adequate or somewhat better. For the rest, there is hardly a scene, a sequence, an image, a piece of business, a speech that is memorable in the way the drunk scene of *The Baker's Wife*, or the wake scene, the saloon scene, the temptation scene in *The Informer* were memorable. The hospital scene in *The Lost Weekend* is more amusing than revealing, the d.t. scene with its imaginary mouse bleeding against the wall is a horror effect made nerve-tingling by sound effects and unabashed yelling. As for the delinquent's motivation—his inferiority complex as a writer—it is a grade-school cliché, and the passages between the big moments are routine. The picture cannot claim even the negative merit of being sordid; the central character hardly ever makes a convincing drunk, except perhaps for the final moment in which he professes to be on the road to health and sobriety! Drunkenness in itself, of course, is hardly a valid theme, and its use here as a big subject hardly achieves greater significance than that contained in the naïve melodramas of the *Ten Nights in a Barroom* variety.

I must reiterate my conviction that basic progress will be made in films when even such gains as adventuresome ideology or political topicality will go hand in hand with more reality on a simple physical level (such as we see in *Open City,* for example), a little more unemphatic honesty, emotional truth and feeling. Most important of all, perhaps, would be to photograph faces that contain the drama of living instead of the tint and gloss of fan magazine portraits.

The emptiness of criticism which limits itself to a declaration that a particular work is good or bad is nowhere more apparent than in the realm of the theatre. Recent reviews of the new Guild production of *He Who Gets Slapped* are a case in point. On the one hand, there were the columnists who were attracted by the play's glamor and therefore pronounced it "good"; on the other, there were those who asserted that the piece was dated, and just as certainly pronounced it "bad."

The argument should not resolve itself to the question of who is right and who wrong, but to the nature of the matter under observation. Even the question of the critic's personal pleasure should be secondary. It is not very important for the critic to tell us whether or not he had a good time at a show (he is not paid for that!) but to understand the character of what he has seen. To put it another way: when we ask a chemist to analyze a new brand of food we are not much concerned to discover whether he enjoys eating it; we want details as to its ingredients. Our reviewers always tend to answer a question they are not being asked and to make their answers in a fashion that relates more to themselves than to the subject they are called upon to judge. Their answers, moreover, betray an undeclared assumption that their taste and constitution resemble ours—an assumption we should immediately qualify as presumptuous.

I do not myself propose to do a thorough review of *He Who Gets Slapped* since it would carry me beyond the plan of the present article. All I need to point out here is that the play is not a fantasy, but a somewhat symbolic drama stemming from the feeling of disillusionment prevalent in a certain section of the Russian intelligentsia between the abortive 1905 revolution and the first World War. This pessimistic mood that permeates almost the whole of Andreyev's work may be regarded as romantic in the slightly deprecatory sense of the word which suggests that we feel it is more of an attitude than a profoundly experienced sense of life. It is as if Andreyev preferred to feel hurt and hopeless, considered it somehow nobler, deeper, almost, one might say, more attractive, than any other way of relating to the world.

It is true, however, that the Russia of Andreyev was a dismal place and the situation of the intellectual class to which he belonged was far from a happy one. So there is more to *He Who Gets Slapped* than color and display. The play is not entirely without psychological perceptiveness or real sensitivity. Nor can we smugly dismiss the play's morbidity on the grounds that in our day we have passed beyond personal depression and moral uneasiness.

The truth is that if the production fails to satisfy, despite the play's best qualities and Tyrone Guthrie's quite original directorial flair, it is due to the fact that the play's style—its emotional core—was not caught. The merits of the production, largely visual and quite real in themselves, are not related to what is significant in the text. The play is neither a love story nor a sad tale of life in the circus. It is a parable of universal defeat, based on a view of suffering as a grotesquely inevitable accident of life which must befall all men, particularly the innocent and fine. If this is spiritually unacceptable to us, there is still no excuse for imagining that it therefore cannot be moving on the stage, or for regarding it mainly as a show competing for the tributes bestowed on *I Remember Mama* or *Life With Father.*

The audience, of course, is not only a vital but perhaps the crucial factor in theatre, a truism that we constantly forget even as we repeat it. Its forcefulness becomes evident as we watch a play like Anouilh's *Antigone* as currently presented by Katharine Cornell. Despite the soundness of its writing and the persistent timeliness of its theme, it remains rather cold and lifeless on our stage. As a play about the need to resist evil, even when evil is armored with logic, and resistance appears almost a vanity, it must have spoken with a special directness in occupied Paris. Even its austerity must have been not only stylistically required but altogether natural in an unheated theatre lacking in all but the barest necessities for physical production. With a virtually martyred audience, the whole performance must have taken on an astringent poignance that it cannot possibly have with us. We see the play done in a plush house by a flush company on a stage handsomely draped to appear unadorned for no reason except "art."

The play, furthermore, has a special interest if we think of a society that makes it possible for a contemporary to take the framework of the Sophoclean drama—far more familiar to the Frenchman out of a secondary school than to a college-graduate American audience—and rework it quite naturally to his own sense of immediate social demands. Despite the play's ambiguities (the tyrant Creon appears more nearly justified than his victim) the play is a challenge delivered in the face of the barbarian enemy. This gives it stature.

It stirred the heart of a French audience then because through it audience and actors were able to communicate a terrible situation they faced in common. As pure text, however, there is something a little depleted about this treatment of the old legend. It appears to be a product of intelligence, culture and will alone. And these are not enough, though perhaps as a worker in the American theatre I should blush to say so.

Perhaps a consideration of individual art works in the light of the civilization that produces them is not altogether fair as it certainly cannot be a complete method of criticism. Nevertheless, when I saw Ray Bolger in *Three To Make Ready*, I could not help wondering why most of our best theatre talent today is almost invariably comic talent. We have practically no so-called "serious" artists in the theatre to compare with Bobby Clark, Fanny Brice, Jimmy Durante, Jimmy Savo, the Marx Brothers. The Lunts are at their best in comedy. Helen Hayes' forte is humor and sentiment. Laurette Taylor is the last of her line, and perhaps she is not altogether a tragedienne. The most fully equipped actor of tragic dimension in recent years was John Barrymore.

Stranger still, our comedians are not "high" but "low" comedians. What they express for the most part is either a crazy inadaptability and revolt against convention or a clownish compliance with it, which comes to the same thing. They are masters of the irrelevant, the empty, the ludicrously and monstrously inconsequent, the nonsensical. Groucho Marx, for example, is the reduction to the absurd of the American small businessman or traveling salesman. Durante is virtually a nihilist, and if he were living on the Continent he would find some interpreter who would demonstrate very artfully that he represented the ecstatic destruction of all values!

Among these men, Ray Bolger alone possesses a kind of classic cleanness of line. He is a spritelike creature of sharpest fancy posing as a humdrum white-collar worker with a yokel background. There was a moment of intense pursuit in *By Jupiter* which was as perfect as anything our theatre has to offer. In the current *Three To Make Ready* most of Bolger's material is poor in relation to his potentialities. The take-off on the soft-shoe routine is exquisitely done, but for a dancer of his fantasy, it is almost too easy.

An eminent American college professor has recently written: "Western civilization is in the midst of a prolonged catastrophic process of dissolution, driving millions to despair, fear and rage, breeding war and revolution, and threatening, if unheeded, to produce even more appalling disasters in the years to come."

As I have pointed out before, the emotional effects of this moral climate are nowhere to be more clearly detected than in the painting of the past few years. Naturally the results are rarely very pleasant, though much of the true meaning of such painting is obscured and disguised by the technique or trick of abstraction.

If we complain that these paintings are distasteful, we may justifiably raise the cry of philistinism. The artist can only reflect the world he lives in. And, ladies and gentlemen, ours is not a happy world—as the professor said! The distinction must be made, however, between material and treatment in a work of art. The destruction that the artist depicts must affect but it should not overwhelm him. Many of the great artists of the past (Goya, Dostoyevsky, Toulouse-Lautrec, Proust) have described corruption. But the clarity, strength, warmth, sorrow, fineness or largeness of their personal qualities as artists creates a balance that redeems what is negative in their material. The artist must not himself be part of what is horrible.

What is often offensive in recent painting is a certain ostentatiousness. I had the occasion recently to see some of the hushed canvases of Albert Ryder. The contrast with the noisiness of what I saw in nearby galleries was a shock. You may say this is a screaming, nervous age so the artists cannot help but scream too. It is not simply the stridency that hurts, but a kind of spiritual immodesty. The artists I am thinking of seem to parade their pain.

Just as bad are those artists who, turning away from the horror of the modern age (and modern art), indulge themselves in a kind of non-objective cheerfulness, the gay decorations of an idiotic playfulness. There is frequently something as willful in their determination to be light and colorful as there is in the determination of the others to be shattering and strong. We are confronted with a stylized grin that bespeaks either a retreat as of a retarded adolescent into a happy playpen, or a device like the commercial smile of a floorwalker.

These attitudes represent an esthetic that is enjoying a considerable success at the moment in the picture galleries. The really good paintings of our day are quieter and are less apt to be violently disturbing when you first behold them. To appreciate their value you will have to look at them again.

This brings me to a discussion of another sin in our cultural life. It is the pressure to express an immediate reaction on every new work presented. At a recent concert of the Rochester Symphony Orchestra, conducted by Leonard Bernstein, I was struck by the critical delight with which Aaron Copland's newly orchestrated *Danzon Cubano* was greeted. The piece is saucy, bright and gay, both dry and delicate, and altogether smart amusement, but the enthusiasm it provoked seemed to me not so much related to the pleasure it gave as to the relief people felt at being able to respond to it immediately. It did not tax their faculties.

When a work of art presents problems to our receptive capacities we are almost annoyed, since it makes it difficult to deliver ourselves of a nice pat opinion. We may be unaware of it but every day we are being pushed further and further into a make-up-your-mind-fast frame of mind. The fact that everybody at a concert, a play, even an art gallery dashes headlong to the nearest neighbor to find out what he thinks, and also to say what he himself thinks, is not a sign that we are becoming more discriminating, but less. The idea that the first task of criticism is to pass judgment is not only false but destructive. The first step in criticism—as in every other kind of appreciation—is to experience. To experience fast is hardly to experience at all. The finer a work of art—the richer an experience—the less likely it is that we will know what we "think" of it right away. Indeed nothing, except a physical shock, can be experienced right away. Bach's *St. Matthew's Passion* is not a "wow."

The pressure that urges us to say something immediately for or against a piece of music or a painting is basically a commercial pressure. It is the enemy of all sensibility and thoughtfulness. It is one of the evil by-products of mass production and cartel civilization. It urges us to see, know, express opinions on everything, so that we finally see very little, know less, and experience nothing but confusion and emptiness. It is fostered by smart weeklies as well as smart parties, and ends with the star-bell-and-thumb system of criticism of tabloid journalism and radio.

Another harmful consequence of all this is the effect on the artist himself. Because the audience strains for a swift reaction—a hit or a flop—the artist becomes intent on producing works that will immediately click. The Copland of such "hits" as *Billy the Kid*, *Rodeo* and the present *Danzon Cubano* is important as well as enjoyable, but no less important, to put it humbly, is the more abstruse Copland of the *Piano Variations*, the *Piano Sonata* and such orchestral works as the *Short Symphony*. If we do not make room for work that is not easy to take we shall never grow up.

Despite all this I must end on a note of acclaim for the hit of the season: the *Airborne Symphony* of Marc Blitzstein, performed at the last of the Leonard Bernstein New York City Orchestra concerts. Perhaps its quality can most readily be characterized by calling it the best show in town. The generative force of this piece is the desire to put it over. This gives it a genuine drive and real sincerity.

It is sincere about making a hit. What does it want to make a hit about? About the wonder of modern times: aviation, anti-fascism, the dangers of the future. If these impulses seem a bit contradictory, they also have their unity. What prevents talented young men from succeeding in this world? To put it baldly: the forces that go to make fascism. The would-be and near-fascists will end by bombing us out of the world as Guernica, Warsaw, London, Rotterdam, etc., were bombed. So we promising young ones must rise and protest.

The text and music of the *Airborne* reflect its dual impulse very well. The words, for example, recall the Second Front slogan as if it were still an issue, but it is only a symbol of something that makes the composer-writer's heart beat faster. It has little concrete political meaning now; and the music here has a young and jazzy success rhythm. The GIs who speak in the narration and chorus are the tough boys with rough vocabularies and good hearts who have become favorite legendary figures. The love song *Dear Emily* is a very effective bit of hokum in the tradition of such popular tunes as *Silver Threads Among the Gold*. The orchestral interludes derive from divers modern masters whose effects are made intelligible here through reference to the works' literary and "story" connotations. There are barber-shop blues, and passages that sound like rousing musical-comedy numbers for a male chorus.

In other words, all the resources available, the classics of recent concert and jazz music, the techniques of what used to be called the left theatre and what might be termed progressive radio, are employed in a febrile eagerness to put everything over: American music, liberal ideas and the piece itself. If there is a certain vulgarity in this, there is also talent. The talent is theatrical, showmanlike, even Broadway, and has a new sophistication— that of the youthful urban intelligentsia nurtured in the thirties. It is urgent, unsure of its true aim, real even if its motives are mixed, expressive of a confused agitation that is energetic, unripe, warmly sentimental to the point of the saccharine, worried, even hysterical at times and, when it is not embarrassing through the obviousness of its special power drive, very engaging withal.

The success of this piece is salutary. It is good for American music. It is good for our public to hear the actual find direct expression in the concert hall as it found expression once in the theatre (*Waiting for Lefty*, *The Cradle Will Rock*, etc.). Should this work prove ephemeral, it is still important as a pioneer piece for those ultimate syntheses which will one day come, perhaps through another generation of artists. There is an aliveness here certainly which didn't obtain in the more "dignified" academic American music of yesteryear. Such work is as important as the minstrel shows, the tall stories and the rest of that humor which

Constance O'Rourke maintained were the true sources of American culture.

The old minstrel shows, it is true, were more innocent. But even what is "corny" and pretentious in the *Airborne* is part of an American consciousness trying to find itself amidst the ubiquitous commercialism in which the ambitious artist must perforce live. Such an artist is useful even to that other type of artist, the semi-recluse who turns his back on the market: Frost, Stieglitz, Williams, Sessions, etc. The success of a piece like the *Airborne* may actually help prepare the way for those other works that have to be lived with and waited for, works that require the effort and patience of the audience.

The *Airborne* finally is emblematic of the values of Leonard Bernstein's contribution to our musical life, perhaps the most important contribution since Koussevitzky and the Boston Symphony Orchestra began to give valiant support to native composers. The performance of the *Airborne* was a triumph for everyone concerned.

—TRW, June '46

IS EVERYBODY HAPPY?

My European friends used to say "If an American has lost his money, been deceived by his girl, had a quarrel with his closest friend, and you ask him how he feels, he will invariably answer "Fine!" It seems that we not only have a tendency to optimism in our country, but that it has actually become a tradition. When we feel low, we not only wish to spare our neighbors the embarrassment of hearing about it, but we virtually hide the fact from ourselves.

Some years ago, Clifford Odets sat in a smart supper club and was belabored by a group of acquaintances because his plays dealt so persistently with unhappy people. "Why don't you write about normal situations? After all, everybody isn't miserable," said a newspaperman with a nervous tic. In reporting the incident, Odets remembered

the argument was eloquently seconded by a gentleman who not long before had crossed the country to threaten his wife at the point of a gun for having announced her intention of divorcing him. Another person who deplored Odets' lugubriousness was a man of unfortunate sexual proclivities, who had accidentally killed a close relative in his childhood. Still another participant in the attack was a successful actor who had, at another time, confessed that he frequently toyed with the idea of suicide. None of these people were being in the least hypocritical. Their habit of mind, formed by the main current of American thought, lent their criticism both cogency and sincerity.

There is historic justification for considering ourselves a happy people. Our country has been a success, and the feeling that things will get better and better for us, if we but play the game and apply our best energy to our enterprises, is not entirely foolish. No amount of scientific, philosophic or economic evidence of disastrous possibilities will actually convince us that we are not destined to continuous well-being. This attitude—implicit in the whole pattern of our behavior—is fundamental, and to voice any different point of view somehow appears peculiar and foreign to us.

For this reason, all our popular arts tend toward comedy forms. The dark strain that entered our recent cultural life with the work of Dreiser, Edgar Lee Masters, Eugene O'Neill, Sherwood Anderson, Ernest Hemingway, William Faulkner, *et al.*, might be termed tragic relief. The preponderant American tradition is happy because it is youthful.

The American artist today seems to be born young and happy! Whatever the detail of crude facts may be, he finds himself, from the first, in an atmosphere that instructs him in a curriculum of unrelenting cheerfulness. A young Frenchman— like Albert Camus, let us say—is born old, that is, he *begins* with the unhappiness of the generation from which he emerges. Hopefulness is something that he struggles to achieve; an optimistic outlook is hard won.

The American artist, I repeat, begins young and happy, even when his work is serious and "strong." *Waiting for Lefty* was an essentially lusty outcry, informed with the enthusiasm of a cheering grandstand. *Awake and Sing!,* sadder and more sensitive, had a certain youthful down on its quivering lip. Marc Blitzstein's work, despite its many moments of acidulousness and portentousness, is redeemed by a very winning boyishness. Saroyan, at his best, has the irresistible charm of a healthy puppy.

I believe the special youthfulness of our artists is not only characteristic but a contribution. What is difficult for the American artist is to avoid having his youthfulness develop into a grinning grimace of empty professionalism and to grow old with a deepening of grace.

At the Ballet Theatre—during its season at the Metropolitan Opera House—one saw happy youthfulness in Jerome Robbins' *Interplay*. Here the training of the classical ballet is made to release the vigorous charm of American boys and girls. How much more alive this is, in its sweet brashness, than the cold contrivance of Balanchine's recent fancies.

This type of American ballet is growing, but not yet as grown up as it possibly imagines itself to be. But even if the young herb springs up a little wild and rough, it is more fragrant than the old plant painfully preserved from some ancient garden of traditional dignity. The humor of the young ballet will go stale if the artists who create it allow it to become a new mode of sophistication.

Youthful charm hardens into an irritating cliché when it becomes a boastful end in itself rather than a spontaneous expression. There is a suspicion of such self-indulgence in Michael Kidd's *On Stage*, although Kidd himself is appealing in his pathetic wispiness. There is some excellent dancing in a show like *St. Louis Woman*. Yet its lacquer of refinement, taste and affluence cannot disguise the fact that in the matter of real spark and vibrancy it is far less notable than, let us say, Lew Leslie's first *Blackbirds,* a crude revue of some seventeen years ago.

With the repetition induced by success, there comes a heightened expertness and a decreased verve. This is true even on the level of the simplest entertainments. I noticed it when I heard Duke Ellington's band at Carnegie Hall in January. It seemed difficult to enjoy this suave craftsman's work now without the aid of a drink, the accompaniment of a pretty girl and a general atmosphere of smoky hilarity. It had become mechanical. When Woody Herman's band put in its appearance at Carnegie Hall in March, it made a noise that sounded like an orgiastic celebration at a crowded Broadway restaurant with everybody suddenly moved to fling hunks of raw hamburger and herring at one another. In the meantime, the audiences' reaction resembled a catalepsy of stupidity masked in jerky movement to lend it the pretense of pleasure. (Into this atmosphere the funeral apparition of a Stravinsky piece, especially written for this orchestra, made a peculiar effect. It was as if the composer, in the guise of a friend of "hot" music, had come to bury his art. In the early twenties, when Stravinsky wrote a jazz piece for piano, it bespoke a fascination with a new musical language, as well as a reflection of the exquisite dislocation of the period. Now it appeared as if the ratio of serious art to the so-called popular art is as Stravinsky's piece to the rest of Woody Herman's program.)

In the light vein, the triumph of the theatrical season is undoubtedly the revue *Call Me Mister*. The show is unified by the energetic candor I have been discussing, given further point here by the fact that all the actors as well as the authors are either returned GIs or entertainers who devoted their services to our armed forces. Combined with a sense of fun, these young people possess a gift for what might be called the tradition of the practical theatre. This theatre has at its core an element of simple instruction such as we found in *One Third of a Nation*, among the best of the old Federal Theater productions. In this tradition—for which we as a young and happy people have a special aptitude—an amateur spirit evolves a hearty style from the desire to communicate socially important information coupled by a sound morality. The medium is compounded of laughter, an innocent shrewdness, childlike wit. This kind of show has little in common with the French political cabaret (which is usually irresponsible and cynical) or the smart English revue, which may introduce an occasional topical number for the sake of hoity-toity banter. Our "practical" revues— of the which the *Garrick Gaieties*, *The Grand Street Follies* and, particularly, *Pins and Needles* were early examples—are flavored with a liberal political point of view (not unduly stressed in this instance) and an optimistic social fervor. There are two or three real talents among the new people of the present show. Such numbers as the one which relates the extraordinary transformations of the *Military Life* ("He went in a slob—he's still a slob!"), *Off We Go*, a lampoon of the motion-picture conception of the Air Force and, above all, the *South Wind* sketch which introduces *The Senators Song*—with satirical compliments to Rankin, Bilbo and sundry legislative Bourbons— are highlights of the season. In this setup anybody over thirty-five would be shockingly out of place. The appeal is to that wholesome section of the public that has not lost its fountain of youth. On this level, we are still happy.

I do not regard such screen shows as *The Kid from Brooklyn*, with Danny Kaye, or Walt Disney's latest cartoon comedy *Make Mine Music* in the same light, that is, as representative entertainment for a still robust people. In fact, both these pictures puzzled me a bit. I was almost about to say that Disney's work at present is almost the only modern art I don't quite understand. It is more than skillful: almost all the adjectives from brilliant up or down can be applied to it. Every device of the abstractionist technique, which bewilders and annoys people at the art galleries, seems to be employed here with the greatest facility. There are notions and fancies that are frequently funny. The results should be more than memorable. On the

contrary, they are equivalent to an utter blank. Ingenuity without personality is like a thousand times zero.

Danny Kaye is equally remarkable. He can be quite funny. He appears able to do a little of everything. He is an effulgent zany with a golem's energy, a sort of perpetual motion of showmanship. It is as if a steel gadget did endless droll tricks. But his performance has no overtones. A complete competence in relating to every kind of audience robs him of savor. One goes away empty. There is no hidden reserve in his work, no enigma or heart. These are as necessary to the clown as to any other artist.

Is everybody happy? The artist may develop after he has reached forty, only if his joy has the same root as his sorrow. Then his gaiety will not become just a more elaborate bag of tricks; his laughter will not become a mechanical guffaw. If "good times" go, and his early success loses its glitter or turns to the dust of neglect, he will not degenerate into a sterile crank.

Think of the fifty-seven-year-old Chagall, whose retrospective show at the Museum of Modern Art is one of this year's delights. He began in Russia with a curiously playful imagination; his fancy bounced with elation in Paris; and his work as a whole, turning from wondrous laughter to a cabalistic contemplation, always retains a unity of humble affection, sensuality, grief. In some of his latest work, the angel of death casts a shadow over his village cosmos, and one becomes aware of tears, that do not cause any distortion but only add a profound note to complete the gamut of his tender music.

Mere richness of color does not signify an agreeable state of mind. Paul Gauguin (in the recent retrospective show at the Wildenstein Galleries) reveals himself as an artist caught in an emotional dilemma that is part pathos and part disease. Out of his deep discomfort, Gauguin created his enchantment. Perhaps intoxication would be the more suggestive word. For there is something both heady and poisonous in the vision that Gauguin wrought. Out of pain came this evil flower—to which we all occasionally come for a momentary whiff to relieve some of our own tension.

Gauguin's sickness may be described as bourgeois surfeit trying to cure itself with greater surfeit. By the end of the nineteenth century, society had produced a wealth of goods for a certain class of people, and with it a great deal of ugliness for the world in general. To a sensitive and sensuous man like Gauguin, the scene he knew was both too rich and too poor—full of all sorts of oppressive luxuries together with a corresponding drabness. He sought an escape to a world better equipped with the power to overwhelm and transport his soul. He wanted an ecstasy of his senses and sensibility that alone might make it possible for him to transcend the prison of the bourgeois life that supported but could not satisfy him. Not having either a belief in God or a belief in man, he craved a universe that would offer more of what he loved in his own despised world—more delicious sensation, more untrammeled embrace of the physical favors of life. In a word, he was seeking a heaven on earth, made up of precisely those goods which had turned his civilization into a suffocating hell. He was seeking a middle-class artist's utopia, a never-never land of superesthetic substance and comfort. He found it in his art. He painted what he looked for. Since it is very difficult to create from within only, he sought the image of his dreams in the world outside. Thus he found the South Sea Islands.

But he saw in this fabulous region only what he needed and had been looking for from the first. The fruity colors and the tapestry, rich textures we see in the later paintings, are all anticipated in the earlier ones. Gauguin was not essentially a painter of nature. His landscapes are inspired by a hunger for an artificial paradise. They are not true, I feel sure, in relation to the places they appear to represent. His women are not so much the real women of any particular place as idols of his imagination, figments of desire—sometimes mixed with fear

and repulsion. This return to the primitive is lacking in naïveté, in freedom, even in passion. Gauguin's Tahiti is an invention—a drug to dull the ache he was suffering.

He concocted his powerful elixir from materials his avid susceptibilities had absorbed in the Parisian upper bourgeoisie from which he ran away, and added to it a few new juices as well as the ceremonial incantations from the tropics to give it its final bouquet.

Back home those who were unconsciously suffering from the same ailments as the artist were offended at first at the exotic remedy which was offered them. Later they developed a taste for its savor, because it had a base that was pretty much that of certain syrups with which they were quite familiar. They took to it as a kind of magic potion. Today some of the first effects of frenzy have worn off, and we take note of Gauguin's sorcery with a sober eye. We see the sorry man, the great gifts, the need he tried to fulfill. We sympathize, appreciate and admire. Gauguin's work is often on the verge of vulgarity. What saves it is its mystery. The whole process of his experience is a strange conjunction of a burning problem and a false solution—resulting in several monuments of modern art.

Altogether different from this European phenomenon is the American eye of John Marin, whose little pen, pencil and crayon sketches of the Brooklyn Bridge, lower Manhattan and other sections of the city were recently shown at An American Place, Alfred Stieglitz' nest on Madison Avenue. Marin—now seventy-six—is generally discussed in relation to his larger pieces. These bits of scratched paper appear so casual in form, so rapid and almost desultory in execution, they passed almost completely unnoticed. For me, however, the whole miracle of Marin may be most quickly surveyed in these shorthand notes of his art. How shall I describe the visionary flashes which, in a few lines, catch the excitement and force of our city? If I said that these sketches convey a sort of effervescent

Arabian Nights concept of New York, it might suggest something romantic and lush, whereas Marin's art is astringent, fresh and thoroughly realistic in spirit.

There seems to be nothing here except a few childish strokes, but these manage to contain the essence of some movement which makes us realize the whole. Here is the power, dash and sharpness that we like to associate with our "new world," but which none of us actually *see*. Marin does see them, apparently without thought or effort—and equally without sentimentality, strain, falsification. This is a lyrical art without tears, a stylized art that strikes us as wholly natural, a lean and pulsating art that catches the structure and spirit of reality without recourse to that abstruse geometry of forms which, in so much latter-day painting, obscures rather than reveals its subject. Marin can show us an array of skyscrapers so that we feel that they are both as light as a dream and as solid as pyramids. It is as if our familiar urban landscape were seen not by a man but by a god, able to seize the fleeting impression while registering the permanent fact, a mirror of the moment and a history of the everlasting.

But this god is a plain American—if there ever was one. This savant of the pencil and the brush is a hayseed. His art makes a comment without ratiocination; it evinces instinct that is at the same time unanswerable logic. This is mastery without pretension. There is greatness in this art. It is fundamentally simple, pure, final. It seems to look beyond the mess of the instant and to exclude most of what concerns and troubles us in our time. Yet it is not at all outside reality. It seems fixed on a point beyond our immediate horizon, without its being in a world beyond our reach. It is a realm of fundamental forces that have grandeur, achieve balance and promise liberation. It eschews exaggeration, hysteria, roaring excess. It is truly happy. It represents the kind of perfection toward which it is natural and healthy to aspire.

—*TRW*, July '46

SHAKESPEARE AND COMPANY

If there is a Shakespeare tradition in our theatre today, it is this: we go to a production of Shakespeare with a slight apprehension of being beneficently bored, and we find ourselves absurdly relieved at finding the experience almost as tolerable as the work of some less formidable classic. Because of this tradition, no one is in a proper state of mind to judge any Shakespeare production intelligently. No one, that is, sees it as a living theatrical experience.

If we did regard the stage Shakespeare in this light, we would confess that in the theatre the fellow is largely unintelligible and therefore curiously empty. On the other hand, because Shakespeare is rarely done in our theatre except as a vehicle for an actor we hope to admire, our criticism of the production seldom considers the play presented as a play, but confines itself to an account of the degree to which the star has lived up to our expectations. Since we do not see the play as a play, we cannot truly estimate the actor whose virtuosity is the occasion for the production.

The fact is that, for at least the past twenty-five years, we have practically no one in our English speaking theatre fit to do Shakespeare at all. For the outstanding and essential characteristic of Shakespeare's genius is his abundance. I refer to an abundance of imagination, color, energy, passion, that no actor or company of actors we possess commands.

I speak of abundance; I might have said excess. Due to his position in our educational system and to the progressive cutting down of forces in our theatre, Shakespeare with us has become an altogether "literary" affair, a matter of more or less lucid or illustrative readings of the big speeches, that is to say, of the words. But this emphasis on the purely verbal and intellectual aspect of Shakespeare is the surest way to denature the sense of Shakespeare as a living dramatist.

Shakespeare is not primarily the archaic and prolix poet of strong and somehow lofty melodramas alleviated by passages of low comedy in prepschool vein that we generally find on our stage, but a bloody, rough, almost barbarically wild Renaissance prince and rowdy—everything but a "gentleman." The Shakespearean spirit is too heroically uncouth, the Shakespearean imagination too explosively riotous for us to capture except in the most timid—I might almost say "sissy"—approximations. Shakespeare is really too physically fundamental in his comedy, too vehement and overwhelming in his tragedy—tending almost always toward the extreme limits of pessimism—for us to cope with. No wonder the French of the eighteenth century were rather revolted by him. No wonder the best Shakespearean actors have evoked such tumultuous phrases as that of Coleridge when he spoke of his experience on seeing Kean as a reading of Shakespeare by flashes of lightning. To make sense, Shakespeare on the stage should serve as a severe shock.

This, at any rate, is the esthetic premise from which I evaluate any Shakespearean production I see. The Old Vic productions of *Henry IV*, Parts I and II, may be fairly described then as a neighborhood or home library version of Shakespeare. It is a pleasant neighborhood and a sound home that give it birth. If it cannot be said to have the size of the older models, it still evinces a sturdiness and stalwartness that mark a continuity from and relationship to its mighty forbears.

No real style—such as were evident in the best European productions I have seen—is achieved. No single performance of the stature and individual savor of a John Barrymore—to mention almost the last English speaking actor *capable* of a true Shakespearean creation—emerges. But there is still the charm of a sweet manliness, a humility in relation to the material, a dignity in the execution, that endow the Old Vic production with qualities which are not only respectable but endearing. Ralph Richardson is not a Falstaff—he has a very engaging humor but he simply hasn't sufficient

exuberance of the senses—nor is even Laurence Olivier quite a complete Hotspur—he has temperament but not quite the sharp flame. Yet both have a humanity and uprightness in their portrayals, a kind of honest appreciation and understanding of their task that cleanse the air of the noxious atmosphere of pretentiousness, foolishness and vain posturing which obtain in nearly all our Shakespearean revivals. One does not feel that the members of the company are trying to make a show of themselves in a sanctified framework, but serving a play for which they have a genuine unaffected fondness and some actual connection.

Though the Old Vic company is closer to the English classic through national and cultural heritage, it is really more suited to Chekhov through human experience. This is not to say that it does one "better" than the other. But it is almost easier for them as people of the twentieth century to translate themselves into the mood of the late nineteenth century than into that of the sixteenth. Even if it is English and not Russian, their Chekhov is entirely sympathetic. It is English—and modern English to boot—by virtue of a kind of introspection, a brittle nervousness and an almost taciturn moodiness that are largely foreign to the Russian temperament and theatre!

Contrary to common belief, the Russian Chekhov is always more robust, more physically effusive, more externally expressive. Thus Chekhov in the Russian theatre always seems "louder and funnier" than he does in most English or American productions. This does not mean that the Russians "play him for comedy," try to convert the situations into a series of shallow jokes, but that their approach to the life of the emotions is more direct and more vigorous.

Despite a certain thinness then and scenes that are uncertain in conception and execution (*Uncle Vanya*'s resort to firearms) Chekhov does come through in the Old Vic production. And he is beautiful.

The daily press reception of *Uncle Vanya* was such that I cannot praise the play without some reference to the dismaying nonsense that most of the reviews contained. One reviewer summed up his impression by declaring that for all the excellence of the Old Vic's performance, the play did not quite make "satisfactory entertainment." As an entertainer poor Chekhov is no match for Lindsay and Crouse! Chekhov is "slow, sprawling, leisurely." The play has no "action"—except for a shooting in the third act that misfires!

The insistent demand for "pace"—rapidity of speech and movement—on the part of all our dramatic critics is composed on the one hand of ignorance as to what constitutes stage direction and on the other of neurosis. The quiet of a reflective art plays havoc with the nerves of our deadline boys. They have no place to go but to their night desks, bars and beds, but they become terribly impatient unless they are jiggled and massaged into the illusion of activity. As for "action" it would surprise them to hear that Chekhov's plays are replete with it. There is hardly a wasted word in any of them. The action, of course, is not that of a Warner Brothers' melodrama, but the action of people waging war against an ever-present antagonist. The fact that the characters are often reduced to a state of muted despair does not make their situation any less dramatic. Chekhov is a master of continuous revelation—and this is true action.

One reviewer complained that Chekhov's characters are "feeble, decadent, frustrated." The truth is that if they appear so, it is only because they are such active and persistent idealists. Aspiration is the very essence of their natures. Uncle Vanya accepts a whole lifetime of obscurity because he believes in the spiritual mission of his brother-in-law. His friend, Dr. Astrov, festers in a remote and backward section of his country to care for his people there, while carrying on a futile defense of the forests which he loves.

What is the evil genius—the antagonist—that dogs these lovely human beings who pursue the ideals they create for themselves with an almost saintly loyalty? Chekhov's plays, written under a very rigid censorship, could not be propaganda. But it must have been clear to his original audience that in a country where, aside from a few artists, no one could exercise any real power or influence except through the officialdom of the aristocracy and the upper military caste that the cause of their unhappiness lay in the whole social structure which subordinated everything to these classes.

The middle class, which never developed in Russia as elsewhere, had hardly much more freedom than any of the classes beneath them. The middle class accepted this situation—was loyal, as Vanya has been loyal to his brother-in-law, the Professor. (We must remember that a professor in Russia was indirectly a government official and thus stuffily representative of the ruling classes.) The Professor of the play—worshipped by his old mother-in-law—unwittingly acts the role of fatuous Fate. He makes his entire family sacrifice itself to him. He reduces his wife to a kind of cowardly and voluptuous impotence. He robs his daughter of every opportunity for self-expression. He relegates the sensitive Vanya to a dismally humdrum life, while he moves about protected, important and unaware of the wreck he causes. At the same time (and this Vanya learns too late for decisive action) he creates nothing of real value, delivering himself of pompous, meaningless forms that have the sanction of an armed and hallowed power which was the semi-feudal government of Mother Russia. All this he does simply by being—the Professor! What do his victims do? They dream, they hope, they try to understand, they struggle against hopelessness and bitterness, they seek to preserve a remainder of moral sanity through human sympathy and brotherliness. Even in their dejection, they retain to an astonishing degree the redeeming virtues of men who suffer innocently but do not altogether break. These people represent a whole generation of the Russian intelligentsia from which issued such people as the backers and the artists of the Moscow Art Theatre as well as Chekhov himself. They were the seed that had to die so that something greater might be born.

The interest of *Uncle Vanya*, however, is not historical. Though none of us lives under regimes like that of the Romanovs, the destiny of many people the world over is not unlike those of Chekhov's characters. The incubus that weighs down upon them may not be any silly Professor, but are there not many men and women—let us say in our own South, for example—whose isolation and sense of being lost, blocked and baffled resembles these characters in a play almost a half century old? May it not even be true that we who live in a land of multiple opportunities are sometimes as defeated by our illusion of freedom as those in Chekhov's world who knew they had none?

That the Old Vic's production of *Uncle Vanya* makes one think of some English country place as much as of a Russian, I repeat, does not diminish but actually emphasizes the play's universality. The English company is rather less virile than any Russian company might be. Still by virtue of his sensitivity, Ralph Richardson, is basically right, even though he somewhat overdoes a certain comic clumsiness in Vanya and seems to fear taking the character altogether seriously as a kind of lost artist. Laurence Olivier plays Astrov with a kind of dry observation that marks him as a thoughtful actor, though his interpretation robs the character a little of some of its underlying largeness and breadth. In view of the notices accorded this production, I must not fail to add that for me it proved the most moving evening spent in the theatre this season.

Most admirers of the Old Vic company reserved this encomium for the production of *Oedipus*. It may appear strange, after what I have said in regard to Chekhov to confess myself a partisan—in theory at least—of a bolder type of dramaturgy than he represents. Abstractly speaking, my personal preference is for the theatre of strong movement, highly graphic or monumental characters, annunciatory even declamatory speech—the theatre of the colorful mask or epic-like affirmation. For this reason, I too enjoyed *Oedipus*. It was perhaps the Old Vic's best show. But I could not regard it as much more than "just a story."

The play itself is, of course, a masterpiece of dramatic construction. Its simple unrelenting line and emotional grip are overpowering. As for the poetry of its speech, I cannot judge the original, and Yeats' adaptation is excellent precisely for its lack of effort to do much more than convey the essential dramatic drive and nobility of the story. But the meaning of the play, in this production at any rate, impresses me only "symbolically." I can show signs of being sobered by the philosophy of ineluctable fate which makes all effort and resistance vain. I can wax intellectual over the demonstration of how Oedipus' very insistence on probing the essence of truth hastens his doom. I can discourse on the discipline and grandeur involved in the acceptance of such a philosophy. But I do not actually believe it; it means nothing to me.

When Nietzsche, discussing *Oedipus*, in his *Birth of Tragedy* develops the thesis that tragedy entails a recognition of life's inherent cruelty (for Oedipus is condemned to destruction by the very quality of his genius, and all his efforts are manifestations of both his vitality and the inevitability of his personal annihilation) I am not only persuaded but experience a kind of awe that is at once sorrowful and exhilarating. But as the Old Vic company tells it—I could not regard any of this seriously: it was a solemn fairy tale that I lent myself to for purposes of amusement. If I believed anybody else in the theatre at the time really accepted it, I should either be revolted or be moved to a kind of scornful laughter. No, I cannot be convinced that the significance of Sophocles' tragedy is really accepted or even understood by a New York audience for this would mean that it acknowledged the truth of a religion of quietistic and pessimistic heroism. I need no second thought to know that this cannot be so.

The present production, of course, may be largely responsible for my benevolent incredulity. A realized work of art can persuade one of almost anything. In relation to its material, this production is respectably amateurish. It is as if a bunch of bright and energetic high-school boys tried to man a battleship. The production is conventionally pretty—statically decorative—rather than dramatically expressive. The quality of a production of a play like *Oedipus* must possess a fierce grandeur. It demands giant personalities in whom the spirit of tragedy is real to the point of the fearsome. (Chaliapin as Boris Godunov may be taken as an example of what I have in mind.) Anything less becomes inferior to the towering marionettes I saw at a performance of Stravinsky's *Oedipus* at the Metropolitan Opera House almost twenty years ago.

Laurence Olivier is one of the finest actors of our English speaking stage today. He has a delightful sense of character. (His Shallow in the second part of *Henry IV* is a capital job.) He has an attractive and winning spirit. He has feeling, even power, but in "straight" roles he is a romantic actor not a tragedian. If he were a Frenchman he could play the heroes of Alfred de Musset's plays magnificently. A romantic actor's strong point is *sentiment* rather than that basic strength of experience that informs the real tragedian like a sap drawn from the earth to give each of his movements the shattering inevitability of a force of nature. The true tragedian portrays the archetypical, something beyond any individual suffering. Olivier at his best is a wounded man, one is tempted to say, a quivering boy. His Oedipus is as good a try at the noble style of tragedy as any young actor of our English speaking stage could make. His almost brutal cry of agony at the moment of self-discovery is daring, almost inspired, but it remains on a level of pathos: a good man is in pain. It is not transfiguration: no principle of life has been revealed.

Olivier manages nevertheless to make the Old Vic season a personal triumph by appearing as Mr. Puff in Sheridan's *Critic*. This piece of theatrical and literary high jinks reminds me for some reason of the kind of boisterous satire that may be frequently seen at the adult camps of our Eastern seaboard states. It represents a kind of sophistication that expresses itself in life-of-the-party pranks.

It is a very cute and jolly romp in which actors and audiences take the opportunity of being decently foolish together. Olivier plays with skill, wit and allowable coquetry.

The real importance of the Old Vic's visit here lies not so much in any single production or in the chance it affords us to see classic plays rarely done here or even in the introduction of such unusual performances as those of Ralph Richardson and Laurence Olivier. The Old Vic's importance derives from its reminder of what a theatre is: a group of dramatic artists devoted through a unified ideal to a continuous program of work in common. If Laurence Olivier has become an actor of enviable achievement, it is not because he is a greater talent than any we possess. Alfred Lunt, in my opinion, is more subtly and richly endowed. But while he will play *O Mistress Mine* for two or three seasons, Olivier, through his association with the Old Vic can employ his talent far more valuably by playing Hotspur, Shallow, Astrov, Oedipus, Mr. Puff, while at the same time doing a motion picture version of *Henry V*, and preparing for the challenge of King Lear.

It is not only significant however that such commercially successful actors as Richardson and Olivier have lent their support to the Old Vic and turned it into a "paying theatre," but that for the past thirty-five years or more England had an Old Vic theatre to which these actors and others like them could come. Unless such a tradition exists, a Theatre can hardly be said to exist. Where no such Theatre exists, an abundance of talent—such as we possess in our country—will lose a great deal of its capacity to make a really effective cultural contribution to society. When the Oliviers and Richardsons leave the Old Vic, there will still be an Old Vic, as there was before they came, and the English stage which, in many respects is far behind ours, will still be able to continue its best tradition. When a brilliant actor or a group of talented theatre people disappears from our scene there is no active tradition to carry the remaining workers forward in the creative paths of those who went before. Thus we are always forced to begin anew with diminished rather than enhanced strength. The spirit of a healthy tradition—which in England, remember, is related to a theatre *at popular prices*—gives the whole of the Old Vic company a professional dignity, an ease, a grace, a sense of participation in a socially useful enterprise that even our very best and most successful actors rarely achieve.

—TRW, Aug. '46

NOTES FOR CONVERSATION

The French Touch: There was much talk before World War II about "French decadence." This was chiefly German propaganda and general ignorance. As World War II approached one heard much less about this famous decadence. Even the shameful collapse of 1940 did not revive the phrase, though it betrayed a condition in certain quarters that might have justified its use.

Now that France is reconstituting herself, sending us a few new paintings—such as those of Jean Dubuffet recently shown at the Pierre Matisse Gallery; new writers—Anouilh, Sartre, Camus; a quasi-new school of thought—existentialism—our minds turn once more to the country and culture of our first enthusiasm.

Early in the year two concerts of French music were given at Hunter College under the auspices of France Forever. Music by Debussy, Milhaud, Poulenc, Satie, Sauguet, and a new composer, Oliver Messiaen, was heard. Nearly all of this music was pleasant or interesting, but I did not feel impelled to discuss it, strangely enough, till I attended the exposition of dress design—and some theatrical decor—given in New York recently as a benefit for French relief under the title *le Théâtre de la Mode.*

I cannot say what the "trade" thought of the innumerable examples of French dressmaking that were shown. They seemed admirable to me, but I might have been a more reliable judge if the dresses had been worn by living models rather than draped on tiny wire mannequins which made them appear more "artistic" but less attractive. What the show served to do, however, was to make me think about certain French qualities, which I had noted at the concerts. A phrase that I had heard in connection with a well-known actress kept recurring to me as I moved through the dimly lit halls of this exhibition: a whim of iron.

There is an almost mysterious mixture in French art of daintiness and strength. It is as if the most delicate expressions of French thought were made of some sturdy substance that cheated time as well as our eye. We associate endurance with gravity and bulk. The French seem to excel in what appears ephemeral and manages to persist. They see no contradiction between what is intended to be only engaging and what proves perennial. The lightest and gayest of modern cultures is for this reason the most "difficult." The difficulty consists in realizing that what is disarmingly easy may at the same time be profound. One of the greatest records of modern perturbation—Pascal's *Pensées*—actually is "quick reading."

I am not a habitual Francophile because I am not a partisan of any People. (I like only my friends!) But I am obliged to confess an indestructible faith in the French. I arrive at this not through an unqualified admiration for all their works, but through the ability of the French to survive in their best and most essential qualities despite the invasion of all our criticism, irritation, condescension, and dismissal of them.

When the sum of all the music I heard at the above-mentioned French concerts seemed to amount to nothing more than an exquisite refinement, my mood grew querulous. The absence of ruggedness, of conflict, of "resistance" in the music struck me as an unpremeditated confession of weakness in the people who made it. The rebellious spirit in French music, I mused, appears only in Berlioz. For the rest there is only the serenity of an old wisdom, gracious sobriety, a muffled brightness, intelligence, wit, and an occasional burst of an insouciant cockiness. Though our interest in these characteristics as they manifest themselves in separate individuals may fade, they remain abiding virtues as they constantly reappear in new forms with new people. They seem to compose a stabilizing body without which our Western culture would be unthinkable. The strength of this art seems to dwell in a perdurable modesty containing in clear solution almost every notable attribute that other people produce to excess. The refinement of the French is thus a kind of universal and spiritually refreshing common sense. It has often succeeded in converting madness into reason.

At the *Théâtre de la Mode* Jean Cocteau has contributed a Tribute to René Clair which, like so much of Cocteau's work, is a visualized metaphor. We see a threadbare room in which a wedding party has been interrupted by the explosion of an enemy bomb. Some of the guests have been maimed or killed; others, apparently unhurt, in clothes that are disheveled but still elegant are writhing about in a kind of horrified spasm. Through the opening of a broken wall we see Paris in the night, silenced by fear, but somehow retaining a stately calm and even chic. The effect of this small tableau—which might be titled France At War—is intimate, poetically plain, ineffably graceful. One is reminded of Gertrude Stein's remark about human nature having gone on for such a long time in France that the French can afford to make their buildings temporary.

French genius consists in the ability to reduce the world's complex experience to usable, one might say, handy proportions. This gift, when it is not revitalized through the upheaval of forces from its own and surrounding chaos, tends to grow complacent and to accumulate on its surface an alarming quantity of dry rot. The latter is often very pretty. Foreigners are frequently unable to distinguish between what is the body and what the parasitical growth in French culture. Thus in much that comes from France today we recognize some of the old intelligence, will, and craft without any truly creative passion. But even in these samples of

ancient decay there is that which promises a future renewal and synthesis.

Slogan for the fortunate: I have no advice for "refugee" artists. It would be presumptuous of me or anyone else to tell those recent arrivals to our country who fled death and destruction through fascism and war what course to take now that Europe has to be rebuilt.

In a sense, of course, the war still rages, and the visage of the bright new world of tomorrow is not only scarred with the wounds of the old battle but marred by the hideous grimace of persistent struggle. A new world always begins as a wilderness or a wreck. No American, I repeat, would dare suggest how or where European artists should face their future. They certainly have not outworn their welcome with us.

Yet as I watched Jean Renoir's latest Hollywood film *Diary of a Chambermaid*—which contains some of the best direction since his arrival—I could not help but observe the anomalous aspect of his position among us. The picture is basically a French product made in America. For this reason it cannot be altogether intelligible to our audience. Yet because it was made to satisfy our audience it will probably seem a bit strange in France. While it is clearly the work of a man of genuine talent it speaks no clear language, being too special for us and too detached from any precise definition for anyone else. As a story of avarice, ambition and hate, evolved in the milieu of a French aristocracy that had finally lost its grip in 1900 not to speak of a middle and working class that in this telling are just as bad, the picture gives little evidence of a particular aim.

The "refugee" artist of superficial abilities makes the transition from one culture to another with little difficulty. The superior artist is deeply rooted and generally loses something essential when he is too long cut off from his natural base. If one were to become absolute about it one would carry this point too far. Yet I am sometimes tempted to reverse the hateful old slogan to a new one which the artists I have in mind may well find equally hateful: if you like it here, go back where you come from. For the artist, the more painful path may well prove the healthier.

Life and letters: One of the nimble wits among our dramatic critics thought there was something hilarious about the woes of the characters in Chekhov's *Uncle Vanya*. What were they all so wretched about? You may recall that the central figure of that play is a man who has wasted his life through sacrifice to a brother-in-law whom he once believed a genius only to discover too late that the man is a selfish fool. Another character is unhappy because she has no hope of winning the man she loves and practically no opportunity to find anyone else. Still another suffers marriage to the aforementioned fool. The community doctor is an idealist isolated in a dreary village among a poor and degraded peasantry.

The other day I entered a fashionable restaurant accompanied by a professional colleague. Sitting alone at a table was a conspicuously unhappy-looking man, drinking hard, outlined as it were by an aura of agony. My companion left me for a moment and went over to the solitary drinker. When my friend returned to our table I asked the name of the man he had been talking to. It was the critic who had not been able to take Chekhov altogether seriously. "What's he so miserable about?" I asked. "Oh," my friend replied, "he wants to be a playwright!"

Art and propaganda: I agree that *On Whitman Avenue,* the play at the Cort Theatre, is a fairly crude piece of writing. When some of the more liberal reviewers were taken to task by their readers for not having supported the play on the ground of its theme and message (the evils of anti-Negro discrimination) the reviewers pointed out that while they were in sympathy with the play's purpose they could not in conscience praise it for that alone. They went on to say that a poor propaganda play might actually do a disservice to the cause in behalf of which it was written.

This is valid, but it would be more so if the plays the same critics were able to accept were truly respectable on a higher level. Between the speciousness of some of our big hits—almost always lauded by these reviewers—and the inadequacies of a play like *On Whitman Avenue* there is perhaps no great artistic difference. If I had to choose between the two, I might say that the rough propaganda play merited more cordial support. For it is surely a moot point whether phoney competence is more valuable than a sincere but inexpert effort to deal with a serious social problem.

When the reviewers expose the obvious flaws of the latter type of play, they imply that such plays are merely propaganda while the others are art or sound entertainment. This, I repeat, is not so. All of us are subject to error, but I notice that our reviewers generally manage to err on the more convenient side. Oh for a dramatic critic who would make the unexpected, courageous error!

How to be right: There is a capable art critic in New York whose pieces on painting reveal a remarkable trait. They are infrequent, and when they do appear they rarely deal with a painter about whom this critic is unreservedly enthusiastic. His reviews usually tend to demonstrate that some highly regarded artist is not quite as good as he is reputed to be. Painter R., he suggests, may have certain merits but he hasn't quite got this, that and the other necessary virtue. Painter G. also has something to be said for him, but he fails in four or five crucial respects. What the painter has is left a little vague, what he hasn't constitutes the body of the review. Almost everything that is said shows both close observation and technical training but the total effect of these reviews is not only negative but empty.

The reader is left with a very favorable opinion of the critic: here is a man who isn't easily fooled. But though almost every statement the critic makes has some basis in good judgment, the subject of his review is never truly revealed, while the reader's appetite for art is weakened rather than sharpened by it.

This particular critic is not an isolated phenomenon. A method of criticism is being developed in certain circles that not only is beginning to affect professional discussion but ordinary conversation among interested laymen as well. It arises where the need to impress is greater than the capacity to enjoy. Its often unconscious proponents are basically timid souls whose mask is one of intellectual independence and lofty discernment. I can give no clearer analysis of their method of criticism—it might be called criticism by subtraction—than by setting down a parody paragraph on a musical "subject."

For instance, one might say that Mozart hasn't Bach's virility; Bach hasn't Mozart's grace; Beethoven hasn't Gluck's tenderness; Wagner hasn't Brahms's softness, Brahms hasn't Wagner's force; Moussorgsky hasn't Debussy's delicacy; Debussy hasn't Moussorgsky's earthiness, so on and on *ad nauseum*. It is a prescription for starvation.

The battle of old and new: Every once in a while the controversy between old and new art bobs up to provide copy for a few Sundays of attack and counterattack. The old painters, we are told, knew how to draw and were devoted to Beauty. The more recent painters are either incompetents, frauds, or plain crackpots. Sometimes the controversy takes subtler forms. In music, for example, we are instructed that while many composers after Stravinsky are men of unquestionable ability, they do not have something that Strauss and his forebears had! It might be pointed out for instance that modern composers make too much use of folk melody or themes borrowed from dance halls and even the musical comedy stage.

Much damning evidence is adduced. The debate proceeds along the lines used by Gordon Craig in his argument about acting. Art, said Craig, has to be fixed in permanent, unvarying forms. The actor cannot help but change his performance to some slight degree each time he appears. Ergo: acting cannot be art. In a similar manner, one demonstrates very easily that photography, being done by a machine, cannot be an art. These arguments are cogent if one accepts their premises. The trouble is that these premises are extremely doubtful.

It matters very little with what tools or through what devices an art object is made. Artists have always used whatever material they found in their environment. I am sure that much of the melody in classic compositions is based on common folk music that is too obscure now for us to recognize as such. Modern paintings reveal more café scenes than cathedrals because our artists frequent the former more often than the latter. It is alleged that Racine's vocabulary was limited to five hundred ordinary French words. Only what is conveyed matters.

Inventiveness may be valued as a quality of an artist's endowment; by itself it does not assure us of anything outside itself—not even originality. I know of a composer whose melodic gift is quite steady and rich. Yet he has not achieved an important body of work. Every artist has a statement to make. We judge him not by the terms employed in making it but by the final worth of his statement.

It is really of little moment whether an old composer—like Chopin—is better than a new one like Roy Harris! Each is as inevitable, unique, and necessary as the other. It is ultimately of very little real interest to be informed that Velasquez was a more gratifying artist than Picasso. No artist takes the place of another for precisely the same reason that it is futile to tell us that people in the Middle Ages were luckier than we because they had faith. We live with and through our times. The conditions of our life today, which must be our major concern if we are to live at all, produce artists that are not going to be Bach, Mozart, or Beethoven. Granting that the latter are "greater" than those of the present, we should realize the urgency of knowing, appreciating and cultivating our own artists on their own grounds, in preference to living in stupefied contemplation of those of the past. (We cannot carry on our life with Helen of Troy!) Roy Harris cannot give us what Chopin does, but

Chopin cannot supply what is in Harris, and to confuse ourselves by comparisons of the two is to misunderstand both.

The fact that there has been a Chopin means that there cannot be another. That job, so to speak, has been done. Every life is irreplaceable; every life has its own function—is lived in some mysterious way under conditions which are always uniquely its own.

This is especially true of the artist. The critic's business is to discover the individual life of the artist he is called upon to consider. The criticism that uses the past as a whip with which to punish the present is plagued by what might be called the trauma of the museum. It regards art not as something to be made but something to be received. It lies back—and waits to be pleased. Even the beholder of art must regard himself as an active witness, a maker. In this sense all art—old and new—is contemporary. We stand before it and ask ourselves "What is this doing to me now? What can I do with it now?" And our present values of life rather than of "art" will dictate our judgment or use of it.

—*TRW*, Oct. '46

PEOPLE FOR SALE

A Night in Casablanca, the latest and probably the last picture to be made by the Marx Brothers, is truer to life than Alfred Hitchcock's *Notorious*! The Marx Brothers are rude, crude, mad and bad; they ruffle your hair, cuff you behind the ears, shake you by the neck, kick you in the pants, insult you and knock you down in a most impersonal spirit of professional absurdity. In the slow spots, when Chico plays the piano, even when Harpo's mature and grimacing puppet face suddenly turns grave to play the instrument which gives him his name, a sense of absolute idiocy emanates from the screen like a deliberate style. When the picture lapses into exposition of plot, the utter staleness with which it is delivered takes on

quality as if this too were part of some all-encompassing mockery. One laughs one's head off, and one is hard put a minute later to remember why or at what. One leaves the picture somewhat exhausted, dizzy, and let down. This is the entertainment of our day. Who shall say that it is not true to life? The screen and the street resemble one another.

The Hitchcock film, on the other hand, is purely a figment of that director's fancy. Unlike the Marx Brothers, he is a conscious craftsman, and he plays with his material, which includes the audience as much as the camera and actors, with an almost unequaled calculation. The story he tells in *Notorious* is next to nothing, and the values it distills are less ponderable than those of the Marx Brothers' show. For the latter, as I have indicated, has a symbolic if accidental accuracy, while the former is no more than an elegant bit of conjuring. Hitchcock makes remarkable patterns of emptiness.

They are worth study. For example, there is the sensational love scene. You know, of course, that kisses on the screen are rationed, that is, they must not exceed a certain duration. The celluloid code of morals forbids it. But it is something for the customers to see Cary Grant and Ingrid Bergman kiss for a good two minutes. Hitchcock provides this special pleasure by interspersing the kisses with casual dialogue. The kisses themselves are varied in time, stress, and savor. There is the near-kiss, the half-kiss, the kiss deflected, and the kiss direct. There is the kiss that is a nuzzle; there is the kiss that is practically a bite. There is the kiss that is a sweep and exploration of the nose and cheek and, finally, the full dive and consummative kiss. This alone, you will agree, is worth the price of admission.

What is curious about this is that the scene is clever rather than sensuous. It piques and titillates without being in the least bit warm. The mind is called into play—not the emotions. The dialogue is used almost mechanically as a teasing device: it both varies the timing and serves as realism. The scene is not a scene about two people in love, but a scene in which the director employs two most attractive screen idols to play cat and mouse with the audience's susceptibilities and inhibitions.

For this reason the scene is basically comic; the audience greets it with gratified laughter of a special sort. The audience is made to feel as wittily sophisticated as the director who arranged it. There is something like collusion here. The result, if not exactly a leer, is like an elaborate wink. It is also a contrivance to replace artificial glamor for the truth of human relationships or even honest sex. In the instance of such a story as that of *Notorious*, the contrivance is quite appropriate. But since such contrivance is made to appear the height of all motion-picture artistry, audiences are apt to forget that it is only contrivance with a connection to life that is chiefly coincidental.

Audiences should make it their permanent motto that in the matter of life, they will accept no substitutes. The function of criticism in our time might well confine itself to one problem: to expose the fraud of all such substitutes. What is wrong with them is that they tend to render life meaningless.

What we increasingly suffer from in our day is what a poet has called "the terror of no meaning." This terror is the subject of much contemporary art. I have seen paintings for which the phrase "patterns of emptiness" might very well be applied as a comprehensive title. But while many such paintings breathe an atmosphere of nostalgia or mournfulness which gives them a certain value, a good many apparently innocuous entertainments are veritable monuments of emptiness and meaninglessness. People who scream against the dangers and abuses of modern art are ingenuous. The harm done by certain abstruse works of art is infinitesimal compared to that wrought by many of our best-sellers and smash hits. What is needed is not so much critics to explain the art we can't "get," but people to reveal the injury done us by the "art" that we get in abundance.

It is not the difficult and complex we should

be eager to understand, but the obvious. This is the case with so common and so little considered a subject as acting. Some of the best acting today may be seen, not in the big climaxes of plays and movies, but in hardly noticeable transitional moments. French movies are built up on the basis of such acting, so that often the most shamelessly sentimental stories become lifelike in comparison with our careful contraptions which try so hard to establish realistic credibility.

An example of what I am referring to was to be seen in *Spellbound*. The two major performers—Ingrid Bergman and Gregory Peck—were called on to tell this picture's unlikely story so that it might be temporarily acceptable and interesting. But though this task was handsomely fulfilled, there was no moment in their acting that was anything more than good imitation. The picture's only vitality was that of Michael Chekhov. He was not a cog in the machine of the story, but a living person.

Chekhov is one of the few great actors of our time. But he has abdicated from creation. What he does in pictures hardly represents even the surface of his talents. (Playing a Russian repertory, he gave us a series of magnificent stage portrayals in a season that passed practically unnoticed on Broadway in 1935.) His film performances—including the one in *Spellbound*—are not true samples of his art. They are routine performances. But with him an entrance, an exit, walking across a room with a glass of milk, lying down, looking, listening, become dramatic. No matter what the scene, we feel ourselves in the presence of human experience. What he does takes on meaning almost apart from the concrete instance of the picture's plot. It is as if he needed no actual role; his acting is a kind of agent of life—focused, pointed, and expressive. He makes the juices of life circulate. Through him we learn once more that we have but to watch any moment of concentrated behavior to be fascinated. The smallest action thoroughly carried out seems to contain a kind of universal essence. This, in little, is the mystery of acting, one might almost say the mystery of life! It illustrates anew that, just as in painting an apple may equal a madonna, so in acting that has living texture there is more real drama than in the most intricate technical ingenuity.

All this might be summed up by saying that in Michael Chekhov—whether or not he creates a character—we are still in the presence of a whole man. With alarming rapidity, our artists are being reduced to the status of functions. Observe our publicity. Actors and actresses are advertised as the Body, the Voice, the Look, the Nose, the Pout, and soon it will be the Bust and the Unmentionable. This is no accident. It is merely a vulgarization of what is happening on a world scale. People are valued for their commercially useful attributes. They are commodities for sale. The part has outdistanced the whole. Our vision of man as a total organism is fast disappearing, and because of this it looks very much as if soon man himself will disappear.

This breakup in our concept of man corresponds to the splitting of the atom. The atom was our last rugged individualist, but we have learned how to disintegrate it. Just as the history of the arts since the end of the nineteenth century—painting for example—may be interpreted as an ever more minute division and detailing of parts, so the human personality today may be said to be undergoing the same process of fission.

The concept of wholeness is breaking down in every phase of existence. It is the great modern catastrophe. In the world of social affairs its danger is more or less recognized. In the world of the arts—which means the world of human relationships—the danger is not only not seen, but its manifestations are cheerfully, even hysterically embraced. It is the ultrafashionable, the smart, the popular. Every faith, thought, idea, word today is fissionable. And how we love the particles!

When life becomes meaningless and only sensation remains, brutality sets in. The fact that overt brutality must go punished in pictures does not prevent its becoming a delectable commodity for the fans. The charm of such typical articles as *The Big Sleep* lies in its assortment of beatings, murders, corpses, and six personable actresses of various flavors. There is intricacy to keep the story moving, but no brains are required to follow it— only an appetite for the slugging and the anticipation of frightfulness, commonly known as suspense. The whole hardly has to be coherent, there is so much delight in the details compounded as they are of clear sadism and spicy innuendo.

Wherever there is a certain type of monetarily-valued power progress, there we will find an intensification of the processes I have described. That is why the country in the greatest peril today is the most powerful country in the world—our own United States. It matters very little ultimately how completely we triumph in the assertion of our power; the threat to us from ourselves is far greater than we realize.

The advantage that certain "backward" peoples hold is their simplicity. I mean by simplicity, regard and devotion to the needs of man as a whole rather than as an instrument whose isolated talents may be subjected to vast exploitation. Our deepest requirement today is to recover the concept of the whole man. We must find new ways of reaffirming the old truths or learn to make fresh truths out of the old banalities.

A delusion of our times relates to acquisition and abundance. An acquaintance of mine, having made a fortune in low-brow entertainment, bought himself a flock of Old Masters. When he showed me the paintings, I was led to imagine a couple who might boast, "We are extremely fertile; we have adopted forty-six children."

That is fiction. It is a fact that, when an artist-aid project was suggested to President Coolidge, he said, "Why worry about art? We can get all we want from France."

Alfred Stieglitz, one of the few major artists that America has produced, died in New York on July 13. Because he was a photographer, his name has not yet taken its rightful place in our culture.

No unified and comprehensive statement on his work and influence has been published. I trust a large show of his work will soon be organized. It would be a task that our most ambitious museums might undertake with honor.

In one of my last conversations, with him, Stieglitz was in a critical and resigned mood. I quote some of the things he said that day as appropriate, final notes to what I have just written. "The supreme American institution is the department store; the great American book is the Sears-Roebuck catalogue; the great American business is advertising." In earlier years he had said, "America starts with the idea of labels—then of price."

A number of recent English films have shown encouraging signs of a desire to preserve freedom from mechanization and their own individual character. Sometimes they fail for special reasons. In Noel Coward's *Brief Encounter*, for instance, a creditable attempt is made to produce an intelligent film about the basic emotions involved in a marital infidelity on the least spectacular level. It is all done modestly enough, but the effect is still a little synthetic, because Coward writes from his ability not from his experience. He does not know: he knows about.

Coward is a virtuoso of the commercial stage and screen—what Broadway calls a genius. Like the actor in *Hamlet*, he can play you anything. He can write and produce any kind of show at all. He knows all the styles, modes, and points of view. In *Brief Encounter* he essays the genuine and humble. Everything in it is just that, in a manner that is something of a relief and nearly convincing. Everything is almost too well done, too conventionally articulate, too much in the proper style of gray and decent realism—and the characters' speech and behavior are abstractly always what they should be. That is what troubled me. The picture is *correct*; its simplicity is not felt. It has no true pulse, no real lift, no surprise—as life, even in its most humdrum aspects, always has when completely seen.

There is less heart in this film than craftsman-ship. Coward always works cleverly from the outside. This is as true here in his renunciation of trickiness as in his patriotic epic of the navy, his historical sagas, his smart revues, romantic musicals, and studies in social decadence. Coward once protested that he was not to be considered a decadent just because many of his plays dealt with corruption. He merely wrote, he said, on any subject the times demanded. This statement merely proved that decadence can be naïve. *Brief Encounter* proves that it can also look innocent.

—*TRW*, Nov. '46

NEW MOON

When the air cools and autumn gray modifies the sun, when, in short, October comes to New York, the tall buildings brood and give promise of something the winter season may never fulfill. The night has a new glow: there is a brightness in the brisk streets that is like the romance of newly conceived plans.

As I sit down to write, I find myself seeking guilelessly to discover or predict the trend of the times. The past year proved nothing. No single new voice emerged to give the day its particular timbre. There was disquiet, cowering, and a babble of trivialities. Everyone guessed that the tiny sounds we heard were like consolatory whisperings in the dark. No one took the pseudo-prosperity either seriously or frivolously. People went about their business without any soul searching: such activity might not only appear futile but slightly ridiculous.

The period of reaction that we entered on Roosevelt's death is not alone a matter of political parties and platforms. Its chief symptom is a distrust of anything uncharted, daring, young, and fresh. It is an angry revulsion against change, a violent denial that the status quo may be altered for something more appropriate to the reality of the new day. There is no new day, says reaction, no discovery, no adventure beyond the law and order of large profits.

We shall be lost if we answer with nothing more than refurbished slogans from the era of the New Deal. We must not fall into the trap, for instance, of replying to demonstrations of the superiority of art to propaganda with equally obnoxious talk about "art is a weapon" or propaganda can be made a paying proposition!

If I begin with such an example, it is because the approach of the new theatrical season has begun with silly but still significant controversies on the social play. What is a social play? It is certainly not the contrary of an "art" play. A play is not entertainment because it is trivial, nor is it art when we find it dull! Every work of the imagination represents a certain sum of life: the life of the individual who made it and the life of the society which made him. We judge these works of the imagination by our measure of the sum of life contained in them. We measure by values which represent our appetites, needs, aspirations, prejudices.

A poetic fable like Saroyan's *My Heart's In The Highlands* is every bit as socially significant as *The State of the Union*, a play about politics; while *Waiting for Lefty,* a propaganda play and virtually a poster, is certainly as much a work of art—by any standards—as the non-political plays of Noel Coward! The fact is that almost all of the plays of Eugene O'Neill, Maxwell Anderson, S. N. Behrman are social plays, but they are rarely discussed in terms of their real (or social) meaning even by critics who like them, while the works of the lesser social writers are always discussed in terms of "art," because in this way critics who are afraid to commit themselves on social problems find it easy to condemn them.

The simplification of which the "left" and "right" are equally guilty in this regard is a symptom that neither side is quite clear as to what is in question. On the one hand, certain "left" writers, when they speak of social plays are referring only to plays on topical subjects or plays of a frankly didactic nature, just as certain "right" critics, when they speak of "art," generally mean, I

am afraid, something that is innocuous and inoffensive. It is ingenuous of such critics to point out that they like Ibsen, Chekhov, or Shaw, who were also social playwrights, when the truth is such critics think of these men as artists chiefly because the problems they dealt with are no longer pressing.

To be sure, I am more interested in honest social playwrights (even when they are misguided!) than in their well-meaning mentors who prate about art. If advice is in order, I have some to offer. Insofar as you wish to express something which runs against the grain of the audience that attends the theatre on Broadway, you are doomed not to be heard. The theatre has at no time successfully housed the work of an author whose ideology opposed that of his audience. (Exception may be made for certain comedies where the dramatist is able to take advantage of an uncertainty or skepticism in the audience to poke fun at its weaknesses, as Beaumarchais did when he made the French aristocrats laugh at themselves on the eve of the French revolution.) If you have something to say to a *new* audience—one that has not yet found its voice in the existing theatre—you must seek to create that audience by creating a new theatre. That is very, very difficult—though not impossible—at the present time.

If you want to say things which you feel the audience really wants to hear but which diverse taboos make it hazardous to say, you must write with the cunning profundity that obtains in a society where there is a rigid and formal censorship. Remember that the works of Tolstoy, Chekhov, Gorky were written under a severe autocracy that stood guard over a state of affairs of which they were acutely critical. If their propaganda had been the facile kind that parades itself, it would never have been able to pass muster. The need to tell the truth despite the possibility of suppression made these men find a method that gave their message both particular point and universal relevance.

The economic structure of our theatre leads to as much repression as that of any censor. The intrepid writer will find a way to speak, and the difficulties that beset him should teach him how to speak well. Defeat through silence cannot be excused.

What is there to say now? Almost everything! A period of doubt, of accommodation, of somnolence or evasion demands greater subtlety and eloquence than any other. We need not advertise our intentions or proclaim programs. Our approach to the big problems need not be direct. They can remain on the most intimate, personal level of human observation. They will not be less but rather more effective if they present small but specific truths rather than labels and large generalizations. Our search for the real and the beautiful will take us on the identical path as long as we allow ourselves to be guided by the deepest springs of life within us.

I must confess myself a propagandist. I seek the genuine in all things. The genuine is my desire, my objective, my norm. The genuine is not synonymous with the "realistic." Realism is only one form of expression. A flight of mad poesy may be more genuine than the most painstaking record of facts; a bizarre mask may be more revealing than a naked face, a buffoon closer to reality than a professor!

Take the case of Bernard Shaw, whose *Caesar and Cleopatra* in Gabriel Pascal's picture version has been condemned as a bore and praised as a delightful example of literary comedy. Both these opinions—like most opinions—are of little intrinsic value. What is important in Shaw is the genuineness of his themes and his attempt to give them scope through the most broadly enjoyable theatrical symbols. He employs traditional types, clown-fashion, to convey what is often the spirit of a devout minister. With all his *gaminerie*, Shaw has a sense of the grand manner—a kind of largeness that is a precious preservative against passing fashion. His education in the Bible, Shakespeare, and the opera help give things like *Caesar* a nobility of line and a gesture of greatness—even though his writing rarely achieves the purity, intensity, and originality of true poetry.

His subject in this instance deals with questions like what is a wise ruler? what makes a man great? what is justice? If we look close, however, we see that, despite this, there is something naïve and old-fashioned in Shaw! There is a boyish prankishness and archness that is a little at odds with the seriousness of his themes. In a curious and not altogether sympathetic sense, Shaw is often sophomoric. There is about his thought something not unlike an argument in a college debating society. His heart, however, is in the right place, and he generally asks crucial questions which he answers in a way that, beneath the apparent audacity of manner, is touchingly idealistic. Yet we cannot help but suspect an immaturity of real experience, so that while our intelligence is set in motion, our flesh is not really engaged, our whole being not entirely held.

Shaw is no more a realistic playwright than Jimmy Durante is a realistic actor. That is why most Shaw productions are stylistically as wide of the mark as are those of Shakespeare. Producers are afraid to use a freely imaginative playfulness with Shaw, and the present picture, with all its supercolossal trappings, is as irrelevant to Shaw's style as acrobatics would be to Ibsen.

Whether or not this *Caesar* is a "good picture" doesn't much matter. Even when it proves itself a little Sunday-schoolish and abstracted from the body of the world, it has at bottom a certain simple and cleansing decency, a basic good will. Above all, it is tonic to hear in it the cry—echoed again in Shaw's most direct and sober play, *St. Joan*—"How long? How long must folly, vengefulness, cruelty, egocentricity, murderous blindness and wars go on?"

Genuineness is the mark of Bela Bartok's *Music for Strings, Percussion and Celesta*—played by the New York Symphony Orchestra under Leonard Bernstein. First performed in 1937, this piece is all direct expression, all sincere emotion. In short, all things which so many people fail to find in modern music.

This failure is partly the result of impatience, but more often due to the expectation of hearing the now familiar emotions of nineteenth-century music. The emotion of Bartok's piece is the emotion of our time—anxiety! Whatever caused the composer's anxiety, this music sounds like a prelude to the era of the atom bomb, and the gaiety of the last movement is like much of the gaiety of our time—a dance over an imminent explosion. The whole suite might have been entitled "Forms of Fear."

This is certainly not the only—or the most desirable—emotion we can experience today, but we cannot fail to acknowledge that it has been clearly, tersely, and powerfully expressed here. Shostakovitch's *Seventh (Leningrad) Symphony*, played at an earlier concert under the aforementioned auspices, expresses another kind of emotion—one which, I am afraid, despite the work's popularity, is much less true to us here in America today than that of the Bartok piece. This Shostakovitch music, written almost literally in the midst of battle, is not as wholly genuine as that of the Hungarian composer. The "war passages" are descriptively exciting, and the end has in it some of the appropriately stirring sentiments that should accompany the idea of victory, but much of the piece, despite the composer's facility, reveals more effort than spontaneous feeling. In a large portion of this symphony Shostakovitch "musicalizes" in the way certain writers "poetize".

Genuineness may be found even in the expression of the chichi. One should not be put off by the prettiness of Florine Stettheimer's paintings, posthumously exhibited at the Museum of Modern Art. They are the work of a real talent.

Their color is like pigmented lace or like crystals of rock candy; the subjects—aside from the flower pieces—are something like fantasies and caricatures on frivolous subjects, and the impression they create generally is of a voluptuous and exquisite spinsterhood. One painting is called *My Birthday Eyegay*, another *Love Flight of a Pink Candy Heart*. But this surface excess of charm is the avenue of entry into a world that is tenderly lyrical as well as sharply witty. The wealthy lady who did these paintings, surrounded and protected by an upper middle-class environment, is a truly sensitive little girl. Her constant dream is of romance and happiness, and her brilliantly effervescent sublimations show that in time she developed to be a shrewd observer and a keen chronicler of the American scene in the twenties and early thirties.

The prosperous land of confections and cordials, Tiffany's, Hudnut's, baseball, Jimmy Walker, modern art that is delivered like an expensive bonnet from the finest milliner, gangsterdom, patriotics, week-end parties, stocks and bonds is described with both a purity and a lack of indulgence that make her painting a valuable social document. Miss Stettheimer was hardly a conscious satirist but she had a true eye and a real sensibility, so that even from her special corner of privilege and luxury—resembling a silken nursery for dolls—she was able to see what was vulgar and what was somehow sweet in the society of her time.

Is her work art, entertainment, or propaganda? It is all these, because that is what products of the imagination are when they truly embody human experience.

—*TRW*, Dec. '46

THE PESSIMISTS

Indeed I think nothing but noise and folly can keep me in my right wits, whereas reason and silence make me stark mad. Sit down discourse to me some dismal tragedy.

—The Duchess of Malfi.

In *Red Rust*, a Soviet play produced by the junior staff of the Theatre Guild in 1929, there was a remarkable scene in which the central character defended himself against the accusation of being a pessimist. It was evident from the violence of his defense that, in the eyes of the Soviet people, to be guilty of pessimism was to be tainted by moral vileness. Though our society is very different from that of the Soviet Union, it is generally considered a shameful blemish among us to admit to black thoughts. Though we may shiver in our boots and quake in our souls, the average American seems constrained to vow that he is content. Pessimism with us must disguise itself in motley. A cynicism that smiles is more acceptable than a thought that frowns.

When confronted with the dogma of cheerfulness, the theory that sanity resides only in yea-saying, I feel impelled to take up the cudgels on behalf of the bitter. There is, I believe, such a thing as a healthy despair. Lamentation may serve as a corrective. Our society is very often like the fool who goes to an early grave because he never admits that he might be sick. In our literature, the tradition of doubt and misgivings that extends from Hawthorne and Melville down through Dreiser and Edgar Lee Masters has been, on the whole, a positive and creative one. The outcry of negation, when it bursts honestly from the depths of the human spirit, is as justified and even remedial as hymns of hope and gladness.

Optimism and pessimism are relative states of mind and relative terms attempting to approximate a reality which is different from either. Life, we know, is neither "good" nor "bad." Our experience teaches us that we are a part and a testimony of something, the pursuit of which is the proof of our love for it. We do not love life because we think it "good," anymore than we abandon it because we learn it is "bad." Mainly, we sense two things about life: that though it be eternal, our share in it is fragmentary since we must die; and that though we are part of its immeasurable wholeness, we are forever lonely within it through our separateness as individuals. This constant knowledge is the core of all our sorrow. The contradiction, which is the very definition of our common concept of life, we feel to be tragic. When man is mature, he regards this tragedy not as an accident of life, but as its very essence.

An optimism that regards pain as an inexplicable intrusion on the normal course of life is stupid-

ity; a pessimism that bemoans the impulse of life itself, madness. For either optimism or pessimism to be part of a real context of life, each must regard itself as comparative to a central fact in which both are contained, as the fruit is contained in the seed. Optimism is valuable when it is able to emerge from a situation which it acknowledges just as difficult as the pessimist would describe it; pessimism is generative when it protests in the name of a promise implied in the optimist's credo. Wisdom lies in the reconciliation of these opposites. Tragedy transcends sadness in its realization of the overall rightness and mysterious unity of life's contradiction.

All this is a necessary preamble to an understanding of Eugene O'Neill's *The Iceman Cometh*. To say that it is bad because it is a thoroughly defeatist play is to assert that a pessimist cast of mind cannot produce valuable works of art. This would be a manifest untruth; there is no need to cite the masterpieces that give an anguished account of life. To believe that the man who curses life is not paying tribute to it in his own way is to have a very poor opinion of life oneself.

O'Neill is America's leading playwright because his plays represent a continuously varied effort to grapple with essential matters. He is deeply in earnest. He always seeks to enter the secret places where basic truths may be found. He pursues this end with a kind of rapt faith, that is in itself dramatic and contagious. It gives almost all his plays—including the present one—an enkindling theatricality and stature, which is the true glamor of the stage.

In their attempt to seize the crucial aspects of life in the particular terms of our American experience, O'Neill's early plays follow the best tradition of our serious literature. Whether he was depicting the innocence of young men lost in the vastness of the seas, or the primitive fears of the still immature-mind, or the pride and terror of man caught as by a dreadful fate in our machine civilization, or the drive of passions that were tortured to the uses of his work, only to explode for want of proper human objectives into restlessness and crime, O'Neill's plays possessed an intuitional power that was often socially illuminating and almost always emotionally stirring. We felt that these plays—no matter how we might define them intellectually—embodied a vivid human experience. In the light of our environment, we considered them all the more brave for being pessimistic.

But alas! though O'Neill's sincere quest continued, the contact or connection with life began to diminish. A special type of analysis set in, a kind of deliberate instrumentalism of the mind, which veered from one question to another, from one solution to another—pantheism, psychoanalysis, Catholicism, sentimentalism. There was not much direction or control, because intellectual control in an artist is determined by an ever-renewed experience of life.

The inevitable result of this floundering in the void of abstraction is *The Iceman Cometh*. In this O'Neill tells us that it would have been better not to have been born (a wag would say that this might be a philosophy for an embryo not for a man!) and that in order to live at all our only refuge lies in illusions, pipe-dreams, lies.

In *The Wild Duck,* Ibsen wrote an ironic play in which the idealistic bringer-of-truth proves an agent of destruction: it is one of his best plays. Many plays of greater violence and more eloquent agony are treasured by us as admirable manifestations of the human spirit. What is disheartening in *The Iceman Cometh* is the poverty of its inspiration, the thinness of its blood, the dryness and banality of its artistic texture.

We are introduced to a variety of characters at the dregs of life. Each of them states the cause of his despair; one no longer believes in the worthwhileness of social struggle; another is the son of an attorney guilty of embezzlement, another has betrayed his mother, still another grieves over the death of a wife he did not love, etc., etc. Hardly a single new facet is revealed once they have declared their problem in the first act. Their background is their mask of characterization which

never alters or grows more meaningful. Their action—an attempt to break the illusion which still sustains them—is mechanically repeated for each character in almost identical terms, so that the pattern of their behavior resembles the movement of marionettes deprived of individual souls.

The whole play thus becomes a repetition of a simple design, set from the beginning in a kind of dull symmetry. That it is a dolorous symmetry instead of a gay one does not make it any more alive. An automatic pessimism is no more profound than a radio announcer's optimism. One can be a Babbitt of dejection as easily as a booster. *The Iceman Cometh* is basically facile and glib and, for all its four hours of playing time, much too short and thin in content.

One cannot, however, deny the old O'Neill seriousness. It demands a response. Here is mine. The world cannot be represented by a bunch of drunks who fail to do anything. Men have done things and we live—even to the writing of pessimistic plays—through what they have done. At no time in history have men as a whole truly doubted the value of living, and no amount of skepticism on their part has lessened their determination to carry out the ends to which they were impelled by the pressure of their lives. Never has man altogether ceased to care, to desire, to love, to act. Any philosophy which overlooks this little thing is silly, schoolboyish nonsense, which can only impress people so unaccustomed to actual thinking that the mere semblance of thought throws them into a state of worshipful amazement. O'Neill's mouthpiece in the play says that he gave up his political activity because he "sees all sides of the question." To some this may be profundity, to me it means only that the man has never been involved. *The Iceman Cometh* is the play of a man who is no longer involved in anything but his own speculations.

The Iceman Cometh should not, in a sense, be termed a pessimistic play. It represents a talent which has become ossified in an attitude. Perhaps it provides safety and comfort to its author. It is certainly not the expression of a real sentience in which there is new suffering and, consequently, some chance of growth. Hence, it barely moves us. A play like Gorky's *Lower Depths* in which many brutal deeds are done, in which people die of fatal disease, others commit suicide while their companions turn away in a kind of irritated revulsion, and some can hardly remember the events of their own lives, ends by being a play that purifies and ennobles us without any recourse to mystic compensation, metaphysical justification, or promise of social reform. *The Iceman Cometh* ends by being a grimacing masquerade, conducted by a man whose reasons for distress seem so remote now as to become practically a matter of indifference to us. A pessimistic play that sprang from an affliction we shared in common as people living actively in our time might be something to cherish.

One has to earn one's right to pessimism. George Grosz, part of whose work from 1914 to 1946 was recently shown at the galleries of the Associated American Artists, has earned his.

Grosz, who called his show "A Piece of My World in a World Without Peace," is a modern master. His drawings have exercised considerable influence on almost all present day caricature. His incisive line, like stabs of pain, creates character with every stroke. As a social seer he had an extraordinarily prophetic vision. Even as peace was being negotiated shortly after the last war, he foresaw the hideous development of German militarism. He predicted the rise of the swastika almost before the Nazis themselves. He understood the meaning of that emblem and the nature of that movement before the optimists in England, France, and America dreamed that they were affected.

He was able to do all this not because he knew politics, but because he had the awareness of the true artist. He read the meaning of the times in the faces he saw on the streets, in places of pleasure, and in casual corners of conversation and pastime. That is where it may always be read. The drawing of Berlin in 1914, called "Pandemonium," reminds me a little of New York today.

Grosz draws with brilliant journalistic and theatrical verve: everything he does in one way or another is effective. He is always trying to say something clear, sharp, pertinent. He has a venomous wit. He hates selfishness, cruelty, brutality. Above all, he has a loathing for certain aspects of German civilization—the aspects which sensitive Germans, like the rest of the world, have always detested.

There is a strange kinship between the artist and what he flays. The latter is like the inner demon of his soul. The title of the watercolor—"Nothing Left but Hate"—gives a clue to the peculiar exaggeration of ire and exacerbation which is so often a characteristic of modern German art. As Grosz moves away from the bare structure of his statement in his drawings and watercolors to the elaboration of his oils, something we suspected at first begins to reveal itself unmistakably. There is a certain ambiguous prettiness in the color, as if the painter were somehow gloating over the horror and rot he is presenting. The color has a crumbly quality, like decayed matter upon which a spotlight had been thrown. The effect is a rather disgusting glow. Grosz's latest painting in oil, a symbol of our world (or his) is a picture of hell which he called "The Pit." It conveys total hatred.

What is disconcerting in this great craftsman's work is that there is no trace of love or warmth in it. When he remembers his friends, they always appear with bloody heads and faces; his comrades are always being annihilated. Grosz sees three basic elements in man: fear, hate, a maniacal will to murder. This, you may say, is the history of 1914-46. But in all that time there must have been some heroic note to strike, some nobility to remember, some sacrifice or aspiration to record—apart from sanguinary martyrdom.

Why should one hate anything if one does not love man? To do this is itself a disease, a convulsion, a self-torturing sadism. There is something melodramatic and false in some of Grosz's latest work. When Daumier, the great satirist of the modern epoch in art, painted oils they were masterpieces of tenderness and devotion. Is the difference between a Grosz and a Daumier simply the result of our progress in savagery between 1870 and the present? Possibly. But I doubt it.

A word about Jerome Robbins' new ballet *Facsimile,* There is a literalness in Robbins' interpretation of the neurotic dallying with sex amongst the young intelligentsia that makes it a little less serious than it seems. It is almost comic at moments and it might perhaps have been more trenchant if it had been done as comedy. Psychologically, it is hardly deeper than the same choreographer's *Fancy Free.* In fact the latter is in some respects more touching than the present ballet, just as a good scene is always more convincing dramatically than a flat statement.

Yet there is something moving and fine in the intensity of the effort which this ballet represents. We recognize both the effort of the choreographer trying to translate his personal experience into new dance forms and that of the dancers themselves. The young people who perform the new ballet are like athletes or soldiers of the new armies, who have retained a sense of line that derives from the older ballets. Their training and strength is amazing, and their ambition to evolve spiritual meanings out of their fresh relation to the world and their new technique is very sympathetic indeed. At times, their effort is too strenuous to achieve beauty in the classic sense. But what they are doing in American terms is perhaps even more valuable for us than that.

—*TRW,* Jan. '47

ENTERTAINMENT: IMPORTANT AND UNIMPORTANT

After a very active month of theatregoing, I find myself confronted by a dismal paradox. It is easy enough for me to name the best plays without being able to say truthfully that they afforded me any deep satisfaction. There were agreeable aspects and points of merit which I might praise

conscientiously. This would act as a reassurance that my disposition had not become too crabbed. I might thus fulfill my journalistic obligation with a measure of good behavior, but I could not honestly affirm that anything I saw on the stage was necessary to me.

Of all the arts the theatre is the one to which my response is most spontaneous. Yet it is not snobbery when I say that only at Katherine Dunham's ballet-revue *Bal Nègre* did I find myself pleasurably at ease. It is true that sex is the subject and center of this show, but that alone is not the cause for my gratification. Miss Dunham's company dances and plays with an animated naïveté and unfettered energy characteristic of some itinerant troupe of olden times. On its own simple level, there is a freshness and purity in the impulse behind this performance, an absence of routine professionalism which give it great zest.

There is something sound, too, in the efforts of the new American Repertory Theatre. It is a valuable contrast to the horse-racing atmosphere of the Broadway theatre. The productions thus far remind me a little of those at Miss Le Gallienne's Civic Repertory Theatre on Fourteenth Street years ago. In those days, I took a harsh view of their inadequacies in view of the great texts that were chosen. Today, I regard their slightly amateur complexion with friendly sympathy.

I cannot say I cared for the American Repertory Theatre's *Henry VIII,* but it is not very much inferior to most Shakespearean productions on our stage. As for Barrie's *What Every Woman Knows,* I do not find it altogether unworthy. Between 1919-39 it might have made sense to gag over Barrie's sweetness, but to do so today is to be futilely sophisticated. Sentimentality is as legitimate a mode of arriving at truth as satire. To believe that Barrie is false because he writes lachrymose comedy is almost as silly as to imagine that O'Neill is true when he indulges in bitter poesy. Finally, *John Gabriel Borkman,* though thinner and more schematic than some of the better-known Ibsen plays, still retains some of its original stature. The acting in the new production is obviously deficient though respectably honest, but the play is clearly the work of a grown-up person—which cannot be said for most of what we ordinarily see. It is pettily barbaric to think of such a play as "outdated." Need I say that the essence of *John Gabriel Borkman*—the relation of the power drive to man's basic humanity and to his women— is not a problem that our modernity has solved.

If my readers should be offended at times by the possibly haughty tone of my judgments on the current theatre, I beg them to remember that there are two levels on which such judgments may be made. There is the judgment which tries to suggest the best buys on the market. It is always a moot question, of course, whether the consumer needs the particular fare that the theatre has to sell. Be that as it may, the province of such judgment is to announce that last night's show is the best of the week, month, or year on this or that particular street! This information may be considered reliable, without its affecting judgment of another sort.

The second level approaches the theatre with the question of a play's worth as nurture for our soul. On this level, it is perfectly proper to say: the highly attractive dish now so expertly served by the town's best caterer is something you will undoubtedly relish—but it is poison! We are living at a time when few people find it seemly to make a distinction between the two levels. It is practical to acknowledge the first level; it is disastrous to ignore the second. Because only the first level is given popular consideration, I am a strong partisan of the second.

This brings me back to the initial paradox of the present article: I do not like some of our best plays. I have already recorded my objections to *The Iceman Cometh,* but, alas, it is indeed one of the best. So, too, are Lillian Hellman's *Another Part of the Forest* and Jean-Paul Sartre's *No Exit.*

In the absence of any "experimental" theatre in New York, the novelty of *No Exit* in form and approach makes it stimulating. If the theatre is to be a little irksome, let it at least be so with a difference. *No Exit* is the "new shudder" of Paris. In New York it has a moderately informative interest, a certain fresh asperity of taste, the attraction of a curiosity. As you probably know, the scene of the play is what appears to be a bizarre hotel room, at once shabby and meretricious. One of the characters refers to it wittily as a self-service cafeteria. This room is Hell. People are tortured in it by being fated to spend the rest of time in constant awareness of each other's misery, pain, and meanness. In other words, Hell is a more concentrated form of life. We are always faced with our own shame and doom through our perpetual relationship with our fellow men. "Hell is other people."

The play is a kind of intellectual allegory written with some of the keenness of a gifted foreign journalist. Its pessimism alone is not sufficient ground for condemnation. What is weak in this play is that its statement is mental and, at best, merely clever. Its people aren't felt, its atmosphere and mood—though possibly effective as showmanship—are forced; its philosophy is mostly a strained and dry hysteria.

One of the signs of the play's emptiness lies in the depiction of its characters. Their story is supposed to be "strong," that is to say, shocking. One is a malicious Lesbian, another a narcissistic doll who has killed her own child, the third a sadist whose least reprehensible act is collaboration. The mere exposition of these facts is expected to move us. The truth is they touch us less than the report of a bus accident. They serve merely to fill out a highly colored pattern that exists only to prove a point. They lack their own eloquence, and, because the point by itself is not convincing one ends by seeing the play as a kind of smartly wicked decoration, not as a valid expression of life—anyone's life, including that of the author. The local production, moreover, though not entirely without merit, tends to emphasize the play's speciousness.

Another Part of the Forest is also strong—and also somewhat shocking. But one asks oneself, "to what purpose?" In *The Little Foxes* one was led to believe that the nasty Hubbard family was typical of a group of capitalists at a pre-liberal period of our history. The play was presumably the indictment of a class. In the present play, more evidence is adduced to prove that the Hubbards were even nastier than we had previously supposed. Let us concede the point—although I cannot say that I truly believe in the reality of the Hubbards, except for purposes of entertainment.

Miss Hellman constructs and writes her plays with a realistic-school solidity and a sure theatrical pointedness which often lends her plays authority. (It is as if she were trained in an earlier tradition of the theatre, somewhere between the Frenchman Henry Becque and David Belasco.) It is not true however that the central figure of *Another Part of the Forest*—Marcus Hubbard—is a richly drawn figure. He has complications, but they do not go to make a basic texture that is more significant because of them. What comes through is only a more involved and therefore better-grade horror. If the play has fascination, it is a little akin to that which the Romans must have experienced in watching Christians thrown to the lions.

Our audiences are perhaps a more genial crowd. Recently, however, I could not help noticing the development of a certain unconscious harshness in them. This is to be observed in the quality of laughter that greets almost every expression of sudden rudeness, irritation, and bald jeering—especially in sexual matters (Do you remember how delighted the audience was when Jimmy Cagney smashed the grapefruit into his girl friend's face in *The Public Enemy*?) There is something of this cruelty in the audience's response to *Born Yesterday*. It is provoked by something in the play. I noticed it again in moments of Miss Hellman's play, and even on more innocent occasions. What frustration, I wonder, what impatience with the fraud of its own life motivates this coarseness in our audience? Its most dangerous aspect lies in the audience's unawareness of it.

Criticism, like everything else, cannot live without its heroes. Thus the audience and the journalists that represent them on Broadway are eager to beat the drum of their enthusiasm at the first opportunity. Weak plays frequently profit by this need to hero-worship actors and, particularly, actresses. When real heroes are not to be found, substitutes are invented.

Helen Hayes has saved *Happy Birthday*, which is a cute vehicle of something like a 1918 make. Much of it is dull, labored, awkward, but there are enough scenic tricks and stock-company pleasantry to be ingratiating now and again. Helen Hayes's enjoyment of what she is doing is quite engaging. The show thus becomes as good as a striped and colored peppermint stick. To call any part of the acting "great"—as some have done—is to insult what Miss Hayes may be able to do on a more substantial level. Permit me to whisper: there are fewer great actors and actresses in theatrical history than great poets and playwrights. Acting is not merely a matter of "personality" and technique, but of interpretation and content.

Ina Claire is an actress endowed with wit, elegance, and a feeling for reality. She is indeed one of the last. It is hard to see how—with the absence of stock companies, repertory theatres, seasons on the road, the ever-diminishing activity of the Broadway stage as well as the disappearance of a studied decorum in our social behavior—stage actresses can be developed to play Miss Claire's type of role with anything like her aplomb. When I saw her in *The Fatal Weakness*, she was not yet in full possession of her part. But even so she was artistically superior to her playwright.

George Kelly is one of our ablest craftsmen (his *Show-Off* is a kind of American theatre classic), but on this occasion he has failed to evolve a clear point of view about the focal character of his comedy. The lady in question is so abstractly romantic and cut off from reality that she sees her husband's affair with an offstage mistress, his divorce, and his marriage to the other woman only in terms of story-book glamor. She could have been made the subject of bantering derision or celebrated as a wonderfully fey poet, but the playwright has taken neither course and decided to be amusing only, so that his comedy—despite Miss Claire—is always tenuous and sometimes tedious.

Ingrid Bergman in Maxwell Anderson's *Joan of Lorraine* has become the sensation of the town. If I were writing a regular review, I should like to analyze the play in detail, since it succeeds in implying a number of important things without saying any of them. It is almost a play about Joan of Arc, but the play is not written—merely discussed and indicated; it suggests thoughts about the theatre which are provocatively slipped in; it states philosophic conclusions without ever dramatizing or actually insisting on them. The whole is bathed in a kind of gentle and benign sadness that is very close to, but not really, defeatism. It is a canny contrivance.

No one particularly cares about all this, because everybody cares so much about Ingrid Bergman. She is worth seeing, as a study in the differences between picture- and stage-acting, as a study in social psychology (the glamor that goes before her through the audience's anticipation of her because of her film appearances), as a sweet, lovely person who, for a variety of reasons, conquers her audience beyond the capacity of the most accomplished actresses. Miss Bergman is virginal in aspect and effect (this gives her an incalculable charm which is in itself a social phenomenon); she is sincere, she is unspoiled, she is devoted and loyal—and if we had a real theatre she might soon learn to act. At present, she is a thrilling novice.

When I grow worried over my own captiousness about the theatre, I realize with some relief that it derives from my expectation of things which, at the moment, it is in no condition to offer. Except for films, which are frequented without being honored, the theatre is the form of expression which makes the loudest public noise. Seen from a broader view, the so-called legitimate stage is at present almost the least significant of all our cultural media.

In terms of meaning, the most important event of the year took place in the halls that house Serge Koussevitzky's Boston Symphony Orchestra. I refer to the first performance of Aaron Copland's *Symphony Number 3*.

It is often said that while much of modern music is technically ingenious, it has nothing to reveal in the way of content. Such a contention flatters our laziness. Listening to new music requires effort: the universe of the "classic" composer is complete; that of the modern is still in evolution.

There is perhaps no modern composer whose message is more clear, unified, and relevant to our home scene than that of Aaron Copland. Copland's work is the dramatization between the composer's need for a solitary inner integrity and the pull of the eternal world, with its complete machinery directed toward apparently impersonal ends.

Twentieth-century man finds the greatest difficulty in striking a balance between his simple requirements of love, work, play, thought, repose, serenity, and the overwhelming force which he has foisted upon himself in his effort to gain power over nature and—through the mechanics of business—over his fellow man. Man needs quiet; the world man has created has been noisy. Man needs contemplation; the world without tends to dispel it. Man needs affection, dream, a relaxed companionship, ideals. The world he faces today seems to foster values in which man's normal goals become merely private—that is, secondary and inconsiderable. Man cannot retire from the consequences of his achievement; yet, if he gives himself wholly to that which is now outside himself, he becomes diminished, crushed, lost. He is thus in continual conflict.

Nowhere in the world is the external apparatus of life more extensive, complex, and powerful than in our United States. We are both proud and frightened by what we have achieved. Before 1861, poets like Whitman spoke with epic fervor of what might be done in the new democracy. At the end of the last century, men like Dreiser grew gloomy because they began to suspect that our success had defeated us. Very few paid attention to these doubts. After World War I, we were both at the apogee of our expansion and beset by a rising clamor of jeers in regard to its values. On the one hand, there were the assurances of the *Saturday Evening Post*, on the other, the laments and lampoons of the Sherwood Andersons, the Sinclair Lewis', the Hemingways. The American arts were thus divided between hoarse hosannas and comedic curses.

Copland's first music (1925) contributed a youthfully excited embrace of the high-stepping twenties, together with a corner of quiet withdrawal in which the artist seems to sing a modest rhapsody—more prayer than plaint. This was the "jazz period" of Copland's work. But Copland was never a jazz composer in the manner of a Gershwin. To have mistaken him for one was to confuse the artist's vocabulary with his content.

Copland's jazz was neither a technique in itself nor an autointoxicated proclamation of well-being. It was a forthright description of the world he saw outside himself and an energetic assent to its attractiveness. Yet, because the inner man stood separate within it, pure, reflective, moral and a little sad, the jazz itself took on qualities of affectionate irony, sharpness, and acidity that bespoke a slight apartness, a margin of reserve.

In Copland's *Piano Concerto* (1927), played last October by the New York City Symphony, the artist's soul seems to take a beating which he feels is somehow good for it. There is a gay acquiescence and even affirmation of the dervish ferocity of the world's mechanics. The small inner voice is the voice of the individual human spirit, and it sounds slightly prophetic. It is never altogether obliterated but, in the end, merges with the rest so that it seems to speak in and through the outer chaos.

In the *Symphonic Ode* (1927-29), recently played by the Juilliard Orchestra, the composer's view of the external world is somewhat more severe, even austere. There is no facile romanticism or decorativeness in the use of the harsh

sonorities. The machine world is no joke or picturesque toy, but an awesome fact to which the final answer can only be "yes."

With the depression of the early thirties, Copland's music becomes flinty and bare, as if descriptive of a new Stone Age in which the depopulated world has either to produce new life or become an eternally condemned planet. Beginning at this point, Copland's music alternates between expressions of hope in the future—sometimes in an annunciatory style—and uncertain returns to a cryptic mood hovering between disturbed resignation and confidence. As the depression receded to a point which permitted some relaxation, Copland turned to dreams of peace and quiet, poetic calm and idyllic gaiety, tender solitude and naïve exhilaration in terms of the halcyon days of the past, the relatively untroubled times of a pre-industrial America. This music—*Billy the Kid* (recently played in a two-piano version by Appleton and Field), *The Lincoln Portrait, Appalachian Spring,* etc.—earned Copland a reputation as a composer of Americana. But, like the previous view of Copland as a jazz composer, this was a superficial application of a deceptive label. This period simply represented Copland in pasture. It was his retreat into another specifically American world in which his soul might rest and derive some renewal and nourishment.

The *Symphony Number 3* (1944-46) is the synthesis of everything Copland has had to say; it is his richest, most mature and varied work. Its importance beyond this lies in the fact that, in this time of increasing and almost fashionable pessimism, it is a work of positive affirmation.

It is one thing to write a symphony of vigorous popular sentiment when one is encouraged by the whole aspiration of a people and the planned support of a self-conscious community, but to declare oneself ready to face the future with simple manfulness in a society where the sincerest speech betrays fear, trembling, and confusion is to achieve genuine heroism.

Copland's new symphony is the music of a

glad resolve, despite the tragedy of our convulsive environment. It is the music of the inner triumph of a man who accepts his world even as he witnesses its apparent madness. It is the music of a man who stands upright and preserves the sacredness of his integrity amidst chaos. He does this because he sees in chaos the pulse and meaning of life, for it is composed of so many other selves equally involved in it. His own self is a fortress that remains pure and strong without turning away from or escaping above the fate of the outer world. This outer world—threatened with doom, everyone says—is seen in all its fierceness as a splendor not without its giddy humor, small compensations, and even light-hearted pleasures. For the man who looks upon this world sees that it is through it that he lives and that salvation cannot come from any other source.

Life, his strong inner self tells him, may be borne just as it is if we carry on with deep determination to persist in it, that is, to be men despite all. Thus we may struggle and transform life, through the innate force of our integrated will. Carried on in this spirit, life must take on grandeur, no matter what our individual destiny may be. That the ultimate issue can prove heroic is attested to by the majestic attitude of the man who in this music is carrying on the battle in our presence.

Aaron Copland is a witness and evidence of spiritual power still residing among us. His work is a proud monument of our day that stands as an inspiration before us without ostentation, boast, facile program, advertisement, or vulgar clamor. It contains the answer to the pessimists. What we need is not optimism so much as strength. Copland's symphony has the kind of strength with which our world must be faced. That is its greatness.

—*TRW*, Feb. '47

DEATH BY ENTERTAINMENT

The dramatic critic is often asked to express his opinion on plays which one should no more be called on to judge than one judges the spit in one's mouth. Dramatic criticism is basically a method of expressing a view of life. A good play contains a sufficient sum of life to make it a proper subject for critical discussion. To speak about it intelligently the critic must address himself to the questions with which the play deals or concern himself with the impulses which the play releases.

Since so few of the plays presented contain any life, the only recourse left to the critic, if he is not to become stupefied by what he sees, is to deal with the living matter which the play suggests, if only indirectly or by distortion. The critic, in short, must seek life in the play or, in its absence there, outside and around it. A poor play which pleases its audience may be treated by the critic as a commentary on the audience.

At the moment I am not thinking so much of a particular play as of *The Best Years of Our Lives.* The terse criticism of the subway review calls it "easily the best picture of the year." Virtually every notice has said the same thing in more extended prose, and I should not be at all surprised—or distressed—if this picture were to win the award of the Academy of Motion Picture Arts and Sciences.

The Best Years of Our Lives has an important subject. It deals with the returned soldier and the psychological and moral dilemma he faces in his renewed civilian life. When the case involves a boy who has lost both hands, the problem has a violent and daring aspect which, though special, must be hailed as welcome material on our screen. Those parts of the film that deal with this boy's adjustment to his family, sweetheart and neighbors and, even more, their adjustment to him, are much the best. It is noteworthy, too, that the agony of the boy's situation—psychologically speaking—is enhanced rather than alleviated by his ability to use mechanical appliances to serve as hands. The wedding scene in which the boy lays his iron "hand" on the Bible and his bride takes it in her own is not only strong as image and symbol, but eminently the kind of thing the motion picture audience needs to see. If the picture contained nothing else, this alone would make it memorable in American film history.

Beyond this there is the suggestion that business and government must give practical aid to the veteran who is now a struggling citizen again. The picture also contains a warning against the type of "Americanism" that is designed to encourage a new war by sowing doubts as to the justification for the last one. While these latter elements are handled so obliquely that they might be construed in a manner less helpful than intended, we must surely set them down as part of the film's assets. For the plain fact is that, aside from technical and journalistic factors, our films are so backward in social and spiritual values that we must be grateful for every tiny step forward. *The Best Years of Our Lives* represents such a step. That we exaggerate and consider it greater makes the film a kind of criticism of its audience.

What is embarrassing about the picture is that, while it heads the list of our good films, it is largely invalidated by all of Hollywood's vices. The banality of most of its devices conspires to destroy its message. It is hard to believe any of the big things it tries to say because so much of its small detail is false. A world where a loose girl is distinguished by her sloppiness from a nice girl who is neat; where the bank employee recently raised to $12,000 a year behaves like a polished man of the world, kisses like an actor and, after several years as a sergeant in the army lives with his family of four like a man of twice or three times his income; where the middle-class wife is portrayed as the ever cool, understanding, chic, and antiseptic Myrna Loy—this is a world of fantasy in which reality enters not only as an intruder, but almost as a mistake. One of the longest sequences in the picture exploits the humor of drunkenness and the hangover, and all through it is evident that the authors of the film felt constrained to make their truths palatable by generous doses of cliché.

Human consciousness, however, is not as shrewd as our purveyors of entertainment. It is not able to convert the kind of showmanship which is merely salesmanship into nutritive values. That is why there is always something a little simple-minded and dangerous in our rejoicing over the triumph of such liberal and progressive art as this. Since its truth is conveyed through a medium of lies—and quantitatively there is more of the latter than the former—it is the lie that is perhaps more apt to stick than the truth.

The creative moment in art occurs when the thing shown makes the spirit leap into that realm where we seem to be set free by the experience of some essence of being. Without this all entertainment—no matter how well wrought—holds us down to a mere exercise of the surface faculties, and offers no release.

With this we enter the world of aesthetics which, to paraphrase Anatole France, is to walk in the clouds. What I found myself reflecting about when I saw Henry Moore's sculpture and drawings at the Museum of Modern Art was not so much the elemental qualities of his work as the pertinence of his pronouncements which serve as a kind of introduction to it.

"A work can have in it a pent-up energy," Moore says, "an intense life of its own, independent of the object it may represent. When a work has this powerful vitality we do not connect the word 'beauty' with it....Beauty in the later Greek and Renaissance sense is not the aim of my sculpture. Between beauty of expression and power of expression there is a difference of function. The first aims at pleasing the senses, the second has a spiritual vitality which for me is more moving and goes deeper than the senses."

I am in sympathy with Mr. Moore's intention, but I fear his statement is misleading. What Mr. Moore means, in the first place, is that prettiness is not his objective. It is wrong, however, to concede that beauty may be the attribute and goal of one kind of art, while "spiritual vitality" occupies another category. Who today would say that the obviously ingratiating music of Mozart is beautiful, while Beethoven, whose music was once regarded as shockingly cacophonous, is not beautiful? I much prefer Ibsen's statement about *Peer Gynt*: "If it isn't poetry today, it will be tomorrow!" Walt Whitman, too, faced this problem when he declared that what he sought was "not beauty but expression." Art that merely pleases the senses is not beautiful, and an art that has a rough and even repellent aspect may be beautiful.

The reason such defenses as Henry Moore's have to be made is that in our time beauty has become synonymous with the pleasing, and vulgarized as the pretty. Art has become a pastime, a salve, an opiate. In these circumstances, art as such must die in either a sterile academicism or a trivial debauchery.

Beauty has many faces. It can inform the glowering Christianity of a Russian icon as well as the graces of a pagan statue. It resides in the gentlest psalm and in the harshest words of the prophets. Whitman's best work is beautiful, with a beauty different from that of Keats. El Greco is certainly as beautiful as Raphael. The "spiritual vitality" that Henry Moore speaks of must be immanent in the beautiful works he refers to or they are not beautiful, and his own work must be beautiful if it has "spiritual vitality." The critic's job is always to discover and define the particular kind of "spiritual vitality," "beauty," or expression that may lie in each body of work that he encounters.

The death of our finest actress—Laurette Taylor—should not go without comment. The perfunctory tributes of the press were dismaying. Perhaps little more could be expected from a theatre which has lost all sense of tradition and all ambition beyond that of profit—and consequently all dignity.

It is not enough to speak of Laurette Taylor's triumphant performances in the manner of a romantic novel or a publicity blurb. What distinguished Miss Taylor just as much in her failures as in her successes was the quality of her talent. She expressed a constantly tremulous sensibility that seemed vulnerable to the least breath of vulgarity,

coarseness, or cruelty without ever wholly succumbing to the overwhelming persistence of all three.

She was staunch even when she appeared broken. She suggested a kind of mute devotion and loyalty to what she loved even when everything conspired to batter her. In her this hurt loyalty took on a particularly womanly significance. Without being especially identified with "mother roles" or the generally disagreeable type of "good woman," she became a symbol of the enduring woman, the very modesty of whose suffering is more personally touching than the martyred mother of heroic myth.

Laurette Taylor seemed to be the victim of a thousand unkind cuts so minute that no word could describe them, no poet make them pathetic. She seemed always to be weeping silent tears, and her slightly bent head or averted eye were unspeakably moving because they were gestures so brief as to appear wholly imperceptible. Her voice was like buried gold whose value we could not guess; her speech flowing and ebbing in strange unequal rhythms was like a graph of her soul in its bursts of tender feeling and recessions of frustration and confusion. A luminous confusion composed her aura. It shone brighter for its ambiguity and its refractions. It warmed us deeply because it was generated from the unrhetorical sources of an ordinary woman's being rather than from any studied glamor. There was always something surprising about it, and no one appeared more surprised by what she sensed and experienced than Laurette Taylor herself. Her face was always suffused with a look of startled wonder, at once happy, humorous, frightened, and innocent.

Laurette Taylor's life was tragic. Her appearances in the past fifteen years were so infrequent that when she arrived in *The Glass Menagerie* most people spoke of her as a discovery. She had made a "comeback." But Laurette Taylor's fate in this regard is very similar to that of many other players—particularly actresses—beaten by the brutal anarchy of our stage. It would be dolefully instructive to draw up a list of the really talented actresses—living and dead—who have been unconscious sacrifices to our mindless theatre. To speak of their personal vices in order to explain their destiny is to mistake the effect for the cause. Most of the actresses who do survive our system of theatrical production, so that at the age of fifty they may be considered at the height of their effective powers, are endowed with a kind of toughness that rarely accompanies the most sensitive kind of talent.

—*TRW*, Mar. '47

MERRY–GO–ROUND

January 6: The paintings by the Frenchman Jean Dubuffet shown for the first time in this country at the Pierre Matisse Galleries are important. At first glance they are literally horrible. The second glance modifies the shock to a more critical judgment which might describe them as brilliant and unbearable. As one considers them more calmly one is likely to recognize a witty intention, a sophisticated playfulness, or one might pick up the professional critics' cant about the influence of Paul Klee. (Nine times out of ten the critics talk about "influences"—that is the definition of one artist in terms of another—if not, deception is mere evasion.) The fact is that Dubuffet, no matter what his conscious intention, has given more striking expression to certain phases of the present French state of mind than any artist we know.

There have been in recent years many attempts to paint the physical and psychological agony of modern life either through symbolic statement as in the work of the surrealists and expressionists or through the balder pronouncements of the social artists. From this standpoint, almost all of them seem to me feeble compared to Dubuffet.

Dubuffet's work expresses the spirit of Europe's delinquent childhood. It is the spirit of the homeless, hopeless, cruel, thoroughly cynical guttersnipe whom the war years, with its occupation, its collaborationists, its starvation, and its cowardice—preceded as they were by years of indecision, spinelessness, indifference and corruption—have brought to new depths of bitterness and degradation. This child has an unutterably obscene contempt for the world of his elders. He sees pimps and black-marketeers flourishing as high officials. He sees ghouls feeding themselves fat at businessmen's dinners. He sees hideous coquettes and their cutthroat "respectable" lovers as the dung of society. He suspects everything, has regard for nothing: birth and death have become a filthy joke....It is not alone this child of our neglect and folly who must be re-educated, but we who must re-evaluate and renew the premises of our beliefs. The criminal kid we have fostered sees through the fraud of our lives and hates us with a ferocity that knows no mitigation.

Technically speaking, Dubuffet may be a "primitive." But he is no naïf. His childishness is more terrible than the wrath of gods or the imprecation of prophets. In his *View of Paris*, the town is exsanguinated, dirty and dead. There is no future here unless a new world is made. Dove is a primitive of the beginning of things; Dubuffet of the end. Dove's world has hardly begun to live; Dubuffet's has been destroyed. Dubuffet's talent consists in his having found his own particular language of color to speak his piece, a color that employs remarkable subtleties and a positive liveliness to convey the contrary. Topicality is not the same thing as contemporaneity. Dubuffet's work, which looks like nothing more than back-fence scratchings, is not topical, but it is more contemporary than this morning's headlines.

January 30: Perhaps the most important aspect of *Street Scene* is that while it is very nearly an opera—in order not to scare the customers the producers call it a dramatic musical—it succeeds in functioning for its audience as a good show. This is important because we have as yet no tradition in our theatre which makes it easy for our audiences to accept a combination of serious drama and song. If the Metropolitan Opera House has never yet been able to make opera in English popular, perhaps our

Broadway may be able to do so.

There can be no question about the desirability of extending the convention of our theatre to include music drama. So far the only successes in this field have been *Porgy and Bess* and Blitzstein's *The Cradle Will Rock*. The former was a little special in its remoteness; the latter was special in being a play for a still restricted audience. *Street Scene* is closely related to our commercial stage.

Beyond this, what interested me most in *Street Scene* is the nature of the audience it attracts. It is not the large hotel and nightclub audience that frequents the hit musical comedies, but a lower middle-class of small businessmen, doctors, lawyers, teachers—the "white collar" clientele. That this audience can afford $6.00 for an orchestra seat is a sign that the depression is still just around the corner.

Street Scene is essentially an old-time stock-company tear-jerker done with a stage shrewdness that makes it appear to be a piece of up-to-date naturalism. As a play it depends for its effect on the shock (or pleasure) of recognition. Everything is delightfully familiar and literal—"just like life." Music lends it a sentimental lift, a kind of unprosaic dimension that surprises and melts its audience.

What lets me down in all this is that when all is sung and said we are not really very far above a rather platitudinous cigar-drug-delicatessen-store level of humor and emotion. Kurt Weill's score is naturally superior in craftmanship to that of most theatre musicians, but it has certainly none of the originality of the same composer's earliest work. Very ably it taps the funds of favorite musical conventions stored in the audiences' memory. It is an amalgam of Puccini, Victor Herbert, modernized Viennese opera, hot jazz. This is fused into a very pleasantly serviceable pap but not into a real musical expression of native feeling. Operas like *Cavalleria Rusticana* or *I Pagliacci* are far more organic in relation to their audiences than *Street Scene* is to ours. Ultimately *Street Scene* is far closer to clever Broadway showmanship than it is to creation.

—*TRW*, Apr. '47

PARIS IN NEW YORK

There used to be a time when we spoke of the "commercial" theatre. Today the expression is almost quaint. What else can there be but "commercial" theatre? Not only has everything outside this category ceased to exist in fact but any conception different from it has disappeared even as an idea. The elimination of the theatre as art has not only taken place in the street, it has been completed in our minds.

At a recent preview of a rather provocative new play I took pains to listen in on a number of conversations during the intermissions. The question that was most frequently asked related to the play's commercial possibilities "Do you think it's a hit?" I could not understand why this problem rather than the play's merits dominated the discussion. This was probably ingenuous of me: the form of the question was obviously the one deemed most conducive to a sound analysis of the play's merits.

Later in the month a new comedy was produced by a very prosperous theatrical firm. As a play the new offering was on the level of a fourth rate movie. Most of the reviewers thought so too. But what was most evident in their reviews was not a determination to emphasize this but the precaution taken not to offend the kind of audience to whom the play might appeal. "I very often found it easier to understand why other people were laughing than to laugh myself," one of the reviewers confessed. Would it not be tantamount to an antisocial act for a reviewer to fight the inanity of a public that responds to such drivel?

In such an intellectual climate no regimentation from the outside is necessary. We freely regiment ourselves. We bow to the inert power of mass-production psychology. "If a man does not act as he thinks," someone has said, "he will end by thinking as he acts." We dislike the play, the reviewers implied, but this is the stuff of which hits are made—so we ought to help make it one!

It is true, of course, that not all generative fire has died in our theatre world. There are people who want to counteract the immense cost and pressure of present theatrical production which render it virtually impossible to put on any play not expected to make large sums of money. People of this kind, contributed to the establishment of an American Repertory Theatre. What is significant, however, is that this money is usually solicited with the assurance that a repertory theatre can be made to pay. Perhaps it can. But one ought never to lose sight of the fact that in a healthy community a good repertory theatre would be supported because of its basic value—whether or not it paid. It must be repeated time and again that the great orchestras, museums, libraries are splendid and necessary institutions even though they never do "pay!" All honor to those individuals and organizations who made it possible for the American Repertory Theatre, on the verge of collapse, to continue—despite its unhappy shortcomings and to produce *Yellow Jack*—its most appropriate revival. Their money was a genuine gift.

The newly organized performances of the Experimental Theatre are also to be commended despite the fact that its approach is vitiated by thinking rooted in premises identical with those of the ordinary—I no longer dare say commercial—theatre. The purpose of the Experimental Theatre is to give new authors a place to see their plays acted so that they may learn to write plays that may reach larger audiences, in other words, plays that pay. This makes a laboratory or studio of the new organization—practical and laudable to be sure—but in no way an experimental theatre.

What is an experimental theatre? It is a theatre seeking new paths, a theatre of spirits so adventurous, daring, subtle that they cannot easily be assimilated by, or adapted to, the conventional channels of popular entertainment. A true experimental theatre is not a tryout for the market but an end in itself. When the old Provincetown Players first produced O'Neill's one-act plays, they were thought to be caviar to the general but also superior to it. When the Group Theatre presented Saroyan's *My Heart's in the Highlands*, it was not because that organization hoped the author would learn to write more profitably but because it believed he was a poet who deserved an honorable place in the theatre. The American theatre needs such work every bit as much as it does the sure-fire stuff of a Norman Krasna.

The theatre is not alone, of course, in showing the effects of a mass-production psychology and aesthetics. Have you ever attended an auction of paintings? The atmosphere resembles that of a snobbish Broadway or Hollywood première. Instead of a simple pleasure we are witness to a sort of contest. Aside from the question of money, competition, purse pride, and similar vices, what is fostered is an attitude that makes the appreciation of painting appear to be a trick. Only the person who is on the "inside" can do it! Worse than this, one begins to believe that the artist painted his picture so that the initiate might judge it. The naïveté of the whole art process has been displaced by a kind of suave trade pact in which all parties have been transformed into sensitive swindlers.

The inroads of publicity thinking are even more invidious than these obvious examples show. At a recent gathering of highly cultivated writers, teachers, critics, and dilettantes, a famous author, recently returned from France, was being pumped for information on his trip. Nearly all the questions revolved around the term "existentialism"—what it was, how it was doing, what its future was. Existentialism had been sold as a subject of discussion through a whole series of special articles in our most widely circulated journals. Everyone had apparently forgotten that no artistic movement is more important than the life of the butcher, the baker, the candlestick-maker which it reflects. The whole discussion was as depersonalized as the statistics on the gross income of a department store.

This is not intended as an attack on anyone. It is a description of an all-pervading atmosphere against which we must protect ourselves as best we can. It is not universal. There are antitoxins. There are colonies and countries in which it has not won total victory. One of the great weapons against it is consciousness—consciousness of one's self.

I have already pointed out in a previous article that "backward" countries are often more hopeful in this respect than those successful dominions where mass and monopoly production have taken possession not only of industries but of souls. Even in the expression of modern distress—that sense of alienation which man feels in a world becoming increasingly unintelligible and remote from him— no better exponents can be found than certain natives of "backward" regions: the Irishman Joyce, the Czech Kafka, the Russian Stravinsky, the Spaniard Picasso.

Many of them came to Paris, which was the crucible and touchstone of western civilization. Now France itself has become a "backward" spot. It has no secure government, no solvent economy, no decisive weight in the balance of political forces. France is strained, sapped, gasping, and weary. It is a depleted and forgotten village in the world's power calculations. Why then have so many of my recent pleasures been of French origin? Perhaps it is precisely because France has been spared some of the worst blights of the postwar era through its failure to achieve big corporation prestige. Old France has not died altogether, and a new one is painfully in the making.

I heard Simonne de Beauvoir speak to a small gathering at the Museum of Modern Art. She is a young and personable lady who is at once a playwright, novelist, critic, and, from all accounts, an effective lieutenant in the existentialist ranks of Paris. She did not even mention existentialism in her talk. She spoke of the writer's responsibility in the world today. How can the writer who realizes his responsibility to his fellow man remain independent of any party with a rigid program was the problem Mlle. de Beauvoir attempted to elucidate.

What she said was not conclusive, it was even unsatisfactory, and one might complain, if one were so minded, that she spoke with little humor and few graces. But what was striking and inspiring was to see the struggle of her search in these fundamental issues. Where there is so much integrity of spirit—even in confusion—where there is such profound striving there is hope, and there will be an "answer."

By pure coincidence I left Mlle. de Beauvoir's lecture to see and hear Lucienne Boyer sing her night club ditties at the uptown Café Society. If Mlle. de Beauvoir was a bit of thinking France, Mlle. Boyer was a bit of Parisian street life. The latter was as real and impressive as the former. Mlle. de Beauvoir's speech had the lean hardness of an inquiring mind; Lucienne Boyer's songs had a rich delicacy, even in their coarseness. If there was fineness in the tension of the young writer's mind, the *diseuse* revealed an equally fine style, which derived from her ability to approach with delight the lowliest banalities of affective diction as part of the whole experience of life. The common level of Mlle. Boyer's interest was no less pure and personal than the "high" realm of Mlle. de Beauvoir's concern.

Both the "high" and the "low" are synthesized in Henri Cartier-Bresson's photography on view at the Museum of Modern Art during February and March. A clear spirit combines realism and intelligence in these photographs. This is first-class work because it is not clever, vulgar, ostentatiously strong, or fashionably suave. It is the work of a man with a lucid eye.

He sees our world peopled by cripples and waifs, a host of the battered and beaten in a landscape that is mostly debris. There are a few tender faces—mostly those of artists or of simple workers. We find no disfiguring prejudice in Cartier-Bresson's work. He is neither sentimental nor cold. He does not assume an "objective" indifference nor make his subjects serve some special aesthetic or symbolic end.

Such photographers as Cartier-Bresson are true historians because they are true artists. He is more complete than a journalist, deeper than a doctrinaire. While he records the world as it strikes the camera, he appears to probe into the very heart of the image he has isolated. There is a potential of real social statement here. Yet how modest is his art: Cartier-Bresson never pretends to the virtues of the seer. Look at the photographs showing the children of Seville playing amidst ruins and at the one of Cardinal Pacelli in Montmartre. They are brief chronicles of our time.

One of Cartier-Bresson's photographs shows Picasso in his studio stripped to the waist facing the spectator like a wrestler. Picasso's works stand high in the world of art because his career is a long succession of bouts with contemporary reality. He is supposed to have said, "I do not seek, I find." Exploration or discovery, conscious experiment or inspired invention, Picasso's work is either directly or symbolically a graph of a highly sensitive spirit and cultivated hand in a series of reactions to what has been happening in the world and in the soul of man from the beginning of the century to the present. Not to understand this is not to understand Picasso at all.

I do not pretend to "get" each and every Picasso canvas. I do not find it necessary to like them all. I do not find myself indignant when I fail to realize their intention. When I find a Picasso harsh, puzzling or even repugnant, I do not believe it is necessarily the artist who must justify himself.

I am confining myself to these generalities not only because Picasso is too vast a subject to summarize in a section of a general article but because the Picasso "craze" has hit the town at a time when only a very limited segment of his work may be seen. The show of nine recent Picassos (1939-1946) at the Samuel Kootz Gallery brought out a row of "standees" that the producers of hit shows might envy. This sudden popularity does not signify, of course, that Picasso has "come into his own": many of the people who saw the recent Picassos were seeing him for the first time—and most of them loathed the paintings. It simply meant that the postwar publicity on top of the old reputation had done its job. At the Paul Rosenberg Gallery earlier and more easily appreciated Picassos (1923-1937) attracted smaller though still sizable crowds.

To know Picasso truly one must study him as a whole. This may be done by reviewing examples of his work from the beginning (about 1901) through all the mutations of the ensuing years. Then and then only can one perceive the human motive that has governed all the apparent accidents and vagaries of Picasso's style. Then we see the amazing and erudite draughtsman who is Picasso as a kind of disenchanted Christian looking with constantly fascinated eyes at the progressive decimation of the modern world.

There has always been in Picasso a somewhat aristocratic but nonetheless genuine feeling for the humble, the impoverished, the dispossessed. We see them first in pictures that resemble a scrubbier, more splenetic Toulouse-Lautrec, in blue pictures of emaciated lovers and housewives, in skeleton-like drinkers warming their carcasses through the camaraderie of the café table. We see them later as exquisite but hungry harlequins deprived of solace or support. Soon these creatures—last remnants of a humanity in which Picasso can believe—disappear altogether or become subjects for weird conjecture, as in some primitive imagery in which the classic sense of man has become distorted either with mystic or impersonal intention. Connoisseurs talk of the influence of Negro sculpture.

Scientific analysis and discovery break the world into fragments with wholly inhumane disinterest and curiosity, finding new patterns and new associations like the cold miracle of machinery designed to fulfill functions that may easily turn out to be fairly useless if not entirely harmful. There is talk of cubism.

Everything is tried since in this new world everything is permissible. The heart tires and the spirit begs for beauty. But "beauty" has now become a banality, and a kind of aloof and almost untouchable linear feminine model appears like a wraith. At almost the same time, the artist is seized with a comic and cold lustiness, a gargantuan rhythmic impulse to fill the human void created by the disappearance of man (or by the artist's disbelief in him), and the paintings become populated by cavorting monsters of monumental dimension whose immense gestures have a Rabelaisian swing at once ferocious and funny. One hears talk of neoclassicism.

Suddenly all becomes wan and still. Nothing at all is left except for the bleached bones of what may have been human, animal, or vegetable life strewn on a shore that is nothing but cold air, emptiness and desolation. This phase of Picasso's work dates from the depression—around 1931. Somewhat later there are scarlet eruptions of feverish though always "classically" ordered dreams—combining several of the former incarnations in one.

This continues till dreams and speculations are exploded in the hideous immediacy of the Fascist raid on Guernica in the Spanish civil war. The result is a shriek, a curse, a howling mockery or savage detestation against a world that could come to this. At the Pierre Matisse Gallery last year I saw a *Still Life with Candle*, painted by Picasso toward the end of the war, which had a glowering beauty. It was colorful in pigment and gaunt in effect. It seemed an image of someone solitary, grim, intense, and strong—awaiting liberation. The *Tomato-Plant* in the Kootz show had some of the same quality. *The Cock* (in the same show) crows a brazenly piercing protest, and some of the portraits give evidence of a savage contempt directed not only against the Nazi invader but against certain gentry at home.

Where does Picasso end? We cannot say. To sum it all up in a catchword is to belie the vitality of a complex evolution the various stages of which we have seen constitute the recondite history of a man and an epoch. In certain of its "movements" Picasso's career is paralleled by the course of other artists: Braque for example. But Braque is French:

always elegant, more soothingly gracious and more ornamental in his melancholy. Picasso's work is more turbulent, more nearly "religious." His talent, more uneven, is also more forceful. It rarely reaches the complete and consummate statement of a whole vision that much less ambitious or disturbed artists like Matisse achieve. If Picasso's work suffers from a spasmodic ebullience and possibly overproduction, it may be as much a sign of extensive genius as of weakness.

—*TRW*, May '47

THE MEANING OF PLAYS: *ALL MY SONS*

A dramatic critic eminent among dramatic critics recently wrote an article which suggested that plays "about something" were generally duds. The article was either very sly or very stupid. It was very sly insofar as it is unarguable that most plays the premise and sentiment of which we do not accept cannot please us. What was stupid in the article was to isolate "plays about something" into a special category of plays that are topical, political, or, in some overall manner, propaganda. Propaganda in the theatre may be defined as the other fellow's point of view or any position with which we disagree.

All plays are about something, whether or not they have an explicit thesis. *Peter Pan* is as much about something as *Candida*. *Cyrano de Bergerac* is as clear an expression of something as *Bury the Dead*. *The Iceman Cometh* is as much "propaganda" as *Deep Are the Roots*. *St. Joan* is as definitely a preachment as any play ever presented on Fourteenth Street by the old Theatre Union.

The critic's first job is to make clear what a play is about. Many reviewers are signally inept in the performance of this simple duty. The reason for this is that they mistake a play's materials for its meaning. It is as if an art critic were to say that Cézanne's painting is about apples, or to suppose that because religious subjects were used in many classic paintings that all these paintings were necessarily inspired by religious feeling.

An artist generally finds it convenient to use the material he finds closest at hand. What he says with his material always reveals something personal and distinct that cannot be described comprehensively merely by stating the materials he has employed. One play about a strike may convey some intimate frustration, another may be a lyric outburst of youthful aspiration. A slight comedy like Noel Coward's *Present Laughter* is not so much a play about the affairs of a successful playwright as a demonstration of a state of mind in which contempt and indifference to the world have been accepted as a sort of aristocratic privilege.

In the Simonov comedy *The Whole World Over*, which I directed recently, the subjects of the housing shortage and the rehabilitation of the veteran are brought into play, but they are not at all the essence of the matter. This comedy is essentially an image of faith and joy in everyday living, told in the folk tradition of those gay and sentimental songs which establish the continuity between what is universal in the spirit of the old and the new Russia.

Another play that has been variously characterized as a war play or as a play about the returned GI or as an attack on war-profiteers is Arthur Miller's *All My Sons*. If I have waited until this date to discuss it, it is not because as one of its producers I might be charged with partiality toward it, but because I prefer to examine it from the particular angle of the present article rather than to praise it as one of the better plays of the season.

The central character of *All My Sons* is a small businessman who during the war sent out defective airplane parts which he hoped would not be used in actual combat but which he would not recall for fear his army contracts would be canceled and his business and his family ruined as a result. The play presents the gradual disclosure of these facts to the businessman's younger son, a former army officer.

The revelation brings with it not only a realization that twenty-one boys were killed as a consequence of the use of the defective material but that the manufacturer's older son—an army pilot—committed suicide because of his father's crime. The younger son tries to make his father and mother understand that nothing—not business necessity nor devotion to family—can mitigate the father's guilt. A man must be responsible not alone to his wife and children but, ultimately, to all men. Failure to act on this fundamental tenet must inevitably lead to crime.

Contrary to what some reviewers have suggested, the author does not exonerate the central character by making the "system" responsible for his guilt. Such an explanation is the cogent but desperate excuse that the guilty man offers, but his son (and the author) emphatically deny his right to use it. There can be no evasion of the burden of individual human responsibility.

The distorted "individualism" of our day that makes the private good of the individual the final criterion for human action is shown to be inhuman and destructive, whereas the true individualism of our early American prophets made the individual responsible to the community. The man who blames society for his betrayal of it is a weakling and a coward. The individual of Arthur Miller's ethic is the guarantor in his own person of society's health. The difference between Arthur Miller's individualist and the believer in "rugged individualism" today is that the latter narrows his sense of self so that it extends no further than the family circle, while the former gives himself the scope of humanity.

What makes the theme of *All My Sons* increasingly talk of "service" and repeat other residual phrases from the religions we inherit while we actually live a daily life devoted to the pursuit of Power or Success, the most unquestioned symbol of which is money. The real war in modern life is between a memory of morality and the pressure of "practicality." We live in a schizoid society. This is an open secret, but everybody pretends not to see it or condemns as "idealism" any attempt to remedy the condition. To understand that our double standard is a fatal disease is, as a matter of fact, the first step in a realistic attitude toward life. We shall see—at a later point of the present article—that it is this realism which a part of our society at the moment wishes to resist.

Some reviewers complain that the plot of *All My Sons* is too complicated. For a while I failed to understand what was meant by this criticism. Then I realized that the whole aspect of the mother's insistence that her son, reported missing, is alive— her clinging to every prop of belief, including the solace of astrological assurance, was what struck some of the reviewers as irrelevant. This is a misunderstanding that derives from thinking of the play as an exposé of war-profiteering.

The war-profiteering aspect of the play, I repeat, represents the play's material, not its meaning. What Arthur Miller is dramatizing is a universal not a local situation. The mother, whose role in the explicit plot of the play is incidental, is the center of the play's meaning. She embodies the status quo or norm of our present-day ethic and behavior pattern. It is on her behalf that the husband has committed his crime. She and what she represents is his defense. But she cannot consciously accept the consequence of the morality she lives by, for in the end it is a morality that kills her children and even her husband. In order to retain her strength she cannot abandon her posi- tion—everything must be done for one's own— and yet it is this position that has destroyed what she hopes to protect. She is a "normal" woman, yet she is sick. She suffers from severe headaches; she is subject to anxiety dreams. She believes in the stars and with fervid complacency maintains that "Some superstitions are very nice."

If there is a "villain" in the piece, it is the mother—the kindly, loving mother who wants her brood to be safe and her home undisturbed. When her husband, who believes too slavishly in her doctrine—it is the world's doctrine, and so there can be no fault with it—when her husband breaks down under the logic of her doctrine, which has

made him a murderer, she has no better advice than: "Be smart!" Yet she, too, is innocent. When her son's friend, the doctor, mumbles: "How many people walking around loose, and they're crazy as coconuts. Money, money, money, money; you say it long enough, it doesn't mean anything. Oh how I'd love to be around when that happens," she answers: "You're so childish, Jim!" She is inno- cent because she cannot understand. Not even in the extremity of her grief does she understand. When her son tells her: "I'm like everybody else now. I'm practical now. You made me practical," she answers: "But you have to be." To her dying day, she will remain with this her only wisdom, her only conviction.

Her son cries out: "The cats in the alley are practical. The bums who run away when we were fighting were practical. Only the dead ones weren't practical. But now I'm practical and I spit on myself. I'm going away." This is the essence of the playwright's meaning. "This is the land of the great big dogs. You don't love a man here, you eat him! That's the principle; the only one we live by This is a zoo, a zoo!" The mother is sorry...deeply sorry. "What more can we be?" she asks. "You can be better!" her son answers, and it is the drama- tist's answer as well.

Arthur Miller's talent is a moral talent with a passionate persistence that resembles that of the New England preacher who fashioned our first American rhetoric. *All My Sons* rouses and moves us even though it lacks the supreme fire of poetic vision. The determined thrust of its author's mind is not yet enough to melt or transfigure us, but in a theatre that has grown slothful it will have to do. Yes, it will do.

What is most significant about certain produc- tions is the public's reception of them. This is especially true of the biggest hit of the season, *Brigadoon*. None of the shows this year—not *Street Scene, Joan of Lorraine, Finian's Rainbow, All My Sons, The Iceman Cometh*—has received unqualified critical and public acclaim. This has been reserved for the new musical about a village in the Scotch highlands that has disappeared from the map and lives one day in each century—or something like that! I am told that the plot is based on an early nineteenth-century German romance—and I can well believe it.

Brigadoon is staged with a pleasant unaffectedness; most of the choreography is trim, sweet, and easy; its actors are engaging. Aside from these elements, I can see little reason for its great success, except that it is entirely without irritating ingredients. I watched the show with a beautiful lady who whispered to me, "My history goes back two thousand years. I have no patience with a play whose characters live only for a day in each century." But such rebellious sentiments are exceptional. *Brigadoon* has enjoyed the only one hundred per cent favorable press (as advertised) because it represents agreeableness abstracted from practically everything. It is so wholly without any "roughage" that it is impossible to call it bad. It is so ineffably bland that it can't even be called boring. To call it treacle is to use too strong a word; to think of it as sugared barley-water is to suggest that it would do for infants. No, it is a kind of air devoid of almost all definable properties—the vaguest of never-never lands, the only place, in other words, that can be guaranteed to produce no tremor of actual life—hence no pain.

For the past two years, I have been looking at paintings that register an increasing apprehension of atomic shock; I have heard forecasts of inflation, depression, rumors of war. The political skies are dark. None of these things impressed me with how bad the psychological situation really is until I saw *Brigadoon*. The derelicts of O'Neill's *Iceman* seek refuge in the bottle; the mother in *All My Sons* turns to the stars to escape from an intolerable reality; the theatregoing public flies to *Brigadoon*. It is the vapid express to nonexistence.

If you listen to people who discuss such matters, you will either hear them say that the new Eisenstein film, *Ivan, the Terrible*, is a bore or that it is great. Both opinions are justified. It is a boring picture that is great or a great picture that is boring.

If it is a failure, it is the kind of failure that only a genius could produce.

In *Ivan, the Terrible*, Part I (I believe the original title was *Ivan the Great*), Eisenstein has attempted to create an epically monumental image of history. Through visual means of the utmost refinement and a thoroughly modern ideology he has attempted to achieve a heroic style that would strike us as primitively simple as an ancient icon. He has aimed at a motion picture that would be the equivalent of the most virile and rooted folk art.

There is almost no story, a minimum of movement. The pace is slow, the acting is exaggerated to the point of what we might call hamminess. Yet to make these observations is to miss the point entirely. Eisenstein assumes a certain knowledge of the facts on the part of the audience—just as the Greek dramatists assumed that the plot of their plays was common knowledge. What Eisenstein wants to do with his characters, his backgrounds, his imagery, and his music is to stamp them indelibly on the audience's consciousness, like the impress of the crucifix on the mind of a devout Christian.

Ivan is the great Czar—historical symbol of a unified Russia—and so his face is juxtaposed in a memorable composition with the image of an endless procession of Russian people whose number reaches to the distant horizon. The watchful eye of the faithful peasant, who devotes himself to Ivan, is photographed again and again to remind us of the eternal vigilance of the people. The antagonists, the Boyars, are veritable mountains of impenetrable and almost immovable flesh, materials, whiskers, and wealth. The weak and handsome countenance of the vacillating prince (divided between loyalty to Ivan and to the class of Boyars to which he belongs) is studied to the slightest quiver of the eyelid. The ancient Russian court is given a substance that is at once sinfully subterranean and bursting with the possibilities of overwhelming fulfillment.

There is magnificence in all this: the faces and make-up alone are triumphs of dramatic meaning. (If only our productions of Shakespeare had some of the qualities of this film!) Yet the picture remains static, not merely in the technical sense but in a spiritual sense. There is something inert here that disturbs us not because Eisenstein is a conscious and masterly craftsman but because we feel in his art more will than feeling, more decision than faith, more plan than inspiration.

The picture fails to be dramatic in the end not because it lacks narrative devices—these devices have been deliberately shunned as extraneous to the director's intention—but because the emotion that the film attempts to convey seems not to have any genuine origin outside the director's determination that it should be there. All art, no matter how subtle, complex, or erudite in conception or craftsmanship, must have its own simplicity, its own spontaneity. *Potemkin* had this naïveté—as did a number of other early Eisenstein films, even when they were marred in spots by a certain aesthetic studiousness—but it is largely absent in *Ivan, the Terrible.*

Despite all we can admire in this extraordinary and valuable picture, we suspect it of being essentially a piece of patriotics, a kind of *Washington Crossing the Delaware!* It is done with utmost skill and workmanlike integrity, but it is basically "official" rather than experienced art.

—*TRW*, June '47

SMILE OF THE REBEL

"The comedian is an iconoclast," Charlie Chaplin said in a recent conversation. The comedian is more frequently a man in disguise. The disguise may even succeed in hiding the wearer from himself. He may not actually know that he has put it on.

The artist may often be observed deriding the values of a society in which he hopes to attain an important position. His criticism of society may be almost wholly unconscious, as in the case of a Groucho Marx whose "act" is a parody of American salesmanship, or it may be so exuberant

an accommodation to a particular social rhythm as to constitute a lampoon of it, as in the case of a Jimmy Durante. Sometimes the artist adopts an attitude of amiable hypocrisy as Oscar Wilde did in most of his plays, where the decorum of the English upper-classes is toyed with so that one is unable to discern whether Wilde was more attracted by the graces than repelled by the absurdities that he perceived in the manners of his time. Where the acceptance of a society is greater than the degree of rejection, you get the kind of flattering satire we find in the librettos of W. S. Gilbert, which are at once a caricature and a celebration of British Philistinism. In all these instances, there is a certain amount of camouflage as to the real meaning of the material. That is why comedy of this type is a sort of social safety-valve, and invariably popular.

When the comedian is conscious that his joke is prompted by a painful state of affairs, we come very close to the tragic artist's confrontation of reality. For this reason, Charlie Chaplin's *Monsieur Verdoux* is one of the most fascinating documents of our day. To question whether it is or is not funny is to discuss it like a cultural moron. You remember the vaudevillian who said about his partner's musical performance: "I wouldn't like it, even if it were good." My feeling about *Monsieur Verdoux* is: Even if it were "bad," I would still consider it a great picture!

Monsieur Verdoux is unique in being the only picture ever made that is truly the expression of the individual who made it. Soviet pictures are unified by an ideology and social demand, which the director may share but which rarely has any special stamp of individuality on it. European pictures generally are made by craftsmen who share a common artistic tradition—naturalism, romanticism, fantasy—to which the individual artist tries to add a slight personal variation. Experimental films (like *The Blood of a Poet*) are usually either dilettante or technical essays to extend the vocabulary of the medium itself. American films pursue the goal of entertainment—a hybrid product, the test of which is box-office receipts. In accordance with this goal, Hollywood films are no one's creation but the result of an attempt to please—or at least not to offend—the producing company, the Johnson office, the State Boards of Review, the foreign market, the representatives of every class, profession, sect, and pressure group—in other words, that conglomerate everybody, which is nobody, called the Public!

Monsieur Verdoux represents the effort of an individual who uses the motion-picture medium to say what he feels about the world he lives in. If the picture has faults, they are faults of conception, spiritual limitations, questions of thought and sentiment. To say this is to recognize that we are dealing with a work of art. To say that a work of art—even a faulty one—has come out of Hollywood is to announce an historic event.

Works of art are not manufactured; they evolve, they have a history. The history of *Monsieur Verdoux* may be traced through the whole of Chaplin's career as an artist and as a man. But the true history of an artist and a man is always more than a personal matter. It leads to an examination of the society in which that artist has lived.

The old Chaplin—the one to which his critics refer as a model for him to follow undeviatingly—was a symbol of an almost innocent epoch: 1913-18. He was the Little Man, a perpetual waif of a world in which there were rich and poor, kings and beggars, in an almost immutable structure ordained by nature. There was nothing to question, and nobody but the sick or the foolish did question it. To be the Little Man was not necessarily a disgrace. He was an accepted character as was the Rich Man—images reflecting the inevitable order of things. An accident—always to be hoped for but thoroughly inexplicable—might transform the Little Man and make him rich, as in the *Gold Rush*. This world was not without its sadness, but because it was accepted by everyone as fact as well as legend, it was as reasonable a world as the child's world—when it is not too violently disturbed.

Chaplin's Little Man was a perfectly intelligible figure that warmed the hearts of the great masses of poor people who did not feel abused even when they were hurt, and that pleased the rich who felt no anger or evil intent in this luckless mite of humanity—only a wistfulness, a hunger for life and light, a seeking for a berth of rest and good fortune. Everyone, in short, could identify himself in his own way with Chaplin's Little Man—a creation brilliant and original without being in the least problematic.

The very early Chaplin pictures are extreme stylizations. They hardly seem to take place in any real place at all; their characters are a fantastic assortment of people who somehow always look foreign. (Chaplin himself arrived in this country in 1910; the plight of the immigrant was one of his first subjects.) The general environment of these films had the aspect of a scrubby slum and the more opulent places were suggested by sleazy sets that resembled the impoverished imaginings of people who possess only a scattered and quaint notion of luxury. The impression of skimpiness and strangeness made by the old Chaplin pictures may be ascribed not only to the primitive technique and low budget of the old days but also to the kind of rough working-class theatre in which Chaplin was trained and whose audience provided Chaplin's earliest public.

The pictures of Chaplin's first period deal with the difficulty of getting jobs—he is unemployed mostly—and while hunger and monetary difficulty with its attendant humiliations recur in the later period (1919-30), most of the problems are those of employment. As they increase in seriousness, the environments come closer to reality and the characters become almost naturalistic, though Chaplin himself remains the stylized spirit, forever solitary but desperately eager to establish some permanent and honored connection with society.

In *City Lights* a picture that anticipated the depression, the first bitter notes are struck. The wealthy wastrel befriends the Little Man when he is drunk and kicks him out when he is sober. There is something akin to cruelty, too, in the scene in which Chaplin mistakes a gentleman's baldpate for a head of cheese.

In *Modern Times*—his contribution to the Thirties—Chaplin shows the Little Man reduced to a gadget of the machine age, and the scene in which he is used as a guinea pig for an eating apparatus is almost savage. A prison is shown as preferable to the hazards of the Little Man's robot life. Most striking is the fact that as Chaplin advances, his pictures are decreasingly "funny"— that is, they become more specific in content, less abstractly comic.

The Great Dictator (1941) marks the beginning of the "new" Chaplin. The unity of the Little Man is broken. Chaplin plays two people: the inflated, hysterical, and sadistic distortion of the Little Man—who is Hitler—and his double, the Little Man who is Hitler's victim. The two figures merge at the end into a voice of protest, prophecy, and broken-hearted plea, a voice that cries out: "Save Yourselves!" In this picture, Chaplin speaks at last—and what he articulates is certainly no joke.

The Little Man has lost his innocence. With the coming of Fascism and the Second World War, he no longer can remain totally unconscious. He no longer can remain the mute fool, the battered darling and beloved burnt offering of the universe. Chaplin himself is no longer the naïve clown from the rough pioneer art of a remote coast. He has become rich, he has been made a famous public figure, he knows the Big People now as intimately as he once knew the little ones. Roosevelt has made the Forgotten Man (the socially conscious appellation for the Little Man) a man who has a right to expect things, a man who must be served. The war ends: a curious tension sets in. Chaplin already "suspect" for having made *The Great Dictator* say something more than a facilely funny poster is now looked upon with a certain distrust. This little man is not pitiful: he seems to have claws. Chaplin makes *Monsieur Verdoux.*

It is interesting to note that while the story of *Monsieur Verdoux* is supposed to take place between 1931 and 1937, the psychological atmosphere of the picture is definitely that of the present. Who is Monsieur Verdoux? He is our old friend the Little Man, who, after thirty years as a small employee (in a bank), has been thrown out in the first crash, cannot "take" it, and decides to go into a business for himself. His business is gruesome: he is Bluebeard—a man who kills his women for the money in it. His troubles now are the troubles of the small businessman. The humor of the situation is based on the tensions of such a person's trying to find security for himself and his family so that he and they may remain rexpected members of the community.

The picture hasn't the simple unity of the early pictures because the mask of Verdoux cannot have the unmistakable definition of the old mask. This is inevitable. The Little Man of bygone years knew his place in the world; we knew his place, and he did not need to be explained. His life was precarious, but his situation was fixed and clear. But Monsieur Verdoux is an uncharted character. He hardly knows himself, and, being so very much like us, we hardly know what to make of him.

Verdoux is a murderer without any special malice. He is an exhaustingly harried man. He has time for a little culture or poetry only between "deals." He is the victim of a depression, but he hates to be depressed by the news of depression! He would rather spend his time quietly within the bosom of his family and chat cozily with his neighbors. He has very little time for them, however— business, you know. Moments of kindness are dangerous for him: they divert him from the strict discipline of his work. He distrusts practically everyone; he warms only to the totally disarmed. He loves women but fears them as peculiarly equipped snares of a rapacious world. (He adores his wife—who is crippled—just as in an earlier picture the Little Man adored a girl who was blind and gave her up when she recovered her eyesight.) He regards most family life as a grotesque battle of egos. Religion offers him no solace. Official justice is beside the point.

He fears poverty worse than disease, but living life in comparative affluence makes him desperate and somehow pitiable even to his friends who knew him in his impecunious years. His ingenuity, resourcefulness, rush, and madness are all for nothing. He loses everything. His destiny is death. He feels free only as he goes to meet his destiny. In the last shot of the picture, he walks away from the spectator like the Little Man of old, but this time he is going, broken and weary, to extinction. The horizon is no longer a mystery or a promise; it is the guillotine. The Little (Business) Man has nothing more to gain or lose.

The mask of Monsieur Verdoux is multiple. The modern man has lost the integrity of a unified personality. The modern man is no man. He is an insincere fop, an impostor, a jumpy marionette, a frightened worm, a would-be genius, an acrobat turning fatal pirouettes over an abyss. He is a shrewd manipulator, a hunted creature begging for time, a smug moralizing papa, a jittering charlatan, a megalomaniac, a lonely mouse.

All this we see in turn in a series of masks on Chaplin's miraculously mobile countenance. His acting now is a startling and almost disconcerting alternation of stylized performance—that has something as cold as a demonstration about it— and authentic emotional realism. The masks change so fast that we seem to be looking at a totally new face (or disguise) at every moment. The effect is like that of one of those strange portraits we see in modern painting in which different planes of the physiognomy are painted in sharply contrasted colors and in strangely arbitrary relationships in defiance of all anatomy or natural law!

The picture is uneven. It must be. Chaplin is trying to say everything he thinks and feels about life today. He is also trying to make entertainment, to put over a good show—with suspense, laughs, tricks, and thrills—so that his picture will earn him a good profit on his heavy investment. If these are slightly contradictory aims, they represent contradictions within the man. He is no longer the lyric poet of his beginnings. He is a major rebel and a major figure in the arts and in the industry of which art is a fragment. He is of this world and against it. He does not know how it can be changed, but he knows that it is killing him and everyone else along with him. He is no rational philosopher; he is an emotional anarchist.

This does not mean his picture is unclear. This harrowing comedy is terribly clear. Its message is not, as some have stated, that the little murderer is no more guilty than the great murderer whom the world condones. That is a banality to make the lazy-minded nod. The picture tells us that we are living in a criminal world; it says we are living a life that makes killers of us all, it says that we have all been denatured through the abandonment of the principle of love and the substitution of the principle of business—and that as denatured people we are all condemned. It says that our efforts to proceed normally along the false path of the money principle is a tragic farce—a Comedy of Murders. Laugh if you like.

It has been objected that Chaplin is not a good writer, that his technique, mechanically speaking, is old-fashioned, that there are lapses of style in the picture, that some spots are dull and others pretentiously verbose. All of these objections—even if true—betray either a lack of understanding or a desire to overlook the core of the picture's significance. The picture as a whole, which is more than the sum total of all its elements, is great. It is great even if we do not like its meaning; it is great even if we find it painful and hard; even if we do not believe its message wholly true. It is great because it reflects, with infinitely more subtlety than anyone has taken the trouble to study, something that exists as the real feeling of an extraordinary, sensitive man, a feeling which in turn mirrors something that exists objectively in the life of our times. Perhaps we should have liked him to say something more than he did or to say it somewhat differently. But that it has been said at all through the medium of the Hollywood film is, I repeat, a revolutionary occurrence.

114

Chaplin does not escape the world through his comic disguise: he faces it. That is why he is an artist of singular force. Those who do not quite decipher his meaning, or who do not wish to fathom it because it disturbs them, would do well to listen and attend again and again. Here is a picture that will not be dismissed or destroyed by a batch of bad notices.

—*TRW*, July '47

LETTER FROM PARIS

I have been in Paris now for only a little over a week, and so I dare not write an article on what I have seen. I can only write a letter. When I was in New York I wrote about France without difficulty, which proves that it is easier to generalize from a distance. When one is in Paris, generalizations become much more hazardous.

The night I arrived, for example, I thought I felt something ghostly in the atmosphere. The city appeared empty, mysterious, still, as if suffering from an unspectacular but severe illness. I went to a de luxe restaurant—and there aren't many Frenchmen who can afford them. It was fairly late, and, as I realized the next day, many people had gone out of town for the Pentecost holidays. A generalization about Paris made that night would have been nothing but a guess based on lack of information. Yet now that I have seen the streets alive with people and traffic and have witnessed the normal activity of the Frenchman at his daily task, I am not sure that my first impression was altogether fantastic.

Paris is still beautiful, though more than ever its beauty is like that of a woman who always appears young even when the marks of age are becoming increasingly noticeable. Indeed, part of the beauty of Paris is now very much related to the signs of its age. Certain scars that are the result of neglect rather than of actual decrepitude take on a frightening charm; but one must beware when speaking of Paris of endowing one's phrases with a certain perfumed ineffability—the traditional tone with which the Bohemian in us responds to the thought of the City of Light. One must try to see Paris as it is today—without glamor.

I was going to call this letter "Paris without Glamor," but refrained from doing so because that, too, would have been a misleading generalization. Paris still has glamor, but it is not the glamor of travel blurbs, lyric sinfulness, emigré carefreeness, aesthetic and political dash and adventure. The glamor of Paris resides in its representing in essence what our Western world has become, what we have to begin with in our journey toward the future. If New York is too protected and blindly energetic, the more devastated areas of Europe may be considered in too low estate to be taken as representative spots. Paris with its black-market millionaires—they are beginning to worry—and its general population with an average salary of eight thousand francs (seventy-five dollars) a month, its excellent restaurants, and its awful food shortages (you hear talk about food—bread, meat, milk—wherever you go), its precarious political situation and rightist parties that favor nationalization, leftist parties that are cautious as well as nationalistic, and centrist parties that hanker for the past and, perforce, accept the present while uttering words of paternal admonition to all sides seems to me to present a fascinating common denominator of our world—from the Rhine to San Francisco!

While the true condition of man is glossed over in the United States by a soothing commercial sheen, in Paris everything is brought into the open—the plight of the nation is frankly, almost triumphantly, admitted. There is very little self-delusion here. In the United States we hear constant vociferation about "free enterprise," with the greater part of the population unaware of what the expression means for the very good reason that, with the exception of some remote and primitive society, "free enterprise" cannot exist. In France, however, no one is interested in such myths. Everyone is engaged in the real and immediate problems that are not merely rumor or subjects for journalistic inquiry. That is why there are constant threats of strikes—including that of small business—and usually a compromise settlement; that is why there is intense political activity here—hundreds of meetings, a vast variety of newspaper discussion, and sometimes a kind of lassitude and total indifference to politics.

I am not chiefly concerned with politics, but it is impossible to understand what is going on here in cultural matters without some examination of the social currents. The reason why Paris is important and exciting (though no longer in the old "lost generation" sense) is that the French are much more conscious of what is going on in their chaos than we are concerning our prosperity; and if anyone in America believes that the European trouble is not his concern, then he is as wise as the man who says: "My legs hurt, but it's no affair of mine."

I heard the novelist Vercors lecture to a quiet little audience of students and poor middle-class folk at the university. The subject was "Morality and the Future." Vercors tried to transcend politics, but he said that for him it was axiomatic that the society of the future would be a collective society (which, he pointed out, did not necessarily mean one that was destructive of individual values), and although it was evident that he is neither a Socialist nor a Communist any more than was his audience, which included several Catholic clergymen, his discussion of the Marxist ethic was lucid and completely devoid of panic. There was nothing very inspired in Vercors' talk, yet there was something reassuring to me in its tone. These people have not lost their heads, though from our American standpoint, they have lost most of their goods.

The same was true of a lecture given by Jean-Paul Sartre on Franz Kafka. It was a very hot night; the small room was packed with some five hundred people—and air-conditioning is virtually unknown here. The room, moreover, was poorly lit. Sartre spoke from notes; he talked without once pausing for a glass of water or to wipe his perspir-

ing brow. After he had spoken for two hours, he interrupted himself to say: "It is getting late, and I see I shall have to end without discussing Kafka's art." (He had confined himself to an explanation of Kafka's psychology and ethical-ideas.) The audience cried: "No! No! Go on!" So the lecture went on for another three-quarters of an hour. When it was over—no one had left during the whole period—a crowd of young people rushed to the platform to ask questions. Questions were very much in order, because although Sartre had spoken brilliantly and had done a fine job of analysis, he had not yet evaluated his subject.

These instances indicate a highly conscious and enlightened community. Such indications may be found everywhere: the great variety of newspapers, whose opinions cover more than those of the four or five important parties; the multitude of weekly and monthly periodicals, covering political, social, and aesthetic subjects with considerable keenness and completeness; the crowds pouring into the great retrospective collection of the Impressionist painters in the museum in the Tuileries as if a popular movie star were on view. The day I went to see the new Braque paintings, I was astonished by the number and variety of visitors. There were artists and critics; there were students in worse than nondescript clothes, and a host of others, who spent a long time actually examining and discussing the paintings. (Smoking, I noticed, was permitted at the private galleries without its affecting the cleanliness of the rugs underfoot.) The Galerie Maeght, where the Braques were shown, is perhaps the finest in Paris far more spacious than any of our private galleries, beautifully lit, very comfortable, with plenty of places where one can both rest and reflect on the paintings one is looking at.

Two things struck me particularly at these various exhibits. One was the difficulty of concentrating on a work of art when the social background for such work is too active in one's consciousness. I mean that though my eye and mind could admire the Braques, the Maillols, the

Suzanne Valodons (Suzanne Valodon—who died in 1938—in her youth a circus performer and a painter's model, was Utrillo's mother and a remarkable painter in her own right), I could not stay with them long because outside the galleries was Paris, which I could not, for the time being, at any rate, take for granted. It seemed to me—emotionally speaking—that I could not really see the paintings clearly unless I had assimilated their background of the moment, which was the city itself.

I was amused, too, to hear that Braque was nervous about his show. "You mean he has 'stage-fright'?" I asked Monsieur Maeght. "Exactly," he answered. Braque is seventy, famous, well-to-do, and, among those who accept the modern school, an undisputed master. He happens also to be about the most handsome artist I have ever met: a patriarchal figure, tall, bronzed, beautifully gray, an aristocrat in bearing, dressed like an artisan-artist, with something hard and tempered in his physique, and with large, dark profound eyes in his fine head. "As long as the artist functions as an artist," I thought, "he always feels himself a beginner."

There is a restaurant somewhere on the Left Bank that saves paper (there is a shortage of that, too) by marking the courses on a blackboard at one end of the room. If you are too far from the blackboard to read it easily, you are handed a pair of binoculars. I could not tell whether this was a gag to amuse the patrons or a humorous accommodation to a difficult situation. It seemed characteristically Parisian.

The Parisian adopts himself to the hardships of his life, hoping for amelioration and making some progress toward it every day. I expected semi-starvation (outside of black-market restaurants, of course), and though the situation is still far from comfortable for the average wage-earner, there has been, everyone admits, a general improvement. I did hear one woman assert surreptitiously to another that she ate better during the war! Most Americans I meet are very pleased with the food they find here.

This capacity for making the best of things, which comes rather naturally and gracefully to the Frenchman, makes the aspect of the streets far pleasanter than I imagined they would be. The Parisian today dresses and behaves with a certain easy carelessness that makes his state of mind as well as his economic status very clear. He doesn't put on any false show. He doesn't cover up to achieve any uniform appearance of middle-class respectability or of well-being. There is very little superficial formality in clothes and deportment. Pierre Levy, who has a very important art collection, was badly in need of a shave and was pushing crates around like a truckman when I entered his gallery.

Albert Camus, novelist, playwright, journalist, and editor-in-chief of the important Gallimard publishing house, wore a blue denim shirt, open at the collar, when I spoke to him in his office. Everybody dresses as best he can and exactly as he pleases. One sees girls in slacks, men in shorts, people dressed as if they had emerged from an 1870 novel, others in clothes that are memories rather than vestments. No one disguises his class or condition. The effect is not shabby but rather friendly and tender. There is a great intimacy about Paris; it is all like a cozy and kindly interior. Paris does not pity itself, but it does little to hide its wounds. This, I repeat, is its glamor.

"What is the average Frenchman thinking about today?" I asked Camus. "He is thinking about the war," said Camus, "about the next war. He may not know how it can be avoided, but he knows that it must be. If there is another war," Camus went on, "there will not be another postwar period!"

Whether this is accurate or not, that is what the Frenchman thinks. He is not a Communist, but he does not want war with Russia or with anyone else. Nothing will be solved by another war: everything will be dissolved. Awareness of this fact—and it is a real and permanent awareness—makes the Frenchman quieter than he has ever been before. For all his dignity and familiarity with the discord of life, he is possessed by a certain fear—

the fear that must have been at the root of my impression of the ghostliness of Paris.

Most Frenchmen do not expect a war in the immediate future, but the point is that they do not want to contemplate any war at all. There will be no civil war in France unless there is a world war. Domestic politics are not altogether "serious" now because all important consequences are limited by the attitudes of and developments in Russia and America. This Camus ironically called the advantage of dependence. It explains what I feel to be a certain atmosphere of spiritual constriction.

One cannot discern any ruling ideology or abiding faith in France. The French may look forward to a "new world," but they see no concrete signs of it yet. They are impressed but not wholly convinced by America. They are respectful but timid about Russia. They are fascinated by American mechanical gadgets that seem new—like a Reynolds pen!

Under these circumstances there can be little real originality in the arts. (I shall discuss some of the individual artists next month.) My impression has been that, on the whole, critical literature is more vigorous than creative literature. There are very few outstanding young men. This, Camus, who as an editor is in a position to know, denies. Yet, when I challenged him for names, he explained that in such a period as this—as during the years of the French Revolution—more good publicists would appear than first-rate poets or novelists. "There is growing doubt as to the value of art. Our writers would like to influence the course of things, but they doubt that they can do this through pure literature." Sartre has said that literature should be involved in the struggles of the day, and so writers have become pamphleteers or critics.

It should also be remembered that very few French writers of value can earn a living solely through their writing. (Camus, himself one of the best-known writers, has to work for a publishing house to afford the luxury of writing a novel. Perhaps this explains why so many writers of distinction have turned to the theatre: Cocteau,

Sartre, Simone de Beauvoir, Francois Mauriac, Camus, and even Gide, are writing for the stage. This is supposed to have a good effect upon the quality of dramatic writing.

So far, however, I have been little impressed with what I have seen in the theatre. There is greater daring and variety of theme than is common on Broadway, but much of the writing seems to me to be factitious, intellectually contrived. Perhaps one can read a symbol or an idea into Cocteau's *Eagle has Two Heads*, but plays, like men, must possess something more than the organ of thought in order to live. At Louis Jouvet's Theatre a one-act play called *The Maids*, by a notorious new writer, Jean Genet, is a kind of effeminately hysterical Strindberg, in which the hate servant girls bear for their corrupt mistress, who has helped corrupt them, is made into a rhetorically poetic exercise. One waits in vain to be either moved or shocked. (Of course, this play, too, can be given an intellectual interpretation: it is about a society which corrupts its workers, who must either rise in rebellion or die themselves!) One wonders what satisfaction the audience is supposed to experience in seeing this play, done against a weirdly pretty but peculiarly ineffective—though original—set by Christian Bérard.

On the same bill Louis Jouvet plays a one-act tidbit by Jean Giraudoux called *The Apollo of Marsac*. Again the set is unusual, striking, and rather irrelevant, and the whole affair is a cleverly written conceit based on the notion that a woman can accomplish anything if she will simply tell the men she meets that she thinks them handsome.

The theatre where I saw these two plays was a very lush ugly-beautiful baroque jewel-box contraption, probably built around 1900. It was in sore need of ventilation, and the scent of a fragrant disinfectant that permeated the auditorium did not help much. I thought the plays and the playhouse went very well together, and I was rather charmed when I noticed during the intermission that half the audience was eating ersatz Eskimo pies. The audience was basically as honest and direct as the plays were phony.

One must always come back to the people. The French are a highly intelligent folk with a strong and cultivated sense of form and design. Their capital is a work of art that has taken many hundreds of years to make. It has a beauty and force of its own. As long as it stands it will act as a kind of guide to its people, leading them in the ways of reason and grace. Parisians have made a city that is the image of their taste and talent for living, and the city itself now acts on the Parisian as a kind of councilor, a norm of civilization, a restorative. The French and the rest of the world are right in adoring Paris: it is itself a constant reminder of the loveliness that the Western world is capable of producing.

—*TRW*, Aug. '47

THE TESTAMENT OF PARIS

Sartre is one of those protean French writers who seem to be able to do everything but sing! He is an extremely provocative critic and essayist; he has written philosophical works, novels, short stories, four plays, and most recently, the scenario for a movie. He is also an excellent lecturer and the editor of a very good magazine.

I shall confine myself to his plays. My personal preference is for the least ambitious and perhaps least highly regarded of these plays: *Death without Burial*. In this two-act melodrama, Sartre has managed to state his point of view in terms of actuality. It is a play of the resistance.

According to Sartre's view, acts alone count. When it is necessary for the resistors, who have been captured and tortured by the Vichy militia, to kill a very young boy of their own group to avoid the possibility of his exposing their leader, they agree to do so. The man who actually does the killing must go on and finish the task he has undertaken despite the mental anguish his act has caused him, just as the girl of the group must continue to

live and serve the movement despite the self-horror she feels at having been raped.

When the man who struck the boy down insists with a terrible sense of guilt that he felt some pride in his act, his comrade says: "You are too concerned with yourself. You want to save your soul. Bah! One must work. One saves one's soul in addition. If you die today, it will be said that you killed the boy out of pride. That will be the final judgment. But if you live? Then nothing is decided. Your acts will be judged on the basis of your whole life. If you allow yourself to be killed as expiation, there will be nothing more absurd than your death." Later on the same character says: "What counts is the world and what you do in the world. Your pals and what you do for them. It is necessary to live."

Sartre's "school" is not only anti-metaphysical but also anti-psychological. Not only is there no God and no abstract moral law, but no general human nature or psychological problem. The individual's life alone is important though every individual feels within himself his responsibility to other men. Man achieves freedom through his own action. In this way, the existentialist philosophy tries to bring hope and courage to a people sick with remorse, shame, fear, guilt, which some regard as the present state of the intellectual middle-class in France. This is the positive function of Sartre's thought in France's present dilemma. It is a philosophy for the trapped. Since Sartre has not yet announced a more specific objective and has not designated a definite area of hope—political or social—we might characterize his philosophy as a tragic pragmatism.

Death without Burial is schematic, like all of Sartre's plays, but at least it says what it has to say in a setting that has living associations for its audience and may therefore stir it. *The Respectful Prostitute*, Sartre's one-act shocker, might be described as an anti-racist play (its scene is the American South), or it might be more properly considered a demonstration of how behavior is shaped by social pressure. *No Exit*, theatrically the cleverest and most striking of Sartre's plays, is a kind of philosophical metaphor signifying less than it appears to and as artificial in its inspiration as in its design.

There remains *The Flies*, the play produced last spring in New York by the Dramatic Workshop. That it is the effort of an intelligent, indeed a brilliant man, and that it tries to use the stage as a medium for mature expression nobody will deny. That it is quite adroit is also a fact, but to take it seriously as art or as thought is to prove oneself somewhat removed from the reality of both.

Eugene O'Neill, a mediocre thinker at best, is far more truly a dramatist than a keen wit like Sartre. For it is not sufficient that a play express a profound thought. Ideas or thoughts in plays function only to the degree that they are embodied in the play. A play acquires substance only through the flesh and blood of its whole texture. There must be a living organism before there can be an idea.

Sartre's conviction that "human life begins on the other side of despair" is impressive and admirably phrased. If one interprets *The Flies* as a play of rebellion against the Nazis or against other tyrannies, then one might credit it perhaps as a shrewd tract. But a gesture is not an act, and a slogan in the void is not a philosophy. "Men are free," says the author's mouthpiece. "I am a man and being a man must invent my own path." In the last analysis, this is no more true—as stated in this play—than it would be to assert the opposite.

The sap of life does not flow through this play. Here despair, freedom, heroic release are merely phrases, for men do not face life in terms of symbols—ancient Greek symbols at that—but in a maze of very specific facts. A philosophy has to be evolved out of the realities with which men actually deal, and to believe that one has said anything at all when one says something through the medium of textbook literature is the disastrous fallacy of people who rarely confront reality except on the ornamental plane of lofty debate.

Since the world is in the state that it is in, since post-war French literature has not yet produced an authoritative voice, Sartre can be accepted as a figure of some importance—not as an artist but as a symptom.

Consider three of the new painters. (There are reputed to be sixty thousand painters in Paris and three hundred and sixty-one publishing houses!) None of these new painters were exhibited at the French show at our Whitney Museum last spring. The latter show was composed of the kind of able, decorative, and even lively, painting that mixes Picasso and Matisse in a sort of cocktail that we might dub "the New Academy."

Dubuffet, whom I discussed in a previous article, is first on my list. He is an original trying to be "ordinary"—direct, unpretentious, and violent. He loves to paint, but he is suspicious of art. ("Art nowadays," he says, "is living on its reputation.") He wants his painting to jump out of the canvas and pursue you. In a crazy way, it very nearly does. He wants his painting to have a palpable body, and he mixes oil, mud, coal, and heaven knows what else. There is a striving for a new vision—angry, brutally childlike, abrupt, as shockingly expressive as a new vocabulary of bad words. Dubuffet is often taken as someone who wants to be terribly clever. As a matter of fact, he is a fanatic whose eagerness to scream some hideous or fantastic insight into reality is a strange amalgam of almost religious hysteria and wicked common sense. His work is an outcry against what has become the modern classicism of such men as Braque. What Braque does is to preserve ancient treasures lost in the disarray of our age like priceless relics taken into exile by an old aristocrat to enrich and grace his declining years. Dubuffet will have no remnant or particle of the old order—no matter how distinguished—but seeks clarity through a savagely destructive barbarism.

Dubuffet's favorite modern painter is another new name in French art: Fautrier. André Malraux speaks of Fautrier's work as the "hieroglyphics of pain." I did not see Fautrier's exhibition but was privately shown some of the paintings in a series called *Hostages*. The title refers to those who were shot down en masse by Germans to curb French resistance. In these paintings men's faces and bodies are no longer anything but a bloody pulp in the mud. Man is reduced to incoherent flesh, to a primitive lump of matter—almost unrecognizable, nightmarishly fascinating, the end of the end—as if perhaps to say: "We must begin all over again and make something different." At the newly opened and very imposing Museum of Modern Art in Paris there are two Fautrier canvases. One is of a man crucified, who looks like an animal struck down; the other is a picture of a wild boar, which looks like a man crucified.

Balthus, the third painter of my trio, is still in his thirties. What is curious about Balthus is that he uses a technique derived from sixteenth-century Dutch and Italian painting to convey an altogether modern sense of frustration and suspense. It is as if something very old in Europe that now feels itself held down in pain were waiting either to disappear completely or to be rejuvenated.

Most of the images in Balthus' paintings are those of young women or little girls. They belong to a formerly prosperous bourgeois environment that now has a faded and lonely look. The children stand sad and tense against this background. The young girl who studies herself in a mirror in one canvas is as old as the ages. She is wise and bold, something of a harlot with a Botticelli face and a great delicacy of being. She is expecting something. A boy with a strong naked back is fixing the fire beside her. There is mystery here—a suspended world in which the future, past, and present is a moment of strange tension and reverie. Another of the pictures is called *Solitaire:* a fourteen-year-old girl is playing that game. How will it come out? Her face is very intent; her body is taut and eager. She appears ready at any second to break off and leave. Very striking, too, is a painting called *The Victim:* a nude woman stretched across a couch in a way that at first blush one would say was wantonly loose but which one discovers is actually tragic as if she were ready for torture.

A fine breeding marks the artist's handling of all his materials—particularly the drawing. There is no point in insisting, as many do, that he is not a *painter*, that he rejects properly pictorial means. His pictures speak—and though the language may be a little archaic, what is being said is still very much of today.

—*TRW*, Sept. '47

PARIS TO LONDON TO NEW YORK

American acting in the last thirty years has drifted toward journalese. The object of the actor seems to be to avoid any shock that will make the spectator suspect that what he is seeing is different from or even more interesting than everyday life. French stage acting tends to more or less subtle patterns in which imagination, energy, and, above all, temperament serve to create a sense of theatrical life. As I remember the acting of the English stage from my last visit to London—1938—it tended toward the American underemphasis, except for a little more precision of projection and detail in characterization. In *The Winslow Boy*—and to a degree in nearly all the plays I saw on this trip—the acting had a theatrical emphasis, a large, full-bodied intention which attempted to retain only a conventional resemblance to naturalism.

The new English stage acting isn't realistic at all in our sense. Much of it is what we would ignorantly call "ham." It shows a desire to recapture some of the boldness of the old nineteenth-century English tradition (Kemble, Booth, Macready, Irving) in a meticulous outline of verisimilitude. One feels that what the actors want is a released kind of acting in which the player might be permitted to tear a passion to tatters—if he has the capacity for it! Added to this is the knowledge that the contemporary play may not be susceptible to such treatment. The actor must, therefore, fit his flame to the proportions of a drawing room. The result is something italicized that looks almost tense—too charged to be casual, too tailored to be flamboyant. Its strength resides in the virtue of theatricality as a form of conscious expression, its weakness in not often being informed with real experience. It is almost always better, however, than the nondescript imitation, which too frequently with us passes as natural acting.

The English still enjoy and respect the theatre as we in America have ceased to do. They do not come to the play to carp. They listen to the actor eagerly; they feel he deserves something like reverence, for they realize that the least important actor is sincerely trying to please them and has taken some pains to learn how. They are rarely impatient with minor flaws—a flimsy set does not disturb them—and in the presence of real talent they are everlastingly elated. Performances of ten or twenty years ago are remembered more vividly by the Londoner than most New Yorkers do the shows they applauded last week. The English audience's taste for movies has not impaired its appetite for the theatre, nor does it confuse the pleasures of one with the glamor of the other. The English audience may take tea or coffee during the intermissions and is permitted to smoke during the performance, but there is very little coughing in the "slow" passages of a play, very little rudeness toward the players, and applause is nearly always hearty.

The London success of a play like Cocteau's *The Eagle Has Two Heads* may be largely ascribed to the English audience's responsiveness to a certain bravura acting as well as to something almost operatic in the play itself. (The play, I might remind you, is at once a pastiche of the French boulevard melodramas of the 1880s and a piece of political symbolism about the decadence of France.) Eileen Herlie, who plays the queen in *The Eagle* (she will also appear as the queen mother in Laurence Olivier's forthcoming screen version of *Hamlet*) is a young actress of promise. What the English have found so attractive in her is her powerful voice, her robust figure, her energetic diction, her authoritative carriage. Cocteau's play

requires everything of the actor that relates to external technique but very little besides. The point is that these externalities still mean much to the English theatregoer and I am the last person to criticize him for it.

There are two ways in which an artist may be neglected. He may simply never be seen or heard of by a large number of people, or he may be widely heralded for the wrong reasons. The latter, it seems to me, is the fate that has befallen Stieglitz. In a sense, the present exhibition perpetuates the misunderstanding. By showing the Stieglitz collection (the European and American innovators of painting whose early work he acquired), together with Stieglitz's photographs, what is emphasized is Stieglitz's role as a pioneer in the modern art movement of America. What is overlooked is Stieglitz the artist.

He was a great artist—one of the greatest, in my view, this country has produced. It is easy to forget this because his art was photography and because his photographs are so modest. They look as if anyone at all might have done them. As a result, it is easy to say that they were remarkable "for their day." After all, he was the first to do a certain type of night photography, and so on.

Such qualifications represent either timidity or insensitivity. When I returned from London and Paris, New York looked to me like a city made not so much for people as for customers. To see Stieglitz's photographs in central Manhattan was to come on a secret oasis in the midst of increasing spiritual aridity.

These photographs have scope without ostentation. They are expressive without pressure. Without self-advertisement they reveal a man. They are a social commentary without proclamation.

Their outstanding quality is tenderness. They are quiet without sentimentality. Only an occasional title—such as *The Hand of Man*—gives any clue to a pretentious meaning. Stieglitz does not impose on his subject matter: his feeling for it is natural, relaxed, spontaneous. His art is a real seeing—without any exultant cry of aesthetic discovery. It derives from understanding. His objects seem to bathe in God's air.

Stieglitz's work is pure in expression and content. He is never angry, vehement, hortatory, or clever. His work is sometimes sad without tears, gentle without softness, almost imperceptibly humorous. Stieglitz saw life as an infinite mystery that reveals itself in clarity. Every object is presented with utter simplicity, while at the same time it seems soaked in experience. Each object has its own deep life; yet there are no mystic fumes—not even in the cloud photographs. There is only steady vision. "It is to be noted that when Stieglitz analyzed his famous *Steerage*, he never specifically referred to its social connotations—only to its plastic problems."

What is the core of Stieglitz's vision, the basis for his sadness, the sum of his solicitude? Stieglitz loved life in its most direct, unmetaphysical sense. He looked at flesh and saw in it what was universally true of all things. Thus, there is an equivalence in his work between the nudes, trees, the look of a house, the flanks of a horse, the shape and texture of the clouds. Human flesh is delicate, lovely, powerful and perishable, unfathomably wonderful. It is changeable, evanescent, capable of creating or sustaining every blessing, effort, martyrdom, and cruelty. Human flesh is spirit; the spirit is human flesh. All things on land, water, or in the sky have similar properties, are, indeed, part of it, as it is part of them. Human flesh is easily destroyed and ever reborn: that is why life is precious, sad, beautiful, ultimately neither good nor bad, so that optimism and pessimism as permanent states are both equally meaningless. Life without labels, life that cannot be characterized as either animal or spiritual, since both are one, life as the source and sense of all strength is what Stieglitz saw in the wispiest, most inconsiderable fragments of reality.

In Stieglitz this personal vision becomes a social vision. The history of our times from 1880 to 1935 becomes an intimate human experience. This is especially important today, because there is

a tendency with our increasing consciousness of the social aspects of art to overlook a basic truth that was implicit in Stieglitz's approach to life: a social point of view is worthless unless it is included in a framework greater than the social. In the end, a correct politics is only possible where a basic position on man's place in the universe has been taken, in short, where a comprehensive philosophy, a comparatively conscious relationship to the whole of life has been assumed.

Stieglitz saw an America in peril of losing its soul—and thus ultimately all its real goods—through a failure to appreciate the true nature of man, the real quality of life. He saw technical energy being cultivated beyond everything else for purposes that hardly seemed to include man. He saw the thinning out of our emotional capacities in proportion to the progress made in our mechanical and monetary efficiency. He saw in America the disastrous triumph of modern cleverness, the trick whereby man could dispose of men, make them unnecessary, render them extinct.

Through the silent report of his eye, with the aid of a soulless mechanical gadget, Stieglitz was able to produce a series of reflections on paper which, for those who really look, contain a great part of the truth of our era and of all time. Stieglitz's work is a repository of joy and wisdom, a priceless signal to mankind. That is why I say Stieglitz was a great American artist—and I do not refer to the graphic arts alone. It is about time we began to discover him.

—*TRW*, Oct. '47

THE DRY SEASON

How a movie critic survives a season is something to marvel over. The difficulty is not that there are so many bad movies but that they are produced in such numbers, and for each one the critic must find something new to say. During the month of August, I saw a selection of the best movies, and I left most of them with the guilty feeling that the challenge of discussing them beyond a word of praise or condemnation would quite paralyze me!

The simple fact is that most of the good movies are on a creative level beneath that of a fourth-rate novel. Imagine a literary critic's never being allowed the opportunity to review anything but slick fiction. This does not mean that one cannot see an insignificant movie without a modicum of pleasure. A pretty face, a trick shot, a clever gag, a certain variety of movement, and a good companion may be enough to make an agreeable evening. Such a combination of merit, however, does not require any comment beyond a nod, a smile, and, for sociability's sake, a phrase. Having to expatiate on the obvious is a form of torture.

The movies themselves are not at fault. American films are products of a giant industry. To expect every movie to be more than a product of mass production is like submitting every chair turned out by a large furniture house to an art critic for extended evaluation. The purpose of the ordinary chair is to provide something to sit on; the purpose of the average movie is to provide something to sit at. In an energetic and exhausted society such as ours this is called entertainment. Entertainment of this kind, therefore, has its positive function, but it rarely calls for criticism.

This is not condescension on my part. On the contrary, professional motion-picture critics often strike me as naïve in their contempt for the average movie. They write as if they were being asked to judge a work of art when they are being invited merely to furnish publicity for a costly commodity. The Hollywood producer who talks in terms of a show to sell rather than in terms of some personal aesthetic is closer to reality than most of his grimly idealistic critics. It is impossible to produce some five hundred pictures a year intended to please at least eighty million people and expect that they will serve a purpose beyond that of entertainment in the sense I have just defined.

What puts us off the track in discussing the motion picture is that a good many people of real artistic capacity are employed in the motion picture industry. Due to the combined efforts of these people an occasional picture or—more frequently—a portion of a picture reveals an actual creative intent. Such moments are happy accidents, but unless we realize they are accidents and not the norm and aim of the industry, we are allowing ourselves to be deluded into a disastrous confusion.

We no longer need proof that the motion picture is a medium with great possibilities. Hollywood has brought us Charlie Chaplin. The point is that Chaplin worked when the industry was small (so to speak, in the handicraft stage) and remained in complete control of his product when the industry expanded. Foreign films, too, have given us reason to hope, because thus far the degree of their industrialization has been comparatively moderate and artists as such have been allowed a certain amount of freedom to realize their objectives. Should the makers of foreign films extend their activities to the point where it becomes financially unfeasible to make films unless they appeal to the hundreds of millions, their product will cease to differ from ours. It must be axiomatic that no society with class divisions can produce art so universally acceptable that it is profitable without being placed on the largest industrial basis. The goals of art and industry, though conceivably compatible, are, for our time at least, fundamentally distinct and generally at odds.

All this makes serious criticism of current motion pictures an arduous task. Technical criticism is virtually worthless for any but the craftsman. General criticism must define its terms at every step since this youngest of arts is inextricably involved in an industry without any tradition. To maintain, for example, that a picture like *Gone with the Wind* is perhaps not the last word in artistic significance is in most film circles to talk gibberish, since the picture was one of the "greatest" (most expensive) and most "successful" (best attended and most profitable) of all time. One must proceed with greater caution in this field than in any other cultural domain. One may talk more rot in a minute's discussion of *The Perils of Pauline* than in an hour of talk on Leonardo da Vinci!

Take a picture like *Crossfire* for instance. Two things are fairly incontrovertible in regard to it. One is that it is an intelligently made melodrama; the other is that it is virtually the first Hollywood picture on the subject of anti-Semitism. In a way, the most sensible review of the picture would stop at exactly this point. Almost everything beyond the basic statement is controversial.

That it is a well-made melodrama using a studied but not obtrusive method of underemphasis is something that may be regarded as high praise in some quarters. Speaking personally, it is a fact that I am pleased to note but nothing over which I rejoice. In short, when a critic writes, "The film X is a corking melodrama," I am not particularly excited by the information; and so we need only reaffirm our first statement: *Crossfire* is an effectively quiet melodrama. Its writing is literately to the point. In the case of one minor and perhaps unnecessary personage the characterization is almost fascinating. The cast is able and well chosen from the standpoint of rightness of type.

The picture's second aspect is its important aspect. The fact that it deals with anti-Semitism at all is even more praiseworthy than the manner in which it deals with it. As to the latter point, I have heard all sorts of conflicting opinions. I am inclined to discount most of the arguments on all sides. Those who complain that the Jew in the picture is made too paternal, too sweet, and generally too "right" or those who complain that he is too smug, prosperous, and unproblematic leave me cold. The Jew has to have some characteristic, and whatever the characteristic chosen would cause complaint in one quarter or another. To judge the picture's value as propaganda, the only testimony I would consider convincing would consist of a record of the audiences' reaction to the picture from all parts of the country.

What was most striking to me in the picture was the fact that it managed to bring up the subject of racial hatred without in a sense ever touching its actual social reality. The postwar frustration and unrest is pointed out as a contributing factor, but this is merely suggested in passing and is hardly given a full dramatic development.

Postwar jitters, however, have merely sharpened the problem of racial prejudice: they are not a cause. What is deceptive in *Crossfire* is that the villain is a kind of maniac, a common enough thug, except that he murders at any provocation—since he not only kills the Jew through a brutal mischance but more deliberately kills his Gentile soldier buddy. If such a figure were a typical anti-Semite, there would be no anti-Semitic problem. The central character of *Crossfire* is more a subject for study by the psychiatrist than by the social psychologist.

Race prejudice is a menace long before it reaches the stage of physical violence. What is peculiar and troubling about it is that many people feel perfectly moral in harboring this prejudice; they very sincerely believe that even if it is immoral, it is one of their "democratic" privileges to permit no law to infringe upon their right to indulge in such immorality. What the nature, quality, meaning of such prejudice is—the crux of the problem—is barely faced in *Crossfire*.

If comparisons can clarify, I might assert that *Crossfire* is superior to a film like *Frieda*. I mean by this that while *Frieda*, which deals with the question of the "good" (non-Nazi) German as distinct from the "bad" (Nazi) German, approaches its theme with a certain dignity characteristic of English films, as differentiated from the characteristically American melodramatics of *Crossfire*, the English picture actually is less relevant to its theme than the American picture. *Crossfire* never comes to grips with its problem on the serious level that it promises, but it does tell its own story convincingly. *Frieda* aims to face its problem squarely, but its story is so contrived that the problem is washed away in pathos. The American picture, moreover, is cinematically more adequate to its purpose: its acting, photography, and direction more forceful and stylistically interesting. The English picture is sober but more than a little banal and strangely enough—compared to *Crossfire*—more like a Hollywood product!

What is good in *Frieda* is that it does essay a real theme and that, on the whole, it avoids cheapness. In connection with *Frieda*, it is noteworthy that the American audience is made a little uneasy by the picture, because despite the war and years of talk on the subject the whole problem of Germany is vague and distasteful to it. The English interest in the subject is based on intimate experience. The American audience reacts like a person who is addressed on a subject he knows should concern him but about which he secretly realizes he is quite ignorant. A disturbing element of bad conscience comes into play. This may relate remotely to our ambiguous political position in Germany.

Both American and English audiences find themselves more at home in the romance of *Great Expectations*. The opening of this picture is both tender and thrilling, and the hero as a boy is utterly winning. He grows up disappointingly—both from the standpoint of the story and the actor who plays him—but what somehow remains attractive in the picture, which is sometimes stuffy and sometimes silly, is that it is a real story, a glorious fiction on the grand scale. Our storytellers nowadays are as timid as we are in the ordinary routine of life, and they stick close to the petty-reasonableness of logic and probability. Not so Dickens, who introduces almost everything into his story: the poetry of adolescence, social pathos, observation, aspiration toward purity and simple heartedness, longing for heroic adventure, the desire for moral retribution, a world of constant wonder. Our audiences, thirsty for more refreshing drink than the soda pop of the usual entertainment, are grateful for this draught from the deeper sources of nineteenth-century genius.

We are definitely tired of ourselves, and this leads to things both good and bad. Good and bad motifs inspire an unpretentious comedy like *Miracle on 34th Street*. Like most Hollywood fare

it is "just entertainment." Hence, its virtues and value are almost unconscious, and its faults fairly inevitable. Its point of departure is a cute idea: Why shouldn't a man who considers himself a Santa Claus really be Santa Claus?

We are so disappointed in the thin sum of our total pleasure in life that we begin to kid all the premises of our normal conduct. Either we believe in Santa Claus, in which case we are crazy, or we don't believe in him, in which case we are dull. Perhaps it is a little better to be crazy with imagination than dull with arithmetic. Since we are afraid to take any position in such a debate, it is best to toy with it as a fantasy, a game that fools all parties including ourselves. (We are afraid of the debate because it might trouble us regarding our social behavior.) If the game were a little more conscious, a very original comedy might result; but since the whole thing arises as a spoof at a Hollywood story-conference, the tale is told in B picture terms and, aside from one or two very funny scenes, no real quality emerges.

What distinguishes European films from those of Hollywood is mainly a result of a higher common denominator in the basic assumptions of the European audience. American films are usually pitched to the juvenile mind. In terms of human experience, they disclose an anesthetic combination of primitiveness and standardization. In almost every respect (subject matter, mental approach, visual treatment) they bear a relationship to reality which is comparable to that of a mannequin to a living person. This is what makes a leading English movie critic, C. A. Lejeune, say, "French pictures with their hard realism are far more to our taste than the modern Hollywood product."

For hard realism, the Italian films are beginning to excel the French. What makes the recent Italian picture *Shoeshine* memorable is just the quality of unadorned realism. It is a picture about the brutal treatment accorded the delinquent children of Rome. The picture is simple, direct, tough, and humane.

All this might be said of other pictures on similar subjects that have been made elsewhere. The Italian picture has something peculiarly its own which is not easy to define. It is a quality that is at once admirably honest and, extraordinarily enough a little disappointing. There is a special lack of emphasis in the projection of everyday reality and an equal lack of reticence. An absence of vulgarity goes hand in hand with a kind of unabashed shabbiness. There is not much light and shade, not much visible style. It is as if the story were told by a good, sensitive man who was too dejected to give his narrative any particular shape beyond the sad recital of the facts. The effect is touching and morose. After hearing the story, one does not experience much beyond a heaviness of soul and a weary pity. Perhaps this is as it should be, but one feels that, considering all the human values that have been conveyed, there ought to be something more. Though everything one has been told is worth our complete attention and respect, no depths or heights of emotion have been reached. Why?

Shoeshine contains nearly every ingredient necessary to the making of a work of art except that transcendent atmosphere that arises when a real philosophy of life, a broad human point of view, a palpable concept and an active direction suffuse the telling of a story. In every work of art there is not only the problem of communicating an immediate subject (story and theme) but the problem of evoking through the subject a universal sense of life beyond itself. This is the essence by which works of art truly move us. Without it realism becomes information, imagination becomes ornament. El Greco's *View of Toledo* is not significant because it is an "effective" picture of a mountain, but because of a vision of life that the artist has somehow succeeded in making the mountain convey.

Shoeshine might move the Italian authorities to ameliorate the lot of the children suffering in their prisons. It is certainly something that adds to the stature of motion-picture history, but it seems to me to fail where a few pictures based on less

ambitious material succeed. For those who have seen the picture, it might make my point clearer to say that the two outstanding moments of *Shoeshine* for me were moments not directly related to the picture's message: the first was the scene in which the two boy protagonists display themselves to their friends on the street, proudly mounted on their newly acquired horse; the second was the image of the boy prisoners seen in the courtyard entering the ancient and imposing hall of justice. Here the picture rose to a truly poignant lyricism. These scenes suggest the picture's basic theme: namely, the contrast between human innocence and the misery of man's present condition. The picture's naturalism—striking in itself—somehow impedes the realization of the possibilities inherent in its theme.

—*TRW*, Nov. '47

PARIS, FRANCE—THEN AND NOW

The first time I saw Paris was in 1921, that is, three years after the First World War. I had gone there to study at the Sorbonne because Paris, it appeared, was the center of the world. The last time I saw Paris was only yesterday, almost three years after its liberation from the Nazi yoke.

The Paris of 1947 is much less "gay." I am not talking in terms of night clubs and dancing. I mean that what is lively, interesting, provocative and characteristic has an altogether new color. It is not a color that might be given the piquant or even eruptive emphasis once conveyed by the word "amusing." Paris today is damned serious.

If Parisians were poor in 1921 they still treasured the dream of luxury. If revolt appealed to them they still believed they might enjoy it in comfort. Today they are very careful about kicking over the traces. Liberation without a plan provides no smiling perspective. To declare oneself "lost" in 1921 was something of a sham. One never believed oneself unprotected. Remember that the dominant political party then was still the Radical-

Socialist—neither radical nor socialist, only anti-clerical, mildly liberal and wholly middle-class. The outstanding writers—Proust and Gide—were still able to live on independent incomes. Their immediate literary progeny—Aragon, Cocteau and others—were either savage juveniles howling their disgust over the breakdown their elders had foreseen or esthetic playboys cavorting about the graceful ruins. "If we can't have anything else," they seemed to be saying, "let us have fun!"

The Paris of 1947 is strangely subdued. Even its hope in the U.S. is filled with misgivings. The base of a solid middle class is almost wholly dissolved. The new generation does not think itself "lost" because that would imply a remembered home. The way back is gone and very few are even looking in that direction. It is the way forward that is not clear. The dominant trait in the youth of the twenties was a horror of the war it had won; the mark of the present youth is its terrible fear of the war that may come.

The basic tendencies are what count. Apart from a study of political programs, a probing of the intellectual and cultural fields becomes an essential activity in relation to the understanding of French life in general. Ideas are explored and the arts practiced more intensely and with greater scope than ever. Despite the poverty of the country, which makes it extremely difficult for even a well known writer to make his living from writing alone, Paris has 361 publishing houses, 45 theaters playing "legitimate" drama in which during the season of 1946-47, 145 new productions were presented—almost twice the number done in N.Y. during the same period. Not only are there some 60,000 professional painters in Paris, but five out of eight Frenchmen paint for their own pleasure. Museums are crowded as never before. The leading literary monthly *Fontaine* has more than twice the circulation of the equivalent publication—*La Nouvelle Revue Française*—before the war. A lecture on a cultural subject that might have attracted 300 listeners in 1938 today will attract more than 1000. Most of the publications do not follow any strict party line, but many are closely allied with the various political orientations. Left socialist and Communist publications are reputed to command a reading public of 5,000,000. Most significant of all is André Malraux's statement that the harmless academicians of old are thoroughly discredited. The adventurous artists are practically the only ones that command attention.

The dadaists and many former surrealists—like Aragon and Tzara—are now Communists. André Breton is the spokesman of the unregenerate anarchist elements within these old movements. These elements are fighting a rear-guard action to preserve their independence of "political" pressure. They are the unresolved and uncaptured spirit of the sensitive Frenchman wandering in space looking for a home—or a form. Their contributions to the arts of painting and poetry are undeniable even though, as in all basically anarchist tendencies, there is a distinct drift toward flim-flam and corruption.

The literary success of the existentialists is significant chiefly because they represent the middle-class intellectual unable to accept the religious premises of the Catholics and unwilling to devote themselves to the concrete aims of the Communists. Existentialism is essentially the attitude of people who recognize that there are no cozy alternatives to modern life, but who assert nevertheless that man must act. Man is isolated, anguished and without assurance of anything but his need to take steps toward a goal that he appoints for himself through the impulse of his need to live. This is a pragmatism for the trapped.

The existentialists do not prescribe a definite line of action or define a particular good except the possibility of discovery. They are without a political program, though Jean-Paul Sartre, the head of the "school," claims to be something of a socialist. An existentialist might become anything, do anything. With the coming of further crises in French life we shall see what the existentialist does become and what he does do. At the moment, I suspect that the best of them are headed for the Academy.

The most significant literary success just now is Albert Camus' novel *La Peste (The Plague)*. Camus is not an "official" existentialist but his book offers a clear insight into the moral situation which gives rise to existentialism. The plague of Camus' novel is an epidemic disease that infests a particular city but it is used here as a symbol of Evil itself. Camus portrays various reactions to Evil. The mediocre, he tells us, will try to wave it aside, the corrupt will traffic with it, the desperate will plunge into it even though it may destroy them, the godly will fight and accept it at the same time (since Evil too belongs to God), the humanist saint will die on the side of the victim and the narrator (Camus), fully aware that Evil as part of the nature of things is ineradicable, will devote himself nonetheless to combating it—finding his only salvation in the struggle itself.

There is something clean and healthy in this grave morality, because while it never specifically defines evil except as that which destroys man, it is both humble and, in the secular sense, devout. It is an attitude which for the moment won't commit itself to anything outside of that which is truly experienced by the man who proclaims it. As a program for the age it is much too abstract, as a statement of a transitional mood it has its dignity and its positive use.

I find the Camus book typical of both the strength and weakness, both the hopeful and dangerous aspects of present-day France. The hopeful and positive features within what appears to be chiefly negative are what I should like to emphasize. I see in France's very pessimism the possibility of a rebirth and a reemergence into sanity. The fierce and sometimes terrifying colors that strike one in French art today signify not only the bitterness of the general situation but also a very acute consciousness of it. It is in that consciousness that I see the particular promise of France.

Amid the troubled faces that one observes in the streets of Paris today, one also sees many that are lean, clear, tempered and uncorrupt. They are generally the faces of people between 20 and 35. They look as if they realize fully that there is as much difficulty ahead as behind. Yet they look calm. They appear resolved to survive the ordeal, however severe, and to discover a real, a satisfying solution in the process.

—*UNW*, Nov. '47

A MONTH IN THE ARTS

October 1

When I look at a painting for the first time, I never ask myself whether or not it is a good painting or even whether or not I like it. It is almost painful for me to answer the question: "What do you think of it?" Thinking of it impedes my seeing it.

At the Museum of Modern Art, Ben Shahn's paintings struck me first by a peculiar edginess, as if the artist felt he lived in a world of permanent discomfort. There is a rawness and frustrated expressiveness in these paintings which I find interesting. These qualities do not represent any technical disability but a special kind of experience. They are interesting qualities because they are conjoined with a kind of anguished delicacy. It is as if we were faced with a man who is far more sensitive than his environment will permit him to be. A unique style emerges. Extreme sensibility in the artist begets a feeling of horror. The artist appears troubled by his own aestheticism. His harsh realism is both a revolt and an adjustment to the malaise he experiences because of the promptings of his own romanticism.

October 9

Seeing *Man and Superman* fortified my conviction that what makes Shaw's work outlast most of the drama of his generation is that his plays are so old-fashioned. Shaw is chiefly intellectual vaudeville. The intellect is sustained by a brilliant rhetoric and the vaudeville is the permanent structure that sustains the whole.

Man and Superman is youthful, enthusiastic, bursting with bright exuberance. It's as cute as W. S. Gilbert, and at least two passages—the speech about moral passion and the one about the artist as husband—are masterpieces of witty eloquence. The play has only a faint resemblance to reality, but it has life—the life of a man enjoying his own intelligence and impudence, his own triumphant emergence into an astonished and delighted world. The effect is utterly charming in its geniality and virginity!

October 15

Picasso rides again! The Buchholz Gallery shows recent lithographs; Paul Rosenberg presents Vladimir Goldscham's collection, which is replete with paintings of the master's latest manner; and, next door, Knoedler presents an array of early Picassos.

There is a tendency nowadays to decry the recent Picasso and to point with pleasure to the early. There is no question that the early Picassos—which the "ultras" like to dismiss as "sentimental"—disclose the excitement of youthful genius. One discerns in these paintings some of the main emotional sources of the artist's work. The influences of Degas, Toulouse-Lautrec, even Renoir, are here, but there is an additional venom and hauteur which indicate that the artist felt the poverty of Bohemia and the society it exemplified more personally, while seeking to free himself of its poison by a dispassionate, aesthetic objectivity. It is as if he were saving himself by assimilating all he saw into universally relevant forms of art that had their origin in "eternal" patterns known to man since the beginnings of conscious design—all of which might be transcribed in the future into distortions that would appear altogether new.

Like other moderns who are classicists of decadence, Picasso reveals both a constantly increasing horror of contemporary life and an adoration of art as almost the only means of redemption from it. The extreme violence of Picasso's work since 1937 is simply an extension of what is inherent in the still romantic first canvases. Picasso's latest work is a brilliantly organized explosion of the world he "enjoyed" between 1901-09. There has always been in Picasso's art something aesthetically exultant as there has always been something morally bitter. The aestheticism today has become demonic; the bitterness a maniacal rage. If you wish to be naïve about it, you can call the first period "lovely," and if you insist upon being superficial, you will call the latest period a brutal fad. If you are a high-brow dope, you may object to both periods as overemotional. For my part, I think the best course is simply to look and to feel...and perhaps—to understand.

October 21

Medea by Euripides through Robinson Jeffers and Judith Anderson attracts our audiences in unconscious revolt against the journalistic theatre. On the Broadway of 1947, *Medea* is a striking novelty. We are sick of seeing people on the stage doing what comes naturally.

I cannot share the general enthusiasm for Miss Anderson's Medea, however. I don't mind at all the fact that she rants, raves, roars, hovers and heaves, sings and soars, whimpers, wallows, hisses and snorts, moans, groans, slinks, slithers, leaps, writhes, and generally conducts herself excessively.

I have three major objections to her performance. The first is that she works too hard. At the end of the play, we experience no Aristotelian purification, only fatigue. Energy is admirable in an actor, but it is not an end in itself. Furthermore, it should not be so evident. The American stage, not so long ago, prided itself on a large number of actresses—Leslie Carter, Margaret Anglin, Margaret Illington, Nance O'Neill, Edith Wynne Matthison, Emily Stevens, Mrs. Fiske, Nazimova, Bertha Kalish, Frances Starr, Jeanne Eagles, Florence Reed (as leading lady)—who, if memory does not deceive me, could do all that Miss Anderson does much more easily. The play as a technical challenge is made much too clear through Miss Anderson's strenuous efforts.

My second objection is that although Miss Anderson is indisputably a theatrically vivid and richly endowed actress with flashes here and there of exciting insight into the various emotional possibilities of her part, her method of approach is chiefly physical. She "uses" her voice. A fine actor does not "use" his voice. When one becomes aware of an actor's use of his voice, it is a sure sign that, theatrically speaking, it is not being properly used.

This is so basic that it applies even to an actor like Chaliapin, who was an opera singer. In admiring him, we did not think of his voice but of what he created. The same point may be made in regard to Miss Anderson's use of her body. Those who saw Pavlova never spoke of her movement as such but of its effect.

Finally, Miss Anderson's Medea is neither a person nor a concept. She fills the stage with her violent illustrations of the text, she overwhelms the house with vocal volume, but none of this is centered in either a specific characterization or the embodiment of a general idea. The play is not illuminated; in fact, no one even mentions it. The realities of mother love, of passion, of grief, are not communicated. Miss Anderson's Medea may very well be a magnificent performance, but I doubt that it is really good acting.

—*TRW*, Jan. '48

STREETCAR

The newest writing talent in the American theatre is that of Tennessee Williams. His *The Glass Menagerie* was a lyric fragment of limited scope but undeniable poignancy. Tennessee Williams' latest play—*A Streetcar Named Desire*—stands very high among the creative contributions of the American theatre since 1920. If we had a national repertory theatre, this play would unquestionably be among the few worthy of a permanent place there. Its impact at this moment is especially strong, because it is virtually unique as a stage piece that is

both personal and social and wholly a product of our life today. It is a beautiful play.

Its story is simple. Blanche Du Bois, a girl whose family once possessed property and title to position in the circle of refined Southern respectability, has been reduced to the lowest financial state. She has taught English in a high school, but when we meet her she has apparently lost her job and has come to stay with her younger sister Stella in New Orleans. Blanche expects to find Stella living in an environment compatible with their former background, but finds instead that Stella is in the kind of neighborhood that playgoers call sordid, though it happens to be no worse than any of the places inhabited by the majority of American people. Blanche is shocked at these Elysian Fields (literally the name of this particular spot in New Orleans, just as the streetcar she took to reach it is actually called Desire). She is even more shocked by her sister's husband, an American of Polish origin, an ex-sergeant, a machine salesman, and a rather primitive, almost bestial person. Her brother-in-law resents and then suspects the girl's pretentious airs, particularly her obvious disdain of him. Slowly he (and we) discover the girl's "secret": after an unfortunate marriage at an early age to a boy who turned out to be a homosexual, the boy's suicide, her family's loss of all its property, and the death of the last member of the older generation, Blanche has become a notorious person, whose squalid affairs have made it impossible for her to remain in her home town. She meets a friend of her brother-in-law whom she wants to marry because he is a decent fellow, but her brother-in-law, by disclosing the facts of the girl's life to her suitor, wrecks her hopes. Drunk the night his wife is in labor, the brother-in-law settles his account with Blanche by raping her. She is ordered out of Stella's house, and, when Blanche tells the story of the rape she is thought to be mad and is finally conducted unprotesting to a public institution for the insane.

Some of the reviewers thought Blanche Du Bois a "boozy prostitute," and others believed her a nymphomaniac. Such designations are not only inaccurate but reveal a total failure to understand the author's intention and the theme of the play. Tennessee Williams is a poet of frustration, and what his play says is that aspiration, sensitivity, departure from the norm are battered, bruised and disgraced in our world today.

It would be far truer to think of Blanche Du Bois as the potential artist in all of us than as a deteriorated Southern belle. Her amatory adventures, which her brother-in-law (like some of the critics) regards as the mark of her inferiority, are the unwholesome means she uses to maintain her connection with life, to fight the sense of death which her whole background has created in her. The play's story shows us Blanche's seeking haven in a simple, healthy man and that in this, too, she is defeated because everything in her environment conspires to degrade the meaning of her tragic situation. Her lies are part of her will-to-beauty; her wretched romanticism is a futile reaching toward a fullness of life. She is not a drunkard, and she is not insane when she is committed to the asylum. She is an almost willing victim of a world that has trapped her and in which she can find "peace" only by accepting the verdict of her unfitness for "normal" life.

The play is not specifically written as a symbolic drama or as a tract. What I have said is implicit in all of the play's details. The reason for the play's success even with audiences who fail to understand it is that the characters and the scenes are written with a firm grasp on their naturalistic truth. Yet we shall waste the play and the author's talent if we praise the play's effects and disregard its core. Like most works of art the play's significance cannot be isolated in a single passage. It is clear to the attentive and will elude the hasty.

Still, the audience is not entirely to blame if the play and its central character are not understood. There are elements in the production—chiefly in the acting—that make for a certain ambiguity and confusion. This is not to say that the acting and production are poor. On the contrary, they are both distinctly superior. The director, Elia Kazan, is a man of high theatrical intelligence, a

craftsman of genuine sensibility. But there is a lack of balance and perspective in the production of *A Streetcar Named Desire* due to the fact that the acting of the parts is of unequal force, quality and stress. To clarify this I must digress here and dwell a bit on the nature of acting in general. What is acting? What is its function in the theatre? How does it serve the goal of art, which is at all times to give flesh to essential human meanings? The digression, we shall see, may lead to a greater insight into the outstanding theatrical event under discussion.

A pedant might characterize the actor as a person endowed with the capacity to behave publicly and for purposes of play as though fictional circumstances were real. The actor knows that the lines he speaks and the action he performs are merely invention, just as he knows the objects he deals with on the stage—scenery, properties, lights—are parts of an artificial world. His acting consists of his ability to make all these things take on a new reality for himself and for his audience. Just as the first step in painting is the "imitation" of an object, so the actor "imitates" a series of human events that in terms of real life are no more true than the apple or flower or horse that we see in a painting.

The actor is himself an instrument, and, if he is able to look right in terms of what he is "imitating," his very presence on the stage is already an accomplishment. Yet we know that an actor of a convincing presence who merely reads his lines intelligibly offers us little more than information, which is the small change of the theatre. The actor who adds visual illustration to what he is saying (beating his breast to indicate anguish!) provides a sort of lamp whereby we read the play more comfortably, although at times the illustration if well chosen may give special illumination. The actor becomes creative only when he reveals the life from which the play's lines may have emerged, a life richer perhaps than the lines' literal significance. The creative actor is the author of the new meaning that a play acquires on the stage, the author of a personal sub-text into which the play's lines are absorbed so that a special aesthetic body with an identity of its own is born. Just as the painter who merely sets down the image of an apple that looks like one is not an artist, so the actor who merely "imitates" the surface impression that we might gather from a perusal of the play's text—an actor who does not create a life beyond what was there before he assumed his role—belies the art of the theatre.

The new meaning that the actor gives to the play emerges from what is popularly known as the actor's personality—not alone his physical "type," but the whole quality of his skill, emotion, insight, sensibility, character, imagination, spirit. These have an existence of their own, which the actor with the aid of the director must shape to the form of their interpretation or understanding of the problem they have set themselves for the play.

There are two things to be considered in any judgment of acting: the material of the actor himself and the use that the material has been put to in relation to the play as a whole. A very fine actor may utterly distort the intention of a play— that is, transform it with as much possibility of happy as of disastrous results. Bernard Shaw tells us that Duse was superior to Sudermann; it was her acting of that dramatist's play *Home* that made it a work of art. In Paris I saw the Laurette Taylor part in *The Glass Menagerie* very ably played in a way that robbed the character of all poetry. In my opinion, most of our highly regarded Hamlets are simply *readings* of the part but rather inferior acting or not acting at all. Katharine Cornell's Cleopatra may be said to have certain attractive aspects (no one need debate Miss Cornell's natural endowments), but, even aside from the question of physical qualifications, she creates nothing with the part, not only in the Shakespearean sense but within her own orbit. On the other hand, I have read that Michael Chekhov's Hamlet was not Hamlet (in the sense that there might be an "ideal" Hamlet) but that it was a true creation, albeit a very special one.

In *A Streetcar Named Desire* all the actors are good, but their performances do not truly convey Tennessee Williams' play. By virtue of its power and completeness the play pretty nearly succeeds in acting the actors, but the nature of the play's reception indicates a prevailing sentiment of excitement and glowing enthusiasm disassociated from any specific meaning.

Jessica Tandy's Blanche suffers from the actress' narrow emotional range. One of the greatest parts ever written for a woman in the American theatre, it demands the fullness and variety of an orchestra. Miss Tandy's register is that of a violin's A string. The part represents the essence of womanly feeling and wounded human sensibility. Blanche lies and pretends, but through it all the actress must make us perceive her truth. She is an aristocrat (regardless of the threadbare myth of Southern gentility); she is an aristocrat in the subtlety and depth of her feeling. She is a poet, even if we are dubious about her understanding of the writers she names; she is superior by the sheer intensity and realization of her experience, even if much of what she does is abject.

If she is not these things, she is too much of a fraud to be worthy of the author's concern with her. If the latter is true, then the play would be saying something rather surprising—namely, that frank brutality and naked power are more admirable than the yearning for tenderness and the desire to reach beyond one's personal appetites. When Blanche appeals to her sister in the name of these values, Miss Tandy is unable to make it clear whether she means what she says and whether we are supposed to attach any importance to her speech or whether she is merely spinning another fantasy. It is essential to the play that we believe and are touched by what she says, that her emotion convinces us of the soundness of her values. All through the play, indeed, we must be captured by the music of the girl's martyred soul. Without this there is either a play whose viewpoint we reject or no play at all—only a series of "good scenes," a highly seasoned theatrical dish.

Marlon Brando, who plays Stanley Kowalski (Blanche's brother-in-law), is an actor of genuine power. He has what someone once called "high visibility" on the stage. His silences, even more than his speech, are completely arresting. Through his own intense concentration on what he is thinking or doing at each moment he is on the stage all our attention focuses on him. Brando's quality is one of acute sensitivity. None of the brutishness of his part is native to him: it is a characteristic he has to "invent." The combination of an intense, introspective, and almost lyric personality under the mask of a bully endows the character with something almost touchingly painful. Because the elements of characterization are put on a face to which they are not altogether becoming, a certain crudeness mars our impression, while something in the nature of the actor's very considerable talent makes us wonder whether he is not actually suffering deeply in a way that relates him to what is represented by Blanche rather than to what his own character represents in the play. When he beats his wife or throws the radio out the window there is, aside from the ugliness of these acts, an element of agony that falsifies their color in relation to their meaning in the play: they take on an almost Dostoyevskian aspect.

For what is Stanley Kowalski? He is the embodiment of animal force, of brute life unconcerned and even consciously scornful of every value that does not come within the scope of such life. He resents being called a Polack, and he quotes Huey Long, who assured him that "every man is a king." He screams that he is a hundred percent American, and breaks dishes and mistreats his women to prove it. He is all muscle, lumpish sensuality and crude energy, given support by a society that hardly demands more of him. He is the unwitting antichrist of our time, the little man who will break the back of every effort to create a more comprehensive world in which thought and conscience, a broader humanity are expected to evolve from the old Adam. His mentality provides the soil for fascism, viewed not as a political movement but as a state of being.

Because the author does not preach about him but draws him without hate or ideological animus, the audience takes him at his face value. His face value on the stage is the face of Marlon Brando as contrasted to that of Jessica Tandy. For almost more than two-thirds of the play, therefore, the audience identifies itself with Stanley Kowalski. His low jeering is seconded by the audience's laughter, which seems to mock the feeble and hysterical decorativeness of the girl's behavior. The play becomes the triumph of Stanley Kowalski with the collusion of the audience, which is no longer on the side of the angels. This is natural because Miss Tandy is fragile without being touching (except when the author is beyond being overpowered by an actress), and Mr. Brando is tough without being irredeemably coarse.

When Kowalski tells his wife to get rid of Blanche so that things can be as they were (the author is suggesting that the untoward presence of a new consciousness in Kowalski's life—the appeal to forbearance and fineness—is a cruel disturbance and that he longs for a life without any spiritual qualms), the audience is all on Kowalski's side. Miss Tandy's speeches—which are lovely in themselves—sound phony, and her long words and noble appeals are as empty as a dilettante's discourse because they do not flow from that spring of warm feeling which is the justification and essence of Blanche's character.

One of the happiest pieces of staging and acting in the play is the moment when Kowalski, having beaten his wife, calls for her to return from the neighbor's apartment where she has taken momentary refuge. He whines like a hurt animal, shouts like a savage, and finally his wife descends the staircase to return to his loving arms. Brando has been directed to fall on his knees before his wife and thrust his head against her body in a gesture that connotes humility and passion. His wife with maternal and amorous touch caresses his head. He lifts her off her feet and takes her to bed.

This, as I have noted, is done beautifully. Yet Brando's innate quality and something unresolved in the director's conception make the scene moving in a manner that is thematically disruptive. The pathos is too universally human (Kowalski at that moment is any man); it is not integrated with that attribute of the play which requires that Kowalski at all times be somewhat vile.

If Karl Malden as Blanche's suitor—a person without sufficient force to transcend the level of his environment—and Kim Hunter as Blanche's sister—who has made her peace with Kowalski's "normal life"—give performances that are easier to place than those of the two leading characters, it is not because of any intrinsic superiority to the other players. It is simply due to the fact that their parts are less complex. Miss Hunter is fairly good, Mr. Malden capital, but both appear in a sense to stand outside the play's interpretive problem. They are not struggling with a consciousness of the dilemma that exists in the choice between Kowalski's world and that of Blanche Du Bois.

As creative spectators, we cannot satisfy ourselves at a play like *A Streetcar Named Desire* with the knowledge that it is a wonderful show, a smash hit, a prize winner (it is and will be all of these). It is a play that ought to arouse in us as much feeling, thought and even controversy as plays on semipolitical themes; for it is a play that speaks of a poet's reaction to life in our country (not just the South), and what he has to say about it is much more far-reaching than what might be enunciated through any slogan.

I have heard it said, for example, that Tennessee Williams portrays "ordinary" people without much sense of their promise and reserves most of his affection for more special people—that minority which Thomas Mann once described as life's delicate children. I find this view false and misleading, but I would rather hear it expressed than to let the play go by as the best play of the season, something you must see, "great theatre."

If the play is great theatre—as I believe—it is precisely because it is instinct with life, a life we share in not only on the stage, but in our very homes by night and day. If I have chosen to examine the production with what might seem undue minuteness, it is because I believe that ques-

tions of the theatre (and of art) are not simply questions of taste or professional quibbles, but life questions. I can think of no higher compliment to the director and actors of such a production than to take their work with utmost seriousness—even to the point of neglecting to make allowance for the difficulties attendant on the realization of so original a play on Broadway.

—*TRW*, '48

THE LOST ART

A friend of mine who happens to be a prominent and talented actor—trained in the old Group Theatre—eagerly picked up *Acting: A Handbook of the Stanislavsky Method* from my desk, examined it for a moment, then let it fall and muttered "The same old....!"

I did not understand the exact significance of my friend's disdainful profanity. Does he consider all handbooks on acting futile? If so, he is right to a degree.

The present book—a collection of papers by Stanislavsky and some of his most distinguished disciples in the Russian theatre—contains one or two pieces that, due to bad writing and worse translation, are almost gibberish, but there are many more that should prove instructive as well as inspiring to those theatre specialists already familiar through practical experience with the subject matter of these essays on the technique of acting and directing.

Why did my friend, who owes so much of his conscious technique to training in the so-called Stanislavsky method, dismiss the very idea of reading such a book at the present time? An examination of my own consciousness as I reread some of the essays—most of which appeared years ago in obscure theatrical periodicals—supplied part of the answer.

The book deals with acting as an art which seems now either to have existed only in the past or to lie ahead in some utopian future. Is there such art as Stanislavsky and his pupils are talking about anywhere outside a handbook? What is this art of acting that grown people should wax so serious and even theoretical over it?

Look at the illustrations in the back of the book. Eleven of them are photographs of Stanislavsky in plays by Pushkin, Molière, Chekhov, Gorky, Turgenev, Tolstoy and others. In each picture Stanislavsky is a new man. This is not merely a matter of contrasting make-ups: each face has a different meaning. Each image reveals not simply a different character but also a world. These pictures are not examples of expert craftsmanship with grease paint, wig and crepe hair, but revelations of genuine artistic perception. They are the fruit of thought, of feeling, of study, of intuition, observation and imagination. These photographs remind us that acting may be an art.

Many actors today have the gifts and even more of them the inclination to work in the vein that these photographs suggest. There still are actors who devour such books as the present one; who, long after they have become "established" in the profession, attend classes like novices. They know that acting with us has become mostly imitation and illustration. They know that to have fundamental theatrical value acting must be creative.

The creative actor—even the actor who simply strives for creation—has become so exceptional in our theater as to seem non-existent. This is not the actor's fault; it is the fault of our stage, which is run as a small-time, hit-or-miss business where study, planning, continuity of purpose and program (not to mention security of employment) are unprofitable and therefore visionary.

The reason you will find only occasional mention of individual actors in my reviews is that most performances nowadays are pleasantly competent without being distinguished. They are rarely related to art: they seldom even begin to set themselves the problems which might lead to art. This, I repeat, is not because our actors are lazy, uninterested, incapable. On the contrary, the majority of our actors today are often quite aware

that they are progressively being cut off from all sources of creative stimulation, all opportunity for creative growth. Directors who demand creative effort from the actor are rare; directors who know how to provoke it are rarer still.

An actor in our theater with a little more "personality," a more engaging or attractive quality than the average, is generally hailed as a master and promptly persuaded (by the nature of the praise, publicity and pressure received) to leave the stage to become a face on the screen, a voice on the air and a mug in the illustrated ads. These actors are generally young people who have been on the stage from two to five years.

Do you remember Barbara Bel Geddes? What will happen to Marlon Brando, Meg Mundy and other discoveries of the season? Will they ponder over the fact that performances such as those of Ronald Colman in *A Double Life* or Loretta Young in *The Farmer's Daughter* are awarded honors as the "Best of the Year"? And will they then some years hence pick up a serious treatise on acting and cry out "The same old...."?

—*NR*, 12 Apr. '48

TROUBLE WITH SHAKESPEARE

When Russell Collins as the Porter in the new production of *Macbeth* spoke his ribald lines about the effects of drink, a lady seated behind me asked, "Did Shakespeare really say that?" The question was more than a tribute to Collins' amusing performance; it was a symptom. Shakespeare on our stage may be many things, but he is rarely a playwright who is permitted to speak directly to us.

Listen to a discussion of almost any Shakespeare production and you will note that practically all the talk relates to some professional aspect of the occasion, very little to the play itself in its emotional bearing on the talkers. The scene changes were accomplished smoothly and swiftly—the performance had a good pace—someone will say, forgetting that in Shakespeare's time the changes were accomplished even more swiftly, since there was no scenery. This or that actor or actress was better than someone else who did the play several seasons ago. The style of one production is preferred to that of another because one was done in the costumes of the eleventh century—the actual historical period of the play—rather than in those of the sixteenth century. The dueling was more convincingly managed in one production than in another. And so on.

This may serve as theatre chitchat; it has little to do with either the artistic or entertainment values of a playwright. Most of Shakespeare's plays as we see them hardly function as plays at all, because—for one thing—in most instances we barely hear the dialogue. (Maurice Evans is pleasurably audible; this alone makes him our leading Shakespearean actor today.) I reread Macbeth a day before I saw the production at the National Theater. I sat in the eleventh row—my hearing is normal—and I missed half the lines.

But it is not this *Macbeth* that is in question here. See it if you like, enjoy it if you can—it is not without its good points and its sympathetic performances. What I should like to stress here is that our whole approach to Shakespeare on the American stage has degenerated into something so remote from the goal of true theatre that most productions have become artistically less nourishing than our good musicals. The Mack Sennett ballet in *High Button Shoes*, for instance, is a completely realized conception, whereas most of the stage interpretations of Shakespeare strike me as empty show, depending for their effect on our reading and the aura of some actor's real or advertised personality.

In the present *Macbeth* some attempt has been made to give the play a wild, shaggy, barbaric aspect. This is all to the good: our usual Shakespeare is much too schoolmarmish. But all that comes of this promising idea is Michael Redgrave's rough costume, his unkempt wig, his wild eye, twitching mouth and his occasionally explosive readings. Redgrave—who is often a sensitive and attractive actor—suggests that Macbeth is obsessed, but the basic problem of showing that this obsession has taken hold of a man of great human stature has not even been worked on. The result amounts to a fitful hysteria.

The fault is not essentially Redgrave's. It derives from the fact that nothing has been thought through, nothing given a real theatrical embodiment. The style chosen for a production cannot simply be applied to one character alone: it must include all. The rest of the cast has not been incorporated into the pattern of the production's ostensible plan: it is treated as conventionally as that of any other Shakespearean show. The backgrounds are sometimes romantically effective without always being relevant to what the production is supposedly aiming to achieve. But effective or not, the treatment of such crucial elements of the play as the three witches reduces everything to the high-school level.

My quarrel, however, is not with this or that detail. I am simply using this occasion to point out that Shakespeare is an extremely difficult playwright for any theatre today, and particularly for our commercial theatre. To take up the challenge of producing one of his plays we ought to be inspired with the sense of the play as something through which we may directly address our audience on a living theme, and we should be equipped with the craftsmanship to shape the play to the meaning we find in it.

Since conditions for the preparation of this kind of production are rare, it is little wonder that our stage Shakespeare is so often what it is—elaborately and expensively amateurish, pretentious and foolish. A propagandist for a true Theatre might suggest a suspension of all Shakespeare till the time when such conditions do prevail. Our hunger and disgrace would then serve as a horrible example of the state of our theatre. We should also be spared many an embarrassing evening.

—*NR*, 19 Apr. '48

EXPERIMENTAL THEATRE

In the halcyon days of the New York stage (1915-28) it was quite exciting to hie ourselves down to the Provincetown Playhouse on Macdougal Street, to the Neighborhood Playhouse on Grand Street, to the Greenwich Village Theater on Sheridan Square, to the Comedy Theater on Forty-first Street, to the Garrick Theater on Thirty-fifth Street, to the New Playwrights on Commerce Street, and even as late as the middle thirties, to the Civic Repertory Theater on West Fourteenth Street. Many of us looked forward to these adventurous jaunts as opportunities to find not only the unusual in stage entertainment but also the best.

It did not matter to us that some of the reviewers at the time took offense at such plays as e. e. cummings' *him*. Or that a number of the "revolting playwrights," as Woollcott dubbed them, were indigestible. The stuff and nonsense of the side-alley theater raised Cain.

The rebellion not only produced a Eugene O'Neill but so influenced the commercial theater that Brock Pemberton, for instance, would present Pirandello's *Six Characters in Search of an Author* fairly close to Broadway at the Princess Theater on Thirty-ninth Street.

We did not altogether appreciate what we possessed in those days because we judged each show on its own merits without realizing that ferment and fertility of production are in themselves a sign of health, a promise of those few fine achievements that are later judged to be emblems of a living theatrical culture.

Monopoly has taken over our theatre. Monopoly shapes the thought of our artists, audiences, critics. The result is that today when the stranglehold begins to bring a new revolt by vigorous young theatre craftsmen, we still think in show-business terms even when we attend performances under auspices that are admittedly noncommercial.

The new organizations now cropping up tangentially from Broadway ought to be encouraged in every possible way, and not only when some of their productions, as in the cases of *Skipper Next to God* and *The Respectful Prostitute*, prove sufficiently sturdy to enter the competitive market. If we demand a hit from every play produced by these new units we shall force a pattern on them that leads to the point where *Strange Bedfellows* is valued above *Galileo*. What is needed to preserve the vitality of the new groups is not only "experimental" plays but experimental audiences. Let us stop thinking like ticket brokers and movie scouts and we may see productions not only of plays like those of Sartre but plays by a far superior dramatist like Garcia Lorca.

These reflections are provoked by the performance of Eugene O'Neill's *Lazarus Laughed*, which the Fordham University players gave at their campus theater last week. Such reflections seemed even more pertinent at the Experimental Theater's fifth bill of its subscription season at the Maxine Elliott—three one-act plays by American authors.

I cannot say that *Lazarus Laughed* offered me much pleasure, since it is not, save for its conception, a good play in any sense of the word. To do it impressively, furthermore, would require the genius of a Max Reinhardt or the nerve of an Orson Welles. Yet I could not help being interested in O'Neill's effort to capture a kind of pantheistic optimism, or being curious about why at that moment of his career—1926—the playwright should have been struggling to sublimate his chronic pessimism. One felt again a genuine respect for the one man among our dramatists whose work represents a persistent quest for faith.

The one-acters at the Experimental Theater were given on a bare stage with a minimum of theatrical allure. The stripped platform seemed a remarkably appropriate environment for the particular plays done. Richard Harrity's *Hope Is the Thing with Feathers* mingles a wry sentimentality with the kind of cockeyed humor that our writers so frequently bring to the subject of hoboes and bums. We can explain this approach by the fact that the play's basic theme is the daring one of hunger and hope. Our theatregoers have never experienced the one and seem to retain only a semblance of the other.

Horton Foote's *Celebration* suffers chiefly from trying to do too much. It attempts a twenty-minute dramatization of an insanity frequently found in the South, where many imagine themselves living in a position they no longer occupy while they dwell in a mess they refuse to recognize. *Afternoon Storm* is a not particularly satisfying illustration of Abe Lincoln's notorious irresolution, by the neglected and talented writer, E. P. Conkle.

I liked the spirit of the Experimental Theater's latest undertaking. It was most in evidence through such sound actors of the younger generation as E. G. Marshall, George Matthews, Lou Gilbert, and the older actor Dan Reed, whose inspired readings of Masters' *Spoon River Anthology* must some day be performed in public.

—*NR*, 26 Apr. '48

A–B–C

Two plays opened during the past fortnight about which I might write as violently deprecatory reviews as my colleagues, but I refrain from doing so. There is little point in specifying exactly how rotten a rotten egg is. It is enough to say that it is inedible.

The New York audience has recently cultivated a keen critical eye—for the inessential. It takes a curious satisfaction in beating dead dogs, and there is a school of criticism that has made itself a reputation for discrimination by indulging the pastime. These observations, stimulated by the unfortunate theatrical exhibits aforementioned, tempt me to set down certain principles upon which some of my thinking as a dramatic critic is based.

It is ordinarily taken for granted that the critic's first job on seeing a play is to state whether or not he likes it. For my part, I suggest that whether a critic likes or dislikes a particular play is almost as much a purely private matter as his reaction to Roquefort cheese or oyster stew—and consequently of small general value or interest. This is true no matter how engagingly the basic sentiments of approbation or disapproval are set forth. Likes or dislikes in themselves may represent no more than an individual accident or personality.

Criticism is not a science, but it should at least attempt to describe something more generally relevant than a whim. The kind of criticism that seeks to win followers for its perpetrator through an enumeration of his peculiar preferences and prejudices often makes entertaining reading, but usually ends by leaving the reader with a sense of merely sharing in the critic's conceit. When the critic says, "I prefer Saroyan's anarchy to Hellman's order," or "Barrie's sweet milk pleases me more than Coward's sour sauce" ("what a clever boy am I!"), it really matters very little whether or not one agrees, though of course it is always flattering to listen to the echoes of one's own notions.

Take the proposition "I like it!" From a critical standpoint, what actually counts here is the definition of the subject and the object: Who is "I" and what is "it"? There are critics whose work is a long essay in self-exposure and self-analysis. When Anatole France urged that the good critic is he who recounts his soul's adventures among masterpieces, he was avowing a penchant for a special category of criticism. What gives it validity is the fact that when you have finished with the critical writings of an Anatole France or a Bernard Shaw you have not only learned to know a man, but a whole attitude toward life which that man represents. The critic's sensibility serves as a magic mirror in which the work of art is reflected.

Another sort of criticism—the one toward which I lean—hopes to define the "it"—the object—with which the "I"—the critic—has been brought into contact. This, of course, may finally prove as personal an activity as frankly subjective criticism, but its aim is to direct the reader's mind to a consideration of the stuff of which the object criticized is composed. Such criticism is not satisfied to indicate that something is "good," but tries to determine in exactly what way the thing under discussion is good, what it is good for, for whom it is good.

This criticism treats the object criticized not as an end in itself but as a key to something that reaches out and encompasses many things not immediately obvious within the confines of the work itself. It sees art in terms of life. Its emphasis is not on the immediate pleasure or pain that the work of art may induce but on an interpretation of the factors which give it birth; the shape, substance and value of the material from which it has been made.

Are *The Respectful Prostitute* and *A Streetcar Named Desire* good plays? The merit of the answer does not depend on its being affirmative or negative or on the eminence or popularity of the gentleman who offers the answer, but on the quality of insight into the plays themselves. I sometimes find it more illuminating to read a critic with whose conclusion I disagree than to read a review in which the critic simply renders the same "verdict" as mine. The measure of a dramatic criticism's worth is not in the bare opinion delivered, but in the degree and extent to which it *reveals* a play as a thing that exists in the world—and I don't mean just the world of entertainment.

—*NR*, 3 May '48

BERGNER

The ten best performances of the season are—or should I say is?—given by Elisabeth Bergner in *The Cup of Trembling*, a new play by Louis Paul.

To dwell on the play's faults would be like complaining that a fire had been a dull spectacle because the firemen and the inhabitants of the burning house expressed themselves in clichés. It is a mistake to watch *The Cup of Trembling* with one's ears.

Of course it is a poor play if we think of it in terms of written words. In a sense, it is hardly a play at all—only an incompletely reported and unimaginatively related case history. It tells of a lady neurotically addicted to drink in a manner that leads one to believe that its author had little more in view than to sell us on the therapeutic virtues of psychoanalysis and Alcoholics Anonymous. Conceived in this vein, no play is possible; the characters involved are not treated as people but as items in a medical chart.

But a play is something other than an illustrated text. It is an entertainment that takes place on a stage where interest may be generated and meaning created by a combination of factors no one of which entirely conveys the effect of the whole. It is true that in many plays our interest derives chiefly from the story told and the words spoken, but in others the value comes from an entirely non-literary source.

Watching Bergner in *The Cup of Trembling* I felt I was in a theatre, and did not at all regret it. This has not been the case on other occasions when reputable texts were presented by performers whose connection with the art of acting seemed to be largely a matter of hearsay. Bergner is an *actress*. The fact that I might wish this actress to come before us under more rewarding circumstances does not diminish my appreciation of her talent.

Because Miss Bergner is an actress—not a megaphone for dialogue—she can be criticized as well as admired. Some people find her irritating. That is because she is somebody and does something. We very rarely think of attacking a story in the *Saturday Evening Post*, but artists like Dreiser, Sherwood Anderson and Henry James are frequent targets. I defy anyone to utter one cogent word of criticism of most of Hollywood's leading ladies.

Bergner is incessant. A fault? No doubt. But she is incessantly interesting. She is interesting not simply as a "personality"—someone we might find charming if we were lucky enough to meet her socially—she is interesting by what she asks you to observe in each scene. Take the moment in which she listens to a friend who urges her to believe in the possibility of a cure. Bergner's concentration, which always rivets the spectator's attention on her, becomes in this scene a moment of intense drama because we see her thoughts—her skepticism, her impatience, her desire to believe, her defiance of false hope, her consideration, her shrewd humor within the orbit of her misery. As she plays it, the scene is as eloquent and gripping as pages of fine writing might be.

The essence of Bergner's technique is the capacity to make every moment she is on the stage dramatic and significant. She makes everything she does theatrically expressive. Every change in tempo, in vocal volume, in physical impulse is the graph of a subtle personal narrative which we see constantly evolving with a basic logic that the lines themselves may not possess.

I cannot evaluate the full measure of Bergner's talent because I was not fortunate enough to see her abroad in any of her famous roles. Nevertheless I venture to say that her art tends to confine our attention to the thing she is doing at each moment. We are satisfied that what we see is being done as completely as possible, but we become aware a little later that there is a whole dimension of experience that she does not reach. She does not evoke the universal from the particular. When she suggests the pain and bewilderment of her situation in *The Cup of Trembling* she does it more convincingly than almost any other actress might do it, but she does not quite give us a sense of something beyond the immediate incident and the individual person involved, a sense of pain and bewilderment as part of that design in life in which we all share.

—NR, 10 May '48

FOR FUN

Since *The Play's the Thing* and *Inside USA* are both designed to amuse, they must be judged as entertainment. On a laugh gauge, I believe the record would indicate that in quality and volume of laughter, the former had, in my case, outdistanced the latter.

I find this a little paradoxical because I can list more objections to the production of *The Play's the Thing* than to that of *Inside USA*. The set for the Molnar comedy struck me as notably ugly. It took me at least fifteen minutes to get inured to it. Imported from England—for economic rather than decorative reasons, I am sure—it is a relic from the theatre of 1914. Even more detrimental to the fun is the style in which the company performs.

The Play's the Thing is done as if Molnar were an Englishman. The essence of English smart comedy is its combination of verbal distinction with intellectual impertinence, while Molnar's comedy is the distillation of a shrewdness of experience. English comedy seems to issue from the lips and the head; Continental comedy—particularly Hungarian—from the viscera and points below. Schmaltz is what the English don't have, and schmaltz—refined by wit—is indispensable to Molnar. Actors in *The Play's the Thing* should not conduct themselves as if they were impersonating epigrammatic butlers out of a piece by Noel Coward.

In itself the company that is performing the Molnar tidbit at the Booth is not at all bad. Louis Calhern is best in the third-act rehearsal scene and Arthur Margetson, as the actor sweating over the pronunciation of multi-cylindered French names, is excellent. They make the play at this point convulsively funny. *The Play's the Thing* survives because it has the mischievous hedonism, the appetite for civilized indulgence and juicy theatre that are characteristic of all the anecdotes told about Molnar.

Despite a dearth of good tunes, a fault common to most of the postwar revues, the Howard Dietz-Arthur Schwartz *Inside USA* at the Century is a thoroughly efficient entertainment. The show moves briskly, it looks rich, it has no unbearably dull spots, it employs the services of attractive and talented people.

Who can fail to admire Beatrice Lillie? Her comedy is a revolt against form, convention, manners, by a lady whose every physical attribute and gesture is elegant. She can play the disjointed clown superbly because she is all precision and subtle balance. She can speak sloppy lines because they acquire a new decorum in her delivery. Finally, there is something about her weirdly decorative in the manner of certain modern objets d'art: she is dry, cool, clear, wickedly impersonal—as if a thermometer were to wink when it registered a fever.

Worth special remark too is Eric Victor, whose insinuating eccentric dance is at once fluent and forceful. Valerie Bettis carries out Tamaris' typically energetic dance patterns with a peculiar mixture of exuberance and an almost neurotic will-to-violence. Miss Bettis' dancing is like a powerful sex impulse that, though released, nevertheless remains unfulfilled. Herb Shriner's monologue is a shy patter—as if a Hoosier boy had many refreshingly "subversive" things to say but had thought better of it. "Forty Winks" is a swift parody on the tendency of our functional civilization to produce useless gadgets—in this instance, a series of aids to sleep that keep one awake. "We Won't Take It Back" provides Jack Haley and Bea Lillie with a song routine full of topical allusions and café ribaldry in the vein of successful popular showmanship. And there is a redhead in the chorus who is a reminder of a better day when show girls couldn't sing or dance but looked gratifyingly stagy.

All this makes *Inside USA* a hit. Yet I found it deficient in an element that *The Play's the Thing* possesses. It has no personality. *The Ziegfeld Follies* had it; so did the *Grand Street Follies*, the

Garrick Gaieties, *Charlot's Revue*, the *Little Show*, *The Bandwagon*, *Pins and Needles*, even *Call Me Mister*. These shows had personality because a dominant mood—both in the people who made them and in their audiences—called for expression. The mood may have been one of luxury, frivolity, sentimentality, snobbism, fashionable eroticism or boisterous proletarianism. No matter: each produced a revue with a distinct character.

Our audiences today are prosperous and frightened, eager for relief through entertainment but uncertain of the prescription for that relief. Such an audience and simple sensuous glamor are incompatible. It is also too confused and intimidated an audience for strong political satire; it is neither corrupt enough nor sure enough of itself to accept straight smut or out-and-out cynicism. It is a worried and impatient audience, so what it finally demands is hard-driving, expert stagecraft without sufficient emphasis on one particular quality to make it much of anything. Such entertainment consequently must lack not only personality but what is almost the same thing—melody.

—*NR*, 17 May '48

O'NEILL AGAIN

We should be grateful to the company at the City Center for the opportunity it gives us to see Eugene O'Neill's early one-act plays. Since we have no repertory companies, nothing resembling a national theatre (our country being too poor to establish one, in contradistinction, let us say, to Palestine), the chance to review part of our dramatic heritage must remain a matter of accident. Our theatre is so organized that O'Neill's part in such a heritage—or even the idea that we possess one—is something of which we must constantly be reminded.

Not that the City Center production of the *S.S. Glencairn* cycle under José Ferrer's direction is entirely satisfactory. In fact it is mediocre. This may be due to the inadequate two-week period allowed for rehearsal. The actors have undoubtedly worked hard to do the plays justice; they nevertheless give the impression of a hasty job.

The company appears to lack that simple faith in the importance of O'Neill's emotions and people which gives these plays dimension. The characterizations in this case become merely a question of accents, and the accents are neither accurate nor convincing. A sense of particularization and close identification with each person is generally missing—though players like Nan McFarland, George Mathews and Harold J. Stone seem on the way to achieve them.

Still, it is a good thing to see these plays again. If we think of the difference between the treatment of the sailors in *S.S. Glencairn* and in such a popular success as *Mister Roberts*, we may appreciate anew the distinction between a real dramatist and the greater number of American playwrights from 1915 to the present. And in this distinction—arbitrary and unfair as it may seem in the present instance—lies a lesson.

I once heard a malicious and witty Irish critic say of O'Neill that he was a great playwright who never wrote a good play. Like the run of such caustic quips, the statement is significant even though untrue. Many Europeans and a few Americans think of O'Neill in just such terms. There is no point in insisting that they constitute a minority, since this minority is a conscious group, while most of us reiterate the opinion that O'Neill is the first playwright of our land in a manner almost as mechanical as our references to that land as the greatest place on earth. We ought to ask ourselves occasionally why we believe—if we do—O'Neill to be our best playwright.

It is a long time since I saw or read *The Hairy Ape* or *Desire Under the Elms;* my discomfiture at *Dynamo* and *Days Without End* is still a vivid memory; and I certainly do not qualify as a champion of *The Iceman Cometh*. Yet I do not hesitate to stand with the majority in my regard for O'Neill. If the *Glencairn* plays strike us today as rudimentary and the later work—including the complex *Strange Interlude* and the monumental *Mourning Becomes Electra*—too dependent on sources that have been imperfectly and rather immaturely assimilated, the whole of O'Neill's work reveals an impressive consistency and unity.

For more than thirty years O'Neill has been genuinely serious. The mood in *The Moon of the Caribbees* is one of nostalgia; the theme of *In the Zone* is the mystery of love; *Bound East for Cardiff* deals with the confrontation of death; *The Long Voyage Home* dramatizes the ironic tragedy of man's fate. O'Neill's career has been a constant quest, a passionate absorption, a rapt struggle to come to grips with a major theme of which the elements I have indicated are varying facets. O'Neill is like the Swedish sailor in his play who, on the point of reaching his peaceful destination, is shanghaied off to renew his long voyage home under the most painful conditions. Only his most negligible work represents conclusions. His best plays are vibrantly disturbing because they strike sensitive fibers within the protected tissue of American life.

O'Neill seems to cry out with Thomas Wolfe—and almost every American writer of stature—that "we are lost!" The range of his search is wider than that of most of our writers and consequently more erratic. He sometimes appears incredibly ingenuous both in his choice of panaceas and in his disappointment with them.

To scorn or mock him because he is insecure in knowledge and unripe in despair is, for an American at least, to betray a sophomoric self-assurance. What certainties have we attained? We live in a country which, though it has inherited the wisdom of the ages, has thus far distilled only the experience of an adolescent. We are even cut off from the past that gave us Emerson, Thoreau, Hawthorne, Melville and Whitman. We have produced no Sophocles, Shakespeare, Cervantes, Tolstoy, Molière or Goethe of our own. If Henry James is a master, he is a little one. We must not deny such men as Dreiser and Sherwood Anderson on the ground of their inadequacies. Each in his own way is, as Whitman called himself, "a primitive surveyor." In the theatre there has only been one such person to render us a lifetime of service: Eugene O'Neill.

—*NR*, 7 June '48

WHAT IS A THEATRE?

I am sure the New York daily press feels it has done right by the visiting players of the Habimah. Most of its productions were praised, and when they were not, the reviewers' ignorance of the Hebrew language or the inadequacies of Calderon and Sophocles were made to bear the blame. But for all the good will manifested, I fear an opportunity has been missed. By not seeing the Habimah's productions within a perspective deeper than their excellence as shows, we fail to reap the full benefit of what they have to teach us.

For those who remember the New York theatre of the twenties, our reception of the Habimah marks a striking contrast. The visit of a distinguished foreign theatrical group in those days was an event anticipated by long historical surveys, followed by critical analyses, debates, challenges, sermons. Our actors felt they were not alert to their profession unless they attended such performances repeatedly. Students of the theatre looked upon their frequentation of the foreign groups as a kind of post-graduate instruction. Books were published on each of the companies, receptions were held, degrees conferred.

All this bore fruit. New schools and studios were set up among us. Daring productions were more frequent even in the commercial theatre. Actors, playwrights, scene designers, directors, audiences and critics evinced greater eagerness and ambition. Today commercial success or failure has become almost the sole measure of value. In the twenties a "flop" like Lawson's *Processional* had greater repercussions than a smash hit like *A Streetcar Named Desire* has today.

No villain is responsible for the change; economic and social factors have brought it about. But theatre devotees are presumably conscious people. They should use their consciousness to act upon the drift of adverse currents. Perhaps it is inevitable that we should have no real theatre today, but it does not follow that we should allow ourselves to forget what real theatre is. If we lose the concept as well as the fact, then there is very little chance of recovery or renewal.

The Habimah is a real theatre. A real theatre exists when a group, united by a common aim, works together to give the most complete dramatic expression to the ideals that inspire it. A theatre works as a unit as any serious artist works individually. A theatre builds for continuity, development, perpetuation of its ideals and its identity. The actors of the Habimah have been working together since 1920. They have produced about 85 plays—modern and classic, foreign and Hebrew—most of which are still retained in their present repertory. The Habimah has its own studio in which to develop a new generation of actors; it has its own playhouse. The Habimah has become an integral part of a culture. It receives community support.

The Habimah's style is predominantly non-realistic. It is capable of other styles as well—my belief is that as Israel progresses toward greater political stability, the Habimah's productions will grow increasingly realistic—but there is no doubt that all its productions are influenced by that heightened and pointed expressivity of speech, gesture, movement, makeup and stage setting that we usually refer to as "stylized."

This does not mean that all the Habimah's productions are alike. Their *Oedipus Rex*—directed in 1947 by Tyrone Guthrie of London—is quite different from the 1922 *Dybbuk*. The reason for this is that *The Dybbuk* was regarded as something out of a directly personal past with a peculiar pertinence for the actors of the company and their original audiences, while *Oedipus* is viewed as an old tale the meaning of which is universal in the traditional sense. *Oedipus* is less emphatic, less savage; it is a classic in the subdued fashion of someone uttering a portentous truth that has become part of an ancient heritage. This is not necessarily the right way to do *Oedipus* any more than *The Dybbuk* must be done as the Habimah does it. The point is that both are sustained by genuine conceptions.

The Golem, on the other hand, is a combination of an almost Gothic symbolism with rather stock nineteenth-century theatricality. Though as a whole *The Golem* is the least carefully wrought of the four Habimah productions seen here, the familiar pattern of its story ("Frankenstein" among the Jews of medieval Prague) as well as Aaron Meskin's touching and graphic performance in the central role has made it almost the most popular.

Just as a single style may have numerous variants, so a single culture may produce divers styles. The Habimah—the theatre of a country about the size of Connecticut—is not the only real theatre in Israel. There are others with different styles. The question to ask ourselves is: what have we—and why?

—*NR*, 14 June '48

A DYING SOUND

The reviews I read of *The Insect Comedy*, the final production of the City Center's six-week season of plays, did not seem to me to convey the nature of the event. They expressed disappointment or faint disapproval of the play and respect for the smoothness with which a rather difficult production had been managed after only two weeks of rehearsal. They omitted to note that the first-night audience was unusually enthusiastic. Nor did they stop to consider why. *The Insect Comedy*: by the Czech writers Josef and Karel Capek, was first given here in 1922 under the title of *The World We Live In*. It is a pessimistic allegory in which man, presented through a parallel

with insect life, is shown as trivial in his love, paltry in his ambition, predatory and rapacious in his social life. The climax of man's struggle is internecine strife, its sum undesired and meaningless death.

Set down this way the play becomes absurd, not because it can be proved false but because it contains the kind of truth that can contribute to nothing except suicide. But *The Insect Comedy* is only partially absurd. There are, it is true, besides moments of sardonic humor, passages in which a kind of Germanic philosophizing is boiled in the heat of that hysteria which prevailed in Central Europe right after the First World War. It represents the combination of despair and fury without any foundation in specific social understanding that inevitably paves the way to another war. The play is nevertheless justified by the fact that it does reflect an atmosphere created by a painfully real historical situation.

The other aspect of the play's significance is that it was written at a time when the Central European theatre was booming with blazing dramatic experiments. It was the time of the theatre theatrical, when plays were scored for the full orchestra of the stage's means: variety of costume, decor, dance, music, characterization. Thus the sting of the play's spleen was sweetened by the glamor of the theatre's magic. The mixture was typical of the twenties, and New York as well as Berlin, Budapest and Prague enjoyed the brew.

Our theatre is now physically impoverished: color and imaginative dimension are relegated either to musical comedy or to essays in Shakespeare. The audiences at the City Center are gratified to see in a straight play something that has a colorful look. It hungers for some of the display and festiveness which our one-set naturalistic drama has all but banished from the theatre. *The Insect Comedy* is a sight for sore eyes.

The audience, in addition, lends a benign intent to the play's rage: it regards it as an anti-war play. I always worry when I see such a play; it is generally followed by a war. But today when anti-war propaganda is almost suspect in many quarters, the good audience at the City Center is to be congratulated on its humane and mildly defiant sentiments.

The production of *The Insect Comedy* is like the reduction of a big score to the range of a harmonica. In this instance, the effect is rather sweet. There is a winning youngness and cordiality about the show.

José Ferrer is amusing when he doesn't act too coquettishly. George Coulouris is at his best when he avoids the rhetorical and discloses the sense of pity within the play instead of yielding to the temptations of the playwright's journalistic declamation. The leading butterflies of the first act are played by two very pretty girls: Rita Gam and Phyllis Hill. Annabelle Lyon, as a Female Cricket, strikes a genuine note of chirping poetry. The direction is proficient, but longer pre-rehearsal preparation might have led the director to further invention with which to give the production more body.

The melancholy fact about the musical play, *Sleepy Hollow*, is that the word "almost" will have to serve as its epitaph. It is by no means reprehensible, but its pleasures are never consummated. Some of Anna Sokolow's dance numbers—particularly the "Couple Dance"—have a lean eccentricity that almost creates a style for the production. Gil Lamb as Ichabod Crane possesses such a style without quite mastering it. He has a strangely pliant body, a sad, sour and somehow friendly face with interesting reserves of quality that might be put to exciting theatrical use. And what is true of him is true of the rest. Everyone gives signs of being capable of offering more than he does. The lack of a strong creative hand at the helm seems to have done the show a fatal disservice.

With *Sleepy Hollow*, the 1947-48 Broadway season "officially" ends. The nature of this production's failings is an oblique comment on the state of our theatre today.

—*NR*, 21 June '48

A CRITIC

To serve as something beyond a privileged press agent with a fancy vocabulary, the theatre critic must be an artist, a historian and a philosopher. Henry James was all of these. It should be no surprise therefore that his admirably edited notes on the acting and drama of his time, collected under the title *The Scenic Art* (Rutgers University Press; $4.50), are a valuable, indeed a delightful, addition to the meager library of enduring theatre criticism in the English language.

Since the articles that constitute James's theatre criticism were written sporadically for diverse journals from 1872 to 1901, they do not have the consistency—stylistically or chronologically—of the equivalent work of Bernard Shaw or Max Beerbohm. The best of the James's pieces are nevertheless just as fine as those of the two younger men who for a number of years were professionally committed to dramatic criticism.

From the pages of *The Scenic Art* we may learn about the creative poverty and the material prosperity of the London stage at the time that Meredith, Hardy, Gissing, Tennyson and Swinburne were enriching English literature. (To inquire why in certain periods and in certain countries the greatest writers devoted themselves to the theatre while at other times they shunned it, would be a worthy task for an ambitious student.) We learn too how the beginnings of English drawing-room realism owed much both to the influx into the theatre of well-to-do amateur actors and to the advance of stage mechanics—all of which, to James's discerning eye, spelled an impoverishment in both acting and dramaturgy.

Among the historical details worth special remark are James's comments on Sarah Bernhardt, whom he describes in 1879 as being a new kind of actress, typical of the age of the advertising genius—"the muse of the newspaper." Bernhardt's success, James points out, "has been in a very moderate degree an artistic success. It has been the success of a celebrity...and Mlle. Sarah Bernhardt is not...a celebrity because she is an artist. She is a celebrity...because she desires with an intensity that has rarely been equaled to be one....She is too American not to succeed in America. The people who have brought to the highest development the arts and graces of publicity will recognize a kindred spirit."

The position of many of our present-day stage celebrities—Broadway geniuses!—is not due any more to their own passion for celebrity but to both our need for hero worship and our loss of the faculty with which to evaluate their work properly. Reviewers, and to a great extent their audience today, no longer see people on the stage in terms of art but in terms of quotes, display ads, box-office reports, interviews, syndicated photographs, contracts and deals.

I have suggested that to achieve anything more than a momentary interest, the theatre critic must himself qualify as an artist. The artist has his own vision, idiosyncrasy, manner of expression. It is real fun to observe the evolution of James's style through the articles in *The Scenic Art*. They begin with a kind of stiff and studious decorum; they progress to an expansive eloquence that seems to break through the writer's many reticences; they go on to the point where we behold a man carrying so precious a burden of gems that he appears fearful of stumbling and scattering them or of making any direct use of them at all.

In regard to style, the paper on the French actor, Coquelin, written in 1887 and rewritten in 1915, is worth close examination. The late manner reveals itself in an ecstasy of virtuosity combined with a prissy meticulousness and scrupulousness, a breathless concern to render the scientifically exact into the most esthetically graceful, an effort to wed exquisiteness of tone with impeccability of taste—leading to something which is at once fascinating and almost unbearable. But James was never meant to be read on the run. In his day the

writer—even the critic—expected to be granted some time.

Perception and felicity of phrase provide pleasure on almost every page of *The Scenic Art*. In speaking of Rostand, James refers to "the bristling bravery of his verse, the general frolic of his vocabulary, especially under the happy crack of the whip of rhyme..."; of Dumas' *The Lady of the Camelias*, James says, "It is all champagne and tears—fresh perversity, fresh credulity, fresh passion, fresh pain.... It carries with it an April air." Of American criticism and the newly discovered writer, James says: "It is solely the manifestation and never the talent that interests us, and nothing is stranger than the fact that no critic has ever explained on our behalf the system by which we hurl ourselves on a writer today and stare at him tomorrow as if we had never heard of him.... We have in England and the United States only the two alternatives of the roar of the market and the silence of the tomb...."

—*NR*, 28 June '48

THE ATOM & COCTEAU

As a further example of militant Philistinism, I say that I almost resent the application of such an adjective as "provocative" to Jean Cocteau's *The Infernal Machine*. It is being given down at the Provincetown Playhouse by a creditable new acting group which might put its fresh talents into far more creative service.

Such groups are always faced with the problem of finding suitable plays in which to present themselves. They hope to avoid the hackneyed, and the more promising new plays are rarely available to them. A play like *The Infernal Machine*, bearing the glamorous name of Jean Cocteau and the accolade of rexpected critics, leads these young people to believe that it will be deemed an attractive as well as a worthy choice. This might be called corruption by the avant-garde, which is perhaps even more corrosive than corruption by commerce.

Cocteau, jack-of-all-arts with a brilliant gift for metaphor in almost every domain, is essentially an esthetic firefly. While his light is sometimes captivating, it is rarely warm or illuminating. The entertainment it offers is chiefly for coterie professionals, tired of the banal and of insufficient spiritual energy to create new values. At best, Cocteau is a kind of ultra-sophisticated decorator whose constant alertness and intelligence made excellent publicity on behalf of composers like Milhaud, Auric, Poulenc, painters like de Chirico and Picasso and certainly—generally minor—poets and novelists.

The Infernal Machine is an occasionally deft literary exercise of a kind frequently indulged in by French literati—the rewriting and "modernization" of classic themes—in this instance, the story of King Oedipus. Though it has a few of the amusing conceits that are to be expected of a bright Parisian poetaster, it has as much valid life as a conservatory student's fugue in the manner of Bach or an Oxford don's tragedy in the mode of Seneca.

—*NR*, 5 July '48

HOT ICE

Have you heard the pleasant anecdote they tell about Virgil Thomson? It seems that, for all his knowledge of the musical theatre, Thomson had never seen a performance of Gounod's *Faust* till his professional duties as music critic for the New York *Herald Tribune* made that experience inevitable. Thomson's review was a rave: he had discovered a masterpiece!

I am in somewhat the same position in regard to the ice show. For most of my colleagues it is a routine affair, a banality. Having seen only one such spectacle before—a soggy performance in Los Angeles—the show at the Center Theatre (*Howdy, Mr. Ice*) proved an enchantment. I shouted my enthusiasm as if I had come upon an utterly new field of entertainment.

Perhaps it is a good thing that a novice like myself should report in all innocence what thousands upon thousands of spectators have been enjoying for many seasons with no concern for what the sages of the typewriter have had to say about their pastime. It occurs to me that many professional students of the theatre are by this time incapable of appreciating the beauties of the ice show. Their eyes have been dimmed, their senses dulled, by the flatfootedness of the naturalistic drama, the airlessness of musical comedy, the constriction of unending streams of prosy dialogue.

I am reminded in this connection of Clive Bell's suggestion that candidates for art criticism ought to be asked to write pieces on familiar objects, like tables, chairs, lamps, door knobs, before they are permitted to discuss sculpture and painting. How can one judge the performance of a play by Shakespeare if one cannot capture the quality of pleasure in an entertainment on ice?

Many of the ice-show numbers are old vaudeville acts—perennially charming and funny—that acquire a new dimension by virtue of the ice skate. It is a dimension of speed and the special levitation that skates give to the human form. The excellence of the skating itself, however, is not what marks the theatrical fun we feel in seeing the show with the detestable name at the Center Theatre. That is an athletic skill, and as we watch the performance we tend to grow less interested in the technique as such.

For this reason the American Olympic star Eileen Seigh, who is no more than a top-notch skater, entranced me less than the Austrian clown Freddie Trenkler. Through his skates, the clown gives wings to his genial impishness. He is no longer earthbound: he races, he soars, he flies, he makes fantastic appearances and disappearances. The skate at the ice show is the comedians' and dancers' magic carpet.

Skippy Baxter, whose face is as finely edged as his skates, dances in ballets that are hardly more trite than many we see in more sanctified areas. Besides the liberating grace of his velocity and the sudden thrill of his triple turns in the air, there is in his work an additional "musical" satisfaction derived from the alternation of the silken silence of dreamlike gliding through space with smart metallic punctuation of the blade as it clicks on the ice to bring us back to the reality of the theatre.

When the choreographer employs imagery that might be likened to a perfume ad with pink-gowned ladies in the lilting ballroom embrace of gentlemen in stylized full dress, the surface of the floor seems to vanish and the dancers to be transported into that realm of black-velvet sheen that makes the wish of all luxury advertisements come true. When a typically old-fashioned number—about the glory of our forty-eight states—is put on skates, the dash and danger involved in the accomplishment of difficult staging (the element of danger is almost as necessary to the theatre as the sports) justify the number's joyous boast.

Part of the show's splendor is the high, wide and handsome theatre, the skating girls' conspicuously fine legs (they're not as lumpishly muscular as the legs of ballet girls tend to become), the exceedingly good-looking juvenile leads—Harrison Thompson and Rudy Richards—the possibility of an occasional spill, the enormous curved stage, the cool atmosphere and the low prices.

—*NR*, 12 July '48

KAY THOMPSON

In the twenties, Gilbert Seldes wrote a book on what he called the "seven lively arts." Some of us were inclined to scoff at his learned lucubrations on lowbrow amusements. We were wrong. If we show no regard for the muses' poor relations, we shall never truly know the family itself.

Kay Thompson was a sensation at the costly Le Directoire night club all season and is now wowing them at the Blackstone in Chicago. She will be equally successful throughout the country. For she is quite literally a "brief and abstract chronicle" of her time. She is a consummate performer. She deserves study.

Do not expect me, however, to follow this statement with a report on the amount and quality of the laughter she provokes. She convulses her audiences—she is greatly aided in this by the presence of the Williams Brothers, a remarkable quartet of bright zanies—but, without putting too fine a point on it, she terrified me. *Sliced Steel* would be a fitting title for her act.

Shortly after I saw Miss Thompson I had to ask the lady who invited me to Le Directoire what the Thompson numbers were about: I had forgotten the words, or rather I barely grasped them, as the performer shot them at us. When Groucho Marx, Fred Allen or even Ethel Merman are called funny, we refer to their material as well as to the manner of its delivery. With Kay Thompson, the manner is all.

One number has to do with the varieties of entertainment that constitute show business. Parodies of burlesque, opera and Noel Cowardish comedy are interpolated. I cannot affirm that any of these were particularly brilliant in execution or content. Another number was a ballad of a Brooklyn floozy that may have been wicked after the fashion of night-club lore, but my memory retains no single gem of epigrammatic buffoonery.

Kay Thompson has a long, narrow head topped by corn-colored hair drawn tightly behind it to emphasize its sharp, incisive lines. Her skin is handsomely burnished by a superb cosmetic job which appears to cover a rather tough epidermis. Her long, lean frame describes a swift, metallic descent to the free points of her high-heeled footgear. This amazing shaft of energy, which resembles a bladelike instrument rather than a body, is accentuated by the shimmering material of her jersey blouse and a pair of ultra-chic black slacks. The waist is as trim as a delicately hard machine part. The effect of this costume is not masculine; it suggests the feminine with a deftly epicene touch.

The approach to the audience is erect and direct with a kind of horizontal thrust like a lightning-fast projectile. The performer hits us like a piston—unyielding, merciless, clean, as if with a series of impersonal, incessant, rhythmically even jabs. There is an ineffable elegance in the operation. There is punishment in this pleasure, but it is all so neatly done that we cannot protest; we can only admire. Efficiency is the ultimate beauty of our society.

Miss Thompson punctuates her numbers by a special glancing slap of her hands. That slap seems at once to conclude the different parts of her act, to polish off her audience, to give the signal for applause. We respond like educated robots. The Williams boys pant, writhe, grimace and grin in what is at once thorough appreciation and calculated mockery of the star. They remind me somehow of the serpents in the Laocoön (only they are college-boy types), while the central figure around whom they twist remains blithe and unaffected. A faint perspiration like an expensive dew glimmers on the lady's intelligent brow and smiling, superior lip.

Kay Thompson's act has the gayety of an electric shock. No lush store beauty she. No sentimental curved doll; no dished-up sexpot. She is far too up-to-date for that. As we are about to conjecture what her appeal might be, she reminds us with acid humor that it isn't the traditional animal allure. Whatever her origin, Kay Thompson is the American pioneer woman become a precision machine of entertainment—all will, energy, shrewdness and speed. She is a streamlined abstraction designed to please the prosperous, '48-model American male, and to serve as a wise fool for his female counterpart. Kay Thompson knows better than anyone what she's doing and where she's going. She makes me a little sad.

—*NR*, 19 July '48

A PRODUCER

I began reading Arthur Hopkins little series of papers on the theatre, *Reference Point* (Samuel French; $2.50), with a slight impulse to quarrel with him. I ended with a great measure of admiration.

The admiration transcends my pleasure in the excellent things Hopkins has to say about the theatre, though the book is replete with memorable aphorisms. It is an admiration for the spirit of the man—a spirit now all but extinct, not only on Broadway but generally in American life.

The producer today is, all too frequently, not even an honest dilettante. He is usually an ignorant hanger-on who caught a free ride on the merry-go-round which the theatre became during the war. In these years, the producer was no longer a man who wed himself to the theatre for better or worse, a man who had paid court to it through many years of apprenticeship; he was only a man who believed he could make a good thing on the basis of a lucky break, a pick-up affair. Producing plays was no longer a profession, but a racket.

The older generation of producers, of which Arthur Hopkins is one of the few remaining, were an altogether different breed. Even when they were not artists themselves, they were genuine show people with an enthusiasm for their work, a kind of imaginative largesse, a rough and ready quixoticism, which made them true personalities and fit companions for the artists of the stage.

As a commercial producer—without the aid of subscription audiences, guaranteed subsidies of any kind or advance critical blurbs—Arthur Hopkins, a recruit from journalism and vaudeville, came to a theatre that had fallen into a style provincialism and gave it a new life. He produced Tolstoy's *Living Corpse* (*Redemption*); a season of Ibsen with Nazimova; an interesting Danish play, *The Deluge*, which failed twice but brought Pauline Lord to New York; Gorky's *Lower Depths*, also twice tried and both times unsuccessful; *Richard III*; *The Jest*; *Hamlet* with John Barrymore; *What Price Glory?*; *Anna Christie*. Under Hopkins' management, Robert Edmond Jones, one of the few authentic scenic artists of the American stage, did his first important work.

I go into this ancient history (theatrically the early twenties seem eons away) because very little is remembered in the American theatre. This failure of memory—which is an indifference to everything that does not produce the immediate buck—is one of the reasons why, despite the never failing flow of talent onto our stage, so little of value is ever built in our theatre, so little remains. We are forever beginning over again from the first step.

Such people as Hopkins, however, are themselves a little to blame for this. He who speaks so beautifully of the past, whose tribute to the vaudevillians is as sound as it is touching, emphasizes "feeling," "inspiration" and other such intangibles above everything else, and speaks almost contemptuously of craft and stage technique. This is destructive doctrine. It represents the "mystic's" (or amateur's) negligence of means. It is a confusion that mistakes the small change of trivial effects and petty tricks for the real technique that helps "love"—rightly stressed by Hopkins—to function.

As long as consciousness in the theatre is regarded as dross, as long as all discipline, method and organization are held to be fruitless, and only "genius" and other God-given virtues are dutifully prayed for, so long will the American theatre continue to deteriorate. Without the "religious" (inspirational) element, there can be no ultimate value in art; with nothing but a trust in this element, there can be neither religion nor art.

Hopkins' sensibility is superior to his mind. Too many in the theatre today have substituted shrewdness for mind and possess only as much sensibility as will pay. My hat is off and my gratitude profound to the American producer who, in 1948, writes in all sincerity, "There is a great difference between feeling that a work must be right and that it must succeed. If success had been the goal, little of the world's art would have been created." All honor to Arthur Hopkins!

—*NR*, 26 July '48

TRYOUT

It was a sad day for the theatre when the populace began to break up into disparate units, some of which might fall into the special category known as the theatre audience. Ideally, there should be no such thing as a theatre public distinguishable from the community at large. The theatre should be a function in which everyone has a part, just as all members of a tribe presumably share a common bond in primitive ritual. We may read the symptoms of the theatre's disease today in the composition and attitude of its audiences.

Two weeks ago I was persuaded to go out of town to see the tryout of a new play. What made the strongest impression on me was the audience on the fourth night of the suburban run. Since this play was being given its first airing in a spot only one hour from New York, the theatre was packed with professionals. A worse audience can hardly be imagined.

The assemblage was bad not because of stupidity, but because it was too interested—in the wrong things. It was so aware of everything that might make the play a commodity that it could not possibly be aware of what might make it a play.

There were prospective publishers; the backers and their representatives; agents for the various participants in the production; producers who had turned the play down; the director's friends, supporters and slanderers; people who hoped the play would prove a hit and those who prayed for a flop; people who wanted to boast they had seen it first; people who were eager to report what some people would say about it—experts all.

An audience aware of the importance of its own opinion can be dangerous. An audience that seeks above all to have an opinion—and to parade it—is a menace. The audience that believes that one goes to the theatre to form an opinion—that opinion is what the theatre aims to create—is destructive of all real values in the theatre even when its opinion is favorable. The theatre is a place for experience rather than for judgment. An audience's merit is its capacity to feel rather than its disposition to hold court.

What was terrible about the audience I describe—to a great degree it was very like most of our first-night audiences—was that it reflected the condition of our theatre. We are all in the position of trying to divide one small loaf of bread among a thousand hungry men. We are living in the theatre under an economy of scarcity. Any production—however modest—becomes a monstrous enterprise, a trial in which verdicts of life or death are pronounced.

To produce a flop in the New York theatre is no longer an unpleasant incident; it is a disaster. The atmosphere of bonanza or bust corrupts everybody: producers, writers, actors, critics, audiences. Up to 1929, when each of our reputable producers could present four plays a season and be satisfied to have one of them a success, work was done in a sane state of mind.

In such circumstances, a producer might be as proud of some of his failures as of his successes. O'Neill could write *Gold*, *Diff'rent*, *The Straw*, *The First Man* (all failures) at almost the same time as the successful *Anna Christie*. Critics were as respectful of a play like Elmer Rice's non-profitable *The Adding Machine* as they were of the same author's smash hit, *Counsellor-at-Law*. Audiences might be disappointed with a poor play, but it did not make them vindictive. Writers and producers were granted the privilege of error without disgrace.

When the orchestra becomes an arena of mortal combat where parasites howl ferociously as they make their bets on the outcome, the theatre is moribund and, by contagion, renders even average audiences parasitically "professional" and thus unworthy of a vigorous theatre. "When joy goes out of the theatre," says Arthur Hopkins, "it is no place to be."

—*NR*, 2 Aug. '48

THE UNDERGROUND

"All men and beasts, eagles and quails, horses, stags, geese, spiders, silent fish that inhabit the waves, starfish from the sea and creatures invisible to the eye, all life completing the dreary round imposed on it has died out at last...."

These are the opening lines of a play that the young poet, Treplev, in Chekhov's *The Seagull* presents to an audience that includes a famous actress and a successful novelist. They don't like it; and the author isn't sure of it himself. He demands new forms for the theatre, but he is still groping. However, the most intelligent member of his audience, Dr. Dorn, is understanding. He calls the boy's work vivid and deeply affecting. "It is only a pity that he has no definite object in view. He creates impressions...and one cannot go far on impressions alone."

I thought of all this when I saw "the interplayers" do e.e. cummings' *him* down at the Provincetown Playhouse. The reaction of the New York drama critics in 1928 when *him* was first produced was very much like that of the highly esteemed professionals at Treplev's play. "What decadent rubbish is this!" Treplev's mother exclaims; our critics were far less polite.

Wasn't it an absurd idea for a young man to write a play about the world's death in Russia at the end of the nineteenth century? And what did cummings mean by writing a raucously orchestrated Bronx cheer at the peak of our prosperity? If one was to express despair—and a certain note of gloom went very well with the cushy Harding-Coolidge era—one ought at least to be serious and dignified about it. There's nothing in the world so exasperating as a gaudy hysteria.

Those who had been to Paris in the twenties and had seen the Cocteau ballets, or those who had read Eliot, Joyce and Aragon, defended cummings. Yet even the writers who supported *him* against the philistines were not in a position at that time to appreciate the play's full import. *him* is essentially a lyric outcry; most of its champions thought it funny.

Rebellion in the twenties reared its head in comparative comfort. The middle class was sufficiently undisturbed to make a game of being disturbed. If a Greenwich Village or left-bank poet felt impelled to give vent to ecstatic gibberish he might go ahead and do so in specially prepared corners that the well-to-do were still willing to provide their poor neighbors, the artists—places like the Provincetown Playhouse for example. Not today! Today no one will even take the trouble to get sore about cummings' play. The production of 1928 was opulent compared to tile bareness of the present one. For if the Provincetown was then the theatre's back alley, today it has become its underground.

him is a coin with two faces: one, that of the poet himself; the other, the face of the world as the poet sees it. The world is an obscene freak show masking a dark realm of brutal hunger that obtrudes only as a ghoulish vision. The poet is uncertain of his own identity. Is he what he appears or what he feels himself to be? He cannot make himself part of the world which is the accepted "reality" of the successful. To live outside of "reality" is torture. The idea "I am an Artist, I am a Man, I am a Failure" obsesses him. The healthy love of his girl is poisoned by this obsession: it leads him to thoughts of suicide. (Treplev in *The Seagull* kills himself, as did Hart Crane, the outstanding poet of cummings' generation.)

After a trip to Paris where the poet encounters a tearful Babbitt suffering very much as he himself does—the frustration of the American businessman and the poet being in the end not very dissimilar—the poet experiences a kind of renewal of spirit. The artist, man, failure, he realizes *"must proceed."* He no longer believes that beauty and the truth are the same. He is now interested above all in finding the truth. The play actually ends on a hopeful note.

cummings did not find the truth in the thirties, though others were sure *they* had. The present period of prosperous doldrums is a time in which the respectable of all classes either will not countenance pessimism of any kind or receive it with indifference, a time also in which even the rebellious have little hope. So MacDougal Street where *him* is being played is now harsh without glamor, the Provincetown Playhouse no longer a center of cheerful obstreperousness but a grimy shed. Here young actors of a theatre world bankrupt with success doggedly proceed before a neighborhood audience of simple folk and those who, like cummings' poet, feel themselves to be artists, men, failures. Yet I feel a truth in their inglorious underground that is somehow more inspiring than the air-conditioned stuffiness uptown where no one would dream of reviving so drunken or so personal a play.

—*NR*, 9 Aug. '48

PLAYS FROM PARIS

If Albert Camus' two plays *Caligula* and *Cross Purpose* (New Directions; $3) were staged in America, I feel fairly certain that the greater part of the public and the press would describe them as cruel and senseless. Cruel these plays obviously are, since they are woven of murder and death, but they are senseless only from a peculiarly American standpoint. With us, only two kinds of plays are easily understood: the play that aims at nothing but "entertainment"—either through a laugh or a shudder or a smirk—and the propaganda play that teaches us a lesson, such as that race prejudice is wicked or that we all share social responsibility.

In the second category the lesson must be of an affirmative or constructive nature. Hardly any American play is conceivable—except possibly as farce—which might suggest that it is better to be bad than good. When the point of a play is tainted by a negative inference, the American audience will generally find it not only unpleasant but senseless. A play like *A Streetcar Named Desire*, for example, pleases Broadway because it is strong (frank, racy, violent) entertainment, but only a minority sees any sense ("lesson") in it, and of this minority many dislike it because they believe its sense to be of a destructive kind.

One reason for this is that Americans rarely talk of art—particularly a play—as a natural outgrowth of a particular environment. They think of a play as something willed by its author. What reason would a man have to will something unpleasant and discouraging unless he were either perverse or crazy?

The French are different. They accept everything they have experienced—including the vile—as part of the fullness of life which they find healthy to contemplate consciously and overtly. When the First World War was over and some of the younger generation realized that the great holocaust had been a contradiction to everything they had been brought up to respect as culture, religion, civilization, they defied culture, religion and civilization with the nonsense of Dadaism. Since the upright world, the Dadaists said, is a malevolent sham, our revenge and pleasure shall be to turn that world upside down.

Though dazed and shocked, the Frenchman after 1918 still preserved a few old-time illusions. Dadaism struck the ordinary Frenchman as a sickness of youth. For all its terrifying grimaces, Dadaism was still fun. There was nothing funny to any Frenchman in the upheaval of the Second World War. Less bloody for the French than the previous war, the psychological impact of the second war was far greater. The younger generation today—of which Albert Camus is one of the most articulate voices—is in no mood for kidding.

Caligula and *Cross Purpose* are reflections of a state of mind that the French public shares with the author. The Roman emperor commits outrageous crimes in the first of these plays in response to the ferocious absurdity of the universe. "If the Treasury has paramount importance, life has none....Since money is the only thing that counts, men should set no value in their lives or anyone else's." Scorn is Caligula's only consolation, and the honest poet in the play—a victim of Caligula's cruelty—is so aware of the causes for the evil in the Emperor that he "can never, never again take anybody's side."

In *Cross Purpose* we are introduced into an atmosphere (somewhere in "Central Europe") in which crime is committed from "force of habit"; a mother kills her long-absent son with the aid of her daughter. This is due to a "misunderstanding": men have forgotten to understand and to proclaim that they are all brothers. Humanity only has a choice between "the mindless happiness of stones" and death; wisdom consists in realizing that "beyond the frontiers of pain lies a splendid, sterile happiness."

Horrible? Yes, but this is what a whole generation has been forced to feel. This exists. Salvation can come only from facing the facts, facing the facts before the salve of a solution is found. It is because Camus is a moralist that he has written these "immoral" plays. Because he is a humanist, a "shameful tenderness" emerges from them. Because he is a Frenchman, *Caligula* is written with an inflamed rhetoric that reminds one of Racine, and *Cross Purpose* with the grave intensity of a theatric Pascal. We need hardly ask ourselves for the moment whether these plays are "good;" it is enough that they are fascinating.

—*NR*, 16 Aug. '48

MORE FRENCH PLAYS

Sad news is the prophet's stock-in-trade. The prophetic spirit is not strong in France, but the moralist's mind, which is akin to it, has always flourished there Rabelais, Montaigne, La Rouchefoucauld, Pascal, Molière, Diderot, Baudelaire—moralists all. Virtue is always the moralist's preoccupation; for this reason sin plays a large role in his thinking. The commercial French stage is frequently frivolous; the serious French theatre—since 1942 particularly—is sinful.

The "decadent" note in the contemporary French theatre is an aspect of its moral preoccupation. A carefree comedy like *Mister Roberts* is actually more wicked than a frightful parable like Camus' *Caligula*. For while the pure entertainment in our typical American comedy shows no awareness of a moral problem, the deliberate terror in Camus' tragedy is wholly obsessed by it. The wretched blasphemer is always closer to God than the lighthearted philistine. A whole group of recent French plays may be listed as the poetics of exasperation.

Americans can learn a good deal from a study of these new plays, not only by what they contain in themselves but by what they reveal by contrast. There are two striking characteristics to be observed in the outstanding examples of the contemporary French drama. First, they are dramatizations of moods and ideas rather than stories. The mood, as I indicated in my article on Camus' plays, tends toward a fierce concern with the question of action in the face of all-encompassing evil. Because this concern is engendered not so much by the dramatists' experience of a single example of evil as by a growing sense that all the springs of life have been poisoned, the plays they write make general rather than specific points. The French are now writing what might be termed "philosophical" rather than realistic or psychological plays.

The philosophical play does not grow out of observation but out of reflection. The immediate reality that inspires the playwright is not dramatized; an indirect symbol is presented. Hence the frequent use of classic plots to convey contemporary significance: Sartre's *The Flies,* Anouilh's *Antigone*, Camus' *Caligula*.

There is something schematic and abstract in the new French plays, even when the subject is contemporary, as in Sartre's *No Exit* or Camus' *Cross Purpose*. The most realistic of these plays— Sartre's *The Respectful Prostitute* and his forthcoming *Soiled Hands*—though melodramatic in plot structure, are rigidly bound within an intellectual

pattern. Americans, more at home with concrete cases than with general conceptions, tend to respond to the plays' stories rather than to their ideas.

The second characteristic of the new French drama is the use of language as a dramatic substance in itself. With us, dialogue is employed chiefly as the conveyor of action with subsidiary functions as a source of color and delineation. The French playwright builds mood, meaning, tension and excitement through language as such. This is evident in *The Flies*, in *Caligula*, and particularly in Jean Genet's one-act play, *The Maids*, which was done in New York for several performances last spring by an organization calling itself The Poet's Theatre. Eloquence and rhetoric—the old-fashioned tirade which may be described as a vehement aria—serve as an instrument of dramatic progression. Such a use of speech ordinarily strikes the American theatregoer as florid and undramatic, and, when passion is added, as either hysterical or hammy.

The Maids is, in a way, the most representative of the plays under discussion. I saw it in Paris a year ago as well as at the special New York performance. I found neither the French nor the American production satisfactory. The difficulty in doing this play is that while it appears to be a realistic piece about two servant girls suffering from a consuming envy of their depraved and wealthy mistress—to the point where they kill themselves because they fail to kill her—it is actually a poetic drama of a kind that our audiences would immediately label "morbid. "

The two girls speak a prose that glows with incandescent hate, demanding the delivery of a Rachel in a play like Racine's *Phèdre*. As realism, *The Maids* is nonsense: the motivation for the girls' hate in everyday terms is insufficient, its degree, monstrous. What is worse, the interpretation to be given the play's symbolism is not at all obvious.

I have heard a critical discussion of *The Maids* in psychoanalytic terms: the love-hate of the oppressed for the oppressor. It might also be viewed as a social allegory: the oppressed unable to destroy their oppressors must destroy themselves. With either interpretation—and I am sure there are others—we are brought back to the question of content.

The "decadent" French drama today is explosive. Heavy with guilt, resentment, self-loathing, yearning for deliverance through destruction, self-immolation, expiation, sacrifice or heroic affirmation, it is an expression of the martyrdom of the French middle-class conscience after the degradation of Munich, the shame of defeat, the conflict between collaborator and resistant, the terrible dichotomy—coupled with impotence—that tears at the country's vitals to this day.

The moral and psychological situation in France is luridly highlighted by the intense level of French consciousness, but that does not imply that this situation is unique. Let us not flatter ourselves that the absence of such plays on our stage is a sign of our moral superiority. A theatre where pessimism is almost completely taboo does not necessarily bespeak a wholesome condition either in the theatre or in the civilization of which it is a part.

The final value of a study of these French plays—none of which is actually more talented than the best we have to offer—is that by understanding them in relation to ours we may be stimulated to seek for greater scope in both the matter and the means of our own theatre practice.

—*NR*, 23 Aug. '48

AULD LANG SYNE

I sometimes imagine that there are no theatregoers over 30. It is true that one occasionally sees people at the theatre who might be old enough to remember Richard Mansfield and the New York of *Life with Father*, but generally I have the feeling that even these people have no memory or affection for any play earlier than *The Glass Menagerie*.

Who but George Jean Nathan or an antiquarian can tell you anything about Bronson Howard,

Clyde Fitch, William Vaughn Moody or Augustus Thomas? Yet these names were once more imposing than those of Maxwell Anderson, S. N. Behrman, Robert Sherwood or Elmer Rice. How many of the audiences that flocked to dote on Ingrid Bergman in *Joan of Lorraine* could tell you anything about Margaret Anglin, Marjorie Rambeau, Margaret Lawrence?

Theatrical opinions consist mostly of chitchat and publicity; they are rarely challenged for more than a season. We have no repertory theatres where the old successes may be reconsidered. The American theatre is always in the process of killing its past. New movies are the gravestones we build over our old plays.

I say all this because last week I attended a showing of Langdon Mitchell's *The New York Idea*, a Broadway success of 1906, given by the group known as On-Stage. In presenting "a cavalcade of great American hits" ranging from Royall Tyler's *The Contrast* (the first American comedy) to *Peg O' My Heart* and *The Bat* in a Fifth Avenue auditorium hardly bigger than your sitting-room, On-Stage is performing a real service.

The original company of *The New York Idea* included Mrs. Fiske, Emily Stevens, George Arliss and Dudley Digges. They were all exciting stage personalities. The show must have been a treat not "for their time," as fools put it, but for any time. Vividness, sparkle, address, are always contemporary. But see if you can list a company today that would match the original cast.

I do not mean that we have no actors now as gifted as those of 1906, but how many young people on our stage at present can command the particular style required for this sort of comedy of manners? When *Lady Windemere's Fan* was done here two seasons ago, there were not more than two or three people in the play who were better than adequate—and they were all English.

In Paris you can still see nineteenth-century war horses—plays like those of Labiche, Augier, Pailleron, the younger Dumas—done in a manner that gives one a sense of their period and of their savor. With us the equivalents of such plays are either never done at all or done as a kind of joke in which we are invited to enjoy our superiority over the past.

As a matter of fact, *The New York Idea* is a frequently witty, literate, urbane stage piece with things to say about American women, marriage and divorce that are not as dated as you might suppose. Of course, it shows its age—why shouldn't it?—but its age lends it a certain charm to which a company of actors as deft as Ina Claire could give a precious glow.

The reason it would be difficult to assemble a company with the bright delivery, grace, humor, attractiveness and poise of an Ina Claire is not that such talent is always rare or that present social conditions do not foster these qualities, but that our stage today has lost the means of *training* people to approximate them. A haphazard theatre cannot perpetuate the feeling for tradition or style.

—*NR*, 30 Aug. '48

CREATION: OLD AND NEW

You might not have guessed it from reading the papers, but the outstanding event of the theatrical season—apart from *A Streetcar Named Desire*—was the appearance of the Habimah company from Palestine in four productions from their eighty-five play repertory.

This was not the Habimah's first visit to the United States. They gave a similar series of plays in 1926. Most playgoers today do not appear to have seen the company at that time. The company was not a better one then (there have been very few changes in the intervening years), but the critical response was more eagerly aware. The reason for this is that the theatre was more alive then than it is today. It was loved for itself. It was not regarded as a milestone on the road to Hollywood.

The Habimah has no actor as glamorous or talented as Laurence Olivier and few that are equal to Ralph Richardson, but the company as a whole

is probably superior to that of the Old Vic in its 1946 season here. However, the excellence of individual actors in the Habimah company is not the salient feature of its importance. What distinguishes the Habimah from practically every company we have seen for years is that it is not merely a collection of actors but a real theatre.

A real theatre is a united collective which develops through a common aim toward a unified achievement. A real theatre is an artistic whole composed of strong separate elements: actors, dramatists, designers, etc., pursuing a course of work as organic and coherent as the work of an individual artist. Just as we can speak of entities named Wagner, Dostoyevsky, Shaw, which represent bodies of thought, feeling, and even epochs as much as they do men, so do we speak of the Moscow Art Theatre, the theatre of Max Reinhardt, the Habimah.

Two forces produced the Habimah. On the one hand, it rose from the nationalistic desire on the part of a group of young Russian, Polish, Lithuanian Jews to form a theatrical unit in which the ancient Hebrew tongue would be used as a living language and cultural medium: on the other, it drew its theatrical inspiration from the Moscow Art Theatre itself in the period that followed the Russian revolution of October 1917. The young men and women who were to constitute the Habimah flocked to Moscow in 1918-19 as the natural Mecca for liberated East European Jews of that era as well as for all idealistic theatrical aspirants.

The director of the Moscow Art Theatre—Stanislavsky—put these people into the hands of his foremost pupil: Vachtangov, a Russian of Armenian lineage and a non-Jew, was no mere disciple but an innovator. His work does not simply continue that of Stanislavsky but marks a new departure. It is exemplified by the Habimah's production of *The Dybbuk* (begun in 1920 and first produced in 1922) and the studio production of *The Princess Turendot* (also completed in 1922), which gave birth to what became the new Vachtangov Theatre—to this day a vital factor in the Soviet theatre world.

Vachtangov died in 1922. The Habimah, however, had taken shape and was able to continue after his death under the guidance of other directors, though it never entirely lost the Vachtangov imprint. The Habimah left Moscow in 1925 for a world tour and in 1928 turned to its natural destination—Palestine. It has flourished there, built its own theatre in Tel-Aviv, established its own studio for the training of actors, added to its repertory modern and classic plays both foreign and native Palestinian. It has produced—besides the plays seen in New York—the work of Bernard Shaw, Romain Rolland, Shakespeare, Schiller, Galsworthy, Maugham, Irwin Shaw, etc.

What was the character of Vachtangov's style? It sought to give a specifically theatrical form to the material it dealt with. This is true, of course, of all genuine stage direction if we take my definition in its general sense, but in this instance we ought both to stress the word "theatrical" and reemphasize the word "form." With such a director as Stanislavsky the form sought was related to a naturalistic conception in the historical and literal sense. In other words, while Stanislavsky knew that Shakespeare and Chekhov were not the same kind of dramatist and could not be produced so that they would look or sound alike, fundamentally he sought for the same kind of reality in both. The result was that in *Julius Caesar* the people behaved "naturally" as Romans, statesmen, soldiers, etc., as in *The Seagull* they behaved "naturally" as Russians, poets, country doctors, etc.

For Vachtangov the question would be: Is there a way of giving what is specifically Shakespearean—the color, melody, language, and basic rhythm—a tangible form for the theatre? Furthermore, is it possible to show not only what is true to Shakespeare's vision of life but to our theatre's interpretation and "opinion" of that way of life? When such a form is found, the result does not simply represent the creation of a different kind of person—as a Roman senator is different from a Russian landowner—but the difference between a real person and a special theatrical creation, which, in a sense, is no "person" at all.

This is the clue to the much disputed "stylization" that is the most striking feature of the Habimah's *Dybbuk*. Stylization by itself does not bespeak a content. What one has to determine in a conspicuously stylized production is the particular significance of the stylization: what aim it serves, what is being said through it that could not otherwise be said.

This exposition is intended for the benefit of those who, when they go to *The Dybbuk*, suppose either that the weird phantoms they see in it are what Jews of olden times were actually like or complain that the acting is too "exaggerated." The Habimah production of *The Dybbuk* must have been a surprise even to its author. For though the story deals with a mystical sect—The Chassids— and is based on a legend, the characters are treated with a special imaginativeness, and what Vachtangov and the members of the Habimah company—as artists of post-Czarist Russia—saw in the play was a phantasmagoria of creatures who by 1920 had become gargoyles and spectres of a bygone civilization. The old Ghetto was viewed as a half world in which the rich were as grotesque as the beggars they bred. A kind of aesthetic detachment mounting from amusement to horrified awe—evidence of a basic rejection—is the chief trait of the production's point of view.

All this is conveyed through fascinating detail in which voices, mask-like make-ups, distorted movement, abstract settings are integrated into a brilliant entity the like of which may be seen in the theatre only once or twice in a generation.

The three other Habimah productions are inspired by a kindred approach. They are far less original but extremely interesting nonetheless. In *David's Crown*, by Calderón, a Greco-Egyptian visual pattern is employed. The production contains a memorable rape scene and a striking bit of staging in a banquet scene among David's murderously ambitious sons. In *The Golem*, Aaron Meskin as the clay monster made by a rabbi of medieval Prague to avenge the oppressed Jews gives perhaps the best individual performance of the Habimah season: pathetic and almost charming at the same time. The Habimah's *Oedipus Rex* recently staged by the English director Tyrone Guthrie, is notable for its comparative simplicity and quiet gravity. Guthrie chose to tell the violent story of the unfortunate king who slew his father and married his mother like an ancient tale seen through a long vista of tradition and philosophic contemplation. It is an unromantic *Oedipus* (as contrasted with that of the Old Vic), comparatively undynamic. Yet it has its own justification and beauty, sustained as it is by a reasoned and dignified conception.

One of the things to be specially remarked about the Habimah's productions is that they bring back to the stage the kind of theatre in which music and movement, visual interest and poetry are envisaged as parts of a dramatic whole. Our audiences—though they may not know it, since they are unconscious of their own needs—really crave such theatre, an appetite which they are able to satisfy only with musical comedy.

When I write about the theatre, I generally dwell on the origin and significance of its productions in terms of the world that fostered them and the audience they are addressed to. The same is true of what I have to say about painting. If we keep thinking of the arts as just a matter of diversion arbitrarily conceived to fulfill the needs of our leisure, we will never know anything about them.

In the recent and constantly raging controversy about old and contemporary art, there is always a tendency for those shocked by what they consider the excesses and disabilities of the modern artist to talk as if he was a perverse creature who suddenly took it into his head to paint disturbing or incomprehensible objects. (I should like to point out in passing that it is a physical impossibility not to paint any object at all, since even a pot of paint hurled at a canvas would produce an effect which, without being art, would still have to be defined as an object!) The truth is that most people who proclaim a priori that modern art is a monstrous mistake rarely understand or feel very much about the kind of art they profess to adore.

To say that a Raphael madonna is altogether clear to you because you recognize her beauty while you rear in consternation at the sight of one of Picasso's misbegotten ladies is really an admission that you are not looking at paintings at all but amusing yourself with a reputable hobby. The fact is that it is not at all easy to comprehend the Raphael madonna, while the counterpart of the Picasso distortion may be seen at almost every street corner!

What I want to know as I look at the Raphael madonna is not whether she is pretty—even if she is, it is no great matter to me, since far prettier ladies are much closer at hand! What I want to know is why Raphael painted her as he did, what world gave her birth, what needs and what forces in the painter, his patron, his admirers were released and satisfied by such painting. This is not a simple thing to discover in a hasty glance. For while I know Picasso's world intimately—it is more or less my own—Raphael's world is fairly remote. In a sense Raphael's "realism" (representationalism) is a stylization for which I need some preparation, while Picasso's ultra-modernism in its closeness to the contemporary scene is a kind of "realism."

When we learn really to see paintings, we shall find that we are not actually concerned with "pictures" as such—for if we were, we should not care much about our preference for one picture to another—but with the experience or "world" that the painting conveys. When this happens—and it is only at this point that we can be said to have contact with art (any art)—we shall understand what distinguishes the old creation from the new.

Is contemporary art more "fantastic" than what we call the classic? A picture like Giovanni di Paolo's sea piece from the life of Saint Clare (15th Century) is as "wild" as anything ever painted by Van Gogh or Chagall! If there is painful preoccupation with the horrors of death in many moderns, we find the same in such work as Carpaccio's *The Burial of Christ*. If there are duds in the modern exhibitions, you find them too in the Berlin museum pieces—even among the Botticellis and the Rembrandts.

There are differences between the older art and ours. They do not consist, however, in the contrast between seriousness and frivolity, sanity and madness. Look at Manet's *The Greenhouse* (among the Berlin paintings) and a very important difference will strike you at once. It can be described in terms of technique, but the technical difference is the surface sign of the real change. The older artists were much more conscious of the world as a whole—of the social and religious as well as physical dimension of the universe which contained them. Our modern artists—since 1870, let us say—are much more alive to sensation. For this reason you can "move around" more in the world of the older artists. Modern man, it would appear, is being bereft of everything but his senses. If you do not like what you see in modern art— provided you are talking about art and not about some lazy self-indulgence—it is not the modern artist who is to blame but modern life. And if you don't like modern life—look to it!

The recent retrospective exhibition of Pierre Bonnard's painting (1889-1947) at the Museum of Modern Art may provide another lesson in how a series of pictures may be appreciated either for attributes of delectability or for their significance as expression. These pictures are as easy to take pleasure in as a table of fruit, flowers, and wine. In fact they constitute a kind of compendium of the sensuous aspects of French painting. Bonnard learned and borrowed from everybody: Gauguin, Renoir, Redon, Degas, Toulouse-Lautrec. Yet he is a master in his own right. It is worth inquiring in what way he differs from those other men whose work he seems to have absorbed.

There is no tension in Bonnard. His art is unmuscular. It does not have the full-bloodedness of Renoir, the daring savagery of Gauguin, the melancholy delicacy of Redon, the bite of Degas or Toulouse-Lautrec, the brain and balance of Matisse. It is relaxed to the point of deliquescence, it is content to the point of dissoluteness. The pictures seem to be compounded of oil and talcum powder. They seem to have the scent of flesh and toiletries, pastry and perfume, sunlight in ordered gardens. Bonnard's art is not chic like that of Dufy: for the essence of the chic is to avoid dwelling upon that which is enjoyed, and Bonnard's art sinks delightedly into its own comfort. Sensation dominates, but it is neither the peasant's animal sensation nor that of the morbid wastrel, but that of the average well-pleased French bourgeois. Only his horses and dogs sometimes look depraved!

Bonnard is a fine landscapist, but his landscape is the image of the world toward which the good Frenchman always aspires rather than nature itself. It is this France that made foreigners think of the French as soft, although it actually represents a certain health. It is a France that was badly shaken but not quite lost after the First World War and now become a dream, a memory, almost a legend. It is on the whole a rather cozy art. It suggests no ultimates and precludes the notion of either stern depths or exalted heights. Exquisite craftsmanship and taste keep this art free of vulgarity. Within its protected confines it is wonderfully sensitive. This should never be designated great art, but those who despise it are wrong.

—*TRW*, Aug. '48

BRECHT: A GOTHIC PRIMITIVE

"In the bloodiest times there are kind people." This line from Bertolt Brecht's play, *The Caucasian Chalk Circle*, might serve as a rebuttal to what I wrote here lately about some recent French plays. There are important differences, however, between Brecht and the Frenchmen. The first is that the French are dominated by a certain type of acid realism, while the German, no matter how much of a materialist he may be, generally moves toward the idealistic and the didactic. The second and more decisive difference is that the French plays are reflections of a basically middle-class psychology, while Brecht is essentially a revolutionary who identifies himself with the dispossessed.

The Caucasian Chalk Circle is now being given at the Hedgerow Theatre in Moylan, Pennsylvania, as its one hundred and sixty-second production in its twenty-fifth anniversary year. The play was translated by Eric and Maja Bentley, and directed by the former in the intrepid tradition of that institution.

Brecht wrote *The Caucasian Chalk Circle* in 1943 and 1944 during what he once called his "exile in paradise" in Santa Monica, California. The play is one of the last in a series of distinguished dramatic works by a man who is undoubtedly the leading poet of contemporary Germany.

The plot is based on an old Chinese play which in turn was a variant of the Biblical tale of Solomon's judicial stratagem in the case of the two women who claimed the same child. Brecht has transferred the locale of his play to Georgia in the Caucasus. In the Brecht play, the wise judge rules that the poor peasant girl who adopted the child shall retain it in permanent custody instead of its actual mother, the governor's wife, who lost it through selfish negligence. The point of Brecht's play is that the revolutionary mind will bring forth new morality:

> ... What there is shall go to those
>   who are good for it,
> Thus: the children to the motherly,
>   that they prosper.
> The carts to good drivers, that they
>   are well driven.
> And the valley to the waterers, that
>   it bring fruit.

There is a certain nobility here. It is a dangerous quality, for lofty sentiments often lead to low art. There is almost nothing more despicable than official "hope," nothing more distressing than courage displayed as propaganda. The nobility in Brecht's plays is fortunately not a self-conscious demonstration of exalted feeling but a quality immanent in his craftsmanship.

No critic of Brecht's work will fail to associate it with his theory of the Epic Theatre. It relates to Chinese as contrasted to Greek poetics. Epic theatre eschews ordinary illusion and suspense, because it does not seek to stimulate the subjective identification of the spectator with the actor on the stage. The Epic dramatist aims to encourage a certain detachment, a kind of contemplative coolness so that the spectator may take pleasure in his *understanding* of what he sees.

But theory does not concern me. I am convinced that Brecht writes as he does, not so much from a predetermined calculation based on what he believes to be the correct goals for the present revolutionary age as from the dictates of his temperament.

Brecht is a kind of Gothic primitive, in whom a rude simplicity is coupled with a shrewd mentality. There is a humorous canniness in his imagery and observation. ("They even have to have their weeping done for them," one of his characters says of the rich.) There is also a kind of ascetic refinement or leanness of line in his work which may be ascribed with equal justification to either the primitive or the modern aspect of his talent. The final impression is that of a great purity of utterance.

Brecht's theatre verse has inspired some of the best songs of our time—those of Kurt Weill and of Hanns Eisler. The songs and choral comments in *The Caucasian Chalk Circle* contain the essence of Brecht's meaning and the peak of his poetic diction. Whether this is proof of his limitation as a dramatist is, at the moment, difficult to ascertain. For the test of Brecht's effectiveness in the theatre must surely come from his audiences.

Except for *The Threepenny Opera* none of Brecht's plays achieved great popularity in Germany before the war. This may have been due to social as well as to artistic causes. Certainly the Brecht style is not easy to render on the stage by actors and directors schooled in an entirely different mode. In any case, Brecht has never been adequately presented in this country, despite Charles Laughton's contribution to *Galileo* and the remarkable intelligence evident in the present production. I have a feeling, however, that postwar Europe may acclaim Brecht. "Terrible is the temptation of goodness," says the narrator in *The Caucasian Chalk Circle*. It is a maxim emblematic of a force that may counterbalance the evil spirits rampant amid the ruins. The virtue of Brecht's plays is good sense carried to the point of grandeur.

—*NR*, 6 Sept. '48

MORLEY AND COMPANY

*E*dward, *My Son* at the Martin Beck, the season's first smash, is presumably about the ruthless father of a stinker son. I say "presumably," because the play might be more accurately titled *Fun with Robert Morley*.

It traces the progress of a lower middle-class rascal to the state of millionaire scoundrel. Every rotten act he justifies as having been done on behalf of his son. We cannot tell whether he really loves his son or whether he simply exults in what he can do for him. Is he a hapless papa or a hypocrite? Is he a man to be derided or feared? If he is merely a "case" to be understood, what exactly are we to understand? Simply that such men exist?

These are all rhetorical questions, of course, because it is plain that Morley, his co-author Noel Langley, and the producers of the play intended nothing more than a fat part for its star—what many people somewhat enigmatically call "good theatre." It would be silly to complain that *Edward, My Son* doesn't "say" anything or that it does not say the things one might like to hear, for in a very concrete sense the play does not even tell its own story—and isn't meant to.

Arnold Holt, the play's central figure, is supposed to be a powerhouse of ambitious calculation. Does Morley (as actor) suggest such a man or try to? Obviously not. At the end of Scene two, Holt-Morley receives word that his son's operation has been successful; at the same time he hears the passing of the fire engines bound for the bankrupt shop he has set on fire in order to collect the insurance money that is to pay for that operation. The joy over his son's delivery from the danger of remaining a lifelong cripple is indicated with the delight one might evince at hearing about the victory of a team one has bet on, and the pleasure at hearing the fire bells is expressed with a kind of boyish glee. It makes a smart curtain.

This is typical of Morley's manner throughout. His effects have never anything to do with the reality of a given situation; they have to do with a rollicking indifference to all moral and emotional reality. Morley's reality is a form of parlor wit in which we take pleasure precisely because everything but the performance itself is negated or dismissed. When Morley makes love, exercises his villainous will, becomes furious, he does only enough to inform us about the nature of the scene he is playing: in any vital sense, his *acting* is chiefly concerned with the joke he makes apropos of love, will, fury, etc.

Does this mean that Morley plays his part badly? On the contrary, he is excellent in clarity and consistency of intention, in diction and crackling delivery. His visible relish in fulfilling his task—which is, above all, to amuse—is infectious. He is constantly telling his audience, "Don't trouble yourself to look for a meaning in this show. It simply affords me an occasion to be terribly bright—and you a chance to enjoy the spectacle."

Peggy Ashcroft, who plays Holt's long-suffering wife, offers a skillful and subtly graphic stage portrait of feminine decay. *Her* reality—the show's nearest approach to verisimilitude—is mainly for the eye, finely vivid without being moving. Under the circumstances, greater emotional depth might not only prove inappropriate but actually ruin the show.

Though the acting of Morley and Ashcroft generates from different impulses, they manage to merge their styles with that of the entire company, which is almost uniformly good, with Ian Hunter deserving special mention. These English actors know how to speak, how to make themselves figure, how to fill the theatre with a sense of story. Their method consists of disguising an old-time theatricality as latter-day naturalism. On the whole, then, *Edward, My Son* is a theatrical equivalent of a 1914 bestseller, and thus entirely worthy of the "four orchids" of 1948.

Time for Elizabeth, by Norman Krasna and Groucho Marx (already closed), a play about the futility of leisure for the "average" businessman, was only slightly inferior to such plays as *Dear Ruth* and *John Loves Mary*. It was simply a little less big city. If the reviewers hadn't been invited to see it and tickets had been sold at a $2 top on the subway circuit and on the road, it might have had a solid run. There is a large public for such things—every bit as estimable as that which applauds the big hits.

The Ballet Russe de Monte Carlo has added Ruthanna Boris' *Quelques Fleurs* to its repertory. With attractive costumes and sets by Robert Davidson it is as delicately fragrant and glamorous as a French playlet of the 1830's à la de Musset. It is better "theatre" than the theatre ordinarily provides.

—*NR*, 18 Oct. '48

MAN WITH A PROBLEM

It is comforting to realize that Tennessee Williams is not a writer of hits, but a writer with a problem. His problem rises from the conflict between the quality of his sensibility and the objective material of his plots.

In *Summer and Smoke* at the Music Box (written at about the same time as *A Streetcar Named Desire*), Williams appears torn between a character and a theme. The character is observed with delicate sympathy, but the theme—too consciously articulated without being mastered—disturbs both the characterization and the play's dramatic clarity. It remains nevertheless a play whose very faults are interesting.

Alma Winemiller, the daughter of a Mississippi minister and his insane wife, is a spiritually energetic girl in love with her lifelong neighbor, Dr. John Buchanan. The young doctor is attracted by the girl's idealism, but he expresses his tenderness toward her by a harsh insistence on its sexual aspects. Shocked, the girl tries to pit her idealism against the boy's boastful sinfulness. ("You're no gentleman!" she cries—and she is right.) Alma wins the "argument" only when John's father is killed in an accident brought about by John's soiled companions. Now redeemed from his carnal course, John does not turn to his savior Alma, but instead marries a buxom little female of coarser background. Alma, in turn, converted to the doctrine of the senses (reversing the pattern of ladies from Thaïs to Sadie Thompson), now seems prepared to indulge in casual affairs.

One of the springs of Williams' inspiration is his fascination with the opposition between the old Adam which tends to keep us mired in a kind of primitive inertia, and our impulse to transcend it. In *A Streetcar Named Desire* this fascination led him almost unconsciously to a social theme: the "animal" in that play is identified with the "ordinary" American. The naturalistic details of portraiture in *Streetcar* are so right that the audience accepts and enjoys them on their own terms whether or not they follow the author's ideological intention, which, to begin with, is intuitive rather than analytic. In *Summer and Smoke* so much time is given to a conscious exposition of theme that Williams loses the specific sense of his people and to a dangerous extent our concern as spectators.

The thematic base of *Summer and Smoke* is rendered ambiguous by being stated through characters that do not properly embody the forces the play is supposed to pit against each other. Is Alma Winemiller "sexually repressed" because of her overreliance on her spiritual nature? Not really, for she loves John Buchanan with an eagerness and a shyness that are both entirely normal in themselves. That she should be repelled by his crudity is also normal. That she should be presented as the champion of the "soul" and he as advocate for the "flesh" is a confusion that derives from the author's inability to know when he is creating character and when he is interfering with the characters by talking—sometimes a little foolishly—in their stead.

The ancient dispute about the polarity of body and soul is mostly a Puritan obsession and a consequence of the abuse of words induced by faulty religious education. Of the two characters in the play, the man, who rationalizes his promiscuity on intellectual grounds, is surely the more Puritan, one might even go so far as to say the more "repressed" and the less normal. His sexual activity does not strike one as a manifestation of natural exuberance but of moral defiance.

It would have been perfectly proper for Williams to present the situation in this light. In that case the play might have suggested that so many American men are Puritans in revolt against themselves that they drive their women to licentiousness. But perhaps a residue of Puritanism in the author prevented him from knowing this.

As a result the play alternates between psycho-analytic hints (never artistically convincing) and what becomes—aside from several fine passages which reveal his natural endowments as a poet-playwright—an almost trite and at moments badly constructed plot line. Fragments of true feeling have been attenuated and vitiated by the author's failure to find a proper form for them, to think his problem through.

It is the function of the director of a play as subtly difficult as *Summer and Smoke* to articulate a coherent interpretation which the audience can actually *see*. It is evident that such an interpretation never existed in regard to this play. The production, in fact, provides an example of how a group of talented people, when there is no firm hand to guide them, may contribute to a play wholeheartedly but without valid effect. As Alma Winemiller, Margaret Phillips, an actress of considerable quality and ability, has been permitted or encouraged by the director, Margo Jones, to overstress such secondary characteristics as a nervous laugh, an affected

speech, super-refinement of manner, at the expense of the main motive of the character, which should be her innate womanly instincts. Tod Andrews as John Buchanan is earnest as well as handsome, but he has been given no real characterization.

Jo Mielziner's setting is not only as pretty as can be, but an honest attempt to capture the play's special style. The setting is nonetheless dramatically unsuccessful because it restricts the free movement essential to the play, and its stylization ends by being almost more confining to the imagination than a realistic set. What would be best would be practically no set at all.

—*NR*, 25 Oct. '48

OFF THE BEATEN TRACK

We suffer nowadays from an inability to play. No people are so lavishly furnished with the equipment of entertainment as the Americans of the big cities, and no people approach the material of entertainment with so little of the spirit which is conducive to real pleasure. We appear to be licked before we begin. Words implying conflict are appropriate in this connection, because we so often enter places of entertainment as if spiritual brass knuckles were as much a requirement for the occasion as formal clothes in the *parterre* of the Paris opera.

A show is not a festivity to which we have been invited; it is a challenge. We doubt the host's honesty. Our wits are alerted; we are ready to administer due punishment if our demands are not met. This is our brand of the critical spirit. We are ready to forgo it if we are sure the host has no serious intentions—if he merely proposes to knock us out with fireworks or narcotics. But let the party be of a quieter nature, where we may retain a modicum of our normal selves, and the relation between host and guest must be stated in terms of combat.

The way we employ our critical spirit is this: we expect in some way to experience some strong physical or emotional shock, after which we want to be assured that we were not being fooled, that the shock had a point. If it is not to be just fun—in the manner of a binge—we demand that our entertainment be worthwhile, "pay off." We hate to be preached at, yet we somehow insist that what we have heard or seen prove itself an asset, something that can be accounted a benefit such as the radio commercials sell with every item.

There is something sound in the instinct that prompts this attitude, but the results are nevertheless meager; they bring no joy. What we overlook is that life itself has no utilitarian value, that everything we hold dear has no end beyond itself. What is the "use" of Man anyway? Love was not created for hygiene. The child plays and strengthens its muscles, but it does not know this. It plays because it is as much the essence of its nature to do so as to feed itself, and in doing both it is innocent of all reason beyond its impulse. This is its need, its goal, its pleasure, its very life. The sane man accepts this fact and says yea to it. His very capacity to reason is based on this acceptance which is an act of faith. He recognizes evil in anything that tends to destroy this acceptance of life. Anything that sets about to "prove" the value of life beyond the evidence of our faith or our experience of it is doomed to sterility.

In art what appears simplest and least demonstrably good is often the most enduring. That art is truest which is closest to a life force. Does a flower, a bird, a river have to "prove" itself? There is in the ability to play something of that same sense of acceptance with which all men in a state of health face the world.

I say all this because during the past month I have noticed that my pleasures at the theatre, at pictures and in the markets of entertainment have come from modest efforts which because of the topsy-turvydom of commerce are often represented to the public as special and abstruse. They are pleasures which we are prone to disregard, because they are not in competition with the entertainment which is advertised as palliative or panacea.

Robert Flaherty, who is one of the fathers of the documentary film and the creator of *Nanook of the North*, *Moana of the South Seas*, *Man of Aran*, has made another picture in a somewhat similar vein called *Louisiana Story*. The difference between *Louisiana Story* and the older pictures lies not only in the fact that it employs speech and a semblance of plot, but that it verges on a "purpose."

The Standard Oil Company paid for the making of *Louisiana Story*. Although it did not issue any orders to Flaherty except to show some of the process by which oil is brought from the earth, one is a little troubled by a sense that in some subtle way we are supposed to decide whether the discovery of oil on the land of simple inhabitants of the bayou country in Louisiana is a boon or a bane for them: we cannot tell which. If the picture has a serious flaw, it is that it seems to have a point which is not demonstrated, a meaning that eludes us.

Nothing in the picture's very bare dialogue would lead us to believe that any sort of "propaganda" is intended, but for the first time Flaherty is dealing with two orders of reality—the industrial as well as the natural. The juxtaposition may in itself provoke an unconscious demand that something be said about it. The flaw we suggest may be due as much to something that we, perhaps unjustifiably, expect as to something that Flaherty actually planned.

If the picture says anything at all on the score of industry and nature, it derives from Flaherty's special vision rather than from anything he may believe. For in *Louisiana Story*, industry is seen as a phenomenon as "natural" as nature itself. If the machinery that the oil company sets up in the waters of the bayou appears a terrible threat to human life, it is less so than the huge alligator that glides through these same waters, fascinating as evil itself. Is Flaherty saying that all life has its innocence and its menace, that the alligator and the oil drill existing side by side with almost equal inevitability are things man may have to guard against equally? This doesn't seem probable, but questions such as these keep obtruding in the spectator's consciousness.

The greater part of *Louisiana Story* is a photographic poem which relates it to the best of Flaherty's work. Flaherty's genius lies in his effort to rediscover nature, so to speak, at its source. This does not imply softness or sentimentality. Struggle and pain are always present in nature and Flaherty observes these with just as patient and loving an eye as its more smiling aspects. In all of Flaherty's films nature is shown in its fathomless loveliness, mystery and grandeur, together with people toiling to live within the pull of its fierce dialectics. Flaherty is so aware of this duality that where nature is at its gentlest, as in the South Seas, he dwells at length on the rite of tattooing in which the natives symbolically enact the pain of life by actually inflicting it on themselves in order to remind themselves that without it men cannot attain their full stature. In the opening sequence of *Louisiana Story*, the camera flows through the inlet and describes its intimacies of strange foliage, delicate wild life, wondrous gestation, beautiful efflorescence of nature's joyous and tender secrets together with the ominous presence of the monster that is as much a part of all this glory as the rest.

Are there villains in biology? Drama there certainly is. The drama becomes most poignant with the entrance of man. A boy of about eleven is the "hero" of *Louisiana Story*—the fleshed counterpart of Flaherty's spirit. He is as beautiful as anything in nature; indeed he and almost all the people we see in the picture are very much like natural objects. Some of these people look like animals, others like trees, still others are akin to stones.

The boy in *Louisiana Story* expresses himself in sounds (part American, part French) that remind us of the birth of speech at a time when man was very close to the other creatures of the earth. The boy is strong, sweet, eager, unafraid, curious, ready to do battle to protect what he loves. The great events of his young life are his fight with the alligator and the advent of that other monster, the machine.

We never see the boy's ultimate conquest of the alligator—only the first thrilling skirmish. We never find out whether the other actor in the drama—the mighty instrument that rises fabulously over the water's surface and digs deep below it—brings the boy the same satisfaction as his triumph over the beast of the bayou. We see unforgettable episodes in the boy's life, and we are left to conjecture if they have any significance beyond the amazement they provide our eyes and the stimulation they offer our imagination.

In the end *Louisiana Story* remains a happy event on the primitive level of Flaherty's pure—we might say boy's—vision that disturbs us by suggesting another dimension which Flaherty either does not recognize or does not consider his province. The miracle of Flaherty's simplicity remains, offering us the opportunity to penetrate where we have long ceased to look, inviting us to journey into a free domain where we may relax our constricted spirits with fresh delight. And Virgil Thomson's superior score helps emphasize what is easy, open, bright, clear and graceful in the film. Without problems or proofs *Louisiana Story* is a treasure.

They say New York is to be without opera this season. Despite all the quarrels one may have with the musty Met, I think such an eventuality would be a disgrace. I cannot believe it will happen. I cannot believe the community will remain so indifferent as to allow it to happen. Yet if it should happen, it may prove a blessing in disguise. For we sorely need to get back to fundamentals in this as in other fields. If we had to begin over again, perhaps some of the snobbism, the claptrap, the false conventions that have parasitically attached themselves to opera might be cleared away.

If we did not already know that opera does not have to be "grand"—expensive, pompous, stuffy and superannuated—the little organization known as the Lemonade Opera that produced Prokofieff's *The Duenna* last spring at their tiny quarters on West Thirteenth Street would serve to remind us of the fact. I cannot tell you the story of the opera except to say that in it parental stupidity and tradesman greed are brought to heel by young love and female strategy. What counts is the vigorous spirit with which the young singers and musicians of the Lemonade Opera proceed to their task: that and Prokofieff's constantly inventive, rich, ebullient score.

Rare pleasures are to be found in New York's amusement fair, but, as I have often said, you must not always seek it where monopoly holds sway, but in the byways where the little people, with undiminished hopes, foregather.

There can be no doubt that there has been a steady decline in the quality of Russian films since the days of *Baltic Deputy*, *The Youth of Maxim*, *Little White Sail*, *The Last Night*. It is difficult at this distance and with the curtain of misinformation that separates us from the Soviet Union to know the exact causes for the decline. It may be due, of course, to the too-sectarian and didactic interpretation of what is socially useful or relevant. Be that as it may, a certain rigidity of subject matter and treatment now mars the product of the Soviet studios.

The Village Teacher is somewhat better than most of the Russian films that have preceded it for a long time. The picture is more satisfying in its depiction of the past than in its treatment of more recent times. This is somehow characteristic. The best Russian pictures are superior in portraying the Czarist era or the early days of the Revolution than they are in the handling of contemporary reality. However, it is ingenuous of the reviewers to complain that the picture betrays the use of propaganda—in showing so many handsome young men as Red Army officers, for example! Do the reviewers expect a Soviet film to foster anti-Soviet propaganda!

A picture rather shabbily neglected by our press was the Danish *Day of Wrath*, directed by Carl Dreyer, who years ago made the memorable *Joan of Arc* in which the faces of the medieval period were set down on film as never before. *Day of Wrath* is not as striking or as important as the earlier film, but it is an impressive work nevertheless.

Many of our reviewers found its pace killing. It does not occur to them that what is killing them is the pace of their own lives. When the reviewer says that a film (or a play) is "slow," it means either that the film is empty, in which case that is what should be said, or that they do not see what is in front of them, in which case they should not be asked to review films or plays.

If *Day of Wrath* is "slow" it is because "slowness" is part of the meaning and quality of what is being said. The picture is a story of religious bigotry, superstition and human passion in a seventeenth-century Danish setting. It is a beautifully wrought picture, completely consistent in style, with many fine performances.

No matter how thorough the research department may be in the making of historical films in Hollywood, the results nearly always look foolish because the historical background is never conveyed through the actors themselves. In *Day of Wrath* the actors look and behave true to humanity in general because they are true to the particular environment and epoch in which the picture is set. The gloom, the probity, the power and the passion of the Protestant religiosity that the film mirrors has never been so nobly re-created as in *Day of Wrath*.

If Kay Thompson, whom I discussed last month, is the new look in night-club entertainment, Mildred Bailey, whom I heard recently at Café Society in Sheridan Square, is typical of what is permanent in American entertainment of this kind. Within the big noise and the brassiness of the popular song environment, she remains intimate. Within the vulgar amorality of the hard drinking crowd she stands smiling and resolutely moral. She does not flaunt her virtues any more than she forces her voice. She is neither priggish nor loose. She is everlastingly and steadily for "what comes naturally."

She advises the girls to have their fun now because it might be difficult to do so in a hundred years, yet she does not forget to warn us that the real thing in love only happens once. Miss Bailey is a classic in delivery as well as in content, for she endeavors to do no more than to hit the spot. Thus she has the advantage of staying old fashioned even while she practices the craft of speaking to the contemporary ear. In this she resembles Irving Berlin, whose perennial popularity resides in his firm attachment to the heartstrings of yesterday and his effortless adjustment to the tricks of today.

—*TRW*, Oct. '48

SEX LIFE

*P*rivate Lives, a sketch with overtones from well-to-do, homosexual Bohemia, masquerades as a marital comedy. It is the kind of play that, as the frayed end of the twenties began to merge with the depression of the thirties, was considered the apogee of effervescent sophistication. Facile and sharp in the contemptuous Mayfair manner modeled by Noel Coward, it is an actors' play to which Gertrude Lawrence and the author brought the perfect tone of combined theatrical scampishness and snobbish high life.

Tallulah Bankhead, who plays the Gertrude Lawrence part in the revival, is an actress of uncommon power. Her vitality now has a slight Benzedrine flavor, but there is no questioning the vivid impression she makes. She is also lustrous with the glamor of that wonderful time when theatre connoted something gay, imaginative, disturbing and sinful. Her wit is malicious and electric. As a personality, Bankhead is phenomenal; as a performer, she is a true professional.

I found Miss Bankhead's performance in *Private Lives* painfully obscene. It is aggressively lacking in charm. Its spirit is snarling, derisive, self-destructive; a sacrilege against sex. Miss Bankhead has become a victim of her legend. She imitates Tallulah. She throws herself away—as if experimenting in how far she dare go. Her adorers seem bent on abetting this self-massacre. If you tell me audiences are wild about her performance I can only reply with Bernard Shaw, "It is the business of the dramatic critic to educate these dunces, not to echo them."

Love Life is an educated musical. Without being exactly pretentious about it, it is an intellectual, philosophical, historical show, exposing the deterioration of American marital relations from 1791 to 1948. Vaudeville numbers of every sort, serving as a choral commentary to the enacted episodes, liven the proceedings with songs about Progress and the inroads of economics on love.

Boris Aronson's sets are fluent, diverse, suggestive, witty and, above all, unhackneyed. Aronson, one of the three or four genuinely distinguished designers of our stage, makes each of his *décors* solve some special theatrical problem he has set himself. There is, therefore, always something fresh in his efforts, though, like most creative talents, he works more unevenly than do the mediocrities. He has done his job in *Love Life* with notable success. No less delightful are Lucinda Ballard's costumes, which leap and glow with bright spirit. The principals are the sturdy and stentorian Ray Middleton, who looks like Walter Huston at the age of thirty-five, and Nanette Fabray, always genial and winning—particularly in the song called "Mr. Right." "Green Up Time" is a nice tune with fresh choreography by Michael Kidd. Etc. Etc.

Despite these assets and the credit deserved by any musical that attempts to be "different," *Love Life* left me a little cold and even weary. Its multiple ingenuity is overstrenuous. It is a gesture without substance; juiceless at its core. It does not seem to spring out of any human source except the resolution to be up-to-date, intelligent and successful. It has ability, but little love.

About *Where's Charlie?*, the musical based on *Charley's Aunt*, I can only say that if you have ever seen Ray Bolger you will want to see him again; if you've never seen him—see him now. *Where's Charley?* is by no means his best vehicle, but even his third-best is the real stuff. Ray Bolger is a performer in the grand line of American players. If we had a real theatre or even a group of solid producing organizations, as in the days from Augustin Daly to Charles Dillingham, special shows would be prepared every season to display the range of Bolger's gifts.

Bolger is the zany drummer of the American small town. He is a kind of hanger-on at the village drug store, possessed of an eccentric, hayseed grace that is akin to genius. This hatchet-faced young man, whose mask is either very dumb or very cunning, suddenly transforms into a benevolently demonic scarecrow in fantastic flight over fields, changes again into a brilliantly lyric Broadway smart aleck. He finally transcends all provincialism so that something is evoked which is like the spirit of pure dance as it exists in the soul of even the most loutish among us. To watch him at work is to have a clean and beautiful experience in the theatre. With Bolger is sweet Allyn McLerie, whose eyes are blue and whose body is a blessing.

—*NR*, 1 Nov. '48

READING SUMMER & SMOKE

The season has slowed down to a walk. Comparatively few plays are being produced, and the mortality rate among the recent productions has been high. As usual, there is some good to be reaped from the evil. The scene builders are in the first stages of a panic: the cost of set construction has gone down. If production continues to decline, the real-estate people will offer better terms for their theatres. It may become a little easier to save a show on the border line between breaking even and losing money. All this has the spasmodic cheerfulness usual among victims of a vicious circle. That is the way of our unplanned theatre.

It is also cheerful to report that mixed notices no longer spell box-office disaster. Brooks Atkinson (of the *Times*) and Howard Barnes (of the *Herald Tribune*) did not care for *Love Life*, but

it appears to be a hit. Only two of the daily reviewers admired *Summer and Smoke*, but it is doing business. The only play thus far that has been accorded a unanimously cordial reception is *Life with Mother*, but one didn't have to go to the Empire to predict that.

This development of a more independent audience reaction is hopeful. When readers learn to understand that the value of a review does not lie in its indication of the odds on a play's success or failure, they will begin to regard reviews not as ticket-broker's copy, but as a possible source of enlightenment. They will then cease to ask shopping advice and demand criticism. Or am I being Utopian?

I have had an opportunity now to read the script of *Summer and Smoke*. It is sensitive, evocative and frequently lovely. Because Williams feels more truly than he thinks, the play has dramatic weaknesses—a certain elusiveness that amounts to vaporousness—which I tried to define in my original review.

Reading *Summer and Smoke*, the faults of the production become even more strikingly evident than they were on seeing the play. The production is an accident. It lacks point. It is without real body—intellectually and even emotionally. The two principal actors (Margaret Phillips and Tod Andrews) are endowed with fine natural qualities—this is particularly true of Miss Phillips—but they are not really used except to play the most obvious aspect of their parts. We are led to think of the central characters as a "cold" girl and a passionate boy, an utter misconception—almost a distortion—of the text.

Margo Jones is apparently one of those directors who believes that to "interpret" a play one has merely to choose able actors who are the right "types" and then set it down on the stage so that it may speak for itself. If it were possible to do this with any good play there would really be no pleasure or need for the theatre at all. To be effective and meaningful in the theatre all plays must actually be given creative translation: the dramatist's words must become flesh in the actors. The two substances are not identical.

Despite the shortcomings of the play and its production, *Summer and Smoke* is a success because it is the only new play this season that addresses its audience in a truly human speech on intimate matters rarely treated on our mechanistic stage.

—*NR*, 15 Nov. '48

LIGHT UP THE BOX OFFICE

Some plays demand thought; others require that you put yourself in their mood. With most shows you have only to decide that you are going to like them. This must be the case with the musical *As Girls Go* (at the Winter Garden). In the sense that a show is an efficient and pleasurable construction of diverse theatrical elements, this new Mike Todd production does not exist. As an excuse to get Bobby Clark and a lot of spectacularly perpendicular girls on the stage, it is a wow. The reviewers and a large public have decided to like it.

Bobby Clark is as much a tradition of the American stage as a Barnum and Bailey poster. He is a funny man. He looks like a vulgar caricature of Harry Truman in the guise of a circus clown. He is the small businessman on a spree. His irrepressible prankishness and almost obscene nonconformity within the lineaments of the "average" Elk or Shriner personality are weird as well as comic. It is as if in Bobby Clark the lower middle-class citizen—like the salesmen or the small manufacturers one sees in the commercial hotels of Cincinnati, St. Louis and Detroit—had found his perfect reflection, so that he might both boast of his absurd good fellowship and apologize for it. In *As Girls Go*, Clark's verbal humor is wretched, the tricks no longer fresh, though still hilarious.

As for the girls, the reviewers and the audience react to them as if they had never seen any before. The reason for this is that Mike Todd, with crass and cunning showmanship, has brought back to the musical-comedy stage the old-fashioned showgirl, unregenerated by the nobler influences of esthetic choreography. After all there are permanent values in the theatre: streamlined lechery is one of them.

To categorize Moss Hart's latest play, *Light Up the Sky*, one has simply to say that it is a hit. This is not an evasion, for there is a distinction between the play that becomes a hit through accident and a play that is a hit by design, a special order of playwriting. If *Light Up the Sky* had not come off, it would have had to be described as a hit that failed—for its aim is pointed only at the bull's-eye. The success of *Light Up the Sky* is essential to its nature.

It is easy enough to recognize this kind of play, but difficult to define it. It is no more sufficient to determine to turn out a hit than it would be to plan to write a great tragedy. In either case one must have a knack for one's job. Moss Hart has the knack for his.

To write a hit one must have above all the desire to please and one must know what pleases one's particular audience. *Light Up the Sky* is about show business in the sense that *Once in a Lifetime* was about Hollywood. Theatre people are represented as lovable rascals, egomaniacs, poltroons, occasionally redeemed by talent, nerve and good luck. Sincere authors are shown to be either willing or reluctant victims of this crazy crowd.

One cannot make much comment on this picture of show business, because while there is enough "truth" in it to win an easy assent, there is so little actual human substance or particularization that one cannot speak seriously of any theme, thesis or point of view. This, however is part of the technique for writing hits. The total effect is to convince us that most of the so-called characters are fairly worthless specimens and that what is lovable is lent them by the actors and by the tolerance (or moral indifference) the audience will always supply when it expects to be repaid in entertainment.

Above and beyond this is the peculiar energy which is the chief characteristic of the hit play. A good-time atmosphere is established like a brightly lit party at which the guests all talk loud, laugh hard, slap each other on the back, exchange bright quips—some of them funny, some of them only fun-loving.

A brisk directorial pace is set so that the audience gets no chance to ask questions, and the actors shout in expert stylization that has the same relation to reality that a brash display ad has to ordinary speech. The company that plays *Light Up the Sky* is good—Audrey Christie, Phyllis Povah, Sam Levene, Barry Nelson and Bartlett Robinson notably so.

—*NR*, 29 Nov. '48

THE THRESHOLD OF A NEW SEASON

The theatrical season of 1948-49 opened with *Sundown Beach*, a first play by the novelist Bessie Breuer, the first production too of a new group calling itself the Actors' Studio. The purpose of the Actors' Studio is to provide "a place where workers in the theatre can perfect their craft. It is not a school. It is, more accurately, a workshop, meeting regularly to discuss the preparation and projection of plays." The leaders of the new Studio are Elia Kazan and Cheryl Crawford.

It is too early to speak of the special significance or value of the Actors' Studio in itself. All such groups—useful even when they endure briefly—acquire an identity through continuity. The general significance of the Actors' Studio, namely the effort to establish such groups in the least adventurous period of American theatre history since 1919, is what matters now.

I believe the very fact of a prevailing depression among theatre workers today will bring about a reaction, an unconquerable desire to break the economic and psychological fetters that hold the theatre in bondage. Young people, and those who have retained some of the fire that gave the theatre its glow in the thirties, will not submit forever to the constriction of a system that permits only those

plays to be done which satisfy the commercial sense of the investment interests. The theatre does not properly belong to small-time gamblers who would make nothing more of it than an adjunct of Hollywood. The young people I speak of know this in every fiber of their being, and this ardent knowledge will soon take the form of an "underground" rebellion against theatrical "monopoly." The Actors' Studio is simply one of the first and most conspicuous examples of what is cooking in the off-center hearths of the theatrical workshops.

If we look at a playbill from Berlin or Vienna today, we shall be astonished and ashamed at the breadth of their theatrical repertories—plays, old and new, from every country in the world are being performed in these ruined towns all the time. If we turn to the illustrated theatre magazines of Central Europe, we shall see that their methods of production are far less standardized than ours have become. The productions in those countries respond to the individuality of the different directors, exponents of a great diversity of styles. The silly argument that we sometimes hear about the richness of the movies as a medium as contrasted to the stage is largely based on the assumption that what we see on our stage today is the theatre's immutable norm. The truth, of course, is that our theatre practice is nothing but one shallow compartment in the treasure house of the theatre's vast construction.

One of the significant features of Brecht's dramatic work is his use of the exotic "costume play" to convey contemporary meaning. We associate plays with choruses, songs, a narrator and the like with a kind of stylization intended to offer us a form of arty escape. Most of Brecht's plays are situated in far off lands at some remote period of time. Thus we might suppose that Brecht's aim is to write poetic pieces to beguile our fancy. But on the contrary, Brecht aims to be more didactic and immediate than are most of our plays on so-called modern or topical themes.

The Caucasian Chalk Circle is based on the tale we find in the Old Testament and again in other ancient texts of the wise king or judge who has to decide which of two women, both claiming a child as their own, is the true mother. In Brecht's treatment, the locale is the Caucasus at some indefinite period in the past. The "twist" in the story is that the judge awards the child not to the real mother, who is unworthy of her motherhood, but to the woman who has cared for the child and has earned motherhood through sacrifice and love. What Brecht is saying is that the new times will bring a new morality in which only work and devotion will confer property rights.

Brecht employs a method of dramatic narration that is related to the Chinese theatre. The emphasis is not on the kind of illusion that induces the spectator to forget he is in a theatre, but one which constantly reminds the spectator of his position as appreciative arbiter. The stage and the audience are not supposed to become suffused in an emotional bath in which both are lost to reason and objective understanding. The actors are expected to illustrate with humor, ease, simplicity and grace the basic meaning of the story being told, so that the spectator may both enjoy these qualities and retain the clarity to measure the value of what is being communicated. Brecht does not want his theatre to intoxicate the mind and the senses, but to act as a noble illumination of ideas that are humanly worthy and socially useful. For Brecht, the theatre is a mask intended not to hide but to reveal the world's true face. He does not seek a theatre hot with indiscriminate passion but cool with choice wisdom. His focus is not on psychological substance or color of detail but on the direction of the structural line. His plays sound a new note in contemporary dramaturgy. There is something unfamiliar and pure in their timbre; at their best, they achieve a new beauty.

At the end of the summer, I was invited to speak at the two-day Art Conference given under the auspices of the Woodstock Artists Association and the Artists Equity Association at Woodstock, New York.

The subject under discussion was Art Now, and the anxiety with which the audience waited—almost implored—for a liberating word, an affirmation of faith or the courage to hope was touching and in itself a kind of assurance. Scratch an American today, and you will find worry! At first it seems only concern about economic security—the fear of hard times, the disgrace of a lower standard of living. Deep down it is a worry about Everything! Personal relations are questioned because they have become unsatisfactory, the meaning and value of life seem uncertain as almost never before. The illusion of security we may have because of a relative prosperity only intensifies the nervousness underneath. It is as if we were thrown back to the beginning—asking ourselves all over again (or for the first time), "Is life worth living?"

In our hearts we know the question to be unnatural. Man in a state of health is inevitably struck by the tragic mystery of life; this mystery, however, does not diminish his appetite for living, but rather heightens his sense of life's grandeur and passion. When life itself is questioned, it means that some poison has begun to devitalize us, that the organism of society has become corrupt and that we are suffering from its contamination. It is part of man's health to seek for a cure, to go to every possible source of inspiration and knowledge for help. Thus, man, knowing that he expresses his essence in art, that art is the evidence of his deepest aspiration, the emblem of his total experience, goes to the artist for a salvaging truth beyond the clamor of editorials or political oratory.

What the reports and credos of the artists at the Woodstock Art Conference showed was that the artists themselves reflect some of the bewilderment of those who come to them for answers. The artists share in the universal instinct which gives us the conviction that what the artist does (creating in play forms of experience through which we both identify ourselves and communicate with others) is perhaps the noblest of man's activities, the one most symbolic of life's aim and meaning. Yet the artist cannot help but realize that his freedom to exercise this faculty is being threatened, that his position in the world is not only becoming increasingly jeopardized, but that he and his work are being rendered unnecessary, almost undesirable. The artist, losing his foothold, begins to wonder whether he is not after all an excrescence, a futile playboy, a pariah, a bum!

My own belief—which I feel it proper to reassert every time I begin anew to "cover" the season in the arts—is that if art has no meaning or value, then man himself has none. Art is the means by which man makes himself visible. Through art man moves toward self-realization; art is therefore a basic product of man's living, the synthesis toward which he inevitably yearns. Contrary to the unwholesome theory that art is a sign of man's weakness, I believe it to be the true testimony of his manhood. All men, whether they know it or not, strive to that condition which makes the artist. Everything that tends to destroy art or the artist in man must be fought. Because nothing human can be alien to art, the artist cannot consider himself outside of anything that is of this world. A distinguished poet has recently said that the artist's values are "not of this world." We all understand what the poet meant, but I think it a misleading statement nevertheless. Whatever values are injurious to the artist are humanly destructive, and should be themselves put out of this world.

I am neither a partisan of "art as a weapon" nor of "art for art's sake" (though I find the latter formulation more sympathetic since I conceive of art as inseparable from a universal human concern). "Pure art" is pure nonsense, and my objection to "art as a weapon" does not arise from a scorn of weapons—they too may be creative instruments— but from a refusal to limit the function of art. "Art as a weapon" is a slogan that usually emanates from the same narrowly utilitarian conception of life which holds that art is justified only as a publicity service for toilet articles, household goods and insurance companies. Art gives content to life itself. The enemies of art are the great betrayers and malefactors of humankind. It is part of the critic's job to praise life where he finds it and denounce everything that conspires against it.

—*TRW*, Nov. '48

MAXWELL ANDERSON

In a sense there is no dramatic criticism in America: all our writing on the subject of the theatre is directed not to the illumination of creative personalities but to the making of reputations. When a dramatist like Maxwell Anderson writes a play that displeases us we make ugly sounds and pronounce it a flop, when another of his plays provides an enjoyable evening we gurgle approval and proclaim a success. The dramatist is never truly seen, defined, situated. Thus success and failure are equally a defeat. The man of talent disappears in a kind of artistic anonymity.

I say this apropos of Maxwell Anderson's latest play, *Anne of the Thousand Days* (at the Shubert), which has been greeted with the kind of acclaim that is good for business. When I left the theatre, I hardly knew what I had seen: I was only certain that the play was a hit. It has a romantic air that captivates, but I had to read the text (William Sloane Associates, $2.75) to discover what it was really about, and what I thought of it. What I found was Maxwell Anderson with his own unique physiognomy.

Anderson deserves to be known. He is one of our few authentic dramatists in the sense that for twenty-five years he has supplied our stage with a steady stream of plays that all—good or bad—bear the stamp of his personality, his reaction to the world. Whether or not one admires that reaction is less important for the moment than to recognize its presence.

The essence of Maxwell Anderson's work is a benevolent indecision. He is a quiescent anarchist. No man or government, he feels, is truly just; we all walk in a painful, glamorous maze: life, as one of H. G. Wells's cockneys would say, is a rum go. Thus all problems are treated with a kind of soft skepticism and considerable affection. The tonality of the Anderson plays usually is composed of a gentle and slightly melancholy moodiness.

Factually and intellectually, all concrete considerations tend to lose their shape and to dissolve in a sad and tender blur with a never altogether extinguishable Puritan Christianity dominant.

If this were all, Anderson could not have gained the position he holds in our theatre. He has a charming and sometimes bawdy humor (as in the first three scenes of *Anne*—the Anglo-historical equivalent of the saltiness in *What Price Glory?*). He has a love of English words, whether it be the American people's slang or the rhetoric of the British classics. He has a real yearning for the heroic days of great gesture, splendid deeds and muscled heroes. This is as evident in a play like *Gods of the Lightning* as in *Elizabeth, the Queen*. Above everything, he is in awe at the phenomenon of two people in love.

My first reaction to *Anne of the Thousand Days* was that it hung in mid-air, that it lacked a basic point—aside from the fact that it was a love story about people (Henry VIII and Anne Boleyn) who spoke good English and were stars of history. This was enjoyable for the early part of the evening and acutely disappointing for the rest. But on reading the play I realized that its point was not to be isolated in a specific theme or even character problem but in the total impression which is the revelation of the Anderson sensibility and talent, the nature of which I have tried to suggest. If that sensibility does not act as a distinct force, it is at least the true image of a man—far more significant of the educated American of good will than many of us care to admit.

What hurts *Anne* as a play is its production—upon which much praise has already been lavished. Though Motley's costumes are opulent and handsome, the production is poverty-stricken. It has no atmosphere of feeling, of period or of theatrical grandeur. The setting is a feeble compromise—inferior, in every respect, to what a good college production might achieve. The acting and direction, in relation to the opportunities the script affords, are merely professional routine, which is another way of saying amateurish with authority.

Rex Harrison, judging from the films I have seen, is an able, attractive and intelligent drawing-room comedian—expert with lines and sharp in the projection of a sort of mental naturalism. He is not romantic in the sense Olivier is; he is not a delineator of character in the sense that Laughton as Henry VIII was. He swaggers a little (the production lacks movement), he assumes the Holbein stance as he wears his Holbein cap throughout, and he works sincerely, but he has no real sinew, sensuality, or emotional dimension.... Joyce Redman is a cunning actress with great performance vitality, a slight pathos, a robust comedy sense, but her portrayal of Anne Boleyn has no center, no depth, nothing queenly beyond a female assertiveness. Not for a moment is she a tragedienne. The effect of all this is a fundamental dryness, and Maxwell Anderson, whatever else he may be, is not dry.

—*NR*, 27 Dec. '48

HARD TIMES

My title suggests poverty. We are not exactly a poor people. But we are living through hard times just the same. There seems to be so little brightness of spirit, joy, love. We have intelligence, but it no longer signifies insight, merely a capacity to maneuver. Talent is not something that springs from the exuberance of our hearts, but from manipulation. Application and shrewdness constitute ability. We are clever and sophisticated when we give evidence that we cannot be fooled by anyone. Everything is so carefully arranged, handled, labeled that little remains which is mysterious, fluid, germinal, fresh or wonderful. A month of nightlife has left me with this wan conclusion. But we must distinguish, and seek oases.

When I was a student in Paris, in 1922, I wrote an essay on Sacha Guitry in which I referred to him as "the minnesinger of the cads." The description is still apt. After all these years his voice is still sweet with a kind of honeyed acid, a humor that is both a twinkle and an insult. If one consorts with him at all—as his many charms lead us to do—one must protect oneself from infection.

Guitry's most recent picture, *Private Life of An Actor*, has a peculiar fascination for me. It is about his father, Lucien Guitry, one of the most skillful actors of the twentieth century, an actor I saw over and over again in the halcyon days. Guitry *père* was a towering figure whose slightest gesture was an event. On Lucien Guitry's stern, massive and monumental face, a smile was like a change of weather. The total impression he made was one of almost institutional dignity and nobility.

Sacha Guitry is also a large man and resembles his father in other ways. Yet Sacha Guitry as Lucien Guitry is still only an exhibition of Sacha Guitry, and not a study of his father, whom he is incapable of portraying. For Sacha is a corrupt romantic whose realism is wit, a classic cynic whose only genuine sentiment is for the make-up box, the footlights, the gossip and glamor of the theatre. He is an accomplished courtesan. He has made a style out of his vices. *Private Life of An Actor* is amusing and amazing as an example of how a film can be concocted from a few anecdotes and some desultory maxims of the theatrical profession.

Fernand Lèger was never one of my favorite painters. But on seeing the small retrospective show (1912-48) given at the new Sidney Janis Gallery, I came to realize that Lèger had a distinct place in modern painting which it would be stupid to disregard.

Aside from the authority of his craftsmanship, Lèger's contribution has been to show how the symbols of modern power—the machine and other industrial forms—could be turned into sweets. In this transformation of things that once seemed extremely unesthetic into the most acceptable forms of ornament we may read a whole social history. It is a story of our times and an American story, but it took the keen intelligence of a Frenchman (who never saw our country till rather late in life) to trace this historical pattern with a sure hand.

From the earliest paintings, which must have been indistinguishable at the time they were done (1912) from the work of the other horrifying "cubists" (to the uninitiated everything that is not representational is "cubist"), we see that Lèger's aim, from the first, was to demonstrate that the new forms that were becoming familiar in the machine age could serve the purpose of prettifying our existence. Looking backward, we see how the abstruse experiments of a Lèger have become the clichés not only of modern art, but of interior decoration, scenic design, household architecture and the businessman's concept of elegance.

Leger's later pieces (1941) painted in New York are so frankly playful that they might be used for magazine covers, perfume advertisements, steamship murals. What might have once been thought austere and scientific now proves itself the entertainment of the well-to-do masses.

Noel Coward is a theatrical wonder boy. He can do practically anything in the way of producing a good show (or movie) except the authentic and the real (though he knows the trick of "realism" as well as anyone). This is not to say that he lacks personality. On the contrary! Not only is his versatility a form of personality—the dyed-in-the-wool theatre man is always loved by everybody, including his enemies—but there is a Noel Coward trait that is unmistakably individual.

Coward is a Piccadilly bohemian whose "ideal" is the fashionable English of the 1918-39 variety. This is an upper class that enjoys its wealth, but has become skeptical of the values that once made it a moral as well as a ruling upper class. It is a class that wields power without a sense of responsibility.

The peculiar variant that Coward gives to his class orientation derives from his being an actor and something of an artist. This inspires him with a certain contempt even for the class he depends on and seeks to flatter. In fact, he has contempt for almost everyone who is not of the theatre, the arts or anything else that is at least amusing. This gives him a certain "freedom" or aloofness, even from those who provide him with his basic social patterns and prejudices. Considering his gifts—wit, capacity to work, awareness of the social currents of his day as it affects theatre audiences—it is not surprising that he has been not only highly successful but for many years—particularly before the war—something of a fetish.

All this is a preamble to a note on the revival of Coward's popular *Private Lives*, which was first produced here early in 1931. The revival was put on as a vehicle for the remarkable and lustrous Tallulah Bankhead.

Gertrude Lawrence, who originally played the role now assigned to Miss Bankhead, must have been charming in it, with the kind of vivacity and sparkle that fits the Coward manner at its most effervescent. Miss Bankhead is a circus—rowdy, bawdy and boisterous. Where Miss Lawrence must have displayed a spirited disregard for everything but her own Coward-ly playworld, Miss Bankhead squats astride it and commits nuisance. The spectacle shocks the audience into riotous laughter.

I believe Miss Bankhead to be a richly endowed actress. She has a frightening vitality, an abundant sense of humor, beauty of face and limb (the near striptease in Act II is unequivocally exciting), a splendid, though abused, voice, expert professionalism and dramatic imagination. But she has allowed herself to become spoiled by her legend: she indulges in flagrant undiscipline and tastelessness, she has turned the sly contempt of Coward's manner into a cackle and belch of disgust.

I realize that *Private Lives* is only a frivolous comedy (and there is obviously a place in the theatre for frivolity along with everything else), but I cannot help thinking that in this play Miss Bankhead desecrates herself, her sex, the relations of men and women generally, even on the level of naughtiness. The producers, the critics, the audience which encourage such human vandalism are either ripe for disaster or not to be taken seriously when they grow solemn on more sedate occasions. The vulgarity of this *Private Lives* revival merits being described as Coward in a disorderly house.

More than ten years ago, I read a play called *Battle of Angels*. In its old version (it has been revised since), I thought it almost absurdly overwrought, but I remember having cited it in a lecture as a bad play that interested me more than most of the good plays that were being produced. The play was subsequently done in Boston, though it has never been presented in New York. Its author was Tennessee Williams.

Summer and Smoke, the latest Williams play to reach the stage, is not a "bad" play, though it is certainly unsatisfactory. It is the kind of unsatisfactory play that deserves our attention and our sympathy. If this sounds condescending, I shall go further and say that many honest and sensitive playgoers will undoubtedly be moved by it: its sources are in life itself, and every whiff of life that blows across our stage is a wind of hope.

—*TRW*, Dec. '48

MOSTLY SARTRE

A fair review of *Make Way for Lucia* (at the Cort) would have something to say about E. F. Benson's stories about English suburban life in the early twentieth century from which John Van Druten made his play. I have not read E. F. Benson. A fair review would also provide an analysis of what might have been done with the script by a more happily chosen cast. I regret not to be able to offer such an analysis. I am probably the wrong audience for this show. I found it insufferably pointless and dull. Not even the pretty colors and cut of Lucinda Ballard's costumes could induce me to make way for Lucia.

Christmas Eve found me in no more charitable mood. I acknowledge that *Jenny Kissed Me* (at the Hudson) will do no one any harm, and that Leo G. Carroll is a sound actor, but it is the kind of play that could only wow them in an old-fashioned girls' school or in a community where the sight of a priest acting as unwilling guardian to a sweet young thing might be considered a merry affair.

Jean-Paul Sartre possesses that gift which enables a writer who is not really an artist (except as a critic-essayist) to turn out respectable and significant work in media—such as the short story, the novel and, particularly, the drama—to which his approach is chiefly intellectual. In other words, though Sartre is not truly a dramatist, he knows how to make a play which will serve the contemporary theatre better than some of his more highly endowed colleagues.

Sartre's plays are all philosophic melodramas. He knows the value of action in the theatre: a forceful story line which makes use of either familiar or topically exciting material. He is intelligent and observant enough to create characters that will function convincingly in the backgrounds within which he sets them. Often these characters are nothing but ideologic counters expressing themselves in a language that is like that of a rhetorical essay, as in *The Flies*, or they are cartoons—half farcical journalese and half sociologic comment—as in *The Respectful Prostitute*.

Sartre knows how to profit by the unstable moral condition of his audience—its potential hysteria—so that a number of symptoms can be passed off as psychological types, as in *No Exit*. In any case, Sartre's characters and situations are so shrewdly selected that they strike the theatre public as acceptable realism or as understandably poetic drama, though in fact they are only tight frameworks constructed to convey a critical perception, a thesis or an attitude which by force of skill and literary agility might be called a philosophy.

Because of its mythlike abstractness, *The Flies* is, for the bookish, the most impressive of Sartre's plays; *No Exit* for Frenchmen, his most theatrical; *The Respectful Prostitute*, for Americans, his most effective. For me, *Les Mains Sales* (not its Broadway distortion, *Red Gloves*) is the most satisfactory. But *The Victors* (*Morts Sans Sépulture*), now being given with textual exactitude by the New Stages, is the most actual of all Sartre's plays. By this I mean that, unlike his other pieces, *The Victors* deals with an environment and an experience with which the French audience has had some

direct connection: the struggle of the French Resistance against the Vichyite police.

What is the essence of *The Victors*, as of all the other Sartre plays? Man is lost and alone, forever condemned to run anguished circles in a senseless universe unless he accepts this basic situation to emerge in a realm "on the other side of despair" where he will defy superstition, dogmas and authorities that keep him in a bondage of fear. He can accomplish this by the exercise of his reason, his decision, his will. He must act and take responsibility for his acts. He must recognize his own uniqueness and at the same time realize the bond of a common human condition which ties him to other unique individuals. He can never achieve a conventional happiness, but only a kind of tragic and splendid freedom, a human dignity beyond tears.

The man who kills his young comrade in *The Victors* suffers a terrible sense of guilt even though the situation in which he is caught obliged him to commit the deed; the girl who is raped can hardly bear the thought of further life. But these inward states (which are themselves a kind of superstition) must not be made the meaning, the guiding force the end of their lives. They must live with their guilt and go beyond it to further struggle in their fight for freedom—both political and moral.

Even so blunt a digest of Sartre's message is sufficient to indicate the appeal that it can have for the educated middle class of Europe and elsewhere. It confesses to the prevalent despair and promises no labeled panacea. It exhorts to action without fixing an absolute or obligatory objective. It attracts the socially conscious and even the radical without any rigid a priori hypothesis.

The trouble with *The Victors* as a play is that its material is too specific for the mental schematism of Sartre's method. The more we believe its characters as people the less patient we become with the playwright's heartless treatment of them. If his idea is what fascinates us, his realism—the harrowing scenes of physical torture—violates the equanimity of our judgment. Thus the play is at once superior, disturbing and unsatisfactory. For these reasons it is extremely difficult to produce. The New Stages company do it as well as they can. They deserve praise for deciding to do it at all.

—*NR*, 10 Jan. '49

POEM FROM PARIS

Paris went crazy over Giraudoux's *The Madwoman of Chaillot*, and so would I, were it not for the production given it at the Belasco Theatre. That made me mad. It was a case of love-hate at first sight.

In all fairness, however, it should be said that, regardless of its production, *The Madwoman of Chaillot* afforded me more pleasure than any other play produced this season. It is a little masterpiece, a model of what the theatre can still achieve in the way of poetic statement on contemporary material.

There are a number of approaches one might take to Giraudoux's gem. In another period, when the purely artistic or theatrical aspects of a play would in themselves suggest its total value, I should have been glad to confine my discussion of *The Madwoman* to its formal beauties. But today when a play is praised, it is usually spoken of as a delight, a hit, a thrill—terms that might just as appropriately be applied to a fashion show, a ball game or a ride on the shoot-the-chutes. For this reason I shall emphasize more than is customary, or perhaps even necessary, the meaning and sense of *The Madwoman*.

Balzac hated the bourgeoisie, because he was a royalist. His novels were at once an apocalyptic picture of the hell the bourgeoisie was in the process of creating and a testimony of the grandiose energy and magnificent scope that went into that creation. A romantic by temperament, Balzac was a realist in his art, because the hell he was describing was in fact a great new world being wrought before his very eyes, a world still destined to a long life. Giraudoux, a witty impressionist and "realist" enough to serve as a minister in his country's government, wrote of the Paris of our day as a fanta-

sist. For Giraudoux was a political conservative, and the conservative, who wants to see the ugliness of our times done away with, can only dream.

The Madwoman of Chaillot is the reverie of an honest, sensitive, wholly civilized Frenchman who at the end of his life (Giraudoux died in 1944) contemplates the world about him and sees that it is fast becoming a moral as well as a physical ruin. His alert eye and probing spirit tell him that the ideology of profit is the chief cause of the growing rottenness. He is a clever man, so he is amused, he is a good man, so he is saddened, he is a peaceful man, so he fancies, "If all the money-bags—the newly rich, the black marketeers, the sinister profiteers, the pimps of capital—were drowned in the sewers like rats...what then? Then the birds would sing again, love would flower, and Paris would once again become the poets' enchanted realm."

But who is to bring about this miracle? Not the government—which is merely the official face of the universal skulduggery; not the socialists, communists and anarchists, for they are either dry doctrinaires or indelicate fanatics. Who then? The old aristocrats, as indigent now and as lacking in standing as the disorganized proletariat of the streets. These aristocrats alone retain a sympathy for the adorable riff-raff of Paris—the ragpickers, the shoe-lace salesmen, the obsolete artists—who would be their natural allies in the annihilation of the filthy bourgeoisie. Giraudoux's play is a prank, a sophisticated Mother Goose tale. Yet, in spite of himself, Giraudoux is a revolutionary. For what his play ultimately says is: to be respectable in France even the conservatives must be revolutionary; and, if their conservatism prevents valid action, the least they can do is wish.

The Madwoman of Chaillot is iridescent with a fantasy that is compounded of sweet memories, ancient wisdom, a tradition that is still vibrant through the survival, amid the debris, of bright mental faculties and keen senses. "Paris is old, very old," says the Sewer-Man, and the romance of this play (like that of the Madwoman herself) is the romance of an old consciousness that seems derelict and grotesque in the linear and soulless new world of slot-machine efficiency. The young lovers have to learn the facts of life and take hope from the maxims of the mad.

Except for Christian Berard's sets (salvaged from the original production), which are on the creative level of the play itself, the current show is like a misguided reading of the script in the early stages of rehearsal. This does not mean that there are no gifted people at the Belasco, but acting talent in a play of this sort is only a first ingredient. It needs transformation into the lyric and modeled texture which the entire production should be.

I found James Westerfield, for example, well cast as the Sewer-Man; Estelle Winwood's mask and adeptness in the delivery of lines are excellent qualifications for the Madwoman of Passy, but her performance is still only a sketch. And while Martita Hunt in the title role is unquestionably an able actress, she plays it on the mistaken assumption (the director's or her own) that its essence lies in a picturesquely eccentric make-up and a stagily romantic "aristocracy," whereas it resides in the profound and almost gross earthiness of the woman's experience, its deep-delved decay. It is that decay which produces the character's and the play's wonderful glow.

—*NR*, 17 Jan. '49

PERSONAL AND PERTINENT

There is an extraordinary quality of salesmanship about *Kiss Me, Kate* (at the Century). Its looks assure a hit. Before we have heard a line or a tune of it, we are gratified by a sense of bright opulence, of mechanically perfect luxury.

A good deal of the credit for this twentieth-century magic must go to Lemuel Ayers whose sets and costumes do far more than merely decorate the stage. They create an atmosphere in which one feels entirely snug, safe and smart, as if one had suddenly entered a world of endless money and convenience, a world in which the real American dream of deathless success has come

true. Once we have become enmeshed in this black-market wonderland, nothing can go amiss, no more questions need be asked.

I found the book of *Kiss Me, Kate*—an amalgam of Shakespeare's *The Taming of the Shrew* in World Fair capsule style with movie and vaudeville shenanigans about an acting couple who are having marital trouble—pretty much of a bore. I thought most of Cole Porter's score and lyrics inferior to "What Is This Thing Called Love?," "You're the Tops," "I Get a Kick Out of You." I was pleased with the song called "Where Is the Life That Late I Led?," and the ensemble number "Too Darned Hot" seemed to me a thoroughly expert job of putting over—through dance, orchestral arrangement and setting—a fairly conventional musical-comedy notion. Alfred Drake worked manfully and engagingly to keep the book lively, and Patricia Morison satisfies.

Lest anyone get the impression these remarks imply some mischief, I hasten to point out that I am more concerned here with general principles than with the nature of an individual offering. It is difficult to render in words the exact quality of any nonliterary art form, and, believe it or not, musical comedy is such a form. The only way to convey what a work of art means to you is to translate your impression of it into terms that are not those of art. The sophisticated musical today of which *Kiss Me, Kate* is an outstanding example—seems to me somehow to have an attractiveness akin to that of a splendiferous bathroom, a top-notch refrigerator or a tony night club. The humor of the new-style musical strikes me generally as an echo of the columnists' gossip, their glamor a reflection of expensive advertisement.

While all these things may be commendable, their sublimation in the shape of a musical show usually strikes me cold; I have a feeling, when I see one, that I am being sold. On the other hand, when I see Ethel Merman in such an old-fashioned piece as *Annie Get Your Gun* I am warmed by a substantial sense of vulgar geniality that might be compared to eating good corned beef at a noisy but friendly delicatessen.

This excursion outside the confines of the straight review brings me to a question which I should like to discuss with my readers. It has occurred to me that some of my recent comments on acting and staging of generally admired productions may have sounded unduly captious and severe. Why shouldn't I agree that Boyer is "superb" in *Red Gloves*, since I admit he is a good actor. Why should I be reserved and even tough with Rex Harrison and Joyce Redman, as indeed with the whole production of *Anne of the Thousand Days*, when they are all undoubtedly better than average? Why am I harsh about the direction of *The Madwoman of Chaillot*, though I am eager to see this delightful play reach a wide audience?

To answer these questions will entail the writing of several articles. For the moment, I mean only to open the discussion. I do not believe in razz reviews any more than I do in raves. Both are closer to gossip and publicity than to criticism. Criticism means, not fault finding, but appreciation. The first step in appreciation is vision—seeing and feeling; the second step is the definition of what has been seen and felt; the final step is to attempt to relate one's opinions and definitions to values outside the theatre—to life itself.

The sharper and more discriminating our appreciation of the theatre, the more interesting the theatre becomes. One of the signs of its deterioration since the twenties can be read in our diminishing concern with everything beyond brute effectiveness, which, put more bluntly, means box-office values. Much highfalutin nonsense was poured out some twenty-five years ago about stylization, new methods of stage setting and lighting, schools of acting, etc., but all of this helped keep the theatre exciting, and stimulated both theatre people and audiences to keener attention. The type of criticism which only slaps a commercial encomium on a production may help someone to a Hollywood contract; it rarely inspires anyone to better work or greater understanding.

If the theatre is an art, then it must be capable of yielding some of the results in human significance that we associate with the other arts. When I speak of the theatre, however, I do not speak of it simply as a subsidiary or annex of literature. When and in what way do acting and directing—the whole process of theatrical production become creative? This is the central issue to which I shall be obliged to return to reply to the initial query apropos of my "toughness," as well as to arrive at some standard for theatrical judgment.

—*NR*, 24 Jan. '49

IN THE GROOVE: RECORDINGS

In a sense little more need be said about these recordings than that they are technically excellent, and that if you admire their material (and who would dare admit that he doesn't?) you should be pleased to have them in your home, school, library, or club. They offer an opportunity to hear the wonderful lines spoken with admirable distinctness and occasionally with distinction. The capacity to make Shakespeare intelligible in the theatre eludes most contemporary actors.

Of the recordings listed above, I should say that Judith Anderson's rendition of Jeffers's *Medea* is the most provocative; the excerpts from Laurence Olivier's motion picture version of *Hamlet* the most likely to succeed; the Shakespeare Memorial Theatre's *Merry Wives of Windsor* the most fun; the *Richard II* of the same series, the most beautiful in its text, and *The Tempest*—also of Stratford-on-Avon Memorial Theatre origin—the least striking.

I have never heard the recording of a whole stage play. I imagine I would not enjoy the experience, for the same reason that I generally abhor listening to excerpts or a condensation of a stage play on the radio. I once attempted to listen to a half-hour version of Odets' *Awake and Sing!* which I had staged. The play is rich in good lines, and the company was the same widely admired one that I had directed. Yet I had not listened more than five minutes when I felt obliged to switch the radio off in embarrassment.

The reason for this is that a play is not simply a matter of spoken lines any more than a man is only his voice and his words. The solitary reading of a well-written play may be thoroughly enjoyable as a self-sufficient literary exercise. Any good play certainly implies and suggests the elements of its possible stage production, but the moment it is *acted* and is carried over to the theatre, it ceases to be a play in literary sense. It becomes something entirely new for which we really have no adequate name in our language except for the cumbersome, ambiguous one of theatrical production.

What distinguishes the play on the stage from the play on the page is, of course, the presence of the actor. Not only does the timbre of the actor's voice become important, the accent, pace, intensity of his speech, but his whole person, his face, manner, thought, the aura of his personality and, above all, his action or movement. But even these do not cover all of the actor's scope on the stage. The space he occupies, his relationship to the audience, his relationship to the company around him, the nature—in shape, color, placement, tone—of the environment that he occupies, all become crucial. Remove all this, and leave only the sound of the actor's voice, and you have only a fragment of the whole and, from the standpoint of the theatre, not always the most significant fragment. I cannot now recall what eminent French critic once pointed out that while the Parisian audience of the early nineteenth century thought it was admiring the classicism of Racine's verse, it was only the romanticism of Rachel's gestures it was applauding.

Let us now turn to a few details in the records at hand. Most of the graveyard scene in *Hamlet*—up to the point of Hamlet's "poor Yorick" speech—is neither very amusing nor significant when all one gets from it is the spoken dialogue. The greatness of the scene is related to the visual shock of seeing the gravediggers jibe and play over the corpses, and Hamlet's contemplation of this in the light of his situation and inner struggle. Or take Hamlet's famous "Oh that this too too solid flesh would melt": what it means in the theatre depends on what the actor intends it to mean. In his motion picture version of the play, Olivier has chosen to make it little more than a stirring of the mind—in order to solve the problem of Shakespeare soliloquies, which might strike the mass movie audience as peculiar and "unreal." The result is that in the recording we hear the speech delivered in a rather uninflected monotone that is justified only by the setting and method of Olivier's presentation. This is even truer of the "To be or not to be" soliloquy, which Olivier reads in the same fashion and largely for the same reason, whereas another actor or even the same one under different circumstances might make the speech highly dramatic and physically active.

Olivier's Hamlet might be called the gray Dane, and the scenes which have been chosen for recording tend to heighten a certain overdelicate, even weak introspectiveness, that is true to *Hamlet* only if we accept Olivier's whole conception of him, which the etching-like quality of his entire production alone can make clear.

It is precisely because the Shakespeare Memorial Theatre series lacks any sense of a specific theatrical interpretation that its recordings are so satisfactory as readings. In a word they recommend themselves to lovers of Shakespeare's poetry rather than to lovers of Shakespeare's plays. That is why the *Richard II* recording which gives the impression of having been done by actors who were less successful in their parts on the stage than were those who did *The Merry Wives of Windsor*, is nevertheless affecting. We think of the speeches only in terms of the beauty of their words, not in terms of their place in a dramatic structure. This is another way of reiterating the thesis that an acted play is not the same as a spoken poem, and that what might be good theatre will not necessarily make a satisfactory recording. "Theatre" for the ear alone demands a specific technique, which may not accord at all with what is scenically interesting.

I am at somewhat of a disadvantage with the recordings of the Jeffers' Euripides piece because I am one of the few who was astonished at Judith

Anderson's Medea without admiring it. As a *tour de force* of performance it left me cold. When I saw it on the stage I thought it mostly vocal—and therefore not the best kind of acting. But as I listen to it now without benefit of Miss Anderson's violent gestures and contorted visage, I find myself stiffening into an attitude of such resistance that I could almost wish *Medea* had been a pantomime; and if Miss Anderson is, as some have claimed, the only American actress nowadays who could do a Medea, I find myself impelled to thank God for it. But this is perhaps unfair, since the declamation of Greek tragedy presents in some respects even greater difficulties to the actor than Shakespeare's verse.

—*SR*, 29 Jan. '49

THE NERVOUS PEOPLE

Before turning to the quiescent stage, let us take note of some pictures that do not move! The latest Chagalls (at the Pierre Matisse Gallery) and some of the later work of Marsden Hartley are worth special attention.

Perhaps I am only imagining it, but there seemed to me to be something not only disturbed but disturbing in the Chagall show. His color, famous for its gaiety—sometimes candied, sometimes jeweled, but nearly always rich and evocative—this time had something crude, raucous, almost cheap about it. It is as if the artist, once ebullient with the memory of his early days in the Russian ghetto and then ecstatic with the energy of Parisian discovery but now cut off from most of his real creative sources, had become too aware of the figure he cuts in the world of painting, and of his own private appetites, pleasures and needs. What was once the dance of youth in love with the life he saw around him, and happy in his jubilant tribute to it, has now become somewhat unpleasantly Narcissistic, self-indulgently autobiographical. Most of Chagall's work has a great tenderness and, despite the rough music of its village fair

merry-making, a certain special repose. The latest Chagalls seem to blare like commercial posters. They have the unquiet and anxiety of the desperate vendor selling in a hysterical market the goods he once offered with a certain humility.

Marsden Hartley—one of the few American painters with an authentically individual speech—is not easily defined. A summary of his meaning must wait on a new and extensive retrospective show. To speak of him as a latter-day Ryder, or, as one critic does, a Walt Whitman of paint, is to miss the fascinating *impurity* of his work.

When I speak of Hartley's "impurity," I do not refer to a cheapness of intention or an effort to sell his work through facile devices. On the contrary, Hartley is almost rigidly and sternly honest in the manner of some of his puritan forbears. His work often has the sharp edge, the cragginess and unrelenting mordancy of a proud man who refuses to give himself easily. But a strange infection inhabits this soul, a secret demon, a spirit torn by the hankering for a kind of continental luxuriousness and indulgence which must turn to lonely places to repress the possibility of its satisfaction. Some of these places—Maine for example—are seen through eyes bloodshot with the strain of the artist's inner duality.

Hartley's landscapes are often majestic and unnatural. His hills, lakes, woods, his fisherfolk and farmers are not entirely of this world. The piece of rope, the rough shoes and other common objects he paints in awe of the common man and his virile ways have something weird, threatening, almost eerie about them.

Hartley seems in love with gloomy power. He is an elegant afraid of the consequences of his elegance. He is a self-forbidding sensualist. Hungry for the graces that the fleshly world offers, he adopts a self-protecting attitude of aloofness before it. He feels he ought to stay within the confines of a simple New England church, but he cannot help turning his gaze in mournful concentration on circus clowns, court and military finery, flowers to which something has been added beyond their natural fragrance. Whatever is carnal and mundane in Hartley is stiffened by a Protestant disdain and a baleful suspicion, whatever is moral and austere is pigmented and softened as if by footlights or the glow of some nether region. Hartley's work is strangely troubled, twisted and uncertain in its beauty.

There is nothing troubled about Ray Bolger. You may find one or two of the tunes in Bolger's new vehicle *Where's Charley?* to your liking—for example, the one that begins, "My darling, my darling, my darling." You will probably enjoy seeing his young leading lady, Allyn McLerie, a winsome pocket Venus who dances nicely. But above all you will appreciate the spare, eccentric gracefulness of Bolger's quality—which is unique.

Bolger is a fantastic figure out of old American funny papers, caricatures and vaudeville, domesticated but not really tamed by Broadway. In addition, he is charged with the electricity of a universally serviceable dance talent. If Bolger were a European—impossible thought!—poets would write surrealistic tributes to him, essayists would find profound symbols in the strange elasticity of his legs and the suppleness of his altogether linear body; his wiry sprightliness would be a perpetual source of inspiration to the draftsman's pencil. Let us make Bolger an American institution.

I would rather see this done with Bolger than with the jokes about the Day clan which are now sold under the title, *Life With Mother.* Mind you, I have nothing against this comic and sentimental chromo—not even its somewhat synthetic flavor. It is knowingly contrived, with several pleasantly managed episodes. I understand its success at a time when so high a premium is put on nostalgia as entertainment. The play is well turned out to look like an album of the "good old days," and, like all pleasant expertness, deserves applause. But I do not entirely understand why *Mother* should become the Sacred Cow of the American theatre. Is it simply because she is not nervous like the rest of us? It is easy for her to remain pretty birdlike and twinkling. She is only a print.

—*TRW*, Jan. '49

FOOTLIGHT CHAT

The events of the past week have been disheartening. *The Shop at Sly Corner*, an English murder thriller, closed after seven performances. *Leaf and Bough*, a kind of Sherwood Anderson-Zona Gale-Eugene O'Neill play of the Middle West by a new writer, Joseph Hayes, closed after three performances. The reports on the new revue, *All for Love*, were so dismal that I haven't yet summoned up enough courage to go to it.

The results of these productions were so negative that there would be little point in investigating the causes for their failure. Yet it is remarkable that the English play was a hit in London, and that the American play not only won a prize in an important contest but was done with impressive effect by Margo Jones in Dallas, Texas. Would it be unkind to point out that the direction of the thriller as done here was hopelessly amateurish and that Hayes's effort was practically invisible in the inept production given it at the Cort?

I say this not to blame anyone, since these plays were probably foredoomed on Broadway anyway, but because they bring up the question of acting and direction about which I promised my readers a series of general articles. This is as good as any to begin.

When that hideously named creature John Q. Public goes to the theatre, what he goes to see is a show. He may sometimes say he's going to see the Lunts or Ethel Barrymore or a play by Eugene O'Neill or Tennessee Williams, but most often he speaks only of seeing a show. In his innocence, John Q. Public is right. He is intuitively and traditionally closer to the truth of the theatre than the more sophisticated playgoer who differentiates among the various elements that constitute a show.

In the beginning, whether the drama was a communal festivity, a religious ritual, public education or a group sport, very little distinction was made among what we would call a "play," the performers and the scenery. They were all organic products of a common impulse that gave the whole occasion a single identity and meaning. Because of the specialization and dismemberment into disparate parts that characterize modern civilization, the theatre is generally organized on an additive basis: we have a promoter, plus a play, plus a director, plus actors, plus a theatre-owner, etc., all of whom present themselves on an independent and almost competitive plane. This does not alter the fact that we see them as a unit. Only by a studied effort can we isolate one from another.

If you look at theatre programs of the period before 1915, you will notice that directors and set designers were rarely mentioned. At a somewhat earlier time, most playwrights were less well-known and certainly less honored than actors.

The theatre—despite our custom of the moment—is not an art in which one element must of necessity take precedence over the others. Shakespeare between covers is always Shakespeare, but Shakespeare on the stage is frequently less valuable than a show based on the work of a writer incomparably inferior. On the stage we do not see Shakespeare's Hamlet or his Cleopatra, but Maurice Evans and Katharine Cornell—and these bring a new substance before us as real as anything that has been written for them to say. If this is not true, there can be no art of the theatre.

My argument is not new; it is something of which we need to be constantly reminded. It would be perfectly sound to discuss a play naïvely as a "show," a performed story, without special reference to its writing, individual acting, direction, settings, etc. Such a discussion would truly relate to what we experience and might thus prove an esthetically valid, because integrated, reaction. In such a discussion one might point out whatever affected him most: the plot, the spoken word, the mood engendered by the background, the beauty of a particular actor's voice or behavior. If it is too late now for us to return to such primitive honesty, if we must continue with criticism in terms of

"departments," it behooves us to make ourselves as sensitive to and studious of every phase of the theatre—acting, direction, etc.—as we have supposedly become about its literary aspect.

Among professional theatregoers (including reviewers), many of whom may be discriminating about the literary value of a play, there exists today only the most rudimentary appreciation of purely theatrical matters. Whereas the layman frequently recognizes his ignorance of the graphic arts or of music, ordinary playgoers as well as many of the theatre's professional judges are ignorant of their ignorance. As a result not only our criticism suffers but also the practice of the art itself. Acting, direction, scene design, etc., have fallen below the standard of former years because, for one thing, our approach to them has become casual, superficial, mechanical and desultory. Very few of us, for example, venture to describe more than two or three plays a season as "superb" or "great," but such epithets in regard to acting are not at all uncommon. In my opinion, however, our better plays are generally superior to our best acting and production. We must try to seek further for the reasons.

—*NR*, 7 Feb. '49

FOOTLIGHT CHAT II

Soon, soon there will be interesting new plays to see and talk about. In the meantime, the City Center offers a revival of the Rodgers-Hammerstein *Carousel* at a $3 top. It is a good buy. *Carousel* is a well-made musical of pleasant complexion. It affects me like a sugared and slightly synthetic wafer. I am certainly not its best audience, since songs that go "This was a real nice clam bake" fail to melt me. *Forward the Heart*, by Bernard Reines (at the Forty-eighth Street), attempts a new slant on the race problem (a blind young war veteran falls in love with a Negro girl). A recent tradition demands that such plays, when they are not good, be given their quietus gently by calling them "honest." The most worthwhile offering in several weeks was a dramatization of Melville's *Billy Budd* by Louis Coxe and R. H. Chapman, creditably done by the (ANTA) Experimental Theatre's invitational series under the title *Uniform of Flesh*.

Last week's chat suggested that the theatre is not a lamp by which a text may be read. The theatre, under favorable circumstances, is a creative art. To be properly understood, the theatre's parts—the dramatic scheme, words, acting, setting, music, etc.—must be viewed as a whole. As we sometimes isolate one element of a painting—composition, drawing, color, subject—as its most telling feature, so in the theatre we may regard one phase of a show the spoken text, the acting, the general pattern of stage movement—as a production's most significant aspect. However, it is always necessary to remember that whatever we may say of the color in a painting or the plot of a play, we perceive the picture and the production as a whole. To regard the theatre as merely interpretive is to misunderstand and ultimately to destroy it.

When Chaliapin entered the coronation scene of *Boris Godunov*, the libretto informed us that he was a Czar and a guilty man. Before a word was uttered, we felt that this Czar was something more than a murderous king. He was a tragic figure, whose sin had a depth that exceeded the individual case. His was the guilt of Holy Russia in all her barbarously majestic splendor, religious conscience, superstition and power. Here was the very presence of something that could hold us in awe as if we were ourselves oppressed and worshipping moujiks. A queer sense of epic grandeur was created as surely as in one of the great Muscovite cathedrals of the sixteenth century. Moussorgsky's score was not only made flesh; it was transcended.

You might say that this miracle was wrought by such details as the wonderful costume, but it was the way that Chaliapin wore his costume that made it seem the spirit as well as the fabric of a world of tortuous magnificence. (I have seen other actors in the same role wear the same costume with only illustrative effect.) How Chaliapin made his Boris what it was is part of the technique of acting, part of that mystery of "personality" which is at the core of all art. My point here is that an appreciation of the opera's music or words would be insufficient to explain or even to recognize the quality of Chaliapin's Boris. Something was made of these elements through the body and soul of the actor that was new and not to be truly grasped by a separate analysis of each element.

What is true of an actor like Chaliapin is true of a director like Reinhardt. Reinhardt worked with first rate actors like Rudolph Schildkraut, Albert Basserman, Alexander Moissi, Werner Kraus, as well as with plays by Shakespeare and other giants. But though these actors were marvelously projected through Reinhardt's direction without the forfeit of their particular contributions, and though the plays were given fascinating illumination, the whole of Reinhardt's creation was marked by that feeling of opulently sensuous rococo characteristic of the cultivated Middle European bourgeoisie between 1895 and 1914.

A knowledge of the texts employed by actors and directors is of course vital to the comprehension of what is being created by theatre artists, but one need not think of these texts entirely in terms of their literary excellence in order to evaluate what one sees on the stage. For example, I no longer recall the lines in the Dunning-Abbott melodrama *Broadway*, but my memory, of the tawdry innocence, shimmer and tension of the speakeasy twenties is still vivid in the atmosphere, images, tempo that were typical of the Jed Harris production. When I saw Charles MacArthur's revival of *The Front Page* two seasons ago, it had lost all the scalawag and brass-knuckle humor that it had originally been given. A play like *Edward, My Son*, if it were to be taken at all seriously, would read like a trashy "social" melodrama, but as played by Robert Morley it is a kind of mischievously cute parlor entertainment. To suppose that Morley conveys any of the play's literal meaning is not only to be blind to acting but even to the merits of Morley's performance itself.

This leads to the conclusion implicit in my premise: that acting and direction possess a content in themselves—that is, they possess it when actors and directors are artists. Appreciation of the theatre bespeaks the audience's capacity to sense the content of what is seen on the stage; the critic's job is to define it. Once we have established that the content of a theatre production is not necessarily the equivalent of what the literary critic may find in the play's written text, we are ready to proceed to a further examination of the interrelation among acting, directing and other elements of theatre art.

—*NR*, 14 Feb. '49

LORCA, SHAKESPEARE AND WEST

Three plays opened early last week: Lorca's *Blood Wedding* (New Stages), Shakespeare's *Richard III* (Booth) and *Diamond Lil* (Coronet). I am not being frivolous when I say that the only genuine theatre among the three productions is to be found in the Mae West revival.

Lorca's *Blood Wedding* is a beautiful play, and perhaps we should thank New Stages for presenting it, though it is sad that the only people who do such plays in our theatre are those unequipped for the task.

Lorca's drama is culturally so remote from us that I sometimes wonder whether any American company can make itself an instrument for his particular music. Profundity, in Lorca, is simple, and passion is so mingled with pride that its blaze bursts forth in a searing white or an imperious black. The peasants of his tragedies, dwelling entirely within their ritual of folk customs and religion, take on the quality of priestly aristocrats. They live close to a harsh earth, but their thought is intertwined with the values of an intellectual church hierarchy. Despite talk of vineyards, hemp and wheat, we feel as though locked within some strange chapel in which freedom exists only through formalism. Moral concepts are both earthbound and godly; there is much concern with

worldly goods, position, money—as if they too were somehow of the spirit and the law. There are drinking, dancing, love making and violence; yet all seem bound in a devout and rigid pattern. No wonder Lorca, whose style is both severely realistic and exultantly poetic, is a challenge that can barely be met by any company of non-Latin breeding. The New Stages group might well have expressed their evident devotion to him by recruiting a few players for the occasion. Though Ralph Alswang's set is a sensitive attempt to solve some of the play's scenic problems on a limited budget, though the direction has dignity and several of the actors are visually well cast, the whole effect is like the playing of the subtlest music on a penny whistle.

The new *Richard III* deserves some of the applause usually accorded Margaret Webster's productions. If it is not Shakespeare, it is at least a performance with a certain amount of youthful brio, a will to be clear, dramatic and effective. This doesn't give the interpretation actual substance, but it makes it something of a show without the stuffiness we get when actors concentrate on their golden voices, their "classically" inspired deportment and the holy burden of the Bard's verse. The present production is not unlike a gangster melodrama with fancy words. As one listens to these words—praise be, one hears a good proportion of them—as one becomes aware of the dramatist's dimension, the actors' impassioned carryings on begin to dwindle until they all become miniatures in pretty costumes.

Mae West is complete. Her Diamond Lil is a genuine creation, and we need not hesitate, because her art is comically low and her aim mercenary, to treat it seriously. Mae West is a consummate technician: she has high visibility, rhythm, a remarkable mimic sense and great guile in self-display. All this is at the service of an image based on the memory of another epoch (that of Lillian Russell) for which most of us harbor an abiding nostalgia, as if it represented a time of less constriction. Mae West's Diamond Lil is not at all of that era, it is only her model. Her art stems from the taste of the twenties, when, because of prosperity and prohibition, the raffish was glorified as the idol of atheists, and the quasi-obscene was venerated as a tribute to license.

Mae West is worth study, above all, as an expression of our attitude toward sex: in the words of Sophie Tucker, "Gentlemen don't love love, they just like to kick it around." A Mae West is unthinkable in France, where sex is *l'amour* and has a good reputation—on both lower and higher levels.

Brooks Atkinson and others are right in pointing out that *Diamond Lil* has very little sex. That is just the point: Mae West will have no truck with such dirt. She knows the Americans' preoccupation with sex and the embarrassment that covers their fear of it. She gives her public what it wants: a glittering facsimile of what it craves and, through laughter, a means of keeping itself free of what it fears. She horses around with sex so that we can have our cake and not eat it.

With all this Mae West is a true theatre artist: almost every detail of her show—including the vulgar sleaziness of its scenery—is right. Look at the stage when she is delivering her songs: the ensemble is wonderfully chosen to evoke the feeling of the Bowery with all it connotes of drab gayety, a depressed, beat-up glamorousness. It is *The Iceman Cometh* turned to farce.

—*NR*, 21 Feb. '49

PORTER ON THE PLATTER

If you are in the habit of collecting recordings of popular musicals, you will get these because *Kiss Me, Kate* is a great hit; the drama critics hailed it as a kind of masterpiece, and very few who see it are inclined to disagree with them. When a show is judged "terrific," when enough crooners put its numbers on their program, enough arrangers and bands play them, and radio repetition in all modes make them like something we breathe,

it becomes difficult not only to resist a total identification with them, but even to ask ourselves whether they are really good or not. They simply exist.

The reviewer's purpose therefore can hardly be to encourage or discourage the buying of such records. He can only muse aloud on what listening to them suggests to him.

I haven't been genuinely taken by a new song for some years now. The reason for this is not that I have grown crabbed or that song writers have all run dry—although at times I am tempted to say so—but that the composers and writers of lyrics, more than any other creators, are extremely dependent for the quality of their inspiration on the mood of the day.

We cannot listen to Offenbach without giving some thought to the frivolity of the "new" Paris of the Second Empire, we cannot disassociate Gilbert and Sullivan from the solidity of the Victorian days, we cannot hear Gershwin without recalling the prosperity of the early Twenties. With the older composers—Johann Strauss, Offenbach and others—we think retrospectively in terms of an era; with our American contemporaries, it seems natural to count in decades. Song writers, it is true, survive their decades, but when they do—have you noticed?—they are very frequently in trouble.

The only striking exception to this is Irving Berlin, whose genius consists not so much in his adaptability to every historical and theatrical contingency, but rather to his capacity to discover the root need and sentiment of all our American lives. You may argue as you will about a Noel Coward lyric, for example, but a line like "…doing what comes naturally" has something one might almost call "cosmic" about it!

Cole Porter seems to me to belong very much to the late Twenties and early Thirties. This was the time when our prosperity had become somewhat overripe with a tendency to mock as well as to enjoy itself. The early Thirties were blue with worry caused by economic despair. Young folks felt abandoned by parents who were going broke, and feared that their student years held very little promise for the future. They wanted to be consoled, they yearned for intimacy and love, the comfort of romance that might compensate for the outer cold.

The Cole Porter touch derives from the feeling of the late Twenties. It is a sophisticated touch, a chic, that expressed itself in a kind of wit that was, to begin with, almost an entirely new phenomenon in American song writing. It has more of the Continent in it—the world as cosmopolis—than was possible before World War I, at which time American provincialism had not yet been breached. This touch is still evident in my favorite number from *Kiss Me, Kate*— "Where Is the Life That Late I Led?" ("And lovely Lisa, where are you Lisa? You gave a new meaning to the leaning tower of Pisa."). It is a style that mixes the highfalutin', the tony and expensive with the almost obscenely common—as in the mixture (in this case unpleasant to me though not at all to its audience) which combines references to Shakespeare with gangster vulgarity.

It is difficult to write good songs nowadays because the late Forties—neither depressed nor confident—have developed no pathos, no enthusiasm, no faith, no conviction commonly shared. So Cole Porter, just like nearly all his colleagues has suffered a partial eclipse in this period—not, I suggest, because he has lost his gifts, but because this period in its colorless confusion gives his special talent very little support.

It is generally accepted that *Kiss Me, Kate* represents Cole Porter's best work in ten years. If this is so, it is a fact that sustains my argument. For I do not consider the score or lyrics of *Kiss Me, Kate* the best Cole Porter—not by a long shot. The brightest spots, I believe, are the plot and story-telling numbers related to the show's book. "We Open in Venice" (the lyrics are cute), "I've Come to Wive It Wealthily in Padua," and the already mentioned "Where is the Life That Late I Led?" These numbers are clever enough, but by no means the kind to mark an epoch or begin a trend. "So in Love" is a slow foxtrot that will probably prove more popular than the pieces I mentioned, because

of its independence of the show's text and its quick availability for diverse use as a dance number, etc. Pieces like "Always True to You in My Fashion" will probably be very well liked, though I find it dull; things like "Bianca" and "I Am Ashamed that Women Are So Simple" seem to me wholly without physiognomy. The delivery and voices of Alfred Drake, Patricia Morrison, Lisa Kirk, Harold Lang are, for purposes of recording, only serviceable. They are more effective on the stage.

If you disagree with these reactions, I might reply, "There is no disputing taste," although I think the remark damned nonsense: taste is the one thing that can and always should be disputed.

—*SR*, 26 Feb. '49

ATTENTION!

"Attention must be paid to such a man. Attention!" The man his wife refers to is Willy Loman, the central figure of Arthur Miller's *Death of a Salesman*. Perhaps the chief virtue of the play is the attention that Miller makes us pay to the man and his problem, for the man represents the lower middle class, the $50-a-week-plus-commission citizen, whose dream is to live to a ripe old age doing a great volume of business over the telephone. It was not unusual to hear of this person in the thirties, but in the theatre of the forties he has once more become the forgotten man.

The play has tremendous impact because it makes its audience recognize itself. Willy Loman is everybody's father, brother, uncle or friend, his family are our cousins; *Death of a Salesman* is a documented history of our lives. It is not a realistic portrait, it is a demonstration both of the facts and of their import. "We had the wrong dream," says Biff, Willy Loman's son, and what Miller is saying in terms few can miss is that this wrong dream is one the greater part of America still cherishes.

"The only thing you got in this world is what you can sell," the prosperous man next door tells

Willy. This is the harsh fact, but Willy, the poor dear fellow, is not satisfied with it. He wants to be well-liked. It is natural and healthy to harbor this desire, but the philosophy of Willy's economic situation denatures this desire to the hope of being well-liked or "known" as a way to security, success, salvation. To be a "personality" is to cultivate those traits which make one sufficiently "well-liked" to do a greater volume of business so that one may achieve a brighter place in the sun.

The competition Willy encounters is too tough for his modest talents; the path he has chosen denies his true being at every step. He idolizes the dream beyond the truth of himself, and he thus becomes a "romantic," shadowy nonentity, a liar, a creature whose only happiness lies in looking forward to miracles, since reality mocks his pretensions. His real ability for manual work seems trivial and mean to him. "Even your grandfather was more than a carpenter," he tells Biff. From this perpetual self-denial he loses the sense of his own thought; he is a stranger to his own soul; he no longer knows what he thinks either of his sons or his automobile (he boosts and denounces them both in almost the same breath); he cannot tell who are his true friends; he is forever in a state of enthusiastic or depressed bewilderment. "That man never knew who he was," Biff says of him. He never owns anything outright till his death by suicide (committed to give Biff a foundation of $20,000); he has never been free.

His sons suffer the guilt of the father: Biff, the older, with increasing consciousness; Hap, the younger, stupidly. Hap seeks satisfaction as a coarse ladies' man. Biff cannot find any satisfaction because, being more trusting and sensitive than his brother, he tries to live according to his father's dream with which he has nothing in common—the boy yearns to live on the land. Only toward the end does Biff discover the spiritual hoax of his father's life, the corruption of heart and mind to which his father's "ideals" are leading him. With his father's death, Biff has possibly achieved sufficient self-awareness to change his course; Hap—like most of us—persists in follow-ing the way of his father. He will go on striving "to come out No. 1 man." The point of all this is not that our economic system does not work, but that its ideology distorts man's true nature. Willy's well-adjusted neighbor "never took an interest in anything" and has no aspiration beyond the immediately practicable.

Arthur Miller is a moralist. His talent is for a kind of humanistic jurisprudence: he sticks to the facts of the case. For this reason his play is clearer than those of other American playwrights with similar insight whose lyric gifts tend to reflect the more elusive and imponderable aspects of the same situation. There is poetry in *Death of a Salesman*— not the poetry of the senses or of the soul, but of ethical conscience. It might have been graven on stone—like tablets of law. *Death of a Salesman* stirs us by its truth, the ineluctability of its evidence and judgment which permits no soft evasion. Though the play's environment is one we associate with a grubby realism, its style is like a clean accounting on the books of an understanding but severe sage. We cry before it like children being chastised by an occasionally humorous, not unkindly but unswervingly just father. *Death of a Salesman* is rational, dignified and profoundly upright.

Elia Kazan's production conveys these qualities with a swift and masterful thrust—like a perfect blow. He has cast the play admirably, and the entire occasion might be cited as an example of real theatre: meaning and means unified by fine purpose. Lee J. Cobb, who plays Willy Loman, is surely one of the most powerful and juicy actors on our stage today. He displays a tendency in this part to sacrifice characterization to a certain grandiosity. Willy Loman's wife speaks of his exhaustion, and Willy himself refers to his having grown fat and foolish-looking. None of these textual indications is taken into sufficient account, and what is gained in general impressiveness is lost in a want of genuine pathos.

Indeed the tone of histrionic bravura tends to make the others in the cast—for instance, Arthur Kennedy, the beautifully sensitive actor who plays

Biff—push a little too hard. The production therefore pays for its virtues by a lack of intimacy, which is the dimension needed to make the event complete. Mildred Dunnock, in her simplicity and delicacy of feeling, is like the symbolic beacon of everything sound in the production. Tom Pedi, as a waiter, is as real and tasty as a garlic salad; Hope Cameron, in the smallest role in the play, suggests a remarkably touching naïveté. Both have a specific reality that I should have liked to see carried through all the longer parts. But virtually everyone in *Death of a Salesman* is better than good; and the whole marks a high point of significant expression in the American theatre of our time.

—*NR*, 28 Feb. '49

FOOTLIGHT CHAT III

The reviewers were quick to register their dissatisfaction with Paul Muni's performance in the revival of Sidney Howard's *They Knew What They Wanted*. What they failed to note is that Muni is one of our most highly endowed actors. He is strong, vivid, emotionally fluent. In the current revival, he plays too directly for the audience's appreciation, as if his every stroke were prefaced with a "See." What he chooses to show the audience, moreover, is often secondary to the significant aspects of his role. One is doubly troubled because there is both a deficiency in the actor's taste and undeniable power in his attack. Yet I prefer the embarrassment of Muni's riches to the blank simplicity that often passes as "natural" acting.

What Muni needs is a good director. It is true that there aren't many directors in our theatre who might command his respect and be technically equipped to guide him. Still I could name six. Excellence in the modern theatre—where a feeling for the play and production as a whole as well as for individual brilliance are essential—demands a creative director.

Robert Morley in a recent talk has denied this, claiming no more for the director than the role of traffic officer. Many directors are hardly more than that; but to take such men as a norm is like arguing about literature or any other art on the basis of its worst examples. And to emphasize the importance of the director does not diminish that of the actor.

In the Theatre Guild's recent production of *My Name Is Aquilon* everything the actors do is negated by actively talentless direction. The play is a bitter-sweet whimsy about the kind of French youth who, having missed everything pleasant in life, compensates for it by indulging himself in fantasy. Though not a good play, it has a certain point and a manner of airily mischievous improvisation. It has been directed "for laughs," that is, for the effects expected from wisecracks. Charm is dispelled: nothing remains but heavy mechanical effort. Even the sets, which, if they had been designed a la Dufy or Matisse, might have indicated a playful intention, are inexpressively literal. In such a context not only is it impossible for anybody to be good, but nothing can be right.

You will observe that the sets in *My Name Is Aquilon* are here judged in terms of direction. Every element in a staged play is part of its direction. The director writes the "score" or "notes" of the theatrical production; the others play them. One might say that the director is the author of the theatrical production, except for the fact that in the collective art of the theatre no one can be more than a crucial collaborator. In the playing of the director's "notes," each of the collaborators— actors, designer, costumer, etc.—brings something of his own individuality or talent to bear.

In *They Knew What They Wanted* Muni is himself the director—in fact if not in name. But he is not a good director, since he plays his Italian vintner with a kind of story-book colorfulness— even to the make-up and costumes—while the rest of the cast plays with the naturalistic approach of the stock production. The result of this is that some fairly nondescript performances seem more "real" than Muni's, which is chock-full of good things. Impatient with directorial discipline and dependent on his own gifts, Muni helps make nonsense of his production and belies the values of his superior talent.

In my last chat, I pointed out that acting and direction must themselves possess a content. Without an awareness of what the particular content of each individual performance is, there can be no valid theatrical judgment. Let us examine a detail of two performances as a study in comparative content. In *Anne of the Thousand Days*, Harrison as Henry VIII looks into his baby's crib only to discover that the child is a girl, not the boy he had prayed for. The same scene was played by Laughton in *The Loves of Henry VIII*. Since both are scenes without words, our judgment of them receives no support from the text. In *Anne* what the actor does constitutes information neatly delivered: the king is disappointed and cold. With Laughton, the moment strikes a note of almost animal pathos, and adds a touch to the portrait of a heroically childlike primitiveness which Laughton drew his Henry.

So true is it that acting has its own content—when it *is* acting—that types, modes, styles and epochs have been set—not alone by the stage but for society at large—by actors. ("They are the brief and abstract chronicles of the time.") Rachel made the French of the 1840's aware of a new attitude toward love through her romantic transformation of Racine's classicism; George M. Cohan for many years typified the American as a shrewdly jaunty optimist; John Drew gave New Yorkers in the late nineties and early twentieth century a fresh sense of their increased urbanity in the Anglo-Continental manner; Pauline Lord introduced to our stage a special feeling for womanhood, akin to that to be found later in the plays of Tennessee Williams.

The art critics tell us we cannot understand painting if we look at pictures in terms of the subjects they depict. Somewhat the same thing is true in the evaluation of acting. Volumes have been written to direct our eyes to what is significant in the graphic arts. For similar training in the appreciation of acting, the first step would be to differentiate among the actor as material, the

nature of acting as function (what it is to act) and the meaning of acting as interpretation. The discussion of these subjects must wait on future chats.

—*NR*, 7 Mar. '49

SINS OF CLIFFORD ODETS

Logic might insist that there are three kinds of plays—good, bad, indifferent—but Clifford Odets' *The Big Knife* is none of these. It represents the state of Odets' soul in 1949; it is exasperating and exciting.

As a mechanism for conveying a definite theme, idea or emotion, *The Big Knife* is misbegotten. Charlie Castle, a top movie star and what is loosely termed an idealist, wants to get away from Hollywood, where he has become so valuable to his studio that he is being offered a 14-year contract worth three million dollars. His wife threatens to divorce him if he signs the contract, because she believes Hollywood has spoiled him: he is unfaithful and generally not the good person he was when they married.

But whatever Charlie's feelings in the matter he can't refuse the contract: the studio asserts that, if he does not sign, it will disclose him as the man who killed a child in a hit-and-run accident. Charlie signs. At this point, a girl who was in the car with him and has been bought off with a contract, seems on the verge of implicating both Charlie and the studio. Refusing to resort to further bribery, the executives contemplate murdering the girl. Charlie revolts; he insults the studio boss. But since he won't take the chance of going to jail—which he says would be to act like a character in a Russian novel—and yet feels horror at the mess of his life, he commits suicide. "He killed himself because that was the only way he could live," says a studio observer.

The ostensible point of this is that a good person in our society becomes the prisoner of forces that will manipulate him as a commodity. Unless he is a saint or a revolutionary he can live only by dying. Apart from any judgment as to the validity of this thesis, the play fails to demonstrate it.

The victim here is a good person because his wife says so, and because he speaks Odets' dialogue. The process of Charlie's deterioration is not dramatized. We never see him in a normal state. He has almost no history or background. When we meet him he is already a bad husband, a coward, a near drunkard and generally wrong at the top of his voice. His wife, who speaks for honesty, is actually his accomplice, and otherwise thoroughly vapid. The other characters (except for the writer-friend who doesn't sell out) have more substance as characters, but we are not convinced that the movie moguls, for example, behave with their native shrewdness in handling Charlie.

The theme cannot function within the story as Odets has seen fit to tell it. The story is largely off-stage, so that the theme becomes mostly rhetoric. Since this rhetoric is applied beyond the point of positive action, much of it is as impotent as the philosophic insults that Charlie hurls against his oppressors. But it is for these insults rather than for the story that Odets has written his play. Due to its faulty construction, much sincere feeling is wasted, many lines that might have been pithy are rendered pompous.

How then can the play be exciting? The subjective turmoil within the author blows gusts of passion through the proceedings and so sweeps the stage that story, characters, lines, no matter how incredible they may appear when isolated, shape to a form—tortured, inchoate, frustrated and rousing—the like of which no other American playwright can produce.

The lack of coordination between plot and theme in *The Big Knife* arises from emotional confusion in the author. It may be possible to write a clear play from a confused source, if one is honest about what actually motivates one's characters. Odets never tells the truth about Charlie Castle, which is that he *loves* Hollywood with a vicious zest, and Odets thinks this love sinful. The conflict between appetite—reinforced by society's

encouragement of it—and the insistent cry of conscience creates self-loathing and conceit. The self-loathing stems from a desire to punish oneself for one's sin, the conceit from an exalted sense of one's superiority in recognizing the sin and wishing to punish oneself for it. "If I didn't love people so much," Charlie mutters, "oh, how I would hate them."

But this is Odets speaking, and one is inclined to answer that if he would stop hating himself so much he would find it easier to get closer to himself, to people, to society. He would not then have to burn himself in effigy by having his heroes kill themselves, and he would not have to cry out, like Charlie's wife at the final curtain, "Help! Help!" It is much better to make the world's sorrow one's own than to try to make one's own sorrows the world's."

The Big Knife is not a play about Odets—it would have been better if it had been so. It is a play in which Odets' confusion about himself has unsettled the foundation of what it is supposed to be about. That is why it is difficult to praise the flashes of character perception, spiritual energy and virile quest that glint within its texture. "It takes tremendous talent to make even a little genius tolerable."

There are good actors in the production and nearly all of them do well. But Lee Strasberg, who is one of the few artists among our stage directors, has, I feel, belied some of his gifts here, and done the play in an improper vein. The direction is smooth enough in its attempt at a cocktail-hour realism, but Odets' play is best conceived as an allegory, and his writing is essentially poetic. To try to make *The Big Knife* acceptable as a literal image of fashionable reality is to magnify its faults and to denature its virtues. Strasberg, whose forte is a kind of sensitized and purified realism verging on the classic, has sacrificed this quality to make the play more palatable—that is, more ordinary. Fear or distrust of audiences is not confined to Hollywood.

—*NR*, 14 Mar. '49

FOOTLIGHT CHAT IV

Melvyn Douglas must be a very modest man. Most actors on their return to the stage from Hollywood insist on a sensational role for themselves in a play they feel certain is likely to create a great deal of talk. Douglas' part in Samuel Spewack's *Two Blind Mice* is genially conventional, the kind of thing he has done with monotonous success in countless movies. The play itself is intermittently funny, an hour and a half skit, that at any given point seems to be only ten minutes long. Nothing distinguishes it except that it kids Washington dunderheads, and thus might be said to have tinkling overtones of importance. If Douglas expects to remain on Broadway—and I hope he does—it was perfectly proper (as it always is for a practicing actor, as differentiated from a Gotham guest) to choose the first pleasant part and play he could find.

Speaking of actors, the other day I came across a statement by Samuel Johnson in connection with David Garrick. "The player," Johnson said, "only recites." Charles Lamb said much the same thing in a famous essay on Shakespeare. Both these eminences were wrong. Being an elocutionist is not being an actor. Acting is not primarily related to words at all.

To act on the stage means to behave under "unreal" or imaginary circumstances as though these circumstances were real. In this definition the word "behave" is crucial. Mimic ability or a capacity to imitate is valuable to an actor, but acting is not imitation. When I speak of "behavior" on the stage I mean that the actor must bring to each moment of his role a sense of fully experienced truth—physical and spiritual—within the circumstances of that moment: he must see, hear, move, react and feel with organic completeness and definite intention. This has little to do with "realism." The actor "forgets" himself in his role, yet always knows that he is playing, and that the object of his performance is to entertain.

There are people of engaging presence on the stage who though they have acquired facility in public deportment are not in my sense actors. They are not transformed by the imaginative reality of the circumstances which the stage calls upon them to face. The play's words and situations and our will-to-believe make them seem to be acting. They are sometimes referred to as "personalities."

Personality in an actor is of two kinds. The first relates to what might be called social personality—such as we remark in a pretty girl, a charming man, a funny fellow, etc.—characteristics which may or may not contribute to acting talent. The second kind of personality has to do with the actor as an instrument. A person of fluent emotional nature, quick sensory reaction, mobility of inner constitution, a person with an expressive voice, striking mask, natural grace, commanding figure, imagination, impressionability and temperament, ought to provide the best acting material.

When Tallulah Bankhead and Charles Boyer are called "superb" what is meant is that they do indeed act, and that they are, in addition to this, striking media or instruments for the stage. For final distinction in acting still another element must be present—illuminating interpretation.

"Interpretation" is a word often loosely used to indicate almost anything the actor happens to do with his part. More strictly, it should apply to what the actor chooses his part to mean. We call a writer "good" not simply to compliment his skill in the use of language but to approve his content. One may agree that an actor shows interesting skill and yet find in him a lack, or a falsity, of interpretation. Boyer's Hoederer in *Red Gloves* seemed to me to have very little interpretation, just as the Morley of *Edward, My Son*—part social wit and part actor—strikes me as amusing and fortunate "misinterpretation."

I have seen actors give remarkable acting performances in plays which they virtually wrecked. Years ago Jacob Ben-Ami played the name part in Giraudoux's *Siegfried*, a play about a Frenchman who, having lost his memory in the war, gains a high post in German diplomacy. Ben-Ami gave an unforgettable portrayal of the tragedy of living one's life without memory of one's past, but the play happened to be a comedy about the delightful difference between the French and German mentality.

The interpretation of a part may sometimes be solely the actor's work. It may even be wise to allow a player of profound intuition to make a part entirely his own. Indeed the very choice of a certain player (Laurette Taylor, let us say) may be a sign that the director has agreed to give his production the stamp of that actor's quality. Yet in sound theatre practice the director should be held responsible for the over all interpretation of a play and its parts. The director should not only set the outline of the actor's interpretation but help him find the method for its concrete embodiment.

Critics often fail to distinguish between the acting and direction of a play because they conceive the director's function as an editorial one, concerned chiefly with technical neatness, pace, mechanics.

In my final chat in this series I shall discuss direction in the light of interpretive content. In the meantime I should like to add that our actors have more real personality than would appear from their performances, and are usually capable of greater interpretive values in their playing than we see. The fault here may be ascribed, to a considerable extent, to our directors, but even more to the chaos of our theatre, which makes a haphazard thing of the relation between actor and director: at the beginning of rehearsals actor and director rarely know each other and are at times even leery of each other.

—*NR*, 21 Mar. '49

FOOTLIGHT CHAT FINALÉ

James Allardice's *At War with the Army* is both funny and fun. We haven't seen an old-fashioned farce of this kind for a long time, and I think it's a pity. We want our comedy more pretentious nowadays, which doesn't signify that we have grown more clever, only more tired. *At War with the Army* is a combination barracks and college-boy show in semi-vaudeville style with rough and ready gags that constitute engaging Americana—part Chic Sale and part Bill Mauldin. It has been excellently cast and ably directed by Ezra Stone. I found William Lanteau, Tad Mosel, Jerry Jarrett and Mike Kellin particularly colorful—affectionate wartime caricature come to life. Gary Merrill as a sorely tried First Sergeant holds the show together. There is about him, too, a suggestion of latent tragic power awaiting the igniting touch of the right part and the right director.

An actor's personality might be said to possess a certain weight. This means a certain degree or quality of human experience. If we think of José Ferrer's facile and amusing performance in *The Silver Whistle* and one that might have been given in the same role by Otis Skinner, we may discover something about the younger actor's limitations. The difference is not in the skill, but in the stuff of life out of which acting is made. John Barrymore was surely the first actor of our stage between 1916 and 1925, not only because of his physical endowment but because of a richness of sensibility, wit, mental force, artistic aspiration, aristocratic soul. Many actors cannot be judged as artists at all because they are composed of thin stuff.

Is not the "stuff" of the actor's nature something he is born with? To a large extent, yes. But I believe it a great mistake to leave it at that. To a great degree, the actor may be made (or unmade) by his social and theatrical environment. What surrounds the actor—his audience, company, playwright, general artistic influences and director—can contribute much to the measure of the actor's personality. I can think of no English-speaking actor with greater natural gifts than Alfred Lunt. Yet Lunt's achievement in the last ten years cannot be compared with that of Laurence Olivier, whose actual talent is not superior to that of the American actor. To understand this discrepancy, we must examine the environment both inside and outside the theatre to which both men belong.

Such an examination would take us far afield. But it is to be noted that no English actor achieves undisputed eminence whose repertory does not include several classic roles. To have played Chekhov, Sheridan, Sophocles and Shakespeare with distinction means more for an actor's prestige in England than the greatest acclaim in an ordinary box-office success. This in itself means that there is a constant challenge to the English actor to test himself in parts which make greater demands on his capacities than do most contemporary plays. It should be remembered, too, that to play Hotspur, Shallow, Dr. Astrov (in *Uncle Vanya*), Mr. Puff and King Oedipus actually serves to educate the actor more than a lifetime in plays like *O, Mistress Mine*.

At this point I should like to stress the importance of the director. The director, as the active principal of a play's interpretation, works through all the elements of the theatrical medium, but primarily through the actor. Many fine individual performances are given without any assistance at all from the director; but rarely is an integrated production with a consistent interpretation by a whole cast given without a director's conscious guidance. Kingsley's *Men in White* was a well-constructed play with an interesting background, but the lofty quality given it by the Group Theatre company was not due to the excellence of its individual members but to the direction of Lee Strasberg.

The style of acting in a production is an interpretive problem which the director alone can solve. The problem is not simply a matter of taste but of meaning. What shall the play say? Is *The Dybbuk*, for example, a play of quaint folk customs regarded with sentimental affection, or a play about a ritualistic world seen as a frightening phantasmagoria of the past? It may be either. The director decides which.

In 1934 I saw a Gorky play, *Igor Buletchev*, in two different Moscow productions on two consecutive evenings. In one production the play was about the spiritual tragedy of a man who has come to doubt the truthfulness of everyone around him. In the second production, it was a play about the necessary decline of a magnificent representative of a class that could not share the needs and hopes of a new generation. There were very few textual variances between the two, but everything else—style of setting, characterizations, make-ups, tempo, etc.—was radically different. Gorky said both productions were "right."

Is *A Streetcar Named Desire* a play about a healthy couple almost wrecked by the intrusion of a destructively neurotic woman, or the story of a woman of fine fiber destroyed by the brutally crude attributes of her surroundings? Whether it is one or the other does not depend solely on the ability of the actors cast for either interpretation, but on the director's choice and his craftsmanship in the realization of his interpretation. A production that achieves meaning by accident is rarely of more than momentary interest.

Shakespeare seldom has significant content in our theatre—despite Shakespeare—because the direction of Shakespearean productions is usually little better than smooth stage management. I could not discern any sustained line of interpretation in Orson Welles's alert production of *Caesar*, but it was a memorable one, because at least two scenes—the opening with its "trouble in the town" atmosphere, and the scene in which the poet Cinna was lynched—gave the feeling of a Shakespeare play seen in a time of political ferment. Without such directorial insights and/or flashes of creative acting, true theatre cannot be said to exist.

—*NR*, 28 Mar. '49

SCENERY

Some years ago Sidney Howard summed up his view of stage setting by saying, "My only rule is—get Jo Mielziner." Howard's rule has been scrupulously followed by many managers. Its chief virtue is that it confesses either ignorance of or indifference to the esthetics of the question. Most reviewers are not so honest. It is obvious from their writing that even where they manifest good judgment on other aspects of theatrical production, their understanding of scenic design is less than rudimentary. More alarming, however, is the fact that a great many theatre people are themselves vague on what they expect from the setting of a play—except that it ought to look "real" and be attractive.

The current exhibition of scene design and costume at the Metropolitan Museum of Art ("Behind American Footlights") suggests a statement of principles in regard to the visual aspect of the theatre to supplement my five *Footlight Chats* on acting and direction. In the early years of this century stage settings had become a combination of academically Victorian landscape painting for exteriors with a kind of tawdry rococo for interiors. Costume plays were done with sets so heavily "historical" that Shakespeare's plays had to be drastically cut: the weight of the sets made quick changes impossible. The setting for the ordinary drawing room was a reflection of the gimcrack modishness of the nineteenth-century French theatre rather than any actual place. To give a production visual interest, producers spent money on some form of gaudy display or on special effects such as a train wreck, a great fire, a chariot race with real horses, as in *Quo Vadis?* or *The Whip*.

Later, David Belasco began to stress meticulous naturalism. A stage replica of a Childs' restaurant became a famous setting; a scientist's library contained all the books that such a person might

own; rainstorms and sunrises were reproduced with astounding verisimilitude.

Around 1915 Robert Edmond Jones, Lee Simonson and others became the pioneers of a new stage craft inspired by European theorists and producers—Craig, Appia, Reinhardt. The stage setting was now conceived mainly as a medium for the projection of a play's essential mood. Between 1919 and 1929, a whole new generation of scene-designers who had learned from Jones's and Simonson's example came to the fore. Reviewers began to devote considerable space to the work of these new men.

Decor, as it was then fondly called, has once more become a routine affair with tasteful and simplified decorativeness, or naturalism as the norm. The reviewers' response to "scenery" has also become routine, with comments that range from the commonplace to the ridiculous. We even hear people affirm that plays might be better done without any "scenery" at all.

Here we have a glimpse of the basic misunderstanding. There is no such thing as a play without scenery. A bare stage is a setting; whatever is seen by an audience is part of the effect of the whole. The stage setting therefore is not primarily decoration, but a function of the play as an organism.

The director may wish his setting or, more accurately, stage arrangement to appear inconspicuous or he may wish it to play a prominent role in the evocation of a particular emotion in the audience, as in the case of the sensuous musical comedy. The director may feel that the place which the setting is supposed to represent must be photographically convincing in order for the play to be interesting, or he may believe that a mere indication of place is sufficient. In certain instances no actual place need be represented at all, and realistic detail is not only irrelevant but undesirable. The choice of setting depends on the director's artistic purpose, his creative idea in regard to the nature, quality or meaning of the entire production.

The director formulates the play's scenic or visual problem; the designer brings his talent to bear on its solution. Exhibitions of scenic art and most criticism of it tend to make scene-design seem an adjunct of painting or decoration to be admired independently of its function in the theatre, where it is meant to serve the play as articulated by actors before an audience. That the set of *Summer and Smoke* looked pretty was of far less significance than that its playing space constricted freedom of movement. That the set of *The Big Knife*, which most reviewers thought handsome, looks like a Hollywood steak house is far less disturbing, than that it makes it difficult for the audience to concentrate on the actors or to conceive of the play's action in any but the most literal terms an approach detrimental to the play's most cogent elements. Even such brilliantly witty sets as those of *The Madwoman of Chaillot* may be criticized for a static quality that reduces their practicability for a kind of "magic" flexibility the play suggests.

It doesn't make good theatre sense for an audience to applaud a set for its abstract "beauty." A set is a utensil which cannot be judged until its worth is proved in practice by the whole course of the play's development on the stage.

—*NR*, 4 Apr. '49

GOOD KISSING

South Pacific, by Rodgers, Hammerstein and Logan, is a good musical. Others call it great. They mean what I do when I call it good. On Broadway, to say that something is good is practically an insult.

As a score and a book, *South Pacific* is highly efficient. Rodgers' tunes are craftsmanlike and pleasant. He knows how to make a little go a long way. Hammerstein's lyrics and his book (in collaboration with Logan) are simple, easy, engaging, not startlingly original but honorably liberal and decent throughout. Mielziner's sets are clean, attractive, gratifyingly without fuss. The real triumph of the show, aside from its unerring sense of trim unity, is the cast. I have nothing but praise for the people

who play *South Pacific* and the manner in which Logan, as director, has handled them.

To begin with, there is Mary Martin. She is the epitome of the show's virtues. "I am as normal as blueberry pie," she sings in one of the show's cheerful numbers. When she tells us with radiant good nature, "I'm in love, I'm in love, I'm in love with a wonderful guy," one doesn't murmur "Who cares?" but, "Congratulations, congratulations, congratulations to you both."

Mary Martin is our ideal, our dream, our faith. She is fresh, lively, humorous, useful and very, very good company. She is delightfully feminine and just a little hoydenish, so that we can enjoy her sex without being oppressed by it. When we take her out, we shall be the envy of all the other fellows, without having to worry. In addition to her shining bright personality, Mary Martin is a grand performer. Entirely without cheapness, stridency, stickiness, she is effortlessly deft. She sings, dances, flirts and acts with a bouncing naturalness that is the happy marriage of hard work and talent.

The quality of healthy Americanism, a buoyant youthfulness still unspoiled by taint of trade, carries through the production. Juanita Hall, who plays a Tonkinese mamma, is as sound and sweet in her delicately racy exoticism as Mary Martin in her native (Little Rock) charm. Betta St. John is poetically dainty and graceful as the Tonkinese sweetheart. William Tabbert, the juvenile lead, has none of the tenor slushiness that mars so many singing actors. He is so admirably right in his quality and performance I kept wishing the authors would not kill him off. That he fails to return to his ivory-colored island love is, for me, almost the only flaw in the plot. Myron McCormick, as an unregenerate gob, plays with a solid, low-comedy relish. Even the "iron belly" officers are excellently cast: Martin Wolfson has a fine astringent dryness; as Henry James once said of an actor, Harvey Stephens gives a loyal performance.

How clever of Logan and his associates to have set Ezio Pinza down amid the resplendent American corn. They show each other off to advantage. Pinza's qualities, including of course his magnificent voice, have been employed with remarkable tact. The producers' shrewdness consists in making this tall, broad-shouldered, mature and cultured gentleman the hero of the show. Men in the audience respond to Pinza's singing and magnanimously concede that he has an impressive figure, but the women, the women, the poor, deprived women in the audience must swoon at Pinza's kissing. Such sincere, appreciative and manful osculation has not been seen in the theatre hereabouts for a long time. Pinza's performance is so infectious in this respect that the younger couple in the show (Betta St. John and William Tabbert) gives almost as good account of themselves as do the more experienced leads. It helps spread a warm glow over the proceedings.

This is not all. The "chorus" of Seabees is composed of boys who can act, and who sound as well as look as if they might all grow up to be men—like Pinza; the girls are real pretty in the best new (un-Ziegfeldian) tradition.

I am off to Paris, Rome, Tel-Aviv. I shall write from those places. I am glad that the last play of the season I was called upon to review was the delectable *South Pacific*.

—*NR*, 25 Apr. '49

THE FIRST PLAYER

Garrick by Margaret Barton

The theatre has a history, but profits have no past. The theatre in our time and place being primarily a business (shoddy), very few people are concerned with its roots and forebears. If our theatre were truly alive, if its workers were inspired to treat themselves as artists rather than as worried job-hunters, if its critics were more than registrars of the play market, they would find theatre history of something more than academic or sentimental interest.

Margaret Barton's book on Garrick, the most renowned actor in English theatre history, is distinctly above the level of most stage biographies. It is not a mushy encomium, a retrospective publicity blurb for a one-time stage favorite; it is a solid documentation of facts eminently worth remembering in considering not only the theatre of old but the theatre today. Though the picture Miss Barton draws is a little undifferentiated, mingling its biographical data, literary allusions, historical color and personal comment without special emphasis on any single element, what stays with us as most significant are the salient features of the eighteenth-century English theatre (1749-1776) and David Garrick's pivotal role in it.

Garrick revived the English theatre audiences' appetite for Shakespeare even though his versions of Shakespeare's plays were only a little less mangled than those of his predecessors. Garrick effected his revolution by the introduction of naturalism into his acting. Garrick's naturalism was not ours, but it served to discredit the idea that acting was synonymous with declamation. Not only was his playing based on an observation of life, but he established a continuity of pattern that gives his interpretations a wholeness difficult to achieve when acting was thought of in terms of separate "arias." It was an innovation in those days to go on acting between one's speeches. "When three or four are on the stage with him," said one astonished observer, "he is attentive to whatever is spoken, and never drops his character when he has finished a speech."

What is remarkable in all this is not simply the reminder that acting was not always what it is today (we need not suppose that it was bad before it got to be what we are familiar with) but that the change in acting was one of the earliest expressions of the new romanticism which was to transform not only the theatre in England and Europe but poetry, art, moral concepts and the mode of life. The new naturalism of romanticism meant that the individual in all the particularity of his private emotions had in every field come to occupy the center of the stage. In the theatre of the eighteenth century it was almost entirely in acting alone that the new romanticism became evident. Even in the early nineteenth century, the romanticism of the English poets had no new literary equivalent in the theatre as French romanticism did in the plays of Hugo, de Vigny and de Musset. (I am not forgetting such things as Shelley's *Cenci.*) It was the actor Edmund Kean who embodied English romanticism in the theatre of that period. Through this fact we learn once more that the theatre in its purely theatrical attributes may be expressive of states of mind typical of a whole epoch.

It is instructive, too, to analyze the elements that went into the making of Garrick's acting. For sometime before Garrick, the French harlequinade which had developed into the English pantomime had been taking popular precedence over Shakespeare in the London theatre. Shakespeare was being stultified in the dreariness of traditional elocution, whereas the pantomime possessed the animal vigor of the streets. Garrick learned from the pantomime how thought could be conveyed through gesture, movement, the physical life of the stage. Garrick discovered what the forebears of pantomime, the Italian comedians, had always known: that the source of the actor's art is not the dramatist's word but the actor's body.

Garrick's peculiar reverence for Shakespeare (whom he "adapted") as well as his actor's instinct led him to such vital reforms as the practice of casting minor parts carefully. He also modified the bull-ring atmosphere of the eighteenth-century stage, got rid of the fops who enjoyed watching plays from the wings, and inspired actors with a greater respect for their profession. He advised a theatre novice "to seek good company *away from the stage*, and to enlarge his knowledge of literature and life."

Miss Barton's book stimulates reflection in all directions: her remarks about the effect of candle-light on the acting of Garrick's time make us think of the relation of the later technics—gas light and electricity—to the audience psychology of later periods. Her comments on the beginnings of naturalism in acting reminds me how the wheel of time

has turned so that today a revolutionary modern, Bertolt Brecht, asks us to create a new anti-naturalism.

It was Garrick's glory to have begun that train of thought in the theatre which might be said to have culminated in the teachings of Stanislavsky. We find Garrick saying with brilliant intuition: "The greatest strokes of genius have been unknown to the actor himself till circumstances and the warmth of the sun have sprung the mine, as it were, as much to his own surprise as to that of the audience."

—*NR*, 30 May '49

THE SUCCESS DREAM ON THE AMERICAN STAGE

When A *Streetcar Named Desire* was first produced, a lady in the theatre asked me what I thought of it. "It is a beautiful play" was my reply. "Is that all?" she complained. She wanted me to say that the play was *great, great, great.*

I have thought of that lady many times since. I imagine that when she saw Arthur Miller's new play, *Death of a Salesman,* she more or less forgot her enthusiasm for the Tennessee Williams play and made a long face when anyone said anything about the Miller play which did not begin and end with a passionate proclamation of its greatness.

I do not believe this mania for the great bespeaks a profound appreciation of the arts or even unusual warmness of heart. The jubilant cries of admiration which will greet Williams' *A Streetcar Named Desire* are more often than not followed by a deprecation of the same author's less successful *Summer and Smoke,* and after that, by indifference, skepticism or forgetfulness.

The American spectator always clamors for new heroes. The hero's glory is a short one. We are so eager to express the intensity of our feeling when we come upon some reason for excited praise that we generally lose sight of what it is that we are praising. I am reminded of the girl who received a box of flowers from a boy friend and exclaimed, "Oh, how lovely!" before she opened the box to see its contents.

Our prepared ecstasies are closer to fadism than to love. They hide an insult to the artist, for what the artist is given is our favor not our understanding. To love is to see and to share. We can neither see nor share what the artist gives us if we are intent only on manifesting our pleasure in bestowing approval. Our mania for the great is a self-intoxicant, an egocentric indulgence rather than a tribute.

Since most of us soon exhaust the pleasure we take in ourselves, we are quick to discard the objects that afford us the excuse for such exercise. We look around for something new to give ourselves a thrill with; we find something else that is "great." The manufacturers of publicity are familiar with this mechanism, and live by exploiting it.

Our mania has two main victims: the artist and the public. The artist, hungry for appreciation, imagines that our enthusiasm serves him. It does serve him commercially—which is one of the reasons why he cannot guess its danger—but it soon becomes a poison. It is a poison when the artist learns—as he must—that the enthusiasm is superficial, ephemeral, made to please ourselves rather than to reward him. He feels more lonely than ever when we have turned to our new enthusiasm. But the most toxic effects of our enthusiasm come from its emphasis, which is not actually on what the artist has made, but on the artist as a subject for flattery.

The artist can grow only when he keeps his sources, his material and the object of his creation constantly before him. The moment the artist puts himself before his work as a thing with a life and dignity of its own, the artist deteriorates. Art is a responsibility as well as a "release." The artist is himself in service—to the things that have moved him and to the thing that has come from him, both of which always exist beyond his ego. By turning the artist's consciousness to his own "greatness" instead of directing it to his task, we who praise

him, in the spirit of a man being congratulated on having made a killing in Wall Street, help to destroy him. The fields of American arts and letters are strewn with the remains of many whom we slaughtered with our "kindness."

The public suffers because its glad shouts separate it from anything but the gratification it takes in shouting. We can receive the full measure of value from a work of art only by possessing it within ourselves, by bringing all our faculties of sympathy, experience and thought to bear upon what has been offered us. Criticism is not a matter of finding fault or of giving credit but of perceiving, testing, weighing, apprehending. We make true contact with what has been given us; we add to it and increase with it. Through this "marriage," we make a world richer by what we have received and returned.

Criticism of the arts—particularly, due to its closeness to the market, the theatre—is becoming increasingly difficult in our country because of our mania for pronouncing judgments in terms of meaningless labels such as "great." Writers, actors, directors are fast becoming incapable of profiting by or even listening to criticisms of any kind, because what they want to know before anything else is what label—one might say price tag—has been placed on their wares, which soon is taken to mean on their own person.

Arthur Miller's *Death of a Salesman* is one of the outstanding plays in the repertory of the American theatre. That its theme is not strictly speaking new to our stage—Arthur Richman's *Ambush* (1921), J. P. McEvoy's *The Potters* (1923), Elmer Rice's *The Adding Machine* (1923), George Kelly's *The Show-Off* (1924), Clifford Odets' *Awake and Sing!* and *Paradise Lost* (1935) being in this respect its antecedents—does not in any way lessen its effect or significance. The value of *Death of a Salesman* lies in the fact that it states its theme with penetrating clarity in our era of troubled complacency.

Death of a Salesman is a challenge to the American dream. Lest this be misunderstood, I hasten to add that there are two versions of the American dream. The historical American dream is the promise of a land of freedom with opportunity and equality for all. This dream needs no challenge, only fulfillment. But since the Civil War, and particularly since 1900, the American dream has become distorted to the dream of business success. A distinction must be made even in this. The original premise of our dream of success—popularly represented in the original boy parables of Horatio Alger—was that enterprise, courage and hard work were the keys to success. Since the end of the First World War this too has changed. Instead of the ideals of hard work and courage, we have salesmanship. Salesmanship implies a certain element of fraud: the ability to put over or sell a commodity regardless of its intrinsic usefulness. The goal of salesmanship is to make a deal, to earn a profit—the accumulation of profit being an unquestioned end in itself.

This creates a new psychology. To place all value in the mechanical act of selling and in self-enrichment impoverishes the human beings who are rendered secondary to the deal. To possess himself fully, a man must have an intimate connection with that with which he deals as well as with the person with whom he deals. When the connection is no more than an exchange of commodities, the man himself ceases to be a man, becomes a commodity himself, a spiritual cipher.

This is a humanly untenable situation. The salesman realizes this. Since his function precludes a normal human relationship, he substitutes an imitation of himself for the real man. He sells his "personality." This "personality," now become only a means to an end—namely the consummated sale—is a mask worn so long that it soon comes to be mistaken, even by the man who wears it, as his real face. But it is only his commercial face with a commercial smile and a commercial aura of the well-liked, smoothly adjusted, oily cog in the machine of the sales apparatus.

This leads to a behavior pattern which is ultimately doomed; not necessarily because of the economic system of which it is the human concomitant, but quite simply because a man is not a machine. The death of Arthur Miller's salesman is symbolic of the breakdown of the whole concept of salesmanship inherent in our society.

Miller does not say these things explicitly. But it is the strength of his play that it is based on this understanding, and that he is able to make his audience realize it no matter whether or not they are able consciously to formulate it. When the audience weeps at *Death of a Salesman,* it is not so much over the fate of Willy Loman—Miller's pathetic hero—but over the millions of such men who are our brothers, uncles, cousins, neighbors. The lovable lower middle-class mole Willy Loman represents is related to a type of living and thinking in which nearly all of us—"professionals" as well as salesmen—share.

Willy Loman never acknowledges or learns the error of his way. To the very end he is a devout believer in the ideology that destroys him. He believes that life's problems are all solved by making oneself *well liked* (in the salesman's sense) and by a little cash. His wife knows only that he is a good man and that she must continue to love him. His sons, who are his victims, as he has been of the false dream by which he has lived, draw different conclusions from his failure. The younger boy, Hap, believes only that his father was an incompetent (as do many of the play's commentators) but he does not reject his father's ideal. (It is to be noted that in a very important sense Willy Loman is sympathetic precisely because of his failure to make himself a successful machine.) The older boy, Biff, comes to understand the falsity of his father's ideal and determines to set out on a new path guided by a recovery of his true self.

There are minor flaws in *Death of a Salesman,* such as the constant pointing to a secret in the older brother's past which is presumed to be the immediate cause of his moral breakdown—the secret turning out to be the boy's discovery of his father's marital infidelity. There is validity in this scene as part of the over-all picture of the father-son relationship. A shock such as the boy sustains here often serves to propel people into the unexplored territory of their subconscious, and may thus become the springboard for further and more basic questioning. Miller's error here is to make the boy's horror at his father's "deceit" appear crucial rather than contributory to the play's main line.

Some people have objected that the use of the stream-of-consciousness technique—the play dramatizes Willy's recollection of the past, and at times switches from a literal presentation of his memory to imaginary and semi-symbolic representation of his thought—is confusing, and a sign of weakness in the author's grasp of his material.

These objections do not impress me. The limitations of *Death of a Salesman* are part of its virtues. The merit in Miller's treatment of his material lies in a certain clean, moralistic rationalism. It is not easy to make the rational a poetic attribute, but Miller's growth since *All My Sons* consists of his ability to make his moral and rationalistic characteristics produce a kind of poetry.

The truth of *Death of a Salesman* is conveyed with what might be compared to a Living Newspaper, documentary accuracy. With this there is a grave probity and sensitivity that raise the whole beyond the level of what might otherwise have seemed to be only agitation and propaganda. Other playwrights may be more colorful, lyrical and rich with the fleshed nerves and substance of life; Miller holds us with a sense of his soundness. His play has an ascetic, slatelike hue, as if he were eschewing all exaggeration and extravagance, and with a sobriety that is not without humor yet entirely free of frivolity he issues the forthright commandment, "Thou shalt not be a damn fool!"

Elia Kazan's production is first-rate. It is true to Miller's qualities, and adds to them a swift directness, muscularity and vehemence of conviction. If any further criticism is in order I should say the production might have gained a supplementary dimension if it had more of the aroma of individual characterization, more intimacy, more of the quiet music of specific humanity—small, as the people in the play are small, and yet suggestive of those larger truths their lives signify.

Mildred Dunnock as the mother embodies the production's best features: its precision, clarity, purity of motive. Someone has said that the part might have been more moving if it had been played by an actress like Pauline Lord with all the magic overtones and "quarter tones" of her subtle sensibility. Concretely such a suggestion is, of course, irrelevant, but it points to a need I feel in the production as a whole more than to Miss Dunnock's particular performance.

Lee Cobb as the salesman is massively powerful and a commanding actor every step of the way. Yet I cannot help feeling that Cobb's interpretation is more akin to the prototype of a King Lear than to Willy Loman. What differentiates Willy from some similarly abused figure is his utter unconsciousness—even where the author gives him conscious lines—his battered pride, querulous innocence, wan bewilderment even within the context of protest and angry vociferation.

Cameron Mitchell as the younger son is eminently likable, but for the play's thesis he ought also to be something of a comic stinker. Arthur Kennedy, who plays the older son, is a truly fine actor, who loses some of his edge, because the general high pitch of the production forces him to blunt his natural delicacy.

Jo Mielziner's scene design seems to me too complex in shape and too diverse in style to be wholly satisfactory for a functional set or for beautiful decoration. Neither this nor any of the other faults that may have been found in *Death of a Salesman* prevent it from remaining a cardinal event not only of this season but of many a long year in the American theatre.

The importance of Clifford Odets' *The Big Knife* derives from the fact that any serious effort such a playwright as Odets undertakes should be a matter of special concern to those who are devoted to genuine expression in the arts of our time. Clifford Odets, in success or failure, is a man grappling with essential moods and problems of our American life. Very few people in our theatre do.

It is easy to spot the technical weakness that invalidates *The Big Knife* as a play. It fails to dramatize the core of its plot. Charlie Castle is an actor with pretensions to serious artistic aims. His enormous success in Hollywood has warped his will so that he begins by becoming a bad husband—sexual promiscuity being the first symptom of his disintegration—goes on to becoming a bad actor, is softened to cowardice (he runs away from an automobile accident in which he kills a child and then allows his buddy to shoulder the blame), drinks heavily to deaden his conscience, and ends by committing suicide when he no longer can bear the burden of facing his life. This story has no before and after. We have to take the author's say-so that Charlie was ever worth bothering about; we are never convinced that Hollywood as such was the decisive factor in Charlie's decay. We never witness the process by which Hollywood reduced him to subservience of body and slavery of soul.

If the play is indeed about Hollywood it is necessary to prove the play's thesis through action. But though Odets piles detail upon detail, which are of specific Hollywood connotation (including reference to its weather), the play omits scenes of crucial action, because Odets really wants to say something other than what his plot and its Hollywood color lead us to believe. Charlie Castle is the symbol of the growing American young man of fine sensibility who struggles for success only to find, when he attains it, that it is a trap which has robbed him of his freedom and his virtue—his power to love, to struggle, to grow.

The grandfather in Odets' *Awake and Sing!* asks his complaining grandson, "That's what you want, Ralphie? Your name in the paper?" and the boy answers, "I wanna make up my own mind about things…be something." Ralphie finds out he can be something by staying at home with "a job to do." "It's no time to die," he exclaims. Ralphie begins "to take inventory." Charlie Castle might be described as a Ralphie who ran away, not "to do a job," but "to have his name in the paper." That is why he finds that it's only a time to die.

There is a confusion in Odets which makes him often unable to distinguish between doing a job and having "one's name in the paper." This confusion is to some extent the subject of *Golden Boy* and *The Big Knife,* but in the latter case the author has become the confusion's victim. Ralphie's background is real, and correct conclusions can be drawn from his struggle with it. Charlie Castle has been given no real background, and is therefore no true or particular person, only a generalized nonentity—part Hollywood image and part self-tortured spirit of Odets himself—and no correct conclusions can be drawn from an examination of his story.

Everything in Charlie's life and thought is an evasion of specific facts. Even his love for his wife must be assumed. Why does he hate Hollywood? That it makes bad pictures is not a convincing reason. One begins to ask oneself the startling question: does Charlie really hate Hollywood? Isn't he in fact hellishly attached to it? Isn't part of the play's venom like a man beating a woman he cannot bring himself to break away from? ("Make a break or spend the rest of your life in a coffin," says a character in *Awake and Sing!*) The "name in the paper" motif is subtler and profounder than we suspected. Perhaps what Charlie (Odets) wants most is not "to do a job" but to be "great"—just as everything and everyone must be "great" in our country from our girl friends down to our symphonies, from our dramatists up to our refrigerators. If Charlie is to be taken literally, he is a pig prodded by Odets' conscience.

The Big Knife represents Odets stewing in his own juices. These juices are rich even when they have turned sour: *The Big Knife* has scenes, characters, lines that are instinct with profound sensibility, sharp observation, wit. emotional force. But the sight of an immensely gifted artist wallowing and thrashing about in a bath of warm and hysterical sentiments is extremely disquieting.

It is simply not true that our society (or even Hollywood) must necessarily defeat the potential human power of all who dwell within it. Such defeat comes only to those who accept our society entirely on its own terms or to those who want to hate it but who actually love it for those things which destroy their sense of responsibility and their need to struggle with it. One cannot be a progressive and believe that the evils of our society must necessarily prostrate us. One cannot believe that we are inescapably doomed and remain an artist. Odets knows this, but he cannot altogether bring himself to accept the guilt he feels at being more eager for his "name in the papers" than for going ahead and doing a job.

The result of this inner conflict makes for a frustrated lyricism of anger without action, a lack of that objectivity which might either enable Odets to write a frank statement of his problem in terms specifically relevant to his own history or, what would be far more useful, a play that really treats of society without blaming it for the personal injustices inflicted on some alter ego like Charlie Castle—a blame and an injustice about which Odets is so obviously uncertain that both society and the character become the targets of an equal hate.

The Big Knife, I repeat, is a mess made by a great talent. It is neither the true story of Odets nor the clear account of a freely conceived Charlie Castle. Its subjectivity is muddled by its pretense of objectivity, its objectivity is compromised by the author's inability to distinguish between his creature and himself. *The Big Knife* in fact is no story at all, but an inchoate cry of anguish, a "Help! help!" from the privacy of an artist's den which no one will heed because no one except the personally interested and the acute of ear will be able to identify or find reason to attend.

The production of *The Big Knife,* despite good actors, "makes" as if it were a tragedy by George Kaufman, and thus magnifies the play's defects without doing justice to its considerable qualities.

—*TRW*, May '49

THE NEW FRONTIER

Had an American visiting California in 1855 sent back East nothing more than his impressions of the San Francisco theatre he would have been justly set down as a fool. Although the analogy is hardly accurate, I feel a little foolish writing on the theatre in Tel-Aviv. Israel as a nation has within a year become a new world in which the theatre plays only a tiny part.

I had little idea when I left on this trip which was to be simply a professional adventure— directing a play in foreign language in a "remote" land—that I was to encounter the spectacle of a civilization and culture in the process of birth. In one sense the making of Israel is more amazing than the 1917 upheaval in Russia. While the latter signified the building of a new kind of society by a hitherto suppressed class within an already formed nation, the Israeli phenomenon involves the making of a new people. It is evident from even the most superficial observation that the mingling, on a new soil and under entirely new social and legal circumstances, of Jews from all the ghettos and concentration camps of the European and Near Eastern world with the native Israelis will produce something hitherto unknown.

The immigrants from developed modern societies must now of necessity become "primitives" on still untried ground. The generation that was born in Israel (called *Sabras* because, like the cactus from which they get their name, they are said to be tough and thorny outside and sweet inside) cannot fail to be affected by the newly arrived settlers who will soon overwhelm them numerically. In the same way the European and Near Eastern Jews (from Turkey, Morocco, etc.) must be renewed not only by contact with the native Israeli youth, but by the marked differences among themselves. The now almost forgotten term, "the melting pot," comes to mind.

The immediate flavor of this new "melting pot" is one of a hard and buoyant youthfulness that seems to possess even the aged. The atmosphere contains ambition, hopefulness, impatience, dissatisfaction, here and there even a raw "disillusion" and something like cynicism. When such fervor characterizes a whole people you have a romantic society in a romantic epoch. To people everywhere—Gentiles as well as Jews—Israel will mean, on a smaller scale, what America meant to some Frenchmen after 1776, what Moscow meant to some Americans in the early thirties.

In the face of such a complex and novel background, it may after all prove safest to proceed from the particular to the general. So I return to the subject of the theatre. The Jews in modern times have everywhere evinced a strong feeling for the theatre, both as professionals and as audience. Tel Aviv, with a population of perhaps 250,000, has three permanent companies operating three separate houses, and in addition a group committed to topical satire in vaudeville form and a recently constituted opera company giving one performance a week in the Habimah building.

The regular companies work on a repertory basis. The oldest—Habimah—has a great success in a new play about the recent military struggle, called *In the Plains of the Negev*. It alternates on the program with *Saül*, a Biblical play just opened. The company is now rehearsing *A Midsummer Night's Dream* under an Anglo-Czech director, and under my direction is about to prepare the French *Montserrat*, by Emanuel Roblès, which New York will see in the fall. The Ohel, a workers' theatre in the sense that it receives its main support from the central trade-union organization, is doing another Hebrew war play and an old-time Yiddish folk-operetta.

The Hebrew National Opera Company (supported in some measure—like the theatres and the Israel Philharmonic Orchestra—by the American Fund for Palestinian Institutions) is presenting Massenet's *Thais* and *Manon*, Rossini's *Barber of Seville* and Offenbach's *Tales of Hoffmann*.

It may take years for full-grown native drama to emerge. (America did not have a three-act O'Neill play till 1920, and there had been precious little worth mentioning before.) The dependence of the Israeli stage on the repertory of the world theatre—both a benefit and a disadvantage—is inevitable. There can be no line yet, no security of approach to the audience, because the audience is culturally so heterogeneous. In the Chamber Theatre some of the actors are still learning Hebrew. While the majority of the audience is familiar with the language, an increasing number will be Jews who know only the speech of their countries of origin—Russian, German, Hungarian, etc.—and Yiddish, the language of the dispersion.

I cannot end this first report without special mention of the opera company's performance of *The Barber of Seville*. I had gone to see *The Barber* chiefly out of curiosity and remained to applaud. The singers, all young, had small but unusually good voices, and what a relief to see slender figures on the operatic stage! The orchestra, too, was small—partly because of the limitation of space in the pit—but it played well.

A youthful spirit was all-pervasive here—in the audience, which included many soldiers of both sexes, in the acting of principals and chorus, in the pleasant settings, in the lively and charming quality of the whole environment. One felt that opera in Hebrew was not only a usual thing but that opera is one of the most popular of mass-entertainment forms. Perhaps it takes a certain innocence to appreciate the sophistication of opera, just as only great naïveté or a profound understanding makes it possible to cope with such a society as Israel in 1949.

—*NR*, 27 June '49

PREFACE TO THE YOUNGER DRAMATISTS

Several friends and admirers of Tennessee Williams (they happen also to be earning impressive profits from *A Streetcar Named Desire*) sent him a set of the press notices on Arthur Miller's *Death of a Salesman* the morning after that phenomenally successful play opened. Was this intended as a warning to Williams that he had better do some fast thinking if he wants to remain No. 1 playwright of the younger generation? I heard the other day of a playwright's wife who developed a migraine headache on her husband's behalf when she was given a report of Miller's triumph.

Some of the market competitiveness of Broadway must have always existed in the theatre. Yet it is hard to believe that the rivalry among contemporary artists ever possessed so specifically commercial a character as it does now in the American theatre. I say "commercial," but that is perhaps a species of highbrow slander. The race between Gimbel's and Macy's, I am sure, does not produce the same psychological tension in the managements of those emporia as is suffered by our playwrights. Perhaps one reason for this is that Macy's and Gimbel's are surer of the worth of their wares.

When Heywood Broun in 1935 wrote that Odets would eventually surpass O'Neill, I thought the prediction a genial expression of faith in a new playwright. When I read a year later that Irwin Shaw, who had just written *Bury the Dead*, was "better than Odets," and a year after, when Shaw had written *Siege*, that he was "finished" (he was then 24), I began to recognize a pattern. Saroyan a few years later was hailed as "the playwright of the forties," and Odets was accused in 1940 of imitating Saroyan. After *Streetcar*, Williams, about whom no decision had been reached on the evidence of *The Glass Menagerie*, became the

great contender for honors which, apart from box-office statements, are rather difficult to define. Today Miller has become the white hope.

Our white hopes darken with the years. Their annihilation is implicit in their glorification. Effusive praise is not necessarily harmful to playwrights or morally wrong of the press. But the basis on which praise is bestowed and reputations made is false. To call an artist the greatest of the year or, before ten years are out, the greatest of the decade, is critically as meaningless as calling him the greatest on Forty-fifth Street. Such encomia can have significance only as publicity designed to stimulate the box office.

Most playwrights recognize this motive, and frequently accept hasty praise with half-defensive, half-gratified depreciation, apologizing to their intimates: "Well, it's good for business anyway." But they do not understand that they are imperceptibly being seduced into a state of being that makes their growth increasingly difficult. The process implies a challenge to the playwright to become "better and better," which makes him demand of himself constant "improvement." But this "improvement" means only growth in relation to the routine salutes that greeted him in the first place—not growth in relation to his needs as a developing artist.

Very few artists in the world have proceeded from masterpiece to masterpiece. The young American playwright is not an artist in an abstract "world"; he is a citizen working in a particular milieu, namely the New York theatre. This milieu sets up standards unlike those obtaining for similar craftsmen in painting, music, poetry or even the novel. The New York theatre obliges the writer to think of maintaining a level of accomplishment not measured by his problem as a creative personality but by the mechanics of a production apparatus which cannot function unless the plays he writes can gross upwards of $15,000 a week. His problem then becomes, far more than is healthy, one of adaptation to a market, an orientation away from his own essence or center. Writing plays becomes a maneuver rather than an expression. We should never forget that Chekhov became a popular playwright in Russia only because the repertory system built up his audience. His plays were not immediate box-office successes even in the Moscow Art Theatre.

After the playwright, who may once have been content as a teacher, a journalist, a small businessman, has tasted success, he is tempted to quit the theatre altogether if his third or fourth play does not live up to the "promise" of his first two or three. (The "promise," I repeat, is almost inevitably interpreted in commercial terms, as is the "fulfillment.") He turns to Hollywood, which is more popular, more commercial, more in line with the kind of demands that seem to be made on him. Or he will pick up cash by writing for the radio or television, and, if he has the capacity, he may attempt a novel. The young playwright is overcome by a sense of fear, frequently followed by a sense of futility. He sometimes accommodates himself to the position of honored hack—he becomes a Successful Playwright—or he succumbs to some other form of depletion. I have always retained the utmost respect for O'Neill, despite disappointment over particular plays, because we can perceive in all his work the determination to say exactly what he has in mind and heart. But O'Neill, apart from his personal qualities, belongs to a generation which had more reason to believe in the theatre than does the present one.

In order to develop as serious craftsmen, Odets, Hellman, Williams, Miller—the outstanding figures of a later epoch—must employ their advantages to dig themselves in against the fierce pressure of the Broadway machine and its poisonous atmosphere. To be blunt about it, I believe it essential that writers of this kind remember they are artists; that they adopt a mode of living—economically as well as spiritually—befitting that humble station in our society. If the huge sums they are capable of earning bemuse them into a belief that they belong to the class of business people who regularly earn more than $25,000 a year, they will find themselves within a few years not only forced to abandon the theatre (which they may not necessarily consider a calamity) but to give up hope of ever achieving full maturity as artists in any field of writing. It is supposed to be not at all nice and shamefully old-fashioned to say, but there is a terribly upsetting wind that blows around the peaks of those higher brackets. To counter with historical examples of contrary evidence from Shakespeare to Bernard Shaw is hypocritical irrelevance. We are talking of our corner of the world in the fifth decade of the twentieth century. A decent poverty, permitting the playwright freedom not to be at all times the "greatest," is indispensable for artistic progress.

The artist—as contrasted to a Broadway genius—does not everlastingly climb upward. His eyes must remain fixed on the real world outside—away from his specialized artistic or theatrical horizon, and his thought must constantly return to what is equally real within him. The artist often needs time to remain silent, time to falter while foraging in the underbrush of strange territories, an opportunity also to be "misunderstood."

A special need of the playwright as artist is to be faced with criticism that does not begin or end with the aim of proving or disproving his eminence. We do not love works of art because they are "great," but because we find them relevant and enriching to us. It would be a real service to younger playwrights if the critic spent more time trying to understand the motive, meaning, source and direction of their talents and less time measuring their achievement.

Perhaps we should remind ourselves that the best of our younger playwrights—Odets as much as Miller, Hellman as well as Williams—are all beginners (Ibsen wrote *A Doll's House*, *Ghosts*, *Hedda Gabler*, *The Wild Duck*, *The Master Builder* after he was fifty). For our beginners to contribute what, let us say, a Dreiser or even an O'Neill has, they have still much work to do. They should be encouraged toward that work, but to pronounce them consummate, as if, let us say, the winning of a prize were an ultimate, is to doom them at their first step.

None of these playwrights is "through" when he writes a bad play. A bad play may even be as significant and, in a sense, as interesting as a good one. An artist, unlike a chain, is to be judged by his strongest link.

These writers have much in common, but they are not alike. Comparisons may be helpful for purposes of definition, but they are truly odious when one writer is used to bludgeon another. The fault of one—a certain impatient rhetoric in Odets, let us say—may be closely bound up with a virtue and cannot be overcome by recommending the logical leanness of another—Miller, for example. Williams, in my view, is as much a "social" writer as Hellman, and the recent tendency to treat him as merely an effective painter of feminine and Southern frustration is only a facile dodge by which superficial judgment seeks to dispose of a talent that does not conveniently fit into a category conforming to the rationalism of certain "progressives." On the other hand, some critics with a disposition to be patronizing toward the rawness of American effort blind themselves to the fact that almost all these playwrights are fundamentally more gifted as dramatists than, for example, the presumably secure Jean-Paul Sartre.

—*NR*, 11 July '49

GOD BLESS AMERICA

Because of my congenital innocence, I am surprised that anyone should express surprise at the mishap of *Miss Liberty*. You mightn't believe it, but Robert Sherwood's book at some point in its career contained a promising idea. Sherwood wanted to contrast the reality of American sentiment and idealism, as manifested in the people's enthusiasm over the symbol of the Statue of Liberty, with the commercial ballyhoo and business skulduggery which often in our fair country muddle and muddy that sentiment and idealism.

Such an idea may be presented with affection, but it is essentially satiric. Satire is not Irving Berlin's forte, and his patriotism is not the kind to suggest any twinge of doubt or intellectual misgiving. Moss Hart's talent is bent toward farce, and what directorial style he has is chiefly unconscious. The fruit of this mésalliance is abortive.

But it would be a mistake to let the matter go at that, for in an odd way the production is an oblique illustration of the vice Sherwood was hoping to poke fun at. In *Miss Liberty* we see what happens to a basically honest conception when it is put through the Broadway wringer.

Producers do not aim to express a feeling of some kind—perchance the playwright's—since that might prove arty and hence uncommercial. And it is every good showman's credo that nothing is anything unless it is ultracommercial. How does one make a show commercial? Give it the best of everything! Hire excellent actors at tempting salaries, even if what they have to say or do has been cut to zero and it will be a humiliation for them to appear in parts that might more gracefully be handled by novices. Get a scenic artist and, for five-minute scenes of exposition that really need no more than an indication of place, have him furnish fancifully lavish sets, each one of which undoubtedly cost the price of a whole production in London. Make everything as expensive as you can (isn't there a supposedly satiric patter in the show called *The Most Expensive Statue in the World?*), spend close to a quarter of a million dollars, shoot the works. In the meantime Sherwood's modest notion has become as inconspicuous as a sparrow around the torch of the statue his play would celebrate. What you get is a golden flop.

Haven't I a kind word for anyone in the show? I would like the reader to believe that kindness is the source of my indignation. I admire practically everyone connected with *Miss Liberty*. I find Mary McCarty most sympathetic; I adore Allyn McLerie, who is as cute as pink and moves like a dream. I consider Jerome Robbins one of the most gifted people in our theatre. Ethel Griffies is a grand trouper, and Irving Berlin is the father and mother of us all—though I couldn't help thinking during the songs about the city on the Seine that he is ill at ease in Paris.

But no matter how you twist its arm, the theatre will have its revenge. To make money is a motive, not an idea. And good theatre—which certainly includes good musicals—springs from ideas. Even in 1949, you can't buy the muses without silencing them.

Am I being sententious? Possibly. But when at the end of this flagrantly wasteful musical, the whole company is made to intone Emma Lazarus' poem, "Give me your tired, your poor," at a time when the first news to greet me on my return from abroad is a rumor of mass deportation of aliens, I feel my gorge rise. And when at precisely the same time I hear of two New York playhouses being leased for a term of years to a broadcasting company by a firm that has just been awarded an honorary plaque for its contribution "to the culture, stability and progress of Broadway," when, at the end of a season which saw fewer productions than any other within current memory, a dauntless old producer proudly announces that he is not worried about the theatre's future, I am impelled to cry, "Damn our optimism; it will end by doing us in." We are supposed to have a sense of humor, but I refuse to drown with a smile, smile, smile.

—*NR*, 1 Aug. '49

THE DIRECTOR'S JOB

*M*ontserrat, the French play I directed for the Habimah Theatre, deals with the problem of choosing a way of life, which, in terms of the play's plot, becomes a way of death. The author suggests that ultimately one's choice is never between something pleasant called "life" and something horrid called "death," but that since death is imminent within life, all choices involve a tragic responsibility.

This abstract statement is made here to indicate only one thing: the play, though brutally dramatic, is a philosophical and not a political play. While his story is of an incident in the period of Bolivar's rebellion against the Spanish (Venezuela, 1812), the playwright's emphasis is general rather than particular. The play has a classic mold; it represents a contemporary effort to grapple with universals.

After what may be called the private work on the script, I began conferences with the scene designer. The play's locale offers the designer ample opportunity to make his setting a riot of Spanish and Italian motifs. Since I was seeking a "classic" style for the play, my first instructions to the designer emphasized that local color would have to be made entirely subsidiary to the structural elements of the setting, so that the characters, each one of whom represents a different approach to life as projected in the dramatist's philosophic scheme, would stand out beyond the accidents of their environment.

Casting a play is a function of its interpretation. The playwright speaks of a young Montserrat, and he is right. The only young man available in the Habimah company has a certain effective theatricality but not sufficient sincerity to carry conviction in a role which demands a person who, without being a fanatic, must seem a man of intense faith. I had to choose between two attributes of the part and, in this case, I sacrificed the outer feature (youth) in favor of the inner quality. The Spaniards were cast with elegant and powerfully built men; the natives, except for the "collaborationist" merchant, with rather spare and not especially attractive people.

It is comparatively easy to discuss scenery or to define certain principles of casting, but the main job of directing, which consists of building scene after scene according to a play's main line and making each character contribute to its meaning and mood, is almost impossible to transcribe on paper. The director's essential work is to set down the "notes"—the moment-to-moment inner and outer action which each actor is to play.

This is the theatre's most intimate and mysterious process. For it is not a matter of *telling* the actor what to do or even of explaining the playwright's and director's intention, but of both firing the actor's imagination and placing it on the right track so that the actor can proceed to the desired destination with an impulse that is as much his own as that of the author's mind and the director's will. Different directors use different methods to bring about that inspired moment when the unity we behold is actually the fruit of a triple generation—the dramatist's text, the director's spirit, the actor's being.

That is what happens, but that is not what the director does. He builds characters through and with his actors.

—*NR*, 15 Aug. '49

STANISLAVSKY IN AMERICA

Americans first heard of the so-called Stanislavsky system when three members of the Moscow Art Theatre—Richard Boleslavsky, Maria Ouspenskaya and Leo Bulgakov—who had come to this country when that famous company played several New York seasons in the early twenties decided to remain here. They became teachers of a technique of acting which they had learned in the Moscow Art Theatre, a technique formulated by its director, Constantin Stanislavsky. Maria Ouspenskaya conducted some classes in the old Neighborhood Playhouse, and a number of young Americans—among them Lee Strasberg, Stella Adler and the present writer—attached themselves for a while to the American Laboratory Theatre under Boleslavsky and Ouspenskaya.

When the Group Theatre was founded in 1931, its directors based their production method on certain aspects of the "system." The Group's first production of Paul Green's *The House of Connelly* made a distinct impression on the New York theatre world, and other Group productions notably those of Sidney Kingsley's *Men in White*

and the plays of Clifford Odets, were not only very favorably received but were considered as evidence that the Group definitely "had something." But it was still a common critical cliché in those days to deny the validity or importance of the "system" whenever a Group production was deemed poor. Frequently, too, suggestion was made that the "system"—a foreign importation—was somehow unsuited to the Anglo-Saxon or, at any rate, the American temperament!

The Group Theatre does not exist today, but if there are any theatre commentators who think of the Stanislavsky system as arty, special, exotic or anything but a basic and universally practicable formulation of acting technique, one ought to point out to them that they are at least twenty years behind the times. Such productions as *Death of a Salesman* and *Brigadoon* owe much to the training their directors received in the Group Theatre, a training by no means identical with that of the Moscow Art Theatre but in a great measure indebted to it. This is true too of actors as diverse as John Garfield, Gregory Peck, Arthur Kennedy, Franchot Tone, Lee Cobb, David Wayne, Karl Malden, Marlon Brando—to mention only a haphazard few. The "system" is not a theory; it is a method of work widely practiced, as we have noted, in the most divergent types of production both here and abroad. It is not a "Russian" system; the actors of the Moscow Art Theatre were at first as skeptical of it as the most hardened commercial showman might be. The "system" has little to do with realism as a style; the purest exponents of the system were not to be found in the more or less realistic Moscow Art Theatre but in the studios or derivatives of that theatre which were preeminently non-realistic. The Habimah Theatre in Israel, having been directed in *The Dybbuk* by Stanislavsky's outstanding disciple—Vachtangov—is supposedly an heir of the Stanislavsky system, but there is actually less Stanislavsky influence in Habimah than there is in *A Streetcar Named Desire*. In fact it is no exaggeration to say that the Stanislavsky influence today is more active in the American theatre than anywhere outside of the Soviet Union.

The most authoritative manual of the system is Stanislavsky's *An Actor Prepares*. But it is important to remember that no book can convey the heart of the subject because it is essentially a matter of concrete work with actors by directors or teachers in rehearsal or classroom. Stanislavsky's recently published *Building a Character* is a supplement to the earlier work, the difference between the two being the emphasis in the first on what Stanislavsky calls the actor's inner technique: concentration, imagination, emotion, etc.; the more recent volume being devoted to external technique; body, voice, speech, etc.

Stanislavsky was never a good writer and as a theoretician he left much to be desired. The present book is spotty and may at times actually prove misleading, with passages that appear to contradict the main trend of *An Actor Prepares*. It is characteristic of the times that the latter book is presented to us now with an introduction by Joshua (*South Pacific*) Logan, an extremely able director, whose work, howsoever amiable and successful, cannot be said to exemplify Stanislavsky.

I enjoyed reading *Building a Character* for its many stimulating and useful pages, but most of all for the image it offers of a man who seems to have devoted twenty-four hours a day and seventy-five years of his life to perfecting a craft every part of which he adored. But I should not bring the book to the attention of the general reader were it not for the opportunity it affords me to point out that now that the Stanislavsky system is a practical success on our stage we have almost no theatre to use it in. Our theatre today consists chiefly of very rich raw material engulfed by an economic organization that seems calculated only to destroy it.

—*NR*, 22 Aug. '49

THEATRE LIFE

It is a common practice in all the arts to arrive at an understanding of a particular artist's work by examining the artist's environment. Because the theatre is thought of chiefly as show business, related to sensationalism rather than to expression, what we usually learn about the life of people in the theatre is the story of their careers in terms of parts played, failures, successes, hobbies and eccentricities. But the environment in which theatre people live is as much part of their quality as their specific stage experience and their talent. Readers may remember my statement here last winter that the superiority of Laurence Olivier over the perhaps more gifted Alfred Lunt is due in good measure to certain traditions of the English theatre world, which demand more of the actor than continuous box-office success.

It is possible for a healthy theatre—a theatre that maintains a continuity of work on the basis of a consistent artistic program—to provide its members with a foundation that will in itself serve as an educational force. The American theatre worker is footloose. He is attached to nothing, and is therefore obliged to spend most of his time either looking for an engagement, worrying about his next one or, when he is associated with a hit, to forget the necessity of considering his future. Our haphazard, accidental production system creates an atmosphere of haste, restlessness, superficiality in our whole theatrical environment. The American actor—most often a decent, likable, eager fellow—rarely possesses any sense of personal dignity, rarely has that appearance of maturity which makes even his less dignified European counterpart more imposing on the stage. Most American actors begin and end as kids.

The American actor before 1919 often seemed stuffy, magniloquently foolish, overawed by the color and glamor of his profession. Yesterday's thespian offered a target for facile jibes. But the background of the old-time actor helped give him a kind of force that the actor today no longer appears to have. Whether or not he was employed, he felt confident that a theatre existed for him to work in. Since the theatre in those days was generally considered special, dangerous, perhaps not altogether respectable, being an actor meant being adventurous, tough, daring, defiantly "gay" or proud with the boldness of one liberated from society's narrow conventions. All this gave the actor then a kind of hardy, dashing quality that made his very presence on and off the stage interesting. Because to survive he had to be one, he nearly always was a personality.

Today the actor belongs to a union, is impressed with his duties as a citizen, tries to make careful business deals and is convinced that he is or ought to be like everyone else. But his profession is not at all ordinary and, in the practical sense of steady work, not a profession at all. Frequently this contradiction produces a frightened, self-conscious, wistful, deluded creature who cannot think or behave with craftsmanlike accuracy or realism in the theatre or in life. His situation deprives him of that independent sense of his own worth which gives man power. If the actor is sufficiently lucky to become efficient and moderately successful in terms of earning his livelihood (through jobs in radio, television, commercial movies and an occasional part on Broadway or in Hollywood), his very commercial maneuverability often renders him as smooth and dull as the "ordinary person"—that rubber-stamp personality that he probably hoped to avoid becoming by going on the stage. If the actor suffers the common fate of his profession—penury—he becomes a lost little man, feeding on nothing much beside the trivialities of his trade: small chit-chat, small curiosity, small drinking and dallying, small pitiful hopes. Such people are incapable of bringing to the theatre anything larger than themselves.

An actor who is called on to play a series of fine plays may acquire a certain stature merely through his contact with such plays. An actor whose theatre comprises a group of serious craftsmen (writers, directors, scenic artists, etc.) is by that fact alone subject to influences that may enrich him in his work. The thinness of so much that we see on the stage today is not surprising when we consider the poor human sources from which it must issue. But the individual as such is not wholly to blame. The theatre is itself a life, and if the theatre's life has a meager or corrupt founda-

tion nothing very inspiring can come from it, regardless of the talent that is poured into it.

That the defects of our theatre as a community institution actually limit even our most superior talents may be seen in the case of many of our stars. Our best directors, too, freer and more aware in most instances than the actors, rarely mount the heights of creative effort and accomplishment that their innate abilities and ambitions might spur them to. How many of our finest productions are on the level of Vachtangov's *The Dybbuk*, Nemirovich Danchenko's *Carmencita and the Soldier*, Meyerhold's *The Inspector General*, Reinhardt's *The Servant of Two Masters*? From the outset our directors are resigned to an excellence sufficient to the standards set by a shackled theatre life.

Is the situation hopeless? It is hopeless only if we allow ourselves to settle into a lethargy of indifference, stupid optimism or routine. Present theatre circumstances demand that the theatre's adherents abandon their playboy giddiness, their café-bar nostalgia and build up within themselves a new *consciousness* of their craft, its possibilities, its requirements, its perils. Simply to wait for a beneficent social-mindedness to descend on men in power so that they may bestow upon us a subsidized "national theatre" is still another fuzzy dream.

—*NR*, 29 Aug. '49

THE ISRAELI THEATRE: A REPORT FROM TEL–AVIV

On the streets of Tel-Aviv, capital of the new state of Israel, the sound that prevails is that of children playing on the piano. I might simply have said the sound of children. I have been to no land where one is more conscious of children. Young people give Tel-Aviv a special tone. To see an aged person in Tel-Aviv who acts and looks it is almost a shock. Not that age is hidden by cosmetics, but a youthful spirit seems to possess all.

Outside Tel-Aviv, all over the country, are the famous *Kibbutzim* (collective farms), the greatest achievement—apart from victory in the war and the elevation to statehood—of the Israeli people. Objection therefore might be made to my using the pianos I hear everywhere as an instrument symbolic of the new nation. This is becoming an agricultural country and more and more of the recent immigrants from central Europe and elsewhere must become farmers. But though the collective farmer has his hard work cut out for him on the land, and the strength of his back and the firmness of his arms are of crucial importance, the *Kibbutz* by no means discounts the need for cultural activities. On the contrary: one might say that the *Kibbutz* aspires toward what the piano represents. At the port of Haifa where I watched a boat being unloaded, I observed the great number of pianos the cargo held. Perhaps the best insignia for Israel would be the plough and the piano.

I attended a concert given by the Israel Philharmonic Orchestra; I visited the Tel-Aviv Museum of Art; I am aware of the unusual interest in music and painting that obtains here. But for the purpose of this article I shall confine myself to the theatre as the particular symbol of the "piano," that is, of the country's cultural life.

I have seen large audiences of soldiers of both sexes watch a play in rapture; and I have seen an equally large audience of children from twelve to sixteen watch the same play with delight. It was a play about the recent war in which Israel defended itself successfully against the assault of seven Arab nations. The play was shot through with Hebrew slang (composed of Arabic words). Such slang is not only new to the stage here but to the language itself. This combination of patriotism in the play and the younger actors of the Habimah—Israel's "classic" theatre—speaking slang was full of meaning.

One cannot understand the theatre here—or elsewhere for that matter—without understanding the character of its audience. The audience in Israel is young, eager, adventurous, impatient, confident, heterogeneous, vital. It is capable of enjoying an American play like *Pick-up Girl* and an opera like *Tales of Hoffmann.*

There are no authorities on the Israeli theatre audience. That is because the audience is changing all the time. An average of nine hundred immigrants a day are arriving. True, they are not able to go to the theatre immediately, but these people coming, I repeat, from many different countries and of different stations of life cannot but quickly influence the composition of the theatre audiences. Every play produced here is a real experiment, because hardly any norm has been established or is likely to be established for years.

There is a new group (five years old) called Chamber Theatre. It is composed chiefly of actors who were not able to get into the venerable Habimah company. For a while the young actors of the Chamber Theatre were not paid salaries, but now that they are in full stride they have become professional in every sense. I met the actors of this company at a party one evening after one of their performances and was struck by the fact that the actress who had played the leading part was a girl from Berlin who years ago had played a child's role in Fritz Lang's picture *M*, while other members of the company were people who had come from Austria, Russia, Bulgaria. Some of the newest members of the company, the theatre's director told me, still speak bad Hebrew, but had to be admitted to the company because they were talented and needed to begin work.

The repertory of the Chamber Theatre includes Beaumarchais' *Barber of Seville*, *I Remember Mama*, Goldoni's *Servant to Two Masters*, a Soviet play, a new Israeli play called *He Went to the Fields*, *All My Sons*, *Pick-up Girl* and *Dear Ruth.* If you are an actor or closely connected with the stage, such a list will make you green with envy, for there is no American company (save perhaps in one or two community theatres) which can boast such a repertory of plays produced within the span of two seasons. If you are simply a cultivated playgoer you may say that such a spotty selection of material makes little sense. But this would merely be an abstract judgment, and abstract judgments in the theatre are rarely valid. The reason for the variegated repertory I have just mentioned lies not in faulty taste, but in the difficulty of measuring a new and ever changing audience hungry for everything and often unacquainted with many things long familiar to residents of big cities abroad.

The Habimah Theatre, which is about thirty years old (it originated in Russia and became Palestinian in 1928), is suffering many a rude jolt from the abrupt social changes that have made the history of the past two years. This can do the Habimah nothing but good. The Habimah repertory, about which I wrote in *Tomorrow* only a year ago (on that company's visit to New York), has been entirely abandoned. It was the repertory of another day.

On its return to Tel-Aviv, the Habimah faced an inner and outer upheaval. The company's contact with the American Theatre made the Habimah discontented with the old collective and cooperative setup of its origins (Moscow, 1919), a setup which called for equal salaries to all members of the company, regardless of parts or talent, and an equal vote for every member of the company on all matters of general artistic and administrative policy. This setup has been altered and will undergo further changes from day to day. Policy is now formulated by a board of six directors, three members of which are not actors and two members of which represent the community.

More important is the Habimah's transformation in relation to its public. The first play to be produced by the Habimah since its New York season was a war melodrama (the war being that between Israel and the Arab nations which began early in May 1948 and which lasted five months). The new play, *In the Plains of the Negev*, represented a complete departure for the Habimah company. Its literary level is low. It does not pretend to be more than a kind of theatrical journalism and a tear-jerker. Its value lies in the fact that it is of today, that it satisfies the audience's need to see its life reflected and celebrated on the stage. The audience cannot wait till its life is remembered in tranquillity so that a dignified work of art, a "masterpiece," might be wrought from it. It wants to relive its experience and to enjoy it now even if the artistic results are raw in form and crude in expression. To the horror of the more staid members of the company and the local intelligentsia, *In the Plains of the Negev* is a hit.

Another reason for its success—aside from its hot topicality and patriotics—is the presence in the cast of a young generation of actors. The Habimah has some excellent actors of middle age and older whom the audience is always glad to see. The younger actors, who have long since been knocking at the Habimah's gates and, up to a year ago, have been refused admittance, have finally broken through in the new production and are in the Habimah company to stay. Two or three of the youngsters are lively comedians—graduates of the Israeli equivalent of our U.S.O.—and they inject into the proceedings the needed ebullience and gaiety of youth which the Habimah so long lacked.

The lesson of the new play was reinforced by the failure of the one that followed. In *Saül*, a play by an immigrant resident of Israel translated from the German, the Habimah went back to an ancient source of dramatic material—the Old Testament. The source is not necessarily exhausted because it served as an excuse for a stuffy play, but the general feeling here—I saw it at its opening which was attended by, among others, the Prime Minister, the Foreign Minister, the Commander-in-Chief of the Army—the general feeling was that *Saül* might do for school children as an illustration in their classes in Biblical history, but not for an adult audience. What the audience wants today in Israel are virile contemporary plays on contemporary subjects or authentic classics on relevant themes.

Another aspect of the production of *Saül* which the audience objects to—though less consciously than to the dullness of the play itself—

is the manner of production. It is a trifle operatic. This is not only a fault in itself but a kind of endemic disease with the Habimah. For the Habimah, which gained its first laurels through the masterly stylization that the Russian director Vachtangov trained them in (when in *The Dybbuk* the company was an amateur group), has never fully recovered from Vachtangov's gift. There is not only always a tendency toward pictorial and vocal stylization but nearly always the same kind of "pictures" and vocal arabesques are repeated. A scene designer said to me, apropos of a play I am soon to direct for the Habimah, "If you can only make them talk like ordinary people, you will have performed a miracle."

This is an exaggeration, no doubt—the company has played Ibsen and Galsworthy and I cannot imagine that these were "stylized" too—but it is one of those exaggerations that highlight a defect. The Habimah is imprisoned in a formalism that no longer has any reason for being. The company is well aware of this by now, but it is not altogether able to free itself without outside help in the shape of new directors who are unacquainted with, inimical to, or not under the spell of the Vachtangov touch.

Even in *In the Plains of the Negev*, which is nothing if it is not realistic melodrama, the staging tends to prettily patterned groups inspired by old paintings. Thus, while most of the acting is conventionally modern—ranging from the impressive to the slightly amateurish—the over-all direction has not yet freed itself from extraneous "aesthetics," falsely noble frames of reference unrelated to the simple truths on which the play's material is based.

At present, a new production of *A Midsummer Night's Dream* is in the final stages of rehearsal and will have opened when you read this. I have seen some of the dress rehearsals and found the production extremely pleasant by virtue of the play's loveliness and the many young people in the cast (including a ballet of girl dancers no older than sixteen or seventeen). There

are also some good comedy performances and a refreshing lightness in the general atmosphere of the production.

A Midsummer Night's Dream was directed by an Englishman of Czech-German origin. His production seems to me influenced by Reinhardt in his more floridly romantic manner. I am not sure that such a style is what the Habimah today needs, for it tends to re-emphasize—in another vein, it is true—the picturesque theatre at the expense of the structural theatre.

The terms I use here are not to be taken literally in relation to stage setting. By "structural theatre" I mean the theatre that goes back to essential elements dramatic material conveyed in the most direct fashion possible by actors on a platform or any other convenient arena—basic theatre. This means that the primary motif of the play be considered before any secondary adornment, and that the actors be viewed as the main instrument, indeed, an organic part, of the play's content. The "picturesque theatre"—to which I have no theoretic or personal objection—tends toward a baroque pleasure in ornament, something added to the play's structure—as if a powder puff an actress used in a bedroom scene were to be made more amusing than the actress herself or the purpose for which the powder puff was employed at that point of the play.

The Habimah, I say, needs to find the solid earth of drama again. It needs to rediscover the sanity of a certain plainness. Another successful play here, *He Went to the Fields*, is popular precisely because its material is the life of the Israeli youth from the *Kibbutz* to the army, and because it is done with a certain primitive simplicity which reminds one of the workers' theatres and the Living Newspaper shows of our Federal Theatre Project in the mid-thirties. The scenery is rough, the scene changes are done as if it were part of the character's toil, the general movement is vigorous, unrefined, and charming withal.

—*TRW*, Aug. '49

THEATRE ROOTS

At about the time—1931—that the Stanislavsky system first began to be a subject for discussion and study in the American theatre, a corresponding and greater impetus was given to the notion that the theatre man had to become a conscious citizen of society. The idea was a fruitful one; it opened the way to vigorous influences that broke down the notion of the theatre as a mere funhouse removed from the world's more substantial interests. Like many beneficent movements, the new tendency did not realize the full scope of its premises. As a result many incipient artists were often deflected from a proper study of their craft only to become puerile sociologists. What was frequently forgotten was that the "good citizen," as such, might have no function in the theatre, but that the thoroughly rounded theatre man would always have an organic and active relationship to the world outside.

What is the first law of the theatre? That it is a collective craft, or, to put it more plainly, that no single force or person alone can make good theatre. The play is indeed the thing, but the play in the theatre is not only the text or the actor or the director, but the thing created when the animating spirit that moves the dramatist is given a concrete body by all the people in the theatre together. Where does the animating spirit or idea of the play arise? From the society of which all the theatre people are parts, in other words from the audience which the theatre people aim to serve.

Because the theatre is by its very nature collective, the highest praise we can bestow on a theatrical production is to say that it has unity, that the theatre collective has achieved a combination of its diverse parts which embodies the play's idea to the fullest extent. At such rare moments we hardly know who is the first, or the most inspired, of the contributors to the production. We simply experience the satisfaction of a happy union of elements, all of which have been shaped to a harmonious statement or expression of an idea or sentiment.

In such a theatre event, the playwright is not king, nor the director boss, nor the actors simply soldiers headed by a star general. What rules is the play idea, greater than the playwright himself, who in actual practice works on his text before and during rehearsal to bring it closer to the consummation which takes account of every part of the theatre, including such physical instruments as the stage setting and even the building that houses the performance. Beyond all this, what dominates is the thought of holding the audience—final touchstone of the play's unity. The audience represents an identity, a state of mind, a philosophy, aspirations and ideals, which the theatre artists hope to intensify, modify or even change by arousing a sense of kinship that will unify all.

In describing this basic pattern of the theatre have we not suggested a process calling for both discipline and a sense of responsibility which in the last analysis, must resolve themselves into a code of behavior and an active morality on everyone's part? Suppose, for example, that a single individual—be he playwright, actor or director—conceives himself as the end and purpose of the theatre's whole endeavor: can we have good theatre? Hardly. But it is precisely this tearing of the individual parts away from the whole which is characteristic of our theatre.

If you counter that this atomization—the degeneration of each part into a self-centered whole—is the rule of our society, and that our theatre simply reflects the ills of our society, you have uttered a truism without arriving at a truth. No doubt our theatre would be healthier if our society were, but the job of the theatre person is not to reduce himself to the role of a mechanism, a cog in the machine, but to elevate himself to the consciousness of a person who exercises his will to make or, at least, influence his own environment, and thus to act socially in what for him is the most immediately effective way, that is, in terms of his own craft. It is true that society produces its criminals, but the same society which produces criminals also produces its teachers and healers. It is a dangerous trend of thought that leads people to think of themselves chiefly as effects or victims and not also as causes and creators.

Theatre people—playwrights as much as. actors or stagehands—must become conscious of what the theatre is and what its correct functioning means in relation to their own individual responsibility toward it.

—*NR*, 5 Sept. '49

VICIOUS CYCLE

To say that the theatre is a collective enterprise may sound arty. But unless this is recognized the theatre will soon cease to be either an art or a business. When a major symphony orchestra, playing to capacity all season long, shows a yearly deficit, no one denounces the loss as a business failure. This does not signify, however, that when a play runs to packed houses for a year and doesn't pay off its cost that the venture necessarily spells art.

Present conditions demand that theatre practice be integrated not only artistically but organizationally and economically as well. Many playwrights and directors will approve this statement, under the supposition that what I have in mind is the elimination of certain onerous rulings made by the stagehands' and similar unions. But playwrights have no right to thrust accusing fingers at the humbler workers of the craft because, organizationally speaking, the playwrights stand as much outside the theatre's interests as do the others. No one is to blame: the theatre will be sick unless *all* its people are joined in a common organizational setup which views theatre as a whole and not as a competition of rival interests.

When a playwright brings his script to a producer today, he begins a chain of exploitation in which each link vies with the others. If the playwright is prominent or if he and his agent can convince the producers that their script is a valuable property, playwright and agent will insist that the best (most expensive) director, the best designer and the biggest star be engaged for it. The best director will demand as his fee what is virtually a producer's share in the profits, and will encourage the expensive designer to be as lavish as possible so that the production will impress a naïve public that what it is getting is truly superior. The cast must also be "tops," so that actors will be chosen for minor roles at salaries that once were paid to leading players. Costs mount to the point where the production will be operated at an intake which allows for a profit of no more than two or three thousand dollars a week for a non-musical play— which means that a play doing sell-out business can hardly redeem its cost for at least six months.

The consequence is that backers who once regarded themselves as gamblers, if not businessmen, unwittingly and unwillingly find themselves playing the role of philanthropists. Theatre owners today are creating an artificial shortage of houses so that rents can be kept high, while producers and playwrights—unorganized in relation to the rest of the theatre—actually avoid any resistance or even overt verbal criticism of the real estate interests lest they find difficulty in getting their attractions into the few houses that still remain or find themselves excluded from the houses on the road, where the theatres are held in monopoly by a single firm. Theatres are more readily available when a play has the protection of a "name star," and ridiculous salaries including a share of the profits are demanded by Hollywood actors. This means that a promising stage actor is encouraged to forsake the theatre to become a Hollywood name in the theatre. And plays must often close prematurely if the name star decides to leave a show after a six-months' run.

When experimental off-Broadway groups begin to show signs of popularity, they are immediately "investigated" and their functioning rendered difficult on the grounds that they constitute a threat to "legitimate" show business in which "experiments"—such as the production of an O'Casey play, for example—are held to be impossible risks. But the discouragement of such experimental theatre—not only in the formal sense of groups committed to "special" plays, but in the sense of anything that does not pretend to compete with *South Pacific*—ultimately means a theatre that kills off all creative endeavor.

The theatre as anything but a series of extravagant private adventures exists so little that even in the matter of public relations—publicity for the theatre as differentiated from publicity for a single show—hardly anything is undertaken. To conduct a successful publicity campaign for the theatre as an institution, the cooperation of all guilds, unions and associations connected with the stage is indispensable, and a factual interdependence must be maintained. But almost all these groups are at present obviously more aware of their separateness than they are of their mutual needs.

Not to be a hit on Broadway is tantamount to moral disgrace, so that everyone engaged in Broadway business seeks to perfect the technique of success. That technique is always associated with the status quo. The Broadway status quo being self-destructive, Broadway's success is indivisible from the theatre's failure. It is ignorance, folly and cowardice for the individual to shrug his shoulder with the rationalization, "What can we do—that's free enterprise." Doesn't that system leave one the will to cultivate a fighting consciousness? Must we enjoy being trapped? It is clear that to create a true theatre one must abandon some of its advantages, allurements and benefits—the "freedom" that enslaves.

—*NR*, 12 Sept. '49

VERY LIGHT

A *New York Times* caption the other day proclaimed, "Country Goes Wild Over Vaudeville." I was glad to hear it. I am always happy to hear that any form of entertainment employing actors in three dimensions is popular.

There is always a better than even chance, too, that light entertainment will be superior to the other kind. How many of our "legitimate" actors can compare in verve, craftsmanship, vividness and charm with Ray Bolger, Mary Martin and Ethel Merman? I am sometimes on the verge of believing that only our light entertainers are to be taken seriously.

They say radio and the talkies killed vaudeville. No. What killed vaudeville was that the best people in vaudeville walked out on it—to earn an easier and more lavish livelihood elsewhere. If the Marx brothers, Jimmy Durante, Ed Wynn, George Jessel *et al.* could be seen at a reasonable price on a bill with other good acts, do you think vaudeville would be dead?

After reading some devastating comments on *Ken Murray's Blackouts* at the Ziegfeld Theatre, I found the second-night audience eating it up. *Ken Murray's Blackouts* is an old-fashioned vaudeville show at revue prices. The only trouble with it is that it is not good vaudeville. Most of it has the hellish quality of one of those huge cut-rate drugstores where every article from sandwiches and malteds to pills and trusses is presented with such lurid energy that one suspects everything—including the customers—of being poisoned.

It is not that all the numbers are bad. There is an eccentric girl dancer I thought quite funny (I am not speaking of the contortionist who got the notices) and I laughed like a fool at some of the smutty jokes. Once in a while I enjoy cheap beauty and don't mind staring goggle-eyed at barroom Venuses. Ken Murray himself, though he always threatens to become monotonous and oppressively vulgar, is a capable performer with a genuine personality—meaning no disrespect—that of a witty bum. But all in all, what comes over is a feeling of damaged goods, as if we had been invited to examine the remainders of show business. Yet because its very tawdriness corresponds to the dejected tastes of many people to whom more pretentious entertainment might prove an effort, these *Blackouts* will find a grateful audience.

Light entertainment is, of course, as much an "expression of life" as those forms we are supposed to approach more solemnly. Take, for example, an entertainer like Maurice Chevalier, whose autobiography, *The Man in the Straw Hat*, has just been published (Crowell; $3.50). Chevalier, who has no "voice" and is hardly an actor—even in the sense that Edith Piaf is—is nevertheless a national figure in France and a source of keen pleasure everywhere.

Chevalier's little book, which is primitively simple, written as if he were talking about himself to a sympathetic visitor in his dressing room, offers some clues to the ingredients that give his artless and beguiling stage work a sense of real style and something that might be called *purity*. Chevalier is a Parisian proletarian kid turned performer and sport. He had no education, a fact about which he neither boasts nor apologizes. He began his career at eleven, and he speaks warmly of Charles Boyer, who in Chevalier's Hollywood days drew up a list of books for him to read.

Chevalier refuses to go beyond his depth in word, thought or sentiment, so that there is a certain innocence as well as wisdom when he tells us that he sometimes wishes his introduction to love had had more to do with love, or when he recounts the moral satisfaction he derived from the aid he was able to give his fellow French prisoners during the First World War when as a medical orderly he devised a method of painlessly administering injections to those who had contracted syphilis. He frankly admits that whenever there was a question involving a choice between his mistresses and his profession, his profession always won. He is naïvely respectful of high authority (royalty, prime ministers and the like) but extremely uncomfortable with it unless it can accept and make itself easy with his own slightly raffish reality.

Chevalier is a "peasant" of Paris. Wine, camaraderie, the lights of gay places, the laughter of friendly women, the excitement of casual, everyday encounters that are viewed as merry adventures—all these, in their most uncomplicated aspects, are what he sings without sentimentality or cynicism. The charm of the ordinary that becomes pure delight through conversation, good humor, a touch of healthy kidding, a sense that there is dance and eternal play at every big-city street corner, restaurant, social gathering—these are what Chevalier communicates in every one of his numbers, regardless of their word content. That is why his "explanations" tickle Americans even more than the songs themselves.

In one chapter of his book, Chevalier describes a nervous breakdown he suffered, accompanied by a nearly insane fear of losing his memory. If Chevalier were an American telling this story, I am pretty certain he would have said it was "psychosomatic," or would otherwise have indulged himself in pseudo-scientific jargon. Chevalier, being what he is, seems at a loss for an explanation, except that he had been drinking too much or eating the wrong things. But he recovered to become riper than ever. No wonder he is a hero to the French and a relief to the rest of us.

—*NR*, 26 Sept. '49

AROUND SHAKESPEARE

Reading Ivor Brown's biography of *Shakespeare* (Doubleday; $4), one begins to think not only of the dramatist himself, but even more of certain basic questions which it was once believed essential for every serious student of the theatre to examine. Brown is a practicing dramatic critic in London. The virtue of his sensible and readable book is that it treats Shakespeare not alone as the shining glory of English literature, but as a man of the theatre. From the latter standpoint, however, Brown fails to take advantage of a subject that might have led him directly into the problem of the relation between literature and the theatre.

Shakespeare's eminence as a poet serves the literary-minded as positive proof that the theatre exists for the writer. "In the beginning was the Word" is, for these people, an esthetic dogma. A true theatre man would alter the dogma to read: in the beginning was the Deed. Actually there is, at least in terms of the theatre, a semantic trick in divorcing word from deed, since words are hardly conceivable apart from deeds or actions, and actions are usually accompanied by words, their symbols and extensions. Historically speaking, it is certain that semi-religious dances, ceremonies that were chiefly pantomime carried out to fulfill primitive needs, lay at the origin of what we now call theatre.

This dispute would have little importance if it were not that in modern times the two schools have developed a deep misunderstanding, one that has the effect of diminishing the theatre's strength. There are critics—and with them playwrights, producers, actors and even playgoers—who speak of the theatre not only as if it were a branch of literature but even as if it were a special philosophical branch. Thus the able and interesting Eric Bentley in his book, *The Playwright as Thinker*, speaks indulgently of Sartre and Cocteau as playwrights because he is interested in their ideas, and waves aside the far more potent O'Neill and O'Casey because they have less intellectual appeal.

On the other hand, there are some critics—as well as playwrights, producers, actors and playgoers—who are so skeptical of "ideas" in the theatre that they would confine Shakespeare between covers and to the classroom. Shakespeare was a man of the theatre who happened to be a master poet, just as Ibsen, another true man of the theatre, happened to be an extraordinarily acute prophet in regard to nineteenth-century society, and O'Neill, the actor's son, a poignant voice echoing the secret grievances of the American consciousness.

On esthetic as well as historical grounds, I am inclined to "favor" the theatre-conscious, rather than the literary-conscious, approach to the theatre. The theatre without the "book" (ideals, ideas and sound literary of "intellectual" values) tends to become shabby and paltry; the "bookish" theatre not rooted in vital theatre qualities tends to anemia and petrification. My chief reason for believing the purely literary approach to the theatre a dangerous one is that it tends to make theatre people think of their work as illustration rather than as creation; it cuts down their ambition so that their standards become those of third-rate journeymen rather than first-rate artists.

The theatre needs great plays (even as the literary folk say), but the better the plays the greater the challenge to theatre folk to make themselves equal to such plays. When actors, directors and scene designers begin to realize that they must be artists in their own right (and when the practical organization of the theatre allows them the freedom to put this realization into effect), the word theatrical will have the same dignity as the word "literary" and not, as now, suggest mere display at the expense of meaning.

—*NR*, 3 Oct. '49

YESTERDAY'S MATINEES

Did you know that "goddam" was uttered for the first time on the New York stage in a play by Clyde Fitch in 1909? That Owen Davis, whose *Icebound* won the Pulitzer Prize in 1923, wrote two hundred Bowery-style melodramas, including one called *Edna, the Pretty Typewriter*? That a musical named *Very Good Eddie* was so popular in 1915 that two companies played it simultaneously on the same block on 39th Street? That the Theatre Guild's first hit, *John Ferguson*, was put on in 1919 for less than a thousand dollars? That on the evening of December 26, 1927, eleven plays opened on Broadway? That the total of 225 productions in New York during the season of 1928-29 was reduced by a hundred in 1934-35?

These facts and many more are strewn helter-skelter through Ward Morehouse's *Matinee Tomorrow* (Whittlesey House; $5), an informal account of the American theatre from 1898 through 1949. The book's assortment of reminiscences, anecdotes, gossip, statistics and illustrations seem wrapped in a shroud of nostalgia.

The last statement may be merely a personal reaction. Morehouse tells his story with confidence and relish. The past is a very living thing to him. He reports the theatre's decline without a tremor of regret or dismay. He anticipates tomorrow's matinees with the same ingenuous excitement he must have felt when he first became fascinated with show business.

I was taken to the theatre as a little boy in 1907 pretty much as kids today are taken to the movies. By 1913 I began to visit the neighborhood stock companies in the Bronx all by myself (there were four within walking distance of my home) and saw many of the old plays that Morehouse mentions: *The Wolf*, *The City*, *Fine Feathers*, *The Melting Pot*, *The Witching Hour*. By 1917 I was a regular Broadway playgoer and an avid student of theatrical lore. That is why Morehouse's book appeals to me more than it may to the reader whose theatregoing days did not begin till after 1929. Yet I could not help thinking as I put this chronicle down, "Where has it all gone? What remains of all the talent, effort, ambition, love, that went into those fifty years of theatre?"

The theatre's ephemeral nature is supposed to be part of its glamor; I am not clamoring for the shows of yesteryear. Odets, Miller, Williams are better playwrights than Augustus Thomas and Clyde Fitch; it is equally undeniable that our scene designers have a more refined sense of the theatre than those who turned out the sets in the days of Belasco, Brady and Woods. But it seems that more should have remained from the past fifty years of theatre than a few good plays and some sweet memories.

Morehouse's book indirectly reveals the reason for the huge waste of talent in our theatre. We proceed wholly from the accident of talent itself—from activity energy, the brute power of movements for their own sake. Our theatre has no social aim, no broad human motivation, no moral foundation. We do not try to build anything except the individual's success and renown. We are interested in "personalities" as in a brilliant display of fireworks—wondrous and momentary. We like to marvel, not to learn. Every day in the American theatre is an entirely new day. It seems to take nothing from yesterday and leave nothing for tomorrow. Our effort—always amazing in vitality and potentiality—mounts to hodgepodge. We are entranced by the myriad aspects of the theatre; we do not conceive it as a whole. We prefer the dazzle of surface color to a knowledge of organic structure. Thus our critics as well as our artists are rarely interested in principles or basic conclusions, in arriving at methods of work or instruction that will be valid for the future.

We are amused by opinions, frightened by convictions. We believe it proper to have tastes, unseemly to foster passion. We will announce what we "think;" if it is understood beforehand that our "thoughts" are not to be considered binding. No one wants to teach because it looks more like impotent preaching than lustrous practice. There is a universal horror of being "wrong." Above all we insist on remaining "private" in thought and behavior responsible to no one but ourselves. But people who are committed to nothing but themselves soon become vacant, empty. Thus we begin with greatness and end in gorgeous nullity.

Some day we may learn that mountains of separate geniuses don't add up to a culture. If France has its Comédie Française, Russia its Moscow Art Theatre, and Germany—even now—a host of remarkable state and city theatres, it is not because these people are cleverer or more gifted than we, but because they are concerned with the force of constellations rather than with the twinkling of stars.

—*NR*, 10 Oct. '49

WITHOUT WORDS

When one repeatedly affirms, as I have, that words are not the essence of theatre, many readers suppose that the critic is indulging in a paradox to make a point. The past weeks' events have served to prove the point. The best words were to be heard in *Twelfth Night* but the best theatre was to be seen at *Les Ballets de Paris*. In between there was a thoroughly pleasant trifle from London—*Yes, M'Lord*—with words so inconsiderable that one could barely remember them ten minutes after they were spoken.

There are people who feel that Shakespeare need only be said intelligibly to provide high pleasure. That may be, but the pleasure is not theatre. If one would leave all to the imagination, as some pedants believe was the case in Shakespeare's playhouse, why do we have to have actors in makeup and costume?

In the current *Twelfth Night* the words are clearly spoken and the actors are agreeable, but all else is lacking. *Twelfth Night* cannot live on the stage today, except as a prettily worded charade, unless a fresh and gay impulse is brought to bear on it. There must be a joyous elation about it, invention and verve—in a word, creation. The director must envision the play as if it were being done for the first time in a spirit of jubilant discovery. To present the text of *Twelfth Night* unadorned is to make it pedestrian and thus to destroy it. All I got from the present production was a strong suspicion that Shakespeare was bisexual.

Yes, M'Lord, by W. Douglas Home, is gentle nonsense apropos of the British election of 1945. This doesn't mean that the play is unintelligent, but simply that Home's "point"—the true English aristocrat doesn't trouble himself over party politics, knowing full well that England under almost any government goes on being the same—is not to be taken seriously. The author merely wants to have a little fun with topical themes.

What makes the play an amiable evening is its lack of strain, its willingness to be brightly yet modestly trivial, and, above all, its old-fashioned and admirably sound acting. A. E. Matthews' maundering lord is a gem in the lightest vein of English caricature, while George Curzon's Tory butler is a color sketch in which the grand manner is put to the uses of a comic "realism." Both these performances make it clear that what we are seeing is to be enjoyed only as make-believe, yet close enough to truth to be part of our appreciation of the amusingly meaningful in life. The source of the robust professionalism demonstrated here by Matthews and Curzon comes from a dignity actors acquire when they are sure, not only of their craft, but of their place in the community.

—*NR*, 24 Oct. '49

ENGLISH VISITATION

The English have a way of turning out dry portraits of familiar and peculiarly British types, which are supposed to be admired for their cool objectivity, but which prove on close inspection to be sentimental, if not secretly worshipful, tributes to British virtues. Galsworthy was a past master at this game. Terence Rattigan is pretty good at it too. In Rattigan's *The Browning Version*, one of the two plays of the double bill being given at the Coronet, Maurice Evans plays a dried-up secondary-school professor of Latin and Greek. Most of his pupils consider him a tyrant, but he is only a scrupulous scholar with high standards.

Rattigan's professor is poky, stiff and humorless, but at the same time a man so basically human that he cries when he finds a student who really likes him, and so truly honorable that he bears his wife no ill will though she constantly cheats him. After all, says the professor, he committed the crime of marrying her. She could not give him the kind of love that was important to him (it is not made altogether clear what sort that is) while he obviously fails to give her the kind of love important to her, about which there can be no ambiguity. At the end of the play, the professor has won a friend—nay an admirer—in his wife's former lover, while the wife is left, so to speak, holding the bag.

I doubt that anywhere in the world but in England and among resolute Anglophiles in America are such portraits taken as probing character studies. They are really salon art with most of the attributes of mature work except reality.

Rattigan has the good sense to wind up his play with a Maugham-like joke. He has also provided good parts for his actors.

What touched me most in *The Browning Version* was Maurice Evans' attempt to *act*. This is perhaps an ungracious way of putting it, but the fact is that Evans is usually less an actor than a reader. Since *The Browning Version* is not especially notable from a literary standpoint, Evans is forced to carry the play instead of depending on the play and his gift for vigorous enunciation to carry him.

His make-up is good, and the moments of emotional embarrassment are extremely well indicated. The particular manner in which Evans breaks down—like a man to whom weeping is a humiliation—so that he becomes somewhat more forcibly childish than moving, proves him an observant and thoughtful actor. Despite this, the part never comes alive, because Evans' technique is calculated only to show his audience what he is experiencing, and he is experiencing little beyond the determination to make clear what he is supposed to be experiencing. Evans' *soul* does not act, and his external technique is not as good as it should be, since it is too strenuously in evidence. He does not possess "the art that hides art."

Evans' faults are aggravated in the company that surrounds him. I have rarely seen anything as un-British as the performance given by this cast of English, near-English and would-be English actors. For no matter how repressed or formal Englishmen may be, they are rarely musclebound. The company acted as if behaving like Englishmen were killing them.

—*NR*, 7 Nov. '49

TWO HITS

As the final curtain descended on *Lost in the Stars*, the "musical tragedy" that Maxwell Anderson and Kurt Weill have made from the material provided by Alan Paton's *Cry, the Beloved Country*, I noticed that many in the audience were misty-eyed and that the applause was loud and long. A few of my friends not only declared themselves unmoved; they appeared indignant. I tried to understand this discrepancy between the general audience reaction and that of my friends.

Lost in the Stars tells the story of a South African Negro minister whose son, having left his home in the country hills for the sinful city of Johannesburg, in the course of a hold-up kills an English boy who was a true friend of the black natives. The minister realizes that his son was a victim of evil circumstances. His religious sincerity and kindness, plus his son's repentance, end by moving the murdered boy's rather rigidly British father to understand, forgive and cooperate with the minister in making a better life for all.

The story, then, is strong, simple and moral. It moves swiftly from one brief scene to another, and those words which are not bare narrative or purely didactic are sung by the individual characters or by a chorus. The words come to us not as precise ideas but as a benign mood. An atmosphere of kindly uplift, of warm dignity and of a nobility that is always on the verge of tears, prevails.

Lost in the Stars is a melodrama in the original sense of a plot play based on popular themes supported by song and instrumental music. In the old days a piano, a violin or an organ would do the trick. Today more fulsome arrangements are required. Such a play makes for basic theatre, and when the social and emotional ingredients are shrewdly chosen, the result is almost inevitably successful.

The Negro actors and chorus of *Lost in the Stars* have fine voices and the numbers are admirably rehearsed. I found Sheila Guyse attractive, Warren Coleman amusing, and Inez Matthews' singing especially good. My objection to the show is not that it is a tear-jerker on the Negro-white theme, but that its creative value is practically nil. I am more than dubious about its "philosophy": it tells us that since man is lost in the stars and nothing else is sure, people ought to

help one another. I hardly believe that such thinking will activate anyone socially, though it may
serve as a softener. Kurt Weill's score is competently synthetic, a kind of oily composition that
smears aromatic musical stuff over the verse in a
manner that may soothe, but will not stick.

To condemn *I Know My Love* as a play and to
indulge the Lunts as performers seems to me an
evasion. Many actors have made art out of worse
plays. While it is always clear when one watches
the Lunts that they are extremely gifted stage
craftsmen, I found them thoroughly irritating in *I
Know My Love*.

Marcel Achard's *Auprès de Ma Blonde*, from
which S. N. Behrman fashioned the Lunts' latest
vehicle, was a sentimental, Paris-made contrivance
for the use of Pierre Fresnay and Yvonne
Printemps, with a dash of bitters to make it seem
something more than that. In the French original,
the ever-loving bourgeois couple, whose marital
career the play celebrates, had their ugly moments.
The husband was allowed his vulgar fling and
wrecked some lives.

Writing for the Lunts, Behrman has had to
pour additional goo into the full measure already
supplied by the original author. Lunt's Thomas
Chanler of Boston never deceives his Emily (Lynn
Fontanne); he is merely enticed by the idea. Her
smiling wisdom deflates his ardor. As in the
French play, the man and wife drive an adolescent
boy to suicide, but the whole thing is made to
appear no more than a peccadillo, the slightest
responsibility for which the good wife must spare
her dear husband. The "first major quarrel in
twelve years" can hardly be described as even a
mild tiff: it is all wreathed in knowing smiles. If
such people were real they would destroy each
other through boredom.

The Lunts are masters of stage cosmetics. In *I
Know My Love* they each put on four brilliant
makeups—giving us a total of eight—and they
dress and characterize accordingly. But, paradoxically, their performance, which is chiefly characterization, lacks character. It is all clever detail,

pigment, graphic flourish—without soul. It is like
suave academic painting at which one marvels
over the technique without giving a hoot for the
subject.

There seems to me little point now in demanding that the Lunts do the kind of plays Olivier,
Richardson and Gielgud usually do in England.
What is important to emphasize is that in what they
do do their quality is becoming increasingly
insipid. I do not ask them to become more aware of
the world which the theatre is supposed to reflect.
If their world were limited to the bedroom, or even
the parlor, it might be sufficient. But their world
now never extends beyond the dressing room.

Two things have hurt the Lunts more than
anything else: the fact that they are treated by their
public as "institutional" ornaments rather than
artists; second, the notion, common on our stage,
that good actors can forgo direction. The outstanding examples of modern theatre practice prove that
the finest actors deserve and need the greatest
directors.

—*NR*, 21 Nov. '49

LOST IN THE STARS OF BROADWAY

Kurt Weill's score for the "musical tragedy"
which Maxwell Anderson has made from the
material of Alan Paton's novel *Cry, the Beloved
Country* is highly satisfactory to the majority of
theatregoers now pouring into the New York
theatre where it is currently being shown. It is an
effective score. This means that it makes Maxwell
Anderson's words go down easily. It helps the
play's sad tale seem elevating as well as touching.
Musically speaking, *Lost in the Stars* is a safe
security.

Under the circumstances, it seems almost
churlish to question if the songs which compose
this solid score are also good music. This is particularly true since the term "good music" is almost
impossible to define. The *Lost in the Stars* score is
certainly good in that it performs its theatrical

function. To those who have seen the play and enjoyed it, the excellent recordings Decca has made of its songs will recall the pleasure of the performance.

The fact that the music is not particularly original—that it is, indeed, full of obvious reminiscence—is not in itself as damaging as certain connoisseurs would have us believe, it is undesirable for a theatre score to be startlingly original. What is wanted in the theatre is a score with a novel twist on the thrice familiar.

Two things have always characterized the best of Kurt Weill's music. He had the faculty of writing scores, every part of which might be proved to lack any striking novelty, but which nevertheless were original in the sense of being *individual*, taken as a whole. The second characteristic of a Weill score was that each section—even the shortest fragment intended to illustrate the briefest bit of action—was written so that it seemed to have the completeness of a little music drama, a thing in itself with a rounded scenic feeling.

The second of these features is still very much one of the assets of Weill's music. No Weill score can be wholly inadequate. On the contrary, it may be safely said that no Weill score can fail to offer a certain degree of satisfaction when the other factors are acceptable. This dependability is an attribute of Weill's unerring sense of the theatre.

But we must come back to the question of the music as music. Though I am vaguely gratified as I listen to *Lost in the Stars*, at no time does the music penetrate my consciousness as a living element. It does not stick. It does not add any new quality of feeling to my being. It does not enlarge my awareness.

An artist friend of mine once told me that in judging new paintings he had one infallible criterion by which he could determine their aliveness: he asked himself whether the paintings helped him see the world differently, whether they had in any way transfigured his vision. Is it not our common experience, when we are under the sway of a real creation, that we begin to see and feel in its vein?

The world takes on Rembrandt shadows after we have seen an exhibition of his work. Even the anti-Wagnerites in the controversial period of that German composer's day had to admit that it was no longer possible to hear and feel except as people who had dwelled in the Wagner world.

By such a test—and I am convinced that it is valid—the score of *Lost in the Stars* is not good music. It creates no world of its own. It is synthetic, not simply because it has been made of borrowed materials—this is true to some extent of all art—but because its materials have not been informed with a new life. This music is pleasant in general, and true art—even the most abstract—is specific. It always reveals its own inalienable soul.

This brings us to the question of Kurt Weill's career. For, obviously, there would be little point to an extended discussion of the present score were it not the work of one of the most gifted and cultivated musicians writing for our theatre. We cannot forget that Kurt Weill composed *The Threepenny Opera*.

It is not my intention to indulge in that other form of critical sadism, which consists of hanging an artist on the hook of his most notable work. I mention Weill's *Threepenny Opera*, which, after all, is less known in this country than some of Weill's more recent scores, because it marks a turning point in a career that had an important preceding history as well as a significant later one.

As a student of the great pianist-composer Busoni, Weill began his career as a composer of what many would call highbrow music, that is, music which, to say the least, was not easy. Two factors altered Weill's musical path. He was temperamentally a composer who preferred to write to order for specific occasions (generally speaking, like Mozart) rather than one, like Beethoven, whose work more often than not seemed to be generated by a spontaneous, inner urge. We must also remember that the early Twenties, the point at which Weill's career began, was a period when even the most serious composers turned toward the theatre as a way of reaching a larger and more alert public than was to be found in the perennially conservative concert halls.

This impulse might lead a French composer of the time to Diaghilev's fashionable Ballet Russe or a German to slightly Dadaistic, occasionally leftish, but certainly unorthodox experimental groups, which combined something of the qualities of the political forum, the artistic cabaret, and eccentric popular tribunes. In such places music could overcome the stuffiness and turgidity or the pained ineffability with which, after Wagner, music became burdened. Music was no longer to be a refuge for solid citizens of slow digestion or for old ladies of both sexes too timorous to face a topsy-turvy world. Music was to go into the market place—laugh, scream, threaten, flatter, amuse, jolt, teach the teeming populace.

Kurt Weill, possessing a keen sense of popular trends, joined in this movement. His associates were lively insurgents among young stage directors and scene designers as well as the best young poet in Germany, Bertolt Brecht. Together they produced a series of tragic shockers or satiric operas bitterly reflecting the diseased society they lived in. Not all these people agreed exactly as to what they were for; they all knew what they were against. It gave them all some sort of emotional line or direction, without which it is extremely difficult for an artist to grow. Out of this movement came *The Threepenny Opera*.

It is too little to say that the Brecht-Weill *Threepenny Opera* was a masterpiece of its time. When one hears the score today, it not only lives again with all its old charm, but it takes on added grace through the flatness, the lack of a particular color, which is the dominant characteristic of the present moment. One is not only delighted by the wit of the Weill score—not to mention the brilliant lyrics—but captivated by its sweet raffishness, its poisonously warm abandon, its drugged back-alley romanticism, its occasional burst of buoyant populism and street-corner bravery. This fundamentally popular score is truly good music. It had an enormous influence in Europe, and in this country, on such composers as Marc Blitzstein.

When Hitler made it impossible for Weill to live in Germany, he migrated to France and then to England. Weill's capacity for change and adaptation evinced in his transfer from the near-Schönbergian mode of his first works to the satirical frivolity of *The Threepenny Opera* displayed itself clearly in his minor essays on the London and Parisian stages. Weill tried hard to be ultra-English and typically Parisian. I have no doubt that had he tried longer he would have succeeded.

When Weill came to this country in 1936 to provide and supervise the score of the Werfel-Reinhardt-Norman Bel Geddes *Eternal Road*, he was little known except by musicians who had been to Berlin and by adventurous spirits who enjoyed picking up exotic flowers in odd byways of the entertainment world or on imported records. Among these were the members of the Group Theatre, and though *The Threepenny Opera* had failed on Broadway (1933)—due to inadequate production, insufficient publicity and bad times—the Group Theatre commissioned Weill to write *Johnny Johnson* with Paul Green.

Johnny Johnson was not a success—although it had its admirers. Only one or two of the critics remarked on the original quality of the score, in which Weill managed to combine elements of a peculiarly sensuous and melancholy nature with typically American musical folklore materials—a strange but affecting mixture, superior, in my opinion, to most of what Weill has subsequently written.

Weill is so much the adaptable artist—he is characteristically twentieth century in this respect—that if he were forced to live among Hottentots he would in the shortest possible span of time become the leading Hottentot composer. Broadway isn't altogether Hottentot, but Weill's career since *Johnny Johnson*, despite excellent work now and again—always on a high level of craftsmanship—has been an adaptation toward an increasingly facile, I might say, artistically nondescript goal. The result has been—not unnaturally—an ever more conventional musicality, a decline in real quality, and an increase in journalistic praise as well as box office receipts.

The score for *Lady in the Dark* was *Threepenny Opera* diluted with Noel Coward and Cole Porter, but it was cleverly suave and fashionable, cutely tough, glamorous music for a cocktail verandah world at 10:00 P.M. I am unfamiliar with the score of *One Touch of Venus*, but no one has recommended it to me. *Love Life* last year had its catchy moments ("Green Up Time") but was hardly as distinguished as the best of *Knickerbocker Holiday*—where Weill tended to mark time by borrowing too much from himself, always a symptom of trouble. *Street Scene* was a smooth amalgam of Puccini jazz, and Viennese operetta for the purpose of putting over the opera form among those prejudiced against it. Now we have *Lost in the Stars*, which is slickly impressive and as basically void as the architecture of our giant movie emporia.

There is nothing wrong in adapting oneself to a new environment, but one must adapt oneself upward rather than downward, that is, to the more challenging and difficult as well as to the simpler and safer. Failing, at least, an occasional effort in the direction of the untried, the hazardous, and possibly even the unpopular, a composer may suffer other than those of the concentration camps. To develop real roots in a chaos such as ours today, an artist must shape some definite ideal for himself of the kind of world toward which he can aspire.

—*SR*, 31 Dec. '49

BEFORE CURTAIN TIME

At the mid-September meeting of the Drama Critics' Circle, some of the members looked glum: nary a show had opened. There had only been *Ken Murray's Blackouts*, which was a collection of vaudeville acts, several smutty jokes and one or two budding Mae Wests. "Is this a season?" the reviewers asked. But there is no reason to worry: in the manner of the radio oracles, I predict that over fifty shows will be produced during the

1949-50 semester, two or three of which will be sufficiently meritorious for the columnists to announce that their faith in the theatre had been restored, and that there had never been cause to fret to begin with.

I should like to make the rhetorical suggestion that a "moratorium" be called on *Hamlet*, *Macbeth*, *Othello*, *Twelfth Night* for the next ten years. If some of the less frequently revived Shakespeare plays were attempted, directors might feel constrained to work out really original production plans. By a production plan, I do not mean a way of expediting scene changes, but the creation of fresh theatrical ideas, without which Shakespeare had best be left in the library.

The fear of old-fashioned theatricality among newly arrived sophisticates is always marked when a form of entertainment doesn't fit into an officially blessed category. Something of the sort has happened, I believe, in the case of Roland Petit's *Les Ballets de Paris*, which the Shuberts have brought from the Theatre Marigny in Paris to Broadway's Winter Garden. Very few dramatic critics were invited to cover this show, or they may have declined on the grounds of an insecurity in regard to their judgment of dance or music. At any rate, the dance and music critics reviewed the imported program, and were extremely gingerly in their praise or showed signs of positive hostility. A more instinctive public, I feel sure, will make the show the hit it deserves to be.

It may be argued that there are few first-rate dancers in the new ballet company, that none of the scores employed are particularly distinguished—except of course for the Bizet excerpts—and that the choreographic ideas in some of the numbers are elementary and, in one instance, almost vulgar. All this may be true, but I should like to submit in the first place that *Les Ballets de Paris* should be seen primarily as *theatre*, and second, that I know no ballet of the past five years more superbly brilliant as a whole than Roland Petit's "Carmen."

What Petit has done with the Carmen story and score is to take its Spanish elements and give them an electrically concise French form. There are music-hall elements in the new "Carmen," but there is also a keen awareness of a certain harsh Spanish formality mingled with a Parisian sense of the raffishness of the streets, a celebration of the color and feel of low-life. It is as if the French appetite for romance in proletarian and criminal dregs (a phase of French art that begins as early as the fifteenth century with Villon) were here given a classic theatric form. The hackneyed story of "Carmen," with its degradation of a simple boy through his fatal penchant for a slut who works in a factory as an occupation incidental to her addiction to outlawed trades, is seen in Petit's ballet as a miniature symbol of sexual passion on an almost heroic scale.

It is snobbish nonsense to approach the present "Carmen" with the jargon of the balletomane—"fifth position," "dancing on the points"—and to overlook what is vibrant, witty, inventive in it. Antoine Clave's settings and costumes are masterpieces. I would counsel all our scene-designers to study this Spaniard's sets to learn how an assortment of separate and ostensibly unrelated realistic elements may be combined to create not only beautiful effects but striking meanings that convey mood, environment, feeling, comment. The wash hanging in front of the Seville factory, the little varicolored lamps of the smugglers' tavern above the large, crooked and broken kerosene lamp which looks like a banged-up Spanish marauder, the white lace curtain that frames Carmen's bedroom with its disordered iron bed on which clothes and a guitar are strewn, the unglamorous washstand at the side, the discarded barouche outside the bullring, are not only memorable in themselves but correspond to and must have stimulated similar "discoveries" in the staging: the flinging of the *aficionados'* hats from the arena onto Carmen's dead body, the animal-like and sexual shiver of her final movement which is preceded by a dance that is itself a mortal struggle that matches but is more terrible than that which is invisible behind the black and bloody fences of the enclosure, the swaying of the wheel from the smugglers' wagon—hanging abstractly and inexplicably with a weapon-like quality from the flies above—the "cavalry" exit of Don Jose and his brigand friends when they dash off to their mountain villanies, the oddly effective business of Don Jose's washing his hands (and being somewhat ashamed of it) amid the carnal play of his love-making: all these make "Carmen" creative theatre—an example, by the way, of what I mean when I affirm that words are not the essence of theatrical art.

I have rarely seen a Carmen who was not to a great extent more a creation of the audience's wish to behold an exciting personality on the stage than the thing itself. Olga Baclanova in that other great version of "Carmen," the Moscow Art Musical Studios *Carmencita and the Soldier* which New York saw in 1925, was extremely handsome, but she merged into the general magnificence of the production as a whole. Mary Garden's Carmen had a steely gravity which was impressive, especially as a contrast to the best operatic Don Jose I ever saw, the lyrically impassioned Lucien Muratore, but generally speaking the Carmens we see—even when she is the voluptuous and merry Viviane Romance of the French films—are only imitations of the Emma Calve Carmen even I am too young to remember.

Renée Jeanmaire, the *Ballets de Paris* Carmen is a treat. Her sexiness is real but unconventional. It is a matter of vivid and poisonously alluring impulses rather than of hippy or bosomy invitation. Her boyishly feminine hairdo, her enigmatic eyes, her pallor, her thin arms and exciting legs, her softly depraved neck and jawline are the physical attributes of her appeal. She is a whirling, flying, fearfully magnetic, circumambient sex wraith.

Roland Petit's Don Jose is lithe, handsome, incisive and innocent through suffering. He has no blue-eyed sweetheart to call him back to a mother he bewails. He wants only to possess his girl, and he triumphs through the price he has to pay for it. At times he huffs and puffs too much, attempting to make up in vehemence what he lacks in other means, but he really knows how to touch a woman—a rare skill among actors on our stage since John Barrymore. Some people, whose demand for restraint in acting is chiefly an unconscious plea to spare their feeble capacities the shock of a substantial emotion, may complain that Petit "hams" some of his acting. Let them not forget that he also lifts his Carmen off her feet and tosses her about with ease and grace and pantomimes his kisses with a greater sense of the brute truth in a kiss than is contained in a season full of moderation as practiced by most of our juicelessly journalistic actors who do not even know how to characterize a man. I always prefer a little hard blowing in the right direction of masculine expression to the victories by default by which polite leading men indicate their neuter modernity.

Yes, it is true: I would make war on the blank simplicity of the latter-day stage (and generally of pseudomodern art) which would deprive the theatre of those attributes of rich expressiveness that are being driven from our increasingly functional existence. The theatre should serve as the arsenal of our imaginative lives. I am against the theatre of the Word alone (the word, in the theatre, acquires its main eloquence through the voice of the speaker); I believe the theatre to be the art of the complete person and his surrounding environment, the art of the body as the flesh of the spirit, the art of things man uses—clothes and "properties"—pageant, game and ritual. I cannot abide the castrated art of the theatre of "ideas" alone, of true-to-the-library and the depressed drawing-room or kitchen life. Such theatre kills all theatre, and the shoddy of even bad movies and the tricks of hideous television will ultimately triumph over such a theatre. There was greatness in the unemphatic gesture of a Duse, poignancy in the tremulous quiet of a Laurette Taylor, but there is little but boredom in the negative naturalism of our hotel customer's drama.

A theatre that still exists without any drama at all is the Yiddish theatre of New York's East Side. Its deterioration, though probably inevitable, is a sad thing. Years ago—approximately between 1890 and 1917—the Yiddish theatre was probably the best in the city. Tribute to the actors of this period may be read in the writings of Norman Hapgood and Lincoln Steffens. I have heard so knowledgeable a judge of acting as Jed Harris say that he considered David Kessler—with Jacob Adler the leading tragedian of the time—the greatest actor he had ever seen. Some of the first productions in America of the plays of Tolstoy, Andreyev, Sudermann, Hauptmann, the nineteenth-century German romantic dramatists, and rousing productions of Shakespeare's tragedies were to be seen in the Yiddish theatre of those days. Even more recently, between 1917 and 1930, many fine artists and productions made a visit to the theatre of New York's East Side a rewarding adventure even to the non-Jewish theatre-lover. But practically all the actors and serious playwrights of these periods have gone. What remains is rarely better than debris.

I was troubled and moved on a recent trip to the theatre once built on behalf of David Kessler to see Molly Picon in her latest musical comedy vehicle *Abi gezunt* (So Long As It's Healthy). For what I saw was a nondescript show which was made cheerful and gaily touching by the wholeheartedly old-fashioned performance of players whose every move, grimace and defect is theatrical in a manner that goes back practically to the origins of continental comedy. These players do outrageous things with such infectious eagerness that, despite the corruption of the language they employ—hodgepodge of Yiddish and Americanese—they create a mood that is unmistakably warming.

Molly Picon is a treasure. She is a sweet scamp of the East Side with shrewd and merry eyes, a great innocence of heart. Her whole quality is a tribute that the shabby present of the depleted American "ghetto" still is able to pay to the wholesome traditions of the theatre and folklife of the generous past.

The Jewish East Side today is a kind of anachronism, an "institution" maintained by the lethargy of old social elements and the nostalgia of people who moved away from it and find themselves unable to rediscover anywhere else in the city the racy saltiness and fervent vitality that were once the East Side's outstanding characteristics.

Molly Picon represents the poetry of everything that is healthy in that nostalgia, together with an indulgent accommodation to what is not so sound in the present East Side. She has become a woman of the world—smart, consummately professional, truly kind—with a never-to-be-diminished loyalty to her roots. She began the best part of her career in 1924, and she stands today as the one truly popular artist the American Yiddish theatre can now claim.

Before the theatrical season got properly underway there were such things to see as the nice performances of the New York City Opera Company, with Offenbach's *Tales of Hoffmann* providing a particularly pleasant example of the company's merits. The reviewers were generally very kind to the Irish film *Saints and Sinners*, the freshest feature of which I found was not so much the famous Celtic charm and the gift of speech that goes with it, but the fact that practically every person in the darlin' village, which is the scene of the film's story, is a bounder of one sort or another.

Less ingratiating but more interesting to me was the new Rossellini film, *Germany Year Zero*. This film about postwar Germany is curious and not entirely satisfactory because it may be regarded as a failure through what it succeeds in accomplishing, or a success through its failure! There is a kind of deadness, awkwardness and distortion about all the people in the picture which is part of its terrible effect. One leaves *Germany Year Zero* uncertain whether the peculiar mutism and ungainly bewilderment of its characters are due to an inability on Rossellini's part to handle Germans as authoritatively as he does Italians, or whether the "frozen" behavior and lame dialogue of his latest film are elements of his calculated design.

One thing is certain: Rossellini has justified the picture's title. The picture is the image of a zero hour of the human spirit, of a world in which all sentiment seems to have stopped. Rossellini's Germany represents humanity at a dead end. In *Paisan,* the brutality of war is conveyed by feeling: a little child cries out heartrendingly in the night against a background of slaughtered bodies. But it is a wholly normal child that cries, and in his shattering cry there is hope. In *Germany Year Zero*, the last remnants of feeling are gone. All is void, there is only death. When the little boy, who is the film's central figure, plays spasmodically amid the ruins, his movements are like the last twitching reflexes of an ebbing life. This is total defeat—moral as well as physical. One wonders whether this is what Rossellini feels not only about Germany but about Europe generally. His camera is pitiless. It has made *Germany Year Zero* a print of a wholly barren world. There is no hope here. All is bleak and gray, and the survivors are more obsolete than the piled corpses of *Paisan.*

The beginning of that process which reduced Germany to the state described in the Rossellini film may be seen in *The Blum Affair*, a new picture out of Germany. It is the story of a frame-up in which a Jewish businessman in pre-Hitler days is falsely accused of a murder because a fascist-minded police and judge hope to find him guilty.

Based on an actual case, the picture is structurally a melodrama, the like of which we have all seen hundreds of times. But intelligence, social understanding, honesty, excellence of dramatic and cinematic craftsmanship render the picture an object lesson in what can be done to give the most ordinary material excitement and meaning, without making either seem like something superimposed on the other. Producers and devotees of "progressive" films, please note!

—*TRW*, Dec. '49

ABOVE: ANTA THEATRE SEMINAR 1950
Lillian Hellman, Fred Fox, Clarence Derwent, Harold
Clurman, Elmer Rice

BELOW: ACTOR STUDIO REHEARSALS
With Elia Kazan and Maxwell Anderson

THE
FIFTIES

CAROL CHANNING IN
GENTLEMEN PREFER BLONDES

Let us, by all means, return to the big blonde— Carol Channing. She has a distinct personality. It reminds me somehow of the Wrigley sign that made the Broadway of the twenties what a French lady of my acquaintance long ago described as "extraordinaire but not very raffinated." Miss Channing is conspicuous, brazen, shimmery and attractive. She is tall and her figure is not dainty, yet there is an odd unreality about her, as if she weren't constructed in three dimensions at all. Her eyes blaze in a vacant ogle that might be lust but is more likely a cunning so dumb that it becomes innocence. One thinks of a gadget too expensive for its parts and too wearing for the fun that one gets out of it, but nevertheless peculiarly precious. For is not all this the symbol of a good time in the vein of those crazy days, when vice was a joke and the city preferred a dandy mayor, who cheated its citizens, to the righteous lawyer who sought to protect them?

The admirable thing about Carol Channing is that she is not a Lorelei Lee, but that she makes one. She is a real actress in the sense that her performance accomplishes a characterization. The high-heeled, squeezed-toe mince, the high-pitched, metallic twang, the fiercely delightful energy combined with the honey-pie slush and gurgle of her speech, are all rendered with absolute and winning authenticity. She delivers "A Little Girl from Little Rock," with its refrain about the guy who done her wrong, in an unforgettable style— which is truly a *style*.

—*NAT,* 2 Jan. '50

FROM A MEMBER

Having directed *The Member of the Wedding*, I am in no position to review it. But my readers might be interested to know some of the things my experience in doing it taught me.

It is impossible to direct a play that has no action. When a play is well acted, it means that a line of action has been found in it. It means that action was in it, however obscure it may have seemed at first sight. Without action, it would not *play*. The reason why Chekhov's *Seagull* did not seem to have action when it was first produced was that the original company had not found it, just as opera singers first thought Wagner unsingable, and a still later generation was to begin by declaring Debussy's *Mélisande* unoperatic. The directors and actors of the Moscow Art Theatre discovered the play in *The Seagull*.

I am convinced that Ethel Waters, Julie Harris, Brandon de Wilde and the other actors of *The Member of the Wedding*, following the line of action I sensed in it as a director, have made a play of *The Member of the Wedding* because it was a play to begin with—albeit of a different kind than any other we had previously done. Ibsen once said of his *Brand* and *Peer Gynt*: "If these weren't poetry before, they have become poetry now." The same may be said of *The Member of the Wedding* in regard to its status as a play. The proof is in the doing of it.

The action springs from the twelve-year-old Frankie Addams' desire to get out of herself, *to become connected* or identified with a world larger than that which confines her to the "ugly old kitchen" which is her world, and to an environment that Carson McCullers (in the book of which her play is a general transcription) describes as "a jungle under glass." Frankie's conflict is with the apparent inertia of the community around her, against which she pushes her adolescent being like a sharp plant struggling upward through the resistant soil.

All the other characters of the play are variants of this struggle for connection—some mature, some stumbling and unconscious, some vaguely groping, some hysterically violent. Every scene is subtly but directly related to the main action. Moreover, the main action, being conveyed through the spirit of a child, is so close to the audiences' secret hunger—for we are a lonely people—that the spectator feels the play's meaning keenly, though he may not be able to explain his response except by saying that the acting and direction are wonderful.

Yet what is the direction of the play but the realization in movement of body and soul of the action I have just indicated? Julie Harris is an actress of inspired invention as Ethel Waters is a personality of profound natural force, so that when I, as director, pointed out that because Frankie was growing with the impulse *to get out of herself* against unyielding circumstances she would inevitably assume queer shapes—twist and turn, run and twirl—Miss Harris had a clue to her characterization and Ethel Waters was able to understand her function in the play and the basis of her attitude toward Frankie. If you observe some of the secondary aspects of Frankie's behavior—her tomboyishness, her "crazy" intensity, her awkwardness, her childish hostilities, her self-absorption, her imaginativeness and the torture that underlies all her efforts—you will see how they emerge from the play's core. The play is the lyric expression of its strong central action; the direction consists of finding a physical or visual equivalent for every emotion that is the concomitant of the action—like the excited hopping of the seven-year-old John Henry when Frankie dreams of her flight around the earth so as to become "a member of the whole world."

If you think that I am simply rationalizing the directorial process, my answer is that just this process, embodied through sensitive actors and all the other means of the stage, is precisely the thing that makes theatre out of the written word. And if such people as theatrical backers and the run-of-the-mill producer who depends on their word for his wisdom, are not able to realize the potentialities of a play like *The Member of the Wedding*, it is because they are not theatre people at all—merely gamblers whose game is the stage. Fortunately there are producers like Robert Whitehead and his associates who are eager to face real theatrical problems because they think of them not primarily in the light of "investments" but as objects of their love. But since art is willy-nilly the theatre's business, it is only through such love that good theatre, and ultimately good business, can be made.

I say this without smugness since I confess that it was the producer, not I, who believed it possible for *The Member of the Wedding* to achieve the box-office success it has. He had faith in the public. I had been on the point of succumbing to a kind of highbrow jaundice which bitterly supposes that truly unusual forms of the theatre are only jeopardized by production on Broadway. A renewal of faith in the sensitivity and awareness of our New York theatregoing public was perhaps the greatest lesson I learned from *The Member of the Wedding*.

—*NR*, 30 Jan. '50

IN A DIFFERENT LANGUAGE

Being a director, it may be assumed that I am prejudiced against the playwright who proposes to direct his own play. If I cited examples of playwrights who had ruined their plays by directing them, I should find myself in the awkward position of also having to list the playwrights who have done very good jobs directing their own plays. The debate cannot be argued on an absolute basis. Obviously a good playwright may prove himself a good director, just as there is no law that says a good playwright may not also be a first-class tap dancer. The point is that one capacity does not necessarily imply the other.

There are people who maintain that all playwrights should direct their own plays. Shakespeare and Molière are there to give the contention historical precedent. It is considered a reasonable premise that since no one can know a play as well as the person who wrote it, the playwright must clearly be the best director for his own work. This is hollow logic. We all know playwrights who are rendered tongue-tied the moment they are asked to deal with a company of actors. Chekhov's answers to questions about his plays were so cryptic that it was practically impossible for his colleagues to act on his advice. His was not an isolated case.

The question is not one of personalities but of principles. How is it possible for a theatre-wise playwright to be a bad director? Why are there directors, far less acute than the playwright whose work they are interpreting, who nevertheless bring this work to life on the stage in a manner the playwrights will readily admit is beyond their ability?

To answer these questions one must go back to the theatre's rudiments. The art of the theatre does not consist in adding actors, scenery, movement and music to a dramatist's text, as one inserts a set of illustrations into a published book. What we call a play in the theatre is something radically different from a play on the page. The dramatist expresses himself mainly through words, the director through *action* which involves people amid the paraphernalia of the stage.

The theatre is a collective art not only in the sense that many people contribute to it, but in the subtler sense that each of the contributors to the final result actually collaborates in his partner's function. The playwright himself is a director when he writes his play; he does not simply set down what his characters have to say, he tries to visualize the effect of his scenes on the stage. The playwright may be described as a writer who has been to the theatre and has a feeling for what will *play*, what will be interesting to see rather than exciting only to hear or to imagine.

What holds true for the playwright holds for the other theatre craftsmen—the actor, the scene-designer, the director. Jokes are often cracked about the vanity and obtuseness of actors, but everyone knows of actors whose intuitive insights not only generate new qualities in a part or in a play but whose feelings—often clumsily expressed by a combination of inadequate words and incomplete gestures—serve the playwright with creative ideas which finally become incorporated into the actual text of the play. There are directors, too,

whose sense of a play's meaning is so acute that they are able to bring elements in the dramatist's text to full fruition chiefly through their own inspiration. I know, moreover, of one very fine play now running in New York which might not have found its present form if a designer had not suggested a scenic method for handling simultaneous action on the stage.

There is nothing exceptional in these instances of cooperative creativity. They are of the theatre's very essence; they have obtained at all times, and in the very greatest examples of theatrical art. What prevents us from being more aware of this constant give-and-take in theatre is the intense specialization of the contemporary stage and the demonic commercial competitiveness that has set in—particularly in our country—during the past ten years.

Still, the functions of playwright, actor, designer, director are distinct from one another. The dramatist usually sets forth the general scheme and theme of the play. (I say "usually" because there have been instances of scenarios and material for plays having been suggested by the director or even a leading actor.) The dramatist's conception—his story-line and plan of action conveyed through descriptive words and dialogue—serves the other theatre craftsmen as the *raw material* from which they make the thing we finally witness at performance.

Before asking why the playwright should not direct the performance of his text, we might ask ourselves why he should not act in it, or at least play the leading part. One might immediately remark that many playwrights, from Shakespeare and Molière to Sasha Guitry and Noel Coward, have been actors. But this would be an evasion of the basic problem. In his heart every playwright is an actor even more than he is a director, but still we rarely think of playwrights as actors because what makes an actor good does not arise from the kind of understanding of a part which is supposedly possessed by the man who first conceived it. The actor's body, his voice, appearance, temperament, imagination, his background and experience on and off stage, are as crucial to the actor as that part of him which is the equivalent of the playwright's mind. There is no theatre without the actor, and when an actor enters upon the stage an entirely new factor has to be taken into account: a human personality, with everything which that connotes in physical and emotional behavior. No longer is the dramatist's character something to be imagined: he becomes a specific person who does not "bring something" to the words he is given to speak, but in a very real sense *replaces* them. Shakespeare's Hamlet we see is Barrymore's, Hampden's, Gielgud's, Evans', Olivier's. What has happened to Shakespeare's creation? He is still there on the page, or in your mind as you read, but on the stage he cannot be other than the actor you see—occasionally an inspiration, more often a duffer. If you deny this, you don't understand the theatre and probably don't even like it.

You would not have a Hamlet without a personality, and the actor, if he is to be anything more than a sound and an image, must always be a personality of some sort; that means a human entity with its own individual color, rhythm, emotional tone and content. In this lies one of the main sources of the theatre's glamor. In the face of it, that playwright is an idiot who cries out: "But all the actor has to do is to 'understand' my lines and repeat them as I wrote them." Any playwright of experience knows that if *that* is all the actor did, he (the playwright) would be induced to commit murder, probably followed by suicide.

Have we wandered far afield from our inquiry? Not at all. The handling of the diverse materials of the theatre so that the parts—actors, stage space, properties, light, background, music, and even the text itself—become a coherent, meaningful whole is the director's job. It is true that the playwright has his scenes, characters and actions in mind, but on the stage all these things have dimensions and qualities which are not of the mind.

That action speaks louder than words is the first principle of the stage; the director, I repeat, is

the "author" of the stage action. Gestures and movement, which are the visible manifestations of action, have a different specific gravity from the writer's disembodied ideas. Theatrical action is virtually a new medium, a different language from that which the playwright uses, although the playwright hopes that his words will suggest the kind of action that ought to be employed. The director must be a master of theatrical action, as the dramatist is master of the written concept of his play.

The playwright may know that he wants a scene to be light, airy, suggestive of a summer day in the country and so forth, but except in a very general way he rarely knows how this atmosphere may be created through the actor's feeling and movement, through the placement of properties or the use of colors and lights. He does not know, because these are not primarily his tools; they are not what he has been trained to deal with. On the stage the dramatist's language must be translated: his spirit must be made flesh.

Composers are not always the best interpreters of their own music. However, when a composer indicates what note he wants struck, he and his interpreters are pretty sure where that note is to be found on a given instrument. The playwright writes for an instrument where the location of the "notes is infinitely variable. It is all very well for the playwright to indicate that a speech be said "angrily" or "with a sob" or in a "high querulous treble." He will frequently find that if his directions are followed literally, the results will be ludicrous. The actor and director generally take the playwright's instructions as a clue to something the playwright is seeking to express. They often find that to express most effectively what the playwright had in view they have to employ quite different means than those which the playwright has suggested.

It is rarely the director's intentions to alter the playwright's meaning. (Of course this has often been done—consciously as well as unconsciously—and occasionally with very happy results.) But it is a mistake amounting to ignorance to believe that the playwright's meaning is necessarily conveyed by merely mouthing the playwright's dialogue and following his stated instructions. In a sense the playwright's text disappears the moment it reaches the stage, because on the stage it becomes part of an action, every element of which is as pertinent to its meaning as the text itself. A change in gesture, inflection, movement, rhythm or in the physical background of a speech may give it a new significance.

The playwright who says, "Just for once I'd like to see my characters as I imagined them," and therefore proceeds to direct his play himself, is more than a little naïve. What he usually means is: "The directors who have done my last two or three plays murdered them. Now I'm going to take a chance on doing it myself." This sort of complaint is understandable and in many cases justified, but it is not craftsmanlike. The playwright can never get the characters he imagined: he gets actors who are always themselves transfigured into stage images which the playwright may feel correspond to a reality he was seeking. How often have we heard a playwright say, "I see the character as a tall, thin, freckle-faced, red-headed man," only to find either that the actor who answered to this description has destroyed what the playwright really felt about the character, or that a short, stocky, clear-faced, dark-haired man has given him more truly what he wanted. The playwright's description of a character is often only a momentary and almost accidental way of expressing a sentiment, the actual embodiment of which has very little to do with the color of a man's hair or the nature of his complexion and figure.

The difference between the dramatist's function and the director's is often revealed when a playwright declares that the director has carried out his—the playwright's—intention to the letter, while a knowledgeable audience discerns that the director, even if he be the playwright himself, has fallen below the play's promise or distorted it. So distinct is the ability to write a play from the ability to judge it in the theatre *as theatre*, that a playwright will frequently fail to realize that what is on the stage is a parody of what he has written.

I have refrained throughout this discussion from becoming personal, since particular instances applied to a theoretical problem usually prove misleading. Yet the reader's experience will bear me out when I say that the playwright-director who boasts that there really isn't much to direction, that "It's a cinch," is nine times out of ten a fairly pedestrian director about whose work as a director one can only say that it is "adequate." Such playwright-directors use their actors as puppets to say their words, and scenery merely to illustrate the place of action. In this way they fashion performances that are not only anti-theatre, but in so doing limit what they might have to say as artists. For when all the elements of a theatrical production are treated as part of a unified but varied creative vision, a play takes on a rich extension of meaning that cannot be achieved when the stage is treated as a platform from which only the solitary voice of the "teacher" (playwright) may be hard.

As a director, critic and above all as a playgoer, I prefer by far the attitude of a Gorky to the productions of his plays to that expressed by the kind of playwright who is eminently satisfied when he has dumped the bare bones of his play on the stage. In 1935, Gorky's play "Yegor Bulichev" was done at two different theatres in Moscow. At one theatre the play was interpreted as the drama of a dying man seeking the truth in a world of liars; at another the play became the drama of a man with the inability to understand a truth which was new and unfamiliar to him. When Gorky was asked which was the true interpretation he answered: "Both—and perhaps there are more."

Gorky knew that a really live play has within it the possibilities of almost as many meanings as there are creative people to find them. The playwright-director who is satisfied with the one little meaning he can register with a kind of sound-recording and demonstration-by-slides of his text is usually a playwright whose play has very little chance of every being done in more than one production, or one who has belied and belittled his meaning even the first time. The written play is not the goal of the theatre—only the beginning. If the play at the end is not something beyond what it was at the beginning, there is very little point in the process of transposing it from the book to the stage; very little point, that is, to the whole art of the theatre.

—*TA*, Jan. '50

INNOCENCE: KLEE & VAN GOGH
R. P. WARREN & G. B. SHAW

There is a quality that relates the three best shows to be seen at this writing in New York. They are the retrospective exhibition of Paul Klee's paintings at the Museum of Modern Art, the Van Gogh exhibition at the Metropolitan Museum of Art, and Carson McCullers' play, *The Member of the Wedding*. The quality is innocence.

Innocence may signify ignorance. Primitive painters may be called innocent on this account. They set down what they see or feel as directly as possible, because they do not know the technique of painting as the schoolmen teach it. Such innocence often goes hand in hand with a general lack of sophistication in worldly ways. But there are "primitives"—such a modern painter as Dubuffet is an example—who are not innocent at all. Their work reflects a revulsion from knowledge of a world which they have found intolerable. The world is too much with them.

The innocence of Paul Klee is neither that of a primitive painter nor that of a person trying to cast out the devils from within him. He is not trying to venge himself on society by painting hateful images of it. Paul Klee is an extremely knowing craftsman, and clearly a person who was able to adjust himself to the complexities and refinements of modern society. His early drawings show the influence of old German painting with its strange mixture of an almost academically meticulous realism and the imaginatively grotesque. His later work proves that he has seen much of the world.

Paul Klee's innocence is something willed even more than something innate. The sensitive man today—and Klee's sensitivity is evident even in his earliest old style landscapes—finds the world and its arts too cluttered and burdensome for comfort. The individual is obliterated by techniques. The soul is crowded into remote corners. Even the simplification of twentieth-century functionalism is as much a threatening presence as the stuffiest of Victorian ornament. The human spirit cries out for privacy. To be alone with oneself becomes as much a need as connection with others.

Paul Klee's work is an effort to renew the sense of a private vision. It attempts to do away with the claptrap of the accidental, the official, the cumbersome. It seeks a purity and intimacy of personal seeing. It would free itself from the jungle of our mechanized view of things. It retires from what we ordinarily call "reality"—which has become a clamor and a blotch—to a world which is closer to the artist's own truth. This retirement is not an escape. On the contrary, escape today is generally sought by the foolish in the noisy madness of the objective. To retire to oneself and to find ourselves clearly and securely is today the more arduous task.

Klee's painting is rarely "abstract" or "nonobjective." It is full of observation and even of reality. It does not say that the world is a horror, and we must turn away from it to seek truth only within ourselves. Its feeling is gentle, warm, humorous, and tenderly attached to the wonders of nature and humankind. But like an uninhibited child, Klee persists in seeing as he sees and feels, not as a pedantic respectability would have him see and feel. This is what I mean by Klee's innocence.

This is a new romanticism—unemphatic and undoctrinaire. It seeks to recover individual truth in a world replete with false and futile knowledge—conventions of thought and behavior that enclose us as in a cell. In a world where people would be permitted such freedom or privacy as Klee found for himself, the relationships of individuals might be kinder, more graceful, more attuned to the measure of love. But since our society is fiercely bent on making us all exactly alike, Klee's image of the world is charming but wistful.

One of the most typical of Klee's pieces is called "Children Before the Town." Children, who are indicated by wisps of ink, sit on a fence gazing at a glowing town—a mysterious blaze that might be electricity, fire or the effulgence of a gigantic jewel. Do the children long to enter the town? Have they been excluded or forgotten—or is the town a great conflagration, which they are lonesomely contemplating? No one can say, but Klee strikes me as having placed himself among the children, watching the attractive and frightening spectacle of modern civilization in a mood of depressed awe and sweet ache.

When man beholds the world with his private eye, the act of seeing becomes a rather lonely one, and what he sees will take on an element of mystery. Even the lightest and gayest of Klee's work is steeped in mystery. Because Klee sees afresh, as a child refusing to trust the tags that adults have affixed to objects, there is also something quaintly funny in his vision. Everything is familiar and odd.

Klee's work might be called "literary" in the sense that he is like a child who has read many things, and what such a child sees is colored by the tales he has read. This work then is also delicately "realistic," for how can we distinguish between what a child honestly sees and what it fancies as it looks at things. Thus it would be absurd to try to disentangle the "literary," "plastic," "romantic" and "realistic" in textbook fashion, since all together they form what is special in Klee's work.

The same is true of the African and Oriental influences in Klee's art. They are there because Klee was entranced by the mystery, silence, feeling of something fixed in patterns of universal meaningfulness that are characteristic of African and Oriental art. The greatest gift of African and Oriental primitives is their sense of man alone with his dreams, fears and naked contact with experience.

As Klee grew older and his imagination traversed freely and fertilely through every kind of spiritual adventure, life in his work becomes less substantial, becomes sheer pattern. In a picture—painted in 1938—called "Insula Dulcamara," nothing seems left but the smile.

In his innocence, Klee smiles; Van Gogh cried aloud, indeed he screamed in his. Van Gogh's innocence was that of the ecstatic and tortured prophet. What he cried about and prophesied was the fact that the world would soon become a desert of selfishness, of heedless movement or "progress" toward a goal where each for himself would build an ugly assertion of nothing but individual willfulness, until the time when each would clash till all would have to succumb to a sort of conglomerate will. In an agonized vision, Van Gogh foresaw the time when a Paul Klee would have to retire from the horrendous chaos of uniformity to redeem his own purity of soul, his own truth.

I am using the word "individual" here in two different senses. When the individual feels himself part of a world which he loves because it nourishes him, a world to which he can give of his strength, then the individual is a *true person,* a person whose connection with the world is a function of his individuality. When the individual feels strength only in an assertion of himself against the world on which he must impose his will or be destroyed, we have a distortion of the person which usually ends in the tyranny of the whole social setup, fearful of its stability unless everyone conforms to a single mold—set up by the most powerful people, themselves just as helpless victims of the setup as the weakest.

Van Gogh's innocence was an impassioned cry at the beginning of the contemporary era. His message declared that men must get together in love and veneration for the beautiful world—which there was still an opportunity for them to enjoy—by working humbly and devotedly in a fraternal spirit on their common task. Paul Klee's innocence signifies that Van Gogh's message was not heeded, that the anarchy of individual wills has produced a world in which it is almost impossible for the *true person* to dwell.

Klee's art is therefore as dainty and delicate as a secret sign or a fetish, to be employed as a protection against the brazen roar around us, while Van Gogh's art shouts with apocalyptic fervor trying to show us some of the wonders of the world he would have us embrace as well as the tragedy of people abandoned by our carelessness. Van Gogh's universe is magnificently illuminated by his ardent faith in it, and distorted by his fear of the approaching disaster. There is something emblematic in one of Van Gogh's earliest paintings in which a large brown Bible is seen side by side with a little yellow copy of Zola's *La Joie de Vivre*. Van Gogh might be called the painter of humanity's last chance. His pictures make one want to weep and to love.

I must add some brief comment to the mere mention of certain films named in this department last month: *The Fallen Idol* is a triumph of technique over matter. Carol Reed, who directed it, is a first-rate cinematic craftsman, but he seems content nowadays to apply his craft to hollow subjects. *The Fallen Idol,* like *The Third Man,* another recent Reed film, is brilliantly made, but it is almost wholly without content and thus, though we must always respect excellence of workmanship, essentially trivial.

It should be noted in passing that there are many people who think more highly of such pictures as *The Fallen Idol* than of any others. These are people who regard pictures, plays and art generally as a kind of superior gewgaw.

All the King's Men has a crude honesty that is arresting, particularly since it deals with a subject based on recent American history and suggests an important theme: the relationship of democracy to "strong" men who would spread its benefits by violently despotic methods. We are obliged to applaud the picture because, as I say, its material is unusual, and its presentation is neither cheap nor frivolous. But after seeing *All the King's Men*

twice, I fail to gather any clear notion of its social message beyond the commonplace that it is dangerous to employ evil for the sake of the good. Nor am I convinced that the public which sees it is politically enlightened by it in any way, since the hero's evil practices are mostly sloughed off— except in regard to the use of thugs to intimidate people, heavy drinking and fornication—while his good is a montage of universities, hospitals and bridges that he presumably had built. In other words, the social, economic and political context in which we see all this is general instead of specific, which makes it difficult to draw any valid conclusions. On the emotional and imaginative side, hardly anything is created, because for one thing the characters are stereotypes, and the acting— with one exception—is illustrative as in a poster rather than significant as in a portrait. The documentary method used by De Sica and Rosselini seems to add life to their pictures; the documentary method in pictures like *All the King's Men* subtly diminishes their life.

Intruder in the Dust is another respectable Hollywood film which, though told as a kind of mystery thriller, gives one a concrete idea of how a lynching in the South comes about, how it is prepared and how its preparation looks. The picture is done with a decent sobriety and lack of sentimentality which make the images stick.

The best things about Bernard Shaw as an artist are his sense of fun, his taste for old theatre forms—opera, pantomime, Punch and Judy shows—large, almost "classic" theatre effects, which he employs to communicate the serious things he has to say. What he had to say in his best years was always worth hearing and much of it is still pertinent.

Shaw always believed in the superiority of the "life force" to a dry philistine rationalism, but his failing as an artist lies in the fact that the "life force" in his work always seems weaker than his wit. A French critic once called Shaw's dramatic work "the theatre without kisses," and this is a clue to certain basic shortcomings. Not that love as sexuality must be considered central to all great drama, but there are in Shaw certain vital lacks which prevent his work from ever becoming truly poetic—which *is* essential to great drama. There is poetry in Shaw only insofar as one feels that he is a man of good will, of vigorous mind (he has more commonsense than profundity) with a gift for clear, clean, sprightly speech.

I say all this apropos of the recent revival of *Caesar and Cleopatra*. The play was once "revolutionary" because it broke with the fustian of the old costume drama, and treated the Caesar-Cleopatra affair with the levity of modern skepticism instead of with the pompousness of romantic awe.

Besides this, Shaw in this play attempted to depict a great man without the trumpery sentimentality common to the nineteenth century. Shaw's Caesar is reasonable, shrewd, aware of economic realities in regard to government, not at all bloodthirsty, free from desire for vengeance, aggrieved at humanity's stupid violence, almost a pacifist, and very much of a Puritan. He prefers sound living to fine art, and esteems law and order more highly than beauty. He has no time and is probably too old for a trifling amorous escapade with Cleopatra which he leaves to the younger, more sensuous and probably more vulgar Marc Anthony. His job with Cleopatra is to transform her from a silly little minx to a serious hardworking socially responsible queen.

Much of this today is still winning, but not particularly impressive as art or thought. But we are so parched for want of anything but synthetic juices in our theatre that many of us will imbibe *Caesar and Cleopatra* as if it were a fresh clear draught of the finest wine. Our theatre audiences, lacking repertory companies in which good plays may be constantly reviewed, are in many respects forty years behind the times.

I cannot accept the present revival of *Caesar and Cleopatra* as a good production of the play. It has no wit, no real definition of approach—only a certain loutish jocosity. The sets are efficient and neat, but have no more style than that of an ambitious amateur group, which has learned stagecraft

from copies of the old *Theatre Arts Monthly*. Cedric Hardwicke (who was very amusing in *Candida* about three years ago) struck me as almost stuffy—a horrible quality for a Shavian hero—and Lilli Palmer as chiefly cute on nice legs.

—*TRW*, Mar. '50

LONDON

Most of the good plays I saw in London were revivals, so that my impression of the theatre there was of an agreeable and lively curiosity shop in which the past was made delightfully present.

Farquhar's *The Beaux' Stratagem* is a box-office success because its writing is still crisp, fresh, bold and brisk, and because its performance is engagingly contemporary; the actors' up-to-date Mayfair style seeming in no way foreign to this eighteenth-century comedy. That is particularly true of Kay Hammond, whose very speech defect—a kind of hot-potato lisp accompanied by a self-satisfied gurgle—contributes a sense of voluptuous gayety to the satisfactions of home comfort. Miss Hammond, who reminds one of a softer, less aggressive Lynn Fontanne, has a way of appearing on the stage as if she were merely visiting it with the intention of giving no more than a few friendly and witty bits of advice to liven things up and make everyone feel cozy before she takes her leave. She gives *The Beaux' Stratagem* the right touch of gentle naughtiness.

At Stratford-on-Avon, I saw an impressively handsome, shrewd and smooth production of *Measure for Measure*. This play, the theme of which may be the evil effects of absolute power, is commonly held to be one of Shakespeare's failures. On the stage of the Memorial Theatre, I found it one of his most stimulating plays, the only one I have seen for a long time that appeared to have any immediate bite. I do not mean by this that Hamlet—which I saw Michael Redgrave play at the Old Vic—or *Macbeth* or *Antony and Cleopatra* haven't any emotional immediacy, but that the manner of their production in most cases makes them seem mere museum pieces—deplorably unstartling.

John Gielgud plays Angelo in *Measure for Measure* with graphic excitement and an almost medieval sense of mystery—but the star of the evening is Peter Brook. Brook strikes me as a highly endowed director, to whom the adjective brilliant might be applied not simply as a compliment but as a definition. I say this first, because I also feel that he is still much too interested in his art to be an artist. This seems a characteristic defect of the present English stage. Many gifted actors, and directors particularly, seem to think of parts and plays as opportunities to display their gifts. The display is often captivating, but it is display—which is not the same thing as art, which is expression.

—*NR*, 19 June '50

THE CONSUL

There is about most plays we see today an air of moral rectitude and a guarantee of noble intention that is faintly tiresome. We live in a world in which there are all sorts of sorry imperfections: yet in the "serious" theatre we are constantly faced with plays that seem to take for granted that both the author and the audience are eminently sound people from every standpoint. There may be something socially constructive in this hypocrisy, but when a writer has the temerity to emit a roaring contradictory laugh, one experiences a distinct sense of relief.

There is a minute gleam of wistfulness in *Now I Lay Me Down to Sleep*, but for the most it is the play's "immorality" that attracts me, its crack-brained heathenishness.

I must call my reader's attention to the reissue of Charlie Chaplin's *City Lights*, the first in a series of revivals of Chaplin's full length films. Chaplin is not only the one great actor our films have ever produced, but possibly the greatest actor of our era. It is not a question of how funny he is or of his inexhaustible inventiveness or even of the pathos of his conception—this is the picture, you remember, in which Chaplin's tramp is joyously befriended by a drunken millionaire, who fails to recognize the Tramp when he becomes sober—it is the poetry and magic with which every action is done, which gives Chaplin his final stature as an actor.

There is a scene in *City Lights*, in which the Tramp is so exhilarated by a few drinks and the sight of people dancing gaily in a nightclub that he grabs a big unsuspecting woman by the waist, and twirls her about in a burst of ecstatic energy that is like the divine assertion of unreasoned joy at being alive that dwells somehow within the least of men.

At the end of *City Lights*, when Chaplin apologizes to the once-blind girl for being no more than he is, the quality of Chaplin's smile though touching beyond description can nevertheless be explained in terms of the situation. But there are things which happen through Chaplin's body in certain of his scenes (as in the sequence where, suspended on the sword of the statue, he tries to preserve his "correct" posture) that are beyond our ability to analyze them logically. They are pure expression, one might almost say as "abstract," as a beautiful melody in absolute music. Here Chaplin is a genius, because what he does transcends the significance of the incident, and extends to some essence of life—concrete as a tear or a laugh yet limited by no meaning that can be measured. This is true art: the mystic moment when the body of the material employed becomes identical with a universal spirit. Such acting as this may be seen only a few times in a generation.

—*TRW*, June '50

ENGLISH ACTING

English graciousness is in evidence these days by virtue of the Sadler's Wells Ballet at the Metropolitan Opera House and in James Bridie's play, *Daphne Laureola*, at the Music Box. Aside from graciousness, there is no resemblance between the two events. Margot Fonteyn, who is the chief glory of the English ballet company, is lyric and lovely as a flower on a beautifully appointed table. Edith Evans, the star of *Daphne Laureola*, hides a formidable robustness beneath her fine manners.

The Bridie play, despite the excellence of the two leading actors, is not well produced. It is set and directed as if it were a ponderously realistic study of an unhappy woman of fifty married to an English peer of eighty-three. Actually the play is a lightly humorous and quasi-poetic anecdote in which Bridie reminds us that many women prefer the pain of loveless domestic security to being the floating image of some mythical goddess in the minds of romantic young men.

Bridie likes to ramble a bit, he doesn't give a darn for structural correctness (he is in no hurry), he may wax philosophical or symbolic with a kind of arch carelessness, but he is nearly always engaging in the manner of a garrulous, good-hearted, crotchety, but still eminently sensible old man. His slight play is civilized entertainment for people somewhat less nervous than our opening-night audiences.

The main attraction of the play for Americans must lie in the acting of Edith Evans. (Cecil Parker as the husband is also first-rate, but his part is relatively small.) I found Miss Evans' performance highly satisfying. You may think this small praise; I assure you that it is not. Most of the good acting we see in New York nowadays is good in the sense that we *like* the people who do it because of some accident of their personality: so-and-so is charming, the other is sweet, the third is warm, etc., etc. With Edith Evans we are in the presence of an actress for whom very little is accidental. She is a professional in the full sense of the word. Her voice is magnificent, her diction powerfully impeccable, her carriage remarkable, her sense of comedy refreshing and her understanding unimpeachable.

The English actor begins with an advantage. He is part of a civilization where a certain grace of

manner is almost universal. English politeness, which usually has something almost tender about it, is a national characteristic that strikes us in the theatre as an attribute of the actor's personality rather than as a cultural trait. This gives the English actor a certain *form*, which, I repeat, is not artistic, but social. An actress like Edith Evans knows how to apply this sense of form to the needs of her role. Her acting, in which every stroke is studied and completely rendered, fills the frame of her part's meaning.

Through technical mastery, then, the form of Edith Evans' acting becomes its content; one may go so far as to say that it substitutes itself for the content. Haven't we always heard that form and content must be one? But form must arise from content, must be, so to speak, its tangible expression. In Edith Evans' performance of the Bridie play there is hardly any content aside from the form. When we see what she does so superbly we have seen all. Her speech, gestures, movement are complete and leave no echo. There are no tones beyond those that have reached our outer ear; there is no residue of feeling beyond what we are asked to recognize. Nothing remains that might grow within us. Nothing is demanded of us except to appreciate the specific matters which the performance presents. There is no element of mystery.

Acting which is all consciously made addresses itself entirely to the consciousness and satisfies the consciousness only. The actor's complete control meets with a response that is equally controlled—that is, confined to what we have been ordered to see and understand. In terms of acting technique, we may say that such acting represents not the behavior of the soul so much as theatrical projection. But perhaps it is even more pertinent to say that the significance of human action—its deepest worth and affective sway—does not derive from the consciousness alone. That is why so much English acting which is very fine (especially where the depiction of minute character traits is concerned) is so satisfactory as craft and so limited as art.

—*NR*, 2 Oct. '50

THEATRICAL CLOSE-UP

Not so long ago, when the practice of debunking was considered a sign of mental superiority, the Messrs. Mencken and Nathan published a book called *The American Credo* wherein the authors listed beliefs commonly held as indications of mass stupidity. I did not care for the spirit of the book, although a critical review of commonplace opinion may often serve a salutary purpose. This seems to me particularly true of the theatre, where because of our lack of sound tradition many unsupported theses are at the base of judgments, which are not judgments at all but reflexes. They might be called clichés of theatrical ideology—common not only with the public but far too frequently among professionals in or around the theatre.

Perhaps the most persistent and mischievous conception—to which most of the others may be traced—stems from the confusion between theatrical practice in New York (show business) and the theatre itself. For example, we often hear it said that the theatre is a dying art, because movies, radio and television are slowly but surely replacing it.

This opinion is based entirely on the shrinkage of production in the New York theatre and consequently in the rest of the country. But production in New York theatre is shrinking on account of economic factors that have little to do with the validity of the theatre as a form of entertainment or with the public's appetite for it. A play that appeals to only $12,000 worth of audience weekly (at present box-office prices) is not necessarily less good than a play that appeals to $20,000 worth of audience. The fact remains that certain plays that can only gross $12,000 a week are forced to terminate their run, because of a shortage of playhouses which our laissez-faire system in relation to theatres has brought about. This was less true before 1943 and hardly true at all in the twenties and thirties. In London and Paris today there are many more theatres devoted to the drama than there are in New York—despite motion pictures, radio and television. In France the government does not permit the sale of theatres for other than theatrical purposes: theatres may not be converted into motion picture, radio or television centers.

There was a time in New York, when a play presented at a tiny theatre such as the old Neighborhood Playhouse on Grand Street would be considered more important than many of the successful shows in the larger theatres of Broadway. But today the fact that hardly any such small playhouses or permanent groups to function in them exist makes us forget that plays done in small houses for a commercially limited public may be as important as most of the successful plays produced in the commercially imposing showplaces that presumably represent the main center of theatrical activity.

Are Sean O'Casey's plays, which have never proved themselves box-office triumphs, a less valid part of the theatre than plays like *The Happy Time*? If this question were answered in the affirmative—as in practice we do answer it—then it becomes exceedingly difficult, not to say impossible, to develop any new playwrights of value. The progress of art depends on the slow and constant nurture of every seed of life which the art may bring forth. How could an O'Neill have developed from the one-act plays to *Desire Under the Elms* without the protective environment of commercially modest organizations like the Provincetown Players? The theatre is not dying in America, but our heedlessness, inertia and ignorance are killing it.

There is a certain type of enthusiast who, faced with such arguments as I advance here, will retort that despite all, we still have great playwrights: Tennessee Williams, Arthur Miller and whoever, tomorrow, makes an impressive and successful showing. Actually, however, this sort of defense of our theatre's present status is a means of permitting the basic and progressive deterioration of the theatre situation to continue.

Readers of *Tomorrow* know that I have a special regard for such plays as *A Streetcar Named Desire* and *Death of a Salesman*, but to speak of young Americans who have written two or three worthwhile plays as "great playwrights," and to confuse the emergence of these plays within a period of less than five years as proof of the health of our theatre is once again to mistake the whole sense of the discussion. Theatre exists where a considerable body of craftsmen make it their permanent job to give dramatic expression to the life of their times. There was a genuine theatre in sixteenth century England not because of Shakespeare, but because of all the other playwrights who, though of lesser genius, were consistently working at the task which was also Shakespeare's. Russia at the beginning of the twentieth century developed a theatre not through Chekhov, who, as a dramatist, was as much a product of that theatre as one of its creators, but because of a body of dramatists (most of them minor in comparison with Chekhov) and a group of actors, directors, designers, etc. whose conscious task it was to speak for the true spirit of their time. They created a tradition which is still being carried on even though the Russian dramatists today are generally inferior writers.

It is not as helpful as one might suppose to call an American playwright, who has written two or three interesting plays, "great." One might almost describe it as dangerous to do so, not only for our critical sense or our cultural perspective, but for the playwright himself. The young playwright whom today we dub "great" because he has pleased us, will be labeled "finished" if he writes two more which fail to please us. In what sense will he be "finished"? He will no longer be in the running as a purveyor of material to supply the Broadway theatrical system, now set up on a disastrously unsound economic basis, a commodity that can be on view long enough for any considerable number of people to judge it. The playwright, who is economically hard-pressed through box-office failure, becomes altogether desperate when he real-

izes that our appreciation for his work is largely limited by considerations of commerce. He becomes so desperate indeed that he finds it unrewarding in every sense to continue as a playwright. With many recent dramatists of talent being a "great" playwright is a career of less than ten years. The beginning is also the end.

O'Neill has always struck me as the soundest of our playwrights, not only for the intrinsic merit of his work but for the consistency and duration of his effort. It would be the most creative as well as the safest policy to think of playwrights like Williams and Miller as beginners who will increasingly need our help. We can help them by working to build a theatrical organization which will permit them to develop.

What I have said of playwrights also holds true for actors, directors and others. A young actress is "great" in one play only to cease being an actress in her next engagement—she has become a movie star or starlet. Success in the theatre is measured commercially and the commercial standard, taken as the norm for all judgment, tends to destroy what it creates. What progress theatre criticism could make if it would forego the use of all blanket epithets of either praise or blame, and aim chiefly at substantive description, a statement of what is actually seen and felt in the presence of a play.

Producers today, reflecting the state of mind of agents, ticket brokers, real estate moguls and petty capital, have established a category unknown to dramatic criticism of any former era—the commercial director. What is a "commercial director?" The director whose name is associated with box-office hits. The belief in the reality of this label makes serious examination of stage direction almost impossible not to speak of certain distinct commercial disadvantages.

By speaking of a particular director as a "commercial director," the producer persuades himself that a particular play is a box-office hit because of a particular director. It would certainly be fatal to deny the contribution of the director to the production of plays, but what that contribution really has been cannot be discovered by merely reading the box-office statement. *The Madwoman of Chaillot* was more successful than many people who knew it as a script guessed that it would be. This despite negative direction. Many other plays which are hugely successful and frequently well directed would probably have been equally successful (box-officewise) in the hands of a merely competent director. There are directors whose reputation for being "commercial" is based on the fact that they never venture to do plays that offer any particular hazard, but this is rarely taken into account in a general estimate of their work.

My point, however, isn't that the "commercial" director is a bad one—most of those who earn this reputation keep it only for a few years after which time they are either said to be "slipping" or are simply referred to as "veterans"—my point is that the conception itself is harmful as well as stupidly erroneous. Besides the directly artistic mischief it causes—since direction under these circumstances is not clearly seen as an accomplishment but only as a fetish—it induces the director labeled "commercial" to be wary of experimenting with plays that may not assist in maintaining the superstition of his dollar-making wizardry. Creative attrition sets in.

The "commercial director" of the moment is virtually the only director certain stars will accept. The result is that the production of certain plays comes to depend on whether such a director will agree to direct these plays so that particular stars will consent to appear in them—so that they may be done at all. When this stage has been reached, the "commercial director" knowing his power may begin to make exorbitant financial demands, demands that are out of proportion to the actual contribution any director can make—since very few plays have been "made" by the director alone. These demands tend to increase the financial unsoundness of the theatre. The director, and very often together with him the star actor, have acquired so large a percentage of the profits that the rest of the people interested in the production (notably the investors) may feel cheated even in

the case of what is ostensibly a success. The theatre then becomes too great a risk for any feasible economy.

What has happened in the case of directors happens in a less spectacular degree with designers. There are designers who are no longer regarded simply as good designers whose particular personality is appreciated at its own value, but men whose name alone for certain producers, investors and critics seem to spell glamor and success. Such designers are allowed every extravagance—sometimes verging on the ruinous—because they too are "commercial." One day someone realizes that the sets designed by these men don't always work: either they are too elaborate for the play or they cannot be moved onto an ordinary stage or cannot be toured, etc. The designer ceases to be "practical."

At this point, the producer seeks out a less well known designer. If a designer who is known to be a real artist is recommended, the producer is both eager and apprehensive: he fears that such a designer may not be "practical." Will this designer's sets work? If the producer's play is scenically complex the first question he will ask of the scene designer, whom he generally treats as an apprentice-applicant to a job, "How will you make the set changes?," putting the technical problem before all others—a procedure that betrays the producer's own uncertainty and artistic immaturity.

The result of this "shopping" for designers is that scene-design for the past ten years has become thoroughly efficient, pretty and fundamentally mediocre—a kind of department store decoration. Between 1919 and 1939, scene design in our theatre was forward looking, experimental, inventive. The sharper the pinch of show business, the more conventional has design become. Our college and community theatres today are often more advanced in their approach to scene design than the professional theatre. All this because the so-called commercial and practical approach militates against basic knowledge or thought, and makes for a theatre that is not commercial, practical or just good fun.

It may be said that all these considerations are the concern of professionals rather than that of the general playgoer or reader. But a refusal to become better acquainted with some of the elements that go into the making of the things we love—the arts, for example—is a way of destroying them. The audience must be an active part of the theatre; when it becomes wholly passive, demanding entertainment without further responsibility, corruption will show itself in both audience and entertainment. The road to genuine enjoyment, moreover, is in a certain awareness.

The spectator who is satisfied that an actor or a play is "great"—and is willing to leave it at that—usually ends as an indifferent spectator, who will easily accept all sorts of sensations at exactly the same value. Even his own enthusiasm will soon become a matter of indifference to him. The role of the critic in the theatre is largely to help make the audience aware of the nature of its pleasure.

What has happened in the past ten years of our theatrical history—although symptoms of the disease were visible much earlier—is that thinking instead of helping to lead or aid the theatre has generally followed it in the decline of all values. One might say that the need for thinking, in good times, is less pressing than in bad, because then action itself sets the example, but where action sickens and grows feeble, a great responsibility falls on thinking—which is another name for criticism and the questioning of all the things we take for granted. Perhaps we can approach the events of the coming theatrical season with this task in mind.

—*TRW*, Oct. '50

A LITTLE ON SHAW

There is something in the current theatre-in-the-round production of *Arms and the Man* which brings out its *Chocolate Soldier* quality in a most agreeable way—although, to be fine about it, the taste of the production tends more toward the blandness of vanilla. The quaintness of the play, which is partly due to its age (1894), the roguishness generally characteristic of Shaw, and his always disarming mixture of bonhomie with shrewdness are highlighted by the toy dimensions and party informality of the Arena Theatre.

Almost every critic who writes about Shaw (and who hasn't?) emphasizes either the philosopher or the artist, but very few have been able to fuse the two aspects into a perception of the whole man. The fact that the critic must have some scope of sensibility and intellect to deal with Shaw completely is perhaps what makes him the outstanding literary personality of the twentieth-century theatre.

This is not the place to undertake a critical summation of Shaw's contribution either to the theatre or to thought. I wish merely to point out a curious contradiction in the criticism of Shaw: when his ideas fail to irritate any of our sore spots, many of us speak worshipfully of his philosophical penetration; when his ideas do manage to hit home, even more of us are eager to pay tribute to his art; but where his art and thought have the least direct bearing on our immediate social situation, there you will find the critics evincing the utmost intellectual awe.

The best of *Arms and the Man* is its delightful third act, a most exhilarating form of mental vaudeville, a composite of sparkling rhetoric with theatre tricks as old and gay as the art of comedy—all based on intellectual hypotheses that are now acceptable without being hackneyed. This is Shaw's intelligent man's guide to bright entertainment and common sense.

Mrs. Warren's Profession (1893) is less characteristically Shavian in its tone, but more essentially Shavian in its social conviction. It is fascinating to observe—even through the crude production at the Bleecker Street Playhouse—how the early Shaw tried to refurbish certain conventions of the late Victorian theatrical and moral tradition by giving them a dry-cleaning of quasi-Marxian realism and his own genial brand of Puritanism and laughter.

The play, by turn charmingly and embarrassingly rickety, still retains a revolutionary core which is lacking in the more accomplished and smiling *Arms and the Man* (mostly confined to the simple spoofing of a now obsolete romanticization of the military). If it is true, as some maintain, that Shaw is eminent chiefly by virtue of his message, *Mrs. Warren's Profession* is the more important play—although its importance will be ducked by those to whom any form of anti-capitalism is abhorrent. If Shaw's manner is what we most esteem, then *Arms and the Man* may be regarded as his first success in the art of making Dutch-uncle preachment both funny and cute.

I managed to enjoy *The Curious Savage* despite my belief that even the best play wrongly done is a bad play. John Patrick's *Curious Savage*, which will undoubtedly fare better in the hands of future amateur and collegiate producers, reveals a talent for an affectionately daft humor. What it suggests in a delicately playful fashion is how nearly impossible it is for good people to live within rational dimensions when the norm of reasonable behavior is stuffy and vulgarly prosaic. On the other hand, the director Peter Glenville's *Curious Savage* is stagy where it should be poetic, stylized in the most pedestrian manner where it should be fanciful and relaxed. All the actors (including Lillian Gish) struck me as rigid with direction. Mr. Patrick's lovable lunatics are turned into puppets without personality. The atmosphere of the home in which his characters carry on their enchanted existence, and which might conceivably be designed in Robert Edmond Jones style as a kind of pearly dreamland of their fantasy, is rendered as an asylum with an expensive and properly institutional look that would drive any sensitive person crazy.

—NR, 13 Nov. '50

TWO LADIES

The lady is not for burning in Christopher Fry's play because, though foolishly held to be a witch, she is life itself.

It would be easy to set Fry's play down as an experiment in euphuism, the perfection of preciosity or just unplain pretty talk. It is something more than that. The literary virtuosity is there, all right, with its constant sizzle and sputter of verbal sparklers. But all this, though it offers its own measure of sophisticated entertainment and novelty, represents a special mood and meaning that are worth study.

There are three basic ways of facing life. One can love it and struggle with it—the creative way; one can loathe it and curse it—the destructive way; one can suffer and accommodate oneself to it—the civilized way. The first way is becoming increasingly rare; the second is a distorted form of heroism made familiar by the grandiose pessimists of old; the third is the prevalent pattern of modern intellectuals.

Christopher Fry is one of those who most delightfully acquiesce. "Has death become the most fashionable way to live?" someone asks in *The Lady's Not For Burning*. Fry's answer, intellectually speaking, is yes. The civilized man is not a humble citizen who tries to make the best of a bad job, for such a person is only meagerly conscious of his position. The civilized man knowingly swears: "Your world history's the fear of a possible leap by a possible antagonist out of a possible shadow, or a not improbable skeleton out of your dead-certain cupboard." He yawns at "mortal life, women, all governments, wars, art, science, ambitions and the entire fallacy of human emotions!" But being civilized—though still very human—he lends himself with wistful humor to "the unholy mantrap of love" and declares "the best thing we can do is to make whatever we're lost in look as much like home as we can."

The epigraph for Fry's art is, "Shall we not suffer as wittily as we can?" Fry is witty. His suffering arouses no tears—he is too conscientiously comfortable to do that—but he is not without tenderness. He wears his rue with a difference—of bright phrases, happy conceits and a rich heritage of English verse. His play contains no character, but he can fashion charming characterizations—the Chaplain, the mother—his plot is haphazard, but he spins some graceful scenes. His writing, marked by an ecstatically twittering indulgence in its own felicity, ranges from poetry to poetastering.

All this is as up-to-date (despite the "fifteenth-century" setting) as existentialism or a Christian Dior gown. For this reason, I do not believe the play is produced in a way to reveal its true spirit. Probably no one in England or America could have done a better job of it than John Gielgud and his excellent company (the best acting is that of Eliot Makeham as the Chaplain), but the production lacks a real style. This requires further explanation, for which, at the moment, I lack space.

—*NR*, 27 Nov. '50

THE FIRST 15 YEARS

The Country Girl is lightweight Odets. That the least meaty of his plays should prove to be almost the most popular is significant of the press, not of the author.

No more gifted playwright has appeared in the past fifteen years. I doubt whether any American playwright at all has a greater talent for living dramatic speech, for characterization, for intensity of feeling. Above all, Odets is a true theatre poet: he is never literal, and his power with words does not represent verbal proficiency but a blood tie with the sources from which sound literature and dramatic action spring.

Apart from a certain romantic afflatus, which is at times an easily discernible defect but more often a virtue, the strength of Odets' work lies in his main theme and the particular quality of its statement. The question Odets constantly asks is: What helps a man *live*? Since we are citizens of the twentieth century, we may translate this as: What today injures man's spirit? What enhances or diminishes the creatively human in him? "It's trying to be a man on the earth," a young boy confesses naïvely in *Waiting for Lefty*. All Odets is a variant on this theme, while the childlike pathos of its utterance reveals the Odetsian touch at its most naked.

Odets' art has an immediacy and an intimacy equaled by no other dramatist of our generation. His plays strike home; they touch us where we live. Though they often shout, they are powerful because, in fact, they speak quietly to our hearts. They are moving because beneath their occasional bluster they sigh and weep with our own unadvertised and non-literary anguish. Their tone sometimes has a slight aura of portentousness, but at bottom they are unabashedly homey.

When at first he emphasized economic pressure as the deterrent to man's development, Odets was considered new, bold and "revolutionary," and his name became consonant with a big social noise. But this was partly due to the mood of the thirties and our foolish appetite for novelty. Later, when he began to explore the depressive effect of the wounded ego on man's soul, he no longer seemed so "new," though in fact he had become subtler and more valuable. The truth is that even "the economic interpretation" of man's unhappiness in Odets' first plays was only an indirect statement of one of the ways Americans feel the injury to their egos.

This confusion in understanding Odets results in part from his immaturity of judgment in regard to his own feeling. Corresponding to the conflict between his inadequate plot structures and his swarming emotion, there has always been a discrepancy between what he is and what he thinks he is, a breach between his consciousness and his actual experience. The most visible dramatic symptom of this was the clash between the story line in some of his later plays and what he expected us to gather from them. This produced an increasing emotional and artistic turmoil which reached its most distressing state in *The Big Knife*.

To evade this dilemma, Odets has written *The Country Girl*, in which he pretends to do nothing but tell a "human-interest" story as effective stage ware. But he is so subjective a writer that he must disclose something of his true feeling. In *The Country Girl* he tells us that the faltering and enfeebled artist (or man) may be restored by the staunch love of a woman if it is combined with the steady assistance of a friend.

To my mind the play is thin in characterization, meager in authentic feeling, shallow in invention. It is by no means dull, because Odets can never be uninteresting. Even his least vital effort smolders unmistakably with the black burn of his not-so-secret hurt—and there are always those flashes of humor and warm understanding that make us realize that we are in the presence of a *person*, not just a showman. This play, then, is a victory by default. By giving up some of his complexity, Odets has, for the moment, ceased to trouble us, even as he has failed to inspire. The negative discipline Odets has here imposed on himself may prove useful to his future even as it has proved profitable to his present.

The production is generally a good one. Boris Aronson has provided evocative sets of the utmost simplicity, and Odets himself has directed with the same careful intelligence with which he has written. I suspect, though, that by his caution he has, in this respect, done himself a slight disservice: much of the acting is more constricted than is necessary, and more might have been achieved with the actors—though the promising Steven Hill is clearly miscast—than they accomplish. In Uta Hagen's case, on the other hand, there is a clean hit. Her impersonation of the wife is a perfect small characterization given stature by the fact that she is, in the personal as well as the technical sense, one of the finest young actresses on our stage.

—*NR*, 11 Dec. '50

GUYS, DOLLS, WITCHES

There are whole families of witches in the fashionable districts of New York. One of them snares Rex Harrison. For witches, love is only mischief: they may be entertained by sex, but they experience no lasting affection and they shed no tears. John van Druten's witch in *Bell, Book and Candle* succumbs to love for Harrison, loses her fell powers, learns to cry and live on as happily as the rest of us. Do you like this? Yes? No? It makes no critical difference.

I found *Bell, Book and Candle* easy to take, like a small cream puff served to look larger without spoiling the stomach. It is very well served. Though Harrison plays a man limited to ordinary faculties, he is the most bewitching person in the cast—intelligent, deft, debonair, unspeakably attractive—the best of drawing-room comedians. Lilli Palmer has an engaging coolness, like white wine and soda; she wears her clothes delightfully and makes Harrison a most natural partner. The rest of the cast is good, and George Jenkins catches the atmosphere of elegant comfort and semi-bohemian familiarity with admirable scenic rightness.

Ring Round the Moon is an exquisitely fluffy comedy spun from very special material. Most of us who write about the theatre have a way of describing the effect of a play without understanding the exact nature of the effect. (Stendhal once pointed out that a pistol shot at a Mozart concert was more "effective" than any of the Symphonies; we are in the position, then, of people who would report the event on the basis of the effective pistol shot rather than on the significance of the music.) A failure to recognize the essential quality of *Ring Round the Moon* is a way of reducing it to a nonexistence it does not deserve.

A Frenchman might call Anouilh, the author of the original from which Christopher Fry made his brilliant adaptation, an anarchist of the Right. Anouilh is both nostalgic and cynical about the past, when wealthy aristocrats could give parties at which a footman might be run through by a haughty guest to the shocked delight of the company. He sees the present as a time when well-to-do society makes a waif and plaything of the artist, when the rich reap little pleasure from their earnings, and love is the last relic in the surrounding devastation. "Every man is quite alone," the dyspeptic millionaire of the play says. "No one can help anyone. He can only go on," and the stage direction reads: "They look straight in front of them, squatting on the ground in the middle of the torn [bank] notes."

Ring Round the Moon represents the lyricism of the French postwar epoch, cruel as a serpent's sting, sweet as a chorus girl's kiss, made gay for the sake of decorum, ballet-like for the sake of culture. All this serves Fry's purpose—though he is actually far less bitter and edgy than Anouilh, being an affable Englishman rather than an exasperated Frenchman—providing the material for a brilliant choreographic presentation by London's most gifted young director, Peter Brook.

The London production heightened the effervescent fun and diminished the acid bite, but a feeling of the grim outline of the original remained within the glow of the added glamor. Gilbert Miller understands only the glamor, so that in New York the play is not so much like bitters over sugar as like maple syrup over candy. The sets are an adaptation but not an improvement on Oliver Messel's jewel-like originals; the Dufy drops are fetching without being necessary. The cast—apart from Oscar Karlweis, whose sickly countenance is significant—is only half as happy as the one it replaces.

The musical *Guys and Dolls* is excellent fun because it is replete with its own character. Its matter is a leaf torn from Damon Runyon, jazz-singer of Broadway's neon personalities. Though its book by Jo Swerling and Abe Burrows follows a more consistent story line than most, its chief

merit lies in the wisecracks that create the authentic mood of the crazy-smart street the show celebrates. Frank Loesser has a real gift for comic recitative that not only composes a song (often musically indifferent) but a real dramatic communication. A number like "Sue Me" becomes an almost poignant scene in a wonderfully screwy way. The crap-game sequence in the sewer is a beaut, and the cast is a perfect ensemble, with top honors for benzedrine-eloquent Sam Levene, wistful-tough Vivian Blaine and the Cary Grant of 46th Street, Robert Alda. Nor must the gravelly B.S. Pully, Stubby Kaye and Tom Pedi be forgotten. *Guys and Dolls* has a real style for the good reason that it is all of a piece in spirit, substance and craft.

—*NR*, 25 Dec. '50

FROM THE SUBLIME TO THE ENJOYABLE

Since ANTA's production of *The Tower Beyond Tragedy* is no longer running, my purpose in discussing it is not that of a reviewer. The nature of the piece and the peculiar tone of its reception—ecstatic praise on the one hand and general indifference on the other—impel me to use the event as a springboard for certain objective considerations.

I understood no more than 50 percent of the Jeffers text. The reason for this was not the difficulty of the verse (one understands almost all of *The Lady's Not For Burning*, even though its verse is not simple) nor was my perplexity a matter of the actors' faulty diction. But it is always easier to understand words spoken from the stage when the players know what they are talking about. This does not mean that the actors in *The Tower Beyond Tragedy* couldn't explain the literal sense of what they were saying or even expatiate on more abstruse aspects of the poem. It means that their understanding was *general* not specifically intelligible to them as living action and direct personal emotion. The word in the theatre comes alive only as it expresses something active in the speaker's whole being. The dramatic word is the vocal sign of the actor's total impulse—palpable in every part of his body and every feature of his face.

Judith Anderson is an actress of immense physical power with an arresting voice of unusual emotional connotations, a strikingly equivocal mask and a complex, eruptive temperament. All this makes her a proper instrument for the projection of such tumultuous states of being as Jeffers' work suggests. But Miss Anderson's work needs *direction* (not merely staging) which will conduct her energies along lines that lead to a clear target of meaning. Without this her entire armament of attributes seems locked in a boiling cauldron that makes a terrific sound without ever forming an esthetically usable object. Her speech is precise, her voice ringing, her fire formidable—yet nothing is clear except that she is *something*.

"Something"—however impressively awful— is not tragic. One difference between the tragic and the melodramatic is that while the second need only produce an effect, the first must have an *irresistible* significance. Jeffers' poem—written in verse that makes a brazenly joyless music-like sound without echo, as if all feeling were buried deep in stone—is an expression of a desire to transcend the pain and violence of ordinary humanity so as to become one with the moral impassivity of nature's eyeless forces. So difficult a design may be carried out in the theatre even though Jeffers did not plan his poem for the stage. But to do so requires more time, thought, knowledge than can usually be commanded under the auspices of our theatrical system. We need not suppose that the problem is simply solved by posing questions about realism versus stylization. I have seen Japanese acting of a most horrifyingly anatomical naturalism that still had artistic shape, as I have seen Chinese acting all symbolic gesture and vocal artifice yet replete with an emotion of its own— just as there is a "realism" which has little life, truth or grace. Miss Anderson and her associates are misguided talents, and such productions as ANTA's *The Tower Beyond Tragedy* belong some-

where in the limbo of the theatre's well-intentioned but unsightly efforts.

Hecht and MacArthur's somewhat inebriate humors, resembling good-natured double-talk over a theatrical bar, make *Twentieth Century* (another ANTA production) an entertaining show. This raffishly sophisticated vaudeville, which was not a huge box-office success when it was produced in the early thirties because its extravagant fable is wholly in the spirit of the twenties, is made altogether cartoonlike by the out-and-out holiday spoofing of Gloria Swanson and José Ferrer. Swanson is a cute trick with an entrancingly stagy personality; Ferrer plays with a kind of hollow gusto, as if his mind were elsewhere, though his body is very actively present. The play runs downhill as the performance tends toward farcical monotony, but still, as the old theatre ads used to trumpet, there are *laffs galore!*

—*NR*, 8 Jan. '51

LEAR AND STOCKMANN

*K*ing Lear is a great play. That it has also been thought absurd or unactable is simply a mark of its difficulty. Seen merely as the lamentable tale of a father abused by his children, it *is* absurd; rendered according to the literal logic of each of its separate scenes, it *is* unactable. For the meaning of *Lear* is not contained in its plot line as one might recount it point by point, but in the total spirit of the work.

Lear is not destroyed by the cruelty of his daughters; this aspect of the drama is almost complete by the end of the first act. Lear's specific folly in the division of his kingdom does not constitute the essence of his tragedy. Nor is the shock of his daughters' disloyalty the core of his drama. Lear's folly lies in the belief that having given away the outer trappings of his regal position, he still possesses power. His tragedy is the searing discovery that everything in life—including the institutions of law and order—is vain show except the fact, rather than the vows, of love. As king, protected by place, he knew nothing of life or even of his kingdom. Alone, like every other man, he finds that "unaccommodated man is no more than such a poor, bare, fork'd animal" as the vagrants and lunatics in the tempest. There is no protection against the ague of life except in love.

Lear is a timeless play: Shakespeare made every effort to situate it at no identifiable moment of history. The story is that of a barbaric king, a primitive man, learning life's hard lessons with a kind of pristine naïveté that is both brutishly savage and frighteningly new, as if the terror of life were being recognized by man for the first time. Lear's "Ay, every inch the king" is either ironic self-contempt or the description of a man who is king chiefly by virtue of his volcanic passion and suffering. Lear is a sacrificial "Neanderthal" symbol portraying the torment of human experience in a world still too raw to offer secondary consolations.

The current *Lear* is better than most of the Shakespearean productions we have seen hereabouts for a long time. Most of the lines are spoken with admirable intelligence and almost every member of the cast is a person of talent and stage attractiveness. The physical production is expert and properly styled for a tragedy in which the accidents of environment are not to be stressed. Louis Calhern gives an imposing reading of the central role, and in the quiet scene with the Fool in which Lear murmurs distractedly, "I did her wrong," he is truly fine. In fact Calhern does everything with Lear that a "prose" understanding of the play can yield, while most of the others—notably Martin Gabel, Norman Lloyd, Joseph Wiseman, Arnold Moss, Jo Van Fleet—supply touches that are valuable or interesting. The fault is not in any individual part or detail, but in the lack of a master conception. For this reason, the production reminded me of the "pony" translations which, as schoolboys, we used to construe our Latin texts. They were practical, but they weren't poetry.

However severe our judgment of any production of a play such as *Lear*, we must not lose sight of the main fact: we are in the presence of something very rare and special in the theatre. The same holds for *An Enemy of the People*, though it is not the best of Ibsen.

It would seem to me a species of hypocrisy to dwell too long on the difference between Ibsen's original play and Arthur Miller's Americanized version of it, or to complain too strenuously that the director, Robert Lewis, has made something of a poster of Ibsen's scrupulous realism. The new production screams and postures youthfully where Ibsen was obliquely humorous, mordant and haughty. Yet what we see now is part of a world where some screaming is in order and where youthful indignation is more tonic than suave resignation.

In its present form *An Enemy of the People* makes the audience the play's protagonist. We catch fire not on Dr. Stockmann's account so much as on our own. The issue is no longer the doctor's fight against the prejudice of bourgeois interests but our own right to hold and express "unpopular" opinions. The audience identifies itself with Stockmann despite the fact that Ibsen's Stockmann felt that he was an individual being stifled by mass stupidity and the fears of the majority, whereas our audience feels itself, if not the majority, at least a powerful mass being stifled by the stupid fears of a hysterical minority.

This leads to a certain amount of artistic and philosophic confusion, but it is inevitable when art is caught in the tempest of social turmoil, and I could not—and for the moment did not wish to—preserve my critical calm, preferring instead to let myself be swept along by the excitement that the approach employed here generates. All values are transformed: Ibsen's doctor is a sweet simpleton who rises to a crotchety dignity and a sardonic, gnarled determination. Fredric March's Stockmann is a moral Lochinvar with a bright face and a splendidly ringing voice, so that at the end I had no patience with a discussion of whether or not Morris Carnovsky as the doctor's brother was too villainous, but wanted to cry out, "Strike! Strike! Strike!" as in the old days when we were all waiting for Lefty. Everything influences the theatre: sex, publicity, escape psychology, snobbism, slothfulness. Why shouldn't the frustration of our silence also find its clamorous voice?

—*NR*, 22 Jan. '51

FROM LORCA DOWN

The most valid drama among recent entries was Lorca's *The House of Bernarda Alba*. Unfortunately, it was presented by ANTA for only a limited run. Unfortunately also, its production, despite the presence in the cast of some talented players, left much to be desired. Lorca is not easy to translate to the stage because his plays involve passion whiter than flame subjected to a discipline blacker than coal. Vocal shrillness will not do to indicate the passion, nor physical tension to indicate the discipline.

While *Bernarda Alba* is in a sense simply a regional play and as strictly realistic as Lorca knew how to make it, and while its ostensible theme might be raucously set down as "sex frustration," it is at once rich in virile emotion, psychological in a way that would delight students of Freud, symbolically sociological in relation to Spain—as a rebel poet viewed it in June, 1936, two months before he was killed by the Fascists.

What I hope to suggest by the foregoing statement is that a work of art contains everything within it: the mood and tone of the artist's feeling as well as the fact and meaning of the artist's environment, the quality of the creative source and the concreteness of the world which is being mirrored, the particular and the general. Philip Barry's *Second Threshold* and Sidney Kingsley's *Darkness at Noon* are not works of art. Though they both treat themes of great contemporary interest, neither gives us a solid sense of either the souls of their makers or of the reality of their material. They are based chiefly on what might be called hearsay.

The subjective aspect of Philip Barry's play is its more important one. A writer of intelligent light comedies, Barry paused periodically in troubled search of spiritual security. It seems natural therefore that his last play should deal with a successful man who, somewhat past the middle years of his life, finds himself with a sense of having nothing to live for. The theme is almost topical. But having once stated it, Barry seems at a loss to carry it forward with anything but the most banal development. The reason for this, I believe, is not that Barry had no "solution," but that the statement of his hero's disillusionment is unspecific, as if Barry, though he knew himself to be morally disturbed, did not know why.

The central figure of *Second Threshold* repeatedly makes glib references to the "state of the world" and one or two other familiar reasons for personal discontent which never have the particular substance or atmosphere of a particular man's problem. Consequently, the play's premise strikes one as thin, the dramatic resolution feeble, and the whole a neatly written improvisation situated between conversational parlor introspection and popular treatises on how to be happy though miserable,

The production of *Second Threshold* is lamentable. The talented Margaret Phillips is miscast; Clive Brook, an expert performer, plays as if he did not want anyone to get morbid over his possible suicide. The director made his people behave as if the homes of the cultured and well-to-do off lower Fifth Avenue were stock-company stages devoted to the revival of plays by Clyde Fitch.

I am confident that most people who hear about *Darkness at Noon* approve of its politics; I am certain that disenchanted leftists, who once looked to Moscow for miracles, will be fascinated by the play's point, which is that the rigid, materialistic functionalism of those misguided humanists, the old Bolsheviks, has led logically to the inhuman brutality of the later Soviet leaders. I am equally convinced that the average sensible theatergoer who sees the play will be left cold, because it is an elaborate mechanism which issues from no central core of real experience or intimate knowledge.

Kingsley has a gift for making theatre out of local color and documentation in such dramatic milieus as hospitals, off-center neighborhoods, detective bureaus. Being a man of the thirties, Kingsley also has a penchant for liberal social preachment. He has, however, no psychological insight, no poetic eloquence, no capacity to convey the quality of any inner state. He has pieced *Darkness at Noon* together from the surface of Koestler's novel, from quotes out of the writings and speeches of various Soviet spokesmen, and from the editorial repetitiousness of innumerable contemporary journalists. The result is a sort of *Reader's Digest* melodrama, intricate without suspense, psychological without characters, philosophical without mind, violent without effect. The total impression is that of cardboard operatics, reminding one both of our old anti-Nazi war films and the propaganda plays of the early Roosevelt era.

Such playwriting is hardly conducive to rich acting. Most of the actors in *Darkness at Noon* are more than competent. Allan Rich, as Prisoner 202, suggests greater reality than the rest. Claude Rains as Rubashov is always sincere, dignified and intelligent. If he strikes one as an impassioned and idealistic English college professor rather than a steel-willed Russian political figure, the fault is not his.

—*NAT*, 5 Feb. '51

CLASSICS, MORE OR LESS

What makes a play come alive in the theatre? The expected and basic answer is: a good text. But this answer, despite its plausibility, is not necessarily true. *Romeo and Juliet*, I venture to say, is a good play, while *The Moon Is Blue* is merely a cute improvisation. Yet *Romeo and Juliet*, with Olivia de Havilland and a cast of quite respectable actors, is barely alive; *The Moon Is Blue* is alive enough to be delightful to many and irritating to a few.

If you have never seen *Romeo and Juliet* before, and its words strike you with a fresh impact, you may find the production captivating. (I once saw a lot of young people in Moscow shaken by sobs at a poorly acted performance of *La Dame aux Camélias*.) But for me the sign that there is little life in the current production is that I had hardly any reaction. It did not even bore me.

I heard all the words distinctly, and the story line was clear (not so usual an occurrence as one might suppose in Anglo-American Shakespeare), but despite these two assets, I cannot report what the play was meant to convey. There was much talk of love, but I felt neither true sentiment nor passion on the stage. The settings were lavish, but I sensed no particular atmosphere. The play takes place in Italy, and might presumably have something to do with the mores or spirit of the Renaissance, but nothing induced my imagination to soar beyond Forty-fourth Street.

For a play (that is, a total stage event) to come alive on the stage it must have *some sort of face*. The present *Romeo and Juliet* has none. It is basically a stock production on which much money and effort have been spent, but it lacks a central conception of any kind, or even the virtue of a simple theatrical naïveté. It was produced as a vehicle for a star without any thought to the problem of how the star's qualities might best be revealed.

The Moon is Blue is popular-magazine romance. Barbara Bel Geddes is an unusually talented actress of considerable charm who, I hope, will someday escape the pseudo-teenage roles in which she has so often allowed herself to be confined as in a downy crib. Barry Nelson is a likable actor of genuine potentialities. Together with Donald Cook, a practiced comedian better in this play than he has been in a long time, these young people make *The Moon Is Blue* a slick piece of bemusement. Whether or not it actually pleases you depends to a certain extent on whether you can prevent yourself from thinking about it. If it should suddenly occur to you that most of the fun is based on a moral premise which makes crucial the problem of when and how a twenty-year-old "good girl" (virgin) is going to turn into either a "bad girl" (unmarried non-virgin) or simply into a wholesome girl with a proper husband, your disposition might turn sour.

Louis Jouvet's production of Molière's *L'Ecole des Femmes*, presented here by ANTA, is a mixture of inspiration and French theatrical routine. Its most creative aspect is Christian Bérard's setting, a fancifully swift, delicate, precise rendering of seventeenth-century classic comedy as seen by a sophisticated modern. The setting is not merely an ornament, but a content: it tells us something of Molière's world and even more about the contemporary Frenchmen who are interpreting him.

There are many bright things in the performance: divinely doll-faced Dominique Blanchar's reading of the maxims for wives, the asthmatic notary's wheezing excitement, Jouvet's idiotically complacent laugh which changes through consternation to a strangled animal's stare. Still I could not help feeling a certain off-handedness in the production, the repetitious and monotonous use of conventional tricks with little true comic invention such as, in terms of the American theatre, we get from Ray Bolger.

Molière suffered real anguish at the thought of being cuckolded and his comedy is as extravagant as his fear was real. The direction and acting did not develop this motif, which constitutes the core of the play. There is too much of the actor's charade in Jouvet's production, not enough of the heart-rending farce, the brilliantly civilized cruelty which represents a large part of Molière's genius. The French today depend too much on the excellence of their classic texts and content themselves too readily with being only appreciative—though often careless—lackeys to their authors.

—*NR*, 9 Apr. '51

TWO MORALITIES

The new Rodgers and Hammerstein hit, *The King and I*, is a pleasant affair. Its story—based on the novel *Anna and the King of Siam*, in itself a nice yarn—is most unusual for a Broadway musical. It has color, sentiment and a quality of good will which, it seems to me, is the source of Oscar Hammerstein's appeal as a song writer.

Musically, *The King and I* is probably the weakest of the Rodgers scores, because the story requires an operetta-like treatment and Rodgers' talent lies more in the direction of the normal American musical, with its bubbling straightforwardness and blithe energy. This story of the education of an obscure Oriental potentate by a proper English governess has in it an element of reflectiveness and serenity which demands what might be called a pastel-like touch or the enveloping atmosphere of a gentle morning song.

That is where Oscar Hammerstein's peculiar gift was able to save the situation. There is nothing English in Hammerstein's style—and Margaret Landon's story is thoroughly English—but there is a warm-heartedness in Hammerstein, an underlying fatherliness of feeling, that lends *The King and I* an endearing tone which triumphs over most of its weaknesses. Hammerstein, in brief, is an unconscious and unpretentious moralist on the level of the simple, honest citizen, and that citizen, though he may not realize it as a member of a New York theatre audience, is eager to be comforted by some form of sincerely meant human affection. Hammerstein supplies sincerity—and we are grateful.

Actually *The King and I* has only two outstanding musical numbers. One of them, "Puzzlement," is more recitative than song; a charming scene, chiefly pantomime and dance, in which the king's children are presented to their new governess. The other is a quaintly humorous ballet; a quasi-Chinese dance version of "Uncle Tom's Cabin" by Jerome Robbins. The rest of the show is mainly expensive decoration and mild convention. The costumes are lavishly handsome without being emotionally communicative. The children are enchanting, a subdued Gertrude Lawrence is gracefully engaging and Yul Brynner gives a more authentic acting performance than one is accustomed to on the musical-comedy stage.

But for me the star of the evening is Oscar Hammerstein telling us modestly that nothing in this world is certain but that it is still wonderful for men to try to learn and for children to begin where their fathers left off.

It may be heresy to say so, but while I am able to accept and enjoy Oscar Hammerstein's popular and oblique homily, I cannot do so with Connelly's *The Green Pastures*. This has nothing to do with the inferiority of the present revival. There are many funny lines in the play and even phrases like Noah's reference to the flood as a complete rain which cannot fail to tickle one, but I am constantly aware in the play that we are being asked to lend ourselves to a simplicity that is not truly folk-like or religious even in the most primitive sense, and to a third-hand appreciation of Negro speech and psychology.

The Green Pastures has always seemed to me a deft, picture-book sort of play for big-city people who are nostalgic about a quality they believe their parents or grandparents once possessed and which they can only recapture in the form of "clever" fun—gay pigment and self-consciously cute drawing. I find no trace of genuine moral sentiment here, only the pseudo-religiosity of the Easter pageant in the larger movie houses—far more skillful and entertaining, of course, but only a little less hypocritical.

—*NR*, 16 Apr. '51

SUMMATION

For six years I have conducted this department devoted to a monthly account of various activi-

ties in the arts—particularly in the theatre. Now that I have reached the coda of my writing stint for this periodical, and feel in the mood for a sort of valedictory address to my readers here, I am struck by a certain ironic contradiction in the general composition of my articles. For while I am technically and professionally best equipped to write about the theatre, some of my most enthusiastic reports have been about work that was not of the theatre.

This does not mean that one enjoys best what one understands the least! The contradiction emphasizes the sorry state of the theatre, which suffers not from lack of talents but from economic constriction and the want of the kind of audience that saner conditions might develop. The organization of the professional theatre in America today necessitates the production of only such plays as may be expected to achieve a certain kind of financial success. Because of this, critical attitudes, instead of guiding the audience to a broad concept of theatre values, tend to attune themselves to commercial standards. The world we live in is hardly recognizable in the plays we see. Acting, direction and the atmosphere of the theatre generally tend toward an efficient stereotype, which has very little to do with the best that is being thought, felt and said in other fields.

If I were to confer my own awards—as distinguished from the many bodies that have now taken to give them—I should turn to painting, music, dancing and the movies to indicate where my imagination, emotion and intelligence were most stimulated. A film like the French *God Needs Men* is incomparably superior to a play like *Darkness at Noon*, the recently suppressed *Miracle* is a far superior piece of work in terms of performance to even the well acted *Rose Tattoo*. How many plays or performances this year could be compared to the profound emotional significance of Aaron Copland's new *Piano Quartet*? Where in the theatre today can one find such a shock and delight as the Toulouse-Lautrec show at the Knoedler Galleries last November provided?

The theatre is capable of offering in the most personal, immediate, inescapable form the equivalent of what we find in the other arts. But to do this, the theatre must be unfettered; theatre craftsmen must be permitted to develop along lines that are still more or less open to other artists. The pitiful thing in the theatre today is that when a superior play is produced—like Lorca's *The House of Bernarda Alba* or *Romeo and Juliet* or *Peer Gynt*, the productions are inadequate to their material, and thus less effective than the productions of rather paltry plays. With all this, as I have repeatedly pointed out, a play like *A Season in the Sun* will be greeted by a majority of the commentators with more applause than a serious and important work like *The Autumn Garden*. An uneven and dramatically awkward work like Edmund Wilson's *The Little Blue Light* which happens to be highly significant will certainly find fewer champions than the flossy show of Christopher Fry's verbally pyrotechnical *The Lady's Not for Burning*.

Let us return, for the moment, to some of the events of the past month. *God Needs Men* is not a picture of the first rank from the standpoint of acting or cinematography. It is intelligently made with honest camera work and sound performances. Its value lies in its meaning, its content in terms of our times.

What the picture says is that men need religious faith, that even the humblest and most sinful folk crave a law beyond their selfish interests by which to guide themselves, to take solace in, something to which they can feel responsibility and, at worst, guilt. Where there are no forms for such faith or where the old forms become neglected, men will improvise new forms. Men make religion, and give substance to religious forms. Where the old forms do not serve in fact, though they are still respected in essence, the forms must be readjusted to the needs of the people—or decay.

What is important in all this is not the bare idea in itself, but that the characters in *God Needs Men* are all devout Catholics, that the picture was made with the approval of the Church and is not considered (in France at any rate) subversive of traditional dogma. The characters many of them pretty disgraceful reprobates—are all submissive to the authority of their church. Yet within this ideological framework, and in a picture that always remains as simple as a folk tale, one can read contemporary history and discern the state of mind of the faithful in Europe today.

The faithful say: we believe—even we who are savage in the discontent caused by our distress and the hard pressure of the world—we believe and shall continue to believe, but we believe only as we find in our religion an understanding of our plight, a sympathy for our needs, a capacity to include within the law and authority of the Church the full embrace of our lives as we actually have to live them.

This indirectly explains certain trends of a quite "radical" complexion which are altering the nature of the European political scene—trends which have created "left" parties composed of orthodox religious folk. For purposes of our discussion it is not necessary to probe further into the questions raised by the film, but it is useful to stress that where art is free, where a popular form of entertainment remains a true expression of experience, profound human values of the widest relevancy will emerge to the benefit on every level of all the living.

In other words, *God Needs Men* has religious, social, political significance, because it is in that vein of human endeavor and feeling from which true art is born. A play like *Darkness at Noon* lacks the political meaning it pretends to because it does not dwell in the province of art—and thus becomes misleading even as a political sign. One can understand very little of life in any direction unless we look at it with the concentration and innocence of the artist.

This leads me back to my original point— perhaps the central thesis of this series of monthly articles—that art must be regarded as man's freest enterprise, the one in which, by facing life with love and in the spirit of play, with that childlike curiosity and openness to experience, which is at the heart of even the scientist's inquiry, we arrive at a true consciousness of ourselves, of the world and of all that we ponderously call our "problems."

The same is true no matter of what art we speak. In Toulouse-Lautrec's work I do not simply find a play of line and color that pleases my eye (this is indifferently true of thousands of pictures of no consequence) but a new kind of beauty, characteristic of our age in which a noisy vulgarity and drabness are combined with an old elegance and transformed into a special big city glamor. Toulouse-Lautrec called one of his famous paintings *Gueule de Bois* (Hangover) and it is symbolic of all of his work. Lautrec coupled a deep-seated attraction and attachment to the derelicts of our civilization with intelligence and mordant observation. Toulouse-Lautrec saw the modern world (basically the world we still live in) as if it were bathed in the sickly sweetness and lonely romanticism of theatre illumination. His color is often frayed and threadbare like old scenery with an odd appeal that may be described as "beat up." When we think of all this—and the particular French "meanness" (witty, unsentimental, aristocratic objectivity) which goes with it, do we not somehow sense more of what is going on in France even now than we do when we read hundreds of reports or editorials that try to explain the present impasse in Europe?

Or take Aaron Copland's *Piano Quartet*: music critics may tell you that it shows the influence of Bartok—as if that were a discovery that matters! In a curious emotional way, I discern through the new piece a kind of "historical" and "psychological" line running from the same composer's *Variations* for piano (1930) to the present. The *Variations* of the early depression era were bare and stark as if all the old life had died off and nothing was left but for new life to bud from the tiny seeds that remained hidden beneath the naked crags of an empty world. The *Piano Quartet* of 1950 is even more disquieting, as if it described the quiet preceding or following an atom bomb attack. The work is the voice of our inner fear, an echo of the secret trepidation in all our

hearts as we look out upon the bleak horizon of a world in bondage to its illusions.

The world today is more terrible, more dramatic and more inspiring than it was when I began writing this record in 1946. We are witnessing epic drama and mad farce, events of literally earth shattering scope and import at every turn. It is a time for saints as well as for scoundrels, for glorious exhortation as well as for hideous braying. A Sophocles, a Shakespeare, a Rabelais, a Balzac, a Dostoyevsky could not cope with all the new mutations of the basic human comedy. But we seem struck dumb not only because we are afraid to look at and to declare what we see, but because we seem to be consciously trained or training ourselves not to see, hear, above all, not to feel— since without feeling there is neither seeing nor hearing. In a time of magnificent invention, we appear to be destroying the instruments of our vision, in a time for eloquence we are gagging ourselves or tearing out our tongues. Our most sensitive antenna—the arts—are being turned to the most frivolous uses. We who could be making history are making jokes.

To judge art from such a standpoint is not so much to be severe with the mediocre as to defend the genuine, not to denounce the inadequate but to forge a path for what is growing, not to be either complacent or captious about what exists but to foster what must emerge—it means to be expectant, courageous, patient and ever mindful of all the great things that gave us being and the desire to speak.

—*TRW*, June '51

FRENCH IMMORALITY

The theatrical picture of Paris, 1951, is easily summarized. There are 47 shows on the boards now—most of them mediocre or worse—rough though lively in acting, unusually ragged in staging though frequently imaginative in setting, playing to audiences that are critically passive but eager for whatever fun the spectacles provide. The French like the theatre even when it is bad.

The outstanding exceptions to the generalization are the productions of the Comédie Française company, which occupies two theatres. The actors have dignity—they speak and move well—even when they lack inspiration, the staging is careful even when it is conventional, and the repertory is varied. Where else today can one see so brilliant and classic an example of the 1910 French bedroom farce as Feydeau's *Le Dindon* ("The Dupe") or such an old war-horse of the late nineties as Sardou's *Madame Sans-Gêne* on the same bill with plays by Racine, Molière, Sophocles, Pirandello and Shakespeare?

Anouilh still turns out acid comedies that are presumably to be taken seriously, but if *Colombe* (with Danielle Delorme) is to become typical of his future work one might as well write him off as a clever but tired confectioner. What is characteristic in Anouilh, and significant of a tendency to be observed in more imposing French writers, is a constant malaise.

La Neige Etait Sale ("The Snow Was Dirty"), the dramatization of a novel by Georges Simenon, is representative of this tendency on a semi-popular level. Its "hero," a boy born out of wedlock and brought up by his prostitute mother, living his adolescence in an "occupied" country, has to give himself, out of an inverted and perverse Puritanism, to filth and crime with the same sense of commitment as a saint gives himself to goodness. In the end, he goes to his death with calm elation because he discovers through his career of sin that love, pity and forgiveness still exist. The play suggests that today heaven is never entered except by way of hell.

Well-staged and acted, *La Neige Etait Sale* is done in an atmospheric style which combines a sketchy naturalism with elements of radio and movie technique. It manages to be effective because it avoids any explicitly moral statement. It plays on the audience's unconscious guilt feeling, its repressed awareness of being soiled yet hungry

for absolution. This shrewd entertainment is part superior horror story and part anxiety dream from which the audience awakes with the thought, "Thank God, it isn't true."

As we ascend to higher levels of creative intention, we must become more severe. There is something in the work of the better French dramatists today (frequently men who are primarily novelists or essayists) that must be characterized as morally and artistically unsound. It must be remembered, however, that when I talk about moral and artistic unsoundness I am not indulging in any disguised squeamishness. In fact, I speak with a certain respect. The "immorality" of the work I have in mind is actually an attempt at purification, an effort to recapture valid ethical truths, a recognition by the French that man cannot long endure an immoral or amoral state.

In Sartre's new (four hour) play *Le Diable et le Bon Dieu*—very badly directed by Jonvet though well cast with the virile Pierre Brasseur—Goetz, a German mercenary soldier of the sixteenth century, acts as if he would be God's rival. He boasts that he does evil for Evil's sake. When he is told by a tormented priest that Evil is not only the easiest but man's inevitable path, Goetz decides to do good as completely as he once tried to do wrong. But he fails even more dismally in his second career—no one loves him for his attempted Christianity. He ends by denying both God and the Devil. There are no absolutes and man must content himself with being human—together with other men in his aloneness—living and fighting without metaphysical guarantees for whatever he believes in and chooses to take responsibility for. Goetz takes up the cause of the downtrodden Protestant peasantry whose rebellion was ruthlessly crushed.

Le Diable et le Bon Dieu has brilliant passages of talk, scenes that bristle with lucid, suggestive and energetic thought, which prove once again, despite long, ineffective stretches in the second and third acts, that Sartre is a writer to be reckoned with. The play is nonetheless a failure because its situations are artificial illustrations ("set-ups") and the mood created is one of neither love nor hate but only of intellection, its approach to life being arbitrary, abstract, fleshless. And here we face the real sin of the French playwrights; their work is about life, but outside it. Their plays do not seem inspired by the passion of an experience, but by the paradox of a debate. Their characters, no matter what they represent are factitious absolutes which seem to move in an airless void entirely surrounded by literature and décor. Our minds finally are mystified because our souls are left vacant. The Greeks were abstract dramatists too, but they spoke with an emotional directness about situations which, although mythical in form, were believed in as the essence of reality. Where there is no immediate connection between the artist and his material, we have a mismarriage—a kind of immorality that is always punished by life itself.

—*NR*, 23 July '51

THE NEW MORALITIES

A play may be well-written, intellectually stimulating, socially significant and still not be good. This is the case with Sartre's *Le Diable et le Bon Dieu*, a big machine, as the French phrase it, which churns up a great deal of interesting and perhaps important matter without ever imparting the feeling of a vital experience.

In any sketch of the contemporary theatre in New York, London and Paris, it is necessary to bear this distinction in mind. There is a type of theatergoer who becomes offended when one appears unimpressed by the ideological content of the literary distinction of certain high-minded plays. Such a theatergoer may become irritating as the more common type who is unaware of any other value than that of the "entertaining." Of the two, the latter type is instinctively closer to the reality of art, although a complete trust in his visceral reactions might virtually end the possibility of all art in the theatre.

What is wrong with Sartre's ambitious play is that nothing within it is motivated except as an "idea" demands it. The central figure arbitrarily switches from evil to good at the point where he has given full literary and philosophic expression to his wickedness. We are thus unable to believe in the evil he rejects or the good he espouses, so that when he takes leave of both to pursue his life as a lonely man (without concern for either category) his choice is practically meaningless: zero can produce nothing but zero.

When characters are set up chiefly as embodiments of general ideas, the ideas themselves begin to lose substance. In Sartre's play, the hero finally decides to identify himself with the historically doomed peasants' rebellion (of the sixteenth century), but the decision seems to be made only because Sartre believes man must choose, not because the character is so presented that any particular choice appears inevitable. Consequently, the play's "philosophy" leaves us exactly nowhere: we do not see on the basis of the play's evidence why any choice is necessary, since—with the negation of the concept of good or evil—all values are destroyed and all choices become matters of indifference.

I am not disputing Sartre's ideas as such; I merely point out that the thinker who exploits the stage for purposes of popular exposition usually defeats his purpose unless he is able to create a true theatrical organism. For this reason some of our less intellectually keen American playwrights are sounder and, in the end, more nourishing artistically than even so brilliant and representative a figure as Sartre.

Subtle psychological character portrayal is not necessarily the key to living dramaturgy. There is very little "psychology" in the Greek dramatists— or in Shaw. Theatrical life is created when the symbols used are adequate to the nature and force of the dramatist's inspiration. Shaw's characters aren't "real" (in a Chekhovian or Ibsenlike sense), but they exactly convey his particular brand of wit, common sense and good will. Sartre himself has been more successful on other occasions in creating effective symbols for his thought.

What is valuable about Sartre's plays and those of the Frenchmen of his generation is that they are attempts to communicate certain peculiarly contemporary modes of French thinking and feeling. For example, in *Le Diable et le Bon Dieu*, Sartre manages to indicate, through the figure of the peasant leader, his attitude toward the Communists, whom he both respects and distrusts, rejecting their outlook on life, though willing to work with them in specific instances. But the most striking feature of the new French dramatic output is the total refusal to profess any sentiment that smacks of "nobility." In fact, there seems to be some compulsion to make the "hero" of the French play today thoroughly bad.

What this means, perhaps, is that the Frenchman, through recent unfortunate experience, has come to distrust all officially noble institutions and personalities. He will accept at face value only one who professes himself more or less damaged and guilty. Think of Camus' *Caligula*, most of Sartre's protagonists and the boy in *La Neige Etait Sale* ("The Snow Was Dirty") who arranges for the seduction of the girl he loves by a criminal. (When her purity is finally established, the boy experiences a kind of exalted humiliation and accepts his condemnation.) The new French "hero" not only expects, permits and does evil things, but when he turns "good" he is so fanatic in his conversion that he simply becomes a monster of another stripe—as is the case in some of Montherlant's plays.

We are not to conclude from this that the French have become corrupt, but rather that the playwrights, still incapable of digesting the complexity of contemporary reality as a whole, are induced to write "morality plays" in which, instead of showing the good (normal) man beset by evil (as in the old morality plays), the bad (normal) man is shown tempted by goodness. There is here an element of intellectual paradox—a game of which the French are very fond—and since the better or more imposing French playwrights are predominantly intellectual in their approach, we get a new dramatic tone which is, to an American

at any rate, fascinating, irritating, false, and still, in a perverse way, meaningful. The drama here mirrors a world that does not know which way to turn and so amuses itself in turning itself, so to speak, inside out.

—*NR*, 6 Aug. '51

CHRISTOPHER FRY

The English, without having any drama, have at the moment a better theatre than the French. I cannot say why the English have produced no group to take the place of Galsworthy, Maugham, Barrie, Pinero, Shaw or even a new Lonsdale, Noel Coward group (Terence Rattigan is not enough), but it is a fact that they haven't. Sean O'Casey is rarely produced, and the plays dealing with contemporary problems are so few that a piece like *His Excellency*, by Dorothy and Campbell Christie, about a Labor man facing colonial issues in an island that might be Malta, becomes an outstanding exception.

This explains, in part, why *The Cocktail Party* and the plays of Christopher Fry occupy their extraordinary position. It is interesting to compare Fry with the French playwrights I have been discussing. The French tone is nervous, debilitated, rather anguished even when it is presumably light. (Sartre, however, has a certain dry energy, and mental vigor.)

There is in Fry something of an affable acquiescence to the prevailing pessimism of the Continental world view. He seems to take for granted that every intelligent person agrees that life is terrible and that to be a blithe optimist nowadays is to set oneself down as an idiot. The characteristic Fry hero either proclaims himself almost eager to die or accepts his own identity only because his neighbors affirm that he has one. The most positive act performed by a Fry hero is to resign from a formerly extensive activity and give his blessings to a son who may possibly find some pleasure in a world become too raw for older men.

But where the French seem sick, bitter or hysterically exalted about the general breakdown, Fry is humorous, gentle, almost sweetly ironic. He is fundamentally undisturbed. His heroes' rejection of life—and their subsequent acceptance or resignation—often seems little more than a series of pretty gestures. And Fry's inherent tenderness is related to an ability to keep himself outside the situations he presents. When he writes what might be called a pacifist play—*A Sleep of Prisoners*—there is a mildness of manner in it that makes the author seem, not above the battle, but one for whom the battle exists. There are two types of men—the play tells us—the doers, who are always getting themselves and us in trouble, and those who only want to *be* (artists, students, simple workers), who bid us cultivate life in all its contradictions with equal love. Perhaps some day the second will influence the first, perhaps somehow, despite the eternal quality and struggle that ensue from it, man will finally come through.

This constitutes a state of being rather than a point of view, so that Fry's plays, even when they deal with hanging, shooting, air raids and other violence, seem almost without action and are always on the verge of becoming literary exercises, comedic incantations, lyric charades, rather than the projections of real conflicts.

But while Fry is at the beginning of his career, which he will undoubtedly center in the theatre, a good many of the French playwrights use the theatre only incidentally. Fry's attitude is that of a man who has managed to find himself a small nook from which he may develop in quiet and safety during a period of transition; the Frenchmen use the stage to achieve a clarity that is still only in the making and which many of them feel may not be of their making.

Fry's use of the dramatic form is rather personal in its offhandedness; the French are more traditionally classic. But both use the medium to embody general ideas. In this they are different from the American playwrights, whose main impulse comes from direct contact with life in terms of character and environment. I am inclined to believe the American dramatists—from O'Neill to Odets, Hellman, Williams and Miller—are working in a richer vein than any other in the contemporary theatre. The present French writing for the theatre, though often related to major problems, seems constantly to carry the spectator away from life to a rather airless realm of speculation—above the crowd and above life itself. Fry occupies a charming niche which the world can regard with pleasure, but which is generally atypical.

American dramatists try to come to grips with the rough material of everyday experience, but only through this often crude, long, apparently wasteful experimental contact with life can the soundest expression be achieved. The fact that the American playwright sticks closer to the form of an old-fashioned realism must not deceive us into believing the Europeans are more admirable. The artistic and cultural timetables of the various countries are different; the more stylized forms employed by the European are as often a sign of a certain attrition of material and emotion as they are of wisdom.

The problems of the American playwright are not only the problems of our culture in general but of our theatre in particular. The danger for the American dramatist is that he will make the defects of our theatre an excuse for abandoning his task. He is certainly not less talented than his French or English like, but he is generally less serious. The American playwright has a predisposition to "spoil" with his theatrical environment—a temptation which is his artistic and human duty to resist.

—*NR*, 20 Aug. '51

BAGELS, BORSCHT, BALLET

Stage shows have been opening since early September, but it would be too much to say that the new theatrical season had begun. Speaking strictly as a reporter and adviser on what is sometimes (laughingly) called "live entertainment," I would say that your best bet now is ballet.

As readers of this department must have guessed, I do not believe the critic's function to be a guide service to practical theatregoing. Such a service is far too personal to be entrusted to a stranger. The critic's function is to be interesting on the subject of his discussion. This is so firmly my belief that I was tempted to title my piece this week "Pay No Heed," and to develop the thesis that any harsh thing that may be said about plays here must not be construed as a warning against seeing them. On principle I am for people's going to the theatre and, if possible, having a good time there—regardless of anybody's critical evaluation. Appetite is far more fundamental than judgment.

These convictions almost failed to stand up against the onslaught of recent evidence. That is why, in order to preserve the cheerful attitude I should like to maintain during the coming months, I begin with a categorical "Go to the Ballet"—specifically, at this writing, to the New York City Ballet, which has developed by dint of devotion and hard work into the finest ballet company we have.

The program I saw was distinguished by unusually good work by the orchestra in the pit as well as by topnotch dancing on the stage. Of the comparatively new works I saw, Jerome Robbins' *The Cage* (to Stravinsky's fascinatingly nervous *String Concerto in D*), though basically naïve and even slight in its fierce conception—the female of the species as mankiller—is brilliantly talented in its total effect. (And Nora Kaye in the central role once again strikes me not only as an admirable dancer but as an exciting actress.) Some day, however, I should like to explain why the American choreographers who employ strong subjects for their material (generically, Anxiety) always strike me as young in their "morbidity," whereas George Balanchine's work seems "old" and deeply sophisticated even in his lightest moments.

Bagels and Lox and *Borscht Capades*, so-called "American"—or "English"—Yiddish revues, are two shows the dramatic critics were mistakenly invited to cover. There are, undoubt-edly, customers for such home-cooked stews—both were reputedly successful in certain summer resorts and other outlying districts—but they are not proper fare for studied notice. However, since my department is as much concerned with generalities as with individual instances, I think there is a kind of ethnological point to be made apropos these revues.

Both shows offer several gifted performers. Both have a kind of good-humored energy and a warmth that ranges from the familiar to the gross, but is warmth nevertheless. What is special here is a peculiar ambiguity which, though rarely discussed by the audience, does not go unperceived by it, because it constitutes the most striking and troublesome feature of both spectacles. They are *not* Yiddish in the sense that good Yiddish theatre was (for that reflected an older and traditionally rooted day), and they are not altogether American in the sense of, let us say, Al Jolson, Eddie Cantor or Lou Holtz, for these comedians felt themselves to be in the strong, sure swim of things.

The present shows are products of a feeling that might be described as a gusty embarrassment, characteristic of people whose world is "local" in the most impermanent sense and whose contact with the community is insecure, flighty, hysterically, though unconsciously and brightly, apologetic. Perhaps they might be set down—in terms of their own particular jargon—as chopped Lindy's.

—*NR*, 1 Oct. '51

PORTRAIT

S. N. Behrman is a playwright in search of material. He has so often been complimented on the felicity of his phraseology that one might suppose such praise a disguised criticism of his content. Behrman does have something to say, but his problem is that he is rarely able to say it "straight out," he always speaks through a mask.

Behrman is a man of rather emotional, almost lyrical and, if you will, sentimental nature, embarrassed by a sense that this nature is not quite smart enough for the society in which he finds himself and in which he would like to occupy a favored place. Thinking of himself—and he is preoccupied with the subject—he is ready to weep, but society, he believes, would consider such behavior unseemly. Looking at the world, he is almost ready to cry out or at least to heave so profound a sigh that the sound might be construed as a protest, so he suppresses his impulse and flicks our consciousness with a soft wit that contains as much self-depreciation as mockery. He tries to chide his world with a voice that might be thought to belong to someone else—a person far more brittle, debonair, urbane than he knows himself to be.

On the surface, then, there is the somewhat Anglicized gentleman gracing a cosmopolitan salon where deft speech and a twinkling eye will lend him a most engaging personality; beneath, there is the "second man," the real Behrman, who is mischievous because he is timid, a sensitive, secretively observing boy nearly always on the verge of sobbing over the spectacle he beholds—of which one of the saddest phenomena is his own discomfort and inability to speak freely.

The sad young man sees that society is mostly harsh, trivial, venal and unkind, but it *is* Society—the world we live in—and who can deny the world, without making himself a fool? The young man's "hero" is always some such fool who defies society—in the thirties it was admissible to treat him as a "revolutionary"—and his foil is always some woman (usually played by Ina Claire) who lent the fool her sympathy, begging forgiveness for not being able fully to share his folly and finally retiring with a smile and a tear to the safety and comfort of a society that the fool scorns. What makes this pattern valuable is that it represents the comic pathos of so many of us.

Behrman's mask—and its motive, composed of guilt and apology, of aspiration and a confession of frailty—is not unfamiliar in dramatic literature. Oscar Wilde wore a similar one. The difference is that Wilde was more genuinely a worldling and more "aesthetic" than Behrman. Wilde really exulted in his mask—although in the end he felt compelled to tear it off. But Behrman, for all his playfulness, is a warm-hearted moralist who wishes with all his (insufficient) might that someone would make a more hospitable and less hypocritical world for him.

As time moved on, the "revolutionists" of the thirties began to seem even greater fools than we first thought them—and dangerous besides. Behrman had some difficulty finding proper symbols to represent either the "naughty" world or the "foolish" rebels. Even the man (or woman) in between was hard to convey in terms that were dramatically cogent and attractive. It was "no time for comedy," and when Behrman undertook more seriously to delineate the "fascist" type (*The Talley Method*, *Dunnigan's Daughter*) there was an indecision in the stroke.

The latest Behrman play to reach our stage, *Jane*, the dramatization of a Maugham story, was written five years ago. Even this slight comedy, observed against the background of Behrman's past work, reveals the basis of his psychology. Its central character is a remarkably frank woman who seems dowdy when she is just plain Jane from Liverpool, but who becomes a sensational success when she is dressed up by a young opportunist in the most dashing London fashion. Jane can't stand the compromise of her life with the opportunist; she retires to the protection and love of an honest, rough-and-ready reactionary.

The play has its pleasant moments of shy jocularity and smoothly worded deviousness, but even so there are faint rumors of a troubled world—quickly suppressed by a flood of strenuous epigrams. The mask has worn thin; the practice becomes tenuous. Behrman's difficulty is not that he cannot tell a story but that he is afraid to tell the real story he has in mind lest it break the myth of his glib affability. Nor has he yet the strength to define himself in less ambiguous terms. Some day he may find it. In any case a good part of the harried public responds to the blandishments of his courteous manner, though one suspects that the author has already outgrown it.

One hopes too that in the future producers and directors will stage Behrman with some recognition of the poet buried in him (that he himself hardly knows) so that even a play like *Jane* is not done in the stiff pseudo-English drawing-room style that encourages most of the actors (except Howard St. John and Edna Best, who are generally excellent) to speak in a manner which, if it were any more "British," would render them unable to speak at all.

—*NR*, 18 Feb. '52

SOMETHING OF ENGLAND

If I had to describe in a word the evening of readings from Charles Dickens given by Emlyn Williams I would say that it was *agreeable*. The quality is not tame; the kind of agreeableness achieved is of that peculiarly English brand which produces a sort of benign, almost enchanted quiet, rest and smiling security. (I could not help remembering, as I sat listening to Williams, that I had experienced something of the same pleasure as a boy, when my father read to me from his favorite authors whenever I grew restless through the confinement of a winter day.) We are all kids as we listen to Williams. Remarks in praise of the actor's shrewd virtuosity are ultimately of secondary consideration; the fact is this evening of Dickens remains childlike and pure.

Dickens himself is not so innocent. He is more or less a radical. The mordancy of his observation of middle-class English life is to be seen even in the fragments of Williams' program. Yet hardly any of the sharpness is communicated—only the charm. This too is characteristic of the English. Their good manners often make even the bitter sound fetching.

Decorum leads to decoration. The motifs of decoration may be similar to those of tragic art. A thorn in decoration loses its sting; a dagger may

become as pretty as a flower. There is something of this transformation in Christopher Fry's work. Its material is often brackish, but the manner is always sweet. If one listens closely to *Venus Observed*, for example, one hears some fairly gloomy sentiments, but the total impression is always *agreeable*—almost delicious.

"The note is loneliness," says the Duke in *Venus Observed*. "So much I delighted in is all ash," he continues. And further: "...I forgive/Both of us for being born of the flesh/Which means I forgive all tossing and turning/All foundering, all not finding/All irreconcilability/All the friction of this great orphanage/Where no one knows his origin and no one/Comes to claim him. I forgive even/The unrevealing revelation of love/That lifts a lid purely/To close it, and leaves us knowing that greater things/Are close, but not to be disclosed/Though we die for them."

All this, as far as sense goes, is in the existentialist vein. But Fry turns it into something elegant, witty, exquisitely sentimental. Better still is a certain gentle, almost tenderly humorous forbearance. Fry's mood is autumnal ("The landscape's all in tune, in a falling cadence/All decaying"). It is autumnal not only in this play, which is an allegory of the passing of old (aristocratic, imperial) England, but even in plays presumed to reflect the atmosphere of brighter seasons.

That is why Fry's plays, even when they contain "strong" action (a pistol shot, arson, a rescue from fire, threatened imprisonment) seem placid and passive. The best days are over; the struggles ahead, we know from the past, are not worth the burning. Let us embrace civilization and forget progress. Since it is their way, the young may toss and turn; the wise will contemplate the universe with an affectionate nod. It all comes to a snore in the end.

Let no one say that Fry's work consists of playful, euphonious words and no more. The meaning is clear to anyone who will pay attention. (The continuous verbal coruscation sometimes makes attention difficult, so that the line of the play—which is usually as pointed as a fable—is obscured.) And the meaning—no matter how one reacts to it—is historically (or socially) revealing. Fry's plays are poems of resignation in which tragic substance is flattened into lovely ornament. The French existentialists (most of whom are poor as creative artists) have a more vigorous intention and an activist temper. Fry confesses here through his leading character, who dwells in the high air observing the stars, "I like to conform."

The challenge of Fry's plays is seldom met by directors because they seem to appreciate him only in terms of quips and fine speeches, and not in terms of feeling, atmosphere, significance. *Venus Observed* is done as a romantic drawing-room comedy rendered limp by literature. Rex Harrison, who is an admirable light comedian—his delivery suggests intelligence—seems miscast in this play. His manner is brittle and worldly in a tripping sort of way, whereas Fry's Duke "dances" to a graciously regretful tune. Harrison stoops and fumbles to convey age: there is no sovereign tiredness or melancholy anywhere in him.

The rest of the cast is careful or valiant—smiling bravely through the hazard of words they have respectfully learned. John Williams, who plays a faltering representative of mercantile England, seems to be having fun—it helps us to enjoy his performance.

—*NAT*, 3 Mar. '52

LOVE'S LABOR'S LOST

A play, in stage terms, is a scenario or a plan of action to be performed by living persons. The basis of drama, then, is action. But action cannot be abstract. It is seen through people who are characters, and in most plays the characters speak words which, though primarily intended to define and carry forward the action, possess a quality of their own. Action is also modified by place—not only the locale of the story itself but the actual place of performance or "stage practice," which must ultimately determine something in the nature of the action. Every character, besides having an ideal identity in the scheme of the play, has a real identity through the actor who embodies him. For this reason the theatre, which is an art of many parts, achieves unity only as one conceives all of them with a view to grasping their central spirit, the root of their organic life.

Love's Labor's Lost, perhaps the first of Shakespeare's plays, is based on a very fragile line of action. Its characters are almost pastel sketches. Yet how lovely and lyric, how bright and gay, youthful and joyous is the feeling of the play. It is all fun and tender merry-making. It bathes blithely in that "sweet smoke of rhetoric" which Shakespeare liked both to laugh at and indulge in. Euphuism and airy conceits, pride in pedantry and glowing satisfaction in new learning—all these Shakespeare affectionately mocks because he knows he is enthusiastically guilty of all of them. He has in him something of the fantastical Spaniard Don Adriano de Armando, lovably mad, who "hath a mint of phrases in his brain," a quixotic loon without a shirt to his name, whom the aristocrats use as a sort of court fool. "The music of his own vain tongue doth ravish like enchanting harmony."

Just as Shakespeare in this early flight spreads his sumptuous plumage of splendid words, so his theme, expressed largely through that happy blade Berowne, is the excellence of love, the pleasures provided by womankind, the primacy of passion. "Abstinence engenders maladies." How this play revels in its own youth, its discovery of language, laughter, and bubbling genius! The play is a harbinger of the Shakespeare to come: it has the glamor of an awakening to a brilliant dawn.

I do not know how the play should be done—except that there must be gaiety and freshness in it. I do not know where it takes place—except on a stage—for the Navarre which is the locale of its action is nothing but the playground of the poet's fancy.

Albert Marre, who directed the City Center production—the first in New York since 1891—has chosen to do the play in an Edwardian mode, which is as quaint and as near or far as need be. To translate the play in this fashion is as legitimate, it seems to me, as to approximate any pseudo-historical time. The "translation" is consistently carried out and certainly amusing. It makes the play a pleasant college boys' romp—and that in a way is just what it is. This *Love's Labor's Lost* has really been directed—which is a rather rare thing in our theatre. It has been given a theatrical form—in terms of the eye and the feeling which goes with what the eye sees—and that, in part, is what we mean when we speak of stage direction. The costumes are charming—as if for a Wilde play done as an operetta; the use of the musical accompaniment is quite winning.

The cast has a young complexion which goes well with the rest. Its diction is a bit over-deliberate, showing a modest caution that is to be recommended even though it constrains and dulls the pace somewhat. But better a hesitant Shakespeare that is heard than a confident one that is blustered or blurred.

The men have better roles than the women. Priscilla Morrill as Jacquanetta has a merry eye, and Nancy Marchand as the Princess of France a good presence. Philip Bourneuf as Holofernes and Hurd Hatfield as Sir Nathaniel are particularly humorous (Hatfield's real talent, I now discover with pleasure, is for character acting), and Joseph Schildkraut is charmingly foolish and forlorn as Don Adriano. Mr. Schildkraut, who it is no news to say is a fine actor, must however overcome one serious fault: he tends to draw his audience's attention to the precise effect he is making so that he seems not only to be acting his part but to be demonstrating how he is acting it. When he is commendably simple, as here, he seems to be asking his audience to appreciate the fact of this simplicity—which makes his performance not quite so simple as he intends.

—*NAT*, 21 Feb. '53

ON BORROWED TIME

Paul Osborn's *On Borrowed Time* (Forty-eighth Street) is a folksy fantasy about the old man who decoyed Death up an apple tree. The play achieved considerable success here in 1938 and was a surprising failure in London. The failure in London was a puzzle to everybody—the play being genial and tender.

Finding myself rather less amused at the revival than the first time I saw the play, and not at all touched—though by no means bored—I wondered whether there wasn't a difference between the American and the English attitude toward death. Americans in the theatre are willing to be saddened by thoughts of death when death is softened with kindly tears or shrouded in heroic cerements, but our audiences dislike thinking of death as a fact of life. For us death must be something romantically spectral, sepulchrally noble, or something so friendly and nice as not to seem to exist at all.

In the Osborn comedy death is a gentleman who means no harm, doing his slightly mysterious job like a decorous process server. If one is clever enough one might elude him, but when one yields to the necessity of letting him do his duty, one finds that one has been summoned to a realm more ineffably sweet than life itself.

I probably would not have thought of the play in this light—no one else does or should—if the playing of it in the present revival were more poetic, charming, tongue-in-cheek, or frankly sentimental. But it is only plain. Victor Moore is perfectly cast as to "type." He is, moreover, a consummately sure and effortless performer. His is the acme of "naturalness." In short, he is everything but interesting. We get very little from him here except the impression of his deftness. Dudley Digges, who played the part originally, worked harder and was not as authentically small-town American, but he had a complete artistic objective in view, whereas Moore simply plays the "notes," but the "notes," even perfectly delivered, do not add up in this case to a captivating spirit.

—*NAT*, 28 Feb. '53

MISALLIANCE
PICNIC

Although Bernard Shaw's *Misalliance* (Barrymore Theater) deals with the same middle-class England which he later characterized as *Heartbreak House*, the earlier play—*Misalliance* was written in 1909-10—might be called the Good Old Days. The young girl chafing at the inane leisure furnished by her papa's prosperity, turning from her hysterical aristocrat of a fiancé to a handsome brute of an adventurer and asking her father to buy him might be considered something to grow melancholy over. But the facts of *Misalliance* are viewed with confidence, humor, and zest. For in 1910 the English middle class was rich, assured, untroubled about the future, and when Shaw complained that it was burying its head in silly illusions while it talked, talked, talked, he was clearly glad to join in the chorus as a brilliantly knowing interlocutor, because there were still ease, freedom, and good fortune to be enjoyed.

The Shavian optimism of 1910 has a tonic effect on us today. It is not only great fun to see *Misalliance* because it bubbles with blarney and mental vigor, does all sorts of verbal nip-ups that bespeak health and high spirits, and practically somersaults with vaudeville tricks that are part of the eternal theatre, but it is also a comfort to our aching souls because Shaw's world is no longer ours, and we are happy to be reminded that it once existed.

It is not true that the play has no action: every scene is based on a fundamentally entertaining, physically projected situation as old as the hills and therefore satisfying. Neither is it true that the play is not about anything—its theme, I repeat, is that of *Heartbreak House* conceived in a gay key—but what carries it along so buoyantly for us is our sense of release in the delightful moral and social landscape reflected in it. This is happily caught in the City Center production with its "crazy" *art nouveau* setting by John Boyt and the very pleasant cast—Barry Jones is best—which conveys the fun of the play while cutting an hour from its text.

The young girl in William Inge's new play, *Picnic* (Music Box Theater), like Shaw's "ingenue," is waiting for something to happen. But the environment of the American play—specifically Kansas—is a place where nothing can happen to anybody. The women are all frustrated by fearful, jerky men; the men are ignorant, without objective, ideals, or direction—except for their spasmodic sexual impulses. There is no broad horizon for anyone, and a suppressed yammer of desire emanates from every stick and stone of this dry cosmos, in which the futile people burn to cinders.

If you read my description and then see the play you will be either vastly relieved or shockingly disappointed. For though what I have said may still be implicit in the words, it is hardly present on the stage. I happen to have read the playscript before it was put into rehearsal, and I saw in it a laconic delineation of a milieu seen with humor and an intelligent sympathy that was not far from compassion. What is on the stage now is a rather coarse boy-and-girl story with a leeringly sentimental emphasis on naked limbs and "well-stacked" females. It is as if a good Sherwood Anderson novel were skillfully converted into a prurient popular magazine story on its way to screen adaptation.

In this vein the play is extremely well done. It is certainly effective. Joshua Logan, who is a crackerjack craftsman, has done a meticulous, shrewd, thoroughly knowledgeable job of staging. He has made sharply explicit everything which the audience already understands and is sure to enjoy in the "sexy" plot, and has fobbed off everything less obvious to which the audience ought to be made sensitive.

All pain has been removed from the proceedings. The boy in the script who was a rather pathetic, confused, morbidly explosive and bitter character is now a big goof of a he-man whom the audience can laugh at or lust after. The adolescent sister who was a kind of embryo artist waiting to be born has become a comic grotesque who talks as if she suffered from a hare-lip; the drained and repressed mother is presented as a sweet hen almost indistinguishable from her chicks; the tense school teacher bursting with unused vitality is fore-shortened as a character and serves as a utility figure to push the plot.

Even the setting, which—for the purposes of the theme—might have suggested the dreary sunniness of the Mid-western flatlands, has been given a romantically golden glow and made almost tropically inviting.

Having seen the play with this bifocal vision—script and production—I cannot be sure exactly what the audience gets from the combination. Lyric realism in the sound 1920 tradition of the prairie novelists is being offered here as the best Broadway corn. In the attempt to make the author's particular kind of sensibility thoroughly acceptable, the play has been vulgarized.

The cast is good—Kim Stanley is particularly talented, though I disliked the characterization imposed on her—and it follows the director with devoted fidelity. There is a new leading lady, Janice Rule, who besides having a lovely voice is unquestionably the most beautiful young woman on our stage today.

Here at any rate is a solid success. But I am not sure whether the author should get down on his knees to thank the director for having made it one or punch him in the nose for having altered the play's values. It is a question of taste.

—*NAT*, 7 Mar. '53

THE MERCHANT OF VENICE

In our times, many things are big, very few have grandeur. We are more familiar with the complicated than with the complex. We have nerves rather than feelings. Our thinking is minute, tight, microscopic: we are able to write the Gettysburg address on a pinpoint and make a camel pass through a needle's eye, but our lives, thoughts, conceptions lack breadth, sinew, scope. Who paints pictures like Tintoretto? What men look like Rembrandt's? What women like Titian's? Who plans novels like *Les Misérables*? Who can act Shakespeare?

The half-pint will not do. Refinement is not enough. Excess must be the norm. We think of the Shakespearean actor of the past as an inspired monster. Look at the portraits of the older players in Shakespearean roles: they all have something *fabulous* about them—the wildness of Kean's eye, the defiant gruffness of Forrest's bearing, the melancholy in Booth, the painful delicacy of Barrymore's profile. Laurence Olivier's best Shakespearean performances are in minor character parts.

The City Center *Merchant of Venice* was a college-educated stock production. It had practically no direction whatsoever. There were some pretty dresses, a bit of haphazard choreography, intelligible diction, a sympathetic Prince of Morocco in Earle Hyman, and now and again a nice reading. In the midst of all this Luther Adler tried to give us a new, thoughtful, and in certain respects a highly original Shylock. No one has yet decided exactly what *The Merchant of Venice* is. It was a farcical melodrama at one time, a humanized melodrama at another. It has been called a fairy tale, a tragi-comedy, an actor's vehicle, an anti-Semitic tract, a propaganda piece for tolerance, an Elizabethan potpourri, a bad play, and a master-piece. It is probably all of these: that is its fascination. But it remains for the director who stages it to determine what it shall be in a particular production.

To me *The Merchant* seems quite clearly a poet's parable on the subject of wealth, justice, and love. Shakespeare's Venice is the city of pleasure and sensual romance rounded on mercantile prosperity. The well-to-do wallow in luxury which verges on corruption. Their morality is Christian in name only. Shylock is the poisoned conscience of Venice. It depends on his services and despises him for it, as he in turn despises it for its hypocrisy. Venice spits on its own face by spitting on Shylock's. Shylock destroys himself by responding to the offense against him in terms of the city's own logic. Shylock's desire for revenge—all his arguments to justify his position—are part of a mercantile triumph in his defeat: Shylock has confirmed his own pessimism and his scorn. He knows for all time now that no one can expect honesty and goodness from the fawning tradesmen of falsely Christian faith.

This Shylock holds the attention. The actor is constantly making a point. He is plastically interesting, and he has real dramatic motivation throughout. There are splendid moments: for example, his anguished cry of "I am content" which reveals the knowledge that he can never win over the cruelty of the vested interests against him. Yet our sympathy is not won; Shylock's resentment does not stir us. We are not touched, exalted, or even—as in the case of the malevolent Shylocks of the past—repelled or horrified by him.

Adler's Shylock has vividness and power but insufficient depth. It is well conceived but emotionally thin. It is impelled by the actor's mind and will, not nourished by his emotions. It is somehow impersonal, lacking in warmth and mystery. It is small. This Shylock loves no one, and though he is vibrantly angry, also does not hate. He seems guilty of nothing—so he cannot suffer. And without suffering Shylock is nothing. For though Shylock must not be guilty in the meaning given to the term by his paltry accusers, he is guilty of a hate as sinful as the vileness that provoked it. The suffering which gave rise to and is the consequence of Shylock's sin is what redeems him for us.

Luther Adler is one of the very few actors among us who could even essay such a part as Shylock. The limitation of his effort here is part of the whole problem of the contemporary theatre. To do Shakespeare on the heroic level one has to reach beyond the measure of the naturalistic, the sensible, the explicit. There must be a kind of metaphysical passion, a reaching inward, outward, upward, beyond the pale of the proved and the defined to music, to poetry, and to the suprapersonal—to that realm of imagination which is beyond formal explanation. But for that one has to have genius—or a director, a production idea, a Theatre to prepare and aid in the quest.

—*NAT*, 21 Mar. '53

WHICH WAY IS HOME?

One playgoer certainly was happier during the past fortnight on Christopher Street (Theatre de Lys), where the Touring Players gave a series of three one-acters by Ellen Violett bearing the collective title *Which Way Is Home?* than he was at the Forty-eighth Street Theater at a revival of the 1937 farce hit *Room Service*. Not that the latter is a poor piece: I still found some of it funny—despite a so-so performance—but at best I was amused as by a rather perfunctory joke that someone might tell me on my way out of a restaurant.

Of the three playlets presented by the Touring Players the most satisfactory by far is *Brewsie and Willie*, based on a story by Gertrude Stein. In this rambling yet unified stretch of dialogue which is both naturalistic and stylized, Gertrude Stein—through her adapters Ellen Violett and Liz Blake—has caught and interpreted for us the basic homelessness of the G.I. at the end of the last war, and through him the basic confusion in all of us.

Tenderly and wisely Gertrude Stein points out the fear we suffer from being at once a pioneer people (yes, even now!), with eager, inquiring, youthful minds, and credulous, gullible victims of ready-made answers which have very little to do with our daily experience. We are afraid of experience, afraid of life, because it baffles and upsets us by being so persistently contradictory to the prefabricated concepts with which we approach it. We are immensely delighted at our shrewd discovery that there is no Santa Claus, and we howl with pain because there is none. We proclaim our virile capacity to face the world, and we shrink like scared children at every actual confrontation. Hogtied by materialism, we are ineradicable idealists. We cannot reconcile our "practical realism," upon which we are constantly urged to rely, with our idealistic impulses, which torture us with their unexpected but unrelenting intrusions.

The sensitive American—he who has not allowed himself to be altogether canned—is an emotional eccentric. His craziness bears witness to his aliveness and is one of his most engaging qualities. He must not be put in a position where he has to beg permission to be pessimistic; he must learn to give his optimism a foundation in fact. He must come to understand life not in terms of "yes" or "no" but in terms of "yes *and* no." Gertrude Stein says all this and more in *Brewsie and Willie* with a curious directness that masks itself behind a studied casualness. I half suspect her of having been a good woman!

'The Touring Players act the Stein play with a certain unvarnished and slightly awkward naturalness which helps it. The company that calls itself Current Stages (Cherry Lane Theater) is well cast as to type for most of the parts in O'Casey's *The Plough and the Stars*, but is frequently unintelligible in its attempt at Hibernian speech.

The play comes off, nevertheless, in its power and poetry. How lucky poor tormented Sean was after all! Life offered him a strategic position amid the Dublin tenements, with their abounding riches of humor, tragedy, and native eloquence, as well as the vantage point of being a witness at the moment of dramatic crisis in the days of the Easter rebellion. Thus he was able to write truly contemporary realistic plays which are passionate in feeling and prophetic in utterance. Here the distinction between prose and poetry vanishes without detriment to either. One is reminded of the lines in Chekhov's *Seagull*: "I come more and more to the conviction that it is not a question of new and old forms; but that what matters is that a man should write without thinking of forms at all, write because it springs freely from his soul."

What most of our playwrights nowadays seem to lack is roots in some reality more fertile and inspiring than their professional world provides. Sprung from a deep soil of reality, the fanatically and explosively honest sensibility of O'Casey was able to produce three or four of the most expressive plays of our time.

—*NAT*, 25 Apr. '53

"PESSIMISM"

What I propose today is to revert to a question which has come up in regard to certain criticisms of *Camino Real*, a recurrent question apropos of plays every season or so. It concerns the issue of "pessimism" in drama.

The word is a vague one, and the author of *Camino Real* might easily argue, if he cared to, that his play is not pessimistic. As I inferred in my own review of the play, the nature of its "philosophy" is somewhat beside the point. No matter what its stated or implied ideology, it is immature art and, in my opinion, inferior to the author's other plays. What is in dispute now is the implication that a play is bad when it is pessimistic—a hypothesis I believe to be pernicious as well as false.

Some of the world's greatest dramatic literature (to go no farther)—*King Lear* and *Oedipus the King*—might reasonably be set down as pessimistic. It is well known, as a French poet once said, that some of the most beautiful poems are pure sobs. And there are others, plays and poems, which amount to curses and imprecations. There have also been plays which might properly be described as "sick"—many of Strindberg's, for example—but which certainly claim our attention and deserve our respect.

Why, then, do we tend in our American theatre to feel that designating a play as "pessimistic" is almost tantamount to complete condemnation? The usual explanation is that Americans are reared in a tradition of optimism. The historically happy circumstance of American life make us shy away from the tragic view of life as from something unhealthy as well as distasteful. This is truer of the theatre than elsewhere. Hawthorne, Melville, Faulkner, even Hemingway are certainly not sanguine figures. But in our theatre of recent years, despite the example of Eugene O'Neill, whose work is tormented by his effort to reconcile himself to the anguish and disorder he has felt and witnessed, there is rarely anything but a grudging or resistant attitude to the play that suggests deep-lying tragedy. Shaw wrote plays pleasant and unpleasant; Anouilh writes "black" plays and "rosy" plays. We insist on sunshine in all our plays just as we recoil from "unsympathetic" characters.

As I am not myself of a gloomy turn of mind and do not accept the rationale of philosophic pessimism, I must hasten to make clear that I believe a certain (unconscious) part of the theatre public's objection to the "unhappy" play is justified on aesthetic, intellectual, and moral grounds. For the state of being a man and the state of negation—what might be called the affirmation of nothingness—are incompatible. But there is in our present aversion to the "pessimistic," our insistence that we always look on "the bright side," a profoundly dangerous element.

We want to protect ourselves from a somber or disturbed view of life not because we cherish life so much but because we fear it. A large part of our program of optimism is dread in disguise. Our faith in life too often depends on our blinding ourselves to misfortune and making ourselves deaf to complaint. The present social atmosphere induces us to seek safety above all by cutting ourselves off from everything contradictory, difficult, untoward. The result is culturally stultifying, morally debilitating, aesthetically annihilating.

There can be joy in life only through contact with it. There can be hope only through the recognition of what may be hoped for in the real world. There can be strength only by the confrontation through intelligence, spirit, and love of everything that life is; no one but an imbecile thinks it is supposed to be nothing but beer and skittles.

There are only two valid objections to "pessimism" in a play: that it is a trivial pessimism—many of our "pessimistic" plays give off the sound of a baby crying because its candy has been taken away—or that it includes too little of the stuff of life. The heroic pessimism which, so to speak, scoops up vast chunks of human experience makes great drama because the acceptance of experience, the painful as well as the pleasant, is the ultimate and real "good" of life. Our unwitting censorship of the "pessimistic" play is a reflection of our reluctance publicly to acknowledge—we may do it privately with a novel—that life is real and life is earnest and that comfort and a streamlined "good time" are not its goals.

Just as the fullness of experience is the true source of happiness in living, so a fullness of life is the basic criterion of excellence in drama. There is more vigor in Hamlet's doubts, more solace in Cordelia's tears, more nobility in Othello's crimes, more dignity in Mephistopheles' denials, more tenderness in Uncle Vanya's frustrations, more relish in the monsters of Webster's *White Devil* than there is gaiety or uplift in a host of our "optimistic" comedies. The man who cries out, "Take him away, he's breaking my heart," ninety-nine times out of a hundred is neither a cheerful nor a kind person.

—*NAT*, 9 May '53

ACTORS—IMAGE OF THEIR ERA

In the theatre this is the time of prizes and awards. The less theatre we have, the more prizes are awarded. Perhaps that is our way of compensating through honor and esteem what we cannot supply in substance. It is certain that among devoted playgoers, the prizes for acting—even more than those for plays—create jubilation, discussion, even dispute. In any case, a good deal of genuine sentiment is expended on the occasion of the various awards.

The most-awarded actress of the past season is unquestionably Shirley Booth. Miss Booth (Motion Picture Academy Award for her performance in *Come Back Little Sheba*; Antoinette Perry Award for *The Time of the Cuckoo*) didn't steal it, as the French say, when they mean that someone got what was deserved. Shirley Booth's success is the opposite of meteoric: she has been working long and hard without ever having achieved the rank of stardom, which nowadays is often accorded to many young people after one or two bright displays. The belatedness of these honors, as far as Shirley Booth is concerned, may be ascribed to the fact that she is no conventional leading lady. Her looks are not "sensational"; her voice and manner are special, but not in a way that is usually deemed theatrically glamorous. This fact has set me thinking.

Is it a mere chance that Shirley Booth's prizes and stardom have come so tardily? Or is there something that makes her eminence at this moment peculiarly fitting and significant? In what way, if any, is she typical of our day? And is there a connection between this typicality and our newly expressed enthusiasm for her?

I have long felt that an actor's popularity is intimately related to the social complexion of an era. This has been true everywhere and at all times, but particularly true here in America because our history may be described as the most rapid in the world. What American over 40 does not realize that a new age seems to dawn every ten years; language, manners, mood and mode undergo a sharp alteration. To speak knowingly today of 1917 is to be regarded as something of an antiquarian.

"Actors," Shakespeare said, "are the abstract and brief chronicle of the time." This is not simply a pretty thought but one which, if carefully pursued, might form the basis of an enlightening social history of our country. Naturally, neither the player nor the playgoer is conscious of their social interrelationship. But each is the image of the other. The lady in the audience begins to dress her hair in the manner of some prominent actress (a coiffeur told me shortly after *The Member of the Wedding* opened that he had several requests for a "Julie Harris hairdo") but the actress probably invented her hairdo in response to some practical necessity dictated by changes in the daily life of the community. (It is said, for example, that bobbed hair became common when the employment of women in business and industry increased.) The stage hero makes the man in the audience give himself new airs and ideas as to proper conduct, dress and deportment. The actor has arrived at this new "manner"—which may become the "rage"—through contact with the same world in which the man in the audience dwells.

There is nothing abstract about this interchange. What we often overlook, because it is obvious, is that the actor is a fragment of the audience. The audience gives birth to the special person who becomes the actor. The actor is the "ape of society," and, if he has a sufficiently striking personality—which means a sufficiently large quotient of that element which society most values in itself—society will soon ape the actor.

The examples of this interrelationship that most readily occur to me are American, although it was the French actress Rachel who, while she achieved her greatest fame in the classic drama of the seventeenth century, represented the new romantic spirit of the Eighteen Thirties in France, and gave me the impetus to begin my inquiry. American actors are also preferable as examples to English actors, because the changes in English society are slower and somehow less drastic, so that the styles of English acting are less subject to change than ours. It should be pointed out, too, that since space permits only a sketch of what might easily be a book, one has to generalize on periods and people to a perhaps unwarranted degree. The ideas expressed here are to be taken as suggestions rather than conclusions. We emphasize highlights and omit the subtleties of historical mutations, which know very few sudden beginnings or endings. One should remember, finally, that in every epoch various and often contrary trends coexist and set each other off.

The theatre had some difficulty in establishing itself in this country. What need was there for entertainment on a professional scale when forests had to be cleared, roads laid, homes built? The Puritan prohibition of the theatre and play-acting may be explained in part by the simple fact that in a wilderness only immediately productive work could be regarded as serious. Our first actors and theatrical entrepreneurs were usually English and their efforts had a limited appeal to a very small audience of the well-born.

Edwin Forrest (1806-1872), who was at the height of his career around 1852, was our first outstanding actor of serious roles. He was not only first in point of time and excellence but in terms of a consciousness of his role as an *American* actor. His was the time when Americans were becoming belligerently proud of their independence of the mother country, and Forrest was an emphatic patriot. The masses, as distinct from the more refined public, looked on Forrest as their champion against English "superiority." (In 1848, some of these masses rioted violently and fatally in New York's Astor Place against Macready, Forrest's "rival," because the English actor tried to play here at the same time and in the same parts that Forrest did.) Forrest was one of the first people in the American theatre to extend encouragement to American playwrights (there were practically none at the time) by giving prizes of $500 to $1,000 for the "best" plays. One of Forrest's great vehicles was the prize-winning *Metamora*, one of the first plays to glorify the "noble red man."

What sort of an actor was our first tragedian, whose emergence was held to be a kind of national triumph, and whose playbills exultantly displayed the American flag as a sign of the actor's pride? He was described by William Winter as "a vast animal, bewildered by a grain of genius." His acting was "bold and forceful" but it lacked "delicacy." Certainly all this is consonant with the ruggedness which we associate with a society only lately free of its pioneer state. No wonder Forrest was accused of "ranting."

Such a man, a kind of rude aborigine with a newly aroused sensitivity and artistic temperament, could not help become truculent and bitter, not only against the still towering prestige of England's important actors, but against the encroachment of Edwin Booth's rising fame.

If Forrest was "nature," Booth represented cultivation. What was incipient and rough in Forrest became informed and tempered in Booth (1837-93). Booth brought to his acting not only something of the English training which he acquired through his father, Junius Brutus Booth, a giant among giants (the rival of the unparalleled Edmund Kean) but a certain depth, delicacy and dignity, bred partly from his inner struggle against the effects of his father's extravagant life, and partly from the growing cultural awareness of America toward the middle of the nineteenth century—to say nothing of the tragic circumstances of his life, which included the struggle within his own family between North and South.

In one sense, however, the truest representative of the spirit of the American people in the nineteenth century theatre was Joseph Jefferson (1829-1905), who played Rip Van Winkle from 1866 to 1880. Jefferson's genial charm, optimistic humor, rural good fellowship and openness of heart represented all the endearing aspects of the American character. His acting had a freshness and innocence the like of which was last seen in our day in the more subdued Frank Bacon of *Lightnin'* fame. Jefferson mirrored an America still untrammeled by the machine age. In our day, the Jefferson stage type is almost extinct—the farm and the village are virtually non-existent in our theatre now—and our present country comedians have something synthetic about them, as if they were more familiar with hotel bars and business men's conventions than with open fields.

Before proceeding to a discussion of the actors of more recent times, I should like to point out that one kind of actor we never produced is the classic actor, typified in England by John Philip Kemble (1757-1823), of whom Forbes-Robertson in a later time was perhaps reminiscent. The stately formal actor in the grand manner who rarely gives vent to any unexpected bursts of passion and yet commands his audience by a studied and steady intensity of feeling can only be fostered by a society of homogeneous culture with few sharp upheavals. American society, as I have already remarked, is constantly simmering, boiling, and overflowing: we have always been in a state of permanent revolution. That is why it is so difficult for us to establish a theatrical tradition.

The nearest thing to a period of prosperous social stability on a broad cosmopolitan level is the era from 1885 to 1914. Although there were counter-currents, the British influence was still strong. The polish and elegance of English decorum were much appreciated and constituted, in an indirect way, our standards of breeding and taste. Most of the favorite actors were educated in England and played in a great many English plays. Even such a thoroughly American actor as William Gillette, the author of popular Civil War plays, made his greatest success as Sherlock Holmes. Characteristic of this era too is the fact that Gillette was college-educated (Harvard *and* Yale), in contrast to the old-timers who were reared, as we used to say, in the school of hard knocks.

John Drew (1853-1927) was the theatrical paragon of the time. This does not mean that he was the best actor. Otis Skinner (1858-1942) for instance, was far more gifted and versatile. The representative actor of a period is not necessarily the finest: the actors I choose to single out here for purposes of illustration are typical of social tendencies in their age; the greatly talented actor also reflects his time, but by virtue of his special faculties he usually has something which eludes and exceeds the common social framework. Most socially characteristic, perhaps, are the popular comedians and vaudevillians (Harrigan and Hart, Weber and Fields, Fanny Brice and so on). But to dwell on them, or on a Chaplin, who, properly understood, is history itself, would lead me too far afield.

President of the Players Club (Booth was the first, Jefferson the second), Drew played polished, sophisticated roles in what came to be known as "dress-suit" comedies. His appeal was greatest for what used to be called the carriage trade, but this group was looked up to by virtually all "average" citizens, because it reflected the specifically new flair of our urban prosperity. He was the top gentleman of our stage, and his appearance every Labor Day at the Empire Theatre marked the "official" opening of New York's theatrical season. He was the genteel hero of the later days of *Life With Father*.

Ethel Barrymore, with her combination of wit, grandeur and veiled pathos was also a great figure of the day, although in certain respects she transcended it, which was, generally speaking, the way of the Barrymores. The feminine essence of those still comparatively innocent years was Maude Adams, whose elfin charm, modesty and sweetness illustrate what well-brought-up Americans thought women should be. To a certain extent, Helen Hayes today is the last of the line to carry on this ideal.

Europe was approaching. Continental influences began to play a considerable role in the life of this period. On the educated level, Richard Mansfield (1857-1907), who was born in Germany and educated in England, showed this influence in a kind of colorfully and romantically eccentric manner by productions of plays like *Cyrano de Bergerac*, *A Parisian Romance* and *Peer Gynt*. The influx into the big cities of poor immigrants found its expression through such character actors as David Warfield and many of the highly gifted music-hall performers whose contact with the new audience was always closer than was common in the "legitimate" theatre. Nazimova, in those days, introduced the intriguing image of the strangely disturbing "exotic" woman of foreign derivation.

Then there were such socially emblematic performers as Lillian Russell and George M. Cohan and William Collier, who were stage types representing the jaunty, sporty, somewhat bottle-happy, small, successful business man—from the snappy salesman to the more firmly saddled executive. To many of us, these actors were for long the perfect image of the "average" American, product of a confident commercial civilization, without malice or doubt.

We are at the threshold of the Twenties—the climactic period of the theatre's success in America. John Barrymore's sudden emergence from 1916 to 1923 as a tragedian (from Galsworthy's *Justice* to *Hamlet*) forms the bridge from the old to the new. Behind the fine romantic brow there was in John Barrymore a painful hypertension, a nervous exasperation and a will to death which had hardly ever been present on the American stage before. This was the first truly "modern" note in our theatre, and it corresponds to the period of America's entry into the world drama of Western culture. For at this point, for all the hectic brilliance and gaiety of the day, the ominous notes of critical and sometimes desperate thinking were beginning to sound in our literature and our life.

On the stage, the Twenties was a time of women. This does not mean that there were no excellent actors, but there was a certain feminine tremor in the distress of most plays, as if the general problems of the day were seen through a woman's person. (The most "virile" of O'Neill's plays, *Desire Under the Elms*, was a play that harked back to the mid-nineteenth-century landscape.) The pattern of a Pauline Lord (*Anna Christie*, *They Knew What They Wanted*), with her half-finished impulses, her fluttering hands and her most casual remarks uttered in a voice that was a king of buried sob, bespoke an aspect of feeling never so magically exemplified in our theatre as in Laurette Taylor's performance in *The Glass Menagerie*. It corresponds to a sense of life that has been most thoroughly developed on our stage in the plays of Tennessee Williams.

The more routine theatrical convention was a type of glamorous neurotic—the beautiful, breached vessel of *The Green Hat*—as presented for a time by Katharine Cornell, whose enigmatic

mask, mysterious voice and suave movement had about them something luxuriously and old-fashionedly theatrical, brooding, chic and up-to-date all at the same time. The human struggle within Jeanne Eagels was more genuine, but she could not "take it" and she, like other such actresses, died before developing all her profound potentialities. Ina Claire, the actress who best revealed the smiling side of this womanly bewilderment, has, to all intents and purposes, retired.

Alfred Lunt was a sort of unconscious but extraordinarily talented compendium of all the tendencies of the Twenties. He was not as sharp or conscious of tragedy as Barrymore; he was softer, more "childlike," but still never without a certain vulnerability that was akin to a threatened heartbreak. He could indicate confusion amazingly well, particularly the confusion between simple emotion and the game of "smartness," the two poles between which many nice people in the Twenties were constantly careening. But just as Barrymore escaped to the movies, Lunt retreated from tragic depth and artistic experiment to ensconce himself in the safety of comedic virtuosity, where, with the brilliantly proficient Lynn Fontanne, he holds undisputed sway. This, too, was typical of the Twenties, which, in the main, flirted with stern realities and heroic enterprises, but stopped short of confronting true danger.

The foundations shook in the Thirties, the theatre was almost totally devastated, as was apparently the whole economic system. There was, in many respects, a real break with the past—the theatre no longer seemed central, and all tradition of loyalty to the theatre, to artistic discipline, to serious standards, seemed to be vanishing. The outstanding form of resistance to this seemed to come from the "barbarians" of the Group Theatre, with their lyrically gruff dedication to forthright expression of unvarnished protest, affirmation of hope and impassioned assertion of youthfully felt knowledge of right and wrong. The Group Theatre actors proclaimed a program for the theatre as the voice of real rather than ornamental experience. These actors attempted to organize their faith, their technique, their managerial administration. Their work bore fruit, but what is to be emphasized here is that their attempt was the concomitant of the general attempt to save something amid the breakdown of the depression—an effort which was to be observed in every field of endeavor—notably in government itself.

The war and the Forties with their haste, the need for new orientations and the shifting of the economic ground (the theatre suddenly became a prohibitively costly luxury) left everything undecided and the moral and artistic needs of the day somewhat vague. The Forties seemed to encompass elements of the Twenties with something of their monetary flush, the fervor of the Thirties and a blurred vision about practically everything. Aside from the need for victory and a subsequent readjustment after the victory, no one was sure of anything—a condition of uncertainty from which we have not yet recovered.

One of the uncertainties of our time is the condition of the theatre and acting itself. Actors do not remain on the stage long enough or appear in enough plays to become representative of anything beyond their momentary brilliance. They flash, and for most critical purposes, disappear. Even as we applaud a Rosalind Russell on the stage (another prize-winner)—and I could name others—we wonder how long, apart from the duration of her present vehicle, we shall be able to hold her and study her as a fixed star. We can never achieve a science of astronomy (or understanding of art) solely through an amazement over comets.

Under present circumstances, who can our representative stage figures be? In my opinion a new sort of "rough diamond"—Marlon Brando, Judy Holliday and, most emphatically, Shirley Booth. In our disturbances and disarray whom can we fundamentally trust! The warm-hearted person without too much bookish sophistication, the person open to experience and willing to learn—all instinct, eager to advance toward understanding

without theories or dogma, skeptical of anything unproved by the intimate daily demonstration of life.

"Classes" have been broken down and "tradition" is mostly highbrow jabber. The new type is just "folks," classless, plain-spoken with the complex commercial jargon of radio, night-club and television slang; pure in heart, wise in the small wonders of the street, anxious to believe but still puzzled, puzzled, puzzled—for the world is too big and there are so many lies in the air.

—*NYTM*, 17 May '53

CAN-CAN

In musical comedy I seek only a few good spots of sight and sound, an occasion to smile, and some pleasant people to watch. The purpose of the musical-comedy form is genial: how can one refrain from greeting it with cordiality? The spirit is what counts much more than the technique. When I like the approach, I like the show.

In *Can-Can* I particularly liked Michael Kidd's dance numbers, which by themselves were (almost) worth the price of admission. Kidd's talent is twinkling as well as energetic. No matter how strenuous the type of movement he may design, the effect has a friendly prankishness, a kind of benevolent teasing or good-natured and humorous mischievousness, always fundamentally delicate and light. In *Can-Can*, moreover, the dancers he has chosen—beginning with the attractive and versatile Gwen Verdon—form a lovable and amazingly agile group.

Not enough attention, it seems to me, or enough tribute is paid to the brilliant training and natural gifts which are shown by the virtually anonymous young people who make the ensemble of our musical shows. No other country possesses such groups in its popular theatre. In Europe these people would be regarded as artists; here, though they have far more craft background and prepare themselves with infinitely more hard work than most of our actors, they are more or less taken for granted as part of the new-fangled "chorus." Dance directors like Agnes de Mille, Jerome Robbins, Michael Kidd, and *their* teachers have made a real contribution to our theater not only through the dances they have staged but through the people they have discovered and helped develop.

—*NAT*, 23 May '53

FROM TEL-AVIV

Two recent experiences have made me think anew about the special nature of the theatre. When I saw *Peer Gynt* two weeks ago in Jerusalem it did not seem to me at all the same play I had seen on several previous occasions.

Though I flatter myself that I can differentiate more accurately than most theatergoers between the word text of a performance and its stage context, I must confess that had I written about Ibsen's play on the basis of my earlier views of it I should not have said any of the things I thought when I saw it recently. The productions were different—so the plays were different.

What, then, is a play? I am now inclined to say, though it may sound like a willful paradox, that there is no such thing as a play apart from its specific performance before an audience. The theatre is always spoken of with a certain deprecation—which I consider philosophically light-minded—as an ephemeral art. What is meant by this is that the only things that remain from a theatrical experience are a memory and a literary text. What strikes me now is that the theatre is even more ephemeral than we had supposed. The play we read in the library disappears in the theatre, absorbed in a context which not only transforms it but can never possibly be wholly the same on two successive occasions. And that, I believe, is an essential part of the theatre's power and glamor.

The book-minded are usually horrified at such a statement. What I am talking about, they may expostulate, are a few decorations, the addition of

living figures to the dramatist's writing, some paltry lights, colors, gewgaws—lamps by which we see the writer's work in what may be gayer and socially more stimulating circumstances than a reading provides. A play to such people is nothing but a text dolled-up.

This does not correspond to the facts. When we see a fool play Hamlet we are that evening in the presence of a foolish play. There is little point in terms of our actual experience to say that *Hamlet* is really a great play, because what we are doing is talking of something we discovered through an experience outside the theatre—which is merely supplementary information in relation to what we have directly perceived. Very few of the "classics" would seem good or even entirely intelligible to us if we came upon them as new plays.

It is certainly not Shakespeare's fault that his plays very often are turned into gibberish on the stage. It only stresses the fact that the play in the theatre is what we actually behold, not what we have read or may later read. The theatrical production has its own identity, always new, and creates its own meaning with every performance.

This momentarily disquieting concept becomes sharply distinct to a critic who also happens to be a director. Some years ago I wrote what many people thought disagreeably insensitive and impudent remarks about Shaw's *Caesar and Cleopatra.* (It is beside the point at the moment that Shaw some time after writing the play said things about it that showed he did not hold it in the same high esteem that most American reviewers do.) What I cannot avoid remarking is that whatever my feelings about the three productions of the play I have seen or about Shaw's script per se, I am now directing the play enthusiastically.

The question suggests itself: why should the critic's point of view be different from that of the director's, particularly when they are the same person? The reason is that the critic speaks only of what he sees on a particular occasion or what he judges the worth of the play text might be if he could possibly contemplate it apart from its production, or what he thought when he read it. The director sees the play script not as a piece of writing with a fixed value but as a *potential*.

The director asks: What can be pleasurable or important in the production of this text for the particular audience to whom I plan to present it? Some texts make better plays in one country than in another; often a text dies as a play in one house and lives in another. What actor, actress, or company will play this text? Have we not seen the life of a play alter through the acting of certain parts by equally talented but differently disposed artists? We have seen texts which might be described as trash from a literary standpoint become truly creative on the stage through the embodiment given them by extraordinarily talented actors or by a director. We remember texts becoming inept plays in the theatre through a so-called excellent (actually ruinous) set. We recall texts which failed to make an impression not because of intrinsic defects but because they did not suit the temper of the time chosen for their presentation.

For the theatre, the fine play on the shelf is only a promise and a hope. What makes a viable stage play is a most complex and miraculous set of circumstances toward which the director advances as to a calculated risk. It is, I repeat, part of the theatre's glory—as it is its very soul—that its delight, inspiration, aesthetic and cultural validity depend on a mysteriously fragile and happy concordance of elements.

—*NAT*, 11 July '53

LANGUAGE OF THE THEATRE

The question most frequently put to me about my work in Israel, where I am staging *Caesar and Cleopatra* in a Hebrew translation, is how a director can put on a play in a language of which he understands no more than a few words. It is not enough to reply that many members of the acting company understand English and that an interpreter translates the director's instructions for the

benefit of those who don't. The question is neither an individual nor a mechanical matter, but involves a fundamental problem of theatre art. How can the director know what is being said at each particular moment of the play, and how can he deal with the nuances of language and speech?

The question becomes particularly pertinent when we consider that Shaw's play is surely more important for its ideas and words than for its plot. Yet even in this case I find that because he was a playwright and not merely a pamphleteer, the problem of directing Shaw in a foreign language is not so difficult as it might seem.

I am glad to take up this problem because it necessitates a discussion of the nature of stage direction. Structurally a play is not a series of speeches but a series of actions. The first question a dramatist asks himself—and this is even truer of the director—is not what do the characters say as they enter the stage but what do they do, what do they intend to do, what do they succeed or fail to do in the course of the scene.

Take, for instance, the first speech of Act I in *Caesar and Cleopatra*—one of the most literary, as distinguished from dramatic, in the whole play: "Hail, Sphinx: salutation from Julius Caesar! I have wandered in many lands, seeking the lost regions from which my birth in this world has exiled me, etc., etc." It reads like the baldest sort of rhetorical exposition—a kind of exalted fanfare to set the tone and introduce the ethical motif underlying the horseplay which follows. Because the actor who plays Caesar usually thinks of his speech as a wordy introduction to the action proper I have often found the speech not only rather boring but hard to "catch on to"—the dignified words, apparently abstract, lull the spectator into a sort of lofty lethargy.

But if we think of the speech as an action we realize that Caesar, curious, eager, energetic, and always mentally alert, is studying the desert, seeking something in it to which he looks forward with the intense pleasure of a man who knows he confronts a great force with which he feels entirely capable of dealing. The riddle of life which the Sphinx represents is no profounder than Caesar's capacity to grasp it, for Caesar identifies himself with the Sphinx, sees it as something akin to himself.

Thus Caesar's speech is a self-explanation effected through an excited probing of the symbol of his own genius which he finds in the Sphinx. When Caesar asks, "Have I read your riddle, Sphinx?" he is glowing with an exultant pride and a (characteristically Shavian) sense of self-satisfaction. We almost anticipate, with Caesar, that the Sphinx will answer with a hearty "Ay!" and wink its approbation. Understood in this light, the scene is not only not oratorically static; it is all drama, that is, action.

Once the director discovers what happens in a scene not in obvious physical terms alone but in terms of the basic human action, the spoken words become instruments of that action and can be heard as such. (Deaf people, it is said, are often much more acute judges of acting than people who hear the words of a play for their surface meaning only, because the deaf try to see what is actually going on. When actors do no more than repeat words— that is, recite their lines—nothing is going on, and the stage under these circumstances becomes dull and theatrically uncommunicative.) The director chases actions for the actors to carry out as notes are set down for the musicians to play. If these notes are clear to the director, and the actors play them well, the director can hear as well as see them distinctly, no matter what language is being spoken.

What I am describing is not a figurative truth but a literal one. As rehearsals progress and the play's actions become ever more sharply defined by the actors' performance of them, my ear becomes increasingly attuned to the exactly proper pitch which their execution requires—visually, acoustically, and even phonetically. Thus without knowing Hebrew I not only can follow practically every word but can detect wrong emphases and even peculiarities or blemishes of accent. In other words, through familiarity with the specific theatri-cal actions of the play I am able to tell what actors have good and what actors have bad enunciation. The language of the theatre, in short, is not so much the language of the specific words being used as a kind of universal language of action; so that the correct use of speech in the theatre is not necessarily achieved by the person with the best diction but by the actor with the clearest dramatic intention.

—*NAT*, 25 July '53

ETHEL WATERS
TAKE A GIANT STEP

Seeing Ethel Waters in her one-woman show (at the Forty-eighth Street Theater) and *Take a Giant Step* with its largely Negro cast (at the Lyceum), I was reminded of a story told about Bernard Shaw in the thirties. A visiting American who went to see Shaw was asked by him about the progress and problems of our Federal Theater Project. The American reported that among other difficulties there was some trouble in certain cities over white actors who objected to appearing with colored ones. Shaw remarked that he didn't blame the white actors. The American gasped at this heresy. "What chance has a white actor with a Negro actor beside him ?" Shaw queried.

Negroes have a vividness and vitality on the stage all their own. They have in addition a remarkable sense of our spoken language, rare among any but a few Irish actors. English actors often speak well, but the excellence of their speech is more a matter of fine articulation and the design of sentences than gusto or the faculty to savor individual words. In the mouth of a good Negro actor English acquires a richness of timbre and a sensuousness which constitute the true music of speech.

Ethel Waters is a formidable woman. Above and beyond the peculiar racial characteristics, she possesses a wealth and depth of human experience more potent than talent itself. There are a goodly number of proficient actors on our stage, but precious few who are interesting people. And in acting, as in the other arts, real quality has its source and acquires significance through the human material from which it emerges. Ethel Waters strikes us not as a "performer" but as a force. She does not need to put anything over; she exists as an element. She is not "natural"; she is nature.

That is why I prefer her least "sensational" numbers. There are a purity of feeling and a subtlety of statement in her rendition of such spirituals as "Motherless Chile" and "Crucifixion"— which she retains in "Cabin in the Sky"—that surpass all her showmanship. In the other numbers she is tremendously clever, even when her vocal equipment fails her; in the spirituals she satisfies something greater than our need for entertainment.

Something of that purity, a reduction to the most artless terms of basic human sentiments, may be found in young Louis Peterson's first play *Take a Giant Step*, the portrayal of an eighteen-year-old Negro boy's first stumblings toward adult consciousness. It may be argued that this play offers nothing new: the scenes with the boy's parents, with the prostitutes, with his first woman, and with his white playmates—all these have been presented before in countless narratives of adolescence. Let those who argue in this vein be satisfied with the correctness of their statistics. They miss the point—and the pleasure. What is fresh and poignant in *Take a Giant Step* is the particular color, immediacy, and urgency of its feeling—a kind of emotional frankness, a wry naïveté, and a rough goodness of heart that smack of something truly native, original in tone, and unmistakably lived.

That there are awkward, unfulfilled, and possibly even trite moments disturbs me very little. O'Casey isn't as adroit as Coward; O'Neill isn't as smart as the writers of our entertainment industries. Plays like *Take a Giant Step* enhance our understanding and love of American life. It is perhaps only a seed, but from such seeds flowers may grow. Most of show business is only window dressing. Our aversion to crudity in the theatre is not a sign of taste; it is a commercial vice— inspired by the psychology of ticket agents and booking offices.

Though uneven, the production of *Take a Giant Step* is basically sound. Its most accomplished actor is Frederick O'Neal, a man of unusual resources, but unfortunately his part here is small. Jane White is handsome and distinguished. Practically everyone in the cast is sympathetic. In the central role Louis Gossett is particularly winning in his quieter and more relaxed moments. He does not command enough craftsmanship to manage the whole range of his difficult part with easy elasticity. But he gives us a warm sense of honesty and cleanness of spirit— invaluable assets in a play of this kind. One leaves the theatre with the reassuring impression that there are still some sensitive and healthy folk among us. Too often we are oppressed by a feeling of being surrounded by abominably suave salesmen and tricksters.

—*NAT*, 10 Oct. '53

THE STRONG ARE LONELY
TEA AND SYMPATHY

From a trade angle there would seem to be little point now in reviewing *The Strong Are Lonely*, which closed after seven performances. But the play was patently superior to most shows we see— including many successes. Apart from an insufficiently integrated production, *The Strong Are Lonely* failed because its subject matter, though based on a fundamentally universal theme, is foreign to our theatre audiences.

Religion in our country is not only separate from the state; it is separate from our lives. The religious impulse, as well as certain consequences of religious training, certainly enters into our thinking and behavior more than we commonly suppose, but we are not used to viewing religion as an active, practical central force of our daily concern. In Europe, where the church has played a vital part in the development of states and cultures, where today there are important parties which to a large extent are secular functions of the church, vying for control of the bodies as well as the minds of entire nations, the problems posed in *The Strong Are Lonely* are almost topical.

To put it as baldly as possible, what Fritz Hochwalder's play—originally called *On Earth as in Heaven*—asks are the age-old questions: Can Christianity serve as a practical doctrine? Can there be a truly Christian state? More specifically, can the church, in the light of the original Gospel, function as a radical or revolutionary political agent? Must the church deal only with men's souls or can it face all man's problems, including the social? Shall the church merely render unto Caesar what is Caesar's?

Hochwalder's play depicts the trials of a Jesuit Father Provincial who wishes to make Christianity a living force on every level of man's activity. As such it is an absorbing and impressive work, though its ending is ambiguous, sentimental, and probably evasive. As a piece of theatre it is unusual and dramatically sturdy in a near-classic vein. It is a pity that it could not be produced here under conditions more favorable to a cordial hearing than those afforded by the Broadway system.

Tea and Sympathy (Barrymore Theater) is a totally successful play because it deals with a theme which has a strong appeal to our audiences and because it is extremely well produced.

I speak of the play's theme, although I was not altogether sure at first what the theme was. Perhaps it would be more accurate to say that the play tells an interesting story which suggests a number of themes none of which are emphasized or probed at any particular depth. The story is that of a sensitive prep-school boy who on very slight evidence is suspected of being a homosexual. The suspicion is furthered because the boy is a shy, introspective adolescent given to playing the guitar, "long-haired" music, and discussion of plays like *Candida*. The main theme therefore is a defense of the special person in a society which tends to look askance at the "odd" individual, even the unpremeditated non-conformist. If the play has a message, it is to the effect that a boy like its protagonist may be more truly a man than those falsely rugged folk who oppress him.

The play also cautions us against prejudice, slander, and false accusation—in a word, is a plea for tolerance. Naturally, we are all for it: every contribution in this direction is more than welcome. Yet in this regard I cannot help thinking that we have arrived today at a peculiar brand of tolerance. We tolerate the innocent! We say "this person who is accused of being off-beat—socially, sexually, or politically—is not guilty; we must therefore be tolerant." If he is guilty, should we then tear him to bits? I should prefer to see a play in which, let us say, a homosexual is shown to be a genuinely worthwhile person and the persecution that he suffers is presented as a disease within ourselves.

This thought leads me to another. In our theatre we are forever beginning all over again. When O'Neill wrote his early plays, we felt we had come of age: we were now free to speak as forthrightly as any of the Europeans. We could be not only frank but, if we pleased, savage or pessimistic. Though now easily acceptable, a play like *Tea and Sympathy* is probably still regarded by many as adventurous and advanced, though it is actually primitive in its theme, characterization, and story development. It is, in fact, a very young play.

This is no adverse comment on it. It is the work of a young playwright, Robert Anderson, whose approach is honorably craftsmanlike and humane. He has been greatly aided by Elia Kazan's production, which represents our professional best. Everything is done with admirable meticulousness and theatric acumen by a finely chosen cast.

Deborah Kerr is beautiful to behold as well as gratifyingly warm and simple. John Kerr is a real find—a delicate, intelligent, handsome, and virile young man. Leif Ericson, who plays the rather obnoxious and underwritten part of a bully-boy husband, is an excellent character actor whose work in pictures is generally an abuse of his talent. All the others, notably John McGovern, are completely right. Mr. Kazan has rendered his author and actors a true service.

—*NAT*, 17 Oct. '53

VICTOR BORGE
THE LITTLE HUT

To put it as succinctly as possible, Victor Borge's one-man show, which he calls *Comedy in Music* (Golden Theater), made me laugh, while André Roussin's *The Little Hut* (Coronet Theater) did not. Yet I have more to say about *The Little Hut* than about Victor Borge.

The success of the Danish-American comic is easy to explain: he is spontaneous, facile, witty—a showman, a clown, and an observer (he imitates pianistic idiosyncrasies marvelously well)—and yet he remains natural and comparatively normal, a rare quality among our native comics, who generally turn to the grotesque. Borge has learned a few American tricks from night clubs and TV, as evidenced by his manner of dishing it out, but what he serves is unusual in its Continental sophistication and sauciness.

The Little Hut, though less than a trifle, has begun to bother me as if it were a problem. I have seen it three times: once in Paris with Fernand Graver, again in London with Robert Morley, and now in New York with its least suitable cast. The play was enormously successful in Paris and London, but I confess that in both these places it amused me almost as little as here.

It is a truism of the theatre that what makes a play, together with the written text, is the actors and, most important, the audience. For if what you have on the stage is not compatible in its premises, atmosphere, and total spirit with the audience's *mores*, assumptions, and modes of mind and feeling, you have no play. That is why it is unlikely that Racine, Goethe, Strindberg, even Pirandello will ever be popular in this country. What is true on this high level is even truer on less exalted levels.

In Paris *The Little Hut* was a somewhat smutty joke—the story deals with a husband and lover who decide to share the wife's favors on alternate weeks during their stay on a desert island where they have been stranded. Jokes about so classical—that is, common and recognizable—a situation as the sexual triangle are welcome to the Parisian theatre audience. But whereas sex—which the Parisian playwright is pleased to call *l'amour*—is an accredited institution in the French theatre, it is not, so to speak, officially received in London. For sex to be admitted and enjoyed by the London theatergoer, he must believe that its existence on the stage is somehow or other fictitious.

Robert Morley's performance in the London version of *The Little Hut* was a triumph of comic make-believe over sex. He simply eliminated it. He was delightfully neuter. He made the whole show into a sort of zany fable having only an oblique and charmingly distorted relation to reality. Oliver Messel's highly stylized setting—a fashionably "primitive" tropical island that looked like a combination of children's book illustration and a travel ad in a smart-set magazine—seemed like the natural habitat for the play's characters.

In the New York production the actors play as English drawing-room comedians, and though the drawing-room is also a theatrical convention, it is too close to actuality to make the play acceptable to us. If it is taken as real it is slightly offensive; if it is taken as spoof it is too long and arduous to be funny. If the joke is supposed to be on the British upper middle class, as at moments it seems to be in the present production, it becomes unbelievable in any vein.

For myself, I find I can take stage sex for its general human or its sensual, sentimental, violent, and sometimes even obscene values; I cannot take it denatured—as mere entertainment. I find Feydeau's farce *Take Care of Amélie* completely engaging in its mingling of crazy ingenuity, social satire, and wickedly frank sexuality. I find fun in Mae West's vulgarly arch play-acting or lampoon of sex in *Diamond Lil*. With a little effort I can be indulgent toward the coyness of *The Moon Is Blue* and benevolent toward the fantasies and fears implied in *The Seven Year Itch*, but I have always been bored with *The Little Hut*, in which sex is treated as if it didn't matter.

—*NAT*, 24 Oct. '53

TEAHOUSE OF THE AUGUST MOON

*T*he *Teahouse of the August Moon* by John Patrick—based on a novel by Vern Sneider—is a hit at the Martin Beck Theater. Of some plays there seems to be little more to say than this. Public and press are so pleased to come upon something agreeable, or at least totally unburdensome, that the sound of their rejoicing renders any further manifestation practically unnecessary, not to say undesirable.

My own reflections on this are only supplementary to the fact. *The Teahouse of the August Moon* is a hit because it is entirely pleasant, benign, and sweet. Didn't William Dean Howells once say that the smiling aspects of life seemed to be the more American? There is something almost traditionally American, or rather American theatre, about *The Teahouse*. It is about the army in a state of peace, it shows us friendly to the innocent natives of a remote culture (occupied Okinawa), its satire of army brass is gentle in the vein of a *Saturday Evening Post* cover caricature—it is good-natured, liberal, and constantly indulgent.

In addition to this, it is delicately colorful: the exoticism lies not only in the subject matter but in the manner of presentation, which is loose, easygoing, and vaguely reminiscent of Oriental tints and pictures, which—one cannot be sure—are either authentic or merely decoratively conventional

simulacra. Robert Lewis's direction is playful and relaxed. A good company—David Wayne, John Forsythe, Paul Ford, William Hansen, and Larry Gates—acts neatly within the scheme designed by the director.

What I like most about the show is that it has a fresh or at least a different look. The clean, almost empty stage with its few odd props and the piquant countenances of a largely Japanese cast are a nice relief from the usual well-made light comedy located in the penthouse of a chic apartment.

The show, in short, is entirely unobjectionable. I do not agree with some of my friends who found it obliquely patronizing to the obscure folk it deals with. It has a story-book and American picaresque tone in which reality is kept at a greater distance than in a fairy tale: its flavor is that of a kindly and limply bemused joke. The writing is journalese, the fable almost immaterial, and the creative content minimal. It is candy concocted with some originality, and easy to take.

What worries me—and this, I repeat, after the fact—is that when it is recommended as a hit, one wonders why so little else is said about it. One asks oneself whether the audience which applauds it doesn't really prefer above all else the totally unobjectionable, uncontroversial, undisturbing, the thoroughly bland.

We used to talk about plays for the tired business man, which perhaps implied that only business men were tired. One begins to suspect that now we are all tired. We agree with those who insist that the theatre should be primarily entertainment. But one is a little perturbed by the thought that we are mostly entertained by things that give our faculties so little exercise. It is perfectly normal to like what is sweet; but must our pabulum contain nothing more than what might please a child? There is a point at which the youngest and tenderest among us must work a little to grow and be healthy. Entertainment and sugared pap ought not to be considered synonymous.

Our reviewers are not to blame. They praise plays like *End as a Man*, they are not generally unkind to things like *Take a Giant Step* or *The*

Strong Are Lonely, and though they frown severely at the inadequacies, presumed and real, of plays like Lillian Hellman's *The Autumn Garden* or Odets's *Rocket to the Moon*, there is something in the way our theatre audiences receive the reviews which makes it seem that there are two sharply contrasted categories of dramatic entertainment—hits and other shows. The second category may include the work of our best writers: these are discussed with all their shortcomings soberly detailed, so that serious people may go to see them if they care to (with due forbearance in regard to the "faults"), while the hits are apparently something that everyone *must see*. The audience that attends the first kind of play goes forewarned; the audience that sees the second goes with the comforting assurance that what it is about to see is hardly to be questioned—it is in fact beyond criticism. The first kind of play usually struggles to keep on the boards; the second is celebrated as a "smash" the moment the press has given the signal, that is, defined the category.

It may be humorless of me to say so, but I am convinced that such a situation spells death to the theatre. The critic is not necessarily an educator, and he probably should not be a propagandist; yet I would be grateful to the man who would constantly tell his readers that while the "faulty" plays—such as those by O'Casey, O'Neill, Odets, and the like—are part of the essential theatre, a great number of the hits, though good to have, are expendable. For entertainment in the sense of titillation is more readily and cheaply come by outside the theatre.

—*NAT*, 31 Oct. '53

THE TRIP TO BOUNTIFUL

How difficult our reviewers have become! They demand impeccable workmanship, masterful literary quality, sovereign artistry. A play with a valid theme, respectable writing, and good acting is slighted on the ground that it is not a "perfect play." Which are the perfect plays? The much-admired plays of O'Casey are far from perfect—and are almost never produced. The "perfect" plays are usually plays by dead playwrights—also rarely produced and successful in our theatre only when "name" actors appear in them, at which times they are discussed as vehicles rather than as plays.

Are we, then, to conclude that only plays which receive unanimously glowing notices, like *The Teahouse of the August Moon* or *Tea and Sympathy*, are the perfect plays? Surely the reviewers do not mean that these plays are perfect—only that they are very nice. The perfect plays—those by Ibsen, Chekhov, Synge, for example—are not very nice, were not so considered when they were first produced, and their contemporary parallels—presuming they exist—would probably not be received with unanimous approval today. There is something wrong somewhere.

The trouble is not that reviewers disagree—this is natural, inevitable, and not necessarily deplorable; the trouble is that no one can be sure of what any of the reviewers are talking about, except that they are pleased or displeased. Values are not made explicit, standards are not defined, prejudices and attitudes of mind are not clarified or defended.

The Trip to Bountiful, by the young Southern playwright Horton Foote (Henry Miller Theater), is criticized for being flatly written, monotonous, and over-extended. On the other hand, Lillian Gish's performance in the central role is highly praised. While all these comments may be substantiated to a greater or lesser degree, their total makes very little critical sense to me.

It is not theatrically sound to speak of a very fine piece of acting as if it were happening in one place, and to speak of the play as if it were to be found somewhere on the shelf of a library several blocks away. True, it is possible, though not always easy, to distinguish among the ingredients of a theatrical production, but they can hardly be departmentalized and pigeon-holed as our reviewers generally attempt to do. If, let us say, a Josephine Hull is less brilliant in *Whistler's Grandmother* than in *The Solid Gold Cadillac*, the difference cannot be explained entirely in terms of the actress.

Lillian Gish seems to me better in *The Trip to Bountiful* than in any other play in which I have seen her. That does not mean, however, that it is the best play in which she has ever appeared. But this little play has an arresting theme and authenticity of feeling and observation, and is at least in the vein of creative expression.

The play tells the story of an elderly lady who wishes to return to the small, now deserted village in which she was born, return even for a brief moment from Houston, Texas, which to her represents the arid mechanization of the big city. Her son and daughter-in-law are denatured specimens of the humanity which the city produces. Contact with land—the earth itself—bespeaks human dignity to the old lady, a dignity she feels she, along with her son and his wife, no longer have. The theme, in short, is our loss of roots in the transition to the industrialized society we live in. The theme, though real enough, is not one that occurs to us often in the homely terms employed by Mr. Foote, because we who go to the theatre have acquired mental habits which reflect a horizon that seems to be bounded on the south by Forty-second Street and on the north by Columbus Circle.

I found the play touching, the characters well drawn, and very well acted not only by Miss Gish but by Jo Van Fleet, Gene Lyons, and the others. I was quite able to bear the play's faults and to be interested throughout, because I heard a sensitive voice communicating something honestly felt. I do not need entertainment to *kill* me. When a neighbor whispered to me during the course of the play, "Don't you think it's too long?" I felt like retorting. "What have you got to do that makes you so impatient?"

—*NAT*, 21 Nov. '53

A MODERN MASTER
(*Aaron Copland* by Arthur Berger)

Music criticism is the most difficult form of criticism. For with music one is, as Anatole France said of esthetics in general, in the clouds. The impressionist is easily tempted to swift departures from the music itself to vaporous realms of conjecture and hyperbole. Technical commentators usually confine themselves to the notation of what one has already heard, a skeletonizing process which takes little account of music's very essence—its texture and spirit. No wonder the annals of music criticism are generally divided between unreliable swooners and unreadable musicologists.

Yet criticism, even music criticism, is inevitable and, believe it or not, necessary. Music is more than effect: it is also a content. We are prone to respond to art works, particularly music, in terms of their ingratiating effect, rarely in terms of meaning. The sound critic is one who attempts to disengage the meaning of the effects which the art work seems to produce. The closer the critic comes to capturing the spirit of the artist, that is, penetrating into the artist's world and making its spirit clear and more significant to us, the more valuable is the critic's contribution to our understanding.

One of the chief merits of Arthur Berger's little monograph, *Aaron Copland*, is its attempt to relate the more popular or readily acceptable of the composer's work to the more difficult work. "Since you get pleasure out of the effect of Copland's folk pieces ("El Salon Mexico," "Rodeo," "Appalachian Spring," etc.)" Mr. Berger appears to be saying, "won't you please take the trouble to realize the true meaning of these pieces by listening more and patiently to those of Mr. Copland's pieces the pleasurable effect and value of which may at first elude you." For Mr. Berger rightly insists that the two Coplands—the popular and the reputedly esoteric—are the same man, and that to "root" for one against the other or to dismiss the one because of the other are equally superficial attitudes.

The first part of Mr. Berger's book deals with Copland the man. It is a concise biographical sketch—not ample enough to constitute a portrait, but sufficient as an introduction. The second section of the book is composed of a very brief description of the sound and "appearance" of Copland's music—its leanness and slenderness which go with a certain economy of means characteristic of Copland both as an artist and man.

Every page of Mr. Berger's book implies that Aaron Copland is an important American artist. This well-tempered composer is a man whose creation synthesizes the tension between the loneliness, isolation, and desire for withdrawal a sensitive person must feel in our stony and increasingly joyless society with the equally strong impulse to affirm and assert with humor and an irrepressible vivacity the age-old aspirations of humankind. Copland is no romantically grandiloquent yea-sayer. Classic in temperament and in his assimilation of all the positive tendencies—artistic and social—of the contemporary world, his music expresses a resignation which eliminates defeat and a humility which need not fear the consequences of courage. In his own way Copland is writing a latter-day variation on the Beethoven motto, "Must it be?" "Yes, it must be."

—*SR*, 28 Nov. '53

PORGY AND BESS

I enjoyed the new production of *Porgy and Bess* very much. In a sense, there is little more to say about it, not only because it has become a kind of classic, but because the quality of its emotion is one which communicates itself easily and directly, and one accepts it without critical cavil.

Gershwin's music has a certain smart sophistication, but its outstanding characteristic, it seems to me, is warm sentiment or a kind of yearning for sentiment. It is as if a skillful popular composer were trying to reach some area of feeling beyond the clatter and glister of "Broadway's" surface, an area purer, richer, more tender than what others were satisfied with.

Everyone in the twenties seemed to be dizzied by the brilliant energy and prosperity of the times, but the more sensitive found themselves lonely and wistful. They were "a-lookin' for a home"—a safe place amid the surrounding jungle in which there might be some repose, sweetness, heart. The music of *Porgy and Bess* voices that quest. It is no accident that George Gershwin, who was Jewish, should have found the material for his masterpiece in what amounts to a Negro folk tale—and that the combination, with the aid of the highly gifted lyrics of Ira Gershwin, should have a lasting appeal for all Americans.

For me the most characteristic numbers in *Porgy and Bess* are not the gay and witty "It Ain't Necessarily So," which has a significantly mock-heroic aspect, or "A Woman Is a Sometime Thing," but the love duets, "Bess, You Is My Woman Now" and "I Loves You, Porgy." They are almost hymns of longing, expressions of desire which transcend their personal objects.

The new production has admirable *brio* and fine touches of color. It is genuinely lively. That its exuberance is sometimes indiscriminate and that the storm scene is awkwardly staged—owing to the scenic arrangement—seem to me minor faults. The director, Robert Breen, is to be congratulated, as is most of the cast. Leslie Scott's Porgy is unaffected and affecting. Leontyne Price as Bess is vocally lovely as well as otherwise attractive, and while Cab Calloway does not make one forget Avon Long's electric Sportin' Life, he (Calloway) has a "classy" musical style which inspires his delivery of the numbers and his acting.

—*NAT*, '53

THE PRESCOTT PROPOSALS
OH MEN! OH WOMEN!
IN THE SUMMER HOUSE

There is an element of topicality and even of propaganda in almost all our current stage successes. *The Prescott Proposals* by Howard Lindsay and Russel Crouse (Broadhurst Theater), for instance, is about the U. N. and international relations: what it means to suggest is that we must not despair of achieving peace, for even the Soviet Russians are human.

But there is so much fear of propaganda among us—while at the same time we remain too moral, idealistic, and practical a people to forgo it altogether—that the propaganda in our plays remains cautious, watered down, and oblique and serves only as a condiment of entertainment rather than as a substance.

Hence it would be simple-minded to speak of *The Prescott Proposals* in terms of social values. Its liberalism provides a slight breeze, but its basic atmosphere is that of a well-mannered melodrama for middle-aged middle-class ladies. It is neatly carpentered, handsomely mounted, well cast—Ben Astar as the Soviet delegate is particularly good—and it brings us Katharine Cornell, as the delegate from the United States, in her perhaps most "realistic" role.

Miss Cornell is not a realistic actress. Hers is a kind of fictional-romantic stage personality, often arresting and glamorous, with a late-nineteenth-century American nostalgia for figures of the theatre and novel of an even earlier epoch. On stage she seems always to be visiting the twentieth century from another realm and another era on a two-hour passport—with only a vague relationship to such humdrum objects as telephones, typewriters, taxis. For this reason her performance in *The Prescott Proposals* is a welcome change—surprisingly and agreeably rooted as it is in the commonplace.

Though the "propaganda" is less obvious in Edward Chodorov's *Oh Men! Oh Women!* (Henry Miller's Theater) we cannot fail to recognize the play's topicality: it deals with psychoanalysis. It is suitably modest on the subject, but it is clearly liberal in its attitude toward a matter about which on the stage and in certain social circles it is usually considered smart to be slightly contemptuous. Its main assets are that it is steadily funny without being gross, and that it is excellently played by Franchot Tone, Larry Blyden, Henry Sharp, Anne Jackson, Gig Young, and the others—all of whom are vivid, ingratiatingly deft, and comically real. Franchot Tone, whose role—that of the earnest, intelligent, and bewildered doctor—is the least grateful of all, is an actor who should be kept in the theatre to play the more ambitious parts for which his ample and subtle gifts endow him.

There is nothing propagandistic or topical in Jane Bowles's *In the Summer House* (Playhouse), which is not the only reason I prefer it to most of the plays I have seen this season. Its author has an original writing talent and a not at all stock sensibility. It may even be deemed a paradox that I like the earlier or wackier part of the play better than the last part, in which the characters are resolved with the aid of a little off-the-cuff psychoanalysis.

The better part of the play—in which an eccentrically proper and severely determined mother berates her perpetually retreating daughter—is written with a kind of airy freedom, humor, and, from the standpoint of conventional stage-craft, unrelatedness; is in fact truthful, sharp, and wittily poignant. Miss Bowles does not trouble to explain why her characters are so fey; those of us who live by labels are tempted to call either the characters or the author willfully perverse or neurotic. But if we listen to them without preconceptions, we understand them very well. Only at the end, when we are favored with an explanation—the mother has a father fixation and has destroyed the daughter's will by reenacting the father's role, thus giving the daughter a mother fixation—do we feel let down, both because the explanation explains nothing and because it is less amusing, moving, and perceptive than what we have seen.

Our contemporary theatre is half dead with "reasons." *Tea and Sympathy* is clear; *Hamlet* is not. The aimless dialogue, the sadly abstract atmosphere of the first part of *In the Summer House*, is lovely, colorful, and strangely evocative: it spins a melody of the trivial and "pointless" which emanates from the semi-consciousness of rather ordinary folk with a primitive directness that is essentially poetic. But where the poetic in the theatre is not sustained by rational crutches, we tend to feel lost and when lost to become irritable.

In the Summer House is a kind of wryly comic lyric poem in a minor key. Its music is that of people isolated in a social world which exists statistically—as a department store exists—but not spiritually in a truly human context. Such people become weird—both sad and funny—and their number far exceeds the few queer creatures Mrs. Bowles presents; or, to put it bluntly, aren't we all?

The play is well produced. The director, José Quintero, has the knack of creating a sort of azure ineffability of mood. Oliver Smith's settings have quality, though I believe they might have been given a little more "surprise," made a little more oddly gay. Judith Anderson, who frequently tends toward too rhetorical a theatricality, has injected into her performance traits of humor and down-to-earth simplicity which are virtually new to her style. Only at the end does she err in the direction of the nobly tragic, a vein foreign to the script—just as the writing itself, I repeat, is at this point tritely psychological.

The most interesting performance of the production is that of Mildred Dunnock as the forever unloved woman whose pathos is mixed with an exhilarating dash of rough comedy. Her drunk scene, in itself an excellent piece of writing, in which the somewhat mad lady she plays drives a "normal" and average waitress—hilariously done by Jean Stapleton—crazy, is one of the best bits of the season.

—*NAT*, 16 Jan. '54

RENEÉ "ZIZI" JEANMAIRE

Several seasons ago when the Ballets de Paris made their American debut, the orthodox dance reviewers were distinctly snooty about the remarkable *Carmen* presented by that company—despite the presence on the stage of one of the most dazzling stage personalities of our day as well as a stage design which was a masterpiece. *Carmen* was apparently not "true dance." Those dramatic critics who attended the occasion seemed equally unimpressed, despite or because of the fact that it was real theatre.

Now that Renée (or "Zizi") Jeanmaire—the outstanding discovery of the Ballets de Paris—is appearing in a singularly inept musical comedy, *The Girl in Pink Tights* (Mark Hellinger Theater), professional theatergoers are hailing her as the toast of the town. Well, better late than never. Only I could not help regretting as I watched *Pink Tights* that regular theatergoers seem to attend the ballet so infrequently—though ballet is nearly always the best theatre to be seen in New York.

For that matter, I mused, it is a pity that so few habitual theatergoers care for music—I have yet to meet a dramatic critic at a concert!—and almost none of them, it appears, care for painting or sculpture.

Jeanmaire is delightfully disturbing, adorably exciting, with a body which is fascinatingly female though its lines are distinctly not those admired in Hollywood. One might speak of her witty, profoundly knowing eyes—brilliant with the crackling wisdom of Parisian streets—eyes set in a head that is a sort of epigram of twentieth-century feminine charm. But all this—even if it were better said—and the considerable technical accomplishment which Jeanmaire's dancing represents hardly explain why Jeanmaire is so alluring and endearing on the stage. Some may think her too slight or too much like the kind of young boy the French refer to as an *éphèbe*—although for all her leanness there is nothing unhealthy in the effect she creates—but the essence of Jeanmaire's hold on the audience is what for want of a more accurate phrase I should call the *rhythm of talent.*

Jeanmaire seems like the embodiment of that mysterious beat or quickening impulse which wherever we find it transforms matter into meaning, acts as a leaven in the inert substance of which most objects are composed. When Jeanmaire rises on her toes, as soon as she begins to move, even to the turn of her head, our breast is constricted with anticipation, our attention is focused, we become alert, concentrated, we begin to seek—we come alive.

How sad that this animating charge of vitality should be entombed in such a mountain of rubbish as the present show. Despite the collaboration of a number of capable actors and designers and the assistance of the ever-gifted Agnes de Mille, one is almost tempted to skip the entire event. Of course, there is nothing so usual as bad entertainment, and a less than mediocre evening in the theatre is no cause for alarm, but one is always uncertain whether it wouldn't be better to pass over such occasions in discreet silence to avoid all further discomfort. That is what I feel obliged to do from time to time—is criticism actually in order simply because a mistake has been publicly made?—but how can one pass Jeanmaire by without recording the gasp of one's rapture.

—*NAT*, 20 Mar. '54

THE THREEPENNY OPERA

Kurt Weill's and Bert Brecht's *The Threepenny Opera* is a masterpiece; in its present production at the Theatre de Lys it very nearly misses fire.

The Threepenny Opera—called that because it is so oddly conceived that it might be a beggar's dream and so cheaply done that it might meet a beggar's budget—sums up a whole epoch and evokes a special state of fraud. The epoch is not just the Berlin of 1919-28; it is any epoch in which a lurid rascality combined with fierce contrasts of prosperity and poverty shapes the dominant tone of society. The state of mind is one of social impotence so close to despair that it expresses itself through a kind of jaded mockery which mingles a snarl with tears. Such in a way was the England of John Gay's *Beggar's Opera* (1728), from which the Brecht "book" derives, and certainly the Germany which preceded Hitler. No wonder the one period produced Hogarth and the other George Grosz.

We do not live in such a time—though people who remember the depression days between 1930 and 1935 will appreciate the mood of *The Threepenny Opera* most readily—but it makes the mood irresistibly present and, strangely enough, induces us to take it to our hearts with a kind of pained affection. There is, despite the sharp sense of period that permeates it, a universal quality in *The Threepenny Opera.* It fosters a bitter sense of regret that we live so scabbily in relation to our dreams and also a kind of masochistic attachment to our wounds, as if they were all we have to show as evidence of our dreams.

This effect is achieved through Brecht's brilliant lyrics rendered with remarkable intuitive insight and witty skill in Marc Blitzstein's adaptation—and through the one score Weill composed which places him on the level of an Offenbach. What bite and tang, what insidious irony, in the clean thrusts of Brecht's verses; what economy and lightness in Weill's songs and orchestration. How poignant is the sullied lyricism of this work with its jeering bathos, its low-life romanticism, its sweetly poisonous nostalgia, its musical profanity, and its sudden hints of grandeur, godliness, and possible greatness. Here in contemporary terms and with a strange timelessness is the ambiguous, corrupt seduction of a submerged half-world akin to that which François Villon sang of long ago.

How disappointing, then, to have so unique a work—acclaimed practically everywhere since its premiere in 1928—reduced to a minor event by so ill-prepared a performance as the one we now see.

Except for Lotte Lenya, who appeared in the original production, the cast ranges from the amateurish to the adequate. Lenya's nasally insinuating whore is superb for its incisiveness and triple-threat innuendo. But the fault is not the actors'—most of whom could do much better—but the director's. Everything seems labored and awkward instead of sprightly and bright. The miracle is that the inherent superiority of the material survives all hazards.

—*NAT*, 27 Mar. '54

ANNIVERSARY WALTZ
BY THE BEAUTIFUL SEA

Supposing a man ran a prosperous notion shop where, among other things, he sold kewpie dolls and fancy chromos. Imagine someone advising him to increase his trade by such publicity as an art critic might be able to give him. Then imagine the art critic coming and being obliged to deliver an opinion on what he saw. Would it help business—or art criticism—if the unfortunate fellow reported that the dolls were inferior to Tanagra statuettes and the postcards not up to the work of Raoul Dufy?

In most European cities there are state theatres, avant-garde theatres, fashionable art theatres, low-down theatres, and general commercial theatres. Entering any one of these theatres, one knows the frame of mind which befits the occasion. With us, practically all theatre works are placed, so to speak, on the same shelf. This is a little confusing for the critic and very bad for business.

What is one to say about a play like *Anniversary Waltz* (Broadhurst Theater)? Shall one compare it to the same authors' (Jerome Chodorov and Joseph Fields) earlier plays—*Junior Miss*, and the others? Those plays were huge successes. It is sometimes held that a play's box-office success is none of the critic's business. I am not so sure. The theatre is a social and collective art, and the audience is a vital—perhaps a prime—factor in its composition.

That there is an audience for a play is not an inconsiderable clue to the play's character; one must be certain, however, to define the nature of that audience. It would be altogether reasonable for a critic to say, "There are thousands of people who will cheer the play which opened last night but I am not one of them. I wouldn't like it even if it were good." Few critics care to place themselves in so "undemocratic" a position. Under these circumstances they are obliged to talk as if they are capable of liking everything "as long as it's good of its kind"—from every standpoint an untenable and misleading position.

Anniversary Waltz is a domestic-relations farce—a sort of stage soap opera. There are jokes about kids who go to progressive school, about papas who detest TV in families who adore it, about in-laws and other aspects of marital relations. On the second night in New York the greater part of the audience laughed uproariously—though several of the reviewers had been severe with it. I have no opinion. I can only report that in one scene Howard Smith as the father-in-law tickled me. I hasten to warn my readers not to attach too much importance to that fact.

It is different with musicals. The very idea of a musical puts most of our New York audiences into a receptive mood. At a "straight" play the audience, unless it has been discouraged by poor notices, is more or less willing to be convinced. At a musical, unless the notices have been positively dreadful, the audiences are happily convinced the moment the band strikes up for the overture.

By the Beautiful Sea (Majestic Theater) is not very much better as a musical than *Anniversary Waltz* is as a farce. But the musical has the advantage of specialty numbers, of scenic variety, and, in this case, of Shirley Booth.

Besides Miss Booth, *By the Beautiful Sea* boasts the delightfully easy and rhythmic Mae Barnes—she is smoothly unemphatic and most satisfyingly precise—and a wittily imaginative bit staged by Tamiris which is a sort of dance-pantomime of the spicy pictures in the old-time penny arcades. There is a saucy and attractively full-bodied dancer named Gaby Monet. The audience also enjoys an effect devised by Jo Mielziner in which a shadowy light gliding along the lines of a scenic railway painted on the backdrop indicates the movement of its cars. It is a quite naïve effect, but it provokes a childlike response of pleasure. When a charming little colored boy (Robert Jennings) dances with Miss Booth (dressed in white) all audience resistance dissolves.

As for Shirley Booth—who makes her plain-Jane quality into something not only reassuring, comforting, and winning but altogether theatrical in a healthy and almost nostalgically old-fashioned way—there remains little more to be said except that she's awfully good. It is amazing how she can make such lines as "I'm a good eater" or "She's brought up lousy" sound clever and heart-warming. She is a superbly effortless professional, and the notion of setting her in the Coney Island of the early 1900's is smart showmanship.

If *By the Beautiful Sea*, while remaining essentially undistinguished, succeeds in being enjoyable, it proves what several dashes of performance skill and genial color will do for a show.

—*NAT*, 24 Apr. '54

ON ANOTHER VIEWING

One need not go as far as George Brandes, but one knows what he meant when he wrote, "If a book isn't worth reading twice, it isn't worth reading at all." With music and with painting one has been made well aware that first hearing and first view are rarely sufficient for a correct, not to speak of a definitive, impression. I am foolhardy enough to suggest at a time when many educated people do not go to the theatre at all that we begin to see the better plays more than once.

We may well repeat a visit to a play which we had difficulty in appreciating at the first go. Within recent memory some of the reviewers have gone a second time to Rodgers and Hart's *Pal Joey*, Maxwell Anderson's *Winterset*, Philip Barry's *Here Come the Clowns*, and might or should have done so with many other plays—for example, Odets's *Paradise Lost*, Brecht's *Galileo*, Hellman's *The Autumn Garden*, Tennessee Williams's *Camino Real*. One can enjoy several looks at even so very simple a play as Saroyan's *My Heart's in the Highlands*. The pleasure to be had from seeing a play for the second—or third, or fourth, or fifth—time is not that of reversing oneself. It is the pleasure of seeing the play in a steady perspective. This season I went to see *Wonderful Town* again because some of my friends thought I had "overestimated" it—I should worry!—and because Carol Channing had replaced Rosalind Russell. I also saw *The Seven Year Itch* again—no "problem" there—because a newcomer, Irene Moore, played Vanessa Brown's part for four performances; and I looked in on *Picnic* once more because Betty Lou Holland had replaced Kim Stanley. And just as four years ago I paid to see a production of *Caesar and Cleopatra* for the second time because my published remarks on it had been deemed impertinently high-handed, so I have just revisited *The Teahouse of the August Moon* because I had seen it at the final New York dress rehearsal—a preview—which happened to be technically rough. On seeing *Teahouse* again, I reread my review of it (October 31, 1953) to determine whether I felt differently about it now. I had said "*The Teahouse of the August Moon* is a hit because it is entirely pleasant, benign, and sweet." Also "it is good-natured, liberal, and constantly indulgent." And further, "There is something almost traditionally American, or rather American theatre, about *The Teahouse*." Finally, "It is candy concocted with some originality, and easy to take."

I have not changed my mind. What may have sounded sour in the first instance was my further comments, which dealt with the hysterically rapturous enthusiasm that almost every pleasantly successful occasion provokes at a Broadway opening—generally reserved for agreeable plays which are conventional at their core and novel on their surface. (About this, I said, "What I like most about the show is that it has a fresh or at least a different look.") My review in a sense represented a reaction to a reaction.

Many differences of opinion in the theatre are not so much that as differences of vocabulary. When I worked in Hollywood, I was asked to comment on the test of a young actress who was being considered for a term contract. "The young lady has a provocative personality," I noted, "in addition to some acting ability. She should prove very useful in secondary roles. I recommend signing her." The executive producer was outraged at my report. "I think she's *great*," he snapped. "We mean the same thing," I answered.

The performance of *The Teahouse* is still in very good shape. What has improved—and increased my enjoyment of it—is the audience. (Preview audiences are notoriously unresponsive both because they are too homogeneous to be representative and because they have not read the notices and are thus loath to have anything but the most cautious opinion.) David Wayne is expert, as we knew from *Mister Roberts*, and very charming, as we had occasion to learn from *Finian's Rainbow*. Robert Lewis's direction is thoroughly stage-wise.

How could the play be anything but the smash it is? It has jokes about the stupidity of the army brass, about the G.I.'s taste for liquor, about our general thick-headedness. (The colonel suspects his captain of making a fortune from the labor of the native Okinawans in his charge. No, the captain explains, the money has been laid aside for them to share and share alike. "That's communism," the colonel roars.) The play voices wholesome sentiments. It pokes (self-congratulatory) fun at our complacency. "I'll teach the natives American democracy," the colonel explains, "if I have to shoot every one of them to do it." A distinction is made between the "democracy" of teaching Okinawans to sing "God Bless America" in English and the democracy of fellow-feeling.

It *is* excellent candy. That's fine. But our diet needs to be extended. And I shall always believe it

my function to be more severe with the "sure things" than with those plays which falter a little on a more hazardous path.

—*NAT*, 15 May '54

REVOLUTIONARY DRAMA

There was a time when we spoke of "revolutionary" drama. What was meant was drama that urged or suggested a change in society. Still the appellation was a misnomer. For in a sense there cannot be such a thing as "revolutionary" drama. The theatre is a communion: no play really flouts its audience. Imagine, if you can, an anti-Semitic play presented by the Habimah Theater!

In the old days—how long ago they now seem—when Odets's *Waiting for Lefty* was the talk of the town, even politically conservative critics were impressed and, better than that, entertained by it, not only because its language of ecstatic slogans was colorful and new, but because its fervent cry for social amelioration seemed justified to practically everybody.

Drama to be effective may anticipate, awaken, and perhaps guide the consciousness of its audience—to a degree. Drama arouses in its audience what is already latent in it; it provokes the response the audience yearns to voice. Drama, in short, lives and is based on the audience's beliefs, it may sometimes appear to, but may never actually, contradict them. That is why it is always socially revealing. *The Seven Year Itch* tells us as much about our society as *The Caine Mutiny*.

A "good play" is not good for all people at the same time. Anouilh's plays are good and essentially popular plays in Paris. With us their appeal is limited. Sartre's *Dirty Hands* (played here as *Red Gloves*) was a smash in France and a flop here, not only because of differences in production and certain alterations in the text, but because the large American theatregoing public, for all its TV habits and excitements, is not intimately and emotionally concerned with politics.

All this comes to my mind now as I read Jean Giraudoux's posthumous play, *For Lucretia*, highly successful at present in Barrault's production at the Théâtre Marigny in Paris. Giraudoux, the outstanding French playwright between the First and the Second World War, is also the foreign playwright who has proved most acceptable to our audiences. The reason for this, apart from the casting of the Lunts in *Amphitryon 38* and of Audrey Hepburn in *Ondine*, is that one of Giraudoux's major themes is the lack of romance, spiritual liberty, and joy in the contemporary world. Stated as Giraudoux states it—with imagination, humorous fancy, and sprightly delicacy—this premise is something we can share.

But not all Giraudoux is so readily assimilable by us. It is the difficulties we might have with such a play as *For Lucretia* that interest me at the moment, because they are typical of certain differences in attitude between the French and us which are cultural as well as social. For though Giraudoux's *Lucretia* is quasi-realistic—its locale is southern France in 1868, and the settings are such ostensibly ordinary places as the *terrasse* of a pastry shop and the home of the province's attorney general—the play is not only poetic in treatment, as are all Giraudoux's plays, but utterly literary in the precise sense of the term.

In our dramaturgy—strongly influenced by the movies in recent years—dialogue is supposed to make the story progress: the irrelevant from the plot standpoint has to be cut. With Giraudoux it is the story which seems irrelevant. When a man in the midst of a scene in which he is led to suspect his wife's fidelity begs assurance that his suspicions are unfounded, the play halts so that the man can deliver what amounts to an aria on conjugal felicity.

Ordinary housewives (French theatre style!) launch into diatribes replete with literary allusions which include references to English novelists of the eighteenth century. "Is man generous and strong?" the heroine asks, and the answer—in the climactic scene—is, "He is above all naive and deluded. To begin with, he believes the world, from nadir to zenith, belongs to him: I speak of the modest. He believes that woman belongs to him, that he owns love: I speak of the intelligent. He is above all pretentious: I speak of the simple."

This is not eloquence so much as rhetoric. Here we are on the threshold of realizing an essential difference between the French and the American theatre. In story, in idea, in language the French are rarely concerned with verisimilitude: the play need not—preferably should not—mirror "real" life, but a *concept* of life. And virtually all concepts are considered valid—even the "immoral"—provided they are expressed with mental agility and distinction or brilliance of speech.

In *Lucretia*, for example, a woman to avenge herself on another because of a sexual slur administers a narcotic to the offending person, stages a false rape to make the victim believe she is no longer pure, and gets the man who is supposed to have committed the rape to attempt one! Such a story sequence would probably either shock an American audience or appear distastefully ludicrous to it—as did certain scenes in *Mademoiselle Colombe*—because the American audience takes them not only as something that is "actually" happening but as something the playwright is pleased to have happen.

The Frenchman regards such scenes primarily as artistic images, metaphors of the stage, artifice (or "theatre"), which need not—and indeed should not—be conceived as literally true events but as meaningful fabrications of the mind and the imagination—related to but deliberately distinct from life itself. Paradox of thought, characterization, event, and language is the norm here. Since, according to French aesthetics, everything is permissible to the artistic imagination (as differentiated from the everyday conduct of life), French drama, aimed at audiences with a more definite sense of moral values than ours—which are fluctuating, sentimental, and "instinctive" rather than reasoned—is more daring, more scandalizing, and at any rate less "natural" than ours. The French theatre is not necessarily better than our own, but because of its departures from what we believe to be aesthetically axiomatic we may learn much from it.

—*NAT*, 5 June '54

BEERBOHM'S CRITICISM

We rarely ask ourselves in the theatre questions about the durability of any given work. The better plays are discussed for a season or two; very few are remembered beyond that. As for dramatic criticism, it expires much more quickly than the plays which are its subjects. It is used nowadays either as a kind of highfalutin gossip column or as a consumers' guide.

The more literate will occasionally remind us that dramatic criticism can endure. Aristotle's *Poetics* is dramatic criticism. Quotations from Lessing, Hazlitt, Lamb, Lewes, or Leigh Hunt sometimes appear in erudite essays. But this is hardly what we mean by dramatic criticism. We mean reviews such as appear in our dailies or weeklies. Can such writing be of any interest twenty-five years hence? Shaw's *Dramatic Opinions and Essays*, reissued in England a few years ago as *Our Theatres in the Nineties*, and Max Beerbohm's *Around Theatres*, reissued this year in a one-volume edition, attest to the affirmative.

I read Beerbohm's dramatic criticism for the first time only six years ago, although I had read Shaw's criticism, the best modern writing on the theatre in the English language, almost constantly since I first encountered it in 1917. I was rather reluctant at first to read Beerbohm because his approach to the theatre, I fancied, would be that of a dilettante. Indeed, Beerbohm's first piece in 1898 as the critic of the *Saturday Review* of London— his forerunner was G. B. S.—was entitled "Why I Ought Not to Be a Dramatic Critic." When I finally got down to reading the pieces I was delighted with them. Rereading them today I find my pleasure undiminished.

What explains the durability of these pieces? (The last one is dated April, 1910.) It is not enough to say they are exquisitely written and enchantingly witty. The important point is—they make *sense*.

I do not simply mean by this that they are "sound." Like all critics Beerbohm made his share of "mistakes." One of them he acknowledges repeatedly: he thought Shaw's *Man and Superman* read well but would not "play" on the stage. He did not care at all for Shaw's *Misalliance*, referring to it as a series of debates. We know better! Beerbohm does not believe acting in a foreign language of which the audience is ignorant can afford any pleasure. Beerbohm need only have turned back to Shaw's piece on Duse and Bernhardt to learn how wrong he was. But then, Shaw's review of Wilde's *The Importance of Being Earnest* was in many respects wide of the mark.

What makes a critic valuable is not his conclusions so much as the texture of his thought and feeling. A critic, Beerbohm says, must be a great man. This is a startling way of suggesting that to have more than a momentary interest criticism must reveal a point of view, a temperament, a reaction to life and to art that may or may not be conveyed in doctrinal fashion, in which the reader can sense the substantiality of a total human personality. Within such a personality the critic's opinions, whether or not one agrees with them, form a living pattern and thus make sense. It is of little concern to me that Mr. X of this or that paper likes the play I do; I am chiefly interested in knowing the channels by which he arrives at his opinion. The critic's opinion is like a single trait in the composition of a portrait: we must see the relation to the whole. If the face portrayed is antipathetic, the cleverness of a single stroke is of little significance.

A special sort of dilettantism is the hallmark of Beerbohm's criticism. One might say that to be a dilettante was his determination and ambition. His elegance and dandyism are a precious creation to the preservation of which he devotes the utmost care and study. He cultivates his foppishness. Though fluent and relaxed, his style is full of artifice and studied effect. Though colloquial, it is at moments coquettishly archaic. It is nonchalant and learned. It appears formless but is most artfully composed.

Beerbohm's attitude is hedonistic without cheapness or depravity. His philosophy is essentially aesthetic; yet he understands the limitations of art. His nature is puckishly skeptical—he calls it satiric; yet he has firm beliefs and moral perceptions. He indicates rather than insists on them. His world is one of decorous reasonableness into which, in his heyday, it was still possible and permissible to make one's own handsome mode of retreat. It was a world of good manners and discreet ecstasies. It was a civilized world as understood by the quietly well-to-do and well-educated in England before the First World War.

No wonder such a man could title a review of Sarah Bernhardt as the hero of Shakespeare's greatest play "Hamlet, Princess of Denmark" and end it by saying, "The only compliment one can conscientiously pay her is that her Hamlet was, from first to last, *très grande dame*." No wonder too that the violently impassioned naturalism of Gorky's *Lower Depths* shocked him to insult, and the inspired and volcanic crudeness of the Sicilian tragedian Grosso disgusted him. Even if we disagreed with these reactions many times more strongly than we do, should we not still admire him for his espousal of the original and his hilariously haughty scorn of the hackneyed, for such quips as "If our English mimes want to improve themselves, let them be born again, of French parents," and generally for justifying Shaw's introduction of him as "the incomparable Max!"

—*NAT*, 12 June '54

AMERICAN MUSICAL COMEDY

Before we had an original and serious American drama, we had an original and "unserious" American theatre in the form of musical comedy. There are pedants who deny that our musical comedy is original, but—no matter! There are others who deny the value of American dramaturgy, even though it is hard to name any other which at present excels ours.

Be that as it may, in speaking of the contribution made by the American theatre beginning with the twenties, we usually fail to point with (a little) pride to the generic masterpiece which the American musical comedy is. Stark Young, our finest theatre critic between 1922 and 1947, hardly ever went to see—and almost never willingly reviewed—a musical.

On those occasions on which we speak despondently about the state of the American theatre most of us overlook the steady excellence of our musical-comedy stage. One reason for this, I suppose, is that if we examine each element of a musical comedy separately and judge it from an exalted standard of ideas, writing, music, and so on, we may find ourselves discouraged. (In these respects our musicals are far inferior to Offenbach's comic operas, which are of course true works of art.) But the sum of our musicals is greater than their parts. I do not speak of individual shows so much as of the long line of musicals from, let us say, 1910 to the present taken as a total body of work.

The other day I noticed an item in a column of theatrical statistics which pointed out that of the twenty-two shows running in New York at that moment eight were musicals, one was the solo Victor Borge, another a revival of *The Seagull*. The rest were straight comedies. The proportion seems typical of the entire period since the war. And I am inclined to think that the musicals—none of which are at this time the most memorable of my experience—probably reveal a greater degree of talent than the "serious" plays.

This may be a warped view, equivalent to my feverish enthusiasm, in 1922, when I returned from a winter in Paris, on seeing the *Ziegfeld Follies*. "This is as admirably American," I told myself out loud, "as the novels of Scott Fitzgerald and Sinclair Lewis." Exaggerated, no doubt, but the point is that the show—among whose players were Will Rogers, W.C. Fields, Fanny Brice, and the

Prettiest Girls in the World—seemed to me symbolical of the energy, humor, silken lushness, cosmopolitanism, and ebullient hedonism of an America drunk with its own youthful success. So, in various ways the American musical manages to express certain basic American gifts and qualities.

One of the most permanent and ineradicable of American ideals embodied in the musicals is the ideal of having fun and a good time. There is a certain innocence—often an adulterated innocence but innocence none the less—in this. But it is so deep-rooted, so historically justified, so physically essential, so desperately sought after, that it has created a host of genuinely expert devotees in the theatrical world.

The demand for real craftsmanship in "legitimate" drama is only sporadically heeded because such drama itself stands on a shaky foundation. One is never quite sure that drama is truly desired, since support for it is so uncertain. But there is little question of our need for the lighter entertainments. And in these fields people learn their business. They have to, the competition is so keen and the audience so aware. Deborah Kerr and Audrey Hepburn are very nice, but can anyone soberly maintain that they have perfected themselves in their craft to the degree that even such a beginner as Carol Haney has in her medium? How many "legitimate" actors are as legitimate craftsmen as Ray Bolger? How many as professionally knowing as Jimmy Durante or Ethel Merman? For that matter, how many dramatists have pursued their careers with the consistency of a Jerome Kern, a George Gershwin, a Cole Porter, a Richard Rodgers? Not many of our directors are as painstaking and artistically ambitious as Agnes de Mille, Jerome Robbins, Mike Kidd.

The retort to these somewhat rhetorical statements and questions may be that in the first place musical comedy pays better than any other "line" in the theatre and that furthermore the problems of the legitimate theatre are intrinsically more profound as well as organizationally and economically more difficult. If so, the theatre worker who pretends to serious creative work must not only

emulate the protracted and strenuous effort of those engaged in musical comedy but even go beyond them. It would not be too much to say, in fact, that the person who enters the non-musical theatre today requires, besides talent, an almost heroic capacity for work and great moral stamina. Perhaps that is why so many of our younger actors are now trying to acquire the disciplines and accomplishments of the musical-comedy performers. For it may take some time for our legitimate theatre to achieve within its own range the completeness of our best musicals.

—*NAT*, 19 June '54

CAROUSEL

In Molnar's *Liliom*, one of the most charming of contemporary plays, the final scene shows Liliom on his return from the "other world" attempting a single good deed in order that he may be permitted to enter the heavenly kingdom. He has stolen a star from the firmament and tries to offer it to his daughter. When she refuses to take it, he slaps her. This bit of tender irony epitomizes the quality of the play. It is very European.

In *Carousel* (City Center), the musical Rodgers and Hammerstein made from Molnar's play, the scene I speak of is retained but it is followed by another. In this, the daughter sits listening to a country doctor's homily at her school graduation. The benign doctor tells the children that no matter how lowly their origin they can all make something of themselves. Billy Bigelow, a rural American Liliom, leans over his daughter's shoulder and whispers fervently, "Listen to him! Listen to him!," while blessing her with a paternal kiss.

The difference between the ending of Molnar's play and that of the American musical illustrates the different spirit of these works. It would be foolish to say that I prefer Molnar's ending to that of *Carousel*, but it explains why, despite the admirable attributes of the musical, I have always found some difficulty in enjoying it fully. A little evil on the stage is a good thing. Molnar's Liliom, for all his inarticulate gentleness, is a rogue. In *Carousel* we are never for a moment allowed to doubt that Billy Bigelow is a wonderful guy. Good nature is unalloyed. If *Liliom* is honeyed paprika, *Carousel* is pasteurized and sugared buttermilk. I have a sweet tooth myself: I do not gag at sentiment or even sentimentality. But to be really nice shouldn't sweets have a little bit of spice?

Still *Carousel* is a delectable show, very near the top of the Rodgers and Hammerstein achievement. The tunes improve with familiarity. Time is needed for music to penetrate into our very bloodstream; when this happens we love it as the best in ourselves. The sound of *Carousel* is a breeze; to say that its melodies are aerated seems not so much a figure of speech as a literal description. In the first act particularly "June is bustin' out all over." Here the show is like a month in the country.

The production, directed by William Hammerstein, who heads the New York City Light Opera Company, is as light and fresh as organdy. The singing is never forced. The total effect is that of a natural *breathing*. Relaxation, affection, smoothness (without slickness) are keynotes. Barbara Cook is a darling Carrie Pepperidge. Chris Robinson is handsome without offense, and sings with an unassuming ease. The whole company is good.

A special word must be said about Bambi Linn and the ballet of adolescent loneliness Agnes de Mille designed for her. Miss Linn's dancing is a golden sunshine that suffuses shore and leafy strand with an energy which renews life and a tenderness which inspires tears. This would not be possible were it not for the delicately humorous awkwardness, the feminine impudence and bravery mingled with childish hurt and pertness which are so characteristic of Miss de Mille's fine talent.

—*NAT*, 26 June '54

JOHN GASSNER

In a way John Gassner has done himself a disservice by having made himself known to that part of the theatre-going public which reads about the theatre as an anthologist and historian. His latest book *The Theatre in Our Times* (Crown Publishers, $5) reveals Gassner as something more than a "scholar"; he is an excellent critic.

We need such a critic in the world of the American theatre. I say this neither to puff him nor to disparage other critics, but to make a point in regard to his particular contribution. The American theatre critic is not only an impressionist in method but because of the nature of our journalism and the nervous taste of its readers is virtually forced into becoming a kind of entertainer, a sort of literary glamor boy. Gassner is never a bright guesser, a self-infatuated phrase-monger, or a ballyhoo expert. His aim is to make sound evaluations on the premises of clearly defined standards and reasoned analyses.

He is not only sober, but forbearing. No writer or actor need fear that he will make him a target or victim. Gassner's manner is always self-effacing, respectful, and, best of all, attentive. When he sees a play he does not think primarily of what he is going to say about it or believe the play was expressly made so that he might voice his opinion of it.

This does not mean that he is the type of professor-critic who is balanced because he never moves for the simple reason that he's not trying to get anywhere. Underneath the rather copious gray garment of his prose, Gassner takes strong positions, affirms and defends opinions which are by no means routine either on Broadway or in the colleges.

In his preface to *The Theatre in Our Times*, Gassner enunciates a credo: "—the American stage," he says, "is most vital when closest to American sensibility and interest, whatever their shortcomings, but the European enterprise in theatre provides a necessary perspective and corrective. I also believe that realism and contemporary interest alone can give us a living theatre, but that realism should not limit us to realistic technique or style while contemporary interest should not limit us to commonplace or topical matters and attitudes."

This sounds reasonable, but it is not, as some might suspect, tame. For what Gassner in the succeeding essays manages to do is to champion the vigorous germination of our young American drama as against certain more civilized and mature continental products which are frequently clever and brittle imitations of past literary modes rather than truly felt reflections of European life. Thus without minimizing the gross defects easily perceptible in their work, Gassner utters a heartening yea to the impulses and achievements of O'Neill, Odets, Williams, Miller among others, and a cordial but quizzical nay to the pretentions of a Cocteau as well as those Gassner, with learned wit, calls epigones in religion and poetic drama—for example, T. S. Eliot.

These opinions do not spring from any esthetic, political, or national partisanship. Gassner speaks with admiration and understanding of Bertolt Brecht whose great talent—essentially poetic, despite its didactic orientation—is so different from that of the Americans. If Gassner recognizes the sweeping power of Sean O'Casey and prizes it above the refinement of certain more shapely dramatists it is not because Gassner espouses emotion for its own sake. He realizes the value of a certain detachment and irony in drama and praises a number of French playwrights who possess this quality. If Gassner tends to favor specific reality and contemporaneity as well as national and even local color as against abstruse mythical and "universal" inspiration—in short if he esteems the concrete above the abstract—it is because as a matter of fact the most substantial and stirring plays of our time—Ibsen, Strindberg, Chekhov, Shaw—have issued from the stimulus of immediate rather than recorded reality.

Thus Gassner is able to make a case for modern drama (including, without apology, the American) even though it has produced no Shakespeare or Racine—dramatists who may appear to contradict his thesis. But what about "high" tragedy, the dicta of Aristotle, Matthew Arnold, and all that? Gassner is, if you like, on the side of the "barbarians": those who are the source and carriers of that living substance which makes art matter. One doesn't grow great by worshipping giants. Beaumarchais, Gassner tells us, once wrote "Only *little* men are afraid of *little* writings." Gassner knows, these things, and his *Theatre in Our Times* is that rare thing in dramatic criticism, a comprehensive book.

—*NAT*, 3 July '54

THE IDEAL AUDIENCE!

All of us agree mechanically that the audience is the theatre's most crucial factor. The thought is hardly valuable if we view the audience as an inert mass. We must regard the audience not as a buyer but as a collaborator. And just as we yearn for good plays should we not also seek good audiences?

Before defining the "good audience," we should perhaps ask ourselves first who the audience is and what its function—apart from its purchase—should be. The audience is, broadly speaking, simply the adult population of any community. Before the dramatist, the actor, the director, the scene-designer become craftsmen of the theatre, they are part of the audience. Their inspiration derives from the language, habits, thought patterns, beliefs aspirations—the whole mode of life which is the audience's.

It would be false, however, to draw an exact parallel between our theatre audiences and our people as a whole. There are innumerable audiences in America as there are in New York itself. The differences are economic, educational, social. It is interesting to note in this connection that certain Broadway productions which are accounted flops sell out their balcony seats throughout the play's run. The orchestra and the balcony at the same playhouse may constitute two (almost) distinct audiences. A prominent New York reviewer told me that he felt more kindly to a play when he saw it away from the main theatrical district. (This shows that the same person under special circumstances may become a different sort of audience.) It explains in part why a play which has been a box-office success below Fourteenth Street may become a box-office failure above Forty-second.

When I speak of differences in education among audiences, I do not refer only to differences in formal schooling. There may be just as many college graduates in the orchestra as in the balcony, and the proportionate relation of these to the audience's general level of intelligence is probably irrelevant. The education I have in mind is education in and for the theatre.

In this connection, we might consider certain aspects of our Broadway audiences with those of other theatrical capitals. One of the most striking differences between our New York audiences and those of the European theatre is our appetite for the "new." The Broadway audience on the whole resists the idea of "revivals." The French theatre lives on them. The British are in this respect somewhere in the middle.

When O'Neill's *Desire Under the Elms* was revived some time ago to a very cordial press reception, I asked various people why they hadn't taken the trouble to see a play which many respected judges considered one of the finest plays ever to be written by an American. The answer was not that they had seen the play before, but that they had not been eager to see an "old play."

The typical Broadway audience is not even interested in Shakespeare—because he is not a novelty, that is, part of the competition, the guessing game as to whether he will hit or miss, establish a new reputation, etc., etc. When I speak of the "typical" Broadway audience, I confess I refer mainly to those who insist they must sit in the first ten rows of the orchestra and more especially those who don't go to the theatre at all unless they buy their tickets through a broker.

The fashionable English theatre audience is sufficiently attached to its leading actors at least to patronize any creditable production of even such "lesser" Shakespearean plays as *The Winter's Tale* or *Much Ado About Nothing* when one of these actors appears in them. The French constantly revive not only their classics but interestingly plays which were first produced only a few years ago. A play's "age" is no deterrent to an audience's desire to see it. This is possible, you may suppose, because there are state theatres on the Continent, and an Old Vic and a Stratford Memorial Theatre in England. The reverse is true: these theatres are possible because the audience makes them necessary.

Another significant difference between the audiences of our theatre and those abroad is the difference of attitude in regard to the "small," the off-center theatres. Though there has recently been some improvement in this respect, most of the "typical" New York theatergoers feel that an off-Broadway production must prove itself worthy of their attention before they will even take notice of its existence. (An off-Broadway play is "worthy" if it resembles or is likely to approximate the box-office success of an "uptown show.") In Paris, prestige—regardless of profits—is conferred by the esteem in which a play is held by the most judicious critics—and these gentlemen expect to find such plays away from the boulevards and the commercial theatre.

This does not mean that the European theatre audience is necessarily brighter or more advanced than ours. In the early Twenties, we too sought some of our most valued theatre experiences in such special places as the Provincetown Playhouse, the Greenwich Village Theatre, the Neighborhood Playhouse, the Civic Repertory. What is characteristic of our New York audiences today is a tendency, and, one might say, a training which induces them to think of excellence in terms of only one value—success on the Broadway theatre market. And this success, let us not forget, is dependent to a considerable extent on severe economic restrictions which are of very recent origin. So fine a play as Clifford Odets' *Awake and Sing!*, never a real money maker, was able to run a season in 1935; under present conditions it would have to close in three weeks.

What are we talking about when we speak of hits and flops? We are thinking in terms of investments; but most of us are spectators, not investors. When an audience, on seeing a play, concerns itself with its commercial destiny—a concern unmistakably audible at previews and during the early stages of the run of a play which has received what the trade calls "mixed notices"—the audience may be said to have become corrupt. It is poisoning its pleasure with sleazily professional considerations which are foreign to it.

A leveling out process is going on in the theatre today, turning our values rigid within a very narrow range. The audience is encouraged to see all the smash hits—but only the smash hits—even though they may all be of very different caliber. (Robert Morley told me he had the suspicion New Yorkers felt that if you could get tickets to a show it wasn't worth seeing—as well as being highly disturbed in the theatre if they found an empty seat beside them!) The audience in Paris which admires Giraudoux, for example, is not at all the same as that which makes the success of an André Roussin (the author of *The Little Hut*).

One typical Broadway audience rushes to every smash—the latest smash, preferably—regardless of the nature and meaning of the plays. In fact, it is often hard to determine whether this audience recognizes any meaning in a play except that it is a smash.

The daily press has willy-nilly played a certain role in the development of this tendency. The reviewers as individuals, no doubt, have their own artistic preferences. But the reviewer for a daily newspaper has a vast heterogeneous audience to which he feels responsible. He is obliged to adjust his writing and thinking to what he believes are his readers' standards. He does not care to be out of line.

He will say, for example, "I like such and such a play, but it cannot be described as pleasant. It is for people who are unabashed at grim thought in the theatre." This is the reviewer's honest and, so to speak, democratic way of warning his readers as to what they may expect.

He does not believe it within his province to educate his "constituents" to his personal taste, as did Bernard Shaw, who wrote about the gallery gods after they hissed what he considered a meritorious play, "It is the business of the dramatic critic to educate these dunces, not to echo them."

The common Broadway emphasis on the latest hit as the only desirable show to see makes for a regimentation of the audience: a routine mind and ultimately what might be called the dictatorship of success. I do not mean to suggest that success is of no account. On the contrary, every success is significant. A play must appeal to an audience—but we should distinguish between audiences. Tell me how and why an audience is attracted to a play and I will tell you the sort of play and audience it is.

It goes without saying that all plays must be entertaining. A dull play never served any purpose. But what's one man's poison is another man's meat; one may be as gratified by a black play as by a pink one.

What then is the "ideal" audience? From what I have already said it must be evident that there can be no such thing in the sense of a universal and identical audience for all plays. That is why in certain European cities there are classic theatres, popular theatres, workers' theatres, avant-garde theatres, each with their own special emphasis, each reaching their own norm and their own "clientele." By an "ideal" audience, I simply mean an audience that is not a cultural automaton, a reflex of prevailing fads and the urge to "keep up with the Joneses," to see what everybody else is seeing, an audience that does not applaud and laugh, as in a radio studio I once visited, by order.

Nowadays we speak, apropos of everything, of the democratic ideal. That ideal, as I conceive it, is to foster and encourage the individual. A good audience has its own taste. That is why on the whole I trust the audience of the off-Broadway theatre more than I do the larger one—the one composed of members who not only want to see the latest smash but often to see it before it reaches Broadway and sometimes to see it no other time than on the opening night. The Broadway audience clamors for an originality that is basically familiar; the off-Broadway audience at its best seeks an unconventional point of view, modes of thought and feeling which depart from the already formulated.

The ideal audience has a certain innocence. It comes to the play anticipating pleasure. It does not fence itself off in a "show me" frame of mind. It opens itself up. It considers it the height of indecorum to arrive late. It seeks an intimacy and sense of sharing with the play.

For a play is not a dead thing; it is a complex—because collectively articulated—human expression. "Behind" the play—if it has any merit at all—are people. The dramatist worthy of the name is telling us what he has observed, felt, dreamed and come to realize—what has made him suffer or given him joy. He is trying to make us take part. The actors are not simply puppets of the author's will or the director's skill: they too bring an individual note to what we see, a note that colors and extends what the dramatist hopes to express.

When Laurette Taylor was on the stage in *The Glass Menagerie*, we perceived not only Williams' chagrin over a certain kind of mother, we were moved by the pathos of a bewildered and pained searching within a simple woman's heart. As we watched, we did not think about the compliments we ought to pay the artisans of our emotions, what prizes they ought to win, what "quotes" would honor them or how long the play would run—all

this should come later, if at all. What we felt was a satisfaction in being with the people on the stage, feeling with them and knowing something in common with them which was related to something first surmised in a life that preceded the play, something which had been brought to a glorious fulfillment by our having seen it.

This is what is often termed a receptive mood. It is also a creative one. It is not passive; it reaches out as much it takes in. It supplies the play with the dimension of our own experience and imagination. It is disturbed but by no means destroyed if our neighbor murmurs "I wish I had gone to a musical": one simply wishes he had. The creative mood is not only not incompatible with a critical faculty but is inseparable from it. To create is to make distinctions, to recognize values—and this is the essence of criticism. For criticism was made not to kill but to enhance and refine our pleasure.

The judgment of a play is not a question of pronouncing an opinion—"It's swell" or "It's terrible"—such statements by themselves are more or less presumptuous no matter who utters them. Judgment of a play is like judgment of a person. If you have some feeling for a person—if you approach the person with love, and in the theatre no other approach is valid—you are disappointed by shortcomings, you are eager to help, you are willing to acknowledge that what you love is more important than what sets you apart—and if finally you are impelled to reject, it is through an awareness of the other person and the difference between your need and what that person has to offer.

A person you care for, you will want to see again. A person who interests you but whom you cannot quite "get" you will want to know better. Certain plays repay repeated seeing. One is no more through with a good play on first acquaintance than with a possible friend on first meeting.

The ideal audience does not cough the moment a play lags or falters. The English audience is exemplary in this respect; the American almost pathological. The ideal audience rids itself of false resistances, freeing itself of workaday haste and impatience. After all, the theatre is a place for a certain repose. In the theatre, we relax through concentration. The place for the "tired business man" is not in the theatre but in bed.

Where there is love, there is also memory. The audience I speak of respects its actors because it remembers what they have contributed to its pleasure in the past. It respects itself; therefore it does not take its pleasure lightly.

The English theatre audience, for example, is known and gratefully appreciated by its artists for its loyalty. An actor, a playwright, who have once made a markedly favorable impression are thereafter regarded with affection and followed with warm attention.

There is a type of audience which hardly remembers anything and is in the same position in relation to its artists ("they're finished," it will say at the first disillusionment) as the person in the familiar joke who asks, "But what have you done for me lately?" Such an audience, because it is a poor collaborator, is destructive. Artists cannot except anything from it except a momentary and mechanical reaction and ultimate indifference.

A collaboration bespeaks mutual respect. Because my subject here is the audience's role in the theatre, I do not overlook the theatre people's responsibility to the audience. It is to some extent due to an indifference to the audience as anything but a customer that our theatre suffers. For the theatre to flourish, people in the theatre must seek by every means—organizational as well as artistic—to make the audience what they would have it be.

Still when we try to excuse our behavior as audiences, it is not enough to speak of the hazardous economic and other external problems: the competition of radio, motion pictures and television, the high price of tickets, the rudeness of box-office attendants, the difficulty of getting seats (to which, in great measure, we contribute), the lack of comfort in the playhouses themselves, the absence of theatre bars.

We must not forget to go to the heart of the matter: the nature of the theatre itself. We must not confuse it with the accidents of show business. We must not forget that we are all part of the audience, and that as such we have a responsibility. We must perfect ourselves as an audience just as we ask our artists to perfect themselves as artists. We should learn rather than complain. The fate of the American theatre is in our hands. We shall make one step forward when we realize that we are not that disembodied "big black giant" of musical fame.

—*NYTM*, 26 Sept. '54

CRITICISM

The critic who reviews a Faulkner novel is rarely the same person who is asked to notice a collection of True Stories. The situation in the theatre is entirely different. It is assumed that all "flesh shows" are somehow "legitimate" theatre and that the man who is delighted by *Anniversary Waltz* is qualified to deal with Strindberg. Such an assumption is no more valid than the opposite belief that a critic who proves discerning about Shaw or Chekhov is necessarily a fit judge of *Can-Can*. It is part of the confusion of our theatrical times that the "ten best plays" of the year—the "Golden Dozen," as they are now being advertised—may include *The Pajama Game* with *The Confidential Clerk*.

All these plays have a right to exist, since, for one thing, they answer specific needs, but it is disastrous to think of them as equivalent merely because they all form part of "show business." One of the reasons we are led to think of these entertainments as items in the same category is that to be socially in the swim we feel obliged to rush to all the hits, in which case *Sabrina Fair* is more valuable than *Ladies of the Corridor*.

—*NAT*, 23 Oct. '54

PETER PAN
THE TRAVELING LADY

Parts of *Peter Pan*, a musical without any music worth mentioning (Winter Garden), are better than the whole. Here the effects, mechanical as well as human, are admirably carried out. It is delightful to watch Peter and three of the children flying ecstatically through the air. And there can be nothing but long applause for Jerome Robbins's choreographic staging, full of brio, humor, and cute playfulness. In addition, Mary Martin, whose courage, proficiency, and charm as a performer deserve our gratitude as much as they compel our wonder, is supported by a carefully selected cast, among whom I choose Sondra Lee as Tiger Lily—Indian chief—as my favorite.

Yet while I left the theatre with a thorough appreciation of the talent displayed, I felt no genuine warmth or real affection for the whole event. *Peter Pan* is a grand show quickened by nothing but ability. It offers skill rather than sentiment. Hardly any of Barrie's sweetness remains. No one, not even the youngest member of the cast, believes in that good Scotsman's fairies. It all happens on Broadway.

Heart is what Kim Stanley possesses. Her flickering but warm glow lends pathos to the awkwardness of Horton Foote's *The Traveling Lady* (The Playhouse). Kim Stanley is the youngest addition to that line of American actresses whose emblematic figures are Laurette Taylor and Pauline Lord. They express the inarticulate but eloquent womanhood of those who have never learned to become ladies. They seem out of step with their environment. They have no "front," no bright armor, no sheen of social glamor. They appear slightly damaged, incalculably hurt, rich in basic human experience. Kim Stanley has amazing naturalness; her speech is real communication

instinct with the unpredictable music and the ebb and flow of a genuine connection with whoever is her partner on the stage. She rarely stiffens with false theatrical projection. Her very presence seems to emanate meaning. She is still far from the mastery which made Laurette Taylor our unmatched example of that humane stagecraft in which artist and person merge in magic integration. Yet if our theatre and her will sustain her, it may be possible for Kim Stanley to progress a long way toward that goal.

My reference to the awkwardness of Mr. Foote's script is criticism and not disparagement. Mr. Foote has talent—true kinship with his material, observation, sensibility, a good ear. But he does not yet know how to pattern his material to his form. There are incidents in the second act which are irrelevant to his story, so that what is essentially a simple tale of a simple soul is made to look like a melodrama which has misfired. The construction of the play, moreover, does not allow the full implications of its characters to become clear. For this reason the audience never quite realizes that the characters represent diverse facets of the play's environment, crucial to the understanding of the play's total significance. As a result, one is not sure whether the play is an extended sketch or a too fragmentary depiction of a world only partly revealed; whether the author is saying too much or too little.

The fact that Mr. Foote has not yet solved his problem—even in his later play, *The Trip to Bountiful*, produced last season—should not disqualify him from our regard. His themes are true themes—and profoundly native. They deal essentially with the difficulty of sinking roots in a soil made barren in the big cities by mechanization and in the country by the dry rot of a dead past. The old mother in *Bountiful* sought to recover the verdure of her childhood home by running away from the big town. The young mother of *The Traveling Lady* wants to find for her child any kind of home which has a chance to endure, but she has to wander all over the largest state in the Union to do so.

—*NAT*, 13 Nov. '54

QUADRILLE
FANNY

When the eminent American actor, William Gillette (1855-1937), was asked what he proposed to do during the period of his retirement, he answered "Act!" On seeing Alfred Lunt and Lynn Fontanne in *Quadrille* (Coronet Theater) I could not help thinking that they had retired to the stage.

To speak ill of the Lunts—Alfred and Lynn—has in the past ten years become tantamount to engaging in a subversive activity. To say that they are "superb" has become as automatic as it is to rise at the first strains of the national anthem. I shall speak no ill of them. I merely wish to point out that the superb couple have been gradually converting themselves into museum pieces. There is a musty odor about their most recent exhibit. Alfred Lunt, though essentially a character actor rather than a tragedian, notwithstanding his unmistakable pathos, is the most gifted and accomplished player of the generation which followed that of John Barrymore. He has that mobility of temperament, that capacity of transformation into the image of what he senses or observes, that nervous humor—with its sudden sting of pain—exploding at the thought of almost any vivid experience which are the marks of the creative actor. Through his long service in the theatre and through association with his wife, who though studiously artificial is a past master in the mechanics of acting, Lunt has made himself into a player without peer on our stage.

An exchange of dialogue between Lunt and Fontanne is a brilliant exercise in subtle rhythms of speech, alternation of tone colors, graceful movement, and a generally witty counterpoint—duel and embrace—of personality. Some of the more ambitious plays of their early years with the Theater Guild seemed to have thrown them, so that with the passing of time, and our lack of any institution comparable to the Old Vic or the Shakespeare Theater of Stratford, not to mention the paucity of fine new plays, the Lunts have chosen to bemuse their vast public with repeated displays of their virtuosity on the most facile level. Their manner now so greatly supersedes their matter that what we get from them is something like masks without faces. There were instances in *Quadrille* when I imagined the actors had disappeared and by some dread conjuration had been replaced by effigies of themselves. That is what happens when theatre, instead of being made from the stuff of life, becomes a substitute for it.

Anyone as prolific as Noel Coward must occasionally turn out sleazy products like *Quadrille*. The plot is hackneyed: an English marquis of 1870 runs away to France with a married woman from Boston; then they are pursued by the Marchioness and an American railroad tycoon, who is the eloping woman's husband; finally the latter two fall in love with each other and are seen in the epilogue bound for bliss on Gallic shores. The background is fake, and the writing, except for a few bright quips, is fairly labored. It is not saved when Coward, to give the railroad man a stature sufficient to merit the favors of the elegant Marchioness, attempts a lyric passage on the beauties of the American landscape in the vein of a Thomas Wolfe. It sounds like a travelogue.

What is sad about all this is not the weakness of their vehicle, but that at a time when the Lunts should be giving us the most exquisite examples of their craft, they are content to parade their ancient splendor in so sterile an atmosphere.

On the subject of *Fanny*, the musical play S. N. Behrman and Joshua Logan (Majestic Theater) have fashioned from the unforgettable *Marius-Fanny-César*-trilogy by Marcel Pagnol, I could easily argue two ways. On the one hand, it is not a successful job because whipped cream should not be thrown over a good piece of meat: the story of *Fanny* is not properly accommodated by the conventional allurements of a Broadway musical, even when they are supplied by the most expert confectioners. On the other hand, the basic situation of *Fanny* is so warm and touching, S. N. Behrman's dialogue so much more gratifying than what one commonly hears in musical shows, Ezio Pinza so engaging in voice and quality, Walter Slezak so pleasingly tactful a comedian, and the whole enterprise so distinct a departure from the routine—the final curtain is a death scene in which no one but the two elderly men, of the story remain on the stage—that I am inclined to overlook the stylistic anomaly of the entire proceedings.

True, the sets have none of the savor of Marseilles, although there is considerable chic in the handsome drop Jo Mielziner has designed for the birthday-party interlude with its flying green cows, pink pigs, blue birds, and yellow fish— Chagall and Klee in a talented adaptation. It is also true that the erotic marine ballet is in somewhat dubious taste besides being banal in itself, and that only two or three numbers are worthy of the voices that sing them. Still, *Fanny* is the only musical in years that has actually moved me for more than a moment.

—*NAT*, 20 Nov. '54

ROBERT EDMOND JONES

Our neglect of the past may be one of the signs of our fundamental disrespect for the living. One of the truest artists the American theatre has known in our generation—Robert Edmond Jones—died on November 27. Too little has been said on the occasion of his passing.

The American theatre can be said to have come of age in 1920—with the emergence of Eugene O'Neill as our only full-fledged playwright. But O'Neill was part of a movement which began to manifest itself shortly before the First World War. The Washington Square Players (1914) and to a greater extent the Provincetown Players (1916), of which Jones was one of the guiding spirits, were early expressions of that

movement. Arthur Hopkins was the first "commercial" manager to bring Jones's work to the Broadway audience.

Technically, Jones's great contribution was in the field of scenic design. There is hardly a designer practicing today who has not learned something from his example. He taught "that a stage setting is not a background; it is an environment. Players act *in* a setting, not *against* it." (I quote from Jones's book, *The Dramatic Imagination*.) "A good scene [set]," he said, "is not a picture. It is something seen, but it is something conveyed as well, a feeling, an evocation. A stage setting has no independent life of its own. In the absence of the actor it does not exist."

Jones never tried to reproduce reality or to embellish it. He reduced stage design to its barest elements of significant and usable detail for the purpose of creating an atmosphere in which the actor's and the playwright's dramatic plan might most amply fulfill themselves. The set for *The Iceman Cometh* was not a saloon; it was the place where O'Neill's meaning could be most appropriately voiced.

But Jones was more than a scene designer or a director. He was a teacher and a seer. He stood for something greater than his own talent, greater than the name he made, the "credits" that might be cited on his behalf. (Many of his imitators received more publicity and made themselves more prosperous.) When Jones said, "Keep in your souls some images of magnificence," he meant it and his work showed it. And magnificence did not signify for him mere opulence or expensiveness. (Today, scenically speaking, we seem to put our faith in furniture.) He spoke of the theatre as a House of Dreams. He embodied the poetic attitude. He never sought to astonish or dazzle. He took technique for granted: he sought to use it in all humility for noble ends.

As a young man in the theatre I was often disturbed by his manner of address. He was not specific enough, not tough enough, or even sensuous enough. He did not appear to take sufficient account of the theatre's "kitchen"—its organizational, administrative, economic sides. But as I contemplate the theatre of today I can only ask myself, "And what have we practical ones, the hard-headed boys, the thick-skinned ones, made of the theatre?"

I do not believe there is less talent in our theatre today than in Jones's best days, but there is a less consistent devotion to it. Jones and his associates made the theatre count for more in our lives, gave it an excitement, a dignity, a force which are now greatly marred. It is not, to be sure, altogether our fault, but neither is it what is shrewd, clever, efficient in us that makes us, even to a slight degree, artists worthy of the theatre.

—*NAT*, 18 Dec. '54

THE BAD SEED

Ordinarily I would have very little to say about such a play as *The Bad Seed*, Maxwell Anderson's adaptation of William March's novel (Forty-Sixth Street Theater). Mr. Anderson has charmingly confessed that it is a pot-boiler. (It goes without saying that a pot-boiler may prove a masterpiece, and a work of more exalted intention a dud.) The fact that Mr. Anderson has succeeded in making the pot boil would not normally stir me to prolonged comment, for *The Bad Seed* is the kind of play that rouses no enthusiasm in me— even when it is good. I take no pleasure in being harrowed to no purpose.

What makes the occasion critically special is that, beside being the first "dramatic smash" of the season, *The Bad Seed* strikes one as a play which, so to speak, makes a comment on its audience. The tale it tells is of a girl of eight who has committed a murder before the play has begun, then kills a little boy because she covets his medal for penmanship, which she had hoped to win, and finally kills the handyman who threatens to expose her. All this killing is done without the slightest tremor—the child, it appears, is congenitally without any feeling of right or wrong, though she was born of respectable and fond parents. The explanation? The mother—unknown to herself—is the adopted daughter of an accomplished murderess of great renown. The little monster's mother attempts to do away with her daughter but fails, though she succeeds in killing herself. The bad seed will thus be perpetuated for the benefit of other melodramas.

In view of the author's usual gift for dialogue, the writing of this play must be set down as mediocre—literate television language. The characters are stereotypes; the plotting is schematic— as clear as a roadmap. There is a touch of comedy relief from a foolish lady who talks penny psychoanalysis all the time, and in such lines as that of an unsuspecting neighbor speaking of the little girl, "She is going to make some man very happy." There is no atmosphere or mood, and very little real suspense. Once the situation is prepared for, the play progresses evenly to its end—except for a clever device at the final curtain—till there is hardly anyone left in the cast fit to kill.

The acting is generally competent. Nancy Kelly as the mother is comely, conscientious, and at moments touching. Patty McCormack as the baby-doll is an excellent vehicle for the story that is being told through her. Evelyn Varden as the lady who spouts Freudian boners is an expert comedienne, and Eileen Heckart, as a simple inebriate woman whose little son was our heroine's victim, plays the same sob scene twice with its effectiveness showing. The direction is slick stage management; the set is as handsomely inexpressive as a department-store display of furniture.

If the play has little real quality—with practically none of the "psychological" fascination of *Angel Street* or the intriguing complications of *Dial M*—how explain its success?

It is "good theatre," you may say. But I have taken some pains to indicate that it is not at all good theatre. (How one comes to detest the phrase when it is repeatedly used to praise the trivial, the sham, the hollow!) The play is as flat and cold as a plate on the shelf. It is essentially incredible and almost entirely pointless. And its emotional after-effect is virtually nil.

It is just this combination of theatrical veneer with meaningless murder which somehow gratifies the audience or flatters it into applauding what it is unashamed to think of as a "swell show." The audience is anesthetized by the standard material bequeathed by the movies, radio, television but more smoothly fabricated here, and then hypnotized as by a snake's eye by the inflamed spot of senseless killing in the midst of it all, a spot which in the circumstances has been made decorative.

In a way the play communicates no horror. The idea of murder with little motive or meaning, murder as an indecipherable X or as a sheer token of human irrationality and misconduct, murder that is abstracted from all reality, has been converted into something reassuring, almost sedative.

So I came from the theatre trembling, not because of the play—which, for my part, you can take or leave according to your disposition—but for the audience.

—*NAT*, 25 Dec. '54

AUDREY HEPBURN

The nature of my reaction to *Ondine* makes it seem proper for me to address an open letter to its star. Therefore:

Dear Audrey Hepburn:

Perhaps it will strike you as unkind if I say that the response of the audience including, of course, that of the reviewers to your performance in *Ondine* is more a private manifestation than a critical judgment. It is as if everybody were asking for your telephone number.

You are enchanting. (How tired you will soon become of hearing this!) You must forgive me if I begin this way, because, though apparently self-evident, it is a statement that cannot be addressed to many actresses of our day. The stage at present has only a few really beautiful women, and most of

the screen beauties resemble posters rather than people. Yours is truly a face. It is a face that has fineness, breeding, grace, and in the large lovely dark eyes there is something that appears to withhold part of yourself for yourself, as well as something that seeks to behold the fascinating world outside. This is rare and precious, and our ecstatic clamor is a cry for the uncommon.

Your delicate apartness shows itself in your choice of vehicle. Giraudoux was a poet and an aristocratic wit: most of his plays are sparklingly veiled proclamations against the crassness of contemporary civilization. The attraction of *Ondine* for an actress like you and for a good part of the public relates to our deep need to get away from the kind of realism that merely mirrors what is ugly to begin with. We are a little like those Frenchmen who at the end of the nineteenth century got so fed up with the naturalism of the *théâtre libre* that they took refuge in tiny theatres where Maeterlinck's hushed and misty symbolism was being revealed or went jubilantly mad when Rostand's *Cyrano* was first brought to them. For somewhat the same reasons there is nowadays a growing appetite for the mood play as differentiated from the plot play.

But young as you are, dear Audrey, you must guess that that is not the whole story, for it is clear that you are as bright as you are sensitive. The audience, while adoring you, coughs a little too much as your play unfolds. For my part, while admiring Giraudoux and enraptured by your presence, I still found that I ceased following the play's text about halfway through the second act, and could never, despite all possible good will, get with it again. It was not that I was bored—how could I be with you on the stage in the third act, modestly weeping and cutting so exquisite a figure?—it was simply a feeling that what the stage was offering no longer engaged my interest.

Ondine is not the best of Giraudoux's work. Charming spirit though he was, Giraudoux was no romantic. His style is opulent impressionism, playful irony, common sense and intellectual paradox appareled as whimsy. Giraudoux's vein is that of a high sophistication, mental refinement, and the ultimate of an ancient—I almost said attenuated—culture, decked out in very light attire. All this is heady and delicious as a wine of superb vintage, but it has little to do with the gravity and thick sentiment of the Ondine legend. Giraudoux can be sportive with Hellenic fable, sparkling about the crazy quilt of France suffering the taint of the twentieth century, but he loses some of his natural grace when he tries to shape the foggy mood of Germanic yearning into a Parisian pattern. There is a basic discrepancy here between manner and matter, and the result is only intermittently harmonious.

The bridge between the two elements can only be effected by the most original and imaginative sort of production. The production you shine in is expensive and old-fashioned fashionable; it is not creative. Instead of evoking a new or different world, it gives the impression of a ballet setting in a post-Ziegfeld musical. It is more pedestrian for all its fancy but essentially conventional air than a bare stage might be.

Still, it is you I am most concerned with now. You are not only beautiful, you are gifted. You have vivacity, your body is trained as well as trim, you are capable of dedication—you follow the director as unselfishly as an actress should—you are, in short, a wonderful instrument with a soul of your own. But, said old Grandpa Ibsen, talent is not just a possession, it is a responsibility. You are at the beginning of your career; because this beginning is so dazzling you must not allow—as so many others do—the beginning to become the end. Your performance in *Ondine* as acting is sweet, young, technically naïve. Your training as an actress is still in its early stages: you do not yet know how to transform the outward aspects of a characterization—the water sprite you play—into an inner characterization. For this reason your performance actually lacks mystery, a dimension beyond your own entrancing self.

You can learn to be a real actress if you do not let the racket, the publicity, the adulation and the false—that is, ignorant—praise rattle you away from yourself. Most young people on the stage have the problem of how to gain an opportunity; for you and all the brilliant youngsters of the present generation the problem is to make something of your opportunity. Keep on acting, studying, working—and not always at your greatest convenience. Play parts that are risky, parts that are difficult, and do not be afraid to fail! Above all, play on the stage—though I do not suggest that you give up films. Do not trust those who tell you that screen and stage acting are the same species or of equal artistic value: it is simply not true even when Jean-Louis Barrault says so.

Devotedly yours,
Harold Clurman

—*NAT*, '54

PORTRAIT OF A LADY
WHAT EVERY WOMAN KNOWS

The week before Christmas offered two new plays which have already closed and a revival of Barrie's *What Every Woman Knows* with Helen Hayes at the City Center.

Only one of the two new plays is worth a backward glance. *Portrait of a Lady*, a stage adaptation by William Archibald of Henry James's novel, was, as everyone agreed, dramatically flaccid, tenuous, and without definite contour. No matter how it had been acted or staged, it was doomed to fail. Yet—and this is the only reason for my referring to it at this date—I was not entirely indifferent to it.

I was somehow pleased and, at odd moments, even moved to find myself in the presence of characters who had some dignity of demeanor, of dress, and of speech. I was glad to be reminded of a world where delicate issues of conscience were expressed in graceful language. People spoke softly and said even inconsequential things with refinement. This manner may often be enervating, but in view of the vulgar clamor, the stupid energy, of so much that is shown nowadays on the stage and heard in the streets, I am grateful for the importance which James's characters, even when presented through the medium of a hapless dramatization, give to their every gesture and reflection.

One character was trying to choose a worthy life; another was capable of love and self-sacrifice; the most trifling of the play's personages was sharp of wit and word. They all looked superb—it is true that sometimes one could not tell whether the actors were wearing Cecil Beaton's clothes or the clothes were wearing the actors; still, it is pleasant to see people look like stage figures—like people worth remark.

The play seemed to lack a story—that is, action and situation; yet the seeds of a grand story were there, a romantic story. The theatre loses much of its attraction when its story aspect is neglected or abandoned. The painter Juan Gris, whose cubism was once deemed as "controversial" as Picasso's, used to beg his artistic mentor to assure him that his (Gris's) "experiments" were truly pictures. A painting, he felt for all his interest in abstraction, had to make a *picture*. In the same way, for all our modern appetite for psychology, atmosphere, and color, we yearn for a play to retain some element of the fabulous, to tell an entrancing story.

There is a good, old-fashioned story in Barrie's comedy *What Every Woman Knows*. When the play was revived in 1946 by the American Repertory Theater—in which Eva Le Gallienne, miscast, gave a most engaging performance as the Comtesse de la Brière—some of the reviewers spoke almost disdainfully of Barrie's sentimentality. They forgot, these up-to-the-minute ignoramuses, that Barrie's sturdy sentimentality has outlasted the spurious realism of most contemporary examples of our ruggedness.

There is nothing wrong with sentimentality: it is one form of emphasis, one way of approaching and telling the truth, or at least a sufficient portion of the truth to be respected. Sentimentality is bad where there is not enough substantial matter in a play to sustain it. Just as romantic heroism is not only tolerable but enjoyable when the nature of an artist's talent proves that this trait really exists in him—through his story, his style, his mode of thinking and feeling—so sentimentality is sound where the artist seems to be able to live, function, and make sense with it. Such was the case with Barrie.

What Every Woman Knows is shrewdly contrived; it says something we recognize as valid; it has a pretty humor, magnetic good nature, and is a wonderful vehicle for a good acting company.

Helen Hayes plays it with abundant skill and sureness. Though she treats her part now with more detachment than she did in 1926, when she was more naïvely involved in it, she is still adorable. To see the play now is like receiving a nosegay in a dismal season.

—*NAT*, 8 Jan. '55

JULIUS CAESAR

I am glad Mr. Kirstein saw fit to call our readers' attention to certain aspects of the American Shakespeare Festival Theater's endeavor—the school or academy directed by John Burrell, etc., (*The Nation*: August 20)—which I omitted in my discussion of their first production, *Julius Caesar* (August 6).

Mr. Kirstein's statement is a respectable one, but it overlooks, I am afraid, the point of my argument, and indirectly emphasizes the fault of which I complained. I wrote "I shall not review the production because what is significant about it is not its badness, but the reason why it was doomed before its first rehearsal was called. The flaws were in thinking and theory—in approach."

My piece was, as noted, not a "review"—if it had been, I should probably have referred to the better performances, those by Christopher Plummer and Fritz Weaver, for example—but an essay on theatre esthetics, more particularly as they relate to the production of Shakespeare. I shall reiterate my point, not because there was any ambiguity about it in the first place, but because it involves a conception of theatre production in general.

Mr. Kirstein tells us that I am in error in having written that the production "aims to reproduce the Elizabethan picture of Rome as the historians and artists of that period conceived it. Why was this approach chosen?" Mr. Kirstein informs us that the costumes were not Elizabethan: "they strive to fulfill what was in Shakespeare's own eye when he thought of Rome." The armor in the Connecticut production, Mr. Kirstein goes on to say, "was the sort of fanciful parade-armor imagined by Piero della Francesca and Paolo Ucello."

I will not dispute this because, for one thing, Mr. Kirstein is a knowledgeable art critic. But I still ask what has this bit of information to do with the production of *Caesar*? How do we know what was in Shakespeare's eye? We do not attempt to reproduce the acting of Shakespeare's day even though that was certainly in his eye. If we did, we should probably find altogether intolerable any production which tried it—despite anything we may surmise to the contrary from Hamlet's speech to the Players.

The production of a play signifies the projection of the playwright's idea in terms that are intelligible, vivid, and stirring to the audience to whom it is addressed. The purpose of a Shakespearean production today—as of all production—is to convey in theatre terms (acting, design, movement, color), the emotional, intellectual, dramatic essence of the play—its body and spirit. What is finally conveyed depends to a great extent on the intention and talent of the actors and their director. My criticism of the Connecticut *Caesar* is not that there was "nothing good in it," but that the approach was basically unrelated to the theatre—Shakespeare's or ours—because it was concerned with matters incidental to the problem of any sort of theatrical production.

In Orson Welles's *Caesar* (for all its limitations) the actual brick stage back wall, painted or lit a reddish hue, was seen throughout. Its use was justified because it was organic to the entire conception of the production, which was inspired by the atmosphere of the thirties. What is crucial in this respect is not what was in Shakespeare's eye, but in ours.

I am perfectly prepared to accept Piero della Francesca or anyone else as a visual model for a Shakespearean play if such a visual style is needed to render its content and impact complete. I may later find fault with the content or declare the style inappropriate, but in the case of the *Caesar* in question I feel that the attempt to produce the play as a theatre piece was never truly begun.

This is not a demand for an "experimental" or "revolutionary" production—these words in this connection are almost meaningless—just as the word "straightforward" employed by Mr. Kirstein in connection with his associates' production is meaningless, for the only thing that could be called that at all in relation to Shakespeare is a simple reading of the text. As I pointed out in my first piece, the recent Old Vic production of *Henry IV* was in no way original in conception but it had immense vigor and gusto which were sufficient to make it enjoyable.

But perhaps I can make my point even clearer by dropping the Shakespeare issue for a moment. When an Odets writes a play which takes place in the milieu of the boxing business, the director does not necessarily try to mirror that environment naturalistically: he tries to communicate a sense of Odets's feeling in regard to certain basic preoccupations in which the fight ring, gymnasium, and dressing room have only a secondary relation.

The playwright's world (Shakespeare's or anyone else's) is not primarily a historical one, but is the spiritual world of his own psychology, temperament, dramatic style—all of which are revealed by the nature of his writing. The job of the director and his company is to convey that world, according to their own lights, to their own kind of audience. This means that every production must possess its own quality and emphasis, not because anyone wishes to distort the playwright's meaning or "star" himself, but because actors, directors, and audience are human beings who are different in every theatrical circumstance.

The Moscow Art Theatre's production of *Caesar* was wrong because it tried to reproduce the Rome of Caesar's time. But we do not get closer to Shakespeare by reproducing what he literally saw in his day—even if we were sure we knew. Only by creative interpretation, that is, by discovering the stage equivalent for what we feel is Shakespeare's impulse, his total artistic personality, can Shakespeare come alive for us in the theatre: We must seek Shakespeare's world in his texts, not in the pictures of his period.

—*NAT*, 27 Aug. '55

MARCEL MARCEAU
THE DIARY OF ANNE FRANK

The new season has begun well. Craftsmanship has been on an impressive plane and content unconventional. In the case of the French pantomimist, Marcel Marceau, who began a limited engagement at the Phoenix and carried on with it at the Barrymore, the craftsmanship is altogether exceptional and the entertainment value of a rare and exquisite quality.

I cannot, however, arrive at any complete estimate of Marceau's total contribution. Beside the craftsmanship displayed—and it is clear that Marceau's accomplishment in this regard is masterly—an artist must finally be judged by the whole weight of his work. By "weight," I mean the import, the human value, the significance in terms of living experience contained and conveyed in an artist's work.

What Marceau has chosen to show us here in New York seems to be only the lighter side of his repertoire. Lightness is in itself an inestimable attribute. Chaplin, to whom Marceau has been compared, is a great artist—but the lightness of Marceau's present program is often trifling. Many of the pieces are admirable exercises that may be studied with care by actors and dancers, and delightedly appreciated by theatergoers in general, but they have very little content beyond their brilliant execution. Some other pieces are pantomimic illustrations of cute observations, enjoyable for their graceful *bonhomie*, but without any substantial creative meaning. Only twice during the evening—in the abstract "Youth, Maturity, and Death" and in the number called "Bip and the Butterfly"—does Marceau transcend the dilettante diversion of his popular bill and enter the realm of poetic expression.

This leads me to believe that Marceau felt he ought to undertake his first American appearance with a showman's circumspection and wait for another occasion to reveal his more ambitious art. In the meantime, we can enjoy the small pleasures of his charming bric-a-brac as well as the picture postures of his partners Pierre Verry and Alvin Epstein, whose perfect miniatures seem to epitomize French art from the eighteenth century through to Daumier.

Frances Goodrich and Albert Hackett have made a decent play from *The Diary of Anne Frank* (Cort Theater), and Garson Kanin, his associates, and cast have made it into an honorable production. I do not mean to qualify my praise of this offering by these adjectives, but to describe the qualities of modesty, wholesomeness, and dignity which characterize the play.

What *The Diary of Anne Frank* does is not to recount a harrowing episode in Nazi oppression, but to suggest the homely beauty of life among simple people under the most dismal conditions. The play is not deeply affecting or profound, but it is constantly sound and most sympathetically sobering. One watches it in the kind of gratifying relaxation one has in the company of honest and humane people who, whether they are glad or troubled, foolish or brave always remain entirely worthy and lovable.

Garson Kanin has directed the play admirably, always keeping its line fluent in a manner which is never dull or undramatic. He has molded the excellent company—headed by a subdued and improved Joseph Schildkraut—into a fine ensemble. In Boris Aronson's consummate set, they keep the tone of the play warm without pathos.

Special mention must be accorded Susan Strasberg, who is not only particularly gifted, but gifted in a way which makes her something other than a child actress. Miss Strasberg is bursting with the potential of her imminent womanliness and acute sophistication. She already has a powerful voice and a manner of delivery which is not of her (teen) age. She possesses a dramatic sense which is not so much Anne Frank's as that of, let us (exaggeratedly) say, a Medea. To put it another way, she is still too young for the parts she is ideally capable of. Never has it been more suitably proclaimed: here is a *promising* actress.

Space does not permit me to expatiate on the special charm of Joyce Grenfell's evening at the Bijou Theater. Her manner is as affectionate, good humored, right as an English lawn, peopled with silly and yet somehow dear people whose absurdity one recognizes with a laughter which harbors no rancor. With slight external resources, Miss Grenfell manages a perfect technique in conformity with her gently intelligent and thoroughly engaging art.

—*NAT*, 29 Oct. '55

WILL SUCCESS SPOIL ROCK HUNTER?

Will Success Spoil Rock Hunter? by George Axelrod (Belasco Theater) is a fantasy disguised as an ordinary farce. All farces are essentially fantastic, but in this case there is almost no pretense that the story is even fictitiously real: the central character is the Devil in the familiar form of a movie agent.

I believe I should have liked the play more if it had been presented as a fantasy—an entertainment

which took even greater liberties with reality than farce permits. But in this I am box-office wrong. Our audiences prefer their falsehoods straight—perhaps because in the theatre at least they are hardly concerned with truth. Here I suspect they are not even concerned with fiction—the play is a series of jokes or improvised gags about Hollywood.

Some of the jokes are funny and there is—helpfully from the standpoint of a certain audience—a bit of rancid ribaldry about many of them. I am a poor audience for these jokes because I consider most of the quips about Hollywood to be based on a lie. The joke about Hollywood's stupidity, madness, and immorality was effective as long as we believed that the people who made the joke had values which were not those of Hollywood—but this is no longer true. Motion pictures are a great industry at which many able people are hard at work, and the product of which most of us patronize. We now realize—if we never did before—that the majority of the people who scoff at Hollywood are extremely eager to become and remain part of its corruption, madness, etc. Martin Gabel, Walter Matthau, and Harry Clark help a great deal through their extraordinarily expert performances.

—*NAT*, 5 Nov. '55

SIX CHARACTERS IN SEARCH OF AN AUTHOR

I have seen Pirandello's *Six Characters in Search of an Author* so many times—in France, Italy, England and here—that I am no longer sure I can evaluate it. What is certain is that it is a play which, to employ a French expression, marks a date.

Pirandello was the first playwright to dramatize the post-1918 sense of the splitting of the ego. Turgenev in one of his novels voiced the nineteenth-century feeling that "the heart of another is a dark forest"—meaning that it is difficult for men to understand one another; twentieth-century literature after the First World War increasingly stressed the notion that men cannot know themselves because man is not one but many; that there is hardly any dominant "I" in any man, but only a collection of disparate and often alien impulses.

Pirandello found an entertaining and theatrically original way of putting this sense of the atomization of human personality on the stage. Men cannot really comprehend one another or even be sure that they exist coherently for themselves—except through a work of art in which the artist, serving as god to his own material, fixes the truth and permits us to see men steadily and whole.

This is an essentially tragic view, although in Piranadello it takes on a hysterical and grotesque aspect, one might say almost a strident "laugh, clown, laugh" quality. Pirandello's work is a kind of tragic *commedia dell' arte*. His characters are puppets, his structure, for all its deliberate mystification, is schematic, and his tone a mingling of sideshow laughter with a shriek. The feeling one is usually left with after seeing a Pirandello play is one of disturbance: the writer appears to have been grinning with pain, and one is chiefly aware of his mordancy.

In the new revival at the valuable Phoenix Theatre, Tyrone Guthrie aims at having fun with Pirandello: the play's tragic center strikes one as an intrusion on a farce. The theatre folk, a director and his company, are rendered as mountebanks, and some of the stage business—particularly in the rehearsal scene in which the director, the most asinine of the lot, is shown to be incapable of entering a set without wrecking it—is hilarious. But though the play lends itself to a great variety of treatments, Mr. Guthrie's seems to me the least relevant. It eliminates almost every vestige of the play's anguish, destroys the tension between two worlds presented—reality and illusion.

I have a further objection to the production. The theatre world itself (the world of make-believe) has its own pathos. A theatrical company is not necessarily composed of imbeciles. Actors are frequently vain and silly people but they nearly always have a certain naive credulity which is

honorable because it is creative. Pirandello's text indicates this, and the actor's fumbling efforts toward understanding make their situation in the play almost as touching as the passion of the "six characters" to make themselves understood.

This is not to say that the production is without merit. On the contrary, it is brilliant. If I were giving a course in stage direction, I would instruct my students to study this production carefully for its resourcefulness and invention. How to make shock entrances and exits while no one in fact enters or exits, how to visualize every line or idea: "Man has dignity" somebody says as he is forced to crawl between another person's legs, "I am master here" the director says as he falls over the furniture; to make more graphic the caged feeling of the older son in the play, Guthrie has him stand under a ladder that somehow seems to imprison the boy in a mesh of taut nerves. All this, and how at all times to keep the stage alive with fluid, expressive movement, may be learned and enjoyed in this production.

But as a critic I am obliged to point out that this directional brilliance is used here for false ends because, for one thing, the director has no true sympathy with his text except as a scenario for his talented exercises.

Individually Kurt Kasznar, Michael Wager, Betty Lou Holland and some others are better than capable. Whitfield Connor in the crucial role of the Father could carry more weight if he were given a little more help. In any case, there can be little doubt that the play's truth has been sacrificed for high jinks.

—*NAT*, 31 Dec. '55

TIME OF YOUR LIFE

William Saroyan's *The Time of Your Life* is a little classic of the American theatre. I do not use the word "little" to indicate any lack of value or the word "classic" to signify any pretension of profundity. The simple fact is that in *The*

Time of Your Life Saroyan has not only given us the essence of his talent, his personality, and his sense of life, but in doing so has expressed in delightfully theatrical terms a certain American dream and a certain American tradition. It is the dream of freedom in an almost child-like aspect, the tradition of a lovable vagrancy.

Americans believe in work, in accomplishment, in success. What we have built as a result of this credo is the most complicated and gigantic civilization the world has ever known. This civilization is at once a smash hit and an unspeakable burden. We are both proud of it and weary; we groan under its duties as we exult in its products. We trumpet its triumphs as we reach for our sleeping pills.

The typical hero of such a civilization is the supercolossal achiever of the greatest amount of financial, social or physical displacement—some sort of personal atomic explosion. But such heroes—and we produce them constantly—soon become as stupefying as the works they create. We seek relief from them in antiheroes—those with whom we can laugh, those toward whom we can feel kindness, those whom we envy not because of their greatness but, on the contrary, because of their littleness, their endearing inconspicuousness.

This sentiment produced such symbols as Chaplin's early pictures and motivates the hobo figure of our popular literature and stage. Saroyan's *The Time of Your Life* is a charmingly effusive, drunkenly dreamy, deft and darling piece of hoboism. We are nuts, but we are good, says the hobo poet; we know that life can be sweet because there is sweetness in all of us, but we allow ourselves to become bewildered—we have lost our "foundation"—through the fraudulent mechanism of the world which has been elaborated around us. People who are full of hate may be brushed aside without malice, like bugs. For the rest we have only to accept the life process—inhale and exhale; there is romance, fun, genius and song on all sides.

Saroyan's play is wayward and airy. It is inspired by the bonhomie of the bar, the mildness, good nature, and cosmopolitan color of San Francisco itself. It moves in circles like a carrousel to beer-hall music spiced with strains of Orientalism and a gently drugged jazz. The dialogue is like a delicious babel of homespun jokes mingled with the strange clamor made by all the languages and races of a port town. There is the constant echo of laughter, and now and again the faint suspicion of a sob. The pervasive quality, as well as the "philosophy" of the play, is one of lyric anarchism.

If I speak with unabashed affection of *The Time of Your Life* it is not without a certain pang of regret. For I must make a public confession now—sixteen years after the event: I once turned down the opportunity to produce this gay and lovely play. It has always been difficult for me to explain or even fully to understand the reason. Perhaps there is in this play, besides the things that endear it to me, a certain cloying infantilism, exemplified by the scene in which the play's central vagabond and his companion vie with each other as to which can consume the greatest number of jellybeans, the "wiser" of the two exclaiming, "I've been wanting to do this all my life."

It is this trait in the play that spoils it for some people and probably spoiled it for me on that lamentable occasion sixteen years ago. But every work suffers from the defects of its qualities, and it is a serious critical weakness to detect the vice before one has a chance to appreciate the virtue of what is fundamentally a healthy, joyous dramatic spree in praise of folly.

—*NAT*, '55

SKIN OF OUR TEETH

Although there are some discriminating judges who esteem the plays of Thornton Wilder above all others in the roster of American drama, his plays seem to stand apart from the main line of our contemporary tradition. One rarely thinks, for instance, of discussing Wilder's dramatic output in connection with that line of playwrights which runs from O'Neill through Hellman, Odets, Miller, Williams, Inge, and so on. Wilder is a unique phenomenon.

The reason for this, I suspect, is not simply that Wilder's plays are more abstract and stylized than the others, but that, while being distinctly familiar in subject matter, they possess a special sort of impersonality, a removal from reality as we actually experience it, a peculiar evasion of the concrete which makes them specifically Wilder without making them altogether individual. Though Wilder, when we look closely, has a mark of his own, his work strikes one as that of an "arranger" rather than that of a creator. His arrangements are artful, attractive, scrupulously calculated, and unmistakably gifted. They are delightfully decorative patterns created from the raw material dug up by other men. To put it another way, he arranges "flowers" beautifully, but he does not grow them. In this sense, he resembles certain modern Frenchmen rather than one of our own playwrights.

What is American in Wilder's plays is their benign humor, their old-fashioned optimism, their use of the charmingly homely detail, the sophisticated employment of the commonplace, their avuncular celebration of the humdrum, their common sense, popular moralism, and the simplicity—one might almost say simple-mindedness—behind a shrewdly captivating manipulation of a large selection of classic elements.

In *The Skin of Our Teeth,* the Robert Whitehead revival first presented in Paris as part of the Salute to France festival, Wilder tells us in a poetic and fanciful charade, which mixes vaudeville technique, historical allusion, timelessness, and the bric-a-brac of time-worn jokes, that life is struggle, that man and all his works are always on the verge of destruction, that his love for his kindred (including evil which is part of him), the steadfastness of woman who keeps him to his promise of binding love, and his pride in his finest accomplishments in the battle against chaos will always save humankind and the world from moral as well as physical annihilation.

There are references in the play to Plato and Spinoza, to beauty contests, the eternal Lilith, the world wars, Aristotle, the cozy charm of American suburbia, refugees or displaced persons—but all this is stated in a winning children's picture-book style which should be comprehensible to virtually every theatregoer. The final effect is sweet, reassuring, now and then sentimentally touching, and for the most part lots of fun—like the deliberate innocence of an intelligent and charming preacher illustrating honorable homilies for kids who might fail to heed the lesson if it were provided in any more severe form.

The new production—and the play merits repeated revival—offers the sharp skillfulness of Helen Hayes' talent, the ringing voice, lovely legs, and charming gusto of Mary Martin. The production errs, it seems to me, in taking the play's trick of willful corniness too literally. The atmosphere of general high jinks was intended by Wilder as a gay come-on to his serious purpose, which is capable of reaching something like exaltation. The production tries for cleverness, rendering the play less stimulating than it might be by making it at moments down-right smug, so that some of Wilder's thought and feeling takes on a kind of complacency which is by no means sympathetic.

Our admiration for the gifted people involved in this production must not hide from our keener sight that they have chosen the line of least resistance, or mistaken one facet of the play's appeal (the "hokum" or jocular) for its essence. Wilder's baby mammoths are reduced to toy baby lambs. There is something vitally wrong in a production of *The Skin of Our Teeth* when its most completely satisfactory moment is the boardwalk seduction scene in which Mary Martin and George Abbott dance in amorous hebetude.

The theatre at its best is either festival or rite. The upstart realistic theatre is only superficially a challenge to this axiom. Chekhov is a poet, Ibsen a priest. The theatre which merely reports or attempts literally to hold the mirror up to nature is a hundred times less interesting than nature.

Because for many years the theatre's festivities and solemnities had become hollow and sleazy, lacking true gaiety or inspired meaning, the naturalistic theatre acquired a certain fascination. The theatre was manacled by a false realism as cheap and trite as the most pompous or meretricious theatricalism.

There are distinct signs of change among us. *The Matchmaker* is a creative adaptation of a play by the "classic" Austrian dramatist Johann Nestroy (1806-1862) which Thornton Wilder wrote in 1938 for Max Reinhardt and called *The Merchant of Yonkers*. It was revised and revived at the Edinburgh Festival of 1954, presented last season at the Haymarket Theatre in London and is now triumphant in New York at the Royale.

Reinhardt's production was impeded by his unfamiliarity with American theatre custom— although his production brought us some delightful settings by Boris Aronson. *The Matchmaker* is directed by Tyrone Guthrie, whom nothing impedes. The most robust and imaginative of British directors—actually he is Irish—Guthrie is a playboy in the healthiest sense of the word. His art has enormous verve, a kind of Tyl Eulenspiegel prankfulness combined with a gusty *désinvolture,* unmindful of decorum or propriety.

The direction of *The Matchmaker* strains a bit in the first act, because Guthrie excels at movement rather than in sentiment, and the play at that point needs warmth rather than impetus, but once the plot begins to twist and turn in its crazy cavortings the show becomes a fetching marathon of joyous inconsequentialities and sweeping slapstick.

Though the entire cast is excellent, the evening is largely Guthrie's and Ruth Gordon's. Miss Gordon has never given a more satisfying performance. Her clowning is impish and abandoned, at once sharp and zestful. She seems to be improvising all the time, but having seen *The Matchmaker* twice I know how much shrewd theatrical calculation there is in her spontaneity. She has herself a ball in the part, and nobody seems to deserve it more.

The play itself is a pure farce, and therefore without verifiable content. Its meaning is in the doing of it, the sheer physical exhilaration of its theatrical pattern. Yet it distills a certain poetry and charm. There is a kind of unsentimental Saroyanesque cheerfulness about it. Saroyan tried to be hearty and gay in the midst of depression; so there is a sneaking little ache in his work which he tried his best to hide. Wilder's play reflects a time of prosperity and innocence. His style—clean, crisp, cool, graceful, all smiles ("The streets of New York are full of cabhorses winking at each other")—shows no trace of shadow. A kind of happy chromo brightness—abetted by Tanya Moisewitsch's settings and costumes which for all their riot manage to be discreet—invites us to pack up our troubles and think back to that old New York—"Father's" eighties—where, so it pleases us to fancy, we might have been truly carefree.

It is a happy condition to be in for two hours or so, but in all honesty it must be said that nowadays not everyone is capable of this sort of levity. I noticed a few people in the audience whom it made restless. There are some who are too attached to the prose of their torment.

—*NAT*, '55

FALLEN ANGELS

Aaron Copland once told how, when at an early age he announced that he intended to become a composer, his friends and relatives asked his opinion of every "musical" manifestation within earshot, including the fiddling of the neighborhood virtuoso, the singing of itinerant tenors, the tunes of the passing hand organ and the harmonica playing of the boys in the candy store. When Copland assured his questioners that he held no opinion on these matters, his attitude seemed particularly insulting to them.

A dramatic critic is likewise expected to pass judgment on practically everything that is exposed on a platform in the way of professional entertainment. I must confess my inability to do so. I harbor no contempt for the spectacles in which I have little interest. My indifference to them is not snobbish: on the contrary, to attempt a close critical scrutiny of them would seem to me like presumption and hypocrisy.

The several plays I saw during the past week do not exactly belong to the category to which I refer, but I find it difficult to develop any strong feeling about them either way. In fact I was rather shocked—though I understood—when I saw a certain critical colleague from a kindred weekly journal walk out after the first act of one of the shows in a state of indignation.

Noel Coward's *Fallen Angels* (Playhouse), a play first presented in New York in 1927 and a failure then, is essentially an extended revue skit passing itself off as a bit of bright sophistication. Hermione Gingold guyed it in its London revival two seasons ago, and Nancy Walker does the same here. The ladies' buffoonery is the only excuse for both revivals, and is undoubtedly a benefit for which Coward, at any rate, should be grateful.

Nancy Walker is funny. She has become increasingly deft since her first success in *On the Town* ten years ago. I prefer her in straight revues and musicals where her material can be terser and more topical than in her present vehicle. It might however be instructive to a student of comedy technique to note the manner in which, bit by bit, Miss Walker makes Coward's dialogue disappear amid her antics. By the middle of the second act one doesn't hear or listen to a word: one simply becomes fixed on the eccentric and disjointed gyrations of this tough and somehow sad lady clown. One laughs and goes home slightly melancholy.

—NAT, 11 Feb. '56

THEATRE IN GERMANY: I

As I remember Berlin—which I first visited in 1922—it was a stuffily comfortable city which gave evidence of a fulsomely prosperous, unmistakably middle-class past. There were marks, too, of shock and despair—a kind of wan astonishment as of a man who, while still surrounded by substantial possessions, discovers that he is no longer solvent.

Berlin today is two towns: the one in the West strikes me like an old-fashioned ice-cream parlor built on a waste land; the other in the East resembles a shabby encampment constructed from the rubble of a formidable city. One can travel without any trouble from West to East Berlin by subway or electric train: yet the effect of the division is to make both sectors seem bloodless, ghost-like, almost unreal. There is a sense of ruin which no one, except the sightseeing guides, thinks it proper to notice or remark upon. In West Berlin people behave as if all were normal or were soon going to be; in East Berlin, as if the shattered streets were a promise of future achievement. Is this the end of a world or the beginning of a new one?

One thing has not changed: the theatre now, as in the twenties, is of the best. There were more ambitious and practiced playwrights then—in fact the German expressionists of those days were auguries, some people believed, of a new and exalted drama—and there were innumerable actors of high rank. Today there are few new playwrights worth special mention, and most of the famous actors whose names were the pride of the European stage have disappeared through natural causes and some through causes which were not at all natural.

Yet there is no escaping the fact: in quality of production, in scenic invention, in variety of repertory, in solidity of organization, the German theatre at this moment (and Berlin is by no means the single nor even the most signal instance of it) makes the American, English, French stages look like little-theatre activities.

I had not expected this because, for one thing, such critics as Eric Bentley in New York and Kenneth Tynan in London had made it appear that the German theatre today was interesting only because of Bertolt Brecht's "Berliner Ensemble Theater" (Brecht is not the titular administrative director, but he is unquestionably its guiding spirit.) While it is true that this East Berlin company represents the most strikingly new development in the German theatre since the Second World War, it is all wrong to suggest that it is the only distinguished theatre in Germany or even in Berlin.

There is, for example, the state-supported Schiller Theater in West Berlin, a modern and handsome construction on the site of the old building which was destroyed in the air raids. It has a seating capacity of 1200, and its management also runs a smaller house in which intimate plays are produced. I did not inquire how large the state subsidy was, but I was informed that in the smaller city of Frankfurt, the subsidy amounts to $1,500,000 a year.

The stage of the Schiller Theater occupies one third of the building's space. (In most American theatres the stage is confined to one tenth of the total area.) It has several revolving tables and is equipped in most up-to-date fashion in regard to lighting, scene docks, etc.

Almost all the actors of the Schiller Theater are employed by the season, which is also true of the imposing technical and administrative staff. The repertory includes at present a German play of the twenties, a play by Calderon freely translated by Von Hoffmansthal, Ibsen's *Peer Gynt* and *Doll's House*, Anouilh's latest play *Ornifle*, Schiller's *Don Carlos*, Goethe's *Faust*, Shaw's *Caesar and Cleopatra*, Büchner's *Danton's Death*, Erwin Piscator's adaptation of Tolstoy's *War and Peace*, Richard Nash's *The Rainmaker*, Arthur Miller's *A View from the Bridge*, Faulkner's *Requiem for a Nun*, and a new play, being given its world premiere here, by Marcel Pagnol.

At the Berliner Ensemble Theater in East Berlin the repertory includes, besides Brecht's plays, versions of Farquhar's *The Recruiting Officer*, Synge's *The Playboy Of the Western World*, a play by the nineteenth-century Russian classic Ostrovsky. Other plays being offered in other East Berlin theatres include Molière's *George Dandin*, plays by Schiller, Goldoni, Lorca,

Hauptmann, Shaw, Shakespeare. All the East Berlin theatres are state supported, as are the opera houses in both West and East Berlin. In West Germany alone there may be as many as 200 state-owned theatres. I paid ten marks for my orchestra ticket at the Schiller Theater: about $2.50. The cost of a similar ticket (in dollars) is less than half that amount in East Berlin.

The audience which attends the theatre in both sectors—it is to be noted incidentally that West Berlin residents may and do attend East Berlin theatres and vice versa, just as actors living in either sector may be employed in theatres of the other—the audience, I say, appears as well "trained" as the companies themselves. They are almost invariably punctual, extraordinarily attentive and quiet during the performance, rarely applaud till the curtain is down and the house lights have been turned up. There is something almost solemn about their behavior in the theatre auditorium—they drink beer or juices and eat sandwiches during intermission in the commodious foyers intended for the purpose. They laugh discreetly, as if laughter might disturb the actors or as if the theatre were not intended for undue levity, although the biggest laugh and applause in a very bad production of *Bus Stop* I saw at one of the "private" (non-subsidized) theatres came just where it did in the New York production.

My purpose in beginning this report on the Berlin theatre with some hasty observations on the physical appearance of the city itself was not simply to introduce a bit of local color into my description. The scarred city and the atmosphere produced by the causes and consequences of its wounds stand in a vital relationship to what one sees in the theatre.

Danton's Death, at the Schiller Theater, is the work of a German dramatist—George Büchner—who died in 1837 at the age of twenty-three. The play was written when he was twenty-one. A medical student, Büchner was a romantic, unhappy with the reaction which had set in Germany after

Napoleon's final defeat. But Büchner's mind had also a critical and realistic bent—he thought of drama as a form of history—and his emotions were torn between the tug of his yearning for freedom, beauty and ethical nobility and the repressive conservatism, which the disillusionment with the French Revolution and the fear of Napoleon—who to most Europeans outside France somehow symbolized that Revolution—had bred.

Büchner was attracted to the purposes for which the revolution had been undertaken—this made him a radical—but he was horrified by the physical and moral depredations of the historical process as it actually works itself out in daily needs. "Freedom has become a whore," one of the characters says in *Danton's Death*; and the play which seems buoyed up by a kind of revolutionary afflatus also has about it a quality of anguish and pessimism which a determined or doctrinaire radical would qualify as counter revolutionary. Throughout the play, a revulsion is expressed at the nemesis of history, which seems to compel its human agents to commit criminal acts.

Because the play is wildly episodic and was utterly impracticable for stage conditions at the time of its composition, it was not produced until seventy-five years later—in 1910. I saw it done in German by the company Reinhardt brought to the old Century Theatre in New York in 1927. The production was extremely picturesque, spectacularly brilliant, but chiefly ornamental, because the play's material served Reinhardt merely as the springboard for a splendid show.

For the present director, Erwin Piscator—some twelve years in exile from Germany and only recently repatriated in West Germany, though still markedly "independent" in his views—the play is something more than an experience in sparkling modern theatrics—though it is that as well. *Danton's Death* is a romantic epic of political turmoil, a grandiose lyric statement of history's heartbreaking contradictions, a song of revolutionary ardor, and a heroic dirge on the personal misery of revolutionary action and the savage errors by which humanity progresses.

How appropriate and meaningful all this is at the state-supported theatre of West Berlin. For everything is here—on the stage, in the audience and in the streets outside: the memory and witness of "revolutionary" faiths of all kinds (we must not forget that for many Germans National Socialism represented a kind of religious revolt against capitalism and the decadent democracies) and the still harassing need to choose between different ideologies each of which is tainted with confusions, compromises and elements of shame.

Beyond all this, the energy, opulence, mechanical inventiveness of the production—which seems to move as easily and colorfully as any movie—serve in sum as an example of the sophistication, resourcefulness and imaginative exuberance of that part of the German theatre which has absorbed all the salutary influences in the world of modern art. Here are ideas, social significance, lavish showmanship, poetry—Büchner was a beautiful writer—free of the shackles of the ordinary commercial stage. The total production is a stage event of which most of us in New York, London and Paris are largely unaware—as if the theatre itself were an experience still to be discovered by us.

There are no great actors in *Danton's Death*, but the company—largely composed of people in their thirties—is virile, well endowed in voice, diction, looks and wholly practiced in the uninhibited use of the stage. A young man, Hans Dieter Zeidler, displays a combination of temperamental dash and solidity which, while it as yet wants the modification of greater subtlety of feeling that may come with a little more living and the opportunity for repose, could well make him another of the big actors for which the German theatre is celebrated.

The setting for *Danton's Death* is a triumph of eclectic methods. Revolving platforms are used, and certain devices of constructivism: the main architectural feature of the setting is a scaffolding which resembles a modified scenic railway, itself frequently in motion, so that when people promenade on it—which is what they do in many street scenes—we get the sense of constant mobility.

Images of places and people are fluently projected against screens on three sides of the stage. The result is a feeling of complete freedom in the background and environment of the play.

This setting is the work of Caspar Neher, the original designer of the Brecht-Weill *Threepenny Opera* and one of the two best designers in Germany. The other is Theo Otto, now residing in Zurich (but employed throughout Germany), who designed Brecht's *Mother Courage* at the Berliner Ensemble Theater. Both men stand among the world's most talented stage designers of our day.

—*NAT*, 23 June '56

THEATRE IN GERMANY: II

Bertolt Brecht's Berliner Ensemble Theatre in East Berlin has been called by one foreign critic the finest acting company in Europe. A number of other critics tend to discuss the productions of that remarkable organization from the standpoint of Brecht's theories. Both these approaches seem to me alien to the value or significance of any artistic phenomenon. The way to understand work in the theatre is to register and measure the effect created and the human, social and (sometimes) technical attributes which render that effect.

I begin my report on Brecht's theatre in this fashion because Brecht himself, as well as many of his admirers, lays so much stress on the unsentimental, didactic, demonstration-like nature of his art. The first thing I should like to note, therefore, is that I found *Mother Courage and Her Children*, perhaps the best of Brecht's plays, very touching.

Brecht is a poet. To overlook the extremely sensitive bareness and strength of his writing is to miss its core. It strikes me as downright silly to talk of Brecht's production methods—the tenets of his so-called Epic Theatre—without realizing that if such methods did not exist, the quality of Brecht's writing would require their invention. Brecht says that his plays may be done in different

ways, but it is clear that they would make no sense if one adhered to the ordinary naturalism of the contemporary stage.

Brecht's plays are morality plays as surely as anything written in the Middle Ages to demonstrate the road to Salvation or to mock the Evil One. There is in Brecht the same basic seriousness, the same need to be clear, popular, real (that is, essential). Those old plays depended a good deal on comedy—often of a primitive kind; so does Brecht, whose shrewd wit and robust humor nearly always assume a rather peasant-like bluntness. The old plays were direct: each scene had its unmistakable comic or pathetic point. They had very little of the ambiguity and indirection of the modern play. Brecht's plays do not attempt to render nuances of personal psychology: they are displays of primary motives. Finally, we are constantly kept aware that we are looking at an artifice, and that helps us to maintain the objectivity and critical sense which Brecht insists is the proper frame of mind for an adult in the theatre.

Mother Courage is the tale of a woman of the people who, with three illegitimate children, follows the troops during the Thirty Years War to sell them liquor and sundry other articles soldiers crave. The play shows us how she is slowly deprived of everything she cherishes: her children, her trade, her reason for being. This woman who takes no sides, who seeks only to live and let live in the most friendly fashion, is swept along by the currents of life in a war period until nothing remains of her native honesty, good nature, moral or material possessions.

There are very funny scenes in the play, dramatic scenes and scenes which for all their brevity give us a remarkably sharp view of the epoch. But what is most important to bear in mind is that, though Brecht always endeavors to keep his writing and presentation dispassionate and rather matter-of-factly quiet—effects of climax, suspense, mood being systematically avoided—what is ultimately achieved is indelibly vivid and emotionally telling. One leaves the theatre with the unalterable conviction that war is nothing less than the greatest scourge of man's making.

In his staging, Brecht doesn't attempt picturesqueness; yet his stage has a constant visual interest. Everything is apparently being done to destroy illusion—the light, for instance, is always bright white, and the electric apparatus always in view; the revolving stage by which Mother Courage's endless wanderings are shown in plainly a stage mechanism. Songs interrupt the action arbitrarily. They sharpen the play's points like epigrams of instruction. (Splendid songs they are too.)

The purpose of all this is to tell the audience that the play is a conscious device to present what the dramatist and his colleagues want the audience to understand—the play's moral point. But, and it cannot be repeated too often, all this does not make the play any the less moving. Everything seems congruous and right. One rarely gets any feeling of a stylistic mannerism, of a trick, labored "modernism."

Brecht is a classicist. He seeks that form of artistic truth which emphasizes the thing created above the creator, a manner which allows the spectator to appreciate the play with that repose and refinement of attention which liberate the spirit without drugging the senses. Brecht's programmatic anti-romanticism is against art as magic as it is against faith as superstition. But, more deeply, Brecht's technique is a form of discipline undertaken by the artist to convey as devotedly and self-abnegatingly as possible his perception of reality. The goal is wisdom rather than excitement. It has always been the aspiration of the highest art.

Brecht's ideas and this theatre are the product of a destroyed world: Germany from 1919 to the present. The landscape of *Mother Courage* (written in exile in 1938) is that of Berlin—particularly East Berlin—today. The audience is part of a world which has been destroyed or one which may be reborn. This is not a metaphor: it is a visible tangible fact. In such a world, one has to get down to fundamentals, everything is truly a matter of life

and death. In these circumstances, an art such as Brecht's is emblematic, necessary, national.

Would Brecht's methods serve all plays? Certainly not. Still Brecht's ideas and practice are stimulating and instructive for an understanding of the theatre everywhere. That Brecht's technique may at times be applied with happy results in certain plays other than his own is attested to by *Drums and Trumpets* (Farquhar's *The Recruiting Officer*) directed by one of the younger men of the Berliner Ensemble Theatre. It has been adapted to the uses of this theatre by making the war for which the recruiting is being done the American war of Independence (the original was written about seventy years earlier) and by making it even more than Farquhar's comedy and occasion for monkey-shines and vaudevillesque lampoon. The result is a hilarious anti-war farce of savage propaganda interlarded with all sorts of theatrical hokum—the whole giving no impression of artiness, strain or falsification.

I say "propaganda," but I must immediately add that it is of a kind which may readily be accepted by anyone at all—except a Junker or a Nazi. This explains why 30 percent of the Berliner Ensemble Theatre audience comes from West Berlin. I have also mentioned a certain primitivism, but should be clear that this is of a highly sophisticated sort. One striking example of this is the music. Much of is by Hanns Eisler and Paul Dessau—Brecht's pre-war musical collaborators. It reminds one very effectively of *The Threepenny Opera* and of that time in Berlin when Marlene Dietrich was driving the Emil Jannings type of boys crazy. It is an echo of the past easing the revolution of the present.

—*NAT*, 30 June '56

THE APPLE CART

I had thought as I sat down to write this review of Bernard Shaw's *The Apple Cart* (Plymouth Theatre) to devote myself mainly to a comparison of the present production with one I saw in London a few years ago in which Noel Coward and Margaret Leighton played the leading roles. But not only would this be unfair to the New York cast and to the reader who had not seen the play in London, but it would be the kind of evasion of criticism which I frequently complain about when revivals of presumably familiar plays are presented on our stage. We must begin with and for the most part stick to Shaw's text.

To focus on the "show" aspect of the production instead of on its content would be to indicate something of which *The Apple Cart* is itself a reflection. Most of us nowadays dislike thinking of politics. We harbor a vague sense of futility about it. Out political talk becomes, even in our own view, mere intellectual chit-chat without much personal or social relevance.

The Apple Cart was written in 1929 when Shaw was seventy-three. England was prosperous with the sort of prosperity about which the king in the play, and Shaw himself, were apprehensive. Shaw had become more than skeptical about the outer forms of democracy. The Labor (or Coalition) government of Ramsay MacDonald was hardly more reassuring to him than a Conservative government might have been. "Breakages, Ltd." (the play's symbol for capitalism) still ruled the roost, and the cabinet in the play suffers a sense of weary or regretful fatalism about it. Contemporary politics, Shaw implies, with gleaming irony and diminishing optimism, is mostly illusion and delusion. Only the philosopher-king—that is, the truly thinking man not engaged in vote catching or momentary local victories—is aware of the operative problems. And he becomes increasingly conscious that his awareness by itself, although irreducible and inalienable, cannot yet move mountains.

The play is beautifully written—it is clear, elegant, pithy, and has a certain aristocratic grace of Anglo-Protestant character. We cannot fail to be charmed by it. It is also brilliantly constructed: for we are given a long series of rather "abstract" discussion—abstract in the sense that there is little plot except as to whether or not the king shall declare himself a nonentity as his cabinet demands—but Shaw, by introducing a delightful episode in which he interrupts the political debate to reveal his own relationship to women, sustains our interest and handsomely entertains us despite what might first appear arid material.

Yet, I ask myself, what does an American (Broadway) audience today get out of all this? When he wrote the play, Shaw must have hoped that, while it would provide an intelligently amusing evening for a civilized audience, the play might also trouble that audience—move it at least to think further of the political dilemmas of the time. But now, I fear, the play indirectly encourages the profound political apathy of our public. When, for example, Shaw quips about the bootlessness of most election results, our audience applauds with a certain gleeful appreciation of his contemporaneity and cleverness. "We really felt all along," the audience seems to be saying, "that all the political stuff we hear about and indulge ourselves in is the bunk—and in this play that wise old bird Shaw tells us that we are right." The only difference is that Shaw was a little sore at heart about it, whereas we simply remain ignorant and complacent. For while it is true that the trappings of politics are generally ridiculous, the core of the matter is of the utmost seriousness.

Yes, it is a good show. The production is good-looking and the actors—Maurice Evans, Signe Hasso, Charles Carson and others—work hard and well at it. Sometimes they work too hard. The long speeches and the need for silken diction are a strain on most companies today; so that the light fluency, the air of superior mental capacity and freewheeling wit are not complete. But we must not be captious. We are lucky to see the play again.

—*NAT*, 3 Nov. '56

AUNTIE MAME
DIARY OF A SCOUNDREL
THE SLEEPING PRINCE
A VERY SPECIAL BABY
L'IL ABNER

Auntie Mame (Broadhurst Theatre) by Jerome Lawrence and Robert E. Lee, based on the novel by Patrick Dennis, is a series of blackouts or revue sketches in the spirit of *New Yorker* cartoons. It deals with an eccentric lady whose dizzy and slightly dazzling career is of little usefulness except for the amusing anecdotes her personality provides. Several of these sketches are funny and the show as a whole—with ingenious sets by Oliver Smith—is well produced, most of the casting being highly expert in its choice of types. I liked best Peggy Cass as a daffy secretary named Gooch and Joyce Lear as a blonde pain-in-the-neck from Darien, Conn.

I found myself somewhat fatigued and depressed after the pummeling of so many gags, even though some were good. I have the impression, when a company of friends spend all their time telling one another jokes, that they have nothing to say to one another. The same is true of a show: this is comedy with a hole in it—where a head or a heart ought to be. *Auntie Mame* is held together by that expert, swanky comedienne and nice girl, Rosalind Russell.

I was interested and entertained by Rodney Ackland's adaptation of a play—*Diary of a Scoundrel*—by Alexander Ostrovsky—"father" of the Russian drama (1823-88). Such plays are very difficult for Americans: their combination of Slavic folksiness á la Gogol with touches of Molière and Balzac are remote in style and point of view from our playgoing public, and particularly from our reviewers.

Considering the hazards, the Phoenix Theatre production, directed by Alan Cooke, was remark-ably good. The entire cast—and particularly Mike Kellin—managed very well the broad, highly colored strokes needed for such comedy.

It seems that the first night audience at Terence Rattigan's *The Sleeping Prince* (Coronet) froze with the kind of special snobbishness which afflicts lowbrows when they are in the mood to be highbrows. They not only refrained from laughter, they behaved as if their common diet was Congreve, Wycherley, Shaw, Sheridan and Maugham. This harrowed the actors—with results which can be imagined.

The Sleeping Prince is a sort of charlotte russe comedy about royalty of a bygone era—I'm sorry I wasn't there—and a chorus girl from the jolly Broadway of 1910. It is certainly inconsequential and at its worst need arouse no one's indignation. I found a good deal of it pleasant and some of it witty. The physical production is not all it might be, and the casting is spotty. Michael Redgrave tends to strain (partly perhaps because of his dual responsibility as director-star) but there is much character sense to be admired in his performance. Barbara Bel Geddes is darling as the chorus girl, though she still has to learn how to employ her endowments to characterize beyond herself. Cathleen Nesbitt as a Grand Duchess has the most deftly written part, and plays it with canny assurance.

The best acting of the season was offered by the cast (Luther Adler, Sylvia Sidney, Jack Warden, Jack Klugman, Will Kuluva, Carl Low) of *A Very Special Baby*—done to death after five performances by negligent reviews. The play by Robert Allan Aurthur (his first) was a rather primitive but respectably honest piece of realism about the effect of a selfish father on his Italian family. I am not much interested in such plays nowadays—for I seek poetry, ideas, theatrical vivacity from my drama—but in this instance I was held by the force, simple truth and palpable humanity of this company's playing under Martin Ritt's sound direction. Elia Kazan's name was mentioned in connection with Mr. Ritt's direction because the actors sometimes raised their voices and were intense. This sort of off-hand comment is irrelevant: one might point out that people even outside of Italian (or Jewish) families have been known to raise their voices and become intense at critical moments of their lives. What I should like to add is that not only many contemporary American plays require such treatment as Mr. Ritt's company gave *A Very Special Baby*, but that elements of such acting might also benefit many a production of Shakespeare. The stage is not a drawing room.

Perhaps it will be no surprise to you, if you know Al Capp's *L'il Abner*, that its characters bear such names as Moonbeam McSwine, Earthquake McGoon, and Appassionata von Climax, or that they are to be found in the town of Dogpatch, U.S.A. A goofy musical has been made of it (St. James Theatre) with a book by Norman Panama and Melvin Frank and lyrics by Johnny Mercer.

It is a paean in praise of backwardness, idleness and general no-accountism. But its distinguishing feature is frenetic energy. As I watched the amazing people who dance, sing, crawl, fly and jump in it, I thought how an English or a French audience would react to it. They would greet it with horrified delight. For it seems that with the energy expended in this show one might build a brave new world overnight. It is almost a pity to waste such whirling power on a mere show.

But it is a good show. Its hero is the dervish Michael Kidd who choreographed and directed it. Everyone is infected by his galvanic humor and contributes to the fun.

—*NAT*, 1 Dec. '56

CRANKS
BELLS ARE RINGING
CANDIDE

Cranks (Bijou theatre) is a little revue from London. The four members of its cast sing,

dance, make fun and change the stage properties. Anthony Newley is the comedian, Hugh Bryant has the voice, Gilbert Vernon dances best, Annie Ross is helpful and owns attractive legs.

I liked the intimacy of the show: our musicals suffer from elephantiasis. A kind of dainty wackiness—including the décor of John Piper and the musical arrangement by John Addison—gave the evening style. There is a certain pleasant amateurishness in spots, there are traces of personal wit, off-beat British humor skirting the fringes of surrealism, which at moments are perilously close to preciosity. All in all—and even with numbers that are totally blank—it was an evening of cordial entertainment.

Bells Are Ringing (Shubert Theatre), a musical about a big-hearted girl in an answering service, shouldn't be a good show but manages to become one. On the debit side are a silly, silly story, some embarrassing dialogue, the lack of any real score. More disappointing than all this, Jerome Robbins and Bob Fosse—who are gifted choreographers—haven't done anything like their best work.

On the credit side is the wholly winning performance of Judy Holliday (aided by the good looking, modest, and sympathetic presence of Sydney Chaplin) and the lovable spirit which constitutes the surprising gift of Betty Comden and Adolph Green.

Judy Holliday has no "voice"; she is no dancer. But she is such a wonderful person on stage that her singing and dancing become more attractive than that of performers technically much better equipped. She combines a feeling for the fundamental cameraderie of the popular theatre—the happy exchange between performer and audience—with the kind of old-time professionalism which distinguished the troupers of vaudeville days like Eva Tanguay, Trixie Friganza, Sophie Tucker: they seemed ready to do anything and everything to give the folks out front a good time. Only Judy Holliday is softer, more touching: she knows something of the shadows of life; her elders knew only the dynamics.

Betty Comden and Adolph Green are frequently crude and gauche. Yet once in a while they can burst into a crazy improvisation which replaces judgment with the bubbling enthusiasm of kids who are wholly delighted to discover that not only the emperor but the entire court is naked. Betty Comden and Adolph Green just can't get over the exhilaration of not being grown up.

Candide (Martin Beck Theatre), labeled "a comic operetta based on Voltaire's satire" with book by Lillian Hellman, score by Leonard Bernstein, lyrics by Richard Wilbur, John Latouche and Dorothy Parker, is very grown up, but unfortunately indecisive in its intention. It felt to me much longer than Voltaire's story, and although many separate bits may be individually admired, the composition of the whole hardly seems to have been planned.

The setting by Oliver Smith, the costumes by Irene Sharaff are handsome and lavish, the voices are superior (Barbara Cook is a charming ingenue who sings exceptionally well), the comedienne Irra Petina is funny, and there are some clever directorial touches by Tyrone Guthrie. Lillian Hellman's tart realism of mind and capacity for sharp statement sometimes serve to focus attention on the point of the enterprise and sometimes—because of the spectacular, extravaganza-like nature of the show—strike one as a wicked intrusion. Leonard Bernstein's music, at times very pretty, runs down all the paths of the production, but there are so many of these that we are left in doubt whether he has captured anything in the process—except for some moments of pure spoof and the exuberance of the race.

In the end I was not certain which of the talented people who fashioned this "operetta" had refused to yield to the other. It looked as if everyone was sticking stubbornly to his own conception of what the production should be. My guess is that in view of the original material (I refer to Voltaire) a sharp, polished, spare, economic "Brechtian" treatment might have served. Instead we have what is probably the most costly production in town.

The total effect of the show—if it can be said to have one—is of an enormous, splendid pastry, at the center of which is a hard, bitter pit. The theatre is a collective art, which is not the same thing as an accumulation of artistic contributions.

—*NAT*, 15 Dec. '56

MY FAIR LADY

My Fair Lady, a musical adapted from Bernard Shaw's *Pygmalion* by Alan Jay Lerner and Frederick Loewe, is a good show; in fact, a very good show—adult entertainment. Yet why, I wonder, are musicals when they are good greeted with more rapturous acclaim and a greater noise than almost any good play? Is it because applause is the natural response to the high spirits of a musical, whereas the reflective nature of drama induces a certain quiet within the marks of approbation? Or are we delighted beyond our knowing when things are made easy for us? We are intrinsically lazy.

These are some of the things which passed through my mind as I watched *My Fair Lady*. What musical does not permit time for our minds to wander?

The show is good, I said to myself, not because of any single element but because of the intelligent integration of all its elements. Shaw's dialogue—much of it has been retained—his basic good humor, health and self-respect cleanse the air. Lerner's lyrics have a certain crispness and quality of urbane banter. The idea of making a triumphant little song and dance when Liza progresses from "The rine in Spine falls minely on the pline," to "The rain in Spain falls mainly on the plain" is theatrically brilliant.

Oliver Smith's sets are festive with a kind of refreshing neatness, and Cecil Beaton's costumes radiate an unoppressive cheeriness. Loewe's music serves—we are glad the music is there; it does not come as a relief but as an extension of the scenes.

How truly Shaw lends himself to musical comedy! (Have any of us seen *The Chocolate Soldier,* which was the musical of *Arms and the Man?)* It took the authors and producers of *My Fair Lady* to remind us that Shaw never was a realist. He often is taken for one, but almost all Shaw productions clinging to a literal representation of the environment in which his plays presumably unfold are as wide of the mark as are most productions of Shakespeare.

Shaw is Punch and Judy, vaudeville and rhetoric informed by paradoxical common sense and joyous wisdom. His speeches are comic tirades (consider Doolittle's contrast of lower-class morality with that of the wealthy) or virtuoso arias in the grand manner—full of humanitarian passion and robust conviction. Shaw's quips, gags, handsprings and somersaults derive from the oldest of old theatre—which is one reason they endure. Shaw's lineage is the "classic" theatre from the street harlequinade to grand opera. That is why he seems very much himself in the new framework.

The cast of *My Fair Lady* is predominantly English. Rex Harrison is a first-rate light comedian. Julie Andrews' face and manner are adorably cameolike in the manner of the musical-comedy heroines of an earlier and happier period when stage faces had a quality of tinkling romance about them. Stanley Holloway as Doolittle is English musical hall with its homey familiarity.

What makes me enjoy all these players most of all is a quality of *bravery,* a certain professional sturdiness and reliability which are characteristic of the English actor at his best. They are disarmingly impudent, self-confident and modest at the same time. They are entirely immersed in the fine task of being entertaining. They are our humble servants and have a grand time at the job which they have taken pains to learn thoroughly. What they bring to the stage is not their private selves, but a craft which has somehow ennobled them for our pleasure and admiration. The total effect is in the honest sense wholesome. It is strange—but that is how I would finally describe the show.

—*NAT,* '56

ON PLAYS NOT REVIEWED

Not so long ago I went to see a play which is tremendously popular. After two acts I felt that I had tolerated enough of this entertainment. As I approached the coat room to get my things a stranger, all aghast, asked, "You're not leaving, are you?" "I've got to catch a train," I hastened to reply.

As a good American, one dislikes not enjoying a play which seems to entertain everybody else. Besides, why spoil someone else's fun? But a critic is supposed to consider all the fare that is offered. This is true only if one views criticism as a kind of penance. Certainly there are men who seem to revel in demolishing trifles. It is a sort of adolescent sadism.

To attack a play, I often think, is to acknowledge that it has some stature, since one has been sufficiently aroused to weigh and condemn it. But a good many plays fail to provoke any desire for such effort. I might go farther and add that there are certain clearly meritorious plays that a critic ought to abstain from criticizing at all. Such restraint should be exercised when the critic senses that he has no natural appetite for or real relation to the material the play deals with or to the point of view it embodies. For he will remain indifferent to such plays even when he surmises that they are good.

Shaw didn't "get" *The Importance of Being Earnest.* Max Beerbohm wrote like a fool about Gorky's *Lower Depths.* Wolcott Gibbs is absurd on Chekhov. None of this necessarily betrays a lack of judgment, only a congenital failure of sympathy with certain modes of experience. Racine is a sealed book to most American critics, as a good deal of Paul Claudel's work is alien to me. When a critic finds himself in such a position, what he writes is usually valueless.

On the other hand, I might say that while I respect and admire and to a degree have a feeling for T. S. Eliot's plays I do not like them. Yet when I "knocked" them I realized that I was still more keenly absorbed by them than I am by a great many quite pleasant plays which I might as well not discuss at all. If I were to write more bluntly than is critically permissible I might say about the first category of play, "These plays make me a little sore—but go see them": about the second, "These plays are, I suppose, very nice, I can't see why anyone should care."

In either case the critic must make clear from what angle he is viewing a particular play, what criteria he has in mind on each separate occasion. I once told a drama critic who complained of the success of a play we both thought cheap that the success of such plays hardly troubled me, while the frequent neglect of certain faulty plays which possessed the dignity of some creative impulse and accomplishment made me boil.

All this is by way of confessing why—apart from my duties elsewhere—I have recently overlooked certain plays in this column, why I have been reluctant to discuss them or in some cases even to see them.

The Tunnel of Love (Royale), for example, is a very successful biological farce of a kind that embarrasses me, although I was obliquely amused by its *Reader's Digest* culture: for while the play might be described as being about a seven year itch to have a baby, it abounds in references to Kafka, Margaret Mead, Thoreau, the *id*, Dylan Thomas, etc. It is obvious that in this instance I had to disqualify myself as a critic.

The case of *Brigadoon* (Adelphi) is different. I know it is a good show—there are several catchy tunes in it, it has twice been a success and many reputable judges have declared that it ranks high among American musicals. Yet now, as at the time of its original production, it made very little impression on me. I cannot for the life of me explain why this should be so except to say rather irrelevantly that I find it too "clean."

I delayed taking notice of *The Duchess of Malfi*—which is not at all clean—till it had closed.

I favor the policy of the Phoenix Theatre which produces plays (at reasonable prices) that are good but not likely to be seen often in the theatres uptown.

Webster's *The Duchess of Malfi* is a man-sized play with great writing, but as done at the Phoenix it seemed pointless—a pretentious polysyllabic horror story: I didn't care how many people died or were tortured in it. The text was cut so that the play's perspective and justification vanished and it was directed and acted (by a company capable at much more) in a nondescript style that might be called unresolved Old Vic—as if the players wanted desperately to escape Broadway but didn't know where to go.

So I didn't write my review, hoping that some of my readers would visit the Phoenix anyway for the sake of the play's renown and the worthiness of the enterprise. It is all very well to say that a critic should not concern himself with the commercial consequences of his notices; I for one prefer to encourage theatregoing.

—*NAT*, 20 Apr. '57

HOTEL PARADISO

Hotel Paradiso is a harum-scarum French bedroom farce—the first, I believe, of thirty-nine pieces in a similar vein by Georges Feydeau (1864-1921). Feydeau has come to be regarded as a kind of classic in France—and rightly. His work embodies the frivolity of cozy middle-class life in that gay, wicked, captivating, creative Paris before the first world war. His dizzy farces typify one aspect of that time as much as Offenbach's operettas typify the Second Empire.

I write in this somewhat schoolroom fashion because in one sense there is little to say about *Hotel Paradiso* except that it is hilarious in a good old-fashioned manner which some of us in the empty-headed sobriety of contemporary theatrical convention might think merely silly.

Feydeau's construction and craftsmanship are masterly: young playwrights ought to make a scrupulous study of his best work. They might observe, for example, how every detail of characterization—each one of them very funny—is used to advance the plot. Feydeau's farces not only served as a model for a whole generation of popular French playwrights, but through the American Avery Hopwood helped shape the technique of several skilled journeyman dramatists of the late teens and early twenties in our country. One could trace the development of Feydeau's fabulous technique by drawing a line back through Scribe and Labiche to Molière, himself largely affected by the ribald and robust itinerant players of the Italian comedy.

Above and beyond this, however, is the Feydeau sense of fun, a kind of shrewd, good-natured, seemingly amoral humor, a combination of street raciness and sophistication which at times skirts the fringes of the great and graver French caricaturists—Daumier, Forain, et al.

This brings us to a point which, in the light of the increasing number of French plays that have been produced in New York recently, is worth repeating. The French think of the theatre as artifice—not as we do as a "mirror of life," but as a game, a playing, a happy distortion in which reality is transformed into new and odd shapes not seen in nature but nonetheless meaningful as poetry or paradox. There is nothing further from realism than the tragedies of Racine written in strictly stylized verse. Most French stage realists have been extremely ephemeral writers, so that it is possible to predict that even Rostand will outlive Henri Becque. In the period between the two world wars the outstanding French playwright, Jean Giraudoux, remained a poet-fantasist, and Jean Anouilh today, for all his approximations of realism, resolutely follows in the same tradition of the theatre of the mask, the theatre which regards all "true-to-life" (documentary) realism as somehow crude and inartistic. It is this difference that makes French drama difficult for us to evaluate.

Alec Guinness was the star of *Hotel Paradiso* in London; here it is Bert Lahr. Since Guinness is a dry-point artist and Bert Lahr an extraordinary clown, Peter Glenville who directed in both cities has wisely made the New York production louder, faster, closer to burlesque. The change, I believe, helps our audiences, which can more readily accept departures from realism when they are unmistakable.

Neither the London nor the New York production is exactly "French." It is impossible for non-Frenchmen literally to reproduce the French theatrical touch—nor is it necessarily desirable.

—*NAT*, 27 Apr. '57

POOR BITOS
ENDGAME

Poor Bitos by Jean Anouilh was interesting to me chiefly as a revelation of how the author has transformed what he hates in himself into an attack against Communists and extreme Leftists generally, as represented in French history by Robespierre. The Communist Bitos is abler, more logical and "purer" than any of his rivals—in this case his former classmates—but he suffered in his youth from being humiliated by his poverty and his class background (his mother was a laundress). His basic impulse, therefore, has become a venomous envy and a desire for revenge, which he translates into political action.

Anouilh himself, once frightfully poor, has never been able to reconcile himself to the rich. He flagellates himself here through his central character, but in doing this he also betrays his ineradicable horror of those who inspired the hatred in him. The result is that, objectively speaking, all parties are derided. The Parisian critics felt insulted by Anouilh's universal contempt but the audiences are held, despite themselves. Aside from Anouilh's skill, they sense in the play an expression of all their tensions—both personal and political—

although, like the author, they imagine that what is presented is a bitter portrait of only one social enemy.

Samuel Beckett's *Endgame* may be said to supply the climax of a tendency in the theatre of negation. Theatrically, the new play is less attractive than the same author's *Waiting for Godot*, because the latter play uses more concrete and colorful symbols: two tramps waiting in a mournful landscape for someone to meet and perhaps help them is an easier image to comprehend than a blind, paralyzed man imprisoned in a bare room with legless parents who remain immobilized and finally die in two garbage pails.

The meaning of *Endgame* is akin to that of *Godot*—though the new play is more savage and hopeless, with little of the tenderness which alleviated the earlier work. It is a poem—at times impassive and drab, at other times snarling through a grin—of the essential meaninglessness of life. Its writing has humor, tang and an obliquely lyric eloquence.

Seeing this play in Paris, I was struck more forcibly than I was at the more entertaining performance of *Godot* in New York, by the philosophical and esthetic flaw in Beckett's work. He wants to essentialize—lay bear to the nth degree—the ground patterns of life's course. But life cannot be essentialized, since the substance of life is not in some supposed abstract design or "secret," but in the apparent trivia which so many philosophers begin by discarding. The surface of life, the myriad day-by-day phenomena, the *illusion* (as some are pleased to have it) is all—*is* life. Not to accept this is sickness.

Pain is certainly real and to cry out with it is right. As one expression of such a cry Beckett may be accepted as a true poet in the theatre of our time; but because of the flaw in what he believes and the art that expresses it, his is minor art.

—*NAT*, 22 June '57

THE MERCHANT OF VENICE

Consider the plot and structure of *The Merchant of Venice* (American Shakespeare Festival; Stratford, Conn.). There is the story of Antonio, the merchant, whose assets lie in the cargo of his ships. To Antonio comes his friend Bassanio, a charming ne'er-do-well to borrow money to finance his courtship of the gilded heiress Portia. Antonio is eager to aid his friend but he has no available cash. He must borrow it from Shylock, who, being outside the rules of the Christian church, is permitted to lend money at interest. Antonio hates Shylock because he is a Jew, which to this Christian is synonymous with usury; Shylock hates Antonio because he is a Christian, synonymous in this instance with a man who despises him for his trade—the only one open to him if he is to be the economic equal of the Christian.

There follows the famous bargain in which Antonio's guaranty for the money borrowed is a pound of his own flesh. Antonio accepts the deal because he is sure he can repay the loan, and Shylock proposes it as a "merry sport" or an act of contempt. We know how Portia manages in the end to crush Shylock.

That is one story. The other is the sentimental comedy of Bassanio's wooing and winning of Portia. This is frivolous and gay, played against the sunny opulence of renaissance Venice.

The problem for the director and the company which present *The Merchant* is to make a meaningful whole of the play's two aspects. It is true that in Shakespeare's time the Antonio-Shylock conflict was something between farce and melodrama because a Jew hadn't been seen in England for several generations and Shylock could be treated as a sort of laughable demon. Still there is the stirring eloquence, the pithy irony of Shylock's speeches: "Hath not a Jew eyes," etc.

So the question remains: aside from the beautiful language, the great quotes, the opportunities for histrionic exercise, what sort of *play* is *The Merchant*? The question applies in varying degrees to most of Shakespeare's works, and I might say that, in view of the manner in which Shakespeare is usually produced in England as well as in America, most of Shakespeare is dramatically bewildering and his glorious work should be left for reading.

This, however, is only my irritated opinion! My poised opinion is that Shakespeare did actually write *plays*—and if they ordinarily seem more like exhibitions of fabulous literary and spectacular wares than the projection of real dramatic ideas, the fault rests in our Anglo-American theatrical Shakespeare tradition which sets all the materials before us, tells tall tales (not always coherently) and leaves them on the stage scattered and unconvincing as living drama.

I wrote an interpretation of *The Merchant* for *The Nation* when it was given at the City Center with Luther Adler as Shylock. What I suggested was that Shakespeare, living in a world that first made the money economy a central historical and psychological factor, wrote a play in which a society heedlessly enjoying the fruits of wealth begins to show the signs of corruption through money.

The rich Christians who gambol and luxuriate in *The Merchant* live a lush life utterly unaware of the means by which their pleasure is supported. They have wealth but they despise money. The Jew's presence makes money ghoulishly real to them. And the Jew, forced to live by traffic in money, hates the Christians for making his livelihood a mark of shame. Thus Shylock, as I previously wrote, is "the poisoned conscience of Venice." He is corrupt with hate, and thus must remain a "black" figure; as Antonio, Bassanio and his playfellows are corrupt in the thoughtlessness—carefree, smiling and spoilt—of their hedonism. The play's fifth act, which would be superfluous if Shylock alone embodied the whole point of the plot, simply shows the "easy life" of Venice continuing when all concern with Shylock has been erased.

I am not saying that this is the "correct" interpretation, or the only possible one. I am saying that it is an interpretation which can be translated into specific stage terms. To do this, however, as in all truly created plays in the theatre, every element—the characterization, setting, by-play, costuming and music—must in some way stem from and contribute to the central dramatic idea.

If this does not happen at the Festival Theatre in Connecticut, it is no exception to the general rule of our Shakespearean productions. Motley's costumes are pretty, the scenic arrangement is delicately attractive, and most of the speech is happily audible, though often too deliberate. Katharine Hepburn looks lovely, and in general no one can complain of the cast. Morris Carnovsky makes a traditional but a sound Shylock, clear in the intent of every word, visually arresting and nearly always impressive. (His mad caper of joy when he hears of Antonio's ill luck is striking and right.) He is a thoroughgoing professional. But he stands isolated.

The prettiness of the production is not thematically related to an articulated intention. It is prettiness for its own sake. The roistering of the young Venetians is a juvenile romping: it is not used to set off the grimness of Shylock's plight. Venice of the sixteenth century—think of its painters and palazzos and what they portended of the extreme material sumptuousness and energy of bourgeois Europe of which Shakespeare was one of the supreme flowers and skeptics—is not even indicated. All has become dainty.

Katharine Hepburn's Portia is a coy debutante in a lesser *Philadelphia Story*. But why shouldn't she be? Has the production any basic form in which her Portia or any of the other roles can play their respective parts?

I dislike being in a position of seeming to discourage any one from seeing a production by the American Shakespeare Festival. Since no one, fortunately perhaps, will heed my advice to call off all theatre Shakespeare for ten years while our theatre folk take time to think it over, I am glad that Shakespeare may be seen in so pleasant an institution as the theatre at Stratford.

I cannot say, for example, that I wasted my time at the *Othello* production. My criticism of it is fundamentally the same as my criticism of *The Merchant*, except that *Othello* having a more compact story line, is easier to assess in its continuity. The Connecticut *Othello* is clearer in speech than any of the other productions I have seen there and can be fairly described as an intelligent reading of the play—and what magnificence there is in that! But I cannot call this seemly entertainment a theatrical presentment of Shakespeare's wildly sensuous, gigantically febrile and tempestuous tragedy.

I admire the devotion and hospitable intelligence of the company which plays at the Festival Theatre. I would enjoin them and their directors, as I would all who undertake the similarly formidable task, to remember that Shakespeare, for all his exquisite gentleness, was part of his times. As such he was not merely a poet-dramatist of inordinate power, but, from the puny standpoint of our day, was uncouth, savage and bloody to a horrific degree—shocking the liberal-minded Voltaire to the roots of his classical hair—an extravagant giant beside whose imprecations, blasphemies and defiance of the proprieties of state and religion, the outcries of our contemporary American rebels are as the gurglings of babes.

—*NAT*, 3 Aug. '57

WEST SIDE STORY

Theatre people, perpetual believers in miracles, clamor for "fair" criticism. The only way for me to be "fair" with *West Side Story* (Winter Garden), the new musical by Arthur Laurents, Leonard Bernstein, Stephen Sondheim, directed and choreographed by Jerome Robbins, who provided the "conception," is to make observations on it from assorted angles. The result will nevertheless remain subjective—criticism is like that, and I would not have it otherwise.

I predict, as certain columnists say, that the show will run a year. At the present time, thanks to the enthusiasm of the majority of out-of-town and local notices, it is nearly impossible to get tickets at box-office prices for the next four or five months.

The reason for the show's immediate success is that it is not only a highly expert production—its various authors and more particularly in this instance the director-choreographer being "tops" in their respective fields—but it may legitimately claim some originality in its domain. For though a "musical," it is not a musical comedy and though it is almost more ballet than play and in some of the duets and "choral" writing approaches the operatic, it remains close enough to the conventional musical comedy form not to suffer the fate of *The Saint of Bleecker Street*.

Important too is the novelty of the show's material: teenage gang warfare, race prejudice in New York where the poor native-born live in uneasy proximity to the immigrants from Puerto Rico. The feud between the two is rather neatly patterned on the struggle of the Montagues and Capulets, with a North American blond as Romeo and an island brunette as Juliet.

The show, I repeat, is as professional as can be and all of the contributions are of a superior grade. Robbins' choreography is not the best he has done—it is occasionally derivative and self-imitative—but there is a great deal of it, and it has his characteristic finish, nervous drive and dramatic instinct. I was not able at first hearing to arrive at any clear estimate of Bernstein's score but one cannot mistake the distinction of its musicianship. Sondheim's lyrics—with one exception which I shall mention again—seemed to me less apt than the other contributions. Laurents' book is admirably serviceable and has several pungent lines; for example, the moment when the apothecary of the story tells the boys they make the world lousy and one of them answers something like, "It was lousy when we got here."

The cast is especially impressive, not through any single performance (I liked Carol Lawrence as

"Juliet" the best) but because, though nearly all its people are dancers, they act and sing creditably during and after choreographic numbers which are taxing enough to kill most European *corps de ballet*. Robbins deserves much credit for whipping these people into their excellent shape.

Oliver Smith's settings, to complete this report, are eclectic for practical purposes and in two instances—the gym scene and the one under the highway where the big "rumble" takes place—quite effective.

If *West Side Story* is certain to run a year, why not two? The commercial limitation is related to an artistic one. People who want to see a Broadway musical do not particularly crave a "*tragedy*" of social significance in which ugly sentiments and violence must play a major role.

My sympathies in this case go with this lowbrow opinion. Although I appreciated the show's merits—and sat in a theatre echoing with "bravos"—I did not enjoy it. In fact, I resented it: I thought it a phony. I am not above enjoying the phony on occasion, but I could not do so here. I do not like intellectual slumming by sophisticates for purposes of popular showmanship. It is vulgar, immature, unfeeling.

The play's best lyric, "Gee, Officer Krupke," is a comic parody by the little "gangsters" of the interpretation that Freudian or social investigators might give to their plight. This would fit perfectly into a skit intended to kid the whole of *West Side Story*. It is used here as comic relief and it works—it exposes the hollowness of everything we see.

Our theatre is too clever by far. Talent we possess to a formidable degree, but in true moral-artistic perception (they are indissolubly linked) we are pathetically underdeveloped. So it is possible for such gifted people as the authors of *West Side Story* to mix the pain of a real problem, penny sociology, liberal nineteen-thirtyish propaganda, Betty Comden-Adolph Green fun and the best of the advanced but already accepted musical comedy techniques into an amalgam which eliminates what is supposed to be the heart of the matter. For above all we want at one and the same time to be progres-sive and to please several million playgoers, the ticket brokers and the movie companies. That is not how *Threepenny Opera* was made.

—*NAT*, 12 Oct. '57

SEAN O'CASEY
LOOK BACK IN ANGER

I have so often written of Sean O'Casey's peculiar genius that there seems little left for me to say about the dramatic reading of *I Knock at the Door* (Playhouse), the first of his six-volume autobiography, than "go and hear it."

O'Casey's genius is "peculiar" because, while almost everything he has written bursts with personal and national character, he has produced only a few entirely satisfactory plays, and nothing in his work is classically coherent. Yet the whole man is always present and a very real man he is—which is not at all as common in books or on the streets as one might suppose. The biographical work, being a form of improvised conversation on specific events in the author's experience, requires less logic or organization than does a play, and is perhaps the most genially representative of O'Casey.

Humor and humanity, indignation and compassion, virility and tenderness, a feeling for the basic sorrows and pleasures of ordinary living are communicated in a style that is at once muscular and melodious, racy, intimate and epic—an exemplary modern prose.

The reading by six devoted and intelligent actors is admirably "orchestrated"; the result is a civilized and heartwarming evening.

John Osborne, an actor still in his twenties, wrote a play two or three years ago, *Look Back in Anger* (Lyceum), which has also knocked at the door—this time at the door of British drama. The knock reverberated momentously through the English theatre, and its echo, slightly muted by its ocean passage, may now be heard on our Broadway shore.

I saw the play at its opening in London, where it was received by the leading critics with an excited gratitude which astonished as much as it pleased me. What the play represented to its English audience was the first resounding expression in the theatre not only of troubled youth but of the tensions within large segments of the middle class in England today. The play is contemporary in a way in which Rattigan on the one hand or Eliot and Fry on the other are not.

The play brings before us two young men of working-class origin in the English midlands who have a candy stand concession in a local cinema. One of them—Jimmy Porter—has had a university education and acts as a self-appointed protector to his Welsh buddy, an uncomplicated person happily free of metaphysical anguish.

Jimmy is married to a pretty girl whom he feels he almost had to steal away from her family, the kind of family whose strength and graces were grounded on England's 1914 Empire. Jimmy not only resents his wife's family and all the institutions that bred them because they led to nothing but the dust and ashes of 1945; he also berates her for having lost the stamina presumed to be characteristic of her background, without having replaced it with any new values of her own—even romantically negative ones like his.

A fourth character, a young actress, represents that middle class which obstinately holds on to its customary traditions, and there is also the wan figure of Jimmy's father-in-law, bewildered and impotent in an England he no longer recognizes.

Jimmy Porter then is the angry one. What is he angry about? It is a little difficult at first for an American to understand. The English understand, not because it is ever explicitly stated, but because the jitters which wrack Jimmy, though out of proportion to the facts within the play, are in the very air the Englishman breathes. Jimmy, "risen" from the working class, is now provided with an intellect which only shows him that everything that might have justified pride in the old England—its opportunity, adventure, material well-being—has disappeared, without being replaced by anything

but a lackluster security. He has been promoted into a moral and social vacuum. He fumes, rages, nags at a world which promised much and has led to a dreary plain where there is no fiber or substance, but only fear of scientific destruction and the minor comforts of "American" mechanics. His wife comments to the effect that "my father is sad because everything has changed, Jimmy is sad because nothing has." In the meantime Jimmy seeks solace and blows defiance through the symbolic jazz of his trumpet, while his working-class pal, though he adores Jimmy and his wife, wisely leaves the emotionally messy premises.

Immanent reality plus a gift for stinging and witty rhetoric are what give the play its importance. It is not realism of the Odets or Williams kind nor yet poetry, although it has some kinship to both. It adds up to a theatrical stylization of ideas about reality in which a perceptive journalism is made to flash on the stage by a talent for histrionic gesture and vivid elocution. While the end product possesses a certain nervous force and genuineness of feeling it is also sentimental, for it still lacks the quality of an experience digested, controlled or wholly understood.

Someone asked me if I didn't believe the play might achieve greater dimensions if American actors were to play it in a manner now associated with the generation influenced by the Group Theatre. The question reveals a misunderstanding of the play's nature. It calls for the verbal brio and discreet indication of feeling which it receives from the uniformly excellent, attractive English cast—Kenneth Haigh, Mary Ure, Alan Bates, Vivienne Drummond.

Jimmy Porter, "deepened" in another vein, would prove an intolerable nuisance, a self-pitying, verbose, sadistic jackanapes. He is a sign, not a character. We accept him because in the final count he is more amusing than real. We can look beyond him and the flimsy structure of the fable in which he is involved and surmise some of the living sources in the civilization from which he issues.

That John Osborne is attached and attuned to those sources is the virtue and hope of his talent. It may take ten years for him to achieve what most people have declared he already has.

—*NAT*, 19 Oct. '57

NANCY WALKER

Copper and Brass (Martin Beck) is a musical with only one virtue—Nancy Walker. She is an actress-clown with a touch of genius. Every year her playing acquires greater ease and finesse. Her art expresses the comic distortion of the unglamorous (plain and unprosperous) city girl amid the grinding traffic of our lives. She is hilarious and unconsciously pathetic without a trace of sentimentality. Some day Nancy Walker will find the vehicle she deserves and, already well known and admired, she will be *discovered*!

—*NAT*, 2 Nov. '57

THE CAVE DWELLERS

I do not particularly admire Saroyan's *The Cave Dwellers* (Bijou) but I shall praise it.

I shall praise it because it is by Saroyan. He is a writer, he is a poet, he is a personality. Among our dramatists he is one of the few who speak in a distinctive voice. It is a gentler voice than that of most others who write for our theatre. It uses a simple, sane vocabulary which refers to smells and sounds and easily identifiable things seen and heard. It is good humored, and slightly inebriate. It has in it a faint flavor of the foreign, yet it is unmistakably American. It reflects the genial aspect of San Francisco where the sea, the harbor, the market place are not overwhelmed by the great hotels, and where the small bars and restaurants have not yet been transformed into machines.

Saroyan's plays have something else that we cherish in the theatre: they have color and fancy—not laid on but organic to his message and his plots. His germinal ideas lend themselves to the *optique* of the theatre. Something in them calls for the magic of stage lighting and the imaginative costumer.

Most of these attributes are present once again in *The Cave Dwellers*. The design of the play is pleasing. A broken-down old actress, a used-up clown, an ex-pug, a pretty young waif, fired from her job in a toy factory, all seek refuge on the bare stage in a soon-to-be-demolished theatre. The three older people have made a little kingdom of their cold, shadowy haven. The actress is the queen, the clown the king and the pug the duke. They adopt the little girl, who becomes an honorary subject.

In their little world these people dream with pleasure or fear of their past, they seek out food for one another and they give shelter to a man who has trained a bear and whose wife gives birth to a child among them. The pug steals milk for the new-born baby; the milkman's apprentice, a mute but prince-like boy, allows these people to keep the milk and brings more because he recognizes their plight and falls in love at first sight with the waif. They all entertain one another with shreds and patches of their talents and when the wreckers arrive—the wreckers too are kindly people—they all depart each his own way into the mysterious night.

What meaning informs this allegory? Its "philosophy" might be called sugared existentialism. We do not know why we are here, we cannot comprehend the universe we are in, we shall never understand the great pattern, if pattern there be, of life. No matter: there is goodness, there is love—even hate is love. We get up in the morning, go to bed at night; in between we play wondrously—and that is enough. We require no more, for the spectacle is bright and even the dark is light enough.

I do not scoff at this, because, for one thing, there is little difference, artistically speaking, between "Life is a dream," and "Life is real." Both propositions may be the seed of beautiful statements. I shall go even further and say that I share Saroyan's sentiments. But *The Cave Dwellers* is still not only slight but I'm afraid somewhat threadbare.

For goodness and love (at times the play reminded me of Chaplin's song about love-love-love-love) have significance only where there is a confrontation with pain and evil. You can have no goodness or true love without a full awareness of the *objects* which are the substance of life. The substance or material of life is always resistant and this resistance—the subject of drama—is what we have so much difficulty in accepting. Saroyan tries nonchalantly to eliminate life's negation: he waves pain away, as in one of the play's best lines, "My cough is simply a language I have not yet learned to understand."

The play—unlike *My Heart's in the Highlands* and *The Time of Your Life*—does not spring from any contact with reality: it is more pose than spontaneous reaction. Its wistful smile is painted on as on a doll. This "poem" is constantly explaining itself—which only a bad poem does. The language, though fluent, is exposition rather than speech. There is a thinness in the writing which comes from a lack of genuine dramatic impulse. As a result, much of what is said and shown, instead of being touching, becomes platitudinous. If there is wisdom here, it is only for hobos.

Yet the play is good enough in concept for us to wish it were much better. A really imaginative production would help. (It is my guess that, because of its remarkable stage potentialities, the play will be produced in many theatres abroad as well as in little theatres in our country.) Not that the present production is bad. The cast (which includes Barry Jones, Eugenie Leontovich, Wayne Morris, Susan Harrison, Gerald Hiken, Ivan Dixon) is in the main well chosen. These actors have nice qualities and act creditably. (I wish Leontovich would remain as simple throughout as she is in her better moments, for a queen—even a footlight queen—is always basically simple, not stagy.) What is missing is true style.

There are two possible styles for this play. One would seek that poetry of the spirit which is evoked when the soul of the actor as a person is stimulated beyond the surface truth of each scene. Another style might be created through delicately but frankly picturesque characterization and stage movement heightened with memorably graphic craftsmanship. At the Bijou, the actors are merely themselves in the least interesting sense of the word. And yet—such is our theatre nowadays—the show has freshness.

—*NAT*, 9 Nov. '57

COMPULSION

Compulsion, the dramatization by Meyer Levin of his own novel (the play is advertised as offering the producer's version of the text) is an arresting show (Ambassador). It also seems to be a success, despite a markedly mixed press reception. One reason for this certainly is the sensational nature of its subject matter—the old (1924) Leopold-Loeb case involving the murder of a young boy by two teen-agers, scions of wealthy Chicago families and *cum laude* university graduates.

I am not fascinated by murders or newspaper accounts of them. I never read any of the reports of the original case, though I heard about it. I can only explain this by saying that I never feel I truly understand anything about any scandal by reading the blunt facts concerning it. I understand things of this sort only through personal contact with people and events or through works of art. When I read in a newspaper about a lurid occurrence my sensibilities may be assaulted but my intuition is not alerted, my imagination not stimulated, my heart not touched, my mind not enlightened.

That violent action is a proper source of drama we know through the whole history of literature. The plot of *Compulsion* is no more ugly than that of *Oedipus Rex*. There is more perversion in Marlowe's *Edward II* than in *Compulsion*, and *King Lear* is not a pretty tale. Camus' play

Caligula—to cite contemporary instances—or Genet's *The Balcony* make *Compulsion* seem like "Home Sweet Home."

Compulsion is no work of art. But that does not altogether condemn it for me, for most of the plays I see—some of which I enjoy—are not works of art either. To assert that one play is entertainment because it deals with pleasant matters and another not entertainment because it deals with unpleasant matters is, objectively speaking, presumptuous—since people in all periods have found certain unpleasant subjects magnetic.

As entertainment, *Compulsion* holds the attention by virtue of three factors: its story suggests various serious considerations—the psychic sources of criminal acts, the importance of psychic disturbance in the administration of justice, the need to view criminality as part of universal rather than special problems. None of these themes is genuinely explored or creatively communicated in the play, but they are brought up. Second, the play has a large canvas of people and places and this is handsomely managed through Peter Larkin's settings and fluent staging by Alex Segal. The economics of our theatre makes such big productions difficult; we are glad to see a panoramic play which moves swiftly from place to place and introduces a great number of types. This is part of the theatre's fun and in the past twenty years we have largely been deprived of it. Third, the actors are well chosen (even the understudies—I saw two at the performance I attended—are good) and Ina Balin stands out in my memory as affectingly right.

I was not moved or even very much excited by the play for reasons I have explained, but I was interested because of the factors I have just noted—though in the matter of acting I must not fail to say that the acting was generally of the literal and illustrative kind which is closer to reportage than to creation. But what really makes me approve of the show is that I believe it worthwhile for the ugly or the sensational (however you are inclined to put it) to be presented in the theatre where in the final count it may have a liberating effect.

Aesthetic sophisticates and moral traditionalists may scorn such a statement—but the theatre would expire if it depended entirely on them. I believe that art is the greatest "propaganda," but propaganda—so feared and shunned these days—also has its place in the theatre, and I think there is a certain hypocrisy in implying that *Compulsion* has no honest effect because it is not artistically composed.

The point that *Compulsion* attempts to make may be old hat to a good number of people but there is a far greater number of people who still need to have made clear to them the social and human value of acknowledging homosexuality, for instance, as something that calls for more than the assistance of a policeman or even of a psychiatrist.

The modern American novel is far ahead of our theatre in scope of theme. Though plays like *Compulsion* are embryonic and crude as artistic expression, they have, beside the fact that they do serve over the protests of the "sensitive" as popular entertainment, a pioneering value: they open the way to plays of a finer vein on similar material. Unless our theatre is made receptive to all subjects and modes it will never attain maturity.

—*NAT*, 16 Nov. '57

THE SQUARE ROOT OF WONDERFUL
JAMAICA
FAIR GAME

Almost all the merit and quality of Carson McCullers' *The Square Root of Wonderful* have become imperceptible in its production at the Lyceum. The scene designer is a gifted man, nearly all the actors are talented and the author is a superior writer. The total is a dud. This is so painful a paradox that I would prefer to skip it were it not for the fact that it illustrates the role of stage direction.

If the play has a thesis it is that love or sex attraction must stop somewhere short of suicide. The play recounts the conversion of a young woman from sentimental sex romanticism to humane common sense. But neither of these descriptions fits the play because Carson McCullers is a poet and her writing is largely an improvisation around characters and a basic situation which are seen in a weblike maze of memory and emotional meditation: an inspired dream at twilight without any precise center or sharp outline. The characters often fall out of focus, and it is one of the mistakes of the play's composition that the author felt constrained to make her story straightforward so that it might appear logical to the prosaic mind. The script might have been better if it had had the faults natural to its author's genius.

No one around seems to have concretely realized the "music"—humorous, eccentric, daft in a way that is both earthy and ethereal—of the playwright's creative bent. The set which needed to be a mere suggestion—veiled and vaporous—is a mess of ugly lumber sufficient to build a cottage in Nyack. The young woman of the play whose sensuality is as innocent as it is direct has been transformed into a "spiritual" creature with a perpetually breathy speech. (Everyone seems to forget Keats's remark that there is no one less "poetic" than a poet.) The husband, a destructive person only because he is destroyed, a lost soul seeking a cocoon, is rendered into a sadistic monster, bursting with aggressive thrust. The suitor, a man whose quiet understanding supposedly stems from tempered power, is pictured as merely soft. The pseudo-aristocratic Southern mother whose middle-class selfishness and obtuseness are protected by an inheritance is played tartly like a George Kaufman "weisenheimer." Only the librarian sister-in-law, reduced to a whisper by her environment, gives a resemblance of what the author intended.

As a result, lyric writing, beautifully awry, and wonderfully intuitive character sense have been flattened into semi-caricature. I mention no names: specific blame would not serve my point.

Jamaica (Imperial), a "calypso" musical wrought by a team of generously endowed theatre craftsmen—E. Y. Harburg, Fred Saidy, Harold Arlen, Robert Lewis—is a somewhat taxing experience. There are however mitigating elements.

The "book" has an "idea": the struggle by simple fishermen of a Jamaican village against the corruption of big-time mechanization. Some of the numbers are lively in rhythm and verbally sharp—with now and again a glance at social significance. But the show progresses to diminishing returns. A lack of spontaneity or genuine invention becomes evident long before the final curtain.

Jamaica's main attraction is Lena Horne. She is a beautiful woman and a highly skilled singer of popular songs. No one can fail to be impressed by her "cool" elegance—the artful cover of a secret flame. But I found myself a little worried by the fact that most of Miss Horne's songs were briskly jazzy with a bit of rock and roll thrown in, whereas her gifts seem to lie in a more sober area; the song of sentiment she sings in the show is one of the weaker numbers. Then too I was slightly put off by the extra fine polish and smoothness of Miss Horne's present technique. She was more touchingly effective some years ago when her style was less burnished.

Josephine Premice is another talented entertainer with a certain charming grotesquerie about her, and Ossie Davis is a winning actor. Yet all these credits hardly compensate for an absence of conviction and joy in the show.

Fair Game (Longacre) is a likably vulgar entertainment. There are people who lament that plays of this sort should draw large audiences. Let them spare their tears. This kind of play has been the staple of the popular theatre for at least a hundred years and will continue to be so.

Fair Game deals with pretty young divorcees among the wolves of the New York garment industry. No problem, you say. You are wrong. The woods are full of them, and there are delighted gasps of recognition in the audience for which the play is intended.

As for myself, I am partial to pretty girls and deft acting. There are several pretty girls in the show and no defter actor is extant on Broadway than Sam Levene. (He is ably abetted by Robert Webber and Sally Gracie.) Levene's concentration is ferocious. His delivery of lines has the shrewd grasp and energy of the biggest operators in any line of consumer business. His work—like Groucho Marx's—is Americana. But while Groucho Marx is a great clown, Sam Levene is a true actor.

—*NAT*, 23 Nov. '57

TIME REMEMBERED
NUDE WITH VIOLIN

I'm afraid I've seen *Time Remembered* (Morosco) too many times. I saw it in London about three years ago, then again in its present production five weeks ago during its pre-opening tour and once more on the second night. I do not mean by this that I have no opinion of it but that my various impressions have given me a peculiarly complex vision—certainly too complex for so simple a play—so that I am obliged to proceed with my comments more analytically than might otherwise be warranted.

Time Remembered is one of the more airily "pink" of Anouilh's plays. It is a nosegay collected from the less bitter flora in its author's hothouse. For that is one of Anouilh's talents: he is able to make sweet stuff from the same roots as produce his more acrid concoctions. In *Time Remembered*, which dates from 1939, he pokes affectionate fun at his own romanticism—his idealization of old loves and dreams—just as in several other of his plays, he flays it. *Time Remembered* is modeled on what Molière called *comédie-ballet*—a gay pirouette of knowing playfulness, gossamer light, admirably written (excellently translated by Patricia Moyes), remarkably gifted.

In London the play was done quite effortlessly and without much surprise. Paul Scofield was the melancholy prince of the fable—mournfully enveloped in the memory of a dead romance—a little limp and almost undramatic. Mary Ure as the *midinette* was simple and direct but so relaxed as the new love—the challenge of present reality—that she appeared almost dreamlike, seen through a mist. Margaret Rutherford as the "lunatic" Duchess was grotesque (Anouilh, with whom I saw the play, said she was doing mad things but that he liked actresses who did mad things) and I was not sure whether her outrageousness was a contribution to the fairy tale quality of the story or a detraction.

When I saw the play in New Haven and was asked my opinion of it I summed it up by saying "almost everything is a little wrong with the production but it will work—the play comes through and it will be a success." When I saw it in New York with an audience which had already read the gushing notices, the reception was cold, almost hostile. I heard people say, "What a shame to waste such a brilliant cast on so slight a play" and others, far less numerous, "The play is charming; something is wrong with the production." By this time I myself was becoming confused.

Normally I would judge *Time Remembered* a good play to produce here in some such small house as the Bijou with very simple, almost paperweight painted scenery giving a water color effect. But if the production in London looked as if it had cost five times what it might in Paris, its New York production looks as if it cost fifty times as much. The production at the Morosco, designed by Oliver Smith, is sumptuous with the gorgeousness of a Fifth Avenue confectioners.

The Americans were out to *sell* the play in a big way. As with the physical aspect of the show, so with the cast: it is studded with great names. And since the actors are all unquestionable personalities, they do have an effect. The effect is sometimes happy and sometimes taxing. To many the total is a triumph. To others—and with such a play much depends on the kind of performance one happens to see on a particular night—the result is this side of enchantment. When I saw the production for the second time, it struck me as heavy.

Helen Hayes, neither "aristocrat" nor "French," is a kind of miracle performer whose resourcefulness in comedy is infectious. Richard Burton, robust in a part of delicately pinched wistfulness, perhaps lends it an interest for Americans which it might not otherwise have. It is a pleasure to hear his fine voice and beautiful speech. Susan Strasberg, with her lovely mask, is vivid, but her quality is essentially dramatic and the timbre of her voice, striking in itself, is as yet unvarying in range. One hopes that although already elevated to stardom she will make due progress as an actress—a very difficult thing to do in the theatre today. The most stylistically consummate performance of the evening is that of Sig Arno as the mock waiter. Amusing too are Frederic Warriner and Glenn Anders.

Noel Coward's *Nude with Violin* (Belasco) is really inconsequential and frequently quite funny. In his frank snobbishness, impertinent levity and *chic* vulgarity, Coward is a distinct figure whom I begin to appreciate more and more (despite the, for me, natural disinclination to do so) as one kind of antidote to conformity. He is a superb performer, a suave and witty showman whose craftmanship must not be dismissed because it is dedicated to the trivial. Like Sacha Guitry, he has a certain wickedness, but there is also a touch of genius in him.

He is helpful to his actors; he writes fat parts for them—thumbnail character sketches, part vaudeville, part shrewd observation around almost traditional stage types—of which experienced comedians can take full advantage as does most of the cast, particularly Joyce Carey, Luba Malina, Mona Washbourne and Morris Carnovsky who as an art dealer in trouble gives a hilarious imitation of a certain apoplectic director haranguing actors of the late-lamented Group Theatre.

By the way, the thread that ties *Nude with Violin* is the anti-modern art joke, but one need take this no more seriously than most other of Coward's "themes."

—*NAT*, 30 Nov. '57

CLÉRAMBARD
THE ROPE DANCERS

In *The Cave Dwellers*, the theatre in which the events of the play take place is described as a "downtown theatre," i.e., south of Forty-Second Street, the implication being that the theatres there are ready to be demolished. Actually the rate of demolition has been higher uptown, where it often takes the form of conversion to radio and television houses. With the relative success of the movement off-Broadway, I am more worried about the "new" theatres above Forty-Second Street, than about the old ones below which are beginning to acquire prestige.

It will be a good day for the theatre when it becomes decentralized, not only geographically but in our psychological attitude toward what makes an "important" show. In Paris the most interesting productions are generally not to be seen on the grand boulevards or on the adjacent streets but, as the French say, *on the side*.

Clérambard (Rooftop Theatre) is certainly as worthwhile a play as *Time Remembered*. In fact Marcel Aymé's play, which is devilishly anti-clerical, is more characteristic of its author than *Time Remembered* is of Anouilh. Nothing in *Time Remembered*—a pretty piece to be sure—is as tartly witty as the scene in *Clérambard* in which all the ordinary folk in a French village are able to behold the miracle of a saintly apparition—except the curé.

The production of *Clérambard*—done with limited means—leaves much to be desired; but so, to anyone who knows the French theatre, does *Time Remembered*. French plays are peculiarly difficult to produce properly outside France—particularly in America. The reason for this is that we are ineluctably committed to a realistic approach in our "serious" contemporary drama. The French, whose Balzac, Stendhal, Flaubert,

Zola (all of them suppressed romantics) have created a great tradition of realism in the novel, have hardly had a strictly realistic drama for any length of time.

Almost the only dramatist who remains of the French realistic school is Henri Becque, whose few plays are almost unknown here. The boulevard society fabrications of Henri Bernstein—half melodrama, half problem play—were popular in this country before the First World War when Broadway, oddly enough, was more receptive to the plays of London and Paris than it is today.

The French theatre, with its spirit bent on close moral scrutiny of the world, nearly always manages to turn its material either to classic abstraction (hence the frequent use of traditional figures—Oedipus, Orpheus, Antigone, Judith, etc.) or to a ballet-like playfulness, with reality paradoxically disguised in "masks" as heightened as those we see in show booths at fairs, or in forms approaching burlesque, vaudeville or operetta which are modernized versions of the Italian mime-comedies.

On Broadway, Morton Wishengrad, the author of *The Rope Dancers* (Cort), is indebted to his producers for having done so much to make his first play a thing some people will enjoy seeing. One is made to watch and listen to the play with respectful attention though it always promises more than it fulfills.

It is about poor estranged parents in New York at the turn of the century who have begotten a child with six fingers on one of her hands. This is a symbol of the physical or moral lesions, the guilts and disabilities which haunt us all. The child dies in the end from an operation which has removed the offending member. This means that we cannot erase the wounds of our bodies and souls in one stroke. Other points are made along the way: about the limitations of a rigid moralism (the wife), the value of imaginative freedom even when it is not crowned with other virtues (the husband), the effect on a child of hostility between parents, the imperfection of all human existence.

The play never gets much beyond intense earnestness, the will-to-create profound truthfulness. What is lacking is language, character portrayal, situations which are sufficient in themselves to embody rather than to symbolize the meaning with which the dramatist hopes to stir us.

The young English director Peter Hall should be accounted the hero of the evening. His cast is good—Siobhan McKenna, Art Carney, Joan Blondell, Theodore Bikel—and he has chosen the right scene designer in Boris Aronson, who knows how to give interest, variety and mystery to what would ordinarily be nothing but a drab background. The lighting (by Hall himself) is superb. But what I would praise above everything is the delicate simplicity—amounting to a subtle stylization—the quiet sensibility bespeaking fineness of spirit with which the director has invested the whole production.

—*NAT*, 7 Dec. '57

LOOK HOMEWARD, ANGEL

The production of *Look Homeward, Angel*, the play by Ketti Frings based on Thomas Wolfe's novel, will strike most spectators as being full of life. It is an excellent production, meticulously articulated in every department and with a practically perfect cast. The direction by George Roy Hill is instinct with theatrical science. There is little doubt in my mind that the show will deservedly become a leading contender for all the prizes.

Yet it did not deeply affect me. Its virtue is the kind of realism which distinguished the American novel in the twenties. It was the realism—extremely valuable in the creation of a contemporary American consciousness—which contrasted sharply with the image of our country as a perpetually smiling community that most of our literature fostered from the Civil War to the early years of the twentieth century.

To this new realism, with its emphasis on the drab and something like pride in a stark avoidance of lyric palliation or metaphysical justification, Thomas Wolfe brought a powerful eloquence containing strains of Whitman supported by the discovery of a richness in language which an extensive reading in the classics of English literature would give a sensitive, enormously energetic young man. The rhetoric sometimes swamped Wolfe's plots—mostly autobiographical recordings rather than inventions—but also gave his novels a gigantic awkwardness which often managed to be inspiring. It is true, as someone has said, that Wolfe was either a giant baby or a baby giant, but his work was significant as an outcry at the anguish and bewilderment of a people newly come to civilized reflection but not yet arrived at ripe understanding.

Ketti Frings in her skillful dramatization, has set the main characters of Wolfe's novel before us in an honestly sober and, except for two brief moments, unexceptionably respectable manner. We are left with the foreground of the novel—all of it interesting, truthful, typical—but with little dimension beyond the notation of the facts on a fever chart. *Look Homeward, Angel* as a play harks back to the realism of the twenties which lacked poetic extension or transfiguration. The shock of recognition is present—and no doubt still valuable—but not the shock of surprise (or illumination) within what one recognizes. We are reminded of what we are acquainted with in life; but we are not transported to any area of feeling or knowledge beyond what our observation—alerted by previous experience with this type of realism—has already provided us. No idea or poetic essence emerges.

It may seem churlish of me to insist on this point, since *Look Homeward, Angel*, is clearly superior to most of what we are usually offered in our theatre. Certainly I must urge readers of *The Nation* to see the play, but I must just as surely try to place it not only in the context of Broadway but in the greater one of serious drama and theatre.

The production parallels the text in its qualities and in its limitations. Anthony Perkins gives a shrewd portrayal of Gene Gant: his technique, in comedy especially, is already well-developed and he uses his very sympathetic personality to make good points with fine economy, but he has not yet learned how to make the ability to communicate human traits the means of reaching our souls in vital contact. Jo Van Fleet as Mrs. Gant seems to me to be an admirable representative of American realism in acting: her points are even more incisively and comprehensively made than Perkins'. And Hugh Griffith as the father brings with the Welsh tang of his background a vividness and a largeness which occur only when an actor by long experience of life and the stage has matured to full manhood. The scene in which Mrs. Gant, exasperated by the failure of her life, is provoked to tear down her home and is jubilantly joined by her husband seems to me the most sparkling moment of the evening—just as the moment which the doctor casually lights his cigar after Ben Gant's death seemed to me the most telling directorial touch.

More should be praised—Arthur Hill, Rosemary Murphy, Elizabeth Lawrence—but space does not permit it, except to add that if a European asked me to point out what the American theatre has achieved in completing one phase of its realistic style I would recommend *Look Homeward, Angel*.

—*NAT*, 14 Dec. '57

THE MAKROPOLIS SECRET
THE DARK AT THE TOP OF THE STAIRS

One might call Karel Capek's *The Makropoulos Secret* (Phoenix) a thriller with a thesis because it purports to dramatize the undesirability of perpetually prolonged life. If that were all there was to it, one would have to find it a pretty silly play. Actually it is quite entertaining.

The reason for this is that the script is cleverly contrived as melodrama up to the moment when its "secret" is disclosed, but more especially because it has been amusingly and artfully directed by Tyrone Guthrie.

The play, written in 1926, takes place in 1911, when most of Central Europe was part of the Austro-Hungarian empire. Guthrie has a penchant for the period—he set his production of Shakespeare's *Troilus and Cressida* in it—a feeling particularly for the theatre conventions of that day. He seems to feel some nostalgia for the innocent and corrupt time before the old continent exploded into its long winter of chaos—a nostalgia mixed with quizzical humor. "How charming," Guthrie seems to be saying, "how foolish, how colorful, absurd and gay it all was. Anyhow the playacting, all the gimcrack 'theatre' of it, was better than the gadgetry we are faced with now." So *The Makropoulos Secret* takes on a kind of greasepaint poetry which is a compound of caricature and tenderness.

The settings by Norris Houghton and the other elements of scenic investiture are most helpful, but best of all is the cast headed by Eileen Herlie as an opera singer with a very much "placed" voice, a persistent voluptuousness and the grand manner of boisterous behavior and ineradicable soulsickness. Very good too are Karel Stepanek as a Baron—impeccably disciplined in his decadence—Eric House, touchingly gaga, Conrad Bain and William Hutt.

If William Inge's *The Dark at the Top of the Stairs* (Music Box) should prove on reading to be less substantial than it seems on the stage, the difference will be attributed to the top-notch production it has received. But that would be unfair to the author, who in his own way is not only a consummate craftsman but a valuable artist.

The mark of Inge's method is its modesty. He never goes beyond his depth, he never promises more than he can fulfill, he ventures only into what he can master. He writes sparsely, almost laconi-cally, but his choice of words and of situations is so shrewd that he makes them go a long way in creating a stage life far more potent than the written page may indicate. His work is very telling for us, too, because it is peculiarly American—in its setting and characters, in its sadness and humor, in its folksiness and in its Freudianism which is never pressed to the point of declamatory "revelation," but is tempered by a certain cautious optimism.

The Dark at the Top of the Stairs is at once the slightest and the most complete of Inge's plays: slight insofar as no single character is more than a thumbnail sketch, complete in that the play covers a sufficient variety of people to give us a sense of Inge's origins.

The father, Rubin Flood, is a gruff, hearty Oklahoman of pioneer antecedents and memory. He is simple, ignorant, honest. His wife is a pure woman, a little too puritanical (from Pennsylvania) for reality. She tends to indulge her children and push her husband overmuch. Their little son clings to his mother's warmth, "hates people," avoids his crude papa and shows artistic tenderness—reciting "pieces" and adoring the movies. The seventeen-year-old daughter is afraid of the world, plays the piano, idolizes her father. The small townsfolk are getting rich and carrying their rickety prejudices over to their prosperity—strongly anti-Catholic and slightly anti-Semitic. The wife's sister is lower middle-class, a little coarse-grained, unconsciously bossy and frigid. Her dentist husband is decent, desiccated, squelched, hopelessly bewildered—he is one of the best-drawn characters of the play, well acted, wonderfully directed.

The play's main incident is simple: an eighteen-year-old boy, whose mother, a small-part movie actress, has abandoned him to the solitude of many military schools, takes the Flood girl out on a blind date. The girl, inordinately shy, tries to avoid going, but is pressed to it by her mother: the boy, half-Jewish, turns out to be well-mannered and thoroughly nice. He is trying to be brave about his loneliness and the anti-Semitism he encounters: he stutters and in other ways betrays an unconscious hostility. But he is fundamentally sweet. At the dance the Flood girl leaves him for a while because she is hurt by the notion that no one but the Jewish boy cares to dance with her. He is then grossly insulted for his Jewishness by a *nouveau riche* idiot, and commits suicide. The shock makes most of the family realize some of their own responsibility in the misfortune, and even more the need everyone feels to find support in the love and respect of another person in the dark that is always before us.

At the end of the play there is forgiveness and reconciliation all around. The father humbly begs his wife's pardon for having slapped her, the wife realizes that she has provoked her husband, the children who have been at loggerheads become tender with each other, etc.

I have oversimplified, but so does Inge—who solves difficult character problems in an almost moving-picture fashion by combining moral good will with gentle doses of psychoanalysis. He has too much taste however to do this crudely, but avails himself of the poetic or showman's license to foreshorten his benign therapeutics by the sympathetic reticence of his nonetheless pointed statements. So we have almost all around happy endings without cheapness or too obvious sentimentality. Yet the play is certainly sentimental in a way that prevents it from taking a more significant place in the realm of that creative realism in which Chekhov was supreme and into which a few other American playwrights have stepped more courageously though often less surefootedly. Inge, I suspect, is intimidated by the inhibitions of our commercial theatre; if he were to dare more—even to fail (the morbid fear of failure is the specter that haunts our stage)—he might rise to the greater stature of which I believe him capable.

His play has the enormous advantage of an excellent cast—Pat Hingle, Eileen Heckart and particularly Timmie Everett merit special mention—and the theatrically astute, admirably observant character direction of Elia Kazan. This production is one of Kazan's finest feats.

—*NAT*, 21 Dec. '57

WILLIAMS & IONESCO
SUDDENLY LAST SUMMER

Tennessee Williams did well to have his long one-act play, *Suddenly Last Summer*—preceded by a short one, *Something Unspoken*—produced at the New York Playhouse. (The two plays are billed under the general title, *Garden District*.) The plays will engender a more sympathetic reaction in the intimacy of an off-Broadway theatre than would have been likely in the greater market.

Not that the plays are negligible. Both plays, representing marginal efforts by a leading dramatist, merit our attention. Though the longer and distinctly more interesting play has about it the fascination of a cleverly contrived horror story, its purpose is more ambitious. Yet I cannot help feeling that it is a transitional piece—an incisive dramatic summation of certain phases of the playwright's thought. It says in somewhat camouflaged symbols what Williams has said elsewhere, notably in *Streetcar Named Desire* and in one of his short stories.

There are two main threads of meaning in *Suddenly Last Summer*. On the one hand, Williams presents a pure person who is victimized and confined to an insane asylum for daring to tell a truth abhorrent and inimical to the powers that be. (This symbolizes the artist in our time.) The wealthy Southern Lady of the play plans to have the poor girl's brain operated on to extirpate from her mind the memory and knowledge of what she has witnessed. This is a more lurid image of Blanche du Bois' history in *Streetcar*.

Then there is the story the girl tells about the wealthy lady's son, an effete "poet," reared in the hothouse of his mother's home, a super aesthete, a weakling and a pervert. (Why must all homosexuality in the theatre always be ascribed to the influence of over-possessive mothers, and why must homosexuals be effete? There are a great many vigorous and creative ones—in the world.) The boy in the play is destroyed by the evil he has fostered: he is literally consumed, *eaten*, by a band of starved little monsters—the delinquent poor of a Spanish beach resort. That is the second symbol—a retributive one.

Williams, it seems, has been made morbidly conscious of the horror and violence of certain of his plays. Has it not occurred to those who find fault with him on this score that some of the greatest literature—Sophocles, Euripides, Shakespeare, Strindberg, Dostoyevsky, etc.—has been far more violent? There is no reason why the blackest violence, cruelty, disease and dismay should not be the subject of drama. What is important, in this area as with other subjects, is the content and ultimate significance of the violence. If critics cannot tolerate unpleasant subjects in contemporary plays, they should disqualify themselves as critics: and if an author feels obliged constantly to apologize for his absorption with the material of his experience or feelings when they are generally harsh, he must despair of maturing as an artist.

Many people who were shocked by *Orpheus Descending*—most of which is characterized by a real pity for people who live in what we recognize as a socially violent environment—are far less troubled by *Suddenly Last Summer* because it is basically abstract and far less real than any of Williams' former plays, except the frankly allegoric *Camino Real*. The present play is undoubtedly very well written—is that anything new for Williams?—and compactly constructed. But there is no character with anything like the richness of Blanche or Kowalski or a number of the minor characters in *Orpheus Descending*. The new play is a product of a general concept and shrewd theatre technique rather than of living experience—except possibly that of the author's experience, suddenly last spring, with the critics. It is therefore melodrama, a recapitulation in sensational terms of themes which have been far more vitally expressed in the author's previous work.

The play is well acted, and so, in a lesser degree, is *Something Unspoken*. This is a sketch of

a strange tie between a woman who compensates for her affective frustrations by collecting provincial honors and by stupidly exercising power over another woman too defenseless to find a means of resistance in their arid world. The play is very slight but not without a meaning which extends beyond its fable. Hortense Alden and Ann Meacham play their leading roles well, and Alan Nixon is very good in a well-drawn bit part. The setting by Robert Soule and the lighting by Lee Watson for the long play are notably good; the whole evening is well managed by its director Herbert Machiz.

Since I wrote here of Eugene Ionesco's *The Chairs*, which I saw in London last June (*The Nation*, July 6, 1957) and which is being presented for two weeks at the Phoenix in the identical production admirably directed by Tony Richardson and acted by the delightfully remarkable Joan Plowright (of the original cast) together with Eli Wallach who does a splendid job, I shall do no more than declare my enthusiasm for this short play.

What Ionesco achieves here is the creation by simple but extremely ingenious means of a sense of the loneliness, the torment, the aching inconsequentiality, the crushed tenderness typical of the ambiance which produced existentialism. Symbols are employed, but they are piquant symbols, fresh and entertaining in themselves. The play is very funny and ineradicably sad. I do not share the author's view of life, but because he is an artist and a master of a novel theatre language I applaud him. The setting for *The Chairs* by Jocelyn Herbert, influenced by certain trends of modern art, is subtly right and inconspicuously effective.

Companion piece to *The Chairs*, *The Lesson* is a sort of macabre farce in which Joan Plowright again appears with charming results. It is a less consummate play than *The Chairs*, but it too has its brilliance. Like *The Chairs*, *The Lesson* is said to be a parable which illustrates man's inability to communicate with his fellow man. That may be so. I also see in *The Lesson* a satire on the lunacy of certain types of learning. I do not insist on this, however, for both plays suggest several ideas—none of them "arithmetically" exact. This ambiguity intrigues rather than irritates me. For I am often inclined to agree with Cocteau's quip, "In art every value which can be *proved* is vulgar."

—*NAT*, 25 Jan. '58

TWO FOR THE SEESAW

William Gibson's *Two for the Seesaw* (Booth) is one of those simple, pleasant plays that obviously belong in the theatre, since they are almost always highly popular. They are the best-sellers of the contemporary stage. No one should cavil at their success. But, I confess with some reluctance, they interest me very little.

The play's sentimental subject holds the seed of a serious theme: this makes it "respectable." A lawyer from Omaha has left his wife because he harbors the feeling that he had been "bought" by her family, that life had been made too easy for him by his well-placed father-in-law. We are told very little else about this marriage—except that the wife is about to marry a more grateful groom. Lonely and wretched in New York, the Nebraska lawyer picks up a little Bronx girl who suffers from ulcers and frequent unemployment. She is a sweet waif, with pathetic ambition as a dancer, sustaining her life through affairs in which she is generous hostess to unworthy males.

The lawyer takes up with this girl, seems to be seriously in love with her (he assures her that she is a "gift"), tries to "straighten her out"—though she is on the whole a far more substantial person than he—is tempted to marry her but finally returns to his wife whom he presumably still loves. The little liaison has perhaps saved his life and, I hope, taught the girl that lawyers from Omaha are no more reliable than bums from the Bronx.

If my account of the play's plot has a certain facetious slant, it is because there is little more to

the play beyond what I have noted except a series of gags—some of them cute, some of them funny—all of them as "typical" as the story itself. The play, in short, is a conventional tale without real characters, cemented by jokes and that sense of recognition which is the recognition of clichés and thus supposed by many playgoers to represent a modest realism.

The one positive value in the play is the discovery of a charming actress, Anne Bancroft. I say this although her characterization of the Jewish girl from the Bronx is far too insistently and constantly characterized. The intonations are right, but such a girl should not be all intonation. I once saw a performance of an American businessman by an English actor in London which I described to my English guest at the show as having the accent of all our forty-eight states. Miss Bancroft, who, besides possessing a touching and lovable personality, really can act, plays her part as if she contained the Bronx in every fiber—which is false.

Henry Fonda is always effective in parts like the Nebraskan of this play, because he is relaxed, concentrated, efficient and honest in the sense that he never does more than is needed and is thus able to suggest more humanity than is present in the writing.

The play is a hit and will run for a long time, not only on Broadway but in every stock company and summer theatre all over the country for years to come.

—*NAT*, 1 Feb. '58

APPEAL FOR A 'REGAL' THEATRE

Theatregoing in London has always been a vast pleasure to me, and, I am sure, to a great many other Americans. I enjoy the audience there. The English are proud of their stars: Olivier, Richardson, Redgrave, Portman, Guinness, Edith Evans, Peggy Ashcroft. These splendid actors are known and admired here as well. We respect—as do the English—such playwrights as Rattigan, Fry, Eliot and now John Osborne. The Old Vic and the Stratford Memorial Theatre on the Avon are held in high esteem among us, as they are very much part of the English national landscape. Yet there are English critics and theatre folk who find the American theatre somehow more vivid, more challenging, more excitingly contemporary. The "rivalry," in so far as it exists, is probably good for both of us.

Still, I find—whatever position I choose to take in this matter—that theatregoing in general gives me greater pleasure in London than in New York. Why should this be so? As I have just noted, I prefer the feeling that envelops me when I sit down to play in an English theatre. The quality of the audience—its attitude toward the stage—gratifies one.

The American audience patronizes the theatre; the English audience loves it. This may be an illusion. In that case, I would still maintain that the English behave as if they love the theatre more—and that alone makes a difference in the effect they produce in their theatre's atmosphere.

Defensive Americans may protest that the Londoner pays less to see a play than we do: it is one of the few relatively cheap luxuries which remain to him. Though the cost of production has risen in England, and money is tighter, the price of the best seat in a London playhouse is hardly any higher than it was before the war. Getting to the theatre—by underground, bus or taxi—in London is also easier than it is in New York. Tickets for plays which promise to be successes are much less difficult to obtain in London than here, because there is a much smaller advance sale, and hit shows are not sold out, as is the case with us, months ahead.

All this, of course, makes theatregoing materially pleasanter in London. Yet these factors alone do not account for the behavior of the English audience. Few people arrive late, and, though Sir Ralph Richardson maintains the contrary, they seem to me to cough less during the slow parts of a show than our audiences do. Still, this is not what I am talking about, though it aids enjoyment.

The English theatre audience seems to be composed of friends rather than customers. A certain benevolence toward the institution of the stage—born of long usage and what might be called historical memory—appears to inform the larger part of the playgoers. True, the opening night "clubs" in the galleries carry on another tradition: a spirit of critical vigilance as if they were the appointed guardians of the theatre's "honor." When there are boos from the gallery on an opening night, London managers fear their play is permanently undermined.

But, broadly speaking, what characterizes the English audience is a patience and an initial warmth of response which are not simply courtesy but marks of respect for the theatre and its representatives arising from some intimate connection and basic reverence. The audience does not seem to have been sold into going to the theatre or captured there; it is prepared, even eager, to give itself to the entertainment before it. When it is not entertained, it strikes one as being sorrowfully silent rather than irritated or hostile.

English audiences have long memories in respect to favorite actors—and not only for the stars. When actors falter or fail several times, they do not lose their hold on the public; they are not considered to be slipping or finished. They may always feel secure in the public's continued devotion. They have but to return once more in a good part, in a reasonably entertaining play, and their position is reaffirmed—and for a long time. Actors are not simply the rage of a season or two; the audience has a genuine regard for them and a kind of affectionate awe which might be accorded a superior person whose merit exists beyond the clamor of the moment, the infatuation of their immediate presence on the night or in the season of their shining.

The London audiences seem to belong to the theatre; it is an extension of their homes. They are not there as suspicious visitors—people who might riot in disgust or raise the roof in jubilation, with no further concern for the cause of their annoyance or their celebration. The playhouses themselves seem to give off the feeling of having been cherished in the past as they are thoughtfully cared for in the present. The English audience reassures one that there always will be a British theatre. Our theatres seem to be hardly anything more than real estate.

What true theatre fan was not touched last summer when Vivien Leigh in the House of Lords and a host of other actors in other ways protested the announcement that the 123-year-old St. James's Theatre, where Oscar Wilde's plays were first produced and Laurence Olivier recently held a lease, was to be replaced by an office building. A drama critic, T.C. Worsley of the *New Statesman*, called the proposed sale "murder for money" and the committee which agreed to the sale "muddled English vandals betraying their heritage." Such a reaction cannot have been an individual one merely and it contrasts with our own tepid and restricted response to the demolition of our oldest playhouse, the Empire. It was part of an abiding sense of the theatre which exists among the English as a need.

When a wrong or a lack is pointed out to an American, he doesn't simply bewail the situation, he wants to *do* something about it. That is why I frequently find myself musing with unabated naïveté about ways and means of restoring some of our theatre's glamor—by making the audience a more active participant in the theatre's function. (It is too often forgotten that the audience is perhaps the prime mover in the making of theatre.) What the theatre brings us is in large measure what we have brought to it. I dream of an audience which is not only less passive, but truly an *actor* in the theatre.

The reader may have noticed that I have just referred to a recovery of the theatre's glamor. If the "pathos of distance" does not deceive me, New York audiences when I went to the theatre as a boy—between 1912 and 1927—were imbued with some of that theatre glow I find more of today in London than here. One of the reasons for this, no doubt, was that there were more plays produced and a more widespread habit of theatregoing. This situation made it possible for many plays to be seen and enjoyed which were not smash hits.

The economic as well as the psychological fever which demands nothing but the smash hit is one of the curses of our present situation. For when we all rush to see a play that gets "rave" reviews, it does not mean that we have all suddenly begun to love the theatre, but rather that we feel it necessary to be in the swim, to be doing and talking about what everyone else will presumably be doing and talking about for the next few months. Robert Morley once said to me, "An American is disturbed if he sits next to an empty seat in the theatre; the Englishman not only doesn't care if the next seat to him is empty; he doesn't mind if the whole house is."

The New Yorker was freer of this commercial prejudice in the old days than now, and consequently had a better time and made a better audience. Now that the theatre has become small—we have fewer houses in New York and throughout the country today—it might help to cultivate some "aristocratic" (or more individualistic) virtues. If the theatre is obliged, as its economists maintain, to charge high prices—$6.90 to $9.90 for an orchestra seat is not a "popular" price—let it at least give itself the glamor of the rare and the treasured.

Let us treat the theatre not as a social chore but as a festivity. Even the unbeliever in a cathedral feels the power of religion because he behaves there according to the code tradition dictates. Ceremonies of all kinds are meaningful to us—despite any skepticism one may harbor—because we act ceremoniously at them. So the theatre will prove greater fun if we train ourselves to behave less casually toward it.

I made this point in conversation recently and brought as evidence the fact that at the opera and ballet, where people "dress" more frequently than they do at plays, where flowers are brought and bouquets thrown, where bravos are less apologetic, where a sense of ritual pleasure and even lavishness are created not only on the stage but in the auditorium, the theatre still has glamor. As I said this, I was reminded of a story about a lady who was preparing to go to one of Odets' later plays: "Shall I dress?" she asked her escort, "or is it going to be a play of social significance!"

The grand manner in public attire may seem out of date for one of the more somber of our realistic plays. This is like saying that we should dress for *Tosca* but not for *La Bohème*, for a Balanchine ballet but not for one by Jerome Robbins. But it is not the black or white tie that makes the difference: Gautier wore a scandalous red waistcoat at the Comédie Française for the opening of Hugo's *Hernani* in 1830 to declare his pride in the advent of the then new romanticism. It was a colorful sign of defiance, too, a symbol that the wearer thought the event a splendid one.

We need to keep our sense of theatre as a place of marvels, of wonder and inspiration—and we ought in some way to show by our manner of entering it what we hope to see there. The theatre at all times—even with Ibsen and Chekhov—was a place to escape the humdrum, a place where we expected to hear better language, see more beautiful people, listen to more elevated or wittier thought than are found elsewhere. Whatever the show, we anticipate that it might somehow prove a holiday.

Even the rough manner of the Thirties—now a woeful affectation with a few—had a kind of dash to it, just as the flowing tie or bobbed hair or extreme décolletage were other expressions of pleasure in an attitude. But our theatre is changing; there is something like a new trend in the air. For conformity will have its rebels, and the newest rebellion will veer toward more rather than less grandeur.

The boundaries of realism are being extended. There is an increasing interest in the more "classical" theatre—of costume, of eloquence, of plastic movement, of color and rhetoric. It is no accident that the production of plays by Anouilh, Giraudoux, Fry, Eliot, Schiller and a return to

Shakespeare, not to mention interesting developments off-Broadway, have become increasingly common in the past few years.

I seem to be harking back to the "old," that is, to the traditional. Sam Goldwyn once asked a famous choreographer why he didn't introduce some "modern stuff" into a picture he was arranging dances for. "But the 'modern'," the choreographer answered, "is so old-fashioned." In the future, I hope to see our audiences advanced enough to be old-fashioned.

This audience will not come to the theatre haphazardly but as partisans of the theatre and its artists. It will not be so concerned with the theatre as show business but hungry for it as art. (How detestable the announcement in theatre columns of the investments made in plays and the degree of profit or loss realized on each of them! It is a thousand times better for the health of the theatre for an audience to view it as an art, which is fun, than as trade which is trouble.) The pride of the artist is always in the quality of his work and the kind of appreciation it evokes. The pride of audience should be in the quality of the appreciation it gives.

Let us cultivate a degree of hero worship for our favorite actors. If we are bold enough, let us become stagedoor Johnnies. Perhaps the glow of our adulation will stimulate actors and actresses to a handsome manner, a finer presence, a more attractively distinctive appearance, princely or bohemian, than has been customary in recent years. If actors imagine the public prefers to view them as just folks, they are sadly mistaken. The actor offstage should either remain invisible to the casual eye or retain something of the fabulous air his profession bespeaks.

Let us emulate the audience which greeted Caruso at his first appearance in *Aïda* in New York when the police on the street dashed into the Met for fear a riot had broken out there or the less fancy but equally fervent audience at the old Civic Repertory Theatre when *Waiting for Lefty* made everyone suspect the day of the "revolution" had arrived. Let us debate things theatrical—be clever, finicky or abstruse about it. Let us encourage people who are never bored at the theatre and find something good in every show. Boredom is boring.

Ask the manager to set aside one evening to be the exclusively dressy one (as is done at the Paris opera) and another evening as the popular-price night—as at the Met. (Both will be successful.)

We need not fear snobbism: I wish an off-Broadway house would hang out a sign, "Only plays for intellectuals and highbrows here," and stick to it, so that many would sneer and cause others to vie with one another to get in. Let us advocate champagne bars in the theatre—gaily decorated. The theatre, Gordon Craig once wrote, is a famous temple. We should enter it in an elevated mood.

Democracy, yes, but let's make our theatre regal.

—NYTM, 23 Feb. '58

THE ENTERTAINER

In writing about *Look Back in Anger*, I tried to suggest John Osborne's importance as a reflection of some of the moral and intellectual doldrums of contemporary England. Added to this is a certain rhetorical gift, an odd combination of witty nastiness, exasperated sentimentality and an histrionic violence which plays well.

The Entertainer—Osborne's second play (Royale)—which he assures us is his "best"—was sold out before the opening of its eight-week run because of an interest in the new author and more especially because of Laurence Olivier's presence in the central role. (If you can't get seats you can read the play which is published by Criterion Books.) It is more ambitious than the earlier play, both in its form and in its attempt to provide us with a wide range of characters as a social background to identify the origin of Osborne's mood.

There is the old music hall comedian who represents the confident England on which the curtain fell in 1914. He tells his granddaughter "You haven't lived, most of you. You've never known what it was like. You're all miserable really. You don't know what life can be like." The girl he speaks to represents that segment of the younger folk, idealistic but uncertain, who suddenly find themselves at rallies in Trafalgar Square because they get "steamed up about the way things are going" and ask themselves, "My own people—who are my people?"

The core of the trouble, apart from the feeling of resentment at the lack of any strong and concrete action to prevent atomic warfare, is expressed by one of the grandsons—the one who refused to go off to fight over Suez (his brother was killed there). "Can you think of any good reason for staying in this cozy little corner of Europe?" the embittered boy asks. "Don't kid yourself anyone's going to let you do anything or try anything here....You haven't got a chance. You'd better start thinking about number one. Nobody is going to do it for you because no one believes in that stuff any more. Oh, they may say they do, and may take a few bob out of your pay packet every week and stick some stamps on your card to prove it, but don't believe it....They're all so busy, speeding down the middle road together, not giving a damn where they're going, as long as they're in the bloody middle!"

The central character—the crooner and hoofer who represents the present and whose lower middle-class wife whimpers in her cups, "Oh Christ, I wish I knew what was going to happen to us!" and sees salvation only in emigration to Canada—this vaudevillian, played by Laurence Olivier, is a mess of vulgarity, bewilderment, heartlessness, seedy and aberrant sexuality, frustration and sentimental artistic yearning. "And do you know why?" he cries out, "Because we're deadbeats and down and outs. We're drunks, maniacs, we're crazy...the whole flaming bunch of us. We have problems that nobody's ever heard of, we're characters out of something that nobody believes in...But we're really not funny. We're too boring...We don't succeed in anything...."

I have quoted from the text itself because whatever value the play has is in its expression, however raw, of the fits and starts that now beset English society. The play is a symptom, and it is right that the English in particular should take it seriously and make a controversial subject of it.

But it is not a good play. (That, however, is no reason for dismissing it.) I do not believe with its author that the music hall, which he may be correct in calling "a significant part of England," can be employed as a symbol for England—certainly not as he has employed it. I believe in the blowsy wife in the play as an authentic character sketch (especially as played by Brenda de Branzie); but generally what is communicated is neither a poetic nor a realistic symbol of a dying society (even decadence may have grandeur or at least pathos), but so many rather grubby, repetitive and, though really explosive, not very sensitive, "slices of life." The fact that these are sandwiched in between music hall turns in which Archie Rice delivers rancid monologues and grinds out soiled ditties on the play's themes does not give the play any larger dimension than the content of the individual scenes.

The Entertainer is the immature work of a gifted, ambitious, battling young man. Because he is one of the very few able writers in England attempting to express something of the present situation there in cogent stage terms, Osborne occupies a more prominent place on the cultural horizon than the actual creative value of his work as yet warrants. A certain crudeness in such a young writer is to be expected, but it may prove damaging to him and to ourselves to mistake his vehement statement of certain facts about which he feels strongly for the revelation of some great truth.

Young writers must learn that the function of the artist is not to produce a sensation but to fashion objects which have an impersonal validity, putting us in contact with both the immediate world and with an overall sense of life we are all happy to share. Chekhov's plays are also about a society in decline, peopled with unhappy, foolish, often reckless people; but they are seen through the eyes of someone who realizes the sources of greatness in all men. Osborne's indignation and iconoclasm often sound like the complaints of youths who fear they may be denied their chance to become men, though they do not yet know what it means to be a man. These are justified complaints, but they are not to be taken either as wisdom or as the voice of humankind.

This spasmodic play is sustained by a brilliant cast and direction which lend a certain sparkle and brio to what might become painfully drab scenes. Laurence Olivier is theatrically consummate without being moving. Only so remarkably endowed an actor could conceive and execute so many character traits (including an unforgettable make-up) with such thoroughgoing dexterity; yet at the end we remain strangely deprived of any unified impression apart from our astonishment at the actor's virtuosity. We do not feel we know Archie Rice or for that matter the actor who plays him. Both have been consumed in the dazzling energy and bravura of the actor's technique—as if a painter in doing a portrait performed so many juggling tricks with his brush, tubes, palette and easel that we forgot to look at the face he had promised to set down on the canvas.

—*NAT*, 1 Mar. '58

WHO WAS THAT LADY
THE WALTZ OF THE TOREADORS

Spectacular melodrama—which offered train wrecks or chariot races as climactic thrills—and riotously improbable farce were absorbed by the movies around the year 1912. As a result the theatre has become an increasingly quieter or less kinetic medium. With a farce like Norman Krasna's *Who Was That Lady I Saw You With* (Martin Beck) it seems that the stunt show has returned to Broadway from Hollywood.

There is probably an audience for this sort of thing—I heard considerable laughter in the house—although I found it forced and tasteless, with a few good jokes but many more that would not pass muster at a varsity jamboree. What interested me, however, was the fact that when the sets were moved backward and forward, or up and down, the audience was highly intrigued.

The innocence of this reaction at this late date made me realize that the mechanical ingenuity and photographic feats of the movies are now so much taken for granted that the manipulation of ordinary settings in full view of the audience has once again become something to gape at. The plaything fascination of the stage seems more enduring than the fantastic inventiveness of the movies just because the former is so childishly candid while the engineering intricacy of the movies is made to appear a matter of fact.

Yet the American audience reacts with a certain coolness, if not a conscious resistance, to any show of artifice in the writing and acting for the so-called "legitimate" theatre. We welcome the conventions or stylization of vaudeville and musical comedy, but for the more sober forms of drama we insist on the "natural," the "true to life." That a play or its performance may be artificial and serious, both slapstick and significant, is a notion we barely comprehend.

These reflections occur to me once more with the resumption of the interrupted run of Anouilh's *The Waltz of the Toreadors* (Coronet) which I directed. The play has been a success from here to Chicago and back, but its critical reception, while generally enthusiastic, has always contained a certain ambiguity.

Anouilh calls the play a farce—which it is. The central character, just before the final curtain, murmurs "What a farce; it's so sad." Yet one critic—a perceptive one—complimented me on having rendered the play funny, while finding fault with the script for not having the texture of a Chekhov play! Another reviewer asks why the play with its new cast (Melvyn Douglas, Betty Field,

Lili Darvas) seems more disturbing than on his first view of it.

The confusion arises, I believe, from the play's traditionally French style to which we are still not wholly accustomed. It is the tradition of the Italian masked comedy—grafted by Molière onto his new "bourgeois" drama—in which important, even tragic, material is transmitted in the guise of a comedy which frequently moves toward the farcical. The French, who in the main have always resisted realism on the stage, prefer the theatre theatrical, the theatre of frank artifice in which even passion is expressed by means that create a certain detachment from it, a slight removal from a sense of the actual. That is why so many French plays—old and new—employ characters and plot devices that are as old as the hills. Henry Miller once called the French the Chinese of Western culture.

The Waltz of the Toreadors is a farce conceived by a romantic to mock and correct his own romanticism. Its characters are not so much "real people" as types, figures, attitudes. Its surface is often hilarious and toward the end deliberately "corny" (the discovery of the long "lost" son is straight out of ancient comedy) but its core is so grim that one's laughter may strike one at times as unseemly.

The second scene of the second act—in my opinion one of the most brilliant in contemporary drama—is Strindberg turned into farce. Its brilliance consists in preventing us from becoming so totally absorbed by its ferocity that we fail to laugh at it and in never letting us laugh so much that we forget its agony. It is in the very nature of the play's construction (its "civilization") that it remains both painful and funny. It is real, but not realistic, it is "superficial" but it probes, it is "heartless" yet it is shot through with sentiment. We are equally wrong if we think of it as a mere joke or if we seek in it the same literalness of statement or the forthrightness of feeling we expect in the plays presumed to hold the mirror up to nature.

Just as *The Waltz* alternates and combines its contrasting features to create something rather new for us, so it is the only one of Anouilh's plays to achieve a balance and conclusion of content. What Anouilh tells us here is that, though nearly all of us must forego the hope of achieving the ideal of our dreams and must learn to accept some sorry compromise with reality, man must ever renew the struggle to attain the very ideal at which he has failed.

—*NAT*, 22 Mar. '58

TWO GENTLEMEN OF VERONA

In regard to the play itself, I am amused by the attitude some reviewers take to the rarely-performed Shakespeare pieces. Perhaps it is intended as a courtesy to the actors, but there is a habit among reviewers, when they do not have a good time at such shows, to dismiss Shakespeare's early plays as "minor" works—which in a sense they are—but the implication is that since they are "minor" they may be airily dismissed. Need I point out that these "minor" works, for all their deficiencies, are packed with genius and are incomparably superior to most of the major works the critics are invited to see most of the time on Broadway.

—*NAT*, 19 Apr. '58

NO TIME FOR COMEDY

I do not particularly concentrate on politics nowadays and I may as well confess that I read history as art and philosophy, rather than as usable knowledge, so that like the average educated American I remain an innocent in world affairs. Still, what with the headlines and an occasional skimming of articles in the daily and weekly journals, some things seep in. Sometimes they make me laugh. I am sure they oughtn't.

Several weeks ago, for example, the Administration acknowledged a recession. A day or two later an official statement assured us that

there would be an upswing during the month of March. Harry Truman made some caustic remarks about the Government's bungling. Then I read a quote from President Eisenhower's speech in which he spoke—obviously referring to Truman and like-minded critics—of "men of little faith." This was followed a few day later by a Presidential statement that things would get worse before they got better. By this time I was grinning, though I know this reaction was absolutely wrong.

Remedies for the bad effects of the recession were suggested. Tax cuts, then no tax cuts, federal spending projects, then no such projects, partial disarmament, no disarmament, and so on and on to an item which announced that our Secretary of State felt there should be no halting of nuclear preparedness since this would impede the work now being done on perfecting the clean bomb. At this point I could not suppress a guffaw—which I am convinced was wicked of me.

Such wickedness never finds itself on our stage today. (There is only the wickedness of total imperviousness to these matters.) Our theatre rarely gnashes its teeth in an indignant smile or hoots with derisive pain. This is hardly surprising: after all we are not Europeans. George Kaufman, who we should remember was co-author of *Once in a Lifetime* and other similar plays, once remarked that on Broadway "Satire is what closes on Saturday night." Most satirical plays on our stage are of foreign origin.

There was some kidding in *The Teahouse of the August Moon*, but it gave offense to no one at all. *No Time for Sergeants* poked fun at the army brass, but this is an almost traditional joke. No one ever asks at the end of such plays, as someone asked me many years ago during a performance of *Waiting for Lefty*, "Say, do they really mean it?" Gore Vidal told me recently, in answer to a criticism in my review of his play, *Visit To a Small Planet*, that he had tried to suggest a point of view but that the audience in the out-of-town tryout froze when it began to suspect a serious intention. The plays of industrial unrest nowadays seem to be typified by *The Pajama Game*. Voltaire's *Candide* became a giant marshmallow on Broadway.

Social satire has always been rare on our stage because satire is the product of a degree of civilized sophistication which our theatre audiences—either literal-minded or frivolous—do not usually possess. (How many plays in the history of our theatre can we compare in purpose with Gogol's *Inspector General* or Beaumarchais' *Marriage of Figaro*?) Even in terms of harmless satire in a gay vein, the last successful show I can recall is the 1946 revue *Call Me Mister*—smoother and slicker than the *Pins and Needles* of 1937-39. What is worth examining however is why there is less satire at the present time than in the twenties—our most self-critical as well as most self-indulgent era—or in the thirties—the period of our most acute social awareness.

To create satire which goes beyond good-natured spoofing of follies and vices that are regarded as peccadilloes, you have to have a community with strong beliefs and convictions. Almost everyone today is uncertain of his beliefs and few are rash enough to harbor convictions.

But when one's beliefs have been shaken, when convictions have been undermined by events, and self-questioning has taken possession of one's soul, the consequences may still bear the marks of the believing personality. The agony which results from the destruction of once firmly held beliefs may take on a dynamic quality apparently destructive but basically the expression of a passion for a renewed faith. Blasphemy is frequently a more telling expression of the religious spirit than piety.

The satire or irony inherent in the plays of many contemporary French dramatists, beginning with Camus' *Caligula* through to Genet, Ionesco and Beckett, is a manifestation of *outrage* and not, as many suppose, the result of a wholly nihilistic attitude. They are at once savage, sometimes obscene, protests against the absurdity of our existence in a world where most of the old faiths have turned to hypocrisy and a (not always conscious) cry for a new one.

These rebels without a platform (except the stage) and without a program (except that of *la farce*: French for a riotous upsetting of the official applecart) are admitted by their very detractors to express something of their country's present spirit. Most of Western Europe (particularly France) knows it is sick, caught in a web of insane contradictions. But being conscious of this and expressing it fully in a mad satire—a comic grimace is noticeable even in the most lacerating and melancholy of their plays—is a sign of vitality.

In the hysterically prosperous twenties we had the energy and wit to poke fun at ourselves and to confess our nightmares—if only as a corrective to our creeping complacency. Besides O'Neill whose realm was the tragic (except possibly for *Marco Millions*), there were such plays, mixing the bitter with the sweet, as *What Price Glory?* by Maxwell Anderson and Laurence Stallings, *The Show-Off* by George Kelly, *The Front Page* by Hecht and MacArthur, *Beggar on Horseback* by George Kaufman and Marc Connolly. The Teapot Dome scandal provided the pivotal theme of *The Grand Street Follies* of 1922. Even *The Garrick Gaieties* of 1925—Rodgers and Hart's first success—contained a number about the Monkey Trial which had some bite. There were occasional rumblings of real dissent—often incoherent or imitative (of the German expressionist dramatists) but nonetheless aggressive.

Very little of all this dug deep because, in a predominantly confident, or at least heedless, time there seemed little need for more than a smiling degree of self-depreciation. When e. e. cummings' play *him* was produced in 1928 in the Village the entire press stood aghast, not recognizing either the play's lyric and satirical quality or its implied prophecy of the coming collapse.

The twenties, theatrically speaking, moved from the sly but painless joke of the Kaufman-Gershwin *Of Thee I Sing* (1931) into the middle thirties when our faces grew longer, and even the essentially conservative Maxwell Anderson mixed some sneers with the chuckles in *Both Your Houses*, which spoke of America's inexhaustible fund of political inertia.

The mid-thirties, as everyone knows, was the Odets period in the theatre, which, lest we forget, was marked by a wholesomely enthusiastic humor as well as the pathos and bathos of our hopes in panaceas we did not fully understand. (Satire mellowed by sentiment was always one of Odets' strong points.) But beyond the "radical," "left-wing," hortatory plays which represented the youthful singing combativeness of the New Deal days, there sprouted on our side streets little political "cabarets" somewhat reminiscent of the *boîtes* in Paris, where the pulse of the people may always be felt beating in ragtime.

The hopes of the thirties were both rebuffed and justified by the war years and their "national unity." Tennessee Williams emerged in his gentlest mood in *The Glass Menagerie*. Saroyan's early plays took the edge off their satirical outline in tender clowning and woozy or boozy kindliness. The post-war forties in the theatre were enlivened by Arthur Miller's *Death of a Salesman* which, for all its tearfulness, contains definite elements of satire and, generally speaking, reveals a more sober and cautious continuance of the New Deal mentality of the thirties. We still produced affably liberal comedies like Thurber and Nugent's *The Male Animal*, Lindsay and Crouse's *The State of the Union* and Garson Kanin's *Born Yesterday*.

The decline of the satiric spirit begins with the fifties. Our hopes were dissipated, rebelliousness was first frowned upon and then squelched. Social criticism now seems to lack a base and the building of positive values appears to lack support in social realities. What new affirmations are made seem to turn inward, are always on a personal level, as if to say "please mind your own business and let me mind mine—and if we are going to take a public stand it must remain within the confines of ideologies and organizations of undisputed respectability and authority." We are not so much frightened, now that McCarthy has passed away, as transfixed, stuck, spiritually immobilized.

We do not know today if we are prosperous or not or exactly what it means to be prosperous—except that to fail to be a success is shameful. We are the leaders of the Western world, but we are not sure whom we are leading or to what. We do not know if we can stop war, though we are rather hopeless of surviving it. We pray that the psychoanalysts will reassure us since the moralists and preachers have not redeemed us. Playwrights who have tried to portray the consequences of this disarray now apologize for their perversity and promise that with some medical assistance they will become good boys. According to our critics *and* audiences it is somehow terribly wrong to be "unhealthy," so that as John Gassner has written, "Health seems to be our brand of decadence."

To be confused is not yet to be damned. An avowal of our confusion even in terms of the comic without fear of some notes of exasperation would be a sign of strength. We live in a challenging time, but we seem unable to take up the challenge. The so-called cynicism of the twenties was creative; the solemnity and some of the immature sloganizing of the thirties and forties were still creative; what is stultifying us now is a failure to recognize and cry out that somewhere along the way our line was lost; that we must go back and find out what it was and what happened to it.

—*NAT*, 26 Apr. '58

BALLETS DE PARIS

Jeanmaire with the *Ballets de Paris* (Broadway Theatre) is jolly, piquant, attractive. The sets by Clave for the company's most successful ballet *Carmen* (sets which one of our daily reviewers once called amateurish) are masterpieces. There are other excellent dancers with the *Ballets de Paris*. The show as a whole is pleasurable.

But the evening I enjoyed most this season—more than all ten of the best plays—was that of the Muscovite Moiseyev Dance Company. My enthusiasm seems to be universal. It has been many years since I have heard such excited applause and cheering at any theatrical occasion in New York. Part of this demonstrativeness may be quasi-political or super propaganda. The audience hopes to make everyone feel that the tensions of diplomatic relations in no way affect the cordiality of its sentiments toward Russians as people—especially when these people are superb artists.

Transcending this cheerful consideration is the fact that the combination of vigor with innocence, perfect technical proficiency with smiling heartiness, physical exuberance with youthful elation releases in our (American) hearts a particular spring of fervor. The qualities which these dancers possess are not only the qualities we most admire but those we like to claim as our own when we feel ourselves to be at our best. It may be said without sentimentality that these Russians on the stage arouse in our audiences a kinship, a certain sense of "brotherhood."

Besides the qualities I have mentioned, which might be achieved by any group of brilliant dancers, there are others even more important. The good humor and healthy playfulness of most of the members are a token of an expansive fresh air humanity which is the most immediate impression one receives. There is also a gratifying (and unboastful) virility in the male dancers conjoined with a rare, robust yet gentle femininity in the women.

In most modern ballet companies the women appear to be trained to function as men. The result is literally overpowering and sometimes frightening. In the Moiseyev company one feels that the women—radiant as apples—are happy to be the more than adequate base for the men's boundless energy. There is no "war of the sexes" here, but a natural consummation and completion. Sensuality as such is wholly absent.

A sense of togetherness is the outstanding virtue of the entire event. I do not refer to the team-work which, it goes without saying, is characteristic of all great troupes. I mean that the distinguishing mark of the company's art is its communality, a collectivism which is not merely organizational but organic: the individuals achieve freedom, power and pleasure through their being a group, sharing common sentiments, living one life, experiencing a creative unity. All the ensemble dances seem to begin or end as if the people who compose the unit did not feel themselves altogether secure or alive until they had touched one another in the proximity of a tight formation—like a fist or a flower.

All this might strike one as a superior sort of folk athletics if it were not for the unerringly picturesque and dramatic sense of the theatre—typically Russian—which the director Ivan Moiseyev has given all the dances.

The high point of his theatrical artistry is the number called "Partisans" which represents people riding to battle in some lonely region at night. We see soldiers moving (as if on horseback) in a strangely fleet and compelling rhythm to the fray. The number is built like a play: mysterious and suspenseful at the beginning, mounting in confidence with always a touch of friendly humor—an all-embracing friendliness informs everything—and ending in a climax of furious power that is an ecstasy of zeal.

This is theatre at one of its true peaks: entertainment which is a dithyramb of movement and meaning, a celebration through the body of a people's soul, a rite, a festivity, an explosive affirmation of fulfillment in the drama of life.

—NAT, 3 May '58

ULYSSES IN NIGHTTOWN

Certainly *Ulysses in Nighttown* (Rooftop Theatre) is a thing to see. Like *Godot, The Chairs, Endgame*, it satisfies our need for "crazy" plays. It is provocative theatre, not merely a departure from Broadway routine, but actually an imaginative venture into a creative domain.

Chief among its assets is its dramatic intelligence. Burgess Meredith who directed with the assistance of Valerie Bettis under the literary supervision of Padraic Colum has taken a section of Joyce's *Ulysses*—barely intelligible to many—and converted it into a fascinating stage piece with a continuity that has both psychological and narrative coherence which can be followed by the audience with interest and, for the most part, pleasure. The focus of our attention is Joyce's bewildered anti-hero Leopold Bloom, embodied in the extraordinary person of Zero Mostel without whose vividly pathetic clowning the enterprise might have proved a calamity.

Meredith's achievement as a director deserves special attention because he makes theatrical sense of material which despite its violence of action and pungent dialogue, is essentially non-theatrical. As I shall explain further on, Meredith did this by examining each scene and almost every line to find out how they might be visualized, that is, lucidly conveyed in stage terms. It is the opposite of what happens with most productions of Shakespeare where familiarity with the texts leads many of us to assume that the play is being staged when it is only being spoken.

It is true that some previous knowledge of Joyce and his great book helps orient the audience in their appreciation of the show—it would be worthwhile to issue a questionnaire to learn how many of the spectators were able to enjoy the performance without any acquaintance with its source. But there can be no doubt that in the main the audience fully responds to this *Ulysses* which can hardly be as well known to it as Shakespeare's plays.

What I have just written is more like publicity than like criticism—the distinction for American writing about the theatre is crucial—and if I have begun my review as though I intended to "push" the show, it is to make clear that what I have to say in a contrary sense is not designed to "knock" it. (Readers of *The Nation* probably have little idea how difficult it is to divorce the theatre world from the concept of reviews as either "raves" or "raps.")

Much of the detail—characterization of minor bits and the stylized movement—is crudely amateurish. This is probably inevitable, since the circumstances of production are even worse off Broadway than on. They do not permit the extended and meticulous rehearsals needed to make a good deal of the performance more than a coarse kaleidoscopic synopsis of the material.

When theatrical expressionism is projected in blunt conventional indications the result is often embarrassing. What is required is sharply etched and originally conceived figures moving with effortless fluency so that they coalesce into a phantasmagoria as authoritative as one of the nightmares of Hieronymus Bosch.

The problem is particularly knotty here because Joyce's *Nighttown* episode, though mainly written in dialogue and "stage direction," occurs in the subconscious rather than in the objective world—even the objective world of dreams. Hallucinations can be staged, but Joyce's writing—even in a realistic play like *Exiles*—is so peculiarly the articulation of an inner state that its outward representation seems somehow to betray its artistic nature. The images, sounds, utterances recorded, though sharp and violent, were never meant to be concretely seen or heard but only sensed as ideas, disturbances of the soul, a forever private or solitary evocation. All the words and the vision emanate, as it were, in silence from silence. Hence there is something aesthetically repellent in presenting *Nighttown* as a public exhibition.

The situation, I repeat, is saved by Zero Mostel who is theatrically as right as can be to the very "boiled eyes" which Joyce gives Bloom. I do not want to see Bloom in the flesh—he is such a character as dreams are made on—but Mostel's "flesh," expanding and contracting like some heartbreaking ogre of human anguish and absurdity, is equivalent to, though essentially different from, the author's more covert and spectral creature.

And now we come to the matter itself—the content of Joyce's so-called novel. As Voltaire said of God, if there had been no such book it would have been necessary to invent it. It represents the end of a line, not only in literature, but in culture. In it all the stuff of our civilization—moral, intellectual, psychological—has been turned into a colossal dung heap. Vastly comic, it is also agonizing, the catastrophic explosion of a guilty conscience. A library of learning is erupted by a volcanic genius, formidable but narrow, making a work which represents either the best-be-forgotten debris of an ancient world or the seething compost of something to be reborn after the final atomization.

Joyce, the spoiled priest, the Jesuit saint whose religion was injected the wrong way, the soiled deity of the contemporary literary intellectual, because he created from a "country full of rotten teeth rotten guts living in a bog swamp, eating cheap food, paved with dust, horse-dung and consumptive's spit" and a classical education tormented by self-accusation and universal doubt (except perhaps for the vaginal affirmations of Molly Bloom) so that in the end nothing was left but a fixation on pure style—this Joyce has fashioned the greatest monument or master tombstone of our time. I have never made up my mind whether I loathe as much as I love him. There is now only a doggedly dissatisfied awe and veneration.

—*NAT*, 19 July '58

JACK
THE BALD SOPRANO

The program of Eugene Ionesco's one act plays, *The Bald Soprano* and *Jack*, at the Sullivan Street Playhouse interested and entertained me. The question raised by most people who have seen Ionesco's plays here, in London and in Paris is, "Are they a manifestation of a significant new dramatic personality or mere French flummery?"

The first thing that strikes me about Ionesco's work is its theatricality. What Ionesco does is to take ideas which are now in the air—some people

would say à la mode—and make arrestingly vivid stage-images of them. The effect in general is usually macabre and witty while the writing is both sprightly and sharp with overtones of pathos.

Overlong, *The Bald Soprano* illustrates the featureless inanity of lower middle-class domestic relations: the lack of connection between man and wife, among neighbors and between individuals and their ordinary environment. Men and women today, Ionesco implies, hardly recognize each other, especially if they have lived together a long time: their homes are blank spots in space and all live in mechanical response to one another and to the world. The fashionable word for this state of being is alienation.

Kafka gave this mood its classically contemporary expression. The surrealists have added something to Ionesco's palette and the perennial Parisian flair for spicy nonsense (nonsense may have meaning) has added to the recipe.

Jack is a fiercer, rather than funnier, variation on the basic theme. It is also more ambiguous, for Ionesco will not be pinned down so that anything altogether precise may be deciphered in his plays. There is a constantly waggish elusiveness to avoid any completely rational or logical connotation. This adds an element of mystery (or mystification) to the picture.

Jack might be called The Family Nags the Son Into Marriage. After the discontented and uncommunicative boy has been bullied into seeing his prospective bride—child of a rich bourgeois household—and he begins to speak with her, she overcomes his reluctance or fear by a wild outburst of erotic wooing to which he finally succumbs. At the end we see him prostrate under the solemnly ritualistic gaze of both families. Has sexual contact with his bride killed him or has he just passed out with passion? The answer is perhaps more pertinent to a psychiatric investigator than to an audience.

All this is very colorfully communicated—the family in this instance are circus folk—and with fundamental (artistic) clarity. My saying this may strike the reader as a pose. *Godot* clear? *Endgame* clear? And now this Ionesco clear? Attentive spectators will find these plays understandable—particularly those I am now reviewing—if they do not seek to grasp every word in a literal or information-bearing sense. What must be followed is what the eyes take in (for example, the weird clock in *The Bald Soprano*) and the *line of action* in each scene. The form of the plays rather than the details of each speech carries most of the message. The speech is understandable too but in a suggestive or "symbolic" rather than a strict sense. The whole is related to meaning as we know it in contemporary painting and in modern verse. What is mainly to be noted in such a play as *Jack*, for example, is that traditional scenes from bourgeois drama with almost conventional action (the mother entreats, the sister reasons, the father moralizes, the boy protests, the would-be in-laws storm, the boy begins to yield, the bride cajoles, love scenes ensue, etc., etc.) are transformed into grotesqueries by the author's thematic intention and poetically stylized dialogue.

It may be difficult to determine at present whether Ionesco's plays will eventually seem more clever than truly felt. His view of life is certainly not mine. But every phase of feeling, every aspect of truth—no matter how strange—ought to find articulation in the theatre. Ionesco utters his truth in specific stage terms which are startling and often brilliant. What he has to say moreover is justified by the routine of our daily living. The lack of spiritual content in our civilization has been the major outcry of European drama since Ibsen. Ionesco has carried this idea to the climactic point of savage caricature.

—*NAT*, 2 Aug. '58

LET'S BE MODEST

Every once in a while when we find ourselves relieved of the tensions of our work in the theatre we joyously announce to the universe that ours is "the best theatre in the world." There are respectable reasons for thinking so. Yet I have never been able to hear such a pronouncement without wincing.

There is something pointless and a little misleading in our optimism. When Helen Hayes a few years ago aroused controversy by implying that American acting was superior to that of the English, my first impulse was to submit that both were good, and both might be improved.

I call these arguments pointless because we rarely define our standard, that is, ask ourselves exactly what we mean by "good," "better" or "best." The state of mind that produces such high flying assertions is misleading because it contributes to what Russell Lynes in a recent article in *The New York Times Magazine* named the besetting sin of our cultural life—complacency.

In the theatre such complacency is related to an ever-present anxiety. For example, if there are no more than seventy new plays produced during a New York theatre season and the figure worries us, we are sure to speak of a "renaissance" if the following season eighty plays are produced. In 1926-27 more than 250 were produced.

A recent trip to Europe disturbed my own complacency. Did I make any momentous discovery? No. Though I saw several pleasant and a few interesting shows in London, there were hardly any "revelations" that might shake my confidence in our own achievements. On the contrary, the fact that Kim Stanley's performance in *Cat on a Hot Tin Roof* was voted by the London drama critics the best performance of the season by an actress was a source of pride to me, while the critics' preference for an estimable but lame effort at musical satire called *Expresso Bongo* in opposition to *My Fair Lady* simply amused me. The most memorable event for me during my visit to London was the Moscow Art Theatre company at Sadler's Wells Theatre in *The Cherry Orchard* and *The Three Sisters*.

I shall not describe the productions here, except to say that they affected me in a very special way. I had seen the Moscow Art Theatre in 1923 and its actors then were superior to those in

London this spring. But there was a perfection of ensemble, a scrupulousness of execution, a clarity of interpretation, an attention to every prop and stage effect so that they all helped create the complete life of the Chekhovian world together with a peculiar lack of haste—which was not "slowness" but something like the natural breath of human behavior that are more than admirable. The audience is not forced to be excited by an effect but invited to share a life experience.

As I reflected on all this I was more and more convinced that we in America were capable of doing as well if we had the means—more even than the money and the time, an *established* theatre—to produce our best plays in a similar manner. Most of the actors of this particular company represented the third generation of the Moscow Art Theatre: it is now 60 years old. The reason why the actors were able to play so beautifully together in an integrated style that was both "real" and as graceful to ear and eye as the performance of any "classic" play might be—is that the actors were trained and supported by a tradition of the theatre initiated before the upheavals of 1917 and continuously maintained since.

Then in drab and impoverished East Berlin in a gem of a theatre—the Comic Opera—I saw one of the most dazzling productions I have ever witnessed on the musical stage—Offenbach's *Tales of Hoffmann*. In polish of stage direction, in lavishness and imaginativeness of costuming and scenic design very little in my theatregoing career could match it.

Not far from the Comic Opera in East Berlin is the Berliner Ensemble Theatre of Bertolt Brecht—where plays are perfectly produced with a marvelous new theatricality by a permanent company that plays in a style altogether unfamiliar elsewhere. It is a style that eschews suspense, the discharge of strong emotions, sentimental identification with the characters—a style presumably akin to the esthetic objectivity of the Chinese theatre rather than to the passion of the Greek, and still for all this, one which ends by affecting us with a sense of nobility and the beauty of free contemplation. In

West Berlin, too, where O'Neill's *A Touch of the Poet* is a great popular success, an astonishing variety of plays—contemporary and ancient—are handsomely and intelligently done. And in the Swedish National Theatre eighteen new productions were carefully staged last season.

When Howard Taubman, whom I met in Spoleto, Italy, told me that the director of the fascinating *Hamlet* he had seen in Moscow had apologized to him for the insufficient rehearsal time allowed for that production—three months!—I began to wonder whether I shouldn't venture further and further into the vast theatre world of Europe and beyond to inoculate myself against the dangerous paralysis of self-contentment.

The Broadway theatre horizon is narrow and its values inadequate for the great world we live in. In Paris, I saw Peter Brook's production of Arthur Miller's *A View From the Bridge*—a smash hit there—a production I enjoyed much more than its original one at home. I asked myself, "When a play is a failure in New York, is it really a failure?" And when I hear the praise bestowed on *The Crucible* in its present off-Broadway production after its cool reception on Forty-Fifth Street several seasons ago, I ask myself, "Is our midtown area really the theatre world's center?"

And then thoughts spark in all directions: When a reviewer says of an actress, "Miss X is the most dazzling find since Miss Y"—(who appeared a season before) and then after that neither Miss X nor Miss Y is heard from again on the stage for several years—what does it mean? Etc. Etc.

Complacency get thee behind me!

—*NYT*, 10 Aug. '58

THE FAMILY REUNION

At the outset of this still young and somewhat laggard season I must confess that I prefer to be strict with plays I respect rather than sharp with those about which I am indifferent. One should contend only with strength.

My preference among the season's early offerings is for plays which may not be seen by the majority of "regular" theatergoers: the Phoenix production of T.S. Eliot's *The Family Reunion* (written some ten years ago but never professionally performed here), which was coldly received by the press; and the repertory of the *Théâtre National Populaire* which is French but apparently not fashionable.

It is easy to spot what is "wrong" with *The Family Reunion*: its plot line does not sufficiently correspond to or embody its theme. The plot has to do with a young Englishman who may have desired or committed the murder of his unbearable wife. The theme has two branches: it relates to the guilt of being man, apart from any specific wickedness (original sin); and to the hope of salvation, not by evading the "furies," but by pursuing and facing them because they are of the very essence of the human condition.

The play then is nebulous as drama, but it has the virtue of being the expression of a real person with a fine stylistic signature. How crisp, skeletally pure and delicately musical is the ruminative melancholy of Eliot's speech. In the presence of such a play—directed by Stuart Vaughan with admirable intelligence and theatrical understanding of Eliot's dramatic mode—one feels oneself an adult again in the theatre and confronted by a man worth a quarrel.

What is my quarrel with Eliot here? It is a double one and relates to the inherent content and attitude of his play. *The Family Reunion* betrays a constant and all-pervading discomfort with the business of living, or to use Eliot's word, the "filthiness" of existence. The hero—like the author himself before his "conversion"—is given to loathing as others are to loving.

This objection may be said to represent little more than a difference of temperaments. My personal bent should not serve as an artistic criterion. The deeper flaw I find is a lack of true pathos—a quality which emerges only when the stuff of life, however abhorrent, is present in a work of art. Chekhov's characters are frequently fools, louts, fumblers, but he gives us a sense of intimate connection with them and makes us discover even in their wounds and fatuity some element of the universally true. In his play Eliot does not seem to have contact with anything but books, ideas and other works of art. His characters at best are witty caricatures. His world is at several removes from life itself, and though it may stink in his nostrils, what we detect is only the ambiguous aroma of decaying documents and moldy screeds. Transcendence (salvation) is not achieved in Eliot's play through a struggle with and beyond the muck and anguish of life: it is chiefly acquired through a graciously diffident and ironic bowing out from the boredom of polite society.

Along with praise for the director, we must compliment the rightness of Norris Houghton's setting, Will Armstrong's costumes and lighting and an excellent cast headed by Florence Reed, Lillian Gish and Fritz Weaver—all of whom speak with exceptional clarity and lucid thought.

I hope at another time to say more about *Théâtre National Populaire*. The actors who compose its company are good-looking, thoroughly disciplined, impeccable in diction. They wear their beautiful costumes as if to the manner born and demonstrate the dignity of people devoted to a fine task—the interpretation of national (French) classics in a simple but strikingly impressive way. There are no stars as far as this organization is concerned, but the company includes Gérard Philipe, an actor no one should miss seeing. As for the two plays I attended—Musset's *Lorenzaccio* and Hugo's *Marie Tudor*—they are much more and much better than the fustian that at first glance they might seem.

—*NAT*, 8 Nov. '58

COCK-A-DOODLE DANDY

Sean O'Casey's career has been a strangely troubled one. His fervid and distinguished champions are to be found everywhere in English-speaking theatre circles, but except for his early plays—*Juno and the Paycock*, *The Plough and the Stars*, *The Shadow of a Gunman*—he has been almost entirely shunned in his native Ireland and largely neglected in his adopted England.

With us in America, where it seems his most appreciative audience is to be found, most of his plays—particularly in recent years—have been produced off-Broadway. This is understandable in view of the fact that, while most of these plays teem with talent, they are uneven in quality and devilishly difficult to present in a key compatible with their content.

Perhaps the most challenging of O'Casey's later plays is *Cock-A-Doodle Dandy*, now to be seen at the Carnegie Hall Playhouse. It is a play a master director might find hard to stage unless he was blessed with a first-rate company of authentically Irish actors. Small wonder then that it is beyond the capacity of the people who present it on Fifty-Seventh Street. They must be credited nevertheless for their valiant effort.

I call the play difficult. The truth is that unless one has read it—and I have not done so for some years—one cannot feel secure in any estimate of it based on a production that is less than marvelously attune to its peculiarly mixed music.

For the play is a poem and a harangue, a bitterly sad farce, a tender fantasy and a savage parody. It sings and preaches, it guffaws and curses. There appears to be too much outright anger in it, and while one is inclined in a certain mood to find its indignation fully justified, one cannot be altogether certain that its anger, if articulated in the proper vein, could not be turned into a beautifully wry melancholy, a heart-broken sweetness.

The play is presumably a paean to the abundant joyousness of life, but the dramatist's heart is oppressed by frustrations, his grin is distorted by outrage at the forces of bigoted religiosity which darken the landscape of his beloved country. There is no patriot more clamorously harsh than the alienated Irishman. He can express his devotion only in a lament that is rendered strident by derision—and while he sheds tears of compassion, one cannot avoid the sense that they are commingled with venom.

The present production is staged in the manner of burlesque. And while the broadness of the play's humor—it is frequently very funny—seems to call for such treatment, I suspect that this approach is fundamentally wrong. Much of O'Casey's action is rough, and many of his characters are both crude and cantankerous, so that the atmosphere verges on that of a pub in which a brawl is in progress. For all that, I believe the play's message and essential quality might be conveyed with a certain reticence in which the basic reality of the environment rather than the ebullient nature of the play's "business" might emerge.

The wickedness or the absurdity of the play's negative characters (those who blemish nature) might then become comically pathetic rather than shrill and cartoon-like. None of the characters—no matter how cruel their stupidity—should in the context of such a play be made hateful. For the hallmark of O'Casey's folk, whether they live in Dublin or in the country, is a certain charming provinciality. They are all *small* people—almost "cute"—and one should laugh or weep over them, not detest them. They are limited, they are blind, they are thick-headed, but above all they are pitiful. They do not know what they are doing—and they would be kind if they were not so foolish. They live in a twilight world in which superstition is as natural as lyricism, a world where vice and terror are somewhat infantile and where beautiful dreams—adorably or distressingly naive—can flourish along with rank depravity of behavior. The soil underneath is confined and boggy.

Set in such a world, the play's conflicting moods—the crazy high jinks and the pain exemplified by the crippled girl who returns unhealed from the pilgrimage to Lourdes—could coexist as parts of a whole in O'Casey's tragi-comic vision of his country's grace and woe.

Since I see the play in this way and since it has been directed in almost every respect in a quite contrary sense, I cannot, for all the honest work proffered in this production, praise any part of it—except for the courage manifested in doing it at all. And, as I have said earlier, for the intrinsic worthiness of the project.

—*NAT*, 29 Nov. '58

DEFENSE OF THE ARTIST AS "NEUROTIC"

When, during the Depression, we read headlines of businessmen who flung themselves from the windows of their office buildings, we were shocked but not utterly surprised. One thing is certain: very few people felt impelled to comment that the nature of business produced madmen.

Many of us have been made uneasy of late to read statements or to hear television interviews in which an artist announced that he was undergoing psychoanalytic treatment. The fact itself is by no means objectionable; we are prepared to believe that such treatment for the artist, as for anyone else, may prove helpful. But this is a private matter. What disturbs us is that such public confessions are presumed to reveal something about the nature of artists and their work. This, I, for one, hold to be entirely false.

Two things are assumed: that art is itself the outcome of some maladjustment or neurosis and that, if the artist were to correct this, he might either function more efficiently or, a more ambiguous conclusion, he might beneficially cease being an artist altogether. In either interpretation, a supposedly normal person might emerge—the prototype of that person probably being the one who reads the confession or hears it on the air.

The reason this view is fairly popular may be set down to our secret envy of the artist who, despite all possible disabilities, is somehow regarded as a special being. The "bohemian"—usually a defective artist—often fosters the myth both as a boast and as an excuse for misconduct, which the community usually believes to be characteristic of him. It has been said that "no man is a hero to his valet," on which Goethe commented, "That is because the valet is a valet."

There may be a more cogent reason why the notion that an artist must be a basically "sick" person is developing into a local cliché. The idea began to gain ever greater acceptance with the spread of the romantic movement in the early nineteenth century. When the artist was no longer ready to celebrate the dogmas of religious institutions or the official policies of the governing classes, his position became more and more precarious. He was regarded with increasing suspicion. He felt himself estranged from the majority—the source of social approval. This was a hard time for him not only materially but spiritually. No man naturally prefers to live as an alien among his fellows.

The artist's defense was, "I am in revolt against the centers of established opinion. They have turned me into a kind of pariah. Very well, I shall be a pariah, cultivate my differences, dwell in an attic, dress and behave in a manner distinct from that of the respectable folk who scorn me and whom I shall now scorn, starve if need be. But I shall persist. If this be madness, I shall nurture my madness and glory in it."

That this summary of a long cultural process is more than a surmise is exemplified in the work of such a master as Thomas Mann, whose *Death in Venice* and other early stories dramatize the artist's inability to cope with society, his morbid sensitivity, his anomalous psychology and behavior. All of which is supposed to explain why a person becomes an artist. Whether this was Mann's last word on the subject I doubt, but, as a description of how many people see the artist, it is not only accurate but by now commonplace.

My criticism of this is first a historical one: the artists in the sturdiest periods of artistic creativity—Greece in the fifth century B.C., the Renaissance, France under Louis XIV—did not think of the artist in this way at all. (Then, and later, the artist who was a general, a senator, a diplomat, a physician, a scientist was not uncommon.) Much more crucial than this, however, is my belief that the whole concept of art as a consequence of some inner disturbance is a distortion of the creative act.

"The nature of man is to know," Aristotle said. Art is a knowing. It arises from our contact with the world outside and within. Life is a challenge from the day of our birth. It is a challenge we accept through every hazard, or we should soon give it up. We face the challenge by a constant effort to understand it, to become, so to speak, intimate with it—to bridge the gap between our individual isolation and everything outside ourselves. The sense of connection we establish through this effort is a source of deep pleasure even if what we discover and the search itself are fraught with anxiety. The most rabid pessimism in art is still an affirmation of life. If it were not, the artist would not trouble to commit his blasphemies to paper, canvas, song or stage.

It is the nature of man, then, to develop and practice the artistic faculty. In this sense, all men are born to be artists. (We observe this in children whose health is judged in the perspective of their play.) The man who is not to some degree endowed with the artistic impulse is a dull, if not a positively maimed one. It is part of the imbalance of our times that we so often view art as an extracurricular activity, marginal to the serious concerns of living, an escape from reality.

"I'm very happy that I had writing as an outlet to my reactions to experience," a playwright recently said in an interview. "Otherwise I would really have gone off my trolley." Hard-pressed in the crisscross of confusions, the modern artist says the right thing. Not to express one's self—the expression need not be professional—not to articulate in some humane fashion what one has witnessed, felt, dreamed happily or apprehensively—that, in the last count, is to be truly unhealthy. Many artists, in defiance of the indiffer-

ence or condescension that often surrounds them, may overstate their case, but I am inclined to applaud when Stanislaus Joyce reports that his brother James believed "poets are the repositories of the genuine spiritual life of their race." And if the English critic Cyril Connolly says too much when he writes, "It is the quality of an artist to be more imaginative than his fellow men," it is nonetheless true that we seek this quality in the artist to echo, enhance and extend our sense of life. If, as I say, art is life-affirming, how to explain to the person who listens, worried or smug, to the artist as he apologizes for his sickness, and who seems thereby to take it for a fact that artists, being artists, must necessarily be sick or, at least, neurotic people?

Before entering a discussion on this phase of the subject, I must begin by voicing serious misgivings about all the terms employed when we speak of "sick" artists as a class. Though there can be no question that many artists are at least as sick as the waiter who is too distracted to remember the dishes we order or the hackie who constantly mistakes the address he is about to drive us to, none of these artists is any more mentally disturbed than the butcher, the baker, the candlestick maker whose irascibility and ineptitude are becoming increasingly evident to the most superficial observer.

Another thing to be noted before we go on to the heart of our discussion is that, with the average neurotic whose inefficiency, rudeness or misdemeanor perturbs us, there is no compensating factor. The sick artist may be a trial to his friends and family but, at worst, his occupation leads to a result which interests or instructs even when it does not produce positive pleasure.

Let us now turn to the "modern" artist, about whom a Viennese doctor, Max Nordau, wrote a book, circa 1890, called *Degeneration*, in which he tried to adduce marks of insanity in such men as the Impressionist painters, Wagner and Ibsen (this book, by the way, was brilliantly refuted in a little-known essay by Bernard Shaw called *The Sanity of Art).*

We may take an indisputably half-psychotic artist like Strindberg as an example. In the sixty-three years of his life, he wrote more than fifty plays, sixteen novels, seven autobiographies and nine other works. He conducted semiscientific experiments, founded a theatre and helped foster dramatic expressionism. Many of his plays—which exercised a considerable influence on Eugene O'Neill—are still produced and read in many parts of Europe. Though this work—all of it beautifully written—veers from the idyllic to the hysterical, from religious exaltation to intellectual rage, the amount of concentrated effort, thought, study expended in producing this work indicates an energy and a creative force far greater than those employed by all the critics who dismissed him as "sick."

Art is *the health* of the artist. Insofar as the artist engages in his art—I do not refer to those who merely hang on to the fringes of the "art world"—the artist is always healthy. Art being a central function of man's life and a prime manifestation of his humanity, the artist is sane as long as he works as an artist. Apart from this work, he shares in the lesions to which all of us are subject. If he is made to appear more damaged than the rest of us, it is because he gets more publicity; the importance of his job makes him an object of greater social concern.

There still remains the problem of those awful, torpid, sordid, morbid plays, novels, etc. These adjectives rarely mean much more than that we do not like what they describe, but to the extent that our dislike is justified, we must remind ourselves that the artist has not created the world into which he is born.

The artist "imitates" nature in a double sense: he reflects society and, through his response to it, helps create a new world—one which may in some way be affected by what he has created. Much so-called negative (pessimistic, destructive) art has a positive purpose and a salutary effect. Can anyone maintain with equanimity that the world we live in today is an entirely smiling or stable one? Show me the person who answers with an unqualified "yes," and I will show you a fool.

Where does the idea come from that a play or any other work of art to justify itself must necessarily be "happy" or "encouraging"? The province of art is the whole range of human experience. Ecclesiastes is as sound Scripture as the Song of Songs. What miserable product of our contemporary dramatists (sometimes referred to as "decadent") matches the horror of the plots of Aeschylus, Sophocles or Euripides? *King Lear,* a black play if ever there was one, is as much a part of Shakespeare's greatness as are any of his comedies.

Our revulsion at certain "morbid" plays is often an unknowing plea for antidotes and narcotics. When the appetite grows for such dramatic sleeping pills—with a generous admixture of sugar—we ourselves become denatured. A quality of sanity is the capacity to endure what is difficult. Hope and faith which shrink from the recognition of evil are merely evasion.

We have heard it whispered, in tones which range from sniggering to indignant, that many of the new actors are "nuts." For that matter, one is often asked, aren't many of the people who are attracted to the theatre crackpots—in some way or other queer? My first impulse in answer to this is "Yes, these people are crazy if they suppose there is enough work to satisfy the needs of all those who would enter the theatre's ranks."

There are two curses in the theatrical (particularly the acting) profession—enough to drive anyone off the deep end: unemployment and the lack of continuity even after merit has been demonstrated. But insofar as acting is an art—and I believe it can be—it, too, shares in art's sanity.

It is true that certain neophytes gravitate toward the stage as a relief from inner pressures, in the expectation of indulging their troubled souls in the theatre's benign masquerade. We cannot blame them for this but, if they succeed in forging a career for themselves, they will learn that the stage, being full of constraints and duties, demands not only real training but arduous discipline. If what finally happens is that they have "sublimated" their personal dilemmas through their craft, we can only agree that they are to be congratulated and the stage blessed for it.

The amateur whose main objective in going into the theatre is self-therapy may arrive but will not long remain there. For every actor who "cures" himself through psychoanalysis in order to be able to function on the stage (I repeat there is nothing wrong in this), I can show you five whose distemper has become controlled or modified because they have made themselves true professionals. One does not enduringly act, write or compose out of mental illness.

The very fact that many of us are inclined to associate the arts with disease is either a sign we know little of the history of the arts or that we live in an environment which is itself tainted. The clamor for "healthy" art in the face of some of the most creative work of our theatre and other arts is frequently a clamor for conformity of the most stuffy sort. Quite apart from the question of dignity and self-respect, the last thing the artist today need do is to apologize either for his vocation or his mental condition. The artist able to work as one is indeed fortunate to be engaged in so wholesome an occupation. Whether he is sick or not, we should all cherish him—as long as he remains an artist, that is, a creator in our society, which wobbles halfway between prayer and destruction.

—NYTM, '58

THE FAMOUS "METHOD"

"A**re you in favor of grammar? Yes or no? God darn it!"

Can you conceive of people engaging in such a dispute? Do you suppose anyone could become fanatic about the subjunctive mood? In theatre circles something almost as absurd as this appears to be going on. The bone of contention is the famous Method—the grammar of acting.

Ordinarily it would hardly seem to me to be worthwhile to write about a matter of stagecraft for the general reader. It is not at all useful or particularly interesting for the playgoer to know how a performance he enjoys was prepared, any more than a knowledge of how pigments are mixed is helpful in the appreciation of painting. But the case of the Method has become a subject of inquiry for many theatregoers for reasons which I intend to explain.

The Method, an abbreviation of the term "Stanislavsky Method," is as its name indicates a means of training actors as well as a technique for the use of actors in their work on parts. This technique, formulated in 1909 by the Russian actor-director Konstantin Stanislavsky of the Moscow Art Theatre, and subsequently employed in the productions of that company, was introduced into this country by three of its actors: Leo Bulgakov, Richard Boleslavsky and Maria Ouspenskaya. After the Moscow Art Theatre had terminated its first Broadway engagement in 1913, these three actors decided to remain in the United States. They became the first teachers of the Method, which they and most other Russians referred to as the "System." Among the young Americans who studied with Boleslavsky and Ouspenskaya between 1923-26 were Lee Strasberg, who today dominates the Actors Studio; Stella Adler, who now conducts a studio of her own; and, a little later, the present writer. The Method had its first real trial and success on Broadway through the work of the Group Theatre (1931-41) of which Cheryl Crawford, Lee Strasberg and I were the leaders. In such productions as those of Kingsley's *Men in White* (directed by Strasberg), Odets' *Golden Boy* (directed by Clurman), Saroyan's *My Heart's in the Highlands* (directed by Robert Lewis), the Method—rarely touted beyond the confines of the Group's rehearsal hall proved its value as a practical instrument in production.

I go into this now familiar history to stress the fact that by the year 1937 the "battle" of the Method had been won. By that time many theatre schools had been set up (among them the

Neighborhood Playhouse whose main instructor, Sanford Meisner, had been an actor in the Group Theatre's permanent company) and an increasing number of well-known players—for example, Franchot Tone, who in 1933 left the Group for Hollywood—had made the Method part of their normal equipment. The Method was no longer a peculiarity of a few off beat or off-Broadway actors.

It is true that a few critics still spoke of the Method and the schools or studios in which it was taught as a foreign excrescence unsuited to the American temperament, forgetting that in Stanislavsky's own company many of the actors had been just as skeptical as people anywhere else might be. But critics are notoriously behind the times. How does it happen, then, that only in the past three or four years there has been such a rush and rash of publicity about the Method? What at this late date causes the endless palaver about Method and non-Method acting in and outside the theatrical profession?

Marilyn Monroe has a lot to do with it! That sumptuous lady in her eagerness to learn had begun to attend classes at the Actors Studio. Since all Miss Monroe's movements are carefully watched, the Studio began to attract attention far and wide. Everybody wanted to know what the Actors Studio was that the phosphorescent Marilyn should be concerned with it. What went on there? Who else participated? Then it was discovered that among other people who had been more or less attached to the Studio were Marlon Brando, Julie Harris, Kim Stanley, Maureen Stapleton, James Dean, Shelley Winters, Patricia Neal—with press emphasis, of course, on the Hollywood names.

If all these people had been adherents of the Studio, then the instruction there—mysteriously called the Method—had a gimmick fascination; there must certainly be something to it. Lee Strasberg might protest all he wanted that the Studio is not a school—nearly all its members had received their basic theatre instruction at schools or

classes for beginners elsewhere—that many of its members were already well-known actors before they were invited into the Studio, that the Studio was simply a place where already trained actors thought particularly promising could pursue what might be called "post-graduate" work. None of this matters to the general public or to guileless aspirants to the stage; all they knew or cared about was the glamor and mystery that surrounded this nest of genius.

Of course, there was a more substantial reason for the Studio's hold on the acting profession. The practical eminence of the Studio's directorate—Crawford, Kazan, Strasberg—led aspirants to believe mistakenly that enrollment in the Studio was a gateway to employment.

None of this would be of much consequence if it did not result in certain misconceptions and confusion both outside the ranks of the acting profession and inside. Most members of the Studio—there is always a tendency in such organizations toward clannishness and cultism—are quite sane about their activities. The damage that is done is in the vastly larger body of "onlookers," actors and those who have a general curiosity about the theatre. This damage ultimately injures the vital elements involved.

The Method, I have said, is the grammar of acting. There have been great writers who never studied grammar—though they usually possess it—but no one on that account proclaims grammar a fake and instruction in the subject futile. A mastery of grammar does not guarantee either a fine style or valuable literary content. Once in command of it, the writer is unconscious of method. It is never an end in itself. The same is true of the Stanislavsky Method.

There was grammar before there were grammarians. Great acting existed before the Method and great acting still exists unaware of it. A theatregoer who pays to see Michael Redgrave or Laurence Olivier cannot tell by watching them in performance which of the two was influenced by the Method.

The purpose of the Stanislavsky Method is to teach the actor to put the whole gamut of his physical and emotional being into the service of the dramatist's meaning. What Stanislavsky did was to observe great actors and study his own problems as an actor. In the process he began to isolate the various factors that composed fine acting. He systematized the way actors could prepare themselves for their task—the interpretation of plays. He detailed the means whereby actors might give shape and substance to the roles they were assigned.

There were acting methods before Stanislavsky, but none so thoroughgoing for the uses of all sorts of plays—from opera and farce to high tragedy both classic and modern. Since the Method is a technique, not a style, there is no necessary connection between realism and the Method. In Russia, more nonrealistic plays than realistic plays were done with the aid of the Method.

Why was it necessary for Stanislavsky to evolve his Method? First, because the organization of knowledge about acting which the Method represents facilitates the first steps, diminishes the fumbling, wear and tear, waste of the apprentice years; and, second, because a conscious technique aids the actor, who has to repeat a part many times at specific hours, in gaining a greater mastery over his interpretation which without some form of conscious control tends to vanish through the capriciousness and fluidity of what is called inspiration.

All this is clearly set forth in Stanislavsky's three books—*My Life in Art, An Actor Prepares, Building a Character*—which have been available to the public for years. It is true that since the first of these volumes is an autobiography and the latter two technical handbooks, no one can learn to act merely by reading them. But the information they contain is neither mystic nor mysterious.

None of the American teachers of the Method (except Stella Adler, who worked with Stanislavsky in private sessions in Paris for six weeks in the summer of 1934) has ever known Stanislavsky personally and only two or three have ever seen any of his productions. I note this because it is always important to remember that just as every actor has his own individual personality which supersedes whatever technique he may employ or aesthetic doctrine he may profess, so every teacher of the Method lends it the quality of his own mind and disposition. There is no longer an "orthodox" Method, only a group of teachers (most of them trained in America) whose lessons derive from but are not limited to the Stanislavsky sources. As so often happens, on some points most of these teachers contradict one another violently. Which of them is in the right? For the layman, it matters very little. Only results on the stage count.

Before abandoning the purely professional aspect of the subject and advancing to what I consider from the viewpoint of the general reader to be the more significant side, I should like to dispel some false notions which have arisen apropos the Method in the past five years or so. Those who are dubious or hostile to it (usually through misinformation) often mock it by saying that "Method actors"—a noxious term by the way—have slovenly diction, undistinguished voices, and conduct themselves on the stage with a singular lack of grace.

Needless to say, neither Stanislavsky nor any of the teachers who claim him as their guiding spirit are responsible for the professional or personal aberrations real or imagined of individual actors who study the Method. I have never heard anyone speak as long and as dogmatically on the importance of the voice and diction as did Stanislavsky to me on the several occasions of our meeting in Paris and Moscow. As for posture, physical deportment, correctness of carriage, discipline of manner: on these subjects Stanislavsky was almost fanatic. The actors of the Comédie Française (famous for fine voices and speech) had an inadequate vocal range of hardly more than three notes, he complained. The actress I most admired in his company was guilty of rather common speech and therefore could not gain his wholehearted approbation. Most actors walk badly, he pointed out. He was not satisfied that *anybody* anywhere had developed a voice to match the inherent demands of Shakespeare's verse.

American directors who were among the first followers of the Method and who have never renounced or denounced it have done shows such as *Brigadoon* (Robert Lewis) and *Tiger at the Gates* (Harold Clurman) which betrayed none of the traits of shabbiness in speech or behavior which many people associate with the Method. Indeed, it should be pointed out that a "classic" Method production, *Men in White,* was notable for a dignity which one critic declared attained a "concert beauty."

How then had this calumny about the drabness, not to say the grubbiness, of "Method acting" arisen? And is it only calumny? Marlon Brando's performance as Stanley Kowalski in Tennessee Williams' *A Streetcar Named Desire* was indirectly a major factor in the development of what might be dubbed a dreadful Method tradition or superstition. Brando's was a brilliant characterization and made a deep impression unexpected as well as undesirable in its consequences.

It is worth mentioning that when I first heard that Brando was to do the part I thought he had been miscast. For I had known Brando, whom I had previously directed in a play by Maxwell Anderson, as an innately delicate, thoughtful and intellectually eager young man. No matter! For an alarming number of young people in the theatre Kowalski was Brando and Brando was great! The fact that Kowalski was largely a mug who frightened rather more than he fascinated the author himself—the play was intended to say that if we weren't careful such mugs might come to dominate our society—this fact escaped the host of Brando imitators. They equated the tough guy, delinquent aspect of the characterization with a heedlessness, a rebelliousness, a "freedom" and a kind of pristine strength which the performance seemed to them to symbolize. In it, they found combined their uncon-

scious ideal: creative power in acting with a blind revolt against all sorts of conformity both in life and on the stage.

In France this is sometimes called *l'ecole Kazan,* although neither the muscularly energetic Kazan any more than the more intricately wrought Strasberg has ever made brutality a tenet of theatrical art. The fact that certain Method novitiates have confused realism with uncouthness in speech, manner and dress is an accident significant of the New York scene, not of the Method.

Too many of our younger actors have come to think of the refinement or decorum of the larger part of dramatic literature as somehow remote, old-fashioned, hypocritical—and alien. Their ideal is honesty, truth, down-to-earth simplicity, *guts.* "Down to earth" eventually becomes down to the gutter, and the only truth which is recognized as authentic is coarseness and ugliness.

This distortion is socially conditioned in the actors I refer to by an impulse to destroy the discipline of a gentility in their general environment, an environment usually without true roots in a meaningful and comprehensive culture. The distortion is also an unwitting protest against the streamlined efficiency of a too strictly business civilization or, so to speak, "Madison Avenue." These young actors fear nothing so much as any identification with the stuffed shirt.

The Method has influenced no theatre as much as the Amercan. I have suggested one reason for this. Another has to do with one particular element of the Method—"affective memory" or the memory of emotions. I need not dwell here on the artistic validity, the use and abuse of this device. Suffice it to say that in the exercise of affective memory the actor is required to recall some personal event of his past in order to generate real feeling in relation to a scene in his part of the play.

This introspective action which—to an unusual degree—rivets the actor's attention on his inner life frequently strikes the novice as a revolutionary discovery. This is particularly true of the

American, who, being part of an extroverted society which makes the world of *things* outside himself the focus of his hourly concern, seems to find in the technique of affective memory a revelation so momentous that it extends beyond the realm of its stage employment.

Most young actors who come upon it eat it up. Some it tends to make a little self-conscious, melancholy, "nervous," tense, producing a kind of constipation of the soul! Those with whom it agrees not only use it but often become consumed by it. With the immature and more credulous actor it may even develop into an emotional self-indulgence, or in other cases into a sort of private therapy. The actor being the ordinary neurotic man suffering all sorts of repressions and anxieties seizes upon the revelation of himself—supplied by the recollection of his past—as a purifying agent. Through it, he often imagines he will not only become a better actor, but a better person. It makes him feel that because of it he is no longer a mere performer but something like a redeemed human being and an artist. In this manner, the Method is converted into something akin not only to psychoanalysis but to "religion."

This was not Stanislavsky's aim nor does it represent the purpose of the Method teachers in America. It is, I repeat, an accident of our local scene to be explained by the psychological pressures and hunger of our youth. Where cultural activities are a normal part of daily life—as in most European countries where self-expression is natural and habitual, the Method is taken as any other form of technical training—something to be learned and then "forgotten" as grammar is forgotten when we have learned to use language properly.

Culture with us is still considered something apart from the main current of our lives. This is especially true of the stage. Since we have no national theatre, no repertory companies, no widespread stock companies, no consistent employment for the actor and since, too, channels for serious discussion, examination and practice of acting as an art are rare, the American actor clings

to the Method and its ever-expanding centers of instruction as to a spiritual as well as a professional boon. It becomes manna from heaven.

I am glad the Method has "caught on." It has been of enormous benefit to our theatre and acting profession. Now that it has been established I hope to see it more or less taken as a matter of course. There is very little that is intrinsically controversial about it.

What the American actor really needs is more plays and productions in which to practice what has been preached. What actors of every kind need is a broader understanding of the Theatre as a whole: a general education in its relation to the world and to art in general. Young actors imbued with the Method have become so engrossed by what the Method can do for them that they forget that the Method exists for the Theatre and not the Theatre for the Method. What they must finally understand is that the Theatre is here for the pleasure, enlightenment and health of the audience— that is to say for all of us.

—NYTM, '58

J.B.
IVANOV

I came away from *J. B.*, Archibald MacLeish's dramatic poem (ANTA Theatre), more indifferent than annoyed; but I reflected, as I thought of how to say this nicely, that such a reaction is no more related to criticism than would be the declaration that the work is one of the outstanding plays of the century.

What is true of art in general is true of criticism as well: conclusions do not matter so much as the process by which the conclusion (if any) has been reached. The what is in the how, the meaning in the body of what has been said.

MacLeish's answer to J. B.'s argument with God—the play is an American parallel of the Biblical story of Job:—

We are, and that is all our answer.
We are, and what we are can suffer...
But...
                what suffers, loves
                        and love
Will live its suffering again,
Risk its own defeat again,
....
Over and over, with the dark before,
The dark behind it...
                and still live...
                        still love.

is at best a kind of truism; but that is really nothing against it. Besides there are other "answers" in the play: that man must use his own right hand, that man's power to understand is paltry compared to the infinite intricacy of creation, etc., etc. In fact there are answers to satisfy almost anyone who might be satisfied with an "answer."

What is wrong with the play is that it contains no people, no true situations and ultimately no poetry. It is an abstraction of drama, as the characters are abstractions of people. The events are as sketchy as the types, but even this might not matter if the main "plot"—the debate of Jehovah, Satan and their victim—were conveyed through language that was specific, vibrant with individual experience and the pulse of life either on the plane of ordinary reality or on that of metaphysical anguish.

To avoid academic dispute we are ready to concede that the verse is good—it is cultivated writing which sounds well, is always very much in earnest, sometimes twinkling with touches of the vulgate; but it remains without an echo of feeling, thought or atmosphere. When I am dissatisfied with the message in one of T. S. Eliot's plays I am still haunted by an insidiously penetrating *tone*— more telling than what he purports to convey ideologically. In *J. B.,* the pleasant knell of the words leaves a sensation of hollowness once it is over. I have been neither roused by the sting of the questions posed nor requited by the replies; neither despair nor solace has been inspired in me.

No doubt it is laudable for an American writer to essay a verse play on a serious theme and I suspect that our theatre public, which so often delights in pap, unconsciously hungers for a kind of absolution, some reminder of spiritual realities. In this sense, it is perhaps proper to welcome *J. B.* But the play is a glittering generality; it offers little but a show of profundity.

It has been directed by Elia Kazan with extraordinary skill. The cast—Pat Hingle, Christopher Plummer, Raymond Massey—is arresting in diction, in energy, in a kind of rapt zealousness. There is a thrilling boldness in the way Kazan has encouraged his actors to cry out with epic vigor when that befits the moment—a boldness our theatre rarely attempts even in the production of Shakespeare whose plays demand it. Boris Aronson's set contributed brilliantly to the atmosphere of magical stagecraft with which everything in the production—even to the stationary posture of the actors in moments of repose—is done.

It is the custom to refer to *Ivanov* (Renata Theatre) as one of Chekhov's lesser plays. He wrote it when he was twenty-seven, and it shows signs of technical rawness as well as a certain vehemence that might be ascribed to the dramatist's youth. Just the same, it is a most beautiful play—rich in character, humor, understanding and a kind of heartbreak that is the opposite of depressing. For there is real love in Chekhov—not of that literary variety which announces itself stentorially with the cloying unctuousness of radio rhetoric—a love which not only endears his characters to us but which also enhances our knowledge of them in their ludicrous as well as in their noble aspects. Chekhov is surely the most human and humane of modern playwrights.

The company for this off-Broadway production has been remarkably well directed by William Ball. Sorrell Booke, Paul Stevens, Jacqueline Brookes give especially sensitive performances.

A robust and tangy bit of realism is to be admired in Brendan Behan's prison play *The*

Quare Fellow (Circle-in-the-Square). The observation is good, the writing has both ease and density, the characters are vividly drawn in swift strokes— eloquent without too much of the Irish dramatists' tendency to over elaboration. In this case, too, the direction by José Quintero is exceptionally fine— and almost the entire cast altogether right. An oppressive atmosphere is rendered without mitigation, yet without either heaviness or bathos.

—*NAT*, 3 Jan. '59

AGES OF MAN

Nothing but good things should be said of John Gielgud's readings from Shakespeare (46th Street Theatre). The program of excerpts from the plays and various sonnets which is collectively entitled *Ages of Man* provides a splendid evening of educational pleasure. Gielgud reads superbly— with clarity, ease, good sense, exemplary phrasing and fine feeling.

The opening night reception was spectacularly demonstrative—and deservedly so. Everyone talked of Gielgud as a great actor; and everyone echoed the notion that such an actor speaking Shakespeare's glorious verse made the trappings of the stage unnecessary. As a mark of enthusiasm this observation was proper as well as pleasant; as theatre aesthetics it is deplorable.

Gielgud is an actor of high rank, but his readings are *readings*: they are not acting. By themselves they are certainly not theatre. This became particularly apparent to me as I listened to a speech from *Measure for Measure*. I had seen Gielgud as Angelo in this play some years ago at Stratford-on-Avon and was much impressed by the insidious, worm-eaten, crabbed "medievalism"—half anguished conscience, half sadistic hypocrisy— which informed his impersonation. In the reading only the verbal sense and the inspiration of language were communicated.

In *theatre*, words are gestures—gestures of the spirit and the body in one organic whole of action,

so that a truly acted play may be largely understood by a person unfamiliar with the language. I agree that very few performances are ever brought to the degree of perfection where this becomes literally true. But that only signifies that what we usually see on the stage is only partially realized theatre. Gielgud's reading is thin compared to his acting at its best. For the text of a play, I repeat and it cannot be repeated too often, is the mental material, the immediate impetus, the germ and the scaffolding of the theatrical life which may finally emerge from its.

This is not to say that *Ages of Man* is not an unalloyed boon and many, many times more rewarding than what often passes for a good show. Shakespeare's words are inspiring music and humane wisdom in one—though even as music their instrumentation suffers when they are not acted and made part of the whole context of drama.

The Old Vic productions are often hardly more than illustrated readings—most charmingly illustrated in *Twelfth Night*—more meagerly in *Hamlet* and *Henry V*. (Young English leading men are very much influenced by their seniors: thus John Neville's Hamlet seems humbly and sympathetically to follow Gielgud's, while, Laurence Harvey as Henry V probably takes Laurence Olivier's Henry as his model.) So powerful and rich are the foundations for these productions—I refer to Shakespeare's plays—and so loyal the spirit in which the Old Vic Company undertakes them that one is glad to see them, if only because they recall the magnificence of the "originals."

Less injury is done to *Henry V* than to *Hamlet* in such productions. For Henry V is a comparatively slight play—an artful bit of propaganda written with amiable grace and fairy-tale simplicity, as if addressed to children or to adults in a sentimentally complacent mood. This is especially true of the acting version employed here which omits certain canny observations on the tricky rationalizations Henry is fed to induce him to go to war with France.

A play on the stage lives through its various organs. Sometimes it is the actors who chiefly count, sometimes direction may project a play to an effective meaning and on many occasions the text itself triumphs, although always there is an interplay of elements, each of which in some particular way sustains the others.

When I belatedly saw O'Casey's *The Shadow of a Gunman* at the Bijou I was aware of a certain over-stressing of characterization in the first act which made the progress of the story slow and the atmosphere somewhat heavy. But as the performance went on I was caught up by the characters, and the situation, the rich, rough humor and pathos of O'Casey's conception and what they reveal of the pitiful foibles and follies of little people in moments of historical stress. The sum of it all was funny, touching, painful and sobering.

—*NAT*, 10 Jan. '59

THE WORLD OF SUZIE WONG
TIS PITY SHE'S A WHORE
THE MARRIAGE-GO-ROUND
A PARTY

The theatre, if you look at it honestly, is a most paradoxical place. When I speak of looking at it "honestly," I refer to a reaction which is immediate and direct and not one based on a preconceived rationale of what we ought or ought not to like and why.

Last week in an effort to catch up on my retarded schedule of play-going I saw *The World of Suzie Wong*, Paul Osborn's dramatization of a novel by Richard Mason (Broadhurst) and John Ford's *Tis Pity She's a Whore* (Players' Theatre), a play written shortly after Shakespeare's death. The first play has been thoroughly drubbed by the press—and no doubt deservedly—while the second is, I suppose, a masterpiece, if only through its endurance in anthologies. But I had a better time with the chaff than with the wheat.

It is easy to discern that the Ford play is tightly written in admirably muscular verse, that its story is arresting (unapologetic incest provides the pivot of the plot), that its author was fascinated by the anarchy of human passions. It is just as easy to detect the slick sentimentality in the story of the whore named Wong. But in the actual circumstances of the theatre I am left cold by the performance of passions by children who have none, and held by the tenacious charm which emanates from lovely Nuyen who plays the Hong Kong bad girl in Broadway's package of oriental corn.

It may he reprehensible to be anesthetized by the inexpressive bareness of the setting employed for the English classic and to be as bemused as a kid at a sideshow by the colorful hokus-pokus of Jo Mielziner's settings which, as reproduction of an environment, are probably bogus. But it is important to note that in the theatre this is the kind of thing that frequently happens to the greater part of the play-going public. We are not to conclude from this that the public is necessarily a lout. It means that in the beginning (of the theatre) was not the word.

This contradiction or paradox may be more complex than my first illustration indicates. If the audience at *Suzie Wong* responds to its color and more especially to the presence of Miss Nuyen and at *Tis Pity* to the boldness of its story and speech (all these related to a sex stimulus), why did I find so little to enjoy at *The Marriage-Go-Round*, Leslie Stevens' comedy (Plymouth) which stars such engaging actors as Charles Boyer and Claudette Colbert and definitely features that sumptuous lady, Julie Newmar.

For me at least—the play is a tremendous success—Charles Boyer and Claudette Colbert remain on a rather facile level of conventional polish (not particularly novel or scintillating) and even the luscious exaggeration of Miss Newmar's physique is not sufficient to supersede the commonplace humors and writing in this play of marital relations. Its attitude toward sex—part Peeping Tom archness, part chromium sophistication, part fake candor, part uncertain virility—makes an embarrassing composite worth sociological study.

Betty Comden and Adolph Green are giving *A Party* (Golden) which consists of a performance of their own comedy and musical numbers. Their fun-making is captivating for a special and again theatrically interesting reason. The numbers from the musical comedies are—as we all had previously known—very good, but Betty and Adolph (a familiarity which seems to fit them) are not, technically speaking, expert performers. In fact, as performers, they are marked by an amateur touch. Adolph is not handsome, Betty is not immediately alluring. Yet Adolph ends by appearing almost glamorous, Betty a true beauty.

The reason for their triumph over their superficial disabilities is, as one of their songs proclaims, that they are "carried away." They are absolutely entranced by what they are doing—entranced not simply by the "ideas" contained in their material but in the frolic of its theatrical point. The little joke, the little sentiment, the little satire each number conveys seem to delight them so much, they are so innocently and wholeheartedly immersed in their "party"—as if relishing it for their audience as well as for themselves—that their little festivity is transformed into theatre in almost its primitive sense—a folk ritual. And the folk they celebrate, the source and object of their inspiration is "New York! New York!"

[*Editors' Note*: Harold Clurman is perhaps the only New York theatre critic who has not had an enthusiastic word to say for *The Cold Wind and the Warm*, the play adapted by S. N. Behrman from his volume of sketches, *The Worcester Account*, and starring Maureen Stapleton and Eli Wallach. Mr. Clurman is disqualified on this occasion by the fact that he directed the play.]

—*NAT*, 24 Jan. '59

MANY LOVES

Arnold Bennett once said that writing a play was much easier than writing a novel. But he wrote better novels than plays. Since the early days of the modern novel—the eighteenth century let us say—more enduring novels have been written than plays. Many excellent novelists (and poets) have attempted the dramatic form with lamentable results. Henry James, who loved and understood the theatre, never could write a play worth a hoot. Joseph Conrad did no better.

These thoughts occurred to me as I watched William Carlos Williams' fragmentary *Many Loves* at the Living Theatre (530 Sixth Avenue). This tiny playhouse is newly, oddly and rather pleasantly decorated by friends of the organization; its atmosphere combines elements of the gravelly aestheticism and mucky mysticism of the "beat" generation in a manner which is not at all unattractive.

The place itself made a greater impression on me than Mr. Williams' play. I experienced a faint hope that in the not too distant future something at least as good as cummings' *him*—an underrated play—might be presented there. In the meantime, besides the present performance, the management announces a series of readings, talks, recitals and film showings which may prove of avant-garde interest. I am not habitually in accord with our American avant-garde but I like to know that there is one. New creation sometimes emerges from its chaos.

The Williams play is a series of thematically related sketches. The prologue and epilogue form one such sketch and describe the effort of a young writer to escape a homosexual attachment to a patron who identifies the writing profession in general with an incompatibility with women. This is a not insignificant thought, worth sociological and psychological observation in regard to the American male as intellectual and artist.

The three other episodes or phases of the play deal with equally troubled "loves" or, more emphatically, lacks of love. The third "act" struck me as the most interesting: it is a talk between a housewife with no maternal feelings whatever and hardly any feminine sensuality and a doctor who might be, in a very minor way something like the play's author—himself a doctor.

The scene is well written and minutely pathetic in a teasing and indeterminate way—as if the dramatist wanted to set down only as much as he could gather from hasty contact with some of his woman patients, without coming to any conclusion about them beyond a sense of their unhappiness. It is an unhappiness that stems chiefly from the absence of a genuine experience of life, the misery of the daily vacuum. This sentiment is the sum of the play's "message." America can never be a truly healthy place till it recognizes the nature and seriousness of its ailments. Its tragedy is the fear of the tragic.

—*NAT,* 7 Feb. '59

RASHOMON

It is perhaps unfortunate in the present circumstance that I saw the Japanese *Rashomon* when it was shown in 1951. It was a beautiful film which combined a pessimistic skepticism with the most exquisitely tender visual artistry. There was a broken-hearted humbleness in the realism with which the beggarly narrator and his two companions—a disaffected Buddhist priest and a dog-like wig-maker—were depicted, a realism coupled by the most acutely sensitive stylization of image in the body of the narration.

The story, you may remember, dealt with a rape and a murder which were recounted in four different and contradictory ways—three of them, fabrications, contained a near-tragic note of epic bestiality or pathos; the fourth in a tone of savagely hilarious irony, established the facts of the case. The final moments suggested that humanity is a sorry species. The bitterness of this conclusion was alleviated by the subtlety of the treatment, an aesthetic relationship to the material that etherealized its brutality with a strange beauty—both painful and sweet—inspiring something between disgust and a graceful though drooping defeatedness. I am also inclined to believe that the makers of the picture were aiming at a satire on the discrepancy between the prettifying tendencies of Japanese idealism and brute reality. One could react to the picture with either some resistance to the bonelessness and cruelty of its philosophic temper or with deep admiration for the extreme refinement of its craftsmanship.

Fay and Michael Kanin have made a play of the film (Music Box) and it has been given an elaborate and intricate production by Peter Glenville who has cast it with a number of good actors.

Why has this stage dramatization been undertaken? The film was not "exotic"—it was organic to a way of life, thought and feeling. The production *is* exotic—but not Japanese; it is American in dialogue, complicated and lush (or plush) in setting, Austrian, Russian, Hebrew, English, mid-Western and nondescript in accent. Except for a sword fight, undertaken by actors who are absurdly amateurish by comparison with Japanese actors, all of whom are thoroughly trained in this almost ritual exercise, the production does not attempt any approximation of the Japanese manner.

What prompted this production was the lure of theatricality, in which no doubt many spectators will be caught. But theatricality—in the positive sense of the word—must have a base in authentic feeling and sensibility. It is something which grows from the nature of a group of artists; it is not something to be applied to material. The specific theatricality of *Rashomon* as a stage piece does not arise from a temperament or a point of view; it is "show"—and ultimately *industry*. We get two visibly revolving stages, an elevator stage, a rain effect on the upper left hand of the stage, a profusion of luxurious foliage, towering bamboo stalks backed by projections of the same on the cyclorama, sound effects indicating animal and bird life, pseudo-oriental music which turns into schmaltzy Western music when the play is supposed to soften to tears, and a great deal of old-fashioned acting.

What beside the possible fascination of its relative intricacy—relative that is to the ordinary Broadway play—does all this mean, what does it convey? Art? But art—even in the most abused of arts, the theatre—must always possess a content, it must signify a sense of life that extends beyond itself into the world and into our souls. This—and I am almost ashamed to point out the obvious—is as true of a canvas by Mondrian as of a statue by Phidias, of a production of a *Noh* play as of a musical like *Show Boat*.

Still, there is the plot and design of the original *Rashomon*: yes, but a story too is only an instrument to communicate an essence which is embodied in it. Very little, if anything, of this remains, it seems to me, in the *Rashomon* play. The heavy production is merely debris and its only end is an effect, which to this observer appears basically childish and coarse.

Cavalleria Rusticana and *I Paglacci* are sometimes brusquely referred to as the ham and eggs of opera: they are staples of the repertory. The American theatre also has such staples: for example, the plays of Lindsay and Crouse. Though they offer only slight nourishment I really have no objection to them and, in some instances, I have rather enjoyed them. They have no positively harmful ingredients, they are wrought from good or, at any rate, safe moral principles, they are energetic and ingenious, though fundamentally simple in construction, they are affable and now and then they are benevolently humorous.

Tall Story (Belasco), a farce about a basketball player and two honest professors involved in a misunderstanding with the athletic interests of their college, is not the best of the Lindsay-Crouse pieces, but it will probably find an audience on Broadway and a far greater one in the movies.

During the first act I failed to laugh because of the too strenuously controlled comedy "readings" with which the actors were saddled, but as the play progressed I began to wonder whether this forced manner of direction (by Herman Shumlin) was not after all the right one, since the play is more cartoon than comedy. I am still not sure because one actor, Marc Connelly, who though slightly self-conscious and not altogether an actor, manages to give the most engaging performance in the show merely by being intelligently himself.

—*NAT*, 14 Feb. '59

REQUIEM FOR A NUN
THE RIVALRY

This is what I wrote here in 1956 about the production of William Faulkner's *Requiem for a Nun* in Berlin. "When I read the play I was certain that it would be unworkable. Most of it is an exposition, through interminably long speeches, describing highly complex situations which have occurred off-stage. With the help of an excellent company the director has made it absorbing. I am not sure I believe the story or trust either its psychology or its morality, but I cannot deny that the play interested me. There is a concentration, a driving intensity...which capture attention."

The play having been produced in most of the great capitals of Europe is now being done here (Golden) where it somehow seems more foreign than it did abroad. The local production is not as arresting as the one in Berlin; our actors seem to lack the density of human quality or the fullness of experience which the European actors possess. And my doubts about the play's morality have mounted to a definite resistance.

But I still found the play compelling. One listens to it with rapt attention, not only because it has some of the fascination of a psychological mystery, a chase after the secret spring of Temple Drake's motivations—she hired a Negro whore and dope addict as her child's nurse, a nurse who finally murders the child—but because one wonders what the author meant to say by his weird story.

The play's plot is the record of a series of sordid deeds, hidden as well as overt violence, anarchy of feeling, an immersion in morbid emotion—and finally a curious act of expiation of a dubious religiosity. The two central characters—the mother and the nurse—climb down to heaven. There is something reminiscent in all this. It resembles the state of mind Europe was in shortly after the war: since everyone felt tainted in some way, cleansing seemed possible only by an admission of one's guilt. The hope was that the evil one had done would serve as a sufficient earnest of one's suffering to merit forgiveness. Sin is a terrible burden and must, when faced, earn some reward akin to the doing of good which carries its own blessing.

Faulkner's play is obsessed by a sense of evil. We have a feeling of being confronted by a race of men who for so long have worn the mask of propriety that it has become unendurable. They deserve the right to besmirch themselves so that on the one hand they may gain some real experience of life and on the other hand learn through contrition something of what might be humanely accounted good. Since respectability has been a spiritually enervating sham, alleviation can only result from a passionate plunge into the dregs.

This state of being is not easily expressed by Americans, who lack a vocabulary for chaotic sentiments. That may be one reason why Faulkner's language, straining to catch the subtlest nuance of contradictory emotion, often seems so tortuous and unnatural. But the general context explains why Europeans have shown greater rapport with the play than we are likely to—even though Faulkner's sources are peculiarly American.

In the final rating one cannot set *Requiem for a Nun* down as an artistically realized play. It is like a graph of a play still to be written. The characters do not speak with their own voices. The author seems to be explaining his characters rather than allowing them to enact their lives. And the morality of the play—that we must "believe," which I take to mean that we must accept life, is a proposition I would not quarrel with in the abstract but which I am certainly indifferent to when posited on the circumstances of this play.

Yet for all its serious shortcomings *Requiem* involved me far more than many a glibber piece: Faulkner is a personality and an artist, whereas what I have seen elsewhere in the theatre this season is for the most part little better than mechanical contrivance.

The Rivalry (Bijou) is Norman Corwin's dramatization and staging of the Lincoln-Douglas debate of 1859 in which the central issue was states' rights versus human rights—a theme, needless to say, still relevant.

The text consists of the debate itself as taken down in a stenographic record, though Corwin does not present the passages in their original sequence. There are short interludes of narrative exposition—spoken by Nancy Kelly as Mrs. Douglas—scenes picturing off the platform encounters between Lincoln and Douglas, and a few comic interludes based on typical campaign speeches by anonymous electioneers of the period.

In short *The Rivalry* is not a play in the usual sense of the term but I found myself following every moment of the performance with eagerness and pleasure.

Medieval English history for most of us is intimately bound up with our memory of Shakespeare's plays. Those celebrated kings, Richard II, Henry IV *et al.,* are enveloped in our minds by a glamor and glory with which the greatest of English poets endowed them. We ordinarily regard our own history as drab—chiefly, I think, because it has almost never been made vivid for us by true artists. What we rediscover with delight in *The Rivalry* is that men like Lincoln and Douglas spoke better "lines" than most of our dramatists seem able to write. Their speech was rigorous, salty, meaningful and could rise at times to an almost epic grandeur.

The Rivalry is very well done. Martin Gabel as Douglas is particularly effective, not only by virtue of his excellent diction and admirable voice but through a genuine characterization. Richard Boone as Lincoln is best in his quiet moments—we imagine Lincoln a grave rather than an impassioned speaker. Nancy Kelly manifests exemplary simplicity besides being very good-looking in a number of beautiful costumes designed by Motley. The bits too are very nicely acted.

—*NAT*, 28 Feb. '59

LES BALLETS AFRICAINS

*L*es Ballets Africains (Lunt-Fontanne) are interesting, stimulating and fun. The over-all quality, surprisingly enough, is a certain sweetness. "Surprising" because from the constant beat of drums which punctuates the evening—now harsh and dry, now frantically exciting—one supposes that the final effect will be either one of "primitive" violence or of ominous mystery. Instead one is captured by a sense of intimacy with nature, a healthy feeling of life accepted with an innocent openness of spirit.

Reita Fodeba, organizer and director of these ballets—chiefly French African in origin—points out that the dances are wholly authentic, even though they are not of purely aboriginal or ancient tradition, because contemporary Africa has been influenced by contact with varying civilizations and cultures. So if we hear sounds that recall flamenco or Calypso song, if we observe a flash of jitterbug cavorting or if occasionally there are Parisian notes in the show, these "Ballets" are nonetheless indigenous to a considerable portion of the Dark Continent today.

The performance is richly captivating. There is a number in which a peasant at harvest time is bitten by a snake as he works in the field. The witch doctor tries to heal the stricken man but fails; the other peasants sing to soothe him in his death throes. This is impressive drama: gentle and touch-

ing. Work, anguish, compassion are depicted with unemphatic simplicity. Episodes based on legend and superstition reflect the inscrutable terror of earth forces with such naive directness that one asks oneself how one could ever think of these phenomena in any other way.

There are exuberant and playful bits that show the citified traits which have been grafted on the primeval roots with quaintly charming results. Oddly handsome instruments with subtly whispering timbres suggest sentiments too delicate for the boldness of speech and soften the effect of love songs shouted in tones of metallic resonance. Girls who should be naked have either taken on a strange elegance in copious finery or struggle in adolescent embarrassment at the predicament of their dress. There are flirtations without sensuality in which sex play is adumbrated with the natural freedom of eddying waters. The only obscenity I should complain of is the brassieres the New York license commissioner has imposed on the women; in every other city they were bare-bosomed.

A word must be said about the settings—graphically modern and wholly right in the use of raw materials consonant with the climate and general environment of the places represented—settings which our designers should study to divest themselves of the stuffy Radio City decorativeness they so frequently employ to convey an exotic atmosphere.

—*NAT*, 7 Mar. '59

GWEN VERDON IN *REDHEAD*

*R*edhead (46th Street Theatre) may not be a good musical but it is an attractive show. It would be easy but not quite accurate to say that its sole attraction is Gwen Verdon. The complete absurdity of the show's plot has been turned to advantage. The more ridiculous the plot became the better I liked it. At the end the show seemed to have developed something approximating a "style" of its own—that of a kid's entertainment akin to the merry hell of a Keystone comedy. The director-choreographer, Bob Fosse, ably seconded by a nice cast and Rouben Ter-Arutunian's clever sets, has transformed what might have seemed hopeless material into stage fun.

None of this could happen without the pivotal presence of Gwen Verdon. She has an extremely ingratiating speaking voice, a lovely figure, fine eyes; she dances delightfully and acts with charming spontaneity. Yet all these attributes, valuable as they are, do not explain the "mystery" which gives her—or any almost similarly endowed player—a *star* quality. Beyond all the separate gifts, there must exist a special element which crystallizes the others and makes them function with a particular fascination.

Ethel Merman, for example, possesses the hearty vulgarity of metropolitan restaurants and night spots; Judy Holliday, the slightly wounded honesty of the half-educated but feeling city girl; Julie Andrews, the dewiness of the old-fashioned music-hall favorite who still retains the fragrant atmosphere of an English garden. Gwen Verdon exemplifies the gay side of our contemporary theatre: she is a gem of light-hearted but consecrated show business—precious through its integrity and its bent toward self-perfection. Hers is a backstage sense of play and romance. Gwen Verdon is a Broadway dream.

—*NAT*, 14 Mar. '59

COWARD & FEYDEAU

Occupe-Toi D'Amélie written by Georges Feydeau in 1908 and revived a few years ago by the Barrault company in Paris was a very funny show. *Look After Lulu* (Henry Miller) the Noel Coward adaptation, follows the play more or less faithfully and is in most respects sprightly enough to correspond to Feydeau's farcical masterpieces.

The production, directed by Cyril Ritchard, is not at all bad: there are some very able perfor-

mances in it; Cecil Beaton's sets and costumes are gay—occasionally even pretty. It should therefore be easy to recommend *Lulu*, as a sort of theatrical desert for the carefree gourmet.

I hesitate, however, because the show doesn't altogether function. I might carp at some of the acting, despite what I have just said in its favor, because in a certain sense it is not "serious" enough. The lovers don't have enough zest, the *cocottes* are not sufficiently *cocottish*, the lechers not sufficiently foolish, the make-believe is too much make-believe.

But the fault, I surmise, is not really the actors as such but in the actors as part of the audience. *We* are to "blame"; we aren't well cast for this play. And the actors—though gayer and more eager than the audience—reflect the audience's unsuitability for its role.

The Parisian audience of 1908 knew the play was nonsense—a machine to make one laugh. But laughter doesn't arise out of a vacuum. The sources of laughter are always in the same appetites, pleasures, flaws and fears as are the sources of tragedy. A farce can strike an audience as funny only when it shares some strict moral code in which marriage, chastity and the recognized proprieties of social behavior are psychologically dominant and operative for the majority. The fun in Feydeau's farces springs from defiance of such a moral code—a defiance by those either rich enough to get away with it or poor enough not to be harmed by it. In either case such defiance is proof that the moral code, though vulnerable to laughter, is still powerful.

Our audience is not the least bit shocked by the Parisian *cocotte* of yesteryear and therefore cannot be truly amused by her. We can be sentimental about prostitutes but hardly entertained. The idea of a whole social category which flourished comfortably alongside, but entirely separate from, the institution of a tight family life isn't either an escape for us or an object of piquant curiosity. Our society today is amorphous: it is on the whole barely conscious of its moral ideas, too vague and general in its notions of proper behavior to become either indignant or intrigued by the middle-class hierarchy of the French Third Republic at its crumbling height.

Thus it is difficult for our actors to be innocent in scabrous ribaldry or charming in smut—the state needed to convey Feydeau's world.

When Arthur Miller's adaptation of Ibsen's *An Enemy of the People* was done on Broadway in 1953, the press and public were cold, and the play failed.

There were, it is true, weaknesses in the production, the worst of which was that while the performance was propagandistic in spirit, its execution was too close to an old-fashioned and half-baked realism. The result was that we had neither a new nor an old Ibsen. But perhaps a more cogent reason for the play's initial failure is that very few serious old plays—"revivals"—ever succeed on Broadway. The audience responsible for success on Broadway's economic terms seeks novelty in entertainment rather than human statements. Unless a configuration of stars can be made to shine over an old play—which by and large means the best drama—the place for it is off-Broadway.

1953 was an inchoate time for public discussion so that *An Enemy of the People* probably discomfited its Broadway audience as something possibly tainted with political infection. Now at the Actor's Playhouse (on lower Seventh Avenue) the play comes to a raw and explosive life as a social melodrama—and none the worse for that. It is a shriek of protest against conformism. The play is vigorous no matter how you view it. The actors in Greenwich Village are very American and forthright, and though it is clearly arguable that their presentation is not "pure" Ibsen I confess—to put it in the mode of their production—I got a bang out of it.

—*NAT*, 21 Mar. '59

SWEET BIRD OF YOUTH

Tennessee Williams' *Sweet Bird of Youth* (Martin Beck) interested me more as a phenomenon than as a play. Its place in the author's development and its fascination for the audience strike me as more significant than its value as drama.

Williams is a romantic; one of the characteristics of the romantic is a pressing need to reveal himself. Though the play's narrative is realistic, the characters are frequently called upon to address the audience directly. Both in its content and its form one senses the author's urgent impulse to say everything he feels right out. Here I am, he seems to be telling us, naked and unabashed, and I am going to speak my piece. At the end of the play the central character turns to us and says, "I do not ask for your pity or even your understanding. I ask you only to recognize me in yourselves."

What is it we are asked to recognize in ourselves? That we are corrupted by our appetite for the flash and clamor of success, that we are driven to live debased existences by the constrictions and brutality which surround us, that the sound instincts of our youth are thus frustrated and turned to gall, and that we have an inordinate fear of age, for the passing of time makes us old before we mature.

There may be truth in this. More important is the manner in which this truth is conveyed. Chance Wayne is an average small-town boy born and reared somewhere on the Gulf Coast. At the age of seventeen he has an idyllic affair with a girl of fifteen. But because he is poor, the girl's father—political boss of the town—calls an abrupt halt to the romance. The boy goes to New York in the hope of becoming enough of a big shot as an actor to impress the folks back home. Because he has good looks but very little training, he gets nothing but jobs in the chorus of musicals. He also gives unbounded satisfaction to numerous women.

He is drafted for the Korean war and he suffers the awful fear that his splendid youth will be cut off by mutilation and his ambition thwarted by death. On his release from the Navy one of his jobs is that of masseur at a Florida beach resort. He earns money on the side as a gigolo. One of the women he encounters is a fading movie star in flight from impending failure. Her terror makes her take refuge in drugs and promiscuity. Chance Wayne brings her back to his home town. He clings to this woman—whose whore he becomes—because he plans to make her the key to a Hollywood career for himself. To make sure that she will live up to her end of the agreement, he uses a dictaphone to blackmail her—she has confessed to having smuggled the hashish they both smoke. In the meantime, he uses her Cadillac and takes her money to spend conspicuously so that his former girl, her father and the boyhood friends will be awed by his "position."

At some point before these latter events, Chance had resumed his affair with the girl who is his true love. Sometime during his career as a gigolo he had contracted a venereal disease and had unknowingly infected his beloved. Her father has her undergo an operation which renders her sterile. The girl bids the boy—still ignorant of what has happened—to leave town for good lest her father have him killed.

There are many more details portraying the girl's despair, the vile hypocrisy of her father, the maniacal vindictiveness of her brother, the savagery of the town's political gang. In the end the movie star, who for a moment had shown signs of compassion for the boy, abandons him because she has made a Hollywood comeback and can think of nobody but herself. By remaining in town after he has been repeatedly warned to get out, the boy virtually invites the castration with which he has been threatened.

I have no categorical objection to this heap of horrors. I can believe that they occur in life, indeed that they have occurred. But the telling of this story is very close to lurid melodrama. What saves it from being just that is the fluently euphonious idiom and vivid grace of Williams' writing. Even more telling is Williams' ache and what might be called his ideology.

Is there any virtue at all in Chance Wayne? Williams names it. Chance has given *great pleasure*. He is consummately male, a wonderful lover. When he hears that a Negro in his town has been castrated for assaulting a white woman, Chance cries out, "I know what that is: it's sex envy"—which is surely the author's comment rather than the character speaking. Sex potency is held forth as a special order of merit bestowing amnesty for every misdeed.

Williams does not ask us to admire the boy, but the whole play suggests that he is sufficiently typical to induce us to share some kinship with him. A nonentity can be made central to a modern tragedy as is Clyde Griffith in Dreiser's book, but the novelist did this by weaving a web of environmental circumstance so complete in each detail that we are objectively convinced. Taken literally Chance Wayne is an atrocity. He is not a real person but a figment of Williams' commanding sentiment.

The simplification and distortion which mark the portrait of Chance are evident in the play's other characters as well—schematic types whose bareness is covered only by Williams' colorful verbiage. The movie actress is the best of them, for there is a grotesque humor about her—a kind of wry pity not far removed from contempt. The most crudely drawn figure is that of Boss Finley, a caricature of a Dixiecrat, a dirty dog beyond compare, more bogey than man. Indeed there is something about all the people in the play which seems calculated to scare us to death.

Much of what Williams has attempted to say here has been implied in some of his earlier plays, but they had more texture in characterization and reality. What we suspect in *Sweet Bird of Youth* is that Williams has become immobilized in his ideology; that it has not been refreshed either by any new experience or by mature thought. He has only become much bolder. The result is that we feel in this play an inverted sentimentality and a willful stress which produce more ugliness than lyricism or credence.

We know that a great part of what Williams feels about American life is valid: many novels and sociological studies in the past thirty-five years or more have helped us recognize its validity. So it is perhaps useful for Williams to cry havoc at theatre audiences still largely protected from the rumor of the real world. Scandal on Broadway may be beneficent. But I observe that the audience at *Sweet Bird* is entertained rather than stirred, piqued rather than sobered. It doesn't truly believe what it sees: it is simply enjoying a show with a kick in it. And this lack of shock may be attributed to something specious in the stage proceedings.

The production, directed by Elia Kazan, is admirably cast throughout: Paul Newman, Sidney Blackmer, Diana Hyland—all are good. Geraldine Page as the movie star creates an especially striking image—more on the comedy character side than on the pathetic. A sure and sharp showmanship is always manifest. The sets, though bare, are prettified by Jo Mielziner's sumptuous lighting.

—*NAT*, 28 Mar. '59

A RAISIN IN THE SUN

A*Raisin in the Sun* by a young Negro woman, Lorraine Hansberry, (Ethel Barrymore) might be called an old-fashioned play—which should not be taken to mean that it is not a good one. It may have escaped our attention that although American drama is very largely realistic, there has been a tendency in the past twenty-five years or so not only to veil our realism with a silk of poetry, a kind of disguised romanticism, but to extend it with a suggestion of social interpretation too bashful to be dubbed propaganda. Our new realism is something more than a picture of a concrete state of affairs. It is a generalization from a commonly known situation heightened by moral fervor and oblique lyric expression.

A Raisin in the Sun shows some of these latter traits but its inspiration is in a certain sense less ambi-

tious and more plainly specific than that of the neo-realist writers, who usually are filled with a desire to express themselves and thus to produce art and literature. Miss Hansberry simply wants to say what she has seen and experienced, because to her these things are sufficiently important in themselves. This is what I mean when I call her play "old-fashioned."

She is right. While the drift away from naturalism in the American theatre is healthy, it is entirely false to assume that we have no further use for the old realism. America is still but little explored as far as a significant stage realism goes. The poetic realism we have been cultivating in recent years often grows fuzzy or mushy. It needs the control of a severe probity in regard to reality and the exercise of discipline in language. The traditional realistic play needs genuine identification with its subject matter (the realist should never be an investigator in the slums) in addition to objectivity and heart.

A Raisin in the Sun is authentic: it is a portrait of the aspirations, anxieties, ambitions and contradictory pressures affecting humble Negro folk in an American big city—in this instance Chicago. It is not intended as an appeal to whites or as a preachment for Negroes. It is an honestly felt response to a situation that has been lived through, clearly understood and therefore simply and impressively stated. Most important of all: having been written from a definite point view (that of a participant) with no eye toward meretricious possibilities in showmanship and public relations, the play throws light on aspects of American life quite outside the area of race.

The importance of the production transcends its script. The play is organic theatre: cast, text, direction are homogeneous in social orientation, in sentiment, in technique and in quality of talent. Without the aid of an aesthetic program or bias of any kind but through cultural and emotional consanguinity— a kind of spontaneous combustion which occurs when individuals who share a common need find each other under the proper circumstances—a genuine ensemble has been achieved.

The acting is robust, sensitive, humorous,

wholesomely impassioned and *popular*. By popular I mean that this acting possesses an innate sense of the stage and of showmanship, a kind of joy in public performance which enhances rather than diminishes our regard for the play's truth. Sidney Poitier, Claudia McNeill, Ruby Dee, Louis Gossett and all the others without exception afford deep pleasure.

There are some *longueurs* in the script, and Lloyd Richards, who has directed the play admirably, has sentimentalized the ending a bit by permitting the actors (Miss McNeill particularly) to become somewhat picturesquely heroic, but such slight flaws are noticeable only because the whole occasion is so extraordinarily gratifying.

—*NAT*, 4 Apr. '59

OUR TOWN

José Quintero, director and guiding spirit of the Circle in the Square, is to be congratulated on another of his modest, honest and sensitive productions—this time of Thornton Wilder's *Our Town*, a play which fits Quintero's manner and his theatre in the round perfectly.

Our Town is a peculiar play: it reduces the majority of its spectators to grateful tears (as if the play and the tears were dew from heaven), but other spectators, a shamefaced minority, are discomfited by its proximity to platitude as well as by its ineffable sweetness. I am not certain that I have ever heard *Our Town* called "great"—though the ecstatic intake of breath and the virtually helpless adoration it ordinarily provokes make one feel that the shopworn superlative is not used only because it is inadequate to express the degree of affection in which the play is held. On the other hand, I heard a lone spectator the other night brutally declare that all the characters spit ice cream!

The play is a classic of our theatre. It epitomizes a distinct aspect of American sentiment—a myth of our folklore. The small (New England) town is presented here as the haven of the humbly righteous, the idyllic symbol of what was friendly, decent,

homey and wholesome in our lives in the days before the taint of corruption by money, machinery, muck-raking, began to darken our horizon.

Romain Rolland once said that there is a bit of Massenet in the heart of every Frenchman; surely there is a bit of this play's snowball purity in the social memory of every American. Even if the glow of that myth is only a nostalgic evocation, it contains an element of reality; whether or not the life of *Our Town* was ever typical we certainly want to believe it was—and that wish is still an American reality. For most theatergoers, anyway.

Wilder was astute enough not to set down his dream as a fact. His play is tracery. What it traces, moreover, is not so much a life—anyone's life—as an attitude. That attitude, the basic reality of the play, might be called a shiningly optimistic Protestantism. Even the least conspicuous person or event, it tells us, dwells in the mind of God; every hour of our lives, though compounded with some speck of sorrow or frustration, is essentially blessed. A benevolent detachment akin to the holy imperturbability of death reveals that every moment we have lived through was precious in its small wound and greater healing. In the final count everything is good.

It requires a very great artist indeed to substantiate this attitude. Wilder is not such an artist, so he spins a frail design of utmost brevity and simplicity to signify his message and to transform our incredulity to profound assent. In this sense his play with its short, unemphatic scenes, its kindly humor, its quiet and plausibly folksy address to its audience, its avoidance of both individual characterization and stage properties (or "scenery"), its monosyllabic vocabulary which is so easily and gracefully phrased that its language never becomes what it resembles—the English of neighborhood drama—is a sort of formal masterpiece. With hardly more weight in content and less specific in incident than a Booth Tarkington tale, Wilder has managed to convert his sentimental idealism into an artful theatrical statement ostensibly as unpretentious as, but even more effective than, *Home Sweet Home*.

—*NAT*, 11 Apr. '59

LONDON:
A TASTE OF HONEY
FIVE FINGER EXERCISE
IRMA LA DOUCE

The three successful plays I went to see on my arrival here seem to me to represent three aspects of the English theatre today.

One is Shelagh Delaney's *A Taste of Honey*. This first play—Miss Delaney is 19—is one of the very few in which the English streets are heard to speak. Though there were realistic plays in England during the days preceding the First World War, they were middle-class plays and, more often than not, upper middle-class. During the twenties and even the thirties—when plays like *Love on the Dole* were presented—the realistic middle-class plays were given a polished stylization in which Somerset Maugham and Noel Coward seemed to have been crossed to make the milieu resemble a charade depicting royalty in *déshabille*.

A Taste of Honey smells of the squalor of Lancashire's industrial towns. It is nevertheless a poetic play because Miss Delaney has a feeling for her characters and a remarkably lively sense of dialogue which is at once pungently theatrical and authentic. She does not sermonize or sentimentalize. Her characters—the mother who is a tart, her illegitimate daughter of seventeen, the Negro, a male nurse in the navy, who becomes the young girl's lover, the homosexual art student from the town's slums who cares for the young girl when she becomes pregnant—are all seen as people of their environment and as people in broader context: the context of common humanity in which, for all the disparities of education, station, or experience, we remain far more alike than we are different.

There is a detachment in the author's approach which is not callousness but the acceptance which rises from a shared experience. Thus the play has no "point" (that is, intellectual bias), but it strikes me as possessing more social significance, because more truth, than it would if it were demonstrating a specific moral idea.

A Taste of Honey is what we used to call a slice of life—its "story" has no ending—with emphasis on the toughness and tenderness of the life rather than on the grossness of the "slice." Such plays represent only a beginning, but a beginning in a vein which may revitalize the chalk garden of the English theatre.

The acting is excellent. The play has been directed by Joan Littlewood, the intrepid young woman whose Theatre Workshop, an organization which has functioned for some years in a working-class district far from London's theatrical center, gave *A Taste of Honey* its first performances. The production shows signs of Brecht's influence, that is to say, Miss Littlewood uses certain of Brecht's devices with a purpose that is not exactly Brechtian.

Though essentially a realistic play, *A Taste of Honey* is given a sort of vaudeville treatment as if the story were part of the jazz world; indeed, jazz music accompanies several of the scenes. The tempo is breathless, actors frequently address the audience, or seem to, and they periodically break into dance steps. For the most part, I found the result effective: it appeared to give the play a certain lightness or effervescence which is probably not inconsistent with the author's brand of impersonality. Still, I could not help wondering what a more traditional realism in direction might do for the play. There is no way of telling unless someone as gifted as Miss Littlewood were to try. This conjecture is made because, as I shall have reason to emphasize later, we all ought to be clear that there is no virtue in the Brecht or any other technique by itself. The novel, the modern, the experimental, the *avant-garde* are all child's play when they are not part of a true content.

Five Finger Exercise by Peter Shaffer is also a first play. It introduces an author who combines the new material of the English theatre with an old mode of statement.

The new material is the sense of impasse in the middle-class family. Father is an ordinary Philistine furniture manufacturer who sees life in terms of solid earnings, small comforts, pub pleasures and homey rewards. Mother, more pretentious, employs her smattering of culture as a club of contempt to bludgeon her husband while she smothers and unmans her son in sugary indulgence. The result is alienation on all sides. The only ones who stand clear of the muddle are a precocious baby daughter who seems free of everything but her charm, and a young German in flight from an ex-Nazi father. The presence of the foreigner brings about a painful explosion of consciousness on everyone's part that nearly makes him its victim.

The play is technically adept—glib, in fact—as if the author were training to emulate Terence Rattigan. Pleasant humors and quips make it agreeable to a West End audience, and its neat explanations of everyone's troubles, its symmetry of plotting, its eloquent but self-conscious editorializing place it in a theatrical category much more conventional than its premise would lead one to expect. The inner turbulence of the young generation is made somehow to echo the complacent moderation of the old. Just so Pinero years ago domesticated Ibsen for the English.

Irma la Douce is a musical comedy (European style) adapted from a great Parisian hit. It is a raffish fable which deals with a *cocotte* and her poor student boy friend who, to prevent his girl from continuing her pavement industry, becomes his own rival by disguising himself as a bourgeois sufficiently well-heeled to support the girl. (He gets a paying job to make the disguise work.) The student becomes jealous of his bourgeois *alter ego* and determines to kill him. He is tried for murder, he is condemned, he escapes, etc., etc.

The score is from the bottom of the barrel, the lyrics are sometimes witty but rarely memorable. What makes the show function successfully is the brilliant invention of Peter Brook's direction. There is no question that Brook's theatrical talent

and a capacity to devise stage business of any sort—plus a highly developed visual sense—are surpassed by no American director and equaled by very few. Yet I came away from the show with the sense of having experienced nothing at all.

—*NAT*, 16 May '59

ASPECTS OF LONDON

The Royal Court Theatre—where early in the century Bernard Shaw and Granville Barker profited theatre art at a loss of $100,000—is once again the site of important activities. For here in this geographically off-center playhouse John Osborne, who looked about in anger, has opened the door to the younger generation's sibilant shouts.

The Royal Court enterprise, undertaken to introduce new playwrights whose realism would be rougher than Rattigan's, has become more than a stage society: it is a gathering place for literary rebellion. One hears talk, half respectful, half grudging, of a "Royal Court crowd" or "clique."

The production unit—under the direction of George Devine, Tony Richardson and lately Lindsay Anderson—has not only produced the three Osborne plays (Osborne began as an actor in the company) but Miller's *The Crucible*, Brecht's *Good Woman of Setzuan* and a number of less well-known plays by English authors. Most of them have been box-office failures, though the last, a war play called *The Long and The Short and The Tall* by Willis Hall, has moved to the West End where it is attracting favorable attention.

Theatre in the West End is conservative to a degree that often makes Broadway look *avant-garde*. The Royal Court and Joan Littlewood's Theatre Workshop are the first concerted postwar efforts to challenge the West End's dominance of the English stage. If Lorraine Hansberry were English, *A Raisin in the Sun* is the kind of play which would have to be done at the Royal Court.

This theatre is a symptom of a wide movement in the arts—particularly in literature. Novelists, poets, critics who are seeking their way out of the morass of yesteryears' Establishment (1919-1945) in the social, cultural, political world are sympathetically seconding the outcry at the Royal Court. One cannot say that all these folk speak the same language or are bent toward identical goals, but they have many characteristics in common. Most of them are better educated than the stalwarts of our 30's and their riot seems more studied and often more snobbish than that of their earlier American counterparts. Because this English radicalism comes at a different time from ours and arises from different causes (ours was rooted in the shock of the depression; theirs in the altered historical position of their civilization), it may strike an uninitiated American as somewhat retarded and its complaints less intelligible or justified than ours seemed to be. (In their recognition of the nuclear horror the English are in advance of us. My impression is that though Americans all talk about it they are not truly alarmed. So long as we are relatively prosperous we think of annihilation by atom power as so much science fiction.)

The latest manifestation of the Royal Court's temper was an evening devoted to the reading of verse by the young poet Christopher Logue—readings accompanied in the San Francisco manner by the playing of jazz. The poetry was followed by the same author's playlet *The Trial of Cob and Leech*. The event as a whole, called "Jazzetry," was presented to select but representative audiences on two Sunday evenings and cordially welcomed by such sedate journals as the *Times* and the *Sunday Times*.

Logue has talent, but since I heard his poems against a background of jazz I am in no position to estimate their worth. What was immediately striking in the verse as in the playlet—which was propaganda in burlesque form—was an addiction to four-letter words, presumably an assault on English prudery, and a loud-mouthed left-wing guying of English politics and sacred institutions. The effect was that of a cultivated collegiate razzberry. The

salient aspect of all this to me was the fact that whatever the audiences' sober judgment may have been they seemed thoroughly pleased that another stinkbomb was being heaved at the bastions of complacent English respectability.

It is worth recalling that in *Journey's End*, the most popular English war play of the late twenties, the leading characters were officers who consoled themselves by quoting *Alice in Wonderland*; the soldiers in *The Long and The Short and The Tall* are working-class men—none of them above a sergeant's rank—from various parts of Britain and each speaks the salty vernacular of his region. The language, frequently unintelligible to older people raised on public school or BBC English, is the outstanding virtue of the play—the language and the virile acting of the young company. The production as a whole, directed by Lindsay Anderson who was previously identified with documentary films, is impressive for its naked and humane realism.

There is nothing actually controversial in this play (nor for that matter in the more lyrically expressive *A Taste of Honey* of which I have already written) but their presence and success indicate progress. I do not believe that any of this work is as sturdy as *Awake and Sing!*, *A Streetcar Named Desire*, or *Death of a Salesman*, but that really doesn't matter. Each community must develop according to its own history and organic needs. There is no doubt, however, that American plays have exercised a certain beneficial influence on English writing for the theatre.

—*NAT*, 30 May '59

MARK TWAIN TONIGHT
ALL'S WELL THAT ENDS WELL
JULIUS CAESAR
THE CONNECTION

One of the pleasantest things put on our stage this season is Hal Holbrook's one-man show, *Mark Twain Tonight* (41st St. Theatre). The evening is memorable because of Mark Twain's tonic writing and Hal Holbrook's acting.

Mark Twain, we all say, is a true American classic. This, however, is a dangerous thing to say. Because a "classic" for most of us is something we refer to, quote and express haphazard opinions about, but which we rarely care for. I know Mark Twain well: did I not last read *Huckleberry Finn* in 1943, and *Tom Sawyer* when I was a kid? I know what Van Wyck Brooks said about the man, and what H. L. Mencken, Bernard De Voto, Kenneth Rexroth and a host of others have said. All this means that Mark Twain is a reputation to me—not a writer. Having seen Hal Holbrook's *Mark Twain Tonight*, the funny man of our literature has become an intimate.

Twain's language is a model of delightfully pithy speech. His "jokes" are refreshing because they embody a particularly American form of non-conformity, a sort of innocently caustic individual-ism. And what is most notable about this traditionally American attitude is that it is now almost extinct.

Hal Holbrook does more than read Twain, as Emlyn Williams reads Dickens or Dylan Thomas: he acts the man. His acting is shrewd and complete. The mischievous twinkle in the eye, the easy, preoccupied gait, the ascetic self-indulgence of the cigar-smoking, the delicate toying with the matches and the ashtray, the handling of the frayed books and scattered notes, not to mention the make-up and the tobacco voice—all form a first-rate miniature portrait.

All's Well That Ends Well (American Shakespeare Festival: Stratford, Conn.) is an agreeable production of a peculiar play. The scenes move lightly, the actors' speech is distinct, the performances are sympathetic, the points for a literal comprehension of the surface humor of the play are neatly made. Thus we get an affable rendition of the play—an ostensibly cute narration out of a naughty Boccaccio tale.

In other words, the Connecticut production takes the play at face value. But Shakespeare was a strange writer. If we are less interested in classics than in communication we may discover that *All's Well* is a deliberately nasty story by a rather embittered man—who didn't always feel kindly toward loyal women, upright kings and splendid soldiers. Some reviewers understood this, but thought it made the play inferior—as if it weren't quite proper for Shakespeare to be acid, after all the nice things we have said about him.

True, the play is not one of his verbal master-pieces; what is distinctive about it is the acid. This is diluted on the Connecticut stage, and we are given an evening of bland Shakespearean fun. Tyrone Guthrie's production of *All's Well*—now playing in Stratford-on-Avon—is a "distortion" which makes the play more meaningful to a modern viewer and less like something out of Charles Lamb.

Julius Caesar (New York Shakespeare Festival: Central Park) is an ironic political melo-drama. It is superbly written, wonderfully constructed, as masterful a stage piece as ever came out of the English theatre. In it—as later in *Coriolanus*—Shakespeare expressed his profound skepticism about the political world and its great figures. Brutus is an idealist who balls things up for himself and everyone else; the others are wily politicos who efficiently wreak havoc. There is not much solace in this for anyone. Besides being a supreme poet and dramatist, Shakespeare was a great spirit; but when he was not merry, he was a disturbing person. Such fellows simply have to be turned into "classics."

The production in the park is robust and—considering the youth of the company—well acted. Stuart Vaughan, the director, has learned several essential things about Shakespeare: he has to be played with great vigor, he has to be made larger than life (that is, unabashedly heroic), his points have to be strikingly visualized. That is what makes Vaughan's park productions good popular shows in a vein that approaches a living Shakespeare. The producer, Joseph Papp, deserves our thanks.

I once heard the composer John Cage speak of the music he and several of his similar-minded colleagues were writing as "non-art." Since I have never been primarily concerned whether any form of communication was "art" or not, the phrase irritated me. But seeing Jack Gelber's *The Connection* (The Living Theatre), I thought the play might fit into the category Cage referred to.

For while *The Connection* may not be "art," it is none the less arresting. The play, which is reportage, rumination and reflection about something that is definitely going on, presents a group of "junkies" (drug addicts) before and after a session given over to their vice. Some play jazz music (quite well), others "philosophize," explain themselves to the audience, tell little stories about their adventures. Though the play's form is unresolved, and some of the writing self-conscious as well as overlong, it is a bit of naturalism not without point and not without talent.

I am not familiar—as some of my friends seem to be—with the goings on in the haunts or "pads" of the beatniks, but *The Connection* creates a distinct sense of authenticity, even in the terrible languor of pace which marks the opening of the proceedings. The actors seem as right for their roles as Kazan long ago did in *Waiting for Lefty* (everyone was certain that The Group Theatre had hired a "hackie" for the part), and the direction by Judith Malina keeps the actors' concentration, their minute activities and physical life, truthful in a way that achieves intensity and casualness at the same time.

The result will surely seem unpleasant for spectators eager for either "art" or entertainment, but there is a sort of melancholy in the event, with touches of genuine pathos and even a wretched sort of lyricism. It is as if one had looked for a moment into a corner of our city to breathe the rank air of its unacknowledged dejection. The play reeks of human beings and if we turn completely away from people of any kind we can know little of anything worth knowing.

—*NAT*, 15 Aug. '59

MUCH ADO ABOUT NOTHING

The strength and weakness of the prevailing tradition in the contemporary English-speaking manner of presenting Shakespeare's plays may be observed in John Gielgud's production of *Much Ado About Nothing* (Lunt-Fontanne Theatre).

The company—particularly John Gielgud and Margaret Leighton—pronounce and phrase all their speeches with admirable clarity, precision, lightness, intelligence, aplomb. In a word, their reading is exemplary. And this, it goes without saying, affords great pleasure.

The pleasure is especially keen in this instance because *Much Ado About Nothing*—though not among the greatest of Shakespeare's comedies—is blessed with some of his most delightful writing, while Benedick and Beatrice are thoroughly charming personages.

The total effect of the production, however, is that of a reading in costume. What is lacking is what the theatre alone can give: a sense of the world from which the figures emerge and in which they dwell. This, technically speaking, is the production idea.

That it hardly exists in Gielgud's *Much Ado* is made evident by two facts: except for Dogsberry, Verges and the watchmen (whose very make ups create identities), there are no true characterizations. And aside from a politely spoofing tone, there is no specific atmosphere.

Benedick and Beatrice are young people of the Renaissance (presumably Italian) "born in a merry humor." They are soldier and lady of a muscular era, cock and hen of high spirits at a time when quarreling, fighting, teasing, torture, dancing, wit, gallantry and lovemaking all were intimately related. The keynote—"man is a giddy thing," Benedick says—is a youthful and externally courtly animality, a joyous vigor which can manifest itself as much in sudden sword play as in enchanting friskiness.

But Gielgud and Leighton struck me chiefly as superbly practiced actors more at home in the smart drawing rooms of Mayfair (or in a Maugham comedy) than in the lusty palaces of Shakespeare's Italy. This tames and reduces Shakespeare to a debonair posture; but Shakespeare, though English, was no "gentleman."

Another failure of style is evident in the treatment of the subplot that centers on Hero and Claudio (though it is difficult to be sure from the structure of the play whether Shakespeare meant the story of Benedick and Beatrice or of Hero and Claudio to constitute the subplot). On the face of it, Claudio's brutal treatment of Hero is melodrama, the amatory turn-about of Benedick and Beatrice is high comedy. In between is the sweet horseplay of the simple folk represented by Dogsberry and his companions.

The secondary plot—the abuse of Hero—has, because of its inherent absurdity, been considerably cut down in text so that it is not embarrassing now—only dull. What remains is done "straight." Gielgud's Benedick challenges Claudio to a duel very nearly in dead earnest. To unify the play, stylistically speaking, all this should be treated with a certain boyish extravagance—mock seriously or, if you will, with comic and "foolish" romanticism.

Little attempt has been made to deal with this problem because the play is done literally on the level of the words alone—as if to make Shakespeare "theatre" it is sufficient to speak his beautiful language with appreciative gusto in a strictly contemporary comprehension of its meaning. That is the common sin of most Shakespearean productions in England and America.

—*NAT*, 3 Oct. '59

THE THREE SISTERS
YVES MONTAND

I seem to have developed a conditioned reflex in the theatre: every time I see a Chekhov play—almost from the moment the curtain rises—I sense tears welling up within me.

The fact that a play makes me cry (or laugh) is no sign that it is good. I am not particularly lachrymose, but I have wept at some fairly bad plays, as I have occasionally laughed at pretty cheesy comedies.

So when I say that the latest production of Chekhov's *The Three Sisters* (4th St. Theatre), a play I have seen more often than any other in the modern repertory, made me cry, I do not offer it as proof that it is a great play. It simply means that, apart from its other distinctions, it is a play which embodies a quality that I always find very moving: *goodness*.

Several of the people in *The Three Sisters* are fools, one is a silly wretch, another irresponsible, still another a selfish hussy. But it is part of Chekhov's genius to make us feel—without indulging in the deplorable theatrical device called "gaining sympathy for a character"—that all his people, howsoever flawed, are entirely human. Which means, because Chekhov is Chekhov, that they are essentially good.

To be human in the Chekhovian sense is to desire happiness, to crave love, to will kindness, to aspire toward an extension of one's faculties—and to be inadequate in all these respects. In one of his short stories a peasant says "A bird is given not four wings but two because it is able to fly with two; and so man is not permitted to know everything but only a half or a quarter. As much as he needs to know in order to live."

A positive character in Chekhov is one in whom the will to strengthen his "wings" is still vibrant. The Prozoroff Sisters are the three purest examples—the archetypes—of this Chekhovian idealism. They want to go to Moscow—another character remarks in passing that if they lived in Moscow they would not "notice" it—but the Moscow they long for is not a city; it is an atmosphere in which they could spread their wings and fly nearer to the high goal which it is the nature of humankind to yearn for. The drama of their failure to make even the first step on the road to this goal is as terrible as, and far more convincing than, anything in the work of our contemporary dramatic pessimists whose theatre imagination is not rooted in common reality but in intellectualized concepts.

What makes Chekhov inspiring in contrast to these other playwrights is that the frustration in his plays—too frequently harped on in popular criticism—is secondary to the fundamental human impulses which make their frustration poignant instead of depressing.

The production of *The Three Sisters* at the 4th St. is decent. The company which plays in it is on the whole intelligent, sensitive and loyal to the Chekhovian vein. If you have never seen the play, you are a retarded theatergoer. To those who have seen it before, I might point out that it is always advisable to revisit a masterpiece.

A Parisian critic, quoted in the program of *An Evening with Yves Montand* (Henry Miller Theatre), praises this French night club singer and actor for his "soul." I should have said *health*. Montand looks strong, sings true, works meticulously. He is virile without ostentation and gives every evidence of being that rare bird, a normal person. He is "proletarian" without crudity, a city fellow without shabbiness, a popular entertainer without cheapness. He is capable of the imagination required for social sympathy, as is witnessed by his song, in flamenco style, addressed to the Spaniard in exile. All this is based on a fundamental attribute: his personal character and professional method express an attitude voiced in one of his songs, *Les Petits Riens Quotidiens* (The Little Daily Nothings) in which he celebrates his love for the inconspicuous pleasures of everyday living: moments of work, a passing smile, a flower, a new necktie, a bright day, a flirtation and anything else you may like. This sentiment represents an essential wisdom—without which nothing can ever be right.

Montand is not "sensational": he is simply sound. He has real gifts as an actor; he is theatrically most effective when he impersonates rather than when he addresses us as himself. His contribution—appreciated all over the world—is that

he emerges from the noisome clamor of everything that surrounds us everywhere, not as a freak of glamor or special accomplishment, but as a whole man. In this he satisfies one of our real needs.

—*NAT*, 10 Oct. '59

THE GANG'S ALL HERE

After seeing *The Gang's All Here*, Jerome Lawrence and Robert Lee's political melodrama (Ambassador), I felt somewhat like the street orator who challenged "Do you believe in God? Take either side."

This does not mean that I had several sharp reactions of divergent nature or that I had no reaction at all. What I felt was a sort of benign neutrality. But out on the sidewalk after the second act a critic I respect indicated that he thought the play unusual—and "advanced"—for these days: meaning something to be encouraged. In the theatre we are constrained to a considerable degree of relativism in our judgments.

The Gang's All Here is the story of a nonentity elected to the Presidency of the United States in the twenties through the machinations of a group of Ohio racketeers who constitute his Cabinet. They hornswoggle the unfortunate man into betrayal of the country and finally into a moment of "greatness"—which consists of committing suicide.

As melodrama, the play, though trim and never uninteresting, is not particularly tense; as journalism it is not sufficiently detailed; as sociological interpretation, primitive with a dash of hortatory patriotics; as character study, thinly sentimental. Yet a theatre critic is disinclined to dismiss the play out of hand. For the earnest professionals and many theatergoers these days seem to suffer a sense of guilt about the backwardness of our stage in reflecting the contemporary scene, particularly in regard to what might be considered controversial matters.

While there is psychological justification for the uneasiness, it does not seem to me concretely sound. Our theatre's impotence to confront reality is surely a symptom of our general shrinking from any public discussion that might involve decided disagreement, but it does not follow that we ought to demand more topical drama—thesis plays about such immediate issues as disarmament, atom tests and the like.

In addition to the fear and confusion which have bedeviled us in the past ten years or more, our stage has been increasingly thwarted by disastrous economics, so that producing a play unconventional in content as well as in form has become almost quixotic. But quite apart from this, there has developed of late something like a rooted habit of discussing everything in swift and facile generalizations—*Time* fashion—so that the high school and college-educated citizen knows something about everything—art, science, politics, medicine, foreign affairs, etc.—and precious little about anything.

Nothing seems to be experienced. We harbor a multitude of opinions and possess almost no convictions. Even our doubts are doubtful. The noise about us—which includes more information in the head of a schoolboy than Aristotle could ever have absorbed or acquired—renders us essentially ignorant even on the one subject with which we might be familiar—ourselves.

Hence American history on our stage is usually juvenile and boring. Our memory of the recent past is so sketchy that not only have most theatergoers forgotten that the material of *The Gang's All Here* was treated years ago in the novel, *Revelry*, and its dramatization, but I heard a middle-aged lady in the audience having a joke in the play explained to her by being reminded that there was Prohibition during the twenties. So that finally a play about such recent events as the scandals of the Harding administration—which I believe did not really shock the country, any more than have more recent scandals—becomes a play about a good-natured boob betrayed by pals with no respect for public office. We look on undisturbed as the poor guy in his death throes voices the sentiment that nothing like his situation will occur in the future.

It is not "daring" themes, the strong stuff of general dispute, we need so much in our theatre as dramatists to deal with what they truly feel and know. They cannot make any real contact with us through research on "important" subjects. Serious drama is not serious through studied hearsay and good intentions. The way to get under your audience's skin is first to get under your own. The American playwright is too often a man whose spiritual range, no matter what subject he has chosen, is confined to the limits of Shubert Alley. He does not seem to be vitally engaged in anything but making a good living at his shrinking profession.

The one thing I unqualifiedly enjoyed in *The Gang's All Here* was Melvyn Douglas in the central role. Douglas is that rare and stalwart phenomenon: a leading player who is always doing his job—on the road or in town, whenever and wherever he has an appropriate role in a play of some discernible merit. This hardy dedication gives the character of President Griffith P. Hastings in *The Gang's All Here* a dimension the authors must have hoped for.

—*NAT*, 17 Oct. '59

THE GREAT GOD BROWN

Praise the Phoenix Theatre for producing Eugene O'Neill's *The Great God Brown* anew (Coronet). George Jean Nathan thought it O'Neill's best play, an opinion I do not share, but one step toward the making of a true theatre in our country is the production of old plays of merit.

It is not sufficient, though, that such plays be seen merely as new "shows"; they should be comprehended as part of a development in their author's work and as part of our own History. It is no longer of first importance that O'Neill used masks in this play, a device considered highly "experimental" in 1926 when the play was originally presented. What is important is the play's theme and the anguish O'Neill imbued it with. The theme is the practical man's envy of the artist and the artist's jealousy of the dominant practical man—a peculiarly American theme in the period of the play's conception.

O'Neill probed further than this bald statement might suggest. He saw the American business-man—for that is what Brown represents, though O'Neill made him an architect—becoming infected with the artist's yearnings, and unable finally to realize himself either as one thing or another. Brown suffers some of the inner dissatisfactions which plague and impel the artist without possess-ing the artist's sensibility or skill. More strikingly, O'Neill portrays his artist, Dion Anthony, as a trammeled human being, really a half-artist with a gnawing sense of inadequacy in his philosophy, his personality and his adjustment to life. That is a crucial American Tragedy: the incompleteness of American civilization as it focuses in the individ-ual.

This sounds old-fashioned. Today only a brief "moment" since the dilemma appeared poignant in the growing American consciousness, terms and circumstances have altered their outer form. The businessman of today is emotionally more compla-cent: if he appreciates the artist's function, collects paintings, attends concerts and reads certain books or book reviews, he expresses his disquiet other-wise than O'Neill's Brown. Similarly the artist today seems to have taken his "proper" place in our society, so that with a little maneuvering, ratio-nalization, psychoanalysis and publicity he can feel pretty much in the same boat as the Browns. The result is that they are both prepared to moan in monotonous chorus about taxes and the threat of atomic extinction.

The core of the matter, however, is not changed as much as we pretend; if we believe otherwise that is chiefly because we rarely think of any "core" at all, except to indulge ourselves in a specious vocabulary of high-brow platitudes. O'Neill was no intellectual; if his play suffers in form and thought as well as in clarity, its impulse and source are nevertheless real and deep.

In O'Neill's work as a whole the theme of *The Great God Brown* recurs again and again in the most diverse guises; and if we refer even cursorily to O'Neill's life we become aware that the conflicts which made the theme urgent were rooted in his relationship to his father, his mother, his brother. A blood tie binds *Beyond the Horizon*, *Desire Under the Elms*, *Marco Millions*, *Long Day's Journey Into Night*, *A Touch of the Poet* into a single underlying meaning: the individual American has not reached fulfillment; he is not full grown, neither as a doer nor as a feeling person has he yet made peace with himself or with the world, and all the blather about the "American way of life" will not heal the sore.

Note too that O'Neill's artist, for all his mockery of Brown, is not presented as a "genius." It is always clear that O'Neill never thought of himself as a master in any way. He identified himself with derelicts and failures. He has no heroes; all his central figures yammer and yearn, curse and are as much lost as Yank the laborer in *The Hairy Ape*. Immature on the level of ultimate power, O'Neill is the dramatic poet of our own immaturity—which in his work is not merely an artistic or an intellectual flaw, but a lacerating wound.

You may be embarrassed by some of the awkwardness and feeble verbiage of *The Great God Brown*; particularly in the last act; and you can if you wish disparage O'Neill, in academic loftiness, by comparing his plays with the best work of the European playwrights of the past forty years. The fact remains that he is not only our most important dramatist, but one whose total product is, even in some of its faults, more truly relevant to the American people—whose "story" after all concerns the whole of modern society—than any other dramatist of this period anywhere.

The Phoenix Theatre production under Stuart Vaughan's direction is much more obviously styl-ized than the original production directed by Robert Edmond Jones. The new production is perhaps more lucid than the early one, or let us say less "mystic." It is intelligently executed throughout. I also believe it likely that the comparatively young actors in the present production—Fritz Weaver, Robert Lansing and the others—"understand" the play and their parts better than did those of the original cast. Yet I cannot suppress the feeling that the emotional resources of our present generation of actors are not as rich as those of former years. The distinction is not one of talent: it has much to do with the times. Today we are perhaps more troubled and possess less actual experience. Our lesions nowadays seem to be chronic, and so to speak automatic, whereas the older actors were more truly engaged in the world and in the living theatre. They had *earned* their neuroses.

—*NAT*, 24 Oct. '59

THE TENTH MAN

Paddy Chayefsky's *The Tenth Man* (Booth) is a curiosity, a strange compost: it will undoubtedly fascinate some; others may well find it indigestible or offensive.

Into a makeshift orthodox synagogue in Mineola, Long Island, one of the communicants brings his insane granddaughter, a girl of eighteen, who he is convinced is possessed by a dybbuk. (A dybbuk, according to the playscript, "is a migratory soul that possesses another human being in order to return to heaven.") In his youth, the grandfather had seduced an innocent girl and it is she who now cries out in agonized protest, "I am the whore of Kiev" from the mouth of the virgin who is brought to the synagogue. Frightened, incredulous and awed, other members of the congregation suggest that the dybbuk be exorcised. The exorcism takes place. Its effect is transfiguring to a passerby—a young lawyer with suicidal tendencies undergoing psychoanalysis. He is "the tenth man" (ten men constitute the "quorum" required by Jewish law for communal prayer). The sick young man, who believes in

nothing, undertakes to care for and eventually to marry the psychopathic girl. He has succumbed to love—the reality of which he had hysterically denied a few hours before—and love, as one character states at the final curtain, is the same as God.

Is this play a fantasy, a folk tale, a mystic parable? No; it is a broad comedy—not through the absurdity of its argument, but through the funniness of its subsidiary characters: the frazzled remnants of Orthodox Jewry in a suburban American community. One is a retired cloak and suiter, another a former journalist, still another an atheistic ne'er-do-well who clings to the congregation for companionship and the kind of guying disputation which is supposed to make Jewish conversation so amusing.

In a word, the play has color—for never have American Jews been represented as they are here. For example, an impoverished old member of the "quorum" comes in an athlete's discarded sweat shirt—the player's number prominent on its back undoubtedly the "gift" of one of the wearer's grandsons. The rabbi of this congregation is a married young man—more social settlement worker than religious leader—trying desperately to raise funds for his synagogue so that it may become something better than a clapboard hole stuck between a grocery and a butcher shop. The rabbi's telephone talk with another young rabbi (he tells him, "You are a truly devoted and pious man and therefore utterly unsuited to the rabbinate") is one of the best things in the play—and central to its serious aspect.

The writing, throughout, is only occasionally that of a recognizable vernacular such as its characters might speak, and it is not a translation from the Yiddish. Mainly it is a studiously stiff language employed either to give these characters "dignity" or a symbolic universality. On the other hand most of them speak with an inflection customary in American Jewish jokes.

The effect of this mixture of ingredients—I shall not dwell on the semi-intellectual dialogue which implies the author's sympathy with the truth immanent in the ancient ritual and faith—is both meretricious and real. The characters are either synthetic or mere caricatural traits; the gags sometimes have genuine savor but they are more often facile. We get the impression of an extremely shrewd showmanship ringing all the changes on the susceptibilities of an audience in which nothing is stable except a kind of foggy benevolence and a faintly aching emptiness which craves laughter to fill the void.

But it is from these latter characteristics that the play's reality derives. Chayefsky is talented; his play is willy-nilly an image of the cultural disarray within a large section of American Jewry and within the souls of the theatre public in general which lives on several different moral levels at the same time without possessing any true base anywhere. For while the play shows signs of vague regret at the loss of tradition and nostalgia for a time when one's community had spiritual unity, the comic tone of the play betrays the predominance of the wry skepticism and cynicism of people who have no firm commitment to anything outside the sphere of success.

The play therefore is not so much a creation as a symptom. As such it is both sweet and revolting: yet it is preferable to many performances which are mere contraptions of the entertainment industry. "Better to believe in a dybbuk," says the play's atheist "than in nothing." That might be the epigraph for *The Tenth Man.*

A dimension of ennobling warmth is given the work by Tyrone Guthrie's direction. Its fluent movement lends the staging naturalness together with a beautiful but unobtrusive pictorial quality— signs of true mastery. Mr. Guthrie has been aided by David Hays's setting and lighting, and an admirable cast whose every member—and particularly Arnold Marlé, David Vardi, Jacob Ben-Ami, Lou Jacobi and Gene Saks—is to be gratefully saluted.

—*NAT*, 21 Nov. '59

THINKING OF SHAKESPEARE

Under the pressure of rehearsal one day, I said to a new playwright who appeared more concerned with the neatness of his dialogue than with the conduct of his narrative, "Remember, Shakespeare was only accidentally a poet!"

"There," he might have replied, "speaks the showman."

There has always been a "dispute" between the stage and literature. What is the *seed* of drama? In the beginning is the word, some say, while others retort, in the beginning is the deed. A play, I recall someone else writing, consists of words on a scaffolding of action.

The dilemma—if it is one—is not resolved in Granville Barker's *Prefaces to Shakespeare*, but I know of no book on Shakespeare which reconciles the two aspects of the Shakespearean "question" more sensibly than this one: "Shakespeare was a very practical playwright."

Granville Barker, actor, stage-director, producer, playwright, teacher, and seer, is one of the very few Englishmen who might be listed among the masters of the European theatre in the twentieth century. In these *Prefaces* he has written about Shakespeare in a manner that marks him as a true professional of the stage who is at the same time attune to the music and passion, the magic and the thought, in Shakespeare.

It may be possible—though I am inclined to doubt it—to understand Shakespeare without reference to the stage, but I am certain that it is not possible to understand him theatrically simply through an appreciation of his quality as a writer. What impels me to speak of a Shakespeare "problem" is the fact that theatre people themselves have for so long been tempted to employ the great dramatist simply as an occasion for personal aggrandizement, with little regard to the significance of his creation as an artist. Or else in petrified admiration of his genius they have neglected to present his works so that their impact as plays or, if you will, as theatre pieces, might emerge in all its dramatic splendor.

For most of us Shakespeare has been a series of renowned "moments" or scenes for histrionic, elocutionary producers' display, or a group of quotable speeches, aphorisms, phrases—grandiose, portentous, mellifluous—isolated from any common reality. In this sense, Shakespeare—more famous than any other single figure in world literature—is still a little-known author, particularly in English-speaking countries. A new sort of interest in Shakespeare has been generated since the two world wars—so that Shakespeare has become the subject of fresh study and of more than library interest.

We all assume when we go to see a play by Shakespeare that we know all about it beforehand. This explains why we permit most theatre critics to omit a discussion of the text when they review a play by Shakespeare, and are satisfied when they speak only of the "interpretation" (the acting, staging, etc.), as if it were possible to interpret anything without having some idea of what is being interpreted. *Hamlet*; is a play about action impaired by thought (yet Hamlet is a furiously active person!). *Macbeth* is about ambition, *Othello* about jealousy, *King Lear* about filial ingratitude. Of course when it comes to *Measure for Measure*, *Coriolanus*, *Cymbeline*, we are not all sure what they are about because they are infrequently read or produced. In short, we—theatre-folk as well as theatergoers—have no intimacy with these plays. We have only habits in regard to them, memories of opinions prefabricated in classrooms, or vague impressions gathered by attending productions presented by people whose sources of inspiration are not much more profound than our own.

Barker asks questions about Shakespeare's plays and forces us to ask our own questions which make us realize how little we have thought about them (we who for so long took our knowledge for granted). The questions he asks, moreover, are pertinent to the plays as living theatre, not simply

as philosophical, historical, or verbal conundrums. He leads us to contemplate Shakespeare, to feel him in terms of our eyes, ears, heart and mind—as works of art in movement and space.

Barker tells us that "dramatic poetry is never to be judged apart from the action it implies." He makes us doubt the validity of any particular Shakespeare tradition (about which we hear a good deal of nonsense) since the original Shakespeare tradition was virtually obliterated after 1660 and his plays were never restored to the theatre in anything resembling their integral form till the middle of the nineteenth century. Shakespeare, Barker also reminds us, is produced too sanely and sentimentally—a reminder which moves this reviewer to loud applause. With all this, Barker measures Shakespeare's sentences, words, and syllables for their weight and sound, their emotional reverberation, and their psychological impact, their color, and their penetrative force.

What we have here, then, in this somewhat neglected masterpiece of Barker is the equivalent for dramatic literature of those recent studies of painters, musicians, and poets which do not simply rhapsodize impressionistically on the beauties of classic creations, but which attempt to cope with them, probing their details in all their aspects.

The result is that for director, actor, scene-designer, general reader, and enthusiastic playgoer, as well as for the literary student, these *Prefaces to Shakespeare* offer invaluable stimulus, enlightenment, challenge, and help. Written in a kind of decorously courtly prose with a certain awkward elegance—pleasurably "old-fashioned"—the book is indisputably something to be cherished in the library of every cultured person.

—*GRIF*, Dec. '59

CANDIDE IN LONDON

Candide (Saville) is a musical composed of superior ingredients. I do not refer to Voltaire's masterpiece, the motifs and the model of which, together with something of the book's picaresque character, supply the basis of Lillian Hellman's adaptation. The ingredients I refer to are Miss Hellman's own seriousness of purpose, the cunning of Leonard Bernstein's musical hand, Robert Lewis's particular humor as a director, and several performers who can really sing. If this *Candide* is to be compared to anything else, it should be to other musicals—from Offenbach to Brecht—which attempt to serve some end beyond titillation. The musical comedy form in our time is bound by severe limitations. The Brecht-Weill *Threepenny Opera*, though a first-rate work, achieves success only at theatres removed from the central market where the majority of playgoers do their shopping. Musical comedy by its label announces itself as something either exultantly trivial or at best—*South Pacific*, *My Fair Lady*, *West Side Story*—charming or sentimental.

Candide attempts something much more difficult: to combine the jocularity which makes the ordinary musical popular and to express Miss Hellman's ineradicable desire to speak her mind. What *Candide* says is that the world is a hell of a place; that no amount of ideological or idealistic whitewash will make it less disturbing, and since we all wish to live we might as well get down to doing our humble tasks with dogged hope and honest hearts.

Miss Hellman can write funny lines, and there are more than a few in her play. What she may lack in this regard Robert Lewis, who commands a mischievous innocence and considerable showmanship, compensates for with bright invention. Leonard Bernstein has also added some tongue-in-cheek humor to the proceedings—the musical numbers are all parodies of operatic forms—while the dancing of Jack Cole's creation is lively and to the point.

Yet there is the question of *style*; here is where the enterprise falters. For whereas Offenbach and Brecht were born with masks and the devilish gift of irony, Miss Hellman has nothing of the hypocrite. There is a fierceness in her nature; she can be mordant but her wit betrays its source in moral sternness and indignation so that we are

made to realize that she gets small satisfaction in cracking jokes for their own sake. That is why *Candide* often seems on the verge of breaking down into something sour, leaden or solemn with spots of vulgarity in the lyrics and occasional strain in the score. The urge towards an organic style is there but not the full capacity.

Still, parts of it are very good. Wholly successful is Mary Costa's Cunégonde, particularly in the hilarious aria "Glitter and be Gay." Denis Quilley's Candide is sympathetic and easy to listen to, Laurence Naismith is an engaging Pangloss and Ron Moody as the Governor is amusing in his grotesque authority. The production as a whole has a discipline and an ensemble flair infrequent in the production of musicals in London.

—*LO*, '59

TYPICAL AMERICAN PLAYS OF THE 1930'S

There is a tendency nowadays to downgrade the thirties. The reason for this is that the prevailing mood of the thirties was what used to be called "left of center." Beginning with the late forties—from the time the phrase about the "iron curtain" became part of the common vocabulary—our "intelligentsia" sounded the retreat. The Roosevelt administration, subjected to sharp criticism not infrequently close to slander, seemed to be in bad odor. "Left of center" might be construed as something worse than liberalism. To be "radical" implied that one might be tainted with some degree of "pink."

A good many of the writers, artists and theatre folk in the thirties were inclined to radicalism. (Had not the Roosevelt administration sponsored the Projects for writers, artists and theatre?) In the early forties the fervor of the thirties was gradually absorbed by the pressures of the war. Since Russia was one of our allies there was less strictly political feeling: everyone was chiefly concerned with victory and the return to peaceful prosperity.

Shortly after the peace conference suspicion of the Soviet Union increased. Radicalism of any sort might be interpreted as "softness" toward the potential enemy. Our artists and writers, including theatre people, had not only shown too much sympathy for social experiment but had also been too emphatic about the real or supposed shortcomings of their own country. At best the enthusiasm of the thirties was now considered a sign of juvenile simple-mindedness, at worst something close to treason.

Around the year 1953 this reaction to the thirties had come close to hysteria. Today there is certainly more calm but the notion that the thirties was a foolish period persists. Presumably we are now far sounder in our thinking and work than we were then.

There is another aspect to the rather low esteem in which much of the dramatic work of the thirties is now held. The immediate past in the theatre always makes a poor impression. Writing about the twenties, which every student of our theatre history regards as a high point of the American theatre both in volume of activity and in achievement, Joseph Wood Krutch in the early thirties said that the record no longer seemed as bright as it once appeared. Very few of the best plays of that time would endure.

What most of us fail to note in this connection is that very few plays measured in the light of decades or generations have ever "endured." Shakespeare as we know Shakespeare is a nineteenth-century discovery! (He was neglected or disgracefully altered during the seventeenth and eighteenth centuries.) The number of plays which have come down to us from the Greeks of the fifth century B.C. and from the Elizabethan era are a paltry few compared to the number produced. How cavalier was the attitude of our drama critics toward Marlowe's *Tamburlaine* because he was not equal to Shakespeare!

We may explain this paradox through our own theatregoing experience. A play may be both enjoyable and important to us at the moment we see it, but when the circumstances of our lives have changed, it may well have lost its appeal. One of the most popular plays the American theatre has ever produced is the dramatization of *Uncle Tom's Cabin*. No one can deny its importance for its day even if we no longer have much regard for it as literature.

It is downright stupid to sneer at our erstwhile excitement over *Waiting for Lefty* because today a good many people (in Europe at any rate) are waiting for Godot. As theatre-goers we are very rarely able to estimate a play in the present as we shall view it twenty-five years hence. What appeared a very inconsiderable play to England's finest dramatic critic, Bernard Shaw, Oscar Wilde's *The Importance of Being Ernest*, has proved durable beyond anyone's belief when it was first presented.

I recall having seen Robert Sherwood's *The Petrified Forest* (1935) in the company of one of our country's most astute men of letters. He enjoyed it thoroughly. A few days later we spoke on the phone. He remarked that the theatre was a hoax: he had been "taken in" by the play as he watched it, he said, but on further reflection he realized the play's flaws in thought and plot. Most readers who are also playgoers are like that.

We enjoy the "show," but we *think* about the play. There is often a disparity of judgment between the two activities. For though we are intellectually aware that literature and theatre are not identical, we are prone to assume that the text of a play is equivalent to the texture of its production. But a play in the theatre communicated qualities beyond—sometimes, in a bad performance, less than—what we find on the printed page. Thus to evaluate the theatre of any period only with regard to its texts is a falsification.

The plays of the thirties sharpen certain tendencies that were already evident, and comparatively new, in the plays of the twenties. For the twenties, which may be said to represent America's second coming of age in literature (the first might be dated around 1850) and its true coming age in the theatre, were marked by a rather harsh critical realism. What such men as Frank Norris and Theodore Dreiser had been saying about us in their novels began to be said somewhat more lyrically (though no less vehemently) in the plays of Eugene O'Neill. The theatre is ideologically almost always behind the times because it is a mass medium. It takes a while for people to acknowledge publicly what a few individuals may think and say privately.

It was the artistic pleasure of the twenties to deride, curse, bemoan the havoc, spiritual blindness and absurdity of America's materialistic functionalism with its concomitant acquisitiveness and worship of success.

Another marked feature of the theatrical twenties was the fact that plays which had previously satisfied audiences with the mere tracing of types (or stereotypes) began to strike them as increasingly hollow. Characters began to show their faces on the stage. Psychology was "introduced." Men and women were no longer heroes or villains but "human," a mixture of contradictory traits. The standardized Puritanism typified by the old anti-vice societies became an object of scorn and ridicule.

The sentiment against war in *What Price Glory?* of the twenties was converted into the poignant and pointed satire of Paul Green's *Johnny Johnson* in the thirties. The sense of loneliness which informs O'Neill's pieces is rendered more acute and more general in Steinbeck's *Of Mice and Men* some ten years later. The plight of the colored people in the Heywards' *Porgy* or in Green's *In Abraham's Bosom* is intensified in John Wexley's *They Shall Not Die* in the thirties. The playful probing of Behrman's *The Second Man* in 1927 is given a social connotation in the same author's *Biography* and other of his later plays in the thirties. The laborer as a symbol of inner disharmony within the apparent health of the American commonwealth which we observe in O'Neill's *The Hairy Ape* (1922) becomes a leading theme on a more concrete basis in the thirties.

The most significant difference between the theatre of the twenties and that of the thirties is the emphasis in the later period on the social, economic and political background of the individual psychological case. The Wall Street crash of 1929, the Great Depression of the early thirties with its attendant scar of widespread unemployment, the hopeful attempt to remedy this bitter condition which ensued are the effective causes for the abrupt and drastic change.

The plays included in this volume are not all necessarily the "best" of the thirties, but all are representative. Space and other factors of publication permitting, I should certainly have included O'Neill's *Mourning Becomes Electra* (1931), an Irish play of Denis Johnston's, *The Moon in the Yellow River* (1932), Maxwell Anderson's *Winterset* (1935), Sidney Kingsley's *Dead End* (1935), Thornton Wilder's *Our Town* (1938), Robert Sherwood's *Abe Lincoln in Illinois* (1938), Lillian Hellman's *The Little Foxes* (1939).

Of the plays included one had to be the work of Clifford Odets. Historically speaking he is the dramatist of the thirties *par excellence*. His immediate sources of inspiration, his point of view, his language, his import and perhaps some of his weaknesses are typical of the thirties.

I am not at all sure that *Awake and Sing!*, first presented by the Group Theatre on February 19, 1935, is the best of Odets' plays. The 1937 *Golden Boy* has a more striking story line and is more varied and personal in its meaning. But *Awake and Sing!* contains the "seed" themes of the Odets plays and indicates most unaffectedly the milieu and the quality of feeling in which his work is rooted. One might even go so far as to say that there is hardly another play of the thirties—except perhaps John Howard Lawson's *Success Story* (1932)—which so directly communicates the very "smell" of New York in the first years of the depression.

The keynotes of the period are struck in *Awake and Sing!* as never again with such warm intimacy. There is first of all the bafflement and all-pervading worry of lower middle-class poverty. This is conveyed in language based on common speech and local New York (including Jewish) idiom, but it is not precisely naturalistic speech, for Odets' writing is a personal creation, essentially lyric, in which vulgarity, tenderness, energy, humor and a headlong idealism are commingled.

What is Odets' basic impulse; what is his "program"? They are contained in Jacob's exhortation to his grandson, "Go out and fight so life shouldn't be printed on dollar bills," and in another reflection, "Life should have some dignity." It seems to me that not only is most of Odets expressed in these bare words but the greater part of the whole cry of the American "progressive" movement—its radicalism if you will—as the artists of the thirties sensed it, is summed up in these innocent mottoes.

The "biblical" fervor in *Awake and Sing!* impels a "revolutionary" conviction expressed in Jacob's comment, "It needs a new world," which leads his grandson to take heart and proclaim, "Fresh blood, arms. We've got 'em. We're glad we're living." This was the "wave" of the thirties. If that wave did not carry us on to the millennium, it is surely the height of folly to believe that it had no vital force and accomplished nothing of value in the arts as well as in our community life.

S.N. Behrman's *End of Summer*, produced by the Theatre Guild on February 17, 1936, gives us the depression period seen from another angle: that of the "privileged" classes. It is a comedy of manners which besides its merits in the way of urbane dialogue, etc., presents a central character who (apart from having a decided semblance to the play's author) is kin to most of the folk who buy the best seats in our metropolitan theatres. Leonie, says Behrman, "is repelled by the gross and the voluptuary: this is not hypocrisy....In the world in which she moves hypocrisy is merely a social lubricant, but this very often springs from a congenital and temperamental inability to face anything but the pleasantest and most immediately appealing and the most flattering aspect of things, in life and in her own nature."

What *End of Summer* presents is the spectacle of such a person confronted by the unhappy phenomenon of mass unemployment, nascent radicalism, specters of fascism and the ambiguities of the psychoanalysts. The treatment is characteristic of Behrman—joshing, debonair, slightly more lighthearted than the author actually feels.

The lady of the play for the first time meets "the young radicals our colleges are said to be full of nowadays." One such radical, a somewhat fictitious Irish Catholic young fellow, tells the lady, "The world is middle-aged and tired," at which the lady queries, "Can you refresh us?" The young man rejoins, "Refresh you! Leonie, we can rejuvenate you." That was another hope of the youth which during the thirties had reached the ages of twenty-five to thirty-five. It was not altogether a vain hope for, as I have already indicated and shall continue to indicate, there was a young and invigorating spirit that relieved the thirties of its blues and led to concrete benefits.

One of the faults easily spotted in *End of Summer* is also evident in Robert Sherwood's *Idiot's Delight*, produced by the Theatre Guild in the spring of 1936. Just as the young radicals of Behrman's play seem to be known by hearsay rather than by intimate acquaintance, so in *Idiot's Delight,* Sherwood's grasp of the European political situation is informed as it were by headlines rather than truly experienced. Thus he makes his French pacifist a Radical-Socialist who speaks of the workers' uprising and alludes to Lenin with reverence, whereas any knowledgeable foreign correspondent could have told Sherwood that the Radical-Socialists of France are the party of small business, abhor Lenin's doctrines and are neither radical nor socialist.

This slight error is worth mentioning because it is symptomatic of a not uncommon failing in American playwrights when they generalize or "intellectualize" on social or ethical themes. It is a species of dilettantism which consists of dealing with subjects in which one is certainly interested but not truly familiar.

More cogent than this flaw is the sentiment which inspired Sherwood to write *Idiot's Delight*. It echoes the American fear of and profound estrangement from the facts of European intrigue which led to war. One merit of Sherwood's play is that it gives us an inkling of the moral climate in our country shortly after the Italian-Ethiopian conflagration and the outset of the Spanish civil conflict—two omens of the future scarcely understood by an average citizen. Sherwood's "solution" to the problem in his play is the idealistic injunction "You can refuse to fight."

This is significant because it shows that the attitude of our dramatists, generally speaking, was fundamentally moral rather than, as some are now inclined to believe, political. This explains why Sherwood, whose *Idiot's Delight* might indicate the opposition to war of the "conscientious objector," took a very different stand when Nazism threatened to engulf Europe and the world. The play also marks the transition from skepticism and pessimism in regard to modern life, suggested by several of Sherwood's earlier plays, to the willingness to be engaged in political struggle and an acceptance of war, exemplified by his *Abe Lincoln in Illinois*.

Sherwood was a shrewd showman: *Idiot's Delight* gives striking evidence of this. He himself is supposed to have said, "The trouble with me is that I start off with a big message and end with nothing but good entertainment." *Idiot's Delight* was good entertainment, particularly in the acting opportunities it afforded Alfred Lunt and Lynn Fontanne, just as Leonie in *End of Summer*, in itself a charming characterization, was given special fragrance by Ina Claire's delightful talent.

John Steinbeck's *Of Mice and Men*, produced by Sam H. Harris on November 23, 1937, is a parable of American loneliness and of our hunger for "brotherhood"—two feelings the depression greatly enhanced. This play, unlike most of the others we have cited, concentrates on the unemployed of the farm lands, the itinerants and ranch workers, while it alludes to the bus and truck drivers whose travels through the country permitted them to observe the state of the nation in its broad horizon.

The American theatre, centered in New York, is on the whole cut off from the rest of the country. The thirties was the time when the theatre, along with the other arts, rediscovered America. *Green Grow the Lilacs* (1931) is one of the several Lynn Riggs Oklahoma plays, Erskine Caldwell's *Tobacco Road* (1933), Osborn's *Morning's at Seven* (1939)—to mention only a few—are among the many which in one way or another perform a similar function. One of the reasons why Steinbeck's parable carries conviction on naturalistic grounds is that the author shares the background and the earthiness of his characters.

Steinbeck knows our longing for a home, not a mere feeding place. He has the same true sympathy for the lonesome devil whose sole companion is a mangy old dog as for the Negro cut off by his fellow workers because of his color. He suggests with something like an austere sorrow that America's "underprivileged" will never reach the home they crave till they arrive at greater consciousness.

Speaking of "austerity" I should point out that one of the ground tones of American art and theatre (particularly the latter) is sentimentality. This is also true of Steinbeck's play, though he tries to control his sentimentality. Now sentimentality is usually accounted a vice, because it bespeaks a propensity to express a greater degree of feeling than a specific situation warrants. But sentimentality need not be a vital flaw; it isn't in *Of Mice and Men*. It is the characteristic of a young and vigorous people whose experience of life is, so to speak, still new and uncontaminated by too frequent disillusionment. In this sense our history makes us a sentimental people and it is only natural that our arts, particularly our folk arts, should reveal this quality.

This brings us to the last play of this volume: William Saroyan's *The Time of Your Life*, presented by the Theatre Guild in association with Eddie Dowling on October 25, 1939. This sentimental comedy is by way of being a little classic. It marks the deliquescence of the aggressive mood of the thirties. For though the moralistic and critical rationale of the thirties is still present in *The Time of Your Life*, it is there in a lyrically anarchistic manner, a sort of sweet (here and there mawkish) dream.

Another way, distinctly 1959, of describing this play is to call it pre-beatnik! "I believe dreams more than statistics," one character says. "Everybody is behind the eight ball," says another. Money appears as the root of most evil—anyway it is the filthiest thing that goes and "there's no foundation all the way down the line," as the old man from the Orient mutters throughout the play.

In a way *The Time of Your Life* is a social fable: it turns its head away from and thumbs its nose at our monstrously efficient society which produces arrogance, cruelty, fear, headaches, constipation and the yammering of millions of humble folk, only to conclude that "all people are wonderful." Though this evinces more bewilderment than insight, it is nevertheless honestly American in its fundamental benevolence.

What saves this play, or rather what "makes" it, is its infectious humor, its anti-heroism (an oblique form of rebelliousness), its San Francisco colorfulness, its succulent dialogue, its wry hoboism and nonconformity. Though it is of another time, one still reads it with a sense of relief.

No account of the theatre of the thirties can convey any sense of its true nature and its contribution to our culture without emphasizing certain purely theatrical factors which played as decisive a role as the plays themselves.

The Group Theatre in certain respects continued a tradition established by such pioneer organizations as the Provincetown Players, the Theatre Guild, the Neighborhood Playhouse. In another way the Group served as a model for such organizations as the Theatre Union, the Theatre Collective, the Theatre of Action, which were "workers' theatres" with a more specifically political orientation. These were valuable organizations (there are none at present) which commit themselves to definite ideals or policies rather than wallowing in hit-or-miss show-shop opportunism.

Far more important than these special organizations was the Federal Theatre Project (1935-1939). Its rudest critics will not deny the interest of such productions as the "Living Newspaper," *One Third of a nation*, the Negro *Macbeth*, Marlowe's *Dr. Faustus*, T.S. Eliot's *Murder in the Cathedral*, and the attempted production of Marc Blitzstein's momentous musical play, *The Cradle Will Rock*—ultimately presented under different auspices.

The Federal Theatre Project brought much excellent theatre fare to a national public at nominal prices, a public the greater part of which was barely acquainted with any form of "live" theatre. This was the first government-sponsored theatre in our history and it indicated how beneficial such an effort could be, even when circumstances were far from favorable.

Orson Welles was given his first opportunity as a director under the Federal Theatre Project. Because of his success there he was enabled to establish (with John Houseman) the short-lived but animated Mercury Theatre which produced a remarkably provocative *Julius Caesar* in the spirit of the times (1937).

Looking back from the vantage point of 1959 we may say that although admirable work still continues to be done on our constantly harassed and considerably shrunken stage, there are two virtues which may be claimed for the theatre of the thirties conspicuously lacking today. The theatre of the thirties attempted to make the stage an instrument of public enlightenment through a passionate involvement with the national scene. It made valiant and, to a remarkable degree, effective efforts to bring order and discipline into the helter-skelter of our theatre's artistic and financial organization.

An intelligent and successful Broadway producer of today recently said to me, "The theatre at present is twenty times more 'commercial' than it was in the thirties. For one thing, you could reach the hearts and souls of actors, playwrights, designers, etc., with good sense and considerations of sound craftsmanship. Today these people, whatever their personal dispositions, appear encircled by an iron ring forged by agents who protect their clients from all thought beyond income, percentages and publicity."

The lean days and hungry nights of the thirties were a brave time. Aren't we a little torpid now?

—Introduction, *Famous American Plays of the 1930's,* (1959)

THE
SIXTIES

TIME OF VENGEANCE

Ugo Betti's *Time of Vengeance* (York Theatre) is a provocative play. I am not certain of its meaning. This is not necessarily a fault: I have never been entirely certain of what *Hamlet*, *Oedipus Rex*, *Rosmersholm* and a host of other world-famous plays mean. I am not suggesting that *Time of Vengeance* is in a class with any of these, I merely wish to point out that intellectual clarity is not the ultimate virtue in art, that in fact a certain elusiveness is characteristic of many masterpieces.

Time of Vengeance is, to begin with, mysterious in the manner of a detective story. I used to think of Pirandello's puzzles as a kind of mordant mystification in which cold calculation was compounded with hysteria, as if a mad logician had tried to turn a tragedy into a practical joke. But just as I realized after contact with certain Swedish novels, films, paintings that Strindberg's plays were not only an expression of his own strange genius but a manifestation of something in the Swedish character, so I am now beginning to suspect that Ugo Betti writes as he does not because he has been influenced by Pirandello but because they both reflect certain traits indigenous to the South Italian environment.

The reader may have seen a French motion picture called *Le Beau Serge* in which a young man from Paris returns to his native village to visit a former schoolmate whom he remembers as a nice fellow, but who has become ruined by the hate, drink, despair, moral indifference and self-destructive brutality that seem to pervade the whole miserable place. When the boy from Paris tries to remedy some of the more flagrant ills he witnesses, his unhappy friend comments, "But he doesn't really understand." What is not understood is that the village is deeply attached to its disease. It is, so to speak, unified and preserved by its pain as if it were a sacred tradition.

So in *Time of Vengeance* a tiny village calls in a police official from Rome to investigate a petty theft. But the villagers and the mayor who have summoned help also seem to fear and resent the presence of the person who has come in answer to their call. There exists in this village a combination of poverty, jovial loquacity, petty intrigue, duplicity, piety, parochial affability, lubricity and shame: qualities we recognize from many accounts of life in the small towns of Sicily and at the bottom of the Italian boot.

What is going on in Ugo Betti's village? A clerk in the mayor's office has a crippled daughter (the "goose") who craves tenderness but is shunned by everyone because of her deformity. The mayor, moved by pity and lewd desire, deflowers the girl. Her father pretends not to know this, for he commiserates with his daughter's loneliness. Other men in the town—themselves bedeviled by hopelessness or meanness—follow the mayor to the girl's bed. The wretchedly poor clerk profits from the situation; he steals from the girl's complacent "lovers." The appeal to Rome for police intervention is the townsfolk's effort to cleanse themselves of the abscess they have created. Yet they fear any change in their condition: they live through their sin. For despite its degradation it represents pity, passion, the sharing of a common secret and hunger for expiation.

Evil as a means to satisfy a need for good of which the ordinary besmirched mortal does not seem capable is the central theme of the play. It is not a social study—though it has social implications—it is more than a naturalistic report. It has religious implications and it symbolizes far more than its surface story or locale. It is not moralistic; it does not preach. It is a parable and possibly a poem without strict definition. The play penetrates one's conscience and troubles it.

The production is unusually aware. If it does not possess all the authentic color it needs—the homely plausibility that lends so much conviction to the best Italian films—it has at least a sense of what such color is supposed to reveal. The cast is a sensitive one—particularly Lou Gilbert as the clerk, Sy Travers as the mayor and Merriman

Gatch as the victimized girl. The direction by David Metcalf admirably brings out the human significance.

—*NAT,* 2 Jan. '60

THE ANDERSONVILLE TRIAL

Saul Levitt's *The Andersonville Trial* (Henry Miller) provides an absorbing evening in the theatre. It is an account of the case brought in 1865 by the government of the United States against Henry Wirz, a Confederate officer in charge of the prison camp at Andersonville, Georgia, where some 14,000 Union soldiers died because of the hellish treatment to which they were subjected.

Wirz's defense is that he was under strict orders from his superior to enforce inhuman discipline. Lieut. Col. Chipman, the Judge Advocate, or prosecuting counsel, maintains—to the discomfiture of the military men who conduct the trial—that Wirz was morally bound to disobey his commanding officer. Wirz is found guilty and is sentenced to death.

In its stage presentation the case is tried with unusual intensity, intelligence and human interest. What is at stake is the still contemporary issue—as the Nuremberg trials showed—of responsibility in the punishment of men whose brutal acts are governed by state authority.

The audience and certainly a critic ought to hold some firm view in considering such a problem, even when it is raised in the theatre. I am opposed to capital punishment under any circumstances, though I should confess that is has not been easy for me to come to this conclusion. I would not have permitted myself to vote for the death sentence even for Hitler—though I believe he is the only man I have ever in my life truly hated.

For this reason I was inclined to feel, or hope, that what *The Andersonville Trial* was saying represented an echo of my own conviction that the execution of Wirz or any such person in a similar situation is wrong. But the play suffers from ambiguities both in its writing and in its interpretation.

The audience at the end of the play also seemed dissatisfied though not, I believe, for the reasons that troubled me. I suspect that the audience was disturbed by the condemnation of Wirz because it felt that he was an ordinary "Joe," very much like the rest of us, and should not be punished for failing to act as a hero. He was pitied because he appeared doomed no matter what course he took.

The play is not sufficiently clear on the main point: we do not know whether the court pronounced its death sentence on the moral issue—as the Judge Advocate demanded—or simply because it had to respond to public indignation and a desire for vengeance against an unfortunate symbol of the enemy's war "crimes." In other words, the play begs the question it has raised, leaves it in fact distressingly up in the air.

Another factor contributing to confusion is the intention of George C. Scott's performance—otherwise excellent—as the Judge Advocate. Though the author makes it plain that Chipman's loathing of Wirz arises chiefly from the advocate's abhorrence of the institution of slavery as part of the Confederate cause, Scott plays the part with a fanaticism that suggests personal sadism rather than the inspiration of a zealot. It would appear that Chipman hit upon the moral issue, not because he possessed a truly Christian conscience, but because he thought he could devise no surer way of getting Wirz hanged.

The production—aptly designed by Will Armstrong, carefully and incisively directed by José Ferrer—is well cast throughout and very convincingly acted by Herbert Berghof, Albert Dekker, Ian Keith and Russell Hardie. It may be objected that several of the actors—Berghof and Scott particularly—force their souls (or strain their muscles) overmuch.

—*NAT*, 23 Jan. '60

PEER GYNT

To do justice to Ibsen's *Peer Gynt* on the stage requires the resources of a great European state theatre—which also includes a brilliant acting company—and the imaginative inventiveness of a Reinhardt, a Guthrie or a Welles. Without such a rare combination of advantages, producing *Peer Gynt* is like playing Beethoven's *Ninth Symphony* with a bull fiddle, a trumpet, a harmonica, a kazoo and a high school glee club.

Having said this, I must admit to having enjoyed the Phoenix Theatre production of the play. For although I am uncertain of the quality of any of the English translations I have heard (the Phoenix uses Norman Ginsbury's 1946 Old Vic version), and despite the apparent unwieldiness of the play's construction, I find this youthful Ibsen work brilliant and beautiful. It has poetic feeling, humor, satiric verve, vigor, intellectual substance. Written in 1867, its implications are not only modern but still entirely pertinent.

Peer is the average sensual man of the bourgeois society which was reaching its apogee in the middle of the nineteenth century. He is a vital individualist of voracious appetite and energy: calculating and eager to amass everything—wealth, women, position, honors. Being the heir of an older society in which the old Adam was tempered by religious faith, Peer still retains enough vestiges of morality to misquote the Bible, of which he has a spotty recollection, at every turn. God too, he is sure, is on his side. Severed from the body of a coherent community, he believes himself unique. "Free," his powers seem to him limitless.

Peer achieves the rewards of his gifts. He seduces women, begets bastards, is loved by a pure girl, traffics in the slave trade, cheats, is cheated only to be favored by miraculous windfalls, makes and loses fortunes and sees the world—a full and adventurous life. He succeeds in his ambition, which is to be himself. What he doesn't realize is

that in his splendidly tempestuous career he has compromised at every point and defaulted before every obstacle which has stood in the way of his presumed fulfillment. Unfettered, he is unwittingly an absurd conformist. He is swindled where he imagines he has triumphed, and in most instances he has behaved either as a monkey or a lunatic. He has served no one, his life has been empty of any enduring value and he dies with no saving grace except in the lingering love of the girl he has deserted. *Peer Gynt* is a prophetic legend of contemporary society.

Needless to say, the Phoenix is ill equipped to deal with the overwhelming challenge of such a play. It would be wholly unfair therefore to dwell on the various shortcomings of its production. I prefer to credit director Stuart Vaughan and his company for understanding the point of every scene so that the play somehow emerges. Since it is a masterpiece, it offers more than many a lesser play which is staged with far greater skill and assurance.

—NAT, 30 Jan. '60

KRAPP'S LAST TAPE
THE ZOO STORY

Samuel Beckett's *Krapp's Last Tape* and Edward Albee's *The Zoo Story* (Provincetown Playhouse) have this in common: both are studies in loneliness. Beckett's play is a sort of marginal sketch in the body of his more ambitious work; Albee's play is the introduction to what could prove to be an important talent on the American stage.

Some may consider it ironic that, whereas Beckett's far more accomplished plays—*Waiting for Godot* and *Endgame*—were generally received here with skepticism, indifference or hostility, this new rather slight piece has been greeted with considerable sympathy. One reason for this is that Beckett's reputation and the respect shown him by many European and several American critics have grown. It is no longer easy to shrug him off. A more immediate reason for the cordiality toward *Krapp's Last Tape* is that a thread of sentimentality runs through its dismal fabric. The play's "story," moreover, is simple, realistic, unelusive.

A solitary old man sits in abject poverty doing nothing but feed himself with bananas that are hoarded in drawers like precious possessions; periodically he washes the fruit down with deep draughts of alcohol. This old man was once an author. He has among the few miserable relics of his past some copies of a book he wrote, a book which sold eighteen copies at the trade rate. "Getting popular!" he mutters.

In the half light the old man listens to tapes upon which he once recorded events now long past. One of these tapes is a memory of love—set down when he was thirty-nine—an apparently sincere love which for some unexplained cause never resolved itself into anything beyond its fugitive existence. The old man, absorbed and yet impatient with himself, listens to the tape, curses and mocks himself—we are not certain why—broods, possibly regrets, suppresses a sob and subsides into what is probably an endless silence.

The atmosphere of the play is grotesque, deeply bitter and yet tender. Beckett is here with something of his sardonic mutism, his mastery of concentrated dramatic image, the determination to wring the neck of his passion. The play is well acted by a young newcomer from Canada, Donald Davis.

The Zoo Story is flawed by improbabilities and perhaps needless notes to provoke shock or outrage—comic and horrifying by turn. Yet the play gives ample evidence of genuine feeling and an intimate knowledge of certain aspects of the contemporary scene, especially of our metropolitan area. If there were not some danger of being taken too superficially, I should say that in *The Zoo Story* certain tragic and crucial factors which have contributed to produce the "beat" generation have been brilliantly dramatized.

The young man in *The Zoo Story*, who intrudes on a respectable and modest citizen sitting on a Central Park bench, is isolated in his poverty, his self-educated ignorance, his lack of background or roots, his total estrangement from society. He has no connection with anybody, but he seeks it—in vain. When he succeeds in approaching an animal or a person, it is always through a barrier of mistrust and in a tension of disgust, fear, despair. When he breaks out of the emotional insulation of his life, it is only by a violent intrusion into the complacent quiet of the mediocre citizen on the park bench; and that unoffending bystander is then forced into effecting the mad young man's suicide. To put it another way: the derelict finally achieves a consummation of connection only through death at the unwitting and horrified hands of society's "average" representative.

This story is conveyed with rude humor—very New York—a kind of squalid eloquence and a keen intuition of the humanity in people who live among us in unnoticed or shunned wretchedness. We come not only to know the pathetic and arresting central figure as well as the astonished stranger he "victimizes," but through them both we also meet the unseen but still vivid characters of a lady janitor, a Negro homosexual neighbor, a dog and other denizens in the vicinity of both the West and East Seventies of Manhattan.

The Zoo Story interested me more than any other new American play thus far this season. I hope its author has the stuff to cope with the various impediments that usually face our promising dramatists.

The play is perfectly cast. George Maharis and William Daniels give admirable performances. Maharis, as the play's interlocutor, is truthful as well as intense. His acting is both economical and gripping. He seems possessed by all the hurts, resentment and compressed hysteria of the bewildered youth we hear so much about, but who is rarely made this real in newspaper reports, editorials, sermons or fictions.

—*NAT*, 13 Feb. '60

THE DEADLY GAME

There are certain things wrong with *The Deadly Game*, a play by James Yaffe based on a novel by Friedrich Dürrenmatt (Longacre Theatre), but it is none the less a better than average Broadway show. These are loose terms: what I mean is that the play is not boring; that, in fact, as a melodrama it offers a touch of excitement and that it piques the mind a little. In its own terms it lacks style both in writing and in production, and the central offstage incident is rather banal. If, however, I feel impelled to dwell on the play longer than I usually would, it is because it provoked ancillary thoughts—which is perhaps also to be counted to the play's credit. The theme is the guilt man feels today in our society. The moral, as the inculpated man screams in this play, is that there is no justice, only law. He is an American salesman who arrives by chance at a house in the Swiss Alps where a retired judge amuses his companions—themselves former jurists—by playing a game of mock trials challenging either legendary "defendants" (Judas Iscariot, St. Joan) or substantial ones when, as in this case, they find somebody willing to lend himself to the fun. The American believes himself wholly innocent of anything worse than infringing traffic laws or the peccadillo of adultery. He nonchalantly agrees to pass time as the "accused" in the old men's peculiar sport.

Very rapidly the prosecuting attorney proves that the salesman induced a fatal heart attack on his superior at the office so that he might take over the dead man's coveted job. Through greedy ambitiousness the salesman is a semi-conscious murderer—though the very notion fills him with horror. He runs from the "trial" in terror, for he (and the audience) are not sure whether the people who tried him are madmen who actually mean to carry out the death sentence they pronounce.

The production is so flatly realistic (except for Claude Dauphin's slightly caricatured but delight-fully humorous defense attorney and Wolfgang Roth's setting, which is in itself a handsomely designed room) that no relevant atmosphere is created. If there is a nerve-tingling ambiguity in the play, the production should convey it, but that it fails to do. Even so, the play itself ought to disturb us, in the way that Graham Greene's entertainments occasionally disturb. Its failure to be more upsetting is the weakness that intrigues me.

The play's material, though superficially unusual, is basically stock. And though it is true that religion, psychoanalysis and latter-day sociology all emphasize the element of guilt in man as one of the prime motives in his behavior, one resists the idea when it is presented in terms that are not in themselves concretely, personally felt.

Differing in origin according to place and generation, the theme of man's sense of guilt exists in Hawthorne, Dostoyevsky, Kafka—to mention only a few. Camus' *The Fall*, though dull as narrative, exerts a strong grip on many of us because it is a naked statement of this sentiment in contemporary middle-class vocabulary. A whole dramatic literature on the same theme has been developed in France since the war. But while most of these writers are truly imbued and oppressed with the feeling they dramatize, others employ it as a device.

The point is particularly worth making because it involves not only drama and art in general, but the whole pattern of our thinking today. At one time we were ashamed of wrongdoing, then we began to confess that our sins were signs of illness—"we are sick," we said—then we began to exonerate ourselves either on the grounds of social pressure or on the fact of psychological traumas suffered in childhood, and finally we have come almost to boast of our delinquencies—either because we say they are universal or on the assumption that our boldness in proclaiming them is a sign of extraordinary moral courage. It has come to pass that in many French plays and movies, for example, the hero has to be a scoundrel lest we mistake him for a hypocrite.

Dürrenmatt's earlier play, *The Visit*, was telling because the author found several striking theatrical images for the corruption he condemns in society. But even in that play one detects a certain facility, an artful glibness, as if its "tragic farcicality" caused no real anguish in its author or in anyone else. Universal guilt is the latest commonplace to which we give automatic consent for the purpose of high-grade discussion and advanced "art forms."

One can lie as much with "strong" drama as with the frivolous; pessimism can be as hollow as commercial optimism. In a play, as in any other work of presumed art, authentic statement is not achieved merely by just conclusions, but by the degree of genuine experience we sense in each moment or detail of the author's expression. The ends are embodied in the means; the immediate action is the clue to the eventual meaning.

—*NAT*, 27 Feb. '60

CALIGULA

Albert Camus' *Caligula* (54th Street Theatre) is replete with atrocities and a profoundly moral play. For Camus was above all a moralist. This does not mean that his play is without dramatic power. But like most parables its interest inheres in its ideological content rather more than in its surface story. That is one reason why the play, for all its record of vice and crime, does not deeply shock or move us. We know that its savagery—though historical—is only symbolic.

Written in 1938—when Camus was twenty-five—*Caligula* reflects a sensitive man who came of age in an epoch of concentration camps and civic nihilism. More important than this is the atmosphere of despair at a time when intelligent and educated people had begun to question all traditional values—when, as I once heard Camus express it, "music had lost melody, painting form, poetry rhyme and meter, thought conviction,

history sense and religion God." Nothing seemed left but a bleak emptiness in which everything is possible because everything is permitted. Expression in this wasteland without limits could become only violent or mad. Fierce and bloody action itself appeared to cause no human repercussion.

The young men of France felt themselves spent. When war broke out in 1939 and France collapsed, shaming itself not alone by defeat but by the behavior of so many of its most respected citizens, there seemed nothing left to do but abandon oneself to the filthy tide or rebel. Many of those who rebelled (like Camus) did so not in the name of their country alone nor in the name of any certified value—for they were skeptical of all explicit values—but from a sense of the spirit within them, a spirit we might call the remnant of human feeling which miraculously (or mystically) rejects the brutal disorder that nature and society perennially foster.

Caligula attempts through an inverted idealism to attain freedom by imitating the anarchic ferocity of life and destroying all that he and the world had hitherto regarded as sacrosanct or proper. He becomes a logical killer by pursuing the illogic of nature and society—archkillers themselves. The end of such action is a secretly desired suicide; for a man cannot deny life without eliminating his own. One cannot destroy others without creating an aloneness more terrible than death. No individual can sever his connection with his fellows; who says connection inevitably says love—no matter how the word may be distorted.

In reviewing Stuart Gilbert's translation of Camus' plays last year (Justin O'Brien's translation for the stage is much better) I wrote that they were important rather than good. I meant that while Camus' plays—to me *Caligula* is the most interesting—are the emblem of a generation and a clue to much that has been thought, written, painted and happened not only in France since the war but to some extent almost everywhere in the West, they are not completely realized works. The writing—while distinguished—does not achieve the white heat or specific imagery of poetry; the characters and scenes attain only a general or moralistic definition.

Camus himself seems to have sensed this, for he acknowledged the play's shortcomings and spoke of *Caligula* as an actor's and director's play. To this and to all I have already said I should add that, for all its flaws, I found that the play merited and got my absorbed attention: that it is in short a superior piece with trenchant passages throughout. The production—simple to the point of emaciation in Paris 1945, where it was a tremendous success with Gérard Philipe—here leans to the spectacular.

I have been told that Camus advised Sidney Lumet, who directed the play, to eschew the obligatory austerity of its original production. Perhaps Camus thought our audiences might find a stark presentation forbidding. But I am not at all sure that there is not some other style for the play which would be neither bare in the manner of an impoverished Paris nor costly in keeping with our prosperity. I am sure that Broadway with its high prices—behind and in front of the curtain—does not provide the most favorable conditions for the mounting of such a play.

Sidney Lumet's direction is intelligent, faithful and sometimes ingenious. Yet all the details of the production struck me as being somehow irrelevant. One cannot help being "held" by the lighting, the set, costumes, etc., but I could not really like them because in some peculiar way they all seemed foreign to the author's idiom. They are too elaborately decorative to suggest classic restraint, too mechanistically modern to be inconspicuously beautiful. Kenneth Haigh's Caligula is creditably, even impressively sincere, and accomplished to a degree. It lacks only the astringency of intellectual anguish and tragic dimension. In the role of a humanist Philip Bourneuf's straightforward intention and diction reach the mind.

—*NAT*, 5 Mar. '60

THE CRADLE WILL ROCK
THE SERVANT OF TWO MASTERS
A THURBER CARNIVAL

If you were thirty and inclined toward radicalism in the days of the Federal Theatre Project, you are likely to call Marc Blitzstein's *The Cradle Will Rock* (recently revived by the New York City Opera) "dated." If in the meantime your radicalism has been transformed into that form of retirement that passes as aestheticism, you are prone to speak of the American piece as an inferior *Threepenny Opera*.

If however you are thirty today—or if the good old rebel time of which *The Cradle Will Rock* was a landmark passed by without your noticing it as anything more special than a period of bad business—you will probably enjoy the Blitzstein opera as a good show with a quality all its own.

The subject matter and plot of *The Cradle*—though crudely cartoonlike—is no more dated than the libretto of *La Bohème*. One is sentimental about "workers," the other about "artists." The charm of neither is specifically related to its surface story. And while it is true that without Brecht and Weill there would never have been a *Cradle*, Blitzstein has given the *Cradle* its very particular quality.

What it typifies is a certain permanent American big-city young-man cockiness, a derisive unwillingness to take any guff—political, social or casual—from anybody. It's the boy in the candy store, the man at the bar, the alert laborer refusing to be hoaxed by any pretension. It is the poor man's perpetual Bronx cheer against complacency that we hear on any city street not yet razed by traffic or the police. The music alternates between a note of vulgar guying and sweet, heart-broken yearning. Blitzstein is less sophisticated than his German models; more acid in anger, more tearful in hurt.

The new production—staged by Howard da Silva with sets by David Hays—is excellent in every respect, though Blitzstein's orchestration—otherwise very effective—seemed too meager at the end to be as rousing as intended. If this opera is retained in the repertory of the New York City Opera, don't let the snobs or the fearful prevent you from seeing it.

The City Center was recently the scene of a perfect theatre event: the presentation by the Piccolo Teatro di Milano of Goldoni's eighteenth-century farce *The Servant of Two Masters*. This production is to tour a number of large cities and if it comes to a town within your compass, don't miss it.

The foreign language should not put you off. The production—including the dialogue—is all action. The players' very volubility is explosively and hilariously theatric, the sense of movement ceaselessly exhilarating. There is a visual histrionic joke (or sight gag) every minute. The precision of each trick or invention sparkles with the freshness of something improvised. The company is one of the finest theatre ensembles anywhere in the world. Such companies are usually associated with "heavy" drama. You will be glad to learn that *The Servant of Two Masters* is all exuberance.

I am a coward: I hate to admit that *A Thurber Carnival* (ANTA Theatre) did not delight me. I was about to write a "rave" review of it saying that I am probably the only person in New York who didn't care for it. Or to evade the issue by saying something cryptic like, "the show is simplicity itself."

Such critical orneriness (or obtuseness) must be explained. Let it be said immediately that this series of Thurber sketches boasts two pretty girls and several admirably cast comedians—Tom Ewell, Paul Ford, Peggy Cass, John McIver—and that the scenery which uses Thurber's now classic (and very individual) drawings is cleverly devised. I laughed too—though not nearly as much as most of the audience.

But I was not happy. There is something arid in this humor. I feel as if I were looking at a caricature of a latter-day *Winesburg, Ohio*, in which every creature was turned into a goon without charm. The world here is dehydrated, deflated, humanly emaciated. There is no trace of affection, joy, even good fellowship. The point of view is so disabused and disengaged as to appear nihilistic. Perhaps we should call it scarecrow comedy. Satire is undoubtedly implicit. But it strikes me as macabre. I am more horrified than amused by it.

—*NAT*, 12 Mar. '60

TOYS IN THE ATTIC

Lillian Hellman's new play *Toys in the Attic* (Hudson) adumbrates a number of themes. There is first the theme of the havoc that a sudden access of money may cause in the lives of those who have always dreamed of money but never got any. When the ne'er-do-well Julian Berniers comes home to New Orleans, his two doting and indigent sisters are thunder-struck by the gifts he pours on them with a triumphant cry that he has become rich. The gifts are showy clothes for which they have no taste—and disproportionate to what they desire.

This leads to the second theme. The sisters have always spoken of a trip to Europe and the eventual purchase of the old house in which they have lived for many years. But these benefits represent fancies, not appetites. What the sisters need—especially the younger one who is incestuously attached to her brother—is the feeling that he depends on them. This theme is related to the one more fully (and convincingly) stated in Miss Hellman's *The Autumn Garden*: one's destiny is fashioned by what one does, and the dream of a goal other than that toward which one's habitual acts lead is mere self-deception. The sisters are upset by their brother's sudden affluence because it threatens to make him independent of them. Their hankering for Europe and the ownership of the house are toys in the attic—playthings that are useful only as psychological ornament.

Then again the play suggests that some people cannot use money. It is not a reality to them; it is the mirage of their suppressed yearnings. Their actual mode of living precludes them from employing money rationally as an instrument to attain ends for which their behavior has prepared them. There are still other strands of meaning in the play: persons denied love grow batty; children whose parents were prevented from giving them love become warped. Others whose need for love is frustrated are rendered demoniacally possessive.

All this is interesting and valid. But the actual conduct of the play's narrative jumbles and confuses the various themes. The play is congested by irrelevantly melodramatic turns of plot implausibilities and jabs of lurid violence. What begins as a fascinating revelation of humble characters in a modest environment turns into a series of hysterical spasms too diverse in motivation wholly to satisfy our aesthetic, or to persuade our moral sensibilities.

The play is signally well written with that combination of selective realism and subtly rhetorical phrasing which gives Miss Hellman's dialogue a distinction approaching nobility. One's attention is held for at least two acts, but the third act, with its exasperating burst of fireworks, creates the perhaps erroneous impression that we have been craftily deceived.

An admirable cast—Jason Robards, Jr., Anne Revere, Maureen Stapleton, Irene Worth—plays with point and precision. Yet I was gnawed by a suspicion that if the direction had been just a little less tightly tidy, if there had been a shade more naturalness or ease of breath, the play might have seemed more truthful.

—*NAT*, 19 Mar. '60

THE BALCONY

In Friedrich Dürrenmatt's brilliantly synthetic play *The Visit* (City Center) the lady who is its prime mover says "The world made a whore of me, so I am turning the world into a brothel."

Jean Genet's brothel in *The Balcony* (Circle-in-the-Square) is a house of mirrors, a temple of illusion, one might say art itself, where things are truer than life. In this brothel—where there is more obscenity than sex—acts turn in on themselves (as in art) and thus achieve a certain purity. They have no practical consequence. What the brothel does is give men a presentiment of their dreams in their essential meaning. The patron who impersonates a bishop realizes and enjoys the cruelty which is at the root of his absolution, the "judge" his kinship with the criminal, the "general" his taste for command.

The ambitious of the world also aspire toward the glorification or perfection of image which is the service the brothel performs. The workers of the world are in revolt. The brothel alone seems protected. The revolution is drowned in blood. When its leader comes to the brothel it is to become the glorified simulacrum of his captors and rulers—and he castrates himself in doing so. The dictator (the chief of police) becomes the new Hero—dominating even legitimate royalty and the lords of religion, justice, war. This Hero—vulgarian without accredited lineage—who has always yearned to become a great figure in the brothel's galaxy—need no longer do the work which has raised him to power. Having established himself and dug the people's faces in the mud with their orgiastic consent, he will now rule by his legend alone—the aura of grandeur which the art-institution of the brothel has given him. Some people still remember their moment of revolt, secretly murmuring "the rebellion was wonderful"—so that despite their defeat they may some day rise again.

Is this confused? Not very. Genet's construction is nightmarish, perverse and chaotic as are the creations of our fantasies, but like them it has its own illuminating vividness, its lurid clarity and a language—as intensely solid as a classic—which gives the play a substance that cuts through the darkness. Since Genet has lived his nightmare and has withal a certain artistic grip on it, he is genuine poet, whereas Dürrenmatt who is only terribly clever is not.

The Visit is clearer—an anti-capitalist parable without real commitment because it is without real identification—a work of shrewd manipulation of materials other writers have originated. *The Balcony* has its obscurities—no explanatory gloss will elucidate its every metaphorical twist—but in this it resembles every true work of art; true art always retains a certain elusiveness because the emanations of the artist's unconscious project beyond the control of his will.

All this does not mean either that I "agree" with Genet or that I consider him a great dramatist. It means that I recognize that he exists in a creative sphere which the more practicable Dürrenmatt does not enter. I suspect that Genet belongs to a category of artists who, while marginal to the mainstream of major work (that which possesses great duration and broad applicability), retain a certain symbolic significance for their time. Such artists act as a ferment, giving rise to what may be described as a salutary disease—through which we recognize what is happening in and troubling the epoch. These artists do not reveal the world as it is or we as we truly are: they isolate and bring into view the symptoms which threaten us. They are portents and protests. Hence their value—for in art everything must be said, everyone must be heard. To feel and understand what is ailing us is more curative than the balm of the bland entertainers or the engaged propagandists.

France has produced more such artists perhaps than any other modern nation. De Sade, Huysmans, Lautréamont, Jarry, Laforgue, Artaud, maybe even Rimbaud, not to mention certain other of our contemporaries in Paris novelists, playwrights, poets, painters—belong to this special artistic manifestation. America is too young for important artists of this sort to emerge. When they appear here they usually seem imitative or phony—bad boys aping mythical monsters. It is true that we are beginning to be so infected, but the circumstances which make a Genet authentic are still a bit remote. So *The Balcony* is mostly an oddity with us, a sideshow novelty.

If José Quintero's production is far from being an organic embodiment of the play, one must at least credit it with earnestness of effort in a supremely difficult task. Resources beyond the capacity of any American management are required. (I have heard that there have been some excellent productions in Germany.) The present production is distinctly superior to the one I saw in London in 1957. Nancy Marchand here plays with authority and intelligence. Salomé Jens is attractive with the ambiguous glow needed for the occasion, and David Hays as designer is appropriately inventive within the limited means available. The cast as a whole plays arduously. But one regrets the opportunity missed to make the production as hauntingly alluring and gravely demoniac as it might be.

In the meantime on Broadway Frank Loesser with *Greenwillow* (Alvin Theatre) offers some pleasant tunes, nice sets, cute choreography and an agreeable cast (Anthony Perkins, Cecil Kellaway) in the kind of pseudo-idyllic Americana to which I fear I am congenitally allergic.

—*NAT*, 26 Mar. '60

BYE BYE BIRDIE

Iam sorry but *Bye, Bye Birdie* by Michael Stewart, Charles Strouse and Lee Adams (Martin Beck), the new musical fun show at which I had a good time, made me think of grave matters.

My pleasure and my sobriety are both rather paradoxical, for when I began to detail the items which had pleased me, I found myself depreciating the show's attributes. There were no voices, I thought. The music, though interestingly orchestrated, did not strike me as ingratiating. The choreography, though animated—and in the instance of the Shriner's Ballet delightfully surprising—was not unusually distinguished. The leading lady, Chita Rivera, hardly beautiful, dances very well but sings only passably; and the leading man, Dick Van Dyke, can't sing at all, though he has an engaging personality and moves with an odd precision which conveys a winning archness.

The plot doesn't altogether cohere and much of the show appears improvised; it is a revue in disguise. But if one were to insist on such negatives the point and value of this entertainment would be lamentably missed. Somehow these negatives compose into a special sort of crazy-quilt spectacle (it reminds me of the blocks on West 52 Street where the theatres housing *Greenwillow* and the *Thurber Carnival*, the fancy honky-tonk Dance City, and an Amusement Center offering a shooting gallery, objects for obscene practical jokes and self-photographing appliances, are all conveniently at hand) that adds up to a positive and peculiarly American quality and dissipates many of our critical demurs. The daily press as a whole described the show as "fresh"—which may be the right word; I think of it as phenomenal.

The "phenomenon" is the satiric vein which at times is so markedly accurate that it becomes painful. At one moment I whispered to my guest, "This is so terribly funny that I feel like crying." What ostensibly is being satirized in *Bye, Bye Birdie* is the teen-agers' craze for the Elvis Presley type of crooner. But the satire extends beyond that: it is a satire on our mass culture, on our all-pervading conformism, our mechanically stratified, almost fossilized infantilism, our public delinquency.

"Satire" is perhaps too specific. Ring Lardner, Thurber and a host of minor American humorists may be thought of as satirists—though their work does not always stand sufficiently apart from the objects of their scorn—but a show like *Bye, Bye Birdie* manifests an energetic innocence which appears quite unaware that its pranks are knocking the hell out of everything in and around us—that if the game were carried far enough the result might destroy us.

This point is best exemplified when the "typical" small-town papa rebels against his house being taken over by the crooner, his manager and the crazy kids who swarm around them. The outraged man is about to throw the intruders off the premises when he is told that he and his family are to be televised on the Ed Sullivan show. This breaks his morale. Consumed in glory, he turns to

jelly. He, his family and the entire community (of Sweet Apple, Ohio) join in a choral hymn—a Missa Solemnis, a Bach Passion—in praise of the grandeur that is Ed Sullivan.

The audience thinks this very funny, which it certainly is; but one doesn't doubt for a second that it also feels about the great television exhibits—Sullivan's or Paar's or any other of a similar category—very much as do the communicants on the stages. Where then is the satire?

Evil or disquieting thoughts broke through to my consciousness, as it may to that of some others. We begin to feel that our countrymen take nothing seriously except financial panic or, more pointedly, the loss of status which would deny them the privilege of remaining comfortably in the swim of a world encompassed and made safe by the benefits that television sells. Such a world is either the peak of our civilization—the goal of all our striving—or the doom. We all know it, laugh over it, fight it, and sometimes turn the occasional nightmare it causes our still sentient souls into such a brightly talented, frightfully ingenious and still youthfully attractive, colorfully frivolous, adulterated expression as *Bye, Bye Birdie*.

The show's theatrical effectiveness is due in large part to the direction of Gower Champion, who also invented the dance routines which compose only one aspect of the evening's ebullience. He is aided by a bunch of remarkable teenagers—one of the most pleasing being the actor, Michael Pollard, who does not however sing and dance as do the others.

—*NAT*, 30 Apr. '60

DUEL OF ANGELS

Jean Giraudoux's *Duel of Angels*, beautifully translated by Christopher Fry, has been given a handsome production (Helen Hayes Theatre) under the skillful guidance of the English dancer-choreographer-actor-director Robert Helpmann.

Vivien Leigh, looking altogether lovely in superb gowns by Christian Dior, speaks admirably in a voice that is both caressing and provocative; she has probably never acted better. Mary Ure is a bit overbleached for my taste, but she also fills the eye with grace.

The text itself—it is Giraudoux's swan song and was first produced posthumously in Paris—has always struck me as somewhat ambiguous. Therefore, though it is certainly one of the superior offerings of the season, I feel slightly ambivalent about it.

The play is another of Giraudoux's paradoxical variations on a classic theme—in this case the legend of Lucretia—and deals, as does so much of his work, with the subject of purity. What is meant by purity in this instance is sexual purity (in *Ondine* and *The Enchanted* the purity is of another kind). One might say that purity here has its most popular Gallic connotation: conjugal purity and its converse, adultery. At the end of the play, with the suicide of Lucile ("Lucretia"), a procuress says something to the effect that purity cannot live in this world, a conclusion which Giraudoux has dramatized before.

What troubles one is that Lucile is made to seem—apart from her beauty—a thoroughly bigoted figure, certainly not appealing. Paola who represents the sophisticated rationalization of the worldly Frenchwoman (the play is set in the South of France in the mid-nineteenth century) makes Lucile appear almost ridiculous, though at the sight of Lucile's dead body Paola is nonplused and admits that Lucile may have been right. We wonder whether Giraudoux meant us to feel that absolute purity must seem either absurd or hypocritical to the normal mentality—as idealism always strikes us in everyday life—because it is so rare as to be out of place in this world. One is not altogether sure where Giraudoux stands. Does he wish to infer that purity by its uniqueness is something of a threat to us and in its own way wrong, even "bad"?

On further reflection, I hardly think this interpretation, though admissible, is what Giraudoux intended. And here a subtle point of theatrical treatment comes into play, one also involving national character. For I am fairly certain that, though the French are usually considered more tolerant than the English or the Americans in regard to marital infidelity, the French audience did not laugh at Lucile as the American, or at any rate the Broadway, audience does. I believe the Parisians must have taken Lucile at her face value as an inspired person (if only symbolically so) whose example of sexual highmindedness was a kind of poetic reproof of their looseness. One is a sinner only if one believes in sin, and the most frivolous French audience is sufficiently penetrated by its cultural-religious tradition to believe in sin. We, on the other hand, are free without foundation; we are not sure of anything either in our orthodoxy or in our emancipation. As a result we laugh at Lucile, whom we take to be a nuisance, and side with Paola, who is shrewd, perceptive and above all gay and amusing.

In this half-spoken and semi-revealed conflict of attitudes, our audience regards *Duel of Angels* as essentially comic, in which case it is very nearly an immoral or a misanthropic play. (Incidentally, Lucile's husband is shown to be a conventional prig, morally entirely inferior to his wife.) But I suspect that for all the play's wit and polished detachment, Giraudoux meant it to have a tragic emphasis: he is *for Lucile*. (The play's original title is *Pour Lucrèce*.)

A striking example of the contradiction between the text and the audience's reaction to it is the last scene, in which the procuress despoils Lucile's corpse of its treasures—the triumph of evil as it were; clearly not a comic moment. But the first-night audience laughed at it, not only because the curtain speech was read with an ineffectual lightness, but because the interpretation of the play as a whole had led the audience to believe that this too was to be taken as a keen joke.

What I think happened is this: the play is difficult because the part of Lucile is not written as consummately as that of Paola. (Also the leading lady—Vivien Leigh—plays Paola opposite a much less vivid actress.) Then the interpreters—the director and the others—like their audience are not impressed by Lucile's (and probably Giraudoux's) moral position. Finally, since the play is so elaborate and elegant in language as to need a special style of presentation to make its particular manner conform with our ordinary demands for "realism," a directorial compromise was effected by placing the emphasis on good looks, suave decorum, salon flair, comedic airiness, a ballet-like picturesqueness in the manner of Constantin Guy's drawings—and a minimum of feeling. The result is civilized, smart, fashionably glacial and—thinking of Giraudoux—perhaps false.

—*NAT*, 7 May '60

A COUNTRY SCANDAL

At the age of twenty-one Chekhov was already blessed with the gifts of observation and understanding that made him one of the masters of late nineteenth-century literature. *A Country Scandal* (Greenwich Mews Theatre), his first play, is endowed with the signs of his genius. It has never before been professionally produced in this country.

Cruder in craftsmanship than his later work—Chekhov's talent grew in subtlety and depth with every play he wrote—less delicate in touch and verbal statement, *A Country Scandal* is none the less a brilliant achievement. The strokes of portraiture are more emphatic, more highly colored with the youthful tendency to exaggerate and overstress, but they are all strokes of the keenest perception.

This is comedy full of hurt, a pathetic work which at times is as hilarious as a French farce. The young man who wrote it understood that the everyday muddle of ordinary folk was a tragedy to those who feel and terribly funny to those who think. Although it reflects perfectly the Russian quality of the scene it describes—reflects too the particular historical moment in which the story unfolds: the eighties of the last century—the play

is universal and its people are more real, more vivid and more intimately known to us than are our neighbors. In fact they are us.

They are a feckless lot. Chekhov makes us laugh at them; yet they are never altogether contemptible. Trivial, they somehow remain worthy. That is why Chekhov's realism is not petty nor what one might call "statistical." He sees that all these people are composed of the honorable traits and needs of more exalted folk. What gives them their aspect of caricature is their lack of purpose: they live in a world without horizon of direction. They move in feverish spasms like members truncated from a body.

As the play progresses we can scarcely fail to notice how much these "benighted" Russians resemble our contemporaries—particularly those who appear most "modern" and sophisticated. There is however this difference of approach: if one of our American realists were to present them, these people would be made to seem abnormal or, much worse, too flat and thin in human texture to touch us, to be poignantly relevant.

The central figure is Platonov, a young school teacher, good looking, idealistic but with no specific ideal to aim at, intelligent but lacking any definite problem with which to grapple. He is moderately sensual and, being aimless, he is intrinsically passive. Attractive to women who live in the same airless environment, he becomes a victim of their yearning; to other men, however, he seems the ravaging pursuer of the female sex. This parochial Don Juan is a lover who experiences little pleasure and whose every adventure renders him more abject—flotsam on a stagnant sea.

Around him are rich landowners with nothing to buy—except women who do not desire them. They are men who seek release in drink or in the fleshpots of Paris (they are ashamed to sin at home), blue-stocking girls who are housewives at heart, married women rendered hysterical by the inanity of their nincompoop husbands, aggressive women who can find no partner or prey equal to them in forthrightness or force. The rich Jew is scorned because he is a tradesman, the aristocrat is spineless, the peasant is brutal and baffled, the doctor, a drunk uninspired by his profession, and the good are simple-minded and utterly lost in a society they cannot comprehend or change.

All this, I repeat, is communicated in heartbreak which is not sentimental, with a sense of the ridiculous which is not patronizing. Chekhov was a fine artist, a beautiful spirit and truly modest.

It is significant that so admirable a play—which by the way offers many first-rate acting opportunities—should be done on the American stage in an off-Broadway production. And it is no criticism of the performance we see now to say that it does not encompass the play's full scope. For it is a very knowing production. The actors are generally well cast; Ammon Kabatchnik's direction, which points up the comedy, is firm and aware; the sets by Richard Bianchi are remarkably apt in relation to the circumstances of playhouse, company and resources.

—*NAT*, 21 May '60

LONDON, PARIS, NEW YORK

The London and Parisian theatres at this moment are healthier than ours. It is pointless to set down the titles and number of our best productions alongside those of London and Paris; the condition of a theatre is not to be measured in such terms. What must be taken into account are the position and function of the theatre in a particular society: the theatre's relation to its audience in respect to demand, sentiment, economic situation.

The French theatre at its best continues a tradition of maturity in writing—often novel in tone and manner—coupled with themes of a certain weight. Even the plays of the apparently anarchistic Jean Genet have potent social implications. His most recent *The Blacks* deals with the tension between white and colored people in a manner that is at least as germane to us as to the French, though its reverberations extend far beyond the reach of civil-rights platforms and liberal legislation.

By comparison, the English plays of similar ambition may be regarded as the work of beginners—often imitative and uncertain—though the English accent justifies them, at least for their own audiences. They also help us understand how the malaise common to the entire Western world expresses itself in one particular segment of it.

What emerges from the new drama in England as well as in France is a desperate cry for help. The stress is different in each country. A character in Sartre's *The Prisoner of Altona* says: "The liquidation of the human species was decided upon in high places. The specific facts and causes don't matter. The main point is that we have a taste for destruction." Speaking of a war criminal, another character says: "He cried to God 'I do not want to do what I am doing,' but he did it." In a word, Sartre says that we are frauds. We refuse to do away with the causes of the guilts that torment us, and linger in willful inertia protected by our temporary prosperity. Aware of our moribund condition, we retreat from historical necessity—that is to say conscious responsibility—which leads to what might be called social incest. Ostensibly about Germany (though some say it alludes to the French in Algeria) Sartre's play challenges all of us. Genet, much less clearly a moralist than Sartre, nevertheless makes his plays resound with corresponding echoes.

The English suffer their anguish more locally. One source of distress is their feeling that they are still constricted by their patient manners, their lack of expressiveness in matters of the heart, that peculiar mutism which is perhaps a vestige of the days of the powerful British Empire. The English dramatist now appears to demand loud denunciation of what may still be remedied, together with outlets for inner turmoil whose alleviation is not readily available because the malady has not been defined.

In this respect there is a division in English about the theatre. It is evident in Kenneth Tynan's resistance to Ionesco as contrasted with his enthusiasm for Brecht. I too am a Brecht "partisan," but let us reflect on this a moment. Ionesco's

Rhinoceros is an outcry against conformism and the dehumanization of the person in our mechanized society. This takes a subjective and romantic form which, beside being bewildered, seems practically impotent. What may be worse, Ionesco often suggests that the process of dehumanization is intrinsic to the human condition. Brecht believes in human intelligence and its capacity to act on behalf of a better life.

What should not be overlooked, however, is that both dramatists represent responses to kindred aches. Western man—to speak only of him—feels himself oppressed and ailing. No artistic (or political) utterance today can be pertinent if it fails to recognize this. Therefore "decadent" writers, insofar as they voice truly experienced reactions to the endemic disease, are being socially creative (or useful) even when their expressions of horror or rage point to no such clear conclusions as are contained in the classic statements of a Brecht.

—*NAT*, 20 Aug. '60

THE ICE CAPADES
MARCEL MARCEAU
H.M.S. PINAFORE

The 1960-61 season begins trippingly. *The Ice Capades* (Madison Square Garden) is no mere athletic event: it is a form of theatre. In it we find not only prowess manifested in grace, but a feeling for the dance. The best skaters make us forget the instrument that serves them: we think only of the line and pattern their bodies trace. The skaters seem to take pride and pleasure in their performance, as if they were as much "carried away" as they hope the audience will be. They slide, glide and coil with a certain aerial ecstasy— and we with them! The effect is smoothly sensuous with barely a trace of eroticism. It is not inappropriate in this context to speak of aesthetic appreciation. "Beauty," Nietzsche wrote, "moves on light feet."

The star is Ronnie Robertson who swirls enchantingly on one leg while, in debonair ease, he appears to lean on the ice with his arm as support. Barbara Wagner and Robert Paul float in a kind of rapturous accord, synthesis rather than unison. The "Old Smoothies"—practitioners of a certain age— bring to their simple ballroom turn a touch of old-time charm that is delightfully domestic. And there are always the comedians, whose antics are rendered exciting as well as hilarious by their terrifying tricks.

As I watched this show at the Garden it occurred to me that what gives any performance that has been brought to the point of perfection its special edge is the presence of danger masterfully overcome. Did not Goethe say that he would like the theatre's platform (he was speaking of the dramatic stage) to be as narrow in a way as the trapeze artist's path, so that those who could not manage to cross it triumphantly might fall—and trouble us no more!

Marcel Marceau (City Center) is an admirable artist whose miming is true theatre. He is a Frenchman, but I would guess that there is a pinch of Russian in his background. This guess is not prompted by the fact that his version of Gogol's short story "The Overcoat" provides the climax of his program, but because there is a certain nineteenth-century romantic melancholy and glamour in his irony that is not unlike the quality found in some of Pushkin's tales, as well as in Lermontov and Goncharov. Marceau is often comic, but his comedy is chiefly that of heartbreak.

His numbers are frequently fragmentary and nearly always of fragile texture, but they are woven out of the poetry of defeat. The momentary victories of the little people who are central to Marceau's sketches are always menaced by disaster and generally end in disappointment if not in dismal failure. The poor clerk in "The Overcoat" is robbed of his single prized possession and disappears from view as naked of hope as he is of vesture. Marceau's china salesman wrecks his wares. (This sketch contains almost the only instance of rebellious outrage.) His acrobat is frightened and, though he avoids breaking his neck, his success is bought at too awful a price in trepidation. There is always the moment of childish glee in (partial) achievement followed by horrible anxiety over the difficulty of the task that he has set himself and finally the anguish of disaster. The balloon always bursts.

Marceau's mask, topped by a wild tuft of russet hair, is mad: the lips are thin, the eyes startled, the face haggard. The body—which through its control seems to be wrought of steel wire—still looks lean, emaciated. The angular movement fashions a picturesque charm through awkwardness and distortion—as in Toulouse-Lautrec and Daumier. The ultimate impression in Marceau is sharp, penetrating, small. Only occasionally does the emotion extend beyond the framework of the "picture." These are the moments which, as Stark Young would phrase it, attain the flower in drama.

The great majority of playgoers pretends to dote on Gilbert and Sullivan. Yet I have a suspicion that the thrice-familiar work of these astonishing Englishmen is not sufficiently understood. What is overlooked, for example, is that Gilbert was not only a first-class literary craftsman—his lyrics are models of compression in parody, of clarity in theatrical communicativeness, of precise vocabulary in dry joshing—but a social critic in the peculiar manner of the English satirist who strangles with an embrace and whose flattery is a sort of slaughter.

We may take jibes at Victorian snobbery and (upper) class consciousness on which *Pinafore* is based as rather mild fun, but we should remember that it was written in 1878 when these characteristics dominated the audiences to whom the piece was addressed. Though Gilbert's thrusts, which are always delivered with the most polite air of innocent solemnity, were a sign of the imminent dissolution of Victorian stuffiness as well as one of the implements which helped the process, the great bulwark has to this day not yet been entirely demolished. To destroy what had become traditionally English required all the cunning and craft which went into the fostering of that tradition. That is why Gilbert's work is as indestructible as Wilde's equally "frivolous" *Importance of Being Earnest*.

Gilbert raised decorum to the pitch of ridicule. Sullivan's melodies—stolen from everyone worth plagiarizing—sweetened and packaged Gilbert's pungent purgatives. Gilbert's "poison" is more invidious than Shaw's; as served up by Sullivan, it reminds one of the varicolored sweetmeats dispensed by London's Fortnum and Mason.

Tyrone Guthrie is just the man to do *H.M.S. Pinafore or The Lass That Loved a Sailor* afresh with the eager and talented Stratford Festival company from Canada (Phoenix). This Irishman has always had a penchant for reducing English pomp and circumstance to priggish nonsense. (His production of *All's Well That Ends Well* is a classic of such treatment.) He is so successful at it not only because of his prankish disposition but because he can at once realize the hoax of English form and exult in it: it makes such a grand show; and form, even when it has become slightly ga-ga, is more attractive than lumpish gray matter.

All the players of this enjoyable production—in which the kidding does not overreach itself—are delightful. My favorites were Douglas Campbell as the Boatswain, Andrew Downie (a lollipop version of John Gielgud) as the Sailor, Harry Mossfield as the Captain, Eric House as the Admiral—and the two leading ladies who sing so pleasingly.

—*NAT*, 24 Sept. '60

GROUPS, PROJECTS, COLLECTIVES...

The very title of this article has an explosive sound. The words crackle like gunfire from a barricade; at the same time they smack of olden days. I almost said the "good old days."

Only yesterday (I mean this literally) in his sumptuous apartment in Paris, Irwin Shaw, whose lyric, antiwar play *Bury the Dead* was first produced by one of the smaller theatre groups in 1936, very nearly sighed as he remarked to his guests, "How exciting the theatre was in the thirties. We all thought of what we wanted to express and what had to be said rather than about success." That was very nearly the truth of the matter.

The Group Theatre—which I founded together with Cheryl Crawford and Lee Strasberg—began its career on Broadway, where it remained for ten years. The Group was the "elder statesman" among the new organizations that gave the thirties its particular theatrical character. But the Group did not represent Broadway any more than the Neighborhood Playhouse, the Provincetown Players, the early Theatre Guild, the Civic Repertory Theatre—organizations typical of the twenties, whose houses were all south of Times Square—were off-Broadway enterprises in the sense that we think of such enterprises today. Even the younger, smaller, less enduring groups of the thirties—the Theatre Union, Theatre Collective, Theatre of Action—though they all functioned more or less in the vicinity of lower Manhattan, were not what we today considered off-Broadway operations. For though most of those brave bands were terribly poor—always on the verge of extinction—they were enormously ambitious. Ambition gave even the least valid of their productions a certain ardor and flare that communicated genuine excitement.

The off-Broadway movement today, though it is growing in importance, is fundamentally a symptom of our theatre's disorder. Many worthwhile productions uptown expire because they are produced at costs—in initial outlay, running expenses, box-office prices—that make the possibility of profit extremely dubious. Broadway theatre rentals, moreover, make the chance of these productions holding the boards for any length of time very slim, even when their producers are willing to keep them going without profit. Contrast the fate of *Summer and Smoke, The Iceman Cometh, The Climate of Eden, A Clearing in the Woods, Orpheus Descending, The Threepenny Opera, The Three Sisters* on and off Broadway.

Off-Broadway is a boon to new writers whose plays undoubtedly hold little appeal for audiences that pay upward of $6.60 for an orchestra seat. *End as a Man* and *The Connection* are typical. There are also the unusual foreign plays, *La Ronde, Endgame, A Country Scandal,* together with "experimental" works like *The Balcony* and, generally, revivals of such plays as *The Father* or *An Enemy of the People,* which are not practicable on Broadway budgets. Then too, young actors and new directors who need an outlet for their talents find their chance more often off than on Broadway.

The ambition I speak of in the theatre of the thirties—whether physically on or off Broadway— was a moral, social, artistic ambition. When Stella and Luther Adler, J. Edward Bromberg, Morris Carnovsky, Margaret Barker, Franchot Tone, Mary Morris, Alexander Kirkland and others joined the Group Theatre's acting company, they were already well known. They chose the Group, and in the main were loyal to it through thick and thin, because the Group's policy in plays, in acting technique, in organizational setup, in social seriousness, appealed to them as artists and citizens. The Group—and most of the other organizations I have named—wanted to make the theatre vitally expressive of the American scene, of the life of the times. They also hoped—this was especially the Group's aim—to develop actors as conscious artists, and eventually to produce new playwrights. They succeeded in nearly all this; I would go so far as to say that Broadway today or, if you like, the "commercial" theatre—is largely composed of actors, directors, playwrights and teachers who were trained or strongly influenced by the groups of the thirties.

Let us examine the record briefly. Franchot Tone began his career with the New Playwrights, a short-lived organization dating from the late twenties, and joined the Group Theatre at its inception in 1931. Clifford Odets, after having played with the Theatre Guild, joined the Group the same year as a small-part actor. Elia Kazan, who was first a stage manager and then an actor in the Group, did some of his first directing with the Theatre of Action in *The Young Go First* (May, 1935). Michael Gordon (director of the movie *Pillow Talk*) first directed some of the Theatre Union's productions in 1934, and later became stage manager for the Group Theatre. John Garfield began with the Civic Repertory Theatre, proceeded to the Theatre Union, and went on to the Group Theatre. Lee Cobb worked with the Theatre Collective and the Theatre Union. (I first saw him in a one-act play produced under the auspices of the New Theatre League, a sort of clearinghouse for the smaller "left wing" groups, which also published a lively monthly magazine.)

Robert Lewis, whom I encountered through a humble production of Maxwell Anderson's *Gods of the Lightning,* a play he later directed (1937) on the West Coast for the Federal Theatre, joined the Group as an apprentice in 1931. He played bit parts at first, then became an assistant stage manager, and directed his first production— Saroyan's *My Heart's in the Highlands*—for the Group in 1939. Charles Friedman, who directed *Carmen Jones,* first worked with the Labor Stage, whose production of *Pins and Needles* was a huge success both then and later on Broadway. Albert Dekker acted with both the Theatre Union and the Group Theatre. Mordecai Gorelik, neglected on Broadway after his outstanding work in the Theatre Guild's production of John Howard Lawson's *Processional* (1925), designed many of the Group's productions (Sidney Kingsley's *Men in White,* for example), and helped found the Theatre Collective. Another frequent Group Theatre designer was Boris Aronson.

I have not yet mentioned—except in passing—the extraordinary phenomenon of the Federal Theatre, which began its career on October 1, 1935, only to end it because of political pressure on July 1, 1939. Under the direction of the doughty Hallie Flanagan, the Federal Theatre Project was the first (so far, the only) nationwide government-sponsored theatre in the United States. This project, born not out of a love or appreciation of the theatre, but as part of the Works Progress Administration, which was established to give employment to needy people in socially useful jobs, made a contribution to our theatre the significance of which has to this day not been fully recognized. For the Federal Theatre, often harshly criticized by professional show folk and politicians who suspected it of being too useful to the Roosevelt administration, proved what might be accomplished in a creative sense by a government-promoted theatre organization in the hands of devoted craftsman.

"Aren't very many of the Federal Theatre productions amateurish?" I was once asked at a lecture I gave at the time. My answer then—as it would be today—was "Yes: and so are many Broadway productions." Though most of the Federal Theatre personnel came from relief rolls, and nine out of ten dollars were spent for wages, the Federal Theatre employed ten thousand people, operated theatres in forty states, published a nationally distributed theatre magazine, conducted a research bureau serving not only its own theatres but twenty thousand schools, churches and community theatres throughout America, and played to audiences totaling millions.

The project invented the "Living Newspaper," a cinematic and journalistic type of production dealing with such subjects as agriculture, flood control and housing. *One Third of a Nation* (designed by Howard Bay) was in every respect a thrilling show, which attracted large audiences on Broadway at something like a dollar top.

It was in the Federal Theatre that Orson Welles first displayed his lavish talent (with the Negro *Macbeth, Doctor Faustus, Horse Eats Hat*). Later, with the indispensable aid of John Houseman, he formed the Mercury Theatre—the last of the outstanding ventures of the thirties. The Mercury's first production, *Julius Caesar* (in which Martin Gabel, Joseph Cotten, Hiram Sheraton and George Coulouris appeared, along with Welles himself), was an example of how gratifying the social enthusiasm of the thirties could be when applied to Shakespeare.

The Federal Theatre produced T. S. Eliot's *Murder in the Cathedral, The Swing Mikado,* a dramatization of Sinclair Lewis' *It Can't Happen Here* (directed by Vincent Sherman, later a successful Hollywood director, whose theatrical "alma mater" was all the organizations of this epoch), the first American performance of Bernard Shaw's *On the Rocks,* and Paul Green's *The Lost Colony.*

Perhaps the most succinct testimony to the swell of fervor the project aroused in the country was published in *Federal Theatre Magazine,* written by a member of the audience: "We're a hundred thousand kids who never saw a play before. We're students in colleges, housewives in the Bronx, lumberjacks in Oregon, sharecroppers in Georgia....We're the Caravan Theatre in the parks, Shakespeare on a hillside, Gilbert and Sullivan on a lagoon, the circus under canvas, Toiler on a truck....We're the Living Newspaper; we're the Negro theatre, the Yiddish theatre and theatres throughout America playing not only in English but in French, German, Italian and Spanish; we're the file, we're the record, we're theatre history."

The theatre of the thirties was often referred to as a "left theatre," a "Roosevelt theatre," a theatre of "creeping socialism" or worse. The record shows that this was mostly eyewash. The theatre then reflected what was going on in the world around it. What was going on affected everybody, and resulted in many changes that are not only permanent but universally approved. The theatre movement of the thirties, often verbose, hotheaded, loudmouthed, bumptious and possibly "pretentious," did not produce communism in our midst; it produced a creative ferment that is still the best part of whatever we have in our present strangulated and impractical theatre.

We should look back to the groups, projects, collectives and "unions" of the theatrical thirties, not simply with nostalgia, but with thoughts of emulation and renewal.

—*TA,* Sept. '60

THE HOSTAGE

The Hostage (Cort) is an improvisation in beat time. Some may see in it a comedy in a semi-Brechtian manner: songs interrupt the dramatic action, actors address the audience and comment on the proceedings. It has already been called a vaudeville, a jig, a romp and a Rabelaisian prank. The audience which is not offended by its "bad taste" (a minority, I would judge) find it grand fun. I myself enjoyed it.

In its exuberance—its blarney—*The Hostage* smacks a little of certain characteristics we find in O'Casey—or in almost any raffishly bright Irishman. It is a product of that state of mind which makes for beatniks the world over. One might say that just as America speaks through plays like *The Connection* or *The Zoo Story*, England through Harold Pinter and John Osborne, France through Ionesco, Beckett and Genet, Ireland now jibes and jokes through Brendan Behan. That is why *The Hostage* strikes a responsive chord in London, Paris and New York.

What is at bottom of nearly all this work—of different artistic nature and merit—is a sense that society today (menaced by annihilation) has no firm values, that though we may despair we actually take very little seriously. Affirmatively the motto of this "school" might well be "Be kind to little animals."

You, I and our neighbors are the little animals—some friendly and pleasant, others mischievous and noisome. There is compassion—for all these writers are good fellows—but there is little belief in man: he stands for nothing. What he claims to stand for is mostly the bunk. Hep folk know it and find great satisfaction in saying or braying it.

This in itself is not without value. In a time of confusion, double talk, hypocrisy, thickheadedness, it may be useful to cry havoc—to laugh at ourselves, to curse, to give ourselves and the world at large the razzberry. The self-mockery does not hide the hurt and disarray. *The Hostage* in its oblique, cock-eyed, drunken eloquence—"Don't muck about, don't muck about, don't muck about with the moon"—is finally a social play in the dizzy mode of 1960. It is the peeling that is coming off the walls of our decaying fortress.

Behan is a talented writer—his *Quare Fellow* (not to mention *Borstal Boy*) in the realistic vein certainly gives evidence of this. But *The Hostage* is a special kind of work. It represents the collaboration of a playwright who furnished a thin thread of plot, some dialogue, a sense of milieu (locally Irish on the one hand and "universal" spirit of the times on the other) with an acting company whose determined and gifted leader Joan Littlewood believes that "theatre should be crude, vulgar, simple, pathetic...but not genteel, not poetical"— in other words *popular*. Most of us are now spiritually dispossessed—out on the streets—so that we must be harangued from the gutter in the voice of a brashly shrewd hawker. This is not Behan's play alone, nor has Littlewood "directed" it in the ordinary sense; they have made it together. It is specifically a theatre creation.

Joan Littlewood's London Theatre Workshop troupe was born for this play, as the play was born for it. The actors make an important contribution: improvisation and the "realism" of the music hall and the hustings are successfully combined. This is true ensemble. Everyone is right: outstanding are Maxwell Shaw, Avis Bunnage, Glynn Edwards, Aubrey Morris, Patience Collier, Alfred Lynch.

—*NAT*, 8 Oct. '60

IRMA LA DOUCE

Everything about *Irma La Douce* (Plymouth) is admirably efficient and pleasantly clever: it suffers only from a malady at its core.

I saw it first in the city of its origin, Paris. It had been running for several years and few, if any,

of the first company remained. That may be why I was disappointed (everyone had assured me that it was utterly captivating). I saw it again in London in the Peter Brook production which is now here and wrote about it in *The Nation* only to convey the same paradoxical reaction: that while I thought it most deftly directed by Mr. Brook, fetchingly designed by Rolf Gérard, nicely adapted by Julian More, David Heneker and Monty Norman (from the original by Alexandre Breffort and Marguerite Monnot), with a group of notably energetic, versatile and engaging performers headed by Elizabeth Seal, Keith Michell and Clive Revill, I forgot the whole thing almost immediately upon leaving the theatre. The event had evaporated.

"Sweet Irma" (for that, in case you didn't know, is one way of translating the title) might be likened to the pink cotton candy I used to see little girls eating when I was a boy. It was pretty and delicately sugary, but the taste lingered only for an instant.

The malady which besets this Anglo-French concoction is an essential nonexistence. It is a sentimental fairy tale which depends on your not for a moment believing in any of it. To illustrate what I mean I should inform you that it is about a *fille de joie*—I cannot in this context use any blunter term—whose *mec*—"guy" or euphemistically "male protector"—is a law student unhappy over his girl's profession. She cannot afford to give it up for lack of what the French call a "serious lover," a man with sufficient funds to support her completely. The law student disguised as a bearded bourgeois undertakes to impersonate the serious lover. He goes to work at a menial job in order to give Irma money enough to turn it over to her protector and "true lover"—himself. The law student is finally not only exhausted by the routine of his masquerade but also becomes "jealous" of his counterpart. The law student murders himself as the bourgeois. He is arrested, etc., etc.

There is an element of fancy in all this which promises the titillation of a frothy dish. But there is no substance anywhere, even if you like the (to me) innocuous music or are taken with the breathless dance numbers or charmed by Elizabeth Seal as Irma. Even in fantasy something must be real. There is nothing sensuous in *Irma*, nothing really naughty (though some may find the line-up outside Irma's professional quarters distasteful), nothing wickedly alluring, nothing genuinely witty, nothing authentically Parisian. It is a make-believe of a make-believe, a decorated vacuum. A musical comedy of the venereal underworld has been made as anodyne as a tourist poster advertising the enticements of exotic places and people.

—*NAT*, 15 Oct. '60

MINSTREL OF AN ODD SONG

Reading Sean O'Casey's latest play *The Drums of Father Ned* and two new books about him reminded me of an incident related to the production of one of O'Casey's first plays which was being revived by an earnest Off-Broadway group. In the course of rehearsals the director and his company were troubled by conflicting interpretations. To settle their argument they wired O'Casey: "What is the significance of your play?" He answered: "The significance of my play is that it is a good play."

The quip strikes me as wholly apposite to the occasion of most O'Casey criticism. The earliest and most famous of O'Casey's plays—*The Shadow of a Gunman*, *Juno and the Paycock*, *The Plough and the Stars*—are pictures of humble Dubliners in the years of internal industrial struggle and of armed strife against the English. These plays are packed with pathos, humor, anger, tenderness, and heartbreak. They are rich in characterization, sweet with human sentiment, hilarious with human fecklessness, yet on the whole quite unsentimental. They are marked by true speech heightened to the pitch of brilliant rhetoric and genuine eloquence. One might say of O'Casey's prose dialogue that at its best it is one of the finest modern examples of folk poetry. These plays expound no thesis and they abound with varied meaning.

Some of O'Casey's later (and possibly controversial) plays are, as a matter of fact, intellectually much simpler, hence much clearer. They are nearly all variations on a single theme: "This comedy's but an idle laughing play," O'Casey writes of *Father Ned*, about the things encumbering Ireland's way. Most of O'Casey's plays are odes to the joy of life and jibes, taunts, hoots, growls, and groans at the puritan bigotry (regardless of denomination), the repressiveness, the folly, and cruelty of those who fear life's splendid anarchy.

"You see, Father," says a girl in O'Casey's new play, "we're fed up bein' afraid our shaddas'll tell what we're thinkin'. One fool, or a few, rules th' family life; rules th' ways of a man with a maid, rules th' mode of a girl's dhress, rules th' worker in fields and factory, rules th' choice of our politicians, rules th' very words we try to speak, so that everything said cheats th' thruth; an' Doonavale has become th' town of th' shut mouth." The accent in O'Casey's play is always Irish but just as Faulkner's and Williams's work is focused on the South but extends beyond its borders, so Dublin (or Ireland) for O'Casey is metaphorically the world's typical parish. And the activity which for O'Casey most thoroughly exemplifies man's insanity or abuse of life is war.

Still there is an O'Casey "problem." He is unquestionably one of the foremost dramatists of our time, yet he is rarely produced. Some may think this is because being inalienably Irish his importance is merely local. Others feel that his plays are misshapen because he exiled himself when *The Plough and the Stars* was booed (for nationalistic reasons) by some of the Dublin audiences, and then turned his back on the Abbey Theatre when its board of directors rejected his anti-war play *The Silver Tassle*. O'Casey, it is contended, lost contact with a working theatre, a contact which might have served to discipline his unruly genius. The result of all this is that a great number of commentators declare O'Casey's work after its initial phase inferior to the three plays which brought him to the world's attention.

To balance the account—to combat its injustice—another group of critics have raised a clamor insisting on a new and perhaps greater eminence for O'Casey's later work of which only *Purple Dust* has had a degree of popular success on our stage. I remember George Jean Nathan, the most persistent and potent of O'Casey's champions, writing me a letter in which he asserted that O'Casey's *Within the Gates* was the greatest play in the English language since *The Tempest*. But Robert Hogan, another partisan of O'Casey's "experiments," considers *Within the Gates* "monstrously dull!" One begins to feel that any defense of O'Casey is rather supererogatory. Do we need to defend Shakespeare because he wrote *Cymbeline* and *Titus Andronicus* as well as *Hamlet*?

An artist is as good as his strongest link. All of O'Casey's plays—regardless of how we rate them—deserve production and are worth seeing. Our theatres are unfortunately unequipped to cope with them so that with very few exceptions all the productions I have seen of his later plays have been inadequate. As for the dispute over O'Casey's "experiments," his extension of theatrical forms, his fantasies and stylizations, I am inclined to stand with Chekhov when he wrote "I come more and more to the conviction that it is not a question of new and old forms; but what matters is that a man should write without thinking of forms at all, write because it springs freely from the soul." O'Casey understood this when he wrote "I'm just a wandering minstrel singing an odd song at all the cross-roads, a song in the form of a play...."

There is an aspect of O'Casey's career which has rarely been noted. O'Casey is indomitable. He has recently completed three more plays soon to be published. Most of our successful playwrights threaten to give up writing for the theatre (and sometimes do) when they are disappointed with the reception of two or more of their plays. O'Casey has never stopped writing his plays though not one of them—to put it mildly—ever made him rich and most of them have been skimpily mounted in tiny theatres. O'Casey is not a "professional." He is an artist and a great spirit.

—SR, 5 Nov. '60

INVITATION TO A MARCH
THE UNSINKABLE MOLLY BROWN

Arthur Laurents is a playwright with attributes of sensibility, wit, observation and sound craftsmanship. Two things, I believe, sometimes impede him. He wants to give his plays a certain "philosophic" stature and he wants to be a highly successful showman. When Laurents writes from the quick of his sympathies and conveys them through a clear plot line, he gives us such effective pieces as *Home of the Brave* and *The Time of the Cuckoo*. When he employs intellectualistic (or psychoanalytic) means, plus stage tricks, the results are dubious as in *The Clearing in the Woods*. When he is an unassuming journeyman he produces such an eminently serviceable "book" as the one for *Gypsy*.

In *Invitation to a March* (Music Box) he reverts to comedy, for which he has a distinct aptitude. There are some good semi-satiric lines and enough nice moments to make pleasant entertainment. But there is a thesis to this play and also an evident determination to make the play work as a smart show. The result is a compromise that dilutes the potency of the author's best qualities.

The thesis is that we all ought to learn to know what we want and then to do it without let or hindrance. But the plot and characters designed to embody this thesis are rather hackneyed and finally conformist. No one today is shocked by the idea of an illegitimate birth and everyone agrees—in the theatre at least—that the safe road of the well-heeled respectability may be duller than that of the freewheeling Bohemian. The play therefore never makes a real point: its challenge is not false so much as it is platitudinous. At best it succeeds only in being cute.

Actually Laurents is hardly lighthearted. There is a streak of sadness and bite in his better plays. There may even be anger. He does not wear the grinning Broadway mask easily. He speaks best when he is sufficiently moved to dispense with theories and theses which only serve to make his sentiments appear less adult than they may be.

As director, Laurents has assembled an attractive cast: in the case of Jane Fonda attractive enough to be worth the price of admission, while Celeste Holm and Eileen Heckart are expert as well. If I have a criticism of the direction, it is one which applies to many other of our skillful directors. Their direction is too meticulously tailor-made; it has too mechanical a precision. Too much pressure is put on the actors to make them give *exact* performances faithful in the last detail to the director's willed intention. While this makes their production ultra-sleek, it also irons out some of the life which may be in the actors and the script—both in need of the freedom of the dance rather than the rigor of a march.

Despite a certain lack of variety, I liked *The Unsinkable Molly Brown* by Meredith Willson and Richard Morris (Winter Garden). This in itself is no special news, but when my readers consider how often I have avowed an imperviousness to the charms of most specimens of stage Americana, the simple declaration of approval should be viewed as a genuine compliment.

The nostalgic Americana of so many of our musicals bores me because they are usually marked by a sort of lacquered complacency without a gleam of reality. In *Molly Brown* there is a historically justified feeling for the fresh-air energy, push and crudity of the lucky Westerner of the old mining days whose wealth was often accompanied by a hankering for (European) polish and sophistication—that in itself being the symptom of an even deeper need for a widening of human experience.

The show's dialogue has American spunk—both true to the material and appealing to a contemporary ear. The music, often in the key of loud and noisy, is not at all bad in the lighter numbers and though slightly dull in the serious ones is very much helped by Herve Presnell's fine voice and pleasing personality. Oliver Smith has contributed some amusing settings and Miles White costumes of character.

Above all I liked Tammy Grimes, who is a clown with a heart, funny-looking and fetching. She sings with point and warmth and she can act. At times she approaches glamor. She will add a further and necessary dimension to her capacities when she learns to love her audience more. At present she seems too involved in her own problems as an actress to achieve the spontaneity, assurance and ease of the true star whose spirit, having become unfettered, magically envelops the spectator's soul.

—*NAT*, 26 Nov. '60

CRITIC'S CHOICE

Otto Preminger was daring: that is his chief asset. He opened *Critic's Choice* by Ira Levin with Henry Fonda, Mildred Natwick and Virginia Gilmore (Ethel Barrymore). These actors are thorough professionals and Miss Gilmore looks yummy in her informal come-hither clothes by Oleg Cassini.

This play is about a critic whose wife writes a play—what a bold subject!—which her husband pans. It has some funny lines, including intramural jokes about the so-called theatre. *Critic's Choice* is not difficult to watch with such attractive people on the stage, but it gave me time to think of contiguous matters.

For instance: why are nearly all plays about the stage so embarrassing? Even people who know the theatre well—say, Clifford Odets in *The Country Girl*—write lines and scenes about stage life which strike one as glaringly pretentious or false. Perhaps it shows that most stage folk are ineradicably romantic, with an attitude toward the stage which is closer to that of the innocent, beglamorized spectator than to that of the sober craftsman. It is as if the American theatre professional never feels himself really part of the theatre (*in* the theatre) but somehow hankers for a theatre that exists somewhere beyond the horizon. (In the same way, many Irishmen living in Ireland seem to dream of Ireland.)

Then, too, I mused upon the sentiment about drama critics which appears to prevail now in theatre circles. I attended a conference on drama criticism some weeks ago and the atmosphere seemed to breathe a kind of tepid adulation toward our drama critics. In this our worst season in recent memory I too am beginning to feel sorry for them. For if our theatre keeps along the path it has taken of late there will be nothing left of it but the critics.

A final observation in this connection: in Mr. Levin's piece a large part of the critic's review of his wife's play is read aloud. It is sensationally funny. Max Beerbohm and Bernard Shaw in collaboration could not have devised anything so funny. Any reviewer *that* funny ought to be fired: he is not a critic at all—he confuses his function with that of the comic.

—*NAT*, 31 Dec. '60

BEEFS AND STEWS ABOUT THE LEGITIMATE THEATRE

When showfolk foregather at bars and restaurants there is, together with the usual kidding, chitchat and gossip, a certain amount of good talk. Sometimes there are complaints—repetitious, dejected, futile—but they nearly always reflect justified grievances. They point to flaws and ills of the profession which may not be easily remedied but which are none the less worth airing.

Yet when these same folks are called upon to speak publicly or to write special pieces for the press they grow benign and disclose a smiling countenance as if all were well with the (theatre) world and they personally were entirely content. So a lot of healthy protest gets lost at the bottom of coffee cups.

Such forbearance is the courtesy showfolk pay to their public. The playgoer should be encouraged to think of the stage as a glamorous place where all is charm, wit, beautiful temperament and lovely elevation. Besides, no one likes to betray private hurt or sound like a gripe. For one thing it may be bad for business, that is, for one's career.

Since here in these pages we are, so to speak, among ourselves, I thought I'd set down a few notes on things I've held forth about at Sardi's, Steuben's, the Russian Tea Room and other quarters cordial to theatrical gentry.

I was not in New York during the actor's strike last Spring. I received news of it while abroad. When it was over I heard that both sides pronounced themselves satisfied: both sides, it seemed, had won. My feeling was that though this was probably true, the theatre had lost.

This feeling was not provoked by partisanship for either side. I am sorry for actors because employment is scarce. I am sorry for managers because they usually own so little of what they presumably produce. The theatre will suffer as long as every category of stage worker—including writers—thinks of his own special field apart from the theatre as a whole. This has very little to do with being idealistic. More than almost every other endeavor the theatre is a cooperative pursuit. No one can really thrive at the expense of the other without doing damage to the entire enterprise.

It is supposed to be thoroughly "realistic" to think of actors and producers as capital and labor because that is what it seems to come to at the moment of "collective bargaining." (Let us forget for the moment that very few producers possess capital.) It all seems very different—does it not?—when a show is in trouble and author, director, producer agree to waive royalties and actors to take cuts—usually without any chance of ever recovering their losses in the future. They all really want the show to go on—not for profit but from an honest regard for their work.

So long as the profession believes itself a business to be compared with the making and selling of shoes, automobiles, cosmetics, etc.—showfolk will be dupes, the theatre will be moribund, and everyone with it sick in every respect. Whatever the theatre has been prior to 1927 it is no proper business now—partly because the theatre was never primarily or essentially meant to be a business and more particularly because of wholly new conditions which have made it an absurdity in terms of serious commerce. The only ones, it strikes me, who have really profited from the theatre in the past fifteen years or so are the big "artists" agencies.

If this is so, whose fault is it? Not with any one individual. We should not think of these matters as a tug-of-war. We must think in new terms in view of the peculiar circumstances today. When I suggested to a manager—oh very tentatively!—that all productions should be truly corporate propositions in which each party began with a certain minimum and each shared in the hoped for profits according to a pre-arranged scale, I was told by some that Equity would never consider the scheme, by others that the managers (or their backers) would refuse. Perhaps so. I am certain however that sooner or later—perhaps through a crisis in which we all shall be involved—some plan now deemed utopian will be adopted to save the theatre from extinction.

Showfolk are the greatest optimists in the world. I say "optimists" but if I weren't one of them I should employ a less complimentary epithet. Despite statistics and yearly experience everyone plans on the basis of success when it is well know that failure not success is—and always has been—the norm. (It's only with success that the question "What happened?!" is appropriate.)

Even publicity men dream only "rave" notices and plan their future campaigns on them. That is why theatre publicity seems on the whole to be routine and ineffective. It is geared to exceptional circumstances: the expectation of the "right" number of favorable reviews in the right spots.

Another effect of the euphoric state which precedes the opening of a play is the contradictory one which makes everyone connected with it unconsciously behave as if there were only to be one performance: the New York opening night.

The second night audience by the way often seems to share the state of mind. If the notices have promised a good time, everyone enters "laughing at the ushers"; if the notices seem mixed or poor the audience seems dreary before the first curtain.

As a result of this confusion of attitude in respect to what the theatre is meant to be and to do, the atmosphere that prevails in it is one of hysteria. Many showfolk enjoy this (masochists!) without realizing that the fevered air in which they live really kills the fun that their hard work should give them. A man who knows his job relies on is craftsmanship, his judgment, his experience and his off-tested talent to produce desired results.

The fact that there is no guarantee that such results may be regularly depended on gives a real professional his deep concentration and concern—even some nervousness—but it will not drive him crazy! In the theatre, one ought to behave like a sound statesman or soldier: they know they are in danger to begin with, but they try above all to preserve their wits. Everyone in the theatre should strive to keep balance, which means, to conduct rehearsals and production conferences in the most relaxed fashion possible. One has to play the "game" well rather than be bent on "winning." "Victory" (or success) is not in our power to command.

With the hysteria that so often obtains among us—particularly during the out of town tryouts (with well received productions as often as those "in trouble") comes superstition.

Showfolk are notoriously superstitious: for they do not know how to placate the "gods." I am not talking of such superstitions as those about climbing over the foots, whistling in the dressing-room, reading the last line of the play at rehearsal, etc. I am talking about the disposition to find a victim, someone to blame, a simple cause for the play's not having done well in New Haven or Wilmington or Boston!

More specifically: the hysteria which demands rewriting before it is determined why an audience's response was unsatisfactory on opening night, the hysteria of replacing actors (or director) on the road before one is sure that what is wrong in a particular actor or director. The hysteria I refer to infects almost everyone: no one seems to be immune—not even the director who often communicates his uncertainty or fear to the cast.

A playwright once asked me shortly before an opening, "Why do you want to relax the actors? They should be kept tense." Perhaps that particular playwright confused relaxation with indifference or drowsiness.

I am skeptical when I hear people speaking of our theatre as a "director's theatre." This is more of a commercial superstition than an artistic fact. Certain directors are supposed to be "top" (money) directors because they have directed several hits. Very few hits have been made from wretched scripts or with bad casts. There is of course such a thing as fine or mediocre direction.

But a play being a hit or a failure isn't a sign of one or the other. But since so few people—even among producers, writers, backers and critics— know much direction (it is not easy to know) the superstition flourishes.

One has heard of stars being coddled. Whoever seems to hold the reins of "power" apparently needs to be coddled or conned. (Sometimes it's the agent!) Hence Boris Aronson's remark, "The theatre is a collective art in which the strongest person wins."

But nowadays I find it's the playwright who needs to be coddled. He is apparently never wrong: it's always his producer or director or designer or cast or publicity man. When a playwright asks me impatiently, irritably and prema-

turely, "Why doesn't X act that scene more forcefully?" I am often tempted to respond uncivilly, "Why didn't you write the scene with more talent?"

There should be mutual respect in the theatre not only for each individual person engaged but for the task and problem that each person's work entails. It all comes down to each worker knowing his job and also knowing something of the nature of the other fellow's job.

The producer can't demand that the playwright be a wonder man grinding out greatness at will, the director can't expect his actors to be inspired at each moment in every circumstance, nor can anyone regulate the bloodstream of every script and personage involved in production.

The theatre in effect must be viewed not as a deal made among a number of craft unions, but as one Big Union.

Failure is always painful. (It may at times also be instructive, even creative.) But nowhere else in the arts but in our New York theatre is it made to seem a disgrace. Our condition might be compared to the plight of fifty starving men who are asked to share or compete for a pound loaf of bread. It is not likely there would be much grace, measure or good will in the environment.

These things might all be more or less taken for granted if the theatre were rationalized in its fundamental organization—a goal it will take a long time to achieve—though, as I have intimated, a severe shock might in the long run help.

Still, in all fairness to everyone, one must admit: the theatre has nearly always (and everywhere) been a little bit as I have described it. Only nowadays with us in New York the mischief is aggravated tenfold.

Don't get me wrong, as the feller said—I speak only from love—and the exasperation that goes with it!

—*VAR*, 4 Jan. '61

DO RE MI

Do Re Mi by Garson Kanin, Betty Comden, Adolph Green and Jule Styne (St. James) is a dandy show; in most respects the best musical of the season. (And think of it, the show was done for a mere $350,000!)

Musical comedy is the theatre form in which we Americans excel. Yet if I were challenged to say which of the musicals in recent years was a masterpiece, in the sense that *The Mikado*, *La Belle Hélène*, *The Threepenny Opera* are masterpieces, I should be hard put to speak with complete assurance.

The reason for uncertainty is that so few of our musicals are altogether of a piece—possessing an artistic identity that may be said to represent a way of thinking, feeling or seeing—emblematic of an individual, a social mode, or an epoch. Our musicals are only generically significant, giving evidence of energy, good nature, intellectual passivity, cleverness and the talent or resourcefulness of particular individuals among our comedians, choreographers, composers, etc. Musical comedies—especially in the past ten years—are successful corporate efforts—generally a trifle synthetic—rather than genuinely expressive works. They are entertainment machines resembling the great national weeklies: triumphs of efficient journalistic organization with a personality that is so to speak more "subliminal" than specific.

Do Re Mi, to use a professional phrase I overheard in the lobby during intermission, is admirably cemented. But when I try to define its essence, I grow doubtful that there is any. The story tells of a ne'er-do-well with ambitions of dazzling success: money in the bank, mink for the wife, name in the newspapers and the best spot on the floor of night clubs. His wife begs him to get an honest job, but he feels that to do so would be an admission of failure. His is the Broadway dream: splash! He goes into the juke box business

with the aid of some old-time buddies, semi-reformed racketeers. He discovers a sensational new singer, gets involved in his partners' shenanigans—they can't abide competition—runs afoul of a government investigation, proves himself a flop as a slick heel, and finally realizes that his wife was right and that if he does his duty as a simple sober citizen and takes time once in a while to dance with her, all will be much better.

A moral tale then, a sentimental plea for modest, lower middle-class, supposedly unspoiled human values. It is all made very amusing until Phil Silvers, as Mr. Jerk Everyman (my name for the character), has to deliver the philosophy of the show in grandiloquent recitative à la Ethel Merman in *Gypsy*. The audience is half-touched and half-embarrassed by the mixture of good will and phoniness. It applauds nevertheless because it feels that it ought to approve the homily—though it does not live by it—and more especially because Phil Silvers, a grand performer (and up to that moment very funny) is likable in every respect.

In sum, the "book" is a mere excuse or framework—and thoroughly serviceable as such—to enable all the contributing forces to do their stuff. In addition to Silvers there is the fantastically down-to-earth clowning of Nancy Walker. Her rendition of the song "Adventure"—in which she uses a blanket and a dressing gown to express the "mad extravagance" of her life with a no account and unaccountable husband—is close to genius and the high point of the evening.

There is, very strikingly, the zany ebullience of the Betty Comden and Adolph Green lyrics, so heightened by the innocent frolic of a headlong impetuousness that they can never seem anything but charming whatever their detail. There is also the unusually good baritone of John Reardon—he must beware of forcing it—and the intriguing range of Nancy Dussault's voice. (This is a season of fine voices in our musicals: for example, that of another young baritone, Ron Husmann. His singing and Eileen Rodgers' good looks are the only things I remember from *Tenderloin*.) There is excellent casting among the minor parts; and

Garson Kanin handles the production as a whole in a way to reveal his friendly kinship with the giddy world the show depicts.

Another feature that is not only superior but extraordinary is Boris Aronson's sets. They make original and varied use, witty and shrewd, of the idiom of modern art—from Kandinsky and Klee to Calder—for entertainment purposes. These sophisticated sets do not obtrude as a "specialty act," but satirically mirror the fabulous vulgarity, the epically electric mishmash of our midtown environment. In them the gaudy decorative patterns of the juke boxes become the stained glass insignia of Broadway religion.

—*NAT*, 14 Jan. '61

THE AMERICAN DREAM

The importance of *The American Dream* (York Playhouse) is that it's Edward Albee's. Edward Albee is the young playwright who wrote *The Zoo Story*—one of the finest of American short plays. A young playwright of genuine talent—that is, one who is not merely clever—is rare nowadays. (I hope I am wrong about this scarcity.) So everything that Albee writes should not be adulatory: it is dangerous to make "stars" of playwrights while they are in the process of growth; nor should our attention consist of slaughtering the playwright's second or third play in behalf of the hallowed first one.

The American Dream is a one-act abstract vaudeville sketch. It purports to typify the well-to-do American middle-class home in this age of automation and mechanized men and women. The excellent little set is hung with frames without pictures; the room itself has expensive furniture hideously gilded, blank prefabricated walls and above them all the Stars and Stripes—in short no intimacy, no personality, no vibrations. Daddy, who earns the money, has had part of his gut removed and of sex there is no question. The family is childless. Grandma who has a remnant of

spunk left in her dry bones is at once a protected and abandoned bit of household crockery—a sort of skeleton in the closet. She says all the right things at the wrong time and the wrong things at the right time. No one listens to anyone else or cares about what is said when they do listen. There is total spiritual, intellectual stasis. The child—called a "bumble" rather than a baby—once adopted by this juiceless family was smashed and dismembered by them.

Into this vacuum enters the "American dream" in the person of a tall, good-looking boy, a perfect juvenile specimen. He has no feelings, no active desires, no real ambition. Passively waiting, he is a prettily furbished shell. He is adopted by Mommy and Daddy—to undergo the same treatment as the earlier "bumble."

The play is funny and horrid, a poker-faced grotesque. It reminds one of Ionesco's one-act plays, *The Bald Soprano and Jack*, although the Frenchman's plays are freer in their extravagance and more devastating. There is no harm in a young writer's being influenced—it is inevitable; besides, one chooses one's influence in the direction of one's sympathies. But there is a certain literalness in *The American Dream*—even at moments a flatness of writing—which makes me suspect that the French influence on Albee (Genet, Beckett, Ionesco and others) is not altogether helpful.

I mean by this that Albee's talent—as with most Americans—lies closer to realism than perhaps he knows. *The Zoo Story* had its "symbolic" side too and was also terrifyingly humorous—as well as obliquely tender—but what abstraction there was in it arose from true observation of specific people in specific environments.

Abstraction becomes decoration when it loses touch with its roots in concrete individual experience; and the word "decoration" is just as appropriate where the abstraction is satirically fierce as where it is beguiling. So while I appreciate the comment and the bitter barbs which *The American Dream* contains, I would caution the author to stick closer to the facts of life so that his plays may remain humanly and socially relevant. For it is easy to make a stereotype from a critical and rebellious abstraction as from a conformist one.

The cast of *The American Dream* is well chosen and ably directed by Alan Schneider.

—*NAT*, 11 Feb. '61

MYSTERIOUS RITES OF THE REHEARSAL

"We're going into rehearsal tomorrow," an actor may say to a "civilian"—if he knows any. (A "civilian" signifies the layman, a citizen with no professional connection with the theatre.) This person will note in the actor's face a mixture of anticipation close to elation and a certain apprehension. He may wonder at the mixed emotions. Year after year—particularly between mid-August and late March—plays are scheduled for rehearsal but, even if he is sufficiently interested to read the item publicizing the event, the ordinary playgoer is vaguely puzzled. What actually goes on at rehearsal? It always remains something of a mystery.

The explanation for the duality of reaction on the actor's part lies in his knowledge that, on the one hand, rehearsal is the crucible of creation for everyone concerned in play production and that, on the other, for all the blood, sweat and tears that will be expended, the play he is in may fail or he fail in it.

When you read a script which will later become the published version of the play, all you have are words suggesting what may happen on the stage. In terms of color, sound, movement, all is shadowy. Hamlet as we see him on the stage is not *Shakespeare's* Hamlet (*he* exists only in the book). What we see is Gielgud's Hamlet, Olivier's, Redgrave's, Evans'. Although all of them speak the same words, none is alike, none has precisely the same meaning. The words are absorbed in the person of the player. The function of rehearsals is to transmute words into a world.

Many dramatists do not even trouble to write stage directions. The indication as to place in Giraudoux's *Tiger at the Gates*, for instance, is "a terrace above another terrace." But this has to be built out of real materials so that people can move on it and certain actions can be conveniently performed on it; the audience, moreover, must be able to sense in looking at it what sort of ambiance and mood they are to dwell in and enjoy for the duration of the performance.

The physical aspect of production, though most immediately striking, is not the most important. When rehearsals begin, the settings and props have already been designed and ordered, though they will not appear till the last four days of rehearsal—usually out of town. What is crucial to the production is the integration of the company of actors in their individual interpretations. It is this that the director must effect so that all the elements—the visual and human—form a coherent and pleasurable meaning.

The director is, to a considerable degree, the "author" of the *stage* play. I qualify, because in the theatre every single element contributes and counts. The director should always be in charge, but he may not always be in control. It is often said that the director "molds" the actors' interpretations. This is largely true—and most flattering to the director—but an actress like Laurette Taylor was herself a creator and every accomplished actor may be one.

The wise director knows and hopes for this; tries to understand his actors and what each has to offer and can be induced to reveal. Hence the most complex and fascinating aspect of rehearsal is the give-and-take between actors and director as well as the relation among the actors themselves.

As every suitor courts his beloved in his own individual way, so each director woos his company in a manner all his own. (He is also different in his treatment of each actor: we are dealing in this instance with a multiple marriage!) Directors often debate the proper method of rehearsal, and it is right that each should speak for himself. But the truth is that there are no absolutes here; no single method is the right one—everything depends on circumstances, the special artistic goal each director sets for himself. Only results—what we finally see on the stage—matter.

Some directors have the company sit and read the play together for three or four days. (It is to be understood that we are speaking of the three-and-a-half-week rehearsal of the non-musical play on Broadway under Equity rulings.) Other directors desire no more than a single joint reading of the play; some—though very few—even insist that actors know their lines before rehearsals have begun.

After the play is read, the company gets "on its feet"; the process of staging—commonly called "blocking"—begins. This involves the placement of actors, the timing and manner of their movements on the stage—in short, the setting of the mechanical or visible patterns of the production.

Sooner or later, the director will in some way indicate not only where the actor is to move—cross, sit, rise, turn, etc.—but why and how. These questions imply others. Is the play to be given a comic or a sober interpretation? What style suits the material? Is a certain character to be regarded as sympathetic or not? Does it hurt or harm for a particular line or bit of business to provoke a laugh?

Many years ago George Abbott had to allow that wonderful actress Jeanne Eagels to leave the cast of *Chicago* because she thought the gamy girl in that play ought to have been treated seriously, while Abbott conceived the character humorously. Again: when this writer undertook his first directorial assignment, Clifford Odets' *Awake and Sing!* he was advised by one experienced colleague to direct the play for pathos, while another equally knowing theatre person insisted it be directed for comedy.

Some directors feel their orders are so explicit that nothing more need be added beyond their simple statement; the actor will supply the rest. Other directors will analyze, philosophize, evoke, suggest, trick, mesmerize, until the actor has attained the proper value or spirit of each moment.

It is told of Sidney Howard—during the rehearsals of his play *Ned McCobb's Daughter*—that, in explaining a certain scene to an old-time actor, Howard delivered a beautifully poetic discourse on what it meant to live all one's life at sea. Everyone who listened was moved. But the actor's only response was, "Do you want me to talk softer or louder?"

The actor may contest interpretations or even refuse to carry out bits of action on the ground that they are false or he does not happen to be able to enact them convincingly. Such crosscurrents are more like the wrangling of husband and wife than the dispute of employer and employee. They generally end by one or the other yielding a point, depending either on the authority and persuasiveness of the director or the humility, receptiveness or status of the actor.

A compromise may be arrived at which will enrich the issue. It is never good counsel to make these occasions a contest of wills. The director who by force of will beats the actor at this game wins a fruitless victory.

Abusive directors hardly exist today. There are, however, tyrannical father-type, or martinet, directors. Such a director must not only be very sure of himself but command immense respect to succeed. There are rather quiet—almost mute—directors who appear to follow (or edit) rather than lead. Some of them, it is said, merely "direct traffic." There are valuable directors whose enthusiasm causes them to carry on like prophets, rabble-rousers, clowns or inspired seers.

Some directors prefer to communicate with their actors rather privately—in odd corners of the stage or in dressing rooms. Others always pronounce themselves within the hearing of the entire company. The director may act a bit himself by way of illustration—rather dangerous if his demonstration fails to be clear and sometimes discouraging if he should be too brilliant an actor. (Max Reinhardt virtually induced histrionic impotence in many of his American actors who felt they could not possibly do his extraordinary demonstrations justice.)

Today's young actors have become somewhat overdependent on the director. They too frequently wait for the director to inspire them. A very fine actress once complained of me that, while I told her what to think in the scenes in which she was involved, I didn't tell her what to think when she was not directly involved. One is never sure with actors who are in the habit of badgering their directors for more direction whether they are trying to attract attention to themselves or are insecure and genuinely in need of help.

But generally speaking there are very few actors who do not wish to be served by the director, while too many hope to be saved. In either case, most actors are deeply grateful to directors who they feel have helped them.

Out in front in the theatre auditorium where, after the first days of "blocking," the director usually sits as he watches and issues advice, all is darkness. And there is not very much more light on the stage where, due to union rulings and costs, a rather evil illumination is projected from a wan worklamp. The production's eventual furniture is suggested by broken-down chairs, uncouth couches, dirty steps and insecure card tables, and crockery by paper plates, cups, knives and forks.

The playwright and producer attend all the first rehearsals. They visit less frequently after the first five-day trial period—when cast changes may be most conveniently effected—and do not make their presence seriously felt until the runthroughs when the play in its entirety is given without interruption.

Then playwright, producer and director consult and their joint findings—when they are in agreement—are passed on to the company by the director. Some playwrights and producers hardly ever leave the rehearsal premises—a constancy not greatly appreciated by directors or actors.

There are generally three to five runthroughs at which the director feels his company is ready to be criticized by "outsiders." A large or small audience of friends may be invited to the last two of the runthroughs. They serve to diminish the actors'

tension before the out-of-town tryout. They may also instruct the actors where laughs may be expected or warn the company of undesirable audience reactions.

Still, these runthroughs are not without their pitfalls. The threat stems from the expert as well as inexpert advice of relative strangers. The chief emphasis in the talk one hears after these runthroughs is on guessing the play's probable success or failure—an utterly futile practice.

A play on the stage is the most elusive of phenomena. After more than thirty years of professional experience, the present writer is quite frank to admit never to have been certain of the success or failure of a play in production. Any professional who claims even a 50 percent degree of infallibility is deluding either himself or others. If one wanted to play it safe, one might take the "realistic" or pessimistic view and always predict failure, since that and not success is the *norm* of the theatre.

At the final New York previews of *Bus Stop* and *The Teahouse of the August Moon* the audiences were so markedly unresponsive that even their sponsors could not help feel thoroughly disheartened. Or take the even more cogent example of *Member of the Wedding*. The play in script form was apparently so unpromising that nearly all house managers refused it tenancy in their theatres. It was unintelligible stuff without action or story.

As director, I was convinced that it was a lovely bit of writing which would probably prove caviar to the general. The reassurance of a few colleagues at rehearsal did not entirely persuade me that my forebodings were unjustified. While the play was greeted with glowing notices in Philadelphia, business was still bad.

Other colleagues who came to see the play there shook their heads and consoled Julie Harris on having to appear once again in a flop. The paid preview audience on the night before the New York opening was distinctly cold. The play turned out to be a solid hit.

All this is relevant to our story because it points to a factor nearly always overlooked by the general observer who asks, "How can so many supposedly knowledgeable theatre folk make so many mistakes?"

A play on the stage is not only different in nature from its point of origin in the script but it is never exactly the same from one rehearsal or performance to another. Most plays at the tenth day of rehearsal are miserably dull. A set which looks "great" may be causing a short circuit in the proceedings—a fact that only the most trained observer may notice.

A fine actor who later will give a brilliant performance sometimes develops rather haltingly at rehearsal (or vice versa). Marlon Brando might have been dismissed after the first five days of the *Truckline Cafe* rehearsals—the first play in which he scored. After the tenth day, it was again suggested that he be dismissed: nothing he did was "getting over." If it had not been for Maxwell Anderson's kindness and co-producer Elia Kazan's support—"if you have faith in him, stick by him"—I might have been pressed into yielding.

The theatre building itself (when too large or small) may modify the impact of a play. A nervous seizure (or "freeze") on the part of a star on opening night (Michael Redgrave in *The Sleeping Prince*) may mortally influence the quality of a production—particularly a comedy—thoroughly enjoyed out of town. The social atmosphere or historical moment (a declaration of war, a stock crash, an economic depression or the weight of a bad theatrical season) may alter the audience's reaction to a play.

The composition of an audience is extremely important to the fate of a play. Hence plays fail in one town and succeed in another. This is true within the boundaries of one country; it is more emphatically evident when one compares reactions to the same play in New York, Paris and London.

We ought also to pause here to ask what is a success? We have all seen plays we admired which did not make the grade. What grade? The accountants'! There was no profit to the play's backers—only a good time for the major part of the audience which saw the play.

The final rehearsals—with settings, lights, costumes, make-up, sound effects—occupy four days before the out-of-town opening. They are often tumultuous and frightening. For the addition of any new element to a rehearsal (even a change of locale) always upsets it somewhat. Though actors have seen models and sketches of the sets at rehearsals, have tried on their various costumes in the costumer's workshop, it takes several days (at least) to adjust to them on the stage. The first dress rehearsal seems to destroy play and production!

It is at this time that leadership—particularly from the director with the support of his producer—is most required. For even when the out-of-town notices are encouraging (they are never decisive so far as New York is concerned) the company tends to become distraught and uneasy as never before.

Rehearsals for four hours a day continue out of town. They are especially useful for the revision of text and the necessary work attendant upon that. This time is also valuable for bringing characterizations to maturity and for polishing scenes which may still be rough in execution or shallow in content.

The out-of-town tryout period is a weird island of time. The world at large has ceased to exist for everyone connected with the production. The atmosphere is intoxicating in both the happy and the forbidding senses of the word. If there is to be trouble—scandalous disagreements, rancorous episodes—here is where it is most likely to occur. Everyone acts as if it were zero hour, not alone for the play—but for survival.

Yet there is joy in creation even as there must be pain. If rehearsals are conducted—as many are—with love and mutual regard on all sides, a wonderful sense of community grows in a theatre troupe that is hard to match in any other collective enterprise elsewhere.

—*NYTM*, 5 Mar. '61

COMÉDIE FRANÇAISE
COME BLOW YOUR HORN

Once again those who are not fortunate enough to be able to see the company of the *Comédie Française* (senior among the French state theatres) on its grounds are privileged to enjoy it in America—this time at New York's City Center and in other cities of the company's scheduled tour. I hope, however, that the future playhouses in which the troupe is to appear will be more intimate, better looking and acoustically superior to the City Center's frightful temple.

At this writing I have seen only the first "bill," consisting of Molière's amiable curtain raiser *Improvisation at Versailles* and the three-act farce *Scapin's Rascally Tricks* (*Les Fourberies de Scapin*). The latter play is undeniably a hit, since it has been running at the *Comédie Française* since 1680. The production we see now was first presented at the *Comédie* in 1956.

These two plays will be followed by Molière's sardonic comedy *Tartuffe*, Racine's tragedy *Britannicus* and a "crazy" bedroom farce *Le Dindon* (*The Dope*) by that master at the game, Georges Feydeau.

Scapin is characteristic of Molière, being all mask and movement with a slyly subversive quality underneath its frolic. Even in Molière's graver plays—like *Le Misanthrope*—one constantly senses the beat of an almost ballet-like rhythm—light, springy, strong. The very words seem to leap from one character to the next; even the long speeches are self-orchestrated *tours de force* for voice and body. It is easy in such a play as *Scapin*—when too furiously paced—to miss some of the folk pithiness of expression which escapes platitude or bourgeois moralizing by virtue of zest and shrewd good humor.

It is necessary to say all this, in passing, because to a playgoer unfamiliar with Molière in

the original (and there is hardly any way of knowing him otherwise) *Scapin* might appear nothing but the silliest kind of burlesque. This impression is heightened in the *Comédie*'s present production, which takes on an added dimension of riot through the acrobatics of Robert Hirsch's Scapin. In energy, agility, invention, speed and general virtuosity Hirsch is fabulous.

This represents one aspect in the art of acting and is certainly to be admired: it is clear that very few actors could emulate it. Still, there must be more to Scapin than that. For somehow, though one is dazzled, there is comparatively little joy in this Scapin. Hirsch's performance seems more a shocking demonstration of skill than of comic (or even farcical) acting. Pyrotechnics supersedes meaning. The "marionette" has replaced the man. The play is no longer a bubbling ballet; it has become a circus.

It has occurred to me that the impression I record here might be due to the fact that the company has been repeating this performance too many times in too many places and that its juices may have dried up, leaving only the brilliant externals. But I am inclined to doubt this because in every (comedy) role I have seen Hirsch play—in France—I have noted his tendency so to overwhelm himself as well as his audience with an effort for effect that astonished delight gradually gave way to skepticism or resistance. There are, moreover, several other highly expert performances in the play—particularly those of Michel Aumont and René Camoin as two miserly old papas, but they too, while offering strikingly vivid images displayed with remarkable technical proficiency, end by becoming monotonously puppet-like. A free comic spirit evades them. There is perhaps a neglected area in the training of these excellent players: craft has lost contact with feeling. Still I look forward to Hirsch and Annie Ducaux (one of the company's prime tragediennes) in *Britannicus*.

Neil Simon's *Come Blow Your Horn* (Brooks Atkinson Theatre) might be called an expense-account show. Apart from musicals like *Do Re Mi*, this is the only kind of theatrical entertainment Broadway nowadays can really afford to produce. If theatre is business, then doing such comparatively successful plays as *The Hostage*, *A Taste of Honey* and *Rhinoceros* is risky to the point of being preposterous.

If this sounds grim I must hasten to add that the theatre in most countries has always subsisted on such plays as *Come Blow Your Horn*. *The Fifth Season* was probably more profitable than *Death of a Salesman* and *Potash and Perlmutter* (way back before the First World War) made more money than Schnitzler's *Anatol* or Shaw's *Fanny's First Play* produced at about the same time. Most theatre in our day has been popular theatre—theatre for the majority at the moment of production. It is a sobering fact which must never be lost sight of by anyone concerned with the theatre financially or artistically.

Although I don't need to be entertained in the manner of *Come Blow Your Horn* I have no real objection to it. There are funny cracks in it and even funnier performances—particularly that of Lou Jacobi, as authentic and flavorsome as a corned-beef on rye.

The play's jokes are largely those of a clever adult-camp comic—topical in allusion, affably vulgar, with the companionability of a lively delicatessen. There is no offense in the play and one is not expected to swallow it whole or to make it serve as a balanced diet. It is trivial and cozy.

Well directed by Stanley Prager, *Come Blow Your Horn* is amusingly played by everyone in the cast. Pert Kelton, as Irish as can be, is still very effective as a (never so labeled) Jewish mama. The Jewish strain in the play gives it its moral anchor and supplies a touch of warmth to its creaky mechanics. The fact that the ethnological note is neither identified nor hidden will give the show its "universal" metropolitan American appeal.

—*NAT*, 11 Mar. '61

THE FRIGHTENED FIFTIES AND ONWARD

When *The Gang's All Here*, Jerome Lawrence and Robert E. Lee's play about the Harding administration, was presented in the fall of 1959, a respected critic murmured to me during the intermission, "We haven't seen anything like this for some time." During the fifties very few political plays had been presented. The critic spoke regretfully, implying that the production of such plays always enlivened, and gave importance to, the theatrical scene. The production of Gore Vidal's *The Best Man* in 1960 is even more to the point because it is topical in its interest. As for *Advise and Consent*, it appears to look to the future. Theatrically speaking, however, we are still living in the atmosphere of the fifties—the most telling plays of this season have been foreign—and the change we hope for probably lies further ahead in the mid-sixties.

It is to be expected that the production of political plays in a heterogeneous society such as ours should be rare. A play that favors a particular political attitude is divisive; it may easily dispel the unity of sentiment in the audience upon which the theatre depends. But what people usually mean when they speak of political plays are what once were commonly termed plays of social significance. The two are not precisely the same. Maxwell Anderson's *Both Your Houses,* written in the thirties, is a political play: it deals with the way bills were passed in Congress; Shaw's *Heartbreak House* is a social play: it deals with the confusion of values among a class of people who have lost the compass of any conviction.

What the critic I quoted was deploring was the lack of social plays—with some sharpness of edge. I add the qualifying phrase because many plays that are fundamentally social—several of Tennessee Williams for example—are usually viewed as little more than the personal drama of disturbed or perverse characters. Their reference to society is sufficiently oblique so that one may easily miss their real point. The sting is there, but it is felt in our private sensibilities rather than in our concern for public welfare.

The thirties, we all know, were pre-eminently the years of the social play. More plays of so-called popular entertainment were presented than plays like Clifford Odets' *Waiting for Lefty* or John Wexley's *They Shall Not Die* (that has always been, and probably always will be so), but everyone agreed that the social play gave the era its particular tone. Even the politically conservative lent a sympathetic ear and followed the new social play with interest. The reason for that is no secret: the depression, which came as the aftermath to the hectic glow of the twenties, was a shock that affected everyone, and induced a *soul*-searching of a *social* nature. Then, too, the facile pacifism of the twenties had given way to considerable uneasiness over the advent of Nazism.

The forties continued some of the social idealism and bravery of the early Roosevelt era. Recall such diverse offerings as *Watch on the Rhine*, *The Patriots*, *The Searching Wind*, *Home of the Brave*, *State of the Union*, *Born Yesterday*, *All My Sons*, *Death of a Salesman*. Each in its own way sought to make us aware of social responsibility; each served notice that Americans were not afraid to regard themselves critically, or to recognize that to be humanly worthy we had to look to our social body as much as to our individual comfort.

The fifties marked a retreat. It was probably not as complete as we might suppose, but there was a distinct modification of approach. Playwrights began to say different things, and say them in a different way. The dominant cause for the change was undoubtedly the cold war. It served no good purpose to complain about ourselves when inimical forces abroad might profit from a documentation of our shortcomings. We were prosperous and relatively strong; it was sinful to rock the

boat: that is, do anything that might weaken our confidence or prestige as a world power—the freest and wealthiest people on earth. McCarthyism became the chilling emblem that frightened and froze us into a kind of tense dumbness. We dared never suggest—no matter what the provocation—that we were not living in the best of all possible worlds. If a peep of protest issued from your lips, you were thought a crank or a neurotic, if not actually subversive.

Arthur Miller's *The Crucible* (1953) was an assault on this new conformity. It did not entirely hit the mark because its argument was stated in terms of the past and its situation was not inescapably analogous to our own. George Tabori's *Flight Into Egypt* (1952) and *The Emperor's Clothes* (1953) were out of focus because they were situated in foreign countries and their characters were ill defined. Lindsay and Crouse's *The Prescott Proposals* (1958) was simply a sedative. John Patrick's *The Teahouse of the August Moon* (1955) implied that we might learn lessons in the good life from so-called backward peoples, but the lesson was administered as candy. Lawrence and Lee's *Inherit the Wind* (1955) was a reminder that bigotry and obtuseness might rear its head in our land, and that courage was needed to combat them. Still, from the standpoint of Broadway, it was a case of it happened "in another country; And besides, the wench is dead." Dore Schary's *Sunrise at Campobello* (1958) was not about Roosevelt as a political force but as a charming man resolute enough to overcome a terrible physical disability. *West Side Story* (1957) was a musical, hence essentially romantic. Lorraine Hansberry's *A Raisin in the Sun* (1959) touched us because it was a tender drama about humble folk who happened to be black—and antiracism is always effective in the North.

Symbolic of the fifties is Odets' *The Flowering Peach* (1954). Noah, the ancient pathfinder-prophet and rebel against inequity, saves himself from destruction because God appreciates his righteousness. He wants to continue to depend on the Almighty's benevolence and the consolation of his wife's love. One of Noah's sons harbors the pioneer spirit: man's fate, he believes, depends on man's action. He disapproves of his father's recently developed passivity. At the end of the play Noah must choose between living with either his "radical" or his rich son. He chooses the second because with him he will be "more comfortable." We were all a little like that in the fifties.

Still, that is not the whole story. With plays like Carson McCullers' *The Member of the Wedding* (1950) and the oncoming of the political and social freeze, many folk began to affirm that drama does not lie in man's struggle with society but in the struggle within himself. Personal problems—one's childhood, one's parents, one's girl, the immediacy of one's emotional (including sexual) life—were the proper domain of the drama. As one critic put it, "Man's conflict doesn't lie outside himself; it dwells between his eyes."

The emphasis shifted to situations that were exposed or solved through a semi-psychoanalytic diagnosis; sometimes—though much less frequently—through a quasi-religious laying on of hands. Some of the plays inspired by this trend were interesting and valuable—nor were they always socially insignificant. (Some of them, indeed, were just as much "propaganda" as any overtly social play.) My intention is not so much to find fault with such plays but to explain that very often their weakness as plays (or, if you will, as works of art) derived from a premise—usually unconscious—that had its roots in the special social climate of the fifties.

If the playwright's inner motivation at the time could be spelled out, it might go something like this: "Since too definite an allusion to the somewhat rotten state of world affairs, as manifested by institutions or customs within the boundaries of our country, is now deemed heinously improper, and may arouse suspicion as to my patriotism; since, moreover and most emphatically, I am not certain of the direction of the most desirable social changes or the political means whereby they may be achieved—I am no longer a loudmouthed kid on a soap-box, and have come to realize that most political messiahs and their nostrums are fraudulent—I ought to delve into myself and study the things that have really been troubling me."

I am not rooting for a particular type of drama. No "type" has merit in itself. A bad social play is just another *bad* play! But it ought to be said that whatever one's personal feelings or religious convictions may be, every man lives in the world—a specific world—and in one way or another must deal with it. A play is always crippled if it neglects the existence of the world (or a particular society) as if they had no bearing on our most intimate thoughts, feelings and behavior. Sartre, Camus, Genet, Anouilh, even Ionesco do not represent social positions or preoccupations primarily—some are, in fact, antisocial—but hardly any of their plays are without some direct relevance to social questions. And the English playwrights—John Osborne, Arnold Wesker, Shelagh Delaney—together with the Irishman Brendan Behan, whatever their particular "message" or lack of it, have their eyes turned both outward and inward.

We are still standing still at this moment. *The Best Man* says some clever and entertaining things about our way of conducting political affairs, but it hardly affects anything very much, nor is it meant to. *Advise and Consent* is not, in my opinion, antiliberal—it might prove more valuably provocative if it were! It is a melodrama which suggests that politicians ought to commit themselves to the truth rather than to party loyalty—certainly a benign counsel stated in a way that need upset no one. Neither play is really much of an "advance" beyond the thoroughly amiable *Fiorello!*

Saul Levitt's *The Andersonville Trial* of last season—though I thought it inconclusive—was a social play with a certain impact. But in a special sense the two most striking "social" plays of the past year were Jack Richardson's *The Prodigal* and Jack Gelber's *The Connection*. What the first play was saying was that the young man of today wants to retire from the turmoil of the political world, and to avoid all commitment to any ideology, but that such subjective inclinations are swept aside by the forces of the world's partisanships. (And what is intimated is that that is just too bad!) *The Connection* shows us a group of men so bewildered, bruised and battered by the noise, gibberish and phony nature of our society that their only escape is through some substance (from narcotics to jazz) that will disconnect them from everything but their dreams. This might be called the sociology of flight.

We have come to this. That is why, apart from the chaos of the theatre's economics, we are at the moment of my writing in the midst of the poorest theatrical season in a good many years. But there will be another change—or our theatre will grow flaccid and decrepit. We will change because the present tension in our world—due in part to our lack of any positive personal or social philosophy—is untenable. The extension of atom power creates an inescapable dilemma; our prosperity, we increasingly sense, is precarious. We are uncertain as to whether we really do lead the expanding world—or are fit to. The pressure of all these worries—if it does not drive us crazy—will finally go to make a social consciousness beside which that of the thirties or early forties will seem so much kindergarten stuff.

We need every kind of play and every kind of talent in our theatre. In the end all the kinds of drama come to one thing: a contribution to our life in the world. But whatever types are written what we ought to demand of all of them is that they express the fullest experience, the most scrupulous probing, the most devoted and challenging thought within the scope of every writer and theatrical craftsman. Without these the theatre is a sham, and, in view of its costliness, both unworthy and unnecessary in the so-called entertainment field.

—*TA*, Mar. '61

NOTES FOR A PRODUCTION OF HEARTBREAK HOUSE

(One of the highlights of the 1959-60 New York season was the revival of Shaw's Heartbreak House *starring Maurice Evans, Pamela Brown, Sam Levene, Diana Wynyard, Diane Cilento, and Dennis Price. The production was directed by Harold Clurman, and TDR is pleased to publish Mr. Clurman's working notes for this production.)*

First Notes:

This *crazy house* is a truth house—for adults.

There is a certain "childishness" in this play.

The play of a bunch of brilliant kids not as old as the people they impersonate—much wiser and gayer and more crackingly articulate than such people would "normally" (naturalistically!) be.

A charming, surprising *harlequinade*. (An intellectual vaudeville.)

Make them funnier—"nuttier"—than Shavian "realism" (or literalism) usually permits.

"The house is full of surprises" the Nurse says. The Captain's whistle, the sudden entrances and exits are Shaw's clues to this.

Another character says "something odd about this house."

The style tends toward a bright-minded wackiness. A puppet show! (Shaw jokes about bowings, introductions, greetings, etc.)

"We are under the dome of heaven."—The garden outside should be very much part of the first act "interior." (Variable nonrealistic lighting.)

Sound—"a sort of splendid drumming in the air." Later the air raid is compared to Beethoven. Ideally the air raid should be orchestrated—use musical instruments—on a Beethoven annunciatory theme—but not the motto of the 5th!

Second Notes (on further reading):

Shaw's characters are ideas—conceptions of people, theatrically and comically colored. The adverse criticism of certain critics who say that Shaw's characters are merely puppets spouting ideas should be made a positive element of the production style.

They may be made as puppet-like as the nature of the play's dramatic structure and the audience's taste will allow.

Mangan says he wants to get "to hell out of this house." Everyone in the play wants somehow to escape his or her condition. All are dissatisfied with it...it's a crazy house, driving them crazy!

All in a sense are "crazy," not true to themselves, not what he or she seems or pretends to be. So that everyone is somehow odd, a *clown*—disguised, masked. Outside is "the wide earth, the high seas, the spacious skies"—waiting.

"In this house," says Hector, "everybody poses." "The Trick is to find the man under the pose."

This is the director's job as well:

a) What is the pose?

b) What is the man or woman under the pose?

More Random Notes (after still further readings):

These English in *Heartbreak House* do not behave as English people do: an Irishman has rendered them! They are more impish, more extrovert, more devilish, devilishly *comic*.

Hesione is a "serpent"—she has mischief in her—not a "proper" lady. She's the cat who swallowed the canary, an intelligent minx. Mentally speaking she *winks*.

An element of "ballet-extravaganza" throughout—as if everyone were "high."

The audience is to enjoy: ideas as color, comedy, and "show," or intelligence as clowning.

They are all aware that they are living in a loony world, which they are expected to take seriously—but can't. As they progress they become aware of the need to act made in order to approximate reality. To achieve their liberation—their world must be destroyed.

Some of the madness demands that they hide it—which is the greatest madness. Thus they speak of "form," of not making scenes—while they are always making scenes. (Lady Utterword.)

They want to burst the bonds of the old times—convention—"to get the hell out." Thus the comic outbursts.

(prelude to England's "angry young men.")

Random Notes Continued:

Shotover roars.

The world's askew (the set to begin with).

They are all flying off the handle: the "handle" being the old steady values, the desire to get the hell out of a situation which no longer supports anybody. The "handle" supplies the form—which these people no longer can grip. Lady Utterword still wants to hold on with her unseen husband Hasting Utterword.

(A "wooden" handle!)

The movement of the play is not placid, polite (or Chekhovian!). It is rapid, hectic, almost "wild." (The actors are asked by Shaw to sit on tables, etc.)

Mangan "not able-bodied." Has aches and pains—presses his liver when he is irritated.

Randall—curly hair ("lovelocks"—like the fop in the film of *Kipps*).

Spine (or Main Action):

To get the hell out of this place.

This "hell" suggests some of the explosive quality desired in the playing—the element of *opera-bouffe* involved.

The Characters:

Shotover: The Sage of Heartbreak House.

This "sage" has fed himself on rum, worked hard with his body, his fists, and his wits. The rugged person on whose hard work and tough life the house was built. But this sage has a mask—a Pose—as important for the actor as his wisdom—indeed more important. It is the mask of the Drinking Devil—almost the "debauchee" with his West Indian Black wife.

Bluff, gruff, hardy—also shut off from anything but his own thoughts and "ways." (Modern England was built by such men: born

1818...in their prime in 1865.)

His dismissal of everything secondary comes from his urge to get at fundamental reality–to run the ship—to find the means to set the boat on its due course. This requires the "seventh degree of concentration."

To drive toward *that* goal (the seventh degree, etc.)is his spine—his prime motive or action. (To scare people into doing what he wants, or to be free of their nonsense, their blather.)

He wants to go on with his quest; his energy is great enough to do so, but at 88 he knows it's late. Therefore he's wistful too. Despite himself he has to relax into a resignation which is a sort of "happiness." This is his pathetic side.

(The clearing and cleaning up necessary to achieve the "seventh degree" will entail a certain amount of destruction—dynamite. He is prepared for that too.)

He moves with nervous energy, sudden shifts of pace, to absolute quiet or concentrated energy—as when he sits down to work on his drawing board.

I'd rather he looked like old Walt Whitman than Shaw!

Ellie: The new life or youth in Heartbreak House.

She wants to find Port (goal for her life).

The Pose is the Sweet Young Thing: the well-bred ingenue.

The real person is eager, intelligent, with a strong will and capacity to fight.

The House is bewildering, heartbreaking: all the facts she learns are upsetting....She encounters hidden or masked wisdom in the Devil—the ogre Shotover. So she ends bravely in a sort of exalta-tion—"greater than happiness."

In the transition between these two aspects of her character she is miserable, hard, calculating.

Then she "falls in love"—differently—with life itself, in all its danger in the person or symbol of Shotover.

This is the Education of Ellie.

Shotover's dreams and ravings—his wisdom and idealism—are the most real things in the world to her—new blood.

She knows her strength (the 1st curtain), so she *looks forward* to another air raid...as toward the prospect of a new world, a fresh start!

Hesione: Heartbreak House is *her* house.

The Eternal Womanly! (And an "actress" by nature.) She wants to make life beautiful, to keep it romantically beautiful.

She wants to get out of the house too (they all do) because she knows its madness...yet she likes it here—the adventure, the uncertainty, the fun...like an actress who understands the theatre's absurdity and deception but at the same time enjoys its warm charm.

She is loving but so intelligent that she occa-sionally is sharp—in the face of hypocrisy, or stuffiness.

Hushabye (the Soother!):. She loves company, the "menagerie." She sees through her husband, admires and laughs at him...

She is active...yet "lazy"...likes to fall asleep when unoccupied because she enjoys all agreeable sensations and experiences. She is not a particu-larly good housekeeper...not thrifty...not very neat (show this through "business" at the very outset)...the maid takes care of "all that."

She likes to gossip...so she's socially endear-ing. Frank, open, enthusiastic, likes to tease affec-tionately.

She's a flirt—for fun. It is also gracious, it keeps things "interesting."

Something of the improvident Bohemian—with very little care for money.

"You are your father's daughter, Hesione." (She's got the Devil in her too.)

She has temperament and temper too—like an actress!

She is changeable—with swift alternations of mood.

Lady Utterword (Addy): The Fine lady of Horseback Hall.

Conventionality is her mask and protection—

447

the sense of "form" in the "Colonel's lady" manner.

Her reality beneath the mask is a hunger for experience...her desire to escape the prison of her class convention. This expresses itself secretly, stealthily, unobserved...except in unguarded moments of hysteria.

"The first impression is one of comic silliness." She has the English "twitter." Her "form" makes her appear more stagy than Hesione (who is real theatre!). Addy is what we call theatrical theatre of the old *very* English school (1910).

She swishes quite a bit.

Her way out of Heartbreak House is to run off to India, to the garden, to tea, to fashionable behavior.

She wants to cultivate, hold on to the "manner" which "saves" her and perhaps gives her the best of both worlds—that of feeling and that of decorum: the one utterly private, the other a "style."

A consciously picturesque *flirt*...but her flirtatiousness rarely goes any further than that–titillation plus elegance, and a slight touch of danger.

When all is said and done she is very practical: she sticks by her husband, Hastings—the "enduring" Englishman.

Hector: The Intelligent Man without Employment in Heartbreak House.

He wants *to get out—somehow*...but there's no place to go. He cannot see the goal. Therefore he wants everything destroyed! He has no task. For this reason he dreams up exploits, philanders, plays "parts," dresses up (in "crazy" costumes), becomes decorative...even in his intelligence.

Like Ellie he's trying to find—port, but he knows of none, foresees none.

"I am deliberately playing the fool," but not out of worthlessness, out of aimlessness.

He's a dilettante—forced to be one—yet he has the energy and intelligence to be something more.

Debonair and cool like a practical madman. A bit of a show-off. this gives him an identity....

But this is his pose...the real man is dissatisfied, unhappy.

A pretty woman is a challenge to him: it leads to an activity of flirtation, the semblance of impressive action. He is telling the truth—or part of it—when he says he doesn't like being attracted—for it arouses him without leading anywhere. He is a civilized person, not a lecher. Thus he is a romantic without a cause.

He sees futility in all positions and arguments—even that of the anarchist...he hasn't even the confidence to feel superior to anyone.

He curses women because they are the only thing left for him to deal with...yet he knows they are only distractions to him.

He wants "beauty, bravery on earth." But he cannot find it around him or in him—except as a senseless activity.

The "saddest" character in the play and he behaves like an ass and a liar...though he often speaks honestly and even wisely.

Mangan: The "Strong Man" of Heartbreak House ("Not a well man").

He wants to get in everywhere—and to get the hell out too.

The big "capitalist"; the sharper, the practical man, the man who counts in business and in politics. All of this is the Pose.

The real man is wistful, twisted, rather frightened and a somewhat resentful child...the most "cheated" or frustrated person in the house.

He's "aggressive"...yet he is always caught off guard. He's sure an aggressive manner is the way to success, but he becomes unsure when his success is challenged or his aggressiveness doesn't impress.

Except in a very limited sphere, he's always out of his element, shaky—unhappy.

So he's always *forced* to pose—except when he believes it's particularly clever of him to tell the truth about himself.

"I don't quite understand my position here"— is the keynote. He never does—anywhere outside his office.

In the end he has a "presentiment" (of death) because he's insecure, a "worrier."

Afraid of women—gullible—an easy prey for them. Shy with Ellie, mooney with Hesione.

Like all lower-class folk who have arrived at the upper middle class he has an excessive sense of propriety—or priggishness.

He's full of unaccountable resentments (a source of comedy in this)—secret and almost ludicrous hostilities. He gets sore and vindictive in spurts. One can hardly discern the source of his irritations.

The craziness (or "unusual circumstances") of this house bursts the bubble of his pose...he collapses into tears, a hurt boy.

Mazzini Dunn: The Ineffectual Intellectual in Heartbreak House.

To be helpful to all (in Heartbreak House) is the "spine." Mazzini has "moist eyes," always smiling—except for moments of total consternation, and even then there's a little smile. He is obliging to everybody.

He feels a bit inferior, insufficient, guilty. Thus he wants to make up for it by being helpful. He regards everyone as somehow better, cleverer, stronger than he. He admires everyone.

(From the actor's standpoint: a sweet zany.) Shy and modest because of all this. But sweet: there is nothing cringing or undignified about him. He accepts his humble position.

He loves his wife as he does Ellie but he feels indebted to them—as to everyone else.

He is credulous, gullible...the world is always a surprise to him; he smiles with wonder and admiration. He really doesn't understand evil.

He thinks all one has to have are the right influences and inspirations to become good, loyal, strong.

(Key lines: "How distressing! Can I do anything I wonder?" "Think of the risk those people up there are taking"—in reference to the bombers in the air raid. "And the poor clergyman will have to get a new house.")

Randall: To act as if he were the one proper—immovable—person. The "imperturbably," the superb English gentleman. Ornament of all diplomatic circles.

That is the Pose. Unruffled, exquisite, the last word in smoothness. Narcissistic.

The real man: a bundle of ragged nerves, a spoiled almost hysterical baby.

He believes himself a romantic character, so impressive in bearing that no matter what he does he must somehow appear dashing and right.

He's always play-acting till his "hat" is knocked off...then he screams like a helpless kid.

The most absurd of all the characters...the most "typically" British—in the old-fashioned comic sense. A "cultured" dandy, super-sophisticated. He will still look and be a kid at sixty-five.

His nerves will always show through his *sangfroid*.

His eyelids flutter...a bit effeminate.

He has no real passions or convictions. Therefore he needs his adoration for Lady Utterword. All his convictions have been absorbed in his pose—which is his class pattern.

Billy Dunn: He reverses all values in *Heartbreak House*.

To get out, make out—anyway he can.

Shaw's intention with this character is to illustrate the total topsy-turvydom of Heartbreak House. Its inhabitants no longer believe in the old justice. The criminal no longer believes in his crime: it's just another way of earning a living.

Because of all this Dunn behaves like a clown—now contrite, now shrewd, now crooked, now pious, now immoral, now joking: for all these poses serve him (A "ham" actor.)

The real man is the poor bloke who couldn't make it either in Heartbreak House or in Horeback Hall, and therefore preys on both—preferably on the former, since he would simply be given a tanning in the latter.

He ends in a terrified attempt to escape—in vain.

Nurse Guiness: The Leveller.

To wait it out—with a minimum of worry.

She's an "anarchist"—she doesn't care because she does get along.

"Quite unconcerned," says Shaw. She's quietly brazen.

A Concluding Statement
(Published in the souvenir program)

Sitting at the back of the auditorium at a Washington performance of *Heartbreak House*, I was delighted to hear a spectator whisper to his neighbor, "Shaw certainly wrote wonderful gags." Why "delighted," why not dismayed? Shaw a gag writer: blasphemy! But I *was* delighted because the spontaneous remark in ordinary American meant that the person who had made it was glad to be attending a "laugh show."

Everyone nowadays refers glibly to Shavian wit. But in relation to *Heartbreak House*—less known because infrequently performed—there is a tendency to become solemn. Shaw himself is largely responsible for this, first, because he called his play a Fantasia in the Russian Manner on English Themes, and, second, because in his preface he cited Chekhov's plays as models.

In directing the play the first thing I told the actors was that both the phrase "Russian Manner" and the name Chekhov were to be disregarded in connection with *Heartbreak House*: they were altogether misleading. True, the name *Heartbreak House* signifies in Shaw's words "cultured, leisured Europe before the (First World) War" and Chekhov's plays deal with the educated middle class of the late nineteenth century. It is also true that in Russia Chekhov's plays—despite their melancholy—are construed as comedies, but there most of the resemblances between *Heartbreak House* and Chekhov ends.

The only other parallel between the work of the two playwrights is that Chekhov's world was destroyed by the Revolution of 1917 and the folk in *Heartbreak House* drifted into the First World War and if not destroyed were terribly shaken. Also the emphasis in this Shaw play—as in those of Chekhov—is not on the plot but on character and atmosphere.

What makes *Heartbreak House* utterly different from Chekhov is its unique style. Shaw's play is extravagant, full of capering humor that verges on the farcical. One of the characters refers to the environment he finds himself in as "a crazy house" in which one's mind "might as well be a football." The fact that this "crazy house" is also a truth house—a sort of distorting mirror which exaggerates the features of the people who enter it gives the play its human and social relevance but it does not distract from the topsy-turvy fun that my Washington playgoer enjoyed so much.

Years ago when there was still some resistance to Shaw—as we all know the greatest playwrights of our time encountered resistance as they came on the scene—certain critics complained that Shaw's characters are not people but puppets. There is no need to deny this. Shaw's characters *are* puppets—unnatural only in the sense that they reveal the truth about themselves more directly, more pointedly, more eloquently, more wittily than people in life are able to.

The director's task then was to combine the "fun" aspect of the play—its arch frivolousness—with its basic intent. The setting had not only to disclose a place but make a comment—smilingly suggestive of the author's mood. The clothes had to be costumes. The characterizations had to be tipped from realism to a kind of gay picturesqueness. Gravity had to be avoided—except as fleeting reminders that we were still dealing with a truth about life—our lives. This slight duality—a sort of "gayed up" seriousness—part game, part prophecy—is only a reflection of the text itself which begins as a comedy of mad manners and ends with an air raid by an enemy never named or even hinted at during the course of the play.

What was Shaw's purpose and why did he write *Heartbreak House* in this peculiar way? The play exemplifies a typical Shavian "trick." *Heartbreak House* is all carefree talk and horse-play—apparently devoid of dark portent; then it bursts for a moment into a scene of shock and ends ironically on a note of almost languid peace. "Nothing will happen," one of the house guests says. Something does happen and something more fatal may yet happen—expected, almost hoped for, by certain of the characters.

These "charming people, most advanced, unprejudiced, frank, humane, unconventional, free thinking and everything that is delightful" are content to drift. No matter what inner qualms they have, no matter what emptiness or discontent they occasionally experience, they have settled for the happiness of dreams and daily pastimes. For all his sharp teasing, Shaw is tolerant with them. Only, says he, in earnest jest, if you go on like this without "navigation"—that is without plan, purpose and preparative action—your ship will "strike and sink and split."

The thought or warning that informs the play—stated in a frolic of entertaining words and postures—is wholly appropriate to our day and our theatre. Though the people of *Heartbreak House* are English it is not merely a play about a certain class or a certain country. Time has turned it into a play about practically all of us, everywhere.

—*TDR*, Mar. '61

MARY! MARY!

Mary! Mary! by Jean Kerr (Helen Hayes Theatre) is a "good show." I put the phrase in quotes not because I mean it to be construed ironically, but because, though I have no need or appetite for the sort of relaxation it affords, I recognize its efficient merits. Since it is well cast—Barry Nelson, Michael Rennie, John Cromwell, Betsy von Furstenberg are all excellent—and nicely directed by Joseph Anthony; and since Barbara Bel Geddes is an actress I adore—

she softens brittleness by the sweetness of her disposition, the downiness of her voice and something tenderly twinkling in her whole person—I am obliged to set the event down with perhaps a casual objectivity as a good show.

Jean Kerr knows how to crack wise. She manages to do so incessantly in *Mary! Mary!* without becoming tiresome. Wisecracking is less than wit: it is as horseplay to humor. It does not illuminate, it surprises. To be continuously surprised is to be burdened. It is like sustaining a hail of kisses. One is not sure whether one is being treated with affection or being made the subject of a practical joke.

Mrs. Kerr's cracks are agile, shrewd, light and literate. They leap effortlessly and gracefully from her characters' lips. They add to their social entertainment value by being archly wicked with numerous topical allusions. They flatter the audience by making it feel hep-to-date. The total effect may be summed up as the charming affability of a hostess who, if she were not so sure of her skill, might dread her guests being unamused even for a moment.

Recalling the play's wisp of a plot, one wonders if there might not have been more to it than meets the ear. The husband in this comedy is a nice fellow but utterly obtuse (though a good publisher!) and a dunderhead in human relations, particularly in regard to women. In a word, he is lovable but dumb, which is how most women seem to regard their "intelligent" mates. The wife is delightful in every way except that she has a quick tongue, a faculty for scalding the blubber of her honest husband's fatuousness—a gift which must gladden everyone except him.

Is the play intended, after all, to make a comment: gentlemen stop being such infernal asses; ladies shut up? Do the ladies enjoy the show because they recognize their alter ego in Mary, and do the men like it because they see themselves forgiven because they are after all necessary? If such thoughts were part of the author's purpose, they are fortunately spirited away by the Bel Geddes glow. The unkind note in Mrs. Kerr's previous play, *The King of Hearts*, is modified here to a girlish laughter in which a feminine caress heals the sting of derision.

—*NAT*, 8 Apr. '61

SHOW BOAT
CARNIVAL

Jerome Kern and Oscar Hammerstein's *Show Boat* (City Center) was first produced in 1927. I saw it then in the company of Lee Strasberg (I cannot help reminiscing in connection with this show) and though we were sitting a long distance from the stage we were both so deeply impressed with Helen Morgan as Julie that most other aspects of the production have faded from my memory. Since then I must have seen this musical on at least five different occasions. I have enjoyed it every time. I doubt whether any other American musical is quite as enduring.

The main reason for this is the nostalgic charm of Kern's score. Almost every song was a hit. To this day the songs retain all the pervasive fragrance and tenderness they had in the old days. I suspect that even in 1927 the score was meltingly redolent of those same good old days—situated not so much in time or place but in some astral area of our national conscience. The music of *Show Boat* seems to create fraternity in its audience.

More surprising is the fact that the sentimental story still brings a lump to our throat and tears to our eyes. The plot includes such ingredients as the abiding love of a white actor for Julie his part-Negro wife (in the Mississippi of the eighties), the epic stoicism of the Negro laborer who slaves on the levee, the romance of Magnolia, the sweet young thing who begins as a rank amateur on the show boat, falls in love with a gentleman gambler deliciously named Gay Ravenal and ends up as a Broadway star in the most sparkling epoch of our theatre. In this span of years Magnolia bears a child (to be convent-educated), enjoys the hazardous good fortune of her husband's game, suffers stretches of rooming-house poverty, is abandoned by Gay (whose act is one of deep consideration and gallant sentiment) and is rejoined by him back on the old show boat when their little girl has grown to be a dewy cutie.

All this is terribly trite, one says to oneself after the fact, but the judgment is mostly self-conscious and hypocritical. The story works: it is basic theatre fable, and he is indeed a cold turnip who can resist it.

Carnival! is a grand *show* (Imperial). "Show" is the exact word, for it succeeds only through its showmanship. Of melodies that might be memorable there are practically none and the nice story about Lili the little waif from the (French) provinces who joins the itinerant circus—which I am told made a nice MGM movie some years ago—fails to be genuinely touching precisely because the talent of this production has been lavished entirely on externals.

Anna Maria Alberghetti as Lili is an unconventional type with her thin body, her pale face, her wide slit of a mouth, her large dark eyes and her admirably delicate singing. (If only she had some real music to sing.) She is dramatically right: her whole being proclaims a true and most sympathetic person. Whatever effectiveness the story achieves—and several ladies near me did weep—is largely her creation.

The wounded hero of the story is the carnival's puppeteer. His puppets are thoroughly disarming and their various voices and words are winning as well as funny. Jerry Orbach is in top form when he speaks through them. He is a handsome young man but he has been directed to be rather monotonously aggrieved or—more accurately—sore. Kaye Ballard as the carnival's Incomparable Rosalie is a robust trouper who brings an old-fashioned comic gusto to the first act number in which she threatens her magician boy friend with the prospect of marriage to a Zurich doctor. There is also a captivating performance by the French actor Pierre Olaf whose mask is that of a philosophic clown—

nimble, intelligent, warm—with an oddly querulous expression that reminds one of a Daumier drawing.

The most notable feature of the evening, however, is Gower Champion's staging. He keeps the performance lively and theatrically glamorous throughout. The movement is always fluid, colorful and continuous. He has been given remarkable assistance by Will Steven Armstrong's mobile and atmospheric settings (in addition to very fine lighting) and by the best costumes of the season (far superior to the much vaunted clothes in *Camelot*) contributed by Freddy Wittop. These costumes are admirable because they have character and are organic to the play instead of being "plates" or display goods for actors to put on their bodies.

Since the girls in the production numbers do not have to be great dancers, they have been chosen with an eye to their looks. Most of them—thank God and Gower Champion—are even sexy, a rather rare quality in our recent musicals. (Flo Ziegfeld would turn over in his grave if he could behold some of the chorus lines recently exposed to view.) The same is true of the men, who are not only attractive but appear virile as well as strong. I told you it was a good show.

—*NAT*, 29 Apr. '61

THE PREMISE

One of the most engaging entertainments in town is to be seen at *The Premise* at 154 Bleecker Street. (Coffee is served.) I enjoyed the evening more than any I have been invited to in many weeks at the more expensive showshops uptown.

Genially directed by Theodore Flicker, four young people—Thomas Aldredge, Buck Henry, Joan Darling, George Segal—enact little skits which, if not entirely improvised, are clearly based on improvisation. Their stage is a platform, bare except for a few wooden cubes. The tradition is that of the political cabarets of Berlin, Vienna, Munich and of the *boîtes* in Paris, but such references to foreign equivalents are misleading. The

spirit of *The Premise* group is wholly American, though we haven't seen anything of the kind in New York since the thirties. The fresh youthfulness, good-humored disrespect, healthy skepticism and wide-eyed shrewdness at *The Premise* are unmistakably native.

The things kidded deserve the treatment they get. Noses are thumbed at the jargon of the Method and psychoanalysis, the antitrust frauds, the mishmash in our minds about the Congo, the cruel antics of the Dixie racists, the cold-war follies—and, best of all, the TV summit conference of David Susskind and Premier Khrushchev, which had me in stitches. Points are made more smartly in all this tomfoolery than in many of the long-faced editorials by our most earnest journalists.

—*NAT*, 10 June '61

BERTOLT BRECHT

The Brechtian catch phrases are well known. For example, in reviewing the New York production of *In the Jungle of the Cities* (first performed in Munich in 1923 when Brecht was twenty-five), Howard Taubman referred to Brecht's theory of the "epic theatre." But there was no such notion in Brecht's mind, nor such a term in his mouth, till many years later. As so often happens when dealing with serious playwrights, we learn to recite the label on the bottle before we taste the medicine. Ibsenism precedes Ibsen; existentialism reaches us before Sartre.

One must realize, in reading Brecht, that his most characteristic plays were written with a special and new type of production in view. Brecht was a master of language, but he was above all a man of the theatre. (He had been trained by Reinhardt, and was himself a director of the first rank.) Brecht's plays are the texts for stage performances that were present in his imagination as he wrote them, and that he worked out with most painstaking care in months of rehearsal with a meticulously chosen permanent company.

The only way to know Brecht completely is to see the productions of his theatre, the Berliner Ensemble. Anything else is of necessity a compromise. Our State Department should be urged to permit the appearance of that splendid troupe on our shores. It would enrich our theatre and afford immense satisfaction to a receptive audience.

We need not fear propaganda. Though Brecht's company is situated in East Berlin, and is supported by its government, only two of his major plays—*The Mother* and *Saint Joan of the Stockyards*—contain anything to conflict with our accepted social ideas. Of those plays I have seen (except *The Mother*), one is an antiwar work of a most unusual kind, since no one in it is against war or intimates that "war is hell"; another is a farce about the rise of Hitlerism: a third is a chronicle concerning the course of science; a fourth is a fable of broad but by no means subversive implications.

I emphasize this because so much has been made of Brecht's didacticism, his (Marxist) doctrines and teaching that it is assumed that one must share Brecht's political convictions (about which there is some ambiguity) to appreciate his plays—an assumption that is largely false. Brecht's work is *theatre* in the most general and salutary sense of the term.

We are now prepared to return to where our discussion might have begun, if there weren't so many misconceptions to dispel. As a writer, Brecht is essentially a poet. Most of his plays—apart from their extraordinary songs—are in prose. It is a prose peculiarly his own: terse, epigrammatic, slangy, concrete. It avoids grandiloquence. The sentences seem to combine a folksy simplicity with bite. One wonders how such "peasantlike" homeliness of expression can make so sophisticated an effect. Brecht's language is at once "classic" in its unaffectedness and thoroughly modern in its directness.

This original mixture is what makes the quality of Brecht's dialogue so hard to render in English. In German, Brecht's dramatic speech has a certain banality of vocabulary (similar in a way to Kurt Weill's musical medium), but Brecht converts its very ordinariness into a thing of continuous surprise and delight. In English this happy paradox is often dissipated so that what was fresh in the original turns flat.

As to what Brecht says in his plays, there has been a continuous change from his early works to the final ones. The first plays, of which *In the Jungle of the Cities,* begun in 1921, remains typical, are despairing and anarchic and what today we might call "beat." It is not essential, it seems to me, to attempt a specific line-by-line interpretation of *In the Jungle;* it is sufficient to sense its mood. (I have read four explanations of this fascinating work—each of them wholly different from the others.) What is important to remember is that the play represents a convulsive reaction to the corruption of Germany after the First World War—a state of mind parallel with that pictured in George Grosz's caricatures of the period.

In the Jungle of the Cities is like a nightmare in which contradictory images are superimposed on one another. The effect is a sort of expressionist (or surrealist) metaphor in which anguish, fear, derision, bewilderment and release all occur, as it were, simultaneously. The play is not intended to be lucid—except as it echoes a chaotic world and an agonizingly turbid inner experience. The final curtain of *In the Jungle of the Cities* suggests that Brecht felt it necessary to live through this time of youthful turmoil so that he might later emerge cleansed of it. And indeed he did. The history of Brecht's career is one of progress from a passionate nihilism to a smiling serenity.

The plays that followed *In the Jungle* are still bitter, but they tend toward irony—a kind of mocking objectivity, as in *The Threepenny Opera* of 1928. Impelled by political and philosophic study, by the reading of Chinese and Japanese literature, and even more by a desire to regulate the contrary pulls of his personal nature, both sensuous and ascetic, added to the need to arrive at the discipline of some moral determination, Brecht finally reached the point, in 1938, where he could compose his dramatic masterworks: such plays as

Mother Courage (1939), *Life of Galileo* (1943), *The Caucasian Chalk Circle* (1944). The tone of those plays, despite the tragic pattern of *Mother Courage,* is that of lofty comedy: modest, restrained, sometimes archly shrewd. There is something about the plays that might be described as a subtle but unmistakable wink of mutual comprehension, as if the author were sharing a self-evident "secret" with his audience.

The last years of Brecht's life (he died in Berlin in 1956 at the age of 58) were devoted to his theatre and the production of his (and other) plays there. For the first time Brecht, with the aid of a complement of associates, including 60 actors and a general staff of 250, among them several highly talented directors, could put his ideas and plans into practice.

Brecht's productions mirror the nature of his spiritual metamorphosis. They are calm, impersonal, deliberately theatrical. Their theatricality, however, is not romantic. They eschew the excitement of suspense and the glamor of illusion. They address the audience directly as *plays.* The narrative is always supposed to take place in a foreign place—largely fictitious—whether it be called Chicago, Soho, the Orient. In these productions, the lighting equipment and other stage devices are always in evidence. The action is frequently interrupted by songs, which comment on the meaning of the play. The delivery of the lines is relaxed. The acting never strives for a fervent emotionalism. Inscriptions, mottoes and sly observations of an expository character are flashed on a screen between scenes. Properties are always substantial and significant; costumes are both expressive and authentic; colors are subdued but always beautifully modulated. All is bathed in a white illumination.

The purpose of these technical procedures is to induce a contemplative and critical state of mind so that the audience may sit back to judge the events they watch. The public is to be persuaded rather than seduced. This should not lead the reader to believe that the plays fail to be absorbing, or that no emotion is created. Emotion is evoked—*Mother Courage* is nobly affecting—but it is a different sort of emotion from that customarily sought in our theatre. It is a *classic* kind: elevated thoughtful, not tearful. It is grandly naïve in the manner of primitive theatre, though the means by which this result is achieved are in no way ingenuous.

The plays tell us that man is responsible for his history, that he is capable of changing it. That he must ever be alert so as not to be hoodwinked into superstition or the docile acceptance of unexamined dogma and custom. The individual alone is helpless, Brecht suggests; men can govern their destiny only if they work together with determined good sense and patient persistence. A tone of genial reasonableness, of humorous canniness, of companionable tact, is always preserved. Hortatory pressure is rarely exerted. We are confronted with a civilized presentation intended to communicate an aristocratic pleasure.

The importance of these productions, if they were to be shown to us in America, would be that they would enable us to enjoy a masterly demonstration of how a contemporary point of view and a realistic ideology may be embodied in non-naturalistic terms. The lesson might serve as a source of inspiration in many areas.

—*TA*, Aug. '61

THE CARETAKER

In its own way Harold Pinter's *The Caretaker* (Lyceum Theatre) is a perfect little play. Like the work of Samuel Beckett, it is a terrifying comedy. I mention Beckett, not only because Pinter has acknowledged his indebtedness to the Parisianized Irishman, but because *The Caretaker* is a variation on the Theme that has begun to haunt the stage since the younger men of the theatre began waiting for Godot. This does not mean that Pinter is not an original talent: the specific English accent of his play lends it its own stamp.

I am sure Pinter detests the reading of symbols into *The Caretaker*. It is written with so much raciness, so definite a tang of British weather that one barely notices the degree of the play's abstractness. Its three characters are named Mick, Aston and Davies; the house in West London where the action takes place reeks of the wet, the slovenliness, the mold and decrepitude of many buildings in that neighborhood. And while the play is streaked with humor, it might appear almost meaningless were it not for the ideological patterns it suggests.

The details are graphic and striking enough to be memorably self-sufficient (which is always true in a work of art). Yet they call for interpretation, even if the author were to protest that a particular interpretation, or any interpretation, belied his purpose.

Aston, a strange young man who dwells in a run-down flat in a battered and leaky house, brings home an old derelict named Davies whom he has saved from a beating in a pub where the old man was presumed to be doing some menial job. The old wretch (ever since the war he has been going under an assumed name: Jenkins) is a malodorous grotesque—craven, boastful, aggressive. He hates foreigners (especially blacks) and is lazy and mendacious. Yet he is pitiful in his stupid pride. Aston sees through the sham and invites him to share the disheveled quarters.

Davies shows little gratitude. He begs for new shoes but is not satisfied with any of those offered. He grumbles over the placement of the bed in which he has been put up. He groans and makes ugly sounds in his sleep—keeping his host awake at night. When he learns that his benefactor was once subjected to shock treatment (Aston was committed to a mental hospital because he was a "dreamer"), Davies abuses him for not treating him as well as he should. Davies also turns for help to Aston's brother, Mick, who actually owns the house which he has bought to keep his brother in safety. Mick hardly ever speaks to his brother, though he seems semi-benevolently to watch over him. Unaccountably, Mick toys with and torments old Davies and threatens him when Davies refers to Aston as a "nut." Ultimately, Aston orders the old man to get out: his complaints, his ungratefulness, his dirtiness are insufferable. Then the old beggar cries out: "What am I going to do? Where am I going to go?"

Each of the three characters seems to dwell in a world apart from the others—and from everything else. They repeat themselves endlessly but never make themselves understood. Each on his own is cruel to the others.

Who are these people? What do they signify? One is not supposed to be entirely sure. But is not Mick, the laconic prankster with his deliberate double talk and barbed mystifications, a kind of godhead—angel and devil in one? May not Aston, crucified for his idealistic dreaminess, be a sort of Christ figure? And could not the curmudgeon Jenkins-Davies, in search of the papers which will identify him and prove who he "really" is, stand for mankind itself? He is asked to be a caretaker, but he has neither aptitude nor appetite for the job. No one knows what his "game" is; the final verdict passed on him in the play is that he must be gotten rid of because he makes "too much noise." The house which he is asked to guard is so run down it is hardly worth the trouble of anyone's care. Aston, who had hoped to make something of it, who tried at any rate to protect the poor, harmless creature whom he has invited to share his digs, now dreams only of building a new shelter of fresh, clean wood—a healthy place somewhere in the nearby premises.

Pinter's refusal to make the play as neatly (or platitudinously) intelligible as this is probably justified. Plays like *The Caretaker* owe some of their fascination to ambiguity. But this ambiguity covers what is inherently a simple—perhaps too simple—design. Hence they disturb without actually moving us. The artistic plan is narrower than it pretends to be; the ambiguity is an unconscious spiritual device whereby the author, uncommitted in his soul in relation to the bewilderment and anguish life causes him, remains congealed in his quandary—a situation which may after all be easier to bear than an outright decision as to how to resolve or change it.

It is a tribute to the talent and value of *The Caretaker*—one of the most representative plays in the contemporary English-language theatre—that it can provoke such thoughts, conjectures and perhaps controversies.

Almost as remarkable as the play itself is its production under the direction of Donald McWhinnie. He has achieved that rare thing in the theatre: a true marriage of text and performance. Donald Pleasence as Davies is funny, obnoxious, astonishing, mysterious. His manner ranges from the fiercely vulgar to the apocalyptic. (How his voice echoes when he utters his last cry of abandonment!) His flailing gestures, frightening and incoherent, seem to beat the air with nameless yet vehement queries and protestations. The emotional result is awesome rather than tragic or even pathetic—in which respect it partakes of the quality of the play itself. This is true too of Robert Shaw as the play's impotent "redeemer," caught in the vise of a pity that fails to console. There is a coldness in Alan Bates's consummate portrayal of the inexplicably good-bad "landlord"—utterly real in its English impassivity, a kind of muted familiarity which in its unyielding objectivity is as fatal as a god's final judgment. Play and production wound and adhere to one's spirit like the impress of a tattoo.

—*NAT*, 21 Oct. '61

DIFF'RENT
2 BY SAROYAN

O'Neill's *Diff'rent* (Mermaid Theatre) was written when the playwright was thirty-two. Its theme is old-fashioned only because it is repeatedly restated nowadays in successful movies, popular novels and well-known hit shows. *Diff'rent* exposes the unhappy consequences of romantic Puritanism, or the repression of sexual instincts through an etherealized idealism, or plain prissiness.

It is a rather crude play—it always was—and yet one is neither irritated nor bored by it. At worst one is inclined to smile, as if the transformation of the 1890 maiden (who conceives of virtue in the manner of a Walter Scott heroine) into the thinly hysterical hot mama of 1920 was intended as satire. One is held, despite the roughness of the writing, the patness of the play's construction, the conventional violence of the conclusion.

One is held because O'Neill's feelings were rooted in his sense of the tragic which, though never intellectually mature, was powerfully personal. It was almost impossible for O'Neill to think about, observe or live through any experience without intense suffering. That is why *Diff'rent*, which might otherwise seem utterly platitudinous by now, still retains a quiver of truth: it is the truth of O'Neill's wounds.

Marian Seldes, under Paul Shyre's sympathetic direction, acts the frustrated girl sensitively (though she has some difficulty in putting on age) and the rest of the cast (Michael Higgins, Robert Drivas and the others) should also be commended.

A thoroughly pleasant evening is provided by *2 by Saroyan* (East End Theatre). I enjoyed it as I might a concert of modest chamber music, the first part of which is tender and melancholy, the second exhilaratingly loco.

Saroyan is not easy to write about, though his plays are simplicity itself. One cannot speak critically, for instance, of *Talking With You* (the first play on the bill) or of *Across the Board on Tomorrow Morning* (the second) without seeming sappy. Saroyan writes deliciously, but if you quote his plays you risk making him appear infantile or pretentious—and he is neither.

There *is* naïveté so genuine that it dissolves all other faults—including the embarrassment of a certain awkward sophistication. Saroyan has the spirit of a healthy child, trapped in a world far too chaotic and burdensome for him to be at ease. The "child" is really sad, but frisks about, smiles, does little tricks, tries to rouse us to play with him and to reassure us that neither he nor we need feel too bad.

This child has significant nightmares. In one such nightmare evil assumes the form of a murderous dwarf who is an expressionless policeman. In the final moment of *Talking With You*, a tiny deaf boy who has run away from home and has lost his last friend and protector whimpers "What's the matter? What's the matter everywhere?"

But the child (Saroyan) cannot long sustain the shock of his dismay: he returns once more to goodness, frolic and sheer tomfoolery—which ring with the laughter of his basic health and basic puzzlement. Unable to understand the world—particularly its discord—he grins wistfully to remind us that somewhere within the turmoil and the tohubohu of our day there remains a certain innocence.

The two short plays are most likably directed by Arthur Storch—*Across the Board* particularly so—while *Talking With You* is lent special warmth through Alvin Ailey's presence as a hapless boxer. Milt Kamen, as waiter and interlocutor in *Across the Board*, creates a thoroughly engaging mixture of intellectual *schmaltz* with all-American bonhomie. James Broderick is purity personified in long pants. Sam Kressen has a wonderful sort of Bert Lahr face as Callaghan, the proprietor of Saroyan's crazy restaurant. Nicholas Colasanto is an endearingly befuddled cab driver, the two Puerto Rican kitchen helpers are very funny and I appreciated the pretty girls amid the charming wreckage. Let us have more Saroyan.

—*NAT*, 2 Dec. '61

BECKET

Readers may have noticed that I frequently omit discussion or appraisal of actors from my notices. In view of my belief that acting is the crucial ingredient of the theatre as theatre, my failure to comment on the acting of many of the plays I see must seem peculiar.

The reason for this contradiction is that in most productions the acting is reasonably competent rather than creative. The actors—usually chosen because they physically approximate the characters the dramatists may have had in mind and because they have formerly proved some ability—illustrate the play acceptably, lend it body. In these circumstances the play presents the actors instead of the actors making the play.

It is not always the actors' fault that they commonly serve chiefly as attractive mouthpieces and models for the dramatist's text. The conditions of theatrical production on Broadway and in the commercial theatre generally are not conducive to creation. The director—even when he is an artist—also is burdened by limitations which make it difficult for him to lead the actor toward creative goals.

There can be little pleasure or gain to the reader of a review to be told that an actor is "O.K." or "will do"—which is how one feels about most performances. Nor does it serve any purpose to make the actor bear the brunt of sharp criticism when he is an actor of middling stamp, chosen for the wrong reasons, directed by a harassed gentleman who is required to deliver a "smash" within three and a half weeks for an audience with few considered standards.

We may learn something about acting, and the critic may usefully spend time discussing it, when the performance is very fine or when a splendid actor fails to act well. This latter is the case of Laurence Olivier as Henry II in Anouilh's *Becket*.

In the first place, the return engagement of this play is something to be studied. Despite a generally enthusiastic press and more or less packed houses, the original (New York) production—with Anthony Quinn as Henry II and Olivier as Becket—lost an estimated $100,000. Olivier generously undertook to do the play on the road to help the producer recoup some of his losses. The actor would also have the opportunity to play Henry, the more colorful of the two leading roles. On the road the show did enormous business; Sir

Laurence won great acclaim. The second batch of notices in New York have been ecstatic and the three-week engagement is a sellout.

The first thing which must strike the most casual eye is that the production now seems shopworn: even the scenery looks shabby. The original director, Peter Glenville, could not have supervised the present proceedings—or if he did, he must have been listless or powerless. I suspect that a stage manager was nominally in charge while the star "arranged" his own interpretation.

Arrangement is the proper word, because Olivier's Henry is a congeries of characteristics or playing points rather than a unified portrayal. Leaving aside the harsh fact that Olivier may be too old for the role—the play is in some measure the story of two young comrades—Olivier has no conception of Henry as a person because he sees him only as a fat part, a series of acting opportunities. Because he is brilliantly endowed, because he speaks beautifully, moves beautifully and has a thorough command of the stage, Olivier enacts some of the part's "moments" with impressive power; but, for lack of direction or thought, he enacts them without much finesse. Here he is coy, there he is fierce, now he is devilish, again he is hysterical. None of these turns are genuine (they are often transparent tricks) because they are not related to a center of meaning.

Anouilh's Henry is a naïve, healthy, natural, instinctive "peasant" with the capacity to grow in understanding. He loves Becket, in whom he beholds the perfection of his own best qualities—a high liver with the education and sophistication of an intelligent and disciplined worldling. Henry's personality is deeply rooted in what we think of as normal. He is innocently and savagely sensuous, he is trusting though wary, he is not at all stupid, he is curious and he is brave. He wants to rule, and despite the impediments of his average selfishness he will become a man of considerable stature. There is no element of caricature in him, for all Anouilh's temptation in the direction of buffoonery, and when he cries out in anger, frustration or pain, his agony is never that of a neurotic.

From all this, Olivier selects the elements of the most conventional comedy and outbursts of emotion (indicated through bold muscular violence and neurasthenic outcries copied from previously praised performances), all of them irrelevant to the composition and intent of the whole play. The result may make the groundlings applaud but must "make the judicious grieve."

I shall say little of Arthur Kennedy's Becket. He is a sensitive actor, but has had scant preparation (or careful guidance) for this part. His long soliloquy proves how little effect sincerity alone can have in such a play without careful training in simple dramatic *reading*.

As to the play itself, now that I have seen it three times, I cannot agree with those who maintain that it is one of Anouilh's best plays. It has many of Anouilh's virtues, as well as some of his worst faults: the Roman scene between Pope and Cardinal is atrociously vulgar.

Those who are respectful of the play on intellectual, moral or religious grounds are fooling themselves. It is intellectually (as well as historically) skimpy; of true religious sentiment there is barely a trace, and its morality is without real commitment. Instead of speaking of the "honor of God," Anouilh might more fittingly have spoken of the honor of one's job. Becket, as Chancellor, had defended Henry (that is what the head of a state is supposed to do); so, as Archbishop, Becket fights for the Church (or God) against the state, since that is what is demanded of a prince of the Church. If the play espouses a precept it is: stand for *some* principle. Perhaps even this is helpful at a time when no principles beyond success and self-interest seem to obtain.

—*NAT*, '61

CRISIS ON BROADWAY

The only conclusion I can come to on reading the six reports which appeared in *The New*

York Times on the Broadway crisis is: "No foundation all the way down the line." This applies not to the *Times'* journalistic efforts but to the thinking about the theatre—in the theatre—which the articles reflect.

To begin with, there is scarcely any agreement as to the facts. What are some of the matters which one might suppose to be beyond dispute? Attendance in the Broadway theatre has fallen from 12,300,000 in 1930-31 to 8,100,000 last season. The theatre's physical plant has diminished from sixty-six houses in 1931 to the present thirty-three. Forty-six new shows were produced last season, a record low, as compared to the more than two hundred produced in 1926-27. Hardly any of the better productions of nonmusical plays were of American origin. Is there a crisis? One of the reporters summed up the reaction of the theatre people he questioned as "absolutely yes—definitely no."

One producer is quoted as having said, "I think Broadway is entering a renaissance. We are on the verge of a boom." (This producer has had an exceptionally profitable year: three musical hits and an English "prestige" play.) Another producer who has lost his backers considerable sums of money in the past but who made some last season with a two-person revue goes so far as to say that "the financial plight of the theatre is exaggerated."

The crisis—acknowledged by the majority— was brought to public attention not because so few plays were produced last season but because so much money was lost. Hardly any nonmusical play, except for *Mary! Mary!,* showed a real profit or even paid all its costs. It is now feared that the conduct of the "legitimate" theatre will soon become a wholly quixotic enterprise and ultimately altogether unfeasible.

The suggested remedies are, first, the elimination of federal and city entertainment taxes; second, adjustments by dramatists, stars, directors, scene designers on royalties, and, third, the abrogation of certain onerous rulings by the stagehand and musician unions. So far only the Dramatists'

Guild has agreed to any concession in the matter of royalty payments—*provided* stars, directors and others follow suit.

The federal and city taxes have not yet been reduced. On the other hand, it is expected that tax privileges on expense accounts for entertainment will soon be rescinded—a severe blow to the sale of orchestra seats bought by so many businessmen whose theatregoing seems dependent on their expense accounts. What is also noteworthy is that the tax on theatre tickets is part of the *entertainment* tax, which places nightclubs on a par with the theatre.

This points to the core of the trouble. Though Senator Javits, in an honorable attempt to aid the theatre through legislation, speaks of it as "a cultural expression," almost everyone else discusses it primarily as a business. For example, one of the arguments advanced on behalf of the community's taking an interest in the theatre's prosperity is that if the theatre were to disappear, other commerce—restaurants, parking lots, garages, taxis, ticket brokers—would also suffer!

There is no question that business organization must play a vital role in the conduct of all theatrical enterprise. But if the theatre is a business chiefly aimed at a profit, then it follows that if a profit is not forthcoming it must and should disappear—unless, like the railroads, its continued life is held to be a matter of public interest and need.

Even the Broadway aphorism tells us that "show business is no business." One of the reasons for the thoroughgoing confusion and muddleheadedness of our theatre world is that willy-nilly the theatre is not *essentially* a business. Even the most hardened or money-minded showman has something of the gambler (that is to say, the artist) in him. We in America have forgotten this or were rarely obliged to remember it—as long as business in the theatre could go on as usual.

The theatre as a private enterprise has existed for at least three hundred years. But almost every country in Europe has recognized that the theatre is part of a nation's patrimony and must therefore be subject to some sort of public control through government (royal, princely, civic or national) agency. Thus in France, Germany, the Scandinavian countries, and now even in England (not to mention most of the Iron Curtain countries even before they were converted to that metal) not only are partial government subsidies provided but regulations as to the number and use of playhouses have been set down. (Napoleon took time on his Russian expedition to rule that the Comédie Française must always keep low-priced—5 franc—seats available for the poorer public.) Some part of the country's theatre establishment—and very often the best—was protected so that it might serve its true function as an expression of the nation's spirit, its emblem. The theatre is one of the means by which a society realizes itself.

In America, for historical reasons, the theatre has never been seriously viewed as being integral with the respectability of our social life. It has been assimilated with our business community, in which success (or profit) becomes the symbolic as well as the effective goal. In a normal economic situation this does not necessarily exert disastrous influence. But when the economic balance in the community is upset, our theatre—now ideologically as well as practically dependent on the profit or pure business motive—must be stricken with paralysis and threatened with extinction.

Talent for the theatre and an appetite for it are still abundant. And theatre folk being what they are, germinal artists, the theatre goes on in our country in a schizophrenic state—half crazy from every point of view and less than half as proficient or useful as it might be.

Let us consider one minor point among the various statements in the *Times* reports by producers on matters of settings and stagehands. Some say that settings should be simplified—to reduce costs, and perhaps also because simplified sets are more "artistic." Others, on the contrary, are entirely satisfied with huge expenditures for "scenery"—when the productions they have spent the money on *prove profitable*. The question of artistic fitness in each instance is gauged by the measure of box-office success rather than by the style of scenic investiture demanded by the text. Certain plays which demand large-scale production—many sets and numerous actors—must virtually be ruled out as prohibitively costly, no matter what their intrinsic merit.

When profit becomes the chief criterion or proof of excellence, understanding of the theatre must become distorted. Business standards replace all others. The preferred actor is the one who will sell the most tickets—if nowhere else, at theatre parties. The most important director is the one who has had the most recent hits. The best scene designers are the ones whose work has graced the greatest number of smashes. This way of thinking makes sane judgment impossible, even *in matters of business.*

No wonder then that the dramatists, presumably the pivot of the theatre organism, are among the most frightened of all show folk. To write a flop is not only an economic blow; it is moral disgrace, a loss of status. Is it possible to write in such an atmosphere? Ah, but the "real" writer will never cease writing. Of course not; the question is what will he write?

Present circumstances—inevitable from the false premises on which the theatre has been obliged to operate—poison the whole theatre: the audience, the critics, the very air of the playhouses. The trauma thus created has made the past fifteen years the age of the middleman, or agent. They are the "victors," the lawgivers. There are now agents for everyone, including the audience. This is the end result of our "realism," "practicality" and nonartiness.

Certainly I favor the reduction of taxes on the theatre. (I also favor special tax benefits, such as obtained in France for accredited theatre folk and artists in general.) Whatever immediately practicable remedies to small specific ills can be achieved must win our unqualified endorsement. But I suspect that very little will get done through ordinary Broadway channels. The provision made by the Dramatists' Guild in regard to the curtailment of royalty payments will not be acceptable to most stars, and certainly not to their agents. The same holds true for most of the others—directors and scene designers—and with a certain justification.

One agent very sensibly says, "I am willing to gamble, but it should be a concentrated effort by everyone. Are the theatre owners ready to make concessions? The unions? The producers? Is the producer willing to let the other people participate proportionately for gambling with him?" The theatre is a collective (or corporate) art. It must be managed that way. It is perhaps the model type of organization for the industrial as differentiated from the craft union. But at present the theatre is being run as a business in which every man looks out for himself as good old-fashioned business dictates. That is why we are at the point of collapse.

Yet in collapse may lie our only hope. Health may be restored through breakdown, as to a degree it was during the thirties. The theatre may have to be beaten into sanity. Reason (or art) may return to the theatre when "business" has done almost everything possible to kill it.

Already there are signs of this even in the very chaos which *The New York Times* series exposes. Our audiences—as developments off-Broadway to some extent indicate—are becoming ever more aware of values different from those which are obtained on Broadway. Community theatres are growing on a more extensive scale than before. Such projects as the civic theatre in Minneapolis and the Lincoln Center in New York may be auguries of a salutary change.

Not everyone inside or outside the theatre today deems it peculiar to think or speak of the theatre in the terms I have so often employed in these pages. My "pessimism" is intended as a creative implement. Before the theatre changes there must be some "new" thinking. We will not go far, even '"business-wise," if we confine ourselves to so-called practical assumptions that are incompatible with the nature of the material at hand. We must be persistent and dogged. Relief will not come overnight. In the meantime we must do the best we can. The first step may be to sharpen our theatrical *intelligence*.

—*NAT*, '61

THE DEATH OF BESSIE SMITH

The Death of Bessie Smith is a notably sharp piece of dramatic writing.

Bessie Smith, a famous Negro blues singer of the twenties and thirties, bled to death after a car accident in Memphis, Tennessee, because she was denied medical assistance in all of the city's white hospitals. Albee has dramatized the incident in an unusual manner. Instead of emphasizing the shameful shock of the episode he helps us understand its human sources.

One never sees Bessie. The play is focused on a nurse who is a receptionist in one of the Memphis hospitals. Her life is a tissue of fear, frustration and sadistic compensations. She loathes her semi-invalid father, whose family was once (long ago) imperiously prosperous in Dixie fashion. He is an idle, shriveled, mean man—disfigured by impotent venom and the ludicrous grimaces of racist superiority. In her own way the nurse continues the paternal pattern, for though her job is ill paid and almost menial, she cracks the whip of her "position" over a colored orderly at the hospital, a young fellow with pretentions to self-betterment. She also teases an intern at the hospital who wants her—even offers to marry her—teases him with calculated provocation without satisfying her own or his needs. In addition, she warns him against any aspirations beyond the bounds of their town's horizon. From her inner constriction and the spite that this begets she mocks and terrorizes the two men; and she does this because she is too weak to fight her way out of the impasse of her life. She insists on accepting the constraints the community imposes. Her dominance over the men embodies the environment's stranglehold on all of them. But just this power maims her as well as her victims;

underneath the grinning grimness of her will she is consumed by self-abomination. It must be clear from all of this that the nurse and the others, even the death of Bessie Smith herself, are peripheral symbols pointing to a tragedy wider than that of one county or segment of our society.

The writing of the play is biting, tensely risible, euphonious—making for heightened speech which approaches stylization. It marks Albee once again as a new American playwright from whom much is to be expected.

The most aptly cast actor in the production is Harold Scott as the orderly, but Rae Allen and the others who are of a softer natural disposition play with professional authority and intelligence, though they are directed a little too "psychologically" for a play in which psychology is implicit in the incisive slashes of the dramatist's "drawing" rather than in an internal probing of mental processes. But perhaps this is only a refined quibble: the production is eminently proficient.

—NAT, '61

RHINOCEROS

*R*hinoceros is Eugene Ionesco's "popular" play, or, as he himself has said, the play he wrote *pour le public*. It has been a success in Paris, in Germany, in London (in good measure due to Laurence Olivier's participation), and now it has been cordially received by a press which was generally indifferent to Ionesco's shorter works.

The play's career makes a lively bit of theatre history. In Paris an American writer of *avant-garde* tendencies assured me that *Rhinoceros* was perhaps the only one of Ionesco's plays which was totally without interest for him, while at the same time an English critic affirmed that it was the first Ionesco play which was not rubbish. Nigel Dennis, English novelist, playwright and critic, complained that the play was too explicit and thus lacked the

imaginative piquancy of Ionesco's *The Chairs;* Kenneth Tynan, in London, where most reviewers favored the play rather than the production (directed by Orson Welles), declared that the production was good but the play bad—but I rather suspect that Tynan's seeming prejudice is dictated by his admiration for Brecht, whom Ionesco scorns. Sartre—another author about whom Ionesco is icy—deems *Rhinoceros* to be a play for the complacent, because it does not really make clear why a man should not become a "rhinoceros!"

With such a background of controversy—and having myself seen the London production—I approach the statement of my present reaction with particular care and caution. There is no use in a critic's pretending that he is never influenced. He would be less than human—therefore a poor critic—if this were so.

I advise my readers to see the play. It requires no courage—at this point—to say that it is the most interesting play of the season. (Of course, like all comparative superlatives the remark is somewhat empty: it has been a dismal season and *Rhinoceros* cannot properly be linked with *A Taste of Honey* or even *The Hostage*.) What may certainly be affirmed is that *Rhinoceros* is entertaining and, whatever one's estimate of its underlying spirit, significant. This is sufficient today to make it important.

The play was originally a short story; it is overlong as a three-act play. Its apparent point is made at least three-quarters of an hour before its final curtain. I speak of an "apparent" point because there is something more in the play's message than is contained in the symbol of men who turn into rhinoceroses—the comedy and terror of conformism. For the play, despite the central figure's ultimate defiance of bestiality, is essentially anarchistic, bitter, very nearly hopeless.

The rational mind and logic are absurd, Ionesco tells us; they have little relation to the truth (which is the chaos) of life. Intellectuals are fools. Most organized radicals are not only clowns but robots—ready under pressure to swing from extreme Left to extreme Right. The conventional middle-class gentleman is a moron; the smooth little subaltern of the business community is a fraud; favored hirelings of the *status quo* are grotesque; the sweet young thing whom we regard as the sweetheart of the world is spineless. Ultimately, they all turn into monsters of blind energy, cruel forces of destruction.

A little man—confused, uncertain, without direction except for some nameless grace of disposition—will resist, though he too is probably doomed. (He acknowledges that the person who wishes to remain an individual always ends badly.) Destined to defeat or not, he does resist—all by himself—which may be described as a *pathetic* absurdity. In almost all the other Ionesco plays the counterpart of Berrenger (the helpless "hero" of *Rhinoceros)* is always done in by the Monster—the mysterious Evil which dominates all. In this sense *Rhinoceros* may be said to mark an "advance" for Ionesco, a stirring of conscience against complete despair, an anguished sign of protest against surrender.

Philosophically this is an unsound, as well as an unsatisfactory, position. Humanly, it is quite understandable: many people the world over feel as Berrenger does, both lonely and afraid of others. Historically, it is typical of the state of mind of a large part of the French intelligentsia today. At worst, its attitude is preferable to the nonawareness and spiritual inanition of, let us say, the ordinary American playgoer. Ionesco's merit as an artist is that he finds theatrically telling means to reflect this contemporary fright. His plays are brilliant statements for the stage; his, therefore, is an authentic and original theatre talent.

Ionesco has said that his work has been stimulated by Kafka and the Marx Brothers: it expresses apprehension through gags. In Joseph Anthony's direction of *Rhinoceros* (more engaging than that of the London production) only the gags are effective. The first act (the most successful of the three) is generally hilarious—though there is a faint touch of college theatricals throughout. The latter

impression is due to the fact that we get very little sense of how the fun and games relate to the central theme, which is not at all funny.

The slightly Disney style at the beginning is not only childlike but rather childish and when protracted makes us surmise that we are witnesses to a one-joke affair. But this is not really the case. From the outset the play's final act and particularly its crucial last speech, which approaches the tragic, should have been kept in view. What is required by the material is not so much "Kafka and the Marx Brothers" as Kafka *within* the Marx Brothers. The present production has no true style because each of its elements apes whatever farcical trick or serious sentiment seems to be indicated moment by moment, and does not convey a sense that all of the play's aspects interpenetrate to form a single Idea with an indivisible meaning. Thus, the last scene of the play descends to the level of a rather flat realism.

Still the "show" makes for a good evening with, as they say, loads of laughs. Complimentary remarks might be made about everyone—Eli Wallach for his bewildered sweetness, Morris Carnovsky for his expertness at rendering innocent idiocy, Anne Jackson for her cuteness, etc.; but the outstanding performance is that of Zero Mostel, whose penchant for Rabelaisian antics of inexhaustible comic verve and inventiveness makes the conversion of his bonehead bourgeois into a roaring pachyderm seem masterfully easy, despite the perspiration. My only reservation on this performance is that the final emergence of the character as a rhinoceros should be indicated by a horn thrust through the bathroom door rather than by the actor's own Gargantuan baby face.

—*NAT*, '61

TO THE YOUNG

The greatest obstacle to creativity in the American theatre is the stereotyped idea that only numbers and size count, that only mass media are important. Only what is "big" matters, has influence. There are perhaps only a million regular theatregoers in this country. Mathematically, then, the theatre with us is not a mass medium. But this does not, therefore, mean that the theatre is without social force.

I might, to begin with, adduce the argument that many plays serve as screen material or are assimilated into television shows—thus becoming part of mass entertainment. Such an argument, however, would not be only an evasion, but a falsification of my thesis.

Every valid expression of a fundamental idea relevant to human personality, to society, to objective fact has life in it which will bear fruit—no matter how special, abstruse, eccentric it may at first appear. Einstein's equations—intelligible at first to only a handful of scientists—have revolutionized the twentieth century. The strange conjectures of a Viennese doctor, Freud, have penetrated all our thinking, not only in the fields of psychology and medicine but in education, law, literature. The patterns of obscure and presumably "crazy" artists in Paris are now commonplaces of household and commercial decoration as well as of architecture—even among people who still regard those artists as phonies.

Bernard Shaw's early plays were hardly noticed when they were first presented in tiny London theatres. (One of them, in fact—*Mrs. Warren's Profession*—was suppressed by the police in its first New York production.) More recently a young English actor of no outstanding histrionic ability, John Osborne, wrote a play called *Look Back in Anger* which was given at a smallish off-center theatre in London; it made a whole generation of Englishmen—in and out of the theatre—conscious of a serious change in their country's social character. The name of the play's pivotal figure—Jimmy Porter—has become a sort of byword in Britain. What is first whispered in secret may one day be shouted from the housetops.

The conventional rejoinder to this is that a play is not like a scientific formula, a philosophic doctrine or a new form in one of the other arts. A play will either please at once or expire. This was not true of Chekhov's, Ibsen's or Shaw's plays. Or, more pertinently, take the case of so well-known a play as Sartre's *No Exit*. It was successfully presented in a small theatre in Paris. (Most of Ionesco's plays are still given in small theatres.) *No Exit* was a failure on Broadway (as was another famous European play: Beckett's *Waiting for Godot*). But *No Exit* has been playing ever since in community and college theatres all over our country.

What is really in everyone's mind when people speak of success is profit. That is the crux of the matter. But even the concept of profit should be debated. Where communities support libraries, opera houses, art museums, symphony orchestras—as in most European countries—there are also theatres that produce plays many of which are recognizably unsuited to a large public. These plays are not necessarily dismissed as less significant or less valuable than the more popular ones. In fact many critics on such occasions maintain that these "off-beat" plays are frequently more useful to the community than the others and endeavor to explain the worth of these special plays in the hope that they may someday command a wider audience.

This, you may object, is a foreign instance. We are concerned with our United States. Failure in the theatre with us is viewed not as a disappointment but as a disgrace. The reason for this is that we equate excellence with success, and success with fortune. In a virtuous mood we deny this, contesting instead that we do not produce plays for our individual pleasure and edification alone. To fight this primary principle is to appear misanthropic, undemocratic and, what may be considered even more horrible, impractical!

This is a half-truth that masks our fixation on large numbers and our appetite for money. A noted playwright, when I suggested that he might invest some of his own funds in his play, exclaimed in sincere consternation, "But, Harold, I have only $250,000 in the bank!" To live as a member of the community with the "best," to feel that he need no longer suffer a social inferiority complex, to maintain the self-esteem he had finally achieved, this artist felt he had to possess a very sizable bank account. If his income or savings were to be reduced to, let us say, that of a college professor he might once again count himself an inconsequential citizen. In our theatre we are a little like Willy Loman, the sorry salesman of Arthur Miller's play: we want not only to be liked, but to be well liked.

I do not recommend as an antidote that we reject "popular appeal." The most "revolutionary" playwright wants to gain the sympathy and the plaudits of the widest possible audience. The quest for publication or production denotes a search for allies. The dramatist who denounces his fellow countrymen does so because of some faith he wants them to share. There is a positive—perhaps even a creative—purpose in plays of seemingly destructive intent. They may finally prove salutary.

The cliché that genuine creativity and popular appeal are incompatible or antagonistic concepts is debilitating. It leads not only to bad business but to artistic incompetence. Let no one tell you that it does not matter that a play is poorly written, awkwardly constructed, sloppily produced and acted as long as it has "something to say" or that its aim is artistic superiority rather than mass attractiveness. This is double-talk. On the other hand, I cannot possibly enumerate the number of plays produced every season which are intended to draw the great public but which fail to entertain or elevate—and therefore "flop."

A normal approach to the theatre may be exemplified in certain of my own experiences. In 1938 a play was submitted to me by William Saroyan, to whom I had previously written, encouraging him to turn to the stage. The play he sent me—*My Heart's in the Highlands*—was by no means a difficult one; if anything, it was over-simple. It was a folk tale—humorous, tender with a loosely articulated ideological point: though the artist may seem an eccentric creature, simple folk need him and will feed him, for he brings them the

solace of his music. Some of my colleagues demurred at the idea of our (the Group Theatre's) producing the play because in those days young folk felt that plays had to be "dynamite!" I felt that Saroyan had a fresh talent, he sounded a heartening note in a wryly smiling manner which deserved to be heard.

I was hardheaded about the project. The play had only a wisp of a plot and though delightful might seem far too slight for Broadway. I decided that it should be very economically presented at five special performances. When the play was given, the majority press verdict was highly favorable. The Theatre Guild, which had previously refused to offer the play to its subscribers, now agreed to do so. It ran for six weeks. To me this meant that the play had been a success—though it had made no money.

I counted the play a success because it had pleased many more people than I had supposed would be pleased; it had also encouraged a new playwright, who was to write a more popular play later on; it had introduced a new director, Robert Lewis, a new composer, Paul Bowles, both of whom initiated their eventful careers with this production. In short, I thought of the play in terms of its function for its author and for our theatre. But others who admired the play bemoaned its "failure" in view of the money "lost." That money, by the way, was supplied from a portion of our profits in Odets' *Golden Boy.*

Then, in 1949, there was Carson McCullers' *A Member of the Wedding,* a play which brought acclaim to one of our finest actresses—Julie Harris. No manager wanted to rent us a house for this play; it was sure to be a dud. It had hardly any story: a twelve-year-old girl insists on accompanying her brother on his honeymoon, to become what she called "a member of the wedding." How silly! It was difficult to raise money for such a play—and at that time Broadway production was approximately half as costly as it is now. But we managed to get it on. It was a solid success.

The point in this case is not that I had any foreknowledge of the play's eventual success. (A conjur man knows as much about what will or will not succeed as any Broadway producer!) In fact, I feared a terrible fiasco. But I did believe it a lovely play—and hoped and worked hard to make it as good as it could possibly be. Had it failed I should have been very sorry indeed, but my appreciation of its quality would have remained undiminished—and I would have continued to produce more such "hazardous" plays.

Then again, in 1955, Jean Giraudoux's *There Will Be No War in Troy*, which we called *Tiger at the Gates*, was offered me for direction. The play had been produced successfully in Paris some twenty years before. It had been available in various translations to both English and American producers who professed to admire it. Their excuse for not doing the play was that it was a so-called intellectual and very "talky" play, besides being in the costume of a place and time not ordinarily associated with popular entertainment. We decided to produce the play in London first, where the audience might prove more receptive than a New York audience. The English manager assured us that the contrary was true: Londoners were more backward in regard to such plays than New Yorkers! The play was warmly received in London and most enthusiastically in New York. It ran six months in the latter city—not as long as certain other plays of lesser merit, but it did show a profit. I was not only satisfied, I was elated.

Instead of dwelling on these comparative success stories I shall speak now of an out-and-out failure: a play none of you ever heard of. In 1931 the Group Theatre chose to do a play, *1931—*, about unemployment. It was not a very well-written play, but it dealt with a crucial problem and lent itself to a fine ensemble production. We believed it our duty to produce it. It ran for only nine performances. Brooks Atkinson of *The New York Times* opened his review of it with this statement: "Seldom has a bad play stunned an audience so completely." In his second review, the same critic added *"1931—*is sufficiently forthright in the

theatre to upset a playgoer's natural complacence and to make the life of these times more intelligible and vivid."

The failure of this play was personally disheartening. But it inspired the organization of several new off-Broadway ventures whose aim was to present plays of a similar nature. It also paved the way for the cordial reception of some of Odets' later and much more successful plays. This forgotten failure exercised more influence than its brief run would indicate.

To cite a more immediate instance, I should mention what was perhaps the outstanding play of last season in New York: Jack Gelber's *The Connection*—a play about drug addicts. It was not written as a sensational piece—Hollywood fashion. The press, to begin with, dismissed it as altogether negligible. If it had been produced on Broadway it would have closed at once. But it was given in a little off-Broadway theatre by a company calling itself The Living Theatre. The reviewers for the weeklies praised it; the play ran all season and continued to run. The author was sufficiently encouraged to write another play.

The history of Bertolt Brecht's and Kurt Weill's musical play *The Threepenny Opera* is also significant. First produced on Broadway in the early thirties, it died unmourned. Produced in a small off-Broadway theatre six years ago it was acclaimed by everyone—ran for years, while one of its tunes became a leader on the Hit Parade! Later produced in larger houses on the road at necessarily higher prices, it was a failure again.

From all this we may learn that even the terms "success" and "failure" need further examination. The honest and truly devoted craftsman may succeed even in these economically uncertain times. Many of our most respected and successful theatre people have not worked with success in mind so much as with the will to create fine things. And since the theatre at its best has always been the bearer of significant tidings—whether of an emotional, psychological or social character—the theatre cannot fail to exercise considerable influence even in our so-called mass-minded civilization. He who speaks eloquently, truthfully, persistently will finally be heard.

The path is not an easy one; it never has been. What has the playwright who was the great hope of the thirties been doing since 1955? One of the most gifted dramatists since O'Neill, he has written several screenplays—none of them to be classed with the least of his stage plays. My considered opinion is that the writer I speak of has been serving Hollywood not only to make more money than he may be able to earn in the theatre but more particularly because he cannot bear the peculiar psychological embarrassment attendant on Broadway defeat. (Even though, be it noted, none of this writer's plays have ever been fiascoes.) The threat to the talented man on Broadway is not so much poverty as lack of plaudits—that esteem which produces favorable publicity and its by-products.

We are back again at the social phenomenon which is at the root of so many fears and subsequent evils: our ideals are directed toward externals, the glaring, the flashy, the noisy, the multitudinous. Money plus popularity have graduated from being conveniences to the point of conferring "moral" status. Herein lies the secret weapon of conformity.

I hope we never have a depression like that of the thirties. But the anguish of the thirties helped form the Group Theatre and Odets, it helped foster the careers of directors like Strasberg, Kazan and Lewis, and finally those of Tennessee Williams and Arthur Miller. If the theatre, the movies, radio and television were to be struck by another wave of economic hardship, they would not go under: they would shrink and become more modest with consequences which might ultimately prove beneficial. There is already evidence of this in the rise of independent movies. The growth of the off-Broadway theatre movement, the extension of community and college theatres, the development of new theatre groups in San Francisco, Washington, Texas may be harbingers of renewal.

The difficulty for the creator in the New York theatre is that production has become terribly expensive, the cost of tickets too high and nothing but smash hits—plays which fill the house immediately after the opening and for a long time afterward—can survive. In London, where tickets today cost exactly what they did before the war, a play which can only fill two-thirds of the house may prove profitable. In New York this is virtually impossible.

This condition fills everyone who works in our theatre with an agony of fear. The game is to the bold, but the boldness now in demand is the speculator's rather than the artist's—so much so that while it is greatly to the credit of the producer and the cast of Ionesco's provocative play *Rhinoceros* to have done it on Broadway, I believe it might have been wiser to have done it elsewhere. Less profits would have accrued to all concerned from such a production, but my guess is that despite a largely favorable press there will be little profit on Broadway to the producer and, in a sense, less honor, because fewer people to whom the play would mean something beyond an evening's fun will be able to see it at Broadway prices.

That is the paradox and the dilemma: if you play for the high stakes of Broadway success—in terms of money—you are limiting yourself in a cultural sense. Your audiences are likely to be less representative of the more serious public. Many of the most significant writers of our time are bad bets commercially under present economic circumstances.

Shakespeare without stars is impossible now on Broadway; so, generally speaking, are Shaw, Ibsen, Pirandello, O'Casey and most of the other classic dramatists. So are nearly most "gloomy" plays. (*The Visit,* a rather "shocking" play, was sustained by the glamor of the Lunts.) Indeed, when we speak of such plays we strike a sore spot of the American theatre.

You may have heard it said that any criticism of our country's procedures, customs, manners or morals lessens its prestige. I doubt the truth of the allegation; Europeans like us best when we do not declare ourselves superior in every way. Boastfulness, even a too resounding pride, gives the impression of complacency—particularly resented when evident in the fortunate. But it is more or less established fact in theatre history since Ibsen that plays critical of the dramatist's native culture have been the most important plays of their time. In America, many of our acknowledged best plays, beginning with Eugene O'Neill, have been "troublesome." As a young and very lucky people it is hard for us to accept what we call the "downbeat." Tragedy is associated in our minds with remote people and epochs: the Greeks, the Elizabethans, the Russians, the Scandinavians.

Despite the success (off-Broadway!) of O'Neill's *The Iceman Cometh,* of Miller's *Death of a Salesman,* of Williams' *A Streetcar Named Desire,* we want our "sad" plays nowadays to possess the sweet balm of Wilder's *Our Town*— which be it noted is situated in a rural vicinity of another era. This peculiarity of ours may not in itself be a vice—though the inability to be objective about pain and evil is not a sign of health—but it does add to our difficulty in presenting somber, bitter or controversial plays on Broadway. Such plays are not necessarily good or "artistic"; but when we shun plays simply on the grounds that they are grim (like the man who left the theatre indignantly five minutes after the curtain rose on Arthur Miller's *All My Sons* when he realized that it was not a comedy) we are perilously close to artistic inanity. The result is the prevalence today of musicals.

Some of the best plays now being written abroad and, to a certain extent, here are declarations of pain of one kind or another. For our theatre to remain vital and to exercise a broad influence it must allow room for such plays. Free speech in the theatre as elsewhere is the surest guarantee of a sane polity.

Some American playwrights have known how to combine the serious statement of major themes with something akin to our popular tradition. This might be said of Thornton Wilder's *The Skin of Our Teeth,* for instance—written with a view to our war-time situation. One of Eugene O'Neill's objectives, I believe, was to encompass the history of America's spiritual struggles in plays with simple, strong plots. Steinbeck's *Of Mice and Men* and Saroyan's *The Time of Your Life* also represent worthy attempts to speak subtly in a folk vein.

We must never abandon the task of essential creation despite all the obstacles in the way. Our very difficulties may force a solution. The problem should not resolve itself to a choice between writing down to the mass audience or shunning it. The answers lie within the conscience, tenacity, fortitude and skill of individual artists. Each man must learn what he wishes to say and work very hard to say it in the manner most compatible with his spirit, taste and inclination. But a resolute objectivity is required; if what results from one's impulse is a play which seems most suited to a small public it is foolhardy to insist that a great public embrace it. Nor, as I have tried to remind you, is the work enjoyed by a small public futile in terms of mass influence. Sooner or later in one way or another the mass will absorb it. The good popular playwright is as devoted to his work and as industrious as the esoteric playwright. Perhaps the musical *Guys and Dolls* says as much about certain phases of big-city life as certain more earnest entertainments.

The so-called masses contain many publics. The practical problem before us is how to reach the right public for each kind of play. The Federal Theatre Project sought and found new audiences all over our country. The warm welcome to Shakespeare in New York's Central Park is another significant sign. The success of plays like Williams' *Summer and Smoke,* O'Neill's *The Iceman Cometh,* Giraudoux's *Tiger at the Gates,* Eliot's *The Cocktail Party,* Fry's *The Lady's. Not For Burning,* when presented under the auspices best suited to them, is also evidence that we need not think of the public as one undifferentiated mass.

Our newspaper and weekly drama critics have of recent years become more receptive to novelty and originality. Although very few critics have assumed the responsibilities of leadership—in the sense that Bernard Shaw as a critic did—some of them give evidence these days of wishing to be of service to the larger and permanent concerns of the theatre. Their hearts at least are in the right place.

Ours is not an altogether homogeneous society. It is difficult to interest everyone in precisely the same way. The only exceptions to this rule may occur at times of national crisis, such as war or a natural catastrophe which affects the whole community. Plays at such times tend to become documentary, propagandistic, overly sentimental. Motion pictures and television usually treat topical material with more immediate effect than the theatre. The theatre in relation to these other media is as verse to prose. The theatre is, so to speak, the "metaphysics" of the news. Plays like *Sunrise at Campobello* and musicals like *Fiorello!* are chromos of popular legend: they have value as reminiscence after the fashion of camp-fire songs.

My message to young people in the theatre today is more than ever "To thine own self be true." In a way the mass you seek to please does not exist—only people do. The "mass" has no face; it is therefore largely inhuman. Discipline yourselves to speak from your heart and from your mind, that is, from your own experience, to the people who have provided you with the ground and framework of that experience. The more scrupulous your effort to make the passage from your conscience and consciousness to theirs the more successful you will eventually be—in whatever way is most important to you. In short, every decade the childrens' call must be raised anew: "Come out! Come out! Wherever you are!"

—*NYT*, '61

THE NIGHT OF THE IGUANA
BRECHT ON BRECHT
PLAYS FROM BLEECKER STREET

Some years ago, defending a novel by a famous writer which had been thoroughly roasted in all the reviews, Tennessee Williams said he liked the book because the novelist had succeeded in thoroughly exposing his inner being. That is a romantic view of the function of art, but since all works of art do in fact reveal the men who made them—though I doubt that it is their main purpose or value—I am not prepared to contest Williams' defense.

Tennessee Williams is a romantic. While his latest play, *The Night of the Iguana* (Royale Theatre), is certainly not strict autobiography, it does give us an idea of how Williams sees and judges himself. At the moment this seems to me the most rewarding aspect of the play, though not the only one. Indeed, it is easy to assert that it is the best American play of the season—since there is nothing else to stand beside it.

There is sentimentality in all of Williams' work, but in *The Night of the Iguana* he is not trying to show himself in a favorable light. The reverse may be closer to the truth. If there is pardon in the play, it results from confession and self-castigation—which is one of the forms a puritanical romanticism takes.

The central character is the still young Lawrence Shannon, an Episcopal minister who has shocked his congregation by denouncing its God and substituted for Him a pantheistic deity, or to put it more plainly, a god as amoral as the forces of nature themselves. Shannon's church is closed to him and he has become a tourist guide in Mexico. He takes pleasure in showing his (American) clients the shady or seamy side of the places they visit, not only because that is what attracts him but also because it fascinates them. He is given to promiscuous fornication—usually with young persons, even minors.

The personal association is clear, is it not? A man of religious disposition desires to spread the Word, but the old God of vengeance is too narrow and shallow for him. Since he cannot renounce instructing and preaching, he must bring to everyone's attention the secret and foul byways of man's experience. Unless these are disclosed life cannot be wholly known or accepted. (This too is what *audiences* hunger to have displayed in a repressed and morally worried community such as ours.) To dedicate oneself to such instruction may have its reprehensible side, but there is a grave mission in it as well.

There is very little indulgence in the portrait of Reverend Shannon. He meets a beautiful and very spiritual New England spinster who travels about with her grandfather, once a well-known minor poet. To support themselves in their extensive peregrinations she paints water colors and he recites his verse in hostelries, restaurants, holiday resorts. The girl is chaste without strain, pure without vanity. She understands all, forgives all. She is the image of what the outcast preacher considers almost sacred. He knows he cannot corrupt, break or defile her. She has her own strength. Nor can he ever measure up to what she embodies. So he reconciles himself to becoming the companion in waywardness of the lewd and gusty lady whose hotel is the scene of the play. Smiling ruefully, Williams must be content (like his poet) to set himself down as "frightened me."

If one does not perceive the drift of *Iguana* in its relation to its author's legend, the play may seem meaningless, shapeless, a little unreal. Every character is more conceptual than specifically true. (I must allow, but find it especially difficult to believe, that Shannon was ever an ordained minister.) Yet such is Williams' talent that the play breathes with its own artistic life.

The writing, to begin with, is lambent, fluid, malleable and colloquially melodious. It bathes everything in glamour. Colored lights seem to illuminate all the play's people, lending them an odd

dimension. I do not care for the hinted psychoanalytic explanation given of Shannon's behavior, but one cannot resist Williams' intuitive invention. For example, cavorting through the seedy Mexican hotel is a chorus of comic maenads in the shape of German (Nazi) tourists—so many fat grubs infesting the place with a sick-making health.

These and the terrifyingly funny secondary characters—the hysterical girl Shannon has seduced (it is interesting to note that he maintains the girls have seduced him), the righteously indignant American schoolteacher infuriated by Shannon—all form part of a picture that not only lends the play credibility but an extraordinary vividness.

A born dramatist, Williams writes wonderful acting parts. The cast has been admirably chosen. Margaret Leighton glows with a subtle flame which conveys a sense of mystery, pity and awe—almost pictorial. Bette Davis, in perhaps the most soundly written part, is ablaze as the sullied bacchante who owns the hotel in which she and the apostate will continue to sin. Patrick O'Neal has the right mask for Shannon—wracked with fever, guilt and a depraved saintliness which somehow resembles asceticism. O'Neal's is a real characterization, though in avoiding gush he appears a little dry, perhaps depriving the personage of lyricism. (It may be a fine point of interpretation whether this is desirable or not.) Patricia Roe and Lane Bradbury are highly effective in smaller parts; Alan Webb who plays the nonagenarian poet is, as always, a complete craftsman. Oliver Smith's set—the seedy hotel rank with undergrowth of strange flora and fauna—is one of his best. The company plays well together, to the credit of the director, Frank Corsaro.

I am pleased that Bertolt Brecht should have a success with the anthology of his writings which a group of zealous actors (Viveca Lindfors, Lotte Lenya, Anne Jackson, Dane Clark, George Voskovec, Michael Wager) are presenting at the Theatre de Lys under the title *Brecht on Brecht*. It lasts a full evening, yet it offers only a smattering of Brecht's scope. Still, it is better to have a bit of Brecht than none at all—especially since we have had so much discussion Brecht while the production of his work is still largely confined to foreign shores.

The better part of the evening is the first—devoted to his "life." Here short poems, anecdotes, a recording of his testimony at he hearing before the House Un-American Activities Committee (1947), passages from diaries, epigrams, quips and several songs are read, recited, played or sung.

Part Two—"Theatre"—is composed of speeches and scenes from plays (also some songs) which fail to contribute much to our appreciation of Brecht as a dramatist. One applauds out of partisanship and as a tribute to the outstanding figure of the world theatre since the war, but one is also frustrated. The longest piece of the evening is a scene called "The Jewish Wife" from one of Brecht's least representative plays, *The Private Life of the Master Race*.

There is a note of nostalgia in the Brecht evening, too, for the material in general recalls a time of strong feeling, witty eloquence, high aspiration, struggle, fortitude everywhere absent now within our domain.

I was sorely disappointed by Thornton Wilder's three short *Plays for Bleecker Street* (Circle-in-the-Square). This distinguished writer is trying to capture certain simple truths and state them in the most rudimentary theatre terms—like so many burlesque skits combined with the bare didacticism of (Chinese?) popular theatre. In *Our Town* this was accomplished by the use of prose that was refreshingly crisp as a snowball and mitigated the oversweet and rather commonplace nature of the play's content. In *The Skin of Our Teeth* the theatre tricks as well as the writing gave a wholesome morality play something like stature. *The Matchmaker* (an adaptation) was a thorough delight that conveyed Wilder's basic geniality and enjoyment of ordinary experience.

These *Plays for Bleecker Street* (part of a long series) strike me in their lighter moments—the first

skit might be called "If Infants Could Speak" and the second "What Children Think"—as false naïveté. They contain only occasional glimmers of original humor. We are aware of a plan and of effort but the pleasure we anticipate after the initial surprise is not provided. Macintyre Dixon and Richard Libertini, who play babies in perambulators, are entertaining.

As for the third piece, which discloses why and how Francis of Assisi came to take the vow of poverty, the less said the better. This is amateur stuff, showing no trace of Wilder's considerable gifts. Dolores Dorn's lovely face (her nun's headdress covers the rest) and Lee Richardson's posture and expression describe the traditional Franciscan line that one observes in Giotto.

—*NAT*, 27 Jan. '62

CREDITORS
LUTHER
WHO'LL SAVE THE PLOUGHBOY?
SECOND CITY

Between mid-December and January seventh I was abroad and saw a number of productions in Paris and London—very few of them of consuming interest. My playgoing schedule since then has been so crowded that I find myself thinking of the performances I have seen in clusters and feel obliged to report on them in jet-propelled disorder.

Strindberg's *Creditors* (Mermaid Theatre) made me recall John Osborne's *Luther* in London, not because they are in any way similar but because each (like Williams' *Iguana*) is wrought from the dramatist's preoccupation with himself. I am not at all sure *Creditors* is a "good" play but it is certainly the work of a genius. Written in 1888, it anticipates Freud, existentialism and expressionism. If the play is "realistic" at all it is so only in its critical and psychological spirit. It is far too compressed, hectic, too consciously analytic, too verbally and explosively expressive to be called realism as we commonly know it. As the play progresses, its story of jealous rivalry between the husband and the ex-husband of an enigmatically fickle woman—it is a question of "revenge" rather than love which motivates the ex-husband—creates the impression that the two men represent two poles of the author's psyche.

Strindberg had something of the scientist's probing mentality—objective, skeptical, "surgical." He was also an unregenerate romantic—impressionable, vulnerable, imaginative and passionate to the point of madness. One part of the man looks upon the woman with merciless distrust, the other is totally infatuated by her. This makes a monstrous mixture, in which a vindictive lucidity is fractured by gusts of feverish feeling, so that in contemplating it we are uncertain whether we are witnessing a clinical exhibition, an opera or a surrealist séance. One is caught in the midst of an unresolved conflict between a coldly enraged mind and a too fervent heart in which woman is the stake and man the victim. The effect borders on the grotesque.

Only a great European (Swedish, German, Russian) company could do full justice to such material. There are some intelligently articulated scenes in Paul Shyre's present production, but the play's extremely difficult style has eluded him. Still it is on the whole a respectable performance in which Rae Allen catches and sustains some of the fascinating ambiguity as the female of Strindberg's fixation.

But what has all this to do with Osborne's *Luther*? Only this: Luther in that play is none other than Osborne himself—an angry young man who, admittedly, hates himself. His rebellion against Rome, the Pope, the Church is a rebellion against all authority—more costive than inspired. Someone says of Luther in the course of the play that he can only love others. That is psychologically untenable: one cannot hate oneself and love others.

Luther is not at all a good play, though by combining powerful quotations from the German monk's life and letters with some of his own gift

for vituperative rhetoric, Osborne has written passages that give the play vigor. But it is mostly a confession of venomous confusion, and its narrow subjectivism distorts and diminishes the name it bears. Still, the play holds its London audience because the English want to see their stored-up bile poured hot on the stage to compensate for a social life that still keeps them under great restraint.

There is a funny side to the turmoil in Strindberg but to think of *Creditors* as a "laugh play"—which is how we often think of comedy—is like equating the humor in Chekhov's plays with gags. It was an unfortunate day when certain critics pointed out that Chekhov insisted his plays were comedies. As a result, many actors and directors do everything possible to dispel the notion from our audiences' minds that Chekhov is gloomy. Labels like "tragedy," "comedy," etc., though useful, often prove theatrically misleading. A situation in a play has its own intrinsic nature and placing it in one aesthetic category or another does not convey its essence.

I was reminded of this on seeing Michel Saint-Denis' painstaking and star-studded (John Gielgud, Peggy Ashcroft) London production of *The Cherry Orchard*. I was put off by the italicization of its "points" in the vein of English (or even French) theatre. For all the delicacy of their creator's perception, Chekhov's characters are earthy, juicy, even peasant-like: certainly not "sophisticated" in the West European manner. But that fact the Saint-Denis company entirely misses.

The French today rarely produce significant realistic plays: they embody ideas, abstract concepts, moods, parables and paradoxes. From Sartre to Ionesco, there are few "real" people in the French theatre—only ideas about people, metaphors in make-up (this is not necessarily a fault). The English are now striving to achieve a new eloquence (and a new—"proletarian"—realism) in their plays, though for security they tend to hark back to Galsworthy rather than to Shaw. In the absence of Rattigan, there is at the moment a staidly intelligent, decorous liberalism in the dramatization of C. P. Snow's *An Affair*—a plea for fairness to the "enemy," tolerance for the unpopular—the application of the English ideal of the Law to every social problem.

The Phoenix Theatre has favored us with a slice of unadorned and bitterly ironic realism in a first play by Frank D. Gilroy, *Who'll Save the Plowboy?* It contains something of the early O'Neill (*Beyond the Horizon*) and perhaps even a hint of the better O. Henry, which is to say that the play possesses a kind of dour trenchancy, as well as pity and anguish over the quirks of fate. This may signify that the occasion marks the debut of a valuable talent.

William Smithers gives an impressive performance, adding a note of subtle feeling to the play which does not, for all its merit, sufficiently resound and echo in our imagination. Still the realistic key is a healthy one which most American playwrights abandon at their peril.

It was said of the youngsters in *From the Second City* during their early season engagement on Broadway that they had been housed in too large a theatre. I prefer to put it that their audience was too small. When they were uptown I enjoyed their genial off-the-cuff humor and oblique digs at the epic mishmash of our time and I continue to be gladdened by their new show at the café-bar at Square East.

The seven players are natural clowns, and each of them has a special and praiseworthy contribution to make. They all give the impression of being intellectuals without wishing to be anything so distressingly highfalutin. I am especially partial to Barbara Harris, whose large eyes within a mask that appears to be composed of rubber and silk, have the peculiar sparkle of a naïveté which is secretly disabused. She is one of those young players for whom one is tempted to predict a Career.

—*NAT*, 10 Feb. '62

ST. JOAN
A GIFT OF TIME

Shaw's *St. Joan* as the Old Vic presents it (City Center) is a reasonable play. It all makes sense. The lines are intelligently spoken (George Howe's Inquisitor, for example, is a model of relaxed speech, as John Clement's Warwick is a triumph of timing) and no point is missed. An assured professionalism is everywhere apparent. As a recorded reading the production might prove first-rate.

One of the chief attributes of Shaw's genius was his common sense. He was also a markedly didactic writer. *St. Joan* may be viewed as a lesson. But what makes Shaw Shaw, apart from the wit and fun in him, is his passion. The passion was moral and, if you will, intellectual, but passion none the less. Joan's peasantlike candor is the mask that Shaw puts on the girl for characterization; all the rest has a frantic fire and the fine impetus of an arrow in flight. Shaw's Joan is irrepressibly voluble, obstinately zealous, impatiently right. She is a saint, and consequently a menace. There is no quelling her except by burning.

To oppose such a force as Joan there must be opposition of equal power and will. There must be conflict between well-matched antagonists. This is lacking in the Old Vic production. Barbara Jefford's Joan is faithful to the direction; that is to say, to the letter of the play. There is no flash or flame. She gives her opponents no trouble, and they are hardly more than slightly disturbed by her. The issues she raises carry little weight. The Church is not shaken; the English commander is able to dispose of the whole matter by a string of epigrams.

The play itself is one of Shaw's most ambitious and most eloquent: it stops just this side of poetry. It is moving not only because of the wonderful story it retells but because its basic quality is a certain sweetness and innocence.

Under the intellection, the quips, the instruction, the classic (sometimes almost corny) stagecraft lie Shaw's kind soul and good heart. Shaw reveals himself as a pure man. The play holds.

What I prefer and respect in Garson Kanin's *A Gift of Time* (Ethel Barrymore Theatre), based on *Death of a Man* by Lael Tucker Wertenbaker, is its theme: the facing of death.

I believe with Spinoza that the wise man does not dwell on the thought of death but concerns himself entirely with living. But to "ignore" death, to fail to recognize its ever-present role in the life process, to fear the very mention of the word is to condemn oneself to perpetual immaturity.

What *A Gift of Time* does is to plant death squarely at the center of the stage and this for our theatre is altogether healthy. Just as a theatrical and cinematic taboo once prohibited mention of venereal disease, so to this day death as anything but a symbol, a hushed mystery, or as an escape to "tragedy" (the suicide which sometimes conveniently ends plays that are in need of strong curtains) is shunned in show business.

For this reason I found myself sympathetic to Mr. Kanin's play even while I felt it slipping away from me, not only into sentimentality (which doesn't necessarily offend me), but into banality. The best thing in the play as it now stands is Henry Fonda. He plays Charles Christian Wertenbaker, the writer who in his early fifties is stricken with cancer and faces it with courage and wisdom till all pleasure in, and hope of, a normal life are gone. At that point he kills himself with the consent and aid of his wife.

What deprives the play of stature (except for its "pioneering") is that, apart from their predicament, we never get to know anything about its two central characters. The death of a cipher is neither touching nor interesting. Wertenbaker and his wife are presented as nice Americans. He appreciates the good things of life—the five senses and the tenderness of women—and when he realizes the imminence of death he bids his family and friends to do likewise: to live life to the full and to cherish

it. His wife is devoted, staunch and sufficiently resolute to bear with her husband's determination to die according to his own code. Still, apart from the rather glib good humor of the jokes they crack and the air of affability with which they surround themselves and which they spread to others, we learn very little about them. They are merely pegs for pathos.

I remember a scene in a Russian novel in which a man in the last throes of tuberculosis curses the world and his comrades because they will continue to live and he must die. He was never a pleasant character in any part of the book nor was there a trace of the benign in the description of his agony. Yet for all its bitterness, his death became an exalted thing; we were made to feel that the expiring man alone seemed to know the value of life, even though his life had never been a happy one. The novelist was able to achieve this by giving the character a real identity with a relation to a fully dimensioned environment. In *A Gift of Time* the characters have the featureless benevolence of stock fiction—even though, as we know, the play is based on actual events and real people.

—*NAT*, 10 Mar. '62

PERIOD OF ADJUSTMENT
THE TEMPEST
A FUNNY THING HAPPENED ON
THE WAY TO THE FORUM

Just before leaving London I saw Tennessee Williams' *Period of Adjustment* at the Royal Court theatre. (It has since moved to the West End.) The play, you may remember, is a little comedy which had a moderate run on Broadway two seasons ago, attracting a few enthusiastic admirers but a larger number of detractors. It has been most cordially received by the London press and is a distinct hit—Williams' first real box-office success in England.

The explanation for this sort of reversal of theatrical fortune is often ascribed to an improvement in production. The London performance, it has been said, is superior to the one on Broadway. I am inclined to doubt that this is the cause for the play's greater appeal now.

It is not the production in London which has turned the play into a success: it is the audience. The audience provides the play's comment. The English stage has latterly become tougher and rougher, its public more eager to see the depiction of working-class people and environments—and provincial ones at that—a milieu that was rare in the West End theatre before 1956. Greater latitude in subject matter, language, moral and social disposition is increasingly manifest. I believe, therefore, that there is going to be a decided "trend" in London toward plays in which sex will serve as a central theme.

But just as Wesker has tried to show in his most recent play *Chips With Everything* that the English Establishment tends to absorb and neutralize "proletarian" protest, so the new sex plays will, to begin with, not parallel Williams' *Streetcar*, *Cat* or *Iguana*; nor will they resemble the sex tragedies of the Continental playwrights from Strindberg and Wedekind to Anouilh.

Williams' early plays may have exercised some influence on a few English playwrights—although that is hardly evident as yet—but it is clear that the playgoing public has not generally been attracted by them. They probably strike that public as too private, unmannerly, extreme and strenuous. They take their "nastiness" too seriously.

In *Period of Adjustment* Williams pokes fun at the sexual timidity, frustration, psychic impotence, gingerliness of the average (Puritan) American—and very few among us have been unaffected in one way or another by our now low-grade Puritanism. The English can appreciate this, for in somewhat different fashion, but even more widely and acutely, they are similarly affected. That is especially true of the educated and semi-educated middle class, if not indeed of large

sections of the working class as well. The generalization may be disputed with respect to the acts and facts of English sexual behavior, but it is true beyond question that frank, open discussion and presentation of sexual impulses in public places like the theatre is still sketchy. The bonds are about to burst.

The breakthrough will at first probably take the form of good-humored comedies like *Period of Adjustment*, in which the Londoners can have their sexual cake and at the same time laugh it off. It is safer that way—and it is especially safe when the play is American—at once racy and sympathetically sentimental.

As a postscript to this, I must add that, just as the London theatre public is now little interested in literary or studiously poetic plays (like those of Eliot or Fry) and prefers on the one hand Osborne, Wesker, Delaney and Beckett, and on the other Pinter, Ionesco and Simpson, so it is possible that America—if any tendencies beyond musical comedy can be discerned in our anarchy—is beginning to hanker after "dignity." *A Man For All Seasons*, an English play, does even better in New York than in London, while *J. B.* fails totally in London.

Back in New York I had a thoroughly good time at the Central Park production of *The Tempest*. This—Shakespeare's farewell to the theatre—is sometimes played dreamily as a philosophical pageant, but there is no reason at all why it should not be done, as here, in the mood of a heavenly farce.

The actors' diction at the New York Shakespeare Festival is rarely "distinguished" and sometimes not even wholly distinct, but the play comes through with youthful bounce and a wild gaiety under Gerald Freedman's well-thought-out and delightfully realized direction. We *see* the play: every speech and scene is translated into substantial physical action. None of the performers is bad and some, like James Earl Jones who plays Caliban, are excellent. Every one has a consistent characterization—sometimes a particularly apt and amusing one. That is the case with Ferdinand of Richard Jordan; he does not hesitate to make this lover a sweet ninny, like so many of Shakespeare's comedy swains.

James Earl Jones is the actor I have seen most frequently on the stage in the past two years. One possible reason for this is that all his acting has been done off-Broadway. He must therefore be more concerned with engaging in his profession than in making good deals and signing careful agent-hatched contracts. Does it follow from this that if one wants to act on the American stage with some degree of continuity one must resign oneself to being poor?

On Broadway, the latest smash is *A Funny Thing Happened On the Way to the Forum*, a respectably rowdy musical by Stephen Sondheim, Burt Shevelove and Larry Gelbart. I can make no extended comment on this entertainment—none certainly is needed—except to say that since my guest and the rest of the audience laughed loud and often, I was impelled to do the same.

There are actually several very funny lines in the show and the plot uses classic farce situations which have served from Plautus (the "book" borrows from a number of Plautus' vulgar comedies) to Minsky. When I had time to think about this—an unnecessary diversion—I wondered who had invented the best lines: the authors or the actors in the course of rehearsals. For there can be no doubt that the graceful Gargantuan clown, Zero Mostel, is a volcano of devilish, almost frightening fun which seems to issue from his lie the gush of a geyser.

Funny, too, but more grotesque are tremulous Jack Gilford and brash David Burns. Without anything in his wide mouth but teeth and tongue, Burns always looks as if he were tormenting a cigar. The show is scenically abstemious. I spotted one sumptuous girl in the small "ensemble." You may find others. What more can one ask of Broadway these days?

—*NAT*, 11 Apr. '62

I CAN GET IT FOR YOU WHOLESALE

I Can Get It For You Wholesale, a "musical play" by Jerome Weidman (based on his novel of the thirties) with music and lyrics by Harold Rome (Shubert Theatre), is curiously uneven: at times one is tempted to go along with it; at others, one wants to retch.

I do not know the novel, but from the evidence of its dramatization it must have exhibited a certain amount of hard-boiled realism in its picture of the petty scoundrels and shabby heartbreak of the ladies' garment industry on New York's Seventh Avenue. Some of this remains in the play, and we have learned from musicals like *Pal Joey*, *Guys and Dolls* and to a lesser extent *How to Succeed in Business* etc., that cynicism, skullduggery and financial low life mixed with Broadway high jinks can make a tasty confection despite the sour center. But the recipe does not go down as well in this case, partly because its central character is distinctly repellent (though Elliott Gould plays him passably and dances even better), but also because a cloying sweetness has been added in an effort to redeem the ambient villainy. Oh those good-hearted, decent, loving, simple Jewish folk who are injected into shows with unpleasant protagonists to minimize the threat of the Goebbels-Streicher shadow—how they sicken us!

Theatrically, the most original feature of *I Can Get It for You Wholesale* is the musical staging by Herbert Ross, whose choreography is asymmetric, informal and woven into the fabric of the play as dramatic action.

The outstanding performance is that of Barbra Streisand, who looks like an innocent Modigliani model. Her Miss Marmelstein—a screaming, hysterical, efficient, harassed, nervously giggling secretary—is a delightful comic miniature. Harold Lang dances with stunning expertness, Lillian Roth has gentle eyes and an appealing manner, and since

I have a perhaps reprehensible taste for flashy voluptuosity (sexiness to you), I enjoy the presence of Sheree North.

Merit badges should also be extended to Ken LeRoy and Bambi Linn, to Arthur Laurents, the director, who must have aided with portions of the script and kept the performances honestly to the point. As for Harold Rome's score, it borrows shamelessly but effectively from Rumshinsky (Second Avenue Theatre sources).

—*NAT*, 14 Apr. '62

NEW ROOTS IN THE CHALK GARDEN

Drama progresses slowly; the theatre is always in a hurry. Whenever two or three young playwrights of ability take the stage, we hear talk of new waves, schools, trends, even upheavals. After five or six years the impetus appears spent, the heat is off. The masterpieces are marked minor, their champions declare themselves let down, the sophisticates shrug and put, while showfolk—forever prepared for miracles—await new wonders.

This is perfectly normal. The eternal theatre is an ephemeral art, an art of presence (this is at the heart of its fascination). The tempo of creation and of its critical appreciation does not correspond to the rhythm of pleasure in the playhouse. In the theatre we enjoy the performance; in the library we review its text. One usually discovers a disparity.

It is not surprising therefore that John Russell Taylor, who speaks in *Anger and After* about "the theatrical revolution we are still living through today" should also remark first that "surely no dramatist can have got further on a smaller body of work than Shelagh Delaney" and, later, that "Arnold Wesker has acquired a greater reputation on the strength of a still relatively smaller body of work than any of his generation."

For a man with an evident enthusiasm for the "revolution," of which he has made himself the first historian, Mr. Taylor is notably reserved in his praise. There is an inevitable ambivalence in his book—I say this to his credit—which makes him less than lavish with encomiums and something more than hopeful. Thus while, to begin with, one is almost grateful for the temperate tone in his judgments of John Osborne, John Arden, Brendan Behan and the never too stringent depreciation of some others, we find him venturing to say not only that Harold Pinter's work is the "true poetic drama of our time," but that "the conclusion seems inescapable...that in the long run he [Pinter] is likely to turn out the greatest of them all"—a statement which might lead one to suppose that of those already mentioned several other dramatists—Alun Owen, Clive Exton, Peter Shaffer—are also great.

Mr. Taylor's book is a good one and particularly informative to someone like myself who has not been able to follow all of the apparently very interesting writing which has been done in this country for television. I like the fact that Mr. Taylor states his opinions without literary artifice or gimmick wit and I can pick very few specific quarrels with his evaluations. He reveals himself generally as a man of taste and respectable judgment. There are, however, certain things to be inferred from his book which he does not say—things which I believe may be helpful to bear in mind when we speak of present-day drama.

A French playwright once commented, "I have written thirty plays—seven of them good," and he quoted a colleague who had described a "great" dramatist as one who had written a number of plays not all of which were bad! To put it another way, I might submit that I can hardly take any playwright seriously who has not suffered a certain number of failures.

The fact is and I regard with favor Mr. Taylor's conveying the point—that virtually all the playwrights discussed in his book are beginners: they have achieved only their first steps in careers which we trust will prove steady, prolonged and fruitful. No flat declaration or assured pronouncement about them as to their staying power or ultimate worth can be made or undertaken at this point.

The importance of the new British drama lies not in its absolute excellence but in the fact that it is clearly the expression of something changing and growing among the people in Britain today. When a daily reviewer cries "masterpiece" because he has seen a performance that rouses him from the lethargy induced by the inevitable mediocrity of theatrefare in general he may, artistically speaking, be acting the fool, but he is being a healthy play-goer within the momentary event which is the theatre's normal atmosphere and life.

The kind of critic, on the other hand, who sneers at a play of some verve and relevance to the time and the audience for which it is written, on the grounds that the play isn't of the first rank—something which meets the standards set by the ages of which he (as critic) is the accredited interpreter—is a snob or a mortician who should not be going to the theatre at all. The theatre has never at any time lived on its masterpieces: it has thrived when the energy of its activity was a response and fulfillment of a people's need. The making of masterpieces is the work of the future.

There is a tendency among many Americans to dismiss the new British drama either because it has been tracing a pattern similar to that which their own playwrights described in the thirties or because some of it is repeating what has recently been better done in France. (This reminds me of a director, a refugee from Nazi Germany, who in 1935 waved Odets aside with the argument that Hauptmann had written *The Weavers* in 1892.) Such criticism is culturally impertinent. We do not live on the flow of other people's blood.

For my part I have been thoroughly interested, entertained and occasionally moved by the work of Osborne, Pinter, Delaney, Behan (I have not seen any of John Arden's plays) not because I find or need to find any of it "great," but because it is the dramatic representation of a world in movement that I sense all about me in Britain. There is plenty of time for "conclusions"—later.

The chalk garden of the English theatre is beginning to grow new roots. It is too soon to dig

them up in an effort to determine immediately if their flower will blossom into things of perennial beauty.

—*LO*, 20 May '62

WHAT DOES THE DIRECTOR DO?

Under the title and the author's name in this program—or any other—you will see a byline which reads, "Directed" or "Staged by." You will probably not pay much attention to this—and you will be right. You have not come to see direction but a play. The play is embodied in a company of actors, and though the actors have been directed (we presume), it is their acting and the words they speak that should entertain you.

Still the name of certain directors—George Abbott, Joshua Logan, Elia Kazan, Robert Lewis, José Quintero, Arthur Penn and a host of others—may have become familiar to you. You know they are important because they are *directors*—a word which has an auspicious ring to it. But do you know exactly what directors do?

The director (in collaboration with the playwright and the producer) usually chooses his cast as well as the scene designer and gives what you see on the stage its overall shape. The *form* of a production is in large measure set by the director. That is why if you have had occasion to see a play in several different productions—*Hamlet*, for instance—you will notice that the play is somewhat different each time: it looks different, it sounds different, it has a different quality and interest.

When a playscript is entrusted to a director, its locale—where the scenes take place—is described in a general way. (In Shakespeare's plays there are no such descriptions but simply indications, such as "Platforms of a Castle" or a "Room in the Castle.") Specific instructions as to the color of the setting, the position of furniture and other objects, where entrances and exits are to be situated, how the sets are to be changed from one scene to another are rarely given. The director with the aid of a scene-designer must decide all this.

The director's decision depends on the sort of impression he wishes the play to make. *The Glass Menagerie*, for example, takes place in a drab living room, but Jo Mielziner's set, while it conveyed the dejection of the environment, possessed glamor—for the play was nostalgic, almost dreamy. Either the director was responsible for the mood created through that particular set or he allowed the designer to make the choice for him. It should be borne in mind that, whatever the actual circumstances of the director-designer relationship, the director is finally responsible for the pictorial side of the production. If he is not satisfied with the designer's guidance, he is in a position to demand another kind of set or another designer!

This is typical of the whole procedure of production. The theatre is a collaborative affair, a give and take between a considerable number of people, hopefully creative; and while the director is officially in charge, he does not and can not function alone. He depends on the talents of all the people he has chosen to work with in the fond expectation that each of these artists will contribute to the total effect he intends his production—the staged play—to have.

The English conductor Sir Thomas Beecham when asked how he achieved beautiful performances answered, "I get good players and let them play." That facetious reply represents a bogus modesty and a partial truth. A stage director might also say, "To be a good director find a good script and choose an excellent cast." But the facts are more complex.

The director is the guide, the leader, sometimes the teacher of his company. Walter Matthau, everyone agrees, is a good actor and he deserves the praise his performance in *A Shot in the Dark* was accorded. I am not betraying a secret, however, in pointing out that the idea for his walk (or gait) in that play was mine as director of that play's production. The manner of execution is due

to the actor's ability to make the detail something more than a trick so that it may be integrated with the characterization as a whole.

In the Paris production of the same play the magistrate's office was (as here) dusty and crowded with sundry paraphernalia of the legal profession. It was not necessary to convince the audience that the play was French and took place in Paris! I decided that a replica of the Paris set would be inadequate to the play's requirements in New York. For us the set had to be elegant as well as shabby like a threadbare suit of clothes made of the finest fabric. So the designer (Ben Edwards) painted the ceiling with its sportive Cupids reminiscent of certain eighteenth-century salon paintings—thus giving the setting a new dimension and style.

The amount and kind of movement required on the stage depends on the nature of each particular play. What if one is called in to direct a play which has many long literary speeches demanding the utmost attention on the part of the audience—as in Giraudoux's *Tiger at the Gates*? A French audience is not made restless by a "talky" play if the talk is witty, well written and full of substance. A French director, knowing this, will reduce movement to the minimum so that not a word will be missed. He "poses" his actors on the flat platform of the stage and has the actors address the audience as directly as possible.

The same objective cannot be achieved in the same way for an American audience. When I directed the play with Michael Redgrave, I had to find some compromise between the rhetorical nature of the text and our audiences' craving for physical action or motion. That is the chief reason I had my designer build a sharply raked stage with many levels to render every step the actors made striking and the visual aspect of the production varied.

These examples are adduced to show that the director's choices are not matters of whim or arbitrary device. They are based on what the play is supposed to "do" to its audience. Entertain them, of course. But in what way? What sort of a play are we to see? Shaw's *Heartbreak House* has often been thought of as a "mood" play in the Chekhovian vein. I conceived it as an intellectual vaudeville—for Shaw was a jester as well as a prophet—so that when I directed it, I sought to make the "crazy" house that was the play's world lively with gay period costumes and an off-beat setting and its people colorful eccentrics somewhat like figures of a sophisticated comic opera.

Tyrone Guthrie's production of Pirandello's *Six Characters in Search of an Author* was a comedy, almost farce. But the play is not necessarily so. Even more pronounced than its comic features are its tragic implications and plot. Guthrie's talent, however, is chiefly fun loving, spectacular, vitally devil-may-care. Thus we learn that a director is up to a point the creator of the play *as we see it on the stage*. He may convert (pervert) a play's meaning according to the bent of his artistic nature or understanding. Pirandello himself once wrote, "In the theatre the work of an author does not exist any longer." The author's work is willy-nilly absorbed by the whole complex of production—its direction, actors, setting, the house in which it is played and last but not least the audience itself.

A great deal of the director's work—apart from suggestions by way of cuts, additions, changes in the text which he may propose to the playwright—is with the actors individually and collectively. Some directors exercise a very strict control over the actors through readings (the manner in which lines are delivered), pieces of "business" (small actions or byplay), placement and movement on the stage. Other directors allow their actors considerable freedom. Most mix the two methods. There is no absolutely "right" procedure, though actors themselves may prefer one kind of director to another, a fact which the knowing director usually bears in mind.

I should like to give a further example of what it means to work with an actor, for it is indicative of the reciprocal creative interaction from which the most fruitful results ensue. When I directed

Julie Harris in *The Member of the Wedding*, I told her that one of the main characteristics in a child's behavior is imitation. Children do not merely speak of objects they see; they try to "become" those objects. When, at a subsequent rehearsal of the play in which Julie Harris impersonated a twelve-year-old girl, she came to the line "And I'll go around the world," the words were accompanied by a sweeping "trip" around the stage—as an "airplane"—sounds, swaying and all. The actress' invention was born of the seed the director had planted in her imagination.

If you read play reviews, you may notice that direction is sometimes (too often) referred to as "slow" or "fast." It is true that pace and tempo contribute to the feeling of a scene or a production. Still critical references to them are hardly meaningful in themselves; the timing of a scene is only significant in relationship to motivation and meaning. *The Cherry Orchard* cannot be played at the same pace as *The Front Page* any more than a funeral moves like a parade.

Having said all this I must reveal the real purpose of my writing about direction for you the playgoer. Generally speaking, I do not believe it very useful to instruct members of the audience in the techniques of production: how a play is made is far less important than what is made. But by giving the spectator some notion of what the director's work consists, an understanding of what is essential in theatrical judgment may be enhanced.

The poet Paul Valéry writing of architecture once said, "Some buildings are mute, others speak, still others sing." True works of art have a character all their own; they speak, they say something. Every stage production, if it is not a haphazard collection of theatrical elements, has a design, a unity intended to impart some attitude or sense of life. The director's main task is to make every ingredient of his production, from the costumes to the most elusive matters of tone and atmosphere, contribute to the core of meaning (or feeling) which the production is to convey.

If the playgoer realizes this and looks in everything he sees in the theatre for the animating spirit, the heart of the play's communication, he will become more discriminating in his taste and will ultimately derive richer pleasure from his experiences there. As we have discovered it is not through words alone that the play speaks but through everything we are made to witness and sense when the curtain is up. That is, as a fine critic, Stark Young, once called it, "the flower of drama."

What happened to your inner being when you saw the play tonight? In what particular manner were you affected?

—*CTJ*, June '62

WHO'S AFRAID OF VIRGINIA WOOLF?

Edward Albee's *Who's Afraid of Virginia Woolf?* (Billy Rose Theatre) is packed with talent. It is not only the best play in town now: it may well prove the best of the season. Its significance extends beyond the moment. In its faults as well as in its merits it deserves our close attention.

It has four characters: two couples. There is hardly a plot, little so called "action," but it moves or rather whirls on its own special axis. At first it seems to be a play about marital relations; as it proceeds one realizes that it aims to encompass much more. The author wants to "tell all," to say everything.

The middle-aged wife, Martha, torments her somewhat younger husband because he has failed to live up to her expectations. Her father, whom she worships, is president of a small college. Her husband might have become the head of the history department and ultimately perhaps her father's heir. But husband George is a nonconformist. He has gone no further than associate professor, which makes him a flop. She demeans him in every possible way. George hits back, and the play is structured on this mutually sadistic basis. The first cause of their conflict is the man's "business" (or career) failure.

Because they are both attracted to what may be vibrant in each of them, theirs is a love-hate dance of death which they enact in typical American fashion by fun and games swamped in a sauce of strong drink. They bubble and fester with poisonous quips.

The first time we meet them they are about to entertain a new biology instructor who, at twenty-eight, has just been introduced to the academic rat race. The new instructor is a rather ordinary fellow with a forever effaced wife. We learn that he married her for her money and because of what turned out to be "hysterical pregnancy." The truth is she is afraid of bearing a child though she wants one. Her husband treats her with conventional regard (a sort of reflexive tenderness) while he contemplates widespread adultery for gratification and advancement in college circles. George scorns his young colleague for being "functional" in his behavior, his ambition, his attitudes.

So it goes: we are in the midst of inanity, jokes and insidious mayhem. Martha rationalizes her cruelty to George on the ground that he masochistically enjoys her beatings.

Everyone is fundamentally impotent, despite persistent "sexualizing." The younger wife is constantly throwing up through gutless fear. Her lightheadedness is a flight from reality. The older couple has invented a son because of an unaccountable sterility. They quarrel over the nature of the imaginary son because each of them pictures him as a foil against the other. There is also a hint that as a boy George at different times accidentally killed both his father and mother. Is this so? Illusion is real; "reality" may only be symbolic— either a wish or a specter of anxiety. It does not matter: these people, the author implies, represent our environment; indeed they may even represent Western civilization!

The inferno is made very funny. The audience at any rate laughs long and loud—partly because the writing is sharp with surprise, partly because an element of recognition is involved: in laughter it hides from itself while obliquely acknowledging its resemblance to the couples on the stage. When the play turns earnestly savage or pathetic the audience feels either shattered or embarrassed. Shattered because it can no longer evade the play's expression of the audience's afflictions, sins and guilts; embarrassed because there is something in the play—particularly toward the end—that is unbelievable, soft without cause. At its best, the play is comedy.

Albee is prodigiously shrewd and skillful. His dialogue is superbly virile and pliant; it also *sounds*. It is not "realistic" dialogue but a highly literate and full-bodied distillation of common American speech. Still better, Albee knows how to keep his audience almost continuously interested (despite the play's inordinate length). He can also ring changes on his theme, so that the play rarely seems static. Albee is a master craftsman.

Strangely enough, though there is no question of his sincerity, it is Albee's skill which at this point most troubles me. It is as if his already practiced hand had learned too soon to make an artful package of venom. For the overriding passion of the play is venomous. There is no reason why anger should not be dramatized. I do not object to Albee's being "morbid," for as the conspicuously healthy William James once said, "morbid-mindedness ranges over a wider scale of experience than healthy-mindedness." What I do object to in his play is that disease has become something of a brilliant formula, as slick and automatic as a happy entertainment for the trade. The right to pessimism has to be earned within the artistic terms one sets up; the pessimism and rage of *Who's Afraid of Virginia Woolf?* are immature. Immaturity coupled with a commanding deftness is dangerous.

What justifies the criticism? The characters have no life (or texture) apart from the immediate virulence of their confined action or speech. George is intended to represent the humanist principle in the play. But what does he concretely want? What traits, aside from his cursing the life he leads, does he have? Almost none. Martha and George, we are told, love each other after all.

How? That she can't bear being loved is a psychological aside in the play, but how is her love for anything, except for her "father fixation," and some sexual dependence on George, actually embodied? What interests—even petty—do they have or share? Vividly as each personage is drawn, they all nevertheless remain flat—caricatures rather than people. Each stroke of dazzling color is superimposed on another, but no further substance accumulates. We do not actually identify with anyone except editorially. Even the non-naturalistic figures of Beckett's plays have more extension and therefore more stature and meaning. The characters in Albee's *The Zoo Story* and *Bessie Smith* are more particularized.

If we see Albee, as I do, as an emerging artist, young in the sense of a seriously prolonged career, the play marks an auspicious beginning and, despite its success, not an end. In our depleted theatre it has real importance because Albee desperately wishes to cry out—manifest—his life. The end of his play—which seeks to introduce "hope" by suggesting that if his people should rid themselves of illusion (more exactly, falsity) they might achieve ripeness—is unconvincing in view of what has preceded it. Still, this ending is a gesture, one that indicates Albee's will to break through the agonizing narrowness of the play's compass.

Albee knows all he needs to know about playmaking; he has still to learn something other than rejection and more than tearfulness. His play should be seen by everyone interested in our world at home, for as Albee's George says, "I can admire things I don't admire."

The production—under Alan Schneider's painstaking direction—is excellent, as is the cast. Uta Hagen, with her robust and sensuously potent *élan*, her fierce will to expression and histrionic facility, gives as Martha her most vital performance since her appearance as Blanche in *A Streetcar Named Desire*. She is an actress who should always be before us. George Grizzard is perfect in conveying the normal amusements and jitters of the mediocre man. Melinda Dillon as his debilitated spouse is appallingly as well as hilariously effective, and though I have some difficulty in accepting Arthur Hill, in the role of Martha's husband, as a tortured and malicious personality he does very well with a taxing part.

A final note: though I believe the play to be a minor work within the prospect of Albee's further development, it must for some time occupy a major position in our scene. It will therefore be done many times in different productions in many places, including Europe. Though I do not know how it is to be effected, I feel that a less naturalistic production might be envisaged. *Who's Afraid of Virginia Woolf?* verges on a certain expressionism, and a production with a touch of that sort of poetry, something not so furiously insistent on the "honesty" of the materials, might give the play some of the qualities I feel it now lacks; it might alleviate the impression of, in the author's pithy phrase, "an ugly talent."

—*NAT*, 27 Oct. '62

BEYOND THE FRINGE

The English topical revue *Beyond the Fringe* is a constant delight. When I say "constant" I speak literally: I have seen this entertainment three times (twice in London) and I enjoyed it more at the John Golden Theatre than on either of the previous occasions.

The reason for this may be that *Beyond the Fringe* seems, amid the native platitude, to possess more literate intelligence and a higher degree of pertinence than any of the "straight" plays now being presented (with the exception of *Virginia Woolf*). Both the language and content of *Beyond the Fringe* are remarkable in aptness, variety and humor.

If you wish to know what the keen-witted younger generation of Britain is thinking today you must see this show. It is not enough to say that it is a hilarious attack on the Establishment. It is indirectly a spitball assault on all our establishments. Its havoc is carried out with wonderful dispatch.

From the moment when, at the show's opening, the four men (who compose the cast and have invented its material) make their patriotic attempt to convert a supposed Soviet citizen to admiration for "our way of life" and are hypnotically altered so that they emit a Bronx cheer for their own government, the entertainment never ceases to speed its barbs into our brain and midriff. Macmillan's adenoidal remoteness from the people (a capital caricature by Peter Cook), the footlessness of the "logical positivists" (professorial inanity), the idiocy of those who would allay our fear of nuclear warfare, the silliness of most Shakespearean productions (this bit is a classic), the sentimentalizing of the war years, the intellectual disarray of the official Church (a masterpiece by Alan Bennett), the sugary culture of Myra Hess's piano recitals during the air-raids (ineffably tinkled by the musical clown Dudley Moore), the foghorn and spastic inexpressiveness of the middle-class business man's conviviality (in which all four men haw and humph with inspiration) and the surrealistic genius of Jonathan Miller's grimaces, movements, fancies and insights: all these are explosions which mow us down in a catharsis of laughter. The gentlemen responsible for *Beyond the Fringe* differentiate themselves from the philosophers, in their "Groves of Academe," by being very fond of real life.

This evening of satire derives an aesthetic dimension beyond its corrective force because the players have an ear for every sort of British speech. The inflection and vocabulary of the various classes are caught and obliquely commented on, so that the show becomes a triumph in the use of language.

The Messrs. Bennett, Cook, Miller, Moore are all well-educated *amateurs* (one is a doctor, another a historian, a third a musician), yet they are many times more accomplished and devastating performers than most professionals.

—*NAT*, 17 Nov. '62

OONA, OXFORD, AMERICA AND THE BOOK
Conversations with Chaplin on the recent past, the present and the near future

Charlie met me at the Lausanne, Switzerland, railway station. I did not see him immediately. I got off the train at the far end of the platform and he was waiting at the central exit. I looked for a shortish man with snow-white hair. When I spied him he looked as he had when I last saw him on a visit to London five years ago—only he had grown a little stouter. He was gleefully cordial as he greeted me and offered to carry my overnight bag before his chauffeur, who was still looking for me, returned to the Bentley, which was parked outside the station. Needless to say I refused this courtesy.

When we got in the car for the thirty-minute drive to Vevey where Charlie lives, I cracked a joke about the honor Oxford University had conferred upon him two days before. "Shall I call you Doctor now, Charlie?" He laughed and then began to tell me with all his old-time eagerness about the ceremony at Oxford and a speech he had made to the assembled dons and other celebrated folk at a dinner after the honorary degrees had been conferred on him, Dean Rusk and the British painter Graham Sutherland.

A few days before this occasion, the historian Trevor-Roper, now Professor at Oxford, had made some public statement deploring the circumstance that an actor—a comedian—was to be tendered a degree in letters by the University. Among other things Charlie told me he had said at Oxford was something to this effect: Astonishment if not indignation has been expressed that a comedian should be named doctor of letters. Of course I am no man of letters. But the title is ambiguous. "Man of letters" may mean a number of things—for example, a postman.

Then Charlie went on to suggest that if a "man of letters" had any significance, it surely must be that such a person creates things of beauty. But this might come about in many ways: humble objects—a garbage can, for instance—viewed in a certain context might be made beautiful. All this and more Charlie reeled off so rapidly that I could hardly follow it all. The tone, however, was good-humored and not in the least pompous. I asked him if he had a copy of his speech. He hadn't; he had spoken extemporaneously.

Charlie had his chauffeur stop at a school in Lausanne to pick up three of his children. Out they came: the oldest of the three a girl about twelve, another, a girl about seven and a boy no more than eight. The younger children had a friend of their own age with them—a Swiss girl—and they all spoke French.

On my quizzing Charlie about his children's education, he said that his elder son had found the studies at the school in Lausanne too hard. "Why don't you have him attend the American school in Geneva," I asked. "I hear it's very good." "Oh, I wouldn't ever send my children to an American school," Charlie answered. "They're too easy. French schools are tough. My children," (and this he almost whispered) "will have enough money to paper the walls with. They must be prepared for life by some form of hardship. They must learn discipline of some kind. French schools make the children really study."

When we reached Charlie's house—it had previously belonged to an American family from New England—I saw at once that it was very large and almost stately without being ostentatious or lavish. It gives onto thirty-seven acres of land—beautifully kept—on which, Charlie explained with something like pride, all his vegetables and fine corn are grown. A long, wide lawn or orchard sloped down to the lake, across which one saw the Alps in France. The prospect was paradisiacally peaceful. Seventeen servants (including gardeners), who occupy a separate dwelling just off the main grounds, are required to take care of the children, the cars and the estate.

I was eager to see Oona, Charlie's wife. I had not seen her since my visit to London at the time Charlie was filming his last movie, *A King in New York*, there. Oona had impressed me from the very first time I met her with Charlie in Hollywood some twenty years ago when we all saw a good deal of each other. She was very beautiful with flesh like soft marble. But even more wonderful than her beauty (her features are reminiscent of her father, Eugene O'Neill) was Oona's repose. I had never been able to tell whether her quietness was due to modesty or discretion, a desire to accommodate herself to Charlie whose ebullience is electric and constant, a natural or an acquired gift on her part developed by having lived in the wake of two overpowering personalities: her father and her husband. Whatever the cause of Oona's effortless ease—her capacity to sit back, listen and absorb—it is a quality so rare in American women nowadays as to seem miraculous.

After Charlie ordered martinis to be served on the terrace facing the lake—he expressed regret that the atmosphere was too misty for one to see the mountain in the distance in all its majesty—Oona appeared, gloriously pregnant with her eighth child (a son who was born eight days later). Still beautiful, the only change I observed in her was an undisguised strand of gray in her jet-black hair. (This gray, Charlie confessed later, had produced a pang in him a few years ago when he noticed it for the first time on her arrival in England after she took leave of America.) Oona can be warm and friendly without being effusive. I felt wholly relaxed sitting between her and Charlie.

During dinner, which we took in the open, Charlie asked me about old acquaintances. I was pleased to notice that none of the people he inquired about were our "famous" or well-publicized friends, but simply people he remembered fondly in the old Hollywood and New York entourage which had been our common meeting ground. And he didn't say "What is so and so doing?" But "How is he (or she)?"

I, on the other hand, was inquisitive about his activities and plans. In the several years since *A King in New York* (a film which he admitted had been a failure, though it had lost no money since it cost only four hundred thousand dollars), he had spent most of the time on his autobiography which was now all but complete—and of which the first one hundred ninety-seven pages were already in galleys. He was soon to begin working on a new farcical film about a crook, the script of which he had written and which he would direct (but not act in) with his son Sydney in the leading role. Charlie and Sydney always seemed to have been particularly chummy. Their "professional collaboration" goes back to the time in Hollywood years ago when Charlie directed Sydney in a tiny theatre-in-the-round production of James Barrie's *What Every Woman Knows*.

I refrained from making any special queries about *A King in New York* because I surmised that it might be painful for Charlie to dwell on a project which had misfired. His film *Monsieur Verdoux* had not been a financial success in the United States, but had been greatly admired and well-attended in Europe. And whatever others thought of *Verdoux*—some of the criticism of it had been anti-Chaplin—Charlie himself, I am certain, was proud of it. But *A King in New York*, I suspect, was something about which he himself had become dubious. It must now seem to him, as it did to me when I saw it in Paris, halfway between excellent slapstick and strained satire. The provocation for that satire—the McCarthy era and Chaplin's brushes with the State Department in the late Forties and early Fifties—was too recent and too particular to himself to be converted into a well-rounded film. Even the general European moviegoer, for whom the picture was presumably made, couldn't have been altogether sure what its target was, while the intellectuals could easily spot the picture's flaws as entertainment.

After dinner Oona retired for the night while I continued plying Charlie with questions. At times, Charlie confessed, he forgot the names of people and places—"One does, you know, as one grows old," he said cheerfully—but he recollection of meaningful experiences remained vivid.

I asked if he would permit me to read that part of his book which had been printed. He consented with some diffidence, for I had remarked that I might like to say something about it for publication and this, he worried, might not meet with the approval of his English publisher, Bodley-Head. (Simon & Schuster are to publish the book in the United States at approximately the same time—in late 1963 or early 1964.) But my keenness to read what was already "visible" of the book—which I said I would undertake the next day—made him impatient to give me a foretaste of it now: so he reached for one of the folders containing the manuscript and began to read passages at random.

One such excerpt dealt with his first marriage—to Mildred Harris—modestly, almost wistfully described. The impression I got from this bit was that he was a confused and bewilderingly successful boy at the time—something of an innocent. He told me he had omitted a detailed account of his second marriage—to Lita Gray—because "She was the mother of my two oldest sons." When I asked if he had written about his encounter and friendship with Hearst, he read some pages dealing with Hearst, Mrs. Hearst and Marion Davies.

When he stopped reading—for a fleeting moment I imagined he was going to read me the entire book just as he had long ago favored me with a "synopsis" of the *Monsieur Verdoux* scenario shot by shot, acting all the parts—Charlie continued to speak of Hearst. Charlie is unable to talk about anyone he knows well without imitating that person—in other words, without acting. Thus he reproduced Hearst's squeaky voice, Marion Davies' charming stammer and, later, the curmudgeonly impact of Winston Churchill's conversation.

How I prodded, had he [Chaplin] incurred Hearst's enmity? It all began, Chaplin answered, with *The Great Dictator* (made before America's declaration of war), a picture Hearst deemed "radical." Hearst had not disapproved of Hitler before 1941. He had asked Chaplin why he was so antagonistic to Hitler. Then, as Chaplin described the scene, Hearst stopped short and exclaimed, "Oh, I understand; it's because you're Jewish." At this point I rather unwarrantedly interjected, "But you're not Jewish." For a second Charlie gave me a look which might be interpreted as quizzical and continued, "That, I said to Hearst, has nothing to do with it; I'm against Hitler because he's anti-people."

After continuing for some time on the subject of his relations with the master of San Simeon, Charlie surprisingly summed it all up by saying that Hearst was an ogre, in many ways a beast, a Fascist, but that "he was also a great man." About Churchill too, Charlie spoke not only with admiration but affection, despite the fact that I gathered Chaplin had not always approved of Churchill's politics, which was to be expected in a way, since Chaplin, I always felt, was somewhat dubious about nearly all politicians. Chaplin, I am convinced, never was politically minded—and now is avowedly apolitical. Chaplin's politics—insofar as they exist at all—are chiefly "poetics." His approach to political affairs is intuitive, emotional, almost one might say a matter of aesthetics.

Our conversation at this point made me realize that the passage of years, the hush of his life in the retreat of his Swiss estate, had not lessened Chaplin's interest in world events, but had made him less apt to arrive at crude conclusions or to indulge in hasty stabs of opinion. ("One gets from one place to another in no time at all," he said in regard to the geographical situation of his home. "The world is small now, and men move very fast. It's a good and also a bad thing. I'm not altogether sure I like it.") Speaking of America and the treatment he had been subjected to, he expressed no bitterness or resentment. "On reading my book," Charlie said, "I'm really surprised how well America comes off!"

I had supposed when I read a press report to this effect that his benign attitude might be a matter of tactics (though Chaplin has never been notably tactful), but face-to-face with him I felt sure his moderation was genuine, a mellowness which is not the sign of any weakening but rather a growth in breadth and wisdom. For the first time in my long acquaintance with Chaplin, I had the feeling that he was not only an artist of genius but a man who might be considered—or had become—wise.

When I speak of "wisdom," I do not mean correct in opinion or even reliable in judgment. I mean that Chaplin's whole personality has become integrated and has attained the finest balance that his talents and nature could achieve—and these are sufficiently rich and human enough to make a man to be cherished.

So when Charlie began to let fly with statements which might be added up to a sort of credo, I had no inclination to contradict him or to test their objective validity. Everything he said— even when paradoxical or perhaps wildly "wrong"—seemed right for him and could be so interpreted that some basic truth, some corrective to his exaggerations might be distilled from his sallies.

I could not quarrel with his concern about the armaments race. I smiled in comprehension of his anarchistically aesthetic declaration, "I can't stand Communists with their *system* and systems. I hate systems." Again and again he exclaimed, "Life is full of poetry," and though this is not exactly a "scientific" statement, his person made his meaning entirely clear.

He went on to discuss matters of acting craft. He had learned much, he said, from his first director. "I believe in theatricalism." (His word, not mine.) "Theatricalism is poetry. I don't believe in The Method." (I did not tell him that I had heard Stanislavsky say to an actress: "If my system"— which we in America call The Method—"troubles you, forget it.") "I believe in theatricalism," Charlie continued, "even in 'tricks'—actor's tricks. I don't like Shakespeare on the stage; he interferes with the actor's freedom, with his virtuosity." And as his spirit almost lifted him from his seat so that I

feared that he might become airborne at any moment, I could see that in his way he was more Shakespearean than many professional Shakespeareans.

What struck me too in this "new" Chaplin (who was still the old Charlie) was that, though I was not at all tempted to interrupt his outbursts, I might easily have done so without offense. In former years I had the impression that, though he was sharply observant, he hardly listened to anyone. He was always "on"—telling stories, doing imitations, recitations, pantomimes, delivering himself of firecracker pronouncements— providing himself and others with a constant spectacle of irrepressible energy and imagination. No one got a chance to speak in his presence. (Hardly anyone desired to.) But now Charlie was also ready to listen.

I was more eager, however, to have him speak his mind than to argue with him about anything, and I felt sure he might have been stimulated to go on talking all night long. His age (seventy-three) has barely modified the speed and bounce of his delivery. (He still plays tennis—"only with Oona," he says as if testifying to his senescence, or perhaps to his isolation!) But for my own sake rather than, I decided to go to bed so that I could get up early to read the opening chapters of his book. It was past midnight anyway.

I woke at six-thirty the next morning, phoned from my guest room (actually a suite) to order breakfast, which was promptly served. Then I plunged into the book, which had been dictated, typed by a secretary and finally corrected by Chaplin.

The opening—the section I read—deals with the period from his early childhood, the years of his parents' poverty and bitter struggle to the days of his first success in Hollywood. I had been told by a friend who had read this part of the book that it was like the Dickens of *Oliver Twist*. (Chaplin, by the way, loves Dickens.) But there is no trace of sentimentality in Chaplin's account of the times he spent in the poorhouse and the whole miserable pageant of his parents', his brother's and his own tortured existence in the London of the late nineteenth century. There is very little editorializing either except for an occasional reflection which tends to be stiffly expressed in the manner of one who has had no schooling, has done little reading and has acquired his vocabulary through contact with more educated folk.

Because of the straightforwardness of the narration, the lack of embellishment or attempts at personal pathos these pages from Chaplin's life story do not make a quick appeal. One is not immediately "carried away." The true quality and nature of the writing begin to reveal themselves when Chaplin interrupts the stream of the book's "action" by listing the violently tragic and sometimes grotesque fates of various music-hall comedians and clowns he knew in his boyhood. (Chaplin began his stage career at the age of twelve.) This somehow is even more moving than learning that his mother went insane through hunger, for it is as if Chaplin took everything which had happened to him and his immediate family for granted—all they had suffered was, so to speak, "natural" and inevitable, about which nothing could be done or complained of. Only the contemplation of other people's destinies—many of them strangers—made him understand the significance of his own condition.

The "triumph" of these opening pages in the Chaplin autobiography—if one can speak in such terms—is the climactic description of his return to New York from Hollywood after the first great splash of his fame had made him not only a rich young man but virtually a legend, the darling of the masses. For though Charlie appreciated and enjoyed his sudden affluence, he had no idea that literally millions of people were almost religiously devoted to him. When this became apparent to him through the thousands who greeted every stop his train made crossing the country and the vast horde which was waiting for him at Grand Central, Chaplin sustained his first major defeat! For everybody knew him, and he knew nobody. He was alone—and lonely.

This, too, is told factually with even less comment than my brief summary indicates, and is therefore truly touching. Chaplin's memoirs honestly convey a *life*—not, as so many actors' autobiographies, a form of curtain call. Chaplin has succeeded in setting himself down on paper "artlessly."

About eight-thirty Charlie sent word that he'd like me to breakfast with him. I said I had had breakfast and was still reading.

I came down to the terrace an hour later. Charlie had finished his breakfast and was poring over a newspaper, of which there were many piled on a chair beside him. I told him at once that reading his book had been a genuine experience for me. His eyes moistened.

I had noticed on the previous day that a trace of tears and a faint reddening appeared in his eyes whenever he heard or spoke of something that affected him emotionally. This, too, was unusual for on similar occasions in the past his head sank a bit, his eyes took on a fixed, grave look and shone with peculiar intensity. This change was the only physical symptom of age (apart possibly from the gain in weight) which I could now observe in him.

After talking about the book in further detail—Charlie seemed to reenact its scenes in his mind as I recalled them—Oona joined us. I asked about personages who might appear in the still unprinted pages, Churchill for example. Charlie did not say whether he had indeed written about the episode he now recounted, but I mused about it after I left both because of the way he mimicked Churchill and the special pleasure he took in doing so.

Chaplin had sent Churchill a print of one of his films (I am now vague about which one, but it was surely one of the last three) and Churchill had written to thank him and to say how much he liked the film. A year or two later Chaplin dined with Churchill in London. The statesman was strangely silent through most of the meal and kept squinting at Chaplin with a rather disgruntled air. Finally

Churchill muttered with a sort of tight-lipped gruffness (which Chaplin aped), "I'm annoyed with you." Surprised, Chaplin asked the reason. "You didn't answer the letter I wrote you about your film," Churchill replied. Chaplin thought it wonderful that Churchill should be so concerned with such a trifle as Chaplin's failure to acknowledge a letter of thanks and praise.

One thing I was most anxious to learn. How exactly had the Little Man—Chaplin's classic creation—been born? It was a question—particularly fascinating to me as a man of the theatre—which had remained unresolved in my morning's reading. The answer was simpler—yet somehow more mysterious—than I expected.

In the days of Hollywood's infancy, Chaplin under Mack Sennett's management turned out one and sometimes two or three films a week. These had no definite scenario: they were simply improvised around some object or theme—a fire, a pawnshop, a police station. Once when Sennett wanted to make a new picture and was turning over in his mind what it should be about, he said, "Charlie, pick out some props and clothes from the stuff.in the costume department...something funny." Charlie searched in the theatrical debris and chose a few articles with no apparent connection one with the other: a cane, a hat, a pair of trousers, some old shoes. As he assembled them, "tried" them, he began to "work" with them—each separately at first and then all together. In a little while, as he endeavored to get the "feel" from the very nature of these disparate materials, the outlines of a character began to compose itself. He continued to experiment and improvise till, out of prop and wardrobe department discards, a new man came into being, a creature that was to make Chaplin world-renowned.

During the course of the morning Oona jokingly issued some stern command to Charlie about how and where he was to sit at the table while coffee and pastry were being served. "What!" I cried mock-seriously. "You let her browbeat you!" "Well, you see, I'm in love with her," Charlie said almost childishly.

Charlie had invited me to stay several days but business obliged me to return to Geneva where I was to board a plane for Paris. "Oh," said Oona, "if you're going to be in Paris you must look up a girl who used to go to school with Geraldine" (the Chaplins' oldest daughter—about seventeen). "The girl's studying acting in Paris: she is half-English and speaks the language perfectly. She's very talented." "Yes," Charlie added, "you must look her up. She's lovely. A Duse!"

Charlie is very tender with the young; he treated the three children I had seen the day before with great delicacy. One of them spoke English with a slight French accent, another hardly spoke English at all. (Charlie's French is practically nonexistent.) The kids have a maid who speaks English to them so they may become or remain bilingual.

The chauffeur who was to drive me to the station is an Italian who speaks French, but no English. The car waited while I exchanged farewell greetings with Charlie and Oona. I wanted to know one thing more: "What's the end of your book like?" I asked. "What's the conclusion?" "That I am content to look out at the lake and at the mountains and feel that, with my family around me, there is nothing more and nothing better," he answered. He pointed toward the sky and the open space around—in a gesture which pleaded to say more than his words might convey, while his expression was one of naïve bafflement at his inability to define the ineffable.

"Would you like to return to America?" I ventured.

"I am very happy here," he answered.

"Well, Charlie," I said, "I've not only had a grand time; this visit has meant much to me."

His eyes twinkled as he said, "I can see in your face that it has. Good-bye."

—*ESQ*, Nov. '62

LITTLE ME

To put it fancily, *Little Me*, the new musical that Neil Simon, Carolyn Leigh and Cy Coleman have based on a novel by Patrick Dennis, mixes Bemelmans with burlesque at the Lunt-Fontanne Theatre.

The "Bemelmans" element is a cartoon satire of the American success story. An unwashed and barefoot baby doll from Venequela, Illinois, seeking to be worthy of Noble Eggleston, the town's rich boy who studies both medicine and law at Harvard and Yale simultaneously, determines to acquire the necessary "culture, wealth, position."

Her rise takes her through marriage to a French hoofer named Poitrine (this gives her the gently Rabelaisian cognomen Belle Poitrine), the making of several idiot Hollywood colossals, the birth of an illegitimate child, First World War service in France, sundry *liaisons* (one with—minor—royalty), and finally the consummation of her romance with the noble Noble. In short, busty Belle has realized the American Dream. She has everything: "culture, wealth, position"—and a pianoforte that serves as a bar.

The first act takes care of the extravagant (or "technicolor") satire; the second act is out-and-out burlesque, each scene being a kind of blackout skit. It might strike the learned that after the first act the authors did not know exactly how to develop their material and therefore decided to run hogwild in the second. They are abetted in this by the peculiar talents of the show's star, Sid Caesar. Lucky authors! For Caesar can be very funny, and this reviewer (to speak like a daily critic) found the silly second act much the better part of the show. The nuttier the proceedings the better he liked it.

Sid Caesar's humor—at least the phase of it he exploits here—has a special Broadway and American-Jewish flavor. (No accent is needed.) It is a subtly "pathetic" humor, the key to which is the ineffable madness of the *accidental*. Every weird hazard—the climactic point of each episode—seems to have appended to it the unspoken but scenically articulate plea, "Would you believe it!"

For example, in one passage Caesar as Otto Schnitzler, a German movie director, demonstrates the action of a film sequence to two dumb actors. From a box containing the props to be used he takes out Cleopatra's "asp" and chucks it at the man playing the Pharaoh. There is a gasp of horror. But, Caesar-Schnitzler chuckles, it is only a fake snake: would he use a real one on a star? Then the Kraut director illustrates Cleopatra's suicidal stabbing on himself with a dagger from the same prop box. He makes a few comments, whereupon, from the flush on his face and an astonished look of slow comprehension, a kind of mute and sad bewilderment, we realize that the hapless Otto has stabbed himself to death with a real dagger!

Caesar, who in this show has seven faces, is always doing himself some injury, coming to grief, *failing* in the most unexpected ways. Life is full of tricky abominations, beyond reason or belief, that balk normal expectations. They leave poor Caesar even more puzzled than pained, but thoroughly obliterated. This is the credulous and usually confident Caesar's perennial cross. Once in a long while—and here we have the ultimate irony—the machinery of fate reverses itself and the accident immanent in events produces a happy catastrophe: someone else is damaged and Caesar comes out unscathed or, better still, crowned with good fortune. The effect is always hilarious and also somehow "frightening." No matter which way the wheel turns, Caesar is dumbfounded—immobilized in metaphysical wonder. Caesar's comedy, strange as it may appear to him and to us, is philosophical! It had me in stitches.

There are few other talents in the occasion of *Little Me* worth separate note. One or two of Bob Fosse's dance routines are clever, Robert Randolph has designed several amusing drops (not "sets"), Swen Swenson's solo dance displays a remarkably trained *musculature*, Nancy Andrews looks right as the mature Poitrine, Virginia Martin has neat legs, a proper figure and a deliberately terrible singing voice as the younger Poitrine. Present, too, are such side dishes as the elegantly attractive Else Olufsen as a tony social catch and Barbara Sharma, a fetching little redhead among the dancers.

But the show belongs to Caesar and to the surrealist antics which do not know their name!

—*NAT*, 8 Dec. '62

THE DUMBWAITER & THE COLLECTION
NEVER TOO LATE

Without being on the creative level of *The Caretaker* or his first play, *The Birthday Party*, Harold Pinter's *The Dumbwaiter* and *The Collection* extend our understanding of this interesting dramatist (Cherry Lane Theatre).

There is a paradox in the combination of these two one-acters. The more effective and the better played is *The Collection*, but I was more fascinated by the not so efficient *Dumbwaiter*. Though shorter than its companion piece (and earlier in composition than either *The Caretaker* or *The Collection*) *The Dumbwaiter* aims higher and its method is subtler. It is written as a comedy sketch, but is nevertheless wholly symbolic. Yet there are no "mists," none of the deeply intoned incantations, commonly associated with symbolism.

Two cockneys, speaking the monotonous, barren language of the uneducated and unimaginative, are discovered to be hired gunmen who kill without malice or personal motive apart from their "profession." (The failure to use an authentic London dialect in the production is unfortunate; it deprives the piece of a needed color.) The gunmen's victims are not only persons unknown to them but "objects" whose identity is hardly distinguishable by them. We see the gunmen in a dismal basement, lying on two miserable cots and waiting for orders to proceed to their murderous destina-

tion. They wait—and here there is an echo of the "waiting" in Beckett's plays—when strange things begin to occur. A packet of matches is suddenly slipped under the door. They do not understand the source or meaning of this "gift," but they decide to use it so they can boil water for the indispensable tea. But the gas range does not work. "Why did he send us matches," one of them asks, "if he knows there was no gas?" And we begin to perceive the play's drift.

Then, just as surprisingly, the dumbwaiter bangs down with a series of orders for all sorts of fancy foods. The place they are in, they surmise, must once have been a restaurant. Though it is now gutted of all provisions, they respond to the peremptoriness of the demand by sending up silly substitutes for the ordered dishes. The orders now come down faster and ever more furiously. They are in despair as they respond with hysterical impetus. They cry out to explain their inability to supply the orders and to find out who exactly is issuing them: "What's the idea! What's he playing games for?" There is no reply. It may be possible that the final order is for one of the men to kill the other: the impulse and tempo of obedience make it not at all improbable that this order too may be carried out.

The intention is clear. (Why does such a simple plot structure baffle so many in the audience—particularly those practiced playgoers who are expected to understand it?) Man immured in penury, discomfort and airless constriction, is bound to carry out the commands of a master whom he does not see, know or fathom—commands he obeys in mechanical haste as if he were gripped by a tic. And if this is not true of man in general, it might be inferred (for Pinter will not say) that it is certainly true of man today; and the play, if one wishes to ascribe to it something less than a metaphysical interpretation, might be set down as a protest, albeit a hopeless one, against the pressure of our industrial civilization.

This, however, sounds more pretentious than is Pinter's spare treatment. His play is a swift image halfway between humor and horror. But its production is imprecise and undistinguished.

The direction by Alan Schneider and the acting—particularly by James Ray and Henderson Forsythe—in *The Collection* are much more pointed and therefore, as I have indicated, make for a better "show." It is unnecessary to summarize the plot of *The Collection*. It too has its ambiguities—does not answer all our questions—but it plays on the themes of jealousy, adultery and the nightmare ambivalence of disturbed marital (or merely sex) relationships, not excluding the homosexual, and is sufficiently clear to almost everyone.

What is astute in Pinter's handling of his subject is that nearly all the impulses involved are only partially expressed, and thus emerge only as possibilities. There can be no Othello or Iago in such a situation because modern man (and woman) disapprove of jealousy and the acts of violence arising from it. They therefore attempt to repress them, so that finally they (and we) begin to doubt the reality of their feelings. Am I really "fit to be tied" because my wife has been unfaithful? Can my contact with that man be really considered "an affair," or did I just toy with the idea of such a contact? If I were certain that he or she has had an affair would I divorce, maim or murder, or would I go on living with my mate in tortured or "sophisticated" indecision, the possible infidelity forgotten or forgiven because I am unsure whether I also "transgressed?"

The Collection reveals another curious aspect of Pinter's technique. His plays work because they are constructed as *melodrama*. They possess a taut, suspenseful quality that serves to give intensity to the suggested emotions. These are rarely probed because, for emotion to be full-bodied and secure, clear values must exist and Pinter's theatre implies that we either have none or that those we have are peculiarly vague. The shadow of the suggested emotions keeps us theatrically excited even before we realize—and even if we don't realize—their specific substance. This technique is so marked in *The Collection* that we are led to suspect it of a certain slickness. The trick may conceivably end by deceiving its author. *The Caretaker*, for all its

effort to suppress it, has feeling; *The Collection*, almost none. As a substitute, it employs tension.

I noticed a high-minded and most intelligent friend leave *Never Too Late* (The Playhouse) after the first act. This was understandable. The farce by Sumner Arthur Long is built on one simple situation: a sixty-three-year-old New England businessman (he is in lumber) learns that his somewhat younger wife is pregnant. The discovery causes consternation in him as well as in his grown-up daughter and son-in-law. It is obvious what sort of jokes will ensue.

Yet I was a little worried by my friend's reaction. This unassuming "commercial" play (a smash hit) is of more respectable stuff than many intellectuals will concede. There is a considerable amount of oblique (though possibly complacent) satire in it. The benign obtuseness (or plain stupidity) of the average American male in regard to his wife and family is exposed in a manner which might be called merciless if *Never Too Late* were anything but an entertainment. The audience recognizes itself (or its neighbors!) and cackles contentedly— I along with it. Lift your nose if you will; the facts are there as surely as in a report on Middletown.

Plays of this kind are not as easy to write or produce as we loftily assume. They used to be a staple of our theatre but our recently acquired tastes have all but driven them from the boards— and good riddance you will say. But you may be mistaken. When they are this well contrived, perfectly cast (with Paul Ford in his eloquent inexpressiveness, his wooden Republican honesty and his thick-headed astonishment playing the lead) and cunningly directed (by George Abbott) they are welcome. They are slight to the point of triviality, funny, and not without meaning. We cannot wholly know ourselves, our people and country, without having some appreciation of them.

I am never unhappy about the popularity of such plays; I am much more troubled by the emptiness of some of our presumably more "serious" plays (there are several on Broadway now which I prefer to ignore in these pages). Deep thinkers of the theatre who refuse to relate to its vulgar pleasures are off balance: they lack that essential ingredient of wisdom—the ordinary.

—*NAT*, 15 Dec. '62

INTRODUCING JOHN BERGER

To readers unfamiliar with the London weeklies the *New Statesman* and *The Observer,* John Berger will be a new name. He is an art critic and a Marxist. Though I do not qualify as either, I recommend this selection of his articles to our American audience. *Toward Reality* is a book I would like even if I did not approve of it.

I have called Berger an art critic and a Marxist, not a Marxian art critic. For though there is undoubtedly an element unifying his craft and his philosophy, one is not entirely dependent on the other. We can appreciate his insights into painting and sculpture without subscribing to his or any other form of Marxism. This is not said as an apology to those for whom any kind of Marxism (which in America is immediately equated with Soviet ideology) is abhorrent. The distinction is made to emphasize Berger's general value as a writer. He is that phenomenon rare in journalism nowadays—a genuine critic. This is particularly true in the realm of the visual arts. His aim, he says, "is to stimulate thought in a field where normally there is very little indeed."

Criticism is not a matter of opinions. To proclaim more or less elaborately: "I like (or dislike) this picture, piece, poem, or play" is hardly criticism: at best it is a label that a critic may affix to his writings; at worst (and rather frequently) it is a presumption.

The first step in criticism is to see, to feel, to absorb the work presented. Here, to begin with, most so-called critics falter. They do not see or sense the specific nature of the artist's material—color, line, shape, composition, tone. They generalize on the basis of an automatic and usually commonplace reaction: "It's delightful, it's horrid, it's tedious, it's immoral," etc. Any or all these things may or may not be so—but no matter! What these utterances fail to provide is any proof that something particular in the artist's work has actually been perceived. We are told that something sweet or sour has affected the critic's taste buds, but we gather little information as to the "chemical" ingredients which cause the critic to complain or to glow. We do not learn what *happens* in the work examined.

The second step in criticism is judgment or evaluation. To be capable of judgment the critic must state or imply clear criteria. He must possess ideas of his own, some personal or traditional scale of values which he can enunciate, elucidate, defend. He may do this analytically or poetically. What must emerge—or it is not criticism—is the critic's own stance, his own world view. In revealing the artist, the critic reveals himself.

One of the supreme figures in modern art criticism, Baudelaire, in speaking of the usefulness of criticism, said: "I sincerely believe that the best criticism is that which is amusing and poetic: not a cold, mathematical criticism which under the pretext of explaining everything, has neither love nor hate and voluntarily strips itself of every shred of temperament. But seeing that a fine painting is nature reflected by an artist, the criticism of which I approve will be that picture reflected by an intelligent and sensitive mind. Thus the best account of a picture may well be a sonnet or an elegy. But this kind of criticism is destined for anthologies and readers of poetry."

At this point Baudelaire appears to be identifying himself as a thoroughgoing impressionist—restricting the domain of criticism to that task of practiced and intuitive vision which I suggested was the first step in any critical approach to art. But Baudelaire goes on—and here we trace our way back to Berger—"As for criticism proper, to be just—that is, to justify its existence—criticism should be partial, passionate, and political—that is, written from an exclusive point of view, but a point of view that opens out on the widest horizons."

Baudelaire's own criticism frequently contradicts his theses—or seems to, which is the artist's privilege. For later on Baudelaire admits that he cannot confine himself to a consistent philosophy. Berger, on the contrary, insists on the doctrinaire bias of his writing. He sometimes seems to adhere to his prejudices by main force as if in protest against both the looseness of the criticism which rides the clouds and the rigidity of the criticism which devotes itself entirely to formal matters.

Berger repeatedly warns us that "Marxist analyses of art have often over-simplified to absurdity." To confuse Berger with the kind of Soviet critic who resolves every problem through the slogan of "socialist realism" or the sort of *New Masses* theorist of the thirties who gratified himself with the assurance that "art is a weapon," would be to do Berger (and ourselves) a grave injustice. There is a coherence in his views but they represent a certain spirit rather than a strict dogma. His Marxism is sincere (possibly romantic) but it does not describe or circumscribe his contribution. A non-Marxist, even an anti-Marxist, can cherish him as a critic.

In a way, painting and sculpture are the most mysterious of arts; and art criticism the most difficult. In writing about literature we seem to be dealing with the medium in its own terms: there is a parallel between the ideas, actions, characters, situations, vocabulary of literary forms and criticism of them. Music is at once so vaporous and so formal, so intangible in its material and so specialized in its technique, that it lends itself either to a verbalization with no ground to stand on or to explication so professional that its "secrets" can be assessed only by the trained.

Painting is primitive in its directness, but in its ultimate effect as remote from the "naturalistic" as music. All painting (and these remarks apply to sculpture as well), no matter how abstract, is definitely "something"—whether it be made to resemble a person, an animal, a flower, or is no more than a splash of pigment. That is why we can "take in" a picture instantaneously—and not see it at all.

The mystery of painting is like that of a dream: it has a manifest content—recognizable in a flash—but its real content, meaning, or value is latent, with no inescapable relation to what is visible. The image very often serves to obstruct one's insight. How in a painting by Soutine does a dead chicken come to look like a passion—or vice versa?

This enigma in painting and sculpture is missed or evaded by many critics either by indulging in what Baudelaire called "studio jargon"—highbrow double-talk—or by situating the painting in some scholarly category of historical origin. When the critic is especially "cultivated" we are treated to a pasty mixture of the two methods. Insofar as the descriptive passages in such criticism have a factual justification they usually put into words what we have already noted; insofar as the historical data are accurate they are generally divorced from any inevitable connection with a specific interpretation of the individual painting—its importance as art, its human meaning.

Berger observes sharply and specifically. His findings are expressed in terse and lucid summations not designed to display his wit but to illuminate the object of his examination and to define what he feels about it. The effect is tonic. The intelligence which guides his sensibility makes for memorable passages on almost every page. When, for example, he discusses Cubism—apart from what he says about individual exemplars—one is instructed in both its technical aim and its relevance to modern expression in general: its origins and its direction, its source in our society and its value for the future.

The concise characterizations of such artists as Matisse, Dufy, Kokoschka, Lipchitz, are remarkable in their combination of precision and suggestiveness. In a series of keen and rapid strokes—which look easy because they have been prepared after long meditation—the artists are revealed to us in the round—in their actual features and in the clarified mystery of their meaning. This is equally true—and perhaps even more striking—in Berger's treatment of the older painters: Piero della Francesca, Poussin, Goya, Watteau. When he writes of Léger (whom he perhaps overestimates) one is exhilarated by a view of an artist presented as he himself must have thought of his work—celebrated with true flair. Berger calls Léger's paintings "flags": and I begin to look at them with a new understanding and an increased sympathy.

It is not, however, with Berger's opinions or preferences in individual artists that I am concerned, nor even with the brightness of his writing. It is his spirit, not his "trademark," which I find immensely valuable. Berger the "modern," who calls himself a revolutionary, proclaims the virtues of a "national materialism," decries the crimes of a decaying capitalism, invokes social rights, and announces his hope for a proletarian socialism, is fundamentally a traditionalist. (In his declaration that "the basis of all painting and sculpture is drawing" he may even be regarded as a conservative.) His inspiration is rooted in a classic foundation.

Berger is himself an artist and is primarily moved by the act and presence of art, but his sights are set not only on art itself but on the world in which art, the artist, and the "audience" at large exist together. ("Art for art's sake?" André Gide once said. "Certainly. But why hold it to so little!") For Berger art is neither an adornment, an escape, a safety valve, a medicament: it is the testimony and insignia of man himself in his personal and social reality. It is his essential *speech*.

This is a cardinally classic attitude. In the times of art's health and citizenship the artist hardly thought of himself as such—indeed "Art" did not exist. It was in the service of—or even more properly, organic with—the all-embracing Idea of a community or a religion. Berger rejects the notion of art as the specialty of a coterie of the defeated, the despairing, the damaged, or the exclusively defiant.

Art, for Berger, is not simply the expression of the isolated individual, but the graph of a relationship between an individual and his fellows. The individual and society constitute a continuum. Art in Berger's view is therefore personal and historical. Man participates in and influences history (the life of his people) through affirmative action. The world "outside" of the individual exists, man's role in it is consented to, his struggle within it and his capacity to modify it are joyously accepted. The continuity of art is made possible through man's constant effort to maintain the continuity of history, of which he is a part.

Berger is one of the few men in the art world today who does not regard science and technology with distrust. On the contrary, he sees them as liberating forces in a future social configuration. He gives evidence of believing—as he declares apropos of Poussin's painting—that man can control his fate. Thus he writes with something like reverence for the masters of the Renaissance.

Berger shares with the romantics "a sense of the future, an awareness of the possibility of a world other than we know." His hopefulness is an incentive to deeds. He may commiserate with contemporary hysteria but is never tempted to succumb to it. "The despair of the artist," he says, "is never total. It excepts his own work." Berger does not scorn the art which is a cry of agony or a confession of panic, but he refuses to acknowledge such art as the peak of creative expression or the last word in the representation of contemporary sensibility. He aspires toward a humane integration of aesthetics and social ethics, and is suspicious of the now prevailing fascination with horror and dissolution. The modernist and revolutionary of Berger's persuasion seeks to achieve an order which will incorporate in new forms what was vital in the old.

The main fault I find with *Toward Reality* is its brevity. It forces Berger to be summary. Some of his explanations are far from complete. This is not a fault due to lack of space alone (though it is true that most of the pieces in the book were published in periodicals which did not allow much room for discussion of the arts). There is in Berger's writing a certain impatience which often marks the committed man, the over-zealous moralist. His dismissal of Dubuffet is understandable but hardly sound; his haste with Klee dismaying. For he slights the liberating effect of Klee's innocence (not to mention his draftsmanship) and the verve of Dubuffet's outrage together with a certain peculiar primitivism which aims at a new richness of color and texture within the mud bath.

Berger will meet with considerable antagonism in America because he opposes the *esthétique* of the Action Painters (or Abstract Expressionists), in which so many now take pride as a peculiarly native product, a mode in which we appear to excel. Berger's objections to this trend follow naturally from the premises of his own faith and temperament. But he is no more given to vulgar abuse of this recent "school" of painters than he is to the pretentious awe which its supporters often voice in gibberish.

It should be noticed not only that Berger speaks respectfully—albeit regretfully—of Jackson Pollock, but that he says in detraction of Pollock's coevals much the same things that Harold Rosenberg (who referred to many of their canvases as "apocalyptic wallpaper") has said in their defense. The difference between the two critics may be that whereas Berger recognizes only the negative aspects in a performance which is usually non-intellectual, anti-formal, largely improvisatory, and almost totally subjective (work which has sometimes dubbed itself "non-art"), the other critic—perhaps another Marxist—may discern in these negations a certain positive side, a possible extension of means and a symbolic content in terms of our civilization—apposite not only to our country but to many in Europe, including several behind the mythical curtain. There may be useful social connotations in these new painters which Berger overlooks.

I have written all this neither to dispute with Berger nor to champion him: only to greet a critic whose challenge is to be welcomed by anyone to whom the cause and existence of art are of central interest beyond the range of so-called art circles. For my part I extend my hand to Berger fraternally, for I find in him a strength of conviction, a

tenderness as well as a virility of feeling, a sturdiness of mind, a succinctness and dignity of style, that is very nearly unique today in writing about art in the English language.

—Introduction to *Toward Reality* (1962) by John Berger

MARCH OF THE MUSICALS

Musical comedy is nothing to argue about: it is to be enjoyed. Yet if you should stop to think about it, you may discover some fascinating and perhaps fruitful opportunities for dispute. It is said, for example, that the American theatre has become a musical-comedy theatre. Some say it mournfully, others with pride and glee. And there are those who deny it fiercely.

The facts favor the ayes. Recent statistics inform us that eleven musicals were produced during the 1960-61 season, fourteen last season, and fourteen musicals, in addition to four revues, have been announced for 1962-63. There are ten musicals occupying the boards at the moment, and only seven plays without musical benefit. As the number of theatrical productions each year diminishes, the near dominance of musical comedy on our stage becomes increasingly evident. As an astonishing corroboration of what one might call the automatic popularity of musical comedy, there is the news item (not mere publicity) that the Lindsay-Crouse-Berlin show *Mr. President* boasts an advance sale before its New York opening of over two million dollars.

Facts, however, are dumb things: they do not reveal the whole truth. The theatre is a place where art, social pattern and economies are inextricably commingled. So if musical comedy is to be discussed apart from its fun, it must be examined in all these lights.

The hastiest and most superficial consideration makes the reason for the box-office potency of the musical quite obvious. Musicals are designed to please practically everyone with the minimum of effort on anyone's part. All possibility of offense is avoided. Every ingredient is scrupulously aimed at ease, comfort, titillation—as with a holiday resort. The musical is a large-scale entertainment package. Won't the man who invites his out-of-town client-friend on a business and pleasure jaunt to New York feel safer in reserving tickets for a splendid musical jamboree rather than for *Heartbreak House* or *Long Day's Journey Into Night*?

Even the weakest musical promises at least two or three good jokes, a talented performer, a bit of rhythm, one or two pretty ladies, a tune one might hum and several nice dresses—or undresses. Musicals are show business' best bet because everyone nowadays seeks relief from real or pretended pressures. A drama might require some strain of nerve or brain muscle. The most resolute theatregoer will vow, in moments of exasperated impatience, that he would rather see a good musical several times than many supposedly earnest plays once.

Though scholarly gentlemen often point out that musical comedy has its antecedents in such European models as operetta and *opéra bouffe,* as well as in certain indigenous entertainments like the minstrel show and burlesque, the bare statement that musical comedy today is the one theatrical form in which America excels seems incontrovertible.

Enthusiasts learnedly explain, furthermore, that musical comedy as we now practice it, is a special and virtually new kind of show, of which Rodgers' and Hammerstein's *Oklahoma!* is often cited as a prime example. This claim of originality for the new musical smacks of hysterical complacency. Whatever fine distinctions are made between the musicals after the great Rodgers and Hammerstein hit and those of Irving Berlin, Jerome Kern, George Gershwin, Cole Porter and Vincent Youmans, as well as those of Rodgers himself (in collaboration with Larry Hart) in the twenties and thirties, it is certain that the work of those early days was of the same nature as, and of

equal (if not superior) value to, that of our more "integrated" musicals today.

To be impressive, one might refer even further back to George M. Cohan, Victor Herbert and Ivan Caryll's 1911 *Pink Lady.* The point is that there always seems to have been a vital and flourishing theatre of light comic character in America. If there is any fixed tradition in our theatre, this is it. The reason is social and historical. The story of America, by and large, has been one of energy, invention, adaptability, youthfulness, buoyancy, optimism, physical well-being and prosperity. No matter what troubles beset us, we try to remain sanguine. ("Pack up your troubles in your old kit bag-and smile, smile, smile!") Despite another strain of American creativity from Hawthorne and Melville to Faulkner and O'Neill, tragedy has been rather alien to us.

Still, there is a correspondence between our so-called serious drama and our lighter musical stage. For all theatre is one: It always reflects—in comedy as well as in tragedy—various aspects of the human landscape. Just as there was almost no important native drama at the time of *The Black Crook* (1866) and precious little during the Floradora days (1900), the sophistication of our musical shows increases as we approach the late teens and early twenties.

It is surely not a matter of chance that our musical theatre burst into effulgent bloom just as our more sober theatre produced its first crop of notable playwrights: Eugene O'Neill, George Kelly, Elmer Rice, Maxwell Anderson, Sidney Howard, S. N. Behrman, Robert Sherwood, Philip Barry. And just before the launching of the Group Theatre we had *Of Thee I Sing.* When we come to observe what is happening to our present musicals, we shall have to judge the situation in the broader context of our theatre as a whole.

There are those who maintain that while our musical-comedy theatre constitutes a masterpiece in the aggregate, very few—if any—of our musicals have achieved the artistic integrity or the staying power of the best in Gilbert and Sullivan,

Offenbach or the Weill and Brecht of *The Threepenny Opera*. (Of course, none of these are, strictly speaking, musical comedy, any more than is Gershwin's *Porgy and Bess*.) Yet, despite such demurs, our attachment to the musical-comedy form is not only understandable but aesthetically justified. For musical comedy is that "mythical" phenomenon—true theatre.

What is true theatre? When still a young man, Bernard Shaw wrote, "The theatre was born of old from the union of two tendencies: the desire to have a dance and the desire to hear a story. The dance became a rout, the story became a situation."

True theatre is the telling of a story or the presentation of a situation through every physical means by which men and women, together in the presence of their community, are capable of rousing its interest and pleasure. Theatre bespeaks human action—movement and speech—raised to an intense degree of eloquence through dance, song, color, spectacle. From ghost stories and tall tales told around a campfire to the austere magnificence of Greek drama, this impulse has always shaped the theatre's essence. It is there in the performance of the Japanese Noh plays, as well as in Shakespeare. We find it in Brecht (at the Berliner Ensemble) as well as in *Pal Joey*. It was what O'Neill always dreamed of achieving.

Where on our stage today is there so much of this true theatre as in our musical comedies? Ballet, which has heightened its appeal for us enormously since the thirties, lacks speech; drama lacks song and (too often) color; opera usually misses acting. The straight play (what a terrible term) often contains ideas. But musicals may possess these as well. At times musicals would appear to be almost the only place in the theatre where ideas may take final refuge!

As we hark back to the past of our musical and nonmusical stages, we fondly recall the personalities which graced both. In the twenties our theatre—the two kinds—was illuminated by splendid constellations of players whose very presence cast a halo of magic over every occasion. In the thirties the stars began to move westward. Now they are mainly to be found on the musical horizon. How many shining bodies have we on the dramatic stage today compared with those we admire in the musicals?

The comparison may be invidious and unfair, but can you, reader, make a list of "legitimate" actors and actresses to set down beside Ethel Merman, Ray Bolger, Mary Martin, Judy Holliday, Julie Andrews, Gwen Verdon, Zero Mostel, Nancy Walker and Phil Silvers—and perhaps Tammy Grimes, Robert Morse, Barbra Streisand and Barbara Harris? (And, oh, if she were only in the theatre—Judy Garland!) What brilliant additions to our stagecraft—not to speak of our satisfaction—have been made by such choreographers as George Balanchine, Agnes de Mille, Jerome Robbins, Michael Kidd, Bob Fosse, Herbert Ross and Gower Champion.

But halt! Some of those named have transferred or will transfer from the nonmusical to the musical theatre as others may take the opposite direction. Everything in our theatre today is in a process of flux and change—some warn of dissolution—and the musicals mirror the alteration perhaps even more strikingly than our drama.

Long ago—for convenience sake, let us say before 1930—what was most important to the musical-comedy audience was beautiful girls (hail Ziegfeld!), comedians (those dear old Ed Wynn days) and, crucially, *music*—real tunes suggesting all the wonderful things the often paltry books of the time could not say. (Think of the *Show Boat* score—one which is most likely to survive.) It did not matter much if you interrupted the story to bring on the girls or to vamp into a bright, consoling melody.

The next musical strives toward "legitimacy." The book, or, more properly, the show's subject matter, must possess a little substance, relate somehow to our normal concerns, edge closer to the contemporaneous and the topical. Due in large measure to the refinement of our taste through the influence of our ballet companies, dancing has developed into a cardinal factor.

Above all, there is now an insistence on "integration"—of which *Guys and Dolls, My Fair Lady, West Side Story* and *Gypsy* supply outstanding examples. Integration demands that all the elements in a musical be thoroughly "cemented." The story, lyrics, music, acting and dancing must not only fit together, but extend or complete each other. The line or fabric of the whole must never appear to break: one part must carry on where the other leaves off so as to compose a closely woven continuity.

This explains, incidentally, why the girls in musicals today are seldom as dazzlingly attractive as they formerly were. All the advantages and talents—the ability to sing, dance, act and to look beautiful—do not often dwell in one person.

The new musical is designed to create a unified impression, a coherent tone, an all-pervasive atmosphere. At times this aim appears to be attained at the expense of melody. The scores of our recent musicals seem to have more utility than inspiration. They have become a means rather than an end. There are signal exceptions to this, as for example the score—which seems to improve with age—of *Kiss Me, Kate.* Still, one might point out that such a stylistic relic as *Kismet* was successful mainly because it was sustained by delightful—albeit borrowed—music.

What strikes many listeners as musical anemia in many recent shows may be explained in another way. It has been widely agreed that our theatre, in general, has become markedly less animated since 1956-57. Certainly there have been good things of various sorts since then, but there has been a definite shrinkage, not only in the volume of productions (and profits) but in every sense in which the word *abundance* may be construed. Our dramatic theatre has thinned out—foreign plays of quality, for example, preponderated last season—and something peculiar has happened to our musical theatre as well.

Serious drama has always encountered a certain resistance in our theatre—more particularly since theatre tickets have become so expensive.

Such drama can exist and thrive only when it is fired by sufficient passion and conviction to make it thoroughly arresting. For the past decade, at least, we have been living in a state of spiritual confusion. Issues are not clear-cut: there has been inner, but hardly articulated, disquiet. Boldness is not feared so much as it is baffled by lack of social support and subjective assurance. We have grown publicly mute on serious matters, for we do not know exactly what there is to be said. We cover up and are not even sure what we are suppressing. Hence the repeated, but rather vague, outcry against conformism.

Yet we do want to express *something* about what lurks in our minds. We do not like to say anything which might be deemed heavy, humorless or offensive—we do not want to rock the boat—so we kid and joke. We mask our misgivings in gags.

The social themes of the thirties and early forties begin to emerge anew as grins and grimaces in the musicals of the late fifties and early sixties. After the war, we appeased our jarred souls with sweet, smiling images of the past (or of remote places): *Oklahoma!, Bloomer Girl, Carousel, Up in Central Park* and *Brigadoon.* With *Finian's Rainbow* we began pushing the present, while *South Pacific,* despite its touch of exoticism, hovered around a controversial subject. Then our present begins to engage us pleasantly with *The Pajama Game,* a "labor" musical without contention, to be followed later by *Fiorello!,* a "political" show without rancor.

The contemporary keynote is struck in *How to Succeed in Business Without Really Trying,* which indicates by its very title the point we have reached. (To begin with, think of the number of musicals which are basically success stories, such as *The Unsinkable Molly Brown.*) We are unsure of our values—at least for purposes of theatrical presentation—so we are both obsessed by the idea of success (and by status or money, which is its goal), and a little ashamed of the obsession. It is no accident that *Do Re Mi, Bye Bye Birdie, I Can Get It For You Wholesale* and even, to some extent, *No*

Strings, are variations on the themes of success, status push and money fixation. These are now what might be called our "social plays." They all deplore our addiction to the success-status-money fetish—but not too emphatically.

Love creeps into these shows, as it were, by the back door. They are only half-heartedly romantic. They suggest that love must ride a rough road in our competitive mechanized world. As a result, the embodiment of glamor, warmth, carefreeness and a poised enjoyment of wealth becomes strained. For shows deficient in these ingredients, it is no easy matter to write free-flowing tunes—melodies with a lift. One might as well try to put double-entry bookkeeping to music.

In *Musical Comedy in America,* one of the best books on the subject, Cecil Smith, clearly a devotee, ends by asserting that while musicals have moved "into an increasingly high plane of craftsmanship and literacy," they are still only entertainments, "and if they are art at all, they are only incidentally so." Though the distinction may be useful, one should be wary of it; it insinuates that art is that which does not entertain!

One might correct a misunderstanding here by remarking that present-day musicals are too often rounded on a sort of industrial calculation, sales gimmicks barely related to true individual or personal impulse. The musical, in other words, far too frequently nowadays is conceived on a mass-production basis as corporate efforts by canny and capable showmen with an eye to profitable enterprise on the Main Stem supermarket. Art rarely springs from such sources. A musical play like the Offenbach and Halévy *La Vie Parisienne,* for instance, was a collaboration of two men who were as much imbued with a feeling—both satiric and gay—about the Second Empire as any artist of their time.

Whatever one's estimate of their separate merits, our musicals at present are as typical of the extraordinary accomplishment and the grave defects as are all the other manifestations of our native theatre. They, too—and perhaps even more at the moment than most other "attractions" our playhouses have to offer—are "the brief chronicles of the time." Indeed, certain knowledgeable folk tell us that the hope of the Midtown theatres lies in our musicals. It may well be so, since they, up to very recently, have proved commercially the most advantageous as well as the most popular of our productions.

Still, the high cost of producing and operating our super-lavish musicals forces them to court disaster. During the past two seasons there have been many more well-liked and lauded musicals which have lost money than we suspect. The relatively small cast and scenic modesty of *A Funny Thing Happened on the Way to the Forum* may be a portent. Should the fate of musicals be threatened by the economic hazards that menace the life of our dramatic theatre, the institution or concept known as Broadway may collapse. This, however, does not mean that the Theatre in our country would die.

One good way to keep musicals lively, at any rate, is to avoid making too sharp a distinction between merit in one category of the theatre and another. A musical must be appreciated according to standards of freshness, imaginativeness and emotional authenticity similar to those we apply to other stage forms. Such criteria may, in fact, serve as a leaven for our theatre generally.

—*NYT,* '62

ABE LINCOLN IN ILLINOIS
THE SCHOOL FOR SCANDAL

In my book *The Fervent Years* I speak of the "high school academicism" of the Playwrights Company during the early years of that organization's activities in the thirties. I had in mind such a play, among others, as Robert Sherwood's *Abe Lincoln in Illinois.* After viewing its new production at the Phoenix Theatre, I find my epithet a little snide. It is true that the play, which many pronounced "great," has about it the quality of a chromo, a sentimentally patriotic backward look that smacks of a commencement-day speech intended to fire students with ardor for the past so that they may rise to the challenge of the present. *Abe Lincoln in Illinois* was written in 1938 when the country was of an emphatically liberal disposition, aware of the Hitler menace and of the imminence of the war to stop him. The historical moment played an important role in the audience's response to the play.

Its simple-mindedness rendered me reluctant to acknowledge the play's merit in terms of the kind of enthusiasm it aroused, although even then I could not but be moved by the eloquence of many of its speeches, which are direct transcripts from Lincoln. Today, when the play, despite the struggle in the South over segregation, is much less "topical," I am touched by the very qualities I previously found juvenile. The play's naïveté is sweet and healthy.

There is here, apart from the Lincolnesque idealism and fond image of our American past, a further and important element of personal pathos. Robert Sherwood was for some years oppressed by a (Spenglerian?) sense of doom as it was set to an American key in Joseph Wood Krutch's *The Modern Temper*. He wrote entertainments (*The Petrified Forest*, *Idiot's Delight*), but running through them was a note of depression never forceful enough to perturb the theatregoer. One remarked in Sherwood a morose withdrawal from the wasteland.

With the advent of Roosevelt, and possibly because of some changes in his domestic life, Sherwood was swept into action. He assisted Roosevelt with his speeches, he became an unofficial member of the administration. Democracy, anti-fascism and the fight against other forms of reaction were causes that now demanded his participation. Thus Sherwood felt a kinship with Lincoln in whom he saw a melancholy man bearing some permanent sear on his soul, a man without much ambition, forced by the pressure of history, conscience, common sense and a decent modicum of vanity into action at the crucial hour

of his time. *Abe Lincoln in Illinois* is therefore the expression of a real experience written by a candid spirit that was not without stamina. The play was well worth reviving and it is well worth seeing.

The Phoenix production, under Stuart Vaughan, sprawls a bit and its cast makes so marked an impression of youthfulness that at times the sense of a spectacle for children is inescapable, though not at all unpleasant. Its most remarkable feature is Hal Holbrook's Lincoln. Holbrook cannot create the feeling of a deep-seated mournfulness which the play demands—a characteristic that Raymond Massey indicated in the original production—but Holbrook, besides an endearing charm, possesses a marvelous faculty of observation, an ability to represent tiny traits of behavior that cumulatively carry immense conviction. There is, too, a quality of *race* in Holbrook, something like an "aboriginal" or typical (early) Americanism, which contributes much to our pleasure in his Lincoln as it did in his impersonation of Mark Twain.

Holbrook's voice pipes a bit, but it ends by exercising an appeal of both innocence and humor. With all this, Holbrook is endowed with an impressive conscientiousness. Each detail in his stage presence is prepared and executed with great scrupulosity. This young man is an actor.

Sheridan's *The School for Scandal* (Majestic Theatre) is the finest comedy I have seen since 1777. Although the author was only twenty-six when he wrote the play, it is not only magnificently witty but endowed with a wisdom that transcends fashion and the cleverness of coteries. The play is as fresh today as it was on that happy occasion when it was first given at Drury Lane (or was it Convent Garden?). A lady of high literary eminence confessed the other night in the lobby of the Majestic that she felt a little self-conscious at the play because the kind of gossip and convivial malice it satirized was exactly the pastime in which she and most of her friends indulge.

The writing is a constant delight—one is tempted to say Mozartian. We enjoy it as a kind of music for the mind. It has sprightly movement, euphony, grace and edge. The play is superbly constructed, with an unsurpassed knowledge of the stage. The slight dust of age that now powders it sets off its magic all the more. Shining through its surface sheen is sovereign good humor and generosity of spirit.

I dwell on the play's text because it is too frequently our custom in the case of old plays to speak of their presentation and little of their matter. Let no one tell me he doesn't like *The School for Scandal* because of some demur over its present production. How often does New York see such a masterpiece? We have as yet no "Philharmonic" theatre.

It is objected by some people that John Gielgud's production is more stylish than sharp, more outstanding for costumes and settings than for concentration on the play's bite. Perhaps there is some justification for this complaint: the English producers and actors may have been more attracted by the play's manners, the quaint stylization needed for its performance, and the polish of their own professionalism than by the human thrust and acid of the play's situations. But I shall not cavil; I confess I was captivated and did not feel that the play had to be any more "real" than the English company makes it. Its removal or distance from me as an actual ("life") occurrence did not prevent me from relishing its artistic truth.

Ralph Richardson as Sir Peter Teazle is gigantically delicious. He is larger than life, a huge comedy doll of genius; playful, pitiful, foolish and adorable, out of this world and close to our hearts. I have seen the production three times (twice in London) and each time Richardson was slightly different, but always irresistible. The first time I saw him—early in the play's run—the moment of his discovering his wife behind the "villain" Joseph Surface's screen was most affecting. The genuineness of Richardson's emotion—its discretion as much as its poignancy—was unmistakable. That sort of truthfulness cannot be repeated at every performance, with or without a Method. But Richardson "dry" or Richardson "full," his Teazle is always a treasure.

John Gielgud, who seems almost too dear a person to play Surface, obscures himself in modest retirement much of the time, but rises to the bait of the screen scene with a great sense of fun. His voice is a bit too evenly and beautifully pitched in its velvet tone for character roles. In contrast, the peculiar reediness of Richardson's voice gives it an arresting oddity within its ingratiating resonance. But both men are a pleasure to hear.

Laurence Naismith's geniality in the role of the Surfaces' beaming uncle is infectious. Geraldine McEwan's Lady Teazle is both tart and tender, her pertness, suavely coupled with a sort of childishly pure uprightness, is very English and very winning. With a generally sound ensemble the production achieves a museum of exemplary stature.

—NAT, 9 Feb. '63

THE COACH WITH THE SIX INSIDES
NATURAL AFFECTION

To the curious and adventurous I recommend *The Coach with the Six Insides* (Village South Theatre), a comedy adapted from James Joyce's *Finnegans Wake*. It may be caviar to the general, but it is worth your pleased if bewildered attention.

It is not a play in any conventional acceptation, but a danced and mimed recital of linked passages from Joyce's recondite and vast nighttime reverie. It progresses to a strange unity in which each part is beginning, middle and end. Perhaps seeing it may serve as an introduction to the book of which Thornton Wilder has said that one must spend a thousand hours to fathom and to appreciate its wonders.

It is not that difficult to enjoy the spectacle shown in the Village. It is generously visual, though perhaps language is its most salient feature—a language as gorgeously melodious as it is distorted and perverted, an erudite pig Latin, hilariously comic, lyric, soothing, frightening, melancholy, obscene and elevating!

I am sure of what I say about *The Coach with Six Insides*, but I have never been sure of Joyce! It needs no insight now to repeat that his was a seminal work with a broad influence throughout the literature of our century; that he, Lord of the Verb, was a fascinating human, as well as artistic, phenomenon. But I have never determined, within my own conscience, whether I am "for" or "against" him. And though the question is of no objective consequence, it has always been important to me so that I might situate myself. For a work of art is as much a test for its beholder as for its creator. Through it we may realize ourselves; that is not the least of its values.

Joyce's work is a repository of the accumulated learning, misgivings, resentments, fears, mockeries, turmoil, triumphs, confusions of our time. In this alone he was a genius. (We must respect all genius—although it can well do without our respect. But must we always *love* it?) Joyce's Jesuit education made, marked and maimed him. That divine in *A Portrait of the Artist As a Young Man* who warned him as an adolescent of the torments of hell that await boys who masturbate put an incalculably damaging imprint on Joyce's spirit. The sermon filled him forever with terror and hate.

He took refuge in exile, in rigorous study, in the constructs of the mind. His thinking was intricate, his aesthetics arcane, his speculations profoundly turned in on himself. He saw and felt deeply but his sight was defective. There was blindness in him. He had a contempt for the world while being attached to every filament of its filth. He tried to save himself through the subtlest games of art: a process which made ash of what he abominated in the sinful world, the while, he secretly hoped, the process would lead him back to what he cherished in the memory of his mother, in his religion and in the Irish earth—all of which he had fled.

One does not know, reading Joyce, whether his work is a dump heap in which lies buried the debris of the past (a wreck he helped make), or an augury of some possible future, the miraculous rebirth of a world no longer soiled by the material, spiritual, intellectual waste which the past bequeathed us. In the awful nightmare of Joyce's inner strife, one does not easily discern which is the greater: the devil of his damnations or the deep blue sea of his purification. ("I done me best when I was let...a hundred cares, a tithe of troubles, and is there one who understands me? One in a thousand of years of the nights? All me life I have been lived among them but now they are becoming loathed to me. And I am loathing their little warm tricks. And loathing their mean cozy turns. And all the greedy gushes out through their small souls ....I thought you great in all things, in guilt and in glory. You're but a puny....") So Joyce sows disquiet in me. A gloomy and grinning giant of our time, he affords me no peace.

As a theatre effort *The Coach with the Six Insides* is not formidable. It is in fact a charming miniature of what in Joyce's poem is both minute and grandiose. The show is youthful, not expert in every detail, but ambitious and talented though not in the least pretentious or heavy. The five players who compose its cast speak well, move well, do everything winningly. The modest costumes are extremely good, the musical accompaniment by Teiji Ito is pleasantly helpful. The whole event, which has been carefully thought out and imaginatively devised by Jean Erdman, gives evidence of impressive devotion and careful training on everyone's part.

William Inge is our dramatist of the ordinary. His people are never deep souls, never intellectuals, artists or even middling middlebrows. They are the common product of American civilization. They are "things," expecting or striving to be born as persons.

Inge's dramatic technique is almost as primitive as the folk he depicts. The people are readily understandable, the technique sure. For these reasons there is a tendency on the part of the presumably more advanced to disparage Inge. This is a mistake. Inge's role in our theatre is a central one; the commonplace is not the obvious.

His plays are deft scenarios. His writing is bare but suggestive. At times it touches the rim of poetry, and the right actors can transport it into that realm. His plays always act better than one would suppose from reading them. They require the extension of the stage.

Natural Affection (Booth Theatre) is his nearest approach to raw realism. I had thought that Inge was capable of something Chekhovian, but *Natural Affection* makes it clear that what he is bent on is a rude lesson which he can best convey by exposing crude facts in swift, blunt, concentrated sketches and rough case histories. The result is not ugly, even when much of the material reeks of the vile.

Freud, plus an innate delicacy and an instinct for the theatre, guide Inge's hand. *Natural Affection* is the most summary of his plays, the baldest, the most banal, and yet in certain respects the most powerful. For the first time his voice is raised in anger, as if he had decided to say something that he had previously hesitated to utter. Our gadget civilization is so without the grace of personal values that it must produce monsters—all the more criminal for having originated in sympathetic human impulses.

The play is too stripped and tight not to reveal its simple monitory purpose and naked Freudian inspiration. Hence, there is a certain poverty and thinness. Yet it provides one excellent figure: the dumb, pathetic, hideously comic car salesman and ex-bartender, a sharp and telling caricature of the average American male, whose mediocrity clings to every semblance of gratification as to a solacing teat in a world too harsh for ordinary endurance. There is also an excellent scene in which a better-off businessman, alcoholic, frustrated, sadistic and nearly homosexual, spews the dregs of his empty being, the misery which is the only warrant of his humanity. All these midges of our urban landscape

reveal some real aspect of the everyday panorama of our native horizon. They make one wince.

The play is very well produced under Tony Richardson's direction. If the production has a fault it is that the blatant coarseness in the play's material is stressed above the vein of decency. (The coarseness is all too patent. Unfortunately, this brutal aspect of the play is what a good part of the audience appears to relish.) A framework of jazz and the stage's exposed electrical apparatus (from Brecht via Joan Littlewood and now a favored stage stratagem in London) adds to the play's liveliness, but does not heal its wounds.

The cast—Kim Stanley in a role not fully projected by the author, Harry Guardino, Tom Bosley, George Rozakis in the detrimentally underwritten part of the delinquent son—is admirable.

—*NAT*, 16 Feb. '63

ASIDES

Before the final push of the spring season (about a dozen new productions are scheduled to appear in March) I take time for several "asides." One does not have the space to say everything one has in mind even in a weekly.

The last paragraph (a sort of post-script) of my *Who's Afraid of Virginia Woolf?* notice suggested that there was an "expressionistic" aspect to the play which might lend itself to another kind of production than the literal one we now have. For example, a different sort of setting might have been designed for it. But more is involved than just a visual manner.

Even those who praise the play frequently voice dissatisfaction with its ending. For two acts husband and wife have been mauling each other to the point of crime; in the last act a reconciliation is hinted at. Very little in the first two acts, such criticism goes, prepares us for the almost wistful conclusion. The more severe critics suspect or accuse Albee of tacking on a "happy ending" to achieve popular acceptance. A *black* play, to employ Anouilh's term, says one reviewer, has been converted into a *rosy* one.

My reason for going into this matter now is that I wish to illustrate how production (staging or direction) actually affects a play's content—a point I have frequently insisted upon because it often appears to be completely overlooked.

If *Virginia Woolf* is naturalism, then its plot premise—two people married for nearly twenty years, invent, imagine and quarrel over a son never born to them—is hardly credible, if not altogether fantastic. But it should be clear that what Albee intends with this device is to dramatize a dream or falsehood which helps keep the couple, at odds on other accounts, together: their marriage is sustained by a lie. Many marriages and lives, Albee may be saying, become miserable because they are based on chimeras, on an evasion of facts. Only when reality, howsoever painful, is faced, when life's wretched disappointments are steadfastly confronted, can there be hope of sanity and strength. George, the husband, breaks through his wife's illusion by the fiercely determined declaration, "Our son is dead": we must kill the lie.

The play, then, is a sort of parable and its savagery is an extravagant heightening of reality. If this is so, the ending is not a trick to soften the play but the essence of its meaning, its moral point.

This escapes us when the play is set, as it is now, in a pedestrian (photographic) representation of a college professor's house. What is required is a set which informs us at once that what we are to witness is super-real, exemplary, if you will, symbolic. A new atmosphere would have to be created in which some of the agonized tenderness of the play's final moments might be anticipated, sensed from the beginning. The acting might then avoid the crackle of its hard-hitting wisecracks and vernacular sadism, would be modified by a mood of pathetic dimension, of yearning and regret. Even now this is perceptible in Shepperd Strudwick's playing of George at the matinee performances (the play, exhausting to the actors, employs two casts).

I feel certain that some such interpretation will be attempted when the play is done in Germany, Sweden or perhaps in one of the new theatres which have been established in certain cities outside New York.

—*NAT*, 9 Mar. '63

BRECHT IS GLOBAL, EXCEPT HERE

Have you ever heard of Bertolt Brecht? If this question were asked of a confirmed English, French, Swiss, Scandinavian, Israeli or even Japanese playgoer, he might consider himself insulted. What lover of the theatre almost anywhere in Europe does not know Brecht as dramatist or director or both?

Similarly, it would be an error and a presumption to suppose that the aware New Yorker is ignorant of the name or the reputation. He may recall Brecht as the original author of the book and lyrics of *The Threepenny Opera* which in Marc Blitzstein's adaptation was a record-breaking hit at the Theater de Lys in Greenwich Village. The passionate playgoer may also have seen Anne Bancroft in *Mother Courage* during its brief run last season.

The historian will remind you that *The Threepenny Opera* was first produced in New York (with Burgess Meredith) at the Empire Theater in 1933, when it flopped without the shedding of any critical tears. Others may discover that Charles Laughton appeared in *Galileo* both in Los Angeles and in an ANTA Experimental Theater production in New York in 1947; among the drama critics, Louis Kronenberger was alone in voting it the best foreign play of the year. The Phoenix Theater also tried without success to convert the unbelievers by a production of *The Good Woman of Setzuan* with Uta Hagen in 1956.

Martin Esslin, who has written the best book in English on Brecht, informs us that there have been more productions of Brecht's plays in the university and community theatres of the United

States than in any other country in the world except West (not East) Germany. Snips and snaps of Brecht's work under the title *Brecht on Brecht* were greeted with pleasure two seasons ago but, once again, off Broadway.

I cite these matters to indicate that while abroad and in certain milieus here Brecht is regarded as a major force in the contemporary theatre, he is still only vaguely known by the mass of New York playgoers. The intrepid will try and try again; no less a main-stem mogul than David Merrick is to present Brecht's farcical fable *Arturo Ui* at the Lunt-Fontanne Theater on Nov. 11.

How explain the discrepancy between Brecht's prestige and our peculiar indifference, not to say ignorance? One is tempted to reply that Broadway does not provide the measure of man in the theatre. But that alone would not represent the case fairly. The fault is not entirely ours.

Before answering the question, we should acquaint ourselves with some basic facts about the man. He was born in Bavaria in 1898. He died, a citizen of Austria, in 1956. He began scientific studies in Munich in 1917 but was called up for military service as a medical orderly a year later. He wrote his first play in 1919, at the age of 21. At the same time he occupied a post as drama critic in Munich, where the following year he was appointed "Dramaturg" (literary adviser) to the Chamber Theater.

His first produced play was seen in 1922. Shortly after, he arrived in Berlin to work as directorial assistant to Max Reinhardt. By the time Brecht fled Hitler's Germany in 1933 he had become a celebrated as well as a notorious literary personality. He was celebrated as the author of *The Threepenny Opera* which created a sensation in 1928; he was notorious as a man of Communist persuasion. His plays of the period between 1930 and 1933 (not to mention his very early semi-expressionist plays) as well as his poems, of which he wrote hundreds, outraged the solid German middle class through their politics, scandalous language and stylistic effrontery.

After some years in Europe, Brecht settled in Los Angeles, Calif., in 1941 and remained around the movie colony until 1947. In October of that year, he went to Washington, D.C., under a subpoena to appear before the House Un-American Activities Committee. His testimony was so casuistic, canny and bewildering that the committee dismissed with thanks for his exemplary behavior as a cooperative witness.

Brecht left immediately for Switzerland, where he wrote his last play as well as his most explicit theoretical work, the *Little Organon for the Theater*. At the Zurich municipal playhouse a revival of *Mother Courage* was staged and in another Swiss town there was a production of Brecht's adaptation of Sophocles' *Antigone*.

Brecht returned to Berlin in 1948, where the great success of *Mother Courage* led the East Berlin Government to offer him a handsomely subsidized theatre. Thus, the organization known as the Berliner Ensemble was founded by Brecht in 1949—an organization which soon earned an international reputation as the finest theatrical company in Europe.

The early plays—of which *In the Jungle of Cities*, produced at The Living Theater on 14th Street two seasons ago, is an example—are manifestations of the frustration, confusion, inner turmoil and nihilism of the young people in Germany after the First World War, that terrible period of inflation, widespread unemployment and gross profiteering. These plays are so full of inchoate despair that they are barely intelligible to those (particularly safe and sane Americans) unfamiliar with the condition of depravity which produced them.

A little later, another of Brecht's plays, *A Man's a Man* (simultaneously presented last season in two off-Broadway productions) began to introduce a note of comic irony. It is a rather sinister parody of the brainwashing process. "You can do with man what you will," one of the play's song interludes tells us. "Take him apart like a car, rebuild him bit by bit." The inoffensive, gullible little anti-hero of the play is turned by swindle, armed pressure and crazy circumstance into a killer.

By the time he was 30, Brecht's mastery became fully evident in *The Threepenny Opera*. Through its sharp wit, there emerged a lofty note of resolution. Written while certain Germans were congratulating themselves on their country's (false) recovery, Brecht exposed the underlying disease of greed, hypocrisy and sloth that the depression of the thirties was to reveal in all its horror.

The most popular of all Brecht's works, *The Threepenny Opera* was made buoyant not only by Brecht's mocking playfulness but by the honeyed poison of Kurt Weill's score. Almost all the music written for Brecht's works was partly inspired by Brecht's nasally defiant way of reciting his poems to his own guitar accompaniment.

During the early thirties, Brecht sought a discipline to counteract both the turmoil within him and the external public breakdown. He found it in Marxism. His plays (not to mention oratorios and cantatas) became didactic. But even these plays rose above politics through a subtle artistry which always says something more than, and different from, their presumed "lesson." That is why they have never been wholly accepted as effective Communist propaganda.

There is a certain ambivalence in most of Brecht's writing which is inimical to strict moralizing. There is always a small "No" or "Maybe" in Brecht's larger "Yes!" No one triumphs easily or irrevocably in his plays.

Brecht is a little contemptuous of Mother Courage for not learning more from her experience: She has not been "converted." Galileo is as much a slob as a saint. Saviors are not noted for skepticism or irony, but these qualities may constitute the spice of drama. Characteristic of all this is the climactic scene of Galileo's capitulation to the Inquisition. Galileo's disappointed disciple says, "Unhappy the land that breeds no hero." To which Galileo replies, "No, unhappy is the land that needs a hero." Brecht has been most genuinely acclaimed outside of East Germany and the Soviet Union.

Brecht's most mature works, written between 1943 and 1949, mark a high point in contemporary dramatic writing. What distinguishes them is not what they "preach" but their universally human import and their theatrical originality. The point of *Mother Courage* is that war destroys even those who would profit from it, but its appeal lies in the pathetic and indomitable nature of its central figure. The theme of *Galileo* is the moral responsibility of the scientist, but its fascination lies in the portrayal of the tension that pulls its all-too-human hero between his duty and his personal convenience.

While Brecht is constantly trying to suggest the direction man must follow to save himself, he never loses sight of the intricate human comedy on the path itself. Brecht's plays are never pills of redemption for the world's ills; they transcend the naked statement of any political panacea.

Whether or not Brecht wrote what are all too glibly called "great" plays (how many such plays are there in a generation, anyway?) it is my conviction that his plays are the most important to have been written anywhere in the past 35 years. Why then, one asks again, have these plays—direct, humorous, pertinent and meaningful—been so little appreciated in our country?

Disregarding the fact, already mentioned, that for the past 100 years we have had no intimate experience of the ravages of war, class struggle, national despair, mass upheaval and savage repression, there are three factors which make quick acceptance of Brecht difficult for us.

The first concerns language. Brecht is essentially a poet, a poet of great stature. His prose—as well as his verse—is not easily rendered in English. In the original German, Brecht's writing is a curiously attractive composite of simplicity and sophistication, slang and elegance, pungency and charm, creating a texture the beauty of which is often hard to appreciate in translation.

A second and more serious obstacle to Brecht's success among us is the special character of his dramatic technique, and the third is the kind of production it demands. Brecht called his theatrical method "epic." By this he meant several things. First, the events (or story) of his plays are to be viewed in the perspective of their historical background. For Brecht, what creates "psychology" in the person is as much a matter of external circumstances as of individual temperament. To understand why a character behaves in a certain way, we must situate him within the larger framework of his social environment.

In Brecht's plays, moreover, events are narrated, rather than shown as action in the immediate present. The audience thus tends to become an observer rather than a "participant." In short, Brecht strives to induce a certain detachment in the spectator, as if he were a god sitting in judgment on what he beholds and preparing himself to come to some decision.

This method serves to diminish ordinary dramatic suspense. Sometimes Brecht tells us what we are going to see before the event itself. He will deliberately interrupt the flow of scenes so that when they seem about to reach a climax, a song—of sly comment or moral exhortation—is introduced as a choral aside.

We are also prevented from effecting any immediate identification with the place of action by its removal from any readily recognizable locale. Most of Brecht's plays are set in the past and usually in some wholly mythical Chicago, China, India or London. The purpose of this removal (in Brechtian terminology, "alienation") is to foster an objective attitude toward the spectacle of the play. All this contradicts our customary habit of mind in the theatre.

You might suppose from the foregoing that Brecht's plays and productions lack feeling. Anyone who has seen a Berliner Ensemble production knows that this isn't so. But the emotion aroused by a Brecht play (as he himself produced it) is more akin to that of the classic theatre than to that of the run-of-the-mill contemporary show. When Brecht says at the end of one of his plays, "Learn to see, instead of watching stupidly," he means that he does not wish his audience to leave the theatre in a frenzy of unthinking excitement.

The Brechtian production style may be summed up as hot under the collar and cool in the head. Its feeling does not sweat. It avoids exertion in the actor and does not aim to induce tension in the spectator. Our attention is invited without clamor. We are stirred without being assaulted. Except for such moments as the hilarious hysteria of *Arturo Ui*, an atmosphere of reflective calm prevails.

This style is real (the surface utterly simple) without being naturalistic. The actors often face the audience and address it. There is so little heaviness in a Brecht production that even *Mother Courage*, among the major plays the closest to tragedy, makes the impression of a picaresque comedy.

Brecht was a great director. The casts in his theatre are drawn from a specially trained permanent company which rehearses each production for periods of no less than three months and often for much more. (The budgets are virtually limitless.) The austerity of the Brechtian productions are deceptive. Theirs is a chastened lavishness.

The Brecht stage—always bathed in clear white light (no moody, atmospheric lighting)—is uncluttered, almost bare, yet it employs the full panoply of modern scenic invention. Solid stage properties are chosen or constructed with extreme care. The unostentatious costumes are works of art. The basic tone of Brecht productions, astonishingly enough, is aristocratic. In comparison with these, hardly any of the Brecht productions I have seen in our country have been adequate.

Though Brecht's material frequently deals with violence and subjects for indignation, he is at bottom forbearing. His final message is affirmative, his ultimate posture a humane assent to life. Even his most brutally pessimistic play—the first one, *Baal*—ends with the line, "It was beautiful...Everything."

His work is full of a horse sense which often mounts to grandeur. "In the earthquake to come," he wrote in an autobiographical poem called

"Concerning Poor B.B.," "it is to be hoped that I shan't allow the bitterness to quench my cigar's glow." He never did. There is always manifest in the main body of his work the determination to face the stress of our times without sniveling, without masochism and without fear.

Brecht might be described as the poet of the quizzical eye. It is an eye which intimates, "I shall doubt, I shall provoke, I shall challenge. Above all, I shall survive." For him the true integer of society is not one person but two. He could say with brilliant ambiguity, "Terrible is the temptation of goodness." He was the kind of revolutionary who could write, "Alas, we who wished to lay the foundations of kindness could not ourselves be kind."

His anti-individualist sense of the world as well as the breadth of his humanity may be deciphered in such lines as "Young Alexander conquered India. He alone? Caesar beat the Gauls. Was there not even a cook in his army? Philip of Spain wept as his fleet was sunk and destroyed. Were there no other tears?"

How telling and significant of Brecht is the verse, "On my wall hangs a Japanese carving, the mask of an evil demon. Sympathetically I observe the swollen veins of the forehead, indicating what a strain it is to be evil."

Brecht is the outstanding figure of the world theatre since 1945. He has already exercised considerable influence on writing and production throughout Europe and beyond—on Robert Bolt, on John Osborne, on Joan Littlewood, on Tony Richardson and on the French director Jean Vilar, to mention only a few relatively familiar names. If Brecht were alive today he might answer, as Shaw did many years ago when asked whether one of his plays would prove a success on Broadway, "Undoubtedly. The question is whether the audience will be."

—*NYTM*, 11 Mar. '63

JACK BENNY

The lean weeks are here; the fat weeks (O'Neill, Strindberg, Zeffirelli-Dumas, Brecht, Hellman) lie ahead.

Shall I speak of Jack Benny? (Ziegfeld Theatre). He is a walking dollar sign; most of his jokes are about money. They are smoothly operated and ring out neatly and impersonally like a cash register. Benny is the businessman's comedian. There is nothing nihilistic about him as there is in Groucho Marx. With him one can indulge oneself in the pleasure of platitude. He makes me laugh occasionally with the automatism of a hiccup. I prefer the two Italian jugglers on his program because I admire training and dexterity.

—*NAT*, 23 Mar. '63

STRANGE INTERLUDE
TOO GOOD TO BE TRUE

In these years of our dismay what has been called "minor Shaw" is fresher than what some may regard as major O'Neill. The lightheaded extravaganza *Too True To Be Good*, a failure in 1931, strikes me as more relevant today than *Strange Interlude*, a most earnest drama and a great popular success in 1928.

Strange Interlude fascinated when it was first produced because it was a pioneer work by America's leading dramatist. It broke new ground, not only by its four and a half hours' playing time, and its use of inner monologue to accompany the traditional dialogue, but also by an attitude its audience found stimulating. The plot of *Strange Interlude* is basically a *True Confessions* story— the revelation of intimacies not ordinarily to be found in American drama before O'Neill. The play, moreover, has a Strindbergian core with a

Freudian slant—still a novelty to theatre audiences in the twenties.

First there is the ideal man with whom Nina (Woman), from Puritan inhibition and her father's possessiveness, never consummated her union. Being ideal, the man is never seen; he has been conveniently disposed of as a casualty of the First World War. Then there are the three substitute figures: the commonplace but decent husband whom Nina loves maternally but with whom she must not bear a child because there is a fatal flaw in his family lineage (symbolic or not, this is indispensable to the dramatist's scheme); next, the virile male most coveted until the woman bears his son; and finally the mother-bound hack novelist, bright, devoted, more or less impotent, in whose arms the resigned woman ultimately rests when they have both passed beyond desire.

This pattern, worked out with the precision of a theorem, is sustained by O'Neill's never-failing soul searching, a genuine anguish primed by his relationship to the various members of his own family. With the aid of his reading (Strindberg and Freud) and the discipline of an attempted objectivity, O'Neill managed to give his abiding romanticism and raw pessimism a quasi-classic dignity. The result is not unimpressive, but even in 1928 I found it humanly immature and artistically unconvincing—defects betrayed by such lines as "sensible unicellular life that floats in the sea and has never learned the cry for happiness!...Oh God so deaf and dumb and blind!...teach me to be resigned to be an atom!"

Such virtues and faults are still apparent in *Strange Interlude*—the first somewhat diminished, the second conspicuously heightened; but new elements have been introduced into the composition, first by the audience, and then by the production.

The audience at the Hudson Theatre, where the play is being given under the auspices of the newly formed Actors Studio Theatre and José Quintero's direction, finds *Strange Interlude*

almost as humorous as it is serious. For this audience, now instructed by plays, films, television, knows all about Freud: that men over-attached to their mothers are unsatisfactory lovers, that women often make an idol of the man they have been deprived of, that a woman seeks lover, husband, friend or father in one man (for lack of which the woman frequently becomes fiend) and that as a mother she sacrifices man to her offspring of whom she in turn becomes possessive till they are strong enough to abandon her, etc., etc. Secure in this knowledge, which it accepts as wisdom, the audience does not reject the play, but laughs contentedly at sharing its "secret." Familiar themes are the most gratifying; the play remains popular. It is now a comedy of complexes.

The production commands a galaxy of good actors, but it is stylistically a hodgepodge. For where O'Neill sharply separates the actual dialogue from the inner thought sequences, the direction takes so little account of this division that the presumably silent speculations are frequently more vehemently expressed than the active speech. But there is a still subtler stylization in O'Neill's text. He maintains a certain loftiness of tone so that the stamp of a grandiose (Greek drama?) elevation will mark the whole. The acting in the new production is lackluster naturalism. What "style" we now find is provided by sets that revolve and drops that change in view of the audience—an increasingly fashionable device, and in this case a silly one, particularly when the sets are as tatty and occasionally as ugly as these are.

Geraldine Page, the new Nina, is one of the most talented actresses in our theatre. Everything she does is true. In each situation her thought and feeling flow freely without the slightest heaviness or strain. (Note the scene in which she hears that she must not have a child by her husband. Or the scornful glance, of fine comic point, which she levels at the sexually quiescent Charley when he intimates that he has had many "adventures.") But Miss Page—except when she is playing such parts as those in *Summer and Smoke* and *The*

Rainmaker—needs a marked characterization or some clearly defined style to be altogether effective. As Nina she has neither. She plays the part as herself (always, I repeat, with touching sensibility), but this only makes the play lose that dimension of grandeur without which it becomes flabby, almost trivial.

Still, Miss Page carries her naturalness naturally! Most of the others—all of them gifted—seem uncomfortable, tense or featureless with it. Ben Gazzara, who plays a tough-minded doctor, makes the impression of a reformed hoodlum embarrassed by his gentlemanly disguise. Pat Hingle as the nice husband does characterize—too much—so that something of Steinbeck's Lennie emerges. In greater repose, William Prince as the neutral novelist misses some of the pathos of his part, but he would still seem in the picture if there were a picture. Though the play merits revival, it has not been given the kind of production that we imagine or hope for from the Actors Studio Theatre.

There is something lacking, for the given assignment, in most of the well-seasoned actors who compose the cast of *Too True To Be Good* (54th Street Theatre). Yet because Albert Marre's direction aims at the right target the production comes off. The play retains its entertainment value without loss of meaning.

Shaw's text was originally overlong. Now, perhaps because some of the actors are unable to deliver very extended speeches with the necessary ease, rapidity and clarity, the text has been cut more than it should have been to attain its full stature. Yet the essence is still there.

Too True To Be Good anticipates the "beat" or the Theatre of the Absurd; Shaw wrote it almost thirty years before that term and practice became the mode. It is a play by a deeply disturbed moralist in the shape of a wacky farce. Its events are as unreal as those of a vaudeville skit, and it is so directed. Its pith is the breakdown of belief in the values held inviolable till the First World War shot them all to hell.

Here are some lines from the great peroration: the characters, says the playwright's alter ego, are all

...falling, falling, falling endlessly and hopelessly through a void in which they can find no footing. There is something fantastic about them, something unreal or perverse, something profoundly unsatisfactory. They are too absurd to be believed in; yet they are not fiction: the newspapers are full of them....How are we to bear the dreadful new nakedness: the nakedness of the souls who until now have always disguised themselves from one another in beautiful impossible idealisms....Our souls go in rags now; and the young are spying through the holes and getting glimpses of the reality that was hidden. And they are not horrified: they exult in having found us out;...we have outgrown our religion, outgrown our political system, our own strength of mind and character. The fatal word not *has been miraculously inserted into all our creeds: in the desecrated temples where we knelt murmuring "I believe...we will not kneel and we do not believe....But what next? Is No enough? For a boy, yes; for a man, never. Are we any the less obsessed with a belief when we are denying it than when we are affirming it?...*

Thus Shaw is seeking a Yes amid the Nos, and confessing at the end that he is empty-handed, that he is "ignorant, intimidated." His last words are that he will continue to "preach and preach and preach no matter how late the hour, how short the day, no matter whether I have nothing to say...." He is waiting (like Beckett's bums) for a new message which will realize at last "the Kingdom of God and the Power and the Glory."

The spark of this pathetic prayer is what keeps Shaw in this play so thoroughly alive: sharp, witty, vigorous and aware as few others in his day or in ours have been.

Robert Preston, an actor of good will, reads with force and sense, Glynis Johns has a contemporary baby-woman appeal, David Wayne as Private Meek, who is T. E. Lawrence affectionately recalled, strikes the proper vein and Cyril Ritchard also keeps in tune. Though very few in the cast are sufficiently "dry British" or nimble enough intellectually, they all (together with the scene designer Paul Morrison) contribute good spirits and go to the occasion.

—*NAT*, 30 Mar. '63

MOTHER COURAGE

Bertolt Brecht's *Mother Courage* is a beautiful play. Written in 1938-39 and first produced in Zurich in 1941, it is one of the peaks of dramatic writing in this century. Its production by the Berliner Ensemble in 1951 under the direction of its author and Erich Engel ranks among the truly great works of theatre art in our time. Done all over the Continent, the play is a modern classic.

I say all this at once because I wish my readers to see the play, despite the severe shortcomings of its production under Jerome Robbins' direction.

I cannot predict what an audience unfamiliar with the play will think of it now, but I hope that the New York production will not be used as evidence that Brecht is the bore that some folk through inverted snobbism (or ignorance) have recently declared him to be, and that he was in certain unfortunate American productions. My guess is that, despite present handicaps, the play still comes through to the audience with some part of its force and grandeur intact.

It requires great artistry for a modern writer to achieve pristine effectiveness and epic scope with apparently primitive means. That is what Brecht has done. There is something almost medieval, peasantlike and penetratingly poignant in the simplicity of *Mother Courage*. Brecht possesses folk canniness and mother wit, a shrewdness of vision based on intimate experience of life's basic realities. He is both skeptical and direct; his language combines the accents and vocabulary of street and stable with the purity and majestic rhythm of Martin Luther's Old Testament German. The play seems massively sculpted in wood.

Mother Courage is not "propaganda"; not an antiwar tract. It is a comic narrative that mounts to tragedy. Its central figure is a woman without a "soul," an earthbound creature astray in the miserable current of history. Virtually illiterate, Mother Courage makes a bare living, supports her three children (each the offspring of a different father) by supplying odds and ends—brandy and belts, chickens and buttons—to the roving armies (Catholic and Protestant alike) during the Thirty Years' War in the seventeenth century. She has allegiance to no cause but survival and the care of her brood. She is a pack horse and a "profiteer" of war. She has not the dimmest idea of what all the shooting is about. Nor does she ever grow wiser, learn a lesson. But the war deprives her of everything—her goods, her children, her indomitable vitality. The only heroic and enduringly innocent person in the play is Mother Courage's daughter, who is a mute. Brecht's use of her in the play is a masterstroke.

The play opens on a note of gaiety—like the exciting, hopeful, first days of war. Mother Courage's two sturdy sons are pulling the wagon which conveys her wares and in which she and her family live. "Here's Mother Courage and her wagon!" the quartet sings. "Hey, Captain, let them come and buy! Beer by the jug! Wine by the flagon! Let your men drink before they die!" It's a lark! Slowly, very slowly over a period of twelve years, Mother Courage and her children cross Sweden, Poland, Germany. The wagon ages, diminishes and ends as a shadow of itself—still a burden to "Courage," who now all alone keeps dragging it through the wasted towns and war-torn countryside.

Much of the play is funny with harsh humor and wry wisdom. There are no villains, barely any sentiment, little pathos. No one preaches, no slogans are enunciated, and even the interpolated songs, which serve as choral comment, might be taken simply as "entertainment." All is impersonal; yet in the end we are moved and feel close to life.

The original text contains nine songs. I have the impression that several of these have been cut in New York—probably because, if they were retained, the time allowed to sing and play them might exceed twenty-four minutes and the Musicians' Union would list the production as a "musical." According to the regulations, this classification would entail the employment of twenty-four musicians at heavy cost.

My supposition strikes me as typical of the obstacles that stand in the way of a fitting production for such a play as *Mother Courage*. But there are obstacles beyond this perhaps minor one: the words of the songs—superb in the original and still admirable in Eric Bentley's translation—are imperfectly heard as they are delivered in this production.

The Brecht (Berliner) production is so intimately related to the text as to seem identical with it. (That is what I mean when I speak of "theatre art.") The actors, the direction, the sets, the props and the time allowed at the Berliner Ensemble for all these to become part of a unified fabric and meaning are what made *Mother Courage* everything I have declared it to be. Very little of this is possible in our theatre.

Anne Bancroft, who plays Mother Courage, is a charming actress with a heartwarming smile and a generous honesty of spirit. She is too contemporary, too locally urban, too young, too soft to do much more than indicate the part. (She puts on age by an obvious change of wig; the later one being much too white.) Of the land, the soil, the devastation of the world she crosses, there is hardly a trace. Most of the company is in even sorrier plight. Zohra Lampert as the mute daughter is appealing. Barbara Harris as a camp follower is an actress of exceptional gifts. Hers is the best performance, and her last scene as the gilded,

disease-ridden whore turned into a puffy "colonel's lady" is, despite a note of burlesque, a treat.

The sets are simplified beyond Brecht, whose visual austerity was so artful that Parisian critics when they saw his production spoke of its several hundred shades of brown. But if Robbins wanted his sets (credited to Ming Cho Lee) bare, why did he have all sorts of journalistic photographs projected against the background to make "editorial" points where none are needed? Indeed, in view of the play's style, they are altogether pointless. A revolving stage is imperative for this play; it evokes the sweep of Mother Courage's endless trek across Europe. Pulling the wagon in circles around a stationary stage, as Anne Bancroft and the others are obliged to do, simply looks silly. The props, themselves works of art and so much part of the play's "feel" in the original production, are now Broadway routine.

The inscriptions introducing the scenes should be shown on a screen if they are to retain their fine gravity; they should not be spoken by actors with little voice or impressiveness of manner. The idea of having all the members of the company introduce themselves by name (Anne Bancroft, Mike Kellin, Gene Wilder, et al.) is a parody of Brecht, whose style, while eschewing the illusionism of the naturalistic, is more *real* as well as more theatrical than most of our so-called realistic productions.

If Robbins wanted to do an original production he should really have been original; otherwise he should have remained as faithful to Brecht as materially possible. In one respect fidelity and duplication proved a mistake: while Paul Dessau's score was ideal for Brecht's words it does not blend happily with Bentley's.

For all that, and though hardly any translation can do Brecht's writing full justice, *Mother Courage* manages to remain impressive.

—*NAT*, 13 Apr. '63

ENTER LAUGHING
THE LADY OF THE CAMILLIAS

The catastrophic deterioration of the Broadway theatre may be discerned in the fact that inconsequential scripts are frequently done more competently than serious ones. An example is *Enter Laughing* by Joseph Stein, based on a novel by Carl Reiner (Henry Miller Theatre). It is composed of the kind of gags the brighter kids on the block used to have fun with at the corner candy stores. The play is not a "comedy," as the playbill notes, but farce-burlesque.

The anecdote is as thin as that of a comic strip. A barely educated Bronx boy, whose parents want him to become a druggist, works as a delivery boy at a one-man machine shop supplying the millinery trade. Our hero dreams of being an actor. I worried during the early part of the entertainment that he might end as another David Susskind, but fortunately this was not the case. The evening concludes abruptly with the boy's hectic debut at a ratty, fly-by-night substock company in a hole-in-the-corner showshop off Broadway.

If you follow the deeper thinking in the drama, you will read that Brecht's theatre aesthetic bids the actor not to *be* the character he plays but to *represent* him. In other words, the actor is not to think "I" am Malvolio or Shylock, but "he"—the character I am playing—is Malvolio or Shylock. There is much discussion in the studios of this presumably abstruse doctrine. But if you watch the comedian Alan Arkin who plays the would-be actor in *Enter Laughing* you will see Brecht's rule popularly demonstrated. Arkin—whose *Second City* skit with Barbara Harris about the Beatnik and the College Girl at a Modern Art Show was a masterpiece—always presents his characters as "third persons," other fellows whom Arkin (of furry voice with nasal twang) is telling you about with brilliant, sidesplitting effect.

Irving Jacobson, a veteran of the Jewish Theatre, is endearingly professional, as is Marty Greene of similar background. Under Gene Saks' witty direction, Sylvia Sidney, Alan Mowbray, Barbara Dana, Tom Gorman also contribute most engagingly to the pleasantry of *Enter Laughing*, a happily integrated show.

The Lady of the Camellias, on the other hand, a "Production Devised, Designed and Directed by Mr. Zeffirelli" (as the Playbill obstreperously proclaimed), was also ruined by him at the Winter Garden. It is difficult—and probably unnecessary—to describe in detail the ineptitude of this event. Franco Zeffirelli conceived the perhaps pregnant notion of following Dumas' novel rather than his play. (Assisting in the dramatization were Giles Cooper and Terrence McNally.) To begin with, two things went wrong: the script that resulted from the collaboration gives the impression of having been written with a club; and the sort of realism Dumas commanded, the novel's intent and style, has been fatally misunderstood.

Zeffirelli's production was vulgar in *Camellias*, a story of true love destroyed by the bad bourgeoisie—a supposedly up-to-date interpretation. But Dumas is much subtler. His bourgeoisie is not villainous but unaware and helpless, so that all its values are accepted by everyone, including Marguerite Gautier, the victim. That is why the scene between Marguerite and old man Duval (who in Zeffirelli's version is presented as a "capitalist bastard" in the manner of the street radicalism of the thirties)—why that scene in Dumas' novel is so touching and why it is, even socially considered, much truer than any tough interpretation could possibly be. This is something the Communist Meyerhold realized in his production of *The Lady of the Camellias* (which I saw in Moscow in 1934) and why the play there succeeded in being both authentic and moving.

Zeffirelli's production was vulgar in conception and amateurish in execution. The occasion proved that a man of undoubted talent (as Zeffirelli's *Romeo and Juliet* showed him to be) will sometimes fail even more disastrously than a mediocrity.

Another point worth making in this connection is that a director cannot function alone. He needs collaborators with whom he must have an intimate cultural and craft relationship. In *Romeo and Juliet* Zeffirelli had the aid of the Old Vic Company, which was itself a coherent unit.

—*NAT*, 20 Apr. '63

A DIRECTOR PREPARES

I have been asked to submit my notes for the production of Giraudoux's *Judith* in the hope that they may be of some interest or use to young directors and to those playgoers who are eager to learn something about the process of production. These notes may conceivably puzzle as much as they enlighten. I must therefore tell you how they fit in to the complex effort which goes to make a production.

First I read the play many times (in this instance at least a dozen) before setting down any specific ideas as its stage treatment. *Judith* is a most hazardous play—which, incidentally, is one of the reasons it attracted me. It is largely verbal: it moves on an enormous vehicle of rhetoric. I say rhetoric, not talk, because its speech is stylized, often close to verse. "Real" characters—in the modern psychological or naturalistic play—do not employ such language. Giraudoux's writing is related to that of the neo-classic French dramatists of the seventeenth century (Racine and others), a style alien to our theatre.

In directing another of Giraudoux's plays (*Tiger at the Gates*) in London and Paris I succeeded in making Giraudoux—undiluted by adaptation—acceptable to English and American audiences. I believed I might do the same for *Judith*, a much more subtle—or possibly abstruse—play.

When I finished my preliminary study I then began to set down general notes—notes I use to guide myself so that I in turn may direct the cast, designer, costumer, composer and others. *I do not read the notes to any of them.* They are, I repeat, statements of intention for myself. They tell me what I am to convey to the cast through explanation, demonstration, exhortation or inspiration.

After I wrote these notes I set down the actual details of direction for each segment of the play's action and dialogue. Every "side" of dialogue is accompanied by a page opposite it on which I inscribe specific directorial notations. These notations are written into one of three columns: the first states as baldly as possible the action which motivates the dialogue and behavior of each character. By action I mean what the speaker's purpose is at each moment of his presence on the stage: what he wants to accomplish. The second column suggests how or in what manner or state of mind the character is to carry out the action. The third column specifies the actual physical behavior in the execution of this action, or what in theatre parlance is designated as stage "business."

Some of this business was planned prior to rehearsal and later adjusted to the needs of the actors and other circumstances (the actual settings, props, etc.). More business was invented by me as well as by the actors during rehearsals and written down in the prompt book by the stage manager. The business (both the actors' and mine) is subject to constant amendment as rehearsals progress. Everything is "set" when the play finally opens. The degree and time for the preparation of business by the director—staging or blocking—is a matter of individual choice, inclination, temperament, judgment and artistic bent.

Just as the road to hell may be paved with good intentions so a bad production may result from a well-conceived plan. My production of Jean Giraudoux's *Judith*, in a translation by Christopher Fry, which was presented at Her Majesty's Theatre in London last June was not at all well received—in a word, it was a flop.

Yet I still hold that production to have been a mirror of my intentions and those intentions to have been *right*—true to the nature of the play. My theory as to why the London production failed—it had its faults!—is irrelevant in the present context. I might point out however that the play failed in its original Paris production in 1931 (directed by Louis Jouvet), and again in South America where Jouvet presented it during the German occupation of France. The play was praised when Jean-Louis Barrault staged it at the Théâtre de France early in 1962 but it was hardly a box-office success.

Despite all this, I believe the play (which also has its flaws) to be a fine one. When certain extremely difficult production problems are satisfactorily resolved—largely a matter of casting—the play may still prove a success somewhere someday. It certainly offers a challenge.

For those who are unfamiliar with the plot, here is a summary:

The Jewish people in ancient Palestine are being attacked by an Assyrian army led by its general Holofernes. The people foresee their doom as their capital is besieged. They have become obsessed with the belief that they can only be saved if the purest and fairest among their women is sent on an appeal to Holofernes to spare them. They have chosen Judith. She is a virgin of twenty, beautiful, brilliant, rich. (In the Apocrypha of the Bible, Judith is a widow.)

At first Judith resists the idea of her "mission" as superstitious nonsense, even though Joachim, the High Priest, and his coadjutor insist that she must yield to the anguished pleading of the community. But the imminence of her country's annihilation—the possibility of which she had not hitherto been able to credit—induces her to undertake the mission to Holofernes. Despite the entreaties of her would-be fiancé, John, a captain in the army, she sets out for Holofernes' camp. But John plans to forestall Judith's arrival there by sending the prostitute Susannah to Holofernes so that she may pretend to be the Judith the Jews have sent to appease him.

However, Judith reaches Holofernes' tent first and encounters his officers. One of them, the pederast Egon, is persuaded by Sara, the Bawd, to disguise himself as Holofernes. When Judith, at first taken in by the hoax, realizes that she has been tricked, she feels desperately humiliated. She has failed miserably. When Holofernes appears she seems incapable of making her plea. He seduces her by his attractiveness, his hedonist reasoning, his splendid pagan regality. He is charmed by Judith's beauty, intelligence and pride. She consents to go to Holofernes' bed. Nevertheless, she kills him.

Homer and other poets of yore told their legendary tales. These myths, Giraudoux implies, did not tell the real story. Yet the myths remain: they have their own truth. But it is not our truth, man's truth. Hence the ambivalence of *Judith*— Giraudoux's most difficult play—in which the precarious balance that Giraudoux usually maintains with wonderful aplomb is constantly threatened. In this play almost all of Giraudoux's preoccupations, obsessions and impulses are woven together to form a complex knot which does not unravel at first reading or seeing.

Here Giraudoux has split himself into two images: that of Judith, the extreme idealist who is also a worldling, the pure young girl (Giraudoux's abiding symbol meant to represent the marvelous potential of a still unspoiled life), the virgin eagerly awaiting some pluperfect consummation; then there is the pagan Holofernes, proud of his consonance with the sensual world. He too is an "absolute"—of ecstatic pleasure in a universe without original sin. Perhaps the third figure which attempts to reconcile or include the first two, the Solider or Guard who proves to be an angel, is even more truly Giraudoux himself.

The legend in the Apocrypha indicates that Judith slew Holofernes because he planned to become the scourge of her people, hence the enemy of God. This, says Giraudoux, may still be true. But his Judith kills Holofernes because, total romantic that she is, her one night of love with him is the highest point of her life, after which everything else must prove mediocre and shabby. Society, history have no regard for such subjective motivations—they have their reasons which the human heart does not know—and Judith herself, imbued with a heroic sense of mission, is persuaded by the Giraudoux imp—the angel of the last act—that she must yield to the wishes of the cunning rabbinate and tell the subjective lie that she killed Holofernes out of patriotism and religious fervor. Judith is thus the whore to whom the angel (in his mundane guise) blows an adoring kiss, and the saint that she finally consents to be. This is Judith's tragedy: that she accepts the role history or the law of man has designed for her despite the fact that the person she is is profoundly committed to the miracle of the flesh by which she was transfigured in Holofernes' arms.

THE NOTES

What the audience is to enjoy: A heroic (and philosophic) tale—told with modern wit and sophistication, in a blaze of beautiful color—sumptuous and noble.

Letter to designer Boris Aronson on the visual aspect:

Dear Boris:
There are indications of the needed props and atmosphere in the script. The first act is a banker's or millionaire's home. ("There are no lack of mirrors in the house.") There may be a fountain of running water (referred to as a "glass of water" in the text) etc., etc. In other words: the first act is a *salon*—the dwelling place of wealth and sophistication as the French might image it—except that the names and locate are semi-Biblical. "You mirror luxury and gold," someone says to Judith. Here all is, to quote Baudelaire, *calme, luxe et volupté*.

The second act is rougher, more barbaric, with an alcove masked by a curtain in which Holofernes presumably sleeps and works and from which, when the curtain is drawn or lifted, he makes his first splendid appearance. Holofernes is the Man of This World—a synthesis of physical and mental keenness.

The most important technical problem of the play is the trick of the Guard's (or Soldier's) trans-

formation into an angel. I would not put him on the bench which the text calls for. He should lie behind a log or some other masking object. One voice should be used, but probably two people or bodies. One body (the Guard's) would have only his legs exposed, while when the Soldier becomes the angel the latter appears in beautiful apparel—the spirit emerging from the rough form of the sleeping guard. In short a *trompe l'oeil* (trick visual effect) must be devised which may not be in the designer's province—though you with the aid of the costumer, or some technician who knows magician's gimmicks might arrive at a solution.

The play is fundamentally French classic—like Racine—stripped, noble, elegant and, so to speak, motionless. But such a style is unacceptable (boring) to the Anglo-American audience.

On its classic purity, savage, violent colors must be splashed in discreet proportion to lend the setting its near-Eastern orientalism and vibrancy. In brief, it is necessary to create a classicism out of decorative and dramatic elements which being somewhat primitive and near-Eastern are not classic at all!

We must avoid a totally flat stage. Perhaps an arrangement of levels or platforms can serve. The play being all rhetoric requires *a stage to move the actors*. Otherwise the play will strike our audiences as intolerably static. (There should be an opulent couch in Act One for Judith to lie down on. And some places to sit!)

A window is called for in Act One for business—the apple—which I may eliminate, but I was thinking of using this window as a possible way of showing the fires of Holofernes' camp in the distance—a starry sky, etc. (The house is presumably on a hill).

The second act requires a throne—a rich, savage-looking affair—in which Egon, parading as Holofernes, sits to make himself look regal. Perhaps some of the second-act tent should show a vista of the Jewish town not far off? When the Jews come and sing their songs I imagine them to be somewhere above Judith or below her but not exactly on the same level. Is this possible?

Above all, the production must be sensuously lovely—most attractive—without giving the impression of compilation or overproduction. We want it to be a joy to the eye in which every figure on the stage may stand out with picturesque impressiveness The play is both virile and *tres raffiné*; it is addressed to the mind and to the senses—a combination of French *espirit* (or intellectual agility) and aristocratic physicality. There is absolutely nothing Jewish in the modern sense or Hebrew in the Biblical sense in the play. Can you be a French (ultracivilized) Assyrian—scenically at least?!

Yours,
Harold

The Main Action of the Play

A struggle with Destiny. In the script, what I call Destiny is called God.

All is Battlefield—in which a girl struggles with Destiny.

Style

The movement of the production should constitute a choreography significant of the gradations, nuances, impulses and suggestions of the dialogue just as dancers graph the music to which they dance. A subtle type of movement is required with sudden and extravagant bursts breaking the calm of the near-classic writing.

The Characters

JUDITH—Her main action: To meet or cope with experience. (To become a woman). "My nature," she says, "is to seek."

The actress is to note the progress of the part from eager anticipation (a kind of waiting) which hides itself in the guise of frivolity to confrontation (in which she is defeated—overcome) and maturity or the realization of her tragic destiny. Giraudoux regards Judith's acceptance as tragic. I prefer to think of it as ironic.

There is always a struggle (and contradiction) in Judith between gentleness and violence, submissiveness and defiance, wildness and passion,

uncertainty and the heroic, worldliness and loftiness. It must always seem doubtful for her—or for us—to know what the outcome will be.

All her life is a seeking and a challenging which sometimes take the form of playing, flirting, teasing (experimenting) for she does not know—this girl of twenty—for what she is destined. She plays with men, with ideas, dreams—to discover which is the "real thing"—that which will consume her, possess her, create a permanent loyalty in her.

This makes her capricious—alternately soft and hard, "unexpected." It also gives her purity, tension and a certain savagery. Disappointment in the expectation of the "miracle"—the great consummation—renders her violent, almost brutal at times. (Thus she says that even before it was required of her she might go forth to captivate, capture, kill or be ravished by Holofernes.)

She has no attachments. She is an orphan. Her uncle spoils her. She acts the adoring ward, the little girl. At first she appears frivolous and flighty—a lightheaded flapper. A "society" girl. She is basically confident—this is what is called her pride.

She cannot bear her fiancé's (John's) softness, his cowardice.

Finally (and fundamentally) she is the great idealist and romantic.

Her purity signifies promise, the promise of being possessed by life. Does she not say, "To be innocent is to hope, to hope to meet one day, among the wretchedness of our time, true human greatness?"

The scene with the Guard is the final struggle: the ultimate challenge of Destiny to her subjective self.

"A woman is a creature who has found her nature." Holofernes says. In the end Judith finds her nature.

HOLOFERNES—His main action: To enjoy, to take pleasure. (That is how he challenges Destiny.) He smiles. He has a sense of irony. People, he believes, are occupied with the irrelevant. He knows the truth: Life is enjoyment and pleasure—which is often coupled with cruelty. (To struggle with Destiny through pleasure—one must be prepared to be "surprised" with an unexpected, a sudden death.)

Those who do not share his "aesthetic" attitude are condemned by life. To kill such people therefore is no great matter, since they have eliminated themselves to begin with, that is according to Holofernes, they prefer not to live. Only the moment (of pleasure) matters. ("How women go away, this I always forget.") He remembers the colors they wear, their teeth, etc.

Holofernes is no mere "leading-man" seducer. He is fascinated and enchanted by the mystery, the challenge of Judith.

SUSANNAH—Her main action: To transform herself. To alter her destiny. To save or redeem herself through an ideal from which she has fallen, the image of which for her is Judith. She wants to be lost—and thus save herself—in Judith. In other words, she is in love with purity.

She weeps—Judith never does. Only when she sees Judith in Holofernes' embrace does she become gruff—the whore! She ends up sacrificing herself to the heroic ideal.

JOHN—His main action: To fight or avoid Destiny. He wishes to balk at heroism, to avoid great issues. (This betrays a certain weakness in him.)

Impetuous—almost hysterical youth.

He feels inferior to Judith—hence his desperation. He's a man, but she is more than a young girl: she's an Idea. He loves her but cannot measure up to her. It makes him feverish.

He fights a war as a brave soldier but he has no conviction about it—therefore his militant impulses are shaky and spasmodic. He represents ordinary intelligence and simple humanity in a heroic situation. He is therefore inadequate to the occasion.

On the simplest level his main action is *to save* Judith, the girl he's in love with for the most sensible and natural reasons.

John is a modern, contemporary character—bitter, confused, "unheroic" as well as anti-heroic. He shuns shibboleth, large gestures, the "transcendental." He would kill fanaticism and "the visionary." And indeed he kills the Prophet at the end of Act One.

JOACHIM (the High Priest)—His main action: To maneuver or force Destiny to his way.

More politician than priest. Grimly realistic. Determined and shrewd. Harsh and decisive in practical action. He calculates. His motto might be—and this might be said, almost is said by the Guard who is very nearly Giraudoux's mouthpiece. "God draws crooked lines to arrive at straight conclusions!" His coadjutor Paul is a fanatic, more rabid than his superior, the High Priest. A distorted personality. He might be a hunchback.

SARA (the Bawd)—Her main action: To avenge herself against Destiny (which in this instance means Judith, the Jews, Holofernes).

She guys without forgiveness. The vengeful woman who has suffered the contempt and neglect of the higher-ups. She in turn has become contemptuous with a rage against all because she has suffered at the hands of all—including her own people—particularly the rich girl Judith, the millionaire's darling. She finds no good except in her own kind—the ordinary folk, the poor, the outcast.

"It's God's injustice that infuriates me." she says.

She might be said to represent the Proletariat. She speaks of Judith, standing pale in Holofernes' camp, "like the boss's daughter amidst the strikers."

GUARD—His main action: To wrestle on behalf of Destiny.

This Guard—who is an angel—is Giraudoux himself; the man in constant debate with himself, the sensualist who enjoys the sensuous spectacle of the world as well as the moralist who speaks for God! (A Fallen Angel!)

He's gentle, eager, full of quirks. He's a good-humored imp, both contradictory and happy in his contradictions.

The Guard's final scene with Judith is a kind of magical nightmare in which he as the angel wrestles with Judith—almost a dance, a ballet, in which he whirls about her in gay persuasion and she suffers and struggles against his hypnotic charm and power.

There are many more characters—Egon, Holofernes' captain who poses as Holofernes, other officers, prophets (who are rendered either as men made mad by grief and fear or sadists). All are made to play their role in the overall pattern of the play.

—*TA*, Apr. '63

DÜRRENMATT & BRECHT IN LONDON

Is there any significance in the fact that the most noted dramatists writing in German today are Swiss? Switzerland, hemmed in on all sides by countries frequently engaged in and always tending toward war, no longer feels itself safe within its Alps. An innocent bystander, it may prove as vulnerable as any other "peace-loving" domain. For this reason, perhaps, its two most prominent playwrights—Friedrich Dürrenmatt and Max Frisch—serve as Geiger counters to Europe. Being themselves without offensive arms, the Swiss are in a position to moralize as well as shudder. Dürrenmatt and Frisch tremble and preach, while their colleagues in the neighbor countries either squeal or despair.

Frisch is prophetic and composes parables; Dürrenmatt, suffering at his ease, grimaces and indulges in gallows humor. Dürrenmatt is theatrically the more deft and the more sophisticated. At a time without fresh dramatic impulse both are outstanding.

The Physicists, the latest Dürrenmatt play, is a continental success. Directed by Peter Brook, it alternates at the Aldwych Theatre with *King Lear* under the auspices of the enterprising Royal Shakespeare Company and is almost as much of a hit as the great tragedy.

More topical than any of Dürrenmatt's other plays (one remembers *The Visit*), *The Physicists* is singularly striking. It is essentially an entertainment, but it has an importance—one which under present theatrical and social circumstances may reasonably be exaggerated.

Technically, the play is a comedy melodrama; it amuses and excites. It provides effective roles for its actors, and Peter Brook has directed it with unfailing skill. The company at the Aldwych—particularly Cyril Cusack, Michael Hordern and Irene Worth who plays a "Teutonic" monster in the guise of a psychiatrist—demonstrates the kind of compelling professionalism in the manner of a superior detective story which is always set down as "real theatre."

Since the play is to be done on Broadway next season, I shall omit its narrative detail and suggest its graver import. It begins with the race of the major powers to obtain scientific supremacy for military purposes. Then the physicists decide to renounce forever their battle of wits which they know can only end in the annihilation of civilization. But, says Dürrenmatt, through one of his physicists, "What is taught cannot be untaught." Those who have learned how to use the new instruments of destruction will not refrain from doing so. The power-crazed will take over; we are doomed.

This is the warning, the lesson. We may shiver; we ought to groan. We should take action. But what we do is applaud a good show. Dürrenmatt is devilishly capable: his play will be a hit everywhere. It will not resolve the issue either in our minds or in our hearts. It is not that kind of play. It is less pessimistic than cynical. The highest compliment one can pay it is to surmise that Shaw might have liked it. It should be seen.

Also worth attention is the production of Bertolt Brecht's first play, *Baal*, acted by the new English star of stage and screen, Peter O'Toole.

The play was written when Brecht was only twenty-three, and is now more dramatic curiosity than event. It reveals the confusion and anguish from which Brecht grew. In the light of the author's development from *Baal* to *Mother Courage*, *Galileo* and the others, we see an artist surmounting vertigo and stupefaction to attain clarity, a passage from romantic floundering to classic authority.

In *Baal* Brecht seems to wallow in the mental and moral muck characteristic of Germany immediately after the First World War. Through his central figure, the poet Baal, Brecht indulges in that "disordering of the senses" which Rimbaud once announced as his aim. In fact, there is a certain imitation of the tortured Rimbaud-Verlaine affair in this play.

Rimbaud ceased writing poetry when he was nineteen; Brecht's poet never publishes at all. In the satirical first, and perhaps best, scene of the play Baal is feted at a dinner party given by would-be patrons, dilettantes and *avant-garde* critics who have heard him recite some of his bizarre verses to guitar accompaniment—verses which the guests compare to Homer, the great decadents and finally agree to call "promising!" But Baal, ragged and filthy, only wolfs his food, asks for a donation of clean shirts and makes flagrant passes at his host's wife.

From this point on Baal (his appearance never less than epically repellent) moves on to a rampage of seduction and near-rape among girls and women who are unable or unwilling to resist the fascination of his priapic confidence. From poetized homosexual adventures and complete besottedness to total depravity and crime, Baal is finally seen crawling like a diseased animal to his death in the open fields.

At one point the poet, thinking back on his wretched odyssey, murmurs "Everything was beautiful." In this one line Brecht characterizes the climate of an era, a state of being which led either to the "reforms" of Hitlerism or to an unconsummated effort to find saner solutions.

Despite its star and a few respectful notices,

the play is not a success. Nevertheless, I suspect that, for all its romantic distortion, it satisfies a need in that part of the younger generation which wonders whether immersion in the mud may not bring it closer to salvation than squatting in the shallows of a stagnant respectability. For many the point of crisis has not yet been reached.

Baal might not have been produced at this juncture—and certainly not in the West End—had it not been for the representative and forceful actor, Peter O'Toole, who seems attracted to those parts which represent "outcasts from life's feast" or, to put it another way, parts which bespeak the chaos that breeds anger.

—*NAT*, 4 May '63

OH WHAT A LOVELY WAR

The English theatre is enjoying a seizure of satire. It all began with *Look Back in Anger*. That play was rhetorically enraged for reasons barely explicit but none the less sensible to its audience. There followed a series of "proletarian" plays—more troubled than affirmative—and to these too an important public was responsive. Then came the intimate revues, notably *Beyond the Fringe* and *The Establishment*, so that even the West End was glad to listen to the wistful lament and mockery of *Stop the World—I Want To Get Off*.

The American tomfoolery of *The Premise* and various editions of *From the Second City* sustained the motion. The drama of Beckett, Ionesco and company also helped to relax theatrical restraints and broaden the perspectives of the permissible.

The English, thoroughly disciplined to decorum, have always found an escape in bouts of eccentricity, low comedy and goofy humor. Now the theatre has begun to run wild in all these directions. There is an air of self-congratulation on this score.

The most generally advanced of the new satirical shows is the "musical entertainment," *Oh What a Lovely War*, the authorship of which is now in legal dispute but which has unquestionably been written and improvised under the supervision of Joan Littlewood, founder of the Theatre Workshop and director of such excellent productions as *A Taste of Honey* and *The Hostage*.

The company in *Oh What a Lovely War* is dressed in Pierrot costumes—as in *Stop the World*. A circus sideshow environment provides the permanent setting. Moving electric tapes flash messages about the accumulation of casualties and futile engagements of the First ("lovely") World War. This device is borrowed from Brecht and Piscator.

On stage are enacted a series of burlesque episodes parodying bayonet drill, meetings of high officials and military personnel in the war zone and in London high society. The bayonet drill under the screaming sergeant who instructs his men in the techniques and manners of murder by cold steel is as grotesquely funny as it has always been. There are other such caricatures—equally laughable without being a bit more novel. Mingled with these are such old-time tunes as Ivor Novello's *Keep the Home Fires Burning*, and these are the only good songs of the evening.

Everyone is "crazy" about this show. Why? The performances on the whole are crude and one is not convinced that the satire bears a direct relation to any present situation. The specific butt appears to be General Haig, who has been under blistering attack since 1918 for his bullheadedness in sending thousands to certain death in senseless "advances" which advanced nothing.

Though it rarely does any harm to scorn the military mind, I suggest that the satire here lacks point. It would not be entirely apposite in terms of the Second World War—except that that war might have been avoided if, for example, Churchill and not Chamberlain had been Prime Minister between 1937-1939. And certainly the prospect of a Third World War has to be treated in quite a different manner. Yet *Oh What a Lovely War* strikes the English as vitally relevant because it emphasizes what the young here cannot repeat too often: that the Establishment was, is, and by inference always will be, irremediably callous and stupid. Even those English who might agree that the show is not strictly applicable to contemporary affairs find in it the pleasure of nostalgia. It recalls a time of innocence when England, the most powerful nation on earth, shed its blood and drained itself of strength in a euphoria of self-confident, heroic befuddlement. At that memory—and in this the old songs are eminently helpful—strong men literally weep.

Whatever our reaction, it is certain that *Oh What a Lovely War* is the most accomplished of recent satires. From this there is a decline to a kind of harum-scarum jamboree of ribaldry and self-abandonment. Some of this is talented and very funny, as in *The Bed Sitting Room*. Its co-author is Spike Milligan, an endearing and original comic. Here we see England shortly after the bomb has dropped. The war itself was of brief duration—a minute and twenty-three seconds. Heaven knows who won it—possibly the Russians—though it doesn't matter; it is clear that England hasn't. Macmillan has turned into a parrot (the resemblance is striking), and a certain Lord into a bed sitting-room!

There is very little politics after this; and there needn't be. Everything has been cut loose from its normal moorings; the ensuing action makes the extravagances of surrealism and Ionesco look sober. The authors have achieved what they intended: to make us laugh at an utterly loony world in which the folk formerly most respected are now the daffiest, because the least endowed with humor and a sense of their own screwiness.

Even this is probably saying too much, for there is no indication that any other world or social order (which Labor might provide, for instance) would prove any less ridiculous. Spike Milligan and his associates may personally support the cause of nuclear disarmament, and their show may represent a gesture on behalf of their convictions, but what is chiefly communicated is a shoot-the-works rapture—anarchist rather than radical.

While this, the prevailing mood, may have its healthy aspect, I cannot help but regard it with some suspicion. For when you revel in turning everything topsy-turvy, jeer at everything and affirm nothing, you may well end by standing still, evading responsibility, sizzling smugly or disconsolately in the same stew as the neighbor you appear to scorn.

The tendency to take these shows, not at their face value but as signs of advanced social consciousness and superior theatrical skill, is complemented by the enthusiasm for spineless dramaturgy couched in literate double talk, as exemplified in such blather as *Next Time I'll Sing to You*, which contains little but the backwash of Pirandello. One critic has called it "the best play in London."

Am I mistaken in noticing a recent falling off in the development of English (and French) dramatic writing? John Osborne's plays since his first three have not revealed any remarkable progress. Pinter is not following upon *The Caretaker* with anything of wider scope. Wesker has turned to other tasks. And how much longer can Beckett, Ionesco and others of kindred temper continue voicing a view of the world which by its very nature has no issue?

This waning of impetus may prove only momentary. But it occurs to me that the low blood pressure may result from a social and moral apathy induced by the fact that nearly all of us fear the future and cannot in good conscience accept the present. However, that is a realm of speculation which leads far beyond, though it lies all around, the confines of the theatre.

—*NAT*, 25 May '63

WARSAW

My first impression of the rebuilt Warsaw—I had visited the city before the war—was that it was like a West European city. "It strikes you that way," a Polish lady said to me, "because you have just come from Moscow. If you had come here directly from Paris you would think it East European."

Specific contrasts revealed themselves at my first conversation. The same lady introduced me to a well-known scene designer at a café where I had pastry and coffee. (The Poles of Warsaw are addicted to pastry, coffee and ice cream—as a sort of *apéritif*, which they consume in honorable proportion to the amount of vodka they drink.) Said the designer: "You have just arrived from Moscow? And what theatre did you see there?" I mentioned the production of *The Threepenny Opera* which I had applauded the night before. My two table companions arched their eyebrows in surprise. "That is progress," they agreed.

I was even more surprised when the gentleman inquired if the saxophone were among the instruments used—and whether the jazz elements of the score had been retained. "Certainly," I answered. "They even did the twist in the prologue." This was hailed as glad tidings. The saxophone, symbol of jazz decadence, had for some time been anathema in serious musical circles in the Soviet Union.

Warsaw, with a population of a million, has twenty-five theatres. Their repertory is of broader scope than that on the Soviet stage. Examining the photographs at the first theatre I went to—a smallish house with a seating capacity of 400—I noted that plays by Beckett, Pinter, Wilder, Anouilh, O'Casey, Brecht, Graham Greene and the *avant-garde* French dramatist Schehadé had all been produced during the past two or three seasons. Many of these plays are still unacceptable in the Soviet Union.

I shall probably have occasion in future issues to refer to some of the contemporary Polish plays (a number of them influenced by the Theatre of the Absurd), since five have been translated into French in the Warsaw theatre magazine *Dialog*—in many respects the best theatre magazine in Europe and perhaps in the world. I shall confine myself now to plays with which I am familiar. The first was a remarkably original production of *The Three Sisters*, directed by Erwin Axer, the guiding spirit of the Contemporary Theatre's widely representative repertory.

The two most striking elements in this presentation were the unit setting and the subdued tone of the acting. The setting, covered by beige cloth with delicate leaflike patterns sewn on its surface, conveyed the feeling of a handsome lace decoration. Even the fourth-act exterior with its birch trees is so rendered. As for the acting, it sought no climaxes or excitement.

The production as a whole composed a tapestry of human relationships marked chiefly by the manner in which the characters *listened* and *looked* at one another. No single person appeared central to the play's development; all were woven into a single fabric of sentiment and meaning clearly legible through what we beheld in the characters' eyes. Presumably minor personages like Solony became as vivid and crucial to the whole as any of the others. It was a marriage of Stanislavsky "psychology" (old style!) with Brechtian objectivity.

The scene of Doctor Czebutykin's (Polish spelling) despair—when he confesses his ignorance and the medical impotence which led to his patients' deaths—usually done as a tour de force of emotional acting, was so casually (almost humorously) presented that without a knowledge of Polish one might suspect that it had been omitted. Yet it moved the audience, as did the entire production, as much as performances elsewhere in which the scene is played with passion.

The most colorful performance was that of Tadeusz Lomnicki, one of Warsaw's best actors, as Solony. In this interpretation, Solony is seen as a suppressed thug, a venomously enamored pig hiding his sick soul behind a mask of eau de Cologne, scented lozenges and "Byronic" verse.

The two old servants, Anfisa and Ferapont (small parts), were brilliantly real; I was told later that the actors who played them are "stars." A very young Tusenbach was admirable in his refinement and sensibility, though the comic inadequacy of the man was overlooked. Among the sisters, only Masha was notable; Kuligin was far more pallid

and fragilely Polish than densely Russian, but still touching; the Vershinin was barely adequate. The love scenes were featherweight in their discretion, the pathos of the play a shadow. The world of Chekhov had become a memory of the melancholy past, still beautifully poignant as it fades.

I admired, rather than warmed to, this reading of the play, but I shall not forget it.

Brecht's *The Resistible Rise of Arturo Ui* is another Axer production, which he is now repeating in Leningrad. I had seen the play (a "history" of Hitler's rise to power allegorically told as the story of a "Chicago" gangster) given by the Berliner Ensemble in a style of grotesque comedy. In Warsaw it was a brutal, Kafka-like nightmare, its setting all lead and steel.

Lomnicki, the Solony of *The Three Sisters*, was now Ui-Hitler. He played it with a savagely stylized harshness, more terrifying than funny. When Ui makes his final speech in a paroxysm of blistering energy, the actor rising to extreme heights of vocal virtuosity, I thought the effect deliberately farcical; but no one, to my initial consternation, laughed. Then I realized the reason: Hitler was never a joke to the Poles. He was a hideous reality, the recollection of which could not be anything but horrifying. During the Nazi occupation of Poland anyone found with a book in English or heard playing Chopin was immediately put to death.

At the Peoples Theatre (all Polish theatres are state-owned) I saw Racine's *Brittanicus*, which I feared might prove a bore. I found the performance more interesting than it had been at the Comédie Française. The setting, a scenic adaptation of *tachiste* painting technique, was barbarously regal and physically stirring; the costumes as well as the make-ups in gold, orange and dark brown had a sinister glamour.

Irina Eichlerowna (Warsaw's "Mother Courage") played Agrippina. Poland's outstanding actress, she possesses formidable authority and commands an arrestingly resonant voice which she controls with utmost ease. Around her, the young actors—Nero, Brittanicus, Narcissus—were handsome, fervid and fluent. The play was no Racine recital or museum piece; it took on its proper stature as a timeless statement of the conflict between will (or politics) and desire.

My only disappointment in Warsaw was with the production at the Contemporary Theatre of Ionesco's *The King Dies*, which I saw at its final dress rehearsal. The setting and costumes were extremely stylish—and entirely misconceived with respect to the play's requirements. (Such a setting and costumes might earn its designer rave notices in New York.) The acting, too, was without point or quality—the fault of the director rather than the cast.

I must add that the original Ionesco text, which I read here for the first time (I had seen the play in Paris and commented on it in *The Nation* last winter), contains its author's finest writing, both witty and touching. The play is not, as I had supposed, an ode to death, but a hymn to life emerging from the troubled depths of existentialist anguish.

—*NAT*, 27 July '63

LETTER FROM TOKYO

Life in Japan today may be viewed as a sort of melodrama, a conflict, not between the "good guys" and the "bad guys," but between the old and the new. Though the upstart new has the clear advantage, the suspense is considerable. As in all instances where a civilization is in rapid transition, there is resistance. Those who fear or resent the passing of the old maintain that change is more apparent than real. It is easier in Japan than elsewhere to take this position, since Japan has always been able to assimilate features of other cultures and to transform them into something peculiarly its own.

Youngsters assure me that the Noh and Kabuki theatrical forms—issue of the fifteenth and

seventeenth centuries respectively—are doomed. Their language is archaic and their pace, particularly that of Noh, intolerably slow. These were aristocratic modes, and are said to have little relation to present needs.

But though the government does not subsidize the theatre in the European fashion, the state financed the Kabuki's American tour; the Puppet Theatre, developed in the sixteenth century, had its career renewed by a grant from the national treasury. These are taken as signs that the old theatre will not become extinct. Yet I found sold-out houses only at contemporary plays. There was greater attendance at the Kabuki than at the Noh, and while the Noh audience was predominantly elderly and the Kabuki audience middle-aged, the audience for the modern was conspicuously young.

A learned devotee of the old theatre made an observation which struck me as especially significant: while the present players of Noh and Kabuki are proficient in the required movement and intonations, most of them lack the "inside feeling" which must animate these forms. Actors in modern plays, it was quickly added, have much more "inside feeling." This says more than any comparative statistics on the two kinds of theatre.

The Japanese film industry, affluent some years ago, is now suffering a decline as sharp as that of Hollywood's. This is supposedly due to earlier overproduction and to the poor quality of many recent films, most of which are as hackneyed as our old "B" movies. The deterioration, according to one gentleman committed to the maintenance of the traditional arts, is turning the interest of the young back to the theatre. But, he added with an enigmatic smile, none of the arts could really attract them because their bent is toward baseball, golf and country outings!

It struck me later that this remark dovetailed with another, by a university student, that the Japanese, "so clever with their fingers," were now reluctant to become skilled workers tied down to permanent jobs. They desire freedom to wander, to have a good time. With employment everywhere at hand, the young are always able to find new jobs.

But labor is poorly paid and most workers live in rather squalid dwellings; that is why, someone explained, so many people crowd the streets, where their eager pursuit of fun gives Tokyo its hectic complexion.

The attempt to resolve the tension between the traditional and the contemporary is most strikingly illustrated in the better films. One has only to think of *Rashomon* and some of Kurosawa's "Westerns" (Samurai adventure stories) to observe how detachment and skepticism allow the modern Japanese artist to celebrate certain perennially admirable virtues while subtly undermining their premises.

Masaki Kobayashi's *Harakiri* is a recent example of the interplay between new and old. Laid in the period of feudalism's decadence, its plot denounces the brutality and futility of that society's codes of honor. By thematic extension the story also casts doubt on adherence to many still prevalent and respected disciplines.

It is beautifully made and superlatively acted, with something of the chastened luxury of ancient Japanese art. Still one recognizes that a good deal of the pleasure of *Harakiri* lies in its cruelty and the gory extravagance of its sword play and fight scenes. It offers pity and terror but little tragic purge because its values are somewhat uncertain.

Other representative new films are Kurosawa's treatment of a murderous kidnapping (a new crime for Japan) and Ozu's homey *Oyaho* ("Hello") which centers on two little boys' desire to possess a television set. That instrument is the hero-image of the film.

The Actors' Theatre—organization and building—was founded some twenty years ago by the actor-director Korea Senda, who learned much from his studies in Berlin in pre-Hitler days. The theatre's auditorium seats four hundred and eighty; it is comfortable, modestly attractive, up-to-date. An orchestra seat costs less than a dollar.

Senda told me that The Actors' Theatre couldn't count on more than five thousand spectators for any of its productions in Tokyo. The most successful of them—*The Threepenny Opera*—had to move to a larger house to accommodate the seventy thousand people who were expected to see it. How, in view of these limited numbers, was it possible to build so fine a theatre? The actors themselves had contributed as much as 70 percent of their earnings from television and movies.

"What idealism!" I exclaimed. "Since the theatre has been in existence for twenty years, one must conclude that there is a certain amount of realism involved as well," said the director. "Has the theatre become profitable?" I asked. "No," he answered, "but the actors now contribute only 20 percent of their earnings."

There is a numerically unimpressive but steady demand for modern plays—as persistent as the political radicalism which is both a force, particularly in the trade unions, and not a force! As a French journalist long resident in Japan put it, there is little "spirit of protest" in the country. The present (democratic) government assumes in the eyes of the people a power as transcendental as the almost religious eminence of the Emperor in bygone days.

There is a theatre school, but I judged the actors insufficiently trained for the modern stage. I inquired if there was any knowledge among them of the Stanislavsky system. Indeed there is, I was told, but there is greater interest in Brecht's methods because "they are closer to the Japanese temperament." This is understandable when one remembers the anti-naturalistic bias of the Brechtian canon with its emphasis on objective detachment. I associated the reference to Japanese temperament with something I read in the program of the Noh theatre. In the Noh play only the main personage (apart from the men who play women's roles) wears a mask—because the tradition has it that *"the mask is more expressive than the human face."*

A conviction grew in me as I was about to leave the country that within these theatrical pronouncements lay hidden some principle or clue which might unify the multiple data of my Tokyo stay. Despite the howlers inherent in headlong generalization, I decided to make a "tableau" of my variegated impressions.

The essential Japanese approach to life is aesthetic. Japanese ethics are aesthetics. Japanese morality is more a matter of balancing courtesies than an effusion or a formalization of sentiments. What we call "heart" is a virtue rarely emphasized.

In an aesthetic world view both good and evil can be made splendid through artistic and intellectual mastery. Ugliness itself needs only discipline to be made elegant. This is pagan, "liberal" and permissive. The Japanese are an ironic people. Irony is a way of checking clashing impulses; it is a step toward balance. To be truly comprehended, life must be contemplated as a lofty spectacle which like all play has a tendency to collapse in farce. The unseemly is often considered more comic than shocking. But a fascination with blood is also clearly marked in Japanese art. Blood is the most specific emblem of life's drama, and the shedding of it (one's own or another's) serves to release the aggressive instincts which must perforce lie beneath a constantly controlled, in this case an aesthetically formalized, existence. The Japanese, polite to the point of courtliness, are prone to sudden fits of nervous rage and hysteria. Where the aggressive instinct does not find physical expression it takes on the guise of another sort of "irony" which is difficult to differentiate from malice.

The Japanese are sometimes accused of hypocrisy, a charge inevitable with the use of the mask which the formalized control of relations entails. The Japanese are eye-minded rather than ear-minded, and the eye is less "soulful" than the ear!

The democracy of the machine is now releasing new forces with tremendous speed and energy. Advanced capitalism is a great leveler. Women, once the glorified slaves and adornment of Japan, are changing their status. Many believe that women are the only ones to have unequivocally improved their condition in the new society, but the women themselves feel that their lot has not been sufficiently ameliorated.

Though homosexuality is still regarded with serene impartiality—the pagan smilingly admits every appetite—the demands of modern efficiency lead to a certain "Puritanism." Did not the Japanese Supreme Court punish the publication of *Lady Chatterley's Lover*? Yet at the same time one finds extreme samples of popular erotica in many book stalls. And Tokyo streets steam with sensuality.

The Japanese intellectual is convinced that in America the artist and the highly cultivated carry far greater weight and are more respected than in his country, where now only the big banker and the monopoly industrialist matter—though they were presumed to have been exorcised during the American occupation. Japan is prosperous, but everyone asks, "will it last?"

—*NAT*, 14 Sept. '63

CLIFFORD ODETS

When Clifford Odets applied for admission into the ranks of the Group Theatre acting company in 1931 my colleagues and I voted to accept him without knowing exactly why. He was not a particularly good actor, I thought, after having seen him play several small parts in Theatre Guild productions, but he had talent. If I'd been challenged to specify what sort of talent I should have been hard put to answer. There was a kind of heat in him, an internal tension and churning which I felt was promising.

Odets lived in a Greenwich Village (Hudson Street) apartment next to a stable just before *Awake and Sing* was produced. He said he wrote it largely because I wouldn't cast him in a decent part in one of our productions. He vowed that if *Awake* was a hit he would rent a nice apartment which we would share. The play did sufficiently well for us to move to University Place.

The first thing Odets did was to buy a huge record player and an enormous number of classical discs. For months, or rather years, the music went round and round. It was better than hearing Odets repeat the same tumultuous minor chords that he used to pound out on the piano at every opportunity. He couldn't read a note.

Odets was generous. He provided his friends with bottles of champagne, books, paintings, and overwhelming dinners. After the opening of *Awake* he gave me money to go abroad. Many years later he bought me a Pontiac. I thought this was excessive. "Harold," he said, "When we were almost starving in 1932 I asked if you would let me have a quarter. You opened your wallet in which there were only two single dollar bills. 'Take one,' you said. I am returning that dollar with interest."

The man had talent—and not just for making potato pancakes, as some people insisted in the dark Depression days when twelve Group actors lived together on West 57th Street. What impelled Odets's talent was a torrent of tenderness, warm and consoling, which when confronted by injustice would turn to an agony of rage.

When he had achieved success—owned a Cadillac and lived in a sumptuous Beekman Place apartment—Odets confided to me that one of his most deep-seated urges was a desire "to reign," to exercise a sort of regal largesse. The one thing he couldn't do was to reign over himself, to dominate the contrary pulls of his nature.

—*SR*, 14 Sept. '63

JAMES GIBBONS HUNEKER: Critic of the Seven Arts.
By Arnold T. Schwab

Unless they be specialists in American arts and letters, very few people under fifty have read or even heard of James Gibbons Huneker. Yet when Huneker died in 1921 at the age of sixty-eight, George Jean Nathan, like Mencken a "disciple," composed a eulogy which spoke of Huneker as "the greatest of American critics, our foremost cultural figure."

Allowing for the exaggeration customary on such occasions, it is still a fact that by 1907 Huneker had become the music, drama and art critic of the New York *Sun* (as well as other journals), that he had written pioneer pieces on what was then ultra-modern music, on still controversial or virtually unknown European dramatists, on "outlandish" novelists, painters and poets. These, together with two biographies, some short stories, a novel and an autobiography, finally came to a total of twenty volumes. Today only *Ivory, Apes and Peacocks*, originally published in 1915, has been reprinted.

If a capsule summation of Huneker's contribution were sufficient, we might call him as others have done, "Europe's artistic ambassador to the United States," except that it might be more accurate to say that Huneker, born in Philadelphia, was America's self-appointed envoy to Europe. As Arnold Schwab's new and only full-scale biography of Huneker puts it, "His ingratiating personality and style captivated so many readers for so long that he was able to acquaint more Americans with European literature [and other arts] than any other critic of his time." To this we might append lines from a review by Edmund Wilson which describes Huneker's letters as "floral bombs...close packed rockets of fireworks." More significantly, Wilson concludes, "If the sparks faded...and left no fixed stars in the firmament, it was not that the fiery beauty had left no colors in our hearts."

Huneker's work evokes an era as well as a personality. Schwab's biography—modest, straightforward, intelligent, detailed—documents that era delightfully and truthfully. We Americans, who are prone to blot out each day in expectation of the next, thereby suffer a failure of pleasure, knowledge and wisdom. We even fail to live fully in the present because we so rarely take pains to preserve our past. Schwab's biography of Huneker is valuable as a reminder of a happy time in the development of our cultural life.

It was a happy time because it was a time of confident rebellion. The bright morning of American literature darkened after 1860. The

Gilded Age (1870-1900) was on the whole an age of artistic mediocrity. The purest and most powerful voices were for the greater part either silenced or unattended. Authority in artistic circles was constricted by the tenets of a silly Puritanism. (*Huckleberry Finn* was welcomed as a kid's book.) The public most steadily appealed to was an audience of proper ladies. Beneath the surface lurked the never wholly absent dissidents who upheld the nobler tradition, men who were to bring fresh blood and sinew to it. "In America," Huneker wrote in 1906, "the eradication of the Puritan microbe will be no easy task, taught as we are in our arid schools and universities that the entire man ends at his collar bone."

So Huneker, whose first book appeared in 1899, dared in 1905 to say of George Moore's *Memoirs of My Dead Life* that it is "a shocking book and its present reviewer delights in the statement"; and of Whitman that he was "a gay old pagan who never called a sin a sin when it was a pleasure." In 1908, Huneker espoused the cause of the "ashcan" (American realist) school of painters as well as of Arthur Davies, who was a mystic. Huneker extolled or aroused interest in Nietzsche, Huysmans, Strindberg, Maurice Barres, Rémy de Gourmont, Edvard Munch, Conrad, Cézanne, Wedekind and Henry James at a time when these men were either scorned or ignored in American journalism. Who beside Huneker could speak or had even heard (except in the "underground") of Villiers de L'Isle Adam, Rimbaud and Laforgue? Who among us in 1915 would have taken notice of Arnold Schoenberg? Though Huneker disliked and feared him, he harbored the suspicion "that in time I might be persuaded to like this music, to embrace, after abhorring it." In any case he could foresee that the "old tonal order had changed forever." that "the tyranny of the diatonic and chromatic scales ...were of the past."

Huneker had an enormous appetite for all of the arts. Some of his long lists of exotic artists sound like items of a menu. He was both gourmand and gourmet. He swallowed and digested all.

But he was not without discrimination and for all his voracious enthusiasm possessed considerable critical insight. He had an infectious exuberance. When he spoke of an unfamiliar artist he made you want to run and look, absorb the new sound and sight of him. The very titles of Huneker's books are glamorous: *Melomaniacs, Egoists, Iconoclasts, Visionaries, The Pathos of Distance, Unicorns, Bedouins.*

There was a Bacchic fervor about him. His frequent references to the joyous and unremitting consumption of Pilsner, his indulgence in a certain snobbery of the bottle, never become offensive because they are not signs of laxity or despair but the celebration of adventure in life and in the arts. He visited many cities—at home and abroad—and savored them as he might a delicious brew, a lovely poem, an exciting symphony. The subtitle to one of his volumes is "A Book of a Thousand and One Moments." Those moments were all the more glorious because he felt himself the herald of a better time and a gayer world than the one into which he had been born.

Without any thesis, social or political, with hardly any determined aesthetic doctrine ("convictions are prisons," he repeated after Nietzsche), Huneker had a sense of mission. It was to bring the glad tidings of colorful and brave human expression to those who still dwelled in the darkness of convention and timid taste. Because he knew himself to be "special" and in the forefront of a doughty group of "anarchs," whose destructiveness was life-enhancing, his work always had about it a triumphantly festive air. Everything becomes indifferent where anything goes, and immediate fanfare turns originality to routine—which is our situation today. Huneker wrote only one extended study—it was on Chopin. For the rest, apart from his fiction and autobiography, his work is made up of brief occasional articles, essays in exhilaration. He had a large, lively vocabulary peppered with exotic coinage: "puissant," "parvitude," "psychologue," "improvisator, "cyclus." He would call a poet "The Buffoon of the New Eternities," and write awkward and nearly meaningless phrases like "cosmogonies jostle evil farceurs." Often in his haste he praised the right people for the wrong reasons, and many of his judgments require the correction of more poised study.

Yet these are the vices of his virtue: that without lacking seriousness he reveled in art, that he was a hedonist of the intellectual life, that he had and imparted fun. So much of our criticism today is academically solemn, severe or sour, while the glossy critics are glib, frivolous, irresponsible, fashionable or just publicity punks. Huneker's laughing ecstasies bespeak the muscle, flesh and blood—the *love*—that was in him. We knew at once when we read Huneker that what attracted him was important.

—*NAT*, 12 Oct. '63

COCTEAU

Learning of the death of Edith Piaf seven hours before his own, Jean Cocteau murmured "The boat is going down." The "boat" was neither her life nor his—this dramatist of Death did not know he was dying—it was the "boat" of an era, the "boat" which sailed elegantly and magically on the painted sea of that fabulous French epoch, Between the Two Wars.

I was a youth drawn to the Mystery of Paris in 1921. During the years when I studied and lived there, and on all the subsequent occasions of my perpetual return, Cocteau remained its emblematic Presence. He shone on the breast of Paris like a gem of strange consistency and ever-changing color. Poet, *causeur*, critic, novelist, playwright, designer, film director, impresario, actor, artist, opium eater, heretic, Catholic and Academician, he was always in the vanguard—a vanguard that had not forsaken the past. He wanted to lead or invent every new game and to refashion all the old ones. He was a dandy and a teacher; Harlequin among the sages, a Character for the ages.

There was a winged intelligence in everything he did and said. He appreciated Picasso,

Stravinsky, Diaghilev from the first. He hailed the advent of the post Debussy-Ravel composers: Milhaud, Poulenc, Honegger, Auric. He brought the boy genius, Raymond Radiguet, to the world's attention. He celebrated Josephine Baker. He sought (and won) freedom from life imprisonment for Jean Genet. He was everywhere by the side of original talent and fixed its image in the public consciousness by the point of his epigrams.

His large jet black eyes radiated a constant sense of surprised glee at the pleasures of existence, joy of the senses, smiling ecstasies of the mind. I saw him take a curtain call on the opening night of his play *Orphée* in 1926. His trim figure flashed toward the footlights as if he were going to fly over the heads of the audience. He wore a huge rose in his lapel. He struck me as a French eighteenth-century sprite in the guise of a twentieth-century intellectual sport embodying the Spirit of Perennial Awareness. From that moment Cocteau and *Tout Paris* coalesced into a single image for me.

—*NAT*, 2 Nov. '63

THE CORRUPTION OF THE PALACE OF JUSTICE
THE PRIVATE EAR AND THE PUBLIC EYE

How tricky is the world of the theatre: profound men may write superficial plays; men not nearly so profound may write clever plays; men neither profound nor clever may write successful plays.

Ugo Betti was a genuinely religious man. His essay "Religion in the Theatre" (which may be read in that excellent collection, *Theatre in the Twentieth Century*) contains passages of soulful wisdom. "I truly believe," he wrote "that if we search untiringly at the bottom of all human abdications, we will end by finding, under so many 'nos,' a small 'yes' which will outweigh every objection and will be sufficient to rebuild every-thing…since in error not all is error."

Betti, a magistrate in the High Court of Rome and a dramatist as well as a Catholic thinker of delicate insight, rarely if ever succeeded in writing a wholly satisfactory play. Like Pirandello whom he followed in time and technique, his plays are usually constructed as mystery melodramas. What is pursued is not a culprit, but the truth which hides like a criminal. The search is carried on in a spirit of zealous anguish and one must be impressed by the "heart" which goes into it. But while Pirandello sometimes managed to find a striking situation or a theatrically fascinating metaphor to dramatize his enigmas, Betti usually employs so much effort in setting up his premises that his final revelation seems unequal to the passion expended to arrive at it.

In *Corruption in the Palace of Justice* (Cherry Lane) we learn that some judge of a high court is suspected of taking bribes from a notorious racke-teer. All six judges of the court are shown to be corrupt, but which one is guilty in this particular instance?

The judges are panic-stricken, in this semi-symbolic drama of conscience, because they all feel culpable of something. Most of them are cowardly crows corroded by malice. The initial point about the universality of guilt is soon made and the suspense is well sustained, but the play's resolution—too simple and not at all inevitable from the preceding matter—makes most of it appear trivial.

What Betti says in effect is that almost no one is wholly innocent and most of us are smeared with iniquity; therefore, if the sinful are often raised to positions of honor, it is finally no great matter: that is the way of the world. "God forgives and forgets." Most of us commit wrongs greater than those for which we may be punished. To achieve purity or absolution the individual can do little more than confess his guilt to the ultimate arbiter, the "Lord High Chancellor" or Supreme Being.

Here, then, we have an unquestionably earnest play, written with dignity by a deeply serious and certainly more than ordinarily intelligent man, which must finally be accounted superficial as art, no matter what our opinion of it is as thought.

The direction of this production, by Richard Kitman, aims at an intensity that will save the play from seeming too "talky"; but the result is to make its contrivance all the more evident. The produc-tion is nevertheless respectable. There are no *bad* performances, and one at least (by C. K. Alexander) adds an individual tang to the general picture.

Peter Shaffer's two one-acters, *The Private Ear* and *The Public Eye* (Morosco), require no extended review from me now since I commented on their London opening last year.

Though I credited the evening's conspicuous merits, I was perhaps mistaken in stressing that it ought not be taken as more than bright, literate, well-bred entertainment.

Mr. Shaffer is a playwright in progress. He is on his way from Terence Rattigan (with somewhat more nerve and sensibility, involving a bit of the latter-day British indignation) to an identity of his own. *Five Finger Exercise*, Shaffer's first hit, was evidence of his ability; if there was anything about it to cause worry, it was its being so thoroughly adept, neat and "finished." I surmise that Shaffer is ambitious, and wishes to go beyond the fashioning of trim Pinero-like packages of what every aware Englishman now knows. If he falters in the future, it will, I trust, be on the road to greater goals.

The Private Ear and *The Public Eye*, in the interim, are engaging comedies of good sense in which Shaffer cuts agreeably shaped patterns from the store of his talent.

Seeing these two short plays again, I was almost exasperated at being so pleased. The play-wright's sure touch in handling their slight materi-als (always suggestive of larger issues) made their surface seem deep enough. But that is the reward of craftsmanship.

Peter Wood's direction is a genuine contribu-tion to the evening's pleasure. Its skill is immensely helpful to the actors—particularly to

Barry Foster and Geraldine McEwan. Without anything being "delved" into, everything clicks. Though the target is small, one is gratified by the marksmanship.

—NAT, 9 Nov. '63

THE BALLAD OF THE SAD CAFE

What may baffle or repel many theatregoers in Edward Albee's dramatization of Carson McCullers' *The Ballad of the Sad Cafe* (Martin Beck) is what attracts me to it. The play is weird and unclear. It is like the little photograph which the hunchback, Cousin Lyman, shows Miss Amelia to prove that he is kin to her: partially effaced, it is barely decipherable. Yet it holds the attention, fascination; it speaks, almost sings.

Most of the plays offered us are so clear that we see through them at first glance; what they reveal, moreover, is unimportant. *The Ballad of the Sad Cafe* may be explained without much difficulty in the jargon of psychoanalysis—in terms of inversion, for example—but to do so would be to render it banal and, by assigning it a seemingly exact meaning, would rob it of its true significance.

The title gives a clue to its artistic form. It is a ballad—perhaps a parable—of the Deep South "where there is absolutely nothing to do....The soul rots with boredom....Somewhere in the darkness a woman sings in a high wild voice and the tune has no start and no finish and is made up of only three notes which go on and on." There is no sustained or shaped melody, except what is heard remotely from a chain gang in the vicinity. The characters are connected through their captivity.

It is not, however, a play of local color. Though specific, its "Southernness" is symbolic. The theme is the frustration of love in a world without horizon or human dimension, a world so bound or "squeezed" in its isolation that all who dwell in it become deformed. The hunchback of the story is the evil which emerges from this constricted world. All the characters are monsters of one kind or another. This evil is also love when love has no natural outlet, no soil to give it nurture. It is a twisted love which forces its way to the light in wild contortion—a kind of noxious weed.

The better people (embodied in this instance by the lonely Henry Macy) are passive, mute, defeated and hardly perceptible amid the rank growth. The others are mean little dwarfs or misbegotten giants, full of an obscene energy that dare not pronounce the word "love," though active with its awkward gestures and an irrepressible, infantile tenderness. Where there is sufficient power the only directed impulse is greed, the only satisfaction acquisition. The result is always destruction. What ties these people together even while it separates them is a loneliness that is unaware of its name.

This is insanity. Most of our fine Southern writers evoke this atmosphere, but here, because of its far-reaching overtones, it becomes, first, generally American, then universal.

The tone of Mrs. McCullers' writing—some of it spoken by the narrator of the play—is spare and almost flat, musical only through a mournfulness and ache that rise to something like nobility by its lack of "eloquence." She avoids explanation. Her story is not "psychological"; she has dreamed it without trying to "understand" it. The narration bears a blank countenance as if its import will either be self-evident or unintelligible—in which case the listener may be someone rendered obtuse by the rattle of commonplace reason.

The tale is plainly told as an event, horrid without being astonishing, a nightmare which, like the environment in which it is set, remains a perennial norm. One cannot think of this as realism. That is one reason why the novella has so little talk. The play must perforce supply dialogue to create a story line, though Albee, through his narrator, supplies background and comment from the original source to circumvent the pitfalls of prosy exposition.

Albee's greatest success for sheer writing is the letter which is momentarily mentioned in

McCullers, but which in the play becomes a searing expression of love-hate, a wrath arising from the lover's inability to affect or touch the beloved except in violence. This, in addition to the bitterness of his comedy, constitutes the mainspring of Albee's talent. He is also a superb dramatic craftsman, as is sufficiently proved by his treatment of this, theatrically speaking, nearly impossible material.

Alan Schneider's production and Ben Edwards' setting are sound enough. Perhaps it is being captious to add that they lack a certain removal from the literal. One misses a mood of pained yearning as if all were being seen through a veil that blurs outlines and dispels our sneaking demand for concrete causation. The "deep unnamable sadness," the essence of the Ballad, is not wholly created.

The cast is well chosen: there are wonderful faces, like that of Roberts Blossom in a subsidiary role. Colleen Dewhurst as Amelia (more attractive and wholesome than McCullers' fright), Michael Dunn, invaluably keen as Cousin Lymon, Lou Antonio as Miss Amelia's wretched husband (though he seems more Mediterranean, lush and warm, than taut and bitingly native), Enid Markey—all these deserve praise. They suffer only to the degree in which the direction has not fulfilled its complete function. William Prince conveys admirably the depressed bewilderment of a gentleness that cannot even articulate its resignation.

—*NAT*, 23 Nov. '63

WHAT'S HAPPENING IN EDINBURGH?

Among the events at the Edinburgh Festival in 1962, an International Writers Conference on the Novel was a notable item. Shortly after their arrival, the guests at this year's Conference on the Drama heard that the novelists' affair had literally become a howling success. A Scottish author

publicly confessed that he had been a drug addict, only to be followed by a Hindu writer who topped this avowal by proclaiming, "I am a homosexual as well as a drug addict."

I cannot say that the report of this incident set the tone for the drama conference, but it must have cast a spell. There were no equivalent revelations—not officially, at any rate—but some of the guests must have felt a certain pressure to say and do things which would be sufficiently sensational to make headlines.

After each day's session—there were six—the organizers and a number of conferees waited anxiously to learn what the press, radio and television had to say about the day's proceedings. The prevailing atmosphere was that of a theatrical company waiting for opening-night notices. When the first day's meeting was received as dull, the sponsors virtually instructed the "delegates" to whoop it up the next day. It became clear to everyone that what was involved was not a serious discussion but a show.

Kenneth Tynan, the conference's general chairman, should be held blameless in this. It is hardly possible for some fifty people to communicate with one another congenially before an audience of at least 1,500 paying persons. The sight of that throng—the best "houses" that some of them had had for a long time—froze rather than encouraged the less frivolous speakers. Some good conversations took place among them between sessions, but there could be little value for them in the open meetings.

When the third day's attendance diminished conspicuously the managers fairly panicked; the conference was expected to pay for itself. "It's all because of that first session," one of the organizers said, referring to the unfavorable press. He forgot to take into account the much more cordial "reviews" of the second day.

In his opening remarks, Arthur Kopit of *Oh Dad, Poor Dad...* fame wondered what the conference was all about. "Why are we here?" (Oh, these candid Americans!) Harold Pinter, most generally admired of young English playwrights, asked the same question. He ventured a simple answer, "We are here because we must all be hoping to become film stars."

The conference was chiefly a spectacle. In that light, the most enjoyable moments were those some might consider shameful or ludicrous. How clever of the Soviet guests to remain silent throughout except for actor-director Zavadsky's formal greeting and somewhat propagandistic expression of good will. The Polish contingent also remained publicly uncommunicative. "What fools these Westerners be" must have been in the minds of both these delegations.

So we yearned for "scandals." The first of these was provided by Bernard Levin, London drama critic, political commentator and one of the "features" of the highly popular satiric television show "That Was the Week That Was." His speech opening the second day's meeting was to be concerned with "What are the principal trends in contemporary drama?" According to the sponsors' bias, the choice was between the theatre of social or political "commitment" and the Theatre of the Absurd; in other words, between Brecht and Beckett. Only Harold Hobson, drama critic of the *Sunday Times,* pointed out that there might be other alternatives. Levin flatly pronounced Brecht bad and the Absurd dramatists absurd. He was clear about what Brecht meant, and he did not like it; while most of the others, he asserted, wrote plays we, the audience, didn't know "what the hell [they] were about." This, despite widespread disagreement, might have passed muster without too acrimonious a reaction if Levin had not also attempted to justify the British Government's refusal to admit into the country members of the Berliner Ensemble, who had been invited to the conference.

What offended many on the platform and a good part of the audience was not so much Levin's opinions as his coolly supercilious manner. Levin is a virtuoso of the microphone; he has an agile mind, his delivery and language are smooth and shrewd, his purpose is invidious. He looks like the youngest and smartest boy in the class, mock inno-

cent and maddeningly plausible. His audience is usually divided among those who wish to laugh with him, to boo him or simply to paste him one on his calm nose.

After a polite interjection by Tynan and some applause and heckling from the house, Wolf Mankowitz, the playwright-producer, intervened hysterically with an assortment of outcries, among which I could only distinguish such expressions as: "Fascist! Parasite! He sucks our blood!" Levin, as usual, remained unperturbed. He had accomplished his provocative mission.

Another highlight was the rude interruption of Joan Littlewood's second speech by James Fitzgerald, the Irish director. When that talented lady described a utopian future in which every man and woman would be a genius and entire communities and groups of individuals would freely make theatre at will, Fitzgerald shouted, "What bloody nonsense!" When Fitzgerald was asked to join Miss Littlewood at the microphone and develop his objections beyond the expletive, he was torn between a desire to apologize and the need to expand on what he had called the Littlewood speech.

This was a setback for Fitzgerald, who had made a hit with the audience on the day censorship had been under discussion by reeling off a series of unmentionable four-letter words, then addressing the public as "You f - - - s!" and finally blurting out, "My God, I'm still drunk!"

The high point of the conference—if its organizers were in earnest about creating a commotion—was the Happening devised by Kenneth Dewey of San Francisco. This was an improvisation ostensibly designed to illustrate one of the possibilities in the Theatre of the Future. The Happening in question began to happen before anyone realized what was happening. First, Arthur Kopit introduced a resolution to hold a handicap contest for all playwrights: Ionesco plus ten, Rattigan minus four, and so forth. Kopit was followed by Charles Marowitz, an American director-critic residing in England, who proposed something equally goofy. He was interrupted by someone in the audience (a conferee incognito) who rose and raged, expostulating madly while Marowitz continued to hold forth.

This went on while, in the organ loft above and behind the speakers' rostrum, a nude girl was slowly wheeled on a dolly from one side of the auditorium to the other. A moment later, some of us could discern a man standing in transparent shorts (tropical kilts, so to speak) while bagpipes began playing merrily. During all this, Carole Baker, a pretty sight in skintight gold lamé pants, moved bewitchingly over the auditorium benches as if in quest of a man, while a woman with a child crying "Daddy" mounted the podium and pointed out the presumably fleeing father. Pandemonium and laughter!

What followed seemed to me more idiotic than the Happening itself. A good (or silly) joke reminiscent of Dada antics in the twenties was denounced as a menace to the theatre, a sign of what the *avant-garde* was coming to, an example of American light-headedness, a symptom of the "totalitarian" mentality, etc.

Whatever one's reaction, the Happening was surely more telling in its pointlessness than Laurence Olivier's contribution on the first day. The audience greeted him like a god, and he spoke like one—in double-talk. On the same day, Judith Anderson averred that she loved the theatre (hear! hear!), and Agnes Moorehead, after the conference had been in session for half an hour, declared that it was an inspiring occasion, a sentiment shared by no other conferee.

Still, it would be altogether wrong to suggest that the conference was entirely on these levels of high-minded or low-grade confusion. In the final moments of the fifth day's windy talks on Naturalism in the Theatre, a significant debate took place. It was set off when an Indian playwright intoned a native chant. Someone complimented him on this charming example of Indian folk art. Wole Soyinka, a Nigerian playwright, in admirably articulate wrath, decried our regard for "local color." The exotic, which always seems to enchant the Occidental, had little merit, he said. Our delight in racial "strangeness" is condescending and cheap.

The English conferees generally spoke modestly and to the point. The most emotionally forceful yet coherent statement was made by John Arden, one of England's vital new dramatists. In appearance he corresponds to the traditional "square" notion of what an artist looks like—long-haired, unshaven, unkempt and possibly ill-washed. Puffing a prohibited cigarette, Arden spoke of the theatre as a life-enhancing "utensil of enjoyment" in a manner which did not make one blush, as Joan Littlewood's effusions did. What was embarrassing about her utterances was not that they were mistaken or pretentious, but that they had no real relation to her actual problems, situation, technique or to those of anyone else.

Arnold Wesker, author of *Chips With Everything,* a definitely "committed" playwright (a term which Americans might translate as left-wing), made remarks which did not particularly please some of his colleagues but which struck me as sincere, intelligent and appropriately personal. The same may be said of occasional comments made by Peter Shaffer, author of *Five Finger Exercise,* and by the amiable Bamber Gascoigne, the drama critic who has taken over Kenneth Tynan's post on the *Observer.* Tynan himself, unequivocally committed to socialism in politics (no sin in England) and to a philosophy of rationalistic humanism, as contrasted with the numerous antirationalists present, conducted himself with restraint and spoke sense. Peter Brook was eminently serious.

Little benefit was to be reaped from such virtues at a conference where the announcement of the imminent arrival of a beauteous film star (who made several appearances in as many sumptuous furs) was repeated over and over again. The quiet simplicity of Joan Plowright and Dorothy Tutin must have gone unobserved in these surroundings.

Among the Germans, the critic Friedrich Luft and the interesting playwright Martin Walser were correct, informative and urbane, very usefully speaking up for better translations of foreign plays. Martin Esslin, a British subject of German origin and author of books on both Brecht and on the Theatre of the Absurd, proved knowledgeable in three languages. An eager Austrian gentleman wanted to rectify all the other speakers' errors, which kept him asking for the floor at all times.

The easiest and wittiest speakers, Ned Sherrin, producer of *TWTWTW*, and David Frost, emcee of the show, did not bring to their allocutions some of the polished rhetoric of the French, whose most prominent representative was Robbe-Grillet, novelist and scenarist of *Last Year at Marienbad.* He found himself attracted, he said—in what is merely a seeming paradox—to the nonrealism or artifice of the film medium, but he also hoped to write plays.

What was striking in his speech, and in those of his compatriots, was that they were all rather indifferent to political commitment in the arts and that they found Brecht a definitely "conservative" influence in respect to aesthetic experiment and new forms of discovery in Existentialism. On the whole, the French, through disdain or discretion, were unusually reticent. The only exception was the Russian-born Arthur Adamov, "renegade" playwright of the Absurd, now emphatically leftist. Adamov, looking like a bedeviled monk, rose several times to praise Brecht (and O'Casey), with an occasional antagonistic reference to General de Gaulle.

The Americans were generally shy of considered thought or positive convictions. Jack Gelber, Arthur Kopit and the perpetrators of the Happening pleased the audience with a certain playful nonchalance, an easygoing anarchism. Alan Schneider's determined straightforwardness was no counterforce to this impression, nor could Edward Albee's platform reserve convince anyone that he was not entirely of an intuitional rather than of an intellectual disposition. Lillian Hellman effaced herself completely, proving how indomitable she is.

The conference adopted a resolution against all censorship and declared itself in favor of subsidized theatre. It also voted approval of Max Frisch's motion that the Rockefeller Foundation establish a bureau of qualified play translators.

The conference proved that under certain circumstances a large number of gifted and intelligent people can resemble a carload of fools. The intellectual import of the conference was nil, the social increment slight, the entertainment value considerable. The public saw a lot of well-known and presumably glamorous show folk at far less than their best (which probably consoled it), while I personally had a good time and tried to acquire a play from a playwright whom, as a critic, I had previously panned.

—*TA*, '63

THE ALCHEMIST
KING LEAR

In the production of old plays theatre folk are almost always concerned with the question of how to make their texts appear fresh. Are we to gather from this that they have grown stale? Hardly. What the producers want is a way to make the classics live as *plays,* plays to stir new audiences with the sense that the masterpieces are truly relevant to their particular and everchanging state of mind. The goal is not to resuscitate (the material is not dead) but to create.

This has been effectively done by Tyrone Guthrie with Ben Jonson's *The Alchemist* at the Old Vic and by Peter Brook with the Royal Shakespeare Company production of *King Lear.* Each play alternates with others on the respective institution's programs and each is a massive box-office hit.

Ben Jonson's bawdy farce is admired for its construction by students of the Elizabethan drama, and its theme is perennially apt: greed and the gullibility of the money minded. A pair of petty racketeers, assisted by their moll, set out to fleece a variety of characters by pretending that they possess the knowledge to turn base metal into gold.

What has kept Jonson's play alive all these years, besides the enduring contemporaneity of its motivations and the juicy roles it offers the actors, is its writing—full of meat, blood, guts, waste matter and vinegar, capped by Latin learning and Elizabethan double-talk—a Gargantuan dish.

Guthrie produces the play in modern dress and has translated the characters into presently familiar prototypes. Certain purists may quarrel with this procedure but this leads to futile debate. Guthrie's direction is comically resourceful, full of brio and high jinks—cold and crazy as the play itself. The byplay is incessant and the pace hectic. All this would be capital were it not for the fact that one's eyes are so wholly engaged in following the stage business that the only words one is sure one recognizes are such solecisms as "travelers' checks," "Lyons" (a London restaurant), "Buchmanism," "Einstein," "Haldane" and "Airwick"—words that Guthrie has introduced to make the play's allusions conform to the new framework. I caught only as much of Jonson's dialogue—by no means easy in itself—as I do language at the opera.

Cocteau once asked Sergei Diaghilev, his mentor, what that great impresario expected of him. "Astonish me," Diaghilev answered. Stagecraft cannot find a more brilliant summation. If Peter Brook's *Lear* could claim no further distinction, it would still be memorable because it astonishes. It astonishes by a magisterial simplification. It eschews all pageantry and, to a large extent, pathos. As Lear is stripped of all his goods and honor, so the production is stripped of pomp. It is a naked production.

The stage is bare. The lights are white. Apart from a minimum of coarse wooden props, two large brown squares of canvas stand isolated on either side of the stage. The backdrop is a chalky gray. In the storm scenes on the heath, squares of black material are lowered from the flies. There is no curtain. The actors enter while the houselights are still on, and these dim only as the action gets under way. At the end of each act, the playing continues for awhile after the houselights

have come up. Costumes look like leather, rough and brown. They are wholly appropriate in the impression they make of a barbaric plainness. The battle in the fifth act is indicated by the clangor of rattling shields: no contestant is seen fighting.

The actors speak with notable distinction. Every word strikes home so that the literal meaning is unmistakable: we know what Shakespeare wrote. The voices are strong; no one rants. Even "Blow, winds, and crack your cheeks! rage! blow," spoken loudly enough to be heard over the not-excessive din, is projected with a certain degree of sobriety.

Paul Scofield plays Lear with a stern, tight, thoughtful impassivity. He looks rather like the wood carving of a hard, peasant forester (slightly Russian!) . He might be compared to a somewhat withered but still sturdy tree. When he dies, he simply ceases to be; he subsides rather than expires. His passing is a period. His speech is deliberate, ringingly precise rather than sonorous or histrionically eloquent. There is no tearing of passion. The only one who cries heartbrokenly is Gloucester as he listens to his king berating humanity.

When Lear is reunited with Cordelia in that wonderful passage beginning "Come, let's away to prison. We two alone will sing like birds i' th' cage. When thou dost ask me blessing, I'll kneel down, And ask thee forgiveness. So we'll live, And pray, and sing, and tell old tales, and laugh as gilded butterflies...," Scoffeld is dignified, poised and explanatory, like a teacher soothing a possibly unnerved child.

All through Shakespeare's text Lear says such things as "I will not be mad" or "O that way madness lies, let me shun that"—and of course he goes mad. Repeatedly Lear also says the equivalent of "Let not woman's weapon, water-drops, stain my man's cheeks," or "You think I'll weep! No, I'll not weep." But we never feel in this production that Lear is ever in danger of either going mad or weeping. He is much too resolute and contained for such frailty or unseemliness.

It would be too easy to say that this refusal of sentiment bespeaks the influence of Brecht, though without Brecht such a presentation might never have come into being. We would rather say that this thoroughly coherent production is in tune with the intellectual and moral climate of our day. It is a reduction of *King Lear* to our size.

Shakespeare's *Lear* is one of the fiercest of all plays: a wild outcry against the human condition and the folly of all our posturing and self-importance. (The play is *not* about the wickedness of ungrateful children!) "Is man no more than this...such a poor, bare, forked animal?" Even the Book of Job hardly expresses more bitterness. "As flies to wanton boys, are we to th' gods: they kill us for their sport." "When we are born, we cry out that we are come to this great stage of fools."

All this we understand, as does Peter Brook. For our time is one in which, with no commanding faith, sensitive souls have begun to spew venom, to mock themselves as the dupes of creation, or to immolate themselves either in inanition or in sadism—for all of which artists have been unable to find any word other than "absurd."

The calm irony of Brecht is not intended as negation but as a purification of the spirit which might lead to the understanding required for sane action. But Shakespeare is not Brecht—nor calm. I do not believe *King Lear* was composed solely as a curse upon all the houses of the Renaissance (or modern) world. *King Lear* is Shakespeare's tortured espousal of the virtue of Love in a civilization given over and abasing itself to the idol of Power. Yes, he seems to be saying, life is cruelly hard and "...Men must endure/Their going hence even as their coming hither," but *"Ripeness is all."* "Ripeness," maturity, manhood, demand a brave acceptance, yea-saying fortitude—not collapse, not a gnashing of teeth nor black despair. Hope is not merely the looking forward to "better things"; it is the motion of life itself, suffered and enjoyed for its own sake.

But should my view of *King Lear* be mistaken it would not alter my interpretation of the new London production. The point is that Shakespeare's immense force, his overwhelming lyric might, the volcanic life that fires his every scene and speech are not to be conveyed in the reasoned, shriveled and bleached terms of Peter Brook's staging—impressive though they be. This "Beckett-like" *Lear* (the production and the play have been compared to *Endgame*) takes place in a realm too blank and airless even for the gesture of suicide. The world of Shakespeare's *Lear* is so rich in substance that one would be glad to dwell in it; we are rewarded for its agony by the fullness of its matter. Such a world may be full of horror; it is not *absurd*. And then, one does not attempt to describe the monumentality of the Himalayas by likening them to the Catskills!

Paul Scofield is a truly fine actor and his performance is consonant with his endowments, as it is altogether loyal to his director's plan. Irene Worth as Goneril and Alan Webb as Gloucester are vivid and individual in a cast almost no part of which is bad. After one has left the theatre one wishes to see the production again—a rare occurrence. Peter Brook is to be congratulated on a *Lear* made to the measure of our day and the circumstances of the modern theatre. For in its own right *King Lear,* as Charles Lamb said, "cannot be acted: the play is beyond all art." Still, in 1935 I saw it in Moscow in a production which Gordon Craig pronounced the best Shakespeare he had ever seen. So Charles Lamb may have been wrong after all.

—*NAT*, '63

DYLAN

Sidney Michael's play *Dylan* is a theatrical bestseller (Plymouth). It is smooth, literate, fashionably sophisticated, entertaining. One watches it unruffled by any of the problems it seems to suggest. It provides "a good evening in the theatre."

Its subject is the poet, Dylan Thomas, part of whose life and all of whose death has been amply publicized. The audience which sees the play knows his "story" much better than it does his poetry. Just as Irving Stone's *Lust for Life* made Van Gogh a famous painter in the United States, so Alec Guinness in *Dylan* may add to the fame of a poet already known to the public through several biographies and the obituaries of larger circulation magazines.

The play occupies itself chiefly with the poet's last days in America, the disastrous tour described in John Malcolm Brinnin's book. The play tells us that though he loved his wife and children, he was a bad husband and an impossible father, deceiving the one and neglecting the others. We see him meandering in self-destructive and irresponsible stupor through a series of public readings, to the head-shaking of thousands for whom a poet's "personality" is more fascinating than his work.

A play with such material might make its theme the drama of the creative man whose talent has begun to fail him and for whom in his own eyes there is nothing more to justify his existence. It might be a study of the poet's plight at a time when he can earn a living only by engaging in activities unrelated to his true function. It could be the depiction of a free (anarchic) spirit in a conformist community, a portrait of a great heart impaled on the gears of the industrial machine, or a psychological treatment of a soul astray in a world in which everyone has become less than half real and very little is worth respect.

A smattering of all these elements does emerge in Mr. Michael's play (this is what, apart from the acting, holds our attention): just enough for gossip, casual "philosophizing" or perfunctory commiseration. A recurring phrase in the play refers to Dylan's "rage." Ah yes, the poet is consumed with rage, it gnaws at his vitals, it makes his life a hell, it drives him to drink, it makes him rude, dissolute, disgusting, it kills him—and is supposed to break our hearts.

But this "rage" in the play is without content, a tag like the flowing tie, long hair, velvet coat and dirty fingernails of the bohemian artist of old.

Dylan recites a few lines of his verse and we hear about his writing of *Under Milk Wood*, but for purposes of any true understanding he remains a "colorful" but meaningless figure. We come away from the play knowing little more than facts we might have picked up at a cocktail party. We are not even impelled to examine the poetry written by this amazing derelict.

There is perhaps no cause for anyone to become "exercised" over this kind of writing in play or novel (*The Moon and Sixpence* was not much better) except that it reflects an audience unaware of the role of the artist in society and a common attitude which makes him a kind of sacred monster, a decorative gargoyle to shatter the monotony of our days, instead of the essential citizen who *through his work* gives consciousness and voice to the fundamental significance of our lives. What happens to the artist in society is happening to us. What he suffers is our pain, what discourages and debases him is what frustrates and diminishes us, just as his hopes and exaltations are ours. Plays like *Dylan*—often quite clever— remove us from both art and life.

Peter Glenville's production is technically expert and Kate Reid as Caitlin Thomas is solid and convincing. Alec Guinness, to whom the play's success is largely due, is exemplary in make-up, voice, speech (wonderfully Welsh in intonation), ease, assurance, and in conveying a sense of utter naturalness and moment-by-moment verisimilitude. There isn't a false note. Yet he cannot supply what the text lacks. His illustration is perfection itself—and a pleasure to observe. But there is no pain or true pathos in it; no single aspect of Dylan's character (he must have had one) is genuinely revealed: there are only traits admirably rendered. The mask is lifelike, the face nonexistent. This is craftsmanship par excellence, but it does not achieve what Lalvini called "serious acting" which for that great Italian actor meant passion and transfiguration, and for the rest of us creation—something which changes us in our inmost being.

—*NAT*, 17 Feb. '64

LITTLE EYOLF

Ibsen is usually thought of as a social critic, but his plays would have been far less enduring if he had been no more than that. They were also self-criticisms. His soul was the battleground of conflicting forces; he was his own grim judge.

An implacable individualist, he was the enemy of social hypocrisy. But the nineteenth century, having proclaimed the individual's inalienable rights, proceeded to shackle the individual in a new class structure which made the wealthy assume a mask of piety and the poor kowtow to the powerful. Ibsen's *Brand* denounces the Protestant compromise of the period which turned religion into a palliative, not to say a humbug. Ibsen admires the "all or nothing" demands of Brand, the harsh preacher, but shudders at his lack of compassion and the bitter consequences of his unyielding idealism. Peer Gynt is the imaginative, resourceful, self-made man, forever eager to get ahead and largely successful at doing so, who ends a betrayer of those closest to him, an empty vessel.

Dr. Stockman in *An Enemy of the People* learns that he must stand alone against the "compact majority" (which Ibsen the self-proclaimed democrat distrusted), and tell the truth, no matter whom it injures. In *The Wild Duck*, telling the truth wrecks a once peaceful home. The drive of reason and the destruction of illusion are means and ends which must be unflinchingly followed, but the results may be as damaging as the pursuit of evil. The unswerving individualist, he who forges the new world, nearly always, in Ibsen's plays, spends his last days isolated, in half-mad doubt and self-reproach.

Almost everything that has been argued against Ibsen—his bleakness, the rigidity of his logic, the constriction and coldness of his craft—was first decried in his own plays. Toward the end of his career he confessed that he was unable to reach the heights to which he had aspired and to which youth summoned him. He had been a self-suppressed romantic. His work, he believed, had a certain brutish bluntness because he had renounced too much, and particularly the yearnings of the heart.

Ibsen's plays are autobiographical in their inner meaning. The tension created by his subjective inspiration and the strict objectivity which he imposed on it give them a mysterious density of mood which preserves them. They do not resolve themselves in any simple ideological proof.

Much of what I have just said applies to *Little Eyolf*, which is being presented by Northwestern Productions (formed by graduates of the drama department of Northwestern University) at the Actors Playhouse. It is rarely done in New York because it is one of Ibsen's most austere plays, one in which we feel that he is trying to say more than his plot will allow. For the tension just mentioned may be defined in another way. Ibsen wanted his middle-class—realistic and functional—constructions to achieve the poetic grandeur of classic drama: he wanted his dwelling places to be monuments. Earth-bound by social and intellectual considerations (one had to be in tune with one's time) he was forever striving, as the last line of *Little Eyolf* has it (in anticipation of his next play, *The Master Builder*), "Upward—toward the peaks. Toward the stars. And toward the great silence."

What *Little Eyolf* literally tells us is that the intellectual as well as the artist of our day, for all his grand talk about "human responsibility," is often a self-centered prig. He marries for convenience—his work—and for sexual companionship. His wife devours him with a love that extends no further than his person. He grows ever less aware of his neighbors, his family, his society; his affections then tend toward the semi-incestuous. He cripples those closest to him; his negligence spells their death. He can save himself only by direct, unequivocal work required by the specific needs of his immediate community.

The flaw and fascination of *Little Eyolf* arise from the interweaving of so many of Ibsen's preoccupations, some of which are merely hinted at. Whether or not we agree with William Archer's estimate that the play is "among the greatest of Ibsen's achievements" (an opinion shared in large measure by Shaw), we cannot fail to be struck by the "something more" in the play's atmosphere. We breathe the very air of one of the Ibsen households—the place, the emotional pressures, the hidden thoughts, the unspoken words, the fate—which exercises a far greater spell than does the bare articulation of the play's structure or thesis.

It is just this substance of reality, this fabric of experience, which the players of Northwestern Productions are unable to create. This, I was going to say, is due to their youth, but it is not a matter of years. Physically the actors correspond entirely to the description of the characters in the printed text. They lack two things: the full technical training for such a play and, even more, the cultural "soil" which gives the European actor a ground wherein his personal knowledge of human relationships may mature sufficiently to express the lifeladen gravity of Ibsen's world. Still, despite their inadequacy as instruments for this task, the Northwestern actors have faithfully followed a director who understands the play so that its lineaments at least are made clear.

—*NAT*, 6 Apr. '64

DUTCHMAN
FUNNY GIRL

It is altogether likely that the folk who go down to the Cherry Lane Theatre to see the three one-act plays now being given there are witnesses to a signal event: the emergence of an outstanding dramatist—LeRoi Jones.

His is a turbulent talent. While turbulence is not always a sign of power or of valuable meaning, I have a hunch that LeRoi Jones's fire will burn ever higher and clearer if our theatre can furnish an adequate vessel to harbor his flame. We need it.

He is very angry. Anger alone may merely make a loud noise, confuse, sputter and die. For anger to burn to useful effect, it must be guided by an idea. With the "angry young men" of England one was not always certain of the source of dissatisfaction nor of its goal. With LeRoi Jones it is easy to say that the plight of the Negro ignited the initial rage—justification enough—and that the rage will not be appeased until there is no more black and white, no more color except as differences in hue and accent are part of the world's splendid spectacle. But there is more to his ferocity than a protest against the horrors of racism.

Dutchman, the first of Jones's plays to reach the professional stage, is a stylized account of a subway episode. A white girl picks up a young Negro who at first is rather embarrassed and later piqued by her advances. There is a perversity in her approach which finally provokes him to a hymn of hate. With lyrical obscenity he declares that murder is in his and every Negro's heart and were it to reach the point of action there would be less "singin' of the blues," less of that delightful folk music and hot jazz which beguile the white man's fancy, more calm in the Negro soul. Meanwhile, it is the black man who is murdered.

What we must not overlook in seeing the play is that, while this explosion of fury is its rhetorical and emotional climax, the crux of its significance resides in the depiction of the white girl whose relevance to the play's situation does not lie in her whiteness but in her representative value as a token of our civilization. She is our neurosis. Not a neurosis in regard to the Negro, but the absolute neurosis of American society.

She is "hep": she has heard about everything, understands and feels nothing. She twitches, jangles, jitters with a thin but inexhaustible energy, propelled by the vibrations from millions of ads, television quiz programs, newspaper columns, intellectual jargon culled from countless digests, panel discussions, illustrated summaries, smatterings of gossip on every conceivable subject (respectable and illicit), epithets, wisecracks, formulas, slogans, cynicisms, cures and solutions.

She is the most "informed" person in the world and the most ignorant. (The information feeds the ignorance.) She is the bubbling, boiling garbage cauldron newly produced by our progress. She is a calculating machine gone berserk; she is the real killer. What she destroys is not men of a certain race but mankind. She is the compendium in little of the universal mess.

If *Dutchman* (a title I don't understand) has a fault, it is its completeness. Its ending is somewhat too pat, too pointed in its symbolism. If one has caught the drift of the play's meaning before its final moment, the ending is supererogatory; if one has failed to do so, it is probably useless.

Dutchman is very well played by Jennifer West and Robert Hooks.

Broadway scuttlebutt has it that $750,000 was spent on the new musical *Funny Girl* (Winter Garden). For all the value in the show the producers would have been well advised to permit its star, Barbra Streisand, to come out and sing some songs on the bare stage—but not the songs she now sings, none of which are any good.

Though Sydney Chaplin has greatly improved since he made his first appearance in new York, and Jean Stapleton and Kay Medford are funny in the few moments they are vouchsafed, there is really nothing to *Funny Girl* but Barbra Streisand. The book if it exists, is phony; there is no dancing to speak of and the music is hogwash, though some of Bob Merrill's lyrics are not bad.

For those who remember Fanny Brice—the show is presumably her "story"—the connection between that great lady, a "funny girl" who at times came close to being a tragedienne, and the star of the present is a little unfortunate. I shall refrain from comparisons because I do not wish to take this occasion to write an appreciation of Fanny Brice, but only to speak of Miss Streisand who is a young woman of unmistakable gifts.

She was brilliantly hilarious in *I Can Get It For You Wholesale*. She manifests new qualities in her present vehicle. She has rhythm—although the rhythm in her numbers now is forced because

supplied by her rather than by the composer; she knows how to color the words and phrases of her songs so as to give each of them their specific emotional quality. She has a disarming directness and a simplicity. Very little is "put on," except where her playfulness is a comic comment, usually a mockery of pretension, plus an apology for having so little to be pretentious about. The nakedness, the flat plainness of the world about her, its fundamental lack of glamour, and her refusal or inability to rise above it—though because she is so talented she feels it more than she shows any consciousness of doing—constitute the essence of her appeal, her pathos. What her acting (even more her singing) says is: "I am a woman; I have imagination. I have spirit, humor, keen common sense, a desire to live a full, vivid life; but I dwell in a place and at a time which really deny and cheapen most of these attributes. Therefore I clown, and you who applaud me so rapturously do so because you sense what I am suppressing—our mutual bereavement from beauty."

—*NAT*, 13 Apr. '64

THE LOWER DEPTHS

Having seen Gorky's *The Lower Depths* in at least ten productions—American, Russian, English, French, German and Japanese—I could not help thinking as I watched the one now being given by the APA at the Phoenix about Max Beerbohm's review of the play when it was first done in London.

The "incomparable Max" found it repellent. It was grubby naturalism, something no person of refined sensibility could abide. We remember artists by their virtues, not their failings: Beerbohm was hopelessly mistaken. *The Lower Depths* is a noble play. It transcends its grime more triumphantly than does Genet.

Gorky was intimately acquainted with the low life of his time. (The play's première took place in Moscow in 1902.) He "hit the road" early in his life; so he really knew the impoverished wanderers, the derelicts, the forgotten men, the prostitutes, the human debris which proliferated in old Russia to an ignominious degree. The use of the play's particular personnel—the denizens of a flop house—was no literary choice on Gorky's part.

The picture is savagely painful. Yet, despite the abject nature of the characters, their cruelty and removal from any possibility of alleviation, one is made to feel kin to them, they become all mankind. This is a depiction of humanity by a writer who was immersed in it, one who succeeded despite every wound and humiliation to retain his faith in it, to struggle on its behalf.

Gorky suffered the ache of existence a hundred times more intensely than any of the dramatists of the absurd (ridden chiefly by a sense of emptiness, life having lost its savor, even its bitterness) and yet his response is affirmative, not from pleasure but from a true contact with experience. Gorky was not "civilized" enough to be world-weary. He is profoundly Russian with the encompassing manliness of Gogol, Dostoyevsky, Tolstoy, Chekhov—all of whom for our time must be regarded, apart from ephemeral politics, as *revolutionary*.

Some may sneer at such key lines as "people live in the hope of something better" and may consider the thief's drunken exaltation sentimental when he cries out "Man—is truth." But look closely at each of the play's defeated persons: the dispossessed nobleman who says, "It seems to me that all my life I've done nothing but change clothes"; at Vaska who became a thief because from childhood he was called one; at the locksmith, crabbed and ugly because his ethic extends no further than his lousy job; at the unimaginative cap maker, sunk, except when in his cups, in the draining dullness of commonplace facts; at the cringing religiosity of the landlord or the sharp common sense of the woman who sells meat dumplings; at the whore who conjures up a past from cheap French novels; at the alcoholic actor, cut off from the stage and no longer able to remember lines from his favorite plays; at the

Mohammedan Tartar sustained and dignified by a fundamental morality. Do not these figures and the others including the canny "pilgrim" Luka, compose a canvas bodying forth a complete world?

All the values of this giant drama cannot be realized by an inspired college performance, which is what the APA gives at the Phoenix. Yet for all those who have never seen or who have forgotten the play I do not hesitate to recommend the production.

—*NAT*, 20 Apr. '64

WHERE ARE THE NEW PLAYWRIGHTS?

The outcry, "Where are our new playwrights?", frequently heard in the last five or ten years, seems to have been uttered with particular intensity during the theatre season that is now drawing to a close. Is it justified?

Insofar as it implies that virtually no fresh writing talent has been emerging in our theatre, it can be refuted by a listing that includes Jack Richardson (*The Prodigal*), William Snyder (*The Days and Nights of Beebee Fenstermaker*), William Hanley (*Mrs. Dally Has a Lover*), Murray Schisgal (*The Typists* and *The Tiger*), David Rayfiel (*P.S. 193*), Hugh Wheeler (*Big Fish, Little Fish*), Lorraine Hansberry (*A Raisin in the Sun*), Jack Gelber (*The Connection*), Lewis John Carlino (*Cages*), Frank Gilroy (*Who'll Save the Plowboy?*), Arthur Kopit (*Oh Dad, Poor Dad*), J.P. Donleavy (*The Ginger Man*), Herb Gardner (*A Thousand Clowns*), Sidney Michaels (*Dylan*). And because he has written one smash hit in addition to some excellent one-acters, is Edward Albee, at the age of 36, a "veteran" playwright?

Yet such evidence somehow does not convince us, nor relieve our sense of frustration about the state of American playwriting. Can these men compare to the writers of the twenties and thirties and forties—O'Neill, Sherwood Anderson, Rice, Barry, Behrman, George Kelly, Sidney

Howard, Odets, Hellman, Kingsley, Williams, Miller, Inge—almost all with a sustained, substantial body of work produced over a period of years? Isn't it a fact that there just aren't the playwrights there used to be?

There probably aren't—but for reasons that in no way negate the real talent or potential of the new writers I have named. The reasons have to do with the changed state of the theatre itself. The number of plays presented on Broadway during the period of 1919-1929 mounted to an average of 200 a season. At present the number has been reduced to about 70.

It is difficult for new playwrights to look forward to a prolonged career in the theatre where the conditions of theatrical productions are inimical to the staging of *many* plays. To put this paradoxically, let us say that to have more good plays, more bad plays must be produced.

Theatrical production today is at least ten times more costly than it was in our "golden age." There were many more regularly active producers then than at present. Each of those producers presented two or more plays every season. A failure was neither a disgrace nor a terrifying financial disaster. Operating costs were so low that profits might be declared within three or four weeks after a play's opening. It was no alarming risk to invest $5,000 or $10,000 in a possibly imperfect play by either a new or a well-known playwright. Arthur Hopkins, a pioneer in the production of sound drama in the twenties, pointed out that he was satisfied if only one of his four seasonal offerings proved a hit; if two of them did, he considered it a bonanza year.

A theatre which depends entirely on the production of immediate smash hits is doomed. The immediate cause for concern over the fate of new playwrights then is related to the defects in the internal structure of our theatre which, without exaggeration, may be described as anarchy. Where there is a free-for-all competition for separate benefits for all the supposedly collaborating constituents (playwrights, actors, directors, designers, agents, real-estate interests), there can be no

security for anyone. The theatre, once a profession, ceases to preserve that status as a business.

Such a theatre does not encourage, let alone support, the new playwright either morally or monetarily. Consider some of the plays in my foregoing list. Many of them are rarely cited as evidence of fresh talent because, having been produced off Broadway or not having been conspicuously successful, they are now held to be negligible and are therefore quickly forgotten. Playgoers, even reviewers, rarely sustain their authors with renewed mention or managers with option money on future work.

A large number of these playwrights and their plays begin obscurely and remain in obscurity because we pay scant attention to that which does not strike us at first flash as complete achievement. Absolute success is the goal.

A large number of these playwrights and their plays begin obscurely and remain in obscurity because we pay scant attention to that which does not strike us at first flash as complete achievement. Absolute success is the goal.

A single play of promise even a single outstanding play, is not the same as a body of dramatic work. We are witnesses to a kind of disappearing act: now we see the new playwright, now he is gone. We tend to forget his presence was once real. The more or less bright beginnings these plays and playwrights bespeak do not assure continuous growth or mature development. The implications of Van Wyck Brooks' symbolic statement that America is the land of first acts become ominous in the context of our theatre. In part, we, the audience, as well as the theatrical profession itself are to blame. We hail the new playwright for his "novelty"! To score a smash, to become the talk of the town, the subject of all interviews the star of all panels and symposia, the cynosure at all parties rattles the successful neophyte and makes the wear and tear of continuous effort required for progress as a writer discouraging. It used to be commonplace to mock Hollywood for its hysterical fabrication of "genius" with every emerging personality. But New York is hardly better.

What happens to the new playwright in such an atmosphere? His first failure discourages him and he vanishes. If his first play succeeds but is followed by several failures, he retires to other fields, perhaps television or movies, which pay more, demand less and induce far less anguish. The nub of the problem is not an absence of playwrights but the state of the theatre itself.

Since we have all come to recognize the sorry confusion which defeats our hopes in the future health of our theatre and to look on it as being in a state of endemic crisis, certain counterforces intended to repair the damaged edifice have begun to operate. This is particularly true in regard to writing for the theatre.

The universities are becoming ever more aware of the services they may perform in this respect. They are doing this not only through courses on the subject but more concretely through productions of the best plays, ancient and modern, foreign and American, as well as scripts by fledgling dramatists.

The Actors Studio Playwrights Unit is now beginning to show results in the shape of various productions on and off Broadway. "Theatre 64" (Richard Barr, Clinton Wilder, Edward Albee) has staged a series of special performances of plays by promising new writers. A group calling itself the American Place Theater, sponsored by Saint Clement's Episcopal Church in New York, has plans for readings of the work of new playwrights and for the full production of *The Old Glory*, a triptych of one-act plays by one of America's foremost poets, Robert Lowell. All over town similar enterprises are being organized.

For the past 14 years, the New Dramatists Committee has done a remarkable job in fostering new playwrights. Among these we find such names as Robert Anderson, Arnold Schulman, Michael Stewart, Joseph Hayes, William Inge, Paddy Chayefsky, William Gibson, Sidney Michaels, Horton Foote. There are 37 playwright members now associated with the New Dramatists Committee. Readings by professional actors are set up, directors are called in for practical advice and criticism in areas with which the new dramatist may be unfamiliar. Run-through performances of untested scripts are given for invited audiences. Permission is obtained for the dramatist members to attend rehearsals of professional productions. An ambiance of fraternal discussion of both general and individual problems is created.

Various foundations (notably Ford and Rockefeller) have of late given serious attention to the needs of the theatre by grants to organizations in and out of New York, to university theatre departments, to individual playwrights, to directors for community theatre ventures.

Still another recent development in theatrical affairs furnishes cause for hope. The growing decentralization of our theatre, the spread of permanent, sometimes endowed, groups all over the country—in Minneapolis, Seattle, Memphis, Houston, San Francisco, Oklahoma City, Milwaukee, Washington, Dallas and New York— is of inestimable value.

All this is certainly helpful but it would be simpleminded to believe that encouraging advice, instruction and monetary assistance by themselves will bring about a flowering of new dramatic writing. While such devices constitute adjuncts to cultural activity, they do not provide dramatic inspiration! Let us agree for the moment that aside from the "accident" of individual genius—for which there is presumably no accounting—an age of splendid drama is the consequence of a series of complex factors. They form part of a "mystery" which patient inquiry may perhaps unravel.

These new organizations should serve to widen our theatre's scope. Broadway has no practical use for most of the world's dramatic masterpieces. A choice of classic plays—not limited to Shakespeare—will become the order of the day on the stages of the new organizations.

Such plays may spur the imaginations of young dramatists because the essential nature of a play which has endured the test of time is its concentration on what is basic and permanent in our lives. It reminds us forcibly of first principles. The importance of the classics as a contemporary contribution to the arts was made brilliantly cogent by André Malraux when he said, "During periods where all previous works are disdained, genius lapses, no man can build on a void, and a civilization that breaks with the styles at its disposal soon finds itself empty-handed."

The classics will also educate a wide audience hitherto unacquainted with them and therefore susceptible to their power. For among the things our theatre suffers from is the lack of an unspoiled audience, that is, an audience free from the poisonous pressures of the hothouse atmosphere of the show market. The audience which will come into being with the rise of the new theatres will in time become committed to them.

Here we approach the heart of our problem. For who says "audience" (or "public") must think of that entity of which they—audience or public—form a part. The theatre's incentive, its reason for existence, derives from the society from the society it serves.

When a society becomes conscious of itself—its needs, aspirations, enthusiasms, beliefs and hardships—the theatre is born. That is why the theatre as an organized institution, being a collective affair, usually develops later than the other arts.

Let us consider American instances. When our civilization was undergoing its early construction (up to 1888, let us say), there was comparatively little native drama. Our typical theatre consisted in great measure of minstrel shows, melodramas and "musicals" staged in saloons and river boats, together with importations from abroad in the wake of foreign—mostly European—stars.

In the late 19th century and in the early years of the 20th, there were modest burgeonings in the plays of James A. Herne, Clyde Fitch, William Vaughn Moody, Percy Mackaye, Langdon Mitchell, Edward Sheldon. (A mid-century piece, important for its time, was *Uncle Tom's Cabin*.)

American drama with any claim to a merit comparable to that of our better literature did not appear—following some "underground" manifestations in Provincetown, Greenwich Village and the lower East Side—until 1920, with O'Neill's first full-length play, *Beyond the Horizon*.

Why this emergence of an American "school" of dramatists at that particular time? With the settling of our land, with confirmed power and self-confidence, we began to look at ourselves with the objectivity which induces both calm and disquiet. Realistic novels were published, notably those of Frank Norris and Theodore Dreiser, beginning a tradition carried on by Sinclair Lewis, John Dos Passos and many others.

With our participation in the First World War and the resultant intimate contact with Europe, the development of new cultural vehicles, the hectic flush of affluence and greater world prestige, we began to divest ourselves of certain past inhibitions. We rejoiced in our success while at the same time we grew more self-critical. We felt we might look forward to a "Renaissance" (indeed, we claimed it was here), yet we suspected that, while our bodies glowed with well-being, our souls were starving. In the theatre, we had the Ziegfeld Follies on the one hand and Eugene O'Neill on the other, George Gershwin's musicals and The Theater Guild. We had come of age. The theatre was saying something.

The depression of the thirties, which struck our country's economy a heavy blow, also affected the arts. The theatre was severely damaged but did not die. In a sense it was stimulated. It brought us the play of social challenge which had, in its sounds of protest, more hopeful rhapsody than denunciation.

Odets awakened. Irwin Shaw, John Steinbeck, William Saroyan and men of the previous generation—Elmer Rice, Robert E. Sherwood, S. N. Behrman—wrote plays which sounded notes largely unfamiliar in earlier American writing for the theatre. The Federal Theater Project, with its Living Newspapers, and such organizations as The Group Theater and The Theater Union, contributed much to the liveliness of our stage. Again the theatre was saying something.

The end of the Second World War brought a reaction against ordinary social or political panaceas. Critical challenge in drama took on a more personal tone. From Arthur Miller, who extended some of the lines traced in the plays of the thirties, through Tennessee Williams who, after the nostalgic melancholia of *The Glass Menagerie* added a certain sexual stress to the social meaning of his plays, dramatists like William Inge began to examine our social environment under the guidance of Freudian doctrine. Our theatre of the forties was still saying something.

The fifties—the period of Eisenhower "normalcy" and McCarthy frightfulness—made conformism the bugaboo of thoughtful folk. There seemed to be no escape except inward—toward an embattled privacy. The refuge of drugs in Jack Gelber's *The Connection* was more symbolic than factual. The lone individual, bereft of any objective ideal of sense of kinship with the mass of his fellow men—engaged in "business as usual"—could make contact with society only by allowing himself to be killed by it, as in the macabre comedy of Edward Albee's *The Zoo Story*.

Only when such preoccupations grip society, only when there is an irrepressible urge within a community—whether it be one of exultation, anger, religious zeal, a desire to remedy an injustice or to celebrate a great deed—is significant drama written. There must be some positive passion, moral principle or triumphant revelation to express.

Shaw, who once said he would destroy all his dramatic work if it had no "journalistic" relevance—that is, application to the preoccupations of the day—could have justified this pronouncement with the examples of the timeless *St. Joan* and the semi-symbolic *Heartbreak House* as much as with any of his earlier and more specifically social plays such as *Widower's Houses* or the later *Apple Cart* and *Too True to Be Good*.

If we ask ourselves, "Where are our new playwrights?" we cannot answer unless we also ask ourselves what we believe, what we are ready to affirm, what deeply in pleasure or pain we truly feel. A stultified society, one that is intimidated, frustrated, uncertain, complacent, conformist without recognizing that such is its condition, cannot produce living drama.

A number of the younger playwrights, however, are imbued with some of the fire needed to rouse us from our lethargy. We are not living in a dull, static period; we are merely evading its challenge. We are, in fact, living in a time of extraordinary, even *revolutionary*, change. The position of the United States in relation to the rest of the world is no longer exactly what it was even 10 years ago. Europe and South America view us in a new perspective, Asia is being transformed, Africa seethes; and we are all faced with a shocking discrepancy between our personal spiritual needs and the ever-increasing mechanization of modern society. We are on the verge of "thinking the unthinkable." All this must inevitably catch up with us not only on a political level but indirectly on a personal one.

Plays do not have to deal literally with these historical phenomena, but they must willy-nilly be affected by them in various subtle ways. English society at the height of the industrial revolution from 1780 to 1890 hardly produced any significant drama but began to do so when the Victorian Era entered its decline, just as more recently the English theatre has taken on a new complexion with the emergence of certain anti-Establishment forces in high places.

If our younger dramatists manage to overcome the disillusionment that followed the extravagant hopes of the thirties and the forties—which led to a retreat or nihilism in the fifties—and if, further, the new forces in our theatre begin to widen the channels of expression so that the Broadway impedimenta are removed, it may not be too "innocent" to suggest that the doldrums of which many of us complain will be dispelled in the future. It will not be necessary, in other words, to ask, "Where are our new playwrights?" We shall be thoroughly aware of them.

—NYTM, 7 June '64

KING LEAR FROM LONDON

The Peter Brook-Paul Scofield production of *King Lear* being presented for a limited engagement at the New York State Theatre at Lincoln Center was a revelation to London and was hailed as an epoch-making stage experience on the Continent. In Moscow, and more particularly in some of the East European countries, it exercised an extraordinarily *emotional* impact. Yet in New York, though the first- and second-night audiences applauded the performance to the echo, a considerable body of opinion described this as a *Lear* without a tear. Expressions of disappointment, though guarded, were not uncommon.

From London I wrote: "If Peter Brook's *Lear* could claim no further distinction it would still be memorable because it astonishes. It astonishes by a magisterial simplification. It eschews all pageantry and, to a large extent, pathos. As Lear is stripped of all his goods and honor, so the production is stripped of pomp....Scofield plays Lear with stern, tight, thoughtful impassivity....We would say that this thoroughly coherent production is in tune with the intellectual climate of our day. It is a reduction of *King Lear* to our size....After one has left the theatre one wishes to see the production again...."

I have seen it again and, to my surprise, I am now inclined to "defend" it rather than to find fault, though my basic criticism remains unchanged.

The New York State Theatre—designed primarily for ballet and musical shows—is much too large for drama. I had specified in my earlier review, "The actors speak with notable clarity....Every word strikes home." At the New York State Theatre anyone seated in the middle or the rear of the house or on the extreme sides may find the actors unintelligible. Thus the actors are obliged to speak with a falsifying deliberateness. But this hardly explains the partially dissident reaction.

If the complaint against the production is its coldness or that it is unmoving, Peter Brook might justifiably reply that he intended it to be so. Why should the play satisfy our conventional anticipation? In general we take for granted that we know what plays by Shakespeare ought to look and sound like; and most of the time we are wrong.

Lear is not about the ingratitude of children. Were it so, it would be over by the middle of the second act. If I were challenged to name the key line offering a clue to *Lear*'s meaning, I would choose Lear's "They told me I was everything. 'Tis a lie. I am not ague-proof." Lear is a primitive, a passionate barbarian who naively believes that since he is a *king*, he has power even when he forfeits the trappings of power. Goneril says of him that he would still "manage those authorities he hath given away!" The Fool admonishes: "Thou should not have been old till hadst been wise."

Wisdom consists in knowing, to cite Goethe, that "against the superiority of another there exists no weapon or remedy save that of love." Only through love can we achieve that "ripeness" which teaches that "men must endure their going hence, even as their coming hither."

A philosophic and (indirectly) sociological extension of the play's basic premise has been given by the Polish critic Jan Kott whose essay on *Lear* guided Brook's production. "King Lear," Kott tells us, "derides the promised heaven on earth as well as the heaven promised after death, the Christian as well as the secular vindication of life, the religious cosmogony and historical rationalism, the gods and the benevolent nature of man created in the image of God. In *King Lear* both orders of value crumble: that of the Middle Ages and that of the Renaissance. When this gigantic 'farce' is over, nothing remains but the empty and blood-soaked earth—that earth which after the storm is left with no more than stones, with a King, a Fool, a Blind Man and a Lunatic to engage in bitter discourse."

Kott calls his essay, "King Lear, or, in other words, Endgame." In content and sentiment

Shakespeare is assimilated with Samuel Beckett! *King Lear*, according to this interpretation, is not so much a tragedy as an epic grotesquerie, the first and greatest of the *absurd* plays.

Borrowing certain technical devices from Brecht (for instance in the use of white light even for night scenes), Brook has sought to accomplish two things: to rid the production of the romantic rhetoric or rant associated with productions of Shakespeare, and to articulate *Lear*'s text and action in the starkest manner possible so that the play's "nihilism" becomes unmistakable. He has succeeded, and much credit is due him for it.

My main criticism of the Brook interpretation was and is that Shakespeare's pessimism is by no means the counterpart of Beckett's. Their styles, hence their content, are at opposite poles. The range of feeling in Shakespeare, the richness of intellectual and emotional substance from which his negations spring, make his world majestic and affirmative even in its imprecations and rejection of life. Shakespeare's world, however deprived of "solace," is one worth living and suffering in; Beckett's is not worth a damn.

Scofield follows Brook loyally and lends the production some of his own innate nobility, a lithic simplicity and an unforced inwardness which compensate in considerable measure for the reduction of Lear's dimension planned in the production. And Irene Worth's Goneril is this Lear's most impressive adversary.

—NAT, 8 June '64

A CRITIC'S CREDO

"Criticism is, has been and eternally will be as bad as it possibly can be." Thus spake George Bernard Shaw, the best theatre critic in the English language in at least the past hundred years. What he meant was that critics will never satisfy everyone concerned, that they will always make horrendous "mistakes," that they are bound occasionally to cause damage, and that the degree of

their benefactions will always fall under the shadow of serious doubt.

What is a critic anyway? For the reader of the daily newspaper he is one who issues bulletins in the manner of a consumers' report. He is a sort of advance man, a freeloading publicity agent charged with the duty of instructing the prospective theatergoer as to what he should or should not buy. He is to tell his readers in no uncertain terms, "I like it" or "I don't like it."

If the reader were as careful in his perusal of printed matter as he is admonished to be about his diet, he would realize that in most cases the inference contained in the declaration "I like it" is of little value, in fact, is nearly meaningless. All three words are vague!

First: who is the "I" that speaks? Why should his assertion carry any particular weight? For him to exercise any decisive influence over me, should I not take the measure of the man, learn something of his intrinsic qualifications, his human disposition, his beliefs, his personal complexion? There are critics whose most emphatic encomia fill me with misgivings.

Second: what does the critic mean by the word "like"? In what way does he like it? I like pretty girls and I do not particularly "like" Samuel Beckett's work; yet I do not rush to a show which boasts a cast of pretty girls (I can meet them elsewhere) and I hope never to miss a Beckett play.

Above all: what is the "it" which the critic likes or dislikes? I like candy and I like meat, but before consuming either I should be able to distinguish between the two. The primary obligation of the critic is *to define* the character of the object he is called upon to judge. The definition itself may constitute a judgment, but insofar as they are distinct from each other the definition should precede the judgment. It is perfectly proper to rave about *Barefoot in the Park* as candy, and I can well understand the critic who damns Wedekind's *The Awakening of Spring*, but I can have little respect for him if he does not recognize that it is meat. It is certainly true that one man's meat is another man's poison, but the manner and reason for the choice may characterize the man.

To put what I have said another way: the reviewer whose reaction to a play is contained in some such ejaculations as "electrifying," "inspired," "a thunderbolt," "a mighty work," "a dismal bore," may in each instance be right, but his being right does not by itself make him a critic. For these epithets only indicate effects: pleasure or displeasure. The true critic is concerned with causes, with the composition of human, social, formal substances which have produced the effect. Strictly speaking, it is not even necessary that the critic name the effect; it is imperative that he take into account the sources from which it springs. In doing this the critic is faithful to the work he treats of, while at the same time he affords the reader some idea of what manner of man the critic himself is—which is a crucial consideration.

In estimating Shaw as a critic it does not upset me that he was captious about Wilde's *The Importance of Being Earnest*—he was wrong—and that he was much more receptive to the same author's *An Ideal Husband*, a play for which I have less regard. In both cases he said things of great interest and moment; I am more impressed by him in my disagreement than I am by the critic who pronounces *Any Wednesday* a "wow"—a statement which brooks no denial.

Theatre having become a luxury commodity with us, the person in quest of entertainment demands instantaneous guidance, and the daily critic is there to supply it with the necessary dispatch. His columns tend to make the pronouncement of opinion a substitute for criticism, so that very few of his readers have any idea of what criticism really is.

Newspaper editors are not especially interested in the theatre. Their views are generally similar to that of the ordinary playgoer. There is, thus, little inquiry into the qualifications of the person who is to occupy the post of theatre critic. If he is a competent journalist, is not so eccentric

in his tastes that his recommendations are likely to disappoint or offend readers, the editor is satisfied. If, in addition, the critic can wisecrack and shape his opinions into formulas as efficient as an advertising slogan, the editor is delighted. What concerns him is circulation.

The daily critic is actually responsible to no one but his newspaper. In the context of our present theatre situation the critics of at least three or four of our dailies (the columns themselves even more than the people who write them) exercise far more power than anyone desires them to—power, that is, which affects sales. The critic may himself be embarrassed by the commercial influence he exerts. He will even go so far on occasion as to disclaim that he is a critic, protesting that he is simply a reviewer, that his word is hardly more important than the next fellow's. After all, as has often been remarked, he is usually constrained to write his review immediately after the performance in less than an hour. While such defenses are largely sincere, they contain some unconscious hypocrisy. The fact remains that most of the daily reviewers mistake their opinions for criticism. They are as much in the dark on the subject as their readers.

Criticism, to paraphrase Anatole France, is the adventure of a soul (or a mind) among presumed works of art. Just as the artist seeks to communicate his experience of life through the use of its raw materials and the specific means of his art, so the critic, confronting the resultant creation, sheds a new light on it, enhances our understanding of it, and finally ends by making his own sense of life significant to his readers. At best, the critic is an artist whose point of departure is another artist's work. If he is a truly fine critic, he will make his reader something of an artist as well. It is not essential that he also make him a customer!

Let us agree that the daily reviewer is rarely a critic of this kind because, for one thing, he has no time to be. One notices, however, that he infrequently has more to say about a play after a week's reflection than he said immediately after the performance. Some reviewers do not even desire more time. They trust that the rush from playhouse to typewriter will furnish them with the impetus to convey hot-off-the-griddle reaction.

For my part, I often do not know what I really think about a play as I leave the performance. Momentary satisfactions and immediate irritations frequently warp my judgment. My thoughts and feeling become clear to me only when I read what I have written! And then, I must confess, I sometimes alter my view, in the sense that I see plays—as I do people—in many different perspectives according to time and circumstance. The critic ought to proclaim the right to change his mind, just as an art work itself changes even for its own creator. Our relation to art ought not be static; it is a very human business.

To be candid, however, let us assert that most daily reviewers are not critics because they are not richly enough endowed with sensibility, thoughtfulness, personality, knowledge of art and life or literary skill to hold our attention for much longer than it takes to read their reviews.

It should not surprise us that great theatre critics—Lessing, Hazlitt, Lewes, Shaw—and even lesser ones of the same line are rarely employed as daily reviewers because men of this rank have prejudices about which they are as explicit as possible—prejudices, moreover, which are rarely those of the casual reader. And one of the authentic critic's main purposes is to enunciate or construct an attitude toward life—if you will, a "philosophy"—and to make it as cogently relevant as possible. This must necessarily scare a newspaper editor whose publication is designed to please "everybody," that is, from 400,000 to a million readers daily.

Criticism can never be wholly objective—though the critic should keep the "object" well in view—but our basic complaint is not that certain daily reviewers are too subjective but that too often they are themselves such puny subjects.

Critics of the mass-circulation weeklies are usually men who write in the vein of the daily reviewer except in that they employ a more specialized or more "pointed" vocabulary. The men who write for the smaller (usually liberal) weeklies aim to fulfill the requirements of true criticism, though too often—as sometimes in the case of George Jean Nathan—they believe they will attain this goal by defiantly reversing the daily reviewers' coin. To thumb one's nose at Broadway values is not in itself an artistic gesture. Still there is a value in upsetting settled and stupid habits of mind.

In the monthlies and the scholarly quarterlies, criticism generally becomes aesthetic debate or exposition, frequently valuable instruments in criticism. (Aristotle's *Poetics* is the classic model for this sort of criticism.) Often this proves to be drama, rather than theatre, criticism. It is necessary to make the distinction because criticism of drama is a branch of literary criticism (though to be sure drama, like poetry and the novel, has its own laws), while the theatre critic, who must be thoroughly aware of literary values, looks upon drama as it historically came into being—as a part of, but not the whole of, the theatre, which is an art in itself. There are men of sound literary judgment who are unattuned to the theatre, just as there are cultivated folk who have little real feeling for music or the visual media. One has only to compare Max Beerbohm's essay on Duse with Shaw's corresponding piece to become aware of the difference between a brilliant commentator on the drama and a complete theatre critic.

In the introduction to my earlier collected volume of theatre reviews and essays, *Lies Like Truth* (Macmillan, 1958), I said: "My notices in the weeklies tended to be milder than those I wrote for the monthly, and I suspect that I should be more careful to be kind if I wrote for a daily."

One may well ask how this statement can be reconciled with "honesty" and high standards. "My years of work as a producer and as a director," I went on to say, "taught me many lessons about snap judgments and the dangers of a too proud or rigid dogmatism....I would conduct myself in criticism...with due regard for immediate contingencies without ever losing sight of the larger issues and aims. Do not, I tell myself, squash the small deeds of the theatre's workers, trials and errors with an Absolute."

Can a person professionally engaged in the theatre also be a reliable critic? The simplest answer is to cite—I have already indirectly done so above—the names of some of the best critics of the past who have been craftsmen and critics in their respective artistic areas—a list I might extend further to include poets, musicians and painters. But I shall once again call upon Shaw to speak for me: "I do my best to be partial, to hit out at remediable abuses rather than at accidental shortcomings, and at strong and responsible rather than at weak and helpless ones....A man is either a critic or not a critic....He cannot help himself."

I shall go further. The fact that I am engaged in active stage work does not render me either timid and indulgent or resentful, malicious and vindictive. It makes me scrupulous and responsible. I am convinced that a critic of contemporary effort owes it to his job to be responsible to everyone in the theatre: the audience, to begin with, as well as to the dramatists, actors, directors, designers. In doing this he becomes responsible to the Theatre as a whole.

George Jean Nathan once cavalierly said that he did not care if every box office in the country closed. I do care. For the closing of the box office bespeaks closing of the theatre, and this would mean that we would end by being more culturally maimed than we are with the theatre in its present deplorable state. There can be no "masterpieces" where there is no production, no routine theatre activity. Even in Elizabethan times, without a box office, no theatre; without a theatre (and inevitably many bad plays), no Shakespeare to write for it.

I would encourage playgoing. (Do not lift your brows too high; it makes you look idiotic.) I would encourage it not by rave reviews of mediocre plays, not by discovering "genius" in every promising talent, but by being wholly committed to saying, with due regard to all the complexity of the elements involved, what I feel at each theatrical occasion I am called on to attend. Such treatment, which arises from a devotion to talent howsoever modest, will arouse interest in the theatre. Making extravagant claims for entertainment which one knows will prove remunerative, with or without critical ballyhoo, depresses such interest as much as does the neglect of promising, but not yet wholly ripe, efforts. I regard the writer to whom the practical economic, social and professional aspects of the theatre are totally alien as at best a curator of the drama, not as a true critic.

As to my own "philosophy" of life and the theatre: it must become apparent with the continuity of my progress as man and critic. It is for that rather than for my incidental recommendations—when I take the trouble to make them—that I write. Just as opinions, yours are as good as mine.

—*NAT*, 14 Sept. '64

A CRITIC'S CREDO (II)

Recently I was introduced to a gentleman as a person about to stage a new play. "What do you think of it?" I was asked. "It's a good play," I answered. "Ah, I notice you are careful not to say it's *great*," he remarked.

I then explained that in the history of the theatre from Aeschylus to Axelrod there were probably less than a hundred plays I would call indisputably great. Not all of Euripides, Shakespeare, Molière, Ibsen or Chekhov is great. Shaw, Pirandello, O'Neill, Brecht, Beckett, Genet are important but I hesitate to call them great.

The use of the designation, needless to say, depends on one's frame of reference. If one believes a play may retain its efficacy for, let us say, fifty years, one may reasonably call it great—though that is not the yardstick by which I measure. In contemporary American theatre criticism the word has come to signify gushing enthusiasm, as similarly indicated by such a phrase as "the best play of several seasons." With us, the superlative is largely an implement of first aid to the box office.

Our theatre and its status among us are in such a sorry plight that when a reviewer labels a play "good" or "interesting," we take it to mean mediocre—hardly worth the expense of seeing it. Only a "money notice" is considered a favorable review—something having at least the force of a full-page newspaper ad. Criticism in such an atmosphere is perilously difficult. Theatre managers who complain about the reviewers do not want criticism; they want praise verging on hysterics. This generally holds true for playwrights and actors as well.

The reaction on the part of some critics to this journalistic inflation is to reverse the process: to preserve their critical chastity they assume an attitude of absolute severity. They will have nothing but the "best"; they insist on "the highest standards." One cannot be too extreme, they feel, in defense of Excellence.

Such a posture strikes me as no less false than the promiscuity of those addicted to raving about any presentation that can decently be commended at all. For while some absolute standard must be latent in the critic's mind if he is to give any play its proper place, it is not at all necessary or desirable to judge every new play on the basis of that ideal. There is even something inimical to art in such a practice.

"Masterpieces," says Auden, "should be kept for High Holidays of the Spirit." That is certainly not to deny that we need organizations to keep masterpieces perennially in view. But what we must demand above all in plays is that they *speak* to us, stir us in ways which most intimately and powerfully stir our senses and our souls, penetrate to the core what is most truly alive in us. To do so plays do not have to have the stamp of universality on them, of impeccable inspiration, or signs of top-flight genius. They have to be the consistent and persuasive expression of genuine perception, individual in origin, social in application. If Aeschylus, Shakespeare, Molière are prototypes of dramatic

greatness, it must be evident that many second, third, fourth and fifth-rate plays may also fulfill the function of usable art.

It is no special feat to determine greatness retrospectively. The critic who implies that nothing less than the absolutely first-rate will do is usually more pedant than artist. Immortality awards are best conferred by our descendants. "A 'high standard,'" said Henry James, "is an excellent thing, but we fancy it sometimes takes away more than it gives." We live more fully on what we create now than on what was created for us in the past. That is as true for audiences as for the makers and doers.

Since we are speaking of the total phenomenon of the theatre, rather than of drama alone, we must remind ourselves that masterpieces badly produced or produced at the wrong time and place cease to occupy their exalted position; in fact they no longer serve the purposes of art. Under the proper circumstances, on the stage and in the auditorium, plays of more modest literary pretensions may excel them. I am often given to understand that Sophocles was a greater dramatist than O'Neill. I need no such instruction. It is none the less true that most productions of Sophocles (and of other Greek masters) have struck me as singularly empty, while certain O'Neill staged plays have impressed me deeply. To make this crushingly clear, on a recent radio program I informed the manager who sponsored both the 1964 Broadway *Hamlet* and *Beyond the Fringe* that I believed the latter contained the greater artistic value.

We have also learned that some dramatists of unquestioned stature—Goethe, Kleist, Racine, Strindberg—do not have the same impact in one country as in another, or make the impression they presumably should, even upon their own people at all times.

Talent of every kind, even small talent, must always be credited. That is particularly so of talent close to us in time and place. I do not suggest that we follow Herman Melville's injunction: "Let America first praise mediocrity in her children before she praises...the best excellence in children of other lands." I submit, however, that a sense of the present and of presence are factors which it is unwise to overlook or underestimate. But the critical faculty does not consist only in recognizing talent; there must be also an ability to evaluate it. The American theatre is richly supplied (I almost said lousy) with talent, but too often talent not worthy enough or put to the best uses.

This raises an aspect of theatre criticism in which we are decidedly at fault. Our praise is usually the response to an effect, a register of stimulation. We applaud the person who produces the effect in an acclaim which ranges from a compliment to cleverness to the proclamation of genius. But what counts in talent is its specific gravity, its meaning, how and in what way it affects us, the human nourishment it offers us. Cyanide of potassium is tremendously effective, but it is not food.

Everything—even the damnable—must be expressed in the theatre. I cannot hold anything to be true unless tested by its opposite. I need Beckett's negations if for no other reason than that they fortify me in my affirmations. I need Genet's "decadence" to sustain my health. I embrace the madness in certain modern dramatists to find my balance. To be sure, there is authentic "far out" writing and there is its fashionable simulacrum; it is the critic's task to distinguish between them. He must sift the stuff which composes each particular talent, assess its value for and in itself, and in relation to himself as a person representative of a certain public. "Entertainment," "good theatre," beauty" are not enough. We must know what these virtues actually do, how they work. The critic's main job, I repeat, is not to speak of his likes or dislikes as pleasure or distaste alone, but to define as exactly as possible the nature of what he examines. It were best to do this without the use of tags intended for quotes to be read on the run.

What I have said about the judgment of texts applies equally to acting and to those other ingredients which go into the making of play in the theatre. ("To see sad sights," Shakespeare tells us,

"moves more than to hear them told/For the eye interprets to the ear....") Most criticism nowadays is even more meager in regard to acting, direction and design than in evaluation of the texts themselves. Merit in acting is weighed chiefly by the degree of personal appeal it exercises. The actor is rarely judged for his relevance to the play as a whole since the play's meaning to begin with is frequently unspecified. To speak to the point about acting, the critic must judge the texture and composition of the role as the player shapes it through his natural endowment and through the authority of his craft.

Perhaps critics should not be held to too-strict account for neglect or oversight in the matter of acting, direction, etc., since most acting and direction on our stage today, for reasons we must refrain from entering into in the present context, is rarely better than competent. In such cases a consideration "in depth" becomes supererogatory when it is not pretentious. Still, even with actors as eminent as Laurence Olivier, Alfred Lunt, Paul Scofield, Jean-Louis Barrault, or with directors as accomplished as Tyrone Guthrie, Peter Brook, Orson Welles, what our critics have to say usually comes down to little more than catch phrases, a bleat of unreserved enthusiasm or regretted disapproval. In this connection I must cite a fact first called to my attention by Jacques Copeau, the actor-director who strongly influenced Louis Jouvet, Charles Dullin and a whole generation of European theatre folk from 1913 to 1941: there have been fewer *great* actors in the history of the theatre than great dramatists.

The new season begins; and no doubt I shall often make hash in my columns of many of my own prescriptions. In extenuation I can only urge that while I am not sure I agree with an admirable literary critic I heard lecture many years ago in Paris who said, "The artist has every right; a critic only obligations," I always bear it in mind.

—*NAT*, 21 Sept. '64

DOCTOR FAUSTUS

Say "classic drama" to the ordinary New York theatergoer and nine times out of ten he supposes you refer to the Bard. (Some years ago on the opening night of a production of Wycherley's *The Country Wife* I heard a fashionably gowned lady, when the word "cuckold" was spoken on the stage, murmur to her companion, "I don't like these Shakespearean plays.") Even Ben Jonson is unfamiliar, and Christopher Marlowe virtually unknown.

We should therefore be grateful to the Phoenix Theatre for opening its season with *Doctor Faustus*. Those who venture to see this play will find that it not only contains elements of a "good show" (apart from the magnificent language) but that it means something!

Faustus' final cry of anguish as he is dragged to everlasting punishment is *"I'll burn the books."* What books? "Necromantic books...lines, circles, letters and characters...O what a world of profit and delight, of power, of honor, of omnipotence/ Is promised to the studious artisan." The doctor has been ravished by "sweet analytics" or what the 16th century called "magic" and we call science.

Marlowe's first play, *Tamburlaine*, told the epic tale of a man who sought to dominate the world by military conquest. He wins all the battles but is defeated by life: his victories are accompanied by personal disaster. Faustus' pride is entirely intellectual. Finding physiology, theology and other branches of philosophy inadequate to his will to power and craving for pleasure, he is bent on breaking through the limits of human (and humane) knowledge. This, he realizes, can be accomplished only by a pact with the Devil.

His every wish is granted. He is made superior to potentate and pope. He is vouchsafed intercourse with the lady whose face "launched a thousand ships." But he is damned. His skills have exceeded the boundaries proper to man.

What makes the play particularly poignant is that Marlowe is on Faustus' side, as he was on Tamburlaine's. The erudite Marlowe was reputed to have been an atheist, and in other respects as well, defiantly exceptional. He knew that a bitter price must be paid for excess, and that man can be no more than man.

Hearing the outcry, "I'll burn the books!," I recalled Galileo's last speech in Brecht's play "...your new machine may simply suggest new drudgeries...The gulf [between progress and the bulk of humanity] may even grow so wide that the sound of your cheering at some new achievement would be echoed by a universal horror."

Writing for the groundling as much as for the elite, Marlowe introduces low comedy which parodies his main theme. There is not only a vein of acid mockery in the play (most pointedly in the masquerade at the Holy See) but many tricks of showmanship. Word Baker has made much hay of this. His direction leads me to suspect that he has forgotten that *Doctor Faustus* is a "tragical historie," not a music-hall pageant.

That, however, may be unfair. While it is evident that Mr. Baker has a flair for cockeyed comedy (even whimsy) and a sharp sense of scenic contrivance, it is also clear that no actor of sufficient stature and scope for the central role was available to him. Because of this alone the emphasis of the production must fall where it does—on the fun and games. It is visually the most ambitious and striking production that the Phoenix has ever undertaken.

The company does not speak well: that is, euphoniously or with the needed authority, but, thanks to care and intelligence, the dialogue is clear. We hear every word, and in the case of James Ray (as Mephistopheles), Tobi Weinberg (as the Evil Spirit) and David Margulies (as the Pope) effortlessly. The nays, you see, have it all their way.

—*NAT*, 26 Oct. '64

THE OLD GLORY

A new confederation calling itself The American Place Theatre has opened its first membership season in a building owned by the Protestant Episcopal Diocese of New York at 423 West 46 Street.

According to the playbill, "The American Place Theatre exists to foster good writing for the theatre. It hopes to accomplish this by providing a place, a staff and a broad program of practical work to American writers of stature: our poets, novelists and philosophers who wish to use the dramatic form, and to serious playwrights."

I heartily approve of this purpose because I always wish to encourage every effort to break the bonds of Broadway. (I am also in favor of increasing production on Broadway by making its organization less burdensome—probably an even more difficult task.) I dispel from my mind the fact that very few modern poets, novelists and philosophers writing in English have written viable plays. Playwrights have often proved themselves poets; poets, novelists and philosophers rarely become effective playwrights. Still, I am convinced that it is highly desirable that writers not primarily identified with the theatre be pressed into service so that they may help freshen the field. One further thing should be said in this connection: just as Mallarmé warned Degas that poems were not made with "ideas" but with words, so drama is not made with ideas or words but through the development of human action given live within certain specific technical limits.

The American Place Theatre has begun its official existence well by offering the work of Robert Lowell. One listens with respect and, in regard to language at least, with pleasure, to every word this poet sets down. Lowell's *The Old Glory* is a triptych of three one-act plays related to early American history from 1630 to 1800. There is throughout a thread of feeling and thought characteristic of the author's spirit.

Since the presentation of the three plays was found to be too long for comfort, the first of the series, "Endicott and the Red Cross," has been dropped. That is a pity because, while it doesn't have the "kick" of the last and longest piece, "Benito Cereno" (from a story by Herman Melville), "Endicott and the Red Cross," as a clue to Lowell's statement, is perhaps the most telling of the three plays.

I cannot say much about "My Kinsman, Major Molineux," the second section of *The Old Glory* (but the first of the evening on 46 St.) because, while its form and import are evident in the production, only one or two of the actors who play it are wholly intelligible. I could make out no more than half of the spoken text.

When the performance of "My Kinsman, Major Molineux" was over, I murmured to a friend who sat in front of me, "This is a subversive play; I'm going to report it to the authorities!" I suspect that my feeble quip represented a certain intuition. There is a subtle and gnawing skepticism in Lowell's soul—and all skepticism is subversive!

After a somewhat extended prelude of talk—*good* talk, though the suspense it is meant to engender verges on the self-defeating because we are not made sufficiently aware of what portends—"Benito Cereno" ends with the slaughter of Negroes on a Spanish slave ship. The Negroes had mutinied against their captors, killed the ship owner and taken over the rule of the vessel. They plan to force the captain of an American merchant ship to sail them back to Africa. When the massacre (at the hands of the American captain's sailors) is over, the leader of the Negro mutiny defiantly proclaims "the future is black." Delano, the American captain replies, "This is your future," and empties all six barrels of his pistol into the Negro's body.

An exciting conclusion. But what is "the future" Lowell suggests? That murderous suppression of Negroes will continue for 160 years and more? History has corroborated this. And it goes without saying that Lowell is a man of good will who abhors violence. Yet the play is ambiguous. It is ironic and disturbed. It is not tragic as much as pained and bewildered. It leaves us shocked and strangely dissatisfied. Lowell, it would appear, is no kin to the American captain; nor, though he understands him, is he really sympathetic to the Negro rebel. Lowell is more like the overpowered Spanish grandee, Benito Cereno, sensitive, lofty, impotent.

—*NAT*, 23 Nov. '64

FIDDLER ON THE ROOF

After seeing *Fiddler on the Roof* (based on some Yiddish short stories; book by Joseph Stein, music by Jerry Bock, lyrics by Sheldon Harnick) numerous members of the audience confessed (or proclaimed) that they shed tears of compassion and gratitude; others have asserted that their hearts swelled in elation, while still others were convulsed with laughter. My own reception of the show was cool.

I too found it endearing—worthy of the affection the enthusiasts had manifested. Yet thinking of it in its detail, the text lacked the full savor of its sources; the music simply followed a pattern of suitable folk melodies without adding, or being equal, to them; Jerome Robbins' choreography, though correct in its method, was not—except for two instances—as brilliant as I had expected it to be. Boris Aronson's sets did not "overwhelm" me; even Zero Mostel's performance, which cements the diverse elements and gives them a core and a shape, was open to objections. Then, too, were not those critics right, in the press and the public, who maintained there was a Broadway taint in the mixture?

Yet the longer I reflected, the greater grew my regard for the show! The steadier my effort to arrive at a true appraisal of my feelings, the more clearly I realized that the general audience was justified. By a too meticulous weighing and sifting of each of the performance's components one loses sight of the whole.

The production is actually *discreet*. For a popular ($350,000) musical there is a certain modesty in its effect. The vast machinery of production—I do not refer to the physical aspects alone—which must perforce go into the making of an entertainment of this sort has by an exercise of taste been reduced to a degree of intimacy that is almost surprising.

The choreography, for example, does not attempt to electrify; though it is rather more muscular, broader and certainly less "cosy" than Jewish folk dancing tends to be, Robbins has, on the whole, successfully combined the homeliness of such dancing with cossack energy. And though Aronson's sets may remind one of Chagall, they do not really attempt to achieve Chagall-like results. (Chagall's art is always more emphatically Russian or French than anything else. Whatever their subject, his paintings possess a certain opulent flamboyance that is hardly Jewish.) Aronson, faced with the need to move his sets rapidly, as well as to give them the atmosphere of impoverishment required by the play's environment without robbing them of a certain quiet charm, has made his contribution to the proceedings relatively unobtrusive—which a Chagall stage design never is. (There is also in Aronson's pictorial scheme a nice contrast between the ramshackle drabness of the places in which the play's characters are housed and the profuse yet delicate greenery of the natural surroundings.) Considering, too, the dizzying extravagance of Mostel's histrionic quality, his performance is remarkably reserved.

None of this, however, goes to the heart of the show's significance, which must be sought in its effect on the audience. That effect comes close, within the facile laughter, the snug appreciation of an anticipated showmanship, to something religious. To understand this one must turn to the play's original material: stories by Sholom Aleichem. Sholom Aleichem (pen name for Sholom Rabinowitz, born in Russia in 1859 died in New York in 1916) was the great folk artist of Yiddish literature—an altogether unique figure who might without exaggeration be compared to Gogol. The essence of Sholom Aleichem's work is in a very special sense *moral*. It is the distillation of a humane sweetness from a context of sorrow. It represents the unforced emergence of a real joy and a true sanctification from the soil of life's workaday worries and pleasures. Although this blessed acceptance of the most commonplace facts of living—generally uncomfortable and graceless, to say the least—appears casual and unconscious in Sholom Aleichem, it is based on what, in the first and indeed the best of the play's numbers, is called "Tradition."

This tradition, which might superficially be taken to comprise little more than a set of obsolete habits, customs and pietistic prescriptions, is in fact the embodiment of profound culture. A people is not cultured primarily through the acquisition or even the making of works of art; it is cultured when values rooted in biologically and spiritually sound human impulses, having been codified, become the apparently instinctive and inevitable mode of its daily and hourly conduct. Sholom Aleichem's characters are a concentrate of man's belief in living which does not exclude his inevitable bewilderment and questioning of life's hardship and brutal confusion.

In the stories this is expressed as a kindness which does not recognize itself, as pity without self-congratulation, as familiar humor and irony without coarseness. This is beauty of content, if not of form. For the Eastern (Russian, Polish, Rumanian, Galician) Jews of yesteryear "would have been deeply puzzled," Irving Howe and Eleazer Greenberg have said in their admirable introduction to a collection of Yiddish stories, "by the idea that the aesthetic and the moral are distinct realms, for they saw beauty above all in behavior."

More of this meaning than we had a right to expect is contained in *Fiddler on the Roof*. Is it any wonder, then, that an audience, living in one of the most heartless cities of the world at a time of conformity to the mechanics of production, an audience without much relation to any tradition beyond that expressed through lip service to epithets divested of living experience, an audience progressively more deprived of the warmth of personal contact and the example of dignified companionship, should weep thankfully and laugh in acclamation at these images of a good life lived by good people? In *Fiddler on the Roof* this audience finds a sense of what "togetherness" might signify. Without the cold breath of any dogma or didactics, it gets a whiff of fellow feeling for the unfortunate and the persecuted. It is a sentiment that acts as a kind of purification.

Is there too much "show biz" in *Fiddler on the Roof?* Undoubtedly. But apart from the fact that dramaturgic and musical equivalents of Sholom Aleichem's genius are not to be had for the asking, is it conceivable that a truly organic equivalent of the original stories could be produced in our time? The makers and players of *Fiddler on the Roof* are not of Kiev, 1905 (except for Boris Aronson, who was born in Kiev in 1900), nor do they live (even in memory) a life remotely akin to that of Tevye the Dairyman, his family and his friends, or of the author who begat them. The producers of *Fiddler on the Roof* are Broadway—as is the audience—and, in this instance, perhaps the best of it. Those who have attended some of the latter-day productions of the Yiddish stage itself will know that they too are as alien to the spirit of Sholom Aleichem as anything we see at the Imperial Theatre.

The name of Chagall has almost unavoidably come up. The nearest thing to that artist's type of imagination dwells within *Fiddler on the Roof*'s leading actor. Zero Mostel has "Chagall" in his head. Mostel's clown inspiration is unpredictably fantastic—altogether beyond the known or rational. One wishes this fantasy were allowed fuller scope in the show, even as compliments for its control are in order. For Mostel too, being part of Broadway, will fleetingly lapse into adulterations inhospitable to his fabulous talent.

—*NAT*, '64

AN ODD HAMLET

I walked out on John Gielgud's production of *Hamlet*. I had followed it attentively for three hours and I could no more. Not that this was the worst *Hamlet* I had ever seen—far from it—but after witnessing countless productions of the play, I could not take another which, apart from commercial considerations, had so little purpose or reason for being.

Almost as taxing as seeing *Hamlet* again under such circumstances is the irritation of reading comments on its leading actor. For how is one to judge a Hamlet unless some idea is conveyed as to what the play itself is supposed to mean. Do we really know what it means?

It is many different things to different people. The "traditional" or schoolboy's *Hamlet* is the story of a man cursed because "the native hue of resolution is sicklied o'er with the pale cast of thought." While this may be generally true, it explains very little. Hamlet in the play is extraordinarily animated, rashly impulsive, even fierce. (He kills not once, but several times.) He turns on Ophelia in passionate scorn; he enters heedlessly into dueling contests, jumps into graves, terrifies his mother. Inactive? Far too active!

Hamlet is the most "interpreted" figure in literature. Among the interpretations in recent critical writing are those of Ernest Jones, Bertolt Brecht, Francis Fergusson, Lionel Abel. Gordon Craig, who directed the play for the Moscow Art Theatre in 1912, thought the play's action signified a search for the truth in a world of gaudy deception. (He covered all the characters except Hamlet in a sheath of gold.) In Moscow last spring, I saw a note in Craig's hand restating the play's theme as a conflict between the material and the spiritual. Underneath it Stanislavsky had affixed *his* comment: "That is *not* the play."

Hamlet has also been called the first "existentialist" play. Hamlet's dejection, his "nausea"

("How stale, flat and unprofitable seem to me the uses of this world") precede his hearing about the murder of his father and cannot be wholly ascribed to his mother's too hasty remarriage.

One of the most startling interpretations, based on a 1956 production in Krakow, is reported by the Polish critic Jan Kott in his *Shakespeare Our Contemporary*. In the Krakow production of *Hamlet* the play was seen in the murky light of Stalin's Russia! The play became preeminently political. The keynote is "Something is rotten in the state of Denmark"—a line three times repeated. Special emphasis too was laid on "Denmark is a prison." Even the Gravedigger's speech "Now thou dost ill to say the gallows is built stronger than the Church" must be stressed in this altered context.

Everyone in *Hamlet*, Jan Kott writes, is *spying* on everyone else—even the dodo Polonius. "Behind every curtain in the Elsinore palace," he goes on to say, "someone is hiding....Fear gnaws at everything: marriage, love, friendship." This may have been directly relevant to Shakespeare, the critic suggests, for the play was written when the Essex conspiracy against Queen Elizabeth was in the making. In *Hamlet*, Kott continues, everyone talks politics. There is no room for love in such an atmosphere. "When politics displaces all other concerns, it becomes a form of madness ."

The various interpretations tend to overlap and merge. So the one just referred to parallels that of Francis Fergusson, who asserts that "the rottenness of Denmark" constitutes the play's central situation. This is faced by two basic postures: that of Hamlet's Renaissance skepticism, which makes him doubt the wisdom or efficacy of revenge, and that of the other prince, Fortinbras, who might be conceived either as a medieval knight or as an ultramodern man who, without metaphysical question, proceeds to get his job or duty done.

I have myself always thought of Hamlet as a passionate person capable of heroic action but "corrupted" by misgivings as to the human worth of such deeds. There is such a confusion of motives in him, because of what he beholds outside and within himself, that though brave enough to undertake anything, he cannot convince himself that any course of action is the just one.

Hamlet is far too rich a work to be wholly clear. (That is why T. S. Eliot accounted it a "failure.") Hence a safe manner to stage it is by way of sheer melodrama, as a glorious showpiece—which may well have been the Elizabethan way. It was certainly Tyrone Guthrie's way in his Minneapolis production. What must never happen with *Hamlet,* if it is to interest us in the theatre, is to produce it in a haphazard, ad-lib fashion. And that is precisely what has occurred in John Gielgud's production.

It is not a "bad" *Hamlet,* but rather no *Hamlet* at all. I was not disturbed or mystified to find the play set in a simulacrum of a New York backstage during rehearsal time, with actors in their work clothes (though the Player King, Queen and their attendants wear costumes). All this may have been intended to show that the play could do without theatrical "trappings," that it is universal. But as the play progressed, with here and there a nice reading and an occasional bright bit of business to illustrate the text—the actors' diction, be it said in commendation, was nearly always intelligible—I could not discern, apart from its plot, what the play was supposed to be about. In what way did it show, as Shakespeare tells us the theatre must, "the very age and body of the time"—except perhaps by its exposure of Broadway opportunism?

We are given little beyond a series of disparate recitations composing no consummate idea or picture. Hume Cronyn's Polonius had its witty points; Alfred Drake's Claudius, within very modest limits, made sense. But the only truly stirring moment is vouchsafed us by the Ghost of Gielgud's voice, which possesses qualities of true characterization, situation, mood and feeling, though I must also add that I detest Hamlet's father taped and sounded on a public address loudspeaker.

I could see little more in Richard Burton than his splendid personal attributes. His voice is powerful: its forte might smash a windowpane; his person is impressively robust, his speech excellent, his readings reasonable, his mask suitably troubled. Yet I could not tell to what creative end this histrionic instrument was being employed. The actor's mind, for all his effort, seemed elsewhere, distracted, as if the challenge of this stupendous role was something he could manage technically but which engaged no part of himself in any profoundly personal sense. As a result, Hamlet's agony and indignation often seemed little more than churlishness. He appeared unhappy enough but not about anything in the play.

Like so many actors today, Burton is now a mere visitor to the stage. Without discipline, without a commanding theatrical structure or institution, without a dominant director, no actor can be used as an artist to the extent of his capacities. There is something "lost," almost tragic, as Burton stands on the stage amid, but distinctly apart from, his fellow actors. He looked altogether uncertain as to whether he wanted to pursue his career as an actor any further.

—*NAT*, '64

CHALLENGE OF THE NEW THEATRES

The "breakdown" of Broadway, the consequent propaganda for the theatre's decentralization, the aid of the foundations, the spread of university and community stages, the "cultural explosion" have all led to the establishment of a number of new repertory or semi-repertory theatres—with more or less permanent staffs—from New York to California, in the South and the Southwest. We have reason to be pleased, but it is too soon to celebrate. As Van Wyck Brooks many years ago said (in effect): America is the land of promising first acts.

An American characteristic which may frustrate our hope in the new theatres is impatience. We must not expect miracles overnight. Time is required to mature all concerned: the directorate of the various theatres, their personnel, their audiences. We have no settled tradition to proceed from. We must learn.

The first step is to define aims. The repertory system by itself is a measure of convenience; it can prove a drawback. A permanent company should be a great asset; it may turn into a deadweight. A subscription audience is extremely useful; it has occasionally acted as a block.

It is not enough to say that the goal of the new enterprises should be to offer "good theatre." As Stanislavsky told Norris Houghton, no one has ever deliberately tried to found a bad theatre. Nor can each of the new companies strive for exactly the same ends. Much depends on where each theatre is situated and the conditions under which it is obliged to operate, the audience it hopes to attract, the very structure of the building it must occupy.

The Repertory Theater of Lincoln Center will serve New York. It cannot do everything for New York which New York needs, nor can it do everything at once. (It promises a studio auditorium for special productions when its permanent quarters have been built.) New York should have several similar theatres, as London at present has three, Paris four, Moscow many. It is a sign of sanity that the organizers of the Repertory Theater of Lincoln Center recognize that even if they play at capacity for fifty-two weeks every season they cannot look forward to a profit! The theatre is not a merchandising business any more than is a library, a museum or a symphony orchestra.

Countries which have long theatrical histories may maintain theatres especially designed to preserve those traditions. That is the chief purpose of the Comèdie Française, and to some extent this was and is the purpose of the Old Vic and of the Shakespeare Theatre at Stratford-on-Avon. It is largely true of the various state or municipal theatres in Germany. Most European countries have produced dramatic literatures rich enough to sustain such theatres over the years.

America has not (though there are more American plays worth revival than we suppose). Certain choices are open to the founders of the new theatres. A choice which is really no choice at all is to announce that one is going to present a series of good plays. The question to be asked is: good for what, good for whom?

A company of actors unprepared—that is, not specifically trained—to do Elizabethan, Restoration or Classic Greek plays deceives itself and its audience when it undertakes to stage them. I could list a whole shelf of masterpieces—by Strindberg, Kleist, Racine, Calderon and others—which would doom any company offering them in the wrong place at the wrong time. Their *audiences* are not prepared! Remember that Beckett's *Waiting for Godot,* eagerly received and thoroughly appreciated in scores of university theatres throughout the country, flopped on Broadway despite an expert cast. The same is true of so relatively forthright a play as Sartre's *No Exit.* The circumstances—costs of production, price of seats, the whole atmosphere and mental disposition on Broadway are inimical to the proper reception of such plays. The audience is a theatre's leading actor!

The Tyrone Guthrie Theatre in Minneapolis made a wise choice of plays for its first season. *Hamlet,* Molière's *The Miser,* Chekhov's *The Three Sisters* and Arthur Miller's *Death of a Salesman* are suitable to any American city of like size. But note in passing that *The Miser,* performed in a sort of enlarged "revue" style, and *Three Sisters* were more popular than *Hamlet,* done by actors not wholly up to the demands of that formidable play. It is a moot point whether it is better to do a great play with mediocre means than to do a lesser but still worthy play more congruously.

It might be desirable to institute a theatre entirely devoted to "difficult" or *avant-garde* plays (a) if the director, actors and others are equipped to do them well, (b) if there is a sufficient number of people in the community who wish to see such plays, and (c) if the financial support at the theatre's command can be counted on for respectable productions of these plays. One must remembcr always that we are speaking not of the desultory production of separate plays but of a continuous program of production.

To present plays by Ghelderode, Beckett, Ionesco, Genet or even more recent examples of "adventurous" drama, in addition perhaps to plays like Büchner's *Wozzeck* and Strindberg's *Dream Play* or his *Ghost Sonata,* without reference to all the above considerations would be as much an artistic misdemeanor as a sign of organizational ineptitude. There is little point in speaking of the theatre as a social art and ignoring in practice the actual society in which the theatre finds itself.

Most of the new theatres—particularly those in cities unused to a steady regime of substantial fare—will, to begin with, have to be eclectic in the manner of the Tyrone Guthrie Theatre of Minneapolis. If a university is able to finance a professional company on any long-term basis—as has occurred to some extent at the University of Michigan—the theatre may take greater risks. No theatre may look forward to a secure future where it is expected to prove a "smash" with its initial productions.

Beyond the practical considerations of the problem there lies the root question of what constitutes a true theatre. The answer once given by the great Russian director Vachtangov was couched in the special jargon of his time and place (Moscow, but it is nonetheless exact: "A theatre is an ideologically cemented collective."

This bespeaks not what we call a "policy" but a fundamental Idea. This Idea—religious, social, aesthetic, political or only "technical"—must inform the entire theatrical community from dramatist to minor player and apprentice craftsman. Such a theatre is not intended as the stage equivalent of a library (offering the Hundred Best Books) or a museum for the display of masterpieces. A true theatre creates from its Idea; it educates its members in the Idea and generates

production methods from it. The Idea is born of an impulse in the society in which the theatre's artists live and is directed toward that society. Dramatists and interpreters are interrelated as kinsmen in a common movement immanent in the social unit of which they are at once the projection and the instrument. Thus the career of such a theatre will take on the kind of character and meaning we find in the work of an individual artist.

Such unity was more or less spontaneously achieved in the Classic Greek, the Elizabethan and the seventeenth-century French theatres by virtue of the homogeneity of their respective cultures. Unity of this kind is extremely difficult to arrive at in our day—especially in America. Still, something of this aesthetic-social concord has been attained.

Besides its purely professional reforms, the Moscow Art Theatre in 1898 declared its purpose to be the creation of serious art for the People. By the "People" the leaders of that famous institution chiefly meant the middle-class intelligentsia and the educated working class. The result was a theatre which explored many avenues of theatrical expression, though its signal contribution was consummated in the production of plays by Chekhov and Gorky. With further development along these lines the studios of the Moscow Art Theatre (virtually new theatres) veered at first toward a sort of Tolstoian mysticism and then proceeded to radical departures from realism, as well as to more pronouncedly social objectives.

By 1935, the Russian theatre had branched out into extremely diverse aesthetic manifestations. Its progress was then impeded by a politically oriented campaign against "formalism," when a very restrictive interpretation of "Socialist realism" was imposed by main force.

Though the Theatre Guild between 1919 and 1929 was hardly a theatre in the sense I have indicated, it did make a valuable contribution in organizing audiences through subscription and in maintaining a fairly consistent program of the kind of contemporary European play which had up to that time been considered caviar to the general. The Theatre Guild represented the new cosmopolitanism of New York's middle class shortly after the First World War. In 1928, the Theatre Guild adopted Eugene O'Neill, scion of another body, the Provincetown Players.

The Group Theatre (1931-41) was the first, and so far the last, conscious effort in America to create a theatre exemplifying both an aesthetic and a "philosophic" attitude. Its first emphasis was on a unity of technique—particularly in regard to acting; its second was the enunciation of what it held to be the temper of American life of the time. The combination resulted in the emergence of a playwright from its permanent acting company: Clifford Odets. He was in effect not only the Group Theatre's typical figure but that of the decade.

What Idea will motivate each of our new theatres? That is for each of them to decide for itself, depending on the composition of the companies. Without some coherent Idea to impel it, an Idea which each group must learn to formulate for itself and exemplify in its action, none will survive beyond the flush of its first flight.

It is my personal conviction that every true theatre must sooner or later produce its own native playwrights. (The Group Theatre presented plays by Paul Green, John Howard Lawson, Dawn Powell, Maxwell Anderson, Sidney Kingsley, before it reached Odets' *Waiting for Lefty* and *Awake and Sing!)* This does not mean that all other dramatists are to be considered "alien"; it means that somehow all the plays produced by a true theatre must more or less serve as "original" expressions of the group (directors, actors and others) who compose its membership.

Such a theatre does not follow fashion, however attractive, up to date, "advanced"; it bodies forth its own spirit. It should be conceived, not as an interpretive vehicle, but as a creative organism. It may find material in old plays of any period from any land, but in this kind of theatre such plays become its own plays, a facet of its own "message." This implies no distortion of revered texts in the manner of certain early Soviet productions. (Though I confess a preference for Meyerhold's staging of Gogol's *Inspector General* or the Jewish Chamber Theatre's mounting of *King Lear* in Moscow in 1935 to most of the "faithful" or faceless Shakespeare productions in America and England.) Classics are produced in my "ideal" theatre, not solely on account of their literary stature but for their relevance to its audience. The outstanding example of this sort of theatre for the past decade or more has been the Berliner Ensemble, whose guiding spirit was Brecht but whose productions have not been confined to his plays. A large community may have several such theatres with differing Ideas. If they are truly theatres each will create its own identity.

For these theatres to exist and flourish, more than a collection of expert professionals is required. The theatre as it develops must *school* itself for the tasks it envisions. We have as yet no single body of theatre craftsmen capable of coping with the wide range of styles which the perspective of our dramatic heritage offers. We must be modest even as we are ambitious. The theatre must not regard itself simply as an arena for the exhibition of a prize "product," but as the ground for the cultivation on the broadest possible basis—technical and spiritual—of the artists and world view it hopes to have emerge.

There are enormous resources of talent in our country, but little coordinating discipline or formative enterprise. That is why the theatre has become a hand-to-mouth business instead of what it was destined to be: a vital expression of adult concern. We are too concentrated on sensations, names, electrifying phenomena, bewitching personalities, and not enough on organic growth. We are eager for the fruit; we do not care about the tree.

With the establishment of the new theatres we have our best chance for a transformation. But we shall miss our opportunity if we think of the new theatres in the light of the old. These new theatres must not be as good or better than Broadway but altogether different. They must forge new paths for actors, dramatists, directors, audiences and the monied patrons. This cannot be done in a hurry. One, two, or even three seasons will not be enough.

—*NAT*, '64

WAR AND PEACE

War and Peace, APA's second presentation of their season at the Phoenix, is an adaptation by Alfred Neumann, Erwin Piscator and Guntram Prufer. I saw the play three times in its Berlin (Schiller Theatre) production in 1956, and the memory of those performances makes it difficult for me to review the play now.

Even then there was something "puzzling" or paradoxical about it. It was scorned by the French when it was shown in Paris and my American friends there taunted me for admiring it. (They condemned it as a radio show.) True, it is no "play"; true also, it cannot be accepted as a dramatization of Tolstoy's book. (An adequate dramatization is almost unthinkable.) It is what I called it in *The Nation* at that time: "a diagram of the novel." It has "little flesh and blood," I wrote, "it contains a minimum of Russian color or Tolstoian humanity."

For one thing the novel's aim extends far beyond the proclaimed purpose of this schematic German version, which is to show that war is a matter of chance, and more pedagogically to prove that war is wasteful, inhuman and ultimately pointless. I don't believe it "proves" any of these things. How then was it possible for me to admire it and return to it each time with undiminished satisfaction?

It is not a play but a *stage piece*. Its attraction owes little to literature and nearly everything to the theatre. It works as a kind of surprise entertainment of "the performing arts." Its lesson teaches us, not about "war and peace," but about the peculiar nature of the theatre. In this spectacle, in which a Narrator in modern clothes not only explains considerable parts of the action but questions and argues with the characters (in period dress)—a spectacle, moreover, in which the logistics of a battle we are presumably "witnessing" are demonstrated by toy soldiers which the Narrator places on the stage floor during a colloquy with the actor playing Pierre Bezuhov—we are taken in, held, even impressed.

The acting in the Berlin production, under Piscator who conceived it, was masterfully evocative. Unadorned dialogue, several simple details of characterization, the discreet sounding of essential tones within a constant shifting of spare scenic elements, and we were in a world that transcended these trifling tokens. This was a game, a trick, which for all its "Bauhaus" functionalism stirred in us a memory of Tolstoy's vast cosmos. It was a creation of striking skill in the manipulation of 20th-century theatrical means.

The APA commands neither the space nor the apparatus to attempt all that the sumptuously endowed Schiller Theatre was able to achieve. Still, Judith Haugan's décor and the director Ellis Rabb's use of it are a triumph of ingenuity in the employment of modest means to suggest an "epic" effect.

The acting of the APA company could not possibly match Piscator's cast. I shall never forget the now deceased Erwin Kalser's Prince Bolkonski. (The part is well roared at the Phoenix.) He gave us a Prince whose great authority, hauteur, *ancien régime* intellectual distinction and immovability were rendered with a quiet delicacy. The formidable power of the man was made to seem impregnable by its very gentleness and silken ease.

Though by comparison the American company seems like an entirely sympathetic body of intelligent, capable, devoted students engaged in the representation of a world remote and foreign to them, they nevertheless manage to sustain a measure of the illusion wrought by the more mature and, through cultural endowment, better equipped Schiller Theatre ensemble.

I cannot be certain what a person who has never read Tolstoy would get from seeing the performance at the Phoenix, but I venture to say it might still be a worth-while experience. Those familiar with book, if they know what not to expect, will find the evening one of genuine interest.

—*NAT*, 1 Feb. '65

THE MOSCOW ART THEATRE

We are more than gratified by the presence at the City Center of forty-nine members of the 140 who comprise the acting company of the Moscow Art Theatre. But there is in America so little knowledge of the Soviet theatre that it may be useful to note a few facts before entering into any consideration of the four productions the visitors have chosen to present.

We frequently speak of the Moscow Art Theatre as if it were the only Russian troupe in existence. By our standards it is certainly a venerable institution—it was founded in 1898—but the august Maly Theatre has a longer lineage in the Russian realistic style, having first taken root in 1824. It is still sturdy.

Strictly speaking, the Moscow Art Theatre is not without cavil the most widely preferred company of the Soviet capital. Some of the younger theatregoers regard it as a kind of "academy," highly respectable but no longer representative of the most vital impulses of the moment. When I was in Moscow two years ago I counted twenty or more major theatre organizations, all of them playing in repertory and offering three or four different plays every week. The recently formed Contemporary Theatre was favored by the youth; the Vachtangov, the Mayakovsky, the Red Army theatres also had their champions. Several Soviet critics were of the opinion that the most interesting of all Soviet theatres today was the Gorky Theatre in Leningrad. Its leading player, Cherkassov, was held to be the finest living Soviet actor.

I set these items down not to argue a point but to establish a perspective. On my first visits to Moscow in 1934 and 1935 the theatres which attracted me most were the Meyerhold and some of the small "Studio" theatres. But that was before an official or state aesthetic had been proclaimed. What I found most stimulating at that time was later attacked as "formalism." In this connection, I might have echoed Jacques Copeau, "father" of the new theatre movements in France, when he said in 1923 on the occasion of the performances given in Paris by Tairov's highly stylized Chamber Theatre and the Moscow Art Theatre: "I am more attracted today to what Tairov is trying to do than to what Stanislavsky has done, but Tairov has not achieved perfection; Stanislavsky has." There can be no doubt that the Moscow Art Theatre occupies a central position in the Soviet and perhaps in the world theatre of our time.

The productions we are now invited to see are "traditional": they do not exemplify the most typical work of the present-day Moscow Art Theatre—as does, for example, its staging of Tolstoy's *Fruits of Enlightenment*. (The company's repertory numbers thirty-three plays.) The dramatization of Gogol's *Dead Souls*, which was first presented in 1932, remains pretty much as Stanislavsky left it. (I saw it first in 1935; several members of that cast are acting the same roles here now.) *The Three Sisters*, directed originally in 1901 by the Theatre's co-founder Nemirovich-Danchenko, was revised by a "disciple" in 1958. That is also the case of *The Cherry Orchard*. Only Nicolai Pogodin's *Kremlin Chimes* is "new"; it was first directed by Nemirovich-Danchenko during the war and revised by others in 1956.

Though the present company is less brilliant than the original one seen here in 1923, which contained at least five actors of supreme rank, it is still superb. (The men are generally superior to the women; this was so from the beginning.) All are consummately trained, dedicated and scrupulous craftsmen, mature in fiber, commanding in experience and accomplishment. What is most immediately striking is the company's natural virility.

Yet it is a mistake at this juncture to judge them—as many are prone to do—singly. To engage in such evaluation, we should see them on their own stage in their complete repertory. Here we must view them—as their best performances bid us—as a unit.

For all its vigor, bounce and color a certain mustiness clings to the production of *Dead Souls*. This may be due in part to the fragmentary nature of Mikhail Bulgakov's adaptation which, while faithful (except for the ending), makes every scene take on a formal resemblance to the preceding one. This is also true of the novel, but the novel is not only sustained by its narrative line but by Gogol's pithy comments on it. They give the book an epic value, a tragi-comic and satiric poetry. *Dead Souls* is not the story of a swindler but a grotesque and heartbroken panorama of Russia. Its central character is not Chichikov but the land itself, contemplated from afar (Gogol wrote the book in Italy) by a wounded member of the "family," derisive and homesick, resentful and hopelessly "hooked" on the place and people whose every idiosyncrasy, enlarged by humorous recollection and spiteful love, he knows as intimately as his own skin and pulse.

Still the play is fun. (The production at the City Center seems to have been reduced by the technical and architectural limitations of the house.) But it is not its frolic which leaves one with the deepest impression, but the sense it imparts of the terrible sadness of provincial Russia in the early 19th century, cradle of odd characters and inspiration of rebel genius. If the play and its playing (some of it delicious) strike us as "exaggerated" to the point of freakishness, much the same may be said of the book—except, as remarked, that the book gives us a large frame of reference which is lacking in its stage adaptation.

Russia had changed considerably by the end of the 19th century but not nearly enough. The educated middle class had a much broader awareness of the dreary backwardness of their country, suffered from it, despaired, often broke down in nervous apathy or wretched nihilism. But at its core there was an undying aspiration, a humanism, which being severely repressed became more thoroughly grounded, more fervent, more truly Christian than any elsewhere extant. It is from this matrix of unhappiness and yearning that Chekhov emerged.

No more telling touching testimony of the Chekhovian legacy—still rich with generative force—may be found anywhere than in the Moscow Art Theatre production of *The Three Sisters*. In it Chekhov asks the specifically native (but still universally applicable) question: "We Russians are peculiarly given to exalted ideas—but why is it we always fall so short in life?" Chekhov doesn't answer the question (is there an answer?) but the manner in which it is asked in *The Three Sisters* makes it a great play. For the humility, the loving observation, the embrace of what is most precious in our lives which inform the play give it a stature far more exalted than its apparent scope.

How quiet is the Moscow Art Theatre production, how delicately quiet. Conventionally speaking, it is "undramatic." Tragedy overtakes all the play's characters; yet it would seem that nothing special happens; everything is done as if part of a humdrum reality. We are in a provincial household with lonely, sweet, surly silly, warmhearted people where life runs an almost uneventful course. How dull it all could be. Yet it goes directly to the heart, stirs the soul, moves the mind, braces the spirit.

There are many ways to produce *The Three Sisters*, and there have been hot debates as to which is the right way. Even Stanislavsky and Chekhov were reputedly at odds on the subject. The production at the City Center is characterized above all by a certain *nobility*. This without strain, without posturing, without "pathos." There is hardly any sentimentality; there is clearly no neurosis.

All is relaxed. There is barely a climax, a marked stress. The action flows like a slightly eddying river of understandable behavior of which we never miss the least ripple. One notices a certain carriage or bearing in the actors which make them immediately impressive. No one is given to eye-catching display. Truculent Solyony hardly ever raises his voice. When he leaves the stage, we notice him crumble in grief for an instant and then resume his destructive bent. Vershinin's idealistic speeches are wistful ruminations, spoken conversationally and given body by the character's warmheartedness. Irina dreams with her eyes constantly fixed on some distant horizon. Olga is restrainedly staunch, truly a general's daughter. Masha is not a hysteric. Kulygin is homely uxorious, honorable, and when affected by truly emotional circumstances reveals sensibility and perception. He is not bright but neither is he a fool; he is mediocre, but a man. The aged servants are not comic relief. Andrei is shy and inadequate within an unrealized strength. The doctor is crusty, gone to seed and cynicism with wasted power. Natasha is an obtuse middle-class upstart and hence something of a coquette, not a bitch or a termagant.

One does not think of "pace" in this production—so often emphasized in our journalistic animadversions on direction. If there is "slowness" one is not conscious of it. There are no pauses because the silences—long or short as the case may be—are also action as absorbingly eloquent as the unhurried speech. (There is for example the moment during which Masha and Vershinin gaze at each other across a room: it is a truly beautiful love scene.) The attitudes, placement and groupings of the characters are natural but they all have meaning, tell a "story." They frequently compose pictures which fix themselves in memory as emblems of a period, of a sentiment, of a human stance. Everything is humanly justified and everything adds up to a virtually musical continuity.

Is this realism? Not as we have come to identify it on the stage. Without being larger than life, it is simple conduct so artfully selected that it becomes symbolic and, subtly, grand. Realism has ceased being casual and becomes style with all the dignity we associate with the classic theatre. The actors are people who really live on the stage—a life purified of accidental and personal dross.

If I am overlavish in my praise of the production, as some will surely maintain, what remains? Chekhov remains. Whatever one may think of this or that actor, piece of stage business or theatrical device, *The Three Sisters* at the City Center communicates what is essential: the image of good people, living an unfortunate existence, isolated in social gloom and individual failure, yet somehow bound together by the savorsome substance of their being—their delight in small pleasures, their consanguinity in play, in pain, in longing, in wonder, in the intimacy of their bereavement couple with their inextinguishable desire for something more, something better, something greater in their lives.

—*NAT*, 1 Mar. '65

ARTHUR KOPIT
THE ODD COUPLE

There's no use moanin': the "best of Broadway" today, the "hottest tickets" in town, are *Hello, Dolly!, Funny Girl, Fiddler on the Roof, Luv, Barefoot in the Park, Any Wednesday*. And now, following this pattern, comes what might be described as the torrid ticket, Neil Simon's *The Odd Couple* (Plymouth Theatre). With the exception of *Luv*, which occupies a category of its own, I prefer the musicals, though they contain very little gratifying music.

'Twas ever thus: popular entertainments as exemplified by the exhibits mentioned have always attracted the largest audiences—whether they were priced a dime, $6.60 or $9.60. Such fare may typify a period and may be even thought of as art. (*Guys and Dolls*, for example, was held to be more than simple fun by a few responsible judges.) I would never raise my voice to dissuade people from attending any of these shows. Occasionally their value is greatly enhanced by brilliant performances.

What troubles me is that nowadays there is so little on Broadway by way of honorable contrast.

Another distressing fact (though I should have become habituated to it by now) is that a sharp distinction is so seldom made between facile showmanship (titillation) and those presentations which offer expression of individual ideas or sensibilities. In the theatre at least, *vox populi* is not *vox Dei*!

If he is to be at all useful a reviewer must take a stand. In the midst of the hurly-burly he must be prepared to go out on a limb and declare flatly that to him even a limited talent such as Arthur Kopit's is more interesting than the very capable and commercially secure knack that Neil Simon displays in *The Odd Couple*.

This "man's show," very well cast at the level of delicatessen jocundity (that excellent actor, Walter Matthau, in the lead) and generously supplied with sight gags by Mike Nichols as director, is a sort of prolonged and fun-raising television sketch based on the proposition that two men living together may annoy each other just as much as any mismated husband and wife. There are other incidental sources of laughter, undoubtedly provoked by the pleasure of recognition, although when it comes down to it I don't meet the fellows every Friday night for a game, nor do I often take part in or enjoy pastrami parties. Snobbish? Certainly. If *you* like it, you're welcome to it, and God bless you.

What I respect in the Kopit double bill of one-acters (Players Theatre) is that these "absurd" playlets are trickily disguised confessions, impersonal expressions of what is essentially personal. One may have been put off in Kopit's earlier *Oh, Dad, Poor Dad*, etc., because what was revealed was an adolescent resentment against a man-eating and child-crippling mama—a rich boy's revenge—but the terms of the confession caught the eye and tickled the fancy: the play assumed a form particular to its author; hence, for all its avowed debt to the French, original.

Similarly, one may think of the brief *Sing To Me Through Open Windows* (the first number) as a boy's memory of a lost "father," whether "he" be a person, a way of life or a dream of the theatre's magic. This may strike one as overly sentimental; but a touch of unexpected color redeems it from banality.

The longer piece with the frisky title—*The Day The Whores Came Out To Play Tennis*—possesses a somewhat vicious extravagance that surprises one into risibility. Behind its nonsense lurks a revulsion from a wealthy Jewish business background. The scene is the "nursery" of a country club. The older folk are confused vulgarians, pathetic empty heads, addle-brained would-be gentlemen of fashion; the younger are impotent nincompoops or potential thugs with savage contempt for their elders. The play develops a metaphor for a rootless urban middle class that is going rapidly to pot in its own inanity, obscenely mocked and ultimately to be destroyed by the whorish world outside—or simply by its women!

You may find this distasteful or little better than fraternity-house Ionesco, but it does exist as a creation, howsoever minuscule. That is why one can occupy oneself thinking about it for a bit, while *The Odd Couple*—which is graced by *one* witty line—can hold us no longer than does a chortle over a parlor-car joke.

The Kopit evening is well staged by Gerald Freedman and in the main shrewdly cast, notably in the persons of Phil Foster and Anthony Holland.

—*NAT*, 5 Apr. '65

JUDITH

I am not at all confident that I can write an "objective" review of the APA—Phoenix production Jean Giraudoux's *Judith*, which I directed unsuccessfully in June, 1962, in London. But since the play is no routine job, I hope I can discuss Giraudoux in a way that may shed a little light on the work itself.

There are more than a few critics in America and England—even in France—who resist even if they don't dislike Giraudoux. An ambiguity, a lack of resolution, is caused in Giraudoux's art (style and content) by the tension in the man himself. For Giraudoux was a divided personality who, it would seem, tried to mask this division from his very self.

He shunned—almost abhorred—naturalistic "psychology"; it entails a degree of self-probing. The opposing stresses of his spirit could be reconciled only through irony. But even his irony was breached, for he had committed himself—as Frenchman, diplomat and bearer of a tradition of playful intelligence, airiness and good temper—to a smiling rather than a bitter irony. Dostoevskian shades do not befit a polite *salon*.

Even his artistic tastes were contradictory. For while he was thoroughly national in his emphasis on clarity, decorum and sparkle, he was attracted by the romantic mists and metaphysics of German literature and legend. His first play *Siegfried* (based on his novel) was the story of a Frenchman who, having lost his memory during the war and having been mistaken for a German, is educated and achieves eminence as one, only to discover slowly and painfully that he is after all irreducibly French. Though I speak of "pain," the tone of the play is bantering. This is true of most of Giraudoux's plays no matter how grave the subject. One might suppose that Giraudoux wished to reconcile the two opposing impulses within himself—a result which he only occasionally achieved.

(This inner conflict extended to his political activities: while he feared the worst, he hoped that France and Germany would remain friendly. He was Minister of Information and Propaganda during the early war years; and it has been whispered in Paris that he was possibly done away with by the Germans.)

Giraudoux fervently desired and dreamed of a spotless spiritual sky—a world of mellow sunlight, generous fruit, lovely girls and bubbling wine! He hankered for some pristine purity—such as the atmosphere of his native home in central France seemed to promise. Wounded during the First World War, Giraudoux grew to be a worldling

attached to various ministries of the Third Republic which, suffering from a sort of political and moral schizophrenia, dissolved in debility and corruption. The darkling clouds of reality obscured Giraudoux's blue heaven. Loyal to his initial impulses, to his tradition and position, he was determined to maintain his affability. His writing—sometimes compared to impressionist painting—seems to float in space without structure; it twinkles, shifts, breaks into hard gemlike fragments or vaporizes in rainbow hues creating a beguiling iridescence in which we are perhaps not meant to discern the essence. For that was drawn from a lacerating experience.

The experience had shattered the myth, it had given the lie to his dreams. There was a worm in all the fruit. The purity of the inherited tradition—the blessed days of France's past—was marred by the intrusion of disgraceful facts. Yet the myth had somehow to be preserved and faith in its eventual justification to be upheld with charm. Virtually all of Giraudoux's stage work is the dramatization of this struggle—sometimes thoroughly abstracted and now and again made more concrete in the social and political implications of *Tiger at the Gates* and *The Madwoman of Chaillot*.

Giraudoux wrote comedies—the gayest being *Amphitryon 38*. Some of them touch the hem of tragedy. In *Intermezzo* (*The Enchanted*) Giraudoux flits from gleeful whimsy to diatribe and violence only to beat a wistful retreat in cozy compromise. But he called *Judith* "a tragedy." It is not a tragedy but it is worth considering the reason for the designation.

Judith, a heroic, voluptuous and vengeful widow in the Apocrypha, becomes a young "society" girl in Giraudoux's play, though its scene remains pseudo-Biblical. She is the somewhat flighty, flirtatious child of a banking family, passionately romantic withal. At first she mocks the idea of the mission assigned her of slaying Holofernes, the oppressor of her people. But when she realizes that hope of military victory is lost, she goes to Holofernes' tent in the expectation of beguiling him by her wit.

Instead of a monstrous barbarian, Holofernes proves a gloriously attractive and intelligent pagan. In ardent trembling Judith abandons herself to him. Then she kills him. Why? Because exalted idealist that she is, she feels that nothing in her life hereafter will ever equal the ecstasy of her contact with him, that all which will follow must prove itself a descent to an intolerable mediocrity.

The rabbis are satisfied with the murderous event which has saved their state and people. But Judith insists on pronouncing the truth: that she killed Holofernes for love. The rabbis will not hear of this; she must be transformed into a national heroine, a sanctified Judge of Israel. Through the sudden intervention of an angel in the body of a drunken soldier (Giraudoux's *deus ex machina*), Judith is persuaded that though she had her own motivation in killing Holofernes, God *used* her action for His superior design. God, in other words, has his reasons which we are bound to obey with as much grace and fortitude as possible. The fallen angel (he is "fallen" because he has betrayed God's secret) blesses "Judith the whore" as she solemnly goes forth to assume her historical role as "Judith the saint."

Underneath all its mystifications—the wry anachronisms, the wordplay, the poetic flourishes and the bright conceits—we find Giraudoux the man in tormented sincerity. Because of the disparity between intention and form—the wish to be fiercely significant and personally prophetic while retaining a paradoxical blitheness—the play leaves a good part of the audience with a disquieting sense of vagueness, pretense and preciosity. The discrepancy also makes the play almost impossible to embody satisfactorily on the stage. Because it has frustrated practically every attempt to find a production style, *Judith* has never been a success anywhere.

In a translation by Christopher Fry my London production—doomed by miscasting—emphasized the play's passionate vein together with the headlong drive and semi-classic swell of its language. Thus much of the humor was sacrificed—though

there is less of this than in most Giraudoux. The APA production, which employs an *adaptation* by John Savacool, attempts to convert the play into an ironic bit of French *persiflage*, almost a "sexy" light comedy. Though Rosemary Harris has appealing qualifications for the central role in either direction, Giraudoux's text, it seems to my probably prejudiced eye, will not yield to the insouciant or relaxed treatment the APA gives it— even with the aid of the adaptation's added jokes. Even if such treatment made the play function satisfactorily as a show, I should be obliged to consider it a falsification of its theme. In any case, the peculiar reception of the play by press and public make it clear that it fascinates some while others it baffles and bores.

—*NAT*, 12 Apr. '65

THE AMEN CORNER

James Baldwin's *The Amen Corner* (Ethel Barrymore Theatre) provides one of the very few evenings which afforded me true pleasure this season. And how surprising. For if I wished to be "real critical" (which means a little foolish) I could easily point out the play's crudities, banalities, *longueurs*, etc. Text and production are marred by many blemishes but the total effect is touching and valuable. Drama does not live by technique alone, nor is art all a matter of "mastery."

What makes *The Amen Corner* gratifying is it genuineness. I don't mean "realism." The play's locale is a "store-front church"—the kind of Harlem church which has no exact denomination or theology except for its own blasted blessedness; and I am not in the least familiar with such an establishment. The sense of genuineness the play creates comes from its sure feeling for race, place and universality of sentiment. It is folk material unadorned and undoctored. It is the stuff which has made the best in Baldwin. It has heart and reaches the heart.

Its crucial passages are beautifully written, wrought of living speech from the mouths of the people whose very clichés somehow transform themselves into poetry. A woman is described as being "full of nature." A man dies and his wife says without emphasis, "My baby. You done joined hands with the darkness." But quotations out of context offer only the barest hint of the sudden poignancy of some of the play's phrases and idioms which are uttered as commonplaces.

The weakest moments are the conventionally comic and the factually "satiric" ones. The play is not "propaganda": it does not insist that religiosity turns the sorry creatures of the community away from reality. There is no glib anti-clericalism here. "This way of holiness ain't no joke," says the unhappy and presumably bigoted woman minister who is the play's central character. "To love the Lord," she learns, "is to love all His children—all of them, everyone! and suffer with them and rejoice with them and never count the cost!" One believes this as one believes a spiritual. In a much simpler, a less probing way, Baldwin has used the material of his past somewhat as O'Neill used his own early youth in *Long Day's Journey Into Night*.

The Amen Corner was written before *Blues for Mr. Charlie*, which is Baldwin in an angrier, more sophisticated, less appealing but perhaps more immediately "useful" vein. But nothing in the later play is as moving as the confrontation of the derelict father and his neglected son, or the minister's "reconversion" (a reconversion to a profounder humanity) in *The Amen Corner*.

It is possible that a great part of my enthusiasm for this production is due to its acting. The play is not well staged or designed. Some of the actors are awkward, insufficiently trained. Yet nearly everything "works" because there is an organic relation between the play's essence and the company. There is little art but much "nature."

Still, Frank Silvera's Luke (the father: a moribund jazz trombonist) strikes home. He may be a trifle soft in his interpretation but there is in him a will to contact the very core of his partners' (his son's, his wife's) being which overrides every other consideration and which moves one inescapably.

Bea Richard's Sister Margaret (the minister) is glorious. Hers is certainly the outstanding achievement in acting of this past season. Again, qualifications which might be damaging in other instances—a rather thin voice and a delivery that threatens to become monotonous, an interpretation that tends to subtract some of the iron and soul-smashing drive of the character—dissolve in the truth of Miss Richards' pathos, the overwhelming fullness of her womanliness in which the sorrow of bitter experience and the abiding humor and tenderness of a total cycle of life manifest themselves effortlessly and yet with electrifying surprise.

After the first week, prices at *The Amen Corner* were lowered from a $6.90 top to maximums of $5.75 on Friday and Saturday evenings, $4.80 on Monday through Thursday and Saturday matinee, and $4 on Wednesday matinee. These are bargain prices for Broadway in 1965 and it will be good news for us all if they bring the play an audience. Show business wiseacres keep repeating that if a play is good, people will pay any price to see it. That is just not so, and the only reason that this truism is rarely contradicted is that our show folks' vision and knowledge of the world is circumscribed by the one street which is their preserve.

—*NAT*, 10 May '65

HAPPY DAYS

The alternate performances of *Happy Days* at the Cherry Lane: Madeleine Renaud in French, Ruth White in English, offered a contrast not simply in languages but of acting styles. One might say that Madeleine Renaud and Ruth White, being separate individuals, would naturally differ in their presentation of Winnie, the lady who speaks with very little interruption by her husband for an hour and twenty minutes in Beckett's play. But the difference extends beyond personalities. There is a difference of approach that is related to national character, to tone and techniques characteristic of the actresses' cultural backgrounds.

Renaud's interpretation made the impression of a remembered performance. She herself does not seem fully there! By this I mean that the French actress went through the part, studied the meaning of its every phase and phrase, and perfected every device of voice and gesture which she might use to convey those meanings. These signs or indications of the character's traits and of the author's intentions are rendered with sharp accuracy, intelligence and polish. The result strikes one as a duplication or copy of something initially conceived and perhaps felt. It is a superb demonstration or explanation, but none of the original impulses seem to be *present*.

This is classically French. For the French—as Diderot once preached and Coquelin practiced—believe that the actor first experiences or recognizes the emotion of his part and then, observing its manifestations, fashions a form that will most attractively embody it. There is of course an intimate correspondence between the actor's first inspiration and the means by which he chooses to reproduce or imitate it. Still, little attempt is made to forge them into an organic unity. This gives the practiced French actor—and Renaud is one of the most accomplished exemplars of the tradition today—a certain objective quality which induces in the spectator a sense of seeing the finished portrait at a distance.

An American actor will aim to make his characterization happen, so to speak, immediately and afresh at each performance, to make it an event being born and living at the very moment we witness it. When the French actor is inferior, we get a disillusioning artificiality or emptiness; when the American actor fails he becomes strained or self-indulgent.

Happy Days changed with the alternation of cast. Renaud made the play crisper, harder, more ironic. Ruth White lent it greater humor, humanity and much more variety. The play thus acquired a tenderness which adds to its stature by making it more complex or, at any rate, less pessimistically unilinear.

If Beckett is at all like Gorky in this respect, he might say, as the Russian dramatist did, of two productions of one of his plays which were produced in Moscow at about the same time: "Both are Right." But my own preference is clear. Ruth White is one of our most talented actresses. Only the sorry state of the New York theatre situation in general has prevented wide recognition of this fact.

After seeing its first production in 1961, then reading the play, then seeing it twice again in the surprise "repertory" scheme of the Cherry Lane, I thought I had had a surfeit of *Happy Days*. I suspected that it was more suited to performance on radio or to disk recording than to the stage. This I now realize is not at all true. Just as there is in its spare writing a wealth of subtle allusion, so every image and stage property—the use of pistol, parasol, lipstick and reticule, etc.—becomes strangely telling, indeed vital to the play's total effect and meaning. It is a bitter, funny, touching work—gratifyingly inconclusive.

—*NAT*, 18 Oct. '65

PLAYS AND POLITICS

To the question, "What has the American theatre to say at the present time about the state of American politics?" the answer is "very little." The question which might then more pointedly be put is "Why?" Those who ask either of these questions are usually more interested in politics than in the theatre. Still, they are good questions for people devoted to the theatre to ask themselves. The effort to answer will momentarily make them ponder politics and also induce them to think a little less superficially about the theatre.

In any discussion of the theatre one of the first things to inquire about is the nature of the audience. On Broadway, where most new plays originate in America, the audience never pays less than $2.50 for the poorest seat, and often more than $6.90 for the best. One can hardly call this a representative audience, even in the era of affluence. It excludes most teachers and students, many professional people who are not in the high income brackets, and what used to be called the "working class." It is an audience of the business community: manufacturers, buyers and moguls of the plushier trades. It demands titillation. Hence musicals and light comedies are almost the only shows which sell out. The economic setup of the New York theatre makes it extremely difficult for plays that don't sell out to return a profit. And what doesn't make money soon disappears. What is believed likely to disappear doesn't get produced.

The facile explanation tells less than half the story. To proceed beyond it leads to perilous ground. I have no statistics, but I venture to say that Americans are not genuinely concerned with politics.

The ordinary American might define politics as something to do with elections and graft. He is convinced that China is a menace, that communism is evil, that taxes are too high, that juvenile delinquency is outrageous, that while the atom bomb is dangerous it is necessary, that our way of life, being the best, must be defended. Politics is something to which one lends oneself for a few minutes a day on TV, or can be disposed of by a cursory glance at the headlines and by gossip about "personalities." Politics is a sort of sport, and no one except a politician needs to devote himself to it.

This view is understandable, given our history. There have been very few deeply disturbing political events since 1865. Compared to its effects on Europe, the First World War was for us a mere scratch. Such scandals as those of the Harding administration or of the Jimmy Walker regime were jokes. A mere handful of people were aware of the implications of Franco's assault on democratic Spain. To judge by the aspect of our big cities at the time, the Second World War was a happy occasion. We disapproved of fascism because of its bluster, and we heartily disliked the Nazis because they produced sick-making sensations in our stomachs. The cause of the war, our

own or our Allies' responsibility in its outbreak, were obscure to us.

The depression of 1929-1939 shook us up. For a time we responded politically although, the crisis once passed, many of us grew impatient with Roosevelt and his reforms. But the depression was a condition no one could overlook, and our theatre gave striking evidence of the fact.

Came Eisenhower, the new normalcy and McCarthy. The Senator scared the wits out of us before he destroyed himself, and we have not yet recovered from the infection he spread. For years, now, not only political discussion but all discussion of vital issues has been timorous or feeble. Such discussion may lead to dissent. Nowadays we hardly know what to dissent from except such enormities as totalitarianism, the insults of inimical powers, narcotics and teen-age killers. Dissent usually involves criticism of our country, than which there is none better on earth. Dissent, moreover, smacks of softness toward foreign ideologies. We had enough of that in the thirties.

Today the civil rights struggle—especially in its painless forms—stirs a great many people. But when prejudice of this stamp is dealt with on the stage it is in a musical like *West Side Story* or in a sentimental play like *A Raisin in the Sun*. Nearly everybody, and especially those who are peculiarly touchy about aesthetics, shudders at the hate in LeRoi Jones's plays. I myself am frightened and mortified by it, but we occasionally need to realize its presence and to see it dramatized in full terror.

We hear that there is a new radicalism in the colleges and among the young who are exasperated by the flatness, the inexpressiveness of our lives. Though the manifestations of this trend are sometimes raw and foolish, it should be viewed as a hopeful sign if it leads to the discipline of study, thought and firmness or conviction. Nerviness is not enough.

The fighting in Vietnam troubles us and we are becoming increasingly vocal about it. The majority of our countrymen react automatically, either approving the government's policy as a matter of simple patriotism, or denouncing it without facing the central issue: whether or not the possible victory of communism in Asia is something that non-Communists are prepared to accept.

If I am only partly right in these assertions, politics as such can hardly be expected to prove a proper subject for American theatrical entertainment. But should I be thought mistaken there are still other phases of the question which the liberal mind often overlooks.

Granted that plays dealing with politics on our stage usually are reduced to such convivial dramatizations of columnist chatter as *The Best Man* or to empty melodrama like the play made from Allen Drury's *Advise and Consent*, one must also recognize that very few political plays of more than momentary value exist in dramatic literature generally. What we sometimes name political plays of social significance or historical plays of broad political application.

Shaw wrote several political plays—*The Apple Cart*, *Generva*, *On the Rocks*—but they are hardly among his best. Shakespeare's Histories possess general political meaning, but they are political only by extension and analogy, as is the case with Miller's *The Crucible*, Sherwood's *Abe Lincoln in Illinois*, Kingsley's *The Patriots*. There are also social-political "allegories," written in various veins, like most of Sartre's play or Genet's *The Balcony* and *The Screens*.

Not long ago a play about the Hiss case was produced on Broadway but, like most such accounts of recent events, it was an inconsiderable piece. Only the Germans and French have thus far accepted a stage version of the Oppenheimer case. Even Kingsley's dramatization of Koestler's *Darkness at Noon*, cited as the Best Play of the Year 1950-51 by the New York Drama Critics' Circle, remained largely inoperative. I could name several other similar plays, like Maxwell Anderson and Harold Hickerson's *Gods of the Lightning* (about the Sacco-Vanzetti case) or John Wexley's *They Shall Not Die* (about the Scottsboro boys) which flashed by without attracting anything but the most limited attention.

Far more effective than any of these were the documentaries presented by the Federal Theatre Project at low prices—*Triple-A Plowed Under* and *One-Third of a Nation*—which produced audience impact through their novel staging and immediacy. But for the popular treatment of topical subjects the movies and television are more appropriate media. Even Odets' *Waiting for Lefty* (about the taxi drivers' strike in the thirties) proved forceful not because of its political message but because of its colorful idiom and youthful fervor. For the rest, with the exception of his anti-Nazi *Till the Day I Die*, Odets' plays are not political at all but social, akin in this respect to O'Casey's early work.

A social play stems from a particular environment which to a degree is a reflection of a political condition. Chekhov's plays and Shaw's *Heartbreak House* are examples. Osborne's *Look Back in Anger* has English social connotations though its political direction is by no means clear. Gorky's dramatic work, rightly held to be inflammatory in Czarist Russia, was not at all propaganda for a particular party or a guide to an unequivocal political solution.

Since all plays are the products of mores and attitudes common to particular sectors of society and are addressed to a public presumed to be attuned to the dramatists' state of mind, one might maintain that all plays are social. (Even *The Ziegfield Follies*, I have often said, could be regarded as a mirror of its times.) The reason why the social basis of drama is not more often pointed out is that audiences and reviewers prefer to think of plays wholly in terms of entertainment or, betimes, of art. In this way they avoid the discomfort of dealing with troublesome matters. They want to divorce entertainment (or art) from their daily concerns. The wish is justifiable, since their concerns are often trivial, but by this amputation they frequently rob both entertainment and art of their primary value.

There is a sense in which the theatergoer who seeks relief from his workaday cares is right. The domain of the theatre is universal, nothing human is alien to it; but the most durable and hence most profoundly influential plays are those which transcend their immediate "journalistic" material. What we seek finally in the theatre is an escape—into reality.

Our ordinary activities are dross of transitory interest even to ourselves. What we truly long for is to be transported to some realm of truth, the purest consciousness. This super-reality which lifts us above the ordinary traffic of existence is what the theatre (along with the other arts and, some may add, religion) aspires to, and in its greatest and rare occasions achieves.

What makes Chekhov's plays so touching is not their depiction of the unhappy middle class of Russia at a certain period, but the use he makes of this subject matter. From it he wrings the "music" of idealistic yearning, the aspiration which both torments and elevates the hearts of not particularly bright folk everywhere. What lends stature to Ibsen's *Hedda Gabler* is not so much the psychology of a lady caught between two social classes, but our recognition that we are all a little like her—unable to find any sphere which satisfies our innermost needs.

Plays of so-called classic breadth, from Aeschylus to Racine, attain such heights. The better realistic plays of modern times move willy-nilly toward the same goals. Patently social plays, like those of Shaw and Brecht, Büchner's *Danton's Death* or Hauptmann's *The Weavers*, are sustained by a similar afflatus. Political plays, if they are intelligent and honest (Hochhuth's *The Deputy*), are to be welcomed even when they do not qualify as art. How many plays of any sort do? Still annals of drama teach us that specifically political plays seldom reach the loftiest peaks—unless one calls *Trojan Women* or *Julius Caesar* "political."

Nearly all social plays of merit exercise political effect, although the degree or exact orientation of such effects are not always determinable. We may cite such old examples as Beaumarchais' *Marriage of Figaro* as relevant to the French Revolution and Gogol's *The Inspector General* as relevant to all bureaucracies. There is no doubt that the naturalistic plays of the middle and late 19th century exerted liberalizing persuasion, first in Germany and Russia, and later in England and France. One the other hand, a sizable portion of the Paris audience just before the Second World War applauded Shakespeare's *Coriolanus* as a reactionary play which others (Brecht, for instance) have interpreted in another sense.

We come now to what for our present purpose is the crucial problem: "How is one to account for the fact," a friend writes me, "that the more dramatic the general political situation becomes, the more intensely private and ingrown are the preoccupations of our more talented playwrights?"

The answer is that the plays referred to in this query, though hardly political, constitute our social drama! There *is* a connection between the theatre and politics. It is sometimes direct and positive; at other times indirect and negative. Today it is mostly negative. The Theatre of the Absurd, seen as a generic phenomenon without judgment as to individual talents, is, whether the writers themselves agree or not, a direct consequence of the social-political climate in most of the "free world." It represents despair and sometimes an oblique protest in regard to the societies from which the plays emerge. They are mockingly bitter outcries signifying a sense of impotence. They present our world as a frightful mess, a ridiculous fraud; a tragic farce. There is nothing left for us to do, they tell us, except to suffer and wait (for what?), jeer and try to avoid hurting anyone or, in extreme instances, burst the bonds of decorum and reason (which have been of no avail) to find some sado-masochistic "mystical" release. America, they intimate, is smug and hypocritical. Britain's stiff upper lip has gone slack with indecision, France poses in a caricature of grandeur. The Soviet Union abides in a strait jacket; China is a threatening tyranny. According to some of these playwrights it is entirely possible that life itself is no damned good and probably never has been. So they turn their backs on all this and now and then seek repose within some no man's land of bleak contemplation or lunacy.

I do not speak in contempt. Today many artist-intellectuals (not to mention others) feel spiritually homeless. They believe themselves deprived of any reliable political, social, religious base. For them all the old faiths are meaningless. That is why in America they appear to take special satisfaction in patronizing the credulous thirties. Their political posture consists of their refusal to assume any. And, one should add, no wonder. The moral and political atmosphere of the world is confusing everywhere. It is easier to assail these new and personally benign nihilists by argument than to reassure them with concrete proposals. The most "advanced" among them are trying to formulate an aesthetics of non-art.

Insofar as these impulses represent protestations against all that is bogus in our society, and if in the process of protest new means of expression are discovered, this anarchic tendency performs a positive function. But a persistent turning away from the world ultimately leads to a conformism as dull and debilitating as accommodation.

Very few of the new plays have any action. Indeed hardly any of them require it, because they deal with states of being in which will power has become superfluous. Since most such plays are based on the assumption that nothing is changeable, they present characters who never bother to change anything. We approach the dead end of drama.

To extricate himself from this dilemma the future playwright must consent to dwell in "error." He must take a walk into the awful world, get to know it ever more intimately and widely. What is chiefly wrong with Soviet realism is that it is not sufficiently realistic. It is usually little more than publicity. Still the aims of that realism, liberated from officious supervision and Philistine dogma, are healthy. They bid the dramatist make contact with society, explore the hardships and triumphs of labor, probe the souls of men and women in the travail of the new civilization as it is being formed, or of the old as it destroys itself. This tradition

gave Russia and the rest of us such writers as Gogol, Turgenev, Tolstoy, Dostoyevsky, Chekhov and Gorky—none of them literalists—and has still much to offer.

As soon as they have attracted notice through early success, American playwrights now tend to become encrusted in professional circles and thus rapidly to detach themselves from their creative sources. They deteriorate into provincials in the sterile ground of fashionable Broadway intellectual coteries.

When we learn to see ourselves and our neighbors truthfully against the broadest horizons of human concern, we shall perhaps not need to clamor for *political* plays; good ones will do.

—*NAT*, 25 Oct. '65

DANTON'S DEATH

A genius, Georg Büchner (1813-37) wrote *Danton's Death* at the age of 22. The play was so far in advance of its time that it was not given a production till sixty-seven years after its composition. Not only were its technical demands beyond the capacities of the 19th-century stage, but its artistic character and inner significance are difficult to appreciate by any audience not profoundly aware through personal and social experience of the contradictions between action and being, feeling and behavior.

"History walks on two feet," in other words, it is man made. Yet the men who make it are different from what they make. The consequences of the historical process exceed the intentions of those who set it in motion. There is an inexorability in the march of history which almost inevitably overwhelms and discards its leading actors.

Though Büchner was himself a radical, he understood the tragedy of revolution. "The Revolution," he has Danton say, "eats its own children." This is not because of the villainy of particular people. There are no heroes or villains in *Danton's Death*. In this lies one of the most impressive attributes of the play. In brief scenes which move hectically and spasmodically like the turbulent events of history itself, scenes dense with characters of crucial importance who are at the same time almost no more central than the passing fragments of the surrounding mob, one senses the palpably human fabric, the very texture of history.

Danton is that complex of traits which mingles the burning idealism, the passionate energy of the dedicated revolutionary with a voracious sensuality which tends toward passivity, skepticism, even corruption. Embarked on the tempest of his political course Danton finds himself weary of its strain, longing for gratification in creature comforts, those things for lack of which he was propelled into action. He is horrified by the cruelty and chaos released by his initial political impulses and commands. Yet he is incapable of believing that similar violence will be done to himself and his comrades. In every fiber of his being he feels the necessity and justification of revolution but he cannot bear to witness the shattering disruption which the revolution entails. What he has done brings about a negation of those sweet and warm satisfactions for which he is so thoroughly endowed and for which he so desperately yearns. He dies in defiance of his executioners and with a sense of relief that his dilemma is being put to an end.

They are all here—the dramatis personae of the French as of most bloody revolutions: the ascetic Robespierre, ruthless in logic, to all intents and purposes immovably convinced of the justice of his dictates, no matter how painful, and still secretly disturbed by doubts and momentary tugs of pity; St. Just, who with suave sophistry, rationalizes terror; Camille Desmoulins, roused by the ardor of his youthful eloquence beyond the recognition of his own vulnerability; the aristocrats turned radical with a haughty disdain which is part sovereign obligation and part cynical indifference to their own safety; the crass bureaucrats, drive without conscience; the women, tender companions who stand by their men to the very end,

encouraging their heroics, suffering their defeats; the sluts who live off the detritus caused by the male-engendered upheaval; the addled populace veering from side to side according to prevailing winds and the pressure of their needs. All are presented as straws in the fateful storm of destiny.

So rich a play, it would seem, cannot but produce a tremendous effect on the stage. But a miracle has been wrought at the Vivian Beaumont Theater (Lincoln Center). The play has not simply been rendered dull but made almost wholly unintelligible, communicating next to nothing.

I am not being supercilious when I speak of this as a "miracle." The truth is that I am not quite certain how the phenomenon has been brought about. The actors have strong voices and articulate clearly enough—in fact they are often given to shouting—but one does not really follow what is being said. Meaning somehow fades in mid-air. One does not even enjoy the masochistic pleasure of being bored or outraged; one is simply reduced to a state of inanition. The performance has no definite *presence*; one sits in the theatre as if enveloped in a vacuum.

I am sure that the director, Herbert Blau, a most intelligent man, understands the play. But his understanding has taken no specific shape. The actors have not been transformed through clearly marked characterization. No character lives as a character. (Perhaps the only exception is Robespierre who strikes one as a Republican appointee to the judgeship of a small American town.) Many of the actors appear embarrassed by the words they mouth as if there were a cleavage separating language from the person. The dialogue, more involved in this translation than in any other and certainly less lucid than the original German, seems to issue from inanimate sources.

The scenic scheme, elaborate and expensive, also fails to register. Some of the most important scenes are played on the forestage (really an apron attached to a proscenium) so that instead of creating any sense of environment we get the impression of actors at rehearsal handicapped by lack of props or proper space. Physically the production is altogether without atmosphere except for the mechanics of a revolving stage floor, sliding panels, set pieces advancing toward us on tracks.

My bewilderment at what was happening or not happening in this notable play (which I had previously seen in two different and thrilling German productions) was so upsetting that I began to blame the very edifice in which I found myself. Perhaps, I thought, the theatre itself, a combination of imposing architectural forms, with large esplanades fronted by a gigantic Henry Moore sculpture and a square pool, with an interior which is neither exactly intimate nor epically sweeping, was at fault. But that is going too far! The trouble lies elsewhere. There is some deep incongruity in the assembled elements: the text, the company, the audience (what's Hecuba to them or they to Hecuba?), the premises and the auspices of the occasion.

I have often asserted that a repertory theatre of the sort Lincoln Center aims to provide must be allowed at least three seasons to prove itself. Thus nothing I have said about the first production of the season under the new management must be construed as a condemnation of the entire enterprise, though it is certainly a cause for worry.

—*NAT*, 15 Nov. '65

BARBARA HARRIS
ON A CLEAR DAY

Barbara Harris waited three years to appear in *On A Clear Day You Can See Forever* (Mark Hellinger). The show by Alan Jay Lerner (book and lyrics) and Burton Lane (music) reminds me of the man who knew a joke and wanted a musical built around it. *On A Clear Day* is about a simple working girl who has extrasensory perception. She is also able to recall a previous life in 18th-century England when she was a highborn lady. That's all. Nothing is added to the "idea" except a lot of expensive scenery. An orchestra seat costs $11.90.

A great deal of money is going to be lost. That's show business.

Barbara Harris is an extraordinary talent. She is all transfiguration. She can make anything of herself. Putty-faced, she resembles a woebegone kewpie doll. But she can make herself look like a romantic star, an exquisite aristocrat, a *femme fatale*. She appears to have no ego or identity of her own: she acquires one through the person she plays. One can see a whole series of instantaneous transformations in her present performance inside a very brief span of time because the character she is supposed to impersonate is nonexistent and she is obliged to replace it with whatever her fancy dictates. She improvises new personalities throughout. A *dybbuk* seems to be in control.

As I watched her in the new show she took on a symbolic dimension. She became young American stage talent in general: charming, mercurial, full of delightful quirks and astonishing leaps of the imagination, deprived of a fixed destination, a secure purpose. It is a state of perpetual dispersal. She is elusive, provocative, funny and ultimately quite sad. Who will write Barbara Harris a real part?

—*NAT*, 22 Nov. '65

THE COUNTRY WIFE

Shall we be grateful to the Repertory Theater of Lincoln Center for having produced Wycherley's *The Country Wife* as its second offering of the season? I am rather inclined to think so, despite the heavy burden of the production's faults. For *The Country Wife* is a masterpiece, champagne of English late 17th-century jest.

Unless you were present in 1936 to see Ruth Gordon's performance in the comedy (I was not), or Julie Harris' in 1957, you could not have seen the play at all, for it is rarely given even in England. Ruth Gordon is said to have been delightful in the role of Mrs. Pinchwife, the lively and candid country girl happily seduced by Mr.

Horner, a London rake who is the greater moral menace for having let it be rumored that he is impotent.

For all the excellence of the cast in which Julie Harris appeared with Laurence Harvey and Pamela Brown, that production failed to come alive. Nor does the present one at Lincoln Center. But somehow we do get a sense of the play's natural vigor beneath the shimmering surface. One is not often provoked to laughter—long sections of the play fall flat—but the audience is at least made aware of the reasons for laughter! It is too early to say what the new company at the Lincoln Center can do well, but its failure with *The Country Wife* cannot be the subject for condemnation. The play's style is no easy one to capture even by an expert English company. While Wycherley's play undoubtedly mirrors the mode or essential tone of Restoration high society and is in that sense "realistic," its artistic character is hardly that. Not only was life itself a game among the fashionable folk under Charles II, but art—particularly the theatre—became a further refinement, a brittle stylization of what to begin with aspired to artifice. The Restoration stage was an exquisite falsification of a reality which aimed at the "false," the un*natural*. Looking at the period drawings in the Repertory Theater program, one gets a vivid sense of the ideal projected by the court and courtesans of the time. The lewd postures and gestures of the figures are rendered as baroque arabesques in finery, foliage and anatomical fantasy more rarefied than robust. It is as if participants in an orgy proposed to cut elegant patterns for a dainty etching of the occasion. It is a mixture of fun and finesse, sensuality whittled to a fine point of irony, high-spirited leer and depreciating grace. It is the metaphor of a haughtily smiling self-consciousness.

That is not at all in the vein of our day. Certainly it has no relation to the company which now plays *The Country Wife* at the Vivian Beaumont Theater, a company which may be called anything but airy or carefree. It is both too young and too old for such dispassionate frivolity. Accord with or practice in the Theatre of the Absurd is hardly preparation for the humors of Restoration licentiousness. That genre was glassily wicked; our counterparts are bitter and tormented, heavy with grim mockery.

So we get a production on West 65 Street which, because the text itself is informed with brilliant verve and is dramatically sturdy, has a few merry moments. The actors are sufficiently energetic; they pound away at all the points with enough intelligence, if not with ease, for all of the play to be heard and, at least theoretically, appreciated. It is wide of the mark to say that they do not speak well; their spirit, not to mention their skill, is alien to the material. Yet I venture to suggest with some trepidation that if you have never seen the play you may still take pleasure in seeing it now—you are not likely to have another opportunity for a long time to come.

All this raises important questions: should such a company choose to do this play in view of its technical and environmental lack of aptitude for it? What sort of plays should a repertory theatre, housed as lavishly and auspiciously as the one at Lincoln Center, produce? There is a trend of opinion in certain critical circles which would unhesitatingly respond—"masterpieces!" Masterpieces of dramatic literature of which *The Country Wife* is no doubt an example. But this answer—like its more modest (and ambiguous) equivalent, "good plays"—seems to me to take little account of the theatre's special nature. The theatre is not a vehicle for the delivery of fine literature; it is the art of making meaning from the concordance of text, actors and audience at a particular time and place. When such a fortunate conjunction occurs a lesser text often will possess richer substance than a masterpiece done at the wrong time and/or place by the wrong group of people for the wrong audience.

The crucial considerations constitute a problem I hope to probe when the Repertory Theater of Lincoln Center has completed its first season!

—*NAT*, 27 Dec. '65

ONE HUNDRED YEARS IN THE AMERICAN THEATRE

Writing in 1869, Walt Whitman in his *Democratic Vistas* complains, "Of what is called drama, or dramatic presentation in the United States, as now put forth at the theatres, I should say it deserves to be treated with the same gravity and on a par with the questions of ornamental confectionary and public dinners, or the arrangements of curtains and hangings in a ballroom—no more, no less."

Seven months after the assassination of Lincoln in April, 1865, the "hit shows" were *Rip Van Winkle,* with the delightful actor Joseph Jefferson, and *The Black Crook,* the first of our big musicals in which "one hundred beautiful girls in short diaphanous skirts and flesh-colored tights" provided an unprecedented sensation.

This came at a time when our literature had already bequeathed to us *Moby Dick, The Scarlet Letter, Leaves of Grass,* not to speak of Emerson and Thoreau. We can sympathize with Whitman's reaction. But we are less astonished. The theatre is almost always a laggard art.

A single reader may be said to constitute an "audience" for a poem or a novel, one viewer may be sufficient to encourage the solitary artist who shows his painting. Theatre requires a larger number of people to convene at the same set time. The theatre is both a public and a composite art, *social* in the nature of its creation as well as in the circumstances of its manifestation. A history of the theatre must comprise not only a study of dramatic texts but an examination of acting, the mechanics and economics of production and, inseparable from all these, the audiences to whom the art is addressed and from whom it derives.

After they had passed through the primitive state of tribal rites the great theatres of the western world emerged as forms of civic and religious celebrations. State and church—in effect the entire community—supported them. Later, when the theatre was no longer an organic part of governing bodies, when indeed it was frowned upon and its suppression was urged by those who held it to be immoral, the theatre still managed to survive through various devices of aristocratic or royal protection. Despite all the vicissitudes of its history, the theatre was recognized as a social benefit meriting special privilege. In a word, a *tradition* developed in Europe which bestowed care for the theatre.

This tradition was lost in the settlement of America. The Puritans thought the theatre sinful. With a civilization to be built there was no time for such frivolity. By the time the educated minority was able to provide for them, a few playhouses were put up in the main cities of the eastern seaboard. Plays and actors were usually foreign. The best fare consisted of mutilated Shakespeare. There was practically no native drama and hardly any native actors.

When preoccupations beyond those of material needs could be entertained, schools and universities were established, important writers and a few signs of original theatrical creation appeared. One of these was Anna Cora Mowatt's *Fashion* (1845), a satire on the American parvenu, which in our present estimation is hardly more than a chromo. Yet Edgar Allan Poe found it praiseworthy.

That Poe should have welcomed so slight a piece, though he probably would not have deigned to notice its literary equivalent, may appear paradoxical. But this paradox repeats itself constantly.

(William Dean Howells in 1891 referred to James Hearne's *Margaret Fleming,* a crude and creaky bit of claptrap, as "epoch-making" because it was the first of our realistic plays.) We may discover a clue in this to the peculiarity of our theatre's progress.

"Hardly anybody listens in the theatre," the Irish dramatist Denis Johnston has said, "to anything he doesn't know already." For a play to prosper it must unite its audience—which to begin with must be homogeneous. A minority attitude, a heterodox premise are divisive, and the theatre's life depends on popularly recognizable interpretations of a common experience. The cultivated handful who were able to appreciate the Brahmins of our literature could not have filled the tiniest theatres of their times.

It has been said—and it is perhaps true—that the liveliest and most representative "theatre" of the period immediately following the Civil War was to be found in the riverboats, in the saloons, in the minstrel shows on the Mississippi and westward. These frolics possessed the rough vigor of their audiences, the hardy folk who were opening the country.

The situation in the East, as we have seen, was that which made Whitman exclaim, "Do you call that perpetual, pistareen, paste pot work...American drama?" Still clinging to his faith in the American dream he was dismayed by a society ever more dominated by money values. Capitalism was set on its roaring course of empire building. Fortunes were being made by and for a most fortunate people. It was the Gilded Age. Theatres attracted folk eager to ease themselves with entertainment inducing the minimum of mental strain. The really poor never went to ordinary playhouses and thus poverty was never made the subject of any but the cheapest tearjerkers. A large part of the audience was beginning to free itself from some of its Puritan inhibitions, though the "upper crust" in press and pulpit hypocritically persisted in upholding the Puritan code. Only the smiling aspects of American life or titillating melodrama were suitable material for such audiences. So rage as intellectuals might, the theatre between 1865 and 1890 was, in its own distorted way, a mirror of the times.

Even the intelligentsia does not go to the theatre for literature alone. Native acting during this period improved steadily. If America did not see any good plays (Shakespeare, remember, was bowdlerized), it had the opportunity of catching glimpses of such luminaries as Edmund Kean and Rachel, and later Salvini and Duse. Edwin Booth refined the red-necked robustiousness of Edwin Forrest, America's first tragedian (1806-1872) .

The actor-manager Lester Wallack, who beginning in 1861 ran a stock company for twenty years, was patronized by New York's gentry. His theatre was something like a London theatre in Manhattan. He never produced an American play because he found none that was good enough. After Wallack the big "name" producer from 1879 to 1899 was Augustin Daly, who had a sound sense of integral play production. Though he produced Shakespeare with excellent actors, the fare at his theatre was more frequently trash. Daly's "discovery," Bronson Howard, the first writer for our stage to become rich from his work, was the author of *Shenandoah* (1889), a Civil War saga which one cannot read today without indulgent laughter.

The theatre prospered, but because of the advent of realism the playhouses were built smaller. Playgoing became respectable; the social elite or "carriage trade" made it customary. Shows toured the hinterland. The theatre became industrialized. Henry James, writing in 1885, found that "scenery and decoration have been brought to the highest perfection while elocution and acting, the interpretation of meanings, the representation of human feelings have not long been the subjects of serious study."

To appreciate the frame of mind of theatrical leaders at this time one may cite the fact that in 1893 the dignified manager Daniel Frohman rejected Pinero's *The Second Mrs. Tanqueray* (about a woman who had been kept by four men before marriage) because it was "too frank." When it was produced, the reviewer of the New York *Herald* spoke of the play as being "for audacity surely without parallel in dramatic literature." Even as late as 1905, when Shaw's *Mrs. Warren's Profession* was produced (and suppressed), it was said by the New York *Sun* "to glorify debauchery."

Clyde Fitch, the most highly regarded dramatist between 1889 and 1909, was entirely sincere when he wrote, "I feel myself strongly the particular value of reflecting absolutely and truthfully the life and environment about us." He had the impulse to confess himself as much as to reveal the environment, but his play *The Truth* (1906), about a compulsive liar, and *The City* (1909), about the corrupting effects of the Big Town, are rather rickety contraptions. After all, plays, like most of the novels of the day, had to please the Ladies or they would incur the censure of the Gentlemen.

While Edward Sheldon may be credited with bringing social themes to the stage—the destitute in *Salvation Nell* (1908), the "race problem" in *The Nigger* (1909) and politics in *The Boss* (1911)—the plays themselves are sophomorically inept and timid. (Stephen Crane, Frank Norris, Theodore Dreiser had already written most of their stories and novels.) Sheldon's true vein was that of *Romance* (1913), about the love of an Episcopalian minister for an Italian opera star. A play which harks back to New York in its Age of Innocence, it is chiefly memorable as a vehicle for the glamorous Doris Keane, rapturously admired by Stark Young. There was artistic substance in the American theatre of the day—not in the plays but in the players. Otis Skinner, Laurette Taylor, Maude Adams, the Barrymores, and later Pauline Lord, Alfred Lunt and numerous others brought life to the boards.

One notes other progressive signs. The actor Arnold Daly champions Shaw, the intrepid actress Mrs. Fisk and the exotic Alia Nazimova do much to convince the retarded, including the shocked William Winter, the New York *Tribune's* drama critic from 1865 to 1909, of Ibsen's worth.

Most indicative of the community's steadily growing sophistication is the effort sponsored in 1909 by J.P. Morgan, John Jacob Astor, the Vanderbilts, Thomas Paine Whitney and Otto Kahn to establish a "permanent national art theatre." A sumptuous house was built on Central Park West between 62nd and 63rd Streets, at this time an exclusive residential section for the well-to-do, and a remote suburb to citizens of more modest means.

Chosen to direct the ambitious New Theatre was the Harvard educated Bostonian Winthrop Ames, a man of ability and taste. He enlisted an admirable company and produced Galsworthy's *Strife* (capital and labor), several plays by Maeterlinck (among them *The Blue Bird)* and Shakespeare. It was difficult to find American plays of corresponding calibre (only three, including Sheldon's *The Nigger,* were offered) because few American plays, with only such possible exceptions as Langdon Mitchell's brightly written comedy *The New York Idea* about divorce among the rich (1906) and Percy MacKaye's imaginative *The Scarecrow* (1910), were anything better than hack work.

The New Theatre collapsed after two seasons. Apart from the auditorium's unsuitability for the presentation of modern drama, its poor acoustics, its high prices and its inconvenient location, the reason for the New Theatre's failure was the absence of an audience great enough to sustain a serious repertory theatre.

Yet forces were at work to bring about a distinct change. Contact with Europe began to exercise a marked influence. The culturally alert became acquainted with stimulating and still unfamiliar dramatists (Tolstoy, Hauptmann, Gorky, Andreyev) on New York's Lower East Side—in both Yiddish and German. Little theatres were spreading all over the country so that by 1915 there were nineteen hundred. In 1916 the attractive comedian John Barrymore proved himself an actor of immense emotional power in Galsworthy's *Justice.* New manager-directors like Arthur Hopkins, inspired by overseas example, ventured into new fields which yielded fresh ideas, unusual plays employing the talent of that fine artist Robert Edmond Jones. A number of discriminating critics—their columns full of intriguing foreign references—began to clamor for a theatre in touch with art, literature and life. Chief among them was George Jean Nathan.

Most important, though little noticed at first, were the activities centered in the vicinity of

Greenwich Village. The year 1915 witnessed the formation of the Neighborhood Playhouse on Grand Street, The Washington Square Players (transformed into The Theatre Guild in 1919), the Provincetown Players, who were to reappear in the early twenties as a triumvirate of the critic Macgowan, the designer-director Jones and the dramatist O'Neill. These new groups planted seeds from which a proud harvest was soon reaped.

In 1920 we became conscious of the flowering with the production—cautiously introduced at special matinees—of O'Neill's first full-length play, *Beyond the Horizon*. That event marks the *birth* of American theatre as a conscious art intended to contribute to our inner life what we expect of the best literature.

This "birth" in the theatre corresponded to a rebirth in American letters generally. For while the years between 1835 and 1850 gave evidence of our native genius in poem, essay, short story and novel, the fortune-hunting years between 1865 and 1913 had very nearly destroyed vital literary expression. During this interval Dreiser, on the one hand, and Henry James, on the other, dwelled in limbo. This is also true of Whitman, Melville and Thoreau, whose work was known to a rare few only. They came into their own just before and immediately after the First World War.

What made the twenties a feverish and wonderful time was our coming of age in prosperity, in power, in self-confidence, as well as in self-consciousness. This made it possible for us to recognize our character and to acknowledge our shortcomings. Our desire to learn and accomplish things as a great nation lent a tremendous impetus to all endeavors. We became cocky and at the same time self-critical. We were prepared to look at ourselves with unrelenting realism. We were rediscovering ourselves as Americans.

Many thought us fooled by the holiday of our success. Others declared our iconoclasm adolescent. The superficial traits of our Puritanism were raucously shed. Freud began to be read by the literati. We rejoiced in our afflatus and jeered at

our rejoicing. Some said that America had become a jungle of competition; others read that Western Civilization was doomed. But whether the diagnoses and prognoses were rosy or black, everything took on a jubilant air.

New York playhouses doubled in number. One hundred ninety-six productions opened in 1920-21; two hundred seventy in 1927-28. The Theatre Guild assembled a loyal body of subscribers which assured its productions a minimum run of five to six weeks. The Guild did many unusual and stimulating plays by foreign authors, as well as by some Americans. After a while it clasped O'Neill to its bosom. Eva Le Gallienne at the Civic Repertory Theatre produced Ibsen, Chekhov and other "standard" European dramatists at popular prices.

Musical comedy, the one theatrical form in which we undoubtedly excel, with truly gifted tunes by Kern, Porter, Gershwin, Rodgers and others, sweetened the surrounding clamor. The Ziegfeld Follies, glorifying the American girl in gorgeous dress and suave undress, served as emblems of our high spirits. Among the lovely faces and the lush furnishings a parade of comedians close to genius cavorted.

The shadowy side of the picture was painted by the uncouth master figure of Eugene O'Neill himself. Apart from his concern with the complexities of personal psychology, O'Neill brooded on the drama of man's soul in America. Something had gone astray. The poet who yearns to explore realms beyond the narrow confines of his job fails to follow his bent and as a result wastes his being. The simple laborer proud of the strength which turns the wheels of our magnificent civilization finds himself scorned and adrift in a mechanism in which he is merely a cog. The artist wishes to attain the effectiveness of the man of affairs; the businessman envies the artist's imagination. Both suffer a sense of incompleteness. The would-be aristocrat from the Old World with his dream of grandeur is rendered absurd in the factory of a materialistic democracy. But without that strain of grandeur the dignity of a true manhood is somehow damaged. The son has little of his pioneering father's grit; the father in his struggle to master the soil of his farm (America?) impairs his capacity to love.

O'Neill dramatizes himself and us as people cut off from but still seeking some principle of coherence. For want of it everyone feels isolated and frustrated. O'Neill's strength lies in the persistence of his quest for a wholeness which has been shattered in the New World. We sicken in detachment from some age-old secret of sanctity. O'Neill is committed to its recovery. He told friends that his never-completed cycle of nine plays would be an epic of America's failure to realize its promise.

The depression of the thirties exposed the moral as well as the social lesion in the national body. Having been wounded where we believed ourselves invulnerable, we began questioning ourselves in new ways. The plays of the depression were not depressed. (Depressed plays appeared in the fifties in a time of prosperity.) The depression was a time of hope. Youth would not accept defeat, would not take "no" for an answer. It condemned the illusions of the previous decade, which had exulted in the fun principle. The thirties sought and found a solution to our dilemma in collective action for social betterment.

The theatre was struck a bitter, though not fatal, blow. The number of productions shrank; playhouses were sold for use as grind-movie emporia and for burlesque shows. Actors left for Hollywood, which prospered because the disconsolate wished to flee the gloom of impoverished homes and streets. The disease wrought its own healing. As Roosevelt aroused the country with his New Deal, so Groups, Collectives, Unions of the theatre were formed. What characterized most of them was the attempt to present plays confronting the times: the condition of the unemployed, the dispossessed, the unprotected worker, the dispirited middle class, the desperate farmer, the threat of fascism. All this was to be done in a new

fashion: through organizations which would commit themselves on a *permanent collective basis to a* disciplined practice of theatrical craft.

The theatre of the thirties was thought to be political—a mistaken opinion. Its impulse was moral—even moralistic. That is the essence of Odets' work. He was the era's representative playwright just as The Group Theatre, of which Odets had been an actor-member, was the representative theatrical organization. That is why after The Group Theatre's dissolution in 1941, it still remained an influence in the ensuing years through its former actors, directors, designers, teachers.

One particular contribution to theatre technique made by The Group was a way of work which was the heritage of the Moscow Art Theatre's New York visit in 1923. This was the Stanislavsky System, which in time—through the Actor's Studio founded in the forties-came to be known as the Method. While the Method is presumed to have narrowed the scope of American acting, though this is not at all its aim or necessary effect, it added a certain vibrancy and density of feeling to our actors' endowments.

With the scattering of forces during the Second World War and its immediate aftermath, in which not only The Group Theatre but the inestimably valuable Federal Theatre Project (the Government's first entrance into the domain of the arts) disappeared, a subtle change took place. As business as usual resumed, there followed a cooling of social fervor which soon turned into a freeze.

This was hardly noticed at first since Arthur Miller's early plays and even those of Tennessee Williams sounded a more subdued and introverted variation on the mode of the thirties.

Social reform had failed to "save" us. Many suggested panaceas had proved delusive (or so it was thought) and some were considered positively treasonable. The source of our ailments, it would appear, lay in our unsatisfactory relations with parents, wives, children. Our traumas—our traumas were to blame! Though Tennessee Williams' work always had discernible social connotations, what public and press chiefly responded to was its private and especially sexual aspects.

The age of conformity and of McCarthy terror drove men of sensibility into themselves. Young folk exiled themselves in the ghetto of their egos. The faceless world, all perpetual motion without any core of meaning, was to be shut out. "Contact," as someone has said about the new dancing, "went out in the fifties."

Connection with the outside world, now threatened with annihilation, became attenuated. Some solace (or drug) which might alleviate the pain of aloneness or sink us more deeply into forgetfulness was craved. To be "beat" became an ideal by default. This laid the groundwork for the dramaturgy of the maimed. The plays of Beckett, Genet, Ionesco, Pinter—usually presented at some distance from the theatre's supermarket—which were expressions of not altogether similar but of equally disabling stresses, became models for American writers. Edward Albee's "permanent vagrant" disturbing the complacent gent on the park bench is a youth who prefers contact through his own violent death at the hand of his neighbor to total neglect. At this moment Albee seems as representative of the early sixties as William Saroyan and Thornton Wilder were, in embodying the spirit of benevolent reconciliation (or "national unity"), in the early forties. Albee testifies to the agony of a society no longer real in which we try to live on debris of exploded faiths, a state which renders us savage.

Though, retrospectively, we may realize that since O'Neill our theatre has turned in earnest to the contemplation of our existence in a manner unthinkable a hundred or even sixty years ago, we remain dissatisfied. Broadway, as the hub of theatrical activity, has become an electrified desert. We still go there though its game is crooked because it is the only game in town! Seventy-five productions a season constitute the norm. At the moment of this writing only musicals and skimpy comedies are produced with much chance of public support. Movies and television are not the cause of the downfall.

It is show business itself which is destroying the theatre. Its arrangements are anarchic; the costs of production are too high, the price of tickets prohibitive. The greedy exactions of the stage-hands' unions are not the sole cause for this. They do what all the others do: treat the theatre as a business, which means every craft for itself, every man for himself. This inevitably becomes destructive to an art, the very nature of which depends on the planned and enthusiastic integration of its entire personnel. We have lost the tradition—indeed have never established one—of the theatre as a service, a social need. When business ceases to be profitable it has lost its reason for existence. There is "no foundation all the way down the line," in Saroyan's words, and it will take more than the Foundations to supply one.

Are we to end with a whimper? On the contrary, we may yet see a new beginning. Observation during my travels convinces me that the country is full of talent and appetite for theatre. Young folk are trying to rediscover a true theatre tradition.

The decentralization of the theatre is not the result of any special "idealism" but the response to a need for using all our unused gifts. In San Francisco, in Seattle, in Minneapolis, in Houston, in Washington, in Philadelphia and elsewhere new professional theatres have been, or are about to be, established. This trend is bound to grow.

These theatres aspire to be more than show shops. We are becoming aware that there are other "classics" beside Shakespeare. Many world-famous plays—ancient and modern, in foreign tongues and in our own—are still unknown to our stages because they do not sit well in the maw of commerce. One hears of productions in university and community theatres, as well as in cafés, of plays so "advanced" and "experimental" that even off-Broadway (now being assimilated into the stream of running rats) dares not undertake them. We are also beginning to get free theatre in the parks and on the very streets of certain cities—both in the South and in the North.

New York itself is now endowed with ambitious new theatre organizations. A heavy load of disdain has been hurled at the first two seasons of the Repertory Theater of Lincoln Center—some of it merited but most of it misguided. To found a theatre is not the same as setting up a series of productions. A considerable time of preparation and at least three years of performance are required as a preliminary test. The demand that these new organizations immediately satisfy our hunger for genuine innovation and artistic achievement is a way of applying the old hit-and-flop criteria of Broadway to enterprises with very different objectives and entirely different problems. The sheer fact of the Repertory Theater of Lincoln Center's having come into existence is a step forward. We must hope that the prolongation of its life, no matter under what auspices, will fulfill its serious artistic function.

If it is correct to speak of our theatre as having been "born" only forty-five years ago, we must agree that compared to the long years which went into the making of the Elizabethan, the French neo-classic stages, the recently founded British National Theatre, our theatre is in its infancy. It is part of our immaturity to expect immediate consummation. The misfortune of our theatre history—due to the absence of a tradition—is its fragmentation. We always seem to be starting from scratch. But perhaps this after all is not the case; there may be a continuity which we do not readily perceive because in our juvenile impatience we are forever grumbling, "Yes, but what have you done for me recently?"

—*NYTM*, '65

TINY ALICE

When Edward Albee's *American Dream* was first produced I presumed to "advise" him. Though the play was specifically American in its humor, I suggested that he eschew the abstract. After the deserved success of *Who's Afraid of Virginia Woolf?*, Albee in his latest play, *Tiny Alice,* has relapsed into abstraction.

Thirty-seven in March, Albee is still the best of our younger playwrights. Since Shaw was forty-five when Max Beerbohm chose to speak of him as "young," I do not feel it improper to refer to Albee as young and to persist in "advice." The kindest way to view *Tiny Alice* is as an honorable experiment. To be candid, the play struck me as the sort of thing a highly endowed college student might write by way of offering us a Faustian drama.

Its locale is generalized (neither England nor America), its action unreal, its speech a mixture of literate vernacular and stilted literacy. The settings (designed by William Ritman) are expensively and toweringly monumental, with a touch of the vulgarly chic. Except for the first scene, they represent the habitat of "the richest woman of the world."

I shall not discuss the plot because that might lead you to believe that I complain of its being too extravagantly symbolic or too obscure. The significance of certain details may elude one—and no harm done—but the play's intention is clear enough. It tells us that the pure person in our world is betrayed by all parties. The Church is venal, the "capitalist" heartlessly base, the "proletarian" cynical and, for all the good he may do, powerless and subservient. There remains Woman: enticing mother image and never-perfectly-to-be-possessed mate. (She may also embody the universal "Establishment.") The crisis in the pure man's life arises when, having found himself uncertain of his faith, he commits himself to a home for the mentally disturbed. Suffering from the need for tenderness and from religious anguish, he dwells in this womb of conscience to emerge after six years as a lay brother determined above all "to serve." But those who rule us—Church, the Economic Forces and Woman—bid him accept the world as it is. Being pure he cannot do so. Isolated and bereft of every hope, he must die—murdered.

Like Picasso, who said that his pictures do not have to be "understood," only seen and felt, Albee has suggested that people need not puzzle over his symbols; they have only to relax enough to be affected by them. There is this difference, however: Picasso paintings, whatever their "meaning," are fascinating on the surface. So too are Beckett's plays, Genet's and the best of Pinter's. Their images hold us; their complexities are compact with material in which we sense substantial value even when we are unable to name the exact nature of their composition. In art, Braque once observed, "It is not the ultimate goal which is interesting but the means by which we arrive there."

The surface or fabric of *Tiny Alice* is specious. The first scene (between "capitalist" and Cardinal) has some of the comic venom of *Virginia Woolf* but—except for those exhilarated by insults aimed at the clergy—it is by no means as apt. There is a certain cunning of suspense in the play, but the clearer it becomes the less convincing it seems. Its artistic method is too generalized to wound or even to touch us. Its pathos is weak, its scorn jejune, its diction lacking in most of its author's personal flair.

I do not ask Albee to stick to realism. *The Zoo Story* and *The Death of Bessie Smith* are not, strictly speaking, realistic plays—nor, in fact, does *Virginia Woolf* belong in that category. But in those plays Albee's dialogue had a true eloquence, a refreshingly dry and agile muscularity because it issued from the concrete. Their vocabulary was grounded in a life Albee had intimately experienced in his environment and in his senses. In *Tiny Alice* all his artful devices leave one impassive. The only moment my interest was piqued, I confess, was in the ambiguously sexual scene when the pure one succumbs to the millionairess' naked body.

Even though the play's terms rather than their meaning are what disconcert me, something more should be said about the content. Though Albee's spirit and gifts are entirely distinct from those of such recent masters of European drama as Beckett and Genet (each of whom in turn is different from the other), there is evidence of a similar "defeatist" strain. I do not share their view of life, but I recognize the aesthetic potency of Beckett's and Genet's work. They speak with genuine originality. They are, moreover, voices revealing of our day. That is their justification and their merit. (It is also to be noted once again that their work, though divorced from realism, is composed of indelibly memorable theatre metaphors.)

We often speak of their work as "negative" or "pessimistic." In a way, however, the pessimism of *Tiny Alice* has an even greater coherence, a more thoroughgoing finality than that of the Europeans. But though it is always easier to adduce evidence for a black view of life, that is, to prove the world an intolerably damned place, than to urge us in any contrary sense, one soon discovers that the conclusions of pessimism have only a minor value. For logic and proof bear little relation to the processes and conduct of reality. The more tightly one argues the futility of our life's struggle, the more futile the point becomes. It is much too simple. Thus the importance of *Tiny Alice* diminishes as our understanding of it increases.

The play is directed by Alan Schneider, and has been cast with such admirable actors as John Gielgud, Irene Worth, William Hutt, Eric Berry and John Heffernan.

—*NAT*, '65

THE WHITE DEVIL

Down amid the roisterers and derelicts of Bleecker Street in the oblong room which is known as the Circle in the Square, off-Broadway's literate audience has made a hit of John Webster's

1612 "tragedy of blood," *The White Devil*. Little wonder: it is a thoroughly contemporary play.

As I left the theatre (unshaken) I asked myself if it is also "great," a masterpiece or whatever it is we usually call a play that has survived the ages. All I felt at the moment was that, with due allowance for near plagiarism from Shakespeare, it is a "well-written" play, as people (critics included) say when they wish to avoid thinking about a play's content. It is better than well written, it is magnificently written. But was it, I put the question to myself, good?

The story is intricate. At times one fails to discern the connective plot tissue. The style alternates between rank melodrama and doleful lyricism, with, in addition, the mad scenes beloved by the Elizabethan and Jacobean dramatists. There are flashes of savage wit; there is chronic anger. I counted at least seven murders. The audience doesn't simply approve the play; it has a ball with it! It is in its element. For *The White Devil* is anti-Establishment: all, any, every Establishment from its time to eternity. Webster based his play on events which took place in Italy, but we know he was thinking beyond the confines of the peninsula.

Paul Tillich called Hamlet the first existentialist hero. For existentialist read "modern." But Marlowe's Tamburlaine and Faustus were already that. Machiavelli had previously dissected, explained and rationalized the anatomy of rule (he is mentioned in *The White Devil*) to the evident consternation of Shakespeare and other sweet souls. The secret was out—government, officialdom, the church, courts of law—were all instruments of a destructive process which Jan Kott in his *Shakespeare Our Contemporary* designates as the Great Mechanism. The Elizabethan and Jacobean dramatists were bitterly skeptical of power, politics and chivalric action. Hamlet doubts the moral validity of the revenge he is enjoined to wreak upon the King. His doubt renders him indecisive, hopeless and great.

Shakespeare's pessimism is mitigated by love. There is no mitigation in Webster. "Blood, Iago,

blood!," Othello cries out in piteous horror. There is no pity in Webster. His heroes are villains. The most fascinating—I almost said attractive—characters in *The White Devil* are a whore and a pimp brother and sister.

What lends the corruption and violence of the play dignity and makes it something more than a butcher's holiday is its social indignation. For example: "Will hear some of my court wisdom? To reprehend princes is disastrous, and to overcommend some of them is palpable lying." Or, "he was a kind of statesman that would sooner have reckoned how many cannon bullets he had discharged against a town, to count his expense that way, than how many of his valiant and deserving subjects he had before it." And again, "I have known men that have come from serving against the Turk, for three or four months they have had pension to buy them new wooden legs and fresh plasters; but after that, 'twas not to be had."

Not only are the aristocracy scorned but the law and religion as well. "...here they sell justice with those weights they press men to death with." And, "The first bloodshed in the world happened about religion." War alone is not feared. "There are mighty strokes come from the hand, But there are killing strokes which come from the head." Princes as well as the people suffer. "Misery of princes, That must be censured by their slaves! Not only blamed for doing things are ill, But for not doing all that men will—" And finally, "O, happy they that never saw the court, Nor ever knew great men but by report."

Retribution is rarely suggested except in such lines as: "Dost thou imagine thou canst slide in blood, And not be tainted with a shameful fall?" Treachery not only commands and prevails but is pictured as inescapable. One suspects that the young man who metes out justice at the end—"Let guilty men remember, their black deeds do lean on crutches made of slender reeds"—would prove still another sanguinary miscreant if he play were to go on.

Here and there as in all plays of this period there are the customary obceneties—as inevitable as the obligatory nudes in present-day films. These too make our audience feel at home. They recognize kinship with this unhypocritical play. It combines features of the play of social protest with those derivatives of the Theatre of the Absurd which extenuate the impulse to protest. But much of these aspects in *The White Devil* remain abstract to our audience. The play is fun, "art"—undisturbing. There is no pain in it at all.

To a large extent this is to Jack Landau's production. It is "well spoken, with good accent and good discretion." In this sense one may commend Frank Langella, Paul Stevens, Erie Berry, Robert Maria Tucci and the bold oddness of Carrie Nye (the white devil) whose diction, voice and carriage of neck and shoulders are equally peculiar. But though continuously interesting it is in another sense hardly a production at all. For economy's sake the characters are dressed in mufti. Modern clothes do not make a play any more contemporaneous than period dress since on the stage everything must be both false and real—in a word *expressive* of a dramatic meaning. For economy's sake too we get no significant sense of place. Imaginative costumes, settings and character make-up would contribute much to the kind of atmosphere this play demands if it is not to be a bare graph.

The production's most serious lack is some "flower of evil." The actor's all struck me as wholly without blemish, even without concupiscence: thoroughly innocent! *The White Devil* becomes child's play. Is it that—together with the painted horror—which pleases its Village audience? Never mind: it deserves its longevity; it is still worth seeing.

—*NAT*, 10 Jan. '66

THE CONDEMNED OF ALTONA

In 1959 when Jean-Paul Sartre's *The Condemned of Altona* was first produced in Paris the audience was deeply impressed and moved. It had cause. This play about a supremely wealthy German shipbuilder and his son was received as a parable. Though contemptuous of the Nazis, the older man had turned informer to get his son out of trouble—an act which led to the murder of a Polish rabbi. The son, who had attempted to protect the Jew and who scorned Hitler, was nevertheless a patriot and later, as an officer of the *Wehrmacht*, had resorted to torture of the enemy.

These events, antecedent to the play's action, establish the premise for the story of guilt that follows. Obtuse Frenchmen in the audience might have taken it as a cautionary tale directed solely toward the Germans; the more knowing saw the play as symbolic of the French condition during the internecine butchery in Algeria of the fifties.

Like the German shipbuilder's son in the play, the French hid themselves from knowledge of crime committed for *la patrie*. Many who protested were tracked down by hatred and violence. Though the vindictive were given to hypocritical rationalization of their brutality, others suffered inner torment and shame. In either case, these sentiments stemmed from two national humiliations: the early capitulation to the Germans and the successful rebellion in Algeria. The country was divided within itself. And, like Germany after its defeat, the French waxed ever more prosperous. It is perhaps no simple chance that the central figure of Sartre's play—the idealistic officer turned torturer—who has immured himself in the family citadel to hide his anguish and to shut out the evidence of his father's and his country's material well-being—is named *Frantz*.

Though the immediate stimulus for writing *The Condemned of Altona* may have been the Franco-Algerian tragedy, Sartre aimed at creating something more than a blunt political parable. The play's final moments reveal the deeper motivations. While father and son are on their way to a double suicide, a taped recording which Frantz had made in his seclusion is played. As the curtain is about to descend on the empty stage we hear:

Centuries of the future, here is my century, solitary and deformed—the accused. My client [Frantz is "defending" himself] *is tearing himself open with his own hands....I will tell you the secret of these multiple incisions. The century might have been a good one had not man been watched from time immemorial by the cruel enemy who had sworn to destroy him—man himself. One and one make one—there's our mystery. The beast was hiding, and suddenly we surprised his look deep in the eyes of our neighbors. So we struck. Legitimate self-defense. I struck. A man fell, and in his dying eyes I saw the beast still living—myself....Where does it come from, this rancid, dead taste in my mouth?...It is the taste of the century....*

We are all guilty. The murderer is identical with the victim. ("One and one make one.") Man must transcend himself. Two people in the play—particularly Frantz's sister-in-law, an "outsider," an artist—appear strong enough to leave the infested family mansion. Perhaps others too may succeed in escaping the vicious syndrome of Frantz's final indictment.

The play proliferates symbols. For example, Frantz and his sister Leni, cynically faithful to the ancestral establishment, have made love together. This signifies that those who bury themselves in guilt and shame, those who fear facing reality, commit a kind of incest.

This is strong stuff. The play abounds in psychological and philosophical convolutions. It is a "think piece." Yet after I had read it twice and then gone to see it some years ago in London I referred to it in *The Nation* as an interesting play which bores or as a boring play which interests! Now that I have seen it at the Repertory Theater of Lincoln Center, the basis for this paradox has become clearer.

Sartre is a brilliant and courageous man. He has an amazing mind, tortuous as often as it is lucid. He has numerous skills, among them the ability to write plays that emit sparks which fascinate and momentarily illuminate. *Dirty Hands*, apart from other merits, is an arresting melodrama.

There are passages in *The Devil and The Good Lord* which might be placed in an anthology of exemplary intellectual dialogue for the stage. Because of the urgent contemporaneity of his thinking, and his gift of statement on subjects of inescapable importance, whatever he writes demands close attention.

In general, however, and more particularly in *The Condemned of Altona*, Sartre is hardly an artist or even a consummate theatre craftsman. His compelling will to stab our conscience creates a certain intensity. At the outset the play induces a degree of suspense. But as it progresses through its three hours of volubility one grows fatigued by the author's strained effort and the inadequate sustenance it provides. The play's personages barely come to life, either as true characters or as powerful mouthpieces. There is no poetry in their speech, no flesh or blood in their contacts, and finally little excitement of drama in their confrontation. They do not make us believe in them on any level. We recognize in the extended dialogue an entirely serious and committed man, a person who, despite his occasional eloquence, in this instance remains only partly articulate.

The complexity in *The Condemned of Altona* is characteristic of Sartre. In many of his essays and critical pieces this complexity produces results that approach genius. At other times—and something of the sort occurs in a few of the play's passages—complexity becomes a pyrotechnic cleverness of rhetoric and debate. The intellect outsmarts itself. One becomes suspicious, feels oneself being deceived. The mechanism of the mind confronting us revolves and gyrates with an agility much too free to be useful. The mental inventiveness surpasses the quality of the insights. We are struck dumb in a kind of confused admiration without being convinced in our intelligence or satisfied in our spirit.

There is little point in insisting that *The Condemned of Altona* is a valuable social document. It isn't for us. Though the play may be assumed to have meaning here in America because of Hiroshima or the war in Vietnam, or because we too engaged in the fight against the Nazis, *The Condemned of Altona* is not written in a vein relevant to our experience or frame of reference. And it is still more futile to say that, for all its defects, it is a more substantial play than any other on Broadway. (That may be so, but who has ruled that we must go to the theatre?)

The French production was galvanized by the lightning shock of Serge Reggiani's acting as Frantz—another factor in the play's Parisian success. We need not to be at all surprised that no equivalent of this exists in the performance at the Vivian Beaumont. The acting ranges from the thoroughly competent to either the somewhat embarrassingly strenuous or the tolerably mediocre. The whole under Herbert Blau's direction is done with determined sincerity and evident understanding, except for the set which does not make complete dramatic sense.

—NAT, 21 Feb. '66

SWEET CHARITY

There is something singularly fitting about the placement of the new musical, *Sweet Charity*, at the Palace Theatre. I do not refer to the Broadway Baroque of the redecorated old vaudeville house but to its location on our "Main Street" at 47th.

Nearby is the "Latin Quarter"—loud, lavish, tough. Less than half a block away there is a poor man's round-the-clock "night club" (formerly a restaurant serving beer and oysters in old-fashioned plainness), a hangout where, accompanied by raucous sound, sparsely clad girls twitch their torsos close to the glass storefront, in full view of the idlers who crowd the sidewalk, bemused for hours by the free display. Also close by is one of those immense drugstores where the sleazy tired of the town appear listlessly to patch their more trifling wounds with plasters and palliatives.

Sweet Charity (Book by Neil Simon, Music by Cy Coleman, Lyrics by Dorothy Fields) is based on Fellini's touching film, *The Nights of Cabiria*, about a perpetually deceived and always hopeful Roman whore. In the musical she has become a taxi dancer in a New York hot spot. She has a heart of gold, aspires to marriage, and yearns for a better life. She wants to be loved and is always dumped.

I can tell you little about the quality of the "book," the score, the lyrics. Yet the show made an impression on me—a strong, rather discomfiting impression. It reflects its immediate environment; that I think is a merit. Willy-nilly, what is expressed is disjointedness—a broken-boned dislocation masquerading as gay energy.

Talented Bob Fosse who "conceived, staged and choreographed" the entertainment has created dizzying patterns of movement out of ugliness. The result is a kind of brilliant and ingenious hideousness which *is* a style—a style wrought from the streets and manners we observe as we enter and leave the theatre. The audience is at home in both. The show, despite quibbles and quarrels as to its various elements—discussion of which seems to me to miss the mark—is a success: it achieves what it sets out to do. It has unity.

The scenery by Robert Randolph is appropriately angular, brittle, luridly "glamorous," clever, like one of those window exhibits where modern ornamentation is employed after a fashion that hovers between a come-hither attractiveness and the nauseating. It works and moves the proceedings with admirable efficiency.

The gem or star at the center of all this is Gwen Verdon—our all-American Toulouse-Lautrec. Miss Verdon is phenomenal. No longer young, she has enormous vitality, a glorious figure, a delightful nature, theatrical radiance, and a mode of dancing altogether suited to the show's salient features. She transforms the inelegant into elegance. Sometimes she appears haggard and then again she becomes beautiful—a light that shines in darkness. She is human enthusiasm emerging triumphant amid the hard and tawdry.

Sweet Charity is Pop Art.

—NAT, 28 Feb. '66

SLAPSTICK TRAGEDY

Tennessee Williams did himself an injustice by having his two one-act plays, collectively entitled *Slapstick Tragedy*, produced on Broadway. They might have gained considerable esteem had they been given in a more modest manner. Their closing was announced after six performances.

A second injustice, almost as great, is the plays' critical reception. *Slapstick Tragedy* is not the author's "top-drawer" work, but he has struck a new note in at least the second of the two plays and both have a peculiarly personal stamp that merits attention.

The plays are melancholy but masked avowals. The first, called *The Mutilated*, might be described as a freakish Christmas Carol. Two whores—the first has had one of her breasts removed, the other has just been released from a short-term jail sentence for shoplifting—become reconciled in wretched companionship one Christmas Eve, because although they have reviled each other through corrupt professional rivalry, they realize that they have only their mutual deprivation, and the understanding of it, to give them solace in their common exile from respectable society.

As in certain of his former plays, Williams in *The Mutilated* reveals his compassion—more, his sense of identification—with the insulted and the injured, the misfits and the maimed. But while the earlier plays were soft in sentiment, *The Mutilated* is savage.

Its "slapstick" consists of deliberate bitchiness. Even the final moments in which the two whores induce a vision in themselves of the Blessed Virgin who will forgive and heal them are bitterly ironic. (This is Williams' squint-eyed flirtation with mysticism.) The intention is to make us see that the two women, one stupidly infantile, the other horribly stricken with shame at her affliction, are as absurd as they are pitiable. Williams refuses to gush over them; they are meant to be both grotesque and ridiculous, and these qualities themselves are to lend the women all the commiseration they need to make them kin to us. The play requires its jokes to be horrible; its horror funny.

To make clear how *The Mutilated* differs from other Williams plays the production should not dodge the play's cruelty. Perhaps the director (Alan Schneider) and the author felt that an emphasis on its savagery would alienate an "uptown" audience.

Margaret Leighton, whose voice touches the heart and who is blessed with the very appealing look of a Pre-Raphaelite beauty in anguish, never for a moment suggests anything but noble sorrow. She doesn't seem to have a bitchy bone in her body. Kate Reid, a gusty and essentially good-natured actress, is amusing but hardly conveys anything soiled or mean. The result is that the play strikes us as a minor repetition of an old Williams theme, when it is really an acid variation.

The second slapstick tragedy, *The Gnädiges Fraulein*, is more interesting in several ways than the first. It is a stylized essay in farcical fantasy altogether new for Williams. It is filled with sardonic mirth at the plight of the artist applauded and glamorized in his triumphs and then repudiated and derided when he fails. The "artiste" in the play is a once celebrated middle-European *chanteuse*, but the inner motivation for the personage is Williams' projection of his present situation. He attempts to ward off self-pity through self-mockery, avenging himself on the "enemy" with satiric lunacy.

The Fraulein earns her keep in a God-forsaken boarding house at the seaboard of the southernmost point of our States by fighting to catch fish in the waters whipped by the hurricanes which harass the place. The difficulty of bringing in the fish (prestige, status, success) is compounded by the jealousy and competition of a bird of prey, the Cocaloony, who not only snatches the fish from the Fraulein's grip but pecks out her eyes in the process.

The play abounds in symbols. The Cocaloony may represent the Critics. The public becomes a Permanent Transient at the boarding house. Certain aspects of the Press appear in the person of Polly, a madcap society reporter who combines impregnable complacency with malice. The clownish lady who runs the boarding house may stand for managerial powers, producers, editors, publishers and the like. There is also a blond Indian who steals and makes a banquet of the fish which the Fraulein has struggled and lost her eyes to catch. Is this meant to stand for one of Williams' directors?

However we interpret this nightmare it is written in an odd but effective mixture of gallows humor and Rabelaisian zest. On opening night the audience laughed uproariously at the broad-stroked slapdash language, but though I was able to appreciate the style I could not bring myself to smile. I was too conscious that its author was in pain.

The outstanding performance in *The Gnädiges Fraulein* was that of Zoe Caldwell as Polly, a truly remarkable creation, all venom and sugar, risible and appalling. Both plays are sure to be seen and acclaimed in future productions at universities, community theatres and in foreign stages.

—*NAT*, 14 Mar. '66

SERJEANT MUSGRAVE'S DANCE
THE LION IN WINTER

Seeing John Arden's *Serjeant Musgrave's Dance* (Theatre De Lys) I was reminded of what Hanns Eisler said of Robert Schumann: "He had more genius than talent"—meaning more inspiration than skill. One cannot see *Serjeant Musgrave's Dance*, or for that matter any of Arden's plays, without realizing that one is in the presence of a real dramatist, a man of passion and power. A cross-grained poetry emerges from his work. Yet one is not wholly satisfied: one is left "holding the bag." One recalls certain aspects of O'Neill and O'Casey.

In this instance one cannot be sure the fault is entirely Arden's. *Serjeant Musgrave's Dance* is particularly difficult to stage. It requires a sweeping flow, a torrential drive in the physical movement of scenes and settings, an authenticity of speech and background in the acting as well as intensity and afflatus, a flashing imagination in the direction extremely rare except in the most accomplished of repertory companies. Such advantages, I suspect, were no more available in the original English production (1959) than they are now in Greenwich Village.

What makes *Musgrave* intrinsically problematic is a certain ambiguity in its content. I say ambiguity rather than unclarity. Musgrave is a fanatic bent on applying a sort of mathematical logic (he calls it religious because its motive is moral) to the problem of guilt and retribution in war. The time is the middle of the 19th century. One of Musgrave's men has been killed during a colonial expedition in the country which the British are fighting to take over. They execute five hostages in retaliation. This so outrages Musgrave that he deserts with three of his men—each of whom has a somewhat different reason for deserting. They all head for a small mining town in the north of England where their murdered comrade lived before he entered the army. Since five men were made to pay for the one boy's death, Musgrave plans to kill twenty-five of the town's leading citizens. This is to be his protest against the madness of war. It supplies the play with a premise only acceptable as hyperbole. Musgrave symbolizes the fallacy of violent action (and strict "logic") as a means of putting an end to war.

The issue is further complicated by the fact that the oldest of the deserters, a man against killing on any pretext, in an apparent accident kills the youngest of the four deserters as he was about to abandon Musgrave's party. Then there are the striking (or locked out) miners whom Musgrave hopes to enlist in his revenge against the town's Establishment, the source, he believes, of both civil and military injustice. The workers fail to see the connection between their situation and the causes of war since Musgrave is himself murderously militant. Thus Musgrave's rebellious ritual or "dance" fails. He is captured while the strike leader, with some sense of fatal misgiving at not having helped Musgrave, goes off to fight the workers' battle alone.

The play is a muddle if we think of it simply as an antiwar tract. But it is hardly that at all. Arden's position is tragic. It might be called anarchist if we divorce the term from any political notion (even though it may at times have political or social consequences).

Musgrave is a hero insofar as he reacts strongly to the villainy of war and wishes to take extreme steps to prevent its recurrence. But he is a flawed hero and a failure because his "logic" leads him to believe that war can be averted by killing its presumed instigators, and that "reason" when backed by force will solve the issue. And for all his noble intentions the pacifist must find himself involved in some phase of the sin he abhors. Thus the tragic dilemma appears insoluble.

Arden finds himself obliged to accept what Yeats once called "the crooked way of life." It is a sentiment which he dramatized in another vein in his *Live Like Pigs*. There the "gypsies," the wayward, the permanent vagrants who want to live in a freedom disruptive to the humdrum order of the welfare state, come into conflict with their humbly respectable neighbors, a conflict as brutally funny and pathetic as the situation in *Musgrave* is painfully somber. Arden doesn't take sides, though one feels his heart is with the determined derelicts. So in *Musgrave*, though one realizes Arden's compassion with the Serjeant's revolt, he indicates no way for his "dance" to arrive at the hoped for consummation. (It is possible that Arden means to suggest that if the workers were to join with the Musgraves of the world, war might be stopped. But this is hardly dramatized.) Arden's play, one must therefore conclude, does not aim at social preachment or philosophical demonstration. It is an attempt to picture the impasse of history in an epic drama.

As such it suffers from characters insufficiently grand or complete and from language which, though it bursts into a kind of rude folk song or verse when prose seems inadequate to express the intended emotion, is rarely eloquent enough to fulfill the author's ambitious design. But we should recognize that design and appreciate the value of the impulse which prompted it.

At the age of 36, Arden is even now one of the few dramatists writing in English today who tries to scale the heights of dramatic expression. Thus far he has succeeded only to a limited degree (I have not seen his latest plays), but his attempt, fortified as it is by an original personality and closeness to a specific soil and to the authentic speech of its people, gives him a unique place among contemporary playwrights.

It is no discredit to Stuart Burge, the director of the present production and the cast he has assembled, which includes a number of interesting actors, to say that under the circumstances of New York production they are unable to accomplish all that is needed to realize the full scope and power of *Serjeant Musgrave's Dance*.

At my grammar school the boys used to tease any fellow who employed unusual words in conversation or composition by saying that he had "swallowed the dictionary"; a taunt which contained a load of derision and a smidgen of respect. The mock compliment of my boyhood schoolmates came back to me at James Goldman's play, *The Lion in Winter* (Ambassador Theatre). Mr. Goldman's vocabulary is not especially extensive but he is noticeably infatuated by the playful surface sounds that phrases can make. His dialogue is ticklingly mellifluous; his play largely patter.

The subject is the struggle between Henry II, King of England at the age of 50 (1183), and his wife, Eleanor of Aquitaine, over the eventual succession to the throne. Henry favors the youngest son, John; Eleanor prefers Richard, the eldest. The two royal personages vie with each other in fierce chicanery. The boys themselves are a trial—the shrewdest and most malign being

Geoffrey, the middle son-for they all scheme treacherously against one another as they do against their father and mother. At moments the quarrels approach tragic violence, but generally they verge on farce. After the paroxysm of one nearly murderous squabble, Eleanor cries out, "Well, every family has its ups and downs," which was the one line in the play I found genuinely funny.

It is not clear to me exactly who Mr. Goldman's influences are, but his writing resembles a glossy mixture of ingredients from all the virtuosi of smooth English prose. This does not constitute a style: it is a pastiche. It has no individual quality; it is gay apparel that belongs to nobody. There are no humans beneath the trappings. Henry, Eleanor and the others are not people but a collection of gestures, improvisations for momentary turns which fail to become true scenes. They emerge from no core which might give the play's line of action a comprehensive meaning.

We hear "nice speeches": for example, about the horrors of history caused, Eleanor explains, not by environmental or social pressures but by what people are; we hear quips that possess a smart conversational edge but which are not expressions of any central idea or part of any consistent conception of events or character. When all is said and done we know very little about Henry or Eleanor except that they are both wily, vigorous and scenically colorful. They are dressed in epigrammatic motley which is not the equivalent of good writing; they carry on in passages of boisterous behavior which is not the same as drama. The play has only the air of wit.

Robert Preston as Henry is endowed with impressive stature and energy, a resonant baritone with something engagingly boyish as well as bullish in his being. Rosemary Harris as Eleanor has a romantic voice, a twinkling eye and a palpitating manner which leaves us uncertain whether we are to expect laughter or a sob. Both players sustain the evening and almost make us forget that they are play-acting around a vacuum.

—*NAT*, 28 Mar. '66

THE CAUCASIAN CHALK CIRCLE

During the first act of *The Caucasian Chalk Circle* (Repertory Theater of Lincoln Center) the title of one of the author's poems recurred to me: "Concerning Poor B.B." Poor B.B. indeed: he has no luck in New York. As the evening progressed, I wondered if B.B. might not be read "Bloody Bore."

The thought shocked me more than it might please those who still resist Bertolt Brecht. For I admire Brecht. He is first among the dramatists of the past forty years, as well as the outstanding theatrical figure and influence since the founding of his Berliner Ensemble in 1949. In a review I wrote of *The Caucasian Chalk Circle* when it was produced at the Hedgerow Theatre, Moylan, Pa., in 1948, I said: "I have a feeling that postwar Europe may acclaim Brecht."

That production, directed by Eric Bentley (his translation was used then as it is now), was wholly unadorned. For that reason, I couldn't approve of it wholeheartedly, any more than I could approve the similarly stark 1947 production of Brecht's *Galileo* with Charles Laughton in the central role. For while Brecht's art has its aspects for austerity, his own productions prove that he means his stylistic reticence to dress itself in an aristocratically subdued splendor.

Galileo is staged in Berlin against a background of burnished bronze that lends the play a ground tone of noble opulence, while *The Caucasian Chalk Circle*—its various scenes played against a scroll painting—is rich in the manner of that Chinese art. To confuse Brecht's sense of the visually pleasurable with the ornate is as aesthetically ignorant as to mistake his restraint for poverty.

The Caucasian Chalk Circle is an epic or picaresque unfolding of the Chinese as well as the Hebrew tale of the wise man who must determine which of two women is the real mother of a "foundling" child. In Brecht's version the rascally but canny judge awards the child to the one who has cared for it rather than to the one who bore it. The moral is stated cryptically yet nevertheless tellingly in the play's concluding lines: "—what there is shall go to those who are good for it, Children to the motherly, that they prosper, Carts to good drivers, that they be driven well, The valley to the waterers, that it yield fruit."

There are many characters and numerous episodes—largely humorous—all of them providing folk-adage comment on government, rule by the wealthy, the law, war and maternal love. The pace is leisurely though the writing is terse; the play seems to approach its destination on a long, circuitous path. But that is Brecht's way: he is not concerned with achieving a sharp, climactic conclusion, or even a compact message, but with the elaboration and scenic visualization of an attitude. That attitude is one of ironic doubt, a shrewd peasant withholding of final assent to accepted dogmas as in such old saws as "blood is thicker than water." Almost every play of Brecht's maturity reveals this trait. I ended that 1948 review of *The Caucasian Chalk Circle* with the observation: "The virtue of Brecht's plays is good sense carried to the point of grandeur."

If we regard *The Caucasian Chalk Circle* as a drama which continuously presses on to an apex of excitement, Brecht's procedure will inevitably seem tedious. Two factors not only circumvent this danger but make Brecht at his best constantly engaging: his writing and his staging. For besides being a poet of great originality, Brecht was a master theatre craftsman. English-speaking audiences rarely appreciate the first attribute because he is devilishly difficult to translate. His writing is a magical transcription of vulgar street lingo into an elevated, almost Biblical purity; it possesses a special elegance. Bentley is faithful to Brecht's text; one cannot blame him for not being altogether successful in recreating this Brechtian transfiguration. What may be required is an "imitation" in the vein of Robert Lowell's treatment of Villon.

Meanwhile, it may be possible to stage fine productions with the Bentley translations.

Brecht wrote his plays with his own staging in mind. He was a great director surrounded by assistants and colleagues of like stature. And in all fairness to the Lincoln Center company, and to other American and English organizations which embark on a Brechtian enterprise, the facilities at the Berliner Ensemble are virtually utopian. For this reason I often despair that any production outside the "parent" institution can do Brecht full justice. Still, I thought well of the Actors' Workshop production of *Galileo* in San Francisco (directed by Herbert Blau) and was very much impressed by *Arturo Ui* as done at the Contemporary Theatre in Warsaw.

The Hedgerow production I have referred to was stripped to the bone. Yet the quality and charm came through: it was in touch with the play's spirit. The production at Lincoln Center's Vivian Beaumont Theatre, directed by Jules Irving, is lavish and diffuse. It is spread all over the stage, making a gaudy show which obscures the impact of the words and blunts the style of the work. The heart of the play—the young peasant girl's feeling for the abandoned child—is absent, if for no other reason than that it is overwhelmed in the general display. The effect produced justifies those who complain that at least the first two acts of the play—except for their broad comic moments—are barren.

In the first place, most of the acting is neutral. There are minor exceptions: the funny Monk, the cadaverous "Bridegroom," one or two others. I am not sure whether the masks (striking as such) that are worn by all the unsympathetic characters hide or heighten the uncommunicativeness of the performances. But it may not be proper to find fault with the players. Just as Brecht's writing requires a certain reserve, so the objectivity or "anti-emotionalism" associated with his theories is not to be equated with inexpressiveness. The greater the formal restraints Brecht prescribes for his actors the greater the need for feeling, power and precise characterization.

The costumes are elaborate but signify little apart from the wealth of the wearers. The musicians and singers are too much in evidence, as is the Storyteller who introduces the scenes and comments on the action, though all are placed at the extremity of stage left. The music itself is fake folksy or "popular" rather than the discreet and delicate framework for the subtle and sage narrative picture of *The Caucasian Chalk Circle*. It is a condiment or side attraction rather than integral to the play.

It may seem that I am being too severe, considering the genuine distinction of Brecht's work and the bravery of the Repertory Theater in undertaking it. But a play does not exist in the theatre except as a performance, a thing done, enacted. And courage is not art. For the most part the production now offered on the stage of the Vivian Beaumont struck me as a spectacular dud.

—*NAT*, 11 Apr. '66

REFLECTIONS ON TRUE THEATRE

There are numerous and complex obstacles to the establishment of True Theatres among us. I do not say repertory theatres because, while I believe the repertory procedure to be the most conducive to rich results, it is by no means essential to the running of a significant theatre organization. The Group Theatre was such an organization but did not function on a repertory basis. What it had, and what counts in this regard was a permanent company of actors and directors with a consistent artistic policy.

I cannot be sure that the terms I have just used, though commonplace, are clearly understood by many who engage in theatre discussion. What, for example, do the words "True Theatre" connote? To define and illustrate them I feel obliged to revert to "ancient history" and first principles.

When the first directorate of the Repertory Theater of Lincoln Center, Robert Whitehead and

Elia Kazan, were dropped or resigned after less than two seasons of activity, the press was packed with surmises and interpretations. Among these the most plausible was the dire failure of *The Changeling* coming on top of the poor impression made by O'Neill's *Marco Millions* and S.N. Behrman's *But For Whom Charlie*.

But it is true that while Arthur Miller's *After the Fall* and *Incident at Vichy* were not "universally" admired, and while the production of Richard Wilbur's translation of Molière's *Tartuffe* was criticized in some quarters, these three productions attracted and generally interested large audiences. The second season which was to wind up with a new staging of Giraudoux's *The Mad Woman of Chaillot* had to be abandoned, largely because of the organizational upset. Speaking professionally, three hits out of six offerings constitute a favorable record in any theatre at any time. The management moreover presented its six plays at less than the originally stipulated budget.

Sharper criticisms on another level were made of the theatre's first two seasons. The Whitehead-Kazan program was almost wholly confined to contemporary American plays which might just as well have been done under ordinary Broadway auspices. It is certainly true that the Behrman piece might more advantageously have been staged at a West 45th Street house.

One aspect of this criticism we shall examine further on, for it is a matter of crucial artistic concern. In regard to the main objection to the Lincoln Center Repertory program or policy, it must be remembered that for its opening season at the Vivian Beaumont Theater the management had announced the following plays: The Belgian Michel de Ghelderode's *Pantagleize*, a difficult but brilliantly provocative "farce," which though written in 1929 has never been given a full-scale production in New York; Robert Lowell's version of the Aeschylus *Oresteia* trilogy (commissioned by the management), and Alfred de Musset's *Lorenzaccio* (1834), to be directed by Zefferelli. Negotiations were also under way to produce

Brecht's *Galileo* (among Brecht's plays the most relevant to our time), and to have the Russian director Zavadsky stage a Chekhov play.

Another complaint was that Arthur Miller seemed destined to become Lincoln Center's "house playwright." Probably so—and others, it was hoped, would join him in this function. But it should be clear that "house playwrights" are not only desirable but necessary to the maintenance of a permanent organization. Chekhov and Gorky were "house playwrights" to the Moscow Art Theatre. Hauptmann was connected with Otto Brahms's renowned "Free Theatre" in Germany as a sort of "house playwright," and what would the Berliner Ensemble be without its "house playwright," Brecht? The fact that Miller is no Chekhov, Hauptmann or Brecht is entirely beside the point. He is one of our best playwrights. And Miller should be esteemed for his willingness to have his plays produced at a repertory theatre; most playwrights prefer the Broadway gamble. There's more money in it for them—or so they suppose.

Whitehead and Kazan, it was also said, represent "the theatre of the thirties" and what was needed was a "theatre of the sixties." Was Erwin Piscator at the age of 70 simply a man of the twenties when he produced Hochhuth's *The Deputy* and Peter Weiss' *The Investigation* at the Berlin Volksbühne during the past three years? Does production of plays by Büchner, Wycherley and Brecht constitute an example of "the theatre of the sixties?" The use of such glib catchwords, though they often issue from high-brow sources, is actually loose talk.

In a similar vein certain critics argued that Whitehead and Kazan were unfortunate choices in the first place because they were part of our theatrical establishment. Aside from the fact that both men had honorable records, one as a producer and the other as director (Robinson Jeffers, Carson McCullers, Inge, O'Neill, Anouilh, Williams, Miller, T.S. Eliot, Marlowe, Wilder were among the writers they had dealt with), the notion of an "establishment" in our theatre is laughable. There is no such thing—would that there were!

The brute fact is that none of the criticism—justified or not—leveled at Whitehead and Kazan were the causes for the overthrow of their regime. The board of directors were eager to retain Kazan and Miller on the theatre's roster. Whitehead was the target. And this was due not to any administrative negligence or to such calamities as *The Changeling* about which Whitehead was as unhappy as anyone else, but to the fact that he had literally forced the board's hand in building the ANTA-Washington Square Theatre, an action to which the most powerful member of the board was unalterably opposed. The complaints I have mentioned and perhaps others more valid were merely convenient pretexts.

The appointment of Herbert Blau and Jules Irving as the new artistic directors of the theatre was undoubtedly encouraged by several critics adverse to Whitehead and Kazan from the outset. Though I was appointed "executive consultant" to Whitehead and Kazan after the organization had been more or less set on its course, I too judged the Blau-Irving choice to be sound. I had written a piece in these pages commending what I had seen of their work in San Francisco: a production of *Galileo* and a rehearsal of several scenes of Genet's *The Balcony*. I knew them to be intelligent, informed, intrepid pioneers. Where else in San Francisco could plays by Beckett, Pinter, Brecht, Genet, Shaw, O'Neill be seen in regular succession? I had no reason to expect the equivalent of a first-rate European company, but it wasn't too much to hope for an organization that might convince the skeptical that a repertory theatre would excite our town with a sense of renewed vitality.

There is no doubt that a lively anticipation of such an eventuality exists: witness the large number of subscribers enrolled from the beginning of the Lincoln Center enterprise to the present. But Blau and Irving's first steps at the Vivian Beaumont have been a sore disappointment.

It is plain that while they are hard workers with the best of intentions, good ideas and courage, they are, to say the least, not mature craftsmen, or even particularly endowed with the ability needed to stage the plays that most interest them. It is still more evident that the company they brought with them from San Francisco, while staunchly devoted to their leaders, is ill equipped to satisfy an audience accustomed in New York to seeing the best American and British actors. The original company at the ANTA-Washington Square Theatre, while generally deficient on the distaff side, gave promise in its male contingent of growing into a better ensemble than any which had been presented in the United States for years.

My purpose here is not to blame or praise any individual or company, though I confess myself reluctant to be harsh with any group that comes to us with something more than pecuniary ambition or snob appeal. My inquiry aims at facing the fundamental question of how a true Theatre is made, what indeed it is. Unless we learn that, we shall be forever led astray in our efforts to establish one.

A true Theatre, in my understanding of the term, is one that plans for *continuity* along well-defined lines, so that its productions may acquire an identity, a face, a style, a fundamental objective beyond the generalization that it be "good." In the 16th, 17th and 18th centuries such theatres came into being, so to speak, "automatically," due to the homogeneity of the societies that bred them and the limited audiences that attended them. And because of the old tradition such theatres exist alongside a thriving commercial stage in most European countries today.

For example, in the Soviet Union there are many different types of Theatre. Since 1936, the authorities have decreed a more or less totalitarian approach known as "Socialist realism" and every Theatre claims the Stanislavsky system as the basis for its actors' training. Yet the Vachtangov Theatre is not at all like either the Moscow Art or the new Contemporary Theatre. Before 1936, the Soviet Theatre was perhaps the most varied in the world: the productions of Meyerhold, of Tairov, of the Theatre of Satire, the Theatre of the Revolution—not to mention those at the numerous aesthetically independent studios—were distinctly different from one another. The Komische Oper in East Berlin and the Berliner Ensemble are not at all similar in style, and there are several other companies in that area that differ from both.

It might be argued that no such Theatres are possible with us because there are no federal or municipal subsidies on the European scale. With us the primary interest concentrates on the construction of new buildings—the edifice complex. True Theatres are not born of preoccupation with real estate. The point of departure must be the desire of actors, directors, dramatists to express something. The impetus arises from the community's need for communication through play.

Blau and Irving's Actors Workshop in San Francisco began that way. It is one reason for the respect in which it was held. In a way, the early Provincetown Players, whose "house playwright" was O'Neill, was also such a group. The same might be said of The Neighborhood Playhouse and The Washington Square Players (1914-17), and even of the Theatre Guild during the twenties. The latter organization devoted itself largely to modern European drama because the production of plays by Tolstoy, Andreyev, and Molnar was still held to be extremely hazardous on Broadway. Eva Le Gallienne's Civic Repertory Theatre served for several years the honorable purpose of presenting plays by Chekhov and Ibsen at popular prices.

It is generally agreed that in more recent years the most productive theatrical enterprise was the Group Theatre (1931-41). It was rounded by three young people of some theatrical experience who, through a long series of meetings from 1928 to 1931, gathered a group of actors around themselves. Most of these were relative beginners though a few had already proved their mettle. Without reputation, funds or aids from foundations, or subsidy of any kind, these actors and directors endured and progressed by dint of sheer will and awareness of their task.

The long period of preparatory work, as well as the "propaganda" among playwrights, was one of the factors that explains the perseverance of the Group in sustaining the hardships of its career. My chief criticism of the Whitehead-Kazan conduct of the Repertory Theater of Lincoln Center when I went to work with them was that they had been hasty in the formation and education of their company. (I refer to education for a permanent Theatre.) "In the theatre, as in so many other things, Americans build from the roof," I said, quoting Jacques Copeau.

There may be a certain ambiguity in my statement that a Theatre must be impelled by an idea. If so I can clarify the point by saying that the Group Theatre aimed first of all at establishing a permanent collective of actors, directors and designers who would develop a common technique and thus engender a coherent body to say the things they felt and believed in. As a group they reacted against the fun principles of the twenties, but at the same time they wanted to raise their voices against the despair of the depression. As they abhorred the fecklessness of Broadway show business, so they espoused an active humanism. They were moral enthusiasts.

Their plays were only occasionally topical, but they always sought those relevant to the temper of their generation. All but one play was by a living American. (The only play they failed to raise money for was Chekhov's *Three Sisters*!) They presented the first work of several new dramatists—Saroyan among them—and Clifford Odets, after four years in the ranks as an actor, emerged to become the representative playwright of the time.

The dissolution of the Group was caused by the fact that no such Theatre can fulfill its purpose if it maintains itself by financing each production separately, as commercial managers do. With the advent of war, a new ideological orientation was required, and in the climate of the time the ground for this was shaky. The end of the war brought a return to "business as usual" in which the cultural atmosphere had altered: the idealistic past was not simply forgotten, it was shunned. We all had to begin from scratch. Today, though there is the will and the possibility of a reformation, our thinking in theatrical matters is more muddled than ever.

It may be wholly fitting for towns like Minneapolis to cultivate a Theatre for plays of classic stature. They have been dismally deprived in this respect. But a true Theatre is not a museum or a library—unless as with the *Comédie Française* its official function is chiefly to serve in these capacities. (The *Comédie Française* has a modern "annex" at the Théâtre de France under Jean-Louis Barrault. The Barrault repertory is largely French; the state also supports the low-priced Théâtre National Populaire where the emphasis is not so predominantly native.) A true Theatre does not simply present plays; it generates them and new concepts for the presentation of old plays. In the main, it does not look backward but forward, not far afield but to its own vicinity.

We in New York can certainly benefit by a theatre for masterpieces of the past—they are impracticable on Broadway unless they are "Burtonized." Such a theatre might furnish us with a beacon to light our way: to provide us with solid standards. But for a truly live theatre we must have something else. The English stage did not quicken with strength in recent years through the Old Vic and the house at Stratford-upon-Avon which had been established long before the war. New action and interest were aroused with the formation of the Royal Court Theatre and the discovery in 1956 of its "house playwright," one of the company's actors, John Osborne. The Royal Shakespeare Company at the Aldwych in London added power to the new wave (here Harold Pinter has become increasingly present), while the British National Theatre attempts to synthesize various theatrical trends by alternating productions of Shakespeare, Congreve, Chekhov, Ibsen, Pinero and early Noel Coward, with plays by Brecht, Beckett, John Arden and other important contemporaries.

There is a kind of criticism that sneers at dramatists whose work does not carry a seal guaranteeing enduring eminence. (This is coterie criticism of which the aesthetic principle is that the more savage the sneer the loftier the critical posture. Such critics behave as if they were the anointed of the Muses, but they are more frequently literary gangsters hungry for power.) This is the antithesis of the creative attitude. John Osborne's eventual status in literary history is far less important to a functioning theatre than his value for its audiences now. The fact that Clifford Odets' plays may prove ephemeral did not lessen their cultural value for the time, place and people of their day.

No great Theatre has been a retrospective theatre only, or chiefly a theatre of foreign imports. The Moscow Art Theatre's fame is not based on its productions of Shakespeare, even though one of them was directed by Gordon Craig; the Abbey Theatre is memorable not for championing Ibsen but for providing a platform to Yeats, Lady Gregory, Synge, Lennox Robinson, St. John Ervine. The Theatre of Louis XIV contributed to the enlightenment of nations not by productions of Euripides or Seneca, though they were imitated, but by the plays of the contemporary Corneille, Racine and Molière. (And the German theatre was weakened for a long time by its dependence on these French masters.) Works of the past and those of strange lands may move us deeply and influence us greatly but we do not mature unless we nurture talents born of contact with our own world. Our grandchildren's children will pronounce on the "greatness" of plays written in our day—and perhaps make as many mistakes as we do. Bernard Shaw thought Ben Jonson, John Webster and most other Elizabethans "a crew of insufferable bunglers and dullards."

It may still be possible to make true Theatres within the monumental new edifices. But the boards who pull the wires within them must include a few people not so abysmally ignorant of the arts that they depend on hearsay from fashionable experts.

The public must be taught that theatre is not entertainment as titillation but entertainment (yes!) as the engagement of the heart, mind, soul and senses. The theatre is not a show shop, where luxury commodities are to be sold piecemeal and haphazardly. As a business it is doomed in our time.

When new theatres are formed their directors must understand that the measure of choice for the repertory cannot be set by an assessment of literary excellence alone. A play is not a document; it is an *address*: the first consideration must be the relevance to the audience for which it is to be performed. It must furthermore be played by actors equipped to do it—by training, feeling, intimate understanding. Chekhov maintained that Russians couldn't do Ibsen properly! The theatre—festivity and ritual—must be a persuasive forum to an audience sought out as its own by those who lead it. One may then organize a theatre of traditional values, a rebellious theatre, a religious theatre, a theatre for farce, musical comedy or tragedy, for realism or poetry, or a composite of some of these, provided there is a central concept to unify the elements into an organic whole. The craftsmanship in each case is to be wrought on the premise of the theatre's purpose. The beginning of such craftsmanship is a secure sense of the desired destination.

—*NAT*, 16 May '66

JOURNEY OF THE FIFTH HORSE
IVANOV

The three plays I attended in the past few weeks were all more or less Russian. As I sit down to write about them I cannot help thinking of a (presumably) Jewish joke I once heard. A man accosts another on the street. "Hello, Goldberg," the man says, "I'm glad to see you. But, my God,

Goldberg how you've changed. You used to be tall, now you're short. You used to be fat and now you're thin. What's wrong, Goldberg?" Excuse me," says the other, "but I'm not Goldberg." "What," says the first man, "You've changed your name too?"

In different ways the Russian plays I've been seeing have changed just as remarkably as Goldberg! The most acceptable change is that effected in Ronald Ribman's *The Journey of the Fifth Horse*, a play drawn in part from Turgenev's *Diary of a Superfluous Man* at the American Place Theatre. This is not so much dramatization as a new play with a contemporary slant, though its locale remains the Russia of the late 19th century. The diary has supposedly been written by Turgenev's sorry protagonist, a shy, self-effacing and constantly depressed young fellow who becomes enamored of, is jealous of, and fights a duel over a girl who does not love him, and whom he is prepared to marry after she has been seduced and abandoned by an aristocratic cavalry officer. In Ribman's transformation the diary falls into the hands of a desiccated editor at a Petersburg publishing house.

The new character, named Zoditch, reads the diary with reluctance and obvious distaste. He finds its author absurdly romantic and stupidly sentimental. In reading the diary, Zoditch is inclined to cry out like Judge Brack in *Hedda Gabler*, "People don't do such things." But dry, niggardly, venomous Zoditch builds fantasies of his own about the robust landlady of his apartment house. In his petty way he is far more sentimental—that is, removed from reality—than Turgenev's superfluous man. Worse still, Zoditch never recognizes any parallel between his own situation and the hapless person whose diary he reads and whom he regards with contempt. He might easily be a critic in one of our highbrow literary journals.

Turgenev's *Diary* is a melancholy tale of failure in love. Ribman has replaced Turgenev's sentiment with modern irony while preserving some flavor of the story's original background.

The play is well written. Though overelaborate in structure (the alternation from realism to stylization is sometimes awkwardly handled) it reveals as a whole a promising talent.

The production directed by Larry Arrick is as forgivably uneven as the text, but there is one excellent performance by Dustin Hoffman as Zoditch, hysterical without feeling, grotesque without bitterness, touching without tears, funny without laughing.

John Gielgud's production of Chekhov's *Ivanov* (Shubert Theatre) made me think of Jane Austen with a bellyache. The atmosphere is not at all Russian and it is barely English. There is a thinness in the production wholly foreign to Chekhov.

Gielgud himself has fine moments as Ivanov. He conveys inner distress truthfully and subtly. He does not "star" himself, which is perhaps a pity. For all his defeatedness, Ivanov should be endowed with the remainders of intellectual pride and vigor added to flashes of fiery despair. We should see that he might have amounted to something in a different environment. That is part of the play's point. Gielgud's monotonous passivity robs the play of definition and backbone.

Still, the fault in the production lies deeper. It may be traced to the latest cliché in Chekhov's criticism, enthusiastically and superciliously embraced by many critics in England and America. His plays are *comedies*, as Chekhov insisted and our critics repeat. Chekhov said Stanislavsky turned his characters into "crybabies." All this may be so—though it should be noted that playwrights are not always right in matters of the stage interpretation of their plays. Certainly Chekhov is humorous, but his plays are not therefore "laugh shows!"

Ivanov has hilarious scenes in the manner of Gogol. The humor is owlish. This does not mean that the play ought to be done in a clipped, matter-of-fact, "common-sense" manner to prove that Chekhov is not conventionally Russian—that is to say, gloomy. Chekhov's characteristic mark is an aspiring soulfulness. His negative characters are gross or pretentiously vacuous or earthbound Philistines. But in almost every case we are attracted to them because of Chekhov's inextinguishable sympathy with them. There is something fleshily warm even in the portrayal of the Estate Manager, the most unpleasant character in *Ivanov*. We recognize this when he speaks of how caviar should be served. (Gorky has described how a bluestocking who bored Chekhov to distraction when she discoursed on lofty matters delighted him after he had induced her to speak about the making of jam.) Whether he be an exhausted idealist, a boor, a pedant or a jackass, one must see in every Chekhov personage the opposite feature, the positive quality that has somehow become flabby, spoiled or debased. No Chekhov character should be made to seem dry or only farcically funny.

There are a number of expert actors in Gielgud's company—Ethel Griffies' energy and sparkle are always gratifying—but most of them strike one in *Ivanov* as only professionally competent. They play their roles with casual ease, as if to remove from Chekhov all taint of Slavic "mystery." They are seen as "people one might meet anywhere"—hence artistically nondescript. For instance, Sasha is made a sort of normal, almost aggressively sporty, college girl; and that deprives her of the inner tension of a virginal being who strives with birdlike anguish to escape a stifling environment. The doctor, Lvov, is converted into a thin-blooded prig, whereas Chekhov means him to be an over-intense moral rationalist whose flaw is the consequence of his incapacity to accept the contradictions of human behavior. In other words, when you omit the complexity, the density of physical life, the combination of the pathetic and the foolish which is indeed comic rather than tragic, you no longer have Chekhov on the stage.

Some years ago William Ball's off-Broadway production of *Ivanov* with a far less experienced and brilliant cast (Vivien Leigh co-stars at the Shubert with Gielgud) was far truer to Chekhov and much more moving than the present one. The play itself, while unripe in comparison with Chekhov's later work, still bears the stamp of the author's genius.

—*NAT*, 30 May '66

THE JOFFREY BALLET

It has been bruited about that I am nostalgic for the 1930s. This is libel: it is the 1830s whose memory I cherish, and even earlier epochs. Witness my fondness for the ballet.

Thus I welcome the City Center Joffrey Ballet in its first regular New York season on West 55th Street. After Balanchine's heavy guns one is exhilarated anew by the light artillery of Joffrey's youngsters. Balanchine has achieved mastery; the City Center juniors are on the exciting path toward that estate. They shine with mounting energy and the results of excellent training under their artistic director Robert Joffrey and their chief choreographer Gerald Arpino.

It is natural and proper to become enthusiastic over the emergence of such a group. "Capitalist competition" among the arts—abundance of production—is beneficial to creativity. (What the theatre needs is more bad plays to open the way for good ones!) But excessive praise is dangerous. It not only warps judgment but leads to later bitterness in those who give it as well as those who receive. Rave notices are good for business; they cripple appreciation.

Apart from its buoyancy, what immediately struck me about the new ballet company is the attractiveness of many of its individual dancers. Thus far I have not been bowled over by any single item of their repertory. *Viva Vivaldi!* is thoroughly pleasant; *Olympics* shows the handsome male contingent to great advantage. *Cakewalk* is an amiable frolic. *Sea Shadow* has a more than serviceable score by Michael Colgrass and two radiant dancers: the incredibly sylphlike Lisa Bradley and the finely wrought Richard Gain.

Among the novelties Lisa Bradley again

excels. She is an ineffable creature of the deep in the earlier ballet, a predatory bird in *Nightwings*, and exquisite in both. But *Nightwings* as a whole is not particularly fresh. Nor was I much moved by Eugene Loring's symbolic *These Three*, which despite its topical subject matter—race riots and the heroics of the civil rights movement—possesses little specific impact or abstract grandeur. There is, however, one effective passage in which the three central male figures dance in concord, a motif repeated at the end by four men who resume the struggle of the martyred three. Loring's intention is bolder than what we actually see, which is surprising in view of the kinetic power inherent in his theme and the gift for incisive visualization he exemplified in *Billy the Kid*.

Moncayo 1, named after its composer, is easy to take, but neither fish nor fowl. The score did not seem to me, though it did to others, much more than routine Mexicana. But evaluations of ballet music must be modified by an awareness that the conditions of orchestral rehearsals are seldom what they ought to be.

The best compliment I can offer the new company at this moment is to say that after visiting it for three evenings I am eager to return for more, not only to reconsider the works I've mentioned and another première (*Vitalitas*) but to deepen the pleasure of seeing my favorite dancers again. These include, besides those previously cited, Luis Fuente, who glows with pride and vigor; Robert Blankshine, a sprite who makes one think of both Puck and Huck Finn; Margo Sappinton, whose womanly magnetism lends a special warmth to the third strophe of the Vivaldi number; Barbara Remington, whose elegant posture bespeaks breeding while her eyes twinkle cool wit. Finally, there is Ivy Clear, demurely funny in the light-minded mockery of *Cakewalk*. But I should not say "finally" for further acquaintance with this most engaging company will extend the list of discoveries.

—*NAT*, 3 Oct. '66

THE KILLING OF SISTER GEORGE
THE ALCHEMIST

They are excellent actresses—Beryl Reid, Eileen Atkins, Lally Bowers—who play Frank Marcus' comedy *The Killing of Sister George* at the Belasco Theatre.

Beryl Reid in particular is a wonder. "Sister George" is her first role in what is loosely called a "legitimate" play. I saw her first in a mediocre English musical revue in which her comic verve and versatility inspired me to a panegyric in the London Observer. What impressed me then, besides her relish and precise sense of characterization, was the tact with which Miss Reid managed to make every trait she drew hilariously vivid without vulgarity and without flagrant caricature. She is both a "born" actress and a highly skilled one. I can think of no one like her at present on our stage.

In *Sister George* Miss Reid's part is an especially difficult one. She is required to be rough, raucous, vicious and funny. With all this she brings a remarkable delicacy to the role, making it at times not only charming but touching. Watch her, for example, as she comments on her girl friend's bare legs.

Eileen Atkins too is very good, bringing a sickly and depraved attractiveness to the (well-written) role of an abjectly dependent, parasitic woman of over 30 who fears any responsibility (including motherhood) and who is indeterminate in sexual inclination because her need for protection is greater than her desire for gratification. (What corruption in her eyes!) Miss Atkins fascinates in a part that might easily have proved to be disgusting.

Lally Bowers plays the part of a television executive as the sort of English lady who combines correct tailoring, maddeningly calculated speech, frigid politeness and iron canniness—all of which is not incompatible with low-grade intelligence.

The three English actresses are ably abetted by the American Polly Rowles, whose Russian accent is disarming because it is so unconvincing.

I begin with the acting because the play's merits are peculiar. It presumes to mock the television business as conducted by the British Broadcasting Company. The joke is that a middle-aged lady who for years has been the central character of a radio serial, the kindly, ever helpful, immaculately and cozily Christian "Sister George" in *Applehurst*, emblematic of a tiny English town, is in private a cigar-smoking, gin-guzzling, tough-tongued, sadistic Lesbian. Also a covert Lesbian is her steely, suave and ever so proper producer who finally abducts "Sister George's" girl friend. For poor "George" has been "killed"—removed from the program—and is now reduced to an engagement in a probably far less remunerative and certainly less glamorous role as a cow.

As a lampoon of the television industry in Britain (or elsewhere) the plot is a *non sequitur*. It is not relevant criticism of the entertainment world to say that among those who become the public symbols of virtue there may be some who are privately scapegraces. This is the kind of attack out of context which seeks to downgrade art by proclaiming that a number of its masters were (or are) homosexual.

Why then was Sister George elected "Best Play of the Year" by London's theatre critics? There is some clever and literate writing (the passage describing "Sister George" scaring the nuns in a taxi), it is stagecrafty, and adopts an ironic tone toward British hypocrisy. In addition, it demonstrates an aptitude for bitchy thrusts beloved in Mayfair coteries.

This has become a favorite vein in London's West End, a reduction to the smartly trivial of the more acrid and occasionally probing jibes initiated in the mid-fifties at the Royal Court Theatre by Osborne and others. It is one facet of London's "sexual revolution."

The first of our own corresponding "revolutions" occurred in the twenties when permissiveness and promiscuity purported to be a protest against a previous "puritanism." This had its English counterpart in the early Noel Coward-Aldous Huxley era, a loosening of morals inevitable after a war, especially since the conflict's aftermath was the beginning of the Empire's deliquescence. Our second sexual seizure began in the fifties as a blatant reaction against conformity. The result with us is to make sex unimportant, conformist and possibly "square." In England, however—specifically in London's more articulate circle—the rebellion is a defiance of the Establishment (which, since the reign of Edward the Seventh, has always masked its licentiousness in cool decorum), a weapon more ostentatious than effective.

The cry for "freedom," D.H. Lawrence once pointed out, is often a mere rattling of chains. The sexual bravado in England today appears to produce little pleasure. There is more leering than lustiness. Such comedies as *The Killing of Sister George* or the more affable but inferior and now defunct *How To Stamp Out Marriage* (a great hit in London) are further from joyous abandon than Harold Wilson's government is from socialism. Though tolerably benign—enjoyable too when acted by such as Beryl Reid and company—the "sexual revolution" is frequently a grim affair which, when prolonged after its simple point has been made, becomes distasteful.

Ben Jonson's *The Alchemist* is "satire keen and critical" in the guise of a Gargantuan farce. Its targets are two of mankind's ruling vices: greed and lechery. One gathers the impression in seeing and more emphatically in reading the play that, while Jonson reviled the lust for gold, he roared with ambiguous appreciation at the other. His construction is tight, his diction obstreperous with lewdness and learning. He was a scholar with a leaning toward the streets, the cribs, the gamblers, the bawds, the duelists, the braggarts, the theives, the pimps, the military swaggerers and finally the librarians of Jacobean London. While London today "swings" in cocky response to Britain's imperial and economic attrition, Jonson's London swells in the savage and overripe abundance resulting from the prosperity gained under Elizabeth.

If it were not for the flush of Jonson's frantic energy, his catchall vocabulary which mingles gems of erudition with the *merdes* of the market place, he might strike us as being as cold as he is sometimes obscure. For all his zest and fondness for stage riot he is as much driven by scorn as Shakespeare, for all his melancholy, was impelled by love. Jonson had a soft spot for the greater bard's basic gentleness, but the world they both inhabited chiefly roused him to anger expressed for the most part through splenetic laughter. Jonson has no faith, little hope, and much less charity. He would not be gulled.

I say all this because it is often charged that the Repertory Theater of Lincoln Center, which has opened its second season at the Vivian Beaumont with *The Alchemist*, has chosen its plays unwisely. It must be repeatedly affirmed that on the contrary most of their texts have been masterpieces which deserve display on our starveling stage. The pity is that these texts have been traduced through their production. The Repertory Theater of Lincoln Center, if it does not soon mend its ways, will succeed in making the classics look bad.

I shall not speak of the acting company for I doubt whether in this instance it is largely to blame. For there is a fundamental flaw in the direction of *The Alchemist* which bespeaks an appalling amateurishness. The actors appear to have been instructed to improvise comedy tricks. The louder they speak the uglier the sound and the more unintelligible they become. Fun in the theatre is created not by aiming directly at its result but by the surprising, illuminating, humorous or witty completion of an authentic human action expressing the will of recognizably real persons. Comedy is an extension of truth and reality to a realm heightened through a special insight provoking, in us a happily renewed recognition. The clowning in this production—extremely pronounced in Michael O'Sullivan—simply obliterates all sense, which is in effect a denial of comedy. We get no relation to time, place, original meaning or adult intention,

only burlesque high jinks as misguided college brats might perform them. What Jonson's characters want—specific desire is the seed of all action—is wealth or women (in Sir Epicure Mammon's case the "women" might also be boys); the actors at the Vivian Beaumont want nothing more than to be madly comic, which is as disastrous for comedy as the headlong efforts to achieve beauty or majesty is damaging to tragedy.

Please, please, Messrs. Blau and Irving, mount a production which I can compliment for something more than its worthy purpose. I'm getting even more sick and tired of recording my complaints than you must be of reading them.

—*NAT*, 31 Oct. '66

UNDER THE WEATHER

It appears that Saul Bellow is now determined to devote himself to writing for the stage. We congratulate him on this resolve, not so much for his sake as for ours. He is a real writer; such men are sorely needed in our theatre. In his "evening of comedies," three one-act plays collectively entitled *Under the Weather* (Cort Theatre), he has chosen to give us something from the lighter side of his talent: the sportive, the odd, the eccentric.

Bellow's Herzog wrote many letters. Some were pathetic or painful, others seriously ideologic. Still others revealed Herzog as a bit of a nut. *Under the Weather* is conceived in the latter vein. The three one-act plays are farces through which Bellow seems to be relieving himself of impulses and anxieties that oppress his spirit. When objectified as "stories" they become laughably "far out." They are like those wild dreams which seem utterly ridiculous when recalled in the light of the morning. Still, they are unaccountably depressing. *Under the Weather* is comic and disturbing.

Part 1, *The weather picture in the Northeast*, is about a middle-aged drug salesman—he has a Bachelor of Science degree—who induces a heart attack in himself to avoid marrying his old sweetheart, now widowed. We are uncertain that this is truly his motive, but it would seem so. Though overabundantly fleshed and no longer young, Flora Sharkey makes the impression of an eminently suitable mate for the complacently ailing (or hypochondriac) Harry Faufill. She is eager, enthusiastic, energetic and hysterically helpful. Despite all this, Faufill wants out and so arranges for his collapse. Laughter and puzzlement!

Part 2, *The weather in the Southeast*, presents Solomon Ithimar, a top-secret atomic scientist on his way to a cosmically significant conference in Geneva. He stops off at a third-rate Miami hotel to see a childhood flame with whom he has since had no contact; she is a respectably married Jewish matron, Marcella Vankuchen. To what end? The memory which has sustained him through his rise from butcher's son to nuclear eminence was the sight vouchsafed him by Marcella during their pre-adolescent sex games of a tiny wen located in the region of her genitals. Nothing since that first intimacy has ever stirred him. The great man pleads in an ecstasy of anticipation and in fear of rejection for permission to behold the magic spot once again and thus regain his capacity for pure elation.

If I am circuitous in stating this circumstance it is probably because Ithimar, like so many mental giants, is given to protracted verbal ejaculations. One is not sure if this logorrhea is simply a form of humor cultivated by Bellow to mock intellectuals whose tensions manifest themselves through an enormous spill of words (he uses the device in several of his novels), or if it is a kind of artful padding—the rhetoric of comedy—to compensate for a lack of characterization through developed action. In any case, what makes this episode memorable is the dry nervous squiggle of the impotent Big Brain whom Bellow, very ably abetted by Harry Towb as Ithimar, caricatures. I should add that the type has become familiar to me through much frequentation of literary parties. On that account alone these events are seldom pleasant experiences. Some of their uneasiness rubs off on this part of *Under the Weather*.

Part 3, *The weather picture for the Midwest*, is

the most telling. Hilda, a prostitute of Polish origin, begs Pennington, an octogenarian millionaire whom she has been serving in monthly installments over the years, to set her sister up in a dress shop. This skit is notable for its exposure of a not uncommon male attitude toward sex. It is crudely functional. Hilda is a domestic personality: she is patient, understanding and in her own way faithful. Pennington pays for her services but resents the intrusion of sentiment or any recognition of her except as an instrument of his need.

Do the three parts of the evening purport to be pencil sketches of grotesque aspects of American masculinity? The gamut runs from fear through employment of neurotic surrogates to cold and unfeeling possession as a touchstone of power. Since the plays on the whole are unpretentious, one cannot be sure that this is the plan. The effect is of a writer of complex talent still insecure in handling a medium to which he is not accustomed. He appears to be expressing fringe facets of his moral and psychosomatic self. We might describe the process metaphorically as that of an artist who took to depicting special portions of his anatomy—the tips of his fingers, the points of his elbows, the space between his toes—rather than his essential being. The result stimulates curiosity without being gratifying.

While Harry Towb in the three roles is offered the opportunity of altering his mask from asinine burgher, to jittery genius, to ludicrously superannuated powerhouse, Shelley Winters is for the most part effectively consigned to the role of feminine victim. It is her most satisfying stage performance to date. She gasps, sighs and moans in a mellifluous monotone which is at once humorous and touching.

The line of Arthur Storch's direction seems too close to "realism" and thus fails to capture the peculiar elements of "fantasy" which are woven into Bellow's writing. But his task has not been an easy one. I believe *Under the Weather* might fare better, commercially as well as artistically, somewhere or anywhere off Broadway. The New York midtown framework is damaging to such enterprises.

—*NAT*, 14 Nov. '66

VIET ROCK

There is a scene in *Viet Rock* written and directed by Megan Terry (Martinique Theatre) which caught my attention. A frightened and grieving mother is conducted into a military hospital to see her wounded soldier son. She bends over to speak to him—he is unrecognizably disfigured—but cannot elicit any response. Horrified at his silence she inspects the boy's identification tag. He isn't her son; the attendant apologizes for the error. The woman bursts into wild sobs as she presses the hopelessly marred soldier to her breast. This stranger too is her son.

The scene—no more than a moment really—is something of an intrusion in the proceedings. It may not be an original dramatic idea but it is vivid and potent. Yet it probably passes unnoticed in the hullabaloo of the proceedings. *Viet Rock* is an irregular chain of improvisations, in feeble rock 'n' roll style, intended to protest and mock the indignity and stupidity of our action in Vietnam.

One would suppose that such an enterprise, however crude, would arouse our social conscience, stir us to applause and shouts of approbation. *Viet Rock* does not propose "art" but propaganda. But we who are not averse to propaganda—particularly in a theatre that offers so little art—are sorely disappointed to find ourselves not only untouched but embarrassed by it. The reaction comes not simply from the ineptitude, the lack of originality in the various parodies (the screaming sergeant in charge of muddled recruits, the barking of inane slogans, the imbecile Congressional hearings, etc.), or a straining after strong effects of satire and caricature. We squirm because of something peculiarly pretentious behind it all. What disturbs is a tone not of youthful bravado or raw radicalism but of a certain artiness and a by now no longer new conformism.

It sometimes goes by the name of "total theatre," an item in "the theatre of cruelty." It aspires to be free and gay, raucous, graphic, topical, improvisational, saltatory, shocking and politically explosive. What is aimed at is not a show but an *event*. Something of this was done with incomparably superior skill in the Brook production of *Marat/Sade*, and it has been brought off in various forms throughout the theatre's history; but in *Viet Rock* we are given the gesture without wit, invention, thought or real point. There is little to indicate that this farrago is propelled by the force of genuine social indignation or understanding. There is hardly any true spontaneity; only untempered ambition and unripe mind. Such exhibits are swipes of *avant-garde*-ism.

Our scorners and jeerers, the would-be rebels in the theatre nowadays, appear to have hardly any artistic or cultural memory. There is only the present, containing no yesterday and looking forward to no morrow. Thus Dada and Surrealism are never recalled, or German Expressionism (Georg Kaiser, Ernest Toller and others), or the genuinely lyric outcries that lent poignancy as well as color to Lawson's *Processional*, Rice's *The Adding Machine*, cummings' *him* of our own twenties, or even the political cabarets of the thirties, and the fun and games of *Beyond the Fringe* and the shows at "The Premise." Some of this is to be found in the smudged plaints and jibes of our solitary "fools": Mort Sahl, Lenny Bruce, Bob Dylan, but the theatre which demands a synthesis and a progression is still barbarously infantile. We are thus made to appear even more abject and impotent by the trappings and parade of a hell-raising "sophistication" which are merely the discarded rags of affectingly ancient and ill-used clowns. Our attempts at liberating laughter and tonic defiance are kid stuff. The only innovation is the lack of heart. We may smile and occasionally guffaw but the consequences are for the most part dispiriting—as with the recent elections. Can we not become a little wiser without all of us first submitting to a real crack on our heads?

—*NAT*, 28 Nov. '66

THE SCHOOL FOR SCANDAL
RIGHT YOU ARE
CABARET
DON'T DRINK THE WATER

The APA returns to the Lyceum Theatre with two items from its "old" repertory: *The School for Scandal* and Pirandello's *Right You Are*. The town—particularly the daily press—has acclaimed them. In part this may be construed as an oblique rebuff to the upstart and more pretentious Repertory Theatre of Lincoln Center whose productions at the Vivian Beaumont have thus far failed to please. A more legitimate reason for the APA's advancement is that its essentially modest performances are pleasantly within the scope of its company's capacities, as well as within the audience's comprehension. (Shaw, for example, is by now more acceptable than Brecht; a schematized Tolstoy and an ever-agreeable Kaufman are easier to take than Büchner or Sartre.) So if New York is to have a repertory company—one that has worked faithfully while enduring neglect, one moreover that has risen from obscurity—the APA must be the public's and the press's choice. What else, after all, is there?

The School for Scandal is a perennial delight. Its theme—the pleasures, absurdities and bloodshed of gossip in polite society—is ever fresh. Its writing sparkles with canny good humor, its spirit is wise, its construction solid.

The APA production begins dully; it grows livelier as it proceeds, but there is a lack of real zest, of effervescence, throughout the first half. The settings are on the drab side, the costumes generally unbecoming. Very little of the acting is bad but the only bit of ingratiatingly sustained playing is done by Keene Curtis as Sir Oliver Surface. We hear all the text except when Dee Victor, in an effort to keep up the required rapidity of delivery, becomes indistinct. There are cute though slightly hokey pieces of stage business in Ellis Rabb's direction and acting.

At the outset, Rosemary Harris as Lady Teazle forces her characterization too much. (This may have been due to opening-night tension.) In the later scenes her natural charm and soothing sense of fun make amends for our initial discontent. Helen Hayes gives us Mrs. Candour, the bitch of the bevy, rather more like a provincial American housewife than a lady of 18th-century London high society—a society which was literally "select" because it constituted a very confined circle immersed in a sea of filth.

Despite my reservations I was pleased to see Sheridan's play once more. It shines on Broadway today like a good deed in a wicked world.

The audience's taste for the APA's program is best illustrated by *Right You Are*. Written in 1917, the play was first produced with Edward G. Robinson in New York by the Theatre Guild some time in the twenties. It was thought to be esoteric, and for that reason was presented at first at special matinees only.

The audience today consumes it like candy. The production is thoroughly lucid: each point is neatly made, each movement, gesture, characterization in Stephen Porter's direction well defined. The setting James Tilton is pleasantly trim and the acting altogether without ambiguity. This is Pirandello without pain.

Right You Are (or literally translated from the Italian *It Is So, If You Think So*) is a comedy, but a Pirandello comedy. It plays an intellectual game with a story wrought from anguish. Its philosophic purport is that we cannot know one another, we cannot arrive at the truth in any matter involving the individual mind. We hardly know the truth even about ourselves. Every person sees us in a different light and we remain unknown to ourselves not only because we are in a state of constant change but because we assume different masks for social convenience.

This thought is no longer vitally impressive, but Pirandello was the first to dramatize it—most brilliantly in *Six Characters in Search of an Author*. He was the first in the theatre to split the atom of the human personality so that in a sense *character*, a coherent whole with its own inner logic, dissolves.

Pirandello wrote play after play on this theme, most of them intriguingly ingenious, a few of them so strained that they verge on tedium. What holds one's interest most of the time is the melodramatic and necessarily unresolved mystery that Pirandello unfolds. From this dramatic pattern and its concomitant psychologic conundrum he wrings a kind of bitter mirth. The Pirandello "trick" might not engage us if it were not for the subjective suffering from which the pattern emerges. This combination of elements makes Pirandello the pioneer in modern drama of the "tragic farce," the precursor of theatre of the absurd.

No production which fails to retain this duality in Pirandello's work can be said fully to represent him. The APA eliminates the play's hysteria and thus reduces it to the grasp of a simple-minded audience. It is flattered by its easy absorption of a "metaphysical" play which has now become a sort of witty suspense show.

In this vein, the production is entirely satisfying. Helen Hayes follows the director's line loyally and expertly; Sydney Walker is more convincing here than in any of his previous roles. But neither stirs in us anything beyond a respectful assent. There are no surprises: Donald Moffat is crisp, Patricia Conolly is sharp, Anita Dangler in a bit part is funny. A sense of cordial give and take ("ensemble") prevails.

Cabaret at the Broadhurst is a show stunning in its ugliness. Based on John van Druten's *I Am A Camera*, itself the dramatization of one of Christopher Isherwood's *Berlin Stories*, it is intended to provide a musical comedy impression of the atmosphere of that town shortly before Hitler's advent.

It was a decadent period and *Cabaret* purposes that we enjoy the spectacle of that decadence. This is not a misconceived plan, for no matter what we

may think of it now, Berlin of the late twenties and early was glamorous. What decayed was an active, complex, sophisticated, cultivated and feverish society. Decay has an aura and where its ingredients are as humanly rich as they were in Berlin the aura glows in hectic hues of an infernal allure. The period produced Erwin Piscator, Ernst Toller, Bertolt Brecht, Georg Grosz, Hanns Eisler, Kurt Weill, Ernst Lubitsch, Emil Jannings, Marlene Dietrich and a host of other artists, actors and entertainers whose various poisons gleamed in the night, smacking of heady and honeyed wickedness.

The authors of *Cabaret*—book by Joe Masteroff, music by John Kander, lyrics by Fred Ebb—had a mine of material to steal from. (The creative artist is always a prime plagiarist.) But *Cabaret* does not afford even a parody of the period. Its tone approximates that of *Sweet Charity*, which has made something of a real style of Broadway jingle-jangle. In *Cabaret* very little is successful beyond the box office. Its decadence is the thinnest sort: that of our night clubs.

Sally Bowles and her lover (now an upright, normal American) become in *Cabaret* subsidiary in interest to the honest landlady (an incipient Nazi in van Druten's play) and a gentle Jewish store-keeper. The lyrics, except possibly for the first one, *Welcome* (in a medley of languages), are flat, the score gratifies the ear momentarily only when it quotes from old German tunes, the choreography is ineffective except in its occasional grotesquerie, abetted by Joel Grey as the M.C. "Les girls" have been chosen with an eye to their thighs rather than to any other portion of their person.

The fabled Lotte Lenya, our heiress of the period, would still be good if she had occasion to display her own tart contemptuousness, but as the benevolent landlady she must act "nice" and though she never loses her directness this quality alone is not sufficiently fascinating. Jack Gilford, always engaging because of his innocence, has a role without much humor, and humor is the greater part of his gift. Bert Convy sings acceptably. Jill Haworth plays Sally Bowles. In the original, Sally was a pathetic and shockingly spoiled waif in deliberate flight from the stuffiness of English respectability. Miss Haworth is brassy. But in shiny black décolleté her back is beautiful: credit where credit is due.

The triumph of the evening is Boris Aronson's scenery, greatly enhanced by Jean Rosenthal's lighting. He seems to have done the work that should have been done by the whole production staff: writers, director, choreographer, cast. His central setting, the cabaret, is a hot spot, burning in low flame within walls of intimate and insidiously suggestive red, surrounded by the sickly window lights of a depressed town. The boarding house and particularly the friendly Jew's fruit shop breathe a cozy air; they are a little tired looking, quaintly tender with a love of homely beauty which barely recognizes its modest appeal. Boris Aronson's work is never mere ornament; his designs are in themselves a text.

Still the fact remains that *Cabaret* invites us to enjoy what it presumably aims to mock and denounce. This makes for a show which, to use the title of one of its numbers, is (in the Yiddish for the thoroughly unattractive) a *Meeskite*. All that remains to be said is that judging by the applause and the full houses at $12 for an orchestra seat, the audience is enraptured.

Here is a paradox: I couldn't for a moment "believe" in *Cabaret*, which deals with supposedly serious matters, but I "believed" the nonsense of Woody Allen's *Don't Drink the Water* at the Morosco. The latter is an anecdote about a caterer and his family from Newark on a visit to a small Communist country. It takes place in an American embassy considerably less "real" than a military musical. How then can I speak of "believing" in such light-headed stuff?

There are funny lines and situations which spring from the reality of odd-ball, carefree, boozy conviviality. Let us tell jokes, helter-skelter. If one of them flops—and a number of them do—we tell another to compensate for the brief lull. Thus: "Years of insanity," shouts the exasperated caterer at the play's frazzled juvenile, "have driven you crazy."

Lou Jacobi speaks such lines as if his life depended on them. For him they contain the most profound truth. He is convinced that their genial foolishness will make life worth living! Thus he wins us. Beside him stands his dryly tolerant but never conceding spouse, played with impassive, nasal tenacity by Kay Medford. The always inept and therefore thoroughly likable ambassador's son, disastrously devoted to diplomatic maneuvers, is engagingly played by Anthony Roberts. If you are prepared to spend a goofy evening at the theatre, *Don't Drink the Water* will serve. It made me laugh on the *right* side of my face.

—*NAT*, 12 Dec. '66

PETER WEISS
Marat/Sade

Everyone should be grateful to the Royal Shakespeare Company of London for bringing to New York its production under Peter Brook's direction of Peter Weiss' *The Persecution and Assassination of Marat as Performed by the Inmates of the Asylum of Charenton under the Direction of the Marquis de Sade*. Whether or not you are going to like it, you ought to see it. For when all is said and done—and much is done and said through the hubbub of the performance—the production is a fascinating entertainment. For scrupulous care in makeup, for subtlety in costuming, for ingenuity in dealing with movement, for the feeling of novelty throughout, New York has not seen the like in a long time. We witness here what a well-organized repertory theatre of talented players and leaders can accomplish.

Much of the talk during the intermission of *Marat/Sade* centered on Peter Brook's "use of space." It is indeed brilliant. So is Richard Peaslee's incidental music. Even more persuasively theatrical are the sound effects—for example, the employment of the wooden platforms as "drums" to be struck by whatever objects are available to the actors. Brueghel, Bosch, Goya have provided models for the visual aspect of various figures. There is a memorable grouping in which the actors' faces alone are seen, their bodies being submerged beneath the stage floor. The impression is that of a heap of severed heads tossed helter-skelter on the ground. There is witty business to match the playfulness of the text, such as the pouring of red paint from a pail to indicate the shedding of the people's blood, changed to blue when the aristocrats' blood is spilled, and then to milky white when Marat finally succumbs to Corday's murderous knife.

More impressive perhaps than all this is the actors' zeal, their unrelenting concentration and byplay so that nothing on the stage is allowed to become static or to fall out of line. Even the musicians in the side boxes participate in pantomime. Voices are resonant, diction is admirable, though I could not always make out the words of the ensemble singing.

The kind of acting demanded, though physically strenuous, is of the simplest sort, requiring attitudes and postures rather than intimate emotional transfiguration. The well-managed trick for most of the cast is to show that the "actors" of the play they are presenting at Charenton are syphilitics, spastics, catatonics, schizophrenics, paranoiacs, manic depressives or otherwise debilitated persons, none of them consistently able to remember the script's lines or to keep within the confines of the author's (de Sade's) scenic scheme. The team work is exemplary.

Of the individuals in the excellent company, Ian Richardson as Marat, Patrick Magee as de Sade, Robert Lloyd as the fanatic Jacques Roux, John Steiner as an aristocrat afflicted with satyriasis, Susan Williamson as Marat's ever faithful mistress, Simonne Evrard, Michael Williams as the Herald (master of ceremonies) deserve special mention, though my particular favorite, an actress of insidious attractiveness, is Glenda Jackson as Charlotte Corday.

Apart from noting "the use of space," the professionally oriented playgoer may speak of Brecht and "alienation" or of Artaud's "theatre of cruelty." The production is punctuated by frenzied paroxysms, as the text is replete with images of extreme violence. There is also—and this is not as noticeable in an English translation as it would be in the original German—a good deal of expressionist hysteria (abhorred by Brecht), a kind of roaring and macabre lyricism.

It should be noted in regard to influences, which though they have a certain interest do not affect the heart of the matter, that while many of Brecht's devices are employed—the most salient being the use of remote historical material to make topical points—certain elements in the production, almost baroque in their profusion and nerve-racking in their intended impact, are antithetical to Brecht. It should also be said of a production in which the staging very nearly swallows the script that Weiss' text might be produced with less emphasis on the hectic and bizarre and that the insanity of the characters need not have been rendered with as much graphic distortion as Brook has employed. In that case, although the results would not be quite so showy, we might more readily discern what Weiss had in mind.

What is certainly untrue, as some have intimated, is that there is no *play*, no meaning or message in Weiss' writing. Here we come to the question of the evening's real worth, of which discussion limited to its stage excitement is actually an evasion. (Do *you* go to the theatre to enjoy "the use of space"?) In Germany, where it was first produced, *Marat/Sade* was preeminently a political play. (To be sure, it also reveals Weiss as a master of the theatrical medium, quite apart from Brook's contribution.) It is a particularly German political play though its author lives in Sweden and stresses his internationalism. There is a reference to the "Final Solution" (the Nazi extermination of the Jews), but the issues raised extend beyond such history. Even allusions to "wars whose weapons rapidly developed by servile scientists will become more and more deadly until they can with a flick of a finger tear a million of you to pieces" are not of the utmost moment here.

Marat/Sade is a debate within its author's spirit. The political issue which gave rise to it is the division of Germany (and the rest of Europe) into capitalist and Socialist camps. In this play Weiss stands between the two camps. He sees fascism beaten and capitalism still oppressively hypocritical. He sees an apparently victorious socialism lead to a crippling conformity. His skepticism turns to bitterness, anxiety to despair. Man is a destructive beast, as Weiss' de Sade (who arrives at his sadism through masochism) says; the people still demand a revolution which will realize the everlasting dream of peace, plenty, freedom of conscience and expression.

Again and again, as the songs in *Marat/Sade* voicing this dream are turned into satires, Weiss mocks the idea that any political action can end oppression. He seems to be saying that all determined struggle in this direction, the promises of all social, cultural and religious institutions, end in betrayal. Remember that all the central characters in the play—including the most articulate, the ultra-radical Marat and the mortified de Sade—are demented, their world a madhouse.

Weiss does not make the Marat/Sade duel a one-sided affair. He tosses and turns in indecision. The final lines of the play are Roux's outcry "When will you learn to see, when will you learn to take sides?"—an outcry stifled by the people's trancelike march and shouts. Yes, one must take sides, but isn't there something futile, Weiss infers, in it all? To which, Weiss or Brook has appended an ironically facetious speech telling us that we can compose our own moral, draw our own conclusions, from the proceedings.

That I am not wholly mistaken in my interpretation I call Weiss himself (apart from his text) in evidence. He has recently announced that since the writing of *Marat/Sade* he has changed his attitude, he has decided to take sides: he has become a Socialist. But for the playgoer or the critic it is perhaps not initially imperative to declare oneself on the validity of Weiss' position in this play but simply to recognize that the play aims to illustrate the anguish of decision, the gravity of the human

problem involved: that social change always entails the possibility of sanguinary upheaval—a price too terrible to pay in view of man's disposition to turn the most high-minded enterprises to mediocrity and, in the end, to perpetuate injustice.

Yet I left the theatre unmoved, almost indifferent. (I was reminded of Tolstoy's quip about Andreyev: "He wants to frighten me, but I'm not scared.") I am moved by the "coolness" of the Berliner Ensemble in Brecht's *Mother Courage*. In like manner, I am truly concerned about Galileo's dilemma in the same author's account of it. With *Marat/Sade* I am left only with a sense of an adult entertainment—surely a precious boon these days—rather than stirred by any vitalizing thought or feeling about the play's subject matter, ostensibly of crucial importance.

It is true that when Coulmier, the asylum's supervisor, jumps up to intervene—after Roux has shouted, "Once and for all the idea of glorious victories won by the glorious army must be wiped out. Neither side is glorious"—with the admonition "This is outright pacifism. At this very moment our soldiers are laying down their lives for the freedom of the world and of our world," the audience applauds (and how delighted many of us are that it does) in recognition of the attack upon a contemporary parallel. Still, I venture to say that it is not really engaged in the play's theme, never truly disturbed by the cardinal question raised, or stimulated to search itself for an answer. LeRoi Jones' savagery (another sort of "theatre of cruelty") appalls us. *Marat/Sade* converts all our political and intellectual concern into display, an artful fun house, a magnificent toy. It is distinguished decoration, first-class theatrical "salesmanship."

Whether or not this is due in part to the sort of brilliant direction Brook has given the play, the fact remains that most of the text, though cleverly or cutely phrased in deliberate doggerel or near verse, is trite. There are long passages popularizing primary existentialist pronouncements as understood in cafés and often reduced, despite

Germanic vehemence, to a facile pessimism very comforting at bottom to the presumably despised bourgeoisie.

Since *Marat/Sade* is a dramatization of political inconclusiveness or nihilism, a position which many smart folk nowadays equate with true wisdom, I shall set down my own sentiments in regard to the misgivings which the play enunciates.

Yes: the French Revolution was followed by Napoleon's autocracy, the hopes of the early Russian revolutionaries were mangled into Stalinism, the war against Hitler has brought Germany, France and Italy to various degrees of stultifying complacency. History offers no guarantees. If pressed hard enough, men will assert their livingness to the point of bloodshed to achieve what they deem to be a better life. Man moves and sometimes fights because he *is* man and wants to make a world according to his material and spiritual needs. This is an impulse, if you will, a fact of nature, to which I say "yea"—no matter how often history appears to negate man's efforts. One does not even have to believe in Progress to assent to and justify the never-ending struggle. As long as there are creatures on earth more sentient than computers, men will, because they must, make choices, and they will not be deterred by what wiseacres in the future may decide as to the sagacity of these choices. When asked, "Is life worth living?" Samuel Butler answered, "That is a question for a foetus not for a man." To despair because man's extreme efforts to modify conditions of social injury or physical misery frequently result in new humiliations is to be either an intellectual sissy or a moral coward.

The best compliment I can tender *Marat/Sade* is that it has provoked me to this declaration. And if anyone argues that in approaching the play in this manner I have exceeded the bounds of the "trade," that is, gone beyond the theatre, I must once again affirm that unless theatre and theatre criticism do this they both become paltry and inconsequential. "He knows no drama who only drama knows."

—*NYT*, '66

MAIN STREAMS OF AMERICAN DRAMA

One of our kindest critics in a survey of the American theatre calls a chapter of his book "Disarray in the Sixties". A more severe critic speaks of the same period as "Seasons of Discontent". Virtually everyone who gives more than a passing thought to the state of our theatre agrees that since 1956 it has been in a bad way. This is particularly true of our native drama.

Still, a word of caution may be necessary. We are an impatient people and frequently forgetful. We burn our credits. We are preoccupied with the latest thing. For this reason there is some danger in making seeping generalizations about so short a time as six or seven seasons. Toward the end of the Twenties and through most of the thirties and Forties, we neglected O'Neill. He was no longer our "hero". With the revival of *Desire Under the Elms* and of *The Iceman Cometh* and the first production of *A Touch of the Poet*, O'Neill's reputation was re-established! We are given to gross exaggeration in enthusiasm as well as in condemnation. We hail able men as masters and when they falter dismiss them as "finished". This is critically and culturally damaging.

Lillian Hellman's *Toys in the Attic* though far from being as sure in craftsmanship as her *Little Foxes* or as unified in theme as *The Autumn Garden* was, despite confusion of aim, still the work of a dramatist of dignity and power. S.N. Behrman's *But For Whom Charlie*, gracefully and wittily written but badly produced, contained a wry irony in regard to the hollow sophistication of segments of New York society and a note of tenderness for inarticulate folk of good will. Tennessee Williams' *The Night of the Iguana* struck chords of personal pathos, and, in the second of his last two plays *Gnädiges Fraulein*, showed him essaying a grotesquely humorous stylization new to his work. In writing and imagination

Gnädiges Fraulein was superior to many of the black comedies produced by our *avant-garde*. William Inge's *Natural Affection*, unfulfilled as a whole, contained excellent scenes and several telling character delineations.

Arthur Miller's *After the Fall* has been the subject of particularly virulent attack in some quarters and so, to a lesser extent, was his latest play *Incident at Vichy*. Both plays, however, interested their audiences and had their partisans. The cause for certain of the harsh things said about these plays—particularly the former—are complex. It was felt that in his self-exposure Miller was not only apologizing but blessing himself for weaknesses which many were not all prepared to condone.

Much of this criticism represented a reaction against a writer the success of whose early plays made him part of an "establishment" which no longer conforms to the latest conformity. Miller was identified with the social realism of the Thirties and Forties, anathema on the whole to many of the younger critics. Others who might have been pleased to see Miller continue the "line" of *Death of a Salesman* and *The Crucible* sensed a defection in the direction of a "soft" existentialism: Forbear because we are all guilty!

Whatever the criticism of Miller's recent plays three points need to be emphasized: (a) that properly produced they are extremely effective stage pieces, (b) that they develop Miller's basic preoccupation: what men owe one another and (c) that Miller is still a force and can be counted on to provide us in the future with provocative drama.

The "softening" in Miller, if it is indeed that, is somehow consonant with the "toughening" of the drama of the Sixties. The two plays which may be said to herald the new decade are Jack Gelber's *The Connection* and Edward Albee's *The Zoo Story*. The title of the Gelber play is significant because the "connection" referred to by the title is an otherwise anonymous character who procures heroin for a group of addicts. He sells a means of escape from a mechanized community. The play

pictures an embattled disconnection. Albee's *The Zoo Story* dramatizes the disconnected youth in a furious and futile attempt to establish a connection with his fellow men. He resolves his dilemma by forcing "society" through the agency of an "average citizen" to kill him. The young vagrant achieves connection by dying at the hand of this unaware gentleman resting on a park bench. Both plays may pass as naturalism, but their effect is symbolic.

It is worth noting that another play of the time, Jack Richardson's *The Prodigal*, retells the Orestes-Clytemnestra story in a manner which denies any values to Orestes' murderous act. The implication is that all positive behavior on behalf of any ideology leads to brutality. A new sort of quietism consisting chiefly of negation (particularly in regard to social affairs) is attained.

These plays were produced off-Broadway in tiny theatres where little money had to be spent in staging and the expectation of profit was, to say the least, modest. Still, though the plays constituted minority expressions, their mood in many variants has become pervasive, so that in one form or another they have reached Broadway's larger audience. The most signal success in this area was Albee's first full-length play *Who's Afraid of Virginia Woolf?* Such success does not denote conscious acceptance of a point of view, for while the "big public" may be fascinated by Albee it is not fully aware of what he means.

Albee is a knowing craftsman, an excellent writer. He has a gift for a distinctive dialogue which sounds "natural" without being naturalistic. It stylizes our common speech into forms which sparkle with venomous wit and hold us by flashes of desperate eloquence of ominous gravity.

Virginia Woolf implies that our lives are based on falsity, that we are corrupt for lack of values or rather that our values are generally confined to status, success, affluence. As a result, Albee insinuates, we destroy one another. Emphasis is on the negative; Albee's mordant talent has been evident chiefly in giving lively voice to a destructive bent. Destruction, however, may be a step on the way to something else.

Albee is only thirty-eight, and his latest play, *A Delicate Balance*, another "domestic" comedy (if we agree that *Virginia Woolf* is a comedy), while more subdued and less sensational than the earlier play, marks a progress in his development. *A Delicate Balance* illustrates our inability truly to like one another. When we profess love or, more humbly, profound friendship, we are rarely able to enact it. We therefore suffer loneliness and find ourselves empty. As the Sartrian formula has it: "Hell is the other."

But Albee also suggests—perhaps as an afterthought—that, though our loneness may always be the curse of our condition, we must make every effort to transcend it. In this we are perhaps philosophically close to Camus.

One of the play's weaknesses may be ascribed, I venture to say, to two interrelating factors. As a young man of our day, Albee speaks from personal hurt as much as from close observation. Though social aspects of the human dilemma are hinted at they are not sufficiently dramatized. Our "emptiness" is not solely an innate phenomenon but is also a sign of the dissatisfaction we feel with our work or, more precisely, with the way we work in our fiercely materialistic and competitive society. Albee never tells us in *A Delicate Balance* how his people earn their living.

To make this clear we might compare Albee's play to Chekhov. Chekhov depicts not only individual sorrow and the inherent pain of manhood but the specific circumstances of his time which intensify his characters' frustrations. Albee has no general social view. One might guess that like most of his generation he shuns such a view because of our common historical disappointments and skepticism about political change. In any case we should not hesitate to affirm, despite a lurking and possibly widespread resistance to Albee, that he is a valuable playwright who is in the process of growth.

—WOR, 1966

MIDSEASON REPORT

I prefer to be an optimist. But optimism which is not based on a firm foundation of pessimism is foolishness. There's no use in asserting that all goes well in our theatre because the weekly gross of the combined Broadway playhouses has, to put it in the words of a certain trade paper, "climbed back to the sunny side of the million-dollar mark." The fact is that hardly any new American play produced this season has induced anything more than mild approval.

Why then go to the theatre? Why if one's livelihood doesn't depend on it be a critic? A poetic answer was given by Ionesco when he said that if only one really good play were produced each season the theatre would still be an institution worth maintaining. At no time in history have the majority of plays been anything but fourth-rate. But there are more cogent reasons for the theatre's perennial appeal. Plays or "scripts" alone do not constitute theatre and certainly do not always provide the greatest pleasure. I am not at all enthusiastic, for instance, about *The Apple Tree* as written, scored or designed, but I am quickened to laughter, dream and desire by Barbara Harris. I am indifferent to the honorable sentiments of *I Do! I Do!* but I admire the skill of Gower Champion's direction, Oliver Smith's settings and especially the performances of Mary Martin and Robert Preston. For those who respond to sounds, sights and personalities of the stage as much as to words I would recommend the show, though portions of its text did intrude on my enjoyment.

There is much more to be said on this matter, things much more helpful than the by now tiresome cry that the Broadway theatre is moribund or dead—even though one frequently relieves one's exasperation by resorting to it. Without further ado then, I submit this survey of the present season's offerings up to the moment of this writing.

The best new play on Broadway is Albee's *A Delicate Balance*. (*The Rose Tattoo* is another play worth seeing but it is a revival, the chief glory of which is Maureen Stapleton.) I speak of *A Delicate Balance* with some diffidence not because certain respectable critics have been strongly averse to it but because I believe its production, though intelligent and generally well acted, does not do it full justice. I must add, too, that the Martin Beck Theater is not a sufficiently intimate theatre for the play. It calls for none of the screaming which characterized *Who's Afraid of Virginia Woolf?* Somewhat more abstract than the latter, subtler in feeling and theme—the difficulty of behaving responsibly according to the friendships we profess—it not only reveals greater compassion than Albee's earlier play but possesses greater variety of characterization and sophistication of statement.

Here I must interject a consideration which playwrights and producers often overlook. Certain plays would gain in longevity, receipts and public appreciation if they were produced more modestly than the Broadway routine permits: in a word, if they were produced *off*-Broadway. Pinter's *The Caretaker* was such a play, so too were Bellows' *The Last Analysis* and *Under the Weather* as well as Tennessee Williams' *Slapstick Tragedy*.

It is true that the plays I have mentioned would not attract "name actors" under off-Broadway's meager circumstances but what may be lost in one way would be more than compensated for in others. In England an Olivier, a Peggy Ashcroft, a Rex Harrison will play at the tiny Royal Court Theater far from the West End because the play and auspices have distinction, but alas! alas! our actors fear a loss of status (as well as earnings) should they appear anywhere outside the midtown ghetto.

I laughed like a fool at the nonsense of *Don't Drink the Water*—it does not pretend to be more than that—and Lou Jacobi and Kay Medford are funny. I wish I could have shuddered at the horrors in *The Investigation* but the accumulation of oft-repeated facts it reports did not have the desired effect. The dramatization of two or three might be moving; with all of them in a lump of testimonies I became inured. There is humor and humane feeling in *My Sweet Charlie* but it is too long for its material and adds little to its subject: the folly of estrangement and misunderstanding between black and white. However, I did like Lou Gossett and the promising and charming, though overdirected, 18-year-old Bonnie Bedelia. *Dinner at Eight* is a play the merits of which may easily be exaggerated, as Tyrone Guthrie has. It is more studded with near stars than with good acting.

A musical of some quality—in certain respects superior to more flashy ones—is *Walking Happy*, based on Harold Brighouse's endearing and enduring *Hobson's Choice*. It too is an essentially intimate show. Its star, Norman Wisdom, combines wistfulness with zest and its leading lady, Louise Troy, can act. There are good dance numbers. The show's tone is old-fashioned but sound. What hurts it is a lack of lightness in the composition of the whole.

Many folk admired *Cabaret* as a brave gesture. Think of it: a musical about the bad days in Berlin before Hitler. For me it is Minsky with a message. The same period produced the Brecht-Weill *Threepenny Opera*. And whatever one may say of the moral wretchedness of the time, its typical girl entertainers were luscious (like the Marlene Dietrich of *The Blue Angel*) not grotesque, and the characteristic music (even in the night clubs) was much, much better than the pastiche of *Cabaret*. It is a show in which the subsidiary characters, though sentimentalized, have a little more body than the supposedly pivotal figures. The only participant in the production who catches the spirit of that corrupt era while rendering it in beauty is the designer, Boris Aronson.

Off-Broadway the things to see are *Eh?* and *America Hurrah!* The first would benefit by cutting but it has at least one sharp performance by Dustin Hoffman in a goofily imaginative treatment of the pixilated little Englishman impishly at odds with the brave new world of industrialism and its concomitant sciences and solaces. *America*

Hurrah! is not literature but its last episode called "Motel," all sight and sound in shattering discord, projects a blinding and instantaneously lacerating image of the world we live in. That takes talent. But it is self-deception to exaggerate its creative import: mediocre shows are not insults; good ones need not be equated with genius.

A fighting general said war is hell. The youngsters of *Viet Rock* agree. As an indictment of war it is not particularly arresting; as a protest against our policy in Vietnam it is feeble. There are momentary flashes of pathos and of satire but in theatrical animation or invention it is not in a class with, let us say, *Oh What a Lovely War*. Still many young people and others who yearn for a theatre which raises Cain will probably welcome it. In so far as it breaks through Broadway barriers, I too am prepared to applaud.

This sketch of the season's prologue is not particularly glowing. We should always clamor for excellence. Still, I believe it vain to be forever pronouncing anathema on Broadway. We must not throw out the baby with the bath nor rejoice in administering still another kick to the notorious invalid's seat. What is most deplorable in the situation is not an absence of gifted or dedicated theatre folk—there are among us far more than we suspect—but our theatre is economically and organizationally set up in what Boris Aronson has called "an organized calamity, a collective art where the strongest force rules." This condition debilitates everything and everyone—including the public and its guides. It also curtails the volume of production and I am often tempted to declare that the staging of even a greater number of bad plays might prove a boon: more good ones might turn up.

In moments of dejection I turn for consolation to Voltaire's ironic wisdom. In his *Candide*, the hero asks, "Monsieur, how many plays have been produced in France?" The man questioned replies, "Five or six thousand." "That is a great many," Candide says, "and how many are good?" "Fifteen or sixteen," the other says. "*That* is a great many," sums up the exchange.

—*WJT*, 1 Jan. '67

THE NEW DRAMA

In recent years respected plays have tended more and more toward abstraction. Realism had become boring. It had deteriorated into "journalism": it did not say enough, merely presented facts, and facts by themselves are dumb. They put out one's eyes. We demand insight and personal statement. We seek a view of life, something which suggests an essence, a core of meaning even if this leads, as so often of late, to a conclusion of meaninglessness. The new drama, we are convinced, brings us closer to the *truth*. It recalls the great classic tradition.

The reason for this reversion to the older style is due not only to the increasing triviality of the naturalistic theatre—with its appeal to a prosperous middle class sodden with property and creature comforts—but to our mounting awareness of crisis. We are on the verge of Armageddon and await an apocalypse. Anything less basic (at least in art) strikes us as deceptive. Literature committed to the study of life as we find it and live it seems paltry, wide of the mark.

Still we are in and of this world, and though we may diagnose our condition as chronically wretched, there is something weak and flabby about our constant attempts to achieve the summits of ultimate knowledge. This groping for divinity bespeaks impotence rather than courage.

—*NAT*, 16 Jan. '67

KEEPING COOL UNDER THE GUN

Some years ago in the presence of George Kaufman and Lillian Hellman, Robert Sherwood and I engaged in a friendly argument in which I decried the American playwright's fear of failure: his inability to contemplate writing a play which he suspected was destined to flop.

Sherwood maintained that such fear was not only humanly natural but artistically justified since a play lives or dies with the immediate audience for which it is first presented. In other words, a play does not have a permanent presence like a poem, a painting or a novel.

I contended that if this were true we might never have heard today of Chekhov, Shaw and Ibsen, most of whose plays at the beginning of their careers had been "bombs." *Hedda Gabler* was greeted with derision at its first performances in Munich, Stockholm, Copenhagen and Christiana. While working on *Ghosts*, Ibsen told a friend that it "will probably cause alarm...but that cannot be helped. If it did not, it would not have been necessary to write it."

Sherwood and I were both correct. I was thinking of the whole history of the theatre—and chiefly of Europe—while Sherwood had Broadway conditions in mind. (Though, for the record, it should be noted that even a musical like *Pal Joey* was far more successful on its revival than at its initial showing with Gene Kelly as Joey.) But conditions may be changed, and it is we who can help change them. But first we must change ourselves.

Most of the productions at the American Place Theater, which is situated in St. Clement's Church on West 46th Street have been received coolly. The organization's one outstanding success, *Hogan's Goat*, was by no means superior to several of its failures. Indeed, I have come to esteem Robert Lowell's *Benito Cereno*, part of *The Old Glory* triptych, more highly than I did on first seeing it. This was partly due to the fact that I went to see it a second time, a practice emphatically to be recommended for any but the most trivial performances. Which is why revivals and a theatre committed to a good many of them are not only valuable but indispensable.

The latest production at the American Place Theater, *The Displaced Person*, an adaptation by Cecil Dawkins of four short stories by Flannery O'Connor, received notices which in the main ranged from indifference to scorn. The play has obvious shortcomings. It does not, for instance, progress with sufficient dramatic tension; the pace of its writing is too even. But it has real characters; its situations are meaningful not only in regard to its environment—the backwoods of Georgia—but to much that is happening everywhere. It is not conceived as a smash; it is written with insight and humor for the compassionate understanding of unhurried folk whose sense of entertainment goes beyond titillation or nervous shock.

Our theatre is governed by hysteria. I do not refer simply to the racing atmosphere characteristic of our first nights in which the audience seems to arrive eager to witness someone win or lose and to bet on the outcome. Opening night excitement is inevitable and may be taken as part of the pleasure of the occasion. But we should come to them as people prepared for feeling and thought, not as gamblers. Only a tiny minority, after all, is materially interested in a play, though one gathers the impression that everyone is an investor with a stake in the show's profits. Ultimately this becomes a disease.

The economics of our present theatre disorganization may be the chief cause of the infection. We cannot be certain who carries the virus: the press or the public. The contagion is probably mutual. When the atmosphere is poisoned everyone ought to take precautions. An antitoxin is called for.

Reflection is a safeguard. It might lead to independence of judgment, a civilized attitude, or at the very least, a measure of forbearance. Alfred Stieglitz, one of the first Americans to acquire a cubist drawing of Picasso in 1912, was asked why he had bought the strange object. His answer was: "Because I didn't understand it; yet I knew there was something about it I wanted to probe." This is not only the proper esthetic position; it is also eminently humane. It makes art a matter of life experience and concern; it gives depth to enjoyment.

What most of us go to the theatre for is fun. That's fine. But we should have our own fun, not merely that of the fold. Fun is real when it stems from personal communications, let us go so far as to say, communion. "The theatre," said Gordon Craig, "is not a bar; it is a famous temple." In it farce and musical comedy may be celebrated as much as tragedy. Slapstick may be as valid as tears; tender sentiment may rank with bitter satire. In every case we must assess the quality and weight at the source of every evening in the theatre. We should know what is being appealed to in us, what is being given us, what chords of our nature are being awakened and touched.

As a playgoer and as a critic I find myself receptive to almost every kind of show. But I try to distinguish between a bullfight and *King Lear*. The first is certainly more "thrilling." The play, well acted and produced (because Shakespeare can be a bore), enriches us in more than one way. After my first contact with a play I do not feel that the most important question I have to ask myself (at least as a critic) is "Did I like it?" but "Did it interest me?" that is, did it rouse my senses, affect my spirit, stimulate my thinking—and how much. I was more interested in *The Displaced Person* than many shows I "liked" better! One doesn't always "like" Pinter's or Beckett's plays but they deserve our utmost attention.

A good critic will speak with conviction but he must always be ready to change his mind—as we do about people as we get to know them. He sometimes needs to be arrogant; he should never lose humility. He must allow for second thoughts and third ones. But none of us should follow any one of them slavishly. Remember that good critics are frequently as notorious for their "errors" as they are famous for their perceptions. "Do not do to others," Shaw said, "what you would have them do to you; your tastes may not be the same."

I speak of critics but it is the audience I have in view. It should not allow itself to be herded into the theatre by crackerjack notices and screaming quotes. It should not be shamed into theatre abstinence by snide reporting. The audience is composed of individuals. They should not allow the morning cry of critics or populace to turn them into a mass-produced jelly.

—*WJT*, 22 Jan. '67

THE WILD DUCK

"No conflict, no drama" is a classic axiom. It seems to be borne out even today when the conflicting forces are not readily identifiable. Protagonist and antagonist appear to merge. *Avant-garde* plays reflect (I can hardly say "dramatize") conditions rather than situations. A man in a state of collapse is in a "condition"; if he does something to recover, or if someone comes to help him, we have a situation. The lack of purposive action makes many contemporary plays on the whole less interesting to wide audiences than the older drama. It is in the nature of humankind to act, and once you begin to do so you are likely to encounter hardship, hence conflict. That is why drama interests us: we participate in its "stories." Quiescent drama is rarely rousing. Yet even in such drama there is some implicit conflict: the conflict may resolve itself to the difficulty of staying inactive.

I have been thinking on these matters because many of the plays I have recently been reading by would-be playwrights are little more than yammers of prostration in which four-letter imprecations are hurled against nothing in particular—not even destiny or God—and I have come to the conclusion that the artists who most firmly hold my attention are those in whom the conflicts they depict arise in the first place within themselves. When such conflicts are settled once and for all, when the warring elements within them are completely subdued, they have for me very little of interest to say. Peace of mind in the artist is gratifying only when we realize the desperate struggle that he has gone through to achieve it. And even then we must not be certain that the battle has come to a full stop.

The impression we gather from most of Ibsen's critics is of a grim and resolute moralist. He was a dogged and implacable warrior who knew what he wanted. When so presented on the stage, he becomes gray and slightly dull, worst of all, "old-fashioned."

There can be no question about it: Ibsen was a severely logical artist. He came of age in the heyday of scientific rationalism. This was the weapon with which to annihilate the hierarchy of bugaboos. He would give no quarter to the constriction of social-ethical notions that no longer corresponded to the facts of the industrial era. He was going to batter falsity down with moral and intellectual rigor. He wasn't joking about it.

Such characters now strike us as unsympathetic, insufficiently human. We prefer greater flexibility. Humor, we believe, is the saving grace. Chekhov maintained that Russian actors couldn't play Ibsen because Russians (those in Chekhov's time at any rate) were more vulnerable, softer, less consistent—delightfully or frantically bewildered. Compared to characters in Turgenev, Chekhov or even Gorky, Ibsen's people are unyielding.

But just as we are eager in our theatre today to discover the comedic aspects of Chekhov's plays so that we may not suffer their intrinsic sadness, so we are beginning to look for Ibsen's lighter side. In both cases we fall into error. For Chekhov's laughter arises from tenderness and compassion; it is not escape from pain. It is an embrace of our total human experience in which the tragic and the comic are complementary, the two being more semantically than substantively differentiated.

Comedy in Ibsen is a symptom of a laceration in Ibsen's spirit. Chekhov smiles because he forgives and accepts. Ibsen is tougher; he is too "logical" for such an attitude. He is fighting all the time, and—this is his pathos—he is generally fighting himself. He says "either, or." Since neither the one nor the other quite satisfies him because he contains both, his laughter is harsh, a godlike judgment, proud and inexorable. Ibsen is relentless, constantly punitive. Neither Chekhov nor Ibsen is "funny."

In a little-known play, *Emperor and Galilean*, Julian the apostate says: "The old beauty is no longer beautiful, and the new truth is no longer true." Throughout his life Ibsen was haunted by a vision of grandeur which was being destroyed and had to be destroyed, while he felt trapped in a world which diminished manhood. He was torn by the conflict between justice and love. He sought the ideal and demanded the practical. He was divided by contrary impulses, and each of his plays is the justification of one or the other of his urges: Christianity and paganism, aristocracy and democracy, individualism and socialism.

Brand insists on self-abnegation and wrecks everyone as well as himself. Peer Gynt wants to be triumphantly independent and constantly compromises with all that stands in his way, finally becoming attenuated into a dry and empty shell, waste matter for the Buttonmolder. Hedda Gabler, a general's daughter, desires a life of glorious splendor and finds herself reduced to a middle-class housewife. Solness dreams of building towering mansions but succeeds only in constructing ordinary dwelling places. In devotion to his art, Rubek in *When We Dead Awaken* renounces passionate fulfillment through the love of a woman and finds that in doing so he has failed both as artist and man. Gregers Werle in *The Wild Duck* pursues truth unremittingly in the belief that it will save, only to find that it may ruin.

All this may explain something about the APA production of *The Wild Duck* at the Lyceum. It is decent and intelligent enough. It is not so trim a production as that of *Right You Are* because the latter is, for all its twists and turns, a simpler, more linear play. *The Wild Duck* demands far more from its actors.

The weakling Hjalmar Ekdal, your "average man," and his sensible peasant-like wife, both brilliantly drawn and on the whole comedic figures comparatively easy to project, never fail to register. But Gregers Werle, presumably the butt of Ibsen's criticism (directed, it may be, against himself), carries the real challenge of the play, and it is rarely met in performance. The reason is that directors try to make a pathetic caricature of him. His idealism is naïve to the point of folly; his motivation neurotic. But though there is a certain mockery in Ibsen's portrait of Werle, he must not be made petty. (Dr. Stockman, the "enemy of the people," may also be given a humorous touch as a fumbling innocent, but in the end he must retain something of the heroic.) The bourgeois realist Ibsen was ultimately interested in nothing less than the grandiose: his "cottages" are really cathedrals. The weakness of the APA production—and one should not be scornful of it on this account—is that its Werle is a slight, almost an inconsequential personage.

Werle may be cramped, even a little absurd, but he is still Ibsen and, despite all, a mighty being. For what does Werle say about himself as the curtain falls: that he is forever destined to remain "*the thirteenth man at the table*." Yes, says Werle-Ibsen, I may be a troublemaker, a spoil sport, even "crazy," but my function is incessantly to go on clamoring for the truth and the ideal, even if I never attain them or am never able to ascertain their exact nature.

I have seen *The Wild Duck* in many different productions. It is still worth seeing at the APA-Lyceum.

—*NAT*, 30 Jan. '67

GUTHRIE!

Allow me to present Tyrone Guthrie as the Playboy of the Western Theatre. Such a designation may strike you as frivolous. For is not Guthrie a Doctor (*Honoris Causa*) as well as a knight of the British realm? Not to mention his being Chancellor of the University of Belfast and director of a jam factory. Is he not furthermore even better known as a director of many Elizabethan masterpieces and as the founder of repertory theatres at Stratford, Ontario and Minneapolis than he is as the man who staged *The Tenth Man* on

Broadway and this season, perhaps more surprisingly, the person chosen to redo Kaufman and Ferber's 1932 comedy *Dinner at Eight*?

The Scots-Irish director is an international figure. He has directed in Helsinki and Tel-Aviv and it wouldn't astonish me if he were soon to undertake a production in Central Africa. Guthrie is an eminently serious and high-minded man. (I do not refer to his six feet five stature.) Yet I insist on "Playboy." I might have spoken of him as Puck but that appellation would not suggest any weight; I might have compared him to Tyll Eulenspiegel and his merry pranks but this might evoke the Teutonic.

A certain sane joyousness and impulse toward frolic constitute not only the essential traits of Guthrie's art but of his personal nature. Their source lies in his inner freedom. It is a quality one notices immediately in his writing, in his conversation and in his comportment. Though he respects tradition, he is unfettered by convention. He is wholly without envy or malice—a rare virtue in the "trade." He has enormous energy without the least trace of strain. He has a boundless and quite salty sense of fun which is more to be prized for being altogether effortless.

He is endlessly inventive. The comic stage "business" or byplay in such productions as Thornton Wilder's *The Matchmaker* and Ben Jonson's *Volpone* at Minneapolis was not only incessant but free-flowing. Watching a Guthrie production one does not suspect him of seeking to enliven the entertainment by trick ploys. His most extravagant inspirations seem to come naturally to him. They do not appear to be the product of brilliant craftsmanship but rather the consequence of his spiritual health and mind's ease.

He is fearless. Though now sixty-six Guthrie has something abidingly youthful in his moral composition. Daring marks most of his activities. He will try anything if it appeals to his imagination and arouses an awareness of the stage as a place of adventure. That is why some of his productions—the modern clothes *Troilus and Cressida* and the liberties taken with *The Alchemist* at the Old Vic in

1963 have offended purists. In his six books Guthrie has said "There is no Shakespearean tradition."

This boldness—the fruit of his freedom—sometimes leads him to the brink of disaster. He once told me that after having staged *A Midsummer Night's Dream* in more or less "orthodox" fashion he decided to do it with an all-male cast. (That, if you will, is the authentic Shakespeare procedure!) "How did it go?" he was eagerly asked. "It flopped," he answered without blush or tremor.

Guthrie's poise in the face of failure does not bespeak unconcern. It arises from a humane largesse, the wit to understand that art and life are a wonderful gambol. One might call such an attitude "aristocratic" were it not for the fact that for all his lordly independence and self-confidence Guthrie is basically unassuming. His not infrequent use of four-letter words sounds almost elegant in his delivery. He used to dress dreadfully. There has been some slight improvement with the years but I fancy he still lives in shabby rather than in fashionable hotels when he is "on the road" with a new show—and when is he not?

Though Guthrie's theatre work has been largely devoted to plays of classic stamp—he is no "modernist"—he is constantly seeking and seeing new ways of doing the old plays. He is particularly interested in new methods of designing and building theatres. His ideas often extend beyond what is deemed practical in commercial circles. That is one reason he has generally shied away from directing in London's West End or on Broadway. He has worked off-Broadway (for the Phoenix Theatre), he has staged ritualistic pageants in churches and city squares, and he will travel to the remotest regions (remote that is from the great centers of show biz) to present plays under the most challenging conditions. He once proposed staging *King John* on a ferryboat.

It so happened that while I served as guest critic for the London *Observer* some years ago my first assignment was to review Guthrie's Stratford-on-Avon production of *All's Well That Ends Well*. The performance was replete with uproarious action calculated to ridicule the military. (Guthrie has no great respect of patriotic pomp and circumstance—or for that matter of any officialdom.) In my review of the production I hailed Guthrie as "the most gifted director of the English-speaking stage"—a judgment I have no cause to amend today.

Still I made one reservation on that occasion—to the effect that the group scenes were more happily conceived than the intimate passages. Loyal and lovely Vanessa Redgrave who played an inconspicuous part in the production called me up to assure me that Guthrie had worked as scrupulously on the "small" scenes as on the "big" ones. I recall this now because it is always useful to stress the fact that even the most generously endowed artists have their limitations: indeed the limitations are concomitant with their talent.

Guthrie is a virtuoso on an epic scale of action—particularly in comedy and melodrama. His is a vaulting theatricality. This does not mean that Guthrie's productions of Chekhov fail to reveal his keen intelligence and shrewd eye in the observation of individuals. But he is not what is sometimes referred to as "an actor's director." He leaves most acting problems—particularly those of a "psychological" and emotional character—to the actors themselves. He works in scope rather than in depth. His forte is the line, pace, structure and mass impact of the total production. The result is often dance-like: fleet, robust, rousingly gay or tumultuously exciting *movement*.

A special characteristic of Guthrie's staging is his use of all areas of the playing space. Stage center is no longer at its accustomed spot. It is located almost anywhere. The spectator's eyes are forced to direct themselves to wherever Guthrie chooses to set the main action and he often chooses the most unexpected areas. Sight lines are not made convenient for the passive or lazy viewer. The audience is put to work.

Young actors adore him; stars revere him. Yet the latter are occasionally hesitant about appearing in his productions. One incident may be cited to shed light on this discrepancy. That excellent English actor Anthony Quayle who played the title role in Guthrie's production of Marlowe's *Tamburlaine* had to deliver an impassioned soliloquy lamenting the agonies of that dictator's turbulent and tragic fate. While rehearsing the passage, Quayle noticed that on both sides of the stage a veritable host of "extras" were carrying on like mad in spectacular gyrations Guthrie had invented for them. Quayle stopped in mid-speech and exclaimed "But Tony if those extras are going to mess about like that no one will ever be able to hear a word I say. Doesn't it matter?"—"not a bit," Guthrie answered promptly. "Carry on." And Quayle did—without a grimace.

—PLAY, Jan. '67

REPERTORY THEATRE

The recent resignation of Herbert Blau as co-artistic director of the Repertory Theater of Lincoln Center calls to mind once again the question of the repertory system of production. It is a matter which should be discussed at this point not solely in relation to the house in mid-Manhattan but in regard to the problem as a whole. Why is a repertory theatre needed? What kind of repertory theatre do *we* want?

The question would be irrelevant, not to say absurd, in Europe. Every large city on the continent has its repertory theatre. There are two in London, three in Paris, at least one in every town with a population over 25,000 in Germany. There are several in Stockholm and other Swedish cities; in the Soviet Union all theatres function on a repertory basis. My queries must therefore be answered with reference to the American and more particularly to the New York situation.

Most actors feel the need for a repertory theatre (composed of a *permanent company*) because it relieves them of the hit or flop tension and because the alternation and variety of roles helps keep their performances fresh while it develops and extends their craft. But it cannot be of vital interest to the community at large to support a theatre for the sake of the actors' well-being alone.

Managers and moguls of the commercial theatre fear the "unfair competition" of the repertory system. (Repertory theatres never pay the high salaries which the individual producer is obliged to offer.) But apart from the fact that in Western Europe commercial enterprises co-exist with the repertory theatres, it is obviously not in the public interest to concern itself with the welfare of private entrepreneurs. From the spectators' viewpoint, theatre is no more a business than is the opera, the symphony orchestra, the museum, the library or the university. What matters is the audience's pleasure.

Virtually the only plays which are prospering today in New York are musicals and farce-comedies. They are not aware of it, but our audiences suffer from the lack of a repertory theatre. (Though they now have begun to have one they approve of in the APA.) Lacking such a theatre, our stage diet is thinned out to the point of undernourishment. We rarely see the masterpieces of drama except in summertime park performances or when on very infrequent occasions some super-star consents to appear in one.

It is a sign of our theatrical ignorance that when "masterpieces of drama" are mentioned we think only of Shakespeare, Ibsen or Chekhov. At a modest estimate there are a hundred plays of the past that might make superb entertainment which as theatre fare would be wholly new to 99 per cent of our theatregoing public.

It is backward of us to believe that a repertory theatre must confine itself to the production of "masterpieces" (a very limited number of old plays) simply because the APA has produced only two "new" plays: a German adaptation of *War and Peace* and Giraudoux's *Judith*. The Royal Shakespeare Theater at the Aldwych in London produces not only Shakespeare in repertory but Pinter, Livings, Dürrenmatt, Marguerite Duras and Peter Weiss.

Our playwrights would be the ones most apt to benefit by the establishment of a truly sound repertory theatre. Still many of them fail to appreciate this because they too are out for the big kill, the vast earnings that accrue from the productions of such plays as *Death of a Salesman*, *Cat on a Hot Tin Roof*, *Who's Afraid of Virginia Woolf?* But the authors of such plays must sooner or later realize that they are not likely to turn out a series of smash hits. The nature of the repertory system makes it imperative that it not only produce the plays the theatre believes in but that it must sustain them. Hardly any of Chekhov's plays were immediate box-office successes in Moscow until they were repeated over and over again in repertory and came to be recognized "classics."

Though it is significant that O'Neill's *The Iceman Cometh* and Williams' *Summer and Smoke* were "saved" off-Broadway, the solution to our dilemma cannot be arrived at through off-Broadway effort. The economics of off-Broadway production make the more than adequate mounting of plays there extremely difficult.

Granted then that unless we are to remain, as we are now, a theatrically backward town as compared to London, we ought to ask ourselves what sort of repertory theatre we want beside the very nice APA. (We would certainly be more than pleased if a number of repertory theatres were founded but such an expectation at present would be utopian.) The difficulties of establishing and maintaining a vigorous repertory theatre are not only external (that is, financial) but internal. Well-intentioned theatre folk and their benevolent patrons themselves are not fully aware of what the formation of such an organization entails.

It is not enough to "hire" good actors. No one ever plans to engage bad ones. The company must not only be capable of dealing with plays in a variety of styles, but it must be a company unified by a common understanding and technique—a moral resolution above all—to travel the rough road of hard work and trials that a repertory theatre

in a city still unaccustomed to this form of organization must endure.

Even this challenge is not insuperable. The leadership of such a theatre must itself have a clear and workable idea as to what *face* it wishes to expose to the public, what it hopes to represent, what its spiritual and social attitude is to be in the context of the community. Merely to declare that its ambition is to provide intelligent and well-acted plays is saying very little. It must not be a theatre for "everybody." It must have some sense of its ideal audience. In a city as large as New York there are numerous audiences.

I know what is generally meant by an *avant-garde* or an "experimental" theatre and I am certainly not opposed to such groups, nor to studios, laboratories, workshops devoted to minority observers. But these are not our most crying need. In fact, I am inclined to regard such enterprises not only as marginal, either needlessly presumptuous or apologetic, but as somewhat old-fashioned in conception. A play designed for the enjoyment of 200 people a night requires as accomplished a performance as the most elaborate spectacle. It must attain its own completeness.

Production in our hypothetical theatre must not aim to be "as good as or better than Broadway" but in its conception and feeling be distinctive in its own right. The idea of such a theatre has nothing to do with bucking Broadway. It need not refuse consideration of a play because it might conceivably be one which a Broadway management would have accepted or a "Broadway audience" (whatever that is) might like. Our new theatre must follow its own line, its own emotional and intellectual bent.

Except for lack of skill, the new theatre must not stress its aversions but its enthusiasms. (I am not impressed by a theatrical leader who proceeds from contempt for *Hello, Dolly!* or *The Odd Couple*. I want to know what he admires.) We should not look to the "brows"—high, middle and low. There is a kind of collegiate dilettantism in this. We need only be concerned with our own minds and how best to address others. It is not "revolution" that should be our frame of reference but revelation. We should have something to say in fun or in frowns but always with a splendid competence, a dedication without visible strain.

Our personal hope is that in the season of four to five offerings at least one new American play (if possible more) and one contemporary European play should find their place on our program. Plays must not be produced simply because they are respected in other countries or conform to a new fashion or "school" but because they are alive and relevant here and now for the folk we plan to serve and whom we wish to communicate. The new theatre must be capable of a certain mastery, convincing to itself and evident to its audiences. It must be self-possessed, confident, of good will and good humor. In a word, it must be theatrically knowledgeable, a body with a keen intuition about the world, city and country it lives in.

—*WJT* 12 Feb. '67

WHO'S AFRAID OF THOSE – – – – WORDS?

The first "God damn" exploded on our stage in the 1909 production of Clyde Fitch's play *The City*. We have no record of the degree of consternation it caused.

The first time I (or possibly anyone else) heard "bastard" used as a descriptive insult rather than as a fact was in *The Hairy Ape* in 1924. That same memorable year a rousing "son-of-a-bitch" thundered off-stage in *What Price Glory?* Jokes were cracked about the influence of such daring on dowager ladies. The new freedom was in the air. So much so that I recall a young stuffed shirt whisper to his next-seat neighbor, "I'm glad I didn't bring my girl to see this show" when O'Neill's Yank vented his profane indignation. By 1928 the final curtain on *The Front Page* came down on a blistering "S.O.B." to the huge delight of the theatregoing multitude.

Who's Afraid of Virginia Woolf? added to the stage vocabulary of impropriety. No one to my knowledge has exceeded the license in this regard of Norman Mailer's *The Deer Park*. The play, remarkably enough, is far more explicit than the 1955 novel of which it is the author's dramatization. The development in colloquial vulgarity from the days when *Desire Under the Elms* (1924) was threatened by the police and *The Captive* (1928), a French play dealing most discreetly with Lesbianism, was actually closed by a special censor, to the present production of *The Deer Park*, has been so steady and inevitable that very few of our reviewers have taken pains to note it, much less to complain. They might be accused of being either prudish or square. Is this progress? Possibly.

In this as well as in other matters our theatre is a backward institution. Nothing we have heard or seen in any of today's intemperate plays approaches the grossness in Shakespeare and his contemporaries. A highly literate editor not long ago expunged the verb "to lay" (signifying to make love) from a review I wrote and was more than a little taken aback when I informed him that the word had been employed in the same manner by Ben Jonson in *The Alchemist*.

European dramatists have always enjoyed a greater latitude in rough speech than ours. This is probably truer of the French than of the others. (Still, when Alfred Jarry opened his play *King Ubu* in 1896 with the excremental exclamation "*Merde!*" it caused a riot.) Yet there is a point easily overlooked in this comparison of continental with our own playwrights. There is a more fulsome use of blankety-blank words in Norman Mailer's play than in any of Genet's plays (*The Balcony*, *The Blacks*) with the exception of the one still unproduced here, *The Screens*, which Barrault presented last year at the nationally subsidized *Theatre de France*.

My reason for going into all this history has less to do with morals than with esthetics, though I do not deny the existence of an interrelationship between them. In reading many play scripts by new writers of the young generation and in seeing them privately acted off-off-Broadway I have come to expect a lavish flow of the most infamous four-letter words. Indeed, the occurrence has become routine.

Where I have occasion to advise young playwrights on this score I begin by chiding them for their lack of originality. We are all living in the same day and in more or less the same environment; it therefore follows that we are all subject to certain common pressures. Artistic originality, I pedantically explain, consists in reacting to them in an individual way. Language must not simply duplicate ordinary speech but assume a personal mode peculiar to the writer. Casual obscenity is banal; it is part of the conformism of high school freshmen—male and female. "I have too much regard for the positive value of profanity, obscenity and blasphemy," I say, "to permit you to rob them of their savor and virtue." Art is never indiscriminate; it is achieved by the disciplined use of its materials, by selectivity. It does not imitate life, it recreates it—into something different and perhaps more wonderful than the original.

We all know that ugliness itself can be the subject of an artwork, that it can be transformed into beauty by the artist's vision. Spanish, Flemish and Dutch master painters provide us with excellent examples. We also know—the whole course of art through the ages proves the contention—that nothing is alien to it. Everything should be said, every subject allowed, every word may be spoken, every thought and emotion, no matter how reprehensible, should be expressed. This axiom is the basis not only for the continued life of art, but a safeguard of morality.

What I have said about art in general applies to the theatre as well—public entertainment though it be. We certainly have the right to reject art we don't care for, including acknowledged masterpieces; we are also free to walk out of a theatre for whatever reason we choose if we are offended by what we hear or see. This does not invalidate our premise.

Irritation and shock may also serve the purposes of respectable theatrical entertainment. The repeated obscenities of *The Deer Park* are not offensive; they are certainly not sexually stimulating. (There is no reason why a play should not possess erotic appeal, though very few, I am almost sorry to say, actually do.) Mailer's hell is arid. His verbal boldness suits his subject. He is writing about the dissolution or impoverishment of the sexual instinct as infernal symptoms where the human being has ceased to be respected and has thus ceased to respect himself. That is the reason why the bombing of "enemy" citizens is brought into the picture, not, as has been suggested, as an allusion to Vietnam. The same references were introduced in the novel written, as noted, more than 12 years ago.

We can no longer regard those - - - - words as special, not even as disreputable unless ineptly used. They are only *words* and like all the materials of art (or the stage) are to be judged only within the context of the entire work's (or play's) import. Years ago I ceased going to burlesque shows because they were so discouragingly unaphrodisiac.

Rabelais is both dirty *and* bracing. Objections to his "novel" were raised in his day on the grounds of his levity in regard to sacred institutions, not to his extraordinary invention of a scatological and veneral vocabulary. There is just as much if not more adultery, vice, crime, filth and foulness in Dostoyevsky as in any play we have yet run anywhere on our stage but his prose, though rather commonplace, is entirely modest, acceptable by any standards. He was writing for adults.

The "revolution" in language in our theatre today is in part a gesture of defiance in the direction of the "established order." It represents eagerness for a break through the constriction of many hypocritical conventions—far beyond the confines of sex. It is also a sign of general and to a considerable extent still unconscious frustrations in the community at large of which the use of four-letter words is the infantile manifestation. It is a kind of "baby talk!" If and when the kids (dramatists and the public alike) grow up, they will, having taken their child-like rebellion for granted, get to speak with a specificity far more potent than the utterance of "forbidden" words, no longer forbidden, but in themselves merely trivial and inconsequential. At present their careless and exuberant use is simply a Happening.

—*WJT*, 26 Feb. '67

SHAKESPEARE WELL SPOKEN

Irecommend Shakespeare! It is true that in many performances he is rendered almost as foolish as the less imposing dramatists encountered in a season of Broadway playgoing. But there is never a time that we can't get something out of the mighty and much abused Bard. If nothing else, seeing and hearing Shakespeare (when we do hear him) recalls the height and scope that writing for the theatre may achieve.

The latest Shakespeare comes to us from the Bristol Old Vic, whose productions of *Measure for Measure*, *Hamlet*, *Romeo and Juliet*, now at the City Center, will tour the country and continent, ending at Montreal in June. The Bristol Old Vic, of which the fixed habitat is the beautiful old Theatre Royal in that city, is one of Britain's six nationally subsidized theatres. It should be noted in passing that the population of Bristol is less than half a million.

The company also runs a theatre for "experimental" productions and conducts a school. "The most important part of the company's policy" the playbill states, "is to build up a permanent ensemble of actors who form a group which stays together long enough to develop a distinctive style. Plays by Brecht, Anouilh, Dürrenmatt and Frisch rub shoulders with Shakespeare."

I shall not attempt to pass judgment on the company on the basis of the first two productions alone (I have not yet seen *Juliet*). The daily press has received them cordially, and perhaps this is deserved, since the less versatile and vigorous A.P.A. is reputed to be "The Best Repertory Company We Possess."

Measure for Measure and *Hamlet* were well staged in what is usually called the traditional style (the first by Tyrone Guthrie, the second by Val May, the company's general director). The actors speak well and make sense. The voices are generally good, so trained as to make nearly all of them sound alike. They bear a standard intonation that holds the right of way from Stratford in central England to Bristol in its southwest. The impression made is that of a first-rate stock company.

I was glad of the opportunity to see *Measure for Measure* again: that "unpleasant" and somewhat ambiguous comedy in which the "hero" is the Duke {whom I regard as the villain), and in which the severely righteous Angelo distraught with lust is the villain (whom I regard as the Duke's chief victim). The "heroine," Isabella, would rather see her brother beheaded than sacrifice her chaste treasure to save him; her brother would rather she made the sacrifice than die, and everyone is willy-nilly forced to marry whomever the Duke orders into nuptial bliss.

This is the sour Shakespeare on his way to majestic pessimism. Very interesting, except that one would like to see the play interpreted, that is, given a point of view, instead of being presented blandly at its confusing face value. As for *Hamlet*—Well, it's *Hamlet*, done better than many I've seen but without the impress of a special, a revealing insight.

What these productions made me think of most is the constant discussion of why we in America don't have our own important Shakespeare productions, the kind that might be taken as seriously as the Hopkins-Jones-Barrymore Hamlet way back in the twenties, productions of which our reviewers might be as respectful as they seem to be of the present Bristol Old Vic season. The critical consensus is that our actors do not know how to speak Shakespeare, that they do not command the "manner." After long and patient reflection I have come to the conclusion that this is sheer rot. Any moderately educated young man or woman, given three years of insistent training with a proper guide (of which there are several among us), can learn to speak Shakespeare and acquire the "manner." The problem is to *act* Shakespeare.

It is because we think of playing Shakespeare chiefly as a matter of voice and speech, and because we harbor an altogether external idea of what constitutes style, that most Shakespeare production for years has been so crucially uninteresting. It is also because of this that the Shakespeare I have found most arresting as theatre, rather than as an exercise in conventional elocution, has been in foreign languages. Lest this be thought a personal whim or extravagance, I report that Gordon Craig assured me that *King Lear* at the Jewish Chamber Theatre in Moscow (1935) was the best production of Shakespeare he had even seen.

Certainly Shakespeare must be magnificently spoken. (Does this mean that contemporary dramatists should be badly spoken?) But good, elegant or virile speech alone does not produce a satisfactory Shakespeare. That is mere reading. Nor will an interpretation that is little more than what an informed college instructor might impart to his students suffice.

Shakespeare requires, apart from proper diction and an understanding of Elizabethan prosody, original imagination, loftiness of thought, boldness of conception, extremes of sensibility and passion from utmost lyric delicacy to that impetuosity, that wildness, grandeur and volcanic intensity which are the marks of Shakespeare's writing.

This is acknowledged today in England itself. The early 19th-century romanticism that had deteriorated into a form of genteel declamation—spiced by occasional bursts of temperament or vocal crescendos which many still think of as the "tradition"—is no longer acceptable. Recent productions of the Royal Shakespeare Company at Stratford and in London follow a new line. Very often this results in a deflation and a reduction of

Shakespeare in an astringent reaction to the grandiose, as in the Brook-Scofield *Lear*, which, though mistaken, certainly possessed its own particular truth.

There is at the very least a freshness in these new productions. They make us watch and listen anew, query and debate, instead of making the greatest dramatist in English sound like a classic-by-rote, a museum piece or a monument we are sufficiently civilized to appreciate without effort and without the excitement, the throb of individual reaction which attends contact with a vital experience.

—*NAT,* 6 Mar. '67

MACBIRD!

If I were interested only in reporting my immediate reactions to stage fare I should have this to say about Barbara Garson's *MacBird!* (Village Gate): I laughed four or five times, I smiled faintly an equal number of times. I thought Jeanne Button's costumes clever, the staging by Roy Levine entertaining, William Devane engagingly like "Robert Ken O'Dunc" in looks and accent, and that Stacy Keach imitated his prototype "MacBird" efficiently. In view of the event, I liked the saloon atmosphere—with drinks at a price. I was unaffected by the show most of the time—neither offended nor elated—but I was pleased that it had happened.

More important than all this—I have often declared that opinions as such are of little moment in criticism—I was interested in the show's origin in the community and how it is received. Let no one say that the play has no political significance. True, the script is a spoof: a parody of the ham Shakespearean manner. The characters, by this time it is almost needless to say, are John Ken O'Dunc, patterned on the late President, Robert Ken O'Dunc, on the Senator, Ted Ken O'Dunc, on his junior brother, MacBird on Johnson, Egg of Head on Stevenson, the Wayne of Morse, on guess who! etc.

It has been said that the first part of the play is better than the second because it deals with things that have happened (the assassination of Kennedy), while the second is fiction or fantasy (Robert Ken O'Dunc aided by his cohorts kill MacBird). To make this distinction is simpleminded. Nothing in this play has happened; the presumption that John Ken O'Dunc was murdered at the instigation of Lady MacBird is not conceivably intended as a serious indictment. Just as a dream bespeaks the reality of a wish or an anxiety, so *MacBird!* indicates what its author and those who in one way or another respond affirmatively to the play feel about our present statesmen and politicians.

They think Johnson an absurd demagogue and hypocrite, that Robert Kennedy's "pulpy heart" is replaced by "a precision instrument apparatus of steel and plastic tubing," that the Earl of Warren, against his conscience, may have served as a scapegoat, that the Egg of Head is a man who, when urged to take a firm stand, wavers and says: "I know you think I'm acting like a toad, but still I choose the middle of the road." And if this isn't what our friends think, it represents how they feel: totally disgusted, altogether distrustful, entirely irreverent or, as the Fugs say about all our leaders, "Nothing! Nothing! Nothing!" Say what you will, and I shall, this is a definite though probably futile political sentiment.

Barbara Garson, who is 25 and part of the Berkeley New Left, is a political activist. Her play is a gesture of the "youth movement." That it amounts to a resounding Bronx cheer or a stink bomb, and that these are less damaging than dynamite, is not very important in itself. What matters is that numerous young people (not to mention many of their elders) believe that such manifestations as *MacBird!* are imperative.

More telling in a way is the fact that certain sophisticated folk approve of *MacBird!*—but somewhat slyly. They speak of Mrs. Garson's satirical faculty (as if it existed in a void), her ability to handle iambic pentameter, both of which talents are on a collegiate level. They praise her theatre sense, which is hardly superior to that of

the lampoons one might see in dozens of American and English universities. Such backbench rebels rarely assert that Mrs. Garson's sentiments find an echo in their own spirit, that they second her motion.

I welcome *MacBird!* for the "subversive" intentions, not because I am opposed to this or that public figure but because what is called "subversion"—sharp and insistent criticism of our society from top to bottom—is a much needed corrective, a purgative of our Stygian world. The play speaks of the "Pox Americana," which is only a passable pun; it also refers several times to our politcos' ambition to devise a "smooth Society," which is much better. What troubles me, however, is that many of our cultivated gentry should express so much glee at the pseudo-brilliance of these schoolboy shenanigans and tomfoolery. Better this than nothing, I agree, but are we so low in precision, daring, and eloquence that we should speak of such trifles as though we were in the presence of Swift, Gogol, Hogarth, George Grosz, Brecht; or even the Village Vanguard revues of the depression years, or more recently, The Premise, the Second City and *Beyond the Fringe*?

I laughed at Mrs. Garson's adept use of two four-letter words; they exploded at just the right spots. I suppose her to be a spunky young woman who might accomplish more in fields outside the cabaret or the stage but, to repeat, I am worried by the kind of accolade accorded her by more adult persons. Seats of power are never shaken by hoots and toy barbs. The show will not be suppressed. Radical changes in our ways of thinking and behavior are a long way off if such things as *MacBird!* inspire us with a sense of being on the road to a new day. Folks who enjoy and applaud the play may well go on voting for people very similar to the objects of Mrs. Garson's derision.

The rebellion of true satire moves us to struggle rather than to sound the breaking wind of impotence. As a symptom of something stirring among the young, *MacBird!* may be encouraging, but I look forward to the day when our good kids will have grown up. Much more acutely, I hope those grownups will not be satisfied with making kids of themselves.

—*NAT*, 13 Mar. '67

THE WITHERING AWAY OF THE AVANT-GARDE

Two recent productions, Lanford Wilson's *The Rimers of Eldritch* and Barbara Garson's *MacBird!*, made me ask myself: is there an avant-garde in the New York theatre today? The tag can not be applied to these two plays unless you dislike them. For that is how some folk describe any manifestation they have difficulty in assimilating and that they therefore find repellent.

What is an avant-garde? To some it is anything off-Broadway. It is the minority or unpopular theatre. But the mere location of the small houses below 14th Street or above Lincoln Square, those too far east or west of the center, supplies no clue to an adequate definition. *The Threepenny Opera* ran five years on Macdougal Street; is *The Homecoming* a "Broadway show" because it is housed on the "street of hits"?

The avant-garde no longer exists in our theatre. One can no longer "startle the bourgeoisie." Your ordinary citizen of modest or more than modest means likes what he likes and doesn't give a hang about the rest. Too much happens too fast nowadays. No sooner has "something different" come upon the scene than there are jokes followed immediately after by facile glosses in *Time*, *Life* and the fashion magazines.

The Rimers of Eldritch presents the material of Edgar Lee Masters' *Spoon River Anthology* (1914) and Sherwood Anderson's *Winesburg, Ohio* (1919) in a collage of rapidly intercut sequences. *MacBird!*, with several four-letter words aptly placed, is a razzberry rather than an accusation directed at the political Establishment. It is hardly more devastating than such informal revues as *The Mad Show*, *The Premise* or *The Committee* of San Francisco.

The playwrights of the Theater of the Absurd constituted the innovation of just a few years ago. But while we have more or less accommodated ourselves to these very different men, Beckett, Ionesco, Genet, et al., one is not certain that they are understood though what they have to say is actually much simpler than the content of Sophocles or Shakespeare.

One reason for confusion in these matters is our propensity to fix labels on new work. Once you attach a "trademark" to an artist—Cubist, Abstract Expressionist, Pop Art, Op Art—there is no longer need for further inquiry. I doubt whether Beckett gives a hoot about the "school" with which his name has become associated. Zola long ago called himself a "naturalist" but he wrote to Flaubert: "I consider the word *Naturalism* as ridiculous as you do, but I shall go on repeating it over and over again, because you have to give things new names for the public to think that they are new."

The poet Rilke once advised young artists "to cherish their obscurity." Jean Cocteau thought this sound counsel but, he added, there can no longer be any obscurity for the neophyte in the arts because the minute an artist gives evidence of originality the "scandal" is shortlived since the glare of publicity begins to shine so intensely that he is clamorously taken "in." An advertised Bohemia is an Establishment.

The cultural explosion has its disadvantages. It may impede the artist's growth because it substitutes curiosity for careful observation. If you read a review, witness an interview or invite someone like Andy Warhol to a party or include him on a panel you really don't have to think much more about him. The process is the same whether the artist is received with philistine contempt or intellectual adulation. It's either "bah" or "ah!" The artist has been had. As far as a genuine understanding goes, he's finished.

Let us briefly examine the significance of our various theatrical vanguards. I shall not discuss the

English or the French although they have exercised a decided influence on our younger playwrights. In the Twenties the attack was on our crass materialism, our success mania, our genteel puritanism. It proved a valuable impulse because its leader—America's first serious playwright, Eugene O'Neill—was not only a truly committed artist but one with a solid grounding in his craft. The attack in the Thirties was on the "contradictions or capitalism": unemployment, the politics of rugged individualism, financial collapse and the consequent spiritual bewilderment. This also gave us some effective writers, notably the lyrically radical Clifford Odets whose contribution was not his "leftism" but the agonized expression of those men who denounced the old order while they still hankered for the fleshpots it had provided. Let us also remember that Odets, who had been an actor, was a seasoned theatre craftsman.

The Forties turned the conflict to the personal, to family relations, to the effects of the environment on sex and on individual integrity. We got Tennessee Williams.

After the freeze of the late Forties, disillusionment with social and political panaceas, the rise of McCarthyite conservatism and the urge of conformism of the Fifties accompanied by the return of prosperity, young men of sensibility gave up altogether. They felt the world had become a gigantic and frightening fraud. They resigned from any vital connection with it. They chose to be immersed in their own private selves. The big public could not discern their drift. It believed Gelber's *The Connection* was nothing more than a horrid play about drug addiction; it considered Albee's *The Zoo Story* a shocking joke: interesting but not particularly related to its real concerns. Still Albee counted because he is canny in stage technique and because his plays, being to some extent a reflection of reality, manage to get under our skin.

At this point the theatre began to shrink markedly, not only in thematic substance but in product and profit. There came a slacking of craftsmanship, even interest in it. It belonged to the past

and the past had proved a curse, leading to the impasse of the present.

Much of today's vanguard theatre writing may be seen off off-Broadway in cafes and obscure halls. It is often compounded from dissolved ingredients of Williams, Albee, Genet and Beckett. The impression it makes is that the writers have lost hope or even the desire for an exit into the abhorred world outside the self. Their egos have shriveled; they hope for its extinction. There are no defiant Prometheuses here. Adventures into space may excite, but their association with possible military use disgusts and frightens the folk of these inner circles.

The plays in such an environment abandon dramatic structure because they reflect a passive condition of being rather than freedom of action. What freedom remains is employed for a plunge into chaos. It is a swamp of impotence only occasionally relieved by mockery.

There are countercurrents. *Happenings* are a means of recovery through accident and improvisation. They arouse spontaneous reactions which may stir fresh impulses, a way through the dark. This may be construed as an oblique form of protest. *America, Hurrah!* is possibly another.

Further attempts to emerge from the slough of despondence are becoming apparent. *MacBird!*, adolescent and raw though it be, may denote a burgeoning of courage to combat our lethargy. Then too such writers as Robert Lowell and others whose plays have been seen at the American Place Theater suggest re-integration through renewed contact with tradition.

—*WJT*, 19 Mar. '67

THE CHALLENGE OF THE HEROIC

In Brecht's play *Galileo*, soon to be produced by the Repertory Theater of Lincoln Center, at the close of the scene of Galileo's recantation a young disciple deeply hurt at his master's defection exclaims: "Unhappy is the land that breeds no hero." To which Galileo replies: "Unhappy is the land that needs a hero."

The implication of Galileo's rejoinder is that only a sick society requires epic effort to heal its wounds. We would exist in comparative tranquillity if nothing were rotten in the State. Though Galileo's maxim is impressive, it is utopian. We doubt man's ability ever to attain so just a balance in social or private affairs that the struggle which heroism entails would become unnecessary.

In writing about the avant-garde theatre (though convenient, I dislike the term) I said that it contained no "*Prometheus*." Even the best of plays in recent years are dramas of defeat. This is not a complaint: everything must be said, and there can be no doubt that very many of us today feel frustrated, defeated, if not altogether maimed. It is inevitable that the theatre should reflect this condition.

If we take Ibsen and Chekhov as classics of the modern era we observe that though their plays are for the most part what the ordinary theatregoer calls "gloomy" (despite their quotient of humor) they speak with a sense of loss which foreshadows the possibility of amelioration. If even this is saying too much, it is still an inescapable inference that these dramatists desired some change from the sorry situations they depicted. That is why Robert Brustein could name them leading figures in *The Theater of Revolt*.

We are not to suppose that such later dramatists as Ionesco, Genet, Pinter or Albee in presenting a demoralized world masochistically embrace the breakdown. Even Beckett's *Waiting for Godot*, in which the outlook is unquestionably dreary, makes the point that the two tramps who are its central characters possess a certain nobility because they know they are bereft of an "answer" and that, despite their every failure to find one, they are actively *waiting*, enduring.

Many young Americans who have been influenced by Beckett and the others give evidence of having become even more devastatingly discouraged. They appear totally flattened. There is a good deal of fashionable imitation in this: they aspire to go their masters one better—or worse. To the charge that I once leveled at a group of such playwrights, that they were all writing the same play as if they not only lived on the same street but in the same pad, they challenged me with the statement that men of my generation still cling to ideals while theirs has been deprived of anything to believe in.

I understood. The young men were, in effect, saying: we live in an age in which the imminence of total annihilation hangs over us; there is hypocrisy in high places, even the prospect of material security is denied us. Promises of social betterment ring hollow; relief from our spiritual depression is a religious concept in which we have no faith. Thus: no exit! For this reason the satire which is now being written has the shrill sound of revulsion rather than of rebellion: it does not mean to affect anything.

While all this is plausible, I do not accept the validity of the argument. It is built on a false premise, a premise which could only be held among people raised on the proposition that well-being is the natural condition of man, his inalienable right. There never has been a "happy time" except retrospectively. The world has always been in jeopardy. The Black Plague of the 14th century and the Thirty Years War of the 17th decimated a large part of Europe. All that men have accomplished has been done in the face of death. It is not the great general, discoverer, scientist who is to be considered a "hero," but, in Emerson's words, "he who is immovably centered," committed to the most deeply rooted impulses of his being. To live is to act, to act is to move toward a greater scope of life. Hope is not a dream of future delight. It is inherent in the very process of engaging in the action of life. Eating breakfast, reading or writing a book, setting up an organization, planning a battle, conducting a scientific experiment are all in themselves hopeful acts. Only the moribund ask "What's the use?"

This is not "optimism." It does not lead to the production of "happy" plays. It is in a sense a tragic attitude, as Walter Kerr in his excellent, soon to be published book, *Tragedy and Comedy*, demonstrates. The tragic involves the heroic. Tragedy posits a freedom to choose our actions without any "guarantee" of success. If anything may be promised for this course it is suffering. But as the French novelist-dramatist Henry de Montherlant says in one of his plays "...one may tremble without being uprooted, just as one may suffer without being troubled." The courage to undertake decisive action is in itself an affirmation of life. That is why tragedy inspires a feeling of exaltation.

We cannot and should not blind ourselves to the evils of our day nor reject their more eloquent manifestations on the stage. We must confront them. What is most alive in ourselves bids us go on with the eternally wonderful struggle to forge a different world. That is what should be meant by the full, the good, life. Tragedy does not exclude comedy: comedy is the record of our ineptitude in the task. Satire too is essential: for if tragedy expresses the defeat of something which should have been saved, satire, an arm of comedy, thrives on "conspiracy"; it deals with something oppressive which should be "murdered." But we must first know and believe in the value for which we employ the weapon.

I am not proposing a return to the social play of the Thirties. Many of those plays were much too limited in their aims. I speak of a quest for restated fundamentals, the bodying forth of our urgent humanity in newly minted language and fresh forms. We can no longer dwell in the dumps or be content with swimming in the swamp. The time has come to abandon a supine position within ourselves and take a walk into the immensity outside.

The enthusiastic reception of such a play as Robert Bolt's *A Man for All Seasons*, a play which I respect rather than greatly admire, indicates our hunger for a reassertion of will and daring. It is a

need which, I believe, is growing and may not too long hence prevail. Young people all over the country are on the threshold of this realization.

The still scattered and often immature efforts to establish organic schools of the theatre and repertory groups (Theatres, not simply buildings) are signs of a still only partially informed and articulate impulse which as it takes firmer shape will also produce a drama of greater heart and sinew than that which we now believe to be the up-to-the-minute vanguard. The theatre's future lies along that path. But it cannot be created by folk whose first concern is ease, comfort, quick returns and a bland "culture." Moral ruggedness as well as genuine craftsmanship are indispensable.

—*WJT*, 26 Mar. '67

ARTHUR MILLER: THEME AND VARIATIONS

*A*fter the Fall, the opening production of the Repertory Theater of Lincoln Center, is Arthur Miller's first play in nine years. When recently asked in what way his plays were related to the events of his life Miller replied, "In a sense all my plays are autobiographical." The artist creates his biography through his work even as the events of his life serve to shape him.

He was born on One Hundred Twelfth Street in Manhattan in 1915. He is one of three children. The Millers were unequivocally middle-class and Jewish. In his boyhood Arthur was neither particularly bright nor very well read. He was a baseball fan. He began to read while working at a warehouse to earn college tuition. He is probably the only man who ever read through *War and Peace* entirely on the subway, standing up. At college he also began to write—plays. One of them won a prize of $1,250 given by the Theatre Guild's Bureau of New Plays. With money from these prizes and $22.37 a week from the Federal Theatre Project, Miller was able to support himself during the early years of his career.

In 1944 while visiting various army camps in the United States, a diary Miller kept as a research for a film, *The Story of G.I. Joe* (the war life of Ernie Pyle), was published under the title, *Situation Normal*. In 1945, Miller wrote his only novel, *Focus*. Its subject was anti-semitism.

That year saw the production of Miller's first play, *The Man Who Had All The Luck*. There were only four performances. His next play was *All My Sons* which was produced by Harold Clurman, Elia Kazan and Walter Fried on January 29, 1947. It was a box-office success and was voted the Best Play of the Season by the Drama Critics' Circle.

Miller is a moralist. A moralist is a man who believes he possesses the truth and aims to convince others of it. In Miller this moralistic trait stems from a strong family feeling. In this context the father as prime authority and guide is central. From *The Man Who had All The Luck* through *Death of a Salesman* the father stands for virtue and value; to his sons he is the personification of Right and Truth.

The shock which shatters Miller's dramatic cosmos always begins with the father's inability to enact the role of moral authority the son assigns to him and which the father willy-nilly assumes. The son never altogether absolves the father for his defection nor is the father ever able to forgive himself for it. Each bears a heavy burden of responsibility to the other. Both may be innocent, but both suffer guilt.

The mother, beloved of father and son, supports the paternal legend of "kingship." She is fealty itself. She is unalterably loyal to the family and the ideal of its necessary cohesion as the basis for the good life, a moral world. Her influence may be constricting, even injurious, though it is never faulted in Miller's plays. Woman in Miller's plays is usually the prop of the male principle without whom man falters, loses his way.

In Miller's view, the family is the "symbolic" cell of the social structure, the dissolution of which is a threat to life itself. It is simply and passionately articulated in *After The Fall* when its central character, Quentin, blurts out, "I can't bear to be a separate person." Separateness from our fellow men is a human *non sequitur*.

What in Miller's experience and thoughts seems the chief cause for the family's crack up? The Depression of the Thirties was the crucial factor of Miller's formative years; it not only brought hardship to his parents and consequently to their children but it made him realize something else as well. It was not financial stress alone that shook the foundations of American life at that time but a false ideal which the preceding era had raised to the level of a religious creed: the ideal of Success. The unsuccessful man who failed in business was a flawed man. Such failure was considered more than a misfortune: it was the sign of a moral defect. It was turpitude.

Miller has often said that as a college student he was very much affected by a performance of Odets' *Awake and Sing!* he saw in Chicago. That play contained a line which struck the keynote of the period: "Go out and fight so life shouldn't be printed on dollar bills," followed by the even more homely precept: "Life should have some dignity."

In *Death Of A Salesman*, Charley, Loman's neighbor, says apropos of Loman, "No man needs only a little salary." And when outraged at Loman's muddle-headedness and feeble sense of reality, his son's basic accusation is that Loman has blown him "full of hot air." It is the hot air of the corrupted American dream, the dream of Success—affluence and status as the ultimate goals of human endeavor.

Willy Loman, seduced by the bitch goddess, Success, by Salesmanship, lives in a vacuum, a vapor of meaningless commercial slogans. Sweet, dumb, nobly ignoble Willy never learns anything. But Miller, and the men of his generation, had begun to. Miller became a "radical." The root of evil was the false ideal. The heart of Miller's radicalism is conservative: it seeks the maintenance of individual dignity within the context of the family which broadens to the concept of society as a whole.

The son becomes the father. He desires to take over authority. The radical becomes the leader, the prophet. Armed with a new insight, arrived at through the father's fall, the son now carries the banner of righteousness and justice. He is no longer simply moral; he is a moralizer, a preacher. Thus he may fall from grace into the pit of self-righteousness.

In *All My Sons* Chris says, "Every man follows a star. The star of his honesty. Once it is out it never lights again." It burns so intensely that Chris virtually wills his father's punishment for having knowingly sent out defective airplane motors to the Army.

The severity of such righteousness often boomerangs. The reforms of the Thirties and early Forties were followed by the repressions of the Fifties. Miller spoke out courageously against the forces of repression. *The Crucible* , written between 1952 and 1953, is still a virile protest against the aberrations of McCarthyism. *The Crucible* shows us a community terrorized into a savagely hysterical fury that is reprehensible whether it is based on fact or on falsehood. The play asks, "Is the accuser always holy now?," a question altogether suitable to the situation of the Fifties. "Vengeance is walking Salem" had become almost literally exact.

The hindsight afforded by *After The Fall* renders perceptible certain secondary aspects of *The Crucible* which passed unnoticed at the time of its production in 1953. Neither John Proctor nor his wife Elizabeth is guilty of witchcraft! Both act in the upright manner we expect of them. (Miller, found guilty of Contempt of Congress in 1956 for refusing to mention the names of people he recognized at a Communist meeting he had attended some years before, was cleared of the charge by the United States Court of Appeals in 1958.) But other guilts are confessed by the Proctors, man and wife, in *The Crucible*. Elizabeth has been guilty of coldness to her husband; John of "lechery." He has been unfaithful. Both suspect that part of their misfortune, the accusation of conspiring with the Devil, and their inability to clear themselves are somehow due to their private failings.

One of the most unmistakable features of Miller's work is its Puritanism. There is a traditional sort of tenderness, even a trace of sentimentality, in the early Miller plays. There is little or no hint of any sensual appreciation of woman. Desire plays little part in the configuration of dramatic elements in any of Miller's plays before *The Crucible* and enters the scene obliquely and, as it were, shamefacedly as a prop to the plot in *A View From The Bridge.*

The Puritan conscience is a complex phenomenon. Even while it holds fast to its conviction of rightness, it is haunted by a need for the expiation of its own sins. There is nothing for which it feels itself entirely blameless. Man must pay and pay and pay—for everything. What the Puritan hankers for is total innocence, and it torments him to understand that it cannot possibly be achieved.

Even the pursuit of righteousness and truth seems to the thoroughgoing Puritan a virtuous aggressiveness which is itself not wholly innocent. It may mask a drive for power. Thus Biff in *Salesman*, as later Quentin in *After The Fall*, questions his own good faith. Sue Bayliss, the down-to-earth doctor's wife in *All My Sons,* wants Chris, avenging angel or conscience of the play, to move away from the neighborhood. "Chris," she says, "makes people want to be better than it is possible to be...I resent being next door to the Holy Family. It makes me feel like a bum." The sentiment is psychologically and sociologically sound—reformers disturb public quiet—but what is especially to be remarked here is that in all his plays Miller gives evidence of wanting to move away from himself in this regard. It worries him that he sits in judgment, that he is placing himself in a position to which he has no right.

The wish to expiate sins of pride, bad faith or moral arrogance are related to a sense of responsibility which lends stature to Miller's work and makes it intimately moving. We are not, we must not be, separate one from the other. Our refusal to acknowledge this and to act upon it is the sin which secretly torments us and causes us profound grief.

Miller harbors an abiding affection for his least striking play, *A Memory of Two Mondays*. This is understandable because in this play he recalls without blame or debate the simple, unde-manding, unselfconsciously oppressed folk with whom he worked at the Tenth Avenue warehouse before he entered the world of assertion and moral combat. Here he dwelled without the exposing glare of critical self-examination. Like infancy, it was free from the burden of ethical choice.

The repose of this short play is followed immediately by the travail of *A View From The Bridge*, the last of Miller's plays before the "silent" years. *A View From The Bridge* dramatizes the passion of betrayal. A decent man is led to squealing on his kin because of jealously Eddie Carbone does not recognize his motivation; this would mortify him. He must rationalize his act on moral grounds. So much is made of Carbone's adulterous and semi-incestuous drive towards his niece that we are apt to miss the fact that what is at stake is not the psychology of sexual turmoil but of duplicity, the man's inability to live up to the obligations of comradeship. We must not force others to pay for the agony of our own weakness.

Miller is compassionate with Carbone; yet he is angry with him. He is compassionate because he feels in himself the bewilderment involved in the sexual impulse, particularly when repressed; he is angry because Carbone is a liar as all men are who conceal their confusion or corruption in an honorable cloak. Miller not only implies that Carbone craves punishment for his delation, he also believes Carbone deserves death. Still Miller, as a humane Puritan, shrinks from so full a measure of condemnation—"an eye for an eye"—and he has his "chorus," in the person of Alfieri, the lawyer-narrator, say, "Most of the time now we settle for half. And I like it better."

To resume a listing of biographical data, Miller was married to Mary Slattery, a fellow student at the University of Michigan, in 1942. She bore him two children: a girl now nineteen and a boy sixteen. He divorced Mary Miller in 1956. He then married Marilyn Monroe. He wrote *The Misfits* for her, a film about the lone worker in a society of industrial mass production. It is a film, he admits, marred by too many cross-purposes. After his divorce from Marilyn Monroe, Miller married Inge Morath, an Austrian-born photographer, in 1961. A daughter, Rebecca, was born to them in 1962.

Two features of *After The Fall* are immediately noticeable. It is the first of Miller's plays where the main emphasis is almost entirely personal. It is also the first Miller play where the largest part of the action concerns itself with marital relationships.

Still *After The Fall* is not only an extension of the themes to be found in Miller's previous plays; it is a reaffirmation through a reversal. The strenuous moralist, the man whose family—the mother in particular—dedicated him to great accomplishments, has come to the middle point of his life and brings himself to trial. He not only confesses, he accuses himself. His self-assurance has gone. As many in our time, he is "hung-up"; he despairs.

He now finds the continuous "litigation of existence" pointless because the judge's seat is empty. There is no "father," no supreme arbiter. He will have to allow us, the audience, to judge him. Why is the trial held? Not so that he may be condemned or that the charges brought be dismissed but so that he regain his capacity to "move on." He is seeking the hope which lies beyond despair, the life which renews itself after the fall, with the death of the sold self. He wants to buy himself as an Idea and find himself as a Person.

The lawyer, Quentin, finds that the examination of conscience through a review of the precise detail in the crisis of his life exposes his self-delusions, hypocrisies, insufficiencies, falterings and confusions. He is now skeptical of abstracts, even the abstract of Despair.

The tangle of lives in the play's broad canvas, the complexity and contradiction of motives in his former search for a moral victory lead him to an understanding of his, and possibly our universal, complicity in wrong doing. We who denounce the hangman are ourselves executioners. We assume powers we do not possess. We undertake tasks it is not within our means to complete. The proposition that we are not separate takes on a new meaning; a new light is shed on the injunction of human responsibility. Each of us is separate and in our separateness we must assume responsibility even in full awareness of that separateness.

Thus Quentin may survive after the fall through a recognition of his own place among the accused, a realization of his role as an accomplice in the misdeeds he has denounced. The judge's bench is not on high; it is in the common court of our lives together. We are all both the jailers and prisoners of the concentration camps. The acceptance of the defeat in this realization may liberate the man dogged by having had "all the luck"—and answers! There are no guarantees for any choice we make, but one is never absolved from the necessity of making choices and of paying for them.

The struggle represented in all of Miller's work, of which *After The Fall* is a central turning point, achieves a special eloquence for us in the American particularity of its tone and speech. Miller is a popular writer. This may be a limitation but it is more probably a strength. Those who wept over Willy Loman, whether his story exemplifies true Tragedy or not, are closer to the truth of our day than those who want it told to them in monumental or quasi-mythical symbols for all time.

There is besides the comforting familiarity of Miller's expression an enthusiasm which mingles a deep-rooted American idealism with an age-old Hebraic fervor, a quality which mounts from hearth and home to the elevations of an altar. Miller's dialogue, coined from the energetic and flavorsome palaver of the streets, is finally wrought into something close to prophetic incantation.

After The Fall is a signal step in the evolution of Arthur Miller as man and artist. The play's autocriticism exposes him to us; it also liberates him so

that he can go on free of false legend and heavy halo. Had he not written this play he might never have been able to write another. We may now look to a future of ever more creative effort.

—*PLAY*, Mar '67

YOU KNOW I CAN'T HEAR YOU WHEN THE WATER'S RUNNING

YOU'RE A GOOD MAN, CHARLIE BROWN

Those who seek entertainment on Broadway will probably find Robert Anderson's four one-act plays collectively entitled *You Know I Can't Hear You When the Water's Running* gratifying (Ambassador Theatre). Its sexual emphasis is constant, it is frequently funny, and its acting is excellent. It provoked me to thought, accompanied by puzzled irritation.

None of the plays was wholly about what it appeared to be about. The theme of the first segment of the quartet, called "The Shock of Recognition," is the disparity between our professed acceptance of bold spectacle and language in regard to subjects once held to be publicly taboo, and our real reaction to these new liberties. The argument concerns a playwright who plans to open his first scene with the entrance of a man in full and unabashed nakedness. He does not propose to arouse libidinous scandal but to awake the audience with "the shock of recognition," a sense of our common nature. The point of Anderson's skit is the discomfort everyone experiences at the possibility of an actual confrontation with the event: the rationale breaks down (even for the playwright) in view of the fact.

The audience titters or laughs at the notion in semi-acknowledgment of its own divided sentiments (at once a kind of prurience and inhibition), but the cream of the jest lies in something else entirely, something which has nothing to do with Anderson's apparent subject. An actor is brought in by the producer to prove that no player would consent to perform the described action. Pathetic comedy issues from the sight of the actor's eagerness to do everything or *anything*, no matter how personally embarrassing, to get the part.

The second "panel" of the series. "The Footsteps of Doves," is a slighter and more obvious bit, taking place in a showroom where beds are sold. The choice of a bed reveals the state of waning desire in the middle years of marriage. The audience's laughter in this instance is both sly and shamefaced: it is giggling with the titillation of recognition.

The third piece (which opens the second and better half of the evening) begins with a discussion between husband and wife about the sex education of their children. The college boy son masturbates; the daughter, the wife contends, should be instructed in the use of contraceptives. The wife is crudely "realistic" in the modern mode; her salesman husband is sensible in his gentle humor and regard for his children's privacy.

A good moment in this episode is one in which we see the hurt the husband suffers when he realizes that his wife, not in the least perturbed, takes for granted that he "cheats" on her every time he goes on the road. Then there is a sudden and rather touching shift of theme at the close when one learns that their son has decided to quit college and (possibly) home because he can no longer bear the stuffy mediocrity of the parental environment. This motif—the misunderstanding or break between the generations—should have been made central to the play's meaning. Instead it bobs up as though an afterthought and thus renders the "daring" of the parents' early colloquy dubiously provocative.

The final and most succinct "movement" (called "I'm Herbert") might be described as a memory of sex. An aged couple are no longer able to remember where and what they did with whom in their several past marriages; they even have some difficulty in knowing whom they are married to now. Having a distinctly melancholy side, "I'm Herbert" is the purest comedy of the lot. It reduces sex to an absurdity, a fleeting and illusory sensation among many which wither and decay along with everything else in the course of time.

I have detailed the four plots to convey the sense of ambiguity the evening creates. Its mental and moral disposition is, I believe, typical of the ordinary middle-class American. (This explains in large measure its undoubted audience appeal.) Its sophistication veils a puerile fascination with sex, a determination to be free and frank in talk about it, together with an equal degree of embarrassment. There is some uncertainty as to whether sex is to be embraced on a biologic level or to be ridiculed as something less significant than what we romantically suppose it to be. There is above all a stubbornly lingering, though now bewildered and apologetic, Puritanism in the attitude. Behind all this is an element of honesty and truthfulness. One feels oneself in the presence of something still unborn, certainly juvenile and consequently somewhat annoying, perhaps even boring, which one still hesitates utterly to reject (much less to condemn) since it does exist on a far wider scale than one assumes. The unbalance in the construction of the four playlets (except for the last rueful farce) reflects a tussle in the playwright's spirit.

There can be no quibble whatever about the acting. Martin Balsam is first rate in the humor of the first two sketches, and moving as the decent father of the third. His is the best sort of simple naturalistic acting. George Grizzard too is fine in the innuendo of the bed salesman in the second piece, both sharp and relaxed in the characterization of senility in the finale. Eileen Heckart is equally good in this, and as always dryly and efficiently to the point in the rest. As performance (under Alan Schneider's direction) the whole evening functions admirably.

There is nothing ambivalent or indecisive about Charles Schulz's musical entertainment *You're A Good Man, Charlie Brown* at Theatre 80

St. Marks: it is wholly childish. We can absorb it without qualm, enjoy it without shame or leave it without discontent. If predictions are in order, it will go on and on like *The Fantasticks*. It appeals to the simple heart.

Based on the comic strip "Peanuts," *You're A Good Man, Charlie Brown* preserves an artless comic-strip discontinuity, each bit leading to a kindly smile or a happy chuckle. It reminded me of what Van Wyck Brooks said about *Huckleberry Finn*: when Mark Twain, a representative of the America of his day, produced his masterpiece it turned out to be a novel of adolescence. (I can't remember now whether the eminent critic also pointed out that the fun in *Huckleberry* masks much savagery and sadness.) The Charles Schulz miniature offers consolation by its benign acceptance of basic human inadequacy and repeated failure. It celebrates in friendly laughter all our frustrations at not being something bigger, better and more glorious than we are.

Here at long last is an *affirmative* statement in the contemporary theatre: it forgives all our shortcomings and tells us we are all good because we are all schmoes! Even the dog Snoopy is a perpetually disappointed and only mildly resentful character. But it is just for that and for his resignation at being forever unable to advance beyond dogdom, that we love him. There is withal a philosophy to the show. "Happiness is finding a pencil...Happiness is two kinds of ice cream, etc., etc." We settle for peanuts: it is enough. The greatest failure, Charlie Brown, is still a good man.

The cast is endearing. The actors impersonate little children and a tiny dog, but their ages do not matter. We take them at their word and applaud them for their charm. Among his other attributes Gary Burghoff as Charlie Brown has a most winning countenance. Bill Hinnant as Snoopy is the most expert player. Everyone satisfies. The evening is delightfully brief.

—NAT, 3 Apr. '67

MADAME SARAH
by Cornelia Otis Skinner

Sarah Bernhardt (born 1844 in Paris. where she died in 1923) played 183 parts during a career which began in 1862. She played Marguerite Gautier in *The Lady of the Camellias* more than 3,000 times. She performed in Paris, London, New York, Albany, Denver, Texas, San Francisco, Mobile, Amsterdam, Zurich, St. Petersburg, Warsaw, Moscow, Bologna, Florence, Rio de Janeiro, Athens, Constantinople, etc., etc.

She was a sensational success everywhere. Her name became a byword. By the nature of the medium it is a simple matter for a film star to achieve universal renown. Bernhardt attained greater fame and notoriety than any other actor in history—with the possible exception of Chaplin—by personal appearances. Among her friends and admirers were Victor Hugo, Emile Zola, Alexandre Dumas *fils*, Gambetta, Flaubert, Pasteur, Renan, Gounod, D'Annuncio and Oscar Wilde, "to mention," as Cornelia Otis Skinner says. "only a few."

James Agate, "dean" of English drama critics between 1907 and 1947, called Bernhardt "the great workwoman." Miss Skinner substantiates this designation by remarking that "at sixty-five Madame Sarah continued to spend twelve, sometimes fourteen hours a day in her theatre, rehearsing her repertory, auditioning players, teaching her pupils, reading scripts." In 1891, on a two-year tour which took her halfway around the world, Bernhardt's luggage (apart from theatre equipment) "consisted of forty-five costume crates and some seventy-five trunks for her off-stage dresses, coats, hats, furs and two hundred and fifty pairs of shoes."

I begin with this data to suggest that *Madame Sarah* is not a book about acting but about an actress; and not so much about an actress as about a dazzling personality. And that personality is an emblem for Miss Skinner of something even more fascinating to her, something which I shall name after we have taken a closer look at the evidence on Bernhardt as actress.

Notable appreciations by contemporary French critics are generously strewn through Miss Skinner's biography. Most of them are ecstatic: they assure us that Bernhardt was an unforgettable phenomenon to those who attended her performances. (When I saw her in my student days in Paris, in the next to last play in which she appeared, I was impressed by the fact that though I sat in the gallery and was still unaccustomed to hearing French spoken from the stage, I understood every word she uttered, while the rest of the cast was wholly unintelligible to me.) I nevertheless remain skeptical about most French criticism of acting: it tends to be effusively impressionistic, a kind of literary swoon adjusted to erotic and visceral reactions, rather than to ideas and scrupulous observation.

Henry James and Shaw, both of whom were well aware of Bernhardt's magnetism, are much more reliable witnesses. Here is what Shaw said about the "divine" Sarah in 1895: "...her acting which is not the art of making you think more highly or feel more deeply, but the art of making you admire her, pity her, champion her, weep with her, laugh at her jokes, follow her fortunes breathlessly, and applaud her wildly when the curtain falls. And it is always Sarah Bernhardt in her own capacity who does this to you...the woman is always the same. She does not enter the leading character, she substitutes herself for it."

In 1879, after pointing out the excellent reasons for her prodigious vogue, Henry James added: "She has to a supreme degree...the advertising genius; she may, indeed, be called the muse of the newspaper...I strongly suspect that she will find a triumphant career in the Western World. She is too American not to succeed in America. The people who have brought to the highest development the arts and graces of publicity will recognize a kindred spirit in a figure so admirably adapted for conspicuity."

Miss Skinner recognizes the trickery and vulgarity of some of Madame Sarah's effects. She has surely read the critics I have just cited; she quotes a complimentary passage from the Shaw review cited above, a review which is on the whole rather devastating. But she is not really interested in weighing the merits and debits of her heroine's art. She does not love Madame Sarah for herself alone (though no doubt the woman's energy, courage, impetuosity and theatrical effulgence deserve her adulation); she loves Sarah as the archetype of *la belle epoque*, that glorious time which the French lived from the mid-nineteenth century through the early years of the 20th.

Historians can detail and diagnose the sores and wounds, the poverty, corruption, follies, diseases, wars, rebellions and sieges, but the fact remains that France danced in those days to tunes, verses, words, arts of fabulous resilience, verve and excitement of the mind and the senses.

Miss Skinner's book, which possesses the twinkling, old-fashioned, discreetly naughty humor of an essentially genteel lady, is a record of fond nostalgia. She who in one paragraph describes "the dear, the wonderful, the glorious comedian Constant Coquelin," and adds that he was "a modest, adorable person," enjoys everything that has to do with the customs, habits, even the vices of the period. Miss Skinner tells us that Bernhardt told countless lies, both in writing and in personal interviews, but she gushes over this too. It is all part of the glamour, the glitter, the bravado. Sarah made lovers of all her leading men and most of her authors: in this too Miss Skinner rejoices, not because she is a lusty lady but because Sarah and France were. They *swung*.

In her imagination Miss Skinner sits in the dressing rooms, in the wings of the auditoriums, goes to all the parties and outings where great artists and mountebanks, seers and courtesans, duelists and drug addicts, radicals and reactionaries commingle, and she can't get over the rapture of it all. Her book is therefore bound to be a bestseller. For we have mechanized everything including our passions and pleasures so that very little of either remains. In the age of conformity we must idealize a time when signal achievements and lurid sins were hardly distinguishable from each other because both were part of the ebullient experience of life. So now we have folk like Cornelia Otis Skinner on the one hand and hipsters on the other, each in their own way seeking release from the dull savagery of our Great Society.

—*NAT*, 10 Apr. '67

BORIS ARONSON: MASTER OF VISUAL ART

Unless you are a theatre buff or a professional you have probably never heard of Boris Aronson, though he designed the settings for *Fiddler on the Roof, Cabaret* and the new opera at the Met, *Mourning Becomes Electra,* for which he also did the costumes. There may be a certain justice in this because though settings are conspicuous they must always remain "subliminal." A stage setting is not a picture but the atmosphere in which a play happens. It is not so much a background as an environment.

Still at the rise of the curtain the audience usually applauds the set. I have sometimes wondered whether such applause is simply a form of congratulation to the company for having arrived at the point of opening the show or a way of wishing them good luck. Otherwise the applause is meaningless. One cannot determine the value of a set at first glance. One must judge it in the light of the action which it houses. At times the audience applauds because the setting is attractive. It is like our expressing pleasure at a store window display or at a publicity layout.

Certain scene designers are merely decorators. They make pleasing arrangements of fabrics, furniture and carpentry. An artist in scene design is one who adds to a play's value as a form of expression.

Between 1915 and the mid-Forties, Robert Edmond Jones was such an artist, the first among his peers. He was recognized as that by his most distinguished colleagues: such men as Lee Simonson and Jo Mielziner. I know of no designer since Jones who more unequivocally deserves the title of master visual artist of the stage than Boris Aronson. Yet as I have intimated at the outset his contribution seems to have received scant attention except from fellow craftsmen in the theatre. Oliver Smith, our presently most employed designer, has acknowledged that he "always learns something from seeing an Aronson set."

One reason for the comparative public neglect of Aronson's work may be ascribed to the fact that it has no immediately identifiable mechanical or esthetic trademark. Most designers' appeal lies in their settings' prettiness: a candy box or calendar picture sweetness. They remind one of travel ads intended to cajole us with the prospect of a dreamy trip. Aronson's sets rarely reach for glamor. They are not fashionable.

I first heard of Aronson through John Mason Brown and Richard Boleslavsky, with whom I studied direction in 1927. They spoke of the remarkable settings at the Jewish Art Theater for an allegorical play called *The Ten Commandments* in which Hell was represented as a place inside the human skull. (Later Aronson designing *Cabin in the Sky* pictured poor Joe's Heaven as a dwelling supplied during the summer with a huge refrigerator!) By the time I got to see a production at the Jewish Art Theater, Aronson had designed a dramatization of stories by Sholom Aleichem. I was moved by the tender quaintness of the settings which looked as if a lively folk tale pigmentation had been infused into a paper thin tissue. I determined that if I should ever get to direct a play myself I would have Aronson design it. That is what happened in 1935 when I staged Clifford Odets' *Awake and Sing!*

By then Aronson had been on Broadway for some time. In 1922 he had arrived in our country from his native Russia where he had studied painting and scene design. His first theatre assignments were performed in an obscure theatre in the Bronx. As early as 1926 Kenneth Magowan had mentioned Aronson's work in the *New York Times Magazine* calling it "futuristic." He subsequently designed for Eva Le Gallienne's Civic Repertory Theater and did the sets for a Sid Perlman-Vernon Duke musical with Beatrice Lillie. He designed several shows for George Abbott (notably *Three Men on a Horse*), as well as for Radio City Music Hall and for a Eugene Loring ballet conceived by William Saroyan which marked one of the first uses on our stage of film projection as scenery. He designed Thornton Wilder's *The Merchant of Yonkers* directed by Max Reinhardt. This was the original play from which *The Matchmaker* and *Hello, Dolly!* were derived. He designed *Coriolanus* for the Shakespeare Theater at Stratford-on-Avon in which Laurence Olivier played the title role. All told he has designed 104 stage productions. "It took me almost 50 years to get to design an opera at the Met," Aronson said the other day with his characteristically rueful humor.

The distinguishing mark of Jones' artistry was its ineffable purity, its pristine, fragrant asceticism, its traditional sense of balance, tact and lack of stress—all reminiscent of an earlier day in our history. Aronson's touch is turbulently dramatic. He sets before us the clash of elements in contemporary society, both the comedy and the excitement of sharp contrasts. His settings for the Comden-Green musical *Do Re Mi* contrived a cathedral-like stained glass effect from the pop-art patterns of a jukebox. He composed an outer space constellation utterly modern in its connotations under the circus tent of MacLeish's *J.B.* The depressed charm of a Berlin rooming house enveloped the action of Van Druten's *I Am a Camera* of which *Cabaret* is an adaptation.

If the settings of *Fiddler on the Roof* bounce with the idyllic distortion of a Russian ghetto village, Aronson is also able to communicate the stone and iron grimness of Fascist force for *Incident at Vichy*. The audience which is astonished at seeing itself in the mirror of *Cabaret* may

fail to notice the homely innocence rescued from drabness in that musical's more intimate scenes.

These settings with their stamp of a certain cosmopolitan exoticism might lead us to suspect that the grandeur of *Mourning Becomes Electra* lies outside Aronson's scope. (He himself repeatedly asserts that an artist's limitations are inseparable from his assets.) But the settings for that opera are a triumph of expressive design. They tell us of the fading venerability of an old New England family, the harsh intensity of the mansion and its inhabitants, the complexity of motives, the cross currents of impulse which create an emotional tangle sufficiently powerful to strangle those trapped within it. The total impression is that of a steel web breathing the ghostly spirit which haunts the entire drama. The contours of the sets are drawn in long lines but no detail within them is smooth. The experience of life has covered every plane with jagged incrustations. The influence of modern plastic and graphic techniques is everywhere apparent. I remember only one Aronson setting (for a posthumous Robert Sherwood play) which was wholly symmetrical.

An original, forever in quest of new means of scenic speech, Aronson as an individual as well as an artist is a true personality. Those who know him well (Brooks Atkinson, for example) love to quote the pithy quips with which he pricks the pretentions of our show business. "What do you consider your greatest achievement?" an interviewer recently asked him. "Some of the smash hits I turned down," Aronson answered.

"The theatre is a collective art where the strongest man wins," is another of his sayings. "The only thing experimental about most 'experimental' organizations is that they don't pay." "I'm not interested in being deep; I'm interested in surfaces where things are seen." "Productions in our theatre," Aronson claims, "are organized calamities."

"Every artist has something essential he wishes to say" I once challenged. "What do you want to say?" "All I have to say," he answered, "is that today everything is *too big*."

—*WJT*, 16 Apr. '67

MOVING BEYOND THE "DRAMA OF THE MAIMED"

Everyone realizes that there is a crisis in play-making. The most obvious causes—the lack of permanent companies with a sustained artistic program, the high cost of production, the price of admissions, the reduction of every aspect of the theater to considerations of business, the lure of films and television—have all been repeatedly set forth.

Though all these explanations may tell us why worthwhile plays are in short supply, they do not make us comprehend the nature of the drama—particularly the portentous drama—we do possess. It is a drama of disturbance. It has been called (by me) the "dramaturgy of the maimed." It is frequently subversive, nihilistic, "absurd." While these designations have a pejorative stress, it is by no means my intention to use them in that sense. Some of the most revealing plays of recent years have been labeled and libeled by one or more of the above tags. Dramatists must write what they see, feel, experience and think. To bid them do anything else is to rob drama of its communicative function.

Two virtually undeniable statements may be made about these plays. They are being produced all over Europe and America, taught in colleges, mentioned everywhere; they are accepted as "representative." Then too, though they have their champions, they do not enjoy wide popular appeal. That such appeal is not a conclusive sign of merit may be true. Yet we ought to understand why a play excellent in its kind and attuned to the times may still not succeed in fulfilling the community's deepest need. There is no use in insisting that the mass is an ass. If this were altogether so there really would be no history of art worth study.

The other day I heard a great admirer of Samuel Beckett say that we are no longer content with images of surface reality; we demand a drama of *essential* (universal) truth. I am inclined to agree, yet I hesitate.

The Greeks certainly attempted to dramatize essential reality but what they had to say was distinctly different from what Beckett (and most "moderns") say. Shakespeare dealt with "surfaces," yet he delved beneath them to disclose essences. More than any of the former, Ibsen and Chekhov depicted immediate aspects of their society and often probed to matters not at all superficial.

What the person cited above meant was that we now desire universal truths or essences voiced in a contemporary idiom. We wish to strip the stage of journalistic and photographic detail, the stuff of humdrum circumstances. We want our truths naked conveyed in theater metaphors inspired by a liberated imagination, and possibly the subconscious. To put it bluntly, we prefer the poetic or "stylized" to the so-called realistic play. Again we agree. But are we satisfied that we have been getting universal essences in the major plays of the past ten years?

Though I admire many of them I doubt that they do what is claimed for them. My skepticism in this regard does not rise because nearly all these plays are "pessimistic"—so is *King Lear*—nor because their stark abstraction makes them difficult to assimilate—that is also true of *Prometheus Bound*—but because their "universal" truth is only a partial and momentary truth. These plays proclaim an immediate ache rather than an enduring condition. Their truths are not those which we must perforce accept if we would be wise.

When young playwrights are asked why they all seem to be writing the same dismal play, their usual reply is "Nothing to believe in." From this they proceed to speak of the war in Vietnam, the prospect of cosmic annihilation, the unresolved struggle for civil rights, etc.

During the depression of the Thirties, the issues were unmistakable: we had to remedy unemployment, feed the hungry, alter the economy, combat Fascism. But ever since the

Fifties we have been living in "the affluent society." Now it would be more appropriate to say with Shaw's genial munitions maker in *Major Barbara*, "Their souls are hungry, because their bodies are full." Yet despite the cultural explosion—more books, magazines, ballets, movies, concerts, exhibitions of art—we complain of emptiness.

Having quoted Boris Aronson's observation that "today everything is too big" as a kind of witticism, I begin to see its relevance to the problem of our playwrights. The spread of communications, the facilities for travel and its swiftness, the bombardment of information which assaults us everywhere, the availability of everything to everybody have destroyed *intimacy*. (Lovemaking is intimate but we now see it projected as entertainment on every public screen.) We live in each other's circle. This willy-nilly tends to render us all alike. The continuous presence of the outside world robs us of personal identity. There is no longer any privacy. Taste is imposed on us; it becomes a matter of hearsay and fashion. The newspaper notice governs artistic perception. Advertisement is our greatest national product.

Watch people at a large social gathering: they can't really be warm with anyone because they are all obliged to be "nice" to everybody. They efface themselves through enforced cordiality. An atmosphere results which is really a vacuum.

One reaction to this oppression is to lose oneself by plunging into chaos, to become one with it. This was the drift of the Twenties; today the pattern is being more desperately repeated in special forms of modern art, including the theater.

The painter Miro once said: "Since the outside world has become intolerable, I paint only what's within me." That is the more common path followed by persons of fragile sensibility. Artists of this kind retreat from the savage proliferation of *things* in the outside world. A degree of withdrawal—call it introspection, call it "silence"—becomes necessary for the artist to discover his own voice.

We may need occasionally to turn off and tune out from the turmoil to find ourselves. One characteristic of the dramatist of the absurd, for example, is his occasionally sorrowful but more often jeering rejection of his public environment. It has become too big for him (and probably most of us) to digest.

Still the world exists, and we in it. It acts upon us no matter how resolutely we flee it. To immerse oneself in it completely, to take "a bath of the multitude" in our present social condition, is to court madness, to become indistinguishable as an individual, to end as a nonentity. To rule the world out as some would have us do is to deform and dwarf ourselves. A good part of the drama of our recent past has suffered intellectual and emotional attrition through its exclusion of the specific, the spectrum and spectacle, the *body* of reality.

To retain our human stature and possibly to enhance it we must learn to walk in the outside world and at the same time find a quiet place within ourselves where consciousness and conscience dwell and develop. This parallels the moral, philosophic, political, some may add, religious task which faces society as a whole: how to keep the vastly incoherent technological advance of our day within human grasp. For man is still the measure—or he is lost. There is no value in saying what some brilliant dramatists appear to have been saying: that indeed all is already lost. In that case even the effort to say it becomes trivial.

When we go beyond the first and inevitable cry of outrage and pain, we may be in a position to recover some of that heroic substance, the optimistic pessimism of the masters which alone is capable of sustaining us. Beckett's bitterness cannot be made to equate with Shakespeare's, as some have tried doing. Despite every terror and hazard we must learn to use our periodic retreat from the horrendous fracas of contemporary civilization as a step forward in it. For the moment attempts to do this in drama may take childishly hysterical forms. There will be a great deal of waste motion but those with the fortitude will come to temper themselves to the discipline of new thinking and accomplishment.

—*WJT*, 7 May '67

GALILEO

Whether because of the pressure of time or of weariness, the daily reviewers are capable of various kinds of injustice. In the case of the Repertory Theater of Lincoln Center's production of Brecht's *Galileo* the reviewers have conceded that it was the organization's best production to date. Even if they had declared it to be the only one of their productions adequate to the material, it would be a slight to Brecht's play of which almost nothing was said. *Galileo* is one of the very few truly fine dramatic works of the past thirty years.

Now once again we hear it spoken of an "intellectual" play. For many theatregoers this spells anathema. One might as readily speak of the Parthenon or of the fugues in Bach's *Well Tempered Clavichord* as "intellectual" (not that Brecht occupies so exalted a level but the comparison makes clear the misunderstanding in the use of the word).

The play's central figure is a scientist. He is, if you like, its "anti-hero." He may be called that because he vilifies himself for having recanted his doctrine in terror and for having too late come to realize that scientific truth is not an absolute value. "I take it," Galileo says, "the interest of science is to ease human existence. If you give way to coercion, science can be crippled, and your new machines may simply suggest new drudgeries. Should you then, in time, discover all there is to be discovered your progress must become a progress away from the bulk of humanity. The gulf might even grow so wide that the sound of your cheering at some new achievement would be echoed by a universal cry of horror."

This is only part of the play's message. But at the moment what I wish to emphasize is that calling a play "intellectual" for most of us implies that it is without "emotion." In his day, Shaw gave vent to a comic exasperation at the fact that we make dramatic heroes only out of hysterical kids like Romeo and Juliet and neurotic maniacs like Tristan and Isolde, never of men like Newton or Darwin!

This was something more than a joke. For when we speak of "emotion" in the theatre we mean visceral disturbance, passion, pathos or just tear-jerking. But there are many kinds of emotion: the grandeur of a conception may inspire the most elevated feeling, as may also the majesty of the mountain or the sea, a courageous act, the recognition of beautiful craftsmanship, the splendor of an abstract design, or what once was called "significant form."

For all its earthiness and humor—the language of the original German is simpler and more robust than the translation—Galileo has a dignity, a loftiness, a purity which moves the spirit and mind in unity. This quality is evident in speech after speech, in scene after scene.

Take the point at which the Little Monk, in humble compassion for his hard-worked peasant parents, speaks of the need for consolation which the Faith provides, and Galileo's deeply felt, lucid and brilliant answer which ends: "I can see their divine patience, but where is their divine fury?" Consider too the scene in which the liberal and knowledgable Pope, the naked man before he is attired in his ceremonial robes, refuses to acquiesce in the threat of torture against Galileo requested by the Cardinal Inquisitor. When finally he stands in full ecclesiastic raiment he pronounces his papal decision. "It is clearly understood: he is not to be tortured. At the very most he may be shown the instruments," to which the Inquisitor replies: "That will be adequate, Your Holiness. Mr. Galileo understands machinery." The eye instructs the mind as to the meaning.

The play is a dramatic paradigm of an idea and the trials it encounters in piercing the inertia and resistance of habit, tradition and interests of established institutions. In the scene in which Galileo is hailed as a "Bible killer," the play shows the distortion of every idea by ordinary folk who seize on its most vulgar aspect. Brecht regarded skepticism, since it counsels caution and therefore balance, as a key to wisdom. His play therefore warns us that any new idea isolated from the broadest human concerns involves us in a new danger.

No word is wasted in the play; no moment is without its contribution to the total effect. The incidental figures (priests and prelates, students, merchants, aristocrats and beggars) are colorful without caricature. A sense of humankind in its most familiar ways informs every character. Galileo—here Brecht drew on several phases of his own nature—is shown as "foxy," even opportunistic, given to creature comforts, gluttony, the ordinary man's sensuality, and the canny playfulness often found in men of common origin. All this is enacted against the pageantry of the Renaissance, all the more impressive because of the restraint with which Brecht employs it.

The last observation is based in part on the memory of the great production by the Berliner Ensemble, in which the scenic atmosphere was conveyed through the deeply glowing bronze which enclosed the entire proceedings. A muted opulence must also exist in the text itself, for when I reviewed the earlier New York production—in which Charles Laughton played Galileo—I complained of its barren asceticism. What I thought the play required was a masculine and severe sumptuousness.

The production at the Lincoln Center (directed by John Hirsch, designed by Robin Wagner) aims at and achieves a little of the necessary magnificence. But I shall try not to belabor the production with my recollection of the Berlin presentation. (No theatre organization in our country, England or France commands the resources in time, money and extraordinary care of the Berliner Ensemble.) In general, the present production is respectable in its intelligence and devotion to the text. This despite the uncoordinated jumble of the carnival procession, much more tellingly managed in Herbert Blau's Actors' Workshop production in San Francisco.

For those interested in "comparative theatre," a paradox may be discerned in the fact that the acting in the Brecht production was much closer to simple realism than the one at Lincoln Center. The Brecht production contained more individual detail and personal savor. Brecht's actors were quieter, more like real folk unconscious of both their roles in history or on a public platform. The small parts at Lincoln Center are all decently done, but they tend to become "block" figures rather than particularized persons.

The sharpest contrast—I speak of style not of ability—is manifest in Anthony Quayle's Galileo. He speaks with admirable conviction in fine voice. Without rant he is more elocutionary than his Brechtian counterpart. As a result the character's speeches sound more like "propaganda" than they do in Berlin. There, Galileo speaks in a tone of the most intimate, man-to-man common sense. Quayle's Galileo is a convincing spokesman for genius; the other Galileo is as unassuming as some little man who might prove to be Einstein! Everything he says and thinks (together with his relish for food) appears ingrained in his entire being. Quayle comes close to this Galileo—in any case never pompous or stuffy—in the last scene where he shows Galileo in his old age and partial blindness. All in all, an honorable performance.

—*NAT*, 8 May '67

COME OUT, MR. KERR, WHERE ARE YOU!

Tragedy and Comedy is Walter Kerr's best book. It is in fact an exhilarating, a tonic book. It may also be an important one.

I must confess that I opened it with some hesitation. There appears to be a plethora of books on the subject of tragedy, by Joseph Wood Krutch, George Steiner, Lionel Abel, Robert Corrigan—to mention only some of the more recent ones. I found many of these informative and occasionally stimulating but rarely relevant to my own disposition.

I am one of those playgoers who, Mr. Kerr properly says, are "interested in plays not concepts." I want a play to move me to laughter, to tears, to thought. My primary concern is not with a play's traditional source, its aesthetic derivation, its weight in the scale of some hypothetical measure. I judge by the value of the play's expressive content.

As I opened Mr. Kerr's *Tragedy and Comedy*, I prepared myself to read another intelligent treatise about which only scholars choose to argue the fine points. What I found instead is a definition of tragedy and comedy seen as a unit, opposite sides of the same coin, a definition which may or may not be "new"—that is a matter of indifference to me—but one which illuminates a central element in our psychology and philosophy at the present time.

"We have a habit of thinking that 'tragic' means 'sorry' or 'doomed' or 'morally guilty': it means 'free'," says Kerr. He defines tragedy as "an investigation of the possibilities of human freedom." Freedom is not to be equated with "liberty" in the social sense although that may be inferred as part of it. Freedom is man's commitment to engage in an action to fulfill a supremely desirable end. "In tragedy man's aim is high and his thrust is strong." Oedipus wants to purify Thebes; Hamlet wants to and finally does set right the rotten state of Denmark. That they suffer and die for these aims, makes their stories not only tragic but heroic. By the nature of his purpose and act the tragic hero's destiny becomes affirmative and inspiring. "At the heart of tragedy...stands godlike man passionately desiring a state of affairs more perfect than that which now exists," Kerr says.

He further notes that "tragedy is inevitably the product of a fiercely optimistic society." "Again and again the Greek chorus cries out the litany of man's aims, adds up once more the conquests made by his astonishing powers...." The disappearance of tragedy in our theatre today is not a symptom of health but of fear. "America's tragedy," the martyred German statesman Walther Rathenau once declared, "is its refusal of tragedy." This retreat is essentially caused by a distrust of life.

I have quoted liberally from the book. If it were possible, I should quote almost the whole of "Tragedy Now," its most brilliant chapter. Here we discover the flaw in the prevalent (almost fashionable) pessimism or skepticism which in the theatre today produces our substitute for tragedy: the black comedy. It is, Kerr says, "a phenomenon of the moment that derives from the complete absence of any tragic aspiration." It dramatizes what Kerr aptly terms "a cringing position."

This may be thought an inevitable historical development. Darwin and Freud among others have shaken our confidence in the *optimism* of tragedy. But Kerr argues convincingly that this need not have been so, that on the contrary, Darwin, Freud, and the others may be interpreted to reinforce man's will to act forcefully and courageously, in Kerr's sense tragically, that is, heroically. He even cites Sartre's existentialism; commonly regarded as a negativist philosophy, it espouses action as the only means of achieving freedom and thus a tragic stance.

Kerr's book contains many knowing observations and comments, but its importance for me lies in its basic thesis. Not only is it helpful but, in my view, *right*. The state of funk we live in today explains the intellectual and spiritual failure of our times. There never was a "happy time." Life has always been a trial and a challenge; for that reason and because of our ineradicable appetite for it, it has always been a glorious adventure, a rousing epic for those with the will to endure it. The wish to make life "easy," which it has never been nor can ever be—our avoidance of moral exertion—is the direct route not merely to flabbiness but to an incapacity to enjoy life, to irresponsibility, to private and social crime.

I cannot leave off at this point without saying something about the book in relation to other aspects of its author's literary character. *Tragedy and Comedy* is admirably written. Its only fault in this regard is its too even flow, which occasionally tends to make for rhythmic monotony. Kerr's aphorisms (such as "Because man can hold his knowledge in his head he holds the cosmos in his hand") pour out in too steady a stream and extend themselves in too many variants.

That he can write fluently and felicitously is no longer news. What is new and surprising is the understanding and respect he displays in dealing with dramatists whom in his regular reviews he has often summarily dismissed: for example, Brecht, Beckett, Genet. In fact all his judgments in the present book show a far greater poise and solidity than he ordinarily brings to his journalistic animadversions.

This suggests several things: that while Mr. Kerr is a master at turning out a readable review in fifty minutes this practice is not a salutary accomplishment for a man who possesses his critical perception, and that as a daily commentary his writing does not represent his soundest thought or the true mettle of his conscience. His daily reviews are patently an increasingly onerous effort to influence the theatre's customers, the folk who read and run to (more often away from) the box office.

The most significant plays are not infrequently difficult plays, particularly at first sight. They rarely please the casual playgoer. As a newspaper critic Kerr sits where he is not at his best, for he is sitting in the ordinary playgoer's seat, and thus too far front: too close to the immediate event to give him the necessary "distance" to allow him to be as good a critic as his new book proves him to be. Where has Walter Kerr, the author of *Tragedy and Comedy*, been hiding?

—*HARP*, May '67

THEATRE IN EUROPE

—Berlin

The theatre in West Berlin is well supplied with new and old texts from the drama of all lands. It is thoroughly sound in orthodox techniques, established and rich with honor in the community. But I was more interested in the theatre of East Berlin because of the sharp difference between what one may see there and what one sees in New York, London, Paris and West Berlin itself. I refer to the Komische Oper ("Comic Opera"), to some extent to the Deutches Theater (whose production of the picturesque Soviet allegory *The Dragon* I saw last year) and, of course, to the world-renowned Berliner Ensemble.

What struck me in the production of East Berlin, as it had in Prague, was the sheer sense of *play*: the exhilaration in the variety of physical action, color and movement, by which meaning may be conveyed. When I saw Topol's *Cat on the Rails* in Prague, for instance, I seemed to "get" even more of its quality and message without knowledge of the Czech language than I did when I read the script in a good English translation by George Voskovec. In Prague and East Berlin the stage action *is* speech.

Hence my conjecture that the great Russian director, Meyerhold, for a long time taboo in Soviet Union because of his "formalism," was probably the indirect influence on the theatres of Prague and to some degree of East Berlin. Meyerhold said that "Words in the theatre are only a design on the canvas of motion." This was not meant to be taken literally (though it is true that he tampered with texts—including those of the "classics"—a practice held to be heretical). It is obvious that Brecht, the founder and leader of the Berliner Ensemble, couldn't have minimized the importance of writing in the theatre (he was above all a poet), but the emphasis on the plastics of movement, the almost choreographic treatment of groups and of individual performances, scenic business, tricks and turns are among the most striking features in the theatre of both East Berlin and Prague. This is theatrical theatre, where playing is the *play* and the text is not altogether the thing.

I attended the first night of a new mounting of Verdi's *La Traviata* at the Kosmische Oper. Its director, Walter Felsenstein, a resident of West Berlin, rehearses his operatic productions for many months. The Komische Oper, like other theatres in East Berlin, is subsidized by the government.

Opera under Felsenstein is endowed with an authentic dramatic life. The actors do not deliver their arias from stage center, face front, with an eye on the conductor. They are characters of a drama which is not sliced into set pieces, and they move and act in accordance with dramatic necessity.

Every role is individualized. In the gambling and ballroom episodes of *La Traviata*, for example, there are no "supers": one can "read" each character among the guests, follow the line of each person's special behavior and yet discern the pattern of the whole. All this in settings perfect in taste, exquisite in opulence (where demanded) and best of all, expressive of style and content.

During the penultimate moments of the death scene in *La Traviata* one catches glimpses of the whole course of Violetta's and Alfred's history—particularly the former festivities—in brilliant miniature. The juxtaposition of these sparkling fragments of the past and the approach of death adds irony to pathos. To see a Felsenstein production is to suspect that opera might be the greatest of theatrical forms. This surely is "total theatre."

The productions at the Berliner Ensemble are no less totally theatrical. Three elements prevail at the Ensemble which we rarely find in Brecht productions elsewhere: elegance, charm and abundantly raffish humor. The actors move in grace and laughter while, at the same time, preserving a certain proletarian plainness without a trace of coarseness.

That such attributes should mark the production of *The Threepenny Opera* is perhaps not surprising, but that they should also appear in *The Bakery*, considering the play's subject matter, is astonishing. The script was composed by Brecht's "heirs" from scenes only partly finished in 1929-30. It is a propaganda play in the playwright's "epic" style, dealing with the economic hardships of the period. The atmosphere is steeped in the dull gray of poverty. Yet there is no heaviness at all in the staging, but great charm, while the drabness of the circumstances presented is transformed into a spectacle of subtle, visual interest, even beauty. In nearly all discussions of the Ensemble its purely *aesthetic* aspect is overlooked. Externally, the Oriental, particularly the Japanese theatre, has served as an inspiration for effects which seem to have been born in Berlin.

My intention at the moment is not to describe the productions of *The Threepenny Opera* or of *Man Is Man*. What concerns me now are matters of principle and instruction which may be extrapolated from the experience of having seen them.

Nowhere in the Western world is such "teamwork" to be seen as at the Ensemble. There are several remarkably fine actors in the company (one of them plays the central role in *Man Is Man*), but the productions are so much of piece that I very nearly forgot to look at the programs to learn their names. The productions are so wholly integrated that one hardly thinks of individual persons or passages. They are "works" in which acting, design, direction, seem to have been created by a single artist—not the dramatist, the director, this or that actor but all of them as One. They have created something greater than the sum of its parts. This is the perfection of theatre craft.

It is important to remember that these productions (*The Bakery*, *The Threepenny Opera*, *Man Is Man*) postdate Brecht's death in 1956. They are the work of young directors trained at the Ensemble. It should be remarked that the latest success at the Ensemble is a production of O'Casey's *Purple Dust*. The Ensemble is not a one-dramatist theatre.

There is a general significance in these bits of information. For what I persist in calling "True Theatre" is not a display of great personalities, geniuses and stars of whatever sort but a unified effort that represents something more than its component individuals. Of geniuses and personalities we in the United States have our share; they come out seasonally. One way of recognizing a true Theatre is that its value extends beyond the brilliance of its immediate personnel.

The Moscow Art Theatre, for example, founded in 1898 by Stanislavsky and Nemirovitch-Danchenko, has exercised an enormous influence on the modern Russian theatre (and elsewhere) long after its prestige was established and after its founders' deaths. This did not come about solely through the eminence of the parent organization (the Moscow Art Theatre is now considered "a museum" by many Russians and others) but through the students of its ideas and practices in many independent and frequently aesthetically divergent groups.

Similarly, the Berliner Ensemble, indisputably Brecht's creation, now retains its vitality through the development of principles and procedures bequeathed by him and put to use by people of a later generation for new audiences. A Theatre is not so much the product of a talent as of a concept, a ruling idea. Through its seminal power it survives those who plant it. A true Theatre inspires not only dedication to its idea but generates a common way of work, a fundamental technique, a characteristic style. A Theatre is the expression of a culture or at least a powerful current within a community. Indeed, it is not too much to say that a Theatre may contribute to the formation of a culture, a statement supported by many historical precedents.

When the Berliner Ensemble moved into the delightful old playhouse where in 1928 *The Threepenny Opera* was first produced, the following lines (written by Brecht) were inscribed on a plaque in the lobby as an indication of the Ensemble's spirit: "The Berliner Ensemble is about to give its plays amid ruins. These performances will be staged in this beautiful building not only for pastime but to have audience and company together establish a harmonious '*us*': so that this House and much else besides may stand fast."

Attendance at the Ensemble is now greater than when I first visited it in 1956. Every performance I attended was sold out. The audience, it seemed to me, was composed largely of young folk. It is also noteworthy that while the people in the streets of East Berlin are for the most part shabbily attired, they come to the theatre almost formally dressed as for a festive occasion.

Another interesting sidelight: the Alfred of *La Traviata* at the Komische Oper was an American from Atlanta, Ga. He is not a "defector" but an alien resident of West Berlin, permitted to work with Felsenstein in East Berlin. The day I was informed of this I encountered Carl Ebert, whom I had first met in Los Angeles where he lives. I asked him what he was doing in Berlin. He told me he was staging Stravinsky's *The Rake's Progress* at the West Berlin Opera House. I inquired whether he was satisfied with his cast. "It's very good," he replied, "the three leads are Americans." Our country, I repeat, suffers no lack of *talent*.

—*NAT*, 31 July '67

THE BIRTHDAY PARTY
THE NIGGERLOVERS

Harold Pinter's *The Birthday Party* (Booth Theatre) is a good and entertaining play. I begin in this blunt and, in certain respects, noncommittal fashion for reasons I must explain.

I saw it first in London after I had seen the same author's *The Caretaker*. That production of *The Birthday Party* (Pinter's first full-length effort) had been staged by Pinter himself, and disappointment led me to suggest that the writer murder the director.

Another reason for advancing circumspectly to a truer evaluation is that a critic, being as lamentably human as any of his fellow creatures, sometimes reacts more to other reactions—especially to those of other critics—than in accord with his own. The critic thus tempted must be sufficiently patient with himself to discover what he really thinks!

The Birthday Party is a good play because it is extremely well constructed, admirably written and the first extended expression of an unmistakably original personality. The play keeps us alert. And it is *not* obscure. Pinter owes much to Beckett and perhaps to Kafka. In a short stretch of dialogue I fancied I heard echoes of Odets' *Paradise Lost*; but this too is only conjecture. The point is that whatever influences have shaped Pinter's work, he has transmuted them into something of his own: stingingly humorous, strangely disquieting, laconically tight to the point of mystification, theatrical to the point of staginess. Occasionally there is a tremor of compassion in *The Birthday Party* though more notably in *The Caretaker*.

Pinter, I repeat, is not obscure: what he intends us to understand can be readily understood. For example, the unctuously plausible and malevolent Goldberg and his thick-headed henchman McCann in *The Birthday Party* may be taken as the police or as wardens of a mental institution or even as Death itself. In effect it doesn't truly matter which; what does matter is that they remove Stanley, the play's anti-hero, to a place where he dreads to go.

Stanley resides at a wretched boardinghouse which its owners, like so many in England who supply digs to touring actors and other indigents, assume to be normal living quarters—and "very nice." (Pinter is a master at making us sense the damp dreariness of such environments, as he is of setting down the speech of the folk who usually run them.) Stanley is something of an artist; at least, a person of sensibility. He has suffered the humiliations which almost inevitably attend such people's lives. (The same is true of the young man in *The Caretaker*). He has retreated from the world to avoid further injury. Even though the hosts of his hiding place are stunningly stupid, they are innocents. But the "furies" (Goldberg and McCann) against which he is powerless catch up with him, take him away and, we presume, destroy him.

The play is a parable placed in circumstances and couched in language that may pass as "realistic." Pinter does not 'however aim' to represent a precise milieu or to depict particular individuals.

He writes to evoke the atmosphere of a widespread modern condition. His style embodies his "message."

The Birthday Party is the simplest of Pinter's plays. It has less scope than *The Caretaker*; it is less cutting than *The Homecoming*. Still *The Birthday Party* is not only a good play but for a "beginner," as Pinter was in 1958 at the time of its first production, a consummate one.

Do I "agree" with Pinter? Is his view of life acceptable to me as a universal truth? No, I do not "agree" with him, and his truth is not universal. But nowadays it is something commonly and very acutely felt by many of us everywhere: the reduction of man to a menaced and quivering atom in a senseless, horribly vacuous world.

Alan Schneider's direction is emotionally pointed. The play might be conceived as a lucid nightmare, but pity is at the core of Schneider's interpretation. There is more pathos than horror in it. His characters are not drained of life; they still retain a degree of vitality. (The Royal Shakespeare Company's production under Pinter was merely inexpressive.) With a touch of mystery melodrama, we are at moments close to a feeling of domestic comedy. Thus, Pinter's dumb housekeeper acquires a distinct sweetness, and her passive husband a benevolence which sadly comes to nothing. What we see at the Booth Theatre is more assimilable and persuasive for our audiences than a colder or more severe English reading of the play might be.

James Patterson projects the mutilated artist's torment convincingly. Always a fine actress, Ruth White makes the housekeeper more touching and less drab than perhaps Pinter's text indicates. Ed Flanders as Goldberg mixes acid and schmaltz in very nearly the right proportions. Alexandra Berlin as a cockney "bird" is juicy, comically affecting and unmistakably present. No one in the cast is bad.

I "agree" with George Tabori's two one-actors which come to us under the distasteful title *The Niggerlovers* (Orpheum Theatre), but I don't care for them.

In the first of these skits called "The Demonstration," a cultivated gentleman named "August" sympathetic to our Southern blacks, goes to visit them on their native grounds. He hopes in some way to be of service to them. He accepts a demonstration of how they are treated by the law in the South. Two black men playfully apply themselves to the task. They give him a brutal going over which makes him cry out "I don't want to be a Negro any more!"

In the second and still more abstract piece called "Man and Dog" a genteel young man of liberal stripe walks his dog along the streets of one of our ghettos. The dog is an aging Austrian bitch (attractive in the person of Viveca Lindfors) and something of a Fascist. She despises "spics" and probably Negroes and Jews as well. She is severely reproved for this by her master. But she is harmless: she no longer has any real bite and she is only moderately randy. Because she still reeks of old-world charm, her "boss" is devoted to her despite her reprehensible prejudices. When, in the course of their walk the man virtually begs to be robbed by two astonished blacks who he supposes intend to "molest" him he ends by calling for the police to take strong measures against his "assailants." At the conclusion of the episode we find him along with his bitch baying at the moon.

The meaning is clear. The liberal minded American, indignant about Fascist traits and behavior in foreigners, is patient, often even affectionately tolerant with them when they no longer constitute a direct threat, but he will clamor for counter-violence to avoid danger from the insulted and injured at home.

This is a good insight. But Tabori's treatment has a counterfeit ring. It is tricked out in the stylistic modes of the "new theatre"—not Brecht, Genet or good red vaudeville but with a smattering of all three. The writer's personal stamp is missing. He has chosen a form alien to him.

Evidence of this is furnished by a passage (almost an interpolation) in "The Demonstration." Here August's lady secretary describes the guilt suffered by a person whose relatives have been done to death in a concentration camp while he (or she) has managed to escape to safety. Such a person constantly tries to assuage his troubled conscience by taking special pains to act kindly toward those weaker or less privileged. This monologue might prove moving in another context. (It might also be more effective if it were spoken by a man.) Set where it is it strikes an incongruous note.

Though it contains a few funny lines, the show remains static. The director, Gene Frankel, has sought to enliven the evening by acrobatics, choreographic stunts, somersaults, jujitsu, chases in slow motion. They are well employed and the players are to be congratulated on their aptitude. But they, no more than the excellent jazz players or the music which accompanies Tabori's lyrics, not even Stacy Keach's ability as a character actor, can turn *The Niggerlovers* into a stimulating event.

—*NAT*, 23 Oct. '67

SCUBA DUBA

At the New Theatre on East 54th Street. Bruce Jay Friedman's *Scuba Duba* is f-u-n-n-y. It is also funny.

I find it difficult to fathom my own reaction beyond the cachinnation which the initial contact with the play produced in me. My funny bone had been struck a considerable whack but I could not make out the exact nature of the effect beyond its immediate physical manifestation. There is laughter and laughter, and though the theatregoer in need of pastime may be entirely satisfied when his risibilities have been aroused, the critic should not content himself with the mere notation of the fact.

In spelling out the key word above I mean to indicate the unease I experienced as I laughed. There was something sad about the play which Peter Larkin's pretty set, the vulgarity of the language, the blatant jokes, the general extravagance of the proceedings did not efface. My head had been hammered, yet I was left with a hole in my heart.

Stripped of theatrical embellishments (Jacques Levy's production is most apt) the play's plot makes a clear point. Harold Wonder, a young New Yorker on his vacation on the Riviera with his wife and two children, strongly suspects that she has run off with a black scuba diver. Frantic with anxiety, Harold spills his troubles out on Miss Janus, a marvelously stacked American neighbor who comes in to visit him in a bikini. He has no eye for her readily available blandishments though he puts up with her simple-mindedness.

He makes an overseas call to his mother, whose consolation consists of a combination of vomitous bromides and aggression. He summons his psychoanalyst, who arrives with Cheyenne, a middle-aged floozy of shameless candor. The doctor's ministrations may be summed up as a kind of Zen doubletalk which drives Harold to the verge of violence. Unable to calm Harold, the analyst takes Cheyenne to bed.

Then Harold's wife, Jean, makes an appearance with her skin diver friend, a clownish black named Foxtrot out of a mental Disneyland accoutered in the devilish paraphernalia of his profession. But Jean is not sleeping with him. Her lover is Reddington, a suave coffee-colored Negro of a very rational demeanor.

Jean tells Harold that he lacks continental delicacy or seductive finesse (she succumbs to his advances only in the bathroom) and that she must leave him. Reddington tries to appease Harold's bewildered fury with the admonition that he ought to accept the situation with civilized poise. At this point Harold goes berserk, strikes the solar plexus of an intruding bore of a tourist, and is ultimately left alone with the children. Though Miss Janus, the receptive lady of appetizing contours invites him to join her in a party at her place, Harold still hankers after his coldly obtuse wife at whom he howls his perennial passion.

In all the simplicity of his soul he doesn't want the dumb siren he can have, only the dumb wife he can't. Pathetic. One surmises that this is not an objective story told for fun but a subjectively painful tale wrested from the author's hectic experience! But it's nuts, and he tells it in maniacal self-derision.

The play is written and directed in a style that might be set down as that of the old *Esquire* and the new *Playboy* blue joke cartoons, raw in color, jocular in design. There are little side dishes. First there is a French cop who instead of arresting a lunatic "anarchist" who nightly robs Harold's house, bawls Harold out for being an American and thus an impostor. (The cop concludes the scene by leading the foreigners in the *Marseillaise*. Then there is the house agent who insists that all of her tenants are famous movie stars (she takes Foxtrot for Sidney Poitier) and acts the *femme fatale* with every male she encounters. The show's every detail is kooky.

But it is not any falsity I fear in this shebang, not the stylization but the verisimilitude. This is not satire, it is naturalism! It is also "nihilism." What Friedman, willy-nilly, is telling us from the frazzled depths of his being is that he, they, *we* are all living in a loony bin in which anything goes. And that there's no use feeling anything about it since nothing is what it seems or is given out to be. We are puppets playing balanced games on a freak stage.

When Harold attacks his wife's companions in the insulting lingo of the gutter he is altogether innocent of any racial slur; he is simply reacting to the turmoil of his cracked brain in which nothing is firmly established or substantial. He is a hobgoblin with straw stuffing where the organs of intelligence and emotion are supposed to dwell. Only enough of the original human is retained to emit squeaks and squawks of distress which remind us of the removed parts. When a Russian long ago wrote such a play (on another level, with a different motivation) he ended by having an actor turn to the audience and cry out: "What are you laughing about, this is you!" We guffaw unabashed: we don't care.

Am I taking *Scuba Duba* too seriously? As I indicated at the outset, I too was jostled into mirth by this uproariously declarative farce. It is a thing typical of contemporary America: spontaneous in a forthrightness whereby the author strips himself and us of all phony pretense of decorum or cultivation. I too admired the free-swinging skill of the presentation. But I left the theatre with a slight ache. The play is more depressing in its hilarity than *Who's Afraid of Virginia Woolf?* in its drama, more devastating in its zaniness than Pinter in his constriction. What troubles me is that so few recognize this.

As Harold Wonder, Jerry Orbach excels because his funny stuff is solidly rounded on the sincerity which the character must have, and which is at the base of Friedman's inspiration. Brenda Smiley's figure commands our scrupulous attention and she has been admirably directed to give Miss Janus the right touch of amiable nitwittedness. Rita Karin is killingly idiotic as the come hither, hip-swaying French housekeeper. Ken Olfson has the suitably glazed solemnity as the head shrinker who recommends that Harold see life "sideways." And Cleavon Little makes a fantastic and agile sprite of Foxtrot. There are a few forced notes and one somewhat dull spot but everyone plays in pitch.

Since early September I have witnessed a number of stage events which I have failed to report and to some of which I may give fuller attention at a later date. Here in the meantime are fleeting notes.

The Joffrey Ballet, a youthfully pleasing and expert company, delighted me in *Cello Concerto* to Vivaldi's score and intrigued me in the mixed media tribute to *Astarte*.

Judy Garland with some vocal insecurity in the lower register still touches me deeply. She is incapable of making a graceless movement. Her dramatic instinct is faultless; her every gesture suggests a large area of never wholly realized power. But this lack of completeness is somehow moving, draws us closer to her.

Marlene Dietrich, pearl-visaged, streamlined phoenix, deserves extended commentary. Do not inquire about her voice or delivery. It is the person herself with her staunch wistfulness, her eyes that gaze at us from the hazy corridors of the past, that matters. She is courteous and aloof; there is a gravity about her now that has little to do with the naughty froufrou of the old days. For all the exquisite flamboyance of her dress, the total impression is of an imperviousness to which one gladly gives obeisance.

After the Rain by John Bowen (Golden Theatre) is a play of so-called ideas. It is a bloodless parable about the rise and hollowness of dictatorship. I did not mind its didacticism but I was anaesthetized by its banality.

At the Lyceum, Max Adrian offers a one-man show, *By George* (Bernard Shaw). The actor's speech is distinct—the hint of brogue in the accent brings out the element of Irish blarney in the master's prose—and his effort is valiant. The selection of material offers us only a tracing of Shaw's career, but even a little of his language and spirit does much to compensate for Broadway.

—*NAT*, 30 Oct. '67

ROSENCRANTZ AND GUILDENSTERN ARE DEAD

Tom Stoppard's *Rosencrantz and Guildenstern Are Dead* (at the Alvin) is *Waiting for Godot* rewritten by a university wit. Based on a nice conceit, it is epigrammatically literate, intelligent, theatrically clever. It marks a scintillating debut for its author.

An English drama critic was skeptical of its success in America because to appreciate it one had to be familiar with *Hamlet*! We may now reassure that critic as to our familiarity with *Hamlet* since Stoppard's play is a Broadway hit and our reviewers, to judge by the ads, have called it "a superb play," "very brilliant, very chilling," etc., etc.

Rosencrantz and Guildenstern are two ordinary youths called to the court of Elsinore to detect what it is that troubles the young Prince. They haven't the faintest idea of the tragedy into the midst of which they have been thrust. They do as they are bid and for their pains meet with sudden death.

This is a parable of little Everyman. We are thrown into a world in which events of great moment apparently take place, have only an inkling of our role in them and in one way or another we are their victims.

As bits of *Hamlet* are enacted in swift and dim outline, the dilemma of poor Rosencrantz and Guildenstern—confused even as to their own names or identities, though one is supposed to be smarter than the other—is immediately clear, and the intellectual pattern of the play is firmly set.

At the outset, all R. & G. know is that "we were sent for." They can't believe that they were "picked out simply to be abandoned, left to find [their] way." Wistfully Guildenstern says: "We are entitled to some direction," and later: "What a fine persecution to be kept intrigued without ever quite being enlightened."

There are jokes about the theatre and amusing cracks about Hamlet himself, who is described as being "stark raving sane." The best of these occurs when Rosencrantz decides what he ought to say to Hamlet, "To sum up: your father whom you love dies, you are his heir, you come back to find that hardly was the corpse cold before his young brother popped on to his throne and under his sheets... Now why are you behaving in this extraordinary manner?"

All this entertaining stuff leads on to the play's profounder purpose, which is to declare that with life, "Wheels have been set in motion, and they have their own pace to which we are condemned." There is no true answer. "Uncertainty is the normal state." "But what are we suppose to *do*?" The answer is "Relax. Respond. We only know what we're told. And for all we know it isn't even true." The only certainty is death. "The bad end unhappily, the good unluckily."

The quips sparkle, the portentous reflections are neatly phrased. The play is civilized pastime,

which is certainly as unusual as it is agreeable, and we are duly grateful. But we need not take the play's "deeper significance" too seriously; it is not thought but student chatter on a brightly dignified level.

I take Samuel Beckett seriously whether or not I think as he does (and I do not) because, for all *his* jokes, there is passion in his plays. But beyond this, I feel bound to submit a subjective comment: I am fed up with the reiteration of life's futility on the ground that we struggle, suffer and die without ever understanding "the meaning of it all." The contemplation of life in the purview of death has produced great art in the past but, generally speaking, I am in accord with Spinoza who thought that the wise man should not be concerned primarily with death. For me, life is enough.

But I *am* taking Tom Stoppard's play too seriously. It is a first-rate spoof and a superior show. Admirably produced under Derek Goldby's direction and scenically handsome, it is generally well acted. I preferred Brian Murray's Rosencrantz to John Wood's Guildenstern, though both are good enough. They might be even better if there was somewhat more genuine naïveté in their ingenuousness. I found Paul Hecht's Player—though American—more impressive than the one I saw in London at the British National Theatre.

—*NAT*, 6 Nov. '67

THE BEARD

Michael McClure's *The Beard* (Evergreen Theatre) is not a play to like or to dislike. To challenge it as a matter of taste would be absurd. It is a phenomenon to be understood.

It has its own completeness, not simply as a text but as a performance. The images projected with apparent incoherence on the irregular walls of the Evergreen, the rock-and-roll ululations which emerge from an excellent trio, the roar of voices and noises heard before any of the play's text is spoken, are not merely preparation for what follows but organic to the short but intense evening, the tedium engendered being integral to the intensity.

What, amid the cacophony, are we able to make out in the all-encompassing projections on the walls? Besides wild fowl and perhaps reptiles, lions, lionesses and full-blown flowers, we catch glimpses of the Pontiff on his papal throne while aurally entwined in the general din are strands of the *Liebestod* from *Tristan and Isolde*.

When this stylistically justified prologue subsides, lights gradually go out and the stage emerges as a sort of blue blank or "heaven" (quite handsome in its soft monochrome) where sit two figures, identified by the playbill as Harlow and Billy the Kid, both wearing small beards of torn white tissue paper. They are at either end of a small table, she in flashy Hollywood array and he in traditional shirt, tight pants and boots. They speak more to the audience than to each other. Harlow begins with the line, flatly drawled and endlessly repeated throughout the evening, and sometimes taken up by her opposite number: "Before you can pry any secrets from me, you must first find the real me! Which one will you pursue?" To which the Kid retorts in a tone equally mechanical and tinny, "What makes you think I want to pry secrets from you?" Then Harlow: "Because I'm so beautiful." The Kid comes back with "So what!" Then Harlow again: "You want to be as beautiful as I am." And the Kid, once more in kazoo defiance, "Oh yeah!"

This teasing refrain of sibylline statement and rejoinder constitutes the keynote of the play. Four-letter obscenities, employed as insult or provocation, are obbligatos to the main motif. All this shapes itself into a kind of nasty love play which is consummated by Billy's tribute to Harlow through *cunnilingus*.

The use of beards for both characters is no idle conceit: the fable may be taken as hetero- or homosexual according to preference. (Didn't a Dadaist of old paint a mustache on the Mona Lisa, and aren't the sexes becoming undifferenti-ated?) The meaning in either case is the same. Is the effect erotic? Not in the least. It may strike some viewers or voyeurs as a pop art celebration of sex: it is actually its put-down. The author's intention may be lyric—I've heard a fine young woman call the show "lovely"—but it adds up to a joke.

If *The Beard* is inconsequential as art, it is not negligible as symptom. Civilization, it is said, has become obsessed with sex. Since little is trusted, since we have no confidence in any faith—religious, social or political—nothing is left but sex. It must take the place of all the exploded values. It forms the life line to continued existence. It alone tells no lies or, to put it in the symbolism of *The Beard*, even its lies culminate in an act, *the* act. So it alone is real.

The trouble is that sex, isolated from every other attribute, ultimately loses its force as a boon. It doesn't, for most of us, pay the rent; it doesn't impede the space race or stand in the way of an outbreak of war. It is not the "answer." It too proves futile, ludicrous. The hippies, for whom I harbor much sympathy as they take ever longer trips to nirvana (they call it love), become increasingly asexual. The inevitable end to the obsession with sex is impotence. Tuning out makes sex unnecessary as well as impossible.

The Beard represents a mockery of sex, a "milestone" on the road to nonentity. We need not despise it. It shows us that our myths (aren't Harlow and Billy the Kid deities of our lowly Olympus?) are in the process of dissolution. Just as the proceedings and debates of the UN are fast becoming caricatures of politics. *The Beard* is a caricature of sex as the saving remnant of our personal lives. To realize this is to comprehend much else about our day.

Seen in this way, the production, directed by Rip Torn, acted by Billie Dixon and Richard Bright, design and media mix prologue by USCO, and lighting by C. Murawski, is perfect.

—*NAT*, 13 Nov. '67

MORE STATELY MANSIONS
THE LITTLE FOXES
HAIR

Ham "saw the nakedness of his father and told his…brothers"—for which he was cursed. In the production of *More Stately Mansions*, sundry Hams commit the sin on the body of Eugene O'Neill (Broadhurst Theatre), for which they must be chastised. Except that they know not what they do.

O'Neill left an unfinished, unrevised script, sequel to *A Touch of the Poet*, which was meant as the first segment of a never completed nine-play cycle, the rest of which he burned. This remnant, which bears the title *More Stately Mansions*, if produced as written would consume ten hours. The Swedish director Gierow cut the script to four hours and presented it in Stockholm, where despite the enthusiasm for O'Neill's work, it was coldly received. For New York, José Quintero as director has cut and rearranged Mr. Gierow's version so that it runs for nearly three hours.

The truncated body, like a gigantic fetus, gives evidence of immanent power and complex interest. There still exist in it various fascinating autobiographical and socio-historical strands. O'Neill writing what he planned as an objective portrait of a family from the time of Andrew Jackson's administration to his own day, a kind of American history, was unable to exclude his subjective nature from it. Thus the huge fragment quivers confusedly but nonetheless profoundly with raw psychological life.

What we discern is the troubled marriage of two strains: the power-deprived and therefore power-hungry impoverished 19th-century immigrant (in this case Irish) and the idealism of the 18th-century tradition with its treasured memories in the refinement of European culture. These opposed forces are more copiously represented in

More Stately Mansions than in the preceding play. Nora Melody, an Irish innkeeper's daughter, becomes Simon Harford's wife; Deborah Harford is his mother. They fight for dominance of Simon's soul.

Simon has something of his mother's spirit, "a touch of the poet" in him, but he is also the son of a Yankee mill owner. He is held in thrall by the earthy strength of his Irish wife, who is possessed of the will to get ahead and make something of herself in the new world. He becomes a ruthlessly ambitious businessman and encourages her (perhaps to humiliate her and to suppress the "poet" in himself) to emulate and surpass him in his drive to material success. In doing this he becomes her "slave."

Still his mother's ever-abiding romanticism, a kind of insanity in her, sways and disturbs his consciousness. He wants to be held by and to hold both wife and mother, and they in turn, while close to each other in their mutual need for the man, vie with each other as antagonists over the booty. He is crushed between his appetite and his aspiration, senses this and begs to be relieved of the insuperable burden of the duality. The mother finally retires from the struggle. In a sense all are destroyed in the conflict.

This is a variation of a constant theme in O'Neill's work: the spiritual tug of war between the potential artist and the man of affairs. It is at the very heart of *The Great God Brown*, but in *More Stately Mansions* it becomes integral to O'Neill's "American history." Here the tension is more emphatically personal, indicating a need on the man's part for a mother and mate in one person with equal devotion and surrender from both, producing a corresponding resentment when neither need is satisfied.

Never a good "writer" and only fitfully a sure craftsman, with ideals often exceeding his grasp, O'Neill groped in *More Stately Mansions* along every path: the script veers from realistic methods to soliloquy and stream-of-consciousness speech (in the manner of *Strange Interlude* and his plays with masks). In addition, passages of ordinary expository writing had not yet been transformed into convincing characters and action.

If this amalgam were ever to be realized as a satisfactory stage entity, a great cast and a director of enormous skill and imagination would have to undertake the task. There are good actors in the production at the Broadhurst, but Colleen Dewhurst is baffled, Arthur Hill is simply embarrassed by his part, while most of the others are hopelessly at a loss in the turbid currents which Quintero was unable to direct.

The audience comes to see Ingrid Bergman in the flesh. The flesh is still beautifully fresh and her spirit is absolutely eager. But she is fatally miscast, not merely in regard to her accent but because she hasn't any of the peculiarly resolute fragility and ineffable dreaminess her role requires. She seems instead to be a fortress of will with not a speck of resignation or renunciation anywhere in her being. She would never be overcome.

The production is not only a botch in itself but a paradigm of what is wrong with our commercial theatre.

Lillian Hellman's *The Little Foxes* (Vivian Beaumont Theater) is not a bad play; indeed it may be called a good one in the sense that it is written with intelligence and economy, that it is admirably constructed, pointed to a sound purpose, and entirely stageworthy. I am reminded of what Meyerhold said when he was blamed for producing *The Lady of the Camellias* in Moscow: "The form is outmoded but the 'stuff' is durable." The fact that the technique of *The Little Foxes* is Ibsen's and it is melodramatic rather than poetic are not truly faults. It is a play about our American past and marks a date in the development of our stage. It served its day well and in some measure may still serve ours.

If *The Little Foxes* is a "well-made play," by which its detractors mean "mechanical," I might say that Mike Nichols' direction of it is too well made. It hews so closely to the literal line of Miss Hellman's script, thus emphasizing precisely the traits we may object to, that all its seams show, all

its limitations are exposed. Mike Nichols is particularly gifted for comedy, so that not only do the comic moments intended as irony make us chuckle but others not so intended positively make us grin.

This tight play, which as social-historical criticism makes one think of Balzac in motivation and of Henri Becque in treatment, needs, if anything, to be "loosened." The more meticulous and efficient showmanship one applies to it (and of that Nichols has a plentiful supply) the more bloodless it seems. The characters do not require sharper etching than the playwright has given them; they call for greater breath and humanity. The play's shortcomings seem to me expertly enhanced by the new production. The characters have become craftily contrived mechanisms. They are artfully manipulated; they barely move with any impetus of their own.

Anne Bancroft, like everyone else, works dutifully as Regina, but strikes me as wrong for the role. (Even her handsome clothes do not "function" for her.) George Scott is very nearly a caricature, extremely deft but still a cartoon. Margaret Leighton is so masterly as Birdie that she seems to stand by herself outside the play. Richard Dysart as Regina's husband is modestly right—simple that is though not as interestingly dimensional as he ought to be; the same might be said of Maria Tucci as his daughter. Only minor roles played by Bea Richards and Austin Pendleton assume a life beyond the production's confines.

The setting by Howard Bay is a valiant and on the whole successful attempt to make use of a stage which is all thrust and no environment. I have still to be convinced that the playing area of the Vivian Beaumont is truly practicable for the purposes it was designed to fulfill.

One thing more must in all fairness be said: for a wide audience in New York and on the road the production works and will "pay off."

The protest theatre of 1967 has already become a stereotype. The "hippie movement," some say, is already showing decrepitude, no doubt petrified by publicity. Too many tourists and jokesters surround the domain. So, at any rate, it would appear in the theatre, where no one has as yet taken the pains to treat the so-called "generation gap" seriously. The trouble is that on the stage we tend to use every new social phenomenon as grist to the amusement industry, rather than as a subject for study and thought.

Hair (at the New York Shakespeare Festival's new Public Theater at 425 Lafayette Street), under the supervision of Joseph Papp and the artistic direction of Gerald Freedman who staged the attraction, takes a swipe at the theme. I call *Hair*, which the playbill describes as "an American tribal love-rock musical," with book by Gerome Ragni and James Rado and music by Galt MacDermot, a "swipe" because it both celebrates the hirsute youth of the moment and kids them. It is well housed in the new building and is thoroughly amiable, but it hardly gets closer to the core of its matter than do the other entertainments in a similar vein.

Except for the musicians, who are enthroned above the colorful pop art background designed by Ming Cho Lee, a professional touch is lacking. This in itself may be no great loss: the young company contains some winsome and pretty players, notably the delicate beginner, Shelley Plimpton, who sings about an impossible but beloved boy friend, Jill O'Hara whose serious face has a slightly Oriental cast, and Susan Batson, a robust and roundish black bundle of sullen mockery and good humor. They and others are very nice to meet and they all cut up with zest. But the show lacks a center: its "book" consists of odds and ends, bits of party fun, a be-in without issue or style.

The red, white and what-have-you squares are gently derided, the friendliness and errant libidos of the young folk are pleasantly touted, political big-wigs are waggishly flouted, and the overhanging threat and presence of war are wistfully deplored. Still, I was left unsatisfied, with only a slight tickle and an expected tear. The music occasionally rises to real lyric expression (the words are not always delivered intelligibly), but rarely to sweeping statement.

I welcome the Public Theater enterprise to which the doughty Papp has added his labors on behalf of New York's public (he will produce contemporary as well as old plays there) and wish it prosperity.

—*NAT*, 20 Nov. '67

IN CIRCLES
HALFWAY UP THE TREE

In the theatre as elsewhere among the industries, more money appears to be spent on publicity than on the product; the ads are more impressive than the ingredients.

Theatregoing is therefore full of surprises. At the tiny Cherry Lane Theatre on Commerce Street, Gertrude Stein's nonsensical *In Circles*, sung to music by Al Carmines, directed by Lawrence Kornfeld, pleased me unexpectedly. The acting of Jacob Ben-Ami and Lili Darvas in a skit (one of a pair) given at the 299-seat Forum—the "studio" of the Repertory Theater of Lincoln Center—struck me as warmer and more vividly genuine than what we get from the dazzling array of "name actors" in more conspicuous places. And up at the Spingold Theatre of Brandeis University (Waltham, Mass.) Morris Carnovsky's gusty clowning in the American premiere of Brecht's *Schweyk in the Second World War* holds more substance than we find in acting of reputed weightiness in most Broadway drama.

Peter Ustinov has written still another comedy. *Halfway Up the Tree* (Brooks Atkinson Theatre), about which you may hear many times a day over the radio. Mr. Ustinov's activities as stage and screen actor, director, playwright, novelist, short story writer, imitator, *raconteur* and linguist are so diverse and ubiquitous—at times so colorfully genial—that we might readily forgo discussion of his latest manifestation without committing any injustice to him or to readers of this journal. The reason for mentioning *Halfway Up the Tree* is not simply respect for its author's gifts but because there is a point to be made about his employment of them.

Mr. Ustinov should be encouraged to remain superficial rather than intellectual. He is bright and brilliantly good-humored, but be becomes embarrassing when he strives in earnest for serious connotations. His froth frequently bubbles; his messages, even when we agree with their general import, are bourgeois banal: their wisdom is the crackling sugar of stage and saloon.

That is much more the case with *Halfway Up the Tree* than with *The Unknown Soldier and His Wife*, which at least moves about quite a bit, is cleverly staged, and has much better jokes. But whether Ustinov treats of the "generation gap" as in his new play, or the recurrence of war in forever similar patterns as in the earlier one, this thinking is merely persiflage, the banter of amiable, comfortable and not really concerned bohemians. Sometimes, as in *Romanoff and Juliet*, the scenic gaiety and buffoonery become captivating, but in *Halfway Up the Tree* I yawned restively between the not so frequent gags. The production is expensive and routine.

Now Gertrude Stein's *In Circles* needs no "meaning" and probably has none, but it charms. Still it must have meaning, though of an astral nature. Whatever Miss Stein's original intention may have been, the result of the Cherry Lane performance based on her "libretto" is an affectionate parody of light opera or musical romance in the days before musical comedy became a big machine. It is more sophisticated and I would judge better than *The Boy Friend*.

The music is delightfully corny, all silly lilt and high-class posturing. The background is fragrantly floral in the manner of a display for the sale of sweets. The direction is an abstract of all the poses and positions of airy musical shows in the halcyon days before the First World War. It is varied, funny, "convincing": we feel that something mock but momentously grand is surely going on to which we owe our confidence for the sake of free-floating merriment. If this is what is dubbed "high camp" it is of the highest, and I am for it. It provides a breather.

Walking to Waldheim, "a comedy almost to the end," and *Happiness*, "a romance in one scene," are the titles of two short plays by Mayo Simon which initiate the series for new playwrights or "experimental" plays imbedded in the bowels of the Vivian Beaumont Theater on West 65th Street.

It is difficult at this juncture to assess the degree or exact nature of Mr. Simon's ability. He seems to be obsessed by the sadness of old age and the emptiness of time passing for people whose lives to begin with were filled with not much of anything. Mixed with this in the first, longer and less satisfying of the two plays is a kind of Jewish comedy writing (American vaudeville type) which alternates between the fairly amusing and the faintly distasteful.

The form of the play—a family riding in a car in a funeral procession, during which we are given glimpses of the six occupants' lives, and in which we also see them move on to their demise—owes something to Thornton Wilder. Oh vain drabness and distress of this world, how we bemoan you!

Much less juvenilely symbolic is the shorter *Happiness*, in which two old people, a widower more aged and debilitated than the widow (either a neighbor or the landlady) cling to each other to console themselves in the penultimate moments of life. This desperate connection constitutes their happiness.

The evening is saved by the acting. Jacob Ben-Ami, a veteran of some fifty years on the Yiddish and American stage, comes into his own once again with a never to be forgotten image of comic-pathetic senescence. (How many theatregoers remember him in a 1920s play from the Danish called *Samson and Delilah* in which he gave one of the most profoundly truthful portraits of the artist's spiritual suffering that has ever been created in our theatre?) Ben-Ami's Old Man is touching without being sentimental. He is grotesque without being offensive and his last spurt of energy adumbrates a vigor in remembered joy, communicating the glow and inspiration of the life force even at its ebb.

Lili Darvas' pulsating heartiness, a kind of paprika which flavors the dismal and obscene with the dignity of sound human instincts, is a cause for rejoicing. The fine interaction of these two admirable players is not only worth a visit to the Forum but is a better example of ensemble acting than is provided by many proclaimed "Ensembles."

—*NAT*, 27 Nov. '67

THE PROMISE
WOLE SOYINKA

People averse to such plays as *The Birthday Party*, *The Homecoming* or even *Rosencrantz and Guildenstern Are Dead*—particularly if the cause for such distaste is either their obscurity or their "pessimism"—may find themselves well suited by Aleksei Arbuzov's *The Promise* (Henry Miller Theatre). Arbuzov's play, a London hit, is replete with sound sentiments which, according to the playbill, have received a warm welcome in Tokyo, Warsaw, Paris, Athens, Tel-Aviv.

These sentiments are loyalty in love and friendship, courage, scorn of middle-class complacency. Perhaps still more fundamental to the spirit of *The Promise* is the conviction that even at the point of death a man may recover and start afresh—or to put it in terms of the old Salvation Army slogan, "a man may be down but he's never out."

Despite the skepticism our brains, blood, circumstances or experience may induce in us, I am ready to subscribe to these notions. I am even willing to serve as their advocate. My hesitation arises from the suspicion that the clever and mean Frenchman who said "with fine sentiments one often makes bad art" may have been dead right.

Aleksei Arbuzov, one of the most prolific and popular of Soviet playwrights, is more or less officially committed to the thesis or "program" suggested in the foregoing propositions. I am certain that he is sincere and that the major part of the Soviet audience shares his commitment with equal good will. The trouble is that it comes to him too easily and that his dramatization of the theme is too pat. His play is sentimental rather than strong. It tugs at the heart with skimpy strings. I could be inspired by Arbuzov's credo only if the play itself convinced me that he had arrived at his conclusion after withstanding a strong temptation to succumb to a contrary faith. Optimism is healthy and artistically operative when it has been attained through hardship.

The Russian people have proved themselves a sturdy lot; they have endured suffering and privation from the earliest days of their revolution, through the years of war, communism, the Second World War and the Stalinist terror. Their generally cheerful outlook, despite the pressures of their existence, is genuine and well earned.

Apart from reflecting this mood of manly confrontation with protracted difficulty, *The Promise* had another asset for its Soviet audience and, to a considerable extent, for the English as well. It reminded both audiences (and apparently all the others) that since their heroic days of trial—the cruel siege of Leningrad or the worst of the blitz—they had become too softly satisfied with petty comforts and mediocre safety. In Soviet terms at least, *The Promise* is self-critical—gently, sweetly, modestly; but still a warning note tinkles. It contains a line to the effect that in victory the winner often takes on the vices of those he has overcome.

For all that *The Promise* is a thin—though not at all a contemptible—piece of work. There is only one thing which can save it for an audience not altogether attuned to its feeling and idea: powerful acting. In London the central role, a young person whom we see progress from a homeless adolescence during the siege in 1942 to the time she becomes a doctor in 1959, was played by the genially robust Judy Dench. The role has been recast in the New York production with Eileen Atkins, who was excellent in *The Killing of Sister George*, but lacks the qualities needed for her present assignment.

In saying this, I have no intention to find fault with Miss Atkins; she is a good actress. My point extends beyond her to the remainder of the cast: the actors who played the two "boys" in London and now play them again here. I do not mean by this that English actors are incapable of portraying Russians, but that the individually sympathetic young actors in *The Promise* must strike a knowing American audience as too correct and "frail" to properly convey the specific nature of the characters and writing of this eminently Russian play. They do not possess, for all their best efforts, that combination of muscular gush and almost peasantlike effusiveness which often strikes the foreign eye as a sort of naïve and rather "butch" eccentricity.

There are many American actors who come naturally closer to this quality; in fact *The Promise* is one of the few plays from abroad which could have been cast here without any difficulty at all—even if "name actors" were sought.

I don't wish to stress the folly of bringing over an English company. I do want to air an old complaint: that so few of our reviewers are competent in the balanced judgment of acting. Several of them have called the acting in *The Promise* "superb." If this is not simply cordiality to visitors it is ignorance.

Ian McShane and Ian McKellen are certainly able, well-qualified actors, of good disposition and pleasant personality. Considering their limitation in regard to the Arbuzov material, they do very well. But the whole first act, which must make us sense the physical facts of dirt, cold, hunger, lack of proper illumination, and every other deprivation, are indicated in the most perfunctory fashion. Because of this we are not only unable to believe in the actors as particular characters, we can hardly credit them as real persons of any kind.

This is as much the director's fault as the actors'. It may escape our critics but the audience, whether it knows it or not, is thus deprived of contact with a basic dimension of the play's dramatic effectiveness. A production which might live on its own level as a "story of true love" and bracing idealism—many a poorer play has done so—leaves the audience dubious if not entirely indifferent.

The acting in Wole Soyinka's two African plays at the Greenwich Mews Theatre is uneven and crude, but by virtue of its energy and relative authenticity works and makes at least the first of the two plays a salty frolic of abundant humor. It is called *The Trials of Brother Jero*, and deals with a man whom the author identifies as a "Beach Divine," in other words, a religious fraud whose Christian evangelism is agglutinated with primitive superstition for purposes by no means sacred.

It is a shrewd folk tale in which enormous gusto is put into service of something more than a piquant exoticism. It reveals an ancient and still unself-conscious tribalism as it begins to pick up, without assimilating, the outward forms of a religiosity outworn in the civilization of its origin and alien to both worlds. The combination and contrast of both elements (European and African) are rendered both picturesque and funny, but one detects in Soyinka's treatment that he could easily transfigure the image that his play offers us into a much more troubled and disturbing picture. Here the colors are brightly laughable and the actors display them with gorgeous good humor and abandon.

With the exception of Harold Scott, who is a cultivated performer, the acting is professional only here and there, but it seems to gain something in this instance from its very lack of "polish." The whole is refreshingly likable.

The second and more ambitious play, *The Strong Breed*, is a tale of sin, suffering and expiation in peculiarly African terms. In this case the lack of adequate means in stage equipment, direction and unity of acting style muddies the impression of the play—mystic in essence—so that one cannot arrive at any confident appraisal. All one is sure of is that Wole Soyinka (now a political prisoner in Nigeria) is a writer endowed with a gift of speech that is both literary and true to the vein of the people he depicts. Soyinka's dialogue is not simply racy but has about it, without the slightest trace of affectation, a mountain-air cleanness and elevation.

—*NAT*, 4 Dec. '67

FOR TRUE TRADITIONS

The Little Foxes is a good show. No one gainsays that a good show is a good show is a good show—always to be welcomed. We have had them before and we shall undoubtedly have more.

Walter Kerr's comment was prompted by the fact that the Saint Subber-Mike Nichols production of *The Little Foxes* happens to be housed on the Repertory Theater of Lincoln Center premises. Neither the production nor its temporary housing has anything to do with the question raised. To think otherwise indicates a basic misunderstanding or ignorance of what is involved.

To begin with, the Repertory Theater of Lincoln Center hasn't been a repertory theatre for the past three seasons. Repertory is an organizational method for alternating performances of different spectacles on a more or less flexible schedule: one play for two nights a week, another for three, etc.

The repertory system provides theatre folk and public many benefits. But repertory as such is not essential to the making of what I choose to call True Theatre. A permanent company with a coherent and consistently enduring artistic policy is. The most valuable contributions to the theatre's history have been almost exclusively the creation of permanent companies from the time of Burbage's Globe Theater to the present. These companies have probably put on as many rotten shows as good ones. The point is that a permanent company sets up a tradition which becomes not only a source or inspiration and instruction to its personnel and public but lays the basis for future growth.

Such companies often outlive the genius of their founders. The Moscow Art Theater not only fashioned and perfected its own style but led to the formation of others in a contrary vein. The Berliner Ensemble is perhaps more active and certainly more prosperous now than it was during Brecht's lifetime. Such theatres may grow stale or expire from lack of new ideas and young blood but they are, if well conceived, rarely sterile. The occasional brilliant "package" we get very rarely has any issue.

There may have been productions in the Thirties as good or much better than *The House of Connelly*, *Men in White*, *Awake and Sing!*, *Golden Boy*, *My Heart's in the Highlands*, but the Group Theater has continued to exercise a real and I believe a beneficent influence while the "packages" of the same period, however brilliant, were good shows without further bearing.

As a director of the Group Theater and a greater number of "one-shot" package deals (*The Member of the Wedding*, for example), I hasten to add that I am for all possible activities in the theatre: new and old American plays, classics, musicals, farces, melodramas, Happenings, documentaries and propaganda shows—both native and foreign. A play is never old when it is brought to renewed life on the stage, nor is a play in the theatre something to be respected because it is a classic on the shelf.

To this day we have very little True Theatre in our country, and one of the main impediments to its creation is the lack of understanding as to its nature. Some folk are only concerned with enjoying the fruit; I am more interested in planting and preserving the tree from which good theatre may grow.

—*NYT*, 10 Dec. '67

IPHIGENIA IN AULIS

I regret not having seen Tyrone Guthrie's staging of *The House of Atreus* because from all reports it was a meaningful as well as an exciting experience. I say this because I have yet to see the production of a Greek tragedy in English which was not a little absurd. On two occasions—one of them at Epidaurus—I benefited by the pathos of distance: ignorance of the language in which the plays were spoken and the distance caused by the great space separating me from the stage.

Despite the disparateness of the various translations, I am nearly always moved by reading the Greeks in English, but I am rarely convinced on seeing one of their plays that I am witnessing anything better than a more or less estimable exercise. Euripides' *Iphigenia in Aulis*, directed by Michael Cacoyannis in an English version by Minos Volanakis (Circle in the Square) and unanimously praised, seems to me no exception.

Though Volanakis' translation possesses a straightforward dignity, I could understand no more than half of the lines assigned to the chorus. It struck me, moreover, as a company of high school girls weaving about in what are presumably pretty patterns of no clear meaning and, for the most part, totally without dramatic impact. We all know or, more correctly, we have all read, that the chorus of Greek tragedy moved in dancelike description, but such movements must have had some relevance to the play's basic argument or significance; if not they must have been as emptily ornamental as what we now behold.

The actors in the Cacoyannis production twist, turn and twirl because, the theatre being in the round (oblong, to be more exact), everyone in the audience must be given a chance to see their faces as often as their backs. But their gyrations struck me as senseless in every other respect. This is not inevitable on a circular or square stage surrounded on three sides by spectators. I was not aware of such distractions in other productions at the Circle in the Square; why should it be so for Greek drama?

Individually, the cast of the new *Iphigenia* is very well chosen. The men (Mitchell Ryan as Agamemnon, Alan Mixon as Menelaus, Christopher Walken as Achilles) are all handsome, virile-looking actors, with fine bodies and powerful voices. One hears everything they say distinctly, though I must add that while their resonance is gratifying their vocal register is limited. They speak on a reduced scale of notes, and being young they might all do further work to remedy this defect.

Jenny Leigh is an appealing actress of promise and Irene Pappas, who plays Clytemnestra, besides being a woman of splendid physique, impressive force and a strikingly beautiful "mask," makes good sense of her lines.

But speaking of masks, one encounters a problem. Greek drama, I am inclined to think, requires the use of masks not because the great size of the amphitheaters in which the plays were performed aided visibility but because there is something superhuman, beyond the common phenomena of earthly life in the very conception and writing of these plays. (In terms of mundane reality most of the Greek tragedies are ridiculous.) For contemporary purposes masks are perhaps not mandatory but a masklike feeling or appearance, something to raise the actor above workaday realism, is essential.

The three men in the Cacoyannis production vociferate a great deal, which helps to give their figures a certain much needed largeness of dimension, but Irene Pappas who acts more "humanly" by that very circumstance seems to diminish her role and the play's legendary scope. She is too much a "real" mother and can't be that to a truly effective or touching degree because the play's style and form defeat the "natural."

This despite the fact that Euripides is the most modern of Greek dramatists, the one whose "realism" and introduction of what we today call psychology in the theatre made him an object of mockery to certain Greeks of his time and the bête noire of Nietzsche in his masterful though perhaps "mistaken" account of *The Birth of Tragedy*. For all his "intimacy," in comparison with his dramatic forebears, Euripides is still thoroughly Greek, a classic in distress and very nearly in breakdown into latter-day protest and pathos.

The "psychology" in *Iphigenia in Aulis* is especially perceptible in the person of Agamemnon. He is accused of being hungry for power—as he very well may be—and he is caught in the toils of fate, which in this case means that he must yield to the pressure of his army which insists that he sacrifice his daughter, Iphigenia, so that it may advance in battle on Troy; he suffers a father's sorrow because of what he feels compelled to do, and is justified by Iphigenia herself, who sees in her father's action and her own death by his hand a triumph of a supreme value: the triumph of Greece. Thus we have elements of social motivation (and critical indignation), personal pain and patriotic fervor, commingled and very nearly at war with one another. This disturbed synthesis was precisely the innovation in Euripides, regarded as a decline by many of his contemporaries, as well as by certain living scholars and aesthetes, but a mixture which brings him closer to most of us.

Still, I repeat, for all his inner struggle with the religion of his state, Euripides remains Greek to the core. What exactly do I mean by this: what trait ties him to his tradition? In Greek tragedy everything is *paid* for. All action is honorable and, in one way or another, doomed. The most terrible destiny is necessary and by that very necessity redeemed. Beethoven asked himself, "Must it be so?" and answered, "Yes, it must be so." So it was for the Greeks, and for all his urge to deny it, Euripides in *Iphigenia in Aulis* accepts tragic destiny and pronounces it glorious.

—*NAT*, 11 Dec. '67

THE AUDIENCE'S JOB

I call it the audience's "job," because, though I hardly wish to suggest that theatregoing should be so onerous, I believe that even its pleasure may be enhanced by assuming something more than a passive attitude toward it. We go to the theatre for fun, yes, but even the fun we get out of a ball game or a tennis match is heightened by watching them with a knowing eye, a certain amount of discrimination.

There are roughly speaking three kinds of audience who go to the theatre nowadays. There is the professional audience—those who work on or around the stage. There is the conscientious audience—composed of folk who think they know all about it through contact with the professional audience. These first two kinds of audience tend to be articulate and often vehement about their reactions. They consider themselves a decisive factor in the making of theatrical opinion. Actually, when a play has been poorly received by the press, these audiences are not able to sustain a Broadway show for more than at best six weeks.

The third audience is what is sometimes referred to as the general public, not to be confused with the total population of any vicinity. At a bold guess this audience numbers a little over a million nationally: people, that is, who are more than occasional theatregoers. This audience, whose number I hope to see increase, is the one which keeps the theater alive.

I do not like to think of this audience as an inert faceless mass. I frequently find myself preoccupied therefore with thoughts about the means of addressing this audience as individuals outside the theatre. I would aim to instruct that audience in the "problems" of the theatre so much as to make it aware of the theatre's greater pleasure, its true glamour.

To this audience I would say first of all: do not

go to the theatre in either a challenging or lazy spirit. The play is not a contest or a duel: it is an invitation. Go to the theatre with the feeling that the actors and their associates are your friends, eager—indeed anxious—to please you. Most of them have trained themselves and worked hard to learn how to do so.

Too many people go to the theatre nowadays as if they suspected something was going to be put over on them or as if the play had to prove itself to them. I am myself considered a rather severe judge, yet I have seen very few plays some aspect of which I could not enjoy—a fine acting performance, an effective scene, a bright passage of dialogue, a lovely setting, an outstanding personality (sometimes in a small part), and I am always grateful for these gifts. I do not think as the curtain goes up: "Show me." I think, "I'm waiting for you—with flowers!"

The audience should put itself in a receptive state. But it should not be lazy. It ought not wander casually into the theatre expecting entertainment in general. The audience should select its entertainment and prepare itself for the play it wants to see. I recall a man some years ago who rose indignantly from his seat after the curtain had been up for five minutes saying "What! This show is a drama? I'm leaving."

The audience may acquaint themselves with the nature of the play they contemplate seeing by reading articles and reviews of it beforehand or better still by listening to the opinion of people whose interests and tastes they share. One should also discriminate among the reviewers themselves: the reviewer to trust is the one whose attitude toward life and the theatre is most akin to one's own.

To see a play well—that is, to get the most out of it—is a process similar in one's experience in meeting a new person. One is attentive and cordial. One observes, one listens, and slowly one arrives at a sense of the other person: he (or she) is interesting, amusing or wise. Perhaps knowing him (or her) will make a difference in our lives—warm, cheer or enlighten us. Perhaps one finds after the first contact that one wishes to know the person better, make friends. Perhaps one is both repelled and attracted: it happens with people, it happens in the theatre. Plays are rarely all good or all bad. I have often returned a second time to plays which at first troubled me, but which I felt might be rewarding on further acquaintance. Critics have changed their minds in this way—and erstwhile "flops" have occasionally been successful in revival. This has been the history of many of the greatest plays and even of certain musical comedies, *Pal Joey* for example.

Snap judgments in the theatre, as elsewhere, are not the best guides. You are under no obligation to make up your mind or have an opinion about a play in ten minutes or even after the first act, and I have known people, like myself, to wait until long after the performance is over to make an estimate of the play, which when all is said and done is almost the least important feature of theatregoing. You must treat the theatre *humanely*, because it is a living thing—and what it offers at best is a sense of human experience, the experience of writers, actors, directors, designers, which is ultimately part of your own.

Because the theatre can do this it is entertainment plus. Pastime is a good thing but what if pastime becomes exhilaration, inspiration, love. Is it then not something infinitely greater? That is why we should look forward to seeing a play with the expectation of a festive or stirring event.

It is not true that people do not wish to be moved or even, as the horrid expression has it, "made to think" in the theatre. We all want to be moved; if we did not we should perish of boredom in a world that would become increasingly unreal and indifferent to us. We all want to think—a phrase which should preclude the implication of pedantry—for when we say we are thinking we mean we are engaged in something of interest to us. That is why tragedy as well as comedy has been popular in every period.

All producers hope to present "hit shows." But from the theatregoer's viewpoint what may be a meat or ice-cream "hit" for one man may be a spinach "flop" for another. We still have individual tastes, I trust, and to go to a play because we have heard it is a hit is to say that what is good for the goose is good for the gander, and some of us, I suppose, do not wish to be confused with either fowl. One ought to choose and champion plays on the basis of a truly *personal* preference. Plays are not mass produced commodities. They represent individual voices addressed to individual beings and the relationship ought to have an intimacy beyond the pressure of any publicity.

This does not signify that I listen to no judgment but my own. On the contrary: I am delighted to hear what thoughtful and alert people have to say about the plays I see. I learn from them even when I disagree. I am stimulated to know and to comprehend more than I may have at first. If you are given to reading reviews of current plays, I suggest you go beyond reading reviews. There are excellent, even profound, books on the theatre. Try them. Serious discussion about the theatre may add immeasurably to your enjoyment of it. The man who *understands* has more rather than less fun. It is either snobbish cynicism or corruption to believe otherwise.

My ideal audience is attune, patient, friendly, keenly observant. It follows the developments in the theatre, its writers and actors particularly. It remembers the new talents which emerge every year and follows their progress. It does not become cold to a person for whom it has had regard when that person falters: artists cannot be at the top of their capacity at all times. (To behave as if they must is subtle slaughter.) This audience goes to interesting productions whether they are given on the main stem or in the purlieus. It comes to the theatre five minutes before curtain time; it tries to suppress its coughing. It remains decently quiet when it is not entertained and applauds vociferously when it is. It does not dash from the theatre when the curtain falls but stays to pay its respects and give thanks to the acting company. It does not pretend that a disappointing play is a crime, though it believes that a good one deserves our devotion.

It attempts to speak intelligently of the theatre instead of just gossiping about it. It will go to a play that isn't sold out, and will realize that if the theatre owes it a glowing sense of life, it in turn owes something to the theatre, beyond the cost of the seats.

—*MUS*, 16 Dec. '67

EVERYTHING IN THE GARDEN
PANTAGLEIZE

Everything in the Garden is important because it is the best of Albee's adaptations and because he is a man of distinct talent. The play is in large degree the work of a now deceased English writer, Giles Cooper, whose play of the same title I saw in London five years ago. Praise or blame must be shared by both. "The voice is Jacob's voice, but the hands are the hands of Esau."

The play is about a lower-middle-class suburban family, English with Cooper, American with Albee. Such a family is usually "comfortable" but perennially haunted by indigence. A foreign lady (possibly Hungarian in the original, English in the adaptation) arrives on the scene and insinuates to the wife that she can earn sizable sums by satisfying sexual needs of proper gentlemen while her husband is at work. At first outraged by the proposal, the housewife finally succumbs. Money begins to pour in; the husband discovers its source, and is ready to kill his spouse. Then he, she and we discover that all the neighbors and friends— husbands and wives—have improved their finances by the same means, accommodating themselves to the situation with satisfaction. When a playfully good-natured, wealthy bachelor becomes aware of what is going on, it becomes entirely possible (because he is a cynical drunk) that he will blab. The husbands strangle the playboy and bury him in the garden.

This is not as farfetched as it sounds: a newspaper item some years ago exposed a parallel instance in the borough of Queens. Cooper told his bitter anecdote in dulcet tones, with a trace of a smile, and one could take it with as much gravity or levity as one desired. The play's fault was that it was virtually over by the middle of the second act. Cooper concluded with a Pirandello-like discourse (out of context) which was as useless and unseemly as a sixth finger.

Albee's treatment is much more virulent. He makes the play a parable of the prostitution of our civilization. He begins quite skillfully. His dialogue is excellent: there are some keen strokes of observation. But as the play proceeds he gets angrier and angrier: the joke has become a scream; we are repelled.

This revulsion, combined with a refusal to believe, is not due to the violence of the play's premise or to its import, which are now clichés. But the dramatic presentation of this message— even in a sardonic comedy—should not be as pat and absolute as Albee has made it. The simplicity of *Everything in the Garden* is adolescent, and when you add grimness of manner to it it becomes false, if not offensively ludicrous. There would be no problem in life if everything were all bad: the difficulty arises from the fact that the beautiful and the damned coexist within each other. Realization of this is what makes both sharp comedy and strong drama. It also makes life interesting.

To clarify my slight preachment, *Virginia Woolf* is engrossing despite its venom because its people are not one-tone types, any more than are the characters in *Bessie Smith* or *Delicate Balance*. In *Garden* there are only stereotypes. These may still serve sound purposes if arresting notes are struck through genuine wit, eloquence or special insights. But such qualities are lacking in Albee's adaptation after the first third of the play. For a bit of constructive criticism, Albee would have done well to drop the murder, which makes the play too neat a syllogism. The man who knows the community secret would then become a mocking threat in a quizzically light-handed vein.

Barbara Bel Geddes has too gentle and warm a nature to engage in the business she is called upon to perform, but she always acts with such complete faith in her roles that one is obliged to yield to her spirit. With an actress of such innate enchantment it is perhaps ungracious to suggest she watch her weight.

The others give competent if routine performances, and Peter Glenville has directed according to the dramatist's specifications.

Michel de Ghelderode—even when exasperating—is one of the most original playwrights of our time; *Pantagleize*, written in 1929, may well be his masterpiece. One of Ghelderode's plays is named *Chronicles of Hell*, and that might be the title for the entire body of his work. He calls *Pantagleize* "a farce to make you sad." The hell of *Pantagleize* is an abortive revolution against capitalism and imperial power. It is a mad venture touched off unwittingly by a puny and sweet nonentity (or "imbecile") named Pantagleize. This wisp of a man is whirled along to his destruction by the absurd tides of a movement of which he is wholly unaware and to which he is entirely indifferent.

Pantagleize is a funny play but as grotesque in its comedy as Ghelderode's other plays are tragic and savage. If Genet had written it he would have called *Pantagleize* a "clown play." All the characters are creatures of a macabre fantasy, but their content is meaningful. They are a disaffected *avant-garde* poet, a wildly naive African house servant full of race hate and credulity, a nihilistic gangster who naturally joins in any destructive activity, a proud, beautiful and militant Jewess with hopes for the redemption of her martyred people. All these, along with the ministers of state, the bankers, the police, the military, are presented like figures in a frieze of gargoyles.

They are typical of Ghelderode's saturnine humor. It is "medieval" and very Flemish. Think of the paintings of Hieronymous Bosch in the 15th century and James Ensor in ours: they are insanely imaginative, distorted, frequently obscene, flushed with hectic color.

Ghelderode is profoundly Catholic, with a faith that verges on heresy. It sees little more in the world than a butcher shop, smelling of decay. The world is an inferno which only faith in God and the Christian injunction to love may redeem. On a first reading of *Pantagleize* the black man and the Jewess may strike one as indications of anti-Negro and anti-Semitic sentiments. (This impression is reduced in the drastically cut APA text.) It would seem that only such inferior people (not excluding the idiotic poet) are both the fomenters and victims or revolution. But the people they blow up are no better. All of us therefore are the broilers and the broiled of hell: that is man's fate in our sinful world.

Ghelderode stands outside politics. Revolutions miss the point. They can be true only if they effect a change of heart: faith in God who is that absolute love to which man can merely aspire and which he can achieve in no more than an extremely modest degree. Thus the most conscious and articulate among the rebels of the play, an educated man who has become a waiter, speaks of his "comrades—whom I despise a little while still loving them a lot." He accepts execution because, "Filled with hatred, I am unworthy to work for the ideal revolution." But none of us may ever be absolved, for "The triumph of noble minds will never come." Beatitude is conceivable only in the beyond.

Yet Ghelderode is fiercely attached to this world in all its foulness, torment and lurid discord. He "loves it a lot." That explains the kind of playwright he is. And that too is why he has written this epic farce of *Pantagleize*. The name is as odd in French, the original language of the play, as it is in English. It is my fancy that it is made up of two French words: *pantin* which means puppet and *glaise* which is potter's clay. This name itself is a clue to the play's style.

It was an act of courage, not to say foolhardiness, for the APA to undertake this fascinating and difficult work. They are not up to it. They provide a few visually exciting moments (a May Day parade just before a riot), and there is intelligence in the overall conception. But the acting is generally at a university-theatre level.

Ellis Rabb, who plays the title role and who with John Houseman staged *Pantagleize*, has been at times an effective character actor, as in Molière's *Scapin*. He is disastrously miscast in the present part. At best he resembles a director demonstrating how the part should be played. He looks and sounds like a sensitive college instructor, not the tiny kinetic clown whose range must be that of a Charlie Chaplin. Rabb hasn't the ebullient imagination, the Puckish freedom and the physical versatility the part demands. And as he fails, so do the others who to a greater or lesser degree remain unfunny and unstirring. Only a supreme actor, a splendidly flexible company and a great director could realize the magically horrendous and Rabelaisian theatricality of this play.

—*NAT*, 18 Dec. '67

A PLAYWRIGHTS' SYMPOSIUM

Reading this book of interviews I am reminded of an incident reported by an American painter some years ago at an artists' symposium. The American, entering a compartment in a French train, found himself taking a seat opposite Henri Matisse. Wishing to profit from the encounter, the American introduced himself to the master. The younger man wanted to talk about painting. Matisse's abrupt response was "An artist who speaks of his art should have his tongue cut out!" After which Matisse talked of nothing but painting.

Artists meditate on their art almost as much as they practice it. They question themselves endlessly about their work, their tradition, their rebellion against tradition, their public, their critics. Beethoven once asserted that he had never given a thought to anything any critic had ever said about his compositions. I don't believe it. Several of the playwrights in the pages which follow aver that, aside from monetary considerations, they don't care whether their plays are produced or not. I don't believe them.

The debate which the artist always engages in with himself is to some extent a debate he is carrying on with a hypothetical audience. In confronting his own work he is also serving the function of an ideal public and critic. For the artist is never a wholly isolated being. The audience is the artist's parents; it has bred him. He may fight the audience—as the offspring often does its parents—but even this conflict is a sign of their intimate relationship.

Though excellent things are said by all the playwrights whose words have been set down in this series of interviews and though they furnish certain insights into the speakers' personalities, one cannot make conclusive inferences about their work from what they say here but only from their work itself. "Artists," André Malraux says, "build theories about what they would like to do, but they do what they can."

Arthur Miller theorizes quite a bit; Albee suggests that he shut up. But Albee doesn't. He expatiates on subjects which are beyond his competence. As a private citizen he has every right to do so, but what he says in these instances has little to do with his status as a dramatist. "Being a writer," Albee goes on, "I don't think very clearly"—which is something of a howler. He amends the statement somewhat by later adding, "I'm not a philosopher. I'm a writer." Still further he makes his real point when he admits that "You get into these conceptual terms and I'm on very shaky grounds. I don't know what I'm talking about half the time."

These remarks apropos of Albee's interview are not meant as criticism. I am simply cautioning the reader not to take general statements by artists as evidence of what they achieve in their work. As Dürrenmatt remarks, "I hope I am interpreting myself correctly. We're often our own worst interpreters." Walter Wager's interviews are valuable in the impression they give of the circumstances and tensions the playwrights endure in the course of their careers.

They are all at different points of their development and generally come from diverse backgrounds. What Ionesco, for example, says both in his interview and his work is hardly relevant to Arthur Miller. Even when Ionesco speaks of Brecht one need not take pains to disagree with him, as I would if I took Ionesco seriously as a critic: one should regard his animadversions simply as additional strokes to his own self-portrait.

What is especially important to remark in reading these interviews is that none of the men interviewed is "finished." Their personalities have already become distinct, the lines of their career indicate a clear direction, but they are all capable of varying, extending, perhaps even of reversing their themes. It would be fruitless as well as presumptuous to predict their future. Ionesco's *The Bald Soprano, Jack, The Lesson* do not lead us to expect *Rhinoceros* and even less *The King Dies*. I once intimated that Pinter and Osborne had arrived at a dead end and indeed they had momentarily done so. I knew I had been mistaken when I saw the plays they had written shortly after I had published my unwarranted misgivings.

One thing all the playwrights here have in common: they are all contemplating the world of our day; each of them after his own fashion dramatizing his findings. Yet none of them, even those who may be called "socialists," is strictly political, a propagandist for a cause.

All are preoccupied with social issues, even Ionesco, whose typical and permanent character "Bérenger" reveals the writer struggling with the nemesis of our time: conformity. The contradiction within each of these dramatists between the reluctance or refusal to be placed squarely in any political category and the realization that his work may ultimately have social-political connotations is not only interesting but moving. It is from this inner conflict that some of the drama in the plays is born.

Arden, for example, says, "I think it is impossible to avoid being a political or a sociological playwright" and at the same time "Playwrights don't solve political problems. If I were to give the answer to *Serjeant Musgrave's Dance*, I would be the Prime Minister—and I am not." Dürrenmatt speaks of the writer's obligation to remain "an anarchist," to place himself between two stools. What all this means is that these dramatists are keenly aware of the complexity of every problem, that they shun simplistic solutions.

Willy Loman is as much an American archetype as Babbitt. To have created Loman is not enough for Miller. His conscience urges him on to something like a messianic posture. I do not mean to suggest that he conceives himself to be a savior but that he is impelled to see his people as actors on the stage of history. In *The Crucible* he deals with mass hysteria and the heroics of resistance to it. There is also a personal note in the play: the sense of guilt the main characters suffer for their own failures in private conduct, a motif repeated in *A View from the Bridge* as well as in *After the Fall*.

There is a semi-autobiographical story in the latter play and an "historical" one. The attempt to combine the two elements has aroused much discussion. Miller seems to be castigating himself for those very characteristics of moral fervor for which he among others once prided themselves. What Miller may be interpreted as saying is that in both personal and other respects he and his like are often self-deluded. Though undoubtedly on the side of the angels, other motives—an appetite for power, self-righteousness, sheer sensuality—often muddle the wisdom and strength such men imagine themselves to possess. They end by injuring themselves and betraying the innocent.

The reaction to *After the Fall* is one of the most curious phenomena of our recent theatrical history. The play didn't simply disappoint many people, it angered them. Miller was accused of having come into a court of his own devising as the guilty party and managed so to arrange the "trial" that he might leave it as a hero. This was in large measure due to the fact that his former wife, the late Marilyn Monroe, was the recognizable model for the girl the central character of the play marries.

There may have been more personal bias on behalf of Marilyn Monroe on the part of those who objected to the play on *this* ground than there was

impropriety in Miller's use of his experience.

A more cogent criticism was made by those who felt that in *After the Fall* Miller was abjuring his early social position, that he had "defected." Whatever our opinion of the play, it does not alter the essential character of Miller's particular bent. He still insists on the imperative of an individual responsibility in the social context. He has only complemented the theme with the admonition that such responsibility misses its aim when the person who exercises it fails to recognize elements of self-deceit in his own presumed moral action. This is an injunction to moralists to practice more honest self-examination and humility.

The Miller canon is given a new form in *Incident at Vichy*, his most compact play, almost classic in construction. It is fashioned as a sort of devotional tablet. Once again compassion is shown for human weakness while our mutual guilt in social misfortune and personal responsibility in combating it are ever more desperately proclaimed.

The austere intensity in Miller's work is that of the impassioned preacher. His passion leads him to the point of poetry. He arrives at it not through what is called the poetic sensibility or through a command of language but through his rigor in pursuit of wholeness.

In considering Tennessee Williams, America's most prolific playwright, so much emphasis has been placed on the sexual aspect of his work that its more general relevance is frequently over-looked. *A Streetcar Named Desire* and *Orpheus Descending*, for example, are more than studies in unhappy personal relations. They are also depic-tions of environments which distort character, places where the lack of cultural nourishment produces bigotry, brutality, madness, a persistent depression of the human personality.

The immediate locale is usually our Southland. This is Williams' native ground; his choice of that setting is particularly appropriate because the symptoms just named are most readily observed there. But they extend beyond that region and are evidences of an endemic disease.

Tennessee Williams does not accuse; he describes. The social atmosphere of his plays is dramatized through characters in whom the social disorientation is mirrored in the frustrations of their love life. This is not the same thing as an obsession with sex: sex in Williams is the focal area at which the deeper trauma reveals itself.

From these premises stems the essential trait of his work: identification with and compassion for victims of our society—the outsider, the shamed, the forsaken, the condemned, the ostracized. He sees such people poetically, at worst sentimentally, never bitterly. He is ambiguous about Stanley Kowalski, certainly a destructive force; yet we sense a certain attachment in Williams' portrait of him. Williams' touch is tender and not infrequently humorous. This is most evident in *The Glass Menagerie*. His thoroughly malevolent characters—the politician and his son in *Sweet Bird of Youth*, the husband in *Orpheus Descending*—are his least realized ones. Lynchers are unseen or only momentarily glimpsed.

The half-light in which Williams' stage seems to be plunged, as if he were writing of secret places of half-sinful and half-sacred sentiments, gives his plays their theatrical glow and appeal. There is a romantic mysteriousness in Williams' treatment of his characters, as if he took a peculiar pleasure in sharing the shadowy world in which they dwell. He is no stranger to their plight. That is why sometimes—as in *Sweet Bird of Youth*, for instance—he overestimates our possible interest in them.

With all this, the puritan streak in Williams is strong. It is present in his characters' constant hankering for salvation, the promise of pardon. He doubts that they will ever achieve a state of grace or what form it may take. But the yearning gnaws at them, as in *The Night of the Iguana*, and there is the abiding hope of understanding and consequently forgiveness.

Death haunts Williams' imagination. This urges him to press on ceaselessly beyond the limits of his past achievements. There is in him the ever summoning challenge to exceed the bonds of realism. His *Gnädiges Fraulein*, as his earlier *Camino Real*—incomplete as they may be—the symbolic strain in all his plays, including the least successful one, *The Milk Train Doesn't Stop Here Anymore*, are signs of this. The impulse suggests possibilities of further development.

When Williams wrote his one "straight" comedy, *Period of Adjustment,* he appeared to be invading William Inge's province. Inge has written a series of comedies about folk less sophisticated in every respect than Williams' characters. The highest in social rank among Inge's people is a dentist. His characters have no pretension at all except the near farcical ones of *Where's Daddy?*

Inge has never been abroad. He writes about simple small-town Midwesterners and writes about them simply, never condescendingly. He is the dramatist of the ordinary. With considerable theatrical acumen he writes sparely. In cold print, his plays strike one as meager, but they take on body, color and dimension on the stage. The weakness in his work, it would seem, is his too obvious Freudian leanings. But to confine one's observation to this trait would be even more banal than the initial objection.

Inge's talent lies in his sympathy with and organic understanding of his people. His light touch and straightforward plots, his clean drawing and avoidance of plumbed depths in no way impair the honesty and livingness of his situations and characters. They are quick and engaging through Inge's kinship with them, and they all tell us as surely as any other American dramatist of their rootlessness, their child-like bewilderment, their profound but hardly conscious loneliness. Inge is a popular writer who has earned box-office success, but he is not a "commercial" playwright. His plays are the expression of a healthy though perturbed spirit, committed to close and kindly observation. They are tender without slush and are forever redeemed from mawkish simple-mindedness through the forbearing grass-roots humor in which Inge invests them.

There are excellent character sketches and poignant scenes even in his less successful plays,

Natural Affection and *A Loss of Roses*, plays which were either improperly focused in the writing or misrepresented in production. That Inge's plays never attain tragic heights or strikingly "original" insights follows from the modest goals he sets himself.

Edward Albee's *The Zoo Story* struck a key note for the American theatre of the Sixties. The alienation of his "permanent vagrant" in that play is not the metaphysical sort to be found in the European dramatists of the Fifties. Albee's savagely frightened folk are severed from even those shallow roots which still hold the people in Williams and in Inge. Albee's people, whether we find them on a college campus, a prosperous suburb or a white hospital, stand naked within an horizon more barren than the empty landscape of Beckett's *Godot* or the mound in which Winnie is sunk in his *Happy Days*.

Whether a bum like the boy in *The Zoo Story* or "cultivated" people like those in *Who's Afraid of Virginia Woolf?* and in *A Delicate Balance*, all his characters are "primitives." They appear to have no past to sustain them or future to which they aspire. The world around them has been consumed in the author's scorn. In the final moments of the last-named plays they are waiting to be born. It is as if they were survivors of some devastation of the moral order and they were too stunned to express anything but a grotesque outrage. They hardly know to what universe or society they belong, the old having been so decimated that their memory apart from ache and disgust has become fragmentary, leaving them without sufficient energy to reconstruct anything new. This is not resignation but spiritual immobility in which the only signs of life are venomous laughter and tremors of hysteria.

Albee has a sharp stage sense, writes acerbic dialogue which ranges from the vernacularly humorous to a tone of disquiet elaboration. His emotional and intellectual range is limited as yet. There is much still to be looked for in scope of subject matter and feeling. But there are evidences of growth.

Dürrenmatt, many of whose plays are still unknown to us, is a dramatist whose work may be said to stand somewhere between valid artistic expression and the virtuosity of showmanship. He might also be described as a popularizer of the *avant-garde* theatre. He has a nose for the topically contemporary, a sense of the modern convulsion. He dramatizes the crisis of the Western ethos in melodrama, satiric allegory and parody. There is something shrewdly synthetic in his work. It is always very clever and frequently more theatrically effective than the dramatic sources from which he borrows, and he borrows from everywhere: the German expressionists, the French existentialists, the Theatre of the Absurd, Pirandello, Brecht, even Mark Twain! He is the Swiss banker of the European dramatic market. He knows how to make negotiable coin out of other people's gold ore. His craft will never fail him even if the winds were to change.

Peter Weiss is a dramatic journalist keenly aware of major issues. He has a remarkable editorial gift in adapting political events and ideas to the stage. His first two plays—*Marat/Sade* and *The Investigation* (the latter an arrangement of trial testimony—a document rather than a play)—mark sensational beginnings.

He is unique among the interviewed playwrights in declaring himself unequivocally a socialist, more inclined to the East European brand than the Western.

Despite the very strong impression his two dramatic essays have made, one cannot yet speak of Weiss as the creator of an original vision. It is true, however, that *Marat/Sade* posits an age old question in a novel manner and that in doing this Weiss has infused the German stage with an enlivening current. He has contributed a special spur of energy which apart from Brecht (whose writing antedates the postwar years) only a few other men—Frisch, Hochhuth, Grass—have thus far done. One looks forward to further manifestations of Weiss' verve.

Ionesco, still poorly represented in New York and not at all likely to become a dramatist for the general public, becomes ever more sympathetic. His range is narrow because his temperament and ideas permit him little more than the improvisations of dramatic metaphors and images. Still most of his short plays and parts of others are surprisingly suggestive and intriguing. Ionesco represents the modern European adrift in a troubled sea. He smiles despite his inability—it may be an unwillingness—to imagine any hope of arriving at a safe harbor. He is a comically pathetic clown of contemporary confusion.

He is sympathetic because for all his obfuscations, his anarchic playfulness and occasional forays into areas of terror, his more recent work, beginning with *The King Dies* and *The Pedestrian in the Air*, reveal a wry tenderness, a shyly desperate clinging to life, an affirmation despite itself. Ionesco yearns for freedom above all. That is why he so insistently balks at the didacticism he finds embodied in Brecht. There is something infantile in this. Still his sense of wonder, his refusal to be held in line by any rational ideology express themselves in odd fancies and stir us to liberating adventures of the spirit. His plays at their best are like mirages sparkling in the dark night of our existence.

Because much of Osborne's output, most of Arden's and Wesker's and even Pinter's (whose *Birthday Party* has been mounted only in regional or university theatres) are still unfamiliar to many of us I treat them as a group, though they do not constitute a "school" of any kind.

The only thing they have in common is their historical position in the English theatre. After the emergence of Noel Coward during the Twenties the theatre in England went into a sort of eclipse as nearly total as the period between Oliver Goldsmith and Oscar Wilde. T.S. Eliot's dramatic ventures are experiments in the "translation" for the popular playhouse of what he had already said far more valuably in his poetry. Christopher Fry furnishes a bridge between the old and the new, though his plays come to us appareled in romantic habiliments. With Osborne, Arden, Wesker and Pinter the England of the past ten years really takes stage center in feeling, in subject matter, in manner.

Osborne is the first to have struck the note of rancor, of satiric or unhappy rejection, generally of disillusionment with the new England. "Everything has changed and nothing has" might serve as the epigraph for Osborne's early plays. The welfare state may look different from yesterday's England, but it is still locked in inhibitions and pretenses more threadbare than the old, which at least possessed the glamour of confident power.

Apart from the first brave gestures of defiance (tempered by melancholy in *The Entertainer*), one isn't certain as Osborne moves on from play to play—nearly all of them interesting—that he has struck any conclusive chord, made an entirely decisive statement besides the sound of discontent. His restlessness, imprecations, blasphemies testify to his versatility. The one sure merit of his plays consists in the embodiment not only of his own sense of oppression but that of a generation dissatisfied and angry without clear aim or positive program. His invective is brilliant, his affirmations troubled and nebulous.

Wesker's initial realism brought the working class onto the London stage as a central subject rather than as colorful background. There is an authenticity of portraiture in his early plays which transcends any propagandistic purpose. He gives us a picture of humble working-class people trying to find themselves, to grow. They create an image of birth in difficult circumstances unfamiliar to the large theatregoing public.

Wesker's latest plays show him groping toward further statements and new forms. What is healthy in him is that he always proceeds from his own associations, the meaning which he attempts to assimilate beyond his subjective perspective. His purview is national.

Arden's turbulent talent approximates genius. He is a volcano whose eruptions vary in substance rarely forming themselves into complete structures which may be readily surveyed. A critical estimate of his work as a whole is therefore problematic. His power is nevertheless unmistakable. We are reminded of certain aspects of O'Casey and O'Neill. He is erratic, shaggy, inchoate at times but always vibrant with creative energy. He is prolific and no doubt my hesitation in "placing" him is due in part to ignorance of his latest plays. One may safely say that he is a *temperament*: one is eager to become acquainted with all its facets.

Pinter has already achieved a certain mastery. He evokes a realm of nameless tenor where no value or identity is substantial or secure. He congeals our bewilderment and anxieties with dramatic images which are usually both funny and horrifying. No matter how puzzling or obscure we may find him we are always conscious of his firm hand: one is convinced that he at least knows what he is about. The strangeness of his method—based on melodramatic suspense—matches the mystery of his message. Pinter's curious imperturbability repels, fascinates, above all imposes. One always watches and listens.

Are any of these playwrights *great*? That is a question college boys and critics who are like them are prone to ask. When it refers to our contemporaries it nearly always strikes me as irrelevant. The playwrights presented here are all men still struggling with the dilemmas of our time. Their goals are consistently serious, they are persevering in craftsmanship and they show a degree of skill worthy of studious attention. That is why I have chosen to speak of them here with positive emphasis.

—Introduction, *The Playwrights Speak*
by Walter Wager, 1967

THE RELIGION OF HAROLD PINTER

Though Harold Pinter has written seven plays and several film scripts I am tempted to cite him as representative of the silent generation.

None of his plays articulates a clear message. It is doubtful whether their author intended them to have any message at all. They are constantly and determinedly ambiguous. That is one reason why certain critics insist that they are "phonys."

Certainly they are irritating. But some of their value and meaning may arise from the irritation they induce. Pinter's plays are silent in that they do not seek to explain the phenomena they set before us. Pinter does not pretend to understand them himself. Like dreams their implications are manifold.

Yet their language and imagery are specific, based as they are on the banalities of contemporary English life. This mixture of the non-realistic and the most commonplace details written with a remarkable ear for the particular speech of different classes and arranged in skillful patterns of melodrama is another reason for the confusion these plays cause. But it is in this combination of elements that their originality lies. That is their contribution to the theatre of our time. Pinter has admittedly been influenced by Samuel Beckett but he has brought something entirely his own to the initial impulse Beckett inspired.

Why is Pinter "silent," and does his silence amount to no more than a trick? It is horror that has rendered Pinter silent: he is aghast, painfully puzzled. One might trace this state back to his early youth. A Jewish boy in a London East End neighborhood bristling with Mosleyite (fascist anti-Semite) thugs, Pinter had to face them with a show of fearlessness. He was afraid but by preserving a cool demeanor—a very stiff upper lip—he managed to get by unmolested. His injuries were internal.

Such subjective data does not suffice for critical purposes. Pinter is "uncertain"; and when one is in that condition one had best keep quiet or assume a degree of evasiveness. Pinter sees himself in a world without values. "God is dead," patriotism is for fools, family relations are shattered or threadbare, politics are hypocritical, sex is marred by its own and surrounding insecurities. Yet we go on using the names and symbols for all these things as if they were valid. What is mere shadow play or fraud is conducted as if it possessed real substance. In the meantime, there is adultery, crime, war, and all manner of moral and physical havoc. How can an aware person make sense of such a world?

To say there are no values left is to subsume them. How would a man without values be able to recognize one? The assertion that our world is without values or that they have all been so compromised as to have become indistinguishable from "publicity" is, in effect, to protest on behalf of values residual in our heritage or grasped by intuition. They are adumbrations of an insistent wish or a hope one hardly dares name. One laughs a bit for clinging to such illusions. One becomes reticent to the point of inarticulateness at the thought of any faith in the old discarded or discredited beliefs. Commitment to any of them is rejected lest one be duped anew. This leads to the discipline of a negative honesty (at least one avoids deception) by withholding any positive declaration which has not been tested by experience and to which one may subscribe with genuine conviction.

Paul Tillich once stated the case of the generation caught in this "Pinteresque" dilemma. "The god," Tillich said, "who is absent as an object of faith is perceived as the source of restlessness which asks the question of the meaning of existence." Folk who find themselves in this case—and they are legion—are all waiting for Godot!

That there is a moral, indeed a religious, aspect to Pinter's work, though he never gives it out as such, may be discovered by a study of at least two of his plays: *A Slight Ache* and *The Caretaker*. In the first of these, a middle-class gentleman is haunted by the sight of a Matchseller who has chosen to post himself outside the gentleman's home on a quiet country lane. No one ever buys any of the old man's matches or gives him alms. Yet rain or shine he remains standing on the road without word or gesture, persistently mute even when directly questioned.

May not this bedraggled figure represent the crude facts of existence itself which the English gentleman tries unsuccessfully to shut out of his mind though they cause him "a slight ache," while his wife responds to the beggar with an instinctive embrace?

May not the still more shabby, definitely nasty "caretaker" in the play of that name embody Man himself, unable to fulfill his duties to tend the house into which he has been invited by a young dreamer so sensitive that shock treatment was once administered to him to make him more "sensible." Despite the caretaker's wrongheadedness, his ingratitude and constant complaints in relation to his benefactors who finally want to remove him from the premises, we feel pity for him because he may forever remain homeless if compassion is withheld. His final words are an outcry, "What am I going to do? Where am I going to go?" in logical congruity with the play's plot but which is also the metaphysical and ultimately religious query we all ask ourselves.

These interpretations are put as questions because I am sure that if Pinter were asked his opinion of them he would reply, "They are interesting," and say no more. I once did ask Pinter if the young musician at the end of *The Birthday Party* were being dragged off to an insane asylum. "Maybe so," Pinter answered. "What is important is he is being *taken away*." The unlikely "hero" of *The Birthday Party*, Pinter's first full-length play, like the lady of a certain American play, counted "on the kindness of strangers" and he is, as was the lady, "taken away." This is certainly the conclusion of an anguished moralist who refuses to be caught sounding like one.

Pinter's *The Dumbwaiter* is a "mystery" play suggesting the misery endured by humble folk through the cruel enigma of existence, in the preserve of a "boss," "governor," or ruling force the identity or nature of which has not been disclosed to them. On the other hand, *The Homecoming*—both naturalistic and abstract in form—is Pinter's most acrid comedy in which the mania and mockery of a world where one thing is said and its contrary done so that action as well as consciousness are reduced to a brutish level. If this is not the vision of an outraged moralist I hardly know how else it may be designated. The "trouble" with this moralist, through shrewd caution or scrupulousness, is that he wouldn't dream of admitting to the role. He persists in preserving a poker face lest a bitter smile which might turn into the contortion of anger or a heartfelt sob disturb the image of his dispassionate irony.

—*DIM*, Winter '67-'68

WE BOMBED IN NEW HAVEN

It has all been Americana for me since the 5th of December, Americana of all shades, stripes and shapes.

To begin with, there was Joseph Heller's *We Bombed in New Haven*, done as part of the Yale School of Drama Repertory season. This is young generation Americana, flippantly derisive and at times quite funny. The fun is not as sustained as in the author's novel, *Catch 22*, and is largely visual in the lively production under Larry Arrick's direction. A good team of actors is most helpful, notably Ron Leibman as a humorously atrabilious sergeant and Anthony Holland as one lunatically eager to replace him. The play's general idea is the obscene pointlessness of military routine and action.

The second act gradually turns to pathos. Here the Captain, well played by Stacy Keach, is obliged to send his own son off to be killed in air combat. In this play, the men thus condemned to death are chosen and known in advance. None of the play is projected as "realism" but as the presentation by actors presenting themselves as both characters and actors—a device which for the most part succeeds—and is called Pirandellesque by folk who think by tags even when, as in this case, the tag is wholly inappropriate.

Most of the audience felt that the second act was a "let down." I found, on the contrary, that its final scenes gave the play a unity it needed to be something more than a series of gags. The situation of a father being forced to sacrifice his son (a role well played by a student actor, Stephen Mills) is a stereotype, but here it is ingeniously handled. And there is an ironic touch at the last curtain in which Stacy Keach asks the audience to contribute to the Will Rogers Fund for tubercular patients.

Two aspects of the play and production interested me particularly. A theatre audience, I have found, is quite willing and able to leap from high jinx to pathos, with no naturalistic bridge between. It is resilient and will play any game theatre artists have in mind, provided each segment of the piece is well contrived. The fact that many members of the New Haven audience failed to respond to the play's last moments indicates that some impediment prevented them from lending themselves to the play's avowed sentiment.

This leads to the second aspect of the play's "problem." The son asks his father why he hadn't done anything to prevent the war, not just before its outbreak but from the boy's birth. The question, a pointed one, is unanswerable because it is "revolutionary." So revolutionary indeed that it demands an altogether different kind of play. Heller's charade and others of similar caliber, despite their "subversive" intention, don't breach our inertia or awake anything in us beyond a mild assent which is little more than complacency at our own inept liberalism. The day of satire which *hurts* has not yet arrived.

—*NAT*, 1 Jan. '68

SONG OF THE LUSITANIAN BOGEY
ST. JOAN

On the many occasions when I have referred to organizations that exemplify "True Theatre" I have had to turn either to the past or to foreign instances. Today I am pleased to note that the recently established Negro Ensemble Company at the St. Marks Playhouse is, or may well become, a True Theatre. Its small permanent company has worked together in training and in performance before the rehearsals of its present and first production. It has a determined policy, its spirit is fervid, its announced choice of plays testifies to the nature and direction of its goals.

The Ensemble will offer four productions in its 1968-69 season, beginning with the current *Song of the Lusitanian Bogey* by Peter Weiss. Though not a conventional "play," but a social tract in a sort of cantata form with passages spoken by individuals and in chorus, dramatic interludes, sound effects, songs and interjections of straightforward information, its performance by five men, four women and four musicians creates in the end a stirring evening.

Neither the text nor the direction is "Brechtian." Brecht is a dramatist, and in this case Peter Weiss does not propose drama in the accepted sense. He has written a recital of facts concerning the Portuguese colonies (mainly Angola), written them in prose and verse which finally impose themselves by the sheer force of their factuality. Weiss's "argument," I am glad to say, is one-sided. One cannot and should not have any doubts about the barbarous cruelty and injustice of the Portuguese presence in Africa or for that matter, about any domination of one people by another. The indictment is not merely against a particular government; Weiss makes it abundantly clear that all governments, or at least all vested interests (industries, banks and certain capitalists) which are influential in their respective countries, are guilty. Ultimately we ourselves are to blame.

I doubt that the strong effect would be achieved—though the argument might still be convincing—if Weiss's text were only read. It is created by the powerful voices, the immense personal dedication of the Negro Ensemble acting company. It is through the actors as a unit—attractive women, men strikingly virile—that the performance becomes theatre. And this acclaim should extend to the musicians and the designer, Edward Burbridge, who has made a set which resembles a tribal totem pole, modern in the vein of the new sculpture, both savage and funny. Michael Schultz has directed to give variety and tang to what may have appeared heavily static on the page. The entire evening is a statement of real force and makes me look forward to the Ensemble's next production, a play by Wole Soyinka who is more truly a poet and dramatist than is Weiss.

Man for man, the actors in the production of Shaw's *St. Joan* at the Repertory Theater of Lincoln Center may be superior to those of the Negro Ensemble, but the production, though by no means bad, is not of one piece. John Hirsch's direction is knowing—he understands, and generally speaking conveys, the intention of each scene and personage—yet I came from the production with little better than a reminder of what a good play *St. Joan* is. It still "holds up"!

Shaw wrote wittier plays, but hardly any in which his temperament and the material furnished him by history were so happily conjoined. In *St. Joan* Shaw revealed something of the child that was in him, for all his cleverness and intellectual capacities, together with the tremendously earnest, understanding and honest puritan he was. The puckish, shrewd and yet somehow "artless" child in Shaw contributes as much as do his ideas to converting his forensics into theatre. An innocence in the playfulness of Shaw's works preserves them against the possible decay of their preachment. And in Joan herself—the image her story evokes in our minds—Shaw found a character ideally suited to his courage, persistence, his certainty of being in the right, his swift and forthright disputatiousness. Like the Joan he portrays, Shaw commands esteem through a candid common sense akin to a mystical trust in life and human destiny. Even Shaw's sexlessness reinforces one's intuition that the dramatist's union with Joan was a blessed one.

A few adults may demur at certain aspects of the play (the first scene, for example, strains toward farce), but youngsters and the pure of heart will always respond to it. If you have never before seen it you should certainly see it now, and if you have seen it before—as I have countless times—you will still like it a lot. I say so at this point because I must now proceed to another phase of my critical duty.

The setting for *St. Joan* by David Hays has a background of slim metal columns circularly arranged. Their height suggests both a cathedral loftiness and the steeliness of medieval warfare. The forestage, where all the action must take place if it is to be fully visible, consists of a number of polished platforms of uneven thicknesses and dimensions. The main properties (throne, table, chairs, etc.) are put in place by costumed supernumeraries. In brief, the setting has a fitting bareness and yet seems to serve the play rather meagerly as a machine for action and as atmosphere. I was aware of "scenery" with a touch of spurious modernity.

Michael Annals' costumes are extremely good-looking, but they are more like plates from an illustrated book of period design than clothes. They are too gleamingly new and rich. The effect is that of a dress parade, and Joan's costume in the cathedral scene is wholly unflattering to the actress' figure—especially in relation to her head.

Diana Sands's Joan has its moments. She is superb in her breakdown during the trial scene and most powerful—gutsy rather than exalted—in her denunciation of the sentence to imprisonment following her recantation. In those passages the actress is wholly in her element. But her speech has not the sharp, crisp stamp of Shavian rhetoric. (Joan was no peasant, the dramatist takes pains to tell us, but a bourgeoisie.) Miss Sands's manner of address is that of a perky maid and not of Shaw's heroic and highly articulate Maid, who at all times speaks the splendidly sane prose of a great statesman. (The play falls short of greatness because the writing, though wonderfully lucid, rarely rises to the pitch of poetry.) Miss Sands fails to achieve the cleansing nakedness and proud loneness when, after the Coronation, the Crown, the Church and the big brass abandon her.

Of all the Joans I have seen, only two seemed to me thoroughly adequate to the challenge of the part. One was that of an actress in Israel, a gentile German girl who had fought in the underground against Hitler and later in the various Israeli struggles; the other was Sybil Thorndike in the first London production. (She was a Fabian Socialist, with some of the wholesome asperity of Shaw himself.)

I mention these actresses not to depreciate the performance of Miss Sands, whose qualities of vibrant strength and pluck I admire and whose undertaking of her present role constitutes a step forward in her development but to emphasize what I have already said about the Negro Ensemble and True Theatre in general.

If a production—especially its acting—is to achieve an artistically communicative entity, it must not only be professionally adept or an assemblage of outstanding talents; it must be lit by a moral energy, a fire that transmutes these talents to a new consistency of idea and belief. That is what gives great theatre its ritual significance. It was present in the early days of the Moscow Art Theatre, in the Berliner Ensemble, in the finer work of the Group Theatre. One also sees it occasionally in a musical where the identification of a homogeneous cast with the material dealt with composes all the details into an exhilarating meaning. Some people found it in *Oh What A Lovely War* and a few of Joan Littlewood's other productions in London's Theatre Royal at Stratford East. It happens now, as I have indicated, in the *Song of the Lusitanian Bogey*.

It does not happen in *St. Joan* because that is not the product of a true Theatre—an aesthetically or ideologically unified company. Yet a word of praise should be said for several of the cast: for the humor of Edward Zang's Dauphin, the pleasant personalities of William Hutt as the Earl of Warwick and of Philip Bosco as Dunois (though both performances are too soft, lacking the soldier's mettle). Mention too should be made of the "masks," voices and demeanor of Tony Van Bridge as Cauchon, Roger De Koven as the Archbishop, John Heffernan as the Inquisitor, Stephen Joyce as Brother Martin. All these, together with the direction, the sets, the costumes, may be accorded some degree of credit, but they do not fuse. Missing is the overall passion of an organic theatre idea to contain and inspire them. For this reason they are not capable of winning our inner assent and are sustained only by the substance of Shaw's capital play.

—*NAT*, 22 Jan. '68

EXIT THE KING

Exit the King (a literal translation of the French title would be *The King Dies*) is for me the APA's most satisfying production: it is in fact a good production (at the Lyceum).

There have been more ambitious APA productions (*War and Peace*, *Pantagleize*); some have been more immediately engaging (*You Can't Take It With You*); some have been somewhat more evenly cast (*The Show Off*); but Ionesco's *Exit the King* seems to me its most complete realization of a dramatist's intention and scenic idea. Ellis Rabb as director has understood the play thoroughly and has found the right means to project it concretely.

The APA production is superior to the one I saw in Paris, though Jacques Mauclair who played the King there and directed it conveyed a childlike pathos that was most affecting. I saw the play again in Warsaw where the director, an intellectual who had a literary understanding of the Theatre of the Absurd, did not know how to direct. In London, with Alec Guinness playing the King in a production staged by the admirable George Devine who did so well with *The Chairs*, the heavy-handed performance conveyed very little. Guinness seemed more concerned with his own characterization than with the play's essence.

Exit the King is Ionesco's most sympathetic work. *The Lesson* and *The Chairs* are perhaps more original, in the sense that they bear the unmistakable stamp of the author's personality. *Rhinoceros* is more acceptable to a wide public—more "entertaining"—but *Exit the King* is the most

integral expression of the playwright's inner being. It is also the closest to our own usually unavowed trepidation.

Ionesco has an ineradicable preoccupation with death. Unlike the Spaniards, it haunts him, not as something majestically awful but almost as a child trembles at the unknown dark. His fear is more akin to a universal bewilderment than to the perception of death so commonly transcribed in literature as something ominous, mournfully, hero-ically tragic, or just crushing. Americans usually evade or gloss over the subject altogether.

The treatment is extremely simple. The King who is dying in this relatively short play is Berenger, the name Ionesco gives to most of his little men, the non-hero. He is not Everyman but Anyman. He exists only for himself; he is central to everything he beholds. In a wonderful passage he is told that he "invented gunpowder and stole fire from the gods....He discovered the way to make steel ...he made the first balloon, and the zeppelin....He built Rome, New York, Moscow and Geneva. He *founded* Paris. He created revolutions, counterrevolutions, religion, reform and counterreform...." To which the King's maid observes, "You wouldn't think it to look at him."

How does His Majesty react when finally convinced that he is going to die, as the Queen remarks, "at the end of the play"? He cries out: "Why was I born if it wasn't forever?...I came into the world five months ago. I got married three months ago." He didn't learn or accomplish what he should have: "I never had the time, I never had the time." He is outraged, inconsolable, amazed and utterly at a loss to conceive of the mystery and meaning of his existence.

The play is a beautifully written dramatic poem. Funny, unrealistic and altogether real. Is it therefore a tragedy or yet another black comedy? The paradox and *charm* of the play are that out of his despair, and perhaps to his astonishment, Ionesco has written a hymn of praise to every instant, event and ordinary phenomenon of life. In a delicious exchange, the King bids the rather downtrodden housemaid to describe her daily routine. The details are drab, but he finds rapture and excitement in each of them. The girl concludes, "a bad life, Sire," to which he replies, "Life can never be bad. It is a contradiction in terms." We must learn to appreciate everything— even to the color of a carrot. In brief, a frightening and lovely play, an inspiration.

Richard Easton is excellent as the King: foolish, terrified, his eyes full of startled incomprehension. He moves from an absurd effort at pride and grandeur to the puling impotence of a sickly baby and again to the recovery of strength in the contemplation of the glory he seems to have missed.

Eva Le Gallienne, the Queen, is all hard reason and an oracle of disaster. The actress' velvet voice and ever-present aspiration to nobility take on tones of tartness and severe irony I have never heard from her before. Pamela Payton-Wright brings plainness, not without humor and buried enticement, to the role of the court chambermaid.

The point to be made clear about the production is not the total success of any of its constituent elements but the soundness in the conception and execution of the whole. This includes Rouben Ter-Arutunian's setting in electrically silvered cellophane which contributes to an atmosphere of lightness within a realm of shades. The "picture" has the bare look of an expiring world where creatures once men have turned into wraiths.

Exit the King may not find as much favor as have other APA productions this season: its theme and form may encounter resistance. But the intelligent playgoer must not fail to see it.

—*NAT*, 29 Jan. '68

THE PRIME OF MISS JEAN BRODIE

With *The Prime of Miss Jean Brodie* (Helen Hayes Theatre) we are clearly in an area of intelligence and good writing. The script which Jay Presson Allen has derived from Muriel Spark's novel is adult entertainment.

I say "entertainment" because I am not at all certain what the real point of the play is and, not having read the novel, I cannot say what its larger intention may have been, if it had one beyond that of depicting a curiously interesting character. Then too there are faults in the production which diminished my pleasure.

Miss Jean Brodie is a Scottish schoolteacher in a conservative secondary school for girls in Edinburgh. At 35 or so and of rather prim appearance, she is bursting with a womanly energy which gives her considerable amorous capacity and attractiveness. She cares little for the strictly academic curriculum; her ambition is to influence her pupils in the appreciation of the sensuous charms of Boucher's paintings, the romance of *La Traviata*, the excitement of Italy, the grandeur of such leaders as Mussolini, Franco and Hitler, and the enthrallment of the sensual life. She wants to stamp her creed and personality permanently on the souls of her students.

Miss Brodie has courage and enormous will. She yields to her sexual drive but refrains from marriage with a timorous colleague. She encourages dalliance in her wards. She abhors Catholicism. She is a Fascist, though she rarely speaks of politics except in epic terms. Being an unconscionable romantic, she does not realize the gap between her convictions and her behavior. She arouses either unbounded admiration or rebellion, but never fails to impress. She is destructive and absurd, drawn here as a comic figure with pathetic overtones. As a fierce egotist, she must finally fail, for the truth is not in her.

One might suspect that Muriel Spark (if not Jay Presson Allen) had in mind a Catholic travesty of Protestant self-deception. But we should not press this interpretation. Her design has broader psychological implications and the play at least does not probe very much beneath its ironically humorous surface. It is sufficient for the occasion.

The production suffers from overemphasis. Michael Langham has directed it with sledgehammer insistence on what the script itself makes abundantly evident and readily enjoyable. Zoe Caldwell, endowed with unusual faculties for vivid projection which include a voice of refined power, great inner force, a natural gift for theatrical delineation, and a healthy sense of fun, is a brilliant actress. But her portrayal of Jean Brodie is much too stressed and studded with obtrusive detail. Even the personage's plainness is overdone by an unbecoming wig and unneeded exaggeration in makeup. Miss Brodie thus becomes freakish. The actress could have gotten twice the effect with half the effort. Proof of this is offered by her best moments in the final scenes, when Miss Brodie, bereft of illusions and her job, becomes simple and touching.

Her earlier overexertion may have been due in part to first-night nerves. Still, other performances—particularly those of some of the girls—showed similar strain. And why, I wondered, did so many of the cast during a large part of the evening stare out front into space? Why also was Jo Mielziner permitted or required to design an abstract set with no trace of atmosphere, a set which doesn't even please the eye?

Lennox Milne is authoritative as the head mistress; several of the children are individually appealing. None of the actors is responsible for the production's limitations. The direction is miscalculated. But for all that, it is certainly superior to most of the season's offerings.

—*NAT*, 5 Feb. '68

THE NEW YORK CITY BALLET
THE INDIAN WANTS THE BRONX

I always enjoy seeing a "bill" at the New York City Ballet. It stimulates me to return: every fine ballet company does. Ballet is the best theatre in town. Balanchine's "Japanese" number *Bugaku*—some of it strikes me as exquisitely Hindu—has an insidiously fragile attractiveness what with David Hay's ascetically pretty set, Karinska's ineffably delicate and smiling costumes and the asymmetrical eroticism of the choreography by way of Suzanne Farrell's long-legged knowledgeability.

I find it difficult—as everyone should—to "judge," that is to declare an opinion of a new ballet at a first view. One doesn't altogether grasp the design of the unfamiliar choreography or hear the surprising (if novel) score. But even without "seizing" either aspect of Balanchine's latest two-part piece of strange title *Metastaseis* and *Pithoprakta* (music by Xenakis), I was sufficiently taken with it to wish to see it again. One doesn't have to know immediately what one thinks of them or what they mean; they have a fascinating look and sound. Judgment, if at all necessary, should come later. The enigma is a pleasure. What amiable frauds some of our dance sages are!

I was amused by those at the opening performance of this ballet who hissed because either they didn't "get" it or because they failed to be ravished on the spot, as they expect to be when that dear devil Balanchine goes to work. I was also bemused by those whose decided opinions were instantly available as if the purpose of art were to furnish an exercise for their insight. The new ballet is a graph of "life" as it impresses a contemporary sensibility, but who can quickly decipher its exact nature or give it a name?

Seeing Jerome Robbins' *The Cage* for the third time—it is a ballet one can readily comprehend, and that may be what is wrong with it—I appreciated the subtle excitement of Stravinsky's String Concerto in D, probably neo-classic if you need a category, but all Stravinsky and irreducibly modern in its tension. Patricia McBride danced in place of the indisposed Melissa Hayden. Miss McBride doesn't "horrify" as the lady spider is supposed to do; she enchants. What a treat it would be, one feels, to be destroyed by her!

As for John Taras' new entry *Haydn Concerto*, I liked the scenery and costumes of

Raoul Pène duBois very much: so serene and gracefully gay. As for the rest it didn't disturb me; I could take it or leave it. As someone much more expert than I in these matters remarked, "The Greek pieces are *avant-garde*, the Haydn is *derrière-garde*."

Israel Horovitz's *The Indian Wants the Bronx*, a one-act play preceded by another, *It's Called the Sugar Plum*, from the same author, merits a visit (Astor Place Theatre). The two plays are ably directed by James Hammerstein and very well acted by Al Pacino and Matthew Cowles in the first named and by John Pleshette, nicely paired with Marsha Mason, in the second.

These plays have the ring of authenticity. *It's Called the Sugar Plum* begins well, goes on a bit too long in respect to its aim and tries to cover too much ground: a youthful fault. But it is a humorous and kindly observation of the grubby and foolish sexuality characteristic of the hip young, nurtured on a sophistication derived from total ignorance and which expresses itself in the verbiage of pop psychoanalysis. The general effect is of a penny-whistle idyll.

The Indian Wants the Bronx is sterner stuff. It is funny and terrifying. Two young fellows harass and mortify an innocent Hindu (they think at first that he might be a "Turk") while he waits for a bus on a deserted city street at night. (Why, one wonders, doesn't he run away?) The boys' malevolence is "play": a consequence of their idleness in an environment empty of any fulfilling contact or purpose. They are not evil: they are stinging bugs produced by the dry rot in the wide fringes of the social structure. They produce shivers because their menace and violence are part of the greater beastliness inherent in our society, which, because it does not inspire creative action based on humane thought and energy, turns to wanton and senseless destructiveness.

The actors in this play brilliantly reveal the incipient ferocity born of moral isolation that can be observed in persons who still possess some of the charming folly of untrammeled youth. In the opening play it is innocence coupled with schooled dumbness that the actor conveys with apt ease.

Horovitz's writing of *The Indian Wants the Bronx* demonstrates a perfect ear for the speech of his two punks. He is not slumming: he has made himself part of their spirit. But like other playwrights of his generation (those between 21 and 30), he should not dwell too long or too lovingly within that sphere; it is narrow and shallow for lack of a more complete understanding of the world outside it. That world may be equally ferocious, but it is nevertheless the *world*, and all of it must be explored to make art splendid and life worth the strife.

—*NAT*, 12 Feb. '68

THE OPEN THEATRE
LES BALLETS AFRICAINS

Look out for the Open Theatre! According to a recent announcement it is "a group of approximately thirty-five: directors, actors and playwrights, who have been experimenting with new theatrical forms for the past five years. From time to time it has given informal programs of improvisations and short plays in various off-off Broadway houses. The off-Broadway productions of *Viet Rock* and *America Hurrah!* grew from our work...." The signatories of this statement are the troupe's director, Joseph Chaikin and Jean-Claude van Itallie, the author of *America Hurrah!*

Though its heart was in the right place I was not enthusiastic about *Viet Rock*, produced independently two seasons ago. I admire the *Motel* episode of *America Hurrah!* which is still running at the Pocket Theatre on Third Avenue. Last week I attended an evening at the Village Gate of songs and skits given as a benefit for the purpose of providing the company with the means to accept an invitation to appear at various European theatre festivals. I paid for my tickets and enjoyed what I saw.

Pleasure was aroused by the company's spirit. It had dedication and vigor. Someone suggested that it promises the recrudescence in the sixties of the "fervent years" of an earlier time. Maybe so. It is, at any rate, a healthy theatre expression of the moment. What its eventual destiny is to be is a matter of conjecture. The theatre, though composed of individuals, does not depend on them alone but on a complex of external circumstances.

The Open Theatre is not literary; it stresses the purely theatrical: sights and sounds, movement, acrobatics, a kind of juvenescent festiveness—not quite "Dionysiac." It is motivated by social as well as histrionic ardor. Besides the songs, rock and roll anti-war doggerel (of which I could not distinguish the words, though the sense was clear enough), the benefit program consisted of pantomime, improvisations and two playlets, one by Ionesco and another by Brecht. Most of this was aesthetically raw but full of Village verve. The effect was tonic.

What is the "message"? Apart from reaching for "new forms"—none of them actually new but a departure from the commercial commonplace—what is revealed are some of the basic tensions of the day. The first number, for example, was a silently rhythmic exposition of our impulses toward fraternity or at the very least the sensory contact people naturally desire to have with one another, followed by an even stronger loathing of proximity. Changes were rung on this motif, for instance in the actors' pleasurable awareness of the audience and then their equal animosity toward it, or again the hope for release from anxiety through exhaustion in unbridled fun and games: in short, the polarity of mutual attraction and revulsion.

Another was a mock doxology with the WASP minister invoking love for man and God while enjoining both to rip the guts out of our enemies. The congregation's "amens" echoed the clergyman's prayer, dutifully or with barely repressed profanities, while an obscene epilogue of almost impersonal sexuality ended the scene.

Later on we were shown synoptic dramatic structures which impugn the male adequacy of our population and the consequent quasi-spastic gyrations of its womanhood. Events were celebrated in songs of dazed sadness accompanied by exhaustingly jittery trances.

Ionesco's skit *Foursome* is an epigram exemplifying the pigheaded hostility within the human species that leads it to battle over often absurdly trivial causes which are utterly forgotten in the ensuing slaughter. Brecht's *Clown Play* is a pantomime illustrating the progressive dismemberment of "Mr. Smith"—little Everyman—to the tune of circus jingles.

In short we are living in a murderous world of shattered nerves and fractured faiths against which we can cry out with lusty imprecations and take hope in our still vibrant capacity for protest. Our very curses, the actors of the Open Theatre seem to be saying, bear witness to our innate appetite for life. They "dance wildly to keep their balance." The Open Theatre's motto might be the line from Aeschylus: "Shout, ye people, the chanting is done."

The actors mix with the audience, join them at their tables (if any), but best of all they throw themselves into their tasks with considerable bodily abandon. In this respect they are children compared to the young folk in certain of the newer theatres in Czechoslovakia and Poland, but then these Americans haven't the facilities for training afforded the stage aspirants of those "backward" countries. The Open Theatre actors signal something *good* taking seed in and out of our theatre, but to grow they will have to develop an authoritative voice, one or more dramatists to give their speech coherence and their thrust effective aim. Otherwise they will remain augurs without artistic issue.

The Open Theatre is one rivulet of a current in dramatic entertainments and demonstrations in the streets, meeting places, union halls and the like. None of this is altogether indigenous with us although it recalls fairs and frolics around campfires, in saloons or boats of our virtually forgotten past.

Les Ballets Africains in a limited engagement at the Mark Hellinger Theatre brings us the real thing from French Guinea. Their ritual dances and festive folklore are the fruit of an age-old tradition. They are truly of the land and of its people and not of a formal boxed-in art we call "theatre." Theirs is a tribal expression which sprang into being in their fields, hamlets, town squares and streets, dating from ancient times down to the present day. At *Les Ballets Africains* we are allowed a glimpse of the theatre's roots as one reads about them in history books or at lectures in drama courses.

What a riotous evening! I cannot say whether the overwhelming exuberance and physical endurance of the company are due to aboriginal racial traits or to these combined with extraordinary practice plus the particular endowment of the participants, but I don't remember ever before having seen such a display of fiercely exultant agility. Here we witness wild excitement, a great rough sweetness, a constantly bounding and bursting drive of irrepressible human energy. The frenzy of our bands, discothèques and dervish hippies are kindergarten merriments compared to this Ensemble Artistique et Culturel de La République de Guinée. The color is amazingly varied, running a gamut from primitive ceremonial dress to the more recent modes—rich and poor—or the encroaching industrial habit.

All this bespeaks a rich, turbulent, still intact nature in vocal and instrumental sound. One seems to hear the hourly voices of the dawn, the dusk and the night, the ululation of strange birds and beasts, the hissing, chirping, cooing to us of unknown fauna which are familiar and almost domestic to the singers, musicians and dancers of these African scenes.

There is no "composition" to them, no center or aesthetically conceived focus. They were not designed for the stage as we know it. they are meant to spill out and to spread through a neighborhood, a country horizon. Go, be astonished and learn there is still lava under the earth's crust and that some of it still courses in some folk's veins—a fact that should awaken us from our lethargy and make us rejoice.

—*NAT*, 11 Mar. '68

OVERTURE

As we approach the final weeks of the season there will be comparatively little for me to review till next fall. You will nevertheless be hearing from me every week during the remainder of the spring session and through the summer when I shall be visiting and investigating many of the world's theatre capitals. But since this piece marks my re-entry into this journalistic area from which I (along with many others) was ejected last May with the precipitous demise of the *World Journal Tribune*, I take this opportunity to establish certain premises of my future writing here.

In stating some of the principles or attitudes which will inform my future reviews I do so in full awareness that principles are one thing and deeds another. D.H. Lawrence once said, "The artist usually sets out to point a moral and adorn a tale. Never trust the artist, trust the tale." It is quite possible that my reviews of particular plays may make hash of my theoretic postulates, but reviews should imply conscious standards, a more or less definite point of view.

A reviewer's basic tendencies ought to become evident after a series of his notices (let's say a dozen) are read. If this isn't so the reader is in trouble who looks to the reviewer for any sort of guidance or illumination. The person who tells you only what he likes or dislikes without suggesting a groundwork from which his preferences or rejections spring leaves one in the void. To say of a play "I love it" or "I hate it" hardly gives a more tangible clue to the reviewer's thought process and even less idea as to the chemistry of what is being endorsed or denounced than if he said "I love lobster" or "I hate chicken."

It is almost an insult to a critic to say that you like his writing because you agree with his opinion.

The Spanish essayist Ortega y Gasset tells us that "writers who have nothing more to convey than praise or dispraise of works of art had better abstain from art." A critic is not a dictator or even an arbiter of taste. The critic should describe, explain, evaluate the *nature* of what he sees to enable his reader to understand the object described and judge the quality or trend of thought the critic represents.

The pressures of theatre production in the U.S. have become so onerous that the function of play reviewing has become distorted. Producers, playwrights, actors, directors and the public want to know immediately—and they seem to want to know hardly anything more—whether a show is a smash or a bust. The reviewer ends by responding in kind; he cultivates a vocabulary which makes his stuff read like a fever chart. A review, in common parlance, becomes a rave or a pan. If it is a "mixed review" (not a "business notice") the effect more often than not is fatal.

Notices during a season follow a pattern very much like this: The season opens around September 25; on, let us say, November 2 someone will write about "the best play of the season"; on January 27 another review will proclaim another show "the first great play this year"; on March 10 we will hear that still another is "the dramatic tops"; April 10 one hears of "a play never to be forgotten," and by May 31 the author or authors of these slightly hysterical encomiums will conclude that on the whole "it has been a lousy season."

Enthusiasm is one of the sentiments that the theatre should engender, but the rave review is generally not so much an expression of genuine feeling as a prop of publicity, a shortcut to the box office, a flattering word (usually suggestive of a limited capacity in the use of language) and a prologue to a capsule condemnation no more justified than the initial frothing at the mouth.

Such writing substitutes gush or bile for discrimination. Criticism is the conscience of art. The savage slam often does little more than gratify the deep-seated hostility immanent today; it offers one more opportunity for malice or loathing.

The rave review—like the ensuing blast—corrupts both criticism and the public. It is the rotten fruit of the theatre's artistically and commercially unhappy condition. It bespeaks no love for the theatre. It is a rush of blood to the head like the impassioned declaration of eternal devotion that an adolescent boy or a tipsy gent addresses to a credulous girl which nine times out of ten leads to disgust or divorce.

I have too much regard for the theatre to *rave* about plays and actors or to wish to assassinate them. I know how difficult it is to produce, write, act or direct a creditable stage piece: how difficult and how rare the occasion. In all its history the theatre may not have brought forth more than a hundred *great* plays. And *great* actors have probably been even less common.

With this in mind you will expect me to be grimly severe. On the contrary, I am receptive to all honestly conceived and skillfully accomplished work (even when faulty), receptive and most attentive to what a play has to communicate. I ask above all that it be something more than a commodity. Plays are respectable solely as testimonies to the joy and travail of humankind.

From high tragedy to low comedy, from Aeschylus to Happenings, there is no form of stage spectacle I reject. Should I call a play "good" or some such adjective nowadays considered lukewarm or dismissive—and even such words will be infrequently employed because they are not specific—I hope no one concludes from their use that I believe a play not worth whatever absurd price is demanded next season for the theatre. There is a vast area, in which most plays belong, between ecstasy and vilification.

An artistic standard is always rooted in a philosophy of life. (Don't let the word scare you.) Do I have such a "philosophy?" I'm not at all sure that what I believe can be qualified as such. But if I have one it rests on four pillars: I believe existence to be essentially irrational but I also believe that man must use his reason (with due recognition of its limitations); I believe that men may not be perfectible but that they must act as if they were; I believe that man may not possess free will but he must behave as if he does; I believe life terrible—and grand.

—NY, 8 Apr. '68

IT'S ALL RELATIVE

On Broadway we don't ask how long a play will last but how long will it run. More solemn thinkers who have heard a play praised will occasionally demand some assurance as to the play's longevity. I was once challenged by a student at a lecture I have at a midwestern university in which I had said laudatory things about Bernard Shaw with the question "But will his work endure?" Somewhat off guard I blurted out "Why does it matter to you?"

No doubt the response was frivolous since the question may have indicated a regard for the highest artistic standards. Yet on further reflection I began to find validity in my answer. The theatre is an art of the moment—the precious moment with its infinite reverberations. We live in history but we do not live historically. The girl we love is the girl we love: it would be folly to ask ourselves if our love is as profound as Dante's for Beatrice.

I remember seeing George Kelly's *The Showoff* in 1924 and not only being entertained by it but impressed. An unpretentious comedy, it teased our prevalent delight at the time in the success of fraud. (Everyone knew our Mayor Jimmy Walker was a crook but we thought him wonderful just the same because of it.) For some of us *The Showoff* like most good comedy possessed an ominous undertone: if that idiot who gives the play its title could finally "make it" how shabby were our values, how doubtful the efficacy of ordinary common sense or humdrum honesty.

On seeing *The Showoff* in the A.P.A. revival this season I was less entertained than I had originally been. I was all too conscious of the cumbersome carpentry of its craftsmanship. The play now seemed thin and rather obvious. Was I wrong then to have thought so well of it in 1924; was it immaturity which had previously misled me? Not at all. The play seemed extraordinarily relevant, eminently to the point in those golden years.

If I am now much less taken with it (though a large body of playgoers still relish it, in part because of their fondness for Helen Hayes) must I consider my past judgment a critical error? The paradoxical proposition that suggests itself is that a "bad" play may also be "good"—not only because it is momentarily enjoyable but because it is temporarily valuable.

Criticism of the arts is a subtle matter and theatre criticism trickier than any other. The effect of a play is instantaneous and the first consideration as we see it is the amount of pleasure it affords. The pleasure may be of various kinds; to begin with we should not reject any of them. there is, first of all, this to remember: a play *in the theatre* is not simply a verbal text, it is also and largely a stage spectacle. *King Oedipus* poorly played may prove a bore or simply ludicrous while *The Lady of the Camellias* ("Camille" to the uninitiate), greatly acted, may move us deeply.

Danton's Death, a classic in Germany, is a play of very considerable stature, but I cannot blame the audience at the Vivian Beaumont theatre three years ago which found it a dud. Giraudoux's *Tiger at the Gates*, both charming and significant in most productions, struck me as amorphous fluff in its revival at Lincoln Center.

Plays change their character for us because we change—and we change because the climate of the time brings about our alteration. I have to some degree begun to doubt that endurance is an impregnable criterion of excellence. I don't mean by this that plays of the past are to be glibly dismissed as "dated." Many of them are more alive than all this season's prize winners. The fact that the wars in Shakespeare's histories cannot be equated with the conflict in Vietnam does not rob them of their force. Nor need we find merit in *Iphigenia in Aulis* solely through discovering a parallel between Agamemnon and L.B.J.! But we must insist that *in the theatre* as distinct from the printed page a play is "good" which speaks to us directly, stirs senses, touches our hearts or stimulates our thinking.

There are, as I ventured to guess in this column last week, perhaps not many more than one hundred *great* plays in all the theatre's history. I hasten to add that I wouldn't care to see a company undertake to present them all if they couldn't be appropriately, not to say, magnificently produced—a consummation hardly to be expected. Produced at the wrong moment in an unworthy manner great plays become less potent—even as art—than presently admired work which in a few years may cause us to wonder what provoked our enthusiasm in the first instance.

Whatever estimate we put on such a play as *The Price* (I liked it) I believe it is more important for me (and you) to appreciate it now than to glow over the grandeur of some reputed or real masterpiece presented as a museum exhibit by a company remote from its substance for an audience in the same condition.

To say that a play is good (or bad) is to say almost nothing at all about it—except as favorable or adverse publicity—unless we make clear to ourselves (or, in the case of the critic, to others) what it is good for (or why bad), what it does to us today and perhaps tomorrow. As for plays which are supposed to endure forever (how long is that?) those who come after us will have their say and they will make almost as many "mistakes" as we now do. The plays that may be set down as worthless in the year 2000 may be very good ones today. All we can hope to do is to try to keep our sights clear as we face them now.

—*NY*, 15 Apr. '68

THE MERITS OF MR. MILLER

Discussing Arthur Miller, author of the current hit The Price, *in these pages last week, Albert Bermel, theater critic of* The New Leader, *argued that the playwright "has not discernibly grown since* Death of a Salesman *and* The Crucible." *Bermel further contended that Miller's heroes do not make decisions based on wisdom and reason but rather on feelings and impulses. He asserted that, far from challenging audiences, Miller "tells audiences what they want to hear." Here, a famous director and critic replies.*

In Bernard Shaw's comedy *You Never Can Tell*, a well-educated man, when asked if he thinks a proposed marriage is unwise, replies, "Yes, I do: All matches are unwise. It's unwise to be born; it's unwise to be married; and it's unwise to live, and it's wise to die." To which the gentleman's unlettered father interjects, "So much the worse for wisdom."

In Arthur Miller's *Incident at Vichy* an Austrian nobleman, Von Berg, offers to sacrifice his life for the Jewish doctor who will certainly be sent to the concentration camp and probably to his death by the Nazis. Von Berg is an esthete: he despises the Nazis in the first place because they are "vulgar." He possesses almost no political insight. When he comes on the scene he is hesitant, embarrassed and on the whole rather unaware of the depths of Nazi depravity. His sudden impulse to self-sacrifice is "unwise."

Von Berg, unlike Chris in *All My Sons*, never preaches. He acts through a rush of feeling which he doesn't question. What he does is not at all "sensible" but we understand its reason.

Shaw, more gifted in ratiocination and argument than Miller, employed reason to justify the irrational—something he associated with Henri Bergson's *élan vital* or life force. Miller, with less philosophy, is similarly motivated. His people often behave like fools but are driven by emotions or instincts they do not comprehend. We, however, understand them.

By temperament Miller is a moralist, even a puritan. In a somewhat different context I once wrote, "The puritan conscience is a complex phenomenon...Even the pursuit of righteousness and truth to a thoroughgoing puritan seems an aggressiveness [of pride] which is itself not wholly innocent...In all his plays Miller gives evidence of wanting to move away from himself in this regard. It worries him that he sits in judgment, that he is placing himself in a position to which he believes he has no right. It is as if Miller felt himself a Reverend Davidson who anticipates and desires his own 'humbling'."

I now retract only one statement in this passage. Only Miller's later plays reveal this trait of self-doubt. In one instance it becomes self-castigation. This turn in Miller's work alters the form of his plays since *All My Sons*. That play and the one that preceded it are conventional realism. *Death of a Salesman* and *After the Fall* tend to reach beyond a narrow naturalism, while *Incident at Vichy* and *The Price* follow the classic model— unity of time and place—and in their continuity and density of action take on qualities of parable.

A close look at Miller's text may cast a new interpretive light on his work. Willy Loman is certainly no "hero." He is surely no "man who seeks or finds the right way to live." In having Loman's younger son Happy say at his father's funeral, "Willy Loman did not die in vain. He had a good dream," Miller is clearly adding an ironic character touch. If the circumstances were different, it would be comic. For Happy has learned nothing from the family tragedy just as Willy's suicide is the climax of his own absurdity. The dream which ruined Willy was to be a success in all the ways which were alien to his nature. Willy's merit is that he was a honest craftsman— he was good at making things—but he bought the latter-day American dream which is to make oneself "well liked" by storing up a pile, riding an expensive car, having one's name in the papers, etc., etc.

Loman has displaced his *self* in an almost universally prevalent falsity. He commits suicide so that his son Biff may have a chance to make good, in other words, to succeed in the same misguided path which has blighted his own and his family's existence. Happy, in contrast to his father, plans to "make it." The "ideal" for which Willy lived and dies, Miller shows us, is a disastrous one, consequently not at all one he asks us to admire.

Carbone in *A View from the Bridge* cannot conceivably be regarded as a "hero." The play is a study in shameful rationalization. A jealous man betrays another and justifies himself on specious grounds: patriotism, horror at homosexuality. Miller's puritan streak—though it is something more than that—consists of having Carbone finally desire his own death: he cannot live with his own lie.

There is a parallel in *The Crucible*. It is chiefly a study in mass hysteria in which superstition conspires with self-interest to incite a society to destructiveness. Proctor accepts death not only as an act of moral defiance but also because he suspects himself of guilt: "lechery."

The change which I detect in Miller (and on the whole it marks a progress) is caused by the tension of an uncertainty in him. I have never believed that Miller proposed to exonerate Quentin in *After the Fall*, or in any way succeeded in doing so. Quentin in that play has always struck me as less honest and likable than his two wives. The play is a moralist's accusation of self-deception and duplicity. Quentin has pretended—with little more than maternal encouragement and a "good head"—to act like a scion of the "holy family." He discovers his fallibility and since the "judge's seat" is empty (there is for him no God to whom he can appeal) he vows, despite the whole world's callowness and brutality, to point no self-righteous finger at others; he must himself first find his way back to a truth which his inner being can substantiate in action. That is *his* morality. It is also new for Miller. The moralist in him now dictates "Put up or shut up."

Does Victor Franz in *The Price* unequivocally assume the status of a hero or a victor? His behavior is hardly "reasonable." He has given up an opportunity for a good career to aid a father he knew or suspected was by no means an exemplary figure. He clings to a deeply rooted feeling that he was bound to act as he did though it may have been "unwise." Miller's sympathy is clearly with Victor, but if he "sides" with him it is not without painful doubt. That is why some folk leave the theatre with the conviction that Walter, the "selfish" brother, is in the right and Victor is indeed a failure.

The play is so written, the ending so understated that its "lesson" is to some extent undetermined. The audience takes the furniture man Solomon to its heart: he is the common citizen, the honest man without pretensions. He is the mediator who sees both sides of the question and is therefore endowed with wonderful humor, the kind of humor that endears him to all of us. It is just this trace of ambiguity—forgoing his earlier dogmatism—which is significant of Miller's development.

More vital than this to an appreciation of the play is that, while it may be well-liked, it also disturbs. It disturbs because it is not exactly what we want to hear. In so far as Miller "irrationally" insists that we follow the rule of responsibility beyond our own immediate or egotistic interests, whether it be the family, a social group or ideal— and all these may also be our *ideals*, representative, in other words, of our professed beliefs—the effort to do so troubles almost more than it reassures us. Most of us are ready to act with a sense of responsibility only when it is easy or convenient.

We live in a world which by its operative custom persuades us to follow Willy Loman's dream and to assent to Happy's apparently ineradi-cable will to imitate it (Goethe said, "You think you're pushing, but you're shoved.") Deny it though we do, Success as the measure of a man still shapes our way of life, and only a memory of another, more ancient faith, and our continued pretense that we abide by it, makes us resent facing the fact that we are doing nothing of the kind.

The power of *The Price,* and it is powerful despite the triviality of some of its details, is that whether we "stand" with Victor or Walter an issue crucial to all our lives is unmistakably posed. Those who "agree" with Victor's self-sacrifice are rendered disquiet because they do not actually live as he has; those who are inclined to Walter's practical mode of thinking are troubled by the suggestion that they are being accused and require defense. *The Price* stirs even those in the audience who may not be "pleased" with it. It pierces our vital centers. That is why some weep and others say, as they did about Willy Loman, that they have a cousin, an uncle, a brother-in-law just like Victor or Walter but very rarely "like me."

Miller's resolution, even under the pressure of some of his own misgivings, to hold fast to a traditional morality is against the grain of our times, against much of our contemporary literature and drama which willy-nilly celebrate cynicism, negativism, collapse, or a comfortable unconcern for responsible ideas sustained by action. This resistance to our souls' sloth dramatized through the humble folk of our land and time defines Miller's signal contribution to the American theatre of our day. About the stage effectiveness of Miller's plays there is no dispute. Our audiences and those from London to Tokyo testify to it.

To point out that Miller is not the equal of Ibsen is irrelevance. It is also an evasion of duty to what is real, immediate and needed in our country and in our lives presumably on the basis of an absolute esthetic purity in which none of us who goes to the theatre dwells or should dwell. Our heirs will draw up the balance sheet—and even they may not be "right."

—*NYT*, 21 Apr. '68

OFF-BROADWAY EXCURSION

I have been impressed recently by the quality of acting in off-Broadway productions.

This in a sense is an insulting observation. As Edward Albee pointed out some years ago when he first made his mark with *The Zoo Story*, *The American Dream* and *The Death of Bessie Smith*, the distinction between an off-Broadway play and a regular uptown production to the detriment of the former is stupidly invidious. It is also vicious. It is a mercenary distinction merely: what you pay little for can't be much good; what is small and publicly obscure can't be important.

The unfortunate circumstances under which most off-Broadway enterprises operate should not make us forget that we owe the re-establishment of *Summer and Smoke* (with Geraldine Page), *The Iceman Cometh* (with Jason Robards) and *The Threepenny Opera* to off-Broadway effort. In addition to the Albee plays, off-Broadway has brought us such provocative pieces as Gelber's *The Connection*, David Rayfiel's *P.S. 193*, William Snyder's *The Days and Nights of Beebee Fenstermaker*, most of Genet, Beckett, Pinter and Ionesco, and if we are to include the American Place Theater in the off-Broadway category, Robert Lowell's *The Old Glory* and Ronald Ribman's underestimated *Journey of the Fifth Horse*, to name only those which I recall at the moment.

It looked for a time as if the rising costs of production were totally to destroy our theatre's safety valve (which is what off-Broadway is) as they have played havoc on Broadway itself. The economic pressure on our theatre generally, with the consequent curtailment of all ambitious production (except for musical comedy) which seems to be leading the "commercial" theatre to extinction, has caused a double reaction: many actors, directors, designers, to some extent even playwrights, have taken to the so-called "regional" theatres (isn't Broadway also a "regional" theatre?!) as well as to university groups. There has also been a renewed spirit of activity off-Broadway extending to the cafes, cellars, lofts and churches, still further "off." Once again we hope for fresh energy from the "underground,"

The acting in *You're a Good Man*, Charlie Brown is of the simplest kind but no less pleasant on that account. It depends on a lack of self-consciousness on the part of the young cast, which is nevertheless more adult than the children they play. The atmosphere created is one of good will and innocence without coyness.

Bill Hinnant as Snoopy is charmingly impish, mildly and thus attractively discontent, at once resigned and resentful, being too adaptable to small comforts and freedom from responsibility beyond cute obedience to rise to rebellion. Hinnant's acting has the most studied characterization as well as the most technical deftness in conveying it. But the others are not far behind in winning our smiling sympathy.

With *Hamp*, the English anti-war play (to designate it in this way is only a matter of identification, not a true description), we reach a more demanding level of acting. One of the things to be noted here in passing is that though all but one of the cast is American, the actors' speech is sufficiently British to fit the occasion.

Most important in this instance is the touching inarticulateness of Robert Salvio as the central character, Private Arthur Hamp. Quite apart from the north country accent employed (which Salvio manages remarkably well), the role is particularly taxing. Hamp is a less than "ordinary" person, indistinguishable except for his inferiority from any other nondescript British soldier. He is not only uneducated but intellectually primitive. He is without the endowment of the most rudimentary words and the capacity for coherent thought: an innocent out of ignorance. A thoroughly good being withal, a blind human soul, he is altogether bewildered, lost in the maze of the army mechanism. He is not only incapable of saying what he feels, being all dumb trust, but he barely knows that he is feeling anything at all. It is we who must feel and speak for him. He himself appears to be making an unduly strenuous effort to bring his experience to consciousness. We seem to be present at the painful mutation of animal life to the human state.

One might expect such a character to become monotonous, even irritating, over the course of a three-act play. But Salvio makes us share Hamp's condition and love him for it. It would seem that we were ourselves not only joining in the struggle to cry out over Hamp's predicament but realizing our own under the mindless incubus of such powerful institutions as the army which we take for granted but do not really comprehend.

Salvio in *Hamp*, a modest and not very "original" play, made me feel more acutely the iniquity of the great machines of our civilization (war and the like), the agony of the individual atom within them, than did Peter Weiss' factual index of horrors in The Investigation.

Fortune and Men's Eyes is not at all comparable to Genet's Deathwatch except that, to its credit be it said, it is a frankly homosexual play. Here the acting is aggressively direct, only occasionally subtle, somewhat unfocused in its interplay (or ensemble) but always arresting.

Terry Kiser, who was frightening in another off-Broadway production of the season, *The Night of the Dunce*, here too brings a sense of secret menace and torture which often emanate from unsatisfied and unconscious impulses within the soul of the common man. Stagnant pools breed poison; a feeling for such effluvia, the sources of which to begin with may be harmless and even healthy, is what Kiser's acting expresses in Fortune and Men's Eyes.

In the same play, Bill Moor as "Queenie" adds virtuosity to his camping—the playwright and director are probably too permissive in this regard—but he does not fail to show us the maleficent violence and the tremendous force of will to destructiveness immanent in the elaborately arch playfulness of the character.

In contrast to these foreboding figures, we discover the fine sensibility of Robert Christian as "Mona," the embodiment of purity within the corruption of imprisonment, a flower of humanity which may emerge in the midst of muck, cruelty and perversion. It is a light which shines in darkness.

Another actor who should be named here— space does not permit me to speak beyond a mention of William Devane's effective sketch as Robert Ken O'Dunc in *MacBird!*—is Dustin Hoffman. I mention him not alone to praise his performance in *Eh?*, second only to my esteem for the acidulous irony he brought to *The Journey of the Fifth Horse*, but to point out one of the most troubling hazards of off-Broadway productions. Hoffman left *Eh?* before it was due to close. He had a film offer. Actors accept off-Broadway engagements because they must act and because off-Broadway is a "showcase." Since salaries off-Broadway are minimal they cannot be blamed for quitting the roles in which they have won acclaim and which lead them to greater monetary rewards.

This once again demonstrates our theatre's most crying need: companies organized for continuous life. These alone can assure sane and fruitful theatre practice for the profession and for the public. A moral discipline is required for all concerned. But such discipline can only result where the artistic clarity and craft stamina of the leadership inspire integrity in the individual members of the group. With this in mind, we must work to establish real Theatres (permanent collective units) to develop actors who will prove something more than flashes in the pan, luminaries of the instant.

—WJT, 30 Apr. '68

COMEDY ABOUT TRAGEDY

In *The Boys in the Band* (at Theatre Four) Mart Crowley, a new playwright, has written an all-homosexual play. It is skillful and amusing in its dialogue, frank in attitude, casually obscene in speech, kind at heart, sentimental at bottom. It is brilliantly cast, very well acted and admirably directed. It's a hit.

Perhaps the writing and production of such a play should be accounted an act of courage. Yet I doubt it. It would be more accurate to say that it is a novelty: no such overt depiction of a homosexual milieu has ever been presented on our stage—certainly not in the London import *Staircase*. Still, the presentation of such a play was to be expected. Tristan Bernard, a pre-war writer of charming French comedies, once said "The audience always wants to be surprised, but surprised by what they're expecting"; and, as an addendum to this, "The principal quality of the successful author is a special gift for handling subjects which are not new but not stale."

Though full of camp fun, *The Boys in the Band* is not a cheap exploitation of its subject. It aims to show the guilt and self-loathing (often masquerading as impertinent and brash self-advertisement) from which many homosexuals, like members of all minorities, suffer.

It is misleading, almost corrupt, to infer that all homosexual circles are peopled by screaming fags who parade their peculiarity as several of the characters in Crowley's play do. It would hardly be true of ancient Greek society or even of such men as Proust or Gide. It is prejudice which obliges the homosexual to become obsessed with his deviation. Any man (hetero or homo) who views himself entirely in the light of his sexual nature is *ipso facto* sick. For while the sexual quotient is central to humankind, it does not constitute our whole life. Would it not be a falsification to treat an Einstein only as a brain?

Within the restricted area of its material (limited, I would suggest, even within the given theme) *The Boys in the Band* is a legitimate comedy whose author should be identified as a playwright to be watched. The criticism I imply here is leveled more on his audience than on him.

Robert Moore, a new director (he played the "interlocutor" in Albee/Cooper's *Everything in the Garden*), has staged *The Boys* with both discernment and discretion, barring only one or two minor "errors." The cast is wonderfully apt. Everyone is to be commended, though I choose Kenneth Nelson, Laurence Luckinbill, Leonard Frey, Frederick Combs and Cliff Gorman for particular mention.

Joe Layton has directed and choreographed the "entire production" *George M!* (at the Palace) splendidly.

I did not really like the show, but credit where credit is due: what I have just said does not mean I was either bored or irritated by this musical. In fact, it fascinated me. Layton has contrived to take a no-account story line (the "book" is by Michael Stewart, John and Fran Pascal) and an accelerated run of Cohan tunes with a cast of young folk wholly unrelated to the tone and temper of the fabulous George M. and make a spectacle which is almost an exemplary reflection of Broadway today.

It is loud and very very fast. Nothing of the past (except by name and citation) is present. Broadway burns its history. Our stage chronicles do not signify love of things remembered: they are not nostalgic. They embody our immersion and pleasure in the chaos of the vulgar now. Everything (including the numerous settings) in *George M!* jumps and flies at a killing pace with as much effort and noise as are humanly bearable for the bravely committed cast and the exultantly frazzled audience. It is not enough that the streets kill us, the show must also do so.

I like the cast. Joel Grey—no more like Cohan than you or I—is a real actor who functions here as a devoted performer of all work. Several of the dancers—Harvey Evans, Gene Castle—also contribute entertaining energy. Bernadette Peters has the right countenance and quality for Cohan's sister Josie—a sweet "period" face! Susan Batson is delightfully impish in a series of bits and I harbor a particular appreciation for Jacqueline Alloway's face and figure which make me recall the girls Ziegfeld glorified.

At the excellent Negro Ensemble Company's house on Second Avenue we were given the opportunity to see Wole Soyinka's *Kongi's Harvest*. Soyinka, now a prisoner in his native Nigeria (for causes unknown to us) in this play as in the others which preceded it earlier in the season writes about life on the African continent.

I speak of Africa in a generalization, though it is cut up into many nations or states each of which has its own specific character and government, because the country dealt with in *Kongi's Harvest* is a typical rather than a particular one. The situation it dramatizes mirrors its author's chief preoccupation: the tragi-comedy of Africa's transition from primitive culture to modern industrial civilization. Terror and actual bloodshed accompany the process but there is also an abundance of sly humor in Soyinka's treatment of the matter. For all the savage beat of its drums, dances and a horrible beheading, *Kongi's Harvest* is often funny.

Psychological and social strands are woven into the fabric of the play's simple plot. There is the old traditional ruler who is skeptical enough about his own so-called reactionary regime. He is too canny to perform its superstitious code with conviction and too human to submit to the maniacal dictator who, now triumphant, stands for the progress of electric and mechanical equipment. Unhappily poised between these conflicting forces we find a representative of a younger generation emotionally sympathetic to the old ways, reluctantly subservient to the new order and chiefly given over to the gratification of his senses. All this, though imperfect in construction and mixed in rhetoric, makes *Kongi's Harvest* a meaningful as well as colorful composition.

—NY, 6 May '68

PLEASURE AND PAIN

Early last fall I told Walter Kerr I thought I'd do a certain amount of movie criticism next season and he said, jokingly of course, that in that case he would have to call me "Judas."

Movies aren't theatre—no art substitutes for or replaces another—but there is a sense in which movies are less like theatre than is ballet. Ballet *is* theatre, so I feel it no sin to assert that I have had more pleasure during the past week at various dance events than at the theatre.

I am thus emboldened to say a little about the first appearance in Manhattan of the Netherlands Dance Theatre. Such mention is particularly appropriate now not only because the Dutch company is entirely new to us and that it is in part American—in one of its founders, Benjamin Harkarvy, and in several of its choreographers—but because at the moment of this week's writing I have seen nothing on the stage which has not been a disappointment or much worse.

What is immediately striking about the Netherlands Dance Theatre is the handsomeness of its personnel, its elegance and its intelligence. Its character is even, to some degree, intellectual. How, you may query, can one speak of "intellect" in the dance? It is certainly not the same thing as in literature, but more like that of, say, Bach's *The Well-Tempered Clavichord* or Beethoven's last quartets. Much of what the Netherlands company does possesses a density of suggestion in its choreographic construction, a contrapuntal design so that we are more engaged in observing various threads or themes woven into the dance fabric than we ordinarily see in more traditional dance forms.

To define the meaning of these ballets, as with "meaning" in music, is an elusive challenge. But watching them one is impelled by a desire and a need to revisit them repeatedly to unveil their mystery, though we know that the mystery in a true work of art can never be finally unravelled. All one is sure of, to begin with, is that we are in the presence of something beautiful which contains in its abstract imagery an experience of life that cannot be summed up in a word. (Rodin once said that to explain one of his statues he would have to fill a book but then he would not have been a sculptor but a writer.) The little descriptive hints apropos the various ballets set down in the program notes by no means cover the subject or are really relevant to what one has witnessed.

There is a special stress of modernity in the company's pieces. This is not only evident in an item entitled *Circles*, choreographed by the American Glen Tetley, with its apparent (visual) machine-age symbolism but also in something in so nearly a classical mode as *Metaphors* choreographed by the company's leading figure Hans van Mansen. Balanchine when asked by Sam Goldwyn to prepare something "modern" for him in a movie, replied "But the modern is too old-fashioned." It is true that much of what is so designated often becomes as stilted and savorless as the most banal imitations of formal 18th century or romantic 19th century patterns. But while the modernity of van Mansen and his collaborators is not "psychological," that is, indicative of the throes of anxiety as much of Martha Graham's art is, it reveals men and women trying to fulfill themselves (and sometimes succeeding) under the constraints of a world in which human beings of another age could not survive.

The most recent Broadway entries are hardly worth discussion in a weekly such as this. There are critical folk who love to beat dead bodies but I see no point to that at all. A play has to possess a degree of merit to be worthy of attack. One can be severe with a fine actor, as I have sometimes been, but how paltry a task to belabor an incompetent one—unless he is taken for something much better. The critic, like the boy we admonish, should take on at least someone his own size.

—*NY*, 13 May '68

SQUEAKS OF ANGUISH VS. ROARS OF PROTEST

The theatre affords numerous pleasures not only different in degree but in kind. Thus at the Public Theatre on Lafayette Street we find Vaclav Havel's *The Memorandum*, at the Sheridan Square

Theatre we are confronted by *The Concept* produced by the Daytop Theatre Company composed of men and women who are being treated for drug addiction; and at the Cafe Au Go Go on Bleecker Street we are aboard an omnibus of eleven short short plays by playwrights whose average age is probably 28 [*Collision Course*]. All these, you notice, are presentations off Broadway where most of the provocative theatre events this season have taken place. I have nothing against Broadway—it is just another foul street in our town—but it is no longer the absolute center of theatre activity in these United States.

Havel is a young Czech playwright who is also the Dramaturg (literary mentor) of the Theatre on the Balustrade in Prague. His play *The Memorandum* is to some extent in the vein of Franz Kafka's novels and short stories. To most of us Kafka represents the key figure in the literature of latter-day alienation. We associate him with a certain horror. But Kafka thought his work funny and it makes the Czechs laugh. *The Memorandum*, a comedy which tickles the Czechs as farce, though in Prague it is played more realistically than in the somewhat stylized production given it by Joseph Papp at the Public Theatre.

Its plot concerns the establishment of a new language ordered by a memorandum from some faceless authority in the silly super-structure. This language is intended to achieve a maximum of efficiency in inter-office communication. In the gobbledygook called "Ptydepe" such expletives as "Ouch? and "Ech? are translated into multisyllabic sounds. It is taught by an effete specialist but no one at all learns or understands it. The order for its study is finally rescinded and those who perpetrated it are punished. We are not surprised that the occurrence is followed by another similarly nonsensical regulation which is to be carried out with the same stringency leading to the same crushing confusion.

It is a well written play of traditional construction, full of tongue-in-cheek humor. Though too long for its basic invention it is by and large quite entertaining. It is well acted by the entire cast (Mari Gorman as a secretary introduces a note of sweetness) and ably directed. It marks another sound choice of the Public Theatre's program. Its relevance extends beyond its Czech boundaries. It recalls the Hollywood hierarchy before its partial fall in the Fifties and certain maneuvers in college faculties. Officialdom everywhere moves toward the ridiculous.

The Concept, though not in any strict sense a play or art, fascinated me more than much which passes as both. It is based on improvisations worked out and composed into coherent shape under the patient, compassionate and astute guidance of Lawrence Sacharow. The cast—there are three, each of which plays at different performances, all of them patients at the Daytop institution and all, I am sure, equally effective. They are less and more than actors. What they reveal is their experiences as people afflicted by the use of heroin, and the stages painful, heroic, touching and unexpectedly humorous—by which they overcome their illness.

The limitation of such a "picture" is that it is not art; art digs deeper, leads to even larger perceptions. With a recital of data—though these as we gather them are rich in suggestion because some of the participants are truly beautiful people—there is a certain surface excitement which fails to convey the full complexity of the subject. I must however add that the interest stimulated is not sordid, not merely clinical but, on the contrary, elevating. *The Concept* is a good deed and it is part of the theatre's glory that it can be seen there and that we can be humanly fortied by being its witnesses.

The value of *Collision Course* is that it informs us as to what a good part of the younger generation of playwrights is thinking about, what it is like. They are not all of equal worth but it would be a distortion at this point to assay a verdict on any one them as individuals or as a group. But they are surely typical.

Several plays exemplify the rapid-fire exchange of "bourgeois" banality, always an easy target. Two other plays are funny/macabre apothegms of race and religious prejudice. Still another play is an instantaneous "shot" of what folk say from habit and what inner considerations really preoccupy them. Then again we see a caricature of American tourists of routine goodwill without any connection with either the foreign landscape or people they come upon or even with their own natures. Young folk today, we learn, literally mean what they say: their ferocity of speech, for example, is no longer metaphoric but actual behavior, that is to say, their talk is not simply savage allusion but the verbal replica of outrageously performed action. The funniest play is a Jules Feiffer cartoon (by the gentleman himself) in which our inverted puritanism finds release and enjoyment only when it is unabashedly accepted as bad, evil, dirty.

I have spoken of these bits of dialogue and monocellular situations as plays; they are skits and exercises. They embody notions and inclinations, trends and velleities rather than substantial ideas. They are all signs of discontent, frustration, anger and mockery generally expressed as gags. Some portend tragedy but none has achieved the maturity which tragedy comprises. They may be regarded as the scratch of vaccines to prevent infection; by themselves they do not assure us of a cure or even a serious hope or desire for health. They are more squeaks of anguish than roars of protest.

Still most of them are well written, occasionally quick with the tremor of talent. They prove that *something* is going on. We can only trust that that something grows to be something more full bodied. They are individually meagre, collectively they promise the emergence of adults. Under café circumstances the company and the director do a snappy job. The evening is never dull.

—*NY*, 3 Jun. '68

BONES WITHOUT MARROW

With the production of Frank Gilroy's *The Only Game in Town* the 1967-68 season comes officially to its close.

Woven into the play's "True Story" fabric one may discern a theme. Joe Grady, a young pianist who regards himself as a loser, works in an inconspicuous Las Vegas joint. He meets Fran Walker, a dancer at a night club. Her father abandoned her as a child. It may be that for these reasons both the man and girl are shy of the commitments of love and more particularly of marriage. Lonely and attracted to one another, they have an affair.

Joe begins to gamble but loses after his most extraordinary winning streaks. He wants to lose because the most modest degree of affluence may tempt him to settle down in a permanent relationship with Fran. When Fran who has had a long-standing but intermittent liaison with a wealthy businessman is offered the opportunity of marrying him (he has just won a divorce) she rejects it.

Joe finally wins enough money gambling to begin a less humble career. He offers to marry Fran. He is willing to admit that he loves her and must accept the responsibility and the permanent hazards which love and marriage impose. These constitute "the only game in town."

What is thematically involved in this is the supposedly typical present-day fear and flight from the trap of love. But the play's characterizations are so slight, the writing, though pleasant enough, so glib that the theme is reduced to the level of soap opera.

Perhaps more could have been done with the material—after all Gilroy is the author of the bitterly poignant *Who'll Save the Ploughboy?* and the decently sentimental *The Subject Was Roses*— but the direction and acting of his new play while entirely agreeable (Tammy Grimes and Barry Nelson are attractive players)—aspire to Neil Simon slickness and speed with little emotional underpinnings.

My hesitant surmise about the play's possibilities somehow brings to mind another kind of play that numerous young people write nowadays which is both more interesting and more frustrating. I refer to the plays which grin, grimace and grind away at the emptiness of our lives. These plays, apart from the occasional novelty of their scenic vocabulary or form, are frequently fascinating (Sam Shepard's *Red Cross* and some of the items of *Collision Course* are recent examples) but what is maddening about them is that they are not only *about* emptiness but they are themselves rather empty. They are afflicted with some of the sickness they excoriate. The patient welcomes and enjoys his illness.

To say this is not to deny their talent. Nor do I fail to recognize the validity of their disillusionment and sense of horror at many aspects of contemporary civilization: particularly its lack of feeling combined with moral hypocrisy, its deep-seated complacency as long as the larder is full. But there is a difference between jeering and hurt, between guying and indignation, between cynicism and anger.

Many of Chekhov's characters are stupid and sometimes callous. His plays verge at times on the desperately sorrowful and their laughter is the comedy of heartbreak but everything in them which is negative or depressing arises from so tender a regard for humanity that they fill us with a deep satisfaction. The most astringent of all living playwrights, Samuel Beckett, still conveys a soul-searing experience of life in which scrupulousness of thought and ascetic discipline of craftsmanship make a statement of severe dignity.

With many of the cutups, spitfires, hellions and imps among our young new dramatists one feels that their scornful japes and stink bombs are all too easily employed. They have not paid the price in the trial of living and the hard labor of artisanship to earn the right to the unpleasant clamor of their protests. Their work is still far too thin.

Neither their youth nor the threat of extinction by atomic warfare quite excuses or explains their state. It has something to do, I venture to believe, with a condition from which society everywhere suffers but nowhere more virulently than with us. We have lost (or are deprived of) direct physical, sensory contact with each other and the *natural* facts of life.

No wonder then that there are therapists who recommend cures by prolonged bodily pressure and group hugs to the point of pain on disturbed persons. The so-called sexual revolution, the love-ins, the be-ins are hysterical antidotes to our ever-increasing estrangement from each other and even from ourselves—antidotes which are further symptoms of our distemper rather than remedies. By themselves they will not work: sexual freedom or abandon do not suffice because they are themselves debilitated by their isolation from a humanly integrated social context.

How then can we produce an art of true marrow, of nutritive substance? We hold in our hands only the instruments and simulacra of a full life, not the intimate knowledge of its wholeness. Our extravagances and outbursts of violence are signs of a wild reaching and groping for something on which to get a sure grip that may sustain us. Our arts and particularly our theatre show that we are still far from the goal. At best we only proclaim and rail at our deficiencies. Like Beckett's derelicts we are waiting. But man is finally as sturdy and durable as he is vulnerable and deciduous. Change is already in the air.

—*NY*, 10 June '68

FROM CRUELTY, EXALTATION

Several catchwords have now become familiar without having become entirely clear. For example: Theatre of Cruelty and Total Theatre. I am interested in them not for their usefulness to candidates for doctorates in drama but in their practical effects.

Total Theatre refers to the kind of production in which all the means of expression available to the theatre—sound, sight, movement, a variety of cinematic devices (not to mention direct audience participation)—are put to the fullest possible aid to the dramatic text even to the point of entirely excluding it. In a sense all good theatre is "total theatre" from musical comedy to the productions of such master directors as Meyerhold, Reinhardt and, at his most adventurous, Orson Welles. Even the ancient Greek and medieval theatres may be cited in this connection.

The fact, if not these labels, is as old as the art itself. When they appear today they denote something rather special. An assault on the senses, a theatre of physical shock is being suggested. The intention is to engage the audience in something more than an intellectual, titillating or melodramatically thrilling fashion. The audience must be overwhelmed, jolted out of its workaday torpor or its cozy after-dinner relaxation.

This "dionysiac" *esthétique* is closely related to the notion of the theatre of cruelty, a phrase introduced into our cultural vocabulary by the French actor, director, poet and sometime madman Antonin Artaud, who died in 1948. He called for a theatre which would affect us like a natural phenomenon: a cloudburst, a hurricane, a sunstroke. It was not a sadomasochistic pleasure he had in mind but a profoundly poetic one. (Poetry was once defined as the language of amazement.) The theatre was not only to remove us from routine but to open us to the wonder and elation, the joyous experience (or suffering) of contact with the suprarational, just as the contemplation of the sea, the feel of the earth, the fragrance of flowers do. The Theatre of Cruelty for Artaud was a theatre of ecstasy and exaltation.

In practice this tends to become a nonverbal theatre; it may be metaphysical but it is surely not logical. It values sensation and feeling above thought. It eschews factual realism, documentary verisimilitude, "psychology." Literature may enter it as an element in its totality but it must never dominate. Music will play a part in it but its use of music will seldom be in the traditional vein but may be wrought of sound from any source whatever through any sort of instrument or object.

Such an approach to theatre may exercise a liberalizing effect and enlarge its boundaries. It corresponds to the contemporary need to escape both the increasing mechanization of our society and the stultification of conventional drama which ordinarily dulls us into a sedative apathy. There *is* an aspect in this theatrical tendency which is thoroughly realistic through a parallel between the seeming chaos of its manifestations and the actual (and inhuman) chaos with which circumstances of our daily lives surrounds us. The intent of *Artaud's* theatre of cruelty however is to free us from the humdrum of commonplace and academically highbrow.

Thus far the "movement" has produced both salutary and frivolous results. If not a prime example of this new wave, Peter Brook's production of *Marat/Sade* certainly rode on its crest. There are palpable signs of it in Tom O'Horgan's productions of *Tom Paine* and *Hair*. In *Tom Paine*, apart from the text's political bias, the results may strike the uninitiated as arty; in *Hair* the straitlaced may think them cheap. The young generally respond enthusiastically; the elderly usually remain unaffected, recalcitrant or take offense.

Papp's *Hamlet* swelled with the undertow as do such productions as *America, Hurrah!* which in its final episode exemplifies a kind of new "realism." To a slight extent *Muzeeka* and more specifically the improvisations of The Open Theatre are similarly inspired. It should go without saying that certain of the more recent ballet and mime companies offer further and sometimes excellent illustrations of the same mode.

Like all, such eruptions or new artistic "shudders" these phenomena are to be embraced even though they will immediately sprout their own clichés, folly and pretentiousness. Above all, such aesthetic "programs" often serve to excuse a great deal of raw incompetence. It is noticeable that in this country the emphasis tends toward the brash, the raucous, the vulgarly untrammeled and, worst of all, to the infantile and vacuous. Artaud took the Balinese dancers as his model, than which there is nothing more exquisite and cultivated in the Western theatre. These Balinese and similar groups in the Far East instead of making a fetish of crudity and the amateurish (which some of the hawkers of the avant-garde espouse) embody the most refined skill and craftsmanship. Erotic, religious or both, they aspire to an almost supernal beauty.

In Europe the best practitioners of this new theatre—in Poland and Czechoslovakia for instance—are not only thoroughly trained in every aspect of acting and production (not excluding Stanislavsky) but their methods are designed to give impetus to significant trends. Acrobatics or, more properly, imaginative patterns of movement are used to create fresh moral, social, political and, if you will, revolutionary urges. They shake audiences *into* their senses; they are humanly instructive.

The goal of the theatre of cruelty is to arouse us to the height of our capacity to be alert in spirit in mind. But that is the purpose and value of all art, whatever its name. To do this we often require an unexpected and probably painful kick. We need to be taken off guard, to be hurtled into the ridiculous and the refreshing bewilderment of non-sense, to be stood on our heads. The nudes rather discreetly revealed in *Hair* (an English critic to his apparent delight imagined he saw the entire cast naked whereas I could discern no more than four of its members in that state) are intended to proclaim a will to freedom and a splendid innocence.

"Damn braces, bless relaxes" (I think) Blake said and, for the time being at least, I am glad to echo the sentiment and to encourage its dissemination in the theatre. But ultimately this tide of feeling must be measured by the test of sound human values which in the arts we sum up by speaking of "content." Content may elude definition by thematic or philosophic verbiage; it is more than and different from the usual limitations implied in the word "propaganda," just as music, the abstractions of the graphic arts and architecture rise above such definition. But our very blood and bones sense its presence and weight, its contribution to the essence of that which makes us proudly men and women.

What must be avoided in the art world's newest waves is their conversion into gimmicks, fashions, fads and sundry trivia. For all great ideas and momentarily heralded avatars are rediscoveries of what make us more fully alive and sane.

—*NY*, 10 June '68

THE PLAY ISN'T ONLY ON THE STAGE

—Munich

On my first night out, university students invaded the 730-seat Kammerspiele (Chamber Theatre) and mounted the stage. They and their champions gathered in the lobby carrying banners, shouting slogans, rushing through the corridors. Can the play be that much of a hit, I asked myself, as I approached the theatre?

My seat—like most others—was occupied by one of the demonstrators. Those who had bought tickets for the play stood by amused or bewildered. Speeches were being delivered from the stage. The theatre's director, laughing through the clamor, and various members of the students "strike committee" alternated in brief statements which were greeted by applause or jeers while expostulations were cracking in all directions. Nothing intelligible was distinctly heard except from those who pleaded or commanded "Ruhe!" (Quiet). Though somewhat chaotic, the total impression was one of obstreperous good nature.

Why, I asked, had the theatre been chosen as a site for demonstration? The students wanted to know what stand the artists and stage crew of the Kammerspiele took in regard to the proposed laws. It was clear that the great majority among them—employees of this theatre—subsidized by the City of Munich to the tune of a million dollars a year—were on the students' side.

Some of the theatre's actors said that they would be glad to discuss the matter after the performance had taken place and that, further, they thought the demonstrators ought to go to the Residenz—a larger federal and state subsidized theatre—where the management had refused to permit a demonstration while the Kammerspiele had agreed to having it.

Finally a vote was taken: did the audience wish to continue the discussion—such as it was—or to let the play begin? The vote favored art: the show would go on. The students left quickly and quietly.

The play for the evening was *Biography* by Max Frisch, a Swiss dramatist whose *Andorra* had a brief Broadway run several seasons ago. Though *Biography* is a great success in many German theatres at the moment, it struck me as far less interesting than the demonstration. It was well acted and well staged but apart from its form—a non-chronological reenactment of a man's life in the presence of a "Registrar" who commented on it and corrected the central character's memory of its events to prove the man was free to choose between various possibilities in this or that turning in his life's course—it was essentially dry. Hardly more was revealed by the play's perhaps ingenious dramatic architecture than that author and audience were well informed on current affairs and literature.

The Kammerspiele, quiet the following evening, gave a new production of the Brecht-Weill *Threepenny Opera* directed by Jan Grossman and designed by the remarkable Svoboda, both Czechs. When the *Threepenny Opera* was first given in 1928, the social order in Germany was on the verge of collapse. The new production is a version of the play for an affluent society. It might be called "The Millionaire's *Threepenny Opera*." The characters all wear evening dress throughout; the extremely stylized set conveys elegance and luxury. The change is not at all incompatible with Brecht's style which almost always has about it a kind of ironic and aristocratic hauteur. This aspect of Brecht's manner is really always missed in productions everywhere outside of Brecht's own Berliner Ensemble.

The departure from the customary norm went beyond the costuming. A toilet was the setting for a prison cell, a dentist's chair was equated with the gallows. Political placards for the parade were scrawls in gibberish. When the millionaire "beggars"—actually racketeers—were told their clothes were shameful (I repeat they were all in black tie and dinner dress)—they changed to hippie attire.

My last evening in Munich proved the most stimulating. I went to a small dimly lit, crowded but attractively appointed underground night club called The Subway, where the girls were young, handsomely clothed and very pretty. This was followed by a visit to a new and quite large discotheque named Blow Up, resembling The Factory in Hollywood and Arthur in New York. Here too the nubile come to jitter in the near-latest modes, but much less brilliantly than we do.

This was less surprising than *Chung!* (which means no more in German than in English) a sort of revue for rebellious youth, which consisted of short, violent exercises meant to express social discontent and protest against the war in Vietnam, the Emergency Laws, racism in America, Lyndon Johnson, Kissinger, et al. The points were not clearly made, but there was no doubt as to the actors' hysterical dedication.

The theatre in which this show was being given is more shack than playhouse and the police threatened to close it on grounds of its being a fire hazard. The theatre is named Action. The influence of the Living Theater once housed in Fourteenth Street and Sixth Avenue, and now rejuvenated in exile, is evident. The best of the Living Theater while it operated in New York was *The Connection* and *The Brig*. Now it produces a new kind of play with which the Europeans are deeply

impressed and which has begun to stir them to unexpected emulation.

—*NY*, 22 July '68

MUST DIRECTORS BE GREAT LOVERS?

In recent times the term "the director's theatre" has come into use. That fine American actor Louis Calhern once declared, "The reason why the director has become so powerful is that there are no more great actors." There is something in this.

The disarray of the American theater economy at present makes the development of major actors extremely difficult. There is not sufficiently sustained employment. Of gifted young people there are enough to establish as many permanent troupes as there are anywhere else. Even the so-called successful actor in America is usually confined to a limited range of parts. He seeks a fat role in a hit show, lest he diminish his market value. He fears for his status as a desirable performer. A good many very able actors in America today are more often active in scene-classes (or "studios") than on the stage. They supplement these "work-outs" with appearances in summer stock, television and films. The young actor perforce remains an amateur.

One of the worst effects of this situation is the actor's loss of confidence in his profession and in himself. Psychologically the American actor under fifty is nearly always a "beginner." By the time he is fifty he is either out of the theatre or a warped person.

Who can encourage, inspire, renew the faith of the actor in this condition? Why, the new medicine man, the well-known, the much-touted director! A superstition surrounds this character. (Superstition, even if only in the form of publicity, is always a sign of a sick state of affairs. Where nothing is secure, magic must work its wonders.) The director, the actor trusts and prays, will sustain him, make him a star. The director as fetish is a symptom; the "director's theatre" is very often little better than a commercial tag.

Capable direction is no doubt a vital factor in the making of a sound production. There is certainly a distinction to be made between the abilities of one director and another. But if we list the plays that have been highly successful on Broadway, we may very well arrive at the conclusion that any number of efficient directors might have returned box-office hits from their scripts. The quality of each production would have been different with each director; however, it is rarely the quality of direction that is perceived by the audience whose spokesman is the run-of-the-mill critic, but rather the degree of monetary success the production may achieve. No matter: when a director has turned out two or three hits, supernatural powers are attributed to him; he is regarded as a "genius," the cause of everyone's prosperity and joy.

Signs of this peculiar syndrome may be observed at early rehearsals of a new Broadway show. Except where a star actor is involved—in which case he has been consulted as to the desirability of a certain director or is aware of his prestige—most of the actors sit in a state of quasi-cataleptic expectancy. They are waiting to be electrified, exalted, transfigured. They seem to have converted themselves into so many vessels into which they hope the director will pour the elixir of his greatness.

At one time I might have agreed with Granville Barker, who said, "The art of theatre is the art of acting or it is nothing." But this is only a partial truth, though it is always worth keeping in mind. Later I arrived at what I was satisfied was a happy formulation that "the director is the author of the stage play," a generalization of which I am now somewhat skeptical. It is deceptive; a good measure of conceit is concealed in it. It may lead to disappointment and trouble for all concerned. The art of the theatre is contained in the entity of the production, in which the director may play a crucial role.

Direction is a job, a craft, a profession, and, at best, an art. The director must be an organizer, a teacher, a politician, a psychic detective, a lay analyst, a technician, a creative being. Ideally he should know literature (drama), acting, the psychology of the actor, the visual arts, music, history and, above all, he must understand people. He must inspire confidence. All of which means that he must be a great "lover."

—*NYT*, 28 July '68

COMPLACENT BUT EMPLOYED

—Vienna

A well-favored actress has said of this city, "The setting is splendid; the cast is bad." When in my younger days I spent four months here I had not appreciated its physical eloquence. But the eyes of youth are not as keen as the eyes of age.

Apart from its looks, what impressed me most at this moment is the city's hospitality to the theatre. The Burgtheater, a magnificent building in itself, has a subsidy of four million dollars a year. The troupe consists of 110 actors. When 60 of them toured last season to New York and Los Angeles, the company in Vienna was able to carry on with its repertoire without difficulty. Members of the staff and players who have served the theatre for 30 years are very comfortably pensioned.

Such statistics make an American theatre person heave a heavy sign of yearning. But here as well as in Munich (in fact wherever such conditions obtain) the complaint is heard that the actors' security in the state or city supported theatres has a stultifying effect on them. They do not develop; they deteriorate into "bureaucrats."

What aggravates this decline, when and if it occurs, is that in such theatres as the Kammerspiele in Munich (which some consider the best in West Germany) the great number of subscribers guarantees monetary stability: there are no flops. Every production is a box-office hit. This, many say, is unhealthy: the keen edge of competition and the critical verdict implied in a resounding "bomb" are dulled.

This may be true but, since no system ever works completely, my preference is for the one I have just noted rather than that of our theatre's freedom. In one case the peril is complacency followed by artistic ossification; in the other it is, in large measure, unemployment. One may be rendered stuffy with too easy a life but that still is better than no life at all—which in the practice of their profession is the lot of most American professionals.

There are two other items worth reporting: the first is that the Austrian government's annual budget for what we call the "performing arts"— chiefly theatre and opera, is $18 million; the second is the spaciousness and beauty of the quarters set aside for the tuition-free academy for actors, directors, designers in theatre, radio and television.

This academy was founded by Max Reinhardt, destroyed during the war, and rebuilt. Students are chosen by competition. The classrooms are large, bright, impeccably clean. There is a fine garden for the students to relax in, a modest area for refreshments which is a sort of students' green room. The building as a whole has a palatial aspect, characteristic of Reinhardt, who as a director was a baroque artist of very high rank.

The theatre of Vienna is conservative in its choice of plays and its methods or styles of production. Munich and West Germany generally are in advance in both respects. At the performances I attended in Vienna the audience was predominantly middle-aged as well as prosperously middle-class.

Altogether remarkable by way of setting and lighting to be perceived as a single visual phenomenon is the second act of *Tristan and Isolde* at the still prestigious Vienna Opera. The design is in itself a play. We see Tristan and Isolde in half light (or hear them in the total darkness) while behind and around them various shapes and

forms of light alternate, communicating the intensities, the ebb and flow of the lovers' passion. The psychological and erotic drama of the duet is conveyed as much through color and scenic mutation as through the vocal line and the surge of the music. It is the painting of sound.

Tristan and Isolde, which usually is burdensome (not to say a bore) as theatre, comes alive as something to see. The inspiration for this magic must have come from Herbert von Karajan, the director and designer: it is perfection.

—*NY*, 29 July '68

PERSPECTIVE

—Salzburg

The 117th session of the Salzburg Seminar in American Studies is the first to be entirely devoted to a consideration of the American theatre. The Seminar faculty—playwright Robert Anderson, Paul Baker, Director of the Dallas Theatre Center, the conductor Lehman Engel, scene designer Donald Oenslager and yours truly—is spending three weeks in explaining the nature of our American stage, its grandeur and gore, to some 60 Fellows from 16 different European countries.

The scene for this happening is the 18th century palace in Salzburg, Austria—Mozart's birthplace. This palace—Schloss Leopoldskron— which is two miles from the center of the very pretty town was once the property of Max Reinhardt. The Schloss has been occupied by the Seminar since 1947. Privately financed by American Foundations and individuals, it conducts academic sessions for six months a year, a period in which various faculties instruct English-speaking Europeans for three to four week terms in such matters as American law, literature, city planning, business management, technology, now the theatre and soon the films.

What has interested me most in my contact with the Fellows—stage directors, instructors of schools of drama, T.V. and radio producers, scene designers, playwrights, literary managers, actors— is the view of their theatres it offers and the light this throws on ours. Most of the theatres represented (unofficially, to be sure) are entirely or largely state-supported—a fact that does not always bring a glow of satisfaction to those who profit from it.

Two facts stand out inescapably: on the one hand, there is astonishment at our lack of permanent acting companies; on the other, a genuine admiration for the richness of the American contribution to the world drama of our day.

In regard to the first item, the question most frequently addressed to Oenslager is "For that theatre do you design sets?" or to me "In what theatre do you direct?" Only Paul Baker can answer unhesitatingly "I direct at Dallas and in San Antonio." Oenslager and I keep making the point that we do not work for any particular theatre but are hired by different managements for separate productions on single contract basis.

This difference between the theatres on the continent and the American situation is an old story. We may grieve over it but we need not do so, for as far as the Fellows are concerned they show much greater respect for the plays we produce—O'Neill, Williams, Miller, Albee *et al*— than most of us at home do. This is not true so much of the English and the French as of the Czechs, Hungarians, Yugoslavs, Rumanians, Dutch, Germans and Austrians. A good part of the repertoire in their countries, apart from the great foreign and native classics, consists of American plays which include not only those of our best known writers but many more "obscure."

It was something of a shock to discover during my eight lectures on the course of American play production from 1915 to the present, that the American playwright has greater stature for foreigners than we assign to him as we dash from show to show in our play market at home. We possess hardly any masterpieces—these are always rare—but in the aggregate our playwrights have told a good deal of the American story with honesty, skill and, occasionally, with considerable force. And this story, of much broader relevance than we suspect, is gratefully received by the Europeans. We have no clear view of our theatre because we have no repertory theatres to preserve the best of what we produce for continued re-evaluation. In this way, we waste our wealth.

Discontent with the theatre is an endemic distemper everywhere. The English at the moment are rather confident about their position. But all the others—Poland and the Soviet Union have no Fellows at the present session—strike notes of discord. The Czechs have reason to be proud of their achievements, but even they clamor for "more"—more and better playwrights, more experiment, greater artistic scope.

One tendency dominates: an opposition to the theatre as the agent or annex of literature. The play, as text, is not the thing. The word must be superseded by action, the markedly articulate physical action of the players. Texts are scenarios with themes on which the theatre team is to ring the changes; they are to be embodied through stage movement, strikingly novel imagery and ringing sound.

The current contributes a special vitality to theatre in many quarters: in some of Peter Brook's recent productions, in odd companies in Poland, the Soviet Union, Czechoslovakia, Yugoslavia and in France. In New York itself, the Open Theatre and the (returning) Living Theatre provide similar evidence. The Public Theatre *Hamlet* was affected by the same trend. O'Horgan's staging of *Futz* and *Tom Paine* at Café La Mama as well as *Hair* on Broadway is also symptomatic. And when Robert Brustein as critic and Dean of the Yale School of Drama champions *Viet Rock* and *Macbird* as examples of a Theatre of Fun, he expresses something of the sentiment and theatrical ideology I have been hearing from several of the Fellows at Salzburg.

—*NY*, 5 Aug. '68

PETER BROOK'S THEATRE OF SHUDDERS

Peter Brook has been greatly influenced by the theories of Antonin Artaud which go by the poetic "trade" name: the theatre of cruelty. "Today the theatre of doubting," Brook writes, "of unease, of trouble, of alarm, seems truer than the theatre with a noble aim." He neglects to add that the noble aim is generally achieved through doubting, unease, trouble and alarm.

His production of Peter Weiss' *Marat/Sade* is well remembered. After a foray into the pop art political theatre called *Us* (about the war in Vietnam) he now brings Seneca's *Oedipus* to the British National Theatre—more abstract in Greek and Asiatic posture than anything he has done.

Brook has always displayed a taste for the theatre of shudders. The best scenes of his early production of *Measure for Measure* and the later one of *Titus Andronicus* revealed his appetite for shattering effects.

As we enter the Old Vic, where the National theatre is housed, the auditorium is half dark. Before the play begins the chorus enters carrying small boxes to be used as stools. At the same time other members of the chorus (more men than women) station themselves against pillars on the orchestra floor, the balcony and the gallery. The boxes are covered with bright tinfoil. There is another box stage center—large enough to hold several people and to serve as an inner podium—silvered in the same way as is the entire background.

The house lights come up and stay lit throughout the evening except for the moment of revelation when the illumination intensifies. The chorus prepares itself by vocal and physical exercise for relaxation. The actors all wear brown pullovers and slippers. When John Gielgud as Oedipus emerges from the big box he wears black jacket and trousers.

The actors of the chorus beat rhythmically on the wooden stools. They hum, howl, hiss, cry, chant as well as speak lines. Slowly the old Oedipus legend unfolds, spoken directly to the audience, always interspersed by wild and often wordless ejaculations. Jocasta, all in black, played by Irene Worth, also recites her part—more impressively than anyone else. The blind seer, Tiresias, is a young man who wears two oblong black glasses over his eyes to indicate his sightlessness. Later, when Oedipus is supposed to have gouged out his eyes, Tiresias places his glasses over Oedipus' eye sockets.

Jocasta commits stylized suicide by driving a sword, conveniently placed in an upright position at stage center by one of the men in the chorus, into her womb. Her face turns into a mask of horror. At the end of the play an object is brought on stage covered by an ornamental sheath. As the sheath is solemnly withdrawn we see that it envelops a golden phallus.

Now the entire chorus, handsomely gowned in gilt and masked, prance up one aisle then into another, in which parade of joyous song they are joined by a jazz band in slacks and sweater—all of them finally frugging around the symbolic penis. For in the ancient Greek theatre the tragedy was followed by Bacchic revelry.

The show plays for an hour and a half without intermission. There are no curtain calls. Rationally speaking the following ideas are expressed: first, the classical Greek one about the danger of any departure from the middle course of action. (There is one good line: "The cure can be so drastic that people will prefer the sickness.") There is also a suggestion that the plague which decimates Thebes is like Hiroshima after the bombing, and that an age old curse is the undisclosed cause of the disaster. Finally we hear the stoic precept that no one can escape his fate.

Brooks aims at a theatre of astonishment. But his possibly piquant scenic vocabularly—including electronic sound—does not in this instance compose itself into a living text. Theatricality is reduced to the superficially sensational and spectacular. (That is perhaps the reason why Seneca's unfamiliar Latin and inferior version of the Oedipus story is employed instead of Sophocles'.) But art is never produced simply by a quest for novelty, but from a genuine human need.

—*NY,* 19 Aug. '68

NEW YORK FILM FESTIVAL

There is often something attractive about even a (moderately) bad film. Its background, for instance, may be nicely photographed. Several of the films I saw during the first week of the sixth New York Film Festival are very pretty. Most of them are regarded as superior. But I soon came to realize that what I enjoyed most was their "landscapes."

They are highly sophisticated films: their boldness about sex and their nudes are immediately striking. (A motion picture nowadays without one or more views of a naked woman is simply not with it.) The films were also very *psychological.* But I find that I prefer their pornography to their psychology.

I relished the Italian lakes, walks, hotels, casinos of *Twenty-Four Hours in the Life of a Woman,* the St. Tropez of *Les Biches.* Even the pigmented *Two or Three Things I Know About Her,* which dwells on the disagreeably altered face of Paris, is somehow made to look delicious. Whatever their subject or message it was the chromatic candy of their images and a sense of luxury in their sites which compensated for my indifference to their content.

Max Ophuls' 1955 film *Lola Montes* is visually exquisite. The director's cultivated eye is everywhere apparent: the composition of a concert in Copenhagen's Tivoli Gardens is a perfect Manet. Anton Walbrook plays the King of Bavaria, Lola's most notable lover; in the very tilt of his top hat one recognizes the director's dash. Yet for all its nostalgic evocation of the early 19th century in Europe—something I especially appreciate—the film is pap.

Orson Welles's sixty-three-minute *The Immortal Story* which takes place in Macao is also a handsome sight. In it Jeanne Moreau, recumbent to receive a passing bedmate supposedly 17—although he looks 35—is rendered more sensuously appealing than ever. The picture is based on one of Isak Dinesen's Gothic tales. It indicates once more Welles' penchant for the mysterious macabre. A program note declares that it is about "the artist playing God" and "that life imitates art with ironic consequences." But the total effect is inconsequential, despite its suggestion of even more portentous meanings.

Though most of these films afford agreeable pastime at least, I had begun to despair of the festival as a source of any great personal satisfaction when I came upon Robert Bresson's *Mouchette.* Bresson's art is a relief from factitiousness. Every shot of his picture is a simple and telling declarative sentence. He doesn't hurry; he looks and sees. He eschews tricks and that "art of the cinema" which so preoccupies the *cognoscenti.* His is an ascetic art, laconic and penetrating. It is deeply human without bathos.

Mouchette is a girl of perhaps 14 who lives in one of those very small French villages in which the inhabitants seem to hide behind closed shutters as if they were keeping watch over corpses. Her father is a hard and soundless peasant worker, her mother deathly ill and her infant brother squalls through hunger and neglect. The family is wretchedly poor. Tenderly she ministers to her mother and fondles and feeds the child maternally. Her schoolmates mock her shabby clothes, her dank complexion. The boys call her "rat face." She revenges herself by throwing mud at them. The town's women are dry; the men, incapable of easy communication, spend their moments of rest in bitter silence at the café *terrasses* after consuming several draughts of harsh liquor. Only when Mouchette's mother dies is kindness shown her by the gift of a free tumbler of coffee and an extra *croissant* which she disdainfully throws away.

There is a gratified smile on her face when a

boy in a miniature auto deliberately and continuously bumps into hers at the fun-fair "race course." Attracted by the boy she follows him, but only to be spurned. And finally when she experiences an intimate contact, the impulse of desire toward her, it is through rape by a drunkard, the town's epileptic poacher whom she later speaks of as her "lover." When her father tells her that her mother was a "brave woman" she responds with *Merde*. When an old woman, enamored of mortality, offers her material to serve as a shroud in which to bury her mother, Mouchette curses the "old witch" and drowns herself, wrapped in a dress from the bounty. It is a terrible story but it sinks into the consciousness as something more than a brutal tale of rural darkness and suffering. It conveys the unnoticed, the unsensational agony, the secret and insidious pain of all human isolation.

It may be concluded from the above that in preferring the black and white *Mouchette* to most of the lush melodramas whose gorgeous males and females suffer the torments of our time—one asks oneself why Bonnie and Clyde didn't go into the movies—that my predilection is for unvarnished realism as contrasted to refined art or camera manipulation. It would be much more exact to say that I am definitely averse to the gay but morally sleazy drapery so frequently used to conceal the diseases it pretends to disclose.

—*NAT*, 7 Nov. '68

CLOWN AND HERO

Let us skip *Cyrano de Bergerac* which hobbles flatfootedly across the forestage of the Vivian Beaumont theatre and prance over to the Biltmore where a young company knocks itself out in a frantic cutup called *Hair*. Rostand was extremely French in an idiom which Henry James described as a "bristling bravery of verse, a general frolic of vocabulary, especially under the happy whip of rhyme"—all absent in its present production. *Hair* is extremely American in its reflection of part of our youth in its "Don't give a damn" mood to the hectic jostle of its rock and roll score.

The new mounting of Gerome Ragni's, James Rado's and Galt MacDermot's musical, containing many new numbers, is far less lyrical than the one at the Public Theatre downtown. The latter was wistful: its emblematic song, the touchingly sentimental "Good Morning Starshine," having been eliminated uptown.

Much else is dropped in the revision—notably its entire story line. The show is now little more than a series of numbers: tunes accompanied by seemingly improvised and corybantic dance dislocations. They all add up to a Bronx cheer to patriotics, aged caution, middle-class restraint, war and all the attributes of white collar respectability.

A moment of tender quiet is provided when Shelley Plimpton (from the original cast) sings "Frank Mills," an oddly tender love ditty, in its very unpretentiousness the most original note in the score. (I also liked the putting to music of "What A Piece of Work Is Man.") But "Frank Mills" is no longer characteristic. Jolly shakes, quakes and perpetual bombination are the rule.

There is gold in the garbage. In a recalcitrant frame of mind one might say that the proceedings were snottily orgiastic. Depending on one's disposition this may repel or attract. Still there is no denying that Tom O'Horgan has a visually inventive stage sense. Though some of his leaps of fantasy fail to take shape and seem like the wild impulses of the fellow who insists at all times on being the life of the party, O'Horgan is talented as only a few of his more composed colleagues among directors are. It may also be true that he would be less representative of his generation if his work were more studied. The essence of his show is tatterdemalion.

The girls are good looking: one of them, Lynn Kellogg, in a fetching Hollywood doll fashion. There are male and female nudes, but this is no novelty: we have all seen naked men and women before—and to better advantage.

When a particularly interesting but to some folk "controversial" play opens, my friends are prone to assail me on opening night with a "Well?!" which is a not-so-oblique request for a summary opinion. It does not matter that I have repeatedly said that I do not see plays in view to delivering snap judgments or to reply to the question "Did you like it?", the interrogator demands an answer.

I understand the query for the requirements of journalism and commerce, but for criticism it leads to distortion. I regard theatre as living matter, like contact with a human being, and except where a play is totally inept or a person hopelessly insufferable, there is little substance in yes or no responses. (Do you like the girl you adore, do you love the girl who gives you a pain?) With honest arrogance, I have frequently told lecture audiences that I am capable of getting more pleasure out of certain plays of which I disapprove than many people do out of plays they profess to be crazy about! The enjoyment comes from the quality of my attention.

Rolf Hochhuth's *Soldiers* (Billy Rose Theatre) held me firmly in its orbit even when at the outset—during its prologue—it bored me. It held me by its subject, by the eloquence of some of its writing (partly quotation), by the author's unmistakable desire to arrive at a decision on momentous problems. That I failed to come to any clear-cut intellectual conclusion is less important than that the play made me concentrate on them. I did not ask myself—as others bid me do—whether I was having a "good time," I was much too engaged by it to notice such things.

Since I have not yet read the complete text (published by Grove Press) I speak only of what the producers and the director, Clifford Williams, chose to excerpt from it. *Soldiers*, like the author's earlier piece *The Deputy*, is an amalgam of dramatic poem and "encyclopedia." Documentation is employed as the basis for drama. Hochhuth is German and there is a German tradition of grandiose historical theatre which runs from

Goethe and Schiller to Brecht; its most recent manifestations are visible in the so-called Theatre of Fact: of which outstanding examples may be found in Peter Weiss, Günter Grass and Heinar Kipphardt who wrote *In the Matter of J. Robert Oppenheimer*.

Like his coevals, Hochhuth is not primarily concerned with art. He wishes to disclose the reality of our time and to do something about it. This, if you like, makes him a propagandist. His effort is not inimical to art; he seeks new resources from which art may spring. This brings fresh forces into play, enlivens the theatre, and thus makes a valuable contribution to its future direction.

Soldiers challenges the morality of aerial bombing of civilian centers and proposes that governments enter an international covenant to outlaw this practice. In following this aim Hochhuth broaches the theme of the means employed in a war motivated by honorable ends, in this case the defeat of Hitler. He is thus led to the depiction of the man, both blessed and blamed, who is caught in the toils of the dilemma: Winston Churchill.

The most convincing achievement of *Soldiers* is its portrait of the celebrated Prime Minister. He is shown as ruthless in his purpose, wracked with humane misgivings, despising and glorying in the valorous savagery of battle, magnificently marred by pride, contradictory perceptions, petty foibles and something of a ham withal—exulting in his own rhetoric and solemnly aware of his place in history. Both spontaneously and consciously given to forthright action, he is torn by moral and metaphysical qualms though he cannot help being, first of all, a fighter. He is driven to risk evil and make a wager with destiny.

Watching this colorful picture, I thought: no amount of fact, no statistical syllabus leads to a true knowledge of history; only great art can do that. I know Napoleon much more profoundly through Tolstoy than through any compendium of facts about him. The reality of history is never known except by God. The great artist ventures to play the Almighty. He chooses and makes us perceive his truth, and in his wake we make our choice, a choice without any guarantee of ultimate verification. The epic wonder of life consists in our acting within that uncertainty and in our determination to abide, that is, to pay the price, of whatever choice we have made.

Because Hochhuth's play—which certainly does not rank in the category of the highest creation—made me think of such things I must pronounce it *good*. And in performance, John Colicos, though I cannot say he moved me, has accomplished a most remarkable feat of characterization, something on which a young actor may well be congratulated and which it is a boon to see. Simpler but also impressive in incisive clarity and intelligence is Tony Church's performance as the logically inconsistent, troubled but nonetheless resolute Bishop of Chichester.

—*NY*, 20 Nov. '68

THE LIVING THEATRE

There are more than a few people in Europe and America who believe that the company known as The Living Theatre (Brooklyn Academy of Music) is making a vital contribution to the theatre. Having seen three of its four presentations I judge that *Le Living* (as the French call it) is more concerned with "living" than with theatre.

The company disarms criticism. Its productions are a way of life, closer to religious manifestations than to either art or entertainment. Though it borrows haphazardly from various arts and artists, The Living Theatre is anti-art. One cannot blandly declare that its performances are boring because they lack measure, every turn, scene and sound being prolonged to our breaking point: "rituals" are always enervating to the uninitiate. "Be bored, you brutes!" the company might retort. "Get sore! Go crazy!—then at least you will be open to emotion!" The usual points made against the "Living's" group exhibits are not relevant to its intention.

My initial impression of seeing *Frankenstein*, the first item in the four-week program, was not of the company's rancor but of sweetness. No matter how absurd the cavortings, I thought only of the company's childlike dedication, the passionate commitment of kids to their games. The sillier the things I beheld the more sympathetically naive and primitively "idealistic" they seemed. People who have suffered ridicule, abuse, penury, perhaps even persecution, and who can still hurl themselves about with wild fury, shrieking apocalyptic slogans in generally untrained voices and worse diction, can't be all bad.

It has been objected that *Frankenstein* is no play. It certainly isn't drama, that is, literature. But it is all *play*, approximating what is loosely termed "Total Theatre." As theatre there were only two effective things in *Frankenstein*. One was the scene in which Man was operated on, all his organs being extracted so as to fashion a new Creature, a dismembered monster. The operation, with its multicolored tubing and electric gadgets crisscrossing in an inextricable tangle over the prostrate body of the victim, reminded me of Matta's paintings of intricate sadism by machinery. When the Creature emerged it was as an enormous, grotesque figure composed by the assembled players in an elaborate acrobatic stunt. That was the second effective moment.

For the rest there was noise, sloppy (though strenuous) movement, caricatural statuesque poses and unsightly exercises for "purification," in the second bill, *Mysteries and Smaller Pieces*; and in Brecht's *Antigone*, the company's third bill, crude borrowings from Brecht, Grotowski, Yoga, Hindu chants, and whatever else might arise from the flotsam and jetsam of improvisation.

If you complain of a dreadful lack of professional skill in these proceedings the answer might well be that professionalism is anathema here: these folk are fanatics of amateurism. I have already suggested that the company is only marginally a theatrical organization. It is a cult and a cult must have a doctrine. What is theirs? It is a utopian anarchy. Its passwords announced (in an incense-filled atmosphere) by the company's high priest, Julian Beck, and chorally repeated by his ragged acolytes, are: Stop the War, Freedom Now, Stop the Draft, Free the Blacks, Free the Poor, Abolish the Police, Open the Jails, Abolish Money, Abolish Banks, Abolish the State.

In *Antigone*, the heroine (Judith Malina) says that it would be better if the victims of tyranny gathered the expression of their protests and did something useful with them. That was the one moment I was inclined to applaud. For what The Living Theatre is now doing is hardly useful, unless one believes that any and all expressions of dissent are valuable and that any departure from convention is a liberating force. I fear, on the contrary, that the basic lack of discipline—of craft and mind—in this as in many other present-day forms of dissent is an invitation to repression, a beckoning to both martyrdom and fascism. For with all the good will of which one is capable, one must recognize mental deficiency in this particular mode of protest. The religion becomes hysteria, the ritual inept, the catharsis flat.

"The horror has failed to horrify," Brecht says in his interesting version of *Antigone*. This applies *a fortiori* to the work of The Living Theatre. The more impassioned it is, the louder its members scream, grovel on the ground, howl, snarl, spit, mock, bluster, fume, pile "dead" body on body, the less we care. And this precisely because there is so little art in it—that is, original inspiration plus thought, rigorous calculation, skill and self-critical application. Boldness is not enough; it frequently turns out to be foolishness.

—*NAT*, 28 Nov. '68

KING LEAR

"Please, please, oh Lord," theatre critics might well cry. "No more classics!" About *King Lear*, Hazlett wrote, "We wish that we could pass this play over and say nothing about it." He meant that it was too great to be encompassed by normal critical standards. I have wished and have been tempted not to say anything about its production at the Vivian Beaumont Theater at Lincoln Center because like 98 per cent of all such productions they make me feel as Tolstoy did with "firm, indubitable conviction that the unquestionable glory of great genius which Shakespeare enjoys…is a great evil."

"About anyone so great as Shakespeare," T. S. Eliot has written, "it is probable that we can never be right; and if we can never be right it is better that we should from time to time change our way of being wrong." The value of being wrong as Jan Kott is in *Shakespeare Our Contemporary* and the way some of the new Shakespeare productions are in England today (not to mention the travesty of Joseph Papp's *Hamlet*) is that they challenge the routine of our reception of the masterpieces. They disturb us into thinking.

It was said of my two separate reviews of the Brook-Scofield *Lear* that they were "unfavorable." Not at all: they were a response to a new statement of the play which stirred me enough to grapple with it as I had done only once before in my long theatre-going habit. Such contention is part of true enjoyment in the theatre. To see *Lear* merely to say that the Goneril is inadequate (or O.K.), that the Fool's lines are (or not) audible, that the leading actor has his good points, that the setting is austere, handsome, unusual or whatever, is not to see the play at all, and has nothing to do with Shakespeare, art or anything else of moment to an adult.

I have just referred to an earlier *Lear* that brought me into a bewildered but rousing contact with the play. It was Michoels' *Lear* in the Jewish Chamber Theatre in Moscow in 1935, a production which Gordon Craig declared to be the best of any Shakespeare play he had ever seen. I could not then understand his enthusiasm despite the original settings.

Michoels was not "every inch a king." He was physically a runt, a poor forked animal, almost a clown. He had very little dignity; the authority Kent sees in him was more an indication of Kent's character than of the king's person. Our audiences and critics would have been puzzled and shocked by that interpretation as I was. But I never forgot it. It was "wrong" in a way that has made me think about the play and led to a further and closer examination of the text.

Lear is a primitive. Shakespeare thought of the story as something that antedates history, timeless. Lear is an emotional savage. He has the furious instincts and wild passion of a primal being. He is like one of those volcanic creatures the rush of whose displeasure may very well turn to murder and just as quickly turn to tearful and equally hectic contrition. The play depicts the development of this man's crude conception of regal majesty to the dawn of his realization that power and nobility do not inhere in the trappings and privileges of kingship, but only in love. Once he is forced into this spiritual crisis even the prospect of imprisonment holds no terror for him so that he tells Cordelia: "We two will sing like birds i' th' cage....So we'll live, and pray, and sing, and tell old tales, and laugh...and hear poor rogues talk of court news; and will talk with them too: who loses and who wins; who's in, who's out...and will wear out, in a wall'd prison, packs and nets of great ones that ebb and flow by th' moon."

Lear is insane long enough before the purgatory of the heath. The shock of his elder daughters' ingratitude drives him mad, but the anguish and turmoil of his madness leads him to wisdom. Before his fall he was all sudden and driving impulse, possessed, as he says, by "*hysteria passio*." Nearly all his previous actions were

choleric, headstrong, grotesquely simple-minded. He is in a constant boil: he is rent asunder by the wrathful elements within him as later he is shaken by the storm without. As the raiments of mundane glory are being torn from him he is only halfway between his old sense of imperial selfhood and his burgeoning humility. So, I imagine him saying: "Ay, every inch a king," beating himself in raging self-mockery, and yet holding to a remnant of that former foolish pride which still dwells within him. The smoothly grandiose Lear of romantic tradition is hardly borne out by the persistent folly of his early behavior. Lear is Man learning through agony and despair the lesson of life: that the most protected of beings is "safe" only through love. It is this progress from uncouth, barbaric passion to the simple dignity of the integrated person which the actor who plays Lear must present.

I am convinced that the ordinary common-sense or middle-class notion of Lear as an irascible dodo of a father who blunders and finds his children unkind not only diminishes the play but makes nonsense of it. Seen conventionally, *King Lear* is just as unworthy a piece as Tolstoy thought it. Shakespeare was no scribe of high-flown homilies; he was a Titan whose conceptions must be embodied with an epic force beyond the confines of familiar rationality.

I shall not blame or praise Lee Cobb. He is an excellent actor of more scope than he is credited with. (For one thing he is a wonderful comedian, as those who saw him in the Turkish bath scene of Irwin Shaw's *The Gentle People* will remember.) His Lear, whatever its faults and merits, is in a vein which I cannot accept as relevant. For the rest, the production strikes me equally inept in setting and in staging they are linked in such a way as to render both feckless. Nor has the direction served the actors. To take only one example: in the speech of Lear's declaration to Cordelia of his new-found insight into existence (it is in fact a beautiful *love scene*) Lear stands—there is no place on the stage for him to sit—and delivers a sweet old papa's consolatory lecture to his child, a benign bit of domestic philosophy.

Therefore: no more classics—unless the producer is impelled by some greater (*personal*) need than that of fulfilling the pedantic requirement to honor the ancients.

—*NAT*, 25 Nov. '68

MORNING, NOON, AND NIGHT

A cast of five—Sorrell Booke, Robert Klein, John Heffernan, Charlotte Rae, Jane Marla Robbins, all good—play the three one-acters *Morning, Noon* and *Night*. The first by Israel Horovitz (whose *The Indian Wants the Bronx* I liked) is an extravagant piece about blacks who swallow some "magic pills" and lose their pigment, with presumably hilarious consequences when a "cracker" comes to kill the black father whose son has knocked up his teen-age daughter, and finds that the family he threatens is white. In the end we learn that the white avenger has also taken the pill and is really a black.

Laughter is provoked by the explosive use of (by now) customary four-letter words. I doubt that a black audience would appreciate the play's fun or approve its liberalism. For my part, I am bone tired of this sort of jape in regard to racism. And I am inclined to feel that with very few exceptions I prefer to see American plays on the subject by blacks only.

McNally's *Noon* is a sick joke in which a tease advertiser invites a group of assorted individuals to indulge in some special sex shenanigans and perhaps a tutti-frutti orgy. A queer, a timid young man, an unappeased housewife whose husband talks and reads more than he does, a flagellant married couple turn up.

It is entirely possible that this play was written with scalding aversion for its characters and situation, and was then transformed into all-out farce by the director, Theodore Mann. In any case, the results for me are some scattered trivial chortles, funny only to the degree that any surprise allusion to sex is risible (the dirty end of the Puritan stick).

I believe Melfi's *Night* is about death and the emptiness of our "official" attitude toward it, or perhaps it is about the equivalence of our mourning whether a burial be that of a man or a dog. If I am not correct in these surmises—the play is "symbolic"—I don't think it matters.

To those who welcome these plays—a few cried "Bravo!" on opening night—I must point out that at best they are *notions*: symptomatic perhaps but inherently of little artistic value. To applaud all manifestations of the tendency they represent betrays a juvenile fear of not being "with it," a callow snobbism. To encourage these playwrights indiscriminately is to do them a disservice.

They should learn that a gimmick is not sufficient for a satisfying theatre event. A short play must have the same substantive quality as one of full length. They write too "soon" and too hastily; they should discipline themselves in self-criticism. They must think and work after their first inspired impulse. They should understand that every shudder of fury, horror, derision or violent dissent must be as carefully calculated and articulated as the most ambitious drama.

A word should be added about the desire to be open, bold, utterly permissive about sexual matters on the stage. The plays of some of those one reviewer ingenuously referred to as our "modernists" are rarely "warm." The obsession with sex today is not like that of the twenties. That was a rebellion against Calvinist repressiveness. Today we reach out lyrically, hysterically, or callously toward some concrete reality. Belief in the older ideas has for the most part proved hypocritical deception. For this reason we grab at what still remains specifically tangible and stirring: sexual connection. It seems to be all that's left.

There is no villain in this situation, and some good has come of it. In several instances, I suspect a certain guilt feeling, a self-punitive strain projected as social castigation in the outrage expressed by our dramatic wild men. But there is another aspect to this trend. We find a statement in two or three of Tennessee Williams' plays which in turn appear to echo D. H. Lawrence's pan-sexuality. This makes passionate sexual experience a total value beyond every other consideration. It represented Lawrence's effort to rid himself and his generation of the prudery, aridity and denial of the instinctual life from which he himself had suffered. It led to wrongheadedness and distortion in several other phases of his thinking. Taken literally, the Lawrence "doctrine" is false. Except in bad art, as in bad biology, sex is not a separate "department" of existence. Isolated from the broad context of life it ends in being ludicrous, unpleasant and destructive.

If what I have suggested is also what our new dramatists have in mind, they must learn to say so with lucid cogency, hold court on themselves, deliberate their way to become artists rather than just clever foundation fellows.

—*NAT*, 16 Dec. '68

FRENCH CHARACTERS
An Impersonation of Angels: A Biography of Jean Cocteau
by Frederick Brown

Frederick Brown does not love Jean Cocteau, whose biography he has written; he is fascinated by him. Or to put it more precisely, he is dazzled by the world and times which Cocteau sparked. *An Impersonation of Angels* is a scintillating portrait of that remarkable period, from 1900 to 1929, which the French have named *la belle époque*.

It was the time "when fashion, politics, literature and journalism milled together with noisy self-acclaim in surrounding cafés, torn by the Dreyfus affair but united by a common passion for theatre on stage and off. Everybody played a role." For all that, there was more to that enchanted day than the twitter of "café society." It was a time of creative ferment in a constellation which included such varied luminaries as Proust and Picasso, Bergson, Valéry and Gide, Stravinsky and Matisse, Debussy and Ravel, Diaghilev and the Surrealists.

What is especially notable in Brown's book is that though he was born in 1934, and could not have seen Cocteau act Mercutio in a dilettante but highly decorative version of *Romeo and Juliet*, his description of the occasion is altogether accurate. This is as true for the figures he discusses. They are drawn with an unfailing eye for the telling detail: we actually seem to be in the presence of these talented men and women.

Brown is severe—at moments almost "bitchy"—with Cocteau, but I regret to say that he is more or less right. He sums up at one point by saying that Cocteau "devoted more of his energy to the persona than to the self." He speaks further of Cocteau's being "fertile in stillbirths," and "opining brilliantly." His more substantial criticism of the Cocteau *oeuvre* is genuinely perceptive, displaying an understanding of Cocteau, not only in his work but in his person. Brown is an acute psychologist whose animadversions are not limited to malicious anecdotes or gossip. While he divests Cocteau of his motley he makes us comprehend the tragic aspect of the naked man underneath.

Why, one may ask, if Brown cannot admire Cocteau, should he have taken the pains to write so thoroughgoing an account of his life? The answer is not only the one I have suggested above: that Cocteau in his incessant activity tried to make himself part of every significant literary and artistic movement but because his undoubted gifts were of a kind—common everywhere among the smart sets—which glitter and flash to the astonishment and applause of all those to whom the arts are a show, a rarefied circus rather than an essential human communication. "He invented a style," Brown says, "a style …melodramatic yet spoofing, wise and wisecracking, irreverent but somehow sadly aware that it lacks the confidence or the energy to make a statement of its own touting and mourning its own sterility." Its spirit tends toward the "sleek and invertebrate, given to cumulus landscapes, ghosts, clowns, pierrots and pale, pale children."

This is well said as is almost everything else in the book. Brown possesses an extensive vocabulary which errs occasionally in the ornamental use of words denoting exotic finery and gems. He also is given to Anglicizing foreign terms. Among other blemishes—the book may arouse resentment in certain quarters—is his inclination to generalize from his subject's particular case to areas where the author is on unsure ground, as in his slighting of certain phases of Picasso's and Stravinsky's art. And though what Brown says in regard to Cocteau's homosexuality is in itself penetrating and convincing, there are misgivings when he extends the diagnosis to homosexuals as a "breed."

Still this biography conveys a sense of Cocteau as a man—versatile, witty, thoroughly aware, deeply troubled: a flawed poet but a poet nonetheless. The reader still cannot help being attracted to the handsome elegant of intense gaze who could say "that the writer [is] a prison from which the works escape, only to be pursued by police the world over." Such a man merits all the attention Brown has lavished on him.

—*NAT.* 20 Jan. '69

MAYSLES' SALESMAN FILM

In mid-March the 68th Street Playhouse will show a documentary film, *Salesman*, by the Maysles brothers and Charlotte Zwerlin, which has given me greater insight into America than all the Broadway shows I have seen this season. To some it will seem a comedy, to others a tragedy.

Nothing is invented: there is not a word in it which was not actually spoken by the door-to-door Bible salesmen the picture is concerned with and the folk to whom they sell or try to sell their $49.95 Holy Book. Seeing the picture one is ready to agree with Francis Bacon that "The contemplation of things as they are...without substitution or imposture is in itself a nobler thing than a whole harvest of invention."

"You can see," says the salesman, as he points to the illustrations in the Book, "how this would be an inspiration in the home," and then explains how to push the three plans of purchase: "Cash, C.O.D. and a Catholic Honor Plan" (so much a month). He continues: "The Bible is still the best seller in the world." The customers are Irish (as are most of the salesmen), Polish, Puerto Rican. They have been recommended by the local Church; the wares to be sold have the imprimatur of blessing of the high clergy. Many of the prospective buyers cannot even afford a dollar a week. The territories covered are New England (seen amid snow) and Florida.

This Bible is a hard sell ("Could you say if this would help the family...? Could you see where this would be of value in the home? A gain to you?"). The sales manager for the company (of porcine countenance) assures his men at a sales convention: "Money is being made in the Bible business...It's a fabulous business...All I can say to people who aren't making the money, it's their fault...The money's out there and go out and get it." One salesman announces he's going to make $35,000 this coming year. To best him another vows to make $50,000. One wants to push his face in. His pals applaud.

At another meeting in Chicago, the designer and theological consultant of the company, Melbourne I. Feltman, Ph.D., tells the assembled flock in an analogy with the Son of God himself that "the good that comes from the selling of the Bible...is definitely identified with the Father's business. Some of you, at one time or another, may or may not have had a higher income, but you have never held a higher position in esteem....God grant you an abundant harvest."

In North Miami, Paul Brennan, the salesman on whom the film makers have concentrated, tries to find 118 Street in the town of Opa Locka (how terrifyingly hideous the architecture of the vicinity). The streets through which he drives are Sinbad Ave., Arabia Ave., Ali Baba Ave., Sesame St., Sharazad Blvd. He calls this "Muslim Territory." He makes no sale that day and we notice that he has become grim. A fellow salesman hopes to encourage Paul by reminding him of the firm's adage: "It's not the bum territory. It's the bum in the territory."

So it goes. We see them pushing, pushing, pushing, talking, talking, telling jokes, exchanging confidences, making philosophical remarks, all to wear down the customers and lighten the embarrassed silences of indecision or resistance. A strained heartiness shields the salesman's anguish as it does the customers' mixture of discomfiture at not being able to reciprocate and an unconscious desire to mollify the salesman's hurt. Often the salesmen are not only depressed by their lack of luck but by the realization of the degree of unemployment and poverty they encounter as they make their pitch.

The salesmen play poker among themselves, do a lot of kidding, make long-distance calls to their wives at home, reminisce. Paul remembers his father who counseled him "to join the police farce and get a pinsion." He imitates the brogue of which there is still a remnant in his own speech. One senses a certain contempt for the accent, the admonition and the "Mickie" breed, mixed with a trace of regret at not having done as his father bade him. These fellows like one another, and when Paul finally prepares to quit the business their compassion is not without some foreboding that Paul's fate may some day be their own.

When we last see Paul mute, immobile and grave, his face is a tragic mask. He has experienced defeat. Through the laughter that the film provokes there runs an ever swelling vein of tragedy. How can these petty people be tragic, purists may ask, remembering Aristotle and his *epigones*. At most they are merely pathetic.

A pox on such aesthetes! The salesmen and their customers are tragic because we can recognize them as kin and they are legion. They are all of us. They are our countrymen caught in the vise of the prevailing religion: utility, business, success—a religion which erodes. We are unable to feel superior. In all of them we catch a glimpse of the presence or potential of something dear. I left the picture in a maze of sentiments and impulses: of suicide, murder, prayer, fraternal embrace.

The film suffers from a certain monotony—it is too long—but that is possibly part of its intended effect and meaning. We are worn out along with its "actors." They are all great, especially Paul Brennan. The stiffly drooping line of his mouth is a study in itself. There is something close to grandeur in his acrid humor, his self-mockery, his realistic perceptiveness, his ultimate stoicism.

The photography and editing are first rate. The producers, I am certain, would like the reviewers to emphasize the film's comedy. I have laid stress on its cutting dreariness, but that does not signify a defect. The combination of all its elements—including the view of its various landscapes—creates its own kind of catharsis. It is a picture for the brave.

—*NAT*, 10 Mar. '69

1776

1776 at the Forty-Sixth Street Theatre is a fine and dandy show. Credit for this must go, in the first place, to Sherman Edwards who conceived the idea of making a musical of the contest, composition and signing of the Declaration of Independence. He was aided by Peter Stone's shrewdly crafted "book," discreetly spiced with sure-fire ingredients of sexual allusion and political joshing, around which floats an aura of residual patriotic sentiment.

It has been expertly directed by Peter Hunt, a gifted newcomer in the field, who knows how to stage the mixture like a legitimate play. Everything is done with the dispatch of musical comedy convention without ever appearing conventional. And Jo Mielziner has done his best settings in years: unostentatiously handsome, efficient, dignified. His lighting too glows beautifully in soft amber. The production benefits from Patricia

Zipprodt's admirable costumes, which avoid calling attention to themselves as special attractions.

Though rarely little better than serviceably bright—with some occasional strain—Mr. Edwards' songs fit neatly into the dramatic context.

The fourth and longest scene of the show is the most accomplished. Here the Continental Congress comes on stage for the first time, the representatives of the thirteen states and their aides in full session. The atmosphere is sticky with heat; there is a pestilence of flies. The delegates are impatient, disgruntled, formally polite with old-time colonial manners which fail to conceal a native crudity that is appealing in its rough humor, earthy spontaneity, unbuttoned forthrightness. We recognize the division and tension of special interests, the Tory recalcitrance to yield to the pressure of the libertarians, the fumbling maneuvers, the obtuseness and chicanery, as well as the downright orneriness of all such conclaves.

Each personage is nicely delineated: Stephen Hopkins, the unreconstructed Yankee villager from Rhode Island who at every turn clamors for rum; John Adams, the voluble and fiery partisan of freedom for the new nation; the genial sophistication of Benjamin Franklin's diplomacy; the decorum of the Reverend Witherspoon of New Jersey; the embarrassed hesitancy of Morris from New York; the baffled timidity of Philadelphia's James Wilson; the haughty aristocracy of John Dickinson, spearhead of the conservatives who insist that "independency" is treason.

If only that scene had been all. But the show goes on with further condiments and charms. There is little that is "bad" in what follows; still as the show progressed I experienced churlish misgivings. I was surprised, almost shocked, to feel something like irritation with the entire occasion. Why, I wondered, should this be so when almost every episode contained some particular pleasantry. Somewhere in the smooth proceedings, I felt, there must be some sort of "swindle."

There is a smugness in *1776*. Its Americanism is complacently synthetic. It is pitted with raisins of such quasi-Shavian epigrams as "Treason is a charge invented by winners as an excuse for hanging the losers." There is a sprinkling of facile witticisms for immediate home consumption about Congress in general and the absurd niggling of the New York legislature. The hypocrisy of the North with regard to slavery is exposed melodramatically in a number called *Molasses, to Rum, to Slaves*, and with levity when Adams says: "If we give in on slavery here there will be trouble in this country a hundred years hence—posterity will never forgive us," to which Franklin replies: "That is possibly true. But we won't hear a thing—we'll be gone."

I appreciate the line, "Revolution comes into the world like bastard children, half improvised, half compromised." But with all this, we find Jefferson burning to get back to his wife and spending nights and days in bed with her instead of getting to work on the draft of the Declaration. This annoys John Adams, who sings to him, "Mr. Jefferson, dear Mr. Jefferson, I'm only forty-one, I still have my virility but life's more than sexual combustibility." While the teasing and gushing ribaldry takes care of one phase of a musical's requirements, Adams' attachment to his wife takes care of another: the domestic-romantic. To mellow it all a Drummer Boy's song *Momma, Hey Momma*, is insufferable in its banality.

The delectable contemporaneity of the show for the audience is evidenced by the first yak of the evening when the silliness of the Congressional goings-on is punctuated by someone muttering, "Sweet Jesus!" In short, nothing is conveyed that will in the least disturb the hazy, lazy view of anything in our past or present, or be incompatible with the comfort and expense of a night out at $15 a throw.

The cast is first rate. I especially liked David Ford's solid John Hancock, the anchor of good sense at the Convention, an effortless performance without a false note; Paul Hecht's polished Dickinson; Roy Poole's tart Rhode Islander. Howard da Silva's Franklin is oily rather than crisp, but technically altogether deft and effective. Clifford David's Rutledge is forceful but because of the song itself or from his anxiety to make it rousingly memorable, he renders the Rum-Molasses-Slaves "waltz" like an operatic ham.

The most generally admired performance is that of William Daniels as John Adams, the story's central figure. Daniels is an intelligent and eminently engaging actor (he was very fine in *The Zoo Story*), but the nearly apoplectic and supposedly spiky Adams is repeatedly referred to as "objectionable and disliked" which was historically the case. Franklin once described him as "sometimes mad." There is hardly a trace of anything like this in Daniels' nature or characterization. He is actually sweet. This sweetness is emblematic of the basic tone of the whole evening; a gruff, hard-bitten Puritan is embodied as an ardent, clean-cut college boy. Perhaps characterization in a musical isn't supposed to conform to the sense of the text? And if the composer or vocal coach doesn't come to his aid, Daniels will soon damage his throat as he struggles with the vehemence of *Is Anybody There? Does Anybody Care?*

Life today is extremely crass and the public harbors a nostalgia for a waning idealism. Thus *1776* is a great and merited hit. It serves our audience as an American "legend" somewhat in the way *Fiddler on the Roof* is a Jewish one, *Man of La Mancha* a "universal" one. I recall a respected New York reviewer who spoke of Marc Connelly's *Green Pastures* as the equivalent of the *Divine Comedy*, and it too was a smash. *Vox populi* !

—*NAT*, 7 Apr. '69

TO BE YOUNG, GIFTED AND BLACK
THE NEGRO ENSEMBLE
AN EVENING WITH MAX MORATH

To Be Young, Gifted and Black has been running at the Cherry Lane Theatre since January. I came to it belatedly, not merely because of the pressure of other duties but because I am reluctant to judge a writer from bits and pieces of her work, much of which do not fall into the category of "theatre" but of "readings." I am glad now that I did not miss it; it constitutes a touching event and provided me with a special insight into the signally honorable personality of its author.

Miss Hansberry's outstanding qualities are sweetness and balance, a healthy intelligence, a secure spirit. She is perceptive, dignified, clear. These are attributes rare in recent Negro writing. Much of the drama written nowadays either by blacks or by white champions of the black "cause" tends to be melodramatic, hysterical or grotesque. It is understandable, perhaps justified, but frequently self-defeating. Miss Hansberry's statements are not soft; they are firmly tempered. In a beautiful letter written in answer to one from a Southern white "fan," she says that the black people must do everything to create a normal situation for themselves by every means from prayer to violent activism in defense of their persons and rights.

She views the crisis of the black man in the white community (or in the community of colonial powers where the black majority dominates the white minority) in the broadest human and historical context. In a brief dialogue from *Les Blancs* the black leader says that it would be simple if he could hate all whites on the ground that they hate all blacks, but having seen how many white hegemonies brutally mistreat their own poor he has come to realize that they have no more love for the white population than for the black. Hansberry's feeling for all people is intimate, rational, compassionate. Because of this her "propaganda" takes on a special forcefulness.

Not all of the original cast is now appearing in *To Be Young, Gifted and Black*, but despite occasional overstress—more often for laughs than from conviction—the performances are good enough, and in the case of Stephen Strimpell better than that.

Maupassant's famous short story, "A Piece of String," has apparently inspired Alice Childress' *String* which opens "An Evening of One Acts" by the Negro Ensemble (St. Marks Playhouse). It is an agreeable piece but Ted Shine's *Contribution* is the best of the three. (The third play is *Mal Cochon* by Dominick Walcot.)

This tells of a black woman in her 70s who has served as a cook and maid-of-all-work to sundry Negro-hating "worthies" in a small Southern town. She is cherished by her employers because her behavior is always "exemplary" in its patient subservience. Her college graduate grandson Eugene, who has been educated in the North, returns home to take part in a sit-in demonstration at the opening of a new drugstore which the town blacks are determined to have "integrated."

At first, there seems to be no special tension in the situation apart from the anticipation of trouble with the sheriff and his cohorts. Eugene patronizes his kindly forebear, but is scornful of her passivity. He talks about the "generation gap." He is shocked when the old lady indulges in hip vocabulary, but this is nothing compared to the horrified astonishment that overcomes him when he learns that she has poisoned the corn bread she has baked for the sheriff, as years earlier she did away with a doctor, a genteel savage who refused to treat her sick husband. As the play ends she is off on a trip to Mississippi where she has been told the governor is being mean to the black citizens. She will bake bread for him too.

Contribution is very funny. Since its joke is the wrapping for an act of vengeance which appeals to us as a sadistic wish fulfillment of an almost infantile sort, it is a wonder that we can still enjoy it. In part, the wryly flippant writing does the trick, giving the piece a peculiar innocence like those cartoons which depict mayhem; but even more it is accomplished by the acting of Clarice Taylor whose gently acid tone, her unquestioning self-assurance that what she is doing is natural and right, creates in the viewer a sense of satisfaction and delight.

An Evening with Max Morath (Jan Hus Theatre) is a one-man exhibit of songs, quotations, anecdotes, colored photos about America at the turn of the century. To be more exact, the period covered runs from approximately 1890 to the mid-twenties.

It is a thoroughly pleasant little show; it is also history. Morath plays the piano well, furnishes appropriate commentary, and generally strikes the exactly fitting note of easy sportiness. His agate blue eyes, his sharp nose, reddish brown hair, shrewd friendly look and snappy suits make you feel that you are *there*.

And where is that? It is the time when the farm boy has become the city slicker and rejoices in his newly acquired dash. The cozy cracker-barrel comic has stepped out of the general store and rides merrily atwinkle on the Broadway electric car, blissfully aware that he is a big boy now amid blazing wonders.

—*NAT*, 28 Apr. '69

BLACK THEATRE

In 1964 I wrote here apropos of James Baldwin's *Blues for Mr. Charlie* that "most of us are not yet burningly aware not only of 'the fire next time' but that the conflagration has already begun." I referred to the seething of black militancy against unkept promises and the extreme tardiness of change.

What is changing rapidly is theatrical silence on the subject. This season alone I have seen

Howard Sackler's *The Great White Hope*; Roger Cornish's *Open Twenty-Four Hours*; Dan Tucker and Jay Broad's *Red, White and Maddox*; McCrea Imbrie and Neil Selden's *Someone's Comin' Hungry* (the work of white writers); Adrienne Kennedy's *Cities in Bezique*; the several productions of the Negro Ensemble Company, notably Lonne Elder's *Ceremonies in Dark Old Men*; Lorraine Hansberry's *To Be Young, Gifted and Black* (by blacks); *Big Time Buck White*, a collaboration between a white writer, Joseph Dolan Tuotti, and a black company from Watts, and most recently *A Black Quartet*, four new plays by black writers Ben Caldwell, Ronald Milner, Ed Bullins and LeRoi Jones.

A Black Quartet was presented by the Chelsea Theater Center, a group, now in its third year, devoted to producing the work of new playwrights at the Brooklyn Academy of Music. (It has already mounted thirty-nine plays.) *A Black Quartet* is given in cooperation with Woodie King, an able black director and writer. The evening in Brooklyn interested me both for the plays' varied merits as drama and for the questions raised by such manifestations.

Caldwell's *Prayer Meeting, or The First Militant Minister* is a farce in which a black burglar rifles an apartment whose tenant happens to be a black minister. On his entrance, the minister begins to pray for forgiveness for one of his race who has killed a white policeman. The burglar, who has stopped outside the door and heard the minister's plea, indignantly answers in the role of the "Lord." He bids the frightened cleric alter his prayer. The minister must support a man who avenged himself on the brutal cop and urge others to follow that example. The minister changes his tune: he prays that his brethren may do as the killer did when their people are abused.

The audience, composed of nearly as many teen-aged blacks as of older white and black folk, laughed and applauded in rapturous glee. The fact that the fake Lord who invokes violence is himself a criminal did not.in the least trouble anyone. The play is, after all, a wry joke. But the pattern repeats itself in Ed Bullins' more sophisticated playlet, *The Gentleman Caller*.

A gentleman caller, presumably a black bourgeois, passively accepts the condescension of a white rich bitch—all mechanical glitter in a stylized make-up and attended by an ominously correct black maid. When the white monster becomes too aggressively haughty the maid shoots her and then the gentleman caller for having been so despicably nice in the face of the woman's insolent cordiality. The maid then proceeds to the telephone, whose intermittent rings she has been bluntly answering throughout the foregoing events. To *this* particular caller she now proclaims that death must be the wages of all enemies of the black people. Again the audience shouts its joyous satisfaction.

Bullins' gifts as a writer have been demonstrated in *Electronic Nigger* and other plays. But despite the comparative polish in the writing and the symbolic stage imagery of the present play, I suspect he wrote it to fulfill a "popular" need. And though this may be laudable, I find that in accomplishing it, he has unwittingly written down to his audience. Even poster art does not have to be as blatant as this play proves to be under its surface gloss.

There are parables which will stir the simplest folk, but these are rarely written by the artfully instructed. If Bullins hopes to help his cause he must do so in his own (more complex) person rather than as a private in the ranks of the committed.

LeRoi Jones's contribution, which he calls *Great Goodness of Life (A Coon Show)*, is written in the same spirit though it is a more compactly accomplished piece. In it Court Royal, who is rather proud of being a post office employee (the audience finds this very funny) and in every respect a blameless citizen, is accused in a Kafkaesque fashion by an unseen Voice (a white judge) of having harbored a black murderer. First he insists on his trusted position as a government worker as clear evidence of his innocence. When this does not avail he asks for his own lawyer. A lawyer is thrust on him as his own, one who snivels, grovels and sneers. He bids Court Royal to plead guilty. Then the accused is promised that if he will fire an emblematic gun at the "shade" of the murderer—who, he is told, has already been executed—he will be allowed to go free. Royal fires: the gun is real, and so is the target. He has killed an unknown man.

This turns out to be a nightmare, the horrid dream of a simple middle-class black man, wracked in slumber with foreboding, and fears which in his waking state he suppresses with apparent complacency.

The point is well made, but the play is not to be compared in intensity or personal meaningfulness with the same author's *Dutchman*. He may well be contemptuous of such criticism because, as I have already suggested, he now proposes, like Bullins, to create the most immediate effects for a still insufficiently aroused or fortified black audience. In both cases, I respect the intention but I doubt the efficacy of such efforts on the part of men whose capacities have more extended scope and deeper roots. Their ambition must reach beyond these self-imposed limitations if they are to confer maximum benefits.

Anger is a fuel which may ignite inspiration, but anger alone will not provoke the proud sense of identity which these playwrights hope to foster. This is done when blacks are revealed as they are in the daily course of their lives. That is why I was most affected by Ronald Milner's *The Warning—A Theme for Linda*. It shows us three generations of black women, grandmother, mother, granddaughter, in their relationship to their men: their hopes in them, their disillusionment and their further demands.

The play badly needs cutting and is somewhat awkward in structure. It is moving because it is warm in its closeness to the real people it portrays. The characters are not being used as instruments to illustrate an "idea." When the young girl around

whom the play centers offers herself to her boy and asks if he will prove a strong person and not the kind of feckless being her once idealized grandfather proved to be, we sense that she is growing up. She wants her man to be strong because she refuses to waste herself on weakness as her grandmother has done, and we feel bound to her and to all her family through an understanding which is in fact consanguinity.

The acting in *The Warning* is especially touching in the performance by Vikki Summers as Linda, Leslie Rivers as her mother, and most particularly by Minnie Gentry as the grandmother. Miss Gentry's long account of her life with her drunkard husband, whose negligence led to the death of their child, is the most powerful expression of pained feeling that I have seen since Bea Richards' great outburst in Baldwin's *The Amen Corner*.

Virtually all the acting in *A Black Quartet* is good and a special word of praise is due Errol Jaye who is entirely genuine as the minister in Caldwell's comedy, as the grandfather in Milner's piece, and as Court Royal in LeRoi Jones's play.

The acting and the audience with its deeply felt—though "intellectually" indiscriminate—cries of sympathy, were for me the most memorable aspects of the evening. For all my misgivings about the nature of the excitation in parts of these plays I could not fail to be impressed. Still, I pray that these representative writers do not fall into the error that vitiated the work of many "left-wing" dramatists of the thirties, that of following a path that too narrowly interprets their mission, and thus seeking to move their audiences by slogans of which derision, hate and self-consuming rebelliousness constitute the main characteristics. Vision with compassion are forever the sustaining and saving ingredients of the most ardent utterances in art.

—*NAT*, 12 May '69

THE YEAR BOSTON WON THE PENNANT
DANCE

Twenty-five-year-old John Ford Noonan pitches wild in his *The Year Boston Won the Pennant*, presented at the Forum of the Repertory Theater of Lincoln Center, but there is promise and poignancy in his play. The loose-jointed awkwardness of the script, the unevenness of its style, the meagerness of emotion and scenic invention in the production rob the event of some of its potential effect and contribute to an impression of obscurity. But the play is not obscure: it leaves its imprint. When and if Noonan arrives at a point of relative mastery, he may write a more successful piece; for he possesses intuitive insight and feeling—attributes rare in the new generation of playwrights who tend to repeat devices familiar in Dadaism, surrealism and the theatre of the absurd.

Put bluntly, what *The Year Boston Won the Pennant* means is that humble, naturally honest and decent folk are not only losers but are buffeted, maimed and destroyed in our society. Characters such as Marcus Sykowski, the central figure in the play, are frequently put on stage as "artists," or as lonely intellectuals, "idealists." But such embodiments sentimentalize their intended message because they posit exceptional people who, to begin with, ought to understand their lot. Noonan's protagonist is a simple man, a warm-hearted guy differentiated from the mass only by athletic ability, the kind of fellow whom we see everywhere and to whom no attention is paid.

A once renowned pitcher for the Red Sox, Sykowski has lost an arm because he refused to accept a bribe to throw a crucial game. The racketeers still pursue and kill him. The preliminary circumstances are never explicitly revealed, only inferred. The mystery of the severed arm is the main reason for the play's supposed obscurity.

Being a good man and thus an irrepressible *believer*, Sykowski dreams that with the aid of a prosthetic appliance (which he is too poor to buy) he may return to his former estate. He tries to earn money for this by seeking a job as caddy at a golf club. He is constantly rejected in favor of the able-bodied. At first he is mocked by his lowly companions at the club because he was once a big shot and is now a nobody like the rest of them. Still, when they decide to help him gain employment by a strike, they are too muddled to win.

A silly homosexual dilettante tries and fails to seduce Sykowski through flattery and cash. He is entirely devoted to his wife (a would-be actress) who, at the suggestion of her "manager," agrees to help by appearing on television to plead for assistance because her husband and their child have supposedly disappeared. Nothing avails; Sykowski's wife leaves him for a television star.

Through the accumulation of these scenes a mood takes form: a sense of painful bewilderment in a world in which ordinary people move through an infernal maze, unaware of what is happening to them. This is the realm of the blind, a place of covered violence unillumined by consciousness. The atmosphere is brutish. The author grapples uncertainly with the monstrous creatures he has wrought. But one cannot doubt that a raw sensibility and a troubled imagination is dwelling within him and his play.

The only area in which the play's quality is realized is in the acting of Roy Scheider as the martyred ball player. The tenderness of a baffled soul, agonizingly aspiring, dumbly courageous and still clean inform Scheider's performance, which needs only the instruction of more knowing direction to make a sharper, more definitive portrait.

Having spent most of the past two weeks of theatregoing at the City Center season of modern dance groups, I look back with particular pleasure to a number based on East Indian and African mating rites called "Doougla," choreographed for the Talley Beatty Company by Geoffrey Holder, and to "Shirah" as choreographed and danced by Pearl Lang.

There is a lovely playfulness in the sensuality of the beautifully costumed Holder piece, in which sex is explicit, fresh and free. This ballet stands in contrast to the cloying prurience of the sexy stuff now prevalent—a by-product, among other things, of a nasty and still immanent Puritanism within us.

Pearl Lang's "Shirah" (Hebrew for "Song") is Middle Eastern in its patterns without being "ethnic." The characteristic trait of Miss Lang's art is graciousness. This is not, as the word often suggests, a matter of decorous breeding but the essence of respect for and joy in life, a celebration of human rectitude, loftiness of thought and behavior accepted as a norm, an elevation with roots in suffering so transcended that it achieves lightness. We observe this again in another form in the final moments of "Tongues of Flame," the mottoes of which are culled from the utterances of the Biblical prophets. After the imprecations, weeping and despair of the middle section, there is a vertical leaping into the air as if a heroic spirit had at last risen like a triumphant flame, with a glow more intense from its previous suppression.

—*NAT*, 9 June '69

BUCHAREST

The Bucharest stage—along with that of Prague—is the liveliest in the Balkan countries. There were no signs of Socialist realism, and there was something "experimental" or adventurous in almost every performance I attended. Literalness or strict fidelity to the texts as the authors may have conceived them seem to be consciously shunned, as if dependence on the play script were a sign of mediocrity or banality. The intention seemed to be somehow to *contradict* the dramatist. Everyone strains for originality. The results were nearly always stimulating even when they failed to be altogether convincing.

The most satisfying of these productions was the least pretentious. It was a production of *Carnival Scenes*, a play written in 1885 by I. L. Caragile, a dramatist highly regarded in Romania, The production, tumultuously and hilariously inventive in the wildest sort of *commedia dell'arte* tradition, is a triumph of gaiety and malice. Where the author was, I am sure, poking gentle fun at local manners, the young and brilliant director, Lucian Pintele, turned the play into extravagantly physical farce in which the scrubby fun of the old days was mercilessly exposed in raffish riot. The acting was superb.

The same director has produced *The Cherry Orchard* in a mode which would bewilder its author and must horrify those Russians who see it today. However, it pleases the Romanians, who have never been particularly enamored of Chekhov. Chekhov considered his play a comedy; Pintele's production verges on farce. The characters are kidded; pathos is almost entirely absent. The atmosphere is bright, sight gags abound, there are quasi-cinematic effects. The achievement here, the actor-director-producer, Liviu Ciulei, told me, was to make Chekhov popular for the first time in Romania.

Ciulei plays Danton in his own production of Büchner's *Danton's Death*. It is scenically so complex a production that it was rehearsed for five months, of which five weeks were devoted to dress rehearsals alone. The most gratifying aspect of this occasion was its detail of characterization. It developed an individual life for each member of the large cast down to the last supernumerary, and there was a wonderfully truthful interplay in the entire company.

The most original production of all was that of *Rameau's Nephew*, a philosophic dialogue by Diderot which was never intended for the theatre as it is wholly devoid of what is commonly called "action." But it is all action and a visual in the amazing staging by David Essig. It employs a battery of man-sized mirrors constantly turned to different angles so that the two speaking characters become multiple images representing many more figures than occupy the stage: they constitute a whole environment, a society. The man who plays Diderot's interlocutor, the no-account, "bohemian" iconoclast who is Rameau's putative nephew, is an extraordinary young actor of fabulous verve, Gheorghie Damisca, who also plays Robespierre in *Danton's Death*. What makes this production important as well as memorable beyond the fascination of its setting and the graphic power of its acting is that it demonstrates how purely intellectual material can be translated into vivid theatre.

A very young director, Andrei Serban, has made a colorfully handsome spectacle of Brecht's *Good Woman of Setzuan* with an excellent student company from the provinces. Serban has taken liberties with the text and has made the play much more of a vociferous social protest than Brecht intended his largely ironical play to be. But even the Belgian Ghelderode, a dramatist who was something of a "maniac" (a creator of enormous seminal imagination), would have been astonished by what another director has done with *Escorial* in which the play's two characters, a king and his jester, are just seen hanging together on the two hooks of what looks like a large anchor. This play, the director explains, demonstrates that the end of the quest for power is always murder.

Those who find literary texts (especially the "classics") stultifying often set up a great clamor in the name of Artaud, whom they barely understand, and talk about "total theatre," "the theatre of cruelty" and the like; or they give themselves up body and soul to the new Magus, the Polish director, Grotowski, whose work they still know only superficially. Courses on Grotowski's methods are already being given in English schools and theses written about it by Americans for academic honors. I saw students in Amsterdam make hash of a Ghelderode play produced "à la Grotowski," in which I was assured they had no real interest.

If the master is inappositely quoted, imitated, falsified, it is certainly not his fault. I look forward to seeing his productions, some of which will be given in New York in September, and I shall not be prejudiced by what has previously been said,

done or written by the hordes of his ready-made epigoni. Everyone knows that Marx was no "Marxist," Freud no "Freudian" and Stanislavsky no "Methodist." Even Brecht finally exclaimed, "To hell with my theories!"

—*NAT*, 28 July '69

A FLEA IN HER EAR

Gower Champion, a whiz at musical comedy direction, has staged Feydeau's (1907) *A Flea in Her Ear* for the second offering in the A.C.T. program. It may please—in fact, delight—some; it oppressed me.

Feydeau was the master mathematician of farce. His plays are perfect mechanisms based on a strict formula. Himself part of the happily corrupt middle class of France's Third Republic, Feydeau wrote plays which are an oblique mockery of it. Their technique, as Feydeau himself described it, consisted in placing ordinary people in extraordinary circumstances. The more commonplace the characters, the funnier the situation. Max Beerbohm's aphorism, "The more somber the background, the sprightlier skips the jest," is applicable to Feydeau.

In the Champion-A.C.T. production all the actors' faces are daubed with white chalk, giving them grotesque masks. Wurtzel's sets and costumes are black and white decorations. The acting is thoroughly camp with added touches of Keystone cavortings. The effect is as chichi as a fraternity romp.

It is not necessarily a fault that the Feydeau ambiance has been annihilated, but the one substituted renders the play infantile. Except at a few moments, the actors' exertions put such a strain on the show as to make it heavy and unfunny. It is all like an elaborate libretto for a *Promenade* sort of musical—without the music.

Michael O'Sullivan's cracked limb and vocal oddity as the cleft-palate secretary provide a few shocked laughs, and Robert Gerringer in that part of his dual role in which he impersonates a half-wit hotel porter is also peculiarly comic.

—*NAT*, 27 Oct. '69

INDIANS
THE THREE SISTERS

As directed by Gene Frankel, Arthur Kopit's *Indians* is an interesting play. There is a semantic ambiguity in this. I might have called it "a production," but then I would have had to differentiate sharply between the text and the performance. That is common practice when we speak, for example, of *The Three Sisters*—which I shall do in a moment. But a theatre event is not two things; it is one: what we perceive with eye and ear at the same time. In short, a play.

That is particularly true of *Indians*. Kopit's scenario is freshly conceived to show how the American Indian was swindled and slain (the remnants sequestered), while the whole shameful process was turned into colorful myth in Wild West shows and movies. In these, the Indians were either glamorous or traduced for audiences who didn't give a damn for anything but thrills.

There is a documentary base to Kopit's stylized account. The facts are presented through a double vision: on the one hand, Buffalo Bill's destruction of the buffalo which was the red man's food, his growing sympathy for the Indians, and his unsuccessful attempt to have the government redress the wrongs that were done them; on the other hand, his showman's desire to cash in on his career through the extravaganzas he packaged for cheering thousands all over the United States and abroad. The two aspects of the story—the cruel reality and the commercial use to which he put it—are deftly interwoven in Kopit's dramatic scheme. What is lacking is eloquence; the writing is thin.

Kopit's plan, to be fulfilled, also needed the flesh of a stirring theatrical embodiment, and it did receive that from Gene Frankel. The result is a play worth seeing. It has the special merit of giving the Broadway stage a "new look." I have heard the complaint that *Indians* is over-produced. The masks and figures which are the spirits of the dead that haunt Buffalo Bill's troubled conscience, the flashes of Indian dances which were performed in his Wild West show, the bucking bronco on which he prances onto the stage, the actors in buffalo skins, the strobe lights, the dummies of the white hero and two of the eventual victims of the army massacre, Sitting Bull and Spotted Tail—some spectators have thought all these excessive. They are in fact essential. Without them there would be no more to *Indians* than a bald historical recital. All Frankel's effects are integral to his creation and constitute its contribution to our stage.

Still, the show rarely becomes enthralling. There are two reasons. One I have mentioned—the lack of verbal power. The other is that, though Frankel's staging is well calculated, visually engaging, rhythmically propulsive, its imaginative and physical resources are limited by comparison with what the scope of the play might have been. When I say this—such a production in our presently restrictive theatre economy is surely very costly—I am thinking of what certain directors in Eastern Europe or even a Guthrie or a Brook might have been permitted to do with the offered opportunity.

While much better than serviceable, most of the acting lacks either epic or comedic stature. Stacy Keach works devotedly, strenuously and well as Buffalo Bill; even more impressive is Manu Tupou as Sitting Bull (his confrontation with the U.S. Commission has the needed wildness of savage pride), and in his baffled and tormented fanaticism Sam Waterston strikes the right key as John Grass, the spokesman for the Standing Rock Reservation.

All in all, a bright evening in the theatre; in the light of what our theatre has to offer nowadays, a momentous one.

There are some good moments in William Ball's production of Chekhov's *The Three Sisters* which is the final American Conservatory Theatre production at the ANTA Theatre.

Ball desires above all to be *theatrical*—a worthy ambition for which he has a distinct talent. But theatricality is not ornament to decorate, supplement or substitute for a text. It is illumination, an added dimension to the implied, stated or potential meaning in the text, creating a new entity for the stage. It is therefore to be judged by the same standards of vitality and significance that we apply to the text itself.

To improve Chekhov's "showmanship," Ball tampers with his text in ways that vulgarize it. One example is the treatment of the character of Vershinin. The subordinate officer, Baron Tusenbach, says of him: "He pays calls and says everywhere that he has a wife and two girls"; when Vershinin in the Ball production enters for the first time and on every other occasion when he is introduced to a new person he automatically blurts out, "I have a wife and two daughters"—which makes him stupid, the one thing Tusenbach says Vershinin is not. In Chekhov's play Vershinin refers to his wife and two daughters only when it is appropriate to the situation. Ball's device gets a laugh; it's a gimmick. There are too many laughs of this kind in the production. That is not what is meant by Chekhov's humor. Ball makes "points" that are often clever but they damage the emotional line of the play, its true tone and value.

Another instance of this is with Tusenbach himself. He is said to be ugly; in Ball's production he is made to look a fright. Tusenbach, as his name indicates, is a Russian of German origin which may explain his romantic idealism (and perhaps masochism), but it is not necessary to give him a thick German accent. Stanislavsky was partly French; he didn't speak Russian with a French accent!

Separate scenes involving various characters in moments of confession are staged before other characters who are extraneous to these intimacies. People in this play, through delicacy, hide from one another rather than expose themselves.

It may be argued that such directorial liberties can intensify or improve a script, as cutting often does. New interpretations of "classic" texts are now and then valid, providing greater insight into them. (The Theatre at the Gate production of *The Three Sisters* in Prague—though it displeased the Russians and troubled me a bit—is a masterly one and theatricality admirable.) Ball's besetting sin is that he makes all his plays, regardless of their style, frisky; he insists on gaying them up. It helps *Tiny Alice*; I doubt very much that it helps *The Three Sisters*.

There are a few sensitive performances in this A.C.T. production; Angela Paton as Olga has quality, so too has Kitty Winn as Irina. Paul Shenar, a handsome man, is more interesting in character parts than "straight" ones (though he served *Tiny Alice* better than did Gielgud). If he were not so absurdly made up, and if the eccentricity of his Tusenbach were less stressed, his interpretation might prove genuinely touching. William Paterson's Chebutykin looks like two different persons who don't get along very well together; a despairing Russian and a rather debonair English clubman.

The play remains beautiful, one of the most beautiful of the 20th century. I have seen it "killed" only once in my theatregoing experience and that, fortunately, was not on this occasion.

—*NAT*, 3 Nov. '69

CRIMES OF PASSION

It has nothing directly to do with the matter, but it struck me as I watched Joe Orton's two one-act plays collectively titled *Crimes of Passion* (Astor Place Theatre) that dramatists often foreshadow their own destinies in their writing. Marlowe's special ferocity presages his death by stabbing; Odets' *Golden Boy* points to his eventual creative collapse; Orton's violent end at the age of 34 complements the horror of his comedies.

He had an unmistakable talent. His pungently derisive dialogue captures the guying tone of contemporary London. There is something at once traditionally elegant and nasally obscene about his manner, as if Oxford had produced an irrepressible guttersnipe. If you open your mouth in laughter at an Orton play, a spoonful of acid is dashed into it. His jokes are a preamble to murder.

In *The Ruffian on the Stair*, the first of the two one-acters, something like a note of tenderness is introduced. But it is muffled either by technical deficiency in the plotting of the play or by some ambiguity of purpose. On the pretext of wishing to rent a room in their apartment, a certain Mike appears at the door of a truck driver who lives with a former prostitute. We do not know at the beginning that the intruder is the brother of a young man whom the truck driver for some unexplained gangster motive has deliberately run over and killed. Mike, the "ruffian on the stair," seems at first to be seeking revenge by harming the truck driver's girl. That, however, is not his intention: it soon becomes evident that he is a homosexual and that his devotion to his brother was more than fraternal. What he wants is to be killed by the very person who killed his brother, the only person he cared about. By pretending to have made a successful pass at the truck driver's girl he succeeds in getting himself shot.

There are in effect two stories here. The first suggests the extreme loneliness of a man bereft of his only beloved and his consequent desire to die. But the greater part of the action concerns itself with the wretched humor of the brutish truck driver's relation to his blowzy, frightened and fundamentally innocent girl friend. In the end they cling to and protect each other because of their desperate mutual need.

If there is unity here, as on reflection there appears to be, it is in the inference that the world is full of foul folk whose only common trait is their aloneness and their shabby groping toward one another to insulate themselves against the chill of solitude. Yet one can hardly say that Orton finds any saving grace in this, because, except for the

"ruffian" and possibly the girl, he sprays everything with a shower of hate-filled mockery. We laugh because Orton writes sharply and can be funny, but the venom scalds. There is no pleasure in the fun.

When Orton turns to thoroughgoing farce, as in the second of his *Crimes*, *The Erpingham Camp* (it takes place in the sort of fun fair now popular in England's smaller towns), he becomes trigger happy, aiming a broadside of buckshot at the entire community, from officialdom and clergy down to the "little people" who frequent such resorts.

The play is too long. It provides moments of acrid entertainment especially through Orton's expert use of the common man's lingo cleverly patterned by his own sophistication—but it all ends by making humanity seem a sorry sell.

The two playlets are done well enough under Michael Kahn's direction by a competent cast of which the ablest are Sasha von Scherler (as the girl in the first play), Richard Dysart as the mucky truck driver and David Birney as the sacrificial "ruffian."

—*NAT*, 17 Nov. '69

JERZY GROTOWSKI

In one of his occasional writings Jean Cocteau cites a Chinese proverb: "Genius creates hospitals." Whenever a towering personality appears, a host of lesser men become warped in imitation of the greater one.

Jerzy Grotowski is a genius, but I shudder to think how many misbegotten "Grotowskis" his Polish Laboratory Theatre will spawn. Peter Brook, being a highly gifted craftsman, knew how to popularize certain aspects of Grotowski's art in his production of *Marat/Sade*. Other such adaptations—most of them inept—are already in use and more are sure to follow. To be influenced by a master is natural, but for the most part the result is dilettantism or disaster.

The reason for all such unfortunate developments is that the superficial characteristics of the original model are mistaken for their meaning and value. The artist's inner history, his basic sources, the social and emotional circumstances of his growth, are very rarely operative in his disciples. Thus a new "manner" is contrived, a fashion sold by the sensitive to the ignorant.

I am sure that Grotowski's methods of training, chiefly designed as preparation for his productions, may prove stimulating and constructive for student actors and other professionals, but they do not constitute the essence of his art. For its better understanding one must turn from the theories and formal techniques (a collection of Grotowski's writings and speeches is called *Toward a Poor Theatre*) to the works themselves. Three of Grotowski's productions (none of them more than an hour long) were staged at the Washington Methodist Church in New York from October 16 to November 26, for limited audiences: 100 at most; in one case, only forty.

The first of these was based on a Grotowski scenario which he made from a romantically baroque adaptation of Calderón's *The Constant Prince*. The second was *Acropolis*, no more than an extract from a play by the 19th-century Polish dramatist Wyspianski; the locale and stress were entirely altered. *Apocalypsis cum Figuris*, the third production, was "evolved by its performers under the guidance of the director by means of acting exercises and sketches." The spoken text was culled from brief passages of the Bible, *The Brothers Karamazov*, one of T.S. Eliot's poems, and from something by Simone Weil.

Grotowski is all paroxysm. Thus his is the most contemporary of all theatres, for it can no longer be denied that we live in a time of cataclysm. Our very entertainments mask the face of agony. In the internal and outer upheaval, forms disintegrate, language decays, communication is conducted in jerks. Electric circuses serve as temples. Flesh is macerated. What is left of the soul goes into hiding or cries out in howls in which the difference between mirth and sorrow can hardly be distinguished. Even the gayest expressions contain the infernal.

These tendencies were already discernible in the expressionist theatre after World War I. But at that time there was an element of journalism and propaganda (especially in Germany) in the outcries of horror. With the end of World War II—in the work of Beckett, Pinter, Genet and others—an element of private anguish became apparent, of withdrawal into secret chambers of consciousness where mainly grotesque (sometimes muted) signs of agony were displayed as if more overt declarations were somehow indecently sentimental.

As we ordinarily understand the terms, story of plot does not exist in Grotowski's plays. There is only a design of fantastically contorted bodies and symbolically violent relationships hardly congruous with realistically purposive action. The figures move in space which with one exception (*Acropolis*) does not resemble any identifiable environment. We are in a fearsomely imagined Gehenna where laws of time, gravity and natural logic have been suspended.

Grotowski's theatre (I speak of it as a unit because he does not consider himself to be its sole creator) is distinct from its predecessors in the vein of modern martyrdom. The tone and inspiration of his theatre derive from the extermination camp. His productions bring us into the realm of the Last Judgment. *Acropolis* takes place on the labor threshold of mass extinction. The figures are last seen descending into a hole beneath the floor and when they have disappeared under its stovelike cover there flows back a final murmur, "Now we die."

Acropolis may not be the "best" of Grotowski's productions, but it is the most representative. Here the prisoners re-enact moments of the mythical past—Hebrew and Greek—distorting them by the use of props at hand—metal pipes, rags—so that a wedding ceremony is made hideous and the cohabitation of Paris and Helen is performed by two men. The lines spoken at incredible speed are not dialogue; they are tortured exclamations projected in the direction of another being, but with no shape as personal address. (It has been said that a knowledge of Polish does not make the lines readily intelligible, but it is evident in *Apocalypsis cum Figuris* that they are not meant to be taken as are the lines of an ordinary play; solemn and poetic passages are delivered in a mode which brutally contradicts and virtually obliterates their initial intent.)

In *Acropolis* the executioners and their victims become nearly identical: they are kin. The rhythm of the meaningless tasks assigned them is set by one of the prisoners who plays a violin while their labors are accented by the drumlike tread of their rough boots. This vision has nothing in common with the factual exposé of the Nazi crimes in Peter Weiss's *The Investigation*. There is no redemption here and except for the closing moment—the march to the holocaust—very little pathos.

What we have seen is the tragic farce of civilization's values utterly despoiled. The prisoners themselves have been reduced to savage blasphemy. They are no longer individuals but the debris of humanity. If pity and terror are evoked in the spectator, if his moral sensibility is affected, it is through a kind of impersonal revulsion, from which he recovers as if from an anxiety dream he remembers as something intolerably spectral. One cannot normally sustain or assimilate such experiences.

Still, there is nothing chaotic in the spectacle. The names of Brueghel, Bosch, Grünewald are frequently invoked for purposes of comparison; but that is misleading, for there was a sumptuousness in those artists. Grotowski's stage, architecture, costuming are bare. Everything has been stripped to the bone. (It is in this regard that his is a "poor theatre.") The structure of the playing area changes with each new play, so that the spectators are always in a different relation to the actors. Sometimes they look down as into an enclosed pit, sometimes they surround the action at stage level, sometimes they are ranged in a tierlike elevation slightly above. The actors are always very close, but they never move into or mingle with the audience.

Much has been made by various commentators of the company's extraordinary technical achievements in the use of voice and body. They are certainly striking and display training, prowess and command of a most remarkable sort. The voices unfalteringly emit sounds which remind one of the strange leaps of the twelve-tone system, with startling crescendos followed by crushed whisperings that do not resemble ordinary speech. They convey an other-worldly sphere *in extremis*. The lament of the constant prince (the play itself might be called the slaughter of innocence) is so desperate and prolonged as to exceed the bounds of human grief. We have arrived at the point of doomsday.

Yet all this has been given precise form. The exercises of Grotowski are intended to make the actor surmount his supposed breaking point, to stretch him vocally and bodily so that he can hold nothing back; to remove his restraints, those "blocks" imposed by his usual social comportment. He is wracked so that he becomes nothing but his id and thus releases what he primally is. Whether he actually succeeds in this, or whether it is altogether desirable that he do so, is another matter which I have no desire to question or capacity to determine at this juncture. One may say that in this respect the outstanding actor is Ryszard Cieslak as the constant prince and as the "simpleton" in the *Apocalypsis*.

To understand Grotowski's form and content as a single process one must consider certain other elements which have gone into its creation. Grotowski is an intensely cultivated theatre artist. He has absorbed Stanislavsky's lessons in regard to acting; he has responded to the impulse in Artaud; he has learned from Meyerhold's precepts on movement, and has felt the impact of the apocalyptic artists already mentioned. In addition and not unlike Brecht, he seeks to establish a certain space between the spectator and the spectacle so that for all their ferocity his plays may be appreciated contemplatively.

Grotowski's art is imbued with strains from

Catholic and other litanies and rituals. In *Acropolis*, especially, one hears echoes of Roman and Jewish services, as well as Slavic melodies. It is inescapable that while Grotowski is not a "believer," his is a ritualistic, indeed a religious art. (He has said that he wished his productions to be received in strict silence.) He seeks purification and salvation through their opposites, a return to the humane through the inhuman. We are to be redeemed through hellfire.

Goethe has said that no man can thoroughly capture the meaning of an art form who fails in some knowledge of the land and people of the art's provenance. Grotowski is a citizen of that Poland which was razed and decimated through the Nazi invasion and by the concentration camps which were its concomitants. Born in 1933 he is the witness and heir—as are most of his actors—of his country's devastation. The mark of that carnage is on their work. It is an abstract monument to the spiritual consequences of that horrendous event.

And that is why most productions done à la Grotowski must be largely fraudulent. His theatre has roots in a specific native experience. It is organic with a lived tradition which was shattered and defamed by unimaginable iniquity and boundless shame. Where an art lacks the foundation of corresponding realities it is ornament, entertainment or mere pretense.

Countless times I have been asked apropos of these performances of the Polish Laboratory Theatre (in existence since 1959 and still engaged "in research") whether or not I *liked* them. My answer: It doesn't matter whether any of us "likes" them. This troupe is what I have repeatedly called true *theatre*. It may always remain a theatre for the few (I do not refer to snobs), even a cult. Its "message" is well-nigh intolerable and its fanaticism forbidding. But its dedication to its vision of life and art is unparalleled in any theatre of our day.

—*NAT*, 8 Dec. '69

ALWIN NIKOLAIS DANCE THEATRE
THE INCREASED DIFFICULTY OF CONVERSATION
PRIVATE LIVES

What I most appreciated among the stage offerings of the past fortnight was the Alwin Nikolais Dance Theatre which, unfortunately, gave only a few performances at the City Center. It is most remiss of me not to have made the acquaintance of this admirable group much earlier. The reason for my neglect may have been that the Nikolais company had for a long time confined its activities to a "remote" part of town (remote from Times Square, that is) at the Henry Street Settlement Playhouse.

The Alwin Nikolais Dance Theatre is one of the best things on our stage. It is more theatre than ballet, but categories be damned. It provides a wonderful spectacle, an experience easily enjoyed but not so readily assimilated. There is a certain mystery to it; while it appears to have no "meaning" beyond its visual delight, one cannot be sure at first view that it is not much more than that. It is an abstract of the pleasures we may still attain in living in the mechanical chaos around us. Nikolais gives the electric turbulence of our civilization—even in some of its destructive aspects— a clear structure very nearly euphoric.

He comes very close to Gordon Craig's conception of a stage director. He designs movement, sets, costumes, lighting, and to a large extent composes the electronic score. All that is lacking to fulfill the Craigian idea is speech (the performers do babble occasionally, producing sounds not unlike the shards of conversation which reach one in the currents of a crowd).

Industrial shapes and noises, with dreamlike visions of other spheres and nonhuman forms (protozoa of another planet), are patterned to create a world of marvels. This is a 20th-century fairy-land relieved of horror. All is metaphor relating to what we have seen and know but cannot define. Is this, as one suspects, merely ornamental show? I doubt it. It may be compared simplisticly to Pop and Op art, but while these are often funny or momentarily fascinating when not depressing, Nikolais' visions are exhilarating even when some sort of doom is suggested. This is the way the world ends, not with a bang but a whoop. There is sophistication in this and even more a redeeming naïveté.

The dancers compose the cheerful focus of the occasion. They blend into the whole, with their gleaming star, Carolyn Carlson, twitching and twinkling as the brightest point of the constellation.

The Increased Difficulty of Concentration by the young Czech playwright, Vaclav Havel (at the Forum of the Repertory Theater of Lincoln Center) is a somewhat elongated comedy skit. It is moderately amusing; on the whole well played and directed by Mel Shapiro, though not quite in the robustly extravagant manner with which such plays are done at the Theatre on the Balustrade in Prague.

What interested me most is that while I speak of the play in terms of mild approval it was an important work for the Czechs. (Here is yet another example of the audience as the theatre's focal source.) The speech that seems almost embarrassingly out of place with us, a speech in which the central character declares his conviction that the truth of life cannot be measured by computers or bureaucratic dictates but only by the motivations of the human heart, is what Havel meant his play to say. That is what gave it social force in his country.

The Increasing Difficulty, etc., like *The Memorandum* (produced two seasons ago at the Public Theatre) is a satire on the rigidity of party "scientism." It is true that Dr. Eduard Huml, the play's sociologist protagonist, is beset by troubles that fall upon men everywhere: wife, mistress and aberrant sexual drives. These supply the play's best jokes, especially since the various episodes are presented out of their normal time sequence. But in addition, the doctor, chosen as a specimen to answer crazy questions addressed to him for purposes of useless classification, by a constantly erratic machine, is badgered by the machine's inane operators and an ominous overseer whose every utterance is at once ludicrous and menacing.

Thus the play, a farce of no great subtlety, becomes something vital to the Czech citizen forever under the vigilant and evil eye of—who can say just what. For us, it offers sidelights on contemporary "history" agreeably mixed with bedroom imbroglio.

There are some who regard Noel Coward's *Private Lives* as a masterpiece on the level of Oscar Wilde's best comedy. It is very neatly constructed, thoroughly apt as a pleasantry, crisply written in an unmistakably personal style. But it provokes in me no great assent in laughter or recognition of experience.

The personal style is important because it represents not only an individual idiosyncrasy—a man—but that of a place and a period: London's stage, café, night club and smart set between 1921 and 1931. It was the time of self-congratulatory flippancy, giddy pleasure in believing in nothing but prickly sensation, and appreciation of one's own appreciation of the dash and swish of it all. Bad manners took on the sheen of the best. Accompanying all this was an undertone of smart music, titillatingly sentimental, champagne induced, as in a wild party where even the knell of doom becomes transposed to a beguiling tinkle. Above all, one senses in all this a total indifference to everyone and everything outside the magic social circle.

It meant that the blithe spirits of the time, enamored of the theatre as superb falsity, had kicked over Victorian restraints as well as ideological solemnity—the previous war above all had to be forgotten. If the revelers had money or proximity to it they could dance in artificial paradises without any thought beyond the luxurious privilege of sparkling in the brilliant atmosphere.

There is no doubt about Coward's special charm. And no one more than Gertrude Lawrence embodied the attractiveness of this lighthearted, romantically scented segment of society which eddied between bright malice and decorative benevolence. Gertrude Lawrence, the first Amanda of *Private Lives*, was the glowing angel of Coward's orbit.

The current revival (Billy Rose Theatre) is directed by Stephen Porter, who has a gift for flighty comedy (à la Feydeau). Apart from the counter effectiveness of its settings, it is certainly a good production, though it has little of that silken softness which in the Coward-Lawrence manner goes along with the crispness. I do not say this in disapproval. It is extremely difficult to recapture a still remembered mood which has passed and not yet acquired a patina.

Brian Bedford is expert in clarity, timing and intelligent delivery of lines, but there is none of Coward's joy-in-wickedness—as if even his flagellant wit implied a caress. And while Tammy Grimes, a pixie if ever there was one, like some oddly fascinating bug or butterfly, is here in top form technically, she is hardly the ideally chic *woman* of Coward's particular fancy. Such creatures have gone with the wind of Vivian Leigh.

Still I must warn the reader that I view *Private Lives* from the "outside." I willingly acknowledge its attractions but I do not care for them. Not even as a youth in the twenties did I share in the myth of the era's lovely frenzy.

—*NAT*, 22 Dec. '69

LILLIAN HELLMAN: A WOMAN IN SEARCH OF TRUTH
An Unfinished Woman—A Memoir by Hellman

Lillian Hellman's book is a record of memories rather than a studied autobiography. Her memories cluster around personalities and events which have impressed her. "I don't want to be a bookkeeper of my own life," she says.

This typical attitude is revealed by the book's title, for Miss Hellman was always slow in development: "It took me a long time to know things" she declares. But she was always engaged in the process of investigation. She has always been on a "find-out kick."

A portrait emerges from Miss Hellman's apparently desultory recollections. Its salient feature is probity. Her probity is something more than "honesty." Its main bent is to examine her reactions and check the least hint of false pride or self-indulgence. Miss Hellman is above all a moral character. Capable of feeling, she is resolutely anti-sentimental. There is something spiritually Spartan about her.

I know something of these qualities because I directed what I believe to be her best, though not her most successful play, *The Autumn Garden*. Three incidents are relevant in this connection. The first concerns her warning that at times she may strike one as harsh and unjust to her collaborators (especially the director) but that her fault in this regard did not signify a lack of appreciation for the work being done. Her apparently sour manner emerged from a desire for a perfection which she realized was virtually impossible to achieve.

Before rehearsals had begun she asked me if I found any serious flaw in her play. I detected no obvious or remediable weakness but on a certain level of criticism I pointed out that while her play dealt with people who were very misguided, feckless or foolish as Chekhov's plays do, one did not come to love her characters as we do Chekhov's. "Ah," Miss Hellman replied at once, "I'm not as good a writer as Chekhov"—a remark which made me deeply respectful of her for all time.

Another memorable moment for me had to do with the writing of the play's final speech. It did not sufficiently clarify the author's basic intent. She worked on several revisions, none of which seemed right. One day late in the rehearsal period she read me a version I found altogether admirable.

"Yes," she said, "it's good: Dashiell Hammett wrote it."

If *An Unfinished Woman* may be said to have a "hero" it is the author of *The Maltese Falcon*. Hammett, with whom for some 30 years Miss Hellman had an intimate relationship, is described by her as "my closest, my most beloved friend." This reticence is characteristic not only of the writer but of her subject. Both of them reflect something of what was in each of them: A determined truthfulness, a tough realism and above all a sense of justice and honor.

She might scoff at the notion but there is in Miss Hellman a certain puritan streak which Hammett (raised as a Catholic) shared. He did not like "soft" talk; neither does Miss Hellman. When either of them was on the verge of expressing emotion too overtly both were inclined to clip the conversation by a curt "I don't want to talk about that." Both had dignity and courage (without rhetoric) as was evidenced in his enlisting in the army as a private at the age of 48 and as she showed in her modestly strong testimony before the House Committee on Un-American Activities. In their relationship with each other both used endearments sparingly. They manifested their feeling for one another with a certain acid bluffness.

This austerity marks Miss Hellman's adjustment to the two women—both black—whom she cared for beyond all others, her childhood nurse and guardian, Sophronia, and later her housekeeper and secretary Helen.

Lillian as a child told Sophronia about when her father had protected a young black girl from a possible rape by two white ruffians and asked, "Papa was brave, wasn't he?" Sophronia, after acknowledging that indeed he had been, added, "Things not going to get themselves fixed by one white man being nice to a nigger girl."

Miss Hellman has always been attracted to proud people of tough fiber and few words. She gives short shrift to fools. She is not ridden with "opinions." Her nature, which, she tells us, has alternated from vagueness to rigid demands, has caused unhappiness in many and, I dare say, in herself as well. The vagueness results, I believe, from the lag between what she experiences and her ability to interpret readily and come to a conclusion about it.

She has a sense of humor but it tends toward sharpness. She appreciates Dorothy Parker, who was another good friend. She speaks compassionately of Scott Fitzgerald for whom she has a higher regard as a writer than for Hemingway, both of whom are vividly etched in several telling incidents. The section on Spain during the Civil War and the pages from her Moscow diaries during and after World War II contain striking dramatic moments which are played down rather than rendered colorfully adventurous.

This brings us to a special sidelight on the book. Miss Hellman is best known to the world as a playwright, the author of such hits as *The Children's Hour*, *The Little Foxes*, *Watch on the Rhine*. Yet there is very little about the theatre in her book. And for a very interesting reason. There can be no question about her talent for the theatre, but she is not essentially a theatre person. She admits this herself: "I have wandered through the theatre as if I were a kind of stranger. I am not good at collaboration, the essence of the theatre."

What then is she if not a genuinely theatre person? She is a woman of excellent intelligence, interested in life in its broadest context. Though not a "preacher" she is a moralist, one who is vitally concerned with the proper conduct of life, making the world "safe" for decency! From her early childhood she has known disappointment and pain (the opening pages of her book indirectly disclose the origins of *The Little Foxes* and her rebellion against the obtuse stuffiness of folk hellbent on the accumulation of wealth and pride in it). All of this, I venture to say, has inflicted a wound (also the cause of periods of excessive drinking), a wound which turned off the easy flow of tenderness, the simple give and take of warm communication, untrammeled love. The word itself must often have seemed fraudulent to her. But she does harbor strong feelings and her heart has always been on the side of the angels. Above all she wants a humane world—and this is what all the best dramatists and artists generally have always aspired to bring about.

Even now she avoids—almost fears—too strong an assertiveness about herself and others. "I do regret," her book concludes, "that I spent too much of my life trying to find what I called 'truth,' trying to find what I called 'sense.' I never knew what I meant by truth, never made the sense I hoped for. All I mean is that I left too much of me unfinished because I wasted too much time. However."

The confession does her honor; it gives evidence of that tremor of humility which approaches wisdom. The final "however" is the sign of a strong spirit still moving onward in its striving for further knowledge, clarity, fullness. One finishes reading the book hoping that one may be able to judge oneself with a comparable probity.

—*LAT*, '69

WITH KIM STANLEY

THE
SEVENTIES

CAMINO REAL

Parents, it is said, are often fonder of their faltering child than of their steadier ones. Thus it may be with Tennessee Williams and his *Camino Real* which has twice before been produced in New York without success. But if the author's devotion to his weakling is understandable, it is sinful for a critic to encourage him in this indulgence.

In my review of the original (1953) production of *Camino Real*, directed by Elia Kazan, I was as cordial as I could possibly be because I admire Williams and was able to acknowledge the validity of certain of the play's psychological impulses. But I did not accept it. An unknown correspondent challenged me, if I were to remain at least an honest person, to see the play again for reconsideration.

With the production now at the Vivian Beaumont Theater of Lincoln Center I have seen *Camino Real* three times—once in London. Its faults have become more glaring for me with each view. This may be due in part to the fact that both the London production and the present one proved inferior to the first production about which I was somewhat severe.

Williams, like the Kilroy of *Camino Real*, is sincere. He wanted, he says, to offer us in free form his vision of the world. He has done so. That is the trouble. For in aiming directly at his statement (the play is not in the least obscure) he is like the artist who proposes to create Beauty head-on (Pascal has said that he who would behave like an angel behaves like a fool.) The attempt in art always results in the amateurish or the juvenile.

Williams proposed, as he has said, to offer "nothing more nor less than my conception of the time and world I live in." It is a brutal world, a police state, where the hungry, the unfortunate, the derelicts and the dreamers—blameless, naive or unwittingly corrupt—are humiliated, mutilated,

hounded to death and consigned to the garbage dumps. Yet it is only such folk, particularly the dreamers, poets and idealists—here represented by Don Quixote, Lord Byron, Dumas' Lady of the Camellias, Proust's Baron de Charlus, Casanova, the wee whore Esmeralda, and Kilroy, the typically ignorant American youth of kind though damaged heart—who, though they struggle vainly against the cold ferocity of the no-man's land they inhabit, may some day manage to break through the stony imprisonment surrounding them or find the route of deliverance precisely through their desire for forbearance, their dreams of freedom, their hope and belief in purity, loyalty and love.

The royal road has become harshly "real." This is romanticism (the hippies presumably espouse it), a perennial gush in humankind. I am altogether willing to flow in its stream for it is part of the body of reality. It has certainly inspired many beautiful works of art as it has been the wellspring of several of Williams' more rewarding plays. But the language of *Camino Real* exemplified in such a line as "We are all of us guinea pigs in the laboratory of God" is not romantic; it reeks of flat sentimentality.

Blanche in *A Streetcar Named Desire*, the unfrocked minister in *The Night of the Iguana*, the stranded actress of *The Gnädiges Fräulein* (a much underestimated play) in diverse ways achieve poignant eloquence because they are depicted as people rather than as mere symbols. The allegoric figurines of *Camino Real* (especially Quixote, Camille, Byron) are sophomoric counterfeits.

There is a further aspect to the play's style. "I am trying to capture the really 'tough' America of the comic sheets," Williams explains, "all the rootless, unstable and highly splendid hope beneath the middle-class in America." When we compare this statement of plan to the actual texture of the play we note once again the slip between the cup and the lip, the aim and the target.

There are elements of the "comic sheets" in the play—the pimp mother, the gosling daughter, their accompanying shill and, to some extent, Kilroy himself. But the overall atmosphere of the play is one of drugged melancholia, a glamorized lower depths of colored lights associated with forbidden places, shadowy, spectral, dangerous and somehow, to Williams and to many of us, poisonously attractive. The comic sheet is raucous; the world of *Camino Real* is a pocket of hell full of the temptations which lure us to nether regions, and to certain entertainments in which we release our hankering for evil. There is a good deal of reverse Puritanism in this.

We touch here on the problems involved in the mounting of the play. The Lincoln Center production under Milton Katselas is a bad one. It lacks sustained mood because it strives to embody some of the rowdy brashness implied in Williams' stated purpose without taking into account the sickly sweet air of corruption with which the play is infused. The dusky figure of death moans "*Muerta*" here as she did in *Streetcar*—but in the stylistic mishmash of this production she strikes one as an incongruity.

Peter Wexler's set, excellent simply as design, suggests the barrenness of the general environment, but it is essential to the play that its hard fundament be masked and saturated with an enticing gaudiness, the dizzying fumes of an artificial paradise, the very stuff which in certain Mediterranean towns and tropical resorts make cruelty and decay appear grimly alluring.

The performance throughout suffers from this lack of a central key so that the actors all seem to be fluttering or flailing about in avoid in which one hears the banality of the play's text all too well. Al Pacino's Kilroy is a tough punk wholly without lyric quality, and hence unsympathetic. We cannot believe that he has a heart of gold "as big as a baby's head." Susan Tyrrell, who was warmly appealing in Gibson's *A Cry of Players*, is made wretchedly funny instead of wryly affecting in her confused yearning for the tenderness she senses in Kilroy. The passage in which Kilroy and the hapless girl try to make contact—the play's best scene—which should be rather more pathetic than comic, becomes sheer burlesque, unfeelingly tawdry.

Jessica Tandy makes a fine appearance but her shrill hysteria never convinces us that in addition to having a secret soul she was once the soiled vestal of many captivated lovers. Jean-Pierre Aumont as Casanova—but why go on? All these worthy actors are forced into strain and vociferation that empty the air—which should be quiet, sultry, rank with languorous debility—of everything but an unresonant emotionalism and the effort to be "sincere."

—*NAT*, 26 Jan. '70

SORROW, FEAR, ANGER, DEATH, POETRY

Listening to the three-album *Spoken Arts Treasury of Modern American Poets*, in which one hundred poets read from their own works, a mental quirk made me recall the Duke in *Twelfth Night* who asks to hear "That strain again!" The request may not be inspired by the pleasure he takes in the music played but by the difficulty of immediately sensing its full import. Very few of the poems in this miscellany may be fully enjoyed on first hearing.

This is not caused by the obscurity of modern poetry, of which many complain, but by the fact that poetry is "the language of amazement." Pertinent to the problem is that statement made by the French poet St. John Perse that "the realm which poetry explores is that of the soul and the mystery in which human beings are enveloped." We today might phrase it differently by saying that poetry is as much the speech of the unconscious as it is of the reasoning mind, and the unconscious is a maze.

Thorough appreciation of these recorded poets is not a matter of a moment or even of hours but of a lifetime! The three albums should induce us to read not only more poetry in general but much more of the poets represented in these recordings by a very limited number of their poems, and those, unfortunately, not always the most characteristic or significant.

Two additional criticisms must be noted. We are not certain, as we listen, whether the aim of the editor, Paul Kresh, who has gone about this arduous task most carefully, was chiefly to present the poems or the poets. (Keats once said there was nothing more unpoetic than the person of the poet.) There is a certain charm in listening to e.e. cummings' velvet voice as he pronounces every word separately as if he were in awe of its wonder, but it is inescapable that many of the poets read their verse badly. Edgar Lee Masters, for instance, gives the impression of hating what he has written as well as the audience for whom he is reciting. Ezra Pound's voice is broken, his dentures impede his speech, though we feel inclined to applaud when we hear, along with his somewhat Irish accent in the *Cantos* replete with Greek, Latin, and probably Chinese, the perfect line, "Asperities diverted me in my green time."

Generally speaking, the poets born after 1929 read more satisfyingly than their elders: there is less archaic intoning. Among the younger men (though none in this *Treasury* is under 40) the attempt is simply to convey the design of their prosody.

It would be presumptuous on the spare evidence here to discuss any of the poets extensively. The range is wide. Yet there are recurrent themes. Apart from the perennial anticipation, sorrow, fear, anger, and at times relief at the prospect of death, there is the everlasting celebration of the phenomena of nature (Stanley Kunitz refers to "a triumph of Chinoiserie" apropos of the dragonfly's wing). But what is strikingly present is an outcry against modern life, particularly life in our country. One poet quotes Henry James, in what might be taken as the motto for this phase of the writing, "I do not fear American savagery, but its civilization."

Since poets are infrequently politically motivated, there is more wailing in this regard than signs of actual rebellion. "The bomb is our child," Brother Antoninus tells us. "History has no truth,"

the suffering Delmore Schwartz cries out in agony. Odgen Nash jokes acidly at our mechanistic society. Kenneth Patchen longs for an absolute amid cruelty and desolation. "Rain is no heavier soaking heavy heads," the sympathetic David Wagoner comments, "than a long party." Denise Simpson observes that, after Hitler, "our education is wasted on the town; we lack enthusiasm." Adrienne Rich says of happiness, "Nowadays no one believes in you," but this is followed by a wistfully encouraging note. cummings, who lives amid "dolls and dreams" salutes the "beautiful anarchist."

The blacks accuse: Langston Hughes with sweet humor, along with James Weldon Johnson in loftier tones. Owen Davidson, rejecting hate in describing the prayer of a black mother whose sons are at war for American freedom, finds that there is "blood in the darkness, blood on the pavements."

Anthony Hecht confesses "that all is not well with a man dead set to ignore the endless repetitions of his murderous blood." Still, affirmations and notes of restorative power are not wholly absent. Louis Untermeyer murmurs, "Ever insurgent let me be, make me more daring than devout." Murial Rukeyser speaks boldly and confidently in the gloom. Richard Wilbur melodiously and manfully bids us "to imagine excellence and try and make it," while Richard Eberhardt, his voice as clear as his message, asserts that though "the human being is a lonely creature...Love and harmony are our best nurture." Allen Ginsburg, whose poems seem to imitate the streets, makes an epic effort at a fundamental statement to "be kind...in the harsh, tangled, confused world, sick, dissatisfied, unloved."

Most penetrating and lucid is Marianne Moore's humanism. ("We devour ourselves," she says) Here we are in the threshold of the masters. (They seem to have been given, or to have taken, less time than some of their inferiors.) T.S. Eliot is delivered in his technically brilliant but lightest vein that reminds one of Edward Lear or even W.S. Gilbert. John Crowe Ransom, while always genteel, is wickedly witty and possibly "anti-woman" in "Captain Carpenter," a note I again find surprising in one of Randall Jarrell's poems. Conrad Aiken speaks with dignity as Robert Frost does in his matter-of-fact way and Carl Sandburg in something like cracker-barrel fashion when he foregoes the prophetic.

Wallace Stevens, like a respected elder statesman (or "classic"), speaks in muted splendor of a fading world. Among his many other virtues Anthony Hecht, a New Yorker who speaks with an English accent, reveals a wry skepticism in his twitting of Matthew Arnold in "The Dover Bitch." Lisping W.H. Auden is above all intellectually acute and contemporary in his spiritual turnings and twistings. We listen with particular attention to Theodore Roethke, his voice adding fineness to the echoes of exquisite sensibility and hurt in his writing ("The leaves, their whispers turned to kissing").

Robert Lowell is delicate, sharp, perceptive, always euphonious. He remains, not unlike George Santayana to whom he devotes a poem, still "unbelieving, unconfessed and unreceived" yet he nevertheless creates a sense of strong inner resolution forever ready to turn to the aid of those who need it. Then, too, there is William Carlos Williams of ringingly youthful voice, a man very much of our world, confronting it in all its pain, ugliness, energy, even in its vulgarity, without fear, indeed with an embrace of sturdy acceptance. It's a pity that no Hart Crane recording was available.

This summary does far less than justice to the diapason of the assembled poets. Their writing strikes me for the most part as far more suited to solitary reading than public address. The Russian poets expect to be heard and listened to; the Americans, fearing the lack of response in a large audience, tend to be much more introspective. But something is saved in our poets by being so "private," that is, removed from the widespread rattle of publicity. Although one hears that the younger generation, torn between a need to act violently upon the world and the impulse to turn from it in defiant refusal, is becoming more aware of poetry as an implement in both exercises.

Poets refresh our feeling for language. More important, they see things we constantly overlook and make us think quietly into ourselves. Long ago Victor Hugo proclaimed, "You say the poet is in the sky; so is lightning." Among us, the excellent Stanley Kunitz restates this warning more simply: "Tears are bullets when they harden."

Envoi: "Play on!"

—*NYT*, 15 Feb. '70

OPERATION SIDEWINDER

It is right for the Repertory Theater of Lincoln Center to produce Sam Shepard's *Operation Sidewinder*. Two such different persons as Edward Albee and Elizabeth Hardwick have praised him. His publishers, Bobbs-Merrill, puff him as the "acknowledged genius of the off-off-Broadway theatre." Most reviewers sympathetic to the new dramaturgy agree. I therefore congratulate the company at Lincoln Center for choosing to set *Operation Sidewinder*, 26-year-old Shepard's most elaborate play, beside those of Saroyan and Williams in this season's all-American program.

For reasons which should be apparent, much of my review here will consist of quotes. The play makes two complementary points: contemporary America is a scene of total madness and brutality, and this is so because a break between spiritual and material values is destined to destroy us.

Two long speeches crystallize these themes. The first is spoken by the Young Man, the play's central figure. He describes the environmental oppression.

The election oppression: Nixon, Wallace, Humphrey. The headline oppression...the radio-broadcast TV oppression. And every other advertisement with their names and faces and voices and haircuts and suits and collars and ties and lies.

And I was all set to watch Mission: Impossible *when Humphrey's flabby face shows up for another hour's alienation session. Oh please say something kind to us, something soft, something human— something different, something real, something—so we can believe again. His squirmy little voice answers us, "You can't always have everything your way." And the oppression of my fellow students becoming depressed. Depressed. Despaired. "We're not going to win. There's nothing we can do to win." We're only losing a little, we say. It could be so much worse. The soldiers are dying, the blacks are dying, the children are dying....*

And then I walked through the crowd of smiling people. They were living and happy, alive and free....You can't always have everything your own way. You'll be arrested. You'll be arrested, accosted, molested, tested and retested. You'll be beaten, you'll be jailed, you'll be thrown out of school....I am a prisoner to all your oppression—I am depressed, deranged, decapitated, dehumanized, defoliated, demented and damned. I can't get out. You can get out. You can smile and laugh and kiss and cry. I am! I am! I am! I am! ...Tonight. In this desert. In this space.

The second big speech is delivered in an "underground" scene among the desert Indians. As spoken on the stage I could understand only bits of it. Here is its essence:

"A great war is about to begin. It will mark the end of the Fourth World and the preparation for the Emergence to the Fifth....Do not seek shelter. It is only materialistic people who seek to make shelters. Those who are at peace with their own hearts are already in the great shelter of life....Those who take no part in the making of world division are ready to resume life in another world. They are all one, brothers. The war will be a spiritual conflict with material things. Material matters will be destroyed by spiritual beings who will remains to create one world and one nation under one power, that of the Creator. The time is not far off...." ·

There are, according to the Indian sibyl who speaks these lines, two kinds of men, those of the Snake Clan and the others of the Lizard Clan. The first represents the spiritual, the other the material—they are the head and tail of one body. Due to the jealousy of the Lizard tail, a cleavage occurred which led to havoc. But the two would one day be joined together in "the night of the great dance." A select few who understand and accept this mystery, "who live in the high mesa of this desert," will be saved from the holocaust which would destroy all others in the Fourth World. And this comes to pass.

These speeches suffice to clarify the play's prophetic, lyric, ideological aspects. But what of the play's body? It is put together in picaresque scenes of boyishly tough American humor. With the aid of his director, and of the lighting and special effects personnel, Shepard employs the full panoply of the stage, including a trick red-eyed snake, gunplay, electric storms, a singing rock and roll band, strobe lights, Indian ceremonial dances—in short, mixed media.

Most of the play's scenes show everyone, including the Young Man, preparing for violence in addle-brained rebellion against the powers that be. The conspirators are whites, blacks and redskins. (But Shepard is certainly not a partisan of violence, no matter how morally motivated.) Other scenes reveal stupid military men, a crazy inventor who has designed a sentient, thinking computer in the guise of a snake (the sidewinder of the title) to explore future possibilities beyond the range of human calculation. There is also an FBI investigator who mouths all the usual denunciations against the disturbers of the *status quo*. (It is not altogether clear why the computer-snake becomes the legendary serpent whose organic unity saves the blessed remnant from universal destruction of which it is also the instrument. Are we to suppose that the machine may also serve to redeem us?) In the surface desultoriness of its scenes the play puzzles the audience at first and thus tends to alienate it.

The evening's final moment—the great destruction, a blinding explosion—is scenic fun. (How pretty the world's devastation is made on stage and in photos.) Still, much of the play is dull. This is due only in part to the impression of aimlessness made by the peculiar sequence of scenes. Contributing even more to a strange boredom is the fact that the play's satire, for all its extravagance and color, is banal. There are random killings, popular obscenities, and a farcically conceived atmosphere of "Wild West" abandon. These are very much like the simplistic blasphemies about the idiotic heartlessness of our reigning mercantile, mechanical and military complex so commonly projected by the juvenile *avant-garde* of stage and screen.

Yes! Our civilization is coming apart at the seams, with its rip and roar becoming sensible even to the deaf. But how tiresome is the announcement of this Armageddon when it is perpetually blared through raucous symbols. Why can't our condition be fleshed in real human behavior, in its subtle as well as in its most patent manifestations, in homes, individual minds, institutions, industries? Luridly generalized, the disarray becomes just display, obstreperous entertainment barely more inspiring than the horrors presumably being lampooned.

Shepard has imagination and a feeling for the theatre. To serve his talent he must become factually more specific and verbally more eloquent. He must discipline himself to sharper thought or cultivate more incisive powers of lyric expression. Has our situation become so hopeless that we can do no more in the arts than rock, roll, rattle and scream?

As a production, *Operation Sidewinder* is physically ambitious, occasionally ingenious and eye-catching. One wonders if because of the pressure of time the gifted director, Michael Schultz, became more concerned with stage paraphernalia than with the acting—none of which calls for particular mention.

—*NAT*, 30 Mar. '70

PURLIE

Purlie, a new musical with book by Davis-Rose-Udell, music by Gary Geld, lyrics by Peter Udell (Broadway Theatre), is based on an amiable play, *Purlie Victorious*, by Ossie Davis, produced in 1961. It is corny, hokey and *good*.

The pejorative adjectives do not truly apply. The corn and the hokum are to a considerable extent desired—a part of the show's style. The intention is to deal with the miserable state of affairs in south Georgia "not too long ago" with teasing cuteness, a sly buffoonery close to fable. There is in it the ambiguous laughter of the presumably compliant black, more watchful than benign.

If *Purlie* is depreciated for its "sweetness," the situation being what it is today, the criterion should be set aside as shortsighted. *Purlie* does not wallop or shove, but its nice nudge is still an unmistakable warning.

If "propaganda" is called for, *Purlie* provides it in the tonic vigor and charm of its performance. It is the most happily cast play in town. Its inner unity is immensely bracing.

I speak first and mainly of the cast because it is the evening's most substantial asset. The book, except that it is too long, is better than most—good-humored, companionably shrewd, something more than a peg for numbers. While the music is not memorable, some of its orchestrations and choral arrangements by Garry Sherman and Luther Henderson are superior. The conducting by Joyce Brown—one of the very few women conductors on Broadway—adds much to the show's musical effectiveness.

That Cleavon Little is a talented actor comes as no surprise; he has been previously admired in a number of Off-Broadway plays. But his excellence as a singer has not been displayed before. His lean, dignified presence as the preacher Purlie, coupled with his natural sense of fun, serve as the "spine" of the show. He seems to acquire stature in the new circumstances of this musical, giving to and gaining from the surrounding company a quality of pride.

The show's triumphal discovery is Melba Moore, a slight young woman, who comes on the stage as if she were an "extra" and then shocks the audience into delighted recognition of a personality of very special charm. Her vocal delivery imparts a wonderful excitement, recalling the early Judy Garland, with a comedic joyousness that is as unforced as it is unassuming. There is a remarkable relaxation and warmth in Novella Nelson's singing and acting, somewhat more "educated" and passive than the others. There are resoundingly uplifting voices throughout.

A word of praise is also due John Heffernan, who plays the derided and quite funny bad (white) man of the piece in just the right "old time" style. Ben Edwards' settings strike the proper note. Philip Rose as producer, director and collaborator on the book, has met with conspicuous success the challenge of transforming the original play.

—*NAT*, 6 Apr. '70

COLETTE

Zoe Caldwell as Colette is fantastic. I use the adjective advisedly. There is an element of fantasy about *Colette*, the theatre piece (Ellen Stewart Theatre), as there was about Colette the writer. The real world of the luxurious Paris of 1912 is now a memory at once artificial and glamorous. Even in its time it was an *ancien régime* enamored of its own dream and reputation. It staged its own actuality. Its appeal lies in its narcissistic image of itself. Even a glimpse of it in the squalor of New York is destined to be a hit.

Colette was a woman avid for sensation and its acute observer. Her work is replete with sights, scents, tactile notations of domestic animals, flowers, plants, birds, fabrics, gems, clothes, gardens, the delicacies of the table and the vine, the delights and torments of the alcove and bedroom hetero- and homosexual. Colette was a hedonist, a taster; she poetized the physical—both the familiar and the cultivated—in an exquisitely iridescent tissue of verbiage, airy, fruity and silken, which retained something of a sharp peasant shrewdness.

Colette is a series of vignettes and tableaux culled by Elinor Jones from *Earthly Paradise*, a collection by Robert Phelps of Colette's autobiographical writings. Either because the precise quality of Colette's prose is difficult to transmit in English or because the excerpts are too brief to weave the necessary spell, the sensuous shimmer of her style is barely communicated in the text of this production.

Thus it is a triumph of stagecraft to make even a little of the Colette world emerge from the skimpy material. Reading the script one would hardly believe that it could be staged at all. Gerald Freedman has accomplished an extraordinary feat in making of these literary cuttings a performance that unquestionably affords pleasure.

He has done it with the aid of a piano (in addition to a bit of singing between episodes) as accompaniment to some of the dialogue. The neat changes in time and place and the expert use of the small cast also contribute to the pleasant effect. Except for Zoe Caldwell, Mildred Dunnock as Colette's wise mother and Charles Siebert as the rascally Willy, who married Colette when she was 15 and claimed the authorship of her early books, all actors play several roles with unobtrusive candor. The tone of the production is nicely stagy in a manner that evokes a period in the theatre untroubled by naturalism.

Still none of this would succeed in making the evening *play* if it were not for Zoe Caldwell's extraordinary verve. Her talent is unique: I know of no English-speaking actress today who has her technical attributes, combined with so much zest, intelligence, humor and sense of performance. Her voice is bronze, which is also how Colette's voice is described. Each word she utters is "sculpted."

Her amazing eyes flash messages, her slightest intention is writ large, though by means which are rarely blatant. Her keenness of observation is sustained by a marvelous mimetic faculty. Without vulgarity she communicates the joys of the theatrical.

Every virtue has its danger: the script of *Colette* being little more than a scenario rendered in thin slices, Miss Caldwell is obliged to make immediately striking impressions—very much as if they were photographic slides or chromos. Because of this, and because too of her special gifts, she injects an element of artifice that is attractive as spectacle but somehow fails to convey a sense of living experience. While I came away from the performance admiring its virtuosity, I could not say I had seen more than a splendid imitation of a woman writer known as Colette. The woman's "life" had entertained rather than touched me.

This, I repeat, may be due in large measure to the nature of the text. Everything is thrust upon us, nothing unfolded. Thus the high moment of the occasion is not, for example, Colette's speech before the Belgian Academy, in which she has some excellent things to say about writing, but the pantomime-melodrama in which she is seen in the variety show into which Willy had forced her for his gain. This is not only very funny but has the genius of histrionic re-creation of a popular old-time way of theatrical expression.

If you really want to know Colette, read her books. For all her refined sensibility—she did learn much from her mother's great lesson to "look, look, look"—they contain something tart, hard and mean, a trait typically French which at times lends French writers their brilliance. I mention this here to differentiate what I feel about Colette as author and Zoe Caldwell as actress.

Colette's love of life has something feline in it. She exposed herself to the delicious bloom of whatever the world offered her, a bounty received with very few "general ideas." But there is another sort of love, not so readily defined in sensory terms which Colette's work does not altogether encompass and for lack of which she remains after all

something less than a master. On the other hand, Caldwell the robust Australian has, besides her tremendous gusto and capacity for laughter, a richer fund of earthy power and greater generosity of spirit than anything one finds in Colette as writer. These will develop further when she has a role in a play which permits the full use of her natural instincts as much as she now exults in her bravura. At the moment she deserves nothing less than our enthusiastic blessings.

—*NAT*, 25 May '70

RABELAIS
THE ME NOBODY KNOWS

Sixteenth-century France produced two great writers: Rabelais and Montaigne. Both were Renaissance humanists. Rabelais, cleric and libertarian, exulted in the pleasure of living—brain, blood, mouth and gut, flesh and genitals. (In Montaigne, Rabelais' ebullience is becalmed in measured wisdom.) Rabelais enriched the French language through his steaming imagination, his all-encompassing gusto. Rhetoric and thought in him were of the same substance: he invented a world.

Jean-Louis Barrault, a Rabelaisian of the head, using segments of Rabelais' prose, has concocted a stage festivity out of the stories of their joyous monsters. In Paris after the student uprisings of May 1968, Barrault's essay in "total theatre" struck its audience as a gorgeous gesture of defiance. It was a quasi-political as well as a theatrical triumph.

Rabelais (recently at the City Center) was designed to be played circus fashion, in the round, in a moderate-sized house. The City Center auditorium is much too large and its proscenium stage altogether unsuited to the planned effects. The actors shout but their voices ascend to the flies, and when they turn their backs to the audience (a few of whom sit in the rear of the platform) the words become totally unintelligible to the audience out front.

But even that is not the worst of it. The production does not embody Rabelais' giganticism. Its style, unusual in Paris, has been made familiar in other European capitals and, to some extent, here. The actors sing, dance, clown, cavort and riot in a manner which in no way turns us on. We have seen all this better done by other companies—especially by our various dance ensembles. Barrault's "choreography" may startle and delight the French because his theatre is associated with the serious, if not the solemn. But for all the frisking about, his *Rabelais* is juiceless and joyless.

Barrault's importance is national. After the war he enlivened the languishing French theatre by employing fine artists to design his settings, by offering an adaptation of *The Castle* and having made a new translation of *Hamlet*, by reviving Feydeau, by encouraging Camus as a playwright, by engaging likable and sometimes first-rate actors in permanent association.

But Barrault's talent is not strikingly original. He is an intelligent and assiduous eclectic, a limited actor and pantomimist. He is no Copeau, Reinhardt, Meyerhold, Brecht or Grotowski. There are lesser men than these in England, Russia, Czechoslovakia, Poland, Romania, who are his superiors in innovation and skill. The best production of Barrault's theatre was that of Molière's *Les Fourberies de Scapin* which was directed by Jouvet.

The Me Nobody Knows (Orpheum Theatre) is based on a series of tiny "compositions," edited by Stephen M. Joseph, written by children between the ages of 7 and 18, attending public schools in Bedford-Stuyvesant, Harlem, Jamaica, Manhattan and the Youth House in the Bronx—in other words, children of our various ghettos. Some of the kids' poems are used as lyrics, and there are others in a more adult vein by Will Holt and Herb Schapiro with well-orchestrated music by Gary William Friedman.

It is not a "rock-musical." It is a staging of the assembled material. The various numbers move smoothly from one to another creating a sense of unity in an architectural setting suggestive of a tenement with projections of children's drawings in the background, all admirably arranged and lit by Clarke Dunham. Patricia Birch has done a good job staging the musical numbers; the whole is under the excellent supervision of Robert H. Livingston.

Ghettos are wretched places; their existence is a shameful blight on our civilization. Knowing this, some may complain that making an evening's entertainment on such premises is a reprehensible exploitation of misery. I can understand the objection, but I am not sure that it is valid.

I myself was born in a ghetto: the lower East Side of Manhattan, and although I witnessed suffering, cruelty, crime and poverty there (albeit different in kind from what now exists) and my father, a doctor, was called upon to heal many of the ill, the wounded, the disabled, I also saw signs of energy, resistance, robust hope and, miraculously, a great deal of fun, a keen joy in living rendered all the more exhilarating by the surrounding squalor. Some of my fondest memories are those of my early years in that "depressed area."

Enjoyment of *The Me Nobody Knows* does not preclude understanding the situation in our ghettos or imply complacency about the need to eradicate it. What I cherished in the show is the talent and vitality of the cast, the bubble of its playfulness, the raciness of its expression which, with or without the advantages of privileged training among the actors, is still the produce of the streets in the dim and sequestered quarters of our town. If I liked the jubilantly aggressive college dropouts of the South in *Stomp* (as I did), there is no reason why I should reject the jaunty youngsters whose laments and frolics are "romanticized" in *The Me Nobody Knows*. The fact is that I had a good time—though I found it a bit too long. The entire company pleased me.

—*NAT*, 8 June '70

THE OPEN THEATRE

I like what the Open Theatre Ensemble is doing. It enacts variations on basic themes—such as the genesis of evil—in a series of interrelated vignettes, with or without words. The manner is akin to that of Grotowski; the tone totally different. While the Pole is tragically exasperated, the American company tends toward humor, irony, a youthful lightness and lyricism.

Such a characterization of the Open Theatre may come as a surprise to some, perhaps even to the company itself. How can one speak of *Terminal* which deals with death as "light"? There is a certain existentialist pessimism in the apparent content of the piece. There is also a quasi-mystic element in it. But when an undertaker's embalming procedure is performed in pantomime the effect is one of a wry kidding rather than of anything horrific or solemn.

Man's inability to understand God or nature's will is made funny. A funeral march is simply the overture to an entertainment rather than a sober moment. The spectacle bespeaks an exercise in theatrical form, not a real connection with the "mystery" of death.

I like *The Serpent* better. That may be because there is something charmingly naive for us in the story of Eve's emergence from Adam's rib, the subsequent temptation of Eve by the serpent and Eve's seduction of Adam. Then graphically and impressively we see Cain's killing of Abel. Following this, there is a mass copulation to the accompaniment of Biblical beats intoned by two ladies. This is amusing enough, though at the end the participants emit agonized groans. The evening closes, in a conceit that is emblematic for me of the Open Theatre's quality, with the company singing "We were sailing along on moonlight bay," after which the actors sit down among the spectators mute and tranquil, as if contemplating the unfathomable wonder of its all.

There are no costumes at the Open Theatre; the actors appear barefoot, in simple work clothes designed for the occasion. Sometimes they speak words written by Susan Yankowitz for *Terminal* and by Jean Claude Van Itallie for *The Serpent*, but it is all a collective work under the direction of Joseph Chaikin and Robert Sklar. Percussive and/or flutelike sound is employed. In *The Serpent* we seem to hear the "music" of plant and animal life in their generative stages. The actors add their own little beastlike bleats, neighs, moos.

At one point the serpent is seen in a swaying tree (composed of the actors' bodies), aglow with glistening red apples. This is one of the most winning stage metaphors in all the Open Theatre's repertory. *Terminal* is a bit too long, while *The Serpent*, which has been rehearsed over a more extended period, possesses a more consistently interesting and richer texture.

I write about the Open Theatre with restraint rather than rapture. Joseph Chaikin and his collaborators are serious and dedicated people. They do not aim to be sensational or "controversial." They are pursuing a course which is theatrically stimulating and valuable. That they are finer in spirit and craft than some of their colleagues in similar areas is certainly true, but to make claims for them without noting their limitations would do them and us a critical disservice.

There are rarely any *individuals* in such ensembles (the Grotowski Company has only one outstanding actor). The nature of this sort of teamwork tends to render special talent almost supererogatory. But even as a group the Open Theatre performances have not yet attained the level of such companies as those of Cunningham, Nikolais and the like. The Open Theatre does not have the time and money required for constant training and practice which alone lead to complete achievement.

More crucial is a lack thus far of really telling thought, cogent ideas suggesting the intensity of experience that is the mark of true creation. Good will, charm and engaging intelligence have been achieved; high artistry or compelling mastery is a long way off.

—NAT, 22 June '70

LONDON THEATRE

They don't play the British national anthem in the London theatres any more before or after the show as they used to. A year ago the expletive "s.o.b." was taboo. Now four-letter words abound. These are superficial signs of change that have been going on since the late fifties.

The anti-establishment theatre is now the popular theatre. Even a thriller like Anthony Shaffer's hit *Sleuth* speaks of such fare—detective fiction—as a symptom of the emptiness of England's old class society.

The deep dissatisfaction with the present state of the nation voiced by all parties is taking anew turn—beyond the merely jocular. A revue like *Oh What a Lovely War* was as sentimental as it was satiric. This is hardly true of such a play as Peter Nichols' *The National Health*, admirably produced at the National Theatre. Here the mockery, despite some alleviation through a travesty of television gush, is bitter. The humor is jaundiced throughout.

On the surface *The National Health*, by the author of *Joe Egg*, is a detailed picture of a general ward in a welfare state hospital. The interns droop with fatigue from overwork; the head physician, while professionally expert, is contemptuous of his rather callous assistants. The seriously ill die; the others are dismissed from care without cure; the prognosis for all is bleak. Few despair but there is little real hope anywhere. Disappointment is chronic.

All this would be unendurable as spectacle if there were not so much levity in the presentation. But it is through this very "fun" that the style of the play and the present mood in the English theatre (and life) become perceptible. The play would be less ominous if it were either more pathetic or more indignant. Danger is inherent in the joke.

The National Theatre, almost eighty actors strong, is talented, versatile, intelligent and attractive. It is especially fortunate in character actors and comedians. The repertory is becoming increasingly far-ranging. The National, together with the other subsidized theatres, the Royal Shakespeare and the Royal Court, are now the focus of interest in London. The West End (the commercial) theatre is in trouble.

But in the West End too the trend is toward sick laughter, grinning discouragement. Though there is less optimism about the state of the theatre now than there was in the early days of Osborne, Pinter, Arden and others, I find that whatever the quality of the particular plays presently on view, there is far more reflection of contemporary life than on our stage or in France. And this, for all the disillusionment that emerges is indicative, at least, of artistic honesty.

The Parisian theatre of the 1950s, in a manner characteristically French, veered to the abstract, the stylized. Though, to some extent this is also true in England, the base is almost always realistic. The English never stray too far from the concrete. There is vigor in this.

David Storey's *The Contractor* is a group portrait of ill-favored (non-union) workers employed by a rough Yorkshire builder. The workers are both wounded in spirit and thick-skinned. There is one rebellious fellow among them—an Irishman—but they are all uninterested in their jobs, unkind to one another, hostile, and unimpressed though outwardly servile to their employer.

Himself a man of working-class origin, the builder (or contractor) is tough in manner, seemingly generous, though his generosity masks a fundamental exploitation of his employees' weaknesses. He is brutal with his family: a daughter eager to escape her home, an educated son he finds soft and useless, a doctor son-in-law for whom he has little respect and who seems to deserve none, a wife whom he bears with and who puts up with him. All are strangers to one another, conscious of little except their shared duress.

The play's language is undoubtedly authentic, the observation literal; the tone is one of mordant amusement and the acting, under Lindsay Anderson's sardonic eye, everything that it should be. The probably intentional effect is somewhat chilling, but this is England looking at itself with rigor. The audience appears to enjoy the sight of this familiar "landscape." But, I wondered, is the truth here sufficiently true. Gorky in Czarist times depicted similar people (and many worse) but there was heart in the Russian's treatment—and I don't mean sentimentality. We do not stand apart from his characters as I felt inclined to do from those in *The Contractor*.

In David Mercer's *Flint*, England's troubled spirit becomes extravagant. Mercer, who wrote the screenplay for *Morgan*, is something of an anarchist. His writing laughs but its laughter bodes no good.

Flint is a 70-year-old Anglican clergyman who drinks, fornicates and values very little apart from such pleasures. He is married to a frigid wife who hates him; he has been his sister-in-law's lover; she is a woman who in advanced age has become savagely eccentric. He takes up with a 20-year-old tart who is pregnant. One wonders how this oddball was able to pursue his duties in the church till we meet his bishop who is himself a man of little faith in anything but his official position.

The play is peppered with obscenities which enliven a highly literary language. Mercer writes to beat the band, but Flint, the man and the play, have nowhere to go but to a fatal vehicular accident as Flint and his girl attempt to ride free of the musty establishment which has for so long been his support. But that establishment, which is treated with so much witty derision in this as in the other plays, is now in visible decay and everyone appears to rejoice in its breakdown.

Reading what I have just said an American might conclude that what England is going through is a moral and social crisis not unlike our own. That would be an error. For even in their present condition the English remain a thoroughly civilized people. Civilization in America has always been unfinished, only partially operative. In England even the hippies, the defectors and the derelicts still manifest the stamp of the original civilizing process. Perhaps this residue of form will serve to preserve the English from the ignominous collapse with which all our civilizations are threatened, seem indeed to "promise."

The sensation of the late London season is the National Theatre's production of *The Merchant of Venice*. The main attraction is Laurence Olivier's Shylock, though there are other novelties in the occasion.

The play has been staged by Jonathan Miller, who was one of the stars of *Beyond the Fringe* and who has recently been marking time by refurbishing Lewis Carroll and Shakespeare with contemporary conceits. The revue touch is especially effective in the casket scene in which the Prince of Morocco is played as a modern African potentate, and the Prince of Arragon is burlesqued as a senile and purblind idiot. But there is less humor in the rest.

Miller mitigates the anti-Semitic aspect of the play. Thus when Bassanio witnesses Shylock's extreme humiliation, he is markedly affected and does all he can to stop his friend Gratiano from viciously guying the suffering Jew. Even Antonio, played as a respectable Victorian British businessman, is shaken when he hears Shylock's terrible sobbing immediately after he has left the court in defeat. The play begins and ends with what sounds very much like a traditional Hebrew chant of lamentation.

I have always thought of *The Merchant of Venice* as an ironic comedy about "capitalist" hypocrisy. Antonio and his companions—their whole society in fact—live on unearned income. Most of them are wastrels parading as gentlemanly gay blades. They hate the Jew for being a moneylender which was virtually the only profession open to one of his religion in the 16th century. But they require his money when they have been profligate in the use of their funds. After they escape the consequences of their improvidence and bankrupted the Jew they turn once more to their thoughtless fun and games. This explains the last act, superfluous even fatuous, unless the play is so understood.

Something of this comes through in Miller's production, but hardly enough. Still I suspect that the interpretation I have suggested is based on the assumption that every one of Shakespeare's plays is a coherent whole. I am not at all convinced that this is so. Shakespeare was a giant among poet-dramatists, but he was also a popular play-maker, and when he wrote *The Merchant* he was dealing with a tricky theme. He planned to write a play with lots of laughs and pretty diversions, a melo-dramatic comedy which would also contain the menace of a fantastic creature, a *Jew*, who in the England of his day was an unknown phenomenon, since the Jews had been banished many years before.

But because Shakespeare was a genius he could not create an entirely false character, and Shylock became a highly complex one: an ogre to the groundlings, a man of fierce and understand-able passion for the more aware. He has been dena-tured by the cruelty of his situation as an "alien" in a corrupt society. On several occasions in these columns I have referred to him as "the poisoned conscience of Venice." He is no "hero" and just as certainly not the laughable villain the Elizabethans must have taken him to be.

What I saw at the National Theatre is a clever show with hints and overtones of contemporary significance and a *reasonable* portrait of the pivotal character. Except for the late 19th-century English mode in which the play is set, the produc-tion marks no startling departure from previous interpretations of recent years.

As performance, Olivier's Shylock is superb. His beardless make-up possesses a striking resem-blance to some Anglo-Jewish tradesmen of Austrian or German origin often seen today in London. His delivery and readings are wonderful in their clarity and eloquence. With great convic-tion he conveys the justified resentment of the persecuted. The famous "Hath not a Jew eyes," is not special pleading but the exasperation of a man fed up to the teeth with injustice. Storming about the stage his protest rises tempestuously from within him but is not addressed to anyone in partic-ular.

Shylock here is reduced to middle-class proportions. The slight Germanic accent conspires to enhance this impression. (There is in the whole idea of making Shakespeare a man of our day, whether in a "Marxist" or "existentialist" vein, something basically middle class.) What is lacking in Olivier's Shylock—and the production gener-ally, more a thing of good and less good bits and patches than a satisfactory whole—is a sense of *grandeur*. Without it Shakespeare's stature is diminished.

I was an interested observer, even at moments an admiring one, at this *Merchant*. But it did not move me nor did it cause me to see the play in a new light. Intelligence and skill had gone into its making, but I felt less involved than I did in the ephemeral pieces I saw on some of the other evenings.

Just as there hardly exists a truly tragic drama in the contemporary theatre, there are virtually no genuine tragedians. The last one I can remember seeing was Chaliapin, and between 1916 and 1922 John Barrymore struck me as having potential. Laurence Olivier is not essentially a tragedian. He is a romantic actor, a brilliant delineator of (often comic) characters. He has extraordinary power, scope and charm, and he is certainly the most dazzlingly accomplished player today on the English-speaking stage.

—*NAT*, 6 July '70

THE NEW YORK FILM FESTIVAL

I saw twenty-three "features" in two weeks at the New York Film Festival at Lincoln Center. Oy! My first reaction was wrath. However, looking back, I find (apart from several entertaining shorts) that I admired four pictures—*The Wild Child, Days and Nights in the Forest, The Scavengers, Tristana*—and had some regard for *Five Easy Pieces, The Butcher, Kes, Street Scenes 1970, Mistreatment, Harry Munter, The Garden of Delights, The Inheritors*. There were two or three others I did not altogether despise. The record did not then seem as abysmal as I had, to begin with, thought it was going to be.

My initial indignation was inspired by the inclusion in the roster of Godard's *Wind from the East*, Dick Fontaine's *Double Pisces*, Jean-Marie Straub and Danièle Huillet's *Othon*. I missed three other presentations, one of which, the Japanese *Chikamatzu Monogatari*, I hope to see at a later date.

The listing indicates at least two prejudices. I dislike esoteric films which, whatever their technical interest, are on their surface (what we actually *see*) immeasurably boring. I prefer straightforward statements (not too remote from "realism") to ambiguity *à la mode*. If these prejudices disqualify me as a movie guide, read no further.

What I object to most of all is the tendency of too many contemporary film makers to imply "psychology" which they do not actually create but assume will be taken for granted because we have all become acquainted with sociological or psychoanalytic tracts and therefore acquiesce in the depiction of sordid behavior as self-explanatory. (A man has been in the Army for fifteen years and, having become a butcher, he is now homicidal. Or since society is now at sixes and sevens, a picture "hero" is understandably, even "forgivably" disaffected from all his fellow men and thus irresponsible.) Then again too many film makers—like a good many "*avant-garde*" playwrights—have retired into ghettos of the mind—which we are presumed to regard as the proper place to dwell.

Godard's *Wind from the East* is filmically a cop-out. If Godard has a message, it is reactionary, no matter what his political position. The title of his latest joke suggests sympathy with Maoism, but Mao would order decapitation for anyone who perpetrated such flummery in his regime. Godard's exhibit is a reversion to the most noxious sort of Dadaism. Our time is too troubled for such farce. *Wind from the East* is wind from the bottom.

Othon is an imbecile "experiment," based on a little-known play by Corneille, and unendurably dull. It is pedantically replete with references to events in the history of ancient Rome—unfamiliar even in France to the general spectator. In the picture, the *dramatis personae* stand in "classic robes on a terrace overlooking modern Rome, where we see, never with any change of the image, the vehicular traffic of the city. The characters hardly ever move (the camera only occasionally) and mouth Corneille's Alexandrines—some of them in foreign accent—at great speed, like kids who have learned the text by rote. If a French boy at a *lycée* spoke the text in this fashion he would be ejected from class.

All this is supposed to suggest a parallel between the situation (what situation?) as set forth in the play and present-day society. A *New York Times* reviewer speaks of the excellent acting which redeems the film. There is *no* acting, and nothing could save the film, except the committee which chose to show it at the festival.

Robert Hatch has already extolled the virtues of Truffaut's *The Wild Child*. Among other attributes it is one of the few films today which speak of something other than the wretchedness of all living things. That is also true of Satyajit Ray's black and white *Days and Nights in the Forest*. It can hardly be said to have a plot. Four young men from Calcutta leave town for a short, carefree holiday in the country. One is a rather foolish, selfish but not ill-natured chap addicted to gambling, another a sports champion; the other two are better-educated fellows of some sensibility.

They encounter members of poor tribes, as well as a family of well-bred and well-to-do folk (a father, his two daughters, a small son) who are also on vacation. One man consorts with a whore; he is also beaten up by a vagrant momentarily employed as a servant, whom he has struck on account of theft of which the miserable creature is guiltless. Another of the four men, in acute embarrassment, fails to accept the offer of her person by one of the ladies who has been a chaste widow for three years. Still another of the four becomes enamored of a lovely young woman in the family which has befriended them. They all return to the city.

That is it: there is no "meaning" apart from the bare facts. But it is enough. For in this there is tenderness without anything in the least maudlin. The misery of the impoverished is casually observed, grace in the various relationships is always present without being stressed. Ray's modest "document" offers an experience, delicately sorrowful, and yet sweetly humorous. We come close to real people, whose flaws and attractiveness are both Hindu and universal. We become more meritoriously human for having met them.

Ermanno Olmi is a director of exceptional integrity. I have admired all his previous pictures—*The Job*, *The Fiancés*, as well as the generally less favored film *One Fine Day*—for the honesty, the sobriety, the quiet observation, personal and social understanding, which are once again evident in *The Scavengers*. Perhaps Olmi, like Bresson, will never be a hit director. His work is always understated and without obvious "point."

The Scavengers is a picture of an Italian village during the 1945 aftermath of the war. Most of the population is jobless. But an old codger, a veteran of World War I, shows a young man just returned from the front how a "fortune" is to be made. Buried in the hilltops are abandoned bombs, grenades, etc., which the Austrians left behind in 1918. These weapons may be dismantled and sold as scrap iron, together with the other valuable ingredients. It is illegal, but the young man engages himself as a partner to the jolly and drunken reprobate, who insists his efforts as a scavenger are preferable to working for a boss. The young man, who had been tempted to leave Italy for Australia, learns the special maneuvers required to disinter the hidden riches. But having recognized the fatal dangers involved, and profiting by his country's partial recovery, he accepts an ordinary job in a mill.

I am not certain what the social objective of the picture is; I am sure that its directness in mirroring the situation, the suspense in watching the several steps in the process of discovering and removing the explosive "treasure" from the earth are absorbing. Art does not readily reveal its subliminal secrets. There is a morose but gentle pessimism in Olmi's attitude to labor in modern times: perhaps what Olmi's picture is saying is that among the choices men must make in earning their livelihood there is only "freedom" through unlawful scavenging or a kind of slavery in the menial tasks of industry. But whether this is so or not the picture is good.

With Luis Buñuel's *Tristana* one enters a more shadowy realm, mysterious and possibly disturbing. Buñuel's nature is complex. Visually he is a superb artist. Every shot is rich with the feeling of place: the locale is probably Spanish Toledo in the twenties. The backgrounds are beautiful with an old beauty which bespeaks an experience of life of profound substrata articulated in grave splendor.

I do not cavil at the ambiguity in this film, if in fact it exists. What is puzzling in it does not arise from a partiality to obfuscation or to supposedly "modern" cinematic gimmicks. Buñuel never deliberately injects difficulty into his pictures as a warrant of sophistication or originality. What is dense is Buñuel's soul, and he can do no other than express it as he does, leaving others to interpret it as they may.

Tristana deals with the tragedy in desire. The film's central figure, Don Lope, is an elderly gentleman with an almost quixotic sense of honor. Though he comes of a wealthy family, his fortune has been rapidly declining, but toward the end of his days he recovers some of it through an inheritance. Don Lope has elevated moral standards in unusual combination. He is a rake, but he believes it wrong to seduce the wife of a friend or a pure girl. He scorns the Church, hates bigotry. He is against the police because it stands for power, while he is always on the side of its victims, the weak. He is a duelist, and something of a "Socialist." But the drive of his sensuality leads him to make love to his ward, Tristana, a beautiful young girl and a virgin. Yet he suffers very little sense of guilt because of this. He considers himself to be her "father" and her "husband," though he does not offer to marry her.

Tristana herself is hardly a simple person. She submits to Don Lope because she has been trained in obedience. When he kisses her for the first time in passionate embrace she does not resist but giggles in surprise. But, while submissive, she hates the old gent who, because of his intense sexuality, is menacingly jealous. She realizes the extent of her abhorrence when she meets Horacio, a young artist from Barcelona, to whom she gives herself. On this affair being discovered, she defies Don Lope who ineffectually challenges his rival to a duel. Tristana leaves Don Lope and goes off with Horacio to Barcelona.

Three years later the artist comes to tell Don Lope that Tristana is terribly ill and wants to come back to his house. Tristana has refused to marry her lover, perhaps because Don Lope has so often repeated that wedding ties are a bondage. It is to be noted that when Tristana is resting at Don Lope's place, she tells Horacio that if he really loved her he would not have consented to bring her to Don Lope's home—nor would Don Lope have acted in like manner under similar circumstances.

Tristana has to undergo the amputation of a leg. She occupies herself by playing a piano Don Lope has brought her. She now moves about on crutches or on an artificial leg. She has become "correct" and hard. She finally agrees to marry Don Lope; when he wishes to sleep with her on their wedding night she ridicules him for it. Still she satisfies a deaf mute boy's lust for her by exposing her bosom for him—at a distance. When Don Lope has a heart attack, he bids Tristana to call a doctor; she only pretends to do so and the old man dies.

Why, one asks oneself, does Buñuel resort to the odd turn of the story—the crippling of Tristana and the various distortions of her later behavior? Must Tristana and the others suffer for their sins, which result from the freedom of their natural but perhaps excessive concupiscence? One cannot tell, but I suspect that despite Buñuel's intense anticlericalism, the residue of his original Catholicism remains implanted in him.

Unabated desire, raw sexuality, though inevitable in nature, poisons the blood. This is tragic because of the inexorability of the impulse, the ineluctability of its consequences. We may deny or dislike this pattern of conscience; it is extremely Spanish and, contrary to the power of his own rationalism, it seems to be very much part of Buñuel.

What is important in this instance is that it is revealed without preachment or explicit doctrine but with pictorial eloquence, emotional reserve, high-born dignity. And, don't be shocked at my saying this: there may be some truth, anyhow *a* truth in Buñuel's view. We always pay a price, in disappointment or pain, for whatever is in us, even when it is not evil.

—NAT, 5 Oct. '70

BOB AND RAY
OPIUM

I don't know if Karl Marx had anything to say about show business, but it is certainly a fact that materialistic interpretation would jibe very well with the theatre's present condition. The uncertain stock market is giving "angels" the jitters. They don't invest readily in anything but musicals, and even in that line things are slowing down.

The one new show on Broadway at this writing, *Bob and Ray—The Two and Only* (Golden Theatre), is radio and television's gift to the "uptown" theatre. Bob Elliott and Ray Goulding are funny fellows and at least one of them can act, but the two make a fine team. Their jokes poke fun at all of us in our crazy society, without being complacent or bitter. They are neither highbrow nor Philistine. Their show is short, and the price of admission is too high—but that is not their fault.

Off-Broadway is more active, but I'm beginning to wonder whether the term still has any specific significance; it no longer accurately indicates location, and the costs of mounting and operating a production are rising to a degree which makes enterprise there as commercially foolhardy as that on Broadway has become. Then too, the scale of off-Broadway ($5.95 to $6.50 and $8.50) is ridiculously high for its audience.

Opium, which opened at the Edison Theatre on West 47th Street—an "intermediary" house, smaller than the ordinary Broadway house and larger than the 299-seat capacity Off-Broadway—is not a play, though it is called that. It is Jean Cocteau's journal of his cure from addiction to that drug, translated and adapted for the stage by Roc Brynner. But everything set on a public platform for purposes of entertainment is now elevated to "play" status. The translation is good, the adaptation intelligent, and Roc Brynner is young and handsome. He speaks and reads well. Time may tell whether he is also an actor.

As to the text, its significance medically, psychologically, poetically is slight. Cocteau was a complex character. He had a certain wit, a gift of smart gab, an alert spirit, flair of a kind and talents in all directions, combined with a compulsion to shine, astonish and show off. He recognized genius in others and followed it worshipfully. All this made him the spoiled darling of Paris in the twenties; an emblematic figure of the City of Light in one of its brightest periods. But at bottom he was a mixed-up kid.

He never evolved a whole personality. He sparkled but he alighted nowhere—not even within himself. To the last, he remained an "amuser" of some brilliance, always promising more than he could produce. He was fun to have around, stimulating rather than substantial—and finally irritating.

Opium is a case in point: it reveals Cocteau's fundamental self-deception. It sounds heady, epigrammatically crackling, even profound, but it is mostly fizz and precious conceit. It did not turn me on.

—*NAT*, 26 Oct. '70

TRINITY
ALICE IN WONDERLAND
TRELAWNY OF THE "WELLS"

Much that is attempted by the "new" theatre is done far better in ballet. In *Trinity*, choreographed by Gerald Arpino for the City Center Joffrey Company, the most appealing aspect of the young generation blazons beautifully before us.

Edwin Denby, former dance critic of the New York *Herald Tribune*, a man of exquisite taste, smilingly murmured to me at the première of *Trinity* that it reminded him of Norman Mailer. I am not sure he meant the remark as a compliment but I, who found the work exhilarating, thought the allusion apt. There is in Mailer at his best the frisky energy of our city's youth and a special sort of romanticism.

The same is true of this propulsive piece to a score (mostly "rock") by Alan Raph and Lee Holdridge. It combines a grotesquerie of movement (which the contortions our civilization imposes on us) with a persistent sentimental dreaminess that persuades us that all is not yet lost. *Trinity* is a charming work, brilliantly projected by very nearly the entire company.

Alice in Wonderland, directed by André Gregory, for the Manhattan Project graduates of the theatre program at New York University's School of the Arts, is being given at The Extension, 277 Park Ave. So. It too is youthfully exuberant. It sweats too much. "Beauty," Nietzsche said, "moves on light feet." But this *Alice* does not aim at beauty. It is *Alice* as street urchins horsing around with her might conceive of it. What we witness approaches fury, an exasperated dervishness. The effect is occasionally imaginative and funny—as in the caterpillar scene—but more often discomfiting.

The six young players are physically strong and courageous in the use of their bodies; they do brave and difficult things; they constantly seem to be in peril. This may be intentional, but it is not sound. Excess in performance is gratifying only when one feels that there is still some reserve of strength. André Gregory, who has worked long and hard on his *Alice*, is earnest and talented. He employs sundry props (kitchen chairs, broken umbrellas, newspapers) with entertaining results. The influence of Grotowski is unmistakable, but in this case, at any rate, Gregory has been misguided by it. The content of Grotowski's art—its apocalyptic passion demands that his actors reach the very limits of their physical and emotional capacities—cannot be conveyed except through the specific means he employs. The same is not true of *Alice*, which is essentially comic.

Alice, it may be argued, is not simply "comedy." It is satirical and perhaps even "mad"—Artaud, who disliked Lewis Carroll's writing, found all manner of perversions in it—but even as "madness" *Alice* is still without patent neurosis or hysteria. The mask of airy playfulness is never discarded. In Gregory's breathless, almost brutal, *Alice* we feel that she is being violated by a treatment that does not befit her nature—even if she is to be seen through a distorting mirror set up by big-city brats gone berserk.

The Grotowski via Gregory method betrays the material. This need not be so. In *The Serpent* of the Open theatre, which is also inspired by Grotowski, there is a gentle lyricism even in moments of conflict and woe.

Still Gregory's experiment is a respectable one and may lead to more agreeably complete achievement later on. It is doing this young director and his arduously committed company a disservice to puff them indiscriminately just because their effort is "new."

Trelawny of the "Wells" is the only one of Pinero's plays which Bernard Shaw liked. It is indeed a delightful thing. Its craftsmanship and its "message" are beautifully blended. Even its hokum—and it is blessed hokum—is translated into art by the happy wedding of Pinero's feeling with professional calculation.

We are in England during the 1860s. Most of the characters are actors and other stage folk. We get a whiff of the upper classes in Victorian society at its stuffiest. The theme is the theatre's perennial hold on those who affect it, which in that era meant almost everybody.

With this there is the pathos of historical change. The play recalls the transition on the English stage from highfalutin melodrama to the realism of Tom Robertson. He was a minor member of such a company as the "Wells," as was Pinero, the "walking gentleman" of Portuguese-Jewish extraction who later became the knighted author of *The Second Mrs. Tanqueray*. In the nineties he was the most successful exemplar of the "well-made" play.

The theatre Pinero sets before us in *Trelawny* is shabby and absurd and yet glamorous because its audience, as well as its manners, had such innocent faith. How stale and profitless our sophisticated stage today seems beside it!

There is a scene in which an impossibly rigid old codger—Vice Chancellor Sir William Gower—who has little but scorn for stage folk (he calls them "gypsies") melts when he hears that a young actress' mother played with Edmund Kean. "Kean! Kean!" he bleats in an ecstasy of memory, and essays an imitation of Kean as Richard the wretched. We dissolve in tears and laughter.

The play caught me by surprise when I first saw it acted by Maggie Smith in London some years ago at the British National Theatre: it "killed" me! Comparisons are odious; so I shall confine myself to the statement that the company at the Public Theater, under Robert Ronan's direction, does a good job. This is not easy on an open stage with an almost all-American cast. The play is eminently English. Nancy Dussault is sympathetically simple and direct as Rose Trelawny. A youngish actor, George Bartenieff, is excellent as Sir William: he makes "overacting" pleasurable. And while Sasha von Scherler's cockney speech is occasionally unintelligible, her robust warmth is endearing. Is it shameful to admit that after attending so many virtuous tries at *avant-garde* expression at the Public Theatre (and elsewhere) one embraces *Trelawny* in relief?

—*NAT*, 2 Nov. '70

JOYCE CAROL OATES

A good cast acts *Sunday Dinner* at the American Place Theatre in Saint Clement's Church on West 46th Street. I was especially impressed by Lois Smith as a panicky sister and Martin Shakar as her feeble-minded brother.

The play is by the generally esteemed novelist and short-story writer, Joyce Carol Oates. She writes with distinction and "temperament," though as yet with an openness of declaration that is not altogether suited to the stage. *Sunday Dinner*, her first play to be given public presentation, failed to please me on two counts: it is a symbolic statement that doesn't really convince in its own specific terms, and it says something which has by now become banal and which in any case I can't accept.

A family, ingrown after its abandonment by the father and the death of an adored mother, goes to her grave every Sunday in a bedraggled cemetery. When they return to the murk of their apartment they sit down to a ritual dinner. They despise one another; each feels he was the most beloved of their mother. They each have a "secret," a sin which they refuse to disclose.

The meal is interrupted by the arrival of a census taker, a blind man in rags. His questions are fantastic and are as oddly answered. He then tells of his unimaginably tortured past and his discovery that we are all part of one another and that all of us are equally guilty. Then one by one the members

of the family confess their own sins, each vying with others to prove himself most culpable. They take pride in their sins, none of which is particularly heinous. Then the youngest of the family, so that he may have *his* sin too—for nothing has ever happened to him—tears the blind man's eyes out. Somehow he had expected to be changed by this, to achieve a new face and higher status in the family. But he finds to his dismay that he is not altered. Sin, you see, does not fundamentally change us, since we are all guilty from the outset.

I have only to add that if everyone is guilty, no one is. And if that is so, there is no point to the concept of guilt and sin is also without meaning. There is something so desolatedly passive and supine in this that it makes its statement hardly worth uttering. Such wisdom leaves us nowhere. We are after all in the world.

The American Place Theatre is devoted to the work of new writers. Therefore *Sunday Dinner*, ably directed by Curt Dempster and atmospherically designed by Kert Lundell, merited a hearing by this organization.

—*NAT*, 16 Nov. '70

ORLANDO FURIOSO

There is something really new in town: the production of *Orlando Furioso* by the Teatro Libero di Roma. True theatre lovers will be glad they saw it, whether or not they liked it.

It is a *show*, a fantastic show, given first in a church in Spoleto, later in the Cathedral Plaza of Milan, then on the floor of the Amsterdam stock exchange, still later at an ice rink in Edinburgh, and in Les Halles in Paris. Here it is being done in a "Bubble Theatre," an inflated dome located in Bryant Park with an entrance on West 42nd Street.

The audience stands and is obliged by the show's action to move about—sometimes in great haste. There are platforms at either end of the free space, and a rostrum in the center. The play is simultaneously enacted on both platforms and often on the rostrum as well. "Horses" (beautifully wrought in metal) dash in from various points of the arena and very nearly run us over, creating hilarious peril. As far as I know, none of the two million people who have seen the show in Europe was ever hurt.

We are, in effect, strollers at a street fair, looking at whatever pleases us most at the moment. I found myself spinning around so I would miss nothing. There are lordly warriors, monsters, distressed maidens, hippogriffs, sprites, crazy friars—a mad panoply of medieval lore. The characters harangue, scream, orate, implore, duel, make love, rape, kill. If you understand Italian you may catch some of the lines, though the theatre is large and the general din is incessant. An outline of the extremely intricate story is printed in the program, but such help is superfluous. What counts is the movement, the color, the atmosphere.

Orlando Furioso resembles the popular (open air) theatre of the Middle Ages, and the parallel offers a clue to understanding this extraordinary event. The production style developed by the young director, Luca Ronconi, is consonant with the material from which it springs. In so much of what is called "new" or *avant-garde* theatre, production methods are imposed on texts that are unrelated to them. The result is distortion or betrayal, which is not the same thing as a fresh interpretation. Those who espouse this strategy say "to hell with the original text: this is *theatre*." But whatever the text, it must be made part of a content; else, why that particular text, or any verbal text at all?

Orlando Furioso by Ludovico Ariosto (1475-1553) is a long epic poem written over a period of ten years beginning in 1505; it is a product of the early Renaissance. The age of chivalry, the poem's subject, was read about in Italy though it had bypassed that country. Medieval romance was something of a joke to the man of the Renaissance. *Orlando Furioso* is essentially comic, packed with hectic incident, antic plot, extravagant invention. It

has the pulse of a wild energy, bursting forth in exultant laughter. It has none of Aristotle's "unity of action."

"The very essence of chivalry," the great Italian critic Francesco De Sanctis says in his *History of Italian Literature*, "is precisely the freedom of the individual, the want of seriousness and order, the want of continuity, the want of a single main action, so that the deeds in chivalry are known as adventures and the knights as 'errant.'"

Ariosto was inspired by the chivalric world because, again to quote De Sanctis, "chivalry was legend and romance, a world of the imagination that is interesting not for its ideals but for the novelty, the variety, the extraordinariness of its chance events. And in proportion as the meaning was empty and frivolous, the content became fantastic and lewd, and all the unity of time and space and verisimilitude were done away with."

In the dawning of the Renaissance, De Sanctis adds, "Man standing in the middle of bewitched Nature was...a primitive, credulous, ignorant being, governed by desires and passions, and moved to action by sudden impulses rather than by reflection; one who has never stopped to look into himself, and lived entirely on the surface, all in the outer tumult and heat of life....Man [was] a force pulled this way and that, confused by the changing play of events, poor in character and autonomy."

This has a contemporary ring. Renaissance man, De Sanctis tells us, had "sensibility more than feeling, impressions and emotions rather than passions...." The aptest criticism of *Orlando Furioso* as a poem is one which also applies to this production as the director and the adapter, Eduardo Sanguineti, has conceived it. "The content is a game of the imagination, and we do not sink into it nor get impassioned over it, for the simple reason that we feel it to be a dream."

The dream is the phantasmagoria of a turbulent society. It is also in a peculiarly naive sense the way the Italians still are and the way we, in our confusion called "sophistication," also are. Ariosto gleefully and ironically gave himself and us free rein to indulge in the fabulous. His poems and the show extrapolated from it are thrilling "camp" and, on the whole, vast fun.

It is not however a show for the aged and sedentary. It cannot be appreciated in the complacent mood of a person down front, goggling at a Broadway musical. Though it runs only an hour and a half, it is too long for non-Italians. Even moderately well-educated Italians are familiar with the poem, and can quickly identify its multiple episodes by sight as we recognize at a glance the characters and scenes from *Pickwick Papers* in Cruikshank's illustrations. Still, I suggest that one remain at *Orlando* until the end of the performance, so as not to miss the final moment when the actors are all enraged and caged in a labyrinth in which they go on joyously hamming it up to the top of their bent. With the single reservation about the playing time, I set the occasion down as a signal achievement in the theatre of our day.

—*NAT*, 23 Nov. '70

HAY FEVER
SLEUTH
LES BLANCS

It was Shaw, I believe, who said that America and England were two countries separated by the same language. I thought of the remark at the performance of Noel Coward's 1925 play *Hay Fever* at the Helen Hayes Theatre. I am not a theatrical chauvinist, but it has struck me on several occasions that certain English plays had best be left to the English. Coward's plays are among them.

The trouble with the present revival of *Hay Fever* is not confined to its lack of English actors, but that is part of it. The proper way to speak Coward's lines is to appear unaware of and superior to them, to pretend that they have not been spoken at all.

The American, no matter how hard he tries to be casual or inexpressive in speaking Coward's

witticisms, can't help seeming to mean them. And they shouldn't be meant: they should, ever so lightly, be "assumed." An American who tries to take on the Coward guise becomes false and hoity-toity. But Coward's artifice is a reality, a habit of mind and spirit so fixed that it becomes not second but very nearly "first" nature.

If any Americans are able to approximate the manner successfully, none of them is in the cast of *Hay Fever*. Shirley Booth is a natural comedian and often a touching character actress, but she is not a *poseuse*, an actressy actress. Her forte is the middle class, and she is out of her element in this play. Worse still, everyone and everything else—including the set and clothes—are misplaced. Carole Shelley, who is English and capable of authentic cockney speech, replaces her person by a characterization which seems to precede her entrance on the stage.

Still, the play retains some of its inherent attributes and arouses occasional laughter. I was shocked some years ago to read in Ronald Bryden's column of theatre criticism in the London *Observer* that he thought Coward England's finest living playwright. In a sense it is so: if the term means to indicate the deftest of stage craftsmen with a marked persona typical of certain aspects of English society and something of a mocking commentary on it. Coward's trick is to mask his own approval and enjoyment of what he is doing in an attitude of indifference. One is never sure how much of this calculated and how much the real thing.

Anthony Shaffer's *Sleuth*, a thriller, was a great London success and will no doubt be one here as well (The Music Box). The management requests the show's patrons not to disclose its plot; I had no intention of doing so, because critically the plots of thrillers do not matter.

Sleuth is written with a certain literary coquetry which the innocent mistake for style. Apart from an initial incredibility in the story's premise—which the audience has to allow in order to have fun with what follows—the rest is clever enough for those who like the game.

There is some stage wit in the recipe, even a dab of social comment. It is suggested that detective stories and thrillers (all except this one, of course) appeal to the privileged of a heartless class society and are to a degree a thing of decadence. This is not to be taken seriously and no one in the audience pays it any mind: it is embroidery. We have all heard that great men (Eisenhower for one) relax from burdensome concerns by conning tons of these fictions.

Having no direct responsibility for the grave matters that preoccupy public men, I am little interested in such toys as *Sleuth*. I do not in the least resent those who like to play with them, but I am a little miffed when reviewers rhapsodize about them. Is it possible that this is the sort of mumbo-jumbo they prefer above all else?

Sleuth is extremely well performed, in a style which befits it, by Keith Baxter. Anthony Quayle is also thoroughly proficient. The direction, the setting, are just what the material demands.

I confess to have been more impressed by Lorraine Hansberry's *Les Blancs* (Longacre Theatre) than I expected to be; more, indeed, than most of the professional theatre-tasters. At a time when rave reviews are reserved for plays like *Sleuth* and *Conduct Unbecoming*, I am tempted to speak of *Les Blancs* in superlatives.

I suspect, too, that resistance to the play on the ground of its simplistic argument is a rationalization for social embarrassment. *Les Blancs* is not propaganda, as has been inferred; it is a forceful and intelligent statement of the tragic impasse of white and black relations all over the world, as well as of the complexity of motivation and effect where European nations colonize undeveloped lands inhabited by blacks.

The play transcends the banalities in the intellectual disputes about this conflict; it clarifies, but does not seek to resolve, the historical and human problems involved. It does not provide an Answer. It is an honest play in which thought-provoking matter is given arrestingly theatrical body.

It is only a few hours since I attended the performance, so I confine myself now to these few generalities. I propose to treat the subject more amply next week. Let it suffice for now to say that *Les Blancs* has been given an admirable production under John Berry's direction, with an interesting set by Peter Larkin. The cast headed by James Earl Jones, who is good enough in himself to make the play worth seeing, also gains much from the acting of Lili Darvas, Cameron Mitchell, Earle Hyman, Clebert Ford and Harold Scott.

—*NAT*, 30 Nov. '70

THE GINGERBREAD LADY

Some years ago I suggested that Philip Barry, a much more serious playwright than Neil Simon, be advised to remain superficial. The same applies to the author of *The Gingerbread Lady* (Plymouth Theatre). Only Simon need not be encouraged to stay light. He always is, and has profited fabulously by being so. Popularity isn't everything, but still....

The Gingerbread Lady is about Evy Meary, a nightclub singer who drinks heavily and hysterically. We meet her first on her return from a cure. Besides her alcoholism she is said to be a nymphomaniac, but there is little actual evidence of such disturbance: she has been divorced, having had a child by her husband. She acquired a heel of a lover, a writer of some sort, who abandoned her and to whom, from what one sees of him, she should have said "good riddance." But she is lonely—she has only two devoted friends—and naturally she would like, is indeed eager, to have a new mate. She is, no quibble on this score, rather foul-mouthed, but today who isn't—on stage and film at any rate?

Evy is tenderhearted; she can't bear to hear about other people's woes. Her two friends cry their pain: one is a rarely employed actor who has just been bounced from a part in a show on the verge of its opening; the other is a pretty empty head whose husband threatens to divorce her. The recital of her friends' troubles drives Evy to an alcoholic relapse. In despair she calls upon her erstwhile lover, the stinker. The encounter is consummated by his punching her in the eye.

Her daughter adores her. She is clean, straight, sensible. Perhaps, it is intimated, the daughter will thenceforth keep Evy relatively sane and sober.

The play then is a portrait in which "psychology" has neither cause nor consequence. The woman who is more or less the model for Evy Meary (and whom I happen to know) is a lovely and profound person. But Neil Simon is incapable of profundity. He has a commonsense understanding of the ordinary citizen's behavior and a knowledge of how to turn received or conventional ideas about such folk into laugh-provoking gags. There is no doubt that he can be funny. It is to be noted, however, that though *The Gingerbread Lady* contains many comic and even clever lines, ten minutes after the final curtain I could remember only two or three of them—and the show contains enough to weary at least one playgoer.

What sustains the evening is the highly charged performance of Maureen Stapleton as Evy. She is one of the four or five outstanding actresses of the day. She is effortlessly humorous; it is virtually impossible for her to strike a false note. Her pathos, too, is unstrained. Hers is a vulnerable nature without displayed neurosis. For all her fragility, there is in her a special womanly strength and pride which eschews the maudlin. She has a vibrant power and a voice (velvet in the low tones) which resounds with it. She is open to all the slings and arrows of outrageous fortune without seeming to beg for them.

The most complimentary thing I can say about *The Gingerbread Lady* is that it elevates Miss Stapleton to stardom. But what in the American theatre does this mean? It should be pointed out in the first place that Miss Stapleton has given even finer—better nuanced and directorially less "pushed"—performances in other plays, but those were not as acceptably box office as is the present one. The hazard of stardom on our stage is not only

that one is stuck with it but that in most cases it has little artistic future.

Miss Stapleton has played Shakespeare and Chekhov as well as Tennessee Williams and S. N. Behrman, and has never been less than admirable in any of them. But now that she has achieved stardom with the stage in its present debilitated condition, how can she develop beyond her momentary station? I do not put the question as a personal challenge. Miss Stapleton has integrity and will always aim at excellence, in material as well as in performance. But our theatre offers very little support to the actor's growth.

In England, to go no further, Maggie Smith, essentially a comedienne, has appeared in *The Three Sisters, Hedda Gabler,* a play by Lope de Vega (adapted by Osborne), and in comedies by Pinero, George Farquhar and Peter Shaffer. Peggy Ashcroft has played not only Shakespeare but Chekhov, Ibsen, Sheridan, Enid Bagnold, Marguerite Duras. The reason for this range and variety of roles is not simply that the English now possess several state-subsidized permanent repertory theatres but that audiences in England will go to see good actors in old plays. Americans, avid for the "latest thing," will rarely do so.

One hears on all sides that the theatre is dead—it has been a long time a-dying—but no one looks further than his Broadway-pointed nose. If our theatre dies—which I don't believe it will, though there is evidence to support the foreboding—it will die a fossilized infant.

—*NAT*, 4 Jan. '71

THE PLAYBOY OF THE WESTERN WORLD

I fully understand why Gordon Craig named John Millington Synge his favorite playwright of the Edwardian era: Synge was a poet. But I also do not wonder that the audience at Dublin's Abbey Theatre in 1907 hissed and rioted at the first performance of Synge's *The Playboy of the*

Western World. This comedy in prose which is sheer poetry is also the sternest realism. For an Irishman steeped in his country's myth, the play's veracity must prove searing.

My own impression of the Emerald Isle when I visited it was that the Irish lived there dreaming of Ireland. For them it is a mystic land, peopled by heroes and saints. Synge suggests that it's a funny and very sad place. There is a "great gap" says the *Playboy*'s Pegeen Mike, "between a gallant story and a dirty deed."

Christy Mahon, the playboy himself, comes to a tiny village and asserts that he has killed his dad, an act that all the villagers deem brave, outrageous and no doubt necessary. He is received as an epic figure of whom the men stand in awe and the women hasten to woo. It is true that he struck his tyrannous father a mighty blow on the head with a farm implement, but on discovering that the old man was not actually killed, these simple folk find themselves sorely deceived. When the father shows up and once more tries to browbeat his son, the young fellow strikes again both to free himself of the parental burden and to establish himself surely as a prodigy. But now the little people turn against him and even Pegeen Mike, who was eager to marry the wonder boy, is fiercely determined to see him hanged. Liberated by his momentary defiance of his da', Christy will now go off to wander heaven knows to what outlandish realms. He will be forever regretted but never again protected by Pegeen Mike.

This hilarious parable, written in plain speech which is all enchanting melody, is a masterpiece because it tells the essential truth of its locale—and thus inevitably about more of the "western world" than County Mayo.

Listen to Bernard Shaw in *John Bull's Other Island* on his countrymen: "Oh, the dreaming! the dreaming! the torturing, heart scalding, never satisfying dreaming....An Irishman's imagination never lets him alone, never convinces him, never satisfies him, but it makes him that he can't face reality nor deal with it nor handle it nor conquer it: he can only sneer at them that do. It's all dreaming, all imagination....Imagination is such a torture that you can't bear it without whiskey. At last you get that you can bear nothing real at all....[Your wife] despises you because you're not a hero....And all the while there goes on a horrible, senseless, mischievous laughter."

Shaw defines the syndrome, Synge embodies it, and Beckett—a far cry from both—symbolizes it in near-abstract, quasi-religious, negations and blasphemies. All of them recognize the same hard kernel of fact: the irreconcilability between the dream and the real which the haze of alcohol makes unbridgeable. O'Casey rendered the picture concrete through the historic events of the 1916 troubles. Denis Johnston in his remarkable *Moon in the Yellow River* limned the same pattern philosophically which resolved itself in the prayer, "Take away this cursed gift of laughter and give us tears instead."

The Playboy of the Western World is a great comedy: its irony is turned to tender mirth without losing sharp clarity of vision. And it should be further noted that though poor Christy never succeeds in doing away with his besotted father, he does strike a blow, and though he may go bewildered into the unknown, torn by both his bereaved heart and failed rebellion, he is ever more the man for that one impulse and stroke of battle.

Though the Repertory Theatre of Lincoln Center at the Vivian Beaumont has mounted many excellent plays, I have enjoyed only two of their productions: *In the Matter of J. Robert Oppenheimer* (which came from the Mark Taper Forum of Los Angeles) and *Playboy of the Western World* directed by John Hirsch.

I do not mean that what we see now is entirely satisfactory—far from it. But it is a much better show than Guthrie McClintic's with Burgess Meredith in 1946 or the later one with Siobhan McKenna. What makes it a pleasure to me are the details of the stage "business" and much of the acting: Martha Henry's Pegeen—though despite her strong voice she is hard to understand at times and is better at scolding than at grieving; David

Birney's Christy, though he is perhaps too soft; James Blendick as Pegeen's sweetly pusillanimous suitor; Frances Sternhagen's sensibly forthright Widow Quin; Ray Fry's humorously crabbed Philly Cullen; Elizabeth Huddle's attractive Sara Tansey, and especially Stephen Elliott's Old Mahon, a veritable archetype of grubby cunning. What the production lacks is an overall style and a sustained mood in which the fun is felt as part of a wistful, almost sorrowful, remoteness of background, the aching haggardness of the boggy horizon. But perhaps under the circumstances of our theatre this is too much to expect. *The Playboy of the Western World* is one of the very few plays now worth seeing in New York.

It is rumored that funds for the continuation of the Repertory Theatre of Lincoln Center are at present exhausted. For all my severity about the quality of its productions I very much deplore this. New York badly needs such an institution. As long as one such remains, is functioning, it may yield to improvement. Without it we have little but promises, promises—a musical comedy theatre with guest appearances from Britain.

—*NAT*, 25 Jan. '71

A DOLL'S HOUSE

If you have never before seen *A Doll's House* I suppose it is proper to recommend your seeing it now. (Playhouse Theatre) If you do, it will confirm the impression you may have gathered through long years of comment and discussion that it is an artfully powerful tract on behalf of "women's liberation." And indeed, through several generations, it did function for many people on that level. Its importance, historically speaking, had two bases. It constituted a revolutionary step in the probing of marital relationships; and it established a form of dramatic construction which became the model in theatre writing to the end of World War I.

But the play is something more than a revelation of the obtuseness of 19th century attitudes of middle-class men toward their wives. If it were that only—though it should by no means be assumed that we have rid ourselves of husbandly blindness and spiritual sloth in regard to wives and to women generally—*A Doll's House* might now seem "old stuff."

What keeps it alive, apart from the grip of its theatrical cunning, is the fact that it deals with all human intercourse. The man who is foolish in his family is usually as unmindful in his contact with everyone else—male or female. *A Doll's House* is a "love story" in reverse. It exceeds the limitations of a social parable about what every husband ought to understand and what every wife should demand.

What is permanently pertinent in the play demands a production which is a subtle and complex study within the rich stuff of human character seen in the atmosphere of a specific environment. The more particularized its delineation, the more "universal" the play becomes. But it is precisely this living texture—truth of feeling and behavior—which is largely lacking in the production directed by Patrick Garland, with Claire Bloom as Nora at the new Playhouse.

The setting by the talented John Bury looks like—a set. It is not a place where anyone might dwell, only one within which actors may perform. This in itself doesn't matter much (though in the theatre everything counts) but it is typical of the whole. The playing is clean, crisp, brisk, intelligible. The play has become a graph, a neat reading, a "radio" recital: it is all smoothly laid out for us as on a platter. It therefore boils down to the old story which everyone agrees is about a conflict long since resolved as to the subjection of women by husbands who treat them as a convenience, a plaything, a footstool, etc.

The performance had not been in progress more than ten minutes when I said to myself, "This is an 'English' production." For the English these days—and they are not alone in this, except that we rarely ever produce the modern masters—are intent on showing that Ibsen (and Chekhov too) are not the musty, heavy-handed old fogies many folk

763

take them to be. So the plays must be given a swift pace and turned out with brilliant precision—no shadows, hesitations, ambiguities, the sharp action rendered with the suspense showing. What we are faced with then in this production is a company of efficient actors who speak will and do everything with dispatch.

Before substantiating this judgment I must pause to say something further Ibsen. He was a priestly poet—at times almost a mystic—with a rationalist bent. His spirit harked back to the times of epic grandeur, but his awareness of the pressures and needs of the mercantile and industrial world which had begun to flourish in the 19th century pressed him toward a realism by means of which he could attack the shallowness, mediocrity and hypocrisy of the ruling bourgeoisie in an "ordinary," commonsense manner that they might grasp.

He who by nature was inclined to portray figures of heroic scope (as he did in his youth) undertook to write plays in which the intensity of his passions was compressed into the more manageable and comprehensible style of the "well-made" play for the prosperous middle class which was the new audience of his day: he wished to show it its tragic dilemmas and wounds. At first they denied and reviled the picture. The strict logic he used, the tight rein he imposed on his eloquence and feeling was an effort to contain as much as possible of those qualities he admired in the classic drama within the restrictions of realism. This resulted in the compact structure of his plays, their fierce economy. But the method had the limitations of its virtue: it led to a certain unreality, almost falsity. He sought to overcome this difficulty later in the more mysterious and less popular plays of his last years.

If any valid criticism can be made of Ibsen's technique it is that the task of being fully expressive, powerful and realistically terse at the same time is well-nigh insuperable. Two examples of the difficulty may be cited: one from *Hedda Gabler*, the other from *A Doll's House*. Immediately after

hearing of Lövberg's death in *Hedda Gabler*, Tesman and Mrs. Elvsted sit down to work on the book Hedda has burned; Hedda, finding herself frustrated and trapped in every way, commits suicide. The structure of the play necessitates this conclusion within less than fifteen minutes of the final curtain. The change of circumstances and action is too great for the short time allowed by "realism." What happens is right, how it happens is not.

In *A Doll's House*, Nora's transformation from the light-minded lark to the conscious person is essentially true, but if we are to consider the events in the mode in which the play is written, the turnabout in Nora's character is much too sudden and hard to credit if we judge it on its face value. The only way this apparent contradiction can be justified is through creative acting. And this is just what is missing in most productions of Ibsen's plays, and lamentably so in the new one which is superficially expert. That it is likely to be praised for its unproblematic nature is a sign of our times. For while the audiences in Ibsen's day were repelled by his content, we are usually impatient with his method: we want everything to be made "clear," snappy and, at bottom, banal.

It is no wonder then that Dr. Rank, the friend of the Helmer family, who on the verge of death caused by tuberculosis of the spine, is played as blithely as possible. We see hardly any trace either in his physical in his physical comportment or in his inner mood to indicate a sense of his fate. The farewell scene between Nora and Rank is thus almost totally without poignancy.

Still this is only symptomatic. What is crucial to the play is the development of Nora's character. In the confrontation scene with Torvald, her husband, she says that she has never been happy, only cheerful. For this to be accepted, we must perceive it at the outset in her very playfulness. There must be some inkling of wistfulness and a kind of buried hurt even as she hops and twitters as a carefree "bird." And when she begins to speak the quietly forceful lines in explanation of her decision to leave her home and children, we must be led to see that she is groping in subdued anguish toward a realization which is just *dawning* on her.

The directorial design of the production makes Claire Bloom's initial sunniness little better than routine jollity, and in her final declaration she is as maturely articulate as if she had always known what she now says. She is as undisturbedly lucid as a well-instructed teacher reading a lesson to an obstinately shocked, slightly backward pupil.

For sheer acting Miss Bloom's best moments are those in which she is frightened by the turn of events and her possible responsibility for them. But the expression of this fear, isolated from the rest, is simply melodrama. All Nora's traits have to be woven into a unified fabric in which her youthful naïveté, her loving dependence, her hopefulness and yearning for something more than what Torvald's kindness dispenses, her agony in the discovery that she no longer loves him, the awful uncertainty within the determination of her leave-taking, her deep-seated idealism and romanticism (as positive qualities) must be envisioned and embodied in a humanly coherent continuum. As the portrait now stands, each element is applied in discontinuous patches forming no organic image, only a professionally adept representation.

Donald Madden is not the comfortable, assiduous, conventionally good-humored, basically blunt and ultimately bewildered and injured "family man": he is a nice fellow and an agreeably romantic actor giving a fluent and sensible reading. As Krogstad, Robert Gerringer plays well with a shrewdly effective staginess which lessens the real despair of the frayed little man unable to cope with unkind circumstances and moral issues. Patricia Elliott as Mrs. Linde, attractive and dignified, has affecting moments with hardly enough of the wear and tear which her unfortunate life struggle would certainly have told on her face and person. But the evening's shortcomings should not be ascribed to the cast: the director has conceived the production as "Ibsen made easy."

—*NAT*, 1 Feb. '71

A MIDSUMMER NIGHT'S DREAM

A Midsummer Night's Dream is Peter Brook's masterpiece. His gift is greatest in stage frolic. Eminently conscientious, he is rarely profound. He is fanciful, colorful, full of merry pranks. He addresses himself almost entirely to the eye. His production of this sweet comedy about the waywardness of love offers no literary satisfaction: it is entirely theatrical. There is little romance in it but much wonderfully bright invention.

Watching it I recalled an anecdote I once heard Henry Kahnweiler, the art dealer who first sponsored Picasso, Braque and Juan Gris, tell. Kahnweiler complimented Gris on his newest cubist painting. "But is it really a *picture?*" Gris worriedly queried. After the passage of several scenes in this production, I asked myself if what I was seeing was a brilliant studio exercise or truly a *play*. A reliable answer could only be provided by someone who had never before seen or read it. It is possible that such a person might not be able to follow the play's argument.

I suppose what disturbed me in the opening scenes was that I heard the lines faintly. The readings were not only dim but rather flat. I noticed that throughout the evening the speeches I never missed were the funny ones. Brook seemed not to be concerned with the play's verbal beauties; dwelling on them might lessen an appreciation of the jest. The loveliness of such a familiar air as, let us say, "I know a bank where the wild thyme blows..." etc., the tender counterpoint to the play's sport, appears to be deliberately eschewed. It would not be in tune with the production scheme or, for that matter, with the temper of the time. Glamor is gone, fun is in.

Of the composition's jocose side, full advantage has been taken, and that with nimble and coruscating mastery. In this respect Shakespeare's text not only serves as an apt scenario but as a justification for some of the play's pleasantest devices. Brook is like Puck, "the goblin" who leads the characters "up and down, up and down." A "man is but an ass, if he go about to expound this dream."

On both sides of the stage narrow ladders rise to a platform high above the stage floor, a platform with a metal railing. On this upper stage we find a small band of musicians who punctuate the action with appropriate percussive sound. Here too the actors who are not engaged in the immediate scenes in progress look on and enjoy the antics of their fellow players. When we enter the theatre, we behold the play's sole scenic background: brightly-lit, white wooden walls on which an immense red feather is attached. This feather, later hoisted aloft, becomes Titania's couch as she lies asleep and falls victim to Oberon's stratagem.

The flower with which Oberon befuddles the various lovers is a silvery plate that can be made to rotate on a wand, a toy we occasionally have seen children play with. Coils of gleaming metal wire hanging from poles manipulated from above represent the underbrush of the woodland in which the love games take place. Oberon and Puck make their first appearance on flying trapezes which descend from the flies. Other characters—Hermia in a rage—also hang or swing hecticly on them.

Extravagant, gimmicky? Certainly, but does not Shakespeare say "All this derision shall seem a dream and fruitless vision"? The lovers' awakening is marked by the ringing of an alarm clock openly displayed by one of the "property men" on the upper stage. When an actor needs a "prop" (such as a calendar) it is thrown to him from the overhanging platform. Brook's motto here is Shakespeare's "And those things do best please me that befall preposterously."

On the nether level a guitarist supplies the sentimental strains which the actors avoid. The costumes are near-contemporary workclothes for the auxiliary players and for the rustics: Bottom and company. The highborn Athenians and the fairyland nobility wear costumes of satin, tulle or voile—their whiteness dappled with green or pink

spots making them look like pantomime Pierrots or circus clowns. Some of the scenic jokes would appear to appeal most directly to affluent "hippies" in their taste for high camp. But in general, there is a healthy exuberance.

This then is a director's rather than an actors' triumphal occasion, except to the extent that the actors are his enthusiastic coadjutors. A youngish, physically well-trained company is bold and agile in movement, sometimes performing acrobatic tricks to superb comic effect. There are dull spots only when laughs are not in order.

Standing out above the company's general competence and good will are David Waller as an authentically humorous and robust Bottom, and the lanky Frances De La Tour as the "painted maypole," Helena, whose every word is funny as well as distinct. Patrick Stewart is a charmingly simple-minded Snout, and little Hermia is well played by pretty Mary Rutherford in her tantrums, though not wholly audible at other times.

Many questions occurred to me as I followed the show, and after I had left I wanted to see it all over again—which I shall probably do in the coming weeks of its limited engagement. That is a tribute to Peter Brook whose *Marat/Sade* and *King Lear* also aroused the desire for renewed acquaintance. Thinking back on these earlier—always interesting—productions, my feeling is that while *King Lear* was most gravely committed to an interpretation of its text (though not altogether satisfactory to me as such) and *Marat/Sade* so devoted to directorial virtuosity that its substance became subservient to it, *A Midsummer Night's Dream* is archetypal of Brook's talent at its most gratifying.

But to return to the questions. It is a good thing that so much emphasis nowadays is put on the quality and originality of theatrical staging; yet one wonders if this is not due, in part, to the paucity of significant new scripts. This production will undoubtedly inspire ambitious theatre folk, but will it not also turn them to much frivolous imitation, more manner than matter? And why does the new stagecraft one hears so much about apply itself mainly to old texts and not evolve new ones? We are constantly required to determine how the classics have been "treated" rather than to judge an organically created work. The marriage of writing and stage work into a true unity has chiefly occurred in recent years only in such productions as Brecht's *Mother Courage*. But consummations of this sort are likely to occur only when truly total theatres are established; where writers, directors, actors, designers are partners who speak together on subjects about which they harbor strong mutual feeling.

These afterthoughts are not for the moment at issue. The simple fact is that Brook's latest production is a signal piece of theatre work in the English-speaking theatre of our day. It will be hugely enjoyed by many, it may puzzle some, it will be condemned by very few—I think wrongly. But there is no doubt that it should be seen by everyone eager for fresh theatre experiences.

—*NAT*, 8 Feb. '71

TROUBLED *PARADISE* MIGHT BE AMERICA

I had heard that National Educational Television was going to broadcast Clifford Odets's *Paradise Lost* with Eli Wallach, Jo Van Fleet and other well-known actors; the news stirred rememberances of things past. I directed the play when it opened in New York on Dec. 9, 1935. The cast then included Morris Carnovsky, Stella Adler, Sanford Meisner, Luther Adler, Elia Kazan, Robert Lewis, and other members of the Group Theatre's permanent company.

In Odets, the Group had found its own playwright, and the thirties its dramatic voice. His first full-length play, *Awake and Sing!*, had been greeted with enthusiasm on its Broadway opening in February, 1935. Some weeks earlier, his *Waiting for Lefty* had created a sensation. A play about a taxi strike, *Lefty* was embraced by nearly everyone, because, at a time of practically universal distress,

its insurgent vehemence radiated courage and good will. *Lefty* literally swept the country, playing to many audiences which had never before gone to anything but a moviehouse.

Tenderly humorous and gently melancholy, *Awake and Sing!* also sounded a note of aspiration, belief in a future in which life might "not be printed on dollar bills." These plays were "antidotes" to the bitter discouragement which prevailed in the land because of the Depression, the most flagrent symptom of which was 15 million unemployed.

Odets's photo bedecked the cover of *Time Magazine*: he was hailed as something more than a stage luminary. *Paradise Lost*, coming a few months after the triumph of *Awake and Sing!*, was considered by his collegues in the Group Theatre his most moving play, rich in characters, eloquent in a special mode of speech, strong in meaning. The noted columnist Heywood Broun praised it extravagantly. After *Lefty* and *Awake and Sing!*, everyone expected further wonders and successes from Odets. But *Paradise Lost*, to the consternation of all, met with a puzzled press reaction followed by a run of only nine weeks.

The Group could not understand why a play utterly clear to it should appear muddy and baffling to the reviewers. The Group believed in the play and fought for it. It ran ads in the *New York Times* and in the *Tribune* to assert its conviction that the play was "great." But while today it may be best to shun that overworked adjective, I am more convinced than ever that *Paradise Lost* still possesses beauty, power and significance.

At the same time, I must confess I now understand why the play initially encountered resisitance. Though its characters are readily identifiable flesh-and-blood creatures, in *Paradise Lost*, Odets piled scene on scene, crisis on crisis in a rapid montage which appeared to have lost focus. To an audience expecting straightforward dramatic narrative this structural peculiarity—part of the play's essence—made its characters appear like figures seen in a distorting mirror.

Much happens, yet there is little formal plot. Its people—they are of the middle-middle-class as contrasted with the workers of *Lefty* and the lower-middle-class of *Awake and Sing!*—are lost in the dissaray of the times, a world falling to pieces. The financial crash, with its attendant moral panic, is swiftly destroying the comfort and confidence which was their paradise. They cannot understand the ghostliness of an atmosphere which covers them like a shroud—for they are nearly all unaware of politics or social currents. They wander about their home in feverish disquiet: they seem to be groping in a dim light, like shades of a previous existence. They lose some of their realistic substance and dissolve. They take on the aspects of portents or symbols. The troubled home they live in might be America itself; they themselves might represent different ways of coping with, or failing to cope with, society's ills.

At the center of the picture stands Leo Gordon, the father of the family. He is an "artistic" type: he designs pocket books, reads Emerson, broods over human destiny and is proud of his daughter's cultivated piano playing. He is an old-fashioned idealist with only a hazy sense of reality. He is a "fool," a fact his cheerful down-to-earth wife recognizes and for which she loves him. For there is purity in his foolishness, an essential kindness, dignity, even loftiness. The Gordon's elder son Ben is an Olympic champion who has never been required to earn his living but imagines now that his days as an athelete are over (due to a bad heart) his early prestige and his good looks will assure his future. Julie, the younger son, dreams of making a forture on Wall Street, but he is ill with sleeping sickness, just as the financial structure of the country has become moribund and the market itself is sinking.

Ben Gordon's boyhood companion, Kewpie, played in 1935 by Elia Kazan, is a tough cabbie who envies the educated and honorable Gordon family but is determined not to suffer its fate: the decline of the genteel middle-class to the state of the impoverished proletariat. Kewpie turns gang-ster so that he may "make" it in a society where, he believes, only the ruthless can survive. Yet for all his brutal drive, he despises himself. There is in this character something of the inner turmoil and bent-toward self-destruction which forshadows the theme of Odets's *Golden Boy*.

Sam Katz, Leo's business partner, besides being desperate over his impotence (a fact we learn through his tortured wife) is tortured by the fear of bankruptcy. To prevent this, he is willing to contemplete crime by connivance with the grotesque Mr. May who practices arson to salvage businessmen in a jam. There is also Gus Michaels, the Gordons' friendly border and father to the hussy Ben Gordon marries and Kewpie possesses. Gus is one of the most charmingly deplorable, laughably and touchingly befuddled characters in American drama. He is typical of an old generation whose exploded hopes make him hunger for the past, and indulge in yearning reminiscence. Such men are taken over by the strong, as Odets phrases it, "like a bulldog takes over a pussycat."

In this strange gallery we also find another wraith-like figure, Mr. Pike, a gritty—"fundamental"—American, down but by no means out. He works at the base of the building: he is the furnace man. A veteran of the First World War, he represents the perennial rebelliousness of our native spirit. His denunciations of war and his anger at the degradation of the American dream have in them the firey sound we hear from our present-day youth but are far more resonant because Mr. Pike makes his outcry from bitter personal experience. On the fringes of these full-sized portraits in *Paradise Lost* we discover snapshots of ridiculous political small fry—a workers' committee from Leo's factory, hardpressed and only half-articulate, demanding more pay and a decent union; and finally the broken men long since counted among the derelict.

There is torment in all this. Yet somehow Odets managed to inform all of it with love, humor, and profound compassion. The language is compact with wisecracks, popular clichés, peppery rhetoric, titles of hit tunes, vulgarisms, exalted and hortatory outbursts of feeling. This mixture—almost a patois—resolves into a sort of song. It is not far-fetched to speak of *Paradise Lost* as a poem, harsh in the concreteness of its details, vibrant with passion, glowing with all the refracted lights of a civilization breaking down, and uncertainly awaiting an apocalyptic awakening, a new dawn.

Dispossessed of his home and most of his belongings, Leo Gordon, in the sweetness of his intellectual confusion, suddenly cuts through the gloom as if purged by the travail of his life and the sorrow he sees about him. In the play's final moment, he cries out, "Everywhere now men are rising from their sleep. Men, men are understanding the bitter black total of their lives. Their whispers are growing to shouts...No man fights alone...Heartbreak and terror are not the heritage of mankind. The world is beautiful...."

We do not speak so today. But surely there is still occasion and need for such ardor. Look around and listen: we may hear renewed reverberations of Odets's romantic summons in tones now more strident but no less urgent.

—*NYT*, 21 Feb. '71

THE NEW THEATRE, NOW

Two attitudes prevail in regard to what is referred to as the "new" or "avant-garde" theatre. There are the unqualified champions and those who are its entrenched detractors. Both are mistaken. In practice, the phenomenon is so diverse in aspect, so eclectic in methods, as to defy categorization.

It is, above all, a reaction against commonplace realism. There is nothing particularly new in this. The realistic theatre is itself a comparatively recent development—hardly much more than a hundred years old. The Japanese Noh, the Kabuki, and the classic Greek theatres were, and insofar as they still exist are, "total theatres." they have little in common with nineteenth and twentieth-century realism.

In the main, new theatre eschews literature as its central factor. Drama as a text which has to be extended, illustrated, interpreted by stage action is not crucial in the new theatre. What we ordinarily call the Play, the work of a dramatist whose language is the core of the theatrical event, is no longer dominant. A respected text may be the springboard for what we see on the stage, but it is employed in a way which its original author might find hard to recognize even acknowledge as his own. The words employed have been absorbed in a context of physical movement, sound, light, improvised episodes, and incidental "business" which, apprehended as a whole, constitute what amounts to a new play and possibly a different meaning.

All drama in the theatre goes through such translation from an initial seed or theme articulated in dialogue into the vocabulary of the stage: acting, setting, and direction. Shakespeare's *Hamlet* exists in print only; what we see in the theatre is this or that actor's *Hamlet* or this or that company's *Hamlet*. Still, in the normal theatre of our era everyone's point of reference is always the original text. Gesture and mime, costume, stage properties, light and sound, improvisations which may include audience participation, may supersede the importance of the spoken word or literary text. In new theatre the Play is the product of a collective "game."

The reduction of the dramatist's work to the function of a scenario within the larger scope of the company's total performance is the new theatre's first and most striking trait. Meyerhold, the great Russian director and to a certain extent the unacknowledged forerunner of much of what is now thought "modern" in the theatre, phrased the new *esthétique* by saying, "Words in the theatre are only embellishments on the design of movement." This was written in 1908 before Gordon Craig, in 1911, published corresponding views.

These pioneers are rarely cited by American devotees of the new theatre, but Antonin Artaud, a

French actor and theatrical prophet, is. Two chapter titles in his book, *The Theatre and Its Double*, have become slogans for the epigones. They are "The Theatre of Cruelty" and "No More Masterpieces."

To make sense of Artaud's ideas, his essentially poetic pronouncements require translation into more sober language. "Cruelty" in Artaud means intensity. He wished theatre to achieve the force of natural phenomena, like lightning and thunder. "This cruelty," he wrote in a letter to a friend, "is a matter of neither sadism nor bloodshed. I do not systematically cultivate horror. The word 'cruelty' must be taken in a broad sense....From the point of view of the mind, cruelty signifies rigor, implacable intention and reason, irreversible and absolute determination."

In certain American new-theatre manifestations, much is expected from elements of chance and accident, things which may happen in the free interplay of performers and public. In Artaud's example of a "faultless performance," that of the Balinese theatre, a theatre of the utmost refinement, he finds "everything...is established with an enchanting mathematical meticulousness. Nothing is left to chance or to personal initiative."

As to "no more masterpieces," it is a summons to replace the preeminence of the written word by spectacle, movement, music, shouts, cries, and other sound effects. Artaud's prescription approximates Gordon Craig's "When literary men shall be content enough to study the Art of the Theatre as an art separate from the Art of Literature, there will be nothing to prevent us from welcoming them into the house."

These quotations belong to the rhetoric of the movement, and such rhetoric, as in politics, is neither illustrative nor conclusive. Craig and Artaud were never fully permitted or able to embody their ideas in actual production. Instances of things actually performed are more illuminating than manifestos.

In "Motel," a segment of the triptych called *America Hurrah!*, staged by Joseph Chaikin and devised in collaboration with the writer Jean-Claude van Itallie, we see a dummy which mouths the attractions of a motel. "Her" speech is a tape recording. While the spiel issues from the mechanism, a man and a woman enter, both grotesquely masked. They are perhaps newlyweds on their honeymoon. They write obscenities on the wall. They very nearly wreck everything in the room just before going to bed. As they proceed to this climax, blinding lights flash in the audience's faces, and a deafening din—the cacophony of our civilization—fill the auditorium. "Motel" is a theatrical metaphor typifying our environment. What is spoken is only significant in relation to what we experience through the aural and visual assault on our senses.

Dionysus in '69, freely adapted from Euripides' *The Bacchae* by Richard Schechner's Performance Group, employs many of the elements suggested in Artaud's program for a "theatre of cruelty." In his book *Up Against the Fourth Wall*, John Lahr, an enthusiastic supporter of the new theatre, describes part of the evening's activities: "[The] theme [is] the new self-consciousness toward the body and the unshackling of the sexual instinct. The actors in 'Dionysus' are trained to a heightened, acrobatic concept of performance. The males stripped to a jockstrap; the females in brief body tunics (sometimes nude) move through a series of carefully disciplined images. Men lie prone on the floor while the women straddle them, fixing their legs tight between groins. Bodies pass under legs and bare backs squirm in a tortuous rebirth. The audience, too, is conditioned to new emotions by an environmental stage, a series of three tiered constructions allowing the audience to watch the performance from a variety of perspectives. They can climb, or hide, or walk about. By making the theatrical expression a physical adventure, Schechner's Performance Group wants to expand the audience's understanding of liberty."

Some of the actors play recorders, others strike drums. They invite the audience to dance with them and trace movements of loving embrace with individual spectators. At times the actors speak lines which relate to their personal lives; on occasions refer to persons in the audience. The night I attended the show there was an allusion to "the great god Harold Clurman." Euripides is not entirely omitted either in theme or verbiage, but Euripides' "message" has been reversed in the light of an ideology consonant with contemporary youth.

Euripides' *Bacchae* dramatizes the conflict between repressive and militant asceticism and Dionysiac license. The Greek dramatist as moderator demonstrates the hazards involved in both extremes. The ascetics tyrannize over the senses and are thus destructive; the passion of the Bacchic celebrants progresses toward murder. But Schechner's "bacchae," handsome boys and girls, win the day: they bathe in the blood of the censorious dictator and march triumphantly through the town. Theirs is "the politics of ecstasy."

The term "environmental stage" in Lahr's description of *Dionysus in '69* is one which will ever more frequently crop up in discussions of the new theatre and may therefore demand further elucidation. The stages long familiar to us are those we contemplate from a distance; we are separated from them. The environmental stage includes and surrounds us; we dwell within it.

All these otherwise dissimilar examples have one thing in common: *abstraction*, or, to put it negatively, non-realism. They do not "hold a mirror up to nature." The path toward abstraction, the departure from realism—to go no further back in time—was first set for us by the previous example of the dramatists lumped together under the tag imprinted on them by Martin Esslin of London: "Theatre of the Absurd." The tag is perhaps unfortunate because it designates such men as Beckett, Ionesco, Genet, Pinter, who are distinctly different from one another.

These playwrights are not to be confused with the new or avant-garde theatre. They are, for all the strangeness or novelty in their manner and meaning, entirely traditional, that is, literary dramatists. If I mention them in the present context, it is simply to indicate that their departure from the techniques of their immediate predecessors served to liberate a later generation of theatre folk from the confines of naturalism, the representation of life as we customarily view it. Their two mottoes might have been that of the French actor Coquelin, who said, "I am for *nature* and against naturalism," and Sartre's, "The Theatre is not concerned with reality. It's concerned with truth."

If any further generalization is to be made about the "absurdists," it is that the truth they perceive is the falsity of appearances, the folly of assuming that our "rational hypotheses" reveal life's essence. What they see is the grotesque paradox of being, which is comic as much as it is dismaying. In Saul Bellow's play, *The Last Analysis*, the prevalent mood of the absurdist-theatre generation is summed up by the line, "Things have gotten all mixed between laughter and insanity."

Another way in which the "rebel" playwrights of the Fifties (at first, mostly Parisian) influenced the generation under consideration is in the depiction of *characters*. These are no longer individual persons but states of mind, ideas, types, symbols, masks. "Psychology" is virtually nonexistent. We cannot speak of Beckett's figures, for example, as we do of Ibsen's Hedda, Chekhov's Gaev, or Othello. What all the new dramaturgy tends toward in this respect is a reversion to the very oldest form of drama. (One might say that Oedipus is a "psychology," but has none!) The intention in such drama is to project basic patterns or structures of human existence. They are parables or "myths."

To a certain degree, this explains another characteristic of the new theatre. Actors often change roles from one performance to another and sometimes within the same play. They are used to perform set tasks. What they do physically and what they say (if anything) constitute their entire "characterization." Individual nuance or subtleties hardly matter: the figure's function in the general scheme of action is what counts. Thus there is usually very little distinction in the acting of new theatre productions. Energy and a willingness to carry out the assignment with fearless enthusiasm ordinarily suffice.

There are gifted craftsmen among the leaders of the new theatre groups, but thus far only one genius: Jerzy Grotowski, founder and director of the Polish Laboratory Theatre. He is the "ace" of the "school" not simply by virtue of his originality, but through the opportunity given him by his government to conduct a workshop where actors may be trained in his arduous system to form a permanent company guaranteed continuous work.

Grotowski forgoes "scenery" and naturalistically identifiable costumes. There is no sensuous appeal in his art. For close contact with the players, the number of spectators is limited to no more than a hundred. At times the audience is seated above the "stage"; the audience witnesses the drama which takes place, as it were, in a pit below. The restricted public surrounds the action.

The texts used are adaptations of famed works, but their words are more incantations or stabs of passion than normal dialogue. Tempos are so hectic that intelligibility becomes difficult, even for those who understand Polish. Vocal tones create the effect of howls, groans, sobs, and imprecations. We are reminded of the dodecaphonic scale. The actors seem to attack rather than to address one another. They grovel, fall or are thrust backward, are carried about and, in the furious course of the proceedings, are thrown into positions which one might consider acrobatic or balletic if their purpose were not entirely different from gymnastics or dance.

The strangeness of Grotowski's art is not dictated by purely formal choice. His theme is the slaughter of innocence. He was a boy of eight during the Nazi occupation of his country; he learned early enough of the world of concentration camps. What we behold in his work in "abstraction" is the torture of humanity. The tormentors and their victims are bound together in mutual horror; all appear equally cruel. Grotowski's inferno is one in which all are as guilty as they are innocent.

Without moralizing or preachment the spectacle suggests purification through martyrdom. Salvation is wrought from suffering. There is a religious strain imbedded in this concept and, though secular rather than denominational, the traces of a special Catholicism may be divined in it. Grotowski's is indeed a theatre of cruelty peculiar to him and to him alone.

In view of this we can understand why the Grotowski system presses the actor through bodily and vocal training of extreme strenuousness. The feats of virtuosity or what strike us as fantastic contortions are such as have hardly ever before been carried out in the theatre. They are calculated to free the actor of his "false face," all the inhibitions, the masquerades, the social reticences and evasions which prevent the actor from yielding the truth of his innermost being. When the actor is able to do this, so the theory goes, we may ourselves be transfigured.

Several of our new directors have been greatly influenced by Grotowski classes in which they have participated in Poland, in France, and in New York. But such influence, we must hasten to add, is more technical than substantive. The context of Grotowski's art is not transmissible, it allows of no duplication.

On this subject, the limitation of masters, passages from Grotowski's book *Toward a Poor Theatre* should be cited:

> *Stanislavsky was compromised by his disciples....When in numerous...theatres we watch performances inspired by the 'Brecht theory,' and are obliged to fight against utter boredom because of a lack of innovation of both actors and producers...[we] think back to Brecht's own productions....They showed a deep professional knowledge....The 'theatre of cruelty' has been 'canonized,' i.e., made trivial, snapped for trinkets, tortured in*

various ways....As for the wretched performances one can see in the theatrical avant-garde of many countries, these chaotic, aborted works, full of so-called cruelty....which only reveal a lack of professional skill, a sense of groping, and a love of easy solutions....When we see these sub-products whose authors call Artaud their spiritual father, then we think perhaps there is cruelty indeed but only towards Artaud himself.

The Living Theatre (now defunct) is the best known or most notorious of the avant-garde groups in America. It had its beginnings in New York as an organization devoted to new playwrights. After a stay in Europe, impelled in part by the Grotowski model, it altered its artistic methods and objectives. Its performances impressed and scandalized many. On their return to the U. S.—in New Haven; Waltham, Massachusetts; New York—the Living Theatre stirred considerable controversy. It had fervent admirers and followers.

Certain elements in the Living Theatre's early productions of Jack Gelber's *The Connection* and Kenneth Brown's *The Brig* were extended in its European phase. Despite its post-Pirandello touches, *The Connection* was not essentially new theatre. Its form was naturalistic, though its effect was quasi-poetic. A play about drug addicts, it raised the curtain on the traumatic symptoms in the social complex of the Fifties. The people in the play wait for the "connection," a person who will deliver the heroin which is their means of escape from the dismal reality of the day. What we were made to feel was their need to be connected with something other than our "normalcy." It was a quest for some sort of inner freedom.

While the most shocking scenes were those in which we saw these lost creatures in the process of injecting heroin into their systems, the most poignant moment was the one where they listen enraptured to the playing of a jazz band on an old phonograph record. There was something ritualistic in this. *The Connection* foreshadowed a rebel-

lion still amorphous, which the Sixties were to make articulate, ardent, combative.

The Brig was very nearly a "documentary." In the depiction of the brutal treatment meted out to the inmates of a Marine Corps brig, one could discern a symbol of the deliberate smashing of human morale by an official arm of the feared and detested Establishment.

In *Frankenstein*, the most coherent of the Living Theatre's later productions, we see Man eviscerated and dismembered, then reshaped as a gigantic robot. The visualization of both these operations was brilliant. These scenic images embodied what the Living Theatre's various manifestations—sketches, songs, direct appeals to the public, incitations to riotous action—were protesting against.

Julian Beck and Judith Malina, the leaders of the Living Theatre, were self-declared anarchists. Their theatre was a forum from which the police, the Army, the banking system, war were denounced. They summoned the audience to storm the bastions of power. As heralds of an anticipated revolt, they engaged in other acts of defiance. The actors lived communally, they dressed more or less strangely, they called on the audience to mount the stage, share their views in conversation, or disrobe with them.

Now and then a satiric skit hit the mark, a song might prove touching, an image (the corpses of the war dead heaped on top of one another and dragged away) struck home. All this went with a kind of willful sloppiness: "professionalism" was taboo. While some of the externals of Brecht and Grotowski techniques were assayed, very little was done with true craftsmanship. The thinking was even more shapeless. While the company invoked a world in which man could be free and loving, the atmosphere of its performances was itself often hostile. There was hardly any pleasure, either in their execution or in the audience's reception of them.

Still, the sincerity evident in the fanaticism of the group—it lived as it preached—commanded a certain respect. Their most valid contribution was something beyond theatre. We may set this down to their credit at a time when out theatre is preponderantly banal and complacent. "What is essential in this time of moral poverty," Picasso has said, "is to create enthusiasm."

If the Open Theatre's *America, Hurrah!* in its first two episodes was closer to the expressionism of Elmer Rice's *The Adding Machine*—itself a derivative from such German playwrights as Georg Kaiser—and the final ("Motel") episode on the threshold of new theatre, the same organization's *The Serpent* may confidently be placed in that category. Indeed *The Serpent*, directed by Joseph Chaikin and Robert Sklar, with a "scenario" by Jean-Claude van Itallie, is perhaps the best single piece that the avant-garde theatre has as yet produced in the U. S. Its aesthetic source is in Grotowski; its manner gently humorous, lyrically wistful.

The Serpent shows Eve's emergence from Adam's rib, her subsequent temptation by the reptile, and her seduction of Adam. Following this there is a modestly indicated mass copulation, to the accompaniment of the Biblical "begats" intoned by two female voices. At the conclusion of this the participants ("all humanity") emit agonized groans: sex isn't all fun! There is a remarkably effective pantomime of Abel's murder by Cain. The play closes with the company humming, "We were sailing along on moonlight bay," after which the actors sit down quietly among the spectators as if ruminating on the unfathomable mystery of it all.

There are no costumes, the actors are barefoot in simple work clothes. Percussive and flutelike sound is employed. There is the music of plant and animal life in their generative stages, to which the actors add their own little bleats, neighs, moos. At one point the serpent is seen in a swaying tree (formed by the actor's bodies), aglow with glistening red apples: an enchanting image.

One aspect of *The Serpent* merits special remark as representative of a particular tendency of the new theatre. It moves toward ritual. Ritual is born of a shared memory of the past or a widely, that is, "tribally" accepted practice. The choice of the Book of Genesis as a framework for *The Serpent* was a happy one: we all know the "story." But many of our latter-day theatre efforts to achieve ritualistic status are abortive because they are not based on a common ground in which multitudes of our fellow citizens feel themselves rooted. Indulgences in pot and other similar pastimes, no more than Macy's Thanksgiving parade, are adequate foundations even for a "youth culture."

Groups, more eruptive and virulent in their methods than the Open Theatre, make sporadic appearances. Their names—like the Guerrilla Theatre—furnish some inkling of their character. The Gut Theatre, directed by Enrique Vargas, addresses itself chiefly to the people of East Harlem and the ghetto (mostly Puerto Rican) neighborhoods. The aim of these theatres is more directly socio-political than that of the Open Theatre. They are usually short-lived because they are rarely sustained by money grants so that they might develop permanent companies. The street-theatre movement extends to the West Coast. When one is liquidated still another crops up. Sometimes they are forced underground.

The furthest limits to which the new theatre reaches are Happenings. They go so far that they stretch the meaning of "theatre" to the point of extinction. (Ionesco has occasionally spoken of his work as anti-theatre but that is a sort of gag to attract attention. His plays are "legitimate.") The Happening sets up conditions in street, playground, subway, anywhere at all, to which those in attendance may react in any way they please or are spontaneously moved to do. In his book *Public Domain*, Richard Schechner gives this description of part of a two-day Happening devised by Allan Kaprow, one of the leading exponents of such experiments: "In the work, a girl hangs upside down from a tree. She is one of five persons dangling from ropes at various spots in the rural New Jersey woodland. From distant places in the damp glen, other persons—searchers—begin calling the names of the five who are hanging. When a name is called, the dangling person who is addressed answers, 'Here.' Homing in on the sounds, the searchers locate each upside-down caller and quickly cut or rip away his or her clothing." The Happening is a game, an amusing or an irritating *folie*, rather than an artistic event. There are some who claim that the socially defiant eccentricities of Abbie Hoffman's public behavior are "theatre in life" or still another form of a Happening.

The various innovations in theatre practice referred to in the preceding account have stimulated the writing of a body of plays which have been produced not only off-Broadway but in the off-off-Broadway theatres. Many of them were first given in the tiny Café Chino in the West Village (the pioneer in the latter trend was the café's proprietor, Joseph Chino) and then in Ellen Stewart's ever-expanding "La Mama" enterprises. The list and relative renown of these plays and playwrights have become impressive. The more prominent among these young playwrights are Sam Shepard, Paul Foster, John Guare, Megan Terry, Israel Horovitz, Leonard Melfi, Lanford Wilson, Terrence McNally. I do not include LeRoi Jones, though his *Slave Ship* is more stage picture and pantomime than written drama and indirectly a new-theatre by-product. He is a genuinely gifted writer inspired by the upsurge of black race consciousness which is in the process of producing ever more significant plays. But these fall outside the range of our present subject. Nor is Edward Albee to be aligned with the people just mentioned. His work is marked by the imprint of Ionesco, Beckett, and Pinter. A few of the playwrights just listed reveal his effect upon them.

One of the traits La Mama's "children" share is a difficulty or an incapacity to write full-length plays. There is nothing inherently inferior in the one-act play as contrasted with the more extended dramatic forms. Still, it is worth speculating on why these young new dramatists appear afflicted

with short breath. Their work usually seems to be sprung on momentary insights, clever conceits, whims, gags, and fancies which are rarely susceptible of development. They are flashes in the pan rather than the seeds of pregnant ideas. They illustrate states of being; they do not build situations. (An invalid in bed is in a certain state of being or condition which becomes a dramatic situation only when he attempts to get out of it!)

The initial inspiration of such plays is often provocative, but their authors show little capacity for prolonged thought and the examination of consequences. Their plays, therefore, result in something like a bright slogan rather than a comprehensive argument. I am reminded of the man who thought of a joke and decided to build a musical comedy from it.

Still, utterly to dismiss these writers on the grounds of their immaturity would be wrong. What motivates them is important and the very crux of the entire new-theatre phenomenon. It is a protest against contemporary civilization, the rottenness of our corporate state, the lethal effects of the consumer society. They are the voices of a youth fed up to and beyond the point of maniacal disgust and violent derision at the hypocrisy, the fraudulence, the stupidity, the asphyxiation, the waste and horror of a world they did not create: the world of the Bomb, of atmospheric pollution, of racial injustice, of ghettos, of religion without substance, of patriotism without heart, of politics without human content, of overkill and oversell, of lovelessness.

Thus "Flout 'em and scout 'em—and scout 'em and flout 'em; thought is free" is the tune to which the new dramatists dance. It is the song of Caliban's mates in *The Tempest*. It is barbaric. Barbarians are upsetting, they make a mess, but they have also been known to eradicate the decay of sick societies. Their depredations may clear the ground for creation. Order is sometimes bred from chaos.

Our barbarians are cursed with the sins of their fathers. They are frequently repellent; their yawps are, in the main, echoes of the vile clamor of which they complain. They have inherited many of the diseases which they wish cured. Their theatrical romps and frolics are symptomatic of the ills they denounce. Their thinking is simplistic, often adolescent. Still, our own health depends on our understanding them.

To the routine playgoer, new theatre evokes the shocking image of nude bodies and the blatant sound of four-letter obscenities. What this bespeaks, however, is something more than a commercial strategy. It is true that merchants of the "latest thing" are always eager to cash in on every device to attract the paying crowd. But at a time when all previously honored values have become hollow and nothing formerly sacred is credited as real, the Body is the one remaining, unmistakable truth. There is no shameful secret in nakedness. It is a symbol of freedom. To exult in sex is an act of liberation. To be stripped is to be honest!

"Dirty" words are employed both in defiance and in joyous confrontation with reality. They declare our courageous acceptance of the "low" as well as the "high" in existence. Nudity, obscenity, even pornography, are exultant battle cries against the false face of our society. Youth and its spokesmen in the theatre want "out," out of the wickedness of the rigidly mechanized status quo. They prefer non-sense to common sense.

There is an enormous amount of self-deception and sheer mindlessness in all this. The raucous hurrahs of deliverance are often little more than a rattling of chains. Despite all his enthusiasm for the new-theatre movement, Richard Schechner admits, "When the lid comes off and we are given the opportunity to express ourselves, we find that we have very little to say. Or, more precisely, we do not know how to say what we want to say. We toy with nudity, sexuality, political organization, democratized artistic creativity. But we don't get very far. Begin to remove...repression and we reveal not the 'natural man' but groups of people who mill about in confusion. It is a desperate situation socially and a distressing one aesthetically."

Another threat to what is valid in the new theatre, particularly in its American component, is absorption by commerce and the "squares" who at all costs desire to prove themselves fashionably "with it." John Lahr recognizes this when he writes, "The avant-garde, far from being the anathema which gives danger (and integrity) to its enterprises, has become an important cultural bric-a-brac. Its newest frustration is to become at once popular and curiously powerless....The Underground life-style, once intended to be a shocking fist in the face of the Establishment, is now predictable because of publicity."

The impetus which has propelled the new theatre will not abate even were it to provoke a backlash. What is more likely to happen, what indeed has already begun to happen, is the assimilation of some of the insurgent techniques by the popular theatre. What is *Hair* but the fabulous hit of the rock-and-roll-theatre ritual?

The man who has profited most by the upheaval in theatre thought and practice is Peter Brook. A cultured person, galvanized by Grotowski, with a sympathetic understanding of Beckett and Genet together with a lively devotion to Shakespeare, he has been receptive to the most penetrating injections of the avant-garde needle. In Peter Weiss's *Marat/Sade* and *Midsummer Night's Dream* (produced in Stratford-on-Avon), Brook has turned some of the "poisons" of the new pharmacopoeia into vitalizing medicine. He has enlivened the English stage, and his example will no doubt help others to further explorations.

The new theatre, in short, has in both its positive and negative phases immediate social implications. It is not, as some believe, an offensively bragging frivolity, a "send up" by aesthetic ruffians, but a mirror reflecting a disturbed world turning a dangerous corner. Aesthetically the new theatre has added a rich and vast vocabulary to the lexicon of stage expression at a time when many affirm that the film alone can hold sway.

"To be new is everything in America," said Ellen Terry in 1883. We have not changed. We are hung up on novelty. It is this drive toward the "different" which constitutes our conformity. Chekhov's aesthetic credo voiced in *The Seagull*, "I came more and more to the conviction that it is not a question of new and old forms, but that what matters is that a man should write without thinking of forms at all, write because it springs freely from the soul," is surely in need of qualification. But it is nevertheless a sound point of departure.

It is as true that there is nothing old in the world as that there is nothing altogether new. Every generation has its particular way of experiencing existence because the world is always in the process of change; and every individual of marked personality originates some special variation on the theme of his time—often in contradiction to it. Therefore art, the most universal form of human communication, changes. But as long as man remains man, his essential needs remain more or less unaltered: health of body and spirit, the hunger to feel and understand his connection with his fellow men and beyond this his dependence on all else to which he owes his being. Judgment in artistic matters must perforce turn back to those sources in man's nature. The biologic and the moral are a continuum.

A true evaluation of the new theatre's products resolves itself to the same criteria we apply to all art, new and old. Otherwise we deal in mere fashion which has only a tenuous, accidental, commercial relation to art. The noisy nomenclature of new artistic movements is helpful to those eager to break through conventional ramparts; they do not in themselves establish values. In a letter to Flaubert, Zola, whose "naturalism" was the *dernier cri* of the mid-nineteenth century, showed how aware he was of the advantages of catch-words. "I consider the word *Naturalism* as ridiculous as you do, but I shall go on repeating it over and over again, because you have to give things new names for the public to think that they are new."

If I were challenged to identify the human core of the new-theatre movement I should mention that it is a reflection of our *estrangement* (or "alienation") from contemporary society and in some instances a defiant response to it. In the first case, it is disheartened; in the second, crudely lyric. Because we have become suspicious of so many words which are now employed to confuse and betray us, the "movement" tends to be anti-literary. For youth especially, action speaks louder than words. And theatre, it has been notably asserted, is to begin with and fundamentally performance, *action*.

Whatever we think of these general aesthetic or craft arguments, in the end we must assign worth to individual offerings within every artistic manifestation in relation to the degree of genuineness, power, breadth, and depth we find in them, that is, to the extent they satisfy our basic human appetites and hungers. All the rest is modishness, and the applied rationalizations, no matter how high-sounding or startling, are fraudulent.

—*HARP*, Feb. '71

THE HOUSE OF BLUE LEAVES

John Guare's most striking talent is for savage farce. There are scenes in Act Two of his first full-length play, *The House of Blue Leaves* (Truck and Warehouse Theatre), in which his fancy boils over into a tempest of hilarity. They are the best things in the play; they provoke wild laughter and merit enthusiastic applause. Still, the play remains unfulfilled; the reasons are worth careful attention.

Guare is not simply a prankster. What motivates him is scorn for the fraudulence of our way of life. In *The House of Blue Leaves* he has been aroused by the obsession with big shots, "personalities," stars, the "in" tribe. That is a way of saying that we no longer see people as human beings; we worship "names." The imbecile, the villainous, the irredeemably mediocre possess glamor (even when we profess to despise them) if they have been sufficiently publicized. No wonder advertisement is the country's prime industry.

The central figure of *The House of Blue Leaves*, Artie Shaughnessy, a man who tends the animals in a zoo, has wanted all his life to be a pop songwriter. His tunes are atrocious. He is not only ungifted—which is no great matter—he is a fool. He is abject in the fetishism of his fellow citizens. The only people who count for him are those who have "made good"; everyone from his wartime buddy who has become a successful Hollywood director to the Pope. His son Ronnie, he boasts, will rise to glory in the Army into which he has recently been drafted. His girl friend, whom he intends to marry when he gets his divorce, is a frisky goose who encourages his idiotic delusions of grandeur. She is a girl who knows everything about the personages celebrated in the gossip columns, television, movie magazines.

Artie really knows nothing about himself or anyone else. His son loathes the Army, goes AWOL—and plans to blow up the Pope on his visit to the U.N. Artie's girl friend leaves him when he proves a bust. His stupidity is apparently the cause of his wife's insanity, though she too is infected with the craving for the smile of the blessed public heroes. Toward the end of the play the Hollywood director—a person of no consequence except there—assures Artie that he is the man for whom all his pictures have been made. Artie stands for the half-wits who constitute the bulk of the audience for Hollywood's typical product.

There is a certain grimness in all this but Guare turns it into a roar of clownish mockery. *The House of Blue Leaves* is crazy fun. But something disturbs it. That "something" may be (this is only conjecture) a personal pain—an autobiographical memory?—which causes Guare to inject elements of cruel sorrow into the proceedings. There is nothing at all mirthful about the madness of Artie's wife nor in the play's final moment when he strangles her.

The play suffers, thus, from a discrepancy of style, but that need not have been fatal. What damages the total effect is that nobody—not the director, the producers, nor apparently the author himself—appears to have been aware of what was required to make the play a workable whole for the stage. It is true that the text itself is deficient in inner coherence, but with some revision and with more knowledgeable direction the flaw might have been overcome. I have just now suggested that Artie's obtuseness may have caused his wife's insanity, but that connection is not made in the writing. As the play stands, she is an unexplained hospital case: a raw wound that cripples the play's comic nature. Insanity, violence, death itself can be—has often been given—a comic, even a farcical mask in the theatre and every other art form.

The play calls for natural comedians. William Atherton as Artie's son, with close-cropped hair, malicious grin and taut nerves—an image of the wild ones of the younger generation—is properly cast. Margaret Linn, pretty, innocently earnest and totally deaf movie starlet, is comic without strain. The same may be said of Alix Elias as a little nun—an endearingly cute character.

The "principals" are far less fortunate, both from miscasting and from a stylistic misconception that mars the whole production. Harold Gould, who plays Artie, is a proficient and intelligent actor: he strikes one as an educated man of the middle class, a carefully groomed professor. But Artie is at best a pathetic "schmo," a well-meaning slob. He should be projected sincerely *as a joke*. Instead, Artie is played dramatically; thus his scenes with his wife are so chilling that at times he appears to be as psychopathic as she.

Artie could be made oddly laughable, if played by an actor in whom a zany naïveté, shrewdness of observation and a bouncing imagination are mingled. Gould is not such an actor. Nor does Katherine Helmond, whose forte is pathos, contribute anything but shock to the role of Artie's wife. The combination of these two players produces the effect of a "psychological" drama. The comedienne Anne Meara, in the role of the dizzy dame whom Artie proposes to marry, is so forced through miscalculated direction that she fails to get the laughs inherent in the part, laughs which should normally come easily to her.

While *The House of Blue Leaves* possesses real and valid content, it cannot, given Guare's gifts, be articulated as realism. Even the setting betrays it. The background for such a play demands some manner of humorous stylization. What one sees instead is a literal replica of a grubby apartment in Sunnyside, Queens. And why, even for "realism," must a set be so detailed in architecture and utilities? The cost of such a set, under present conditions, must exceed a sensible budget for off-Broadway. Plays of this kind are more readily enjoyed when unburdened by the needless (and inartistic) ponderousness of the scenic trappings which most managers associate with first-class production.

Long ago I came to the conclusion that within the disastrous economics of show business there lies a more destructive factor: the lack of basic theatre understanding.

—*NAT*, 1 Mar. '71

ALL OVER

Because Edward Albee's latest play, *All Over* (Martin Beck Theatre), is one which many people may have trouble appreciating, I feel constrained to begin by saying that it is the best American play of several seasons—a manner of speaking of which I disapprove! The play comes to us, moreover, in a remarkably fine production, one that is so much a part of the total impression of the event that one is not sure in discussing it whether one is referring to the text or to its stage embodiment. John Gielgud as director has given Albee his most thoroughly realized interpretation.

To quote one of the characters in *All Over*, Albee is shocked by the "sad and shabby times we live in." Though wholly immersed in the present, he appears to be withdrawn from it, to set himself apart. He "alienates" himself. *All Over* seems written from a tomb, a world on the other side of existence. Its people, though recognizably contemporary, produce the effect of wraiths recalled from a bygone life. The play conveys an existential shudder which has its origins in the soul's dark solitude.

The theme is man's relation to death. Americans tend to shy away from the very thought. When death is dealt with on our stage it is nearly always in a sentimental, pseudo-religious or sensational vein, any of which betrays evasion. This indicates a spiritual error. Death is a definition of life, and life is made precious by an acknowledgment of its containment within the bounds of death. Maturity is possible only when death is fearlessly confronted and freely accepted. Without such acceptance, life itself ceases to have dignity.

All Over is a view of American life (or certain salient aspects of it) in the perspective of death. A wealthy lawyer—many honors have been bestowed upon him—has been brought home to die. "Brought home" not only because he is said to prefer dying there than in a hospital but because for many years he has been living with a mistress and away from his home. The play takes place around the unseen deathbed. Gathered there are the man's wife, his mistress, his son and daughter, a lawyer who is his best friend and partner.

Little love is lost among them. The wife is contemptuous of her children. The son is a weak incompetent, rapidly going to seed; the daughter a venomous woman who is having an affair with a racketeer. She scorns her mother, who despises the daughter for her crude impatience and failure to understand the older generation's way of life. The daughter hates the mistress because, so she rationalizes, the mistress has robbed her of her father. The mistress, a sturdy counterpart of the more delicately fibered wife, is strong, realistic, unsentimentally humane. There is a bond of understanding and sympathy between the wife and mistress because they have shared a love for the same man. The best friend is an average intelligent citizen who tries to mediate in the family's contentious.

The play offers little of what is usually called "action." Instead, there is a constant revelation of character and idea through the interplay of motivations and the clash of temperaments. At first one

779

tends to see the play's personages as heartless and loveless, hence unworthy of interest. There is a steady exchange of insults, with the daughter pitted against both mother and mistress. There is also some acid scoffing about the son: the rich boy spoiled by paternal indifference and a cushy job in his father's firm for which he has no particular aptitude. Only the old doctor and the attending nurse, both of whom have long lived with death, are entirely without rancor or despair. The characters reminisce (there is a passage about a garden that should be abbreviated); they joke, indulge in trivialities and engage in an exchange of barbed sentiments as if they had forgotten that they are in the presence of death.

Listening attentively, as one must to understand this largely verbal play, one comes to recognize that it contains not only feeling but pathos all the more poignant for its severe repression. Albee is saying that, despite all the hasty bickering, the fierce hostility and the mutual misunderstandings which separate us, we need one another. We cry out in agony when we are cut off.

On close examination, the bitterest dramatists today prove to be the most moral. Albee condemns the vulgarity of an age that refuses to perceive the sanctity of the human condition and the responsibility for mutual respect. Instead of struggling for balance amid the conflicting drives within us, we retreat to hypocritical subterfuges. Albee decries the younger generation not for its well advertised "sins" but because it refuses to comprehend the validity of tradition which the past has so valiantly fashioned to convert chaos to order. He also accuses the older generation of having depleted tradition of its content by neglecting to persevere in the arduous task of maintaining it. Tradition has been reduced to the mouthing of its nomenclature: loyalty, honor, home, country, etc.

So much may be agreed upon in the abstract. But what about the play itself? It is not important in this instance that, as some insist, the dying man be seen. His person is not the issue. All we need to know of him is the part he played in the history of the living: the two women who loved him, the children, his friends. The play is their drama, not his. Nor does Albee mean to "move" us in the sense of eliciting tears. (Art is not for crying.) He wants to show how these apparently cold and selfish people, the damage of their souls expressing itself in malice, sum up their experience in a confession of searing unhappiness and sense of loss when their connection with a fellow human being is severed.

It is a stylized play; its characters do not speak "naturally." The language is that of an artist who sees things through the peculiar spectrum of his brooding spirit. His is a frozen fire. No one else in our theatre writes in this particular way. That makes Albee truly original.

I must cavil, in passing, on a matter too often overlooked in the consideration of theatrical events. The choice may be no one's fault, but the Martin Beck Theatre is too large for so intimate a play. Unless one is sitting up front, one is likely to miss important points in the closely woven fabric of the dialogue.

John Gielgud has staged *All Over* as a "ritual." This treatment is not arbitrary; it is suggested by Albee's style and meaning. The setting, which might have been realistic (a paneled bed-sitting room, tapestried walls, family portraits, etc.), is admirably rendered by a sepulchrally diagrammed space, bare of everything but indispensable furniture, in which the figures stand out in emblematic isolation.

The pace is deliberate rather than "slow," with every phrase carefully shaped in congruence with Albee's writing, a vernacular artificial as verse is artificial. It is the prose of a man who desires to restrain the too overt expression of the extremity of his passion and pain and yet purposes to be stringently honest. A strange wit flickers over the dark background.

The acting company is well chosen. There are no bad performances. Colleen Dewhurst as the wise and earthy mistress is seen here to better advantage than perhaps ever before. Betty Field as the nurse manifests a delicate and charming astringency of humor. As the wife, Jessica Tandy possesses the right air of intelligence and breeding, together with inner firmness. Madelaine Sherwood is somewhat more adept at conveying the daughter's resentments than her hurt. (Her voice carries best in the large house.) Neil Fitzgerald as the doctor, James Ray as the son, George Voskovec as the best friend bring to their assignments something more than skill.

Gielgud has not attempted to make his players "profound"; he has sought to present them in sharp outline. The play's transcendent message is thus projected in a memorable pattern or picture.

—*NAT*, 12 Apr. '71

FOLLIES

I shouldn't enjoy the new musical, *Follies*, but I do (Winter Garden). Like most of the musicals since, let us say, the 1940s, this one lacks "heart." The old ones, though they too were commercially oriented, appeared to mean what they said. They were usually sugary and silly, but they seemed candid. Their foolishness lent them innocence and thus made children of us. The musicals now are mechanisms, designed like ads to seduce us into purchase.

Still there is no denying the splendid skill of such a spectacle as *Follies*. Some people speak of "movie movies": this is a "show show." Its incontestable talents are admirably packaged. The assembling of the ingredients amounts to a science. As such it is a triumph.

Follies combines the "best features" of the old and the new. It has a touch of humorous nostalgia. Former stage, picture, television and radio "names," appearing in energized parodies and near replicas of old musical song-and-dance routines, contribute to the remembrance of things past. Jonathan Tunick's orchestrations are adept enough to add the zip of modernity to the convention of the tunes. Similarly, there are excellent costumes by Florence Klotz, and Stephen Sondheim's lyrics

are more tautly clever than those of the past. The whole show is synthetic but it is accomplished with such dispatch that one cannot fail to applaud its bravura.

According to James Goldman's "book," we are on the stage of an old theatre—the Palace, perhaps, or the Winter Garden itself—now in the process of demolition. The owner has invited the stars that once shone here—most of them now 50 or older—to a farewell party. They remember their early romances, their struggles, their successes. As they recall their hits, we see them shadowed by the mirage of their former selves.

The two main couples who met, wooed and wedded in those days are no longer connected with stage. They are now rich—unhappy. They seem to have been mismatched. Divorces appear imminent but all are reconciled before the party is over. Notes of bitterness, dissolution and regret are sounded in their meeting in the night but dawn brings sweet resignation and promise of hope. This—the failure of marriage—is another of the story's "modern" touches. We are no longer supposed to believe in the possibility of marital harmony or wise maturity.

There's one brief episode in which a youth who serves drinks at the party is picked up by one of the ladies. Nothing happens but the young fellow's casual acceptance of the situation—almost equally indifferent as to whether the encounter does or does not develop into sexual intimacy—has a certain truthfulness about it.

Though negligible, the "book" does supply a link for the numbers and they, I repeat, are thoroughly effective. As directors, Harold Prince and Michael Bennett, have helped make them so. They have chosen the right cast, and with Sondheim's astuteness in writing apt lyrics for each of the principals, they all show to their best advantage.

Alexis Smith, who has never before appeared in a New York production, is handsome, intelligent, direct, dignified and has long legs withal. She sings and dances most agreeably. Dorothy Collins has quiet passages of real acting. Mary McCarty is robust and funny; Ethel Shutta, a luminary of the twenties, is very funny in a song in which she tells how in her heyday she was eager to give body and soul to play *any* part in a *"Broadway Show."* (The term had real glamour then.) Gene Nelson is exciting in a dance routine in which he expresses his discontent. The show girls are, one way or another, swell lookers. My one complaint—but it is a compliment to the old-timers; Yvonne De Carlo and the others—is that the young people chosen to represent their senior counterparts are not nearly as attractive or as interesting as the originals.

Added to all this, Boris Aronson once again demonstrates the multiplicity of forms his imagination can assume. His decayed and gutted "backstage," in which a constructivist design is not only evocative but theatrically furnished—a machine for movement—together with the airy frivolity which gays up the "Folly" numbers at the end, create a masterpiece in decor. Tharon Musser's lighting is a notable contribution to the acting company as well as to the designer.

—*NAT*, 19 Apr. '71

70, GIRLS, 70

*7*0, *Girls, 70* does not contain that many females; the title refers to the age of various members of the cast (Broadhurst Theatre). It is a musical show with a book by Fred Ebb and Norman Martin; music by John Kander and lyrics by Fred Ebb.

It is a loony, corny, untidy affair and, to use Broadway lingo, "I loved it." The sillier it became the fonder I grew. This was a surprise to me. When the curtain rose and I saw the large company of gray heads, each of whom announced his or her advanced years, I found myself on edge. Why, I began asking myself, do elderly Americans feel they must ape the young? Why can't they act their age? If they were bouncy and foolish in their youth, must they persevere in this to the end? Why in our land is seniority so often regarded as inferiority? Because the young are quicker, are readier

with the action that spells commodities? It is related to salesmanship, gross national product, getting ahead. Being is less valued than doing. It is a matter of economics!

These dark musings were soon dispelled by the show. There was a freshness of feeling in it, a satisfaction in play, an elation of craftsmanship characteristic of our theatrical age of innocence. It is said that actors are children; if so, it is one of their most endearing traits. With the withering away of confidence in the theatre through its desperate commercialism actors lose the particular naïveté without which they cannot take pleasure in their profession or give it.

The old time trouper had "style," a certain elegance even when his material was raffishly popular. An exceptionally accomplished actress, Mildred Natwick, is the star of *70, Girls, 70*; by her breeding, poise, intelligence and constant humor she gives the entertainment backbone. How earthy and strong, how assertive in her doubt, is Lillian Hayman. What verve and salt, together with trim articulation of movement, in Henrietta Jacobson. There is hearty vigor in Lillian Roth whose bumpy career has not diminished her ability to gobble life as if it were edible. Lucie Lancaster's present characterization combines an old-maidish timorousness with a wicked cuteness. But then the entire company is delightfully at home within the proscenium. One does not have to summon "nostalgia" as aid to the appreciation of these players: they are all aglow today.

This histrionic festiveness is based on a farcical notion borrowed from an English play, *Breath-of-Spring*. A gamesome widow suggests to a group of indigent companions that they may brighten their late years by a corporate engagement in shoplifting. In *70, Girls, 70* it becomes the peg for a number of "crazy" scenes and numbers. The lyrics are pleasant, the music supports them, the direction of Paul Aaron and Stanley Prager uses the cast well, but the roster of performers makes the show. One must be heavily uptight not to enjoy the fling.

A reader, Frieda Arken, has written me a nice letter suggesting that Albee's *All Over*, which she "unhesitatingly labeled a meretricious bore," might be something to read but not suitable to the stage. Her letter gives me an opportunity to comment further on the play to which the reactions, with a few exceptions, have ranged from boredom to sadistic hostility.

I find *All Over* every bit as *theatrical* as Pinter's *Landscape* and *Silence*, Marguerite Duras' *A Place Without Doors* (now being admirably played in French at the Barbizon-Plaza Theatre under its original title *L'Amante Anglaise*) or Beckett's *Play*—all of them pieces I have reviewed favorably. Indeed, what isn't "playable" nowadays!

Still that is not my point. The truth is that what I prefer is a "swinging" theatre, by which I mean—Shakespeare! I love movement, color, physical excitement, bravura as much as "thoughtfulness." Since Ibsen, drama has become ever more introverted: this tendency has now reached the static. The atmospheric or social oppression of our day has brought about an explosive reaction to this: a theatre that is chiefly movement, sound, hectic imagery, in which ideas, when they exist at all, may be inferred. We are bound to accept these opposing trends in the theatre—they both mirror realities—providing we find them in one way or another meaningful.

What I seek in art are personal statements or manifestations of human experience. I wish to be convinced that the artist has really felt something about the world in which he lives and has found his own way of expressing it. I have often written that what Beckett says is alien to my nature but that I respect him greatly because his is a real experience (akin to one we all share at times) and that he has found his own special mode of expression. Most of what is seen in the theatre—even when agreeable—has a "ready-made" quality of secondhand content and form.

My temperament is totally different from Albee's. I find that, having become increasingly dour, disheartened and withdrawn, he nevertheless expresses a genuine response to the aridity of much that we now sense about us. There is a terrible tension in his work, as if he were about to howl his distress but somehow does not dare to do so. It "screws" him up—his language gives evidence of this—but there is an emotional significance in his writing that I find moving.

The result, theatrically speaking, is a degree of abstraction which emaciates his characters and makes "patterns" of them. Still there is more body in *All Over* than in *Box-Mao-Box* which was a graph of Albee's discouragement. For this reason, while I approve of John Gielgud's attempt to visualize the structural element in *All Over* through a thoroughly nonrealistic setting as though a place in which corpses were to be dissected and through acting which may be too formally verbal, I conceive another sort of production. It would still be stylized, but a precise environment would be suggested and the play's characters, somewhat less obviously isolated from one another than they are now, might take on more body.

Most damaging to the play in its present "format"—I wager it will be seen elsewhere in the country and more especially in many cities throughout Europe—is the size of the Martin Beck Theatre. *All Over* demands intimacy of presentation, a small house.

Finally in reply to my correspondent I feel obliged to repeat a tenet basic to my and, I hope, to all criticism: what counts in criticism is not agreement in opinion—in terms of "yes" and "no." What is important is how and why a critic arrives at his opinion, whatever it may be.

—*NAT*, 3 May '71

LONG DAY'S JOURNEY INTO NIGHT

In the last act father-and-son scene of O'Neill's *Long Day's Journey Into Night* (Promenade Theatre) James Tyrone says, "The praise Edwin Booth gave my Othello! I made the manager put down his exact words in writing. I kept it in my wallet for years. Where is it now, I wonder? Somewhere in this house. I remember I put it away carefully—." To which his son Edmund replies, "It might be in the old trunk, along with Mama's wedding dress."

In the play's final moments the mother, benumbed by morphine, enters dragging a wedding gown on the floor. She doesn't recognize it as hers. James, her husband, takes it from her, pointing out that she might get it dirty, and she murmurs, "I remember now. I found it in the attic hidden in a trunk. But I don't know what I wanted it for. I'm going to be a nun—that is, if I can only find." She breaks off and then resumes, "What is it I'm looking for? I know it's something I lost."

The four Tyrones are bedeviled by a terrible unnamed loss. The loss inspires guilt in them; they thrash about in a vain effort to identify it, though they hardly realize the nature of their quest. They blame one another for the absence of what is essential to them, and immediately thereafter apologize, knowing that the accusations are misdirected. Each is isolated in his or her sorrowful guilt. Only one of them, Edmund, may emerge from the morass—as Eugene O'Neill did later, through his plays.

The long day's journey is a bitter self-examination into the darkness of the self. The journey for the dramatist constituted a process of self-discovery. But the play's characters, bound together by their dilemma, which makes for a kind of tortured love, are rarely able to touch one another. Each suspects the others of being the cause of his sufferings. An audience sufficiently attentive, and aided by a wholly sound production, should comprehend the source of the Tyrones' tragedy.

They have lost their faith. Loss of faith is the main theme almost throughout O'Neill's work. For him it was more than a personal tragedy, it was *the* American tragedy. As individuals and as a nation, we have lost that spiritual coherence which makes men and societies whole. O'Neill declared that his *magnum opus*—the nine plays, of which he completed only *A Touch of the Poet*—was the

dramatization of the question, "What shall it profit a man if he gain the whole world and lose his own soul?"

What innocent and trusting Mary Tyrone has lost is her religious faith, a faith in God which sustained her in the genteel home and the convent in which she was raised. She fell in love with James Tyrone, a star actor of romantically heroic roles, "and was so happy for a time." Her husband believed in the theatre, especially in Shakespeare; "I studied Shakespeare," he says, "as you'd study the Bible." Shakespeare was central to his religion, on whose account he rid himself of the brogue of his Irish birth.

His many years of immigrant struggle against poverty had made him acutely aware of "the value of a dollar." This turned him to a miserliness to which his sons ascribe all the family's misfortunes. His anxiety to avoid the specter of the poorhouse caused him to abandon his deepest desire to be a great Shakespearean actor and give himself to the exploitation of the box-office hit which he played for more than twenty years to the exclusion of everything else. He betrayed his religion. "What the hell was it I wanted to buy that was worth—" He falters as he asks the question.

The vagrant life of the road led to Mary's intense loneliness (James's boon companions, his fellow actors, were no fit company for such as she) and so unwittingly she became addicted to drugs. On this account, her older son, James, Jr., lost faith in his mother, becoming a cynical drunk and patron of brothels, a blasphemer against his mother's religion and his father's profession, always a little jealous of his younger brother whom he also loves. Edmund is a seeker after truth. He declares himself not so much a poet as a faithful realist. Still, he feels that he will forever be less than whole if he is unable to recapture that sense of belonging to something "greater than my own life, or the life of Man…to God, if you want to put it that way…." He experienced such a state at moments in his year at sea. It is this ecstatic relation to existence which Edmund says he lost—"and you are alone, lost in a fog again, and stumble on toward nowhere…."

If the desolateness of this condition in the Tyrone household and the agonized quest for a light beyond the dark are not present in the production, it becomes only the chronicle of an unhappy family—though, even as such, very moving. The triumph is that here a solidly constructed realistic drama is rendered integral with social meaning as well as the soulful poetry of despair and forgiveness. That is what makes *Long Day's Journey Into Night* O'Neill's masterpiece.

The sympathetic production under Arvin Brown's direction should be seen. Its actors are intelligent and personally winning. What is missing is a grand design wrought of deep inner characterizations and understanding of the play's basic mood—its tragic essence. As it stands now, the production is only a good domestic drama, though it is impossible to overlook the elements of grandeur in the wonderful scenes preceding the play's end.

Robert Ryan looks right as Tyrone. He has a mildness of temperament that is appealing without actually being impressive. (But where on the American stage today is the heroic tragic actor?) Geraldine Fitzgerald, who properly enough stresses the childlike side of Mary Tyrone and is by nature a sweet and sensitive woman, does not sufficiently convey the unfathomable bewilderment in suffering which is at the heart of the role. A promising young actor, James Naughton is a straightforward Edmund. He reads the cardinal speech of his part well: only there should be much more to it than that. Stacy Keach alone brings the searing torment of the play to the role of James, Jr. There is fire in him but perhaps not enough of a certain boyish candor, which also exists in the character's spoiled nature.

To achieve an "ideal" production for this play directors and actors must not shy from the painful, as Arvin Brown willy-nilly appears to be doing. There is a bit too much standing and walking about on Geraldine Fitzgerald's part—particularly in the third act—in order, I suppose, to avoid her having to sit quietly while speaking what amounts to a long sequence of monologues. (Morphine reduces energy in movement, but the character here, supposedly deep in her drugged musings, acts as if she were merely overtalkative.) To eschew the "heaviness" of serious drama everyone smiles too much, tries to keep things light, "natural," unemphatically simple. How afraid we are today of emotional power, of magnitude! We make everything "clear" and small. "The tragedy of America is its fear of tragedy."

—*NAT*, 10 May '71

ANTIGONE

We are at sea when we discuss the staging of old Greek drama. Despite all the explanations and illustrations in textbooks: masks to make the actors more impressively superhuman, more visible and possibly more audible; *cothurni*, built-up shoes, to make them more formidable in stature; *periaktoi*, painted prisms to serve as "settings," we know little about ancient Athenian production.

The acoustics were perfect—I have had occasion to verify that in the edifices which are still usable—but we are largely ignorant of how the language was pronounced, how it sounded. In short, we can be sure of scarcely anything except the impressive spectacle of the vast areas which the theatres occupied. They had a seating capacity of more than 10,000 and the *orchestra*, that is, the main stage space, was about 80 feet in diameter.

What we call the Greek Theatre tradition is mostly modern German. Max Reinhardt's *Oedipus Rex*, first seen in Vienna in 1910 in a "circus," became a model for many of the later productions in this "Greek" tradition.

For years I read Gilbert Murray's translation of Euripides, only to learn from T. S. Eliot that they were closer to Swinburne than to the original master, whom Nietzsche accused of having introduced personal psychology into the majesty of tragedy and by so doing diminishing its nobility.

Though one of the fundamentals in the Greek philosophy of behavior was "Nothing in excess," extremes of pain are voiced in its drama. Edmund Wilson once remarked on this, finding in Sophocles not the godly calm that is generally ascribed to Hellenic art but fierce torment and rage at man's fate, aggravated rather than lessened by the ineluctable compulsion to accept it. What modifies this terror of Greek drama is the sublimity of its music: the lyric diction, the dance, the ritual, the "distance" between the bestiality of the action and one's contemplation of it.

Now the Repertory Theatre of Lincoln Center has chosen to do Sophocles' *Antigone*. Why? The play's theme at present must appear similar to that of *The Trial of the Catonsville Nine*! Creon, the anti-hero of the venerable play, sets the law of the City above that of human conscience. "The State is the King!" Creon proclaims; to which Haimon, Antigone's betrothed, replies: "Yes, if the State is a desert." There is much more to *Antigone* than that and if a reader would care to understand its full and almost inexhaustible content I should be obliged to refer him to the writings of the British scholar-critic H. D. F. Kitto.

My purpose for citing the foregoing data is simply to indicate the gap between a New York (or any American theatre) production and the immense complexity of the problem if it undertakes the presentation of a Greek tragedy. It is almost unbridgeable.

The acting at the Vivian Beaumont is not at all bad. Reasonably read, nearly all the lines come through distinctly. Philip Bosco's Creon is convincing enough as "realism" and wholly "sincere." Martha Henry makes a good appearance as Antigone and has a voice which carries effortlessly. David Birney's Haimon is engagingly credible. The dance and musical elements, which played a crucial role in the Greek theatre, here amount to very little: the chorus has been rendered visually and dramatically neutral. Jane Greenwood's costumes are good-looking without fuss. Douglas Schmidt's setting, consisting chiefly of huge shattered images of Attic derivation in sculpted relief, is striking.

Yet I was left untouched, never for a moment vitally concerned. The production is a parade of isolated fragments from an august history. It may be virtuous to assay such a production; it is not conducive to pleasure or even edification. The basic reason for the failure is not "aesthetic" or technical—there is nothing terribly wrong with Lincoln Center's *Antigone*. The reason is that there is no inner necessity for it, no human pressure within our community to demand it, no real subjective, personal "push" in the players and producers to do it. It is fundamentally aimless. So we are once again faced with the dilettantism that makes so many "educational" dramatic institutions discouragingly anti-theatre.

—*NAT*, 31 May '71

REFLECTIONS ON MOVIES

It is widely held that movies nowadays are much more interesting than the theatre. Arithmetically speaking, it is a fact. It should be immediately admitted that a moderately entertaining film is much more attractive than an indifferent play.

The reason for this is simple enough: there are the *pictures*. Most films today are admirably photographed. The pictures' locales are diverse, often exotically fascinating, bold in the maneuvers of their execution. The faces and bodies we see are, with the cameraman's aid, more sensuously gratifying than those beheld at present on the stage. Physical beauty, which should be one of the theatre's lures, is now sadly lacking.

While the theatre for centuries has been taken as an adjunct of literature, its very name derives from the Greek "theatron," which connotes seeing. In our country at least, the theatre has become visually impoverished as well as verbally depleted.

Drama signifies action. In this respect also, the theatre has become poor. It is generally deficient in movement. By their very nature, films, even if we think of them only in regard to editing, are all movement. In pictures we are present at the accidents of daily living, the disasters of war, the upheaval and wreckage of nature. Movies act directly on our senses. Because of all this they "grab" us more readily than any other art.

Have I, who began my playgoing career at the age of seven and spent over forty-five years of my professional life in the theatre, then turned movie buff? Have I lost my appetite for stage spectacles? The debate over or contrast between the two media is specious. I have been going to the movies since the days of Bronco Billy Westerns. I did not give them much thought then, I just went. It never occurred to me, later on, to engage in any argument over the comparative merits of theatre and cinema. Such discussion is usually more a matter of pragmatic or commercial than of aesthetic concern. No art replaces another. My addiction to the theatre and my growing interest in the movies have never interfered with my reading poetry and novels, my love of the dance, my attentiveness to painting and sculpture, my enjoyment of old and new music.

Films are a new and exciting mode of expression. They do not, I repeat, render any other medium, however ancient or neglected, obsolete. What we are called upon to enjoy and evaluate in all the arts is the weight and quality of what they express.

The film, I have always believed, is an essentially silent medium. I found myself disturbed at first by the third dimension of speech which intruded on the two dimensionality of the screen image. I held John Ford's *The Informer* in special esteem because he used so little dialogue. (I can remember only two or three lines of the spoken text.) But we have talkies and screenwriters now, and they have added a great deal to the scope of the cinematic form.

Another addition to film vocabulary is color. Its employment has become virtually mandatory not only because of the TV companies' insistence upon it. Still, I cannot help but feel that in this way many pictures lose something of their truth. This is a paradox because we do perceive objects in a variety of shades. There are certain films the effects of which are thus enhanced. But the tints employed in most films are more pigment than true color. Faces are too often drenched in an intensity of hue which makes them look glazed in a bath of cosmetics, as if they were on sale.

Many scenes photographed on big-city locations (including the slums) become glamorized to the detriment of the film's artistic intention. Paris in René Clair's *Soux les Toits de Paris* or Agnès Varda's *Cleo from 5 to 7* appears more truly itself than do the usual film images of that town which look like ads for travel agencies. One could hardly believe in the wretched garishness of the dance hall in *They Shoot Horses, Don't They?* because of the chromatic lushness of the photography.

It is possible that, in time, greater delicacy in this regard may be achieved. In any case, except for travelogue enchantment, we have more or less ceased to notice color in films: it is just there. The subliminal effect of its use is to make the world appear opulent, which is perhaps a solace for a fatigued population.

I am now chiefly concerned with the intrinsic content to be found in the films seen in the past two or three years. As I choose only those recommended by people I respect, I can honestly state that I have had a pleasant time at most of them. If I enjoy fifteen or twenty minutes of any film, because of a sequence made exhilarating through an actor's personality, interest in the subject matter, or directorial ingenuity, I do not feel myself cheated.

Though it is entirely proper to speak of the art of films, I find very little art in films except when artists make them—and they are exceedingly rare. I view most films—especially the American—as *documentaries*. They tell us more of the time and place in which we dwell than any of the other media. As fiction, drama, or art, they lie. They are primarily designed as diversions, games, toys; yet they are willy-nilly full of instruction. The response they elicit from their vast audiences is as much part of their message as their material—often more telling than volumes of statistics. Thus, no matter how frivolous they may be, I take them seriously.

Cultured folk, when I began seeing movies, held them in contempt. This was so for many years. Not only were movies primitive in technique, they were also paltry in content. They were kid stuff and as such may have done more harm than good. Even when they became more sophisticated, educated people rarely regarded them worth adult consideration. The big studios made them conform strictly to the myth of America as the land of the pure, the brave, the just, and above all, the happy. There was no ill that our benevolence could not remedy. Love conquered.

All this has changed in the past fifteen years. The increasing interest in foreign pictures plus the breakdown of the old Hollywood system—the dissolution of the monopoly by which producers controlled the industry through ownership of the movie houses—the ensuing financial panic, forced the remaining film entrepreneurs to meet the challenge from Europe and that of the ever increasing number of independent filmmakers and theatre proprietors. At last freedom was attained. No holds are now barred. Everything may be shown or said. Should the new films be deemed too licentious, the release may be marked R (restricted) as a warning to parents and a caution to the squeamish.

This newfound freedom has, in my view, opened the way to a new sort of falsity, a fresh factitiousness, a special type of opportunism more dangerous, though more masked, than the old. There is no less distortion and sentimentality in today's daring films than there was when the heinous movie moguls reigned. While the sweet and soupy product of former days was debasing through its avoidance of real issues and facts, the recent spate of knock 'em dead or gut movies blows our brains and hearts through benumbing sensationalism. To expose vice and corruption as a spectacle for fun, no matter how well decked out in psychoanalytic hearsay and radical palaver, is just as corrosive of sensibility and intelligence as the indulgence in vacuous daydreams of well-being.

Stag films have become superfluous. Ever since *Hiroshima, Mon Amour*, scenes of nude bodies in tight embrace followed by explicit images of sexual activity have become almost obligatory as emblems of filmic emancipation. But this is a minor matter. The erotic has always occupied an important place in the world's treasury of the arts. There are masterpieces of pornography. I am always gratified by the sight of a beautiful nude body—though such sights are vouchsafed us under much more favorable conditions elsewhere. The issue now is what role such images play in the context of the complete picture.

I do not refer to films primarily intended to arouse desire or to shock or to serve as a come-on to the prurient, although such purposes are by no means overlooked by the film's purveyors. I speak of so-called socially significant films, often praised by film critics in good standing.

Take, for example, *Getting Straight*. It is a picture about the formal education of youth, in other words, about college life. Youth is represented in this movie by a great lummox (supposedly very bright) in the shape of a popular favorite, Elliott Gould, who is probably about thirty. He has great appeal because he is like "everybody": coarse in manner, somewhat thick-tongued in speech, generally crude and blunt. The fellow he plays—like presumably so many of the young—believes our educational institutions to be little more than factories for the production of degree. (Some of them are just that.) He is, we are to assume, an advanced student, eager for knowledge. His problem is that the college doesn't provide it. What do we get to know of him?

Apparently he spends every night "sexualizing" with his girlfriend, a typical co-ed in the person of Candice Bergen. When he behaves boorishly, she forbids him her bed. This is too great a deprivation for him to bear. He immediately compensates for it by sleeping with a beauteous black girl who asks if he finds this novel experience especially pleasurable.

There are funny scenes—mostly caricatures—showing how dumb the academic doctors are, and there are others in which police brutality on an "epic" scale is photographed: half-measures never suffice in such pictures. Thus the film is not only topical but "revolutionary."

The principal characters in many of these films are shown to be "alienated" when they are not just morons. *Easy Rider*, made at a relatively low cost and so successful that it inspired a "trend" in the big studios, introduces us to several nonconformist youths: which of us is not sympathetic to their like? How do they use their liberty? To profit from their freedom they undertake to transport drugs from Mexico to California.

The best thing in the picture, apart from Jack Nicholson's performance as a drunken dude, is the sight of the landscape. Nicholson is beaten to death because he taunts some red-necks who resent the free life of the long-haired youths. Later the two boys are wantonly shot down by passing red-necks for no reason except that they are hippies. There is a moral to all this: one of the boys, before his death, murmurs "We blew it." In other words, he now realizes that he and his buddy muffed their chance at a good life. Nevertheless they are presented to us as folk heroes of a sort.

The filmmakers are always on the side of the angels. In the supposedly satiric *Bob & Carol & Ted & Alice*, four nit-wits experiment in wife-swapping. But they can't make it after all. They are basically "beautiful people." Aside from a few hilarious bits (one of them in a psychoanalyst's office), the picture is a setup for jokes about permissiveness in promiscuity in which little else (children, work) comes into play. One might conclude, then, that this is a picture about sex, but it is really nothing of the sort. Sex is something more than a physical function. Emotions are taken as a matter of course, real sentiment is never suggested, except that the couples do not consummate their cross-copulation. Given the circumstances and the nature of these citizens, this is rather stupid of them.

One of the most engaging among recent films with some truly amusing scenes and several excellent performances is *Five Easy Pieces*. Its central figure is a man who might have been a musician (he was reared in a musical family) and, when we meet him, is a totally disorientated person. He is without any specific direction or impulse, except to drink, fornicate, and run away. He is loyal to pals and is capable of momentary affection but has no regard for women, though he makes passes at all within his reach. At best, he is sorry about his state. He is to be accepted as the maimed hero of our subculture. To see him in this light is surely to indulge in wishy-washiness, a widespread trait in a society in which an understanding of human frailty means to exonerate ourselves from all moral judgment.

There is considerable validity in the theme posited in *Joe*. Racists and reactionaries, the film implies, well-heeled businessmen as well as uncouth hardhats, lacking the sustenance of sound values, are, when balked, impelled toward murderousness. But the plot has it that a "respectable" commercial executive who earns $60,000 a year will go back to the squalid quarters of a vicious drug addict to pick up his daughter's things—she being the fellow's girlfriend—things which consist of a few odd and soiled rags. Here, in his fury at being scoffed at by the derelict youth, he knocks the boy's brains out. Skeptical of the picture's initial steps, we are led from one lurid improbability to another in support of a thesis based on a loosely held ideology which demands proof. Everything finally is made subservient to the fabrication of a bloodcurdling movie replete with thievery, sexual "orgy," drunkenness, playing with pot.

Minute clues reveal the meretriciousness of the whole. Bonnie and Clyde in the picture of that name are played by two spectacularly good-looking actors who needn't have gone hungry even in the darkest days of the Depression. Hollywood was prosperous then; they could have gotten jobs in the movies. More folk heroes? A jolly ballad?

Seeing this film and several others less craftily made reminded me of the old cowboy song: "There was blood on the saddle, blood on the ground...blood all around." Blood? No, ketchup and Technicolor, as unbelievably fake as the vitals which, along with all manner of high jinks, are supposed to provide a sharply satiric comment in *M*A*S*H*, a movie practically everyone acclaims because we are all against war and especially ashamed of the Korean and Vietnam adventures, aren't we?

Everything in these films is spelled out. There is, for example, Clyde's impotence and his recovery from it through his loyal and gorgeous mate Bonnie-Dunaway. What a thrill in the mowing down of the two hapless marauders: the girl's body riddled with bullets bounces voluptuously from their impact. When that presumptuous idiot and distinguished novelist in *Diary of a Mad Housewife* disrobes Carrie Snodgress, we observe each separate article of her clothing slowly drop from her body. Then, as a clincher, we are favored in an isolated shot with an ample view of the actress's glowing bottom. If it hadn't actually been shown, we might not have known that she had one. There is more decency in the filth of *Trash*.

Is it really possible to give credence to the extremely pretty and healthy Jane Fonda as the haggard, half-starved, hopelessly beat victim of the dance marathon in *They Shoot Horses, Don't They?* followed by her inviting death at the hands of her sweet partner? For all the degradation through which her miserable life has dragged her, she cannot bear the thought that even such as he may have "deceived" her. Because of this, her contempt for life and love expresses itself by the exercise of felatio on the master of the sordid ceremonies whose normal approach she refuses in horror with the fierce command, "Don't touch me!"

Our behavioristic flicks tend to assault: they conspire to kick the stuffings out of us. They are unabashed in the use of four-letter words—the more the merrier—though this will soon prove ineffective as an instrument of titillation. The earth shakes, the heavens howl, the beasts yowl and clamor, walls crack and crumble, the world's chaos is magnified tenfold. Calm is unknown, contemplation impossible. For the quiet and calm we find in the films of Bresson, Ozu, Bergman, Satyajit Ray, Olmi, the early Antonioni, Renoir, or the Fellini of *I Vitelloni*—the repose essential to perception—our big audiences have little patience. Truffaut's unemphatically tender *The Wild Child* is a flop. Attention to the little pleasures and the unexplosive dramas of daily life is ignored. The tumult of our civilization has become our films' drug on the market.

Sentimentality may be defined as the disproportion between the reality of feeling and the means employed to convey it. To present reality as a charnel house and a bordello for the sake of arousing superficial shock is as sentimental and as poisonously misleading as to jerk at our tear ducts on behalf of motherhood or the Stars and Stripes. Ugliness, like beauty, is in the eyes of the beholder. The ferocious realism of our tough new pictures is as bogus as the sweetness and light of the old.

No matter how savage their imagery or high-minded their ostensible purpose, most of the new filmmakers treat us as though we were morbidly spoiled children who will heed nothing unless whipped. Their protagonists are themselves nearly always infantile or persons of low-grade mentality. With a slight insinuation from sub-Freudian social psychologists we are, for instance, called upon to understand and therefore to care for and forgive the sadistic hustler of *Midnight Cowboy*. It may be argued against Eric Rohmer's *My Night at Maud's*, or his latest picture, *Claire's Knee*, that they are too verbose and thus insufficiently cinematic. But they are remarkable in one thing at least: they deal with grown-ups whose preoccupations reach beyond the realm of thugs or fatuous slobs.

The rediscovery of sex in recent films—sex without affection, love, or even joyous sensuality—is something more than mere exploitation; it is a sign that we are in doubt about everything else.

These films possess one positive asset: they compel a realization that our values are not simply all in question, but that they have never previously been confirmed in us by profound experience or probing inner examination. We have ceased asking ourselves fundamental questions when we satisfy ourselves by predigested answers. These are supplied by "those who know," usually members of various Establishments—right and left—whom at the same time we profess to scorn. Those who shout the loudest are the only ones heard. We will not take pains with anything which demands protracted study, concentrated effort, time.

The great mechanism of our society, in which we jiggle and are flung about, wearies us. We do not in consequence demand privacy and peace of mind or socially useful action, but even more of the brutal battering of body and spirit which is driving us senseless.

There is something to ponder on in *Gimme Shelter*, no matter how contrived it may be thought to be. The killers and the victim, lawyers, arrangers, impresarios, agents, publicity men, and crazed acolytes of the Rolling Stones *are* our neighbors and kindred. Little wonder, then, that we accept the roughhouse improvisations of *Husbands* as a huge joke or as a faithful picture of marriage and homelife in America today. Still, a little sober reflection should make us aware that even the stupid and stupefied, the crass and the cruel, the fools and the criminals, are something more than what such films represent them to be.

We shall never be any wiser if we seriously believe that all the new pictures to which we are now asked to pay tribute are truly examples of films coming of age in a new realism. They are the product of gifted, well-intentioned craftsmen in the service of the same old profit-oriented movie industry they and we imagined had been destroyed and abandoned. In the toils of this Moloch, it is all but impossible to preserve genuine thoughtfulness, insight, stouthearted integrity. With the general acceptance of the platitudinous notions that the modern world is nothing but a stinking stew, an acceptance which has become a complaisance (often disguised as a denunciatory judgment), most filmmakers with the backing of the corporate powers have been sucked into the surrounding bedlam. Their pictures are not antidotes to our diseases; they are both the symptoms and among the most potent of their conveyers. Hence for me they are eloquent documents and documentaries of our time; they require scrupulous study. One should see them and see them again!

—*HARP*, May '71

A REPLY TO OUTRAGE

Indignation is often a vitalizing force. It may also obfuscate vision. Professor Richard Hornby's spirited response to my short account of "The new theatre, now" is such a case. He hardly appears aware that his comments are an outraged addendum to my article rather than a correction of it. He implies that I was formerly "against" the new theatre—he takes Richard Schechner's review of my book *The Naked Image* as evidence of this—and that now I am "for" it.

Allow me, for the sake of those readers who have not seen my piece to quote its first sentence: "Two attitudes prevail in regard to what is referred to as the 'new' or 'avant-garde' theatre. There are the unqualified champions and those who are its entrenched detractors. Both are mistaken."

The professor enjoins me to remember the interrelation of moral issues and aesthetics. The concluding paragraph of my article reads, "...in the end we must assign worth to individual offerings within every artistic manifestation in relation to the degree of genuineness, power, breadth, and depth we find in them, that is, to the extent they satisfy our basic human appetites and hungers. All the rest is modishness, and the applied rationalizations, no matter how high-sounding or startling, are fraudulent." And preceding these lines is a half-column statement of my (humanistic) position made as explicit as possible in so brief a space.

If he has previously read me, Professor Hornby should know that, though I am not certain that consistency is an unmixed blessing, as a man of the theatre—director and critic—I have never "changed sides." I have always insisted that a critic's foremost task is to describe, understand, and elucidate rather than praise or blame. Value judgments come later. That is why I rarely indulge in "raves" of enthusiasm or howls of condemnation. Such outbursts are alien to the core of criticism.

The point of my piece was that the new theatre is in large measure a critical expression of the *mores* or the customary behavior of our day, and that there is a positive usefulness in their being expressed even when the way they are embodied goes against our grain, and that, furthermore, some of the techniques and vocabulary employed may serve to broaden and enrich the theatre.

Professor Hornby abhors sadism, violence, license, and morbid titillation. So do I. In my quotation from Schechner's book, I cite exactly that passage in which he admits the artistic and ideologic inadequacy of much that has been done thus far in the new theatre. For my part, I reserved most of my "compliments" for the serious emotiveness in the Open Theatre's production of *The Serpent* and for Grotowski, whose "cruelty" is a function of his quasi-religious motivation.

Respectfully I suggest that the good professor, now that he has rid his chest and typewriter of his ire, reread my piece with calm, and, if he will, delve further into other of my writings on the theatre, old and new.

—*HARP*, May '71

THE HOMECOMING
THE BASIC TRAINING OF PAVLO HUMMEL

Seeing Harold Pinter's *The Homecoming* (Bijou Theatre) I was reminded of Jean Genet's reaction at a rehearsal in London of his play *The Balcony*: "It's obscene!" he cried. (He was refused further admission to the theatre.) What Genet meant was that in the staging the brothel which is the play's locale had been too explicitly revealed.

I cannot similarly object to the new production of *The Homecoming*, but it is far more specific (less "mysterious" and menacing) than that of the original Royal Shakespeare Company. The English cast did not stress the "points"; there was something noncommital, almost frozen-faced in everything it did. One was not certain whether what one surmised was literally intended: whether, for instance, Ruth, the professor's wife, really proposed to set herself up as a public tart as well as a family concubine. Vivian Merchant, who played the role, then acted like a business woman driving a hard bargain, and as if this were a normal arrangement for her.

One did not know whether she despised her husband; Janice Rule who plays Ruth now makes it utterly clear that she does. Her husband in the earlier production looked imperturbable as his pugilist brother all but raped her in full view of everyone in the room. Lawrence Keith, the new professor, perspires a bit as he observes the event. The whole clan now seems more rapacious, more sensuously involved. What was coldly implied in the first production becomes unmistakable in the second.

It is a moot point which of the two treatments is the more meaningful. Perhaps the play, as it is done now, can be more readily understood by an American audience; is "funnier." Its black humor is more blatant. The original production was precisely "Pinteresque": its manner bore a marked resemblance to Pinter's own personal demeanor. No matter what he actually says, his facial expression hardly ever betrays his feeling. It is with the same apparent impassivity, I suppose, that he prefers to have his plays acted. But, I imagine, he would not insist that "his" way is the only way they ought to be done. In any case, Eric Berry, Tony Tanner, Norman Barrs, Danny Sewell, as well as Janice Rule and Lawrence Keith, intelligently directed by Jerry Adler, give the play its due.

Understated or stressed, *The Homecoming* remains more frightening than funny. It presents a world totally insensible to everything except the appetites of the flesh, and even these have become mean and mournful.

Believe it or not, like or not, it constitutes a powerful statement wrought by a master hand.

I understood little more than half of what was spoken or shouted by the actors in David Rabe's *The Basic Training of Pavlo Hummel* (Public Theatre). But though I gathered the impression that much of its text was well written, I was not troubled by missing so many of its lines. The pace had to be hectic, the scenes had to overlap, the sounds needed to be raucous: here was inferno.

It is supposedly a simple matter to write or stage a play depicting the horrors of war. That is not so. People screaming in agony, bodies flung about, wounds inflicted, harsh words yapped, ruthless cruelty on all sides nearly always become commonplace and boring in the usual anti-war play or picture. They are piteous preachments thundered at us in sham stage hyperbole; we do not believe them. This is not the case with *Pavlo Hummel*. The staging is largely stylized (without artiness), the gunfire is not deafening, no blood spurts out from the injured, but the sense of real men at war is present. We come to know the human abjectness of it all. It is haunting in its personal challenge.

Pavlo Hummel is a dumb kid who doesn't wish to go to war but once there he wants to fight it "like a man." He prefers combat duty to work as a hospital orderly. He's a fool, almost crackers, an amalgam of the innocent vices and stupid virtues of the universal unknown GI. He's good-natured and atrocious. Around him are the other clumps of recognizable humanity, reduced to the point where they lose any identity except that of soldiers, food for slaughter, self-killers, ridiculous and terrible, victims who are also venomous. War makes them so; they are totally immersed in a "planet" where everything has turned to filth.

The First Sergeant bellows a spiel of oaths and exhortations which are projected like bullets: they cause laughter and hurt. The phantomlike enemy is fierce and unfathomable. The savagery of "our" men is visited upon one another almost as much as on those of the opposite side. At the end of the play it is a shock and yet no surprise when we see that Pavlo Hummel has not been killed by an enemy raid but by a drunken U.S. sergeant who vied with Hummel over a girl inmate of a cathouse. The murder has nothing to do with the issues of the war, but much to do with war itself.

Is then *The Basic Training of Pavlo Hummel* a "good" play? The answer hardly concerned me. It strikes home as very few "better" plays do. It is the first play provoked by the Vietnamese disaster which has made a real impression on me. The author, David Rabe, was there, and we are there with him. The large cast—notably William Atherton, Joe Fields, Albert Hall, Lee Wallace, Bob Delegall—is excellent throughout in type and performance, and the direction by Jeff Bleckner has the right overall sweep and smash and is often truly felt in detail. The setting by David Mitchell solves a knotty scenic problem with forceful simplicity.

—*NAT*, 7 July '71

LENNY

Will you enjoy *Lenny*? Who are you...? Though nowadays everything set on a stage is called a play, *Lenny* is barely one (Brooks Atkinson Theatre). It is however a show of considerable interest for those capable of viewing it in its own special light. A compound of Lenny Bruce's routines, it has been pieced together by Julian Barry with thin slices of personal information about Lenny Bruce's marriage, his arraignments before the law on the ground that his "act" was obscene in language, scurrilous and blasphemous in content. His death through an overdose of heroin is summarily visualized.

There is no probing of character beyond what the routines themselves reveal. The event is sustained by Cliff Gorman's performance as Lenny, by an elaborate scenic investiture, sideshow clowning, nude male figures, masked players as "tribal" zombies prancing about to nondescript music which never registers. All this has been devised by Tom O'Horgan who is best known as the director of the uptown *Hair* and many off-off Broadway exhibits.

The virtue of O'Horgan's staging is that it makes you aware that you are in a theatre, really seeing something happening. Since very little actually is happening, one is led to expect something sensational at any moment. The eye is engaged; one remains curious. The most attractive sight for me was Jane House's nearly naked body (for the greater part of the evening she plays Bruce's wife), especially as she not only appears in this state as a stripper, which is her profession, but also when she visits her mother-in-law who, judging from what we see, is herself a highly seasoned lady.

The defect of O'Horgan's staging in this instance is that much of what is shown is irrelevant to the verbal context. Exceptions, perhaps, are the huge ("Mount Rushmore") effigies of Presidents Eisenhower, Kennedy, Johnson and Nixon, which Lenny supposedly confronts as a hapless rebel. For the rest, the decoration (Robin Wagner did the "scenery") seems like monkeyshines and special effects brought in from another show.

That impression is made, I am inclined to believe, because the story of Lenny and even his "numbers" are not essentially funny. His exacerbated spirit, his extreme susceptibility to the injuries of our society, his violent disgust and anger, coupled as they were with a self-destructive bent, produced a peculiar wit and, most extraordinary of all, a fantastic inventiveness of speech. Many of his sallies missed fire, but when he was in form his words struck home with savage satiric impact. The effect was more surprising than shocking, and the result was the relief of laughter.

But Bruce was not a funny man, nor was his career anything but painful. On seeing Lenny in London, I thought him haunted and tormented, and

when I was asked to comment on his "act," I could say no more than that there was "gold in the garbage."

Very little of this aspect (the laceration) of Lenny Bruce's history is in the play. Even the mention of his child (to whom he was greatly attached) has been excised, no doubt because it would prove a disturbing factor in the entertainment. The play thus becomes an exploitation of a personality that deserves something more. There can be little question that Bruce's "crazy" spiels from 1951 to 1961, in their undisguised contempt and derision of every phase of our mores (political, Spellman-ecclesiastic, sexual, linguistic) had explosive social value, but today these protests, especially as here presented, are almost commonplace—except perhaps on the *Broadway* stage.

What adds to this taming of Bruce is at the same time the show's chief asset: Cliff Gorman. He is remarkable in his vigor, his versatility, his honest and likable commitment. (The episode in which he projects Nixon as a dummy in the ventriloquist Eisenhower's lap is one of the most successful moments of the show.) But no character of person is really created—perhaps under the circumstances cannot be created. There is no center from which the acting can emerge; what Gorman presents is a most capable, indeed an admirable performance. Lenny Bruce still remains to be truly embodied, interpreted.

—*NAT*, 21 June '72

OLD TIMES

At Harold Pinter's new play, *Old Times*, given by the Royal Shakespeare Company, I was reminded of a quip: one man asks another, "Have you seen *Last Year in Marienbad*?" The other answers, "Perhaps."

Meticulously written, with an odd lucidity in which every speech is shiningly clear and at the same time, in its context, bewilderingly ambiguous, *Old Times* suggests (it never says) that the past is a kind of palimpsest, so that one's memories overlay one another and one can't be sure which of them really happened and which are in fact dreams.

However, there is more to the play than that rather familiar proposition. The mind in which events are chiefly recalled is that of a man tortured by sexual apprehensions which he cannot resolve because his recollections as to what occurred or may have occurred twenty years ago are troubled by contradictory testimony from his wife and from her long absent friend, now living in Sicily and come to visit the couple in a quiet English village by the sea. At first he appears to know nothing of the visiting friend (she is called Anna), but later he says that he had stared at and presumably desired her when they sat opposite each other in a London pub in the bygone days. Anna does not refute this; indeed, she affirms that she knew him, remembers him well.

The foregoing is complicated by puzzling corroboration followed by contrary evidence. Husband and wife had met for the first time at an old movie, *Odd Man Out*, and he was immediately attracted to her. Anna professes to have met the man's wife at another showing of the same picture. (Were they all there together? It is possible but by no means certain.) What disturbs the man is that the friendship between Anna and his wife was so uniquely intimate that he somehow feels shut out, excluded, by their mutual reminiscences of the days and nights of their former companionship. He even suspects that their relationship may have been something more than girlhood camaraderie. They say nothing to allay his jealous fears. Perhaps his troubled state in this regard—hurt and anger—stems from a sense that he is or was sexually aroused by both women and thus in some way frustrated by both.

I am not positive I have all these twists right and, to a certain extent, it hardly matters. The main point is how difficult it is to recapture old times and how evanescent is the substance of reality. And since so much experience is centered in sexual longing, our lives tend to move toward a

never fulfilled yearning for the satisfaction of some true knowledge, a confirmed consciousness of what life has been to us, an unequivocal grasp of its meaning. However, all that is left to us are imprecise but haunting "old time" melodies, songs that linger in the air.

Is it so? For Pinter it is. Subtle craftsman, shrewd dramatist, he builds his plays as metaphysical melodrama, their ambivalences fostering suspense. Nor does he omit the irony and surprising comedy of the situations he posits. With all this, Pinter remains a master of contemporary theatre writing with something more than a "manner"; he is no mere trickster or aesthetic tease.

Having acknowledged that much, I must extend my review with a few subjective notations or statements of personal prejudices. My tastes veer toward a less ascetic art. I favor fullness; I enjoy rich surfaces, greater body, broader canvases. Hence my attachment to Shakespeare, and among novelists my preferences are Dickens, Balzac, Tolstoy, Dostoyevsky. These men lived in more spacious epochs. We have "conquered" space and have become dismally constricted. Each of the artists mentioned above was in one way or another also a moralist, but their creations were founded in flesh and the boundless miracles of action amid a world of color. Perhaps there is no help for it, but I am discomfited by the bleakness of so much of the "modern." Why, I ask myself, must our own art be so sedulously "minimal?"

There are too many things around us and we are overwhelmed. We move too rapidly, cover too much ground, rest very little. We find it difficult to cope with the environment. Serious artists experience a tendency to withdraw from the external tumult, to make ever more abstract graphs of reality, to dwell within themselves.

In drama, Ibsen occupies a middle point between the prodigality of the "old" and the narrowness of the "new." With Pirandello, we arrive at the desperate skepticism of our age. We can no longer be sure of anything—not even for the hell or the fun of it. Certainty eludes us. We are in a grotesque dreamland. Shakespeare, toward the end of his career, seems to have arrived at a similar state, but how much more ample, colorful, zestful the journey. Now the stage of our insights and perspectives has shrunk: we have become very small. This, as I say, may have been inevitable, but should we take pride in it?

To return to Pinter's *Old Times*: it is called his first "full-length play" since *The Homecoming*, though it runs only eighty minutes. Directed by Peter Hall, the production of the Royal Shakespeare Company is especially fine. Like the text itself John Bury's sets and lighting are spare and yet utterly telling of place, time and atmosphere. Their simplicity and neatness are somehow eerie, chilly in the sense they create of vacancy and isolation.

The acting is beautifully precise, with an edge of cruelty and pain. It seems perfect in its verbal and intellectual articulation: its form completely conveys Pinter's essence. Vivian Merchant as Anna, Dorothy Tutin as the wife, and Colin Blakely as the husband not only express the play but seem to contain it in its incisiveness, its own kind of elegance and its brilliant mystery.

For all my alienation from the Pinteresque "landscape," I nevertheless admire *Old Times* for the probity of its delineation, the authenticity in the projection of an individual vision—which is part of the truth of our day. The play will be produced in New York before long, where, I venture to say, its press reception will not be as wholly enthusiastic as it has been here.

—*NAT*, 28 June '71

NE REVEILLEZ PAS MADAME

Jean Anouilh's latest play, *Ne reveillez pas madame* ("Madame is Not to be Disturbed") is another of his successes. It has already run more than 250 performances, and the night I saw it the house was sold out. It has been awarded the Paris Critics' Prize as the best creation of the season.

It is ostensibly about the private lives of stage folk in relation to their profession or vice versa. "Don't wake mother," the little boy who is to become a director and the play's central character is told; being an actress, she works late at night and needs to rest mornings. She rehearses during the day. So, the boy sees only his neglected and intimidated father to whom his wife is indifferent because he is not of the theatre. Besides, mother has lovers as the boy's actress wives will have when he grows up. The play repeats the usual Anouilh theme: the deception and despair of the decent person in a corrupt society; the fragility of human relations, especially the marital ones. Women are fickle but perhaps they have a right to be: they endure childbirth and sustain the race. On that account they are sturdier than men. Then again, the wholly earnest male is something of a brute, frequently puritanical and yet himself far from consistent in his morals. This situation is aggravated when the man and the woman belong to the notoriously unstable and disruptive world of the theatre, and perhaps more especially that of the French theatre.

This is another version of the same author's *Colombe*. But, whereas the earlier play (which I directed in 1954) possessed a certain emotional authenticity, probably because of personal circumstances, the attitude has now become a complaisant cynicism. There is a commercial taint in it. Anouilh's pessimism is how he makes his living. The Paris theatregoing public enjoys his witty denunciation of its vices. It somehow finds itself absolved by it. *C'est la vie, quoi!* I find the trick the more offensive because Anouilh manages it so skillfully.

The acting of the play is typical of the present-day Boulevard—professionalism gone rotten. It reeks of staginess. Some of the actors, genuine enough in films, carry on in the theatre with a facile and flagrant falsity of which they seem absolutely proud. One is very nearly persuaded to admire their confident effrontery.

There is something more to this than just over-acting: it is shameless exhibitionism. Heavy "characterization" takes precedence over character. Every point is hammered out; stereotypes abound. One has the impression that each of the personages has put on many times more makeup than is needed for visibility or credibility. Scenes in which the players caricature the extravagances of a former stage generation (the old "Sarah Bernhardt" days) are hardly more absurd than what they do as pretended naturalism during the ordinary course of the evening's drama. (Sarah Bernhardt had a temperament that justified her giddy excesses.) Anouilh, in the person of his protagonist, says that audiences don't listen to or understand most of a play's lines: they care only about situations. So exposition is rattled at a dizzy pace, after which the actors pause to mark their "big moments," so that no one can fail to notice that that is what they are. The audience responds to these florid or hysterical declamations—the writing has a certain brilliance—with gratified rounds of applause. This is "theatre!"

I do not scorn artifice. It may convey grace, wit, elegance, polish—bespeak refinement of manner and delicacy of sentiment. One finds this in such an actor as Pierre Fresnay and among a number of English and German actors. But, though the kind of acting we see in Anouilh's play has its origins in the French inclination toward flamboyance of the romantic age and the modified bombast of the neo-classic, both have become infected by a vulgar showmanship, a phony and clamorous "Frenchiness" which the best representatives of Gallic excellence from Copeau to Vilar abhorred. These men were purifiers of the theatre of their time, the last and finest examples of which in acting was Gérard Philippe.

Acting too is rooted in the social environment. The bad acting I speak of is a sign of the decline of the French tradition through the grossest, most self-indulgent elements in the newly fattened French bourgeoisie with its greedy eye on the tourist trade. In the classless American world, with its vast variety of backgrounds ("high society" has vanished), the stage has developed an honest, truth-seeking actor—often blunt and insufficiently discriminating in matters of style and interpretation—impeded chiefly by lack of broad artistic training, wide repertory and continuity of practice. The English actor has gained something from the decorum imposed by the class breeding of former generations, and now with the liquidation of the Empire is being refreshed by the emergence of articulate forces from the working, regional or rural strata of the country.

I now find American and English acting of sounder and more vigorous fiber than present-day acting in France, once held to be the most dazzlingly admirable in the Western world.

—*NAT*, 2 Aug. '71

BUTLEY AND ENEMIES

Simon Gray's *Butley* does not trouble the audience at all: it delights it. The comedy proliferates funny verbal twists, a medium for irreverent levity. It also enjoys the advantage of Alan Bates' easy and expert performance in the name part. But if one chooses to think about it a moment (the audience apparently doesn't), one must realize that it is even more devastatingly nihilistic than the Osborne play. Harold Pinter, who directed *Butley*, was surely aware of this.

The English theatre public will let a playwright get away with anything if his text flashes with humor and is cultivated in texture. *Butley* has little dramatic core. It is the pen portrait of a college professor (his specialty is T. S. Eliot), a man who has forsworn all concern for education and his pupils, for whom he evinces nothing but scorn.

Butley drinks. He is altogether pleased to do so; the audience in consequence does not worry about him. He neglects his person—is in fact a slob. This also amuses. He is predominately homosexual, though given to wounding remarks about homosexuals. He has been married, has a child, doesn't like it that his wife is divorcing him, resents her marrying someone he says is a bore, and does nothing to prevent either move. His chief victim is his homosexual consort, formerly a student, whom he has contrived to have appointed to the faculty of the same college. At the end, even this weak young man quits him.

What is it about Butley that, apart from his jokes, "gets" the audience? He despises everything with which it has itself become disenchanted. Everything, even sex, bores him. Butley is dismally tired. He will die from exhaustion with his own viciously corrosive banter. But there is a certain relief from spiritual depression in *Butley*. Its protagonist makes inconsequentiality, disinterestedness, deliberate folly appear acceptable through laughter—and not only acceptable but somehow damned clever.

In contrast to such fare is Maxim Gorky's *Enemies*, admirably produced by the Royal Shakespeare Company, an organization which in recent years has covered itself with ever more merited honors. Written in 1906, immediately after the suppressed uprising of 1905, *Enemies* was forbidden performances by the czarist censorship and was not staged until in Leningrad and at the Moscow Art Theatre two years later.

Gorky was socially prescient. At a time when most of his literary cohorts, disillusioned by the 1905 debacle, were writing works of dejected mysticism or of a turbidly desperate sexuality, Gorky predicts in *Enemies* the ultimate triumph of the oppressed. That alone would not cause me to like the play; a dramatist need not prove himself a political seer. The play is absorbing through the compression of its characterizations which are subtle, rich, compassionate and alive with social insight.

Almost the whole society is limned in brief strokes. There is the doggedly brutal boss, determined not only to squelch all signs of independence in his subordinates but also to take over the factory from his more refined partner. (The play's action is sparked by the murder of this bourgeois

ruffian by a worker whom he has kicked in the stomach during a labor dispute.) There is the soft and easily swayed liberal owner of the factory, who wants to be fair to all parties and cannot understand the reasons for the fierce hostility which surrounds him.

His brother has taken to drink because he has sensibility and understanding without specific talent or a capacity for action. The man's wife is an actress who is drawn to the rebellious workers—it is she who foresees their ultimate victory—but who, despite her sympathy, makes no positive move on their behalf. She is a bystander, a witness, an artist. Her deepest concern is to be cast in plays that will be earthshaking or ennobling.

The most winning portrait in the play is that of the liberal boss's orphan niece. She is ardent with love of decent people and causes. Gorky had a special empathy with such young girls who, in the midst of moral desolation, strive toward a radiant future. Of this particular 18-year-old girl the actress says, "If you begin asking yourself questions you'll become a revolutionary...."

Then there are the workers, some craven, some brave, some consistently loyal, others innocently trusting, and a few supported by peasant shrewdness. When the actress asks the oldest of the men what remedy he would apply to the evil of their lives, his answer is "we've got to do away with the kopek...once the kopek's gone why should we push each other about?" The actress challenges "And that's all?" to which the old man replies, "It's enough to begin with."

I found myself positively refreshed by this play. The fact that the revolution it presages has led to a new tyranny does not diminish my accord with its spirit. There is heart in Gorky's "politics." It epitomizes the warm humanism of the Russian intelligentsia in its purest phases—something which still remains inspiring and exemplary.

Adding to the pleasure I took in Gorky's "script" was my admiration for the acting company; many of the players were the same as those who had performed with so much physical agility and gaiety in Peter Brook's *Midsummer*

Night's Dream. Especially notable in this respect was Mary Rutherford. In the *Dream* she was Hermia; in *Enemies* she plays the fervent answer-seeking Nadya, seen by her friend (the actress of the play) perhaps rightly as being overwhelmed and finally crushed by future eventualities. The entire company is excellent, projecting by its own special means the essence of this eminently Russian play.

—*NAT,* 27 Sept. '71

WHERE HAS TOMMY FLOWERS GONE?

The answer to the question implied in Terrence McNally's *Where Has Tommy Flowers Gone?* is *nowhere* (Eastside Playhouse). I say that not so much as rebuke as diagnosis of what ails "Tommy," both as a person and as a play. For though it is written—in spots brightly written—in a manner resembling a series of revue skits, it *is* a play with that beginning, middle and end upon which pundits insist.

Tommy, the flower boy, hails from St. Petersburg, Fla., a town which, from his earliest age, he has found deadly dull. In a sort of color TV monologue we meet his mother who is sweet and indistinguishable from other "hinterland" mothers and therefore, it seems, ridiculous. Similarly we meet his big brother who is a harassed, cuckolded salesman. So Tommy escapes to where life really is: New York.

Here at the age of 30 we find him panhandling: he wouldn't dream of working. Of course, he smokes "grass." He is personable and thus finds girls easy to get. He befriends an old vagrant who for a while pretends to have been an actor. Tommy also protects a woolly but amazingly passive dog. He swindles a ride in a taxi driven by a classically garrulous hackie, dishonest and down on everything (the scene is funny); he steals stuff from Bloomingdale's and hides in the ladies' room where he encounters a girl cellist, also a shoplifter. They have an affair which terminates when she is jailed for her complicity in Tommy's misdeed. Everywhere, in short, Tommy is faced with stupidity, passionless promiscuity, brutality: it is what every young man is supposed to know today and ultimately to expect. Roughed up slightly by a cop, Tommy kills him with a blast of dynamite.

Is Tommy a good or a bad boy? He is neither. Tommy registers our society, typifies disoriented youth. But the "registrar" is as dumb or as banal as everyone he contacts. One cannot accept him as a product of our society, because his good nature, projected chiefly through the actor who plays him and McNally's jokes, evinces nothing propulsive in any direction: he neither learns nor protests, he does not yearn or despair. In a word, he is not a true person. He is a peg on which to hang all the clichés about our shabby time. No community whatsoever would make Tommy anything other than what he is, because he is a lump incapable of the volition needed for good or evil, the human material to develop toward a meaningful purity or a damnable baseness.

I stress all this in what is after all only a light entertainment (not without its laughs and clever twists) because the play is meant a little more seriously than it would appear. It belongs to that taken-for-granted criticism of the *status quo,* in which so much of our "new theatre" and New Left politics indulges, where the tag or verdict precedes and supersedes thought.

It would be unfair on this account not to recognize the appeal of Robert Drivas' versatile performance as Tommy, Wallace Rooney's easy candor as his deadbeat companion, F. Murray Abraham's risibly able assistance in a variety of bits (also true of Marion Paone) and Barbara Worthington's debut in which she displays, besides lovely golden hair, luscious legs, inviting navel, a delightfully sunny smile. There is also "Arnold," already acclaimed as the finest canine actor seen hereabouts for years. As a show under Jacques Levy's direction *Where Has Tommy Flowers Gone?* works smoothly and—barring some extra goodies in the way of preposterous puns and special comedy routines—rapidly.

—*NAT,* 25 Oct. '71

NEW YORK THEATRE
UNLIKELY HEROES

It is surely no secret: since 1955 at least, the New York theatre has been deteriorating. This alone should not cause alarm because the theatre has been in trouble through most of its history. But the situation today is truly alarming.

The cost of Broadway production for plays without music (a play with a small cast and one set) is upward of $75,000; for a musical, it exceeds $300,000. Operating costs are extremely high; the price of tickets ranges from $8 plus to $15 plus. A play must run a very long time to play off the initial investment; few of them ever do. Off-Broadway production costs and ticket prices have mounted to where they were on Broadway between 1940 and 1950. The rate of unemployment for actors in the theatre is cruelly high. More actors are working as taxi drivers, cashiers, waiters and restaurant hostesses than in what they hoped would be their normal profession. Playwrights suffer acute depression and live in fear!

The New York Times is well aware of the crisis; its regular critic is eager to help salvage the expiring patient. Wherever there is the least trace of merit, the slightest possibility of praise, he takes pains to emphasize it. I find this sympathetic, though it is hardly likely that his method of resuscitation will avail. On today's Broadway stage only certain types of musical comedy (*Applause, Promises, Promises*), sentimental comedies like *Butterflies Are Free* and a thriller like *Sleuth*, the plays of Neil Simon, and a very few plays by notable writers can maintain themselves. It is significant that so much that is now offered is not original theatre material but adaptations and dramatizations. These are symptoms of exhaustion.

I bring all this up as a preface to my remarks on *Unlikely Heroes: 3 Philip Roth Stories*, adapted for the stage and directed by Larry Arrick (Plymouth Theatre). I must begin with a generalization: it has never been my belief that we ought to go to the theatre only to see plays of the first magnitude. If we did, the theatre would have disappeared long ago. The critic pleased by nothing but the first rate in the theatre should ensconce himself in the library. I do not mean that when there is a dearth of truly valuable plays, the fourth and fifth rate should be greeted with the acclaim deserved by masterpieces. That is the impression many reviewers give when a pleasant performance is hailed with the rapture show folk call a "business notice." That such a notice is required to rouse people to see a play is itself evidence of a morbid condition.

Unlikely Heroes constitutes a nice evening in the theatre. The Roth stories, to begin with, are amusing, well written and intelligent; one of the three, "Eli, the Fanatic," is something more than that. Moreover, they are well acted and suitably staged. Much of Roth's writing is retained.

The first story, "The Defender of the Faith," lends itself most readily to dramatization. It is the wry tale of a GI who uses a pretended devotion to his Judaism to curry favors from a modestly upright sergeant, also Jewish. It takes the sergeant some time to discover that the GI is a wheeler-dealer who will use all means to gain the advantages of convenience and pleasure.

Roth tells the story without bitterness or wrath but with engagingly sly humor. The playlet is admirably acted by David Ackroyd—bright and crisp—as the sergeant, and by Jon Korkes—plausibly engaging, without mitigating the basic obnoxiousness of the private's character—and by all the others, with special service rendered by George Bartenieff as a chaplain.

The second story, "Epstein," is essentially a monologue. It deals with a successful manufacturer of paper bags, a man of fundamental good will and mediocre virtue, heir to the disquiet and disappointments common to men of his class and disposition. The most agonizing episode of his life is the occasion when, after his one and only deviation from marital fidelity, he develops a rash around his crotch and is suspected by his horrified family of having contracted syphilis, though in this respect he is unsmirched. We last see him in an ambulance, being transported to a hospital after a heart attack. As a stage piece "Epstein" is sustained by Lou Jacobi's direct, unforced and unsentimental delivery (in speech rather than in action) of Epstein's plight.

There is much more substance in "Eli, the Fanatic." Here Lou Jacobi, as the "headmaster" of a school for refugee Jewish children who are to be raised in orthodoxy, achieves greater dimension in characterization: a concise performance. Michael Tolan as a capable middle-class lawyer is also convincingly effective.

The theme of "Eli, the Fanatic:" is the troubled conscience of the assimilated Jew who has lost virtually all sense of connecting with his origins as a Jew and the fate of "his" people. When a bearded Jew in ghetto garb (wide-brimmed black felt hat and long kaftan) appears in a respectably aseptic, predominantly Protestant, small suburban community, the Jewish residents are upset. The anomalous figure disturbs their sense of security: he is a stain on the immaculate conformity of the town. He makes "Jewishness" unsightly.

As a lawyer for the Jewish contingent, Eli is sent to see Mr. Tzuref, the head of the religious school who employs the unnamed Man to do odd jobs on behalf of the institution. Eli begins by asking Tzuref, on legal grounds, to move the school away from the residential sector of town. When Tzuref refuses, and Eli suggests that the school may be allowed to remain where it is if only the Man can be made invisible by having him change his startling attire, Tzuref explains that the man possesses no other clothing, that he is entirely alone and utterly without means. More telling than all this, Tzuref reminds Eli that he himself is part of that Man's world and people, and that they are a part of him.

Eli effects a compromise: he will give the Man a suit of his own. The gift is accepted. But when

Eli approaches the Man, now transfigured by the commonplace and, to him, sacrilegious dress, the latter shuns him in fear and trembling: the change of apparel has been a humiliation to him, another injury added to his lifelong suffering.

An ancient guilt wills up in Eli's soul. He dons the Man's discarded hat and coat: his friends and wife believe him struck by madness. "Recovered, " Eli tearfully begs forgiveness of God, beating his breast in orthodox lamentation, and vows to resume the rite of putting on the Man's old habit one day a year to commemorate what has happened; he will never again avoid identification with his forebears, their tribulations and grief.

It is a fine concept; the story as story is a brilliant allegory. Though its meaning still remains inescapable, reaching beyond its specific ethnic framework, it becomes rather too concrete, and therefore not altogether credible and less poignant than it should be, when it is translated in realistic terms to the stage. (David Ackroyd, who plays the Man, should be provided with a proper beard; it is far more important to the play than the elaborate setting. At present, he is made to look liké an extra in a stock company too poor to supply adequate make-up.) For all that, I repeat, "Eli, the Fanatic," is *something*.

—*NAT*, 15 Nov. '71

ON THE TOWN
STICKS AND BONES

On the Town, the hit musical of 1944-45 with book and lyrics by Betty Comden and Adolph Green and music by Leonard Bernstein, has just been revived at the Imperial Theatre. It is not the equal or the equivalent of Offenbach, Gilbert and Sullivan or *The Threepenny Opera*. So what? Kurt Weill is not the equal of Schubert, Sullivan of Lecoq, Offenbach of Mozart: one might go on like that forever till all were eliminated.

On the Town is dated. So too is Johann Strauss. Stravinsky is not as up-to-the minute as Stockhausen. Again: so what? All art is the product of a specific time and place. True quality, on the exalted or on the modest level, is never replaceable. The simple fact is that Bernstein's music for the show, whatever one's estimate of it, is in every way superior to virtually every score of the successful musicals which have reached Broadway for years. It *is* music.

I found the show fun. Its chief attraction is its bounciness. It leaps, giggles, cavorts, grows dreamy with youthful zest and innocence. It doesn't do these things as we do them today. One can nonetheless savor its quality anew—especially as there is very little in musical comedy at present which has any savor at all beyond the undifferentiated scuffle of rock and roll.

Such a number as *Carried Away*, with its delightfully childlike abandon, contains the very essence of Comden and Green's ebullient good nature. And Bernstein has known how to translate it into sound, similarly fresh. One needn't be nostalgic about it. Its very difference from the contemporary brouhaha is a mark of its individuality.

Comparisons are odious. What I remember most vividly about the original production, which was more lilting and relaxed in its sportiveness than the current one, is the enchantment of Sono Osato's face, physique and dancing. It is not Donna McKechnie's fault that she is only very nice when viewed in the light of Sono Osato's very special being. Miss McKechnie, who dances admirably, could be dressed and given a hairdo which would set her off to greater advantage: she is certainly attractive enough.

The men—the three sailors on the town—are adequate. The most "romantic" of them, Ron Husmann, has an especially good voice. Phyllis Newman has an alluring figure, beautifully bright eyes, a gift for mimicry of the absurd.

Bernadette Peters as the eager, down-to-Tenth-Avenue-earth girl hackie is priceless: she has exactly the right kind of prettiness, the saucy verve and, despite all the stress on the character's New York raciness, something so close to purity that it approximates pathos.

I noticed Miss Peters first in *George M.*, as Cohan's sister Josie. She seemed then to spring right out of the Cohan epoch—America's more recent age of innocence (1900-17). After *Dames at Sea*, which was a parody, and as an acting "problem" a pushover for this comedienne, she appeared all too briefly as the little Italian waif in a musical version of Fellini's *La Strada* in which she revealed a lyric quality within the "peasant" gamine that might be developed to greater importance and qualify her for roles with larger demands than those provided in light entertainment.

I mention this because Miss Peters is now only 23 and I observe that she is pushing or being pushed toward making her various charms into an unmistakably reliable commodity, something to be advertised even when the rapture is gone. That is the danger: that she may become a perfect "type" and cease being an actress. When a player rises to the status of a Broadway or a Hollywood "personality," he or she ceases to be a person: the counterfeit steps in. It happens again and again.

Last season I voted a special award to *The Basic Training of Pavlo Hummel* and marked its author, David Rabe, the most promising new playwright. I am glad to report that his second play, *Sticks and Bones* (Public Theatre) confirms my favorable opinion of his talent.

Sticks and Bones, though written in a vein different from that of the earlier play, is a kind of sequel to *Pavlo Hummel*. It is bitter and powerful, peppered with acrid humor and all the more disturbingly impressive on that account. It appears at first to be a realistic drama, but is in fact a grim "fantasy." It reminded me to some degree of the expressionist plays the Germans were writing after the First World War. But the Germans were apocalyptically hysterical; *Sticks and Bones* is savagely ironic. It has a cold, hard bite. With very little outward violence, it stings and wounds.

It might be called "The Soldier Returns." Into the cartoon family headed by Ozzie and Harriet of TV fame, the elder son David comes back from Vietnam blind. Papa Ozzie and Mama Harriet epitomize the happily average American Lower-middle-class couple. They ignore their son's injury as if it were a trifling disability, hardly more than a scratch. It would seem that they are duty bound to be perpetually "glad." At first one is incredulous: no such family exists. But soon enough it becomes evident that this picture of the "booboisie" is satirically symbolic.

Mama is devoutly Catholic and always as sweet as pie; papa is addicted to the "box," though its sound apparatus never works. Rick, their younger boy, strums the guitar and is forever consuming fudge and milk. His home life consists chiefly in a dash to the kitchen, a hurried meal and out again to the street. His only positive contribution to the family's well-being is to photograph everything, including his brother's tragic homecoming as if it were a sport.

David is haunted by the memory of the girl he left behind, a serene Vietnamese, the only solace from the hellish cruelty which has scarred him for life. Dumped back into the domestic lap, he feels isolated. His parents are strangers to him. His boyhood, he now realizes, was a construct of deceit. For papa, superficially a most humdrum and foolish citizen, is as frustrated and made as miserable by the platitude of his life as David is crippled by the experience of war.

The portrait of Ozzie—profoundly alienated from his wife with whom he has no contact apart from routine amenities, unable to address anything meaningful to Rick's nonentity, and resentful of David's contempt—is one of the play's most original strokes.

Ozzie, Harriet and Rick want above all to avoid hearing anything about the war, or about any other unpleasantness, including all mention of intimacy with any of the "filthy yellow race." David's insistence on bringing home to them the unspeakable brutality of what he has seen in Vietnam becomes a sadistic reprisal against his family, the emptiness of their lives and their obdurate evasion of everything real. His new consciousness, ruthless in its violence, drives them frantic.

The final scene is the most telling. As "realism" it is quite impossible; it a ghoulish metaphor stated as a kind of joke. In a tone of affable reasonableness Rick advises David to commit suicide. Since the blind youth offers no resistance, his brother does the job for him very carefully by cutting his wrists. David is not dead, Ozzie says, only "nearly dead." David's Vietnamese girl, present as a wraith throughout the play, whom Ozzie has finally been made to "see," is laid prone on the floor covered by a blanket. Vietnam is erased from the family's conscience.

The play is well cast with Tom Aldredge as Ozzie, Elizabeth Wilson as Harriet, Cliff DeYoung as Rick, and David Selby as the soldier—the slight smile under the dark glasses which cover his blinded eyes is like a hurtful gash across his face. Charles Siebert is effective as a priest in a stabbingly comic scene in which the man of God tries to maintain his clerical largesse while David repeatedly hits him with the stick by which he guides himself.

Jeff Bleckner has directed the cast with fine intelligence, but I am not sure that the almost naturalistic setting and lighting are exactly right for the play: one is led to suspect that what occurs is to be taken literally, in which case some of the play's writing becomes too self-conscious, too overtly expressive. Perhaps some oddity of design might have established its proper key. Still, I am not certain on this point. It may be that the play's transformation of a commonplace environment into a chamber of shocks and hallucinations does after all induce the more insidious shudder. In any case, *Sticks and Bones* offers an unusual evening in our theatre; it is unlikely that we shall have others of the same nature or distinction this season.

—*NAT*, 22 Nov. '71

EL HAJJ MALIK—THE DRAMATIC LIFE AND DEATH OF MALCOLM X

El Hajj Malik—The Dramatic Life and Death of Malcolm X is a theatrical collage by N. R. Davidson, Jr., based on the extraordinary destiny of the heroically tragic figure of the title (Martinique Theatre).

There are pantomimically abbreviated episodes of Malcolm's life: scenes of his father's murder by the K.K.K., of his mother's humiliation by welfare investigators, scenes from his Harlem escapades, his imprisonment and his final emancipation as a leader, to the moment of his assassination. Many of the "tableaux" are accompanied by or composed of direct quotes from Malcolm's autobiography, with additions from the author's gnomic verse and hortatory prose. There are music, dancing and acting in which Malcolm's avatars are enacted by various members of the cast, male and female, who also alternate in other of the play's parts. The result is a group expression, almost a rite. It is always interesting, sometimes exhilarating, occasionally funny, and at the end disturbing.

The most successful scenes are those suggesting life in Harlem. The segment in this sequence which satirizes the black entertainer is especially effective. He is mocked because he is today the emblem of Negro toadying to the befuddled white man's comforting image of the black man as a blessed fool, compact with rhythm, song and carefree laughter. We have often been told to view the black entertainer's "act" as a disguise for his contempt of the role the white man has imposed on him. But what struck me in this episode was that the black people in the audience, as well as the white, responded to the scene with rapturous recognition, not simply on account of its satirical bite but because it is actually an expression of what was and is creatively valuable in such entertainment: its irrepressible energy, its joy in play, its full-blooded affirmation of the ecstasy of living.

This scene and others with almost equally sharp comic verve filled the house with unanimously delighted approval.

But it would be less than honest or critically intelligent to be content with the successful show-biz aspects of the event. Indeed it would not even be respectful of the author and the company. For the evening concludes with what used to be called "agit-prop" harangues on the subject of black nationalism. To neglect the import of this coda to the evening's pageant, to pass it over with a casual nod of acquiescence or dignified acceptance, is to castrate it.

Much in the closing section of *El Hajj Malik* is a celebration through quotation of Malcolm's eloquent speeches. We hear him denounce the black man's fate in America with the passion proper to the subject. He speaks of his early devotion to the black Muslim leader and of his defection from that movement because he began to suspect the leader of a self-centered will to power, and later because after his visit to Mecca, Malcolm realized that human brotherhood could be achieved beyond the separation of race and color. He did not want, Malcolm emphasizes, his change of heart in this respect to earn the white man's approbation and thus be used as an argument against his fundamental mission to liberate the blacks from their abject condition.

So far, very good. But then we hear a zealous roar of slogans which are of dubious value and veracity. A revolution on behalf of black nationalism is called for, a bloody revolution. "Revolution does not sing, it swings." Blood, blood, blood we hear time and again. Coming after what has preceded, the effect is unconvincing, confusing, wrong.

I am not conversant with the politics and ideologies of the various trends which the shameful race situation in the United States has called forth. But amid the hue and cry which closes this dramatic life of Malcolm X, questions arise that disturb my sense of participation in the play.

Who is responsible for Malcolm X's assassination? No answer is forthcoming. It may have been a police plot abetted by a white conspiracy of some kind. In Malcolm X's autobiography, a stirring book which left me with veneration for the man, it is suggested that the murder was committed by henchmen of his former master. I venture no opinion, but the book didn't lead me to believe that Malcolm's message was blood, blood, blood.

Revolutions do indeed shed blood, but this play manages to overlook the fact that *counter-revolutions* shed much more. It may seem trivial to remark—but I cite it simply as an example of what I am objecting to here—that in the hot lava of the play's final outcry, "We shall overcome" is denigrated as a symbol of softness by contrast with the sanguinary resolve demanded by revolution. It should be pointed out that, contrary to what the sloganeers scream, *every* revolution sings. *La Marseillaise*, now a national anthem, was not originally a lullaby.

I am ready to listen respectfully to every appeal and argument, no matter how personally dismaying, but I am alienated when calls to arms, to terror and bloodshed are hurled at me in doses of hasty shibboleth rung from premises not truly established by what has been set forth in the name of a great man.

El Hajj Malik is a presentation of "the Afro-American Studio for Acting and Speech which is dedicated to providing quality theatre training and production within the Harlem Community. All members of the *El Hajj Malik* company are members of the Studio's advanced theatre workshops." More power to them.

—*NAT*, 20 Dec. '71

THE SCREENS

"Hello! I'm laughter—not just any laughter, but the kind that appears when all goes wrong." That is a line from the Mother's soliloquy in Jean Genet's *The Screens* at the Chelsea Theatre Center of Brooklyn.

The Mother's greeting may well be the open sesame to a sense—I do not say "understanding"—of a play which may be set down as a terrible masterpiece. Its running time is four and a half hours, and if you seek strict coherence, you are lost. The scenes are scattered, confused, frightening, absurd and ultimately no more nefarious than a nightmare. The play's very explosion constitutes its meaning. "Everything wicked in the vegetable kingdom," the Mother goes on to say, "was won over to me." That is Genet's insignia, his contribution. If evil and hatred must have a conscious voice in drama, let it be Genet's.

The outraged patrioteers who rioted in Paris at the Roger Blin/Jean-Louis Barrault production of the play several years ago, because it insulted the French Army fighting the Algerian rebellion, were quite mistaken. The French presence in Algeria is not the butt of Genet's venom, nor is French officialdom the object of his mockery and wrath. His real target is civilization itself—all of modern civilization. He despises everything that it has spawned; he is no more pro-Algeria, as a social interpreter might read him, than he is anti-French. His scorn is all-embracing; it aims at universal devastation. The agony within him and the residue of a profoundly Gallic cultural heritage are wrenched from him in immense gusts of grotesque laughter. They echo like reverberations from Rabelais and Rimbaud.

As long ago as 1915 James Huneker wrote, "Foul is fair in art today." If, as some assert, we are entering a new dark age, it will surely produce its saints as well as its victims. Sartre has called Genet a saint. He is a saint who would purge us in a reversed morality which scours our hypocrisy, deceit and violence in an acid bath of loathing. (The play's title is not a reference simply to the screens that are used as "scenery" but to the symbols of the false front behind which we hide our villainies. Evil be thou my savior is Genet's prescript, an outcry which has in it almost as much mephitic irony as anguish.

The play's "story" is a springboard for an apocalyptic vision which contains the essence of Genet's *esprit*, and makes it more stage poetry than dramatic narrative. The pivotal figures are Saïd, an Algerian youth, and his mother, both at the bottom of the social scale. Saïd is so poor that to earn some money he marries the most hideously ugly girl (her face throughout the play is covered by a hood), a girl whose father pays a pitiful sum to get her off his hands. Saïd mistreats her; for sexual satisfaction he frequents a brothel (a prominent and tell-tale locale in this play as in *The Balcony*). But Leila, Saïd's abject wife, develops a slavish devotion to him, apparently thriving on his cruelty. She follows him like a whipped dog and joins him in his every misdeed. To escape Algeria, where he works as an abused farmhand under international capitalist ownership, he steals and Leila abets him in his thefts. Both are frequently jailed.

Saïd turns traitor to his countrymen. It isn't clear whether he does this because of a desire to escape the misery of his condition as an oppressed worker or because he has become a stooge of Genet's ideological bent: he says, "What can I sell out on, so as to be a complete louse?" When finally he is hunted down and the French authorities want to make a hero of him—with song, decoration and statue to celebrate his betrayal—he refuses the "honor," with his mother's blessings, and allows himself to be shot down. He is an adherent to no political cause, a patriot of no land—in which respects he imitates Genet himself.

In and around this bit of plot is a vast panorama of scenic flashes in which the foreigners' orange groves are burned by the natives, the elegance of French military splendor is burlesqued, together with the stupefying decadence of the *haute bourgeoisie*. Then, too, one glimpses the hilarious unconcern of the afterlife, the demystified exchanges between the living and the dead, and one hears voices from "nowhere." There is always the return of the whores—who know everything, for in their company men reveal their true feelings.

Through all the long parade of vicious insult, scatological rhapsody and infernal scurrility, Genet provides such keynotes as: "I want you to plunge into irrevocable grief. I want you to be without hope. I want you to choose evil. I want you to know

only hatred and never love." A local sibyl, now deceased, calls out, "Saïd, Leila, my loved ones. You realized that in evil lay the only life." Then, addressing the others, she asks, "What have you done for evil to prevail?" Then, too, we hear the Cadi confess: "All I brought from life is my trembling. If it's taken away from me, I lose everything."

All this builds to a strange, often bewildering and always arresting eloquence. Unlike his imitators (how I shun them) Genet, through the world's early rejection of him and through his subsequent suffering, has earned the right to his epic nihilism. He bears his humiliation like a defiant badge. And yet I find his outrage somehow cleansing, almost an alleviation in a world of half measures, cautious distinctions, "reasonable" remedies and timid compromises.

The very vehemence and savagery of Genet's ribald imprecations have something unutterably comic about them. They transform the insane turmoil of modern society, of life itself, into farce. Now everything has been said, every condemnation, every superlative of obloquy has been voiced; now we know how bad, and badly off, we are. We are shamelessly unmasked, but on beholding our shamefulness we can emit a roar of relief that we have been told the worst. Pushed beyond the edge of despair, we may realize all that has been left unsaid, all that is still good in the Gehenna in which we dwell. Genet flagellates himself and us into a new purity through the excess and sullied grandiloquence of his derision.

Only a true poet, a man possessed of verbally imaged artistry, could write such a play as *The Screens*. In one of his earlier pieces, Genet spoke of "a truthful idea born of an artificial show. The use of the screens in the present play to obviate all traces of realism, the instruction he gives for devising weird masks, costumes, sounds, reveal a fabulous theatrical imagination, a joy in the creation of stage hyperbole. And when one acknowledges the joy in spectacle added to the thrills of language—colorful, adventuresome, astonishing and dense in allusion—it can no longer be maintained that the end result or even the purpose of the whole enterprise is to depress or destroy. Genet is one of the few creative dramatists of our epoch. From the holocausts of the day he lights his own flaming torch. It illuminates what we are, what we have wrought, what we must renounce.

Minos Volanakis' direction is admirable in its fidelity to and understanding of the script, its treatment of the actors, its skill in the use of the limited technical resources available at the tiny Chelsea quarters. Speeches and scenes, which in reading one might suppose unplayable, become clear; no intention or nuance of action is left recondite, as literature. Everything is theatrically visualized. Watching the play, I speculated on how much more tricky and costly Tom O'Horgan would have made the production if he had been given the opportunity: there would have been more lavish expenditure with much less point. I also wondered why, if we dare cut Shaw and Shakespeare, Volanakis did not venture to abbreviate Genet. But perhaps without the license of length Genet's play would lose some of its dynamism.

The cast too merits much praise. The list of players who warrant compliments is too long to be included, but some words of special commendation are due Julie Bovasso for her shrewd humor and bite in the acting of the Mother; to Grayson Hall for the acrid clarity of the plays emblematic prostitute Warda, and to Joan Harris as Malika, who seconds Warda; to Robert Jackson for the tortured fervor of his Saïd; to Martin Garner for the canny and touching skepticism of the Cadi; to the physical and vocal versatility of Barry Bostwick's showoff sergeant; to James Cahill as a Mouth for the dead; to Janet League for the accomplishment of her arduous task as Leila; to John Granger for the pathetic fatuousness of his French lieutenant.

Robert Mitchell has used every possible foot of space and remarkable ingenuity to accommodate the multiple effects called for by the play. Especially gratifying are Willa Kim's costumes, among the best of the season; they speak of something more than the money spent on them.

—*NAT*, 27 Dec. '71

THERE'S ONE IN EVERY MARRIAGE

Georges Feydeau's *Le Dindon* ("The Turkey," which in French slang means "sucker" or "fall guy") dates from 1898, and is one of many bedroom farces with which that brilliant contriver supplied the Paris stage from 1886 to 1921. The pattern of his plays was imitated by a host of entertainers, but none could match him in technical excellence or in the invention of situations. An American, Avery Hopwood, whose best play, *Fair and Warmer*, was a Broadway hit in 1915, modeled his output on Feydeau, but was unable to keep up the pace, and declined from the naughty to the silly-dirty.

From the 19th century up to the early twenties such fare was favored, because the French bourgeoisie, though already infected by the laxity which inevitably ensues from the ideal of luxurious pleasure, still preserved its strict sense of propriety, while the Americans were only just shedding their Puritan heritage. To be altogether effective, bedroom farces must be based on middle-class standards of decorum. Their upset is a shock which strikes respectability's funny bone. Since society manners and mores are no longer "correct," the bedroom farce is an obsolete mode and when produced is usually regarded as quaint.

When we do this sort of farce now—the last one here was Gower Champion's production of Feydeau's *A Flea in Her Ear* at the ANTA Theatre in 1969—it is staged as a wildly eccentric, extremely "stylized" piece having little relation to actuality. And that is wrong. For Feydeau, a bitter man, was willy-nilly a mocking moralist. He stated his formula thus: "I set about looking for characters in living reality, determined to preserve their personalities intact." He placed their personalities in absurd situations and made them swirl about in an inextricable trap. The environment for these crazy misadventures is always that of well-to-do middle-class reality, familiar to the audience for which the plays were written. To produce them as if they were an extension of commedia dell'arte is not only to falsify them but also to render them less funny than they should be.

Le Dindon, now being presented at the Royale Theatre under the title *There's One In Every Marriage*, is a production which originated at the Stratford National Theatre of Canada. Under Jean Gascon's direction, the cast performs like a company of grotesques. Without being as fantastically distorted as in the above-mentioned Gower Champion production, the characters are kidded, as if to say that playwrights, actors and directors in the old days neither knew nor cared about "truth to life." (The asides are shot out front, whereas in the best French productions they are deftly thrown away, as if the characters were swearing in exasperation to themselves.) The actors at the Royale work too hard to get all the laughs they should.

Still, Feydeau is not to be drowned. His pace, his adroit plotting, the surprise of his complications, the constant introduction of new and always delightfully unexpected types, the special energy of his theatrical tricks are achieved with astonishing skill. They cannot fail to produce hilarity. The flourish of his craftsmanship, together with his note of scorn, make Feydeau a "ball" in Paris today and in London, where Jacques Charon of the Comédie-Française has directed him. It is still pleasant to attend his inventions in New York.

There are some good performances in the present production. Roberta Maxwell does not overdo her role: she looks and acts like a human being rather than a cartoon. Marilyn Gardner brings considerable zest to the part of a Swedish lady bent on amour in Paris (the character was English in the original play); Tony Van Bridge displays robust humor as a Major in the army's medical corps; Joseph Maher is merrily "Irish" as a senile French caretaker.

—*NAT*, 24 Jan. '72

MOONCHILDREN

I liked Michael Weller's *Moonchildren* (Royale Theatre). I begin thus bluntly and, from a strictly critical viewpoint perhaps irrelevantly, because I shall say things which may give the opposite impression.

There is vitality in this comedy though its characters bombinate without direction. We do not know at the outset what these college kids want, we are not at last certain where they will "end." They are on no determined path, they are not headed toward any clear goal. Their humorous behavior is self-destructive. We nevertheless feel that life forces are stirring within them. This inner whir and roil is a kind of rock and roll which has some positive meaning. Young Michael Weller doesn't tell us what it is—he doesn't know—but he sets forth the surface phenomena vivaciously.

Boy and girl students about to graduate, they all live together in a single apartment, share a common refrigerator and meals, some share each other's beds. (Such eccentrics do exist in universities, but are rarely to be found together in one residence.) They put each other and everyone else on, they tease and taunt all outsiders as squares. They are contemptuous of the faculty; they are bright but do not respect the subjects they study. The most earnest of them is puzzled by his own assiduity in reading; he ends attempting to set fire to himself in the Buddhist fashion as a protest against what, we surmise, is the war, but we are not sure even of that. There is a girl who hides—we don't know exactly from what—under tables.

The most cynical of the lot—two brothers—are the best students, probably destined to be "successes." One student gives evidence of "heart," but is incapable of giving it a voice. He gives up the girl he cares for because he cannot bring himself to declare his attachment to her. He loves his mother, but the sight of her dead body arouses his disgust. There is sex play but no passion. In the funniest of scenes the landlord who comes to collect the rent (always in arrears) envies his juvenile tenants their "freedom": they are bound by no rules such as those which govern his life.

Jokes are cracked (too many and too extended) and constant activity is engaged in but nothing *happens*. When they all depart hardly anything is resolved; they are left up in the air, empty. No point is made, but that is the point. There is an oblique pathos in this, but we are not moved to tears, nor does the author expect us to be. We cannot forget that the youth most endowed with sensibility, verbally eloquent but emotionally mute, skeptical of all values including his education, throws in the towel by announcing that he will accept being drafted though he is surely indifferent to the issues involved. The students all join in an anti-war demonstration, but even that is more a lark than a gesture of conviction.

What the play expresses, in a sequence of scenes which makes it appear to straggle rather than progress, is that while there are brains, talent, energy and good will—all those assets we think of as "human potential"—in our youth and in our country, there is no faith, no guiding and binding moral principle to structure our lives, give it dignity, and creative force. There is inner chaos which I, rather than the author, infer must lead to social cancer and dissolution.

In a way the play is a cartoon. It deals with reality but it is no more "realistic" than is Hogarth if we think of his work as a true representation of England's 18th century. Though the play is unified in its scenic locale, it is serial in construction, one comedy turn after another, creating the effect of caricature. Yet there is truth in it, symbolic rather than literal.

I mention Hogarth's England possibly because seeing Weller's play I was reminded of *Look Back in Anger* which was significant of the English young in 1956, while *Moonchildren* speaks of our youth in the late sixties, though in both cases the time and the class have further extension. Osborne's world was both regretful and scornful of the past, but even more irate about the lethargy and dead end of the present. It was frustrated and confusedly wrathful because the road ahead appeared cut off. Weller's world is seemingly without a past and apparently no redeeming future. Weller's world is more frivolous, hence more damned.

Weller, like Osborne, can write. He is less rhetorical than Osborne, less "cultivated" and perhaps less conscious, but in his clownish swipes he cuts even more sharply to the bone. We know what has happened to Osborne—with a more ample vocabulary and greater sophistication he is now possessed by a morbidly impotent rage; I look forward to Weller's development and wonder where (and if) he will "come out."

Under Alan Schneider's direction, the company, which originally played *Moonchildren* at the Washington Arena Stage, acts well and forms a lively and truly coherent team. (Only the opening night audience, I felt, was miscast.) There are no bad performances and some, like those of Kevin Conway as a roguish gadfly, Cara Duff-MacCormick as the girl who seeks refuge under tables, Robert Prosky as the befuddled landlord, Christopher Guest as the "Parsifal" and would-be martyr of the group, Salem Ludwig in an almost inconspicuous bit are the ones I especially appreciated.

—*NAT*, 13 Mar. '72

TWELFTH NIGHT

*T*welfth Night is not one of my favorite Shakespeare plays. Still I have seen productions of it that were replete with poetic enchantment and comic zest. But now at the Vivian Beaumont Theatre I do not know what the play means or is supposed to mean in sentiment, thought or entertainment. Irate after the first act (the second is a bit livelier), I came out with the cruel determination to declare that the Repertory Theatre of Lincoln Center is boredom institutionalized.

In bewilderment I turn for enlightenment to Harold C. Goddard's excellent *The Meaning of Shakespeare*, with its sometimes farfetched but always stimulating interpretations. (Goddard, now deceased, was head of the English Department at Swarthmore College from 1909 to 1946.) He states that "if in *The Merchant of Venice* [Shakespeare] exposes the hollowness and even cruelty lurking under the silken surface of a leisured society, if...in *Much Ado About Nothing* and *As You Like It* he tears the mask off wit and word play, he does all these things at once in *Twelfth Night*...but does them so genially that his very victims were probably loudest in their applause...." Going even further, Goddard suggests that "The theme of the main plot as well as that of the enveloping action...is rescue from drowning: drowning in the sea, drowning in the sea of drunkenness and sentimentalism."

This may or may not be so, but such a reading of the play might possibly lead to a fascinating stage embodiment. What distressed me about the *show* at Lincoln Center is that there was no way I could "read" it. There were some pretty pictures, some good-looking costumes (without real character), two engaging performances, several fatal pieces of miscasting, and a lot of quite listless acting. But there was no core of intention, no clear line to hold the play together. It was just another item in the season's program. There is no justification for producing Shakespeare (or any other dramatist, for that matter) unless one hopes to say something, to achieve something—even if it be merely boisterous fun or extravagant romance.

Only four actors were wholly intelligible in speech: René Auberjonois, Leonard Frey, Stephen McHattie and Philip Bosco. (Clarity of speech is not a matter of technical proficiency alone: it also results from definiteness of dramatic impulse.) Blythe Danner, usually a most delectable actress, besides having some vocal trouble of probably recent origin, appeared almost insipid, as if uninterested in the role of Viola. Martha Henry, customarily decisive, did little, as Olivia, but

recite. Moses Gunn, ordinarily forceful, seemed to be directed toward a characterization which, whatever it may have presumed to connote, denatured him. Cynthia Belgrave as Maria drew a blank. Sydney Walker's Sir Toby hardly existed except for effort and words.

Auberjonois as Malvolio had energy and a degree of comic verve, but there is more to the personage than that: Malvolio should be as pathetic as he is silly, more worthy of respect than the ribald creatures who beset him. Leonard Frey's Aguecheek traced a certain woeful depletion that makes the poor sap touching. George Pentecost as Feste sang nicely (though I prefer the simplicity of authentic Elizabethan tunes and a less framed staging of them) but needed a more defined character impress to provide the melancholy note which, within the merriment, exists in the part.

I often fail to notice productions—even when they are hits—when my reaction is entirely negative. That is not due to any supposed "kindness" but to indifference, distaste or dejection. (One show some people liked I could only describe as "nostalgia for ugliness," another is a thriller which failed to thrill me. In any case I don't care to be "excited," shocked or frightened unless the occasion provides some merit or value over and above these sensations.) I have expatiated on *Twelfth Night* because it is time that utterly superficial or routine productions of important texts be denounced as such, precisely because they come wrapped in an aura of "culture," education and serious artistry. They add nothing to the gaiety of the nation—except perhaps to kids, old or young.

—*NAT*, 20 Mar. '72

THE COUNTRY GIRL

Though *The Country Girl* (Billy Rose Theatre) is not as "characteristic" a Clifford Odets play as *Awake and Sing!*, *Paradise Lost*, *Rocket To The Moon* or *Golden Boy*, it is one which has most frequently been revived. I have now seen four New York performances of it and one in Paris. The reason for the special interest, apart from any other merit, is that it provides three fat parts for personality actors.

When Odets wrote *The Country Girl* in 1951 he wanted and needed a *commercial* success. He wrote the play with less spiritual energy than he had spent on the previous ones. But he was too creative a person to set aside the man he was, the subjective self. Aiming at an effective story with opportunities for histrionic virtuosity, he wrote a play as much about his inner self as the personally prophetic and successful *Golden Boy* or the rather muddled *Big Knife*.

A play's plot is not its theme. Objectively, *The Country Girl* is about Frank Elgin, a once renowned actor now alcoholic and very nearly derelict. He is "finished." His wife Georgie has stood by him despite his aberrations and the lies he tells himself and others to explain his decline. An energetic and gifted young director, Bernie Dodd, in desperate need of an actor to replace a star who has quit a production during the second week of rehearsal, remembers Elgin, who was one of Dodd's boyhood idols. He calls him in as a replacement for the defector. The producer is horrified at the thought of taking a chance with the notoriously unreliable Elgin, but Dodd persists; he offers Elgin the difficult assignment.

Dodd questions Elgin as to the causes of the actor's downfall. Elgin blames it on his wife's disturbed state of mind; she had once tried to commit suicide after the loss of her child. He has had to be forever watchful to prevent a relapse. So he took to drink, that made him inept at learning lines, etc. Dodd is suspicious, even hostile, toward Georgie, whom he declares a bitch. He presumes that she has been taking advantage of her neurosis to emasculate her actor husband. She will prevent her husband, the director fears, from making the grade in his forthcoming production.

But we soon learn that Elgin's story is pure fabrication: it is Georgie, his wife, who has sustained him. He is talented but grievously lacking in self-confidence, and she does everything possible to fortify his tremulous ego. He has a morbid need of reassurance at every step and constantly rationalizes fantastically to mask his insecurity, his fear of failure. Through infinite patience and nerve-racking struggle with Elgin's always imminent breakdown, she finally succeeds in seeing him through to a triumphant opening night.

The play's action is transparent; its "psychology" simple. What is essentially conveyed is that the deepest desire of such an artist as Elgin ("Odets") is the support of an immovably devoted, ever understanding and forbearing woman and the unshakable confidence of a fellow artist, to guide him in the pursuit of his profession. Such a person was what Odets in private called a "loyal witness."

There has always been something to me embarrassing in the sentimentality of the specifically theatrical facets of the play, its picture of stage life and "politics." But that is hardly important. The audience responds to the human interest of the story, which is real enough, and the play works to the degree that it is well acted.

It is very well acted in the present revival. Frank Elgin is certainly impressive only when played by an actor of heroic compass, as was Michael Redgrave in the London production. It is nearly always Georgie who most firmly captures the audience's imagination. There are several reasons for this: one is of course that the staunch, put-upon woman is more sympathetic than her selfish and errant husband. It is possible to that Odets saw himself, symbolically, in the woman role, and his various wives as her irresolute mate! It is therefore essential that the person playing Elgin convince the audience that he was formerly a great actor and that he may once again become one.

For such an actor's play as *The Country Girl* the director (John Houseman in this instance) need only supply intelligent guidance. Houseman has done so. The creative impact of the play is entirely Maureen Stapleton's. George Grizzard makes a sensible Dodd, playing the role honestly and simply. Jason Robards is a proficient and credible Elgin, showing considerable craft ease and insight. He is an admirable foil in the scenes of hectic conflict between Elgin and Georgie. What we do not sufficiently get is the sense of a lost grandeur and a stirring belief of the man's inner anguish, the excruciating lesion of self-doubt.

Maureen Stapleton is so moving because we perceive in her Georgie an extreme vulnerability that is transformed into great strength. What lends her strength is richness of feeling, always a source of power. Maureen Stapleton has enormous resources of sentience, the only treasure a person must possess to achieve truly human worth.

A number of reviewers have commented on the good old-time histrionic "fireworks" to be found in this production. Why "old-time?" Because it *is* acting, the use of the entire emotional organism—rather than just peripheral physical capacities—in the presentation of character. Because *The Country Girl*, through Stapleton in the interplay with Robards and Grizzard (in addition to a delicate performance by Joe Ponazecki as a young playwright), gives evidence of articulated personal experience, the play becomes a more rewarding theatre event than most others of the Broadway season.

I should also point out that within his text Odets indicates the exact nature of the play. Speaking of the vehicle in which Elgin is appearing, Georgie asks Dodd whether he really believes it to be "literature." No, Dodd answers, but with fine playing, which full-blooded actors may bring to it, it may assume a life on the stage of unmistakable potency. Odets was right and the present cast, in large measure, justifies him.

—*NAT*, 3 Apr. '72

SMALL CRAFT WARNINGS

In a generally laudatory article on Tennessee Williams three years ago, I said that he was fascinated by sin and had an affinity with sinners. I am impelled to revert to this old statement because his *Small Craft Warnings* is an "old" play (Truck and Warehouse Theatre).

I refer not only to the date of the play's composition—which, I surmise, was sometime before his breakdown in 1969-70—but to the nature of the play itself. It is old in the sense that it repeats the mood and mode of much earlier work. Williams has been there before—and so have we.

Then, too, the play is overextended. It was originally conceived as a one-act play called *Confessional*: much of the exposition and character delineation of *Small Craft Warnings* is semi-soliloquized. Williams was subsequently persuaded to expand it, thus compounding its faults. That also happened with *Camino Real*, an overdeveloped fantasy.

Williams' penchant for the compassionate depiction of damaged souls is as much part of the moralist in him as it is a sign of complicity, and I am sympathetic to it. Everything must be said, especially if it is well said. Williams is gifted with a superb instinct both for the stage and for certain aspects of our people and civilization. What he has had to say, therefore, was not only interesting but, in our fretfully and skittishly puritanic society, important. There was, and still are, elements of pity and terror in his work (combined with humor), which at all times saves it from being scabrous. At worst it was sentimental, but sentimentality itself may be a positive quality, if it is supported by the evidence of convincing fact and honest feeling—in other words, where expression does not exceed what we recognize as genuine experience.

In *Gnädiges Fräulein*, part of his "Slapstick Tragedies," Williams translated his hurt into an original symbolism, in which bitterness was masked and alleviated by strange laughter. In the most subjective of his plays, *In The Bar of a Tokyo Hotel*, his sense of personal collapse was almost shamefully exposed, but in a manner painfully impressive because of its very abjectness. In both these plays the author's self-laceration, though shocking, might still inspire a certain respect. *Small Craft Warnings* does not offend, but neither is it moving. It strikes one as a demonstration of an old posture, an overcalculated litany now bereft of poignancy.

In a bar along the coast of Southern California we meet once again Williams' entire menagerie of derelicts. There is Violet, the most bedraggled and woebegone of them all, whose only relief from her wretchedness is manual contact with the genitals of whatever compliant male may be sitting beside her. (The first act ends with this dismal observation on the woman: "She's got religion in her hands.") There is Leona Dawson, a beautician wandering from town to town in a trailer, who half out of commiseration and loneliness, takes on a lover, a fellow who employs his sexual prowess as insurance against participation in any other effort. There is a homosexual screenwriter who bewails the increasingly deadening callousness of his passing encounters with the youths he picks up. There is Steve, almost cretinous in his accommodation to the mire of his existence. The bartender, Monk, is a bachelor content to eke out a living from his shabby establishment. He is resigned to bleak isolation and to probable sudden death from an expected heart attack. Under the circumstances, he is a decent enough person whose kind response to the lowly Violet's plea for tenderness may to some extent redeem both of them in their loveless lives. The doughty beautician, Leona, on the other hand, after giving her feckless lover the go-by, concludes that the greatest strength consists in being able to bear living by oneself alone.

Williams always writes well, but because the characters in this play are little better than tokens of the author's preconceived canon—there is also a still pure youth, questing for the surprise or poetry of life—the writing seems studiously "correct" and unanimated. It gives the impression of an attempt to formulate as lucidly as possible a considered credo. Even in its dialogue, the play suffers from lack of spontaneity.

This, I am inclined to believe, is not the Williams of today, whatever his spiritual condition may now be. The play is an encapsulation of past history, which in its original telling possessed authentic vitality. We can only hope that, when the playwright gets the residue of his toxic affections out of his system (I refer to the plays of his period of exhaustion), he can give fresh voice to whatever his recovery may dictate. No artist ever completely alters his nature, nor have we the right to expect such a change, but when the initial sources of creativity are deep, a vivid and varied florescence may occur. We owe it to Williams to trust that this will prove the case with him.

—*NAT*, 24 Apr. '72

THE CRUCIBLE
THE REAL INSPECTOR HOUND
AND AFTER MAGRITTE

Arthur Miller's *The Crucible* is almost twenty years old. Since its first performance I have seen it in an intimate off-Broadway presentation, then in London at the Royal Court Theatre and again in Paris in an "operatically" elaborate mounting that starred Yves Montand and Simone Signoret. Now at the Repertory Theatre of Lincoln Center, under John Berry's direction and with sets of exemplary simplicity by Jo Mielziner, the play stands forth for what it is: a work of impressive dramatic and moral strength.

When it was presented in 1953, its "topicality" alienated some people who saw in it little more than "propaganda." *The Crucible* was viewed chiefly as a protest against the plague of McCarthyism. With the play's outcry, "Is the accuser always holy?" it was to some extent what its adversaries accused it of being, a denunciation of the causes and a treatment of the effects of the disease that poisoned the atmosphere in which we lived. The play was misleading, so the criticism went, in suggesting an analogy between the McCarthy terror and the hanging of the Salem witches, because we know that witches do not exist, whereas Communists do. What the play does in fact depict is the way in which hysteria can confuse and drive a community to crime, when special interests foster it and when its citizens are too ignorant to combat it. Yet even that is not the play's chief issue.

Now that McCarthy is gone and the wound he inflicted is largely healed, *The Crucible* may be viewed in its true light. It is a link in the chain of Miller's main theme: we are all responsible to one another and to that truth within us which we hold most worthy. Only in the preservation of our "name" (our true being) do we acquire dignity in our own and our neighbors' eyes. This constitutes the highest fortitude and honor.

The honest farmer John Proctor, susceptible to temptation, fearful of death, no "hero" to his wife or friends, chooses to die rather than sign a false confession, one assenting to betrayal of truth and treachery of his fellow citizens. This "gratuitous" sacrifice to a sense of inner, and ultimately social, rectitude is at the core of *The Crucible* and several of Miller's other plays.

The play's language is at once formal and pristine, stalwart as an oak without losing any of the grace of nature or the tongue of those who for generations have read the Scripture and spoken in its rhythm. The play's structure is tight, steady and clean as the 17th-century New England which is its scene.

The Crucible is the best of the Lincoln Center's productions at the Vivian Beaumont Theatre. It has unity. All the players give better than adequate accounts of themselves and of their roles. The newcomer, Robert Foxworth as Proctor, is attractively strong in physique, forthright in delivery, genuine in sentiment. Pamela Payton-Wright, an actress who has hitherto impersonated only gentle and reticent young women, here lends her delicate sensibility to more dangerous employment as the minx whose desire for Proctor and jealously of his wife light the fire that inflames the town. Philip Bosco is an almost prissy Puritan reverend who, through tormented conscience, becomes as passionately eloquent in

his contrition as the monk Stogumber in Shaw's *St. Joan*. Stephen Elliott, in the difficult role of the deputy governor, finely engraves a semi-stylized portrait of the self-assured ruler of his narrow realm.

One serious flaw, however, must be mentioned because it pertains not only to this production but to a general criticism of present-day American acting. Too many of our actors—especially the younger ones—who are intelligent and probably gifted, seem unable to convey the expression of heightened emotion in clear speech. We see them undergoing tremors of violent feeling but we do not understand what they are saying. Even some of the more experienced actors become unintelligible when the lines they are called upon the utter require especially rapid pace.

To remedy this defect, as Tyrone Guthrie once pointed out, requires daily work for at least four years. And long ago Stanislavsky, the "father figure" for most young American actors today, told me he found that actors who would earnestly devote themselves to the discovery of a true inner life for their parts became lazy when the incessant work on proper diction was involved. It was a patter on which he was insistent to the point of fanaticism. Actors should never forget how frustrated the spectator becomes when gasps of excitement issue from the stage with no distinct verbal meaning.

The Real Inspector Hound by Tom Stoppard, together with his shorter, one-act *After Magritte*, have found favor with a majority of reviewers and perhaps with many other theatregoers (Theatre Four). Stoppard is the author of *Rosencrantz and Guildenstern Are Dead*, a winner of several awards during the 1967-68 season. It was a clever play—a sort of witty appendix to *Hamlet* that rang changes on a Beckett-like theme.

After Magritte is a quasi-surrealist parody of the English police melodrama. It has its amusing moments, but for the most part I found it heavy going. *The Real Inspector Hound*, which offers more entertainment, is a mockery of a routine murder mystery, accompanied by caricatures of dramatic critics whose professional behavior, lack of literary style, vanities, ambition, jealousies and private peccadilloes are facetiously drubbed as they sit in a side box—where critics never sit.

The gimmick in the play is that the critics become fancifully mixed up in the action of the murder mystery they are reviewing. The second-string critic is gnawed by envy of his superior and other journalists more favorably placed, and finally murders one of them who may have been having an affair with the leading lady in the show—and so on and so forth in salty extravagance.

This is "university wit," which is another way of defining undergraduate pranks seasoned by latter-day airs of sharp sophistication and British toniness. I tried hard to enjoy the event, but found it trivial and arid. The satire of old-fashioned mysteries and of theatre critics—all very "in" jokes—interests me hardly at all. I write about these at best slight offerings out of deference to those who have a taste for such things—their number may be greater than I suppose—which I shall refrain from designating as silly ass snobbery. David Rounds as the second-stringer and Tom Lacy as the more fully established critic are both effective.

—NAT, 15 May '72

AN EVENING WITH RICHARD NIXON AND— THAT CHAMPIONSHIP SEASON

There are various kinds of merit to be found in a theatre event. Gore Vidal's *An Evening With Richard Nixon And*— is not "drama" but I favor it (Shubert Theatre). There are obvious criticisms to be made—where's the surprise, the tension, etc.— but I enjoyed the visit. All the speeches given George Irving to speak as Nixon are verbatim quotes. Isn't that enough to cause shudders and laughter?

It may be old stuff to you, but not to me. I listen to very few political speeches. With most noted figures in so-called statecraft I am as I am with actors at an audition. The actor has only to read several lines for me to assess his quality and suitability for a role, though out of courtesy I may permit him to read further. I once heard Jimmy Walker for about five minutes: I recognized him at once as an affable and possibly companionable rogue. As for our dear President, I have seen and heard him on television, observed him on the street; his *opinions* after these brief encounters have become supererogatory: I know the man.

Still I didn't recall his prose in its specific content. He is, after all, part of history's comedy, and history is serious. I therefore found all he said in Gore Vidal's transcription fascinating and frequently funny. The historical context from the man's green youth through to his present high estate is rapidly processed, the montage witty, the staging by Edwin Sherin sufficiently deft and George Irving's impersonation amusing. The total account is summary, biased—the basic attitude disheartened, but the picture on the face of it befits the facts. Contemporary politics in general is a self-made mockery—to some a comedy, to others a tragedy. Other attitudes may be assumed but, to begin with, the first impression is natural. In any case, for all its frivolity, *An Evening With Richard Nixon And*—has more substance than most of the "art" Broadway now has to offer.

I also liked Stephen Newman's George Washington and Philip Sterling's Eisenhower. I must report, too, that on opening night several people in the balcony hissed; if Nixon had no supporters there would be little interest in the lampoon.

That Championship Season by Jason Miller at the Public Theatre is a good show. Many habitués of that peppy institution have expressed surprise that the new play was old-fashioned realism rather than "experimental." There may be a sense of relief in this astonishment: we really haven't changed as much as is supposed; we are not altogether "new."

The play concerns five men in a small Pennsylvania town who gather for a reunion at the house of their old high school basketball coach. They come at regular intervals to reminisce and rejoice at their boyhood triumph as winners of the trophy which attested to their championship. The coach is their idol and they the living witnesses of the rightness of his stern discipline and "philosophy." Religiously, they cling to the memory of their adolescent splendor.

We soon discover that, apart from the fact that the famous championship was won by dirty tactics, each of these men is an empty, a damaged bag.

These men are all practicing Catholics without a speck of true faith: all that is left of their religion is clannishness and ritualistic gesture. The coach is a racist and an anti-Semite: his heroes are Joe McCarthy and Father Coughlin. He is a sincere hypocrite; his goal is absolute domination in the petty puddle of the township.

The points made smack of a boldness readily acceptable to all but the most backward or totally indifferent among us. Why then the pleasure with which this play has been received? It has vigor, its dialogue is salty and its unmasking of the contradiction between mask and face, myth and reality is heightened, to speak in the play's vein, by a "no bullshit" forthrightness.

The play's attraction goes even deeper; there is something hammy in it. This is not altogether a detraction. Most hamminess in writing and acting turns us off; but there is also such a thing as talented hamminess, just as there is melodrama which provokes resistance and melodrama which grips us, as in the novels of Dickens and Balzac. *That Championship Season* is "ham" with talent. Its story and "message" is by now largely old stuff, to a considerable degree imitative, but real blood flows through it. The author's sentiments are authentic, his conviction streaked with acrid humor, genuine. The play affects us less than it entertains. The mixture assures audience enthusiasm.

On the whole, with moments of not too reprehensible overacting, the play is well cast and well acted. Walter McGinn, Charles Durning, Michael McGuire, Paul Sorvino, Richard Dysart, under A. J. Antoon's knowing direction, acquit themselves admirably.

—*NAT*, 22 May '72

SHAKESPEARE: YOUNG AMERICAN PLAYWRIGHT

There was a time when many Americans thought of Shakespeare as an author whose works were entirely composed of quotations. Too many had read rather than seen his plays and, what is worse, read them as high school texts. A much older generation saw the plays as "vehicles" for star actors with lines, even whole scenes, deleted. The cuts were made because there were many "improprieties" in them and because it took so long to move the heavy "realistic" scenery. Shakespeare's plays are intended to move as swiftly as a film.

Shakespeare today is no longer viewed as a "classic" to be pondered, but as a dramatist to be enjoyed. His plays are not museum pieces. No one was puzzled when in 1964 Jan Kott, a Polish critic—now an American professor—wrote a book called *Shakespeare: Our Contemporary*. At present Shakespeare is played all over the U.S.; he is, numerically speaking, our most popular playwright. We have come to appreciate him as a living voice, which speaks to us of our own experience.

At a performance of *Macbeth* some years ago I heard a lady, picking up the Porter's joke about man's natural functions, murmur "Did Shakespeare really say that?" And the other night at *King Lear* in New York's Central Park when Lear, in his misery, says "Thou hast seen a farmer's dog bark at a beggar…And the creature ran from the cur? There thou mightest behold the great image of authority: *a dog's obeyed in office*," numerous people in the audience reacted as though the lines referred to current events.

The stress in Kott's book is in large part on Shakespeare's pessimism, which nowadays is often equated with wisdom. To support his point, a line from *Lear*: "Men must endure their going hence, even as their coming hither" is set down as one example of the Bard's "blackness," but Kott does not complete the citation by its afterthought, "Ripeness is all." Shakespeare recognizes the tragic facts of life, but he also affirms that "ripeness" (maturity) requires that instead of collapsing beneath them we face them with fortitude. Shakespeare's greatness lies not alone in his recognition of life's terror, but in his capacity to rise above its disillusionments.

Shakespeare is our contemporary and has much to say to us in America, because he is universal. He is a world which contains all. "What fools these mortals be," the sprite of *A Midsummer Night's Dream* observes blithely, and "We are such stuff as dreams are made on" the wizard Prospero muses in *The Tempest* in melancholy yet benign resignation. On these foundations Shakespeare creates fantasy, frolic and farce not unmixed with license of words and behavior as well as romance both smiling and tearful, bitter comedy, horrendous melodrama, epic tragedy, life-questioning drama.

Ours is a political day. Many of Shakespeare's royal chronicles are not so much history as vital dramatizations of political destiny not at all limited to the blood soaked flux of the middle ages: they stand for all time. They mirror the shifting of fortunes in the struggle for power: the "Grand Mechanism," to use Kott's phrase. Rulers are elevated to high places and then viciously deposed: revered, celebrated, vilified, executed. "Uneasy lies the head that wears a crown" says weary Henry IV, he who earlier as Bolingbroke craftily plotted to do away with a former head of state. Newspaper headlines today help us understand this all too well.

Shakespeare knew the rot in all parties and political partisanship. It is not in *Coriolanus* that he has a character call down "A plague on both

your houses," but that is a conclusion that play suggests. The turmoil in periods of political and moral uncertainty which many recognize in the troubled atmosphere since the fall of the first atom bomb is given vivid imagery in the second act of *Richard II*: "The bay trees in our country are all withered, and meteors fright the fixed stars of heaven. The pale-faced moon looks bloody on the earth, and lean looked prophets whisper fearful change. Rich men look sad and ruffians dance and leap, the one in fear to lose what they enjoy, the other to enjoy by rage and war..." A figure called Rumour in the second part of *Henry IV* states: "Upon my tongue continual slanders ride, the which in every language I pronounce, stuffing the ears with false reports. I speak of peace while covert enmity under the smile of safety wounds the world."

What American does not hear the like, in language much less gracious, through all the media. And what about this, which all our journals might have employed for editorial use as the curtain fell on the last act of the conflict in Vietnam: "A peace is of the nature of a conquest, for then both parties are subdued and neither party loser."

It is no secret to anyone that movie production nowadays is sex saturated. There is more love than sex in Shakespeare, but the glories, grandeurs, follies and falls of carnal appetite are fully explored in Shakespeare's happy and sorrowful plays. He was the singer and dramatist of every sort of passion. He was no prude or puritan. He was often merry in ways which the Victorian age considered unseemly and gross. Even the matter of "censorship" is broached by the greatest writer of the English tongue: "Tis needful that the most immodest word be look'd upon, and learned; which once attained...comes to no further use but to be known and hated."

No latter-day Jeremiah has inveighed against the disorderliness of the times as does expiring Henry IV: "For the fifth Harry (the royal heir) from curb'd license plucks the muzzle of restraint, and the wild dog shall flesh his tooth in every innocent...O my poor kingdom, sick with civil blows, when that my care could not withhold thy riots...O! thou wilt be a wilderness again, peopled with wolves..." But the old man deceives himself, for his riotous son as Henry V will prove a shrewd politico and learn how to rationalize an unwarranted war.

There's no theme so trifling or incidental of which Shakespeare has not something pithy to say. Take the fetish of astrology. Thus, the wily bastard Edmund in *King Lear*: "This is the excellent foppery of the world, that, when we are sick in fortune—often the surfeits of our own behavior—we make guilty of our disasters the sun, the moon and the stars; as if we were villains on necessity, fools by heavenly compulsion, knaves, thieves and treachers by spherical predominance...."

One is always reminded of the majesty, muscularity, sinew and wit of Shakespeare's speech. But he, who probably died wishing he had been a poet exclusively, was primarily a maker of plays. His plays were written for seeing: "To see sad sights moves more than to hear them told, *for the eye interprets to the ear*. "That is one reason he is as popular in foreign countries, where his plays are only known in translation, as in England and America. Shakespeare's plays, for all their splendid panoply of words, are wrought on a motor of constant *action*.

"For our giddy world, is there no play"—to make a "montage" of the dramatist's lines—"to ease the anguish of a torturing hour?" Yes, there is: Shakespeare's. His are plays to catch the native conscience. As Americans we hear them afresh with the spectacle of our "reeling world" nakedly visible before us to give them new meaning to add to the pleasures they afford.

—*STGB*, '72

THE CHERRY ORCHARD

It was Horace Walpole who said that the world is a comedy to those who think and a tragedy to those who feel. Chekhov was both a feeling and a thinking man. I read an article somewhere which set out to prove him more deeply pessimistic than any of the dramatists of the absurd. He has also been called an optimist. All such definitions are beside the mark: I mean the mark of the plays themselves. They are at one and the same time funny and sad. Chekhov sees what is comic in his sad people and what is pathetic in their absurdity. He objected that Stanislavsky had made his characters into "cry babies," but his texts are replete with stage directions which read "weeping," "sobbing." His plays are comedies that provoke tears.

Chekhov's attitude toward his people is at once objective and tender. He recognizes the nobility of their aspirations and the poverty of their actions. He portrays the contradictions in all human behavior. Madame Ranevskaya, the central figure of *The Cherry Orchard*, is generously profligate with her money at the very time when she is most in need of it. Knowingly, she returns to a lover who has betrayed and robbed her. Her brother, Gayev, a man of sweet nature, is spoiled, incompetent, hopelessly sentimental. Lopahin is a gruff capitalist, tasteless, good-hearted, uneducated, respectful of learning, humble and self-assertive. He pleads with the owners of the estate on which the cherry orchard is located to take decisively practical steps to save it for themselves, but when he acquires it he exults in this sign of his wealth and power. In the latest Soviet production he is portrayed as the play's only positive character, because capitalist industry in Russia was a historically necessary development at the end of the 19th century. Some have gone so far as to suggest that Lopahin is in love with Ranevskaya. But he is far too concentrated on his work to be in love with anyone.

Trofimov, the perpetual student, is sure he knows the answer to everything, but he is idealistic to the point of foolishness. The silly housemaid thinks of herself as a delicate flower. The coarse valet, Yasha, is contemptuous of Russian ignorance, and speaks enthusiastically only of France, where all he has learned is to drink champagne and be forward with guileless girls. The thick-headed Pishchik borrows money from everyone but he repays it. (He is probably also being swindled by English business people.) The aged manservant Firs thinks the emancipation of the serfs a misfortune. He takes care of everyone with utmost devotion, but is left alone to die in the deserted house. As he sinks into unconsciousness he murmurs, "Life has gone by, as if I had never lived," which is what many of the moribund probably feel. And he calls himself, as he has called almost everyone else, a "nincompoop," a "clumsy fool," a "good-for-nothing." Both sentiments dwell in the recesses of Chekhov's spirit.

The Cherry Orchard is a personal play, a "parochial" play (since it deals with a specific moment of Russian history and a particular class) and a widely social play. It is also universal: it is appreciated practically everywhere in the civilized world. What makes it universal is Chekhov's vision of the bitter folly of life and the compassion of his acceptance of that condition as a given fact. What binds all his characters together is love, the same rueful love he himself feels for them. Chekhov does not prate or prophesy, but he is fortified by the knowledge that the young will always place hope in the future, something which it is inevitable and right that they do. The speechifying and somewhat ridiculous student says: "Humanity is marching toward a higher truth, to the greatest happiness that it is possible to imagine on earth." "And will you get there?" he is asked. "I shall," the young man answers. "I shall get there on my own or show others how to get there." And Anya, Ranevskaya's daughter, cries out as her mother and the others leave the ancestral home, "It's a new life that's beginning." The youthful

sunniness in the dark resides in all of Chekhov's most beloved characters: it was part of himself. Nearly all Chekhov's major plays end with a young person, heartbrokenly or joyously saying very much the same thing. Chekhov's "optimism" is imbued with true wisdom: it is based on a profound substratum of tragic perception. That is what makes his plays reach beyond his time and place.

The Cherry Orchard is now being played by an all black cast at the Public Theatre. I am not sure I'm able to judge its production without preconceptions: I have seen the play countless times, going back to 1923, when the original Moscow Art Theatre presentation with Stanislavsky and Olga Knipper (Chekhov's widow) and the entire cast which first acted it in 1904 was being shown in Paris. I would nevertheless say that the Public Theatre effort is a creditable one and that in it the play still lives.

There are several readily discernible flaws. It is a mistake, for instance, to have various characters use Russian expressions and sing songs in Russian. It is also false to have Chekhov's people speak of the French capital as "Paree." (Only Yasha with his vulgar Francophilistinism uses French in the original.) Also, little bits of contemporary emphasis are tastelessly introduced, as in the scene where the passing wayfarers are made to appear menacing, to suggest the rebel poor of the future in relation to the rich. In this scene, Lopahin (as a "liberal" capitalist!), believing that the gentry are being threatened, draws a pistol—an entirely gratuitous and improbable gesture.

These are minor blemishes: there are others. Firs, for example, though very old, need not be played as if he were 150. I might go on to indicate other misguided interpretations, but this would be unwarrantedly captious: the play calls for the most careful staging and that requires many months of meticulous rehearsal. What this and other non-Russian productions. I have seen most crucially lack is a quality of soulfulness which makes even a life of dismal failure take on a dignity and grandeur beyond its pettiest pains. It is a quality often found in Russian (and Negro) folk melodies.

Gloria Foster as Ranevskaya plays in a muted key which lends a special warmth to her performance. Ellen Holly as Ranevskaya's adopted daughter, Varya, who desires but misses marriage to Lopahin, is touching. Earle Hyman makes a sympathetically fragile Gayev. Robert Jackson brings an unusual eloquence to the role of Trofimov. Suzanne Johnson is pretty and sweet as Anya, and James Earl Jones is an excellently ingratiating Lopahin.

—NAT, 29 Jan. '73

ENDGAME

Beckett's *Endgame* is neither tragedy nor comedy. It is too devastatingly bleak for comedy; it mocks itself too much for tragedy. It is a heartbroken chuckle in an infernal cave. Beckett is entirely modern and yet fits into no category except perhaps that of certain early medieval scribes.

If Beckett were less contemporary he might have called his play "World's End." In the gray region where his piece takes place "nothing stirs" but the remnants of three men and a woman. When the earth is viewed through a telescope it is "corpsed." "And the sea the same." Inside the breast of Hamm, the play's central personage, is a "big sore." Life has ebbed away and to the anguished cry, "What's happening?" the brainwashed answer is—as in *Waiting for Godot*—"Something is taking its course." Life is forever going on, but we do not know exactly what it is.

Mankind has been reduced to those who cannot stand—the masters; and those who cannot sit—the servitors. And then there are the legless parents on the dump heaps. Hamm has a father whom he calls "accursed progenitor." What keeps humanity going? Beckett's brilliant answer is "The dialogue." How do we know we're alive? We cry. One asks the other, "Did you ever have an instant

of happiness?" The reply is, "Not to my knowledge." What life there is proceeds along "the same insanities." And "we do what we can." It appears that isn't much. No, *Endgame* isn't comedy.

There is pathos in it, and, remotely, a plea, a hope. "Ah, yesterday"; "formerly" things were easier, better. Does Beckett mean that, or is it another of his ironies, a jibe at the sentimentality of nostalgia? (This note is struck also in *Godot*.) We are not wise enough, Beckett implies, to deal with the dismal riddle of the universe. "Imagine," he has Hamm say, "if a rational being came back to earth, wouldn't he be able to get ideas into his head if he observed us long enough?" Is a savior (a "Godot") then possible? But he is not God: "The bastard! He doesn't exist!"

For all his severity, Beckett, like Hamm, has a "heart in his head." That is what makes him moving; also why he (and we) cannot be entirely rational. For a head without a heart is lifeless, and in life we must suffer. The only way this can be mitigated is to know and accept it. Beckett's plays are the dramatization of the perennial struggle which causes us to storm against our sufferings and to find some inner or supernal way of relieving them. *Endgame* is not a declaration of total negativism; it may be drama of resistance to that state. If Beckett's nihilism were his "last word" we should be obliged to question his intelligence and conclude that his is an unnatural wisdom. For my part, I welcome the chaos into which we are all plunged and I believe it our task courageously to forge paths within it. Beckett is doing that—by writing plays bodying forth the terrible trials involved in the effort.

Though I prefer *Waiting for Godot*, I consider *Endgame* a masterpiece. (I did not fully realize this when I saw its original 1957 production in Paris.) It is a complete theatre statement of a consummate poet's experience. Its writing is endowed with a marvelous musicality which, while mordant, is graced by subtle repetition and thematic variations.

"Nothing is funnier than unhappiness," is one of the *Endgame* lines. This may have served André

Gregory as a warrant for his treatment of the play. He has jazzed it up. Unlike Roger Blin's Paris production (*Endgame* is dedicated to that actor-director), Gregory's is done under bright lights. The speech, the tempos, the stage business are pop American. Everything is forcefully projected and italicized by incessant by-play or stage business. It is nearly all set in a single key, at the sacrifice of the mood and modulation of Beckett's writing. I am at present somewhat at a loss to define my impression. That the production is not what Beckett envisaged, I am certain. But no matter! Only those who have never before seen the play can say what Gregory's production means to them—that is, whether it makes sense and, if so, what sort of sense? What I have attempted here is to convey what the script contains and my reaction to it.

—*NAT*, 26 Feb. '73

MACBETT

About his *Macbett*, which is now being given at the Yale Repertory Theatre in New Haven, Ionesco writes that he spells the title "with two t's, so it wouldn't be confused with the play by Shakespeare, which I expect many people know." It is also possible that his (Ionesco's) spelling corresponds to the French pronunciation of the play's original name.

The intention of this most recent of Ionesco's pieces is, in his own words, to show "straightforward and honest revolutionaries [becoming] tyrants, dictators, assassins....So it is the problem of power, ambition and action which is evil, that I am discussing in this play. All dictators become paranoiacs. The world will be peaceful only when we are no longer ruled by the state, that is, by other men. Never have I written about such sinister themes with so much pleasure."

The play has nothing to do with "Watergate"! Still I fancy that some of the young people who see

it in New Haven must find a parallel, as French youth undoubtedly related it to de Gaulle. I have quoted Ionesco's little "foreword" to indicate the element of quirky playfulness, a charming fuzziness of thought and deliberate inconsequentiality, combined with a deadpan irony, which characterize much of his writing.

Ionesco works within a narrow range of ideas. In fact, he does not care about ideas as instruments for use in the conduct or interpretation of life. His "ideas" mirror a mood or an attitude of oppressed bafflement in the face of the impenetrable mystery of existence, especially in its contemporary phases. He holds no hope of a solution, he offers no remedial source of alleviation. Instead he has given himself, in surrender, to playing games. All his plays, including *Macbett*, are comedies. Yet there is nearly always a touch of melancholy in them. The melancholy results from his resignation, his inability and unwillingness to contend with the universal dilemma. Despair takes refuge in wry jokes.

Ionesco's plays are especially notable for his feeling for farce and his theatrical inventiveness. The limited range of his themes—he commands only two or three—is compensated for by the many shapes and twists he is able to give them. His many variations always work; they surprise, arrest and amuse. Sometimes they touch us too. For Ionesco is neither petty nor malicious; his is an essentially benevolent nature. He yearns above all for freedom; he knows it isn't to be found, not, at least, in the childlike, almost infantile mode he imagines. So he spins fantasies and devises quaint yarns wrought from his sense of loss, which relieve him and in a way console us who are in a similar quandary.

Within the fun one often hears a note of anxiety. Though there is something tart and mischievous in Ionesco's humor, even at moments a touch of the macabre and frightening, the whole of his work breathes a pathos which is at the core of its subjective origin. The hard edge of the French Existentialist posture, its acid anguish, is lightened and softened in Ionesco—of Romanian birth and background—resolving itself in a colorful game consisting of tall tales for the stage. It is through a play-booth prankishness that Ionesco's theatre lives. In this realm he is a poet I find sympathetic as well as deft. He is certainly much simpler than his own or other people's explications would lead us to believe.

There is little point in listing all the ways *Macbett* transforms its Elizabethan model. It is Lady Duncan, in Ionesco's play, who tempts Macbett to murder her cowardly, imbecile husband. She and her lady-in-waiting are the weird sisters. Banco is Macbett's fellow conspirator. Fragments of the war episodes become hilarious vignettes, very close to vaudeville turns. Inflated descriptions of bloody battle which are repeated verbatim by two different "sick" characters—Glamis and Candor—produce oddly comic—quasi-Rabelaisian—effect. The banquet scene becomes a lampoon of conformity and court servility in which the participants and the king (Macbett) himself break into operatic parody. When Macbett is finally knocked off, it is Lady Duncan (now presumed to be Lady Macbett) with her accomplice, the lady-in-waiting, who do the job. Banco's son, hight Macol, replaces Macbett as ruler. He promises to be more tyrannically homicidal than any of those who have preceded him.

The Yale company—Alvin Epstein, Eugene Troobnick, Stephen Joyce in the "leads"—is well suited to the improvisatory and burlesque manner of the play. One does not mind certain crudities: after all, the show is a charade. And the director-actors—William Peters, John McAndrew and Alvin Epstein—move the play at a larkish pace and have added some good gags of their own to the text.

—*NAT*, 28 May '73

ROMBERG 1887–1951

A Broadway gag years ago had it that "the sun never sets on *The Student Prince*." Not long after its opening in New York on December 2, 1924, for a run of 608 performances, nine *Student Prince* companies were touring the country. It has had numerous revivals since then and its songs have never been forgotten. This despite the "competition" of other forms of popular music—jazz, boogie-woogie, rock. What is the explanation for *The Student Prince*'s longevity? To answer this we should know something of its composer's history.

Sigmund Romberg was born in 1887 in a small town in Hungary when it was part of Franz Josef's Austro-Hungarian empire. His father was a cultivated man, conversant with many languages, an amateur pianist and composer. His mother wrote and published several short stories. Sigmund's parents wanted him to study engineering, but he, who had begun playing the violin at the age of six and was admitted as a member of his school orchestra when he was ten (and had also learned to play the piano), dreamed of other things. He was obliged to conform to his parents' wishes. He prepared himself for an engineering career, first in his native town, and between the ages of eighteen and twenty-two, in Vienna.

In the waltz-saturated city when Gustav Mahler was the chief conductor at the imperial Opera House and Bruno Walter his assistant, Romberg began to study composition "on the side." Vienna was then not only the gay capital of which Johann Strauss was the "patron saint," but also a flourishing theatre center. Romberg's love of music—especially waltz music and gypsy rhythms—was coupled with and heightened by an infatuation with the stage.

In 1909 Romberg arrived in America with three hundred dollars for what was planned as a brief visit. It was intended to heal the rift with his father who insisted that his son abandon the idea of becoming a musician. He settled in the Bronx, then a wilderness. The three hundred dollars were soon spent—mostly in theatregoing. Romberg got himself a job at seven dollars a week wrapping pencils. He gave this up when he was hired as a pianist at the Café Continental on Second Avenue at fifteen dollars a week. He improved his situation by playing harmonium at Pabst-Harlem restaurant on West 125th St. which paid him first thirty dollars a week and later, forty-five. He learned a good deal at this job by plugging songs for neophyte tunesmiths. One of these was a skinny fellow who asked him to play *Alexander's Ragtime Band*; his name was Irving Berlin.

Romberg did not soon return to his folks in Hungary. In 1912 he applied for American citizenship. For a while after that he conducted his own orchestra in a super-elegant restaurant on 39th Street just off Broadway where he introduced dancing, an exercise not considered quite the thing for the clients of a fashionable dining place. His salary had risen to a hundred and fifty a week.

Romberg's first Broadway musical was produced at the Winter Garden on January 10, 1914 and had 161 performances. He was then twenty-seven. He was never to stop working after that; but one cannot describe his progress as meteoric—not at least in his view. He wrote music for fifteen productions in the course of twenty-two months. Many of these were Winter Garden revues which were called (and indeed were) *Passing Shows*. The snooty dubbed him a "Shubert hack." Though in 1917 he achieved some success with *Maytime* and wrote a number of memorable melodies, which added to his reputation by adapting Franz Schubert's music for *Blossom Time* in 1921, it was not till 1924 with *The Student Prince* that Romberg struck musical gold and became a big name in his own right.

After that, *Desert Song*, another fabulous and virtually "universal" hit in 1927 might be designated as the high point of Romberg's career. But as late as 1945 he contributed a charming score to *Up in Central Park*, a musical about New York in the

heyday of Tammany Hall. All in all the list of Romberg's musicals mounts to the staggering number of sixty-seven, and the songs written for them cover two columns of eighteen book-size pages. We need not supplement this record with an account of Romberg's ventures in radio, film, concert tours, foreign productions and appearances with the Philadelphia orchestra and with his own orchestra at Carnegie Hall.

There is a certain "mystery" in this tale. It relates to the fact that Romberg's music came to prominence at a time when it must have struck people familiar with the shows of Irving Berlin, George Gershwin, Cole Porter and Richard Rodgers as "old-fashioned." But it was just because it was old-fashioned that Romberg's music was so successful. When Romberg's producer J.J. Shubert found the audience at the try-out of *The Student Prince* indifferent to it, he wanted to remove one of its most beloved numbers, *Serenade*, because it was too "Metropolitan Opera House." And indeed compared to what had then begun to be written and was to continue being written, Romberg's music had about it an air of reminiscence: it recalls calmer and more fragrant landscapes than those of the hectic twenties and the years which followed.

In an epoch of jitters and rattle, love songs which verge on fainting spells, references to one's heart in a dying fall, expressions of devotion to one's girl friend through gifts of flowers and candy, carousels voiced in drinking songs without drunkenness, nostalgia for romance and young dreams could not but soothe the souls of folk not altogether satisfied by feverish movement and brash sound. Romberg's tunes sneaked in on one's unspoken yearning for idealistic aspiration, for tenderness and, amidst so much contemporary coarseness, for something which we might call "princely," though it is only another word for handsome *dignity*.

We recognize the influence in Romberg's music of Strauss and Lehar, touches of Bizet, Mascagni, Leoncavallo and Puccini. But all these borrowings from Europe are scented and lightened by the youthful geniality of our American environment in a bygone era. Listen in repose to the pattern set by such numbers as the ever-attractive *Deep in My Heart, Dear*: it is an echo of the golden days of the regretted past. The music sinks down somewhere below the solar plexus, gathers inspiration there, then rises for a longed-for ecstasy and sinks back for another scoop of sentiment, then to smooth itself out in the lilt of a waltz.

To those who might at present consider themselves too hip for Romberg's innocence, one can only say: put aside the cosmetic of your recently acquired smartness and enjoy, enjoy!

—*STGB*, '73

A MOON FOR THE MISBEGOTTEN

To say that *A Moon for the Misbegotten* is the best production of the best play of the season is to say very little. One might ask why it has taken so long for the reviewers and the public to recognize its unique distinction in O'Neill's work. For the play, written in 1943, failed dismally at its tryout tour under the Theatre Guild's auspices in 1947 and was still held weak when it was done on Broadway in the spring of 1957 with Wendy Hiller, Franchot Tone and Cyril Cusack. It achieved acceptance in its revival at the (old) Circle-in-the-Square in 1968, but only now at the Morosco Theatre has it become an unqualified success.

The play's initial failure was to some degree the fault of its author and producers. They insisted that the girl in the play, Josie Hogan, be acted by someone of Irish blood who is "almost a freak—five foot eleven in her stockings and weighs around one hundred eighty." These physical attributes were considered so important that the actress who played the role—tall, but not heavy enough—was asked to sign a contract which read "the artist agrees to gain the necessary weight

required for the role." This stupid and horrible clause may very well have led to the actress' death shortly after the play's production. None of the actresses who played it subsequently answered the playwright's description of the character's size nor were they, as far as I know or as anyone could tell, Irish.

Both Wendy Hiller and Salome Jens are good actresses, but the productions in which they were cast were either not successful or only partially so. I am rather pleased to relate that Colleen Dewhurst, now in the role, was asked to play it for me while she was still a beginner, in one of my private classes, before I had ever seen the play. She played it in Spoleto (Italy) during one of its summer festivals which, for all her suitability to the part, was not enough to render that production impressive. In such a play the entire cast, its direction and the spirit of the whole must be coherent, unified. A play on the stage is not a good play simply because it may be one in its text. Theatre is something different from literature. It may be more or less, but is not the same.

The historian Henry Steele Commager, writing about O'Neill, complained that he was obsessed by sex—and he was not the only one to do so. (As a joke, I once said that since there are only three or four things a person can be obsessed by, sex obsession might be considered as good as any of them.) But the truth is that O'Neill was ambivalent in the matter—it could be maintained with sufficient evidence that he had a certain horror of it. *A Moon for the Misbegotten* is a love story—almost the only one O'Neill ever wrote. Because it is that, *sex* occupies a peculiarly oblique role in it.

The love story in this play is a thwarted one. Yet that, in a certain sense, (O'Neill's sense) is one of the reasons why the love is realized. For the two people involved are "misbegotten." Josie Hogan believes herself unattractive because she is physically lumpy and perhaps even more because she is the daughter of a widowed and indigent farmer, working unyielding soil in a vicinity where the neighboring males are louts. She is ashamed of her condition and tries to mask it by pretending to a promiscuity which her natural fineness and pride shun. She is in fact a virgin. Old man Hogan understands Josie's plight and goes along with her game, while he sorrows over it. With all his being, he wishes that she may find a good man whom she might love and who would love her.

James Tyrone, Jr. is such a man, but he too is "misbegotten." He is an actor's son, morbidly attached to his now dead mother; his father's profession and person both alienate him, to the degree that he has become an alcoholic who finds little gratification in life except through the frequenting of "Broadway tarts." His experience with these creatures makes him regard sex as dirty. In Josie, he finds purity, the maternal tenderness, the loving sensibility which reaches out to comfort him in his hurt.

Their love is a "moon"—a romance, an ideal, a dream, the opposite of a reality by which they might live. Thus, they cannot consummate a union of the flesh. The perfection of love to which they both aspire is impossible for them: he is too far gone in self-abasement, in his death-in-life; she perceives that the last remnant of his manhood resides in his enraptured regard for her and that she must forgo any expectation of redemption for him. Yet in their momentary contact they fulfill something of their dream by knowing they have experienced love in their one ecstatic and fleeting moment of mutual recognition. She knows that in a special way she has been truly loved; he knows that selfless love is possible, and what he desires even more, forgiveness, which he had never believed would be vouchsafed him.

What makes the play so absorbing and affecting is that O'Neill, without preachment or turgid poetizing, has poured into it all the ache of his confusion, all his drive toward perfection. He longed for the "absolute" in everything, strove toward it wildly, felt his inadequacies for achieving it and understood that only in his impassioned reaching for it did he attain the stature he hoped for.

O'Neill said his plays dealt with man's relation to God; what he meant was that he was concerned with purity, a life without taint or compromise. His weakness in confrontation with the circumstances of his own existence made him feel disgraced in his own eyes, so that all that remained to him was to pray for forgiveness as he himself, after his long day's journey into night, managed to forgive those who he imagined, despite himself, were responsible for his failings and wounds.

There is an affinity in Jason Robards with O'Neill's spirit. That is why he has reached the apogee of his career here in the role of James Tyrone, Jr. He was a perfect Hickey in *The Iceman Cometh*, admirable as the same but younger James Tyrone, Jr. in *Long Day's Journey*; but Hickey is limited compared to Tyrone in *The Moon*, and the junior Tyrone of O'Neill's masterpiece is caught within the complexities of that play's other personages. In *The Moon*, James, Jr. is both subjectively and objectively essentialized. Objectively, he is O'Neill's brother; subjectively, he is O'Neill himself. (One wonders if O'Neill realized this.) And Robards is able, through inner motives and analogy, to convey the cracked vessel that is Tyrone, Jr. Robards' voice, with its buried sob and its suppressed laughter, its drunken despair so close to cynicism, its Broadway randyness and its shamefaced apology, the "hamminess" of it all, together with its humanity, go to the heart of O'Neill's creation. Robards and James Tyrone, Jr. are one.

Colleen Dewhurst brings a powerful womanliness to the part of Josie. She is of the earth, warm and hearty. She looks and sounds a person who can do her own and her father's hard work; one, moreover, who possesses the vast sexuality she boasts of, as well as a woman chaste through the very force of that sexuality.

The play begins as comedy—very old-fashioned comedy at that—and it is an aspect which could mislead an audience into expecting something other than what follows and which therefore doesn't often come across as part of the play's deeply affectionate quality. In Edward Flanders' performance, dryly understated yet sharply indicative of stout fiber, bereftness, sorry slyness and fatherly devotion, Hogan becomes, for the first time, wholly alive and integral to the play's texture and scheme.

José Quintero's direction is his best. The play flows in easy and precise rhythm. There is no impediment, wasted movement or ponderousness in it. Without being "stylized," it is free of petty realism and without rhetorical inflation, rises to its own inherent grandeur. The direction is well aided by Ben Edwards' setting and lighting, which combine poetic theatricality with the specificity of the play's environment.

A Moon for the Misbegotten has at last become a wonderful evening in the theatre.

—*NAT*, 19 Jan. '74

RICHARD II
MEASURE FOR MEASURE

The difficulty in judging a production of a Shakespeare play is that we know either too little or too much about it before seeing it. If it is one of the "histories," we are confused by information and charts culled from the program which graph the intricate family relationships within the royal lineage. Then, too, there are many contradictory critical essays. We may have also seen a number of earlier productions which set up preconceptions. What is more confounding still is that if we read the play before or after seeing it, we find it not readily "decipherable," apart from the beauty of the verse, as literature.

All these hazards beset me when I came upon the Royal Shakespeare Company's *Richard II*, now being shown at the Brooklyn Academy of Music. For this reason, I shall merely summarize what I specifically observed in it, without much reference to my previous acquaintance with the play as text or theatre event.

On the stage, two long flights of steps of silvery hue lead to the upper playing level. These are placed on either side of the main stage space. They may be said to have a symbolic significance: they are the two paths followed by the play's principal antagonists, King Richard and Henry Bolingbroke. They give the setting a distinctly "modern" look; they resemble department store escalators.

The upper stage descends and ascends from time to time, like a lift, effecting a certain visual excitement. Potted plants at the far right and the far left represent a garden; a bit of earth on the forestage, the English soil. The colors throughout, except for the royal robes and crown of gold, are a dull brown or black, with occasional bursts of gleaming white in the costumes. Though I looked upon this chromatic scheme with approval at the start, it soon tends to monotony.

John Barton, the company's Shakespeare scholar, who serves here as the play's director, quite clearly means the production to illustrate what Jan Kott has called the "great machine" of history or politics. At the end of the play, after Bolingbroke (now mounted on the throne as Henry IV) has taken on the robes of his position and expressed his intention to journey to Jerusalem in expiation for his role in Richard's murder, he turns back to us and we see his face or mask transformed into a skeletal death's head.

There are other bits of business which excite momentary pleasure. When, for example, Richard is shot by one of Bolingbroke's crossbowmen, he is hoisted into the air by the chains which bind him, and swings before us in the posture of crucifixion. Another typical moment: Richard, after looking at himself in a mirror, does not simply hurl it down but breaks it by thrusting his head through the glass.

But in this, as in nearly all theatre, the crucial element is the quality of the acting and, still more important, the interpretation of the roles. Ian Richardson and Richard Pasco play Richard II and Bolingbroke respectively. (Both are good actors.) On certain evenings, they switch their assignments—to demonstrate, the director explains, that both represent two sides of the identical royal coin: each in different modes is equally reprehensible, equally pathetic. To make this aspect of the "history" clear, a scene from Henry IV, Part II ("Uneasy lies the head that wears a crown") has been redundantly interpolated.

I saw the play with Ian Richardson as Richard. He played him in a manner which strictly adhered to the director's production idea—as an insincere, prating politico and absolute ruler. No matter how lofty his verbiage, one could see that the character means much less than he says. Bolingbroke, on the other hand, was matter of fact, hard and much more credible, though he also must be accounted crafty and devious.

This reading of Richard is troublesome; for in his fall he becomes an increasingly moving figure, and his words—in some of the most beautiful lines Shakespeare ever wrote—should not fail to go to one's heart, but on this occasion I was not touched by them. The two aspects of Richard's character were not shaped into a whole. Just as Lear is a fatuously innocent and primitive creature who grows ever closer to us as he suffers humiliation, so Richard, I take it, is at first a vain, self-infatuated young sovereign who believes in his divine right. On no account must he be viewed as a fraud—as historically he may have been, and as he is here played. For in that case, he cannot possibly enlist the sympathy his lines are unmistakably intended to evoke.

W. B. Yeats has spoken of Richard as an artist, a sort of narcissistic Hamlet. And as we all know, many persons of "artistic" disposition make rotten statesmen. That does not mean they are hypocrites. Shakespeare undoubtedly harbored grave misgivings about political leaders, but being of his time (not ours!) he shared some of his countrymen's regard for royalty and portrayed a number of virtuous princes and kings.

In other words, Shakespeare's Richard is much more humanly complex than we in our facile iconoclasm are quick to understand. The "showing up" (or denigration) of Richard, Bolingbroke and the others of their court in the Royal Shakespeare Company's production robs the play of its poetry, of its pathos, of its subtlety and deep pain. It has flattened the insights of a profound creator to something like a poster. There is a certain "modernism" which arrives at "truth" by emptying experience of most of its content, its flesh-and-blood reality.

What may be overlooked in a description of such a production as this Richard is that many of its lines as spoken are unintelligible. Some may say that this is to be ascribed to the acoustics of the Brooklyn Academy, a hall larger than the Aldwych Theatre in London, where the production is usually given. But I sat close to the stage and yet missed a good deal of what was said. Most of the company's actors, having been instructed in a technique designed to create chest tones of velvet and oil ("piped-in voices"), do not command a truly *dramatic* speech naturally responsive to the ebb and flow of genuine feeling. Many of them sound as though they were "reciting," though they know they shouldn't and don't wish to.

The old-fashioned "emotionalism" of Tony Church's John of Gaunt is more telling than the vocalization in several of the longer roles. The cold acid of Clement McCallin's treacherous Northumberland drives an unerring shaft through the proceedings. He is properly dry, but this should not apply to the production as a whole, which I'm afraid it does. And certain short scenes are wretchedly acted.

I understood every word of *Measure for Measure* in John Houseman's production with the City Center Acting Company. In this regard, as well as in movement, the actors have been well trained. They achieve their distinct articulation by speaking somewhat more deliberately than is perhaps "normal." But it *is* a pleasure to hear what Shakespeare wrote!

In the company's treatment of *Measure for Measure*, the play is transformed from a "black" comedy into a cute one. Perhaps this befits the American youthfulness of its players. In its present stage of development, the company appears too dependent on its directors—which may be the directors' fault. I speak not only of *Measure for Measure* but of the two other production I saw: *The Three Sisters* and *Beggar's Opera*. It is time for the actors to be allowed greater freedom, more breathing room. They often seem to be toeing a prescribed line, and that makes them seem like "beginners." Their productions might be more advantageously seen in other than a large Broadway house. but they are an *ensemble*—which is very much in their favor. I hope I cause it not hurt by saying that David Ogden Stiers now seems the "ripest" in the company. His Kulygin in *The Three Sisters* is one of the best I've seen.

—*NAT*, 26 Jan. '74

CLARENCE DARROW

Clarence Darrow, programmed as "a new play by David W. Rintels," isn't one—unless you accept the thesis that anything with live actors which interests an audience is a play. But play or not, Henry Fonda, speaking on the stage of the Helen Hayes Theatre as the legendary lawyer, Clarence Darrow, is well worth listening to.

I call Darrow "legendary" though he was a real enough figure. Some may not know of his 1894 connection with Eugene V. Debs (several times Socialist Party candidate for the Presidency) or with Peter Altgeld, from 1893 to 1897 the great liberal Governor of Illinois. More theatregoers may remember that Darrow served as attorney in 1924 for Leopold and Loeb, the two Chicago boys who committed a "perfect" crime to prove their superman intelligence. By introducing a quasi-Freudian interpretation of perverted mentality into the case, Darrow saved the two from execution. Perhaps even more vividly recalled is the absurdly notorious Scopes (or monkey-trial) case in 1925 at which Darrow knocked William Jennings Bryan's Fundamentalism into a cocked hat. Darrow died in 1938 at the age of 81. We were reminded of him in

1955 through Lawrence and Lee's dramatization of the Scopes trial, *Inherit the Wind*, in which Paul Muni and later Melvyn Douglas starred on stage and Spencer Tracy in the film.

Darrow was nearly always the defender of those who through bigotry were socially unpopular: the poor, the black, Anarchists, Communists—all, in brief, commonly designated as "the underdog." None of the more than 100 alleged murderers whom he defended was ever sentenced to death. He was opposed to capital punishment.

Yet though most of the audiences who will attend the Henry Fonda performances will have some knowledge of these facts (at least by hearsay) I still think of Darrow as a figure of legend. Now that his battles are more or less won, it is easy to agree that Darrow's ideas, actions and career were admirable, but what is far more crucial for us to understand at present is not the history of his achievement but its *spirit*. It can hardly be said of it—as of John Brown's body—that it goes marching on.

Darrow's liberalism was a grass-roots force. It was at once trusting and skeptical, gentle and gruff—traits characteristic of people close to the soil who had to work doggedly to make it flourish. Theirs was an active liberalism, not an academic posture, a matter of benevolent verbiage. It was tough, resistant, vigilant, and it produced a plain and powerful breed of men.

The educated among them, like Darrow and Lincoln, were largely self-taught. Their speech had a simple, rugged yet lofty eloquence consonant with the arduous tasks and goals that lay before them. With it all went a homely and not infrequently salty humor bred of a realization of the limitations of human capacities.

An agnostic, Darrow was nevertheless a man of faith, and his court addresses rang out with a noble common sense based on a direct experience of the basic phenomena of existence. That is why they moved juries to just decisions, even against their selfish interests.

We do not have to agree with Darrow that there is no such thing as crime; we are not obliged to acquiesce in the belief that man is fundamentally "good" or perfectible (many keen minds have held contrary views), but we are convinced, as we listen to Darrow, that we ourselves become better people and incidentally more truly American in sharing his beliefs. That is why, though *Clarence Darrow* is not a play or theatre or art, one still relates to it heartily.

Henry Fonda is the right actor to deliver Darrow's message, which I would not call a "performance." There is no elaborate characterization, no great elocutionary passion, no effort to tug at heartstrings. We are faced with the essential matter at stake: we are placed in a position to reflect, to think, to judge. And since virtually every word spoken is Darrow's, it is enough.

—*NAT*, 13 Apr. '74

JUMPERS

The seeming contradiction in my review of Tom Stoppard's *Jumpers* last week may require further elucidation. I called it "an exceptional and superior entertainment," while also saying that I could not take Stoppard seriously as an important dramatist. *Jumpers* is superior by virtue of felicitous wit and its cleverness in making bright stage fare of its ideological content. But it fails to turn its material into true drama; its point or "thesis" is not revealed through action: it is only *stated*. There is no basic confrontation, conflict or delineation of real characters. What keeps the show going, apart from the amusing "mask" of the author's spokesman and his brilliant verbiage, is mere window dressing: acrobatics, pastiche mystery melodrama and dollops of nudity.

The intellectual substance of the play hardly ever challenges one's mind, nor is it made emotionally penetrating. What, in sum, does the play tell us? As against the so-called "radical-liberals" of Stoppard's invention we are told that God exists. "*Cogito, ergo Deus est*," Stoppard's professor says. I am pleased that he takes this positive position at a time when most drama and literature are hell-bent on negation. But to assert rather than to make manifest God's existence is to go no further than does any sensible humanist, not specifically a "believer." There is more of God in the tragi-comedies of Chekhov, in the murk of Gorky's *Lower Depths*, even in Beckett's bleak despair or in Shaw's cheerfulness than in all Stoppard's literary exercises.

I might also ask what a faith in God's existence makes us do, know or experience that any good person cannot do, know or experience without such faith. What does Stoppard's moral philosopher, George Moore, tell us has happened to him or will happen to us—what change is wrought in him or us—as a result of his recognition of God's being? Or perhaps *Jumpers* is only another bit of Stoppard's irony, meant to show the absurdity of trying to prove God's existence.

I do not pose these questions to suggest any philosophic antagonism to Stoppard's views and certainly not from any "liberal-radical" bias against a belief in God. I am bringing up a matter of theatre criticism and theatre critics. They write chiefly about effects—of laughter, thrills, fine language, prettiness, etc., etc.—with very little reference to the roots, causes, intents and consequences of these effects. If a play is presumed to have a genuine intellectual import, then one would suppose that intellectual discussion—expository, corrective, adverse or supportive—was called for. But that is usually considered outside the province of theatre criticism, which is what makes so much of our criticism and our theatregoing provincial and fruitless.

—*NAT*, 18 May '74

WORDS AND MUSIC
WILL ROGERS

It has surely been apparent to readers of *The Nation* that I regard the theatre as my way—or one of my ways—of gaining insight into the state of the world. It must also have become clear that, apart from such revivals as *A Moon for the Misbegotten* and certain foreign pieces, few new American plays this season have significantly served my search. They are *Boom Boom Room*, *Creeps*, *My Sister, My Sister* and *Short Eyes*.

But on the whole I found the season rather dry. Other presentations only obliquely "theatre" have provided me with further occasions for speculation.

Words and Music and *Will Rogers' U.S.A.*, apart from the affable entertainment they offer, strike me as worth discussion as Americana. The "words" of the first of these are by Sammy Kahn, who is central to the evening. Kahn has written lyrics a list of whose titles would fill a column. These were composed to tunes by Jule Styne, Jan Van Heusen and many others; among Kahn's many hits, the best known perhaps were *Three Coins in a Fountain*, *Bei Mir Bist Du Schön*, and *Call Me Irresponsible*. In the course of the evening Kahn sings a number of these songs with no apologies for his voice (Kelly Garrett is on hand for the really tough scores) and tells many jolly stories about the circumstances connected with their writing. As narrator, Kahn is wholly engaging, in the manner of a peppy dinner guest or a table companion at one of Broadway's or Hollywood's expensive but "homey" eateries.

Like many show-biz lyricists and composers, Kahn is an East Side Jew; once very poor and now very rich. His approach to his work is frankly commercial, which does not necessarily diminish its merit. He boasts of his success; there is no offense in this, since making money in our society is, generally speaking, a sign of virtue and a proof of excellence. All through the evening I had the impression that behind the words and music, I heard the satisfied tinkling of a cash register.

There is honesty in the man, the honesty of one whose whole nature and practice is in accord with the environment in which he lives: the world of mass entertainment which runs in a swift flight from Times Square to Sunset Boulevard. There is never a dissonant note of differentiating personal-ity, of eccentric stress or insistence on the specifically individual. There is in him a spirit of friendliness, of conviviality, a nudging intimacy among like-minded men and women who are successful or who regard success and prosperity with all their perquisites as the universally agreed-upon American goal.

There is no shadow of doubt here. "Is everybody happy?" The question need hardly be put, since it might suggest that some aren't. This is the popular mainstream. It offers many benefits; it contains certain unmentionable dangers. It is largely reassuring and, though I smiled throughout the evening, I could not quell a slight uneasiness—I almost said queasiness—somewhere within me.

Will Rogers' U.S.A. might be considered the polar opposite of the spirit evident in *Words and Music*. Will Rogers (very agreeably projected by James Whitmore, who gains a good deal from the adaptation of Rogers' spiels made by Paul Shyre, who also directed the actor with modest discretion), Will Rogers, I say, was a semi-literate "critic" of our civilization. Born in the Indian Territory in 1879 (he died in 1935) and himself part Indian, he was wholly American, but at the same time, because of his background, somewhat askew of the main current of our native push and hurrah. A "cowboy," there was something of "Mr. Dooley" and even a little of Mark Twain in him; something, too, of the cracker-barrel philosopher who frequently in our history has added salt and yeast to the dough of widespread complacency.

There is plenty to arouse laughter in the collection of quips and jokes. What is especially valuable in most of them is the parallel they offer to the condition we are in at present. The short-sightedness, skullduggery and downright stupidity of much of our political life, plus the intellectual innocence and plain ignorance characteristic of public attitudes which support social and governmental fraud, were the main targets of Rogers' seemingly off-hand remarks. The audience applauds and in doing so feels itself absolved from any further commitment or action.

It is no doubt salutary for social criticism to be couched in humor. It may lead to further reflection, to study and to judgment, rather than to mere noisy sloganizing and objurgation. But there was another side of Rogers' joshing, something endemically American. We are a nation of good-natured cusses. We are not used to rocking the boat; we are confirmed kidders. Kidding, so we imagine, will blow trouble away; we hope we can laugh sin out of court. For all his acute sense of the national diseases, Rogers as professional entertainer kept assuring us that we are, after all, O.K., a wonderful nation, and that he never met a man he didn't like. This benevolent anarchism is sympathetic, but does it not in the end lead to social and political passivity, to something less than valor? It may even turn in times of sharp distress to a limp or even corrupt pessimism.

Perhaps I exaggerate. To a degree my reaction to the show, at which I had a good time, is due to Whitmore's grinning much more and differently than Rogers himself ever did. There was something insinuating in Rogers' smile. Since he underscored his remarks by casually enacted rope and lariat tricks, which moderated the pace of his delivery (Whitmore only "plays" at these exercises), Rogers took more time to allow his comments to sink in and thus made them more meaningful.

But the deeper reason, I believe, that such popular community critics as Rogers do not have more incisive effect on us is that America has been and still remains a wealthy country. So long as that is the case, our complaints will be muffled in a habitual and seemingly obligatory hilarity.

—*NAT*, 25 May '74

THE FROGS

The most gratifying aspect of the Yale Repertory Theatre production of Aristophanes' *The Frogs*, as adapted and directed by Burt Shevelove with music and lyrics by Stephen Sondheim, was *physical*. During its first thirty minutes I was ready to cry out like a "regular" reviewer: "Sheer delight…smashing…a hit, etc., etc."

Here, I was going to say, is the latest thing: multi-media theatre (which is, of course, at least 2,000 years old); dialogue in prose and verse, music, choral speech and song added to natation in the large pool of the Payne-Whitney Gymnasium at Yale. The entry of twenty-four splendid swimmers—the "frogs"—was truly joyous. Gliding through the waters of the Styx, their bodies described lovely patterns as they accompanied—gaily mocking—frightened Dionysus on his expedition to the blessed and damned in Hades. Sixteen hundred spectators roared their pleasure at this hilarious festivity.

What followed was, on the whole something of a letdown. Aristophanes' comedy is an aesthetic and political jape of propagandistic intent. (Athens was engaged in a fatal war at the time of its writing.) The Shevelove adaptation eschews politics entirely and is weak in its literary phase. In the original, the main situation centers on a debate between Aeschylus and Euripides, which was doubly meaningful to the audience of 405 B.C. because the two dramatists represented not only differences of style but differences of moral and social attitudes. At Yale, the confrontation was one between Shakespeare and Shaw, and all they did was exchange contrary (sometimes insulting) quotations from their writings that were not particularly relevant at the moment to any essential issue.

Larry Blyden's relaxed manner, good nature and coy brightness made him a most engaging Dionysus. He was always intelligible, as were Michael Vale as his slave; Alvin Epstein, grotesquely funny as the guard at Hades' portals; handsome Dan Desmond as Herakles, and Ron Recasner, who spoke the introduction to the *parabasis* with winning elegance. An added asset was Carmen de Lavallade's ravishing physique.

Balancing the pros and cons, which include several college-oriented jokes, a few Broadway-tinged ribaldries (by no means as pointed as those in Aristophanes) and, to repeat, the marvelous corps of swimmers, this production, perhaps the most ambitious the Yale Repertory Theatre has undertaken, turned out to be an event which the company may properly regard as earning congratulation.

—*NAT*, 15 June '74

OVERNIGHT

U.R.G.E.N.T. (Universal Relevance Group Enterprise in a National Theatre) under the direction of Ronald Muchnick and Nathan George is an organization devoted to the production of worthwhile plays—new and old. The group occupies the 15th floor of an office building at 151 West 46 Street. It is a pleasant space.

Among the plays produced there was Ray Aranha's absorbing *My Sister, My Sister*, which subsequently moved to Broadway. U.R.G.E.N.T. initiated its activities two years ago with a revival of William Inge's *Natural Affection* which in its 1963 production at the Booth Theatre met with a harsh press reception and consequently suffered a short-lived run there. Though no doubt faulty, it deserved a better fate. Now U.R.G.E.N.T., for the first time, is showing one of Inge's posthumous plays called *Overnight*, a piece which should interest scrupulous theatregoers.

It is one of a series of Inge's plays in a different vein from that of his accredited hits: *Picnic*, *Bus Stop*, *The Dark at the Top of the Stairs*. The later plays have little of the gentle humor and ameliorativeness of the former. The first in Inge's more severe manner was the 1959 *A Loss of Roses*, and the last one vouchsafed an off-Off Broadway production in 1970, was *The Last Pad* (Inge died, a suicide, in 1973). Nearly all these "unpleasant" plays take place in a sordid atmosphere—which is perhaps the chief reason for the reviewers' and public's aversion to them. They require a subtly superior kind of acting and direction to make them more acceptable. But what I wish to stress here is that these plays reveal the sorrow, pain and protest which were always latent in Inge's spirit but which

for a while he succeeded in tempering with benign comedy and with perhaps too heavy a dependence on the therapeutic aspects of Freudian psychology.

The American theatregoing public more than any other is repelled by the expression of raw hurt, the anger of wounded souls—especially when, as in Inge's case, it sometimes lacked clear focus. The original title of *The Last Pad*, which deals with prisoners awaiting capital punishment, was *Don't Go Gentle*, to signify the character's (and Inge's) need to cry out in violent desperation against the cruelty in man's fate.

Of these plays (several are still unproduced) *Overnight* is perhaps the most balanced and assimilable. It does not go to the savage extreme that *The Last Pad* does. But before I speak further about *Overnight* I believe it appropriate to say something more about Inge's work in general.

For all the good notices in the dailies, the box-office success and the Pulitzer Prize the first plays won, I am convinced Inge was underestimated. Serious critics thought the early plays too sweet, sentimental, facile. But whatever justification there may have been in such pejorative judgments, they were rarely set in a just perspective. Fault was found with Inge for not measuring up to standards he never set himself.

Inge was the dramatist of the ordinary. He plumbed no great depths, but this limitation does not negate the honesty or genuineness of his endeavor. Inge really knew and felt his people; he was kin to them. His plays provide insights into their childlike bewilderment, their profound if largely unconscious loneliness. His touch was popular, but never "commercial." His plays reflect a perturbed spirit modestly but nonetheless authentically groping for alleviation from the burdens of our society, particularly as they affect simple or unsophisticated citizens outside our big cities or on their fringes. As such, Inge's plays are perceptive and touching. The narrowness of their scope, their American "provincialism" is in his case an asset rather than a liability. There was very little synthetic in what he had to say; his plays were born of his own distress.

Overnight is centered on Muriel, a young woman from a "white trash" family out of Waco, Tex. She thinks of herself as an actress because back home she appeared in high school productions and was told she possessed conspicuous talent and high promise. Like thousands of others of her kind she hied herself to Hollywood to realize her aspirations as an actress. There she married a physicist in government employ, a decent fellow with no particular interest in acting or films and therefore unable to help advance her career. This arouses intense marital dissension which leads to a divorce in which she vindictively claims not only the custody of her child but a financially ruinous settlement from her husband. Then she takes up with a lawyer who is probably close to the film world. Though no "villain" he is a man of coarse fiber, typical of an environment where the pursuit of women as objects of sexual appetite is permanent and aggressive while sympathy for them is rare. Muriel falls into the usual rattrap in which sex is the bait and its exploitation the poisonous consequence.

Late one night Muriel returns to the husband she has divorced, who is at first most reluctant to receive her. We soon become aware of the ignorant little girl from the "sticks" who is reaching for something real in herself which her men do not recognize or are indifferent to and the vicious hysteria, a destructiveness of the self and of others, to which the obfuscation of her nature has led.

Without going into further detail, it is sufficient to say that *Overnight* dramatizes the havoc caused by the frustration of creative impulse, especially in people lacking in personal or cultural support.

The character drawing in this play, though somewhat thin, is firm in outline and intention. The husband, too tame to deal with the turbulence wracking his wife's being, the lover too unfeeling beyond his desire, are essentially well observed. But the play's full effectiveness largely depends on the kind of acting which embodies Muriel. For as a "type," she is all too common throughout our land (especially in the movie colony) but nearly always conventionally seen in stage performance.

Nathan George has directed the play with intelligence and drive. The two men in the cast—Arthur Roberts as the divorced husband and William Mooney as the lover—respond very well to the requirements of their roles. The woman's role calls for a very special sensibility. Carol Potter acts the play with passion but it is more willed and muscular than spontaneous and free flowing. Muriel's hysteria is not to be conveyed only through noisy gusts of vituperativeness or outcries of disillusion but by a constant tremulousness so subtle that it might be overlooked by the superficial observer. It is a ripple of nervous energy streaming out from the abscesses of the spirit so delicate that rather than being obviously disagreeable contributes to the woman's fascination; even in considerable measure to her physical appeal for many men. A native innocence and great vulnerability are involved in the ache and sickness of such creatures. I can think of very few actresses among us equipped to satisfy the deep demands of the role. It would be unfair to blame any actress however capable and attractive who fails to do so.

Still, despite all reservations, I was glad to see *Overnight* and thus to reconsider Inge's honorable contribution to our theatre.

—*NAT*, 3 Aug. '74

ABSURD PERSON SINGULAR
THE NATIONAL HEALTH
THE MEASURES TAKEN

A curious thing occurred as I watched Alan Ayckbourn's *Absurd Person Singular*: I experienced a sense of seeing two plays at once (Music Box Theatre). The first was an *effortlessly* wacky send-up of British middle-class characters—fools and eccentrics all; the second, a grotesquerie by Americans aping the English. I found the result drearily funny.

I began to speculate as to the reasons for this impression. The play presents three couples: an eagerly servile small businessman pushing his way up the social and mercantile scale, a fellow who bulldozes his wife, an even more ignorant cockney with a mania for domestic spotlessness; a negligible architect whose wife has been rendered nearly cataleptic by her husband's persistent philandering; a stuffy banker who confesses that he doesn't understand what women are all about and whose main endearment to his former wife and to the present one is "ole sausage," so that the latter combines catty snobbishness with alcoholism.

The play certainly does not aim at realism: it is a spoof rather that a satire on the pottiness of the English. Poking fun at their own special peculiarities—the capacity to maintain their wavering endurance despite a built-in obtuseness—is an old English tradition, and Alan Ayckbourn is its latest and, in a harmless fashion, its most successful practitioner. To carry this off well it must be done lightly, offhandedly. For the English take this aspect of their silliness for granted; at bottom they are fond of their foolishness and are happy to rig themselves, on the assumption that both their absurdity and their easygoing tolerance of it are virtues and somehow marks of strength.

The excellent American cast—Larry Blyden, Sandy Dennis, Richard Kiley, Geraldine Page, Tony Roberts, Carole Shelley—most of them wearing fright wigs, work madly to prove that they are the mad English. This strains the joke. The characters should be played as if their battiness were the most natural thing in the world. Is it possible that the director, Eric Thompson, who staged the play in London, wished to make his American actors behave exactly like the English cast, thus achieving something close to the comedy of a burlesque skit? Many English plays can be very well played by Americans, but *Absurd Person Singular* does not appear to be one of them. I laughed less than I had hoped; the audience laughed as much as it was expected to. The daily press raved.

Peter Nichols' *The National Health* (Circle in the Square) takes place in the men's ward of a British hospital. Most of the men are seriously ill—three die in the course of the play—and very few are convalescent, yet the play is a wry, but not at all heartless, comedy. The theme is life and death among the economically ill-favored. Death has no longer any sacramental dignity: it is as bureaucratized and mechanized as almost everything else today.

The theme is not spelled out; it is only inferred from the conversations, the complaints, outcries, benevolences and despairs among the patients, the orderlies, matrons and chaplain of the hospital. The dramatist's attitude is mordantly disenchanted—very British, after the fashion of the postwar generation. (Peter Nichols is now 46.) We cannot help but laugh at the crotchets and even at the pathos of what we hear and observe. What strikes us is the contrast between the mystery of life and death and the triviality or littleness within which most of us dwell.

Also recorded with tart humor is the paltriness in the routine of welfare hospitals. The chaplain, a functionary like the others, often arrives to offer his consolations after a patient has died. The adjunct medical attendant is so exhausted by her long hours of work that she drops off to sleep on the body of a moribund patient. One of the men suffers an ulcer chiefly on account of work in which he has no interest. The elderly are "Tories" who detest the present condition of their environment. Some are essentially decent people still eager for life despite the dismal quality of their existence. There is the permanent callousness of institutional behavior within the agony of individual fates.

I saw it first when it was the hit of the 1969 season at London's National Theatre. It was an excellent production with every role played with utmost authenticity as to type and with a dryness which befitted the writing. At the Circle in the Square, under Arvin Brown's inventively deft direction, the acting is also very good. Such actors, among others, as Emery Battis as a dying man who sees no good at all in our time; John Braden as a largely illiterate man now deprived of his alcoholic crutch; Richard Venture as the gentlest of the stricken; George Taylor, a victim of a coronary ailment who accepts his life with kindly patience; Louis Beachner as one of the men who recovers and longs to go home to his wife and his spot of tea—all these merit praise.

Yet the production is afflicted by a determination to soften its hard edge with ha-ha comedy— visual and verbal jokes added to turn the evening into a "fun show." In the London production there were moments when the telly was turned on to point out the irony in the central situation—imbecile programs to alleviate the patients' pain. Now these moments are elongated into minutes in which live actors perform vaudeville skits about some of the doctors and nurses. The protracted monologues and antics by the chief orderly, though brilliantly done by Leonard Frey as a burlesque "Mefisto," degrade the play. Our national weakness is the refusal to confront the "unpleasant" right-on. It is a detriment to our national health.

In the tiniest auditorium of Joseph Papp's Public Theatre, the touring Shaliko Company, a group of young players, all of whom, including their director, are alumni of New York University's School of Performing Arts, are presenting Bertolt Brecht's didactic play, *The Measures Taken*, in Eric Bentley's translation.

It was first given in Berlin in 1930, two years after Brecht had turned from the wily satire of *The Threepenny Opera* as he had also from the hectic anarchism of his youthful work. Brecht had become a Marxist and, whether or not a "certified" communist, wholly committed to the cause and the party. *The Measures Taken* was designed to teach workers the tenets of Marxist ideology and the discipline it entailed.

The German Communist Party found fault with the play and requested its withdrawal; the Soviet party condemned it utterly. The reason was that it seemed to rationalize or justify the murder of one of the party's own members because of an emotionally motivated breach of revolutionary conduct. Like several other Brecht plays, *The Measures Taken*, so bold in its espousal of presumed Communist doctrine, was a double-edged sword. It became, indirectly and unconsciously, an exposé of the party's ruthlessness—as the Stalinist trials of the old Russian revolutionaries were to reveal.

The Communist agitators in the play kill one of their comrades during a secret mission to pre-Mao China because, as they explain, "He often did the right thing, several times he did the wrong thing. but in the end he endangered the movement. He wished the right thing and did the wrong thing." The killers ask to be exonerated by the party's "Control Commission," and in the end they are.

The commission's central doctrine of revolutionary action is enunciated in these words: "Who fights for communism must be able to fight and not to fight, to speak the truth and not to speak the truth …to keep promises and not keep promises….Who fights for communism has only one of all the virtues: that he fights for communism." More explicitly, at a later moment: "What baseness would you not commit to root out baseness? If, finally, you would change the world, what task would you be too good for? Sink down in the slime, embrace the butcher, but change the world: it needs it!"

On the surface this is "dated" stuff, but something deeper is involved that makes the play contemporary and of worldwide significance. A tragic dilemma is implied: the conflict between means and ends—no matter what ideology is in question. Some would die to avoid a humanly heinous action. Others would not hesitate to carry out any vileness for what they are convinced are righteous and just ends. It was ever so and probably will ever be. The decision is not only a matter of individual conscience or group faith but a response to the crucial pressures and realities of given circumstances. It is the hideous tragedy of history, which only poets can ennoble.

The play resembles an oratorio. Originally it was done in an enormous hall with orchestra and a chorus of 400 in the background, while on the bare forestage, with very few properties and little movement, the actors demonstrated what had occurred. The play's basic form remains intact in the present production: each of the four agitators who tell the story changes roles continuously, taking on the guise of one or the other of the conspirators or of the various oppressors, speaking or singing individually or in unison. Much of the writing is in Brecht's characteristically terse and telling verse with its glancing shafts of sly humor. Hanns Eisler's songs mingle snarling vehemence with gruffly heroic stalwartness.

The means available to the Shaliko Company is in every respect minimal: one piano must do the work of an orchestra. But there are effective players in the company, and all shine by virtue of their energetic determination. The director has done well within the microscopic dimensions provided for this fundamentally massive and imposing play.

—*NAT*, 2 Nov. '74

EQUUS

In *Equus* Peter Shaffer has conceived something like a detective story with philosophic implications (Plymouth Theatre). The detective story—in which the "detective" is a psychoanalyst—is brilliantly crafted, handsomely written and unusually compelling.

The salient feature of the play's craft is its construction. The stage is as bare as a surgical arena. Around it are several tiers of seats on which student members of the audience are placed, as if observing a lecture-demonstration. On the left and right sides, close to the observers, are seated the play's characters; they leave their positions only when the script calls upon them to enact their parts in the drama. A battery of powerful lights shines down on the platform to lend the proceedings an atmosphere of scientific precision. Horses play a crucial role in the story; actors are clearly visible within the horses' heads of hilt metal, and their hoofs of similar material not only give them great height but contribute an ominous effect by the clatter they make on the burnished wood floor.

Very few props are employed; the scenic style is generally non-realistic except, curiously enough, when a boy and girl of the play set about to make love, at which time they are seen in total nudity. While the overall impression is one of severe functionalism, an air of spectacle, of *theatre*, obtains in which dramatist, actors and director display their skills with gratifying aplomb.

Alan Strang, a youth of 17, has gouged out the eyes of six horses; he is saved from prison by an intelligent woman magistrate who insists that he be put in the care of Dr. Dysart, a psychoanalyst, who may discover the cause of the boy's insane act and thus cure him. By a slow process of discovery—confrontation with the boy, who at first responds to questions asked of him by singing television advertisement slogans; meetings with the boy's parents; the use of truth pills, etc.—the inner story is artfully unfolded.

Though his mother was a schoolteacher and his father a printer, Alan is semilliterate. There is something of a "Parsifal" about him, all instinct and juvenile candor. Mrs. Strang is a religious woman; her husband, a Socialist and atheist, strongly objects to his wife's religious bent. She had once put up an image of the Crucifixion in Alan's bedroom—a rather lurid one, she admits. He had become fixed on the sight of the suffering in the picture. His father, appalled on seeing Alan kneel before it in an attitude of prayer, tears it down and replaces it with the picture of a horse. Alan comes to regard this new image with some of the same fascination and sense of worship that he had brought to the previous one. The horse, with a bit in its mouth and a steady stare of bafflement and powerful rebellion, exercises a magnetic effect on him.

One day on the beach when Alan is 10, we learn in a flashback, a man splendidly mounted on horseback almost runs him down. Alan is scared, so the rider, to assuage his fear, invites him to join in a ride behind him. Mr. Strang happens to see this and angrily pulls Alan from the horse, reproving the rider for having endangered his son. (Mr. Strang's interference at this moment corresponds with all the repressions to which he has subjected Alan, including the removal of a television set which Alan, in his withdrawal into solitude, loved to watch.) After Mr. Strang's departure from the encounter on the beach, in which the horse's mouth has been injured through a sharp pull on the bit necessitated by his father's sudden intervention, Alan in a gesture very like an embrace "consoles" the horse, and the animal responds in a movement of its head toward Alan resembling a kiss. This vision of the boy and the animal "kissing" repeats a previous flashback which might be taken as the play's insignia.

After he has worked for a while in a dull shop, a young girl employed in a stable invites him to join her there as an apprentice. He eagerly accepts and is quick to learn. But at night, secretly, he occasionally takes one of the horses called Nugget out for a wild dash, an excursion which fills him with almost erotic joy, although it was thought that after the episode on the beach he never rode again.

The girl is attracted to Alan. She asks him to take her to see a porno movie—which neither of them has ever before attended. Ironically enough, they discover Alan's father there, and he pretends he has come to investigate and protest such exhibitions. Alan and the girl go back to the stable where, both sexually aroused, they are about to make love. Alan feels he is being watched by the horses, as it were, censoriously. He very much wants to go through with his love-making but the suddenly insistent beat of the horses' hoofs in their stalls, which sound as if they were threatening him, shatters his desire. It is then that he grabs a sharp instrument and blinds the horses.

What is the meaning of this queer tale? Dysart's own situation provides the answer. He is unhappily married but is still bound to his boring wife. Enamored of Greek art and ancient lore, his medical practice does not permit him freedom to follow his bent. Like most other "normal" (or socially conformist) people, he has been frustrated from fulfilling himself in his most personal need. So as a parallel instance we see Alan's savage gesture as a contradictory outburst against the repression of his deepest instinct for worship—which many would consider abnormal. Alan was unable to consummate his fleshly urge for the girl because of his more fundamental devotion to the (symbolic) "Equus" (horse), so he is prompted to violence on the object of his truest love. In this Dysart reads a lesson: the futility of any attempt to convert profoundly rooted "mystic" instincts—even more tenacious than earthly appetites—into the usually mediocre and stultifying channels of the so-called normal citizen.

When the good and ever-so-earnest doctor cries out in anger and agony at the fact that he, who in his therapeutic task on Alan may be eliminating what is actually creative in the boy, is at the same time freezing his own best impulses, a good part of the audience applauds. The inference is that, once cured, that is, rid of his "divine" suffering, Alan will become a dullard like most normal people. Such applause is an echo of the new cant: that the schizophrenic is closer to the truth of life than the ordinary citizen. But positing such an alternative is false. One need not be "crazy" to live untrammeled by conventional proscriptions. Most of the insane (I have seen them in hospitals) are in every way far more wretched and pitiful than the average man in his quiet despair or humdrum gloom.

As dramatized, I find the play's "philosophy" bogus. Dysart himself needs to be cured of his faulty reasoning. The playwright needs a more fitting "objective correlative" or story analogy for his defense of the irregular or anomalous person. The production is superbly managed: John Dexter's direction is adroit in every respect and the acting thoroughly persuasive. Peter Firth (Alan Strang), marvelously right in type, plays with an intense sincerity which crushes all possible cavil. His future work will show whether what is now said in deserved praise of him is true. Anthony Hopkins, compact and sturdy in physique, displays that sweeping professionalism, resounding in elocution, heroic in energy, eloquent in rhetorical vigor which is the envy of so many American theatre folk and the admiration of our audiences.

Frances Sternhagen plays Mrs. Strang with a forthright and touching truthfulness. As the woman magistrate, Marian Seldes is more convincing in her firm delivery of her intellectual argument with Dysart than he is in his heated protest and plea. Michael Higgins too merits kind words in the ungrateful role of Alan's father. And Roberta Maxwell as the girl who doesn't get the boy is as sympathetic as she is attractive.

—*NAT*, 16 Nov. '74

LOVE FOR LOVE
SHERLOCK HOLMES
BATTLE OF ANGELS

I love *Love for Love* (Helen Hayes Theatre). William Congreve wrote it in 1695, when he was 25, and he set it forth as satire. But there can't be much satire in it for us today. It is now pure fun, a glittering frolic. There is wisdom in its wit, but we are not compelled to weigh or assess it. It sparkles before us and transports us to a realm essentially aesthetic. It triumphs in images which provoke wonder and delight; language is its chief glory.

The feast of words does not smack of "quotation"—as Shakespeare does! It is modern language, on the whole free of obscurities and odd locutions. All the words strike our ears as if they were never before spoken or heard. They retain a marvelous freshness; they are of the finest vintage. Even the slightly starched or stiff structure of the period rhetoric enchants through unfamiliarity.

The Phoenix production is one of the best in that company's history. Harold Prince, who staged *Love for Love*, has since *Candide* shown himself a happily inventive master of "ceremonies." He gives the play an American, almost musical comedy reading. Songs by Hugh Wheeler and Paul Gemignani, more or less in the mode of the time, have been added. No English director would have done the play quite this way, yet the American funhouse note does not abuse Congreve; it accommodates him to our temper.

Douglas Higgins' setting is a jolly collage of late 17th-century objects; all the bric-a-brac and furniture are admirably chosen without giving the impression of being on display. Franne Lee's costumes too are not merely pretty; they are right.

The actors do themselves proud. John McMartin is very funny in crackpot senility—such roles are his forte—Charles Kimbrough is grotesquely amusing as the eloquently egregious Tattle, George Ede as the stodgily shrewd and yet foolish Sir Sampson serves as an anchor to the flighty proceedings, and Mary Beth Hurt, as the sexual novice, Miss Prue, is cutely captivating.

An even more masterly production is the Royal Shakespeare Company's *Sherlock Holmes* (Broadhurst Theatre). Here again we are summoned to a realm which is, in a very different sense, most ingratiatingly *theatre*. We lend ourselves to its make-believe as to a fantastic fable and, as with all good fables, there is something real in it.

The *Sherlock Holmes* of Conan Doyle and William Gillette offered in 1899 that indispensable quality of suspense expected from plays of crime and its detection. (Conan Doyle was in his own fashion an innovator. He brought a late Victorian modernity, a touch of "science," the semblance of deductive wizardry, to the long-established English tradition of the romantic thriller.) What is suspenseful to us now is not the artful tracking down of felons by a super-clever gentleman sleuth but the histrionic ingenuity and stage devices by which Holmes's exploits are carried out.

Still, something of the reason for the original Conan Doyle fascination remains. The London of Conan Doyle's day was in the main correct, orderly, genteel. How wonderful, then, to show its underside, its dark secrets, its nefarious mysteries, its corruption. (*The Yellow Book* was also part of the period's "subculture.") Inside, solid wooden comfort and wooden people; outside, fog and frightful doings. The English and the Americans (who to some extent were also then brought up to profess, and as much as possible to practice, rectitude) developed a semi-surreptitious appetite for its opposite. One aspect of the novelty in Holmes is his addiction to morphine. What a shiver that must have given the audience in 1899! It was not a social or a clinical matter to them: it was awful wickedness. With all this, Holmes is a moral person! He upholds the law and virtue itself. Cynical and almost misanthropic on the surface, he is ever on the side of the right, always gallant, imperturbably British, a knight in mufti.

A production of *Sherlock Holmes* might be converted to parody. This the Royal Shakespeare Company avoids. It chooses to be *seriously* stagy. Everything is sharpened and heightened enough for us to assent to it as if all were "real," while we are never allowed to forget that it is all a splendid game. Everything takes on a special glamour: the glamour of the brown and misty London of another day, the day when we treasured the good and were appalled by the bad, and hoped to see it eliminated. Above all, there is a feeling of the theatre as a place where things, whatever else they are, must be *extraordinary*.

What is especially engaging in the play as here done is that its substantive interest is not the trapping of the guilty and the rewarding of the blameless, but the "intellectual" battle between the hero and his antagonist, the redoubtable and ghoulish Professor Moriarty. They are pitted against each other like two principals of life—both brainy, both powerful of will, both enduring.

And how they are played! With humor, with a precision that renders them picturesque in every turn and grimace and in an astonishing boldness of projection, orally and graphically.

John Wood of the equine head, is lean, towering, unflappable and pale with mental tension and professional purpose, a demon of benevolence; Moriarty, cadaverously thin, is the fantastically elongated demon of malevolence. Philip Locke plays that part in a manner which might be hilarious—it is certainly witty—if it weren't so consummately spectral. Both actors have resounding voices, exaggerated for characterizations by Locke, but it is part of the production's style for almost all the actors to employ a tone several decibels above the naturalistic.

The entire cast is excellent and very large. There are also many sets, just as there used to be in the good old days! The actors are members of a company which has played together for some time now in a varied repertory. They have been directed by Frank Dunlop who has a genius for outlandish comedy and theatrical extravagance. (*Scapino* was his achievement.) Much of the brilliance of *Sherlock Holmes* is due to Dunlop's talent, although it would hardly have emerged if he had had a less "prepared" roster of actors. The Royal Shakespeare Company has no equal on the English-speaking stage, except perhaps the British National Theatre.

Together with these assets Dunlop has benefited by the collaboration of Carl Toms, whose sets and other scenic effects are ingenious and at times sensationally apt.

Tennessee Williams' *Battle of Angels*, which he wrote in 1939 (never before done in New York), is related to his *Orpheus Descending* of 1957 as, *mutatis mutandis*, Chekhov's *The Wood Demon* is to *Uncle Vanya*. There is a similarity in story line, many of the characters appear in both plays, several speeches recur, yet they are different plays. Having directed *Orpheus Descending*, I shall refrain from a comparison as to the relative merits of the Williams plays. Suffice it to say here that more than the seeds of Williams' talent are already evident in the early play. What is more pertinent for me to say at this juncture is that I believe everything Williams has written or writes for the theatre is worth seeing.

The production of *Battle of Angels*, directed by Marshall Mason for the Circle Repertory Company, now housed for its main events at the Sheridan Square Playhouse is marked by considerable animation and is well set by John Lee Beatty. The production's weakness is the inappropriate casting of the central roles. The best acting is in some of the minor parts—especially that of Conchata Ferrell, who seasons the role of a woman painter subject to "visions" with an odd note of comedy.

—*NAT*, 30 Nov. '74

SIZWE BANZI IS DEAD AND THE ISLAND
SATURDAY SUNDAY MONDAY

Athol Fugard's two one-act plays *Sizwe Banzi Is Dead* and *The Island*, presented in alternating evening performances at the Edison Theatre, are important—not simply because they provide an insight into the life of the blacks in South Africa but because in writing and in acting they are examples of original theatre. By "original" theatre I mean drama which has grown organically from a condition of existence common to its several creators. Though Fugard is white and the two men who act in both plays are black, the identification of the writer with his subject and with the actors who embody it is complete. All three are fundamentally of one stock.

Fugard, whose *The Blood Knot* and *Boesman and Lena* I reviewed enthusiastically, has made the black South African cause his own. More, as director, he has worked with his cast since the 1960s in an organization which has produced not only his plays but also several by Brecht, Genet, Strindberg, Sophocles, Euripides. Their association spells a *theatre* unit inspired by a basic sympathy in sentiment and method of work.

Sizwe Banzi Is Dead begins with a long harangue addressed to the audience in which a man named Styles (John Dani) describes his life as an employee in the Port Elizabeth Ford factory. He is derisively eloquent about the hectic preparations for a welcome to be accorded the big U. S. boss, and the gruffly abrupt nature of his visit. In this recital Styles takes the audience into his confidence, as if it were a boon companion. It conveys a vivid impression of what it means for a black man to be working in such a place as a South African factory.

After this, the story of Sizwe Banzi (Winston Ntshona) unfolds. He hasn't the papers required to live or hold a job in Port Elizabeth. Without such papers he will be obliged to leave the city forthwith and return to his wife and children in a miserable and distant village. He explains his plight to Buntu (also played by Kani), a chance acquaintance. Walking along together, they happen upon the corpse of a black man on whom they find the papers needed for residence and work in Port Elizabeth. Sizwe is reluctant at first to take the dead man's papers and thus to forgo his own name. But Buntu manages to convince Sizwe that he should do so. We last see him being photographed in a new suit, now that he has a job. He looks positively jaunty, very much as if he had struck it rich, but we know from what Styles has told us that he will be no better off than the hard-pressed and humiliated worker at the Ford factory.

Sizwe Banzi is a wistful comedy which stems from a painful situation. Shot through with humor, *The Island* is essentially tragic. But because of its objectivity it never becomes oppressive; the harshness of its events is made to appear casual.

The locale is a small island in the Atlantic Ocean about 7 miles from Capetown. It was once used as a leper colony and a lunatic asylum and is now South Africa's maximum security prison for political offenders. The play begins with two silent men shoveling heavy loads of sand into barrows and then dumping them along a beach. (Very effectively done without the use of props.) This is a special assignment, probably even more exhausting and injurious than their normal task: cutting stone in a quarry. Sand gets into the men's eyes and lodges in their skin; their efforts to remove the sand from their bodies are almost as hurtful as the initial damage done them.

When they retire to their cell we learn that the two men have promised to appear at a prison "concert" in their own version of *Antigone*. One of the men, Winston, who is to play Antigone, has great difficulty following the plot line and learning the words. On finding that his wig and costume send his cell mate, John, into fits of laughter, Winston refuses to undertake the travesty. But John, who is to play Creon, argues so heatedly that the story of *Antigone* has great significance for them and the other prisoners that Winston consents to go on with the show. The performance is given before the prison's authorities and its inmates.

When the two men get back from the "concert" they learn that John, who had been sentenced to a ten-year term (he has already served three) is to be set free in three months. Jubilation! Suddenly Winston turns bitter: he is to remain in jail for a long (unspecified) time, he will probably die there, while John will forget he had ever known him. John promises that he will always remember Winston. For a moment John seems to regret that freedom will separate him from his pal. There are occasional flashes of hatred between the two, but we also recognize that their mutual suffering has forged an unbreakable link between them.

This bare summary of their plots is insufficient to suggest all the subtle gradations of feeling which give the two plays, and especially *The Island*, their substance. A fierce compassion and a rude tenderness mingle in a way which makes an exact definition of the plays' qualities extremely difficult. A naked humanity is in them without any overlay of civilized distinctions.

The acting is the word become flesh: we are hardly able to differentiate between text and performance, yet the actors have dissimilar personalities. John Kani, in both instances, plays the "leader," the more knowledgeably articulate one; Winston Ntshona the more naively puzzled one.

Kani is all driving impulse, which might render him breathless if he were not propelled by extraordinary energy. His many expostulations ring with the sounds of a soulful plea, an absolutely convincing earnestness, a cry that is ecstatically hopeful while verging on despair. The effect of his passion is joyful. It inspires confidence, not only in him but in mankind itself.

Ntshona is charming in his confusion; though he must struggle to understand, we are sure that his instincts will lead to the right actions. Technically he is more a character actor than Kani, but his characterizations spring spontaneously from his inner being, so his effects are as natural as Kani's. Both these men have acted together since their boyhood. They are now more than a team; together they have become emblematic of a people. Such acting carries primitive force; it is clear, sharp, seemingly free of any "aesthetic" premeditation.

I harbor a certain affection for Eduardo de Filippo's *Saturday Sunday Monday* (Martin Beck Theatre). I am always moved by the depiction of people who love one another in a family or community context. Since New Yorkers live in a graceless city whose neighborhoods, except for its ghettos, are fast disappearing, and with them the sense of family, the kind of fellow feeling one gets from such a play as de Filippos's exerts a special hold on my spirit. I laugh because its absurd people are at bottom such innocents, and at the same time I find myself disarmed—in fact, close to tears!

De Filippo's plays—several of which have been seen here as film vehicles for Sophia Loren—are folk tales permeated with the spicy flavor of Naples. Since ethnic characteristics—especially in Italy—are inevitably associated with local dishes and wines which create as much of binding tradition as intellectual or artistic pleasures, there is much talk in *Saturday Sunday Monday* about ragouts and particular assortments of pasta. But to believe its theme is culinary misses the considerable charm of the play. It is about the ties which hold families together, of which one of the main ingredients is the things they mutually enjoy. The ritual of the special Sunday dinner is the domestic and social symbol of a tightly knit community where the very upsets and quarrels serve as evidence of deeply rooted devotion.

The play is funny: besides his unerring eye for the idiosyncrasies of local types, de Filippo has a consummate knowledge of the popular stage. (He is himself one of the best of living actors.) For their perfect realization his plays demand an evenly matched company. This does not mean that all the actors ought to be Italian: the play reportedly was well done at the National Theatre with an all-English cast (Laurence Olivier, Joan Plowright, et al.). The New York cast is not that coherent in national or environmental derivation; it is distinctly variegated in accent, tone and individual stress. Still, it works, largely because of Franco Zeffirelli's direction (he did the staging in London as well) and the excellence of Sada Thompson and Eli Wallach. Ms. Thompson is especially successful in finding the right pace and rhythm of Neapolitan speech without resorting to a fake accent. And she lends a kind of matriarchal size and dignity to her part without missing any of its wit. Eli Wallach's own vein of frustrated candor, with occasional outbursts of ineffectual outrage cut short by immediate contrition and sweetness, also fills the group portrait with the needed color and "temperature." To deny oneself so pleasant an entertainment on the ground that it is old-fashioned is to impoverish oneself through a juiceless pseudo-sophistication.

—NAT, 14 Dec. '74

THE RULES OF THE GAME
ROSMERSHOLM
OF MICE AND MEN
WHERE'S CHARLEY?

It is a sad circumstance that some of the masterworks of dramatic literature are produced on our stage by companies ill-equipped to do them justice. We have none of those well-established theatre organizations which most European countries possess where means and ends are artistically compatible. Audiences at such plays as Pirandello's *The Rules of the Game* or Ibsen's *Rosmersholm* in New York must make "allowances"—an unhappy state of mind for pleasure or enlightenment.

The Rules of the Game, which the New Phoenix Repertory Company put on for a brief run at the Helen Hayes Theatre, is not as "difficult" a play as his *Six Characters* or his *Henry IV*. The passion which is present in all Pirandello's work burns more palpably in the earlier play (written in 1918) than in the later ones. And the passion here is not intellectual but erotic, the passion of jealously.

Pirandello was a Sicilian with the torrid nature which we associate with that island. His marital sorrows and, I imagine, a great amount of philosophical reading, which led him to speculate on appearance and reality, the lack of a clear focus in human consciousness and the consequent split in individual personality, congealed Pirandello's hot temperament so that it often appears icily cerebral. That is one reason his plays, both madly intense and strangely constricted, sometimes leave one puzzled, even frustrated, unless they are superbly projected.

They are constructed like mystery melodramas: neither realistic nor, with a few exceptions, overtly stylized. They are colorful and somehow stark; emotion is held in check but because there is at bottom so much of it, it creates a fierce tension through which a malicious irony spreads an uncanny sense of mystification.

The Rules of the Game is about a man so hurt by his wife's equivocal romanticism and infidelity that he seeks to protect himself from his pain by cultivating a frigid objectivity. To no avail. Beneath his cold calculation, he is consumed by a thirst for vengeance, a murderous plan to rid himself of his wife's lover, toward whom he always maintains a posture of sedulous politeness.

The Phoenix Company simply lacks the actors for such a play. Someone like a 40-year-old John Barrymore is needed, and all the Phoenix can provide is John McMartin, a character actor best in the impersonation of clowns, weaklings and dotards. Joan van Ark is nice and pretty in a role requiring the most bewitching and exasperating sensual allurement in a sinuous grand manner. So for all the company's good will, we do not really see this very interesting play.

Ibsen's *Rosmersholm* (Roundabout Theatre), from the master's late period (1886), is one of his most complex creations. When Duse undertook to act it she engaged Gordon Craig to design it. On seeing his setting—abstract and grandiose—she thought it alien to Ibsen's world of provincial domesticity. But perhaps Craig was closer to the play's spirit than she or anyone else at the time could have understood. *Rosmersholm* is a "confessional" play in which Ibsen dramatized his self-doubt, the essential fissure in his soul, the never quite resolved contradiction which underlay the course of his whole career.

The grim puritan Ibsen yearned for a moral perfection which his inexorable conscience never permitted him to feel that he had attained. The anarchist in him was suspicious of all statehood and governments, but he insisted that he receive medals and decorations from them. He clamored for obedience to the precepts of an austere and absolute ethic, but he craved the warm indulgence of a pagan world. He believed in democracy but demanded that it be aristocratic. He gave himself unrelentingly to the discipline of artistic effort but was embittered by the tardy realization that it led to the sacrifice of his more fundamental need for personal love. The revolutionist in him began to doubt the premises of his ardor for progress and reform. This scrupulously determined realist came to aspire to an ineffable mysticism. He wished to construct monuments that might reach to the heavens and found that he had built no more than convenient dwelling places.

Ibsen wrought the Rebecca West of *Rosmersholm* out of his subconscious self. She is a woman of doubtful origin, ambitiously forging ahead with ruthless power to beat down reactionary prejudices, only to find herself through contact with the noble Rosmer guilty of baseness approximating crime, for she has desired him and helped drive his wife to suicide. Ibsen is also Rosmer become unsure of his mission as either pastor or political leader; he finds the first narrow and confining and is disqualified for the second by confused motivation. Neither Rebecca nor Rosmer can go on; they must die—a symbolic rather than a factual necessity. Ibsen accuses himself in this play of being, like all the people of the Rosmer line, too controlled to cry and too appalled by his own shortcomings to laugh.

To bring life to such involuted characters in an environment that is only ostensibly related to conventional naturalism is a task of utmost delicacy and difficulty—a formidable challenge to actors, director, designer. All that can be claimed for this performance is that it is earnestly and intelligently spoken, a sort of staged reading in a confined space.

John Steinbeck's *Of Mice and Men* is now being given a sound production at the Brooks Atkinson Theatre. The play, which as editor I included in an anthology of *Famous American Plays of the 1930s*, strikes me in retrospect as one of the best pieces of dramatic writing since our country's coming-of-age in the 1920s.

It is something more than a rugged tale of itinerant agricultural workers during the Great Depression. It is a sort of American "legend." There is a mythic simplicity about it. What emerges is not only a sense of the loneliness of American existence, the separation between persons, the lack of brotherhood, our incapacity to fructify our vast continent with the warm blood of fellow feeling, but an inference to the effect that until brawn and brain become one in our land we shall suffer the dumb ache of isolation, a perpetual state of partial being.

It may well be that Steinbeck did not think of his story in these terms, but that is nonetheless what he created. Its moral point lies in the telling. There is no artifice or "aesthetic" design in it; it is rather stark. The mood and meaning spring naturally from the authentic Americanism of the language, the spareness of the character delineation. Even those who do not get the play's "message" as conscious content must be touched by direct contact with the naked material. The play is modest in form and large in emotional implication.

James Earl Jones as Lennie and Kevin Conway as George are excellent and most of the others, particularly Stefan Gierasch as the old and disabled farm hand whose only companion is a decrepit dog, are also good. Jones does not play Lennie as the cretin he so often seems in most performances; he endows the man with a sort of primitive mystery resembling certain pieces of pre-Columbian sculpture. He stares out at the incomprehensible universe in blank wonderment, alive only to the realities of tactile connection, food and kindly care. Kevin Conway is perhaps a bit too energetically assertive, not himself sufficiently "lost" (in his own way George is as bereft of support as Lennie, and needs his animal-like fidelity).

And despite its general merit I found some lack of encompassing poetic mood in the production. I'm not sure I can ascertain the exact cause for this, but I shall set down some of my misgivings.

The actress who plays Curley's wife is miscast: she lacks the body and the unaware sensuality of the girl, a heavily brooding dreaminess within the vacant intelligence. The sadistic ferocity of Curley's impotence (a negative sensuality) is missing, and the pathos of the black man excluded because of his color from the company of the other hands fails to register because Jones, too, is black. There were other impediments to my total involvement: the use of soft music not only between scenes but at the fearful climax when George prepares to kill Lennie; petty "realistic" details—

water splashing off stage, birds and animal sounds in the bushes—are all antithetical to the play's epic lineaments. The staging of Lennie's scene with Curley's wife seems to diminish its poignancy: they are seated too far apart; their inner apartness can be made evident only by physical proximity. There is something a little studied in the overall performances.

Despite these reservations, *Of Mice and Men* is something assuredly worth seeing, a most honorable effort on everyone's part.

It is truly a holiday occasion when an actor like Raul Julia appears on the scene. He *communicates*. He has charm, imagination, good humor, zest, the courage of a clown, a perpetual sense of comedic opportunity. He brings all these qualities to his singing and dancing.

He is now appearing in a revival of *Where's Charley?* (Circle in the Square Theatre), the George Abbott and Frank Loesser musical produced in 1947 based on the perennial *Charley's Aunt* (1892). Deep thinkers in the theatre pooh-pooh this chestnut but I found it innocently diverting in its old-fashioned but still pleasant tunes, lyrics, dialogue. But if there were nothing more to the show than Raul Julia (supported by funny Tom Aldredge and an engaging company), I should still recommend it.

—*NAT*, 11 Jan. '75

A DOLL'S HOUSE

See Liv Ullmann in *A Doll's House* (Vivian Beaumont Theatre). I put it that way with some misgivings, because a staged play is never to be regarded as a one-star show; it must be collectively coherent. In that respect the production at Lincoln Center fails.

The audience today assumes, since *A Doll's House* was written in 1879 and has been produced innumerable times, that it is "old hat": that, for instance, Torvald Helmer is a male chauvinist pig and that Nora is a pioneer of women's lib; or that all males who now see the play are free from Torvald's taint and all females wholly liberated. The play's thesis or "message" is taken for granted, and at present held to be supererogatory.

Quite apart from my conviction that very little of that is true, one should consider Ibsen's view of the play. In a speech delivered in 1898, he remarked: "I must decline the honor of being said to have worked for the Women's Rights movement. I am not even very sure what Women's Rights actually are." More important than that, Ibsen asserted at an earlier date that "the play is not a mere realistic drama, but a poem, and...its poetry should be emphasized to give it full effect."

This quiet drama has nothing declamatory in it, little of the hortatory or tendentious. It dwells on relationships between individuals, regardless of sex: the true marriage of souls. In most intimate human contact there is a tension, most often unconscious, between the one who is dominated and the one who is dominating—in extreme circumstances, an aggressor and a victim. This happens even when it may be said that love exists between them. What Ibsen asks is how people shall live together in humane responsibility to one another.

More than love is involved. The impediments to a balanced togetherness are numerous: economic factors, social prejudices, religious concepts and habits, community attitudes; all impinge on personal connections. There is also considerable uncertainty as to whether we truly understand or believe in what we accept, because we rarely examine the premises of our customary actions. All these matters very subtly come into play in *A Doll's House*.

Torvald is depicted as a decent, kindly man; he is no household tyrant. He doesn't "stand for" anything. When Nora tells him that it is petty of him to resent his former schoolmate Krogstad, now his business subordinate, Torvald doesn't become furious (as Sam Waterston does in the role); he is simply hurt. He dotes on Nora. He never "bosses" her. When he finds out that she has committed what is technically a crime, he doesn't pounce on her or bellow; he is frightened and shocked.

He is a home-loving, almost uxorious, mildly self-assertive, middle-class husband, neither gross nor stupid. When Nora calms him and explains why she must leave him, he admits that there is "some truth in what you are saying"—and when he adds, "under all the raving exaggeration," he is more or less right. Nora acknowledges that she doesn't know anything about the world she lives in. She wants to learn. Perhaps it is true that she is unfit to educate her children, since she has never been given the opportunity to discover things for herself. She is as bewildered as Torvald and hardly more "sensitive." She is only much more *innocent* or ignorant. The play's drama lies in the progression to an awakening of consciousness—his as well as hers. His last line expresses the possibility that the "miracle of miracles"—"the wonderful" in Christopher Hampton's translation—that Nora has spoken of may occur. It is the hope that, after the crisis and the test of further experience, a healthy union may be established between them. The play, judged in this light, is just as much one of "male liberation" as of its counterpart. It does not seem to have occurred to those who believe Torvald a paltry creature that if this is so, Nora herself becomes a goose and the play itself lame.

The audience at Lincoln Center laughs scornfully at Torvald. This is not only a symptom of its New York, mid-20th-century complacency or phony sophistication but also a sign that Torvald is being played falsely—that is, without proper realization of the play's meaning or mood. And that mood, I must emphasize, for all the play's dramatic force, is reflective and subdued.

I am not blaming Sam Waterston, though I believe him miscast. The production's fault is recognizably in virtually all its major performances—except that of Liv Ullmann. The Norwegian director Tormod Skagestad has clearly aimed at a straightforward, unromantic, no-nonsense interpretation. This, like Santo Loquasto's nicely functional setting, is entirely justifiable. But either because the director is unfamiliar with American actors, or because the company is ill cast, the result in most cases is dry and coarse.

Krogstad is a crushed and deeply embittered man, but he is played here as a vociferously vindictive villain. Mrs. Linde is a disillusioned woman who has grown "sensible" or down-to-earth; still there must also be tenderness in her, which is little evident in Barbara Colby's performance. Dr. Rank needn't be played sentimentally, but there must be an abiding thoughtful sorrow, a mellowness in his pained irony—largely lacking in Michael Granger's interpretation.

The entire production misses the discreet gravity, the contemplativeness, the modest temper and tone of the play's (provincial) environment, in a word, the *poetry* that is peculiarly Ibsen's; without that, the play is indeed "propaganda" now supposedly hackneyed. The cast plays moment to moment for "points," now melodramatically loud, now weakly soft; it fails to communicate a unifying through-line, what some call the characters' "spine."

Liv Ullmann is almost embarrassingly a real person among figureheads. She plays Nora with unadorned simplicity, a touching innocence, a snowdrop purity. Avoiding all strong "effects," she is so much part of the total Ibsen creation that the completeness of her art may easily be missed by those who view acting as display. In the climactic revelation scene she doesn't proclaim a new determination; instead we see her struggling for clarity and a growing into a fullness of being which foreshadows the possible achievement of the "wonderful," the miracle of miracles.

—*NAT*, 22 Mar. '75

SUMMERFOLK
THE ROCKY HORROR SHOW

Summerfolk is one of a group of plays Gorky devoted to the unnerved and disheartened middle class of Russia between 1902 and 1917. There are at least nine of them, of which only two have been seen in prominent New York productions: *Enemies*, written in 1906, and *Summerfolk*, written in 1904. (Another such play, *Odd Play*, 1910, one of the most "amusing," was very well done by the Long Wharf Theatre of New Haven under the title *Country People*.)

All these plays—especially *Summerfolk* and *Enemies*—point to an inevitable revolution. But they are not, as some now maintain, "propaganda pieces." Gorky knew the milieu intimately and was not "antagonistic" to its people. If his portrait is cruder and harsher than Chekhov's, it is not simply because he was not so fine an artist as his senior but because Chekhov wrote of an earlier period and Gorky of a time when the disarray of the middle class and Russian society in general had become much more shattering.

Summerfolk, Gorky is careful to stress, is not a play about the Russian intelligentsia (*Country People* is that) but about men and women who, once poor, have grown moderately prosperous. They now find themselves with nowhere to go; the road ahead is blocked by state and church. They are bored, distempered, without real hope or fresh ideas. They hardly even dream; they drink, philander, relieve themselves in cynicism or in a rootless mysticism. A writer, vigorously aspiring in his youth, has lost his faith and with unconcealed shamelessness mucks about in his own and his friends' melancholy puddle. An engineer is totally uninterested in what he has built and neglects his work. His wife deceives him without pleasure. The young become destructively restive. Faithful wives are overwrought because of the stupid, complacent inertia of their husbands. An aging maiden comforts herself in a cushion of boneless poetics and musical reverie. A wealthy peasant landowner from Siberia combines muscle with horse sense because he has labored on the land of a still undeveloped area, and a woman doctor retains her sanity and urges escape into constructive paths away from the morass of mediocre safety; though she too suffers, she works usefully. There is a ludicrous move toward suicide and murderous gestures are adumbrated.

The canvas is overcrowded and diffuse, so that it appears to want focus. Yet everything rings true. The play's acrid humor provokes laughter as much as pain. Gorky's compassion is unsentimental. Above all, we find a wealth of observation and sentience in the almost documentary notation of personal and social facts. We very nearly cry out for an alteration of the described condition and one senses that Gorky, while "philosophically" awaiting change, does not distort his vision or mock his people because of impatience.

There was much to praise in the Royal Shakespeare Company presentation, especially in the performances by Margaret Tyzack as the hard-pressed woman physician, Susan Fleetwood as the unhappy lady poetaster, Tony Church as the bibulous engineer, Estelle Kohler as the martyred wife who finally breaks through her bonds. During the first act I had been seated in the sixth row of the "mezzanine," deep in the immense space of the Brooklyn Academy of Music, from which all the actors looked like midgets and all I could be impressed (or depressed) by was the dim sonority of their over-precise diction. When I moved down to the orchestra floor, close to the stage, I observed the excellence of certain details of David Jones's staging and of the acting. But what struck me most throughout was that the play's mood had become entirely British.

I do not refer to the English speech but to a certain hard-edged brittleness in the overall effect. This was especially marked in Ian Richardson's much lauded characterization of the disillusioned writer. He seemed to have stepped in from

Bloomsbury! There was something thin, bloodless, pettily superior and altogether disobliging about him. True, the man has lost his nerve and marrow, but he was once the hope of those who sought a breakthrough into spiritual and social freedom. An artist, though perhaps essentially a "romantic," his depressed readers were justified in expecting and demanding from him a liberating call, an enhancement of being. Richardson's writer was simply nasty. And that, I believe, is counter-indicated by the text and, more decisively, by the Russian temperament.

The most "pooped out" person in Gorky (or Chekhov), even the rare villain or the vicious, has more fiber and heart, more density of "flesh" and soul, more vulnerably quivering humanity, than Richardson's writer possesses—and this holds true for many of the other characters. The Russian, even in his disquiet, in his decline into rottenness, is still a creature who once was a man. He is hardly ever defective through lack of substance, but through a diminution or corruption of a total virility; he almost always remains *full bodied*. This basic quality—ever present in Gogol's satires, in Dostoyevsky's lacerations, in Tolstoy's cautionary lamentations and "anti-heroes," and still there in Chekhov and Gorky—was for the most part missing in the RSC's *Summerfolk*.

But then—and here is the paradox—the production is quite right for the situation and temper of present-day England. Far more "picturesquely," metaphorically and convincingly, it does what most of the "angry young" English playwrights have been trying to do since 1956. *Summerfolk* as given here is the best "English" play of the past two decades.

To descend from the comparatively sublime to the utterly ridiculous—to the bottom of the barrel in fact—it is worth being reminded that *The Rocky Horror Show* (Belasco Theatre), which I thought originated on Sunset Boulevard, actually is an English product.

The Rocky Horror Show is deliberately sloppy: tackiness is its style. Compared to this most recent expression of English collapse, the "Beats" were idealists and poets. They wanted to remove themselves from the suffocation of middle-class conformity. The creators of this piece—*The Rocky Horror Show*—Richard O'Brien, the director Jim Sharman, and the leading player Tim Curry, who made the show a huge success in London and Hollywood, have cut themselves off from any sort of dream to sink in raucous abandon to a realm without memory of anything more elevated than the old-fashioned science-fiction thriller. It is a domain of little joy though much ambivalent sexual activity, where little distinction is made between male and female and where refuse is the natural resting place. Costumes are by choice ugly and tattered, music is pointedly jagged, aural and visual shock is supposed to make for a special sort of euphoria. There is no protest in this: it is embraced as a fact, something that irremediably *is*, a celebration of garbage. And note, furthermore, that the show as offered at the Belasco is arranged, cabaret style, with separate tables at which drinks, peanuts and popcorn are served (some food and dancing follow the performance) and the whole is relatively tidied up. It is all perhaps an image of where civilization has landed itself.

—*NAT*, 29 Mar. '75

DEATH OF A SALESMAN

What is most important in the revival of Arthur Miller's *Death of a Salesman* (Circle in the Square Theatre) is not the merits or faults of the production but the text itself. Despite its initial success in 1949 and widespread reputation for high excellence, there have been and probably still persist in the byways of critical opinion those who cavil at the general acclaim.

The play, it has been said, cannot be a tragedy because its central personage, Willy Loman, is more or less a fool, almost literally a "little" man whose aspirations are mediocre or trivial. The question whether the play is a tragedy or not has

never occupied me in the least. For purposes of appreciation it may just as well be dubbed a comedy: aesthetic nomenclature doesn't help understanding.

The play is neither an attack on the "system" nor a cautionary tract. Its comedy and pathos arise from the depiction of people detached from reality. Willy Loman, in particular, is nowhere; he flies through an ether of illusion because he and the world in which he dwells lack truly human values. Yet he believes in that world and dies without ever becoming aware of its emptiness. For want of recognizing the unsubstantiality of his condition he, with all the good will possible, destroys not only himself but his almost equally benighted family.

Willy's economically luckier neighbor, Charlie, speaks in specifics when he says, "Willy was a salesman. And for a salesman, there is no rock bottom to life. He don't put a bolt to a nut, he don't tell you the law or give you a medicine. He's a man way out there in the blue, riding on a smile and a shoeshine." But what should be evident through the play is that in our civilization we are all somehow placed in Willy's position: we all become "salesmen!"

Willy does not possess his soul. Or if he conceives of one, his notion of it is based only on concern for his family's well being—that is, its prospering, its gaining position and power in a society which is itself very nearly a spiritual vacuum.

Willy is better than most because he is a dreamer. His dream is a false one because it corresponds only to what is immediately given as the object of dreams—swell jobs, fat incomes, splendid accouterments, splash and display. Yet all the while we perceive in Willy's funny and dismal twists and turns, his perpetual mouthing of vapid slogans culled from commercial publicity and received doctrine, a reaching toward something that might nourish the hunger of his inmost being. He envies the success of his neighbor's lawyer-son who is to argue a case before the Supreme Court; he idealizes the phantom of his brother who went into a jungle and achieved a fortune—in diamonds. He cannot know that such envy and "ideals" are the very crystallization of his folly. His unconscious integrity as a true person has been dissolved in his fantasies. Because of them he cannot discover his deepest needs, his native aptitudes or the full treasure of his love.

Willy Loman is no special case, nor is his plight merely a sad story: his number is legion; I almost said, universal. Hence the power, the stature of the play. Not to recognize this is to put oneself in the category of the man in the audience who on seeing the original production summed it all up by muttering, "That New England territory [where Loman plied his trade] always was a bitch." Miller's details are commonplace, chosen as they are from the routine of a petty existence, but they add up to something far greater than the particles. In more ways than one, he was right: attention must be paid!

One might say of the new Loman, George C. Scott, that he is an actor of tremendous clout. He is always vivid, never less than arresting. He is one of the few American actors who create the impression of a mature manliness: most others strike me as grown-up boys. Scott understands Loman but he gives him almost too much personal dimension. That is a matter of personality, rather than of interpretation. He is more the boss or the man who might have been the boss. What he and the production he has directed miss is a pervasive tone of lyricism, subdued but nearly always present. Despite fitful explosions of temper which should never be abrasive, the characters all move in a realm of "romanticism"—yearning, laughable, touchingly tender. For all that is humdrum about the play it is not matter-of-fact naturalism; it has its own special poetry. The production suffers from a certain dryness, overcome only by the intrinsic spirit of the text.

There are other shortcomings, some of them technically unavoidable. In the last scene—the Requiem—for instance, it is impossible for the people to stand in line together over Willy's grave—impossible because the theatre's structure does not allow the necessary sight lines for such an arrangement. The characters are, therefore, dispersed on the stage in a manner which makes the funeral ceremony casual and haphazard rather than solemn, as it should be.

I was rather disturbed by the casting of two black actors as Willy's next-door neighbors—though both of them are good. James Farentino as Biff, Willy's older son, is too mature-looking and blunt, lacking the fineness of personal texture which the character must have, though he plays the climactic confrontation scenes (between himself and his father) with the proper hurt and dramatic passion. Harvey Keitel has a sweet callowness in the first act but unaccountably fades out in the second. Teresa Wright is a little too forthright as Mrs. Loman; she makes the woman more sensitive than brokenly staunch in the limbo of crushing melancholy which is the Loman household.

But none of these demurs diminishes my conviction that one should see the play—certainly one of the signal best in the entire American repertory.

—*NAT*, 19 July '75

ORSON WELLES

I found myself caught up in Orson Welles's *F for Fake*, not for its cinematic virtues but on account of my interest in Welles as a person.

The film concerns itself with such self-declared frauds as Clifford Irving, author of the bogus biography of Howard Hughes, who also wrote a biography of Elmyr de Hory, the fantastic forger of Matisse, Modigliani and Picasso paintings. The picture, shot in semi-documentary form, mixes fact and fiction—an exercise in filmic prestidigitation.

Welles has always practiced tricks of magic. Part of his artistry lies in his use of "mystery." He has sought to transfigure himself and his work into something strangely out of this world. He has delighted in subterfuge and imaginative deceit, in alternation from Jekyll to Hyde, in masks. He launched his career by a now self-confessed lie: at an early age he told the credulous people in the Dublin theatre that he was a famous American actor and, having been cast in several good parts there, he was received in America as an actor of considerable repute in Ireland.

He has always played with the media of radio, stage and screen as with gigantically astonishing toys. He thinks fantastically and big. An arch-showman, he doesn't wish to be known for what he is but for what he might appear to be. He is a charlatan of genius, committed in life as in art to the theatre which tells lies to reveal truth. In his new film, he celebrates with intriguing candor the fake and the faker. He is so devoted to the psychological *double entendre* that he frequently outsmarts himself and very nearly nullifies his enormous talent. He has fashioned a fabulous persona for himself behind which lurks a greater degree of vulnerability than we might suppose.

He has always created new faces for himself; one of them was that of a bohemian clown of Falstaffian disposition, posture and weight. But lo! now that he exposes in *F for Fake* this inner compulsion to parade his dazzling ambiguity, he looks as if he had come into his own more fully than ever before. There is something impressively complete in his present disguise. He was handsome in his youth (in the first part of *Citizen Kane*, for example) but there was something unformed, unborn in his countenance. Now he is a man, a very special man, but a whole man. He has developed into himself.

—*NAT*, 19 Oct. '75

TRAVESTIES

I confess to have betaken myself with reluctance to the two most recent major theatre openings: Tom Stoppard's *Travesties* and Robert Patrick's *Kennedy's Children*, for I had recently commented on both. But on seeing them again, I noticed things I had not previously perceived. Which goes to show....

About *Travesties* (Ethel Barrymore Theatre) I had written that its author is "brilliantly adept as well as highly cultivated. He is certainly entertaining. Besides his shrewd theatrical sportiveness there is in him an itch to communicate matters of philosophical import." I failed however to grasp exactly what the import of *Travesties* might be. I supposed it to be contained in the play's concluding lines—"You're either a revolutionary or you're not, and if you're not you might as well be an artist as anything else...If you can't be an artist, you might as well be a revolutionary...."

I realize now that this aphorism sums up an attitude that informs Stoppard's other plays: *Rosencrantz and Guildenstern Are Dead* and *Jumpers*. This attitude—in its context it cannot be called a "philosophy"—is one of almost total skepticism: we can be sure of nothing. Humankind is tossed about in a storm of experience with no certainty as to its origin, direction or outcome. The thought may cause us to shed tears or arouse laughter. Stoppard laughs.

The joke in *Travesties* is that the memory of our own past is as unreliable as everything else. In the play is Henry Carr, who was British Consul in Zurich in 1917. There he met James Joyce who had undertaken to produce *The Importance of Being Ernest*, in which Carr was to play Algernon—or, as he repeatedly says, "was it the other one?" Carr also supposes that he encountered Lenin, resident in Zurich at the time, as well as the Dada poet Tristan Tzara. If he had stopped Lenin from boarding the sealed train which took him to Russia, Carr might have foiled the Bolshevik seizure of power. but, he speculates, that probably isn't so, since Marx himself had maintained that the doom of capitalism was inevitable and, in that case, the revolution would have taken place if Lenin, or for that matter Marx, had never existed. Ergo the individual person can't alter the course of history. It's a rationalization for social passivity— or for becoming an artist!

For purposes of theatre criticism it is not essential to dispute the point. What I must assert, however, is that in this play Stoppard is neither a revolutionary nor, except in a most limited sense, an artist. The play is a charade, full of antic capers, educated allusions and bright writing in high-grade English. As such it is a superior show not entirely without significance. Its amused skepticism suggests flaccidity of will, the weakening of moral sinew characteristic of our time. It gratifies those for whom a jocular literacy and a modicum of theatrical and intellectual glitter are sufficient.

The Royal Shakespeare production is also attractively clever, though John Wood, a versatile and gifted actor, pushes his characterization too hard. It is an excusable fault, since his role and all the others in the play are cartoons.

—*NAT*, 22 Nov. '75

AN IMPOVERISHED STAGE
A MUSICAL JUBILEE

To be proficient in the craft, the actor must have more or less steady occasion to practice it. Sometime appearances on or off Broadway, a soap opera, a shot in the dark of cinema, a summer stock engagement, a TV commercial, may provide a livelihood for the actor; it will hardly extend a capacity for acting on the stage.

The actor must of course earn a living; the shrinkage in stage production for at least the past thirty-five years has made the possibility of doing so extremely precarious. Apart from musicals, very few productions are undertaken here, most of our plays being imports from London performed by their original casts. Off-Broadway production has become as commercially hazardous as the large-scale enterprises. The result is an artistic as well as economic crisis. And while I am chiefly concerned with the first, it is imperative to begin with the statistics of the second. But, as we shall

see, something even more fundamental is involved—a social and cultural condition crucial to the whole.

I return now to the question I raised here (*The Nation*, November 15): why in recent years has the quality of acting become impoverished? The obvious answer is that our most notable talents (among the men, at any rate)—Marlon Brando, Paul Newman, Al Pacino, Dustin Hoffman, Jack Nicholson and others—abandon the theatre soon after their abilities have been recognized in New York. That is easily explained: there are too few worthy scripts to provide continuous employment, the stage offers only limited "exposure" and as good Americans our actors must not only be well off, but very well off.

But this plausible explanation does not go to the heart of the matter. There might be almost enough plays of, let us say, modest merit, to offer desirable acting opportunities for players who have not yet achieved "names." But producers and their backers demand "stars" to protect their investment, although the truth is that there are today fewer than ten actors who can by their attractiveness or renown sustain a play that doesn't in itself interest an audience. This fact is generally overlooked by the folk responsible for New York play production because most of them are dilettantes, amateurs or nervous speculators rather than knowledgeable and committed theatre people. They are rarely able to judge a script.

In the aforementioned column I suggested that for the younger actors there has been an overemphasis on one or the other aspect of the craft of acting: the so-called emotive or the so-called technical. In the first instance, acting often becomes self-indulgent personal effusion without consideration for interpreting the inherent content of the script, of style and of external skills. In reaction to this, a system of training is often pursued which takes for granted acting talent (the faculty of embodying total human behavior within the artifices of the stage) so that the stage aspirant need only be perfected as an instrument in movement (including dance) and speech (in addition to singing) with grace, clarity and volume of articulation. But to separate these elements is to think of the body without a soul or vice versa. Even the Japanese teachers of the Noh, one of the most "stylized" of theatrical modes, complain that most of their younger actors who have mastered its external forms lack inner motivation for it, so that the result is "traditional" but no longer a living art.

What brought this most sharply to mind was seeing *A Musical Jubilee* (St. James Theatre) and remembering the Rodgers and Hart package last season. It hardly need be said that neither of those shows called for "deep emotion." The voices in both instances ranged from fair to very good; the actors were certainly engaging—Tammy Grimes in *A Musical Jubilee* brings an impish humor to everything she does—but there was something of inert window display in both shows. The spirit which had originally brought those very winning songs into being, the animating motive, the period atmosphere of which they were an expression—in short, their style—was almost entirely missing in these performances. Every show—be it Wilde, Shaw, Ionesco, Beckett or *Hellzapoppin'*—must have its own special "soul" (or style) as much as Chekhov, Shakespeare or Sophocles, for they all have roots in a manner of being, a way of life. Lacking this, they leave us unstimulated, dispirited. The "nostalgia" is arid.

To venture a broad metaphorical generalization, I might say that the scores of most recent musicals are usually their weakest ingredient because there is no music in the air! And for a somewhat similar reason most acting now is quite competent—and uninspired. We are living in an era of conformity through commercial need or pressure. Adventure and direct challenge is in the making of money; if possible, a fortune. (A New York director on arriving in Hollywood observed "Actors here talk more about their contracts—options, residuals, billing—than about their parts.")

The actors up to the time of such men as Alfred Lunt and Fredric March inherited something of the "pioneer" stamina which characterized their profession from Edwin Forrest in the mid-19th century through the second decade of this one. Many of those actors were knockabouts and a little disreputable: they lived in a rather strenuously reckless manner—largely because they were obliged to. It was a rougher and a more spacious time than ours. To be an actor then was to be something of a sacred monster, an "outlaw," generally distrusted in polite circles. Now they are citizens like the rest of us, bent above all on security and success. Our progress in technological or prefabricated comfort has whittled us all down.

There is only a little extravagance in saying this. What actors today are full-grown men or women, robust, awe-inspiring personalities? John Barrymore and Laurette Taylor may have been exceptional even in their day, but I could name many or equal stature whose careers were as much brave as brilliant struggles from beginning to end. (Barrymore was as sparkling in comedy as he was magnificent in drama. The same was true of Taylor.) In their blemishes as well as in their powers such actors were of a dimension beyond the rather hearty audiences for whom they played. That is why they were revered. They had "muscle," they were larger than life. There was adventuresomeness in them and danger. Most of plays were written with such actors as his father in mind, the father of whom he disapproved as a person but whose authority as a player he thought heroic. The ideal sought after was grandeur. Actors were then tremendously virile; actresses inescapably enchanting goddesses! Today we see too many historically notable plays—classic or near classic—acted by casts which strike me as kids in knickerbockers and pinafores, parading as giants.

I am not clamoring for the shows of yesteryear, but the theatre can flourish only when it is not viewed or conducted chiefly as one business among others. Nor is it—as what I have just said might lead some to believe—a place for "wandering minstrels," though I prefer such characters to entrepreneurs on a holiday from more humdrum occupations. The theatre must exist and be thought of first of all as "a factory of thought, a prompter of conscience, an elucidator of social conduct, an armory against despair and dullness, and a temple of the Ascent of Man." That is how in 1906 Shaw put it. I think of it as a necessary, an essential organ of a community's consciousness. That is how in every civilized country it has been maintained even in periods of hardship and distress, even in times of revolution.

Today, under extremely onerous economic circumstances, the English Government supports three theatres for drama in London alone, theatres which never function at a profit. That is also one of the reasons why English dramatists have not defected, as many American playwrights do when their plays flop or are no longer held to be safe investments. (One thing that may be said with some assurance about the better English writers for the theatre is that they have not evaded but have dramatized the bitter burden of living in our day.) And almost all the best actors are ever eager to appear in their plays.

Most of our playwrights fade with failure. (The great exception was O'Neill.) Our younger playwrights are satisfied with being promising, innovative and shaggy. They rarely learn to discipline themselves, to think their problems through, to strive for genuine mastery, and their well-wishers or advocates do not constrain them to do so. The entire theatre situation is too unstable, too loose, too haste-ridden, too sloppily permissive.

The underlying ailment we suffer is only indirectly economic. Till we come to understand in practice, not just in theory, that theatre is theatre and not an adjunct of financial interests, that its values are not inevitably connected with the accountant's ledger or one's personal bank account, there can be no excitement, glamour or mature interest in the art. Even a state-subsidized theatre in the United States would at present prove of only slight benefit if what was sought were only more of the same conventional or success-oriented standard which obtains commercially or in our partially subsidized theatre institutions.

I have said all this before: it should be said thousands and thousands of times. Must everything collapse before such proclamations are heeded?

—*NAT*, 6 Dec. '75

THE MISANTHROPE

There are a host of figures in literature which, though created as individual persons, have in the course of the ages taken on significance as universal types. Hamlet, Don Juan, Don Quixote are names which readily come to mind. What is remarkable about them is they are all ambiguous: neither entirely virtuous nor wholly wise.

Though of noble mind and princely vigor, Hamlet is weakened by both his impetuosity and by his questioning the value of an assigned duty. The great lover, Don Juan, may be impelled by his inability to love or by a fear of impotence. Don Quixote is a headlong idealist whose deportment is barely distinguishable from a befuddlement of the brain.

So, too, Molière's Alceste, the misanthrope. If he is at all a hero, he is an absurd one. A rebel against society, he is vulnerable in his private life. He accomplishes nothing by his harangues against dishonesty; he abdicates. We view him with respect—we may even think him our spokesman—and yet we recognize in him something of a comic dupe.

Alceste's ambivalence has, therefore, lent itself to diverse stage interpretations. In Paris many years ago, I saw the renowned Lucien Guitry play Alceste with a gravity and spleen which caused most of the critics to complain that he had divested the play of its fun. Guitry in an interview countered with, "If you see anything funny in Alceste's situation, you are free to laugh. I don't see it that way." Though *The Misanthrope* is generally held to be Molière's supreme masterpiece, it was not as successful in its day (1666) as most of Molière's previous plays. And no wonder! If Alceste's diatribes against hypocrisy are sufficiently tempestuous to appear ludicrous, they still found their mark during Louis XIV's reign: the audience of the time must have found many of Alceste's barbs hurtful. Courtly manners spelled flattery toward those in positions of power and moral frivolity, masking itself in attitudes of superb sophistication and elaborate displays of malicious wit. Alceste is not only unwilling to flatter anyone, but eager at the slightest provocation to flay all and sundry for the least sign of polite prevarication.

When Alceste's friend, Philinte, asks him, "Wouldn't the social fabric come undone if we were wholly frank with everyone? Suppose you met with someone you couldn't bear; would you inform him of it then and there?" Alceste's blunt answer is "Yes." Society as a whole then (as now) would agree with Philinte that Alceste, or his like, should forget the follies of the times and pardon mankind for its petty crimes; let's have an end of ranting and of ravings, and show some leniency to human failings. The world requires a pliant rectitude; too stern a virtue makes one stiff and rude; good sense views all extremes with detestation, and bids us to be noble in moderation...I take men as they are, or let them be...."

Alceste's obstreperous uprightness can and often does provoke laughter. "If people heard you talking so, Alceste," says Philinte, "they'd split their sides. Your name would be a jest." To which Alceste's tart reply is, "So much the worse for the jesters." And because of an uncertainty as to Molière's own view of Alceste—did he believe Alceste a fool?—many critics and audiences have been troubled because they believe he did not make himself entirely clear in the matter. Some have maintained that Philinte is Molière's mouthpiece, or what may be worse, that Molière was protecting himself against the suspicion that *he* is Alceste, and that his view of seventeenth century Paris was that of the misanthrope. That, in fact, was what Jean Jacques Rousseau in the eighteenth century accused Molière of doing, and

though he harbored the almost universal French veneration for Molière, he scorned the play. But then Rousseau himself was something of an Alceste.

There is another side to the picture, more personal and human than any of these socially controversial considerations. Alceste is enamored of a girl who is extremely flirtatious and playfully insincere, certainly as devious as any of the fops he reviles. Alceste admits this with the lame (or sufficient) excuse, "Reason doesn't rule in love." Cupid has brought the arrogant sermonizer down.

This, in more ways than one, brings us to the heart of the matter. Alceste is perhaps a man of forty (like Molière, who first played the part) and his beloved Célimène only twenty. In the seventeenth century, a man of forty was considered older than we do a man past sixty today. This discrepancy of age in Alceste's marriage was regarded as in itself ridiculous. (One remembers the same discrepancy and the jokes which derive from it in Molière's earlier play, *The School of Husbands*.) But in *The Misanthrope*, he was not aiming at any sort of "propaganda" in this regard, though he was one of the "liberals" of his time in relation to women. Molière, at forty, had married the leading lady of his company, Armande Béjart, who played Célimène to his Alceste, and who was exactly half his age. Their marriage was far from calm: she was a terrible coquette and probably unfaithful. Molière was no more capable of leaving her, than Alceste, till the very end, is able to give up Célimène.

Alceste's rule of absolute integrity and consistency of behavior is breached by his infatuation with the flighty Célimène and it is through this contradiction that the play completes itself and exemplifies one of the issues very much in the air of Molière's time, and of all time. For the conflict between personal sentiment and classical order represented secularly by the all dominant King and his court was the subject of the tragic drama of the era: that of Corneille and Racine. Desire, fierce to the point of sinfulness in Racine, had to give way to the dictates of reason. Reason and order were equated with the fixed principles of the epoch, the ethical foundation of the Sun King's monarchy. In the eighteenth century, natural feeling laid siege to the fortress of the old morality.

Molière was not an aristocrat, but a *bourgeois*—a tradesman. He was a forerunner of the humanistic opposition (which eventuated in a Revolution) pitted against the old regime and the moral authority which was integral with it. But Molière, dependent on Louis XIV's favor and frequently protected by him, never openly defied the prevailing doctrine. He mocked clerical cant, he derided the licentiousness of the nobility, he ridiculed the obscurantism of the medical profession, he espoused the cause of youth against the rigid prejudices of their elders, he lampooned the stupidity and avarice of parents in *Scapin*, he satirized the wealthy businessmen who aped the highborn in *The Bourgeois Gentleman*, he poked fun at blue stockings along with the pretensions of boring intellectuals. In short, he was the dramatic gadfly of his day, but though there was a serious and stern element in all his jibes, he never more than momentarily forsook the amiability of the comic muse. All his plays grin, even when they suggest a grimace. He was committed to sanity, so that he could serve at once as a social castigator and as a benevolent healer of the ills which beset his world. And of all his plays, *The Misanthrope* most strikingly reveals his mind and method. For there can be no doubt that Alceste says much that Molière felt. Does not the most sympathetic character in the play, Eliante, declare, "The honesty in which he (Alceste) takes such pride, has its noble, heroic side." Molière had less egotism than Alceste, and a more smiling and accommodating forbearance.

This salutary duality makes *The Misanthrope* forever and everywhere contemporary. That is why there is nothing at all forced and gimmicky in the British National Theatre's setting of this masterpiece in the France of a more recent regime.

—*STGB*, '75

SUMMER BRAVE

William Inge's *Summer Brave* is no *Picnic*. *Picnic* is a comedy providing many laughs with an underlay of sadness. Indeed it is all "opposites". It deals with "ordinary" folk, but Inge's attitude toward them is by no means ordinary. It ends happily but a note of skepticism may be detected in the future of this happiness. This note of skepticism was deepened considerably by Inge when he rewrote *Picnic* shortly before his death and retitled it *Summer Brave*.

Inge was wholly aware of the grim realities of existence but he was equally conscious that patient understanding might relieve them and render them benign. Without being sappy, running through *Picnic* we discern a romantic affirmation. Love, Inge implies, is an unquenchably imperious instinct, in which we must believe for life to be made bearable.

First produced in 1953 (under Joshua Logan's direction), *Picnic* is situated in a Kansas town. It is an environment which Inge, Kansas born in 1913, knew more intimately than any other American playwright. His play is a piece of grass roots Americana. The date of production suggests that the author was writing of his homeland in the Forties or perhaps even earlier but the sentiment of the play has something about it of permanent native relevance, something, in other words, which holds true of our experience now as much as of then. *Picnic* is another depiction of "our town" seen more ruefully and thus more realistically than viewed in Thornton Wilder's idyll.

There is another aspect of *Picnic* which is characteristic of its several contradictions. It reads almost too simply or simplemindedly but it plays beautifully; all its various roles are so finely shaded that they offer wonderful opportunities for superb performances as well as for audience appreciation. The laconic, underwritten, dialogue is typical of midwestern speech, but it sounds notes deeper than its plain vocabulary might lead us to suspect. The "simplicity" of the play is not so "simple," which is one reason why there was a tendency shortly before Inge's death in 1972 to underestimate his contribution to our drama.

On the surface *Picnic* appears casually cheerful but its over-all atmosphere—most delicately indicated—is one of loneliness. Hardly any of the characters complain of isolation or the constriction of their lives: they are not articulate people. They accept their situation or repressed mode of living as completely natural. Indeed they seem to enjoy it. When eighteen-year-old Madge "the prettiest girl in town" cries out, "Oh, Mom, what can you do with the love you feel? Where can you take it?," her widowed mother replies, "I...never found it." Those bare words strike the keynote of the play. The train whistle in the gaunt landscape supplies the orchestration for it. The heat of the seemingly endless late summer day stresses the surrounding aridity. Still from the pain or melancholy of ordinariness there emanates a kind of stifled poetry.

Lacking both cultural aid to self-knowledge and normal emotional outlets—Kansas is a state bound by numerous written and unwritten blue laws—the impulses the "picnic" people sense are a puzzle to them. Though Madge is called "Delilah" by her boyfriend and the fresh newspaper delivery boy is constantly whistling at her in adolescent lust she nevertheless wonderingly confesses, "It seems like when I'm looking in the mirror that's the only way I can prove to myself I'm alive." And yet she also asks, "Mom, what good is it to be pretty?" and later on adds, "I get so tired of being told I'm pretty." Kindly Mrs. Potts, in thrall to an ailing and commanding mother, shows intuitive insight when she declares, "We plan picnics just to give ourselves an excuse to let something thrilling happen to our lives."

When Howard, the forty-two-year-old bachelor who runs a little "notions, novelties, and school supplies" shop finally consents to marry Rosemary Sydney, the pathetically and hysterically eager

shorthand teacher at the local school, he apologetically explains his taking so bold a step, "A man's gotta settle down sometime" and adds more self-assuringly, "And folks'd rather do business with a married man."

All the people suffer difficulty in either loving or receiving love. Something about love apart from its connection with marriage is somehow found embarrassing. Young men are categorized as either good boys or bad boys. The good boys are reticent and inept, the bad boys uncouth and dangerous. As a result "sex" is in the air manifesting itself in peculiarly oblique, slightly comic or grotesquely masked forms. And when passion emerges it bursts forth like a twister, the sort of tornado that overwhelms and sometimes devastates the central states. But it is just such passion that Inge sees as a saving grace, a human need, especially when circumstances are set up to impede or deny it.

The middle west, which diversE writers speak of as quintessentially American, has often been painted in gloomy or drab colors and not infrequently in derision, is viewed by Inge in his early plays—*Picnic, Bus Stop, The Dark at the Top of the Stairs*—with compassion and benevolent humor. (In fact, though the characters in *Picnic* frequently behave in a manner quite different from the perfect "respectability" they profess, they are not really hypocrites and throughout remain entirely sympathetic.) That is why despite the critical implications these plays contain they achieved popular success as entertainment. One has to regard them with some thoughtfulness to realize the "warning" lurking in their shadows. When the more sombre significance of Inge's ostensibly lighthearted plays was overlooked and he was downgraded as a mere purveyor of hit shows, he and his work turned shatteringly bitter. This change can be seen clearly when the sunny *Picnic* is compared with the more bittersweet *Summer Brave.*

—*JFK*, '75

STARK YOUNG—A LIFE IN THE ARTS: Letters, 1900-1962

In the history of the earlier 20th-century American theatre, there have been only two critics who have strongly impinged on its literature: George Jean Nathan and Stark Young.

Through his education, his European travels, his knowledge of foreign languages and his histrionic sophistication and flair—he was something of a showoff—Nathan made the more alert public aware of the world of the theatre beyond the Broadway horizon. He was in no sense a profound critic but he championed Ibsen and Shaw when they were still caviar to the general, and he was the first to beat the drum for O'Neill. He began writing his most valuable reviews in 1905; their impact began to diminish by the end of the 1920s.

Stark Young, who began his career as a theatre critic in 1921 at the age of 40, brought a refined aesthetic disposition to his view of the theatre. Most important, he knew that it was a single art of which all the components had to be judged as integral to the whole production or performance. Himself an occasional painter (he exhibited his pictures at various galleries in 1946-47) he had an especially keen appreciation of décor and costume. His observation of acting and directing was more particular and probing in its sensibility than that of any previous American critic and to this day he has not been surpassed in this regard. He was a man of considerable education and culture—deeper and more extensive than Nathan's. While Nathan was a hornblower for artists he admired, Young's criticism moved toward poetry. He had an ear for the *tone* of each production, and sought in each staged play the soul which imbued it and the "music" it created.

One reason why so few of our theatre critics have achieved any true distinction is that hardly any of them are men of stature, interesting individuals apart from the temporary and limited prestige of their jobs. "If you amount to nothing," Young says, "your art in the end amounts to nothing." Stark Young was *somebody*.

The best of an artist is in his art. The rest is only the sediment of his mundane behavior. No biography of Stark Young exists as yet. But perhaps none is now needed because the most complete view of his personality in its flaws as well as in its admirable features is to be found in the vast collection of his letters recently issued by the Louisiana State University at Baton Rouge, splendidly edited by John Pillington. They have, besides other assets, a special documentary value as Americana.

Not that Young wrote great letters as did Shaw, though the extent of his correspondence was extraordinary. Even so, much is omitted: love letters, for example. It is also evident that Young did not intend his letters to be published; in fact, he frequently apologizes for their "dullness" and for the desultoriness of his hastily written, poorly typed or pen-scratched messages. Still a picture and a feeling of the man emerge. Besides letters to near relations, there are many to Julian Huxley, Ellen Glasgow, Allen Tate and to a host of editors, teachers, poets, actors and critics.

Young was pre-eminently a Southerner. Not simply because he was born one—so were his fellow critics Joseph Wood Krutch and John Mason Brown—but his sense of life, his nostalgia, his hope for the perpetuation of something he once knew in the native landscape, even to a considerable degree his style, all stem from the southland. Though he enjoyed some of the razzle-dazzle of New York, he never felt really at ease anywhere far from his birthplace—except possibly in Italy and there mostly in Florence. He recognized the inevitability of industry's rampage but he could never be reconciled to it. New York which "points to what the world is going to be," he wrote in 1921, "leaves one longing for the dream of something smaller and seemingly more complete at least in its meaning." His roots were close to the traditional, classically oriented, Southern aristocracy: the planting class. Though not a committed "agrarian," he wished that some of agrarianism's fundamental values could be retained as a corrective or guide to offset what he called "trashimindedness" which the proliferation of the machine plus business had fostered.

What in Young's estimation was Southern? He speaks of Poe as Southern in "the formalism of his tone, the drift toward rhetoric, the aloof or elusive intensity." What he most intimately associated with the South was "the life of the affections in some beloved air." The salient feature of his letters is his great capacity for friendship. He calls the people he cares about and who care for him "cousin" whether or not they were so related. He hungers for the comfort and solace of graceful manners, a lordly warmth. "The strong belong to the weak through love," he writes.

No wonder then that in the midst of Manhattan he came to feel that "the whole world is getting cheap" and that "sometimes I feel that America is unbearable." As a theatre critic for *The New York Times* he lasted one season—1924-25—because its publisher thought his reviews "too abstract."

Yet—very humanly!—he desired general acceptance in the vulgar marketplace in which destiny had placed him. How desperately he craved praise from his inferiors, almost as much as from his peers. He tries to disguise the pleasure he feels at being wanted by Paramount Pictures. He hoped in 1922 to do "something distinguished with his reviews" and adds "at any rate the theatre will know I am in town…for I try to say what I think aesthetically, which is something they are unaccustomed to." But in 1939 he writes, "I have used a great deal of good taste with a very small reward, and neglected to use some good old bad taste, that might have worked wonders."

Broadway might have mistaken his manner for prissiness, though such an allegation would have been false, but misunderstanding was in any case unavoidable. There were other reasons to for his separation from the tendencies of his day, many of which he found abrasive, causing pustules of malice and spite to show on the skin of his politeness.

Philosophically, Young may be described as a Platonic idealist. His style often suggests a reaching for the ineffable, an ascent toward a star of meaning which must forever elude definition. The result is often stimulating as well as beautiful and occasionally gaspingly unfulfilled. The effort, when it was pursued without the encumbrance of untranslated quotations in Latin, Greek or Italian, made his theatre criticism genuinely significant. For opinion alone is not criticism. But it was precisely the genuineness of the kind of criticism he wrote that puzzled those persons who must be persuaded by an author who seeks general popularity. It is perhaps not a paradox that Young's civil war novel, *So Red the Rose*, published in 1934, was much more transparently written and partly on that account became a best-seller and material for a movie.

Young eschewed the admixture of social and political comment which characterized the writing of many of his colleagues in the weekly and monthly journals during the 1930s. This was a further factor in his estrangement from his contemporaries. He was not so much stupid about politics as essentially unconcerned with them, and in one instance so unknowing that he was able to write in 1931, "I saw Mussolini who was very warm and intelligent, and several times saw their remarkable Minister of Foreign Affairs, Grandi, who had me to dine." In addition he wrote with palpable pride that he had "just received a decoration from the King of Italy and the government, *Commander of the Crown of Italy*." But in this I see his thirst for important recognition rather than a strong reactionary bent. He frequently speaks as if he were unsure of his position, indeed as though he were a failure.

At times his insecurity rendered him almost laughably ingenuous. He deplores literary "wire-pulling," the use of complimentary citations from his friends on the publication of his novels, plays, memoirs, translations, but he is constantly requesting them. At every turn he explains and all but puffs the virtues of his writing. He cherishes those who praise him and becomes mean when he detects even mild resistance to his work.

Though certainly no anti-Semite, he is led to refer to several adverse reviewers of his section as "young Jews" or "New York Jews." And once writing to a priest in Rome he points out that his ancestors could be traced back to a lady who came to our country with the lost colony of Virginia in 1580, and tongue in cheek adds, "so I am really more American than Irving Berlin." He was wrong about that! But it was his wound and alienation from his immediate environment that is the source of such breaches of his high-mindedness.

At his best—and human being should always be judged on that ground—he was one of those distinguished figures in our culture most often forgotten, especially in the theatre. He maintained lofty standards, and if he had limitations, they were the vices of his qualities. He stood for something, and so he wrote with some bitterness, "in New York nobody represents anything." (In our society a point of view is a dangerous thing.) Because he was what he was his criticism is not only readable, as is that of very few others, but often inspiring. I still recommend him to students to acquaint them with the nature of criticism in the theatre—which in the course of their reading of current theatrical journalism they might never get to know. Besides their other assets, his *Letters* offer a broad view of the cultural spectrum in the years between the 1920s and the mid-1940s.

—*NAT*, 20 Mar. '76

THE LADY FROM THE SEA

On seeing Ibsen's *The Lady From The Sea* (the Circle in the Square) I asked myself why, though it is almost the only Ibsen play with a happy ending, it is so rarely produced. The answer, I believe, is that if it is not to seem somewhat banal it needs very special playing. (Of past performances we hear only of Duse's magic.) Despite its apparent transparency, *The Lady From The Sea* is elusive.

It is often referred to as the first of Ibsen's "mystic" plays. Its central figure, Ellida Wangel, harbors a constant yearning for the sea and is haunted by the memory of a sailor to whom she was once betrothed. After committing a crime, he escaped and disappeared. Some years later, Ellida marries a doctor, a widower, the father of two children. He is a kindly, intelligent, in all ways honorable person who offered her security and release from the confinement of the lighthouse of which her father was keeper. The special circumstances of her marriage have left her in a state of disquiet. She has not been able fully to accommodate herself to domesticity. When the sailor, "The Stranger," who had been thought drowned in a shipwreck, reappears and asks her to leave her husband and go off with him, she is tempted.

The special hold that the Stranger seems to exercise on her and the peculiar restlessness which troubled her before his return are the factors which have led to the play's reputation for "mysticism." But all of its elements are materially and psychologically concrete. Her birth in the lighthouse and her long years of proximity to the sea make life with her husband in a tiny, dull seaside resort, unnatural to her. The doctor's elder daughter also longs to get away from home to enter the wide world, an indication that there is nothing specially peculiar in this aspect of Ellida's dilemma.

There is a correspondence between her nature and Ibsen's. He too sought escape from the backwater of the Norway of his time and left it for many years of exile abroad. He too was a romantic who found intolerable the narrow and retarded middle class of his country. Ibsen's protagonists are all romantics of some sort, bent on breaking their bondage to the limitations of their condition. They stifle under the external discipline of custom or place. The "miracle" Nora hoped for in her "doll's house" happens when Dr. Wangel allows Ellida to choose freely between himself and the Stranger, who after the passage of time is more illusion than reality. (He represents boundless freedom.) Absolved from marital constraint, she chooses to remain with her husband, and to become a mother to his younger daughter. Just so, Ibsen himself returned to the cold north of his birth, though he felt himself deeply drawn to the Mediterranean sun.

Wangel says of Ellida that her mind "is like the sea. It ebbs and flows." The same is true of Ibsen and it made him something very different from the stable, dogmatic and rationalistic moralist he is commonly taken to be. His work ebbs and flows, his plays contradict one another, his duality continues to the end. His most steadfast conviction was what Ellida herself learns: that *one can only be free with responsibility*, and that whatever choice one makes in life one must pay for; free will has its price.

Vanessa Redgrave, lovely in person, idealistic, graceful in manner and movement, enchanting in voice and speech, lacks only one trait to render a complete Ellida: she has no "lostness." To the very end—even after the sensible and right reconciliation to her lot—Ellida must not appear settled. She will wander forever in a mist of profound spiritual uncertainty, wavering between life's manifold possibilities, all of them perilous. So while Vanessa Redgrave outlines a creditably engaging Ellida, she misses the darkling poetry essential to the part.

Pat Hingle's Wangel is honest enough, but too literal and stodgy, too much the staid citizen, benevolent but very nearly obtuse. The role requires a modest delicacy, an intuitive and sad awareness of Ellida's ineffable sensibility and pain. For he himself experiences the bewilderment and mystery of her nature and in his own way shares it.

The Stranger is lamentably miscast in the handsome, almost "aesthetic" looking Richard Lynch. The man should be a lean, bronzed, taut-muscled, hard-grained seaman and not the pretty, white-faced hero of a young girl's imagination. He must embody the reality of his experience: a sailor who murdered his captain, suffered a shipwreck,

and who, seasoned character that he is, goes off alone when he sees that he is no longer desired.

This miscasting is no accident. The play has been directed by Tony Richardson entirely for its surface story and "message," with touches of ill-conceived theatrics as in the sharp dimming of the lights when the Stranger—awesome creature!—appears.

These are not the only reasons why for me the play drew a "blank." The oblong three-sided structure of the theatre diffuses one's view of the play. (The actors seemed remote from where I sat in the center of the house.) The background, a veranda and an arbor, are attractive enough, though behind them is a smudgy wash on a canvas backdrop to suggest sea and mountains. In the foreground are several flat stone mounds, used as seats. As for the rest, the actors are obliged to go up into the "hills" (the aisles) through the audience, which destroys all illusion. If it is held that no illusion is needed, since audiences are prepared to adapt themselves to any scenic scheme the director and designer may choose to employ, why use any setting at all? Here it is a mishmash of elements conveying very little except the inadequacy of the house for this particular event.

—*NAT*, 10 Apr. '76

EDWARD ALBEE

There are too few new "straight" plays nowadays to keep our theatres warm. Most of the big hits are musicals. There are occasional light comedies—farces really—and, for the rest, London imports. As a result, managers cast stars in revivals of the better examples of yesteryear. Theatre criticism is thus obliged to become retrospective.

Though an unqualified box office success, Edward Albee's *Who's Afraid of Virginia Woolf?* caused a certain amount of controversy when it was first produced in 1962. Whether one liked it or not, there is no question that to a considerable degree it set the tone for American drama in the 1960s. Playwrights of the 1920s were more or less critical realists, with dabs of quizzical comedy or near satire; the writers of the '30s voiced their dismay at the economic state of the nation and its attendant human disarray and pointed their thoughts toward a (sometimes innocent) remedial hopefulness. The '40s and '50s repeated the theatric material of the earlier periods with greater emphasis on the personal, familial and "psychoanalytic" aspects of the situations they treated. Shock and despair were the keynotes of the late '50s and the '60s. Plays turned savage and nihilistic and—in certain instances, under the influence of Beckett or Pinter—to metaphysical or existential groping. The pervasive tone was somber, the comedy black. This led me then to call the tendency "the dramaturgy of the maimed."

Virginia Woolf was played practically everywhere: it was a smash, despite all objections, even in Israel, and when I was in Japan most of the questions put to me concerned Albee. His "poisons," it seems, were more antitoxin than noxious.

My usual answer to questions asked me about the new dramatic wonder boy was that I could speak of him with greater assurance in ten years: Albee was still a *young* playwright, and while I had hailed his advent on seeing *The Zoo Story* and had been impressed by *The Death of Bessie Smith*, all I could assert with any certainty about *Who's Afraid of Virginia Woolf?* was what I had written in *The Nation*—it was a play "packed with talent."

My review also contained such further notations as "the pessimism and rage of *Who's Afraid of Virginia Woolf?* are immature. Immaturity combined with a commanding deftness is dangerous." To this I added "[the play's] inferno is made very funny. The audience ...laughs long and loud—partly because the writing is sharp with surprise, partly because an element of recognition is involved: in laughter it hides from itself while obliquely acknowledging its resemblance to the couples on the stage." But most of the comments

were tentative as compared to my conviction that "at its best, the play is a comedy."

There is very little I would now revise in my praise or in the fault finding of that early review. But the two things which struck me most on seeing the play in its present revival at the Music Box Theatre were first, the brilliance of a dialogue that has very few equals in the American theatre, and second, that in certain respects Albee had grown.

I was not much concerned on this occasion with the play's "meaning." The parallel with Strindberg's *Dance of Death* seems to be an otiose consideration, the speculation as to whether the husband and wife of the play might be substitutes for a homosexual couple or the unlikelihood that any married pair could maintain the fantasy of having had a son who serves as a subject for their contention didn't matter much to me. There is in the writing a constant crackle of invention, a fluency, a leap, that are delightful in themselves, cleansing the play of many of its less fortunate elements. What is to be especially noted is that the writing is not, as, for instance, in Tom Stoppard's plays, merely clever, a matter of epigram, wit or fine language, but that it is speech of the theatre, a give-and-take of human exchange which is dramatic in itself. The dialogue is shaped into a maliciously sparkling dance; a duel of mind and will. If the play contained very few other merits, this alone would make it extraordinary, affording a special theatrical pleasure.

The touch of pathos in the play's coda led me to believe, as I said in my 1962 review, that it "indicates "Albee's will to break through the agonizing narrowness of the play's compass." *A Delicate Balance* in 1966 justified the surmise: there is more compassion in it, a deeper sense of characterization, a fuller understanding, a broader significance than in *Virginia Woolf*, though it is not as sure-fire in immediate resonance. Then too, the ruminant drama *All Over* had a steadiness and objectivity of observation which surpassed all Albee's previous plays, except that the writing, as in most of the plays since *Virginia Woolf*, tended toward a studied quality bordering on stiffness. And the humor in *Seascape* was gentle and pointed toward humanistic sentiments. If none of Albee's plays exceeds *Virginia Woolf* in pungent force, all of them prove that he is by no means "finished."

—*NAT*, 24 Apr. '76

DANTE

Because its season was brief at the Brooklyn Academy of Music, the Warsaw Teatr Studio performances of *Dante* will no longer be on view when this review appears. Another of the company's productions, *Replika*, may still be seen, and, though I cannot say anything about it at this moment, I recommend that people genuinely interested in the theatre attend.

The reason for this peculiar recommendation is that the company and its director, Jozef Szajna, offer exemplary models of a meaningfully new and powerfully suggestive current in the contemporary theatre. *Dante*, which I saw in Warsaw last June and mentioned briefly in my report here, was first presented in Florence in 1974; and the earlier *Replika* originally was given in Nancy (France). Both plays have subsequently toured many of the world's capitals.

To say that these productions represent what nowadays is frequently referred to as "total theatre" is to emit hot air. Musical comedies as well as the classical Greek theatre answer to the same designation: a combination of speech, stylized movement, dance and striking visual effects are common to them. In regard to *avant-garde* productions we also hear much blather about "audience participation"; no theatre has ever existed without it! Nor is the "theatre of cruelty" a particularly descriptive term, unless we are thinking of the atrocities perpetrated in its name. And while some critics have asserted that such a production as *Dante* does not require knowledge of the language employed to be appreciated, and therefore set it down as "nonverbal," the allega-

tion leaks. Many words assail the ear in *Dante*—words, I venture to judge, quite distinctly pronounced, sung or spoken—and I regretted not knowing exactly what they meant. The fact that many of them were presumably culled from *The Divine Comedy* is also somewhat misleading, for it is clear that, while the Polish text is "based" on the Italian masterpiece, it can hardly be said to follow it. Virgil is absent; Dante is the central figure in the play, whereas in the *Commedia* he is more or less an observer (almost a "visitor") with Virgil as his guide. In the *Purgatorio*, Dante moves "so that untired [he] follows the swift spirits up with ease." In the play, the poet, bearing no resemblance at all to the traditional profile, suffers as much as do any of the condemned in the *Inferno*. A Beatrice is very much present in the production, but she is by no means the Beatrice of the book.

This *Dante* has its source in the director's, Jozef Szajna's, experience in the concentration camps of Auschwitz and Buchenwald where he survived at the age of 22. Originally a scene designer, Szajna conceives his plays in visualizations. His images are related, but hardly correspond, to those in the *Commedia*: for all the parallels with those of the original work, they are images of an inferno and a purgatory which only a latter-day Surrealist artist of the theatre could create. They are eclectically nightmarish, eminently picturesque and excitingly kinetic. They move all over the theatre space, from the lobby through and over the auditorium onto the stage—with some of the actors in agonized contortions, suspended above the heads of spectators in the front rows. Accompanying every episode are expostulations, outcries, groans, wails of derision and pain—a few in Latin and Italian. Lights and stage properties play their part in the phantasmagoria. Though the play ends with the *Commedia*'s closing line—"The love that moves the sun and the other stars"—there is in the spectacle more evocation of fear, anguish and violent passion than of beatitude.

Yet on the whole I was rather more absorbed and stimulated than truly stirred by what I saw, and for several reasons. But before stating them, it is only just that I repeat the play's central virtue: Szajna's vision is propelled by an emotionally authentic impulse. *Dante* does not emerge, as so often occurs in American and other imitations of a similar mode, as a mere stylistic or "aesthetic" exercise. The same is true of the actors, who give themselves to their arduous tasks with a dedication that only an organic connection with the play's *idea*, the spiritual and existential material of the background, could foster.

Months, perhaps years of thought, training and disciplined work on every level—acoustic, mechanical, physical—must be expended in the making of such a play. The actors' bodies are mature, handsome, strong, agile and pliant; the voices supple and sonorous. (The Beatrice of Anna Milewska is especially fine.) The sense of an integrated corps is utterly convincing. And there is a vein of full-blooded sexuality that "subliminally" courses through the event, relieving it of all sickly strain or ostentation.

And yet, one misses a sustaining text, one that might give "music" to what we see and hear, an extension into a realm which the images alone fail to provide. This does not mean that the visual cannot rise in the theatre to heights of supersensual values, values beyond their concrete embodiment. But much of what we behold in *Dante* tends to be either a little too simplistic or the product of private metaphors which do not really communicate what the director and various ecstatic critics suppose they do. They do not possess the sort of universality which penetrates beyond ordinary intelligibility as does the poetry of the *Commedia*, or as do the works of great artists in other realms—even on rare occasions in the theatre.

Yet the exploration merits respect and gratitude. More than that, it broadens one's sense of how widely theatre art may range and what it may achieve in fresh domains.

—*NAT*, 12 June '76

THE ARCHITECT AND THE EMPEROR OF ASSYRIA

Fernando Arrabal's *The Architect and the Emperor of Assyria* is a "big" play (La Mama Annex). I do not refer to its length—in a cut version it runs three hours—but to its sweep. It is a vast "send up" of modern civilization—"Christian capitalism"—a play of gargantuan blasphemy.

It is not to be readily categorized. Arrabal himself has referred to it as a panel in his "theatre of panic." He and his audience are under a similar spell. He saves himself and us from its brutal blows by a sort of hideous humor; his total disgust is spewed out in raucously derisive laughter. It may be called a sado-masochistic farce. But no conventional epithet quite fits it. It is surely an original play, even if the pigeonhole purposes we invoke the names of Ghelderode, Genet, Goya and Buñuel.

The influence of Spanish Catholic atmosphere and upbringing are strong in Arrabal. "In Spain," he wrote, "children are cruel…in my childhood, everything was sin and I wonder to what degree the idea of sinfulness does not still haunt me." It certainly does! But added to this there is the actual experience of the Franco years, during which his father disappeared from jail never to be heard from again. Arrabal's investigation into the condition of Franco's prisons and his brief incarceration in one of them contributed to his education in horror.

Because his father had been a traitor to the regime, Arrabal's mother abjured her husband. It was on a search for his father that Arrabal set out for France, where he settled in 1960 and began to write most of his plays in French. First produced in Paris in 1967, when he was 35, *The Architect and the Emperor* was not an easy play for me to grasp when I then saw it. Nor is it now wholly transparent—one may ask oneself why the "Architect," why "Assyria," etc.?—but its mood, its sentiment, its special eloquence and its basic thrust make it unmistakably powerful. Like it or not, it is one of the signal plays of our time.

A "gentleman" falling to earth from an airplane accident, lands on an unknown island of which the sole inhabitant is a savage. In that isolation the man of the world teaches the native barbarian the speech and facts of the outside world. The instruction is a process of fun and games: the games of justice, war, religion, love, marriage, filial attachment and duty. Our culture's representative becomes the "Emperor" as the native is the "Architect," the creature of work and constructive action or, if you will, master and slave. And what does the Architect gather from the Emperor's discourse? At first the Emperor speaks of the blessings of the world which made him. "Ah philosophy! Ah music! Ah monuments!" he periodically exclaims. "Civilization? What a wonder!" he goes on. "During thousands of centuries man has stored knowledge and enriched his intelligence until he has attained this marvelous perfection that has become life. Everywhere, happiness, joy, tranquillity, laughter, understanding. All is conceived to render man's life easier, his happiness greater, and his peace more durable. Man has discovered all that's necessary to his well-being and today he's the happiest and most serene being in all creation."

But around the very ecstasy of his praise there is nothing but destruction, frightfulness, venom, slaughter, obscenity. "All that is atrocious, nauseating, putrid and vulgar is contained in one word: God." As for justice: "What justice? What is justice? Justice is a certain number of men like you and me who most of the time escape this very justice by hypocrisy or subterfuge—I don't give a damn for your courts, your operetta judges, your puppet tribunals and your prisons of vengeance." He quotes a great poet: "Little bastard, big bastard, we are all bastards."

These are the least of his imprecations. The hot line between Kennedy and Khrushchev is alluded to, the unspeakable curse of the bomb is part of the panorama, the ghastly idiocy of war reports in which the casualties of the opposing powers are triumphantly trumpeted are given their due in this message from hell. The Emperor recalls the memory of his adored mother, reviled and decapitated! With all this there is an ambiguous savor of the homosexual. And the play ends in a satanic ritual of self-immolation. The Emperor bids the Architect to kill and eat him. "I want you to be you and me at the same time." Perhaps, to begin with, they were two sides of the same entity: humankind. For at the end we witness the repetition of the initial pattern: the Architect returns in the person of the Emperor, the Emperor in that of the Architect.

The writing is sometimes cast in the mode of surrealist "automatic" composition, wildly incoherent and yet astonishingly lyrical, with a sort of madly orgiastic afflatus and hurricane giddiness in which everything from Coca-Cola to world literature revolve in a giddily grotesque dance: "We'll erect palaces with labyrinths," the Emperor shouts, "we'll dig pools for sea turtles to bathe in, I'll give you an automobile so that you can tour through all my thoughts and pipes steaming liquid smoke in spirals that change into alarm clocks. I'll drain the swamps and out of their mud will emerge a flock of pink flamingos with tin-foil crowns, etc. etc." Everything is desecrated in an appalling circus.

Yet one cannot say the play's ferocity voices an all-consuming nihilism—no work of art ever does—for even the Emperor says to the Martian of his imagination, "I want to stay on earth....We have just reached the point where we can sustain grief...What, I'll die an atrocious death during a war, burnt by radiation?...In spite of the fact that I don't know and have no desire to know Mars, I a thousand times prefer to live on earth in spite of our wars and difficulties, rather than on your dream planet." The play, is at once a howl of anguish, a hysterical prayer, and a protest.

Tom O'Horgan has directed the play with epic glee on Bill Stabile's fantastic set, which we look down on from the height of several tiers. There is picturesqueness and ingenuity in his direction though his extravagance leaves too little to the imagination. He errs in matters of taste and his desire to find a physical equivalent for the author's every idea and metaphor sometimes obscures the text, which in this case is of the first importance. For all that, I consider his production one of the most outstanding of several seasons. Lazaro Perez as the Architect and Ronald Perlman as the Emperor (all other "characters" are mimed as part of the games played by the two principals) are loyal to and efficient in their formidable tasks.

Time and space do not permit me to expatiate on the other performances I have seen in the flurry of activity as the season nears its end. The best of them is still Ntozake Shange's *for colored girls who have considered suicide when the rainbow is enuf*, which I reviewed here in April on the occasion of its earlier production at the Federal Theatre on Grand Street. (It is now at the Public Theatre.) The show consists of sung, danced and spoken pieces in verse and prose given exaltingly touching impact by six captivating black women, including its author.

It is part of the movement of black expression by which the black theatre has imbued our stage with a fresh spurt of life. It is an important movement, not only because it has helped the black community to a further awareness of itself but because, through it, all of us may come to know about a people; ignorance of or indifference to them is a peril to our entire society. Whatever the merits of the individual plays may be, I nearly always find that they interest me.

Livin' Fat by Judi Ann Mason is black folk-farce which reminded me of one of Sholom Aleichem's droll stories, except that the personnel in *Livin' Fat* is all black. (Negro Ensemble Company at the St. Mark's Playhouse.) It has some deliciously funny lines and I enjoyed the spirit of the acting.

—*NAT*, 19 June '76

HEINRICH VON KLEIST

Heinrich von Kleist who died a suicide in 1811 at the age of 34 is a classic author of German literature. His life was agonizingly hectic, but though he wrote several heroically tragic plays his work also contains a brilliant comic vein. "Man can be great in grief," he wrote, "but only in happiness is he a god." In *The Marquise of O—*, one of his finest stories, humor subtly tinged with irony proclaims his ambivalent genius. There is a sort of "Mona Lisa" smile about it: affection, mockery and a faint note of anguish are all contained in it. The result is a clear, classic surface which induces chuckles and yet remains unaccountably disturbing. The French director of *My Night at Maud's*, Eric Rohmer, has literally transcribed the story to the screen and in doing so has wrought his best film.

I have used the word "classic" in several of its connotations. There is still another I would apply to it here: it is a work of art so limpid and serene that one can hardly tell what it is about! Though there is no obscurity at all about the plot, the final impression created is not of a tale but of a mood or "music." The classic in this sense hides itself, it does not declare its point. It simply is.

Yet much happens. Kleist both accepts and teases the moral standards of the time. Ever so gently set forth is the incalculability of human destiny and the childishness of our behavior in regard to it. What gives the picture its special quality is the sober beauty of every shot, movement, setting, costume, performance. There is hardly any emphasis of detail: every moment is complete in itself. If the narration were to be suddenly arrested we would still feel that we had become part of a living experience, equivocal and fascinating like so much which goes unnoticed in our day-to-day traffic.

A German critic has found something of Kafka in Kleist. For my part, I find the film's "surface," pictorially and dramatically, so direct, burnished and *light*, that it eludes explanation while it says all. The acting by the entire company is flawless. Besides the excellence of each of its individual members, all of them have been associated in a permanent theatre ensemble. It shows.

—*NAT*, 6 Nov. '76

EUGENE O'NEILL'S JOURNEY INTO CLARITY

Long Day's Journey Into Night is perhaps the greatest of American plays. I say perhaps because there is a fallacy and an ambiguity in the designation "great." Even Shakespeare was denied the encomium by Tolstoy. Greatness for the individual critic, reader or spectator is measured by what he or she finds personally vital or profoundly meaningful. Apart from this there is only tradition. But in any consideration of the American theatre what plays may be thought deserving of the highest praise to the same degree as O'Neill's masterpiece?

The greatness of *Long Day's Journey Into Night* (written 1940-41 and first produced in 1956) consists of several elements. In it our foremost dramatist—foremost in his seriousness, power, ambitiousness of content and variety of form—has woven two of his major themes into a pattern of extraordinary emotional penetration and clarity. The play is autobiographical, a passionate probing of the author's own self. But if it were only that, its scope might appear limited. But one of the most remarkable features of O'Neill's writing is that from the stuff of his own experience he fashioned a body of work significant of America's human history.

Before explaining this last statement something should be said about the *clarity* of *Long Days Journey*. Much of O'Neill's output was derivatively "experimental." In *Strange Interlude* there was the experiment of inner speech in counterpoint with normal dialogue. There were experiments

with masks as in *The Hairy Ape*, *The Great God Brown*, *Days Without End* as well as with choral effects in *Laughed*. O'Neill "borrowed" from the Greeks, he occasionally leaned toward Strindberg and he undertook Freudian ventures of vast extent. But in *Long Days Journey* O'Neill's view of himself in the matter of compositional method is voiced by Edmund (the youthful O'Neill) in reply to his father's judgment of him: "There's the makings of a poet in you." "The makings of a poet," Edmund says, "No, I'm like the guy who is always panhandling for a smoke. He hasn't even got the makings. He's only got the habit. I couldn't touch what I tried to tell you just now. [O'Neill's feeling about the sea]. I just stammered. That's the best I'll ever do....Well it'll be faithful realism, at least." *Long Day's Journey* is the least diluted example of O'Neill's realism. And realism, be it noted, is the dramatic mode at which America's playwrights have thus far excelled. There is nothing plainer and more thoroughly real in our theatre than this play.

We find very little symbolism in it—except for the title. It may be construed this way. *Long Days Journey*—self examination, *Into Night*—the darkness of self. In the self-examination which the play dramatizes, and through which all the characters reveal themselves, O'Neill achieves utmost clarity. Through probing into his own and the other selves O'Neill has elucidated himself and in doing so attained crucial insight into a large part of American inner experience of the past hundred years.

O'Neill insisted—it was his main theme—that America's fatal flaw is its failure to hold to a deep faith, the kind that maintains security in a person despite the buffets of adversity. He said this in so many words when he spoke of the nine play cycle he had begun to write, of which *A Touch of The Poet* was the first completed part. The American tragedy, he said, was that America neglected to heed the sacred admonition "What shall it profit a man if he gain the whole world and lose his own soul?" America had triumphed materially—in the myriad spheres of technical and industrial progress and thus in property and power—but had lost the integrity of a binding faith.

Mary Tyrone, the mother in the play, wanders through day and night seeking something. "What is it I'm looking for? I know it's something I've lost." And she answers herself without being conscious that she has done so when she murmurs "If I could only find the faith I lost as a girl." She had dreamed of becoming a nun.

Her husband, the actor James Tyrone, had his own faith, a faith in his art, which if not entirely shattered in his advanced years has certainly darkened and become enfeebled. His god was Shakespeare. Just as Mary's lost innocence is suggested through the wedding dress abandoned in a trunk in the attic, so Tyrone's belief in his calling is a tribute from Edmund Booth who once said of him "That young man is playing Othello better than I ever did!"

Tyrone tells us how he betrayed *his* religion: the theatre, Shakespeare and Booth. "My good bad luck made me find the big money-maker. (The play) was a great box-office success…and then life had me where it wanted me." Because the play made him a fortune, he could never relinquish his part in it, nor, after his success, did the public wish to see him in any other. "What the hell was it I wanted to buy, I wonder, that was worth—" and he breaks off because he can't bring himself to formulate the answer. He is only lucid enough to confess "On my solemn oath, Edmund, I'd gladly face not having an acre of land to call my own, not a penny in the bank—I'd be willing to have no home but the poorhouse in my old age if I could look back now on having been the fine artist I might have been."

Tyrone's betrayal of his art was not the consequence of a vulgar money grubbing nature. It sprang from a fear of poverty. And here O'Neill weaves into the web of the play the second of his major themes. Tyrone's fear was not the common one, but that of the immigrant to a new land. America was a country in which everything had to be built from "nothing," a country to which poor and otherwise hard pressed immigrants had to fight for subsistence. They were forced to think first of all about material security. The younger generation which profited by their forebear's victory in this struggle did not appreciate its hardships. The second theme referred to then is the generation gap, the misunderstanding between fathers and sons as a permanent lesion in America which obtained from the mid-nineteenth century through the years following the Civil War. The theme is present in *A Touch Of The Poet* and also, though rarely recognized in *Desire Under the Elms*, as well as in *Long Day's Journey*.

James Tyrone had been an Irish immigrant. From the age of ten he had to work under the most wretched conditions for wages of no more than fifty cents a week! As the "man of the family" he had helped support his mother who "Worked and scrubbed for the Yanks" and his older sister sewed, and the two younger stayed at home to keep house. They never had clothes enough to wear, nor enough to eat. No wonder then that Tyrone developed an all consuming mania for saving money and owning land. He had learned "the value of a dollar." He was unable to unlearn the lesson even when he had grown affluent.

His sons realize very little of this. They think of him as the most miserly of men. They believe him responsible for the crippling torment in their lives: their mother's addiction to morphine. Did he not try to save money by calling in an inferior doctor to ease her pain following Edmund's birth. That is merely their supposition; in fact Tyrone was guilty of ignorance rather than avarice. What emerges from the long confessional scene in the most moving last act in all of American drama is that Edmund (O'Neill) comes to understand his mother, his older brother James and, to a considerable extent himself. He now sees the true nature of his father's "sin" along with it's sad consequence. He absolves his father and the others from condemnation.

Rather than being the "villain" of the piece, Tyrone is an honorable character, a hearty, affectionate, stalwart pillar of the family, trying desperately to hold it together. Though remiss in some of his duties, he still, as he says, *Believes*. His most damaging weakness is intellectual: he is confused as to the cause of his fall. He doesn't understand exactly how his career as an actor has affected other aspects of his life. It is only in response to Edmund's accusation of him as a skinflint and the family's wrecker that Tyrone is forced to wrest the truth about himself from his muddled consciousness. His good intentions had paved the way to the family's hell.

Tyrone's original sin was the abandonment of what was best in himself for the pursuit of material success. It led, among other things, to an immersion in the shabbier sides of the theatrical profession: travel to one night stands throughout the country, companionship with drunken, footloose cronies, lack of any genuine stability, no real home. Sick and isolated, his wife is bereft of close ties to her husband and sons. Her older boy James Jr. is incurably wounded by what he considers his mother's dereliction and defection as well as by a loss of respect for his father. He wastes his days in dissolute behavior, justifying it on the grounds that his parents had "betrayed" him. Edmund's drive to discover the truth underlying his unhappiness leads him to its alleviation through understanding and thus to forgiveness.

This explains why O'Neill who was the first to make the tragic acceptable on our stage insisted that tragedy is not "pessimistic" but joyful. This belief sustained him and made him one of the very few American playwrights who in times of public neglect as well of acclaim never wavered in his task: unremittingly to express what he had learned through his own agonized existence much that was crucial to his nation's life. In that sense, he is still the greatest among us in the theatre. And *Long Day's Journey Into Night* is the most cogent statement of his findings.

—*STGB*, '76

A COMEDY OF MAD MANNERS

Heartbreak House might be described thematically as a picture of the educated middle class in the limbo of their waning power and effectiveness in England. But the same with the exception of locale might be said of *The Cherry Orchard*. The spine of *Heartbreak House*, that which sets all the characters in motion, is this desire "to get the hell out of this place"—the place being the condition of a particular social group.

So far, so good! But such a spine might be treated somberly, lyrically, naturalistically, or, as some critics, taking Shaw at what appeared to be his word, in a Chekhovian key. What struck me, however, in reading *Heartbreak House* was its extravagance, a manner very close to comic opera! In intellectual purpose the text is entirely serious but in its body or mode it is akin to what the French call *vaudeville*. As a stage piece it is a lark and almost as remote from Chekhovian realism as Gilbert and Sullivan. Therefore in its stage treatment, I believe, it has to be made as playful and gay as if it were a fashionable bit of camp.

Apart from the parallel with Chekhov which Shaw mentions in his preface to *Heartbreak House*, it may be worth considering how he envisioned his plays on the stage. There is a strong indication in his letters to Granville Barker, his managerial partner and frequent interpreter as actor-director, that Shaw's theatre taste inclined to the theatrical rather than to any of the modified forms of naturalism which the work of Ibsen, Galsworthy and Granville Barker himself called for. In a letter to Granville Barker Shaw wrote, "When will you understand that what has ruined you as a manager is your love for people who are 'a little weak, perhaps, but (have) just the right tone.' The right tone is never a little weak perhaps; it is always devastatingly strong. Keep your worm for your own plays; and leave me the drunken stagy, brass-bowelled barnstormers my plays are written for..." And again to Barker, "You hate the thing (barnstormers' acting) because it is so blatant and unreal...my plays are built to stand that sort of thing."

In one of his little essays Shaw said, "I went back to the classical style and wrote long rhetorical speeches like operatic solos, regarding my plays as musical performances...As a producer (the English theatre word for our director) I went back to the forgotten heroic stage business and the exciting of impressive declamation I had learned from the old-timers."

In the same piece Shaw tells of an actor playing Burgess in Candida "who after rehearsing the first act in a funereal mute, solemnly put up his hand as I vengefully approached him, and said 'Mr. Shaw: I know what you are going to say. But you may depend on me. In the intellectual drama I never clown.' And it was some time before I could persuade him to clown for all he was worth."

What makes Heartbreak House utterly different from Chekhov is its unique style. Shaw's play is extravagant, full of capering humor which verges on the farcical. One of the characters refers to the environment he finds himself in as "a crazy house" in which one's mind "might as well be a football." The fact that this "crazy house" is also a truth house—a sort of distorting mirror which exaggerates the features of the people who enter it gives the play its human and social relevance but it does not distract from the topsy-turvy fun.

Years ago when there was still some resistance to Shaw—as we all know the greatest playwrights of our time encountered resistance as they came on the scene—certain critics complained that Shaw's characters were not people but puppets. There is no need to deny this. Shaw's characters are puppets—unnatural only in the sense that they reveal the truth about themselves more directly, more pointedly, more eloquently, more wittily than people in life are able to do.

The director's task then is to combine the "fun" aspect of the play—its arch frivolousness—with its basic intent. Gravity is to be avoided, except as fleeting reminders that we are still

dealing with a truth about life—our lives. This slight duality—a sort of "gayed up" seriousness, part game, part prophecy—is only a reflection of the text itself which begins as a comedy of mad manners and ends with an air raid by an enemy never named or even hinted at throughout the course of the play.

What was Shaw's purpose and why did he write Heartbreak House in this peculiar way? The play exemplifies a typical Shavian "trick." Heartbreak House is all carefree talk and horse-play—apparently devoid of dark portent; then it bursts for a moment into a scene of shock and ends ironically on a note of almost languid peace. "Nothing will happen," one of the house guests says. Something does happen and something more fatal may yet happen—expected, almost hoped for, by certain of the characters.

These "charming people, most advanced, unprejudiced, frank, humane, unconventional, free-thinking and everything that is delightful," are content to drift. No matter what inner qualms they may have, no matter what emptiness or discontent they occasionally experience, they have settled for the happiness of dreams and daily pastimes. For all his sharp teasing, Shaw is tolerant of them. Only, says he, in earnest jest, if you go on like this without "navigation"—that is, without plan, purpose and preparative action—your ship will "strike and sink and split."

The thought or warning which informs the play—stated in a frolic of entertaining word and postures—is wholly appropriate to our day and our theatre. Though the people of Heartbreak House are English, it is not merely a play about a certain class or a certain country. Time has turned it into a play about practically all of us, everywhere.

Random Notes: Shaw's characters are ideas—conceptions of people, theatrically and comically colored. The adverse criticism of certain critics who say that Shaw's characters are merely puppets spouting ideas should be made a positive element of the production style.

This may be made as puppet-like as the nature of the play's dramatic structure and the audience's taste will allow.

Mangan says he wants to get "to hell out of this house." Everyone in the play wants somehow to escape his or her condition. All are dissatisfied with it...it's a crazy house, driving them crazy!

All in a sense are "crazy," not true to themselves, not what they seem to pretend to be. So everyone is somehow odd, a *clown*—disguised, masked. Outside is "the wide earth, the high seas, the spacious skies"—waiting.

"In this house," says Hector, "everybody poses. The Trick is to find the man under the pose."

(a) What is the pose?
(b) What is the man or woman under the pose?

More Random Notes (after still further reading): These English in *Heartbreak House* do not behave as English people do: an Irishman has rendered them! They are more impish, more extrovert, more devilish, more devilishly comic.

Hessione is a "serpent"—she has mischief in her—not a "proper" lady. She's the cat who swallowed the canary, an intelligent minx. Mentally speaking she *winks*.

They are all aware that they are living in a loony world, which they are expected to take seriously—but can't. As they progress they become aware of the need to act mad in order to approximate reality. To achieve their liberation—their world must be destroyed.

Some of the madness demands that they hide it—which is the greatest madness. Thus they speak of "form," of not making scenes—while they are always making scenes. (Lady Utterword.)

They want to burst the bonds of the old times—convention—"to get the hell out." Thus the comic outbursts.

—*PDG*, '76–'77

G.B.S.

What word supplies a key to the treasure house of Bernard Shaw's accomplishment? He was ninety-four when he died in 1950; by that time his name was possibly as familiar as Einstein's. That is not the same as saying he was well known. Only a very few specialists understood Einstein, and the diversity of opinion and information about Shaw made any security of judgment about him difficult.

Shaw or G.B.S., as he was commonly identified in London's political and literary circles, was a man of many—some might say too many—parts. There was Shaw the vegetarian, the teetotaler, the socialist, the speaker at public meetings, the journalist, the (unsuccessful) novelist, the art critic, the music critic, the theatre critic (probably the best in the English language for the past hundred years) and finally the playwright, though he did not enter the arena in this capacity till he was almost forty. The prefaces he wrote to his plays are occasionally as long as the plays themselves. They deal with love, theology, politics, history, economics, biology, medicine, literature. The thirty-six volume English edition of his work still does not include all his writing. He was awarded the Nobel Prize in 1925.

The question still remains: how to define the core of the man's genius. In the briefest of his prefaces which he called "a warning," Shaw wrote, "Now it may be that a pen portrait of an imaginary monster with my name attached to it may already have taken possession of your own mind through your contact with the press. If so, please class it with the unicorn and the dragon...a character perhaps amusing but certainly entirely fabulous. If you are to get any good out of me you must accept me as a quite straightforward practitioner of the art I made my living by...(playwriting)."

But even this statement does not tell the whole story. For Shaw was not a "straightforward practitioner" of his art. If he had been, he would have been less stimulating and less successful. Though he has often been pronounced passé, his plays are constantly being revived in England, in the United States and virtually everywhere else. The detractors have never been able to explain Shaw's theatrical longevity.

He came close to revealing his secret when he wrote, "that my business as a classic writer of comedies is 'to chasten morals with ridicule,' and if I sometimes make you feel like a fool…I never do it without giving you laughing gas."

There is a *clown* in Shaw which explains much of his dramatic vitality. This does not mean that he is not entirely in earnest; on the contrary he is as serious as the Fool in *King Lear*. Royal fools serve to breech the armor of prejudice, pretense and hypocrisy by which the mighty protect themselves. Most of us are reluctant to swallow Truth— we find its taste unpleasant—but if we can pour it down our gullet while we are in our paroxysm of hilarity.

In his youth Shaw championed Ibsen as he later professed an immense admiration for Chekhov. But his art is unrelated to either one of those dramatists. He is much more akin to Molière, whose zaniest comedies imply social criticism and whose more sober plays skirt the fringes of farce. A man of intellect with something of a scientist's rigor, Shaw always retains the simplicity of a natural man.

It is the quality which enabled him to see through the shams of official insignia and ideologies. Thus the little "pagan" of *Androcles and the Lion* in his unaffected humility and kindness is the true Christian and the professed Christian in that play is a bully. In Shaw's "American" play *The Devil's Disciple* the clergyman is the fighter; the "revolutionary" trouble-maker is a man of peace and the general (Bourgoyne) the civilized skeptic. Shaw is both the clear-sighted "old gentleman" Caesar who perceives in the girl queen Cleopatra the forceful woman she becomes under his tutelage, and the inspired peasant Joan, who despite

the weight of all the hierarchies which impede and oppress her, remains true to her "voices," preferring martyrdom to betrayal. So too the more fortunate Anglo-Irish dramatist. In Shaw, as in Molière, ideas become animated and personified. They are, if you will, the "puppets" of the clown's manipulation and imagination replete with smiling wisdom and noble purpose.

The spirit of inquiry and contradiction which always bespeaks a challenge to our complacencies and outworn modes of thinking are often resisted as not only impolitic but as a form of bad manners. Thus the Shavian "paradox"—a way of saying the right thing at the wrong time—was frequently dismissed as frivolity or mere witticism. Yet truth is always imbedded in the Shavian joke, sparkling, clear and firm.

The clown in Shaw masked the Puritan. Early in his career he referred to himself as an "atheist" but his basic disposition was religious; he sought a binding faith, something that might dispel despair and make us trust life. At the end of one of his lightest comedies *You Never Can Tell* a father asks a hard-headed lawyer whether his son's proposed match to a very uppity young woman is unwise. "Yes, I do," the lawyer answers, "all matches are unwise. It is unwise to be born, it is unwise to be married, it is unwise to live; and it's wise to die." To which, the lawyer's father, a waiter, interjects, "So much the worse for wisdom!"

Shaw employed reason to defend instinct, the "worthwhileness" of living. This he expressed in a prose so resilient, energetic, euphonious and fervent that it often enters the realm of poetry. But his idea of living was not a mere trudging or skating haphazardly on the surface of existence. "Life with a blessing! That's what I want," exclaims young Ellie in *Heartbreak House*. Such a life cannot be achieved by willessly relying on luck. The liberal gentleman of that play confesses, "Though I was brought up not to believe in anything, I often feel that there is a great deal to be said for an over-ruling Providence…" To which Captain Shotover (one of Shaw's many *alter egos*) replies, "Every drunken skipper trusts to Providence. But one of the ways of Providence with drunken skippers is to run them on the rocks." "Very true, no doubt, at sea," says the benign philosopher. "But in politics, I assure you, they only run into jellyfish. Nothing happens." To which Shotover retorts, "At sea nothing happens to the sea. Nothing happens to the sky...Nothing happens...nothing, but the smash of the drunken skipper's ship on the rocks, the splintering of her rotten timbers, the tearing of her rusty plates, the drowning of the crew like rats in a trap...Let a man drink ten barrels of rum a day, he is not a drunken skipper until he is a drifting skipper. It is the man who lies drinking in his bunk and trusts to Providence that I call a drunken skipper, though he drink nothing but the waters of Jordan." "What then must we do? What are we to learn?" Shotover's answer comes back like a shot, "Navigation. Learn it and live; or leave it and be damned."

The liberal persists, "I thought all that once, Captain, but I assure you nothing will happen." And then bombs begin to fall! The play, conceived and largely written before World War I, was prophetic. Shaw's plays were nearly always prophetic. England's time of troubles (right now) is clearly perceived in *The Apple Cart* of 1929. Shaw called for the world to shape up, and indicated a direction—which it has yet to embark on.

He was a democrat who believed in brains, in philosopher-kings. He was never a routine or dogmatic propagandist. No matter what cause he espoused, he never argued it with a sledge hammer. No character in his plays is entirely wrong, no point of view entirely unjustified. Shaw is never truculent; his amiability, his pure-hearted clowning give his plays a grace which captivates even when we feel the sharp edge of a prodding elbow. *Common sense* permeates the jest. But common sense in a crazy world is uncommon, and Shaw's shifts of posture from comedian to preacher could puzzle and irritate almost as much as it could charm. Had he not written, "The plain

truth is that it is not only good for people to be shocked occasionally but absolutely necessary to the progress of society that they should be shocked pretty often."

None of this means that Shaw was in any sense an unperturbed optimist. (The Fool in *Lear* dies of grief.) In one of his last plays *Too True to Be Good* Shaw detected a gradual surrender to nihilism in our civilization. In the closing speech his spokesman proclaims, "The fatal word NOT has been inserted into all our creed...But what next? Is NO enough? For a boy, yes: for a man, never...I must have affirmations to preach. Without them the young will not listen to me, for even the young get tired of denials. ('The negative-mongers') way is straight and sure; but it is the way of death; and the preacher must preach the way of life...All I know is that I must find the way of life, for myself and for all of us, or we shall surely perish...."

—*STGB*, Jan. '77

A SORROW BEYOND DREAMS
HOLD ME!
MY LIFE
THE CRAZY LOCOMOTIVE

The press has been much more cordial to Peter Handke's *A Sorrow Beyond Dreams* (Marymount Manhattan Theatre) than it was to any of his plays previously offered in New York, the most recent of them being *Kaspar*. That is understandable because the earlier plays were more or less avant-garde and rather "difficult," while *A Sorrow Beyond Dreams* is simple, straightforward and "theatre" only by our latter-day extension of the word.

It is a "confessional" short story that lends itself to spoken monologue. In it a writer tries to set down his recollections of his mother, who had committed suicide some months earlier. He tells her life story: that of a simple woman born in a province of what used to be the Austro-Hungarian Empire among the humblest of uneducated folk. She, however, had a healthy appetite for life, learns to read good books, and gives promise of becoming a well-rounded human being. But an unfortunate affair, followed by marriage to a stupid man, the narrowness and hard domestic work of her environment, the advent of Hitler and all that bespeaks of constraint, lead to quiet despair, inanition and finally suicide.

I am not telling this very well because, to be frank, at this writing ten days after the first night I have forgotten most of the details. The writing is truthful, sound, sympathetic (in an excellent translation from the German by Ralph Manheim) but I was not affected by it. Such histories are legion and always cause for a generalized regret, but that indicates the limitations of this sort of retelling. Perhaps Handke knew this; at the end of the piece he suggests that he may return to the subject when he feels he can do it greater justice. He may be reiterating one of the major themes of his work: the inadequacy of language to communicate reality of thought, feeling and behavior. But it is precisely the function of art to make the general particular, illuminating and moving. Handke's effect is only that of benevolent, rather than eloquent sentiment.

The most telling elements in the presentation are James Tilton's remarkably well-chosen photographic projections, which picture the mother at various stops of her life: the man she lived with, the townships, the Hitler period, the progressive decay of her features, etc. These give the story more body than the text. Its playing or, more exactly, its reading by X, a well-equipped actor, is manly, intelligent, spoken in a good voice and entirely creditable; it has been hailed as a remarkable piece of acting—which it is not; it is hardly acting at all, but what I have called it: excellent reading.

What strikes me most is the enthusiasm with which the event has been received. Is our stage now so arid that any meritorious expression of thought or sentiment becomes worthy of special celebration? Has the drought in serious theatre become so extreme that a reminder of the ordinary facts of life, even in their most modest manifestations, has become *important*? Or are we only rejoicing that Handke, a presumably advanced and not easily accessible writer, here proves himself a regular fellow?

Hold Me! An Entertainment by Jules Feiffer is being given (until February 21) in the basement of the Sub-Plot Cabaret of the American Place Theatre. It is composed of short skits, most of them based on the author's well-known cartoons. They have the original Feiffer stamp: wry humor stemming from the moral discomfort of modern American civilization. Much of it is enough to make me wince even as I laugh out loud. Most of these pills of acrid jocularity work well and are in fact quite funny in their three-dimensional presentation: that is, with live actors. Some of them seem to require the dry thin line, the quick stab, of Feiffer's drawing.

The best way to convey the nature of the show's fun is to quote a few lines from among numerous examples. A self-confessed "rotten kid" has been so transformed by therapy that he becomes "nicer and nicer," so "hung up on nice" that he "gave (his) analyst guilt feelings."...A woman enters a department store to return a Christmas present. "My husband gave it to me," she says. "It's the wrong color. It's the wrong size. It's the wrong present. And he's the wrong husband. Every Christmas I realize that."

The incompatibility of the sexes receives the sharpest treatment. A bright woman who talks too much says men feel challenged by her and grow hostile. "So when I'm very attracted I make it a point to talk more slowly than I would to one of my woman friends...(So) he tells me I'm the first woman he's met who's as interesting as one of his boy friends. That's love."

The briefest bits made me laugh the most. A boy speaks—in every possible rhythm and tone— "ME. ME. ME. ME. ME. ME. ME. ME." The Girl: "I." The boy yawns. The overall mood is summed up by a man who reports, "I wake up singing...I sing on the bus to work…I sing on the street and a stranger puts a dime in my hand and asks how in a world full of misery are you the one man who's happy? 'Who's happy?' I reply to the stranger. I sing to drown out my screaming."

Five actors—Geraldine Brooks, Michael Tucci most notably—though not especially adept at this sort of comedy, are nevertheless thoroughly engaging.

Corinne Jacker's *My Life* (Circle Repertory Theatre) is a memory play in which a young man, confused as to "where he's going," recalls his boyhood, adolescence, his grandfather, his parents, a girl he once loved, his forays into radical activity. It ends in reconciliation with his family and acceptance of the girl with whom he and apparently his father have had an affair.

This is told in a convolution of flash-backs with two actors playing several of the parts at different ages. Nearly everyone in the cast plays well, especially Douglass Watson as the father (past 50), William Hurt as the pivotal young man after adolescence, Jo Henderson as his mother, very pretty Nancy Snyder as the young man's first love, and Claire Malis as the later one. All are well directed by Marshall Mason in David Potts's ingenious setting, which includes a "real" swimming pool in which almost every member of the company is obliged to immerse him or herself. There is good writing in the play on a level of respectable sophistication; there is very little that is unbelievable or false.

Why then was I left indifferent? And with a feeling that the piece might go on forever? In the manner of many plays of recent years, characters seem to indulge in a perpetual process of psychic nitpicking. But few interesting *events* result from it. What is crucial in the best novels and plays is not only the inner landscape depicted but the *action* which both embodies and follows from it. *My Life* is mostly rumination.

A good deal of the latest avant-garde drama is literary imitation or illustration of readings from the latter-day philosophic writings. The anguish and soul searching that are to be found in Strindberg's "experimental" plays, praised now as forerunners of the "absurdist" drama, were real; that is, experienced, *lived* by the author. This too— almost more historically or politically than personally—may be said of the dramatic writing of S.I. Witkiewicz, who was also a novelist, painter and philosopher. He was, says the critic Jan Kott in his *Theatre Notes*, "the most original man of letters in Poland between the two wars. The combination of cold blood and lunacy," Kott goes on to say, "had much greater density in Witkiewicz than in Artaud."

Witkiewicz, who was born in 1885, committed suicide in 1929, largely because of the double invasion of his country—first by the Germans and then by the Russians—but his despair at the state of the modern world and the catastrophe toward which it was leading had begun in him much earlier.

His *The Crazy Locomotive* (Theatre Four) written in 1923, shows a corrupt civilization being conducted by criminals who are driving our "train" straight ahead at top speed to an inevitable smash. There is much surrealistic imagery, characterization and incident in the presentation of this parable, but the intent is clear.

A very promising 24-year-old director from Canada, Des McAnuff, has staged the play as a sort of 1920's film thriller, which makes it less hallucinatory than it must have been in the author's imagination. The American style used at Theatre Four demystifies the play and makes it humorous; however, it is probably the style most suitable to present-day presentation here. Within the chosen mode, everything is skillfully done in Douglas Schmidt's admirably designed set—it is in itself an "actor"—and there is excellence, too, in Carol Oditz's costumes, in Pril Smiley's electronic music and orchestration, and in the devoted, hardworking, able group of actors.

—*NAT*, 12 Feb. '77

OTHERWISE ENGAGED

No country today seems more honestly represented by its playwrights than England. Their reports are by no means complete, but the attempt to reflect the "state of the nation" is often theatrically adept as well as humanly forthright. I refer not only to the generation of the late 1950's and early 1960's: Osborne, Pinter, John Arden, Arnold Wesker, Ann Jellicoe, Henry Livings, Keith Waterhouse; but to more recent men: Edward Bond, David Rudkin, Joe Orton, David Storey, Trevor Griffiths and Simon Gray whose *Butley* and now *Otherwise Engaged* (Plymouth Theatre) brings the list more or less up to date. (Tom Stoppard occupies a special niche.)

The report is definitely "negative": the colors range from a murky gray to black amid flashes of abrasive laughter. It is right that this should be so. England is not a happy country; it is in economic and spiritual disarray. There is sanity in revealing the facts.

Simon Gray is both the most forthright and the most equivocal of the playwrights named. There is in Edward Bond a pained and savage indignation, in David Storey (*The Contractor, The Changing Room, Home*) compassion, in David Rudkin (*Ashes*) a grim determination to persist and hold on. Simon Gray displays a grin that masks something not far from disgust and perhaps a narcotized hate.

Most of our reviewers have found both *Butley* and the present *Otherwise Engaged* funny. That's good for the box office. The English also laugh at Gray's work because the poison in his plays draws off some of their own venom and thus possesses the properties of an antidote. They also see irony and even a certain pathos, if not exactly commiseration, in Gray's picture. I find hopelessness and something close to complaisance in it. Gray seems to be very much part of what he mocks. He grins as he spews the toxic matter within him. I refuse to swallow it.

Otherwise Engaged (which won a prize in London as the "best play of the season") is deftly written with that facility in adroit bitchiness of which many young Englishmen have become masters. It contains sharp quips, gracefully worded snarls of contempt, self-vilification and outright malice. The play is certainly effective; we are caught up by clever jabs that elicit a gasp of amused surprise before we wince and gag at the thrust.

Butley taught English; the Simon of *Otherwise Engaged* is a successful publisher of nearly 40. As he prepares to listen in calm solitude to a recording of *Parsifal*, he is interrupted by a series of intruders. One is a shabby young man to whom Simon has rented a flat in his house. The fellow doesn't pay his rent, borrows money for liquor and girls, cadges whatever else he can from his "landlord," envies and resents him. The lout calls himself a sociology student but one sees at once that he is totally ignorant of that, or any, subject. So much for the radical younger generation!

Simon's brother, Stephen, a graduate of one of the red brick universities, now an embittered schoolteacher with a large family, suffers a sense of inferiority induced by the class of arrogance of the Oxford-Cambridge clan. He has never risen above a drab mediocrity in his career, for he has neither the brilliance nor the material ease of his brother. Still another visitor is Jeff, a drunken, boorish, derisively "superior" critic, given to womanizing in indiscriminate confusion. He proclaims his thoroughgoing Englishness, professes discomfort with foreigners, and curses England because it is done for, *finished*.

Enter a woman writer (she once had an affair with Stephen) who in an effort to get Simon to publish her book bares her breasts. An old secondary schoolmate phones up; after reminding Simon of the homosexual escapades of their boyhood days, he tries to find out if Simon has laid his fiancée. (He did—once.) The man threatens suicide over the phone; we never learn if he goes through with it, because Simon cuts him off: he doesn't wish to know.

Simon's wife has been unfaithful. He has known this from the outset and done nothing about it. What good would it do if he made a fuss? He is willing to go on with their marriage as if everything were normal—it *is* normal in this environment—and is only slightly shaken when his wife tells him she is pregnant, but is uncertain whether by Simon or by her lover.

Simon's "virtue" is that he remains unruffled through all this. He is a snob about everything—especially the use of the English language—and is unfailingly well-mannered. He takes life as it comes, and it comes rough and dirty. As the play ends we see him going back to dosing himself with Wagner. I found him, for all his forbearance, which is hardly more than decorous cynicism, the most obnoxious personage of the lot. Is he meant to be the butt of the author's anger or dismay? Simon Gray will not say: he is writing a play, an entertainment. The "verdict" is up to us.

This is not "objectivity." The fact is I don't believe any of it, even though it may be said "to hold the mirror up to nature." That such people exist, even that they may be common in certain "sophisticated" English circles (and elsewhere), I have no doubt. But the detail of their behavior is not the truth about them, nor is the author's imperturbability in presenting them an artistic merit. There is always something more to be conveyed about stupid or corrupt people than evidence of their stupidity and corruption. The artist, in this case the dramatist, must not only display what we already know but impart a sense of his own attitude and, if it is not considered sentimental to say so, to allow us to look into his own heart and discover the values to which he is loyal. I discern little heart in *Otherwise Engaged* and certainly no wisdom.

Tom Courtenay, who plays Simon, is an actor of quality. He was especially affecting in some of his early films, especially *The Loneliness of the Long Distance Runner*. There is something fey, hurt and bewildered about him. Perhaps this softening is an advantage in his present role, but it struck me as somewhat misplaced. The play's style

requires a more cutting edge, for I am inclined to think its texture had best be kept superficial and glib. The shadow of real, though crushed, emotion in Courtenay emphasizes the play's essential hollowness.

The rest of the cast—especially John Horton as Simon's brother—is rather better than adequate, but I found Harold Pinter's direction strained and, in physical staging, almost ungainly. Greater fluency, even frivolity, would better suit the occasion.

—*NAT*, 19 Feb. '77

AMERICAN BUFFALO
THE CHERRY ORCHARD

David Mamet is a talented young American writer. He is not yet a complete dramatist, but may become one. One of the impediments to his progress is Mr. Puff, a generic name for most journalist reviewers.

Mamet's talent, at present, is for colorful (cartoon) characterization. There is content in his drawing as well as originality. He employs the language of people who have not yet arrived at the stage of integrated personality; they are void of coherent inner experience. Words, barely assimilated, casually picked up from the public media, rattle around in their consciousness only to come out in half-finished, involuted and convoluted spurts of verbiage, more gibberish than meaning. The effect is sometimes very funny and strangely disheartening. Millions speak so.

Mamet's latest play is *American Buffalo*. The title refers to the now rare five-cent coin. In the play, a man who wanders into a junk shop offers $80 for one such nickel. He is therefore presumed to have a large collection of valuable coins, and Donny Dubrow, the junk-shop boss, plans—with the aid of his juvenile assistant, Bobby, a subnormal fellow who serves as his surrogate son—to rob the wealthy customer of his treasure. To do this efficiently they call on a friend whom they call "Teach" (for teacher) to execute the proposed heist. The job never comes off for reasons that are ambiguous or deliberately left unclear. The situation hardly matters: hence a lack of dramatic fiber.

Look at the face of the coin, as reproduced on the show's playbill. The buffalo looks stunned, baffled, dejected, ready for slaughter. The animal is antiquated, and the would-be robbers are a mess. The combination is symbolic.

Donny is the gang's solid base. He lives in soiled passivity amid the debris from which he earns his living. He tries to "educate" Bobby, to whom he is paternally and possibly homosexually attached, correcting, reproving and protecting him. Bobby, without independent resources, is benevolently enslaved. On this account, he may have plotted the projected theft on his own, with the help of an unseen ally who is later reported to have had his jaw broken.

Teach is the "brains" of the outfit. He repeatedly speaks of sensible business practice, totes a gun, and is maniacally frightened, hysterically hostile and, through essential impotence, violent: he smashes things. Donny somehow likes him. None of these men has warm ties with any women; a consciousness of love hardly exists among them. They are close only through their proximity in the same muck heap. They are dissevered from the world; they are aware of the police, a few women whom they despise, and several other men of their own kind, mentioned but never present.

The fragmentation and vagueness of the play's plot and dialogue constitute its meaning. The characters' lines have no "body": their behavior is a series of obscene spasms, all of them abjectly pathetic. The play's incompleteness, though suggestive, demands something more, which the author's future work may provide.

A junk shop is usually a crummy hole. Santo Loquasto's setting is immense, a massive edifice of refuse, the *disjecta* of a chaotic civilization. The cast, under Ulu Grosbard's intuitive direction, is excellent. Kenneth McMillan plays Donny with a sense of the sad, slow, still sentient humanity that resides in the thickness of his mind and flesh. John Savage makes lamentable but sympathetic sense of Bobby's victimization, and Robert Duvall as Teach has the menace which makes our streets, with the short-circuited energies contained in them, terrifying.

Splendidly graphic, *The Cherry Orchard* at the Vivian Beaumont Theatre is a Chekhov charade. I doubt that anyone who had not already seen or read the play would understand it as now produced. For while the entire text is used in a colloquially American version by Jean-Claude van Itallie, it is not so much the Russian writer's play as Andrei Serban's.

A young director from Romania, Serban is among the most gifted theatre people now resident in this country. I liked one of his productions I saw in Bucharest some years ago, I greatly admired his *Medea-Trojan Women* cycle at La Mama, and was pleased with his *Good Woman of Setzuan* at the same theatre. With *The Cherry Orchard*, I find him pursuing a false track.

It is an exuberant show. For a student of stage direction it is, in one particular respect, exemplary. Everything is visualized: the eye reads the scenes. And very handsome they all are in Santo Loquasto's setting and costumes. The cast too is most likable. It enthusiastically fulfills every one of the director's instructions. Yet the playful result doesn't add up to a play. It makes very little Chekhovian sense or even, except in a limited way, Serban sense.

Chekhov conceived his play as a comedy. He found Stanislavsky's interpretation too tearful. Right or wrong, however, it proved extremely affecting and meaningful. Serban's production is an exercise in theatrics: a mishmash of vaudeville turns interlarded with poetic tableaux and picturesque effects for social symbolism. The actors vociferate at the top of their bent to emphasize absurdities in their characters' attitudes or come forward to stage center at serious moments which become soliloquies or "arias." Nearly every scene is a set piece. It is all very much like an operetta of indeterminate style.

This is so-called "director's theatre" with a vengeance. The text goes hang. We are already familiar with the play's subject or theme: the dying of a futile but still amiable class in the old Russia and the lyric prediction (or hope) of future renewal. To make this inescapably apparent, some characters behave clownishly, others speak like revolutionary orators, and in one scene there is the shadow of a huge industrial plant, representing the days to come. At the end of the evening a pretty maiden comes to lay flowers on the old servant, Firs's, dead body to mark the burial of the old order and the dawn of a new age!

I do not object to free adaptation or departures in the treatment of "standard" plays. In one of the most outstanding of these, Meyerhold's production of *The Inspector General*, the great Russian director took more liberties with Gogol than Serban does with Chekhov. But the play's essential significance was rendered more incisively than in any of the traditional productions I had seen. Peter Brook de-romanticized *Midsummer Night's Dream*, but it came through with Shakespearean zest and point. Serban's *Cherry Orchard* is based on a misconception of "new theatre."

Every element employed in the theatre must support the whole. A unified, self-sufficient and intelligible meaning (not dependent on prior knowledge) must be achieved. With or without verbal text, no part should supersede the central intention. We might suppose from the present *Cherry Orchard* that the director dislikes the text and used it only to display his artistry.

In the third act, for instance, in which Ranevskaya is on tenterhooks to learn whether her beloved home and estate is to be sold, guests are dancing at a family party. In the old days, the senile man servant says, the guests used to be generals, barons, admirals; now they are the station master and a post office employee and even they do not come willingly. The dancing is supposed to be seen in the background through most of the act. At the Vivian Beaumont now, the dance becomes a miniature ballet in fancy costume, which takes place in a circular enclosure that occupies three-quarters of the stage. The main action and important dialogue are crowded onto the forestage. When Ranevskaya refers to the noisiness around her, the dancers have disappeared, so that she can be heard. The byplay takes precedence over the play.

Here Chekhov comedy becomes stuff for gags, thought is speechified and moments of tenderness or psychological subtlety are scotched by burlesque business. Many scenes alternate among obvious "symbolism," parodies of sentiment, or mere frivolous gamesmanship, in a "modern" or sophisticated manner.

In brief, matter and method must always be honestly wed in the theatre, so that what we hear and see are in consonance with some intended statement, as they are, for example, in Brecht's productions. I found no such statement in this *Cherry Orchard*, except that its director is a superb craftsman. Acknowledged masterpieces may be reinterpreted but not trifled with for the sake of theatre aesthetics and dilettante exegesis.

Still, Andrei Serban's *Cherry Orchard* should be seen.

—*NAT*, 12 Mar. '77

MR. PUNTILA AND HIS CHAUFFEUR MATTI

Yale Repertory Theatre in New Haven is presenting Bertolt Brecht's *Mr. Puntila and His Chauffeur Matti* as part of its present repertory season. The new production is lively and affords a most pleasant evening.

It has been staged by a talented young English director, Ron Daniels, who sets the play in a carnival or traveling fair environment. The text itself is a folk comedy with rural underpinnings. The direction transforms Brecht's intention intelligently; a writer's work in the theatre must take account of the actors who play it and the audience to whom the production is addressed. In this respect, Yale's *Puntila* is a success.

The play was written in Finland in 1940-41, when Brecht was resident there en route to America. It is the story, told in free and swinging style, of Puntila, a wealthy Finnish landowner. The play's sources were some popular Finnish tales and the draft of a script by Hella Wuolijoki (Brecht's hostess at the time). By design or by choice, Puntila resembles the millionaire in Chaplin's *City Lights*: he is generously liberal in his cups, unfeeling and greedy when sober.

Matti, his hired man and chauffeur, shrewdly copes with his boss' ambivalence. Puntila first plans to marry his daughter off to an attaché of the diplomatic corps, but the enlightened perception of his inebriety makes him realize that the fellow is a nincompoop. Puntila then resolves to give Eva to Matti, a "real man." She herself appears to prefer Matti but, because of class differences, Puntila doubts that she will make him a good wife. Matti asks Eva to show him how she would behave in key circumstances of a workingman's life: when he takes her home to live with his poverty-stricken mother, when he comes tired from his labors. Can she stand the diet of poor people (herring every day of the week)? Does she know how to darn socks properly? Though she fails with the socks, she does well at most of the examination. Nevertheless, she proves herself unsuited to fill the job of becoming Matti's wife when she takes offense at his slapping her encouragingly on the behind.

Puntila sober, once again becomes niggardly with his employees and threatens to fire Matti. But becoming drunk in the process of swearing off liquor, he begs Matti to remain by his side, promising all sorts of advantages. Matti refuses and leaves. Whatever benevolence Puntila may show from time to time, he is still a capitalist, therefore untrustworthy.

The play (*Mr. Puntila and His Chauffeur Matti*) is humorous and witty with a racy and hearty joviality which is thoroughly endearing. But Brecht didn't write it just for fun! Puntila contains a warning: the working class should never depend on its masters, no matter how good-natured they

may appear. The abyss between them cannot be bridged.

Still, the character of Puntila comes through with great charm. Brecht, mistrusting the general freshness of feeling that pervades the proceedings, went so far in the later German productions as to put masks on Puntila and his minions (a judge, a lawyer, a parson): this would make them look menacing or at least much less "sympathetic."

D.H. Lawrence once said—I paraphrase—that every narrative tells a tale and conveys a moral: one should not heed the moral but put faith in the tale. So it is with *Puntila*, as it was with *Mother Courage*. Brecht did not wish his audience to think well or warmly of that woman but it did, and while the "moral" of *Puntila* is militant, the man Puntila, as written, remains a delightful creature.

—*NAT*, 26 Mar. '77

THE NEW YORK IDEA

Shortly before he died in 1933, Langdon Mitchell said: "The plays of today are better than the ones we fellows wrote." It is true that the number of American plays of any lasting merit before 1920 can be counted on the fingers of one hand. Mitchell's own 1906 play *The New York Idea* (it played in repertory until April 10 at the Brooklyn Academy of Music) was among those rare exceptions.

The idea referred to by the play's title is crisply stated by one of its characters, a visiting Englishman: "New York is bounded on the north, south, east and west by the state of Divorce!" Its the facetious Britisher's little joke, but Mitchell took the subject seriously. "I wrote *The New York Idea*," he said, "because I think the subject of divorce is the most important question in this country at the present time...."

Oh happy 1906, when divorce was the most important question in this country! Fortunately his play is not as earnest as it is humorous. It is thoroughly amiable, felicitously written, charmingly sophisticated, admirably crafted. In it, Mitchell, a physician's son born in Philadelphia in 1862, reveals himself as a gentleman of refined and witty disposition in whose company we may still delight.

The play's radiance is not so much in its quips—the aforementioned Englishman, Sir Wilfred Cates-Darby says; "Some of your American gals are the nicest boys I ever met"—but in its tone. It is distinctly upper class in a day when there really were classes. (Today, class lines are blurred.) The rich then were mostly business tycoons and their heirs. If they were educated, they became lawyers for the wealthy, or judges who went into politics. They were painted by Sargent, collected pictures and other *objets d'art* picked up in European travel, went to the races, often to watch their own horses run. They were rarely as neurotic as the rich today; they valued leisure and, unless they were boors, used it gracefully.

That was the New York which Langdon Mitchell viewed with a pleasure both critical and cordial. This is how he describes some of his characters: "Miss Heneage is a solidly built, narrow-minded woman in her 60s. She makes no effort to look younger than she is...She commands her household and her family connection, and on the strength of a large and steady income feels that her Opinion has its value." William Sudley, an oldish gentleman, "is and appears thoroughly insignificant, But his opinion of the place he occupies in the world is enormous. His manners, voice, presence, are all those of a man of breeding and self-importance." The bridegroom's mother, at a wedding for which the woman her son is to marry is late, voices her discontent in this fashion: "I don't wish to be censorious or to express an actual opinion, but I must say it's a bold bride who keeps her future mother-in-law waiting eight hours."

Every role in the play is an actor's holiday. And Frank Dunlop, of Young Vic and *Scapino* fame, has chosen a perfect cast. Everyone shines, above all, Denholm Elliott as the priceless Sir Wilfred Elliott, who has improved with age (as John Gielgud has done), brings a mischievous bounce, a shameless bonhomie, a nonchalant and engaging rudeness to every movement in the best conceived part of the play. Dunlop's staging is light, breezy, scrupulously exact and happily free of directorial exhibitionism.

Several members of the cast—Rosemary Harris, René Auberjonois, Margaret Hamilton, Stephen Collins—will also appear in Dunlop's next production at the Brooklyn Academy of Music—Chekhov's *The Three Sisters*. We shall then not only have the opportunity once again to see that beautiful play but to measure Dunlop's scope as a director. If *The Three Sisters* proves nearly as good as *The New York Idea*, we shall have reason to hope that he is well on the way to establishing an excellent resident company. In any case, it would be a boon to playgoers if *The New York Idea* and *The Three Sisters* (assuming it lives up to expectation) were to tour the country.

—*NAT*, 16 Apr. '77

ANNA CHRISTIE
WHITE MARRIAGE

"None of us can help the things life has done to us. They're done before you realize it, and once they're done they make you do other things until at last everything comes between you and what you'd like to be...." Mary Tyrone says this in *Long Day's Journey Into Night*. It is the feeling which sets the tone and creates the pervasive atmosphere of O'Neill's writing. It defines the fate which weighs down and imprisons most of his characters.

In *Anna Christie*, O'Neill associates this fate with the sea. The play's last lines, spoken by Anna's father, Chris Christopherson, a Swedish-born captain of a barge anchored in a New England harbor, are "Fog, fog, fog. All bloody time. You can't see where you vas going, no. Only dat old davil sea—she knows." It is the impenetrable mystery, the essential tragic force which Chris (through O'Neill) perceives in all occasions. In the evocation of the mood which results from that soul-burdening perception we recognize the O'Neill signature.

In his best plays the dramatic material suits his "music." In *Anna Christie* (Imperial Theatre) the plot is banal, as in fact are most of the characters: Anna, the blameless sinner; the Irish steamship stoker, muscular, loose-living, bragging, guileless, decent, superstitiously Catholic, and the confused, hard-drinking, regretful father. In 1921-22 those who found fault with the play, that season's Pulitzer Prize winner, did so only on the ground of its "happy ending." Others, "the discriminating playgoers," to quote a prominent reviewer of the time, "who had learned what to expect of O'Neill were enthusiastic in their endorsement. It is a rough play....Much of its dialogue may prove offensive to super-fine sensibilities. (The characters) do not speak the language of the drawing room. But it is also one of the big dramas of the day, soundly human..." etc., etc.

It requires no particular acumen at present to dismiss the play as corny, but it is important to understand that in 1921 it proved effective because crucial to it is the O'Neill spirit, that low-keyed but inescapable inner intensity which lends even his weakest plays an impressiveness that very nearly overrides many of our objections. In 1921 that spirit was embodied in the person of Pauline Lord, one of the most moving American actresses of the past fifty years or more. From Pauline Lord, who was by no means a pretty woman, there emanated a sense of a hurt and sorrowful consciousness, the counterpart of the persistent fatality that hangs over O'Neill's plays. She was not dramatically "exciting": hers was a seemingly mute presence, ineffably touching because it contained all the unshed tears in the common heartbreak of existence.

Liv Ullmann, who now plays Anna, is beautiful and remarkably resembles O'Neill's description of the character: "She is a tall, blonde, fully developed girl, handsome after a large, Viking-daughter fashion...." There is a muffled pain and yearning in Ullmann's voice, a kind of northland bewilderment in her blue eyes, as though her gaze had been forever fixed on a far-off but not quite discernible horizon. She also acts the part, line by line, scene by scene, quite well. Yet she does not express the quintessential Anna. As she enters the stage, she indicates the ill health Anna has suffered, but it is only a temporary indisposition. Anna's sickness is the ache of a soul, an unromantic existential pain which is exemplary and not only due to the accident of present circumstances. Ullmann, whatever her immediate ailment and trouble, strikes one as healthy at the core. O'Neill's Anna is something more than a figure in a particular, lamentable and not very original story. Only with an Anna such as I have suggested through the image of Pauline Lord can the play today truly affect us.

The rest of the cast, like Ullmann, may be set down as "good." John Lithgow is certainly engaging as the boastful Irish swain, but somewhat callow in the torment of his discovery that Anna has been a prostitute. Robert Donley is descriptively right as Anna's father, but his is impeded by the nature of the production as a whole. It is faithful to the action and the events of the play; it does not evoke the underlying sources from which the play must draw its power, and without which all O'Neill's work may appear shoddy. José Quintero's intelligent direction is in line with the play's overt course; it is external, which makes it vehement, professionally sound and, at bottom, ordinary. Good settings (especially that of the barge) by Ben Edwards and other assets do not overcome the basic deficiency. The production does not speak with the inner voice which alone could save it.

Were I to recite in full detail all the elements which compose *White Marriage* I would still not convey its extraordinary quality (Yale Repertory Theatre, New Haven). Its author, Tadeusz Rozewicz, born in 1921, is today one of the leading Polish playwrights. The play has been directed by Andrzej Wajda, best known in this country for his film *Ashes and Diamonds*. (He also heads what many consider the best theatre in Poland, situated in Krakow.) His wife, Krystyna Zachwatowicz, has designed the scenery for the Yale production, as she does for most of her husband's many films and plays.

When *White Marriage*, which Wajda calls a "fairy tale for adults," was first mentioned to me it was described as a highly erotic piece. Eroticism is virtually taboo on the Soviet stage and, though Poland is free of many Soviet artistic inhibitions, *White Marriage* when it was produced three years ago in Poland aroused controversy there on that account. But though it is true that the erotic sensibility is part of the play's texture and theme, *White Marriage* encompasses a wider range of feeling and answers a broader purpose. It is at once satire, fantasy, poem.

The play, in thirteen "tableaux," pivots on two young girls who are approaching their "spring awakening," a sensual awareness of their femininity. The younger one is unrepressed, charmingly forward; the second, extremely shy, is already nubile and is in fact being prepared for marriage to a youth who, though a student at Heidelberg, is still a virgin. But all three are in almost every respect innocents. The action takes place at a country estate in the early years of the century.

What is pictured is bourgeois society (with peasantlike underpinnings), especially in regard to sexual relationships. The young are kept uninformed of such matters; most of the married women have been subjected to unions with men who treat them as properties. The men chase their female servants—cooks, maids and other such—like brutes. They reduce these women to wildfowl and they display little warmth to or understanding of their daughters. Thus, on the one hand we observe the silly decorum of pseudo-cultivated society (piano playing, amateur theatricals, poetry recitals); on the other, the manners and morals of the barnyard.

One might suppose, then, that all this would be transformed into a sort of women's lib parable, an earnestly fanciful denunciation of the old-time Polish bourgeoisie. Instead, along with hilariously phallic humor, deft stabs of ridicule, the play is suffused by a very special delicacy and tenderness, a kind of comic benevolence, a purity which dissolves derision and dispels any suspicion of preachment. There is an insinuating mockery here but it always remains joyous, sane and surprisingly touching. At certain moments a somber note is struck to provide a framework for and a contrast to the general airiness. The loveliness of both adolescent girls bathes the crudities inherent in some of the proceedings with a light which turns all to serene beauty.

As director, Wajda has captured the intent and spirit of the play to perfection. The production, in setting, movement, characterization, is an unostentatious gem. Everyone is in tune. Carol Williard has the vulnerable fragility and the sweet bewilderment of Bianca, the girl bride; Blanche Baker, as her younger companion, is luminous with the wily candor, the seething energy of a child on the verge of becoming a glorious woman. Alvin Epstein is very funny as the toothless satyr of a grandfather, the apt progenitor of his untamed bear of a son played by Eugene Troobnick.

—*NAT*, 30 Apr. '77

SOMETHING ROTTEN IN AMERICA: INNAURATO

A book which in publication fails to appeal to a large public still remains alive for the few who read it; it may endure for future appreciation. This is rarely true of plays. They must immediately succeed in attracting a wide audience or forever pass from notice.

Theatre therefore lags behind literature. Social readiness and a degree of homogeneity in the community must be obtained for a theatre piece to gain general acceptance.

Realism in the American theatre—especially realism of a "disagreeable" sort—lagged behind literary realism. William Dean Howells (1837-1920), one of our first modern realists in the novel, was faulted in the thirties for being much too genteel. Had he not said, "the more smiling aspects of life are the more American?"

Before 1915, the number of American plays with unhappy endings could be counted on the fingers of one hand. Tragedy was foreign! It was not until 1920 with Eugene O'Neill's first full-length play, *Beyond the Horizon*, that plays of unhappiness were allowed honorable entry on our stage.

O'Neill did still another daring thing: he made a stoker on a transatlantic liner (in *The Hairy Ape*), a black Pullman car porter (in *The Emperor Jones*), and other such untoward characters central figures in several of his plays. He opened the doors to "guests" almost never before admitted to our tables of entertainment.

Tennessee Williams went further than O'Neill and the playwrights of the thirties (Clifford Odets and others). He called our attention to the "somehow unfit," people in limbo who were in one way or another defective, delinquent, or unglamorously sinful. By the fifties many plays had become infernal. We had gradually become aware that there was something rotten in Denmark!

The English theatre has evolved along similar lines (although for different reasons). But in the great number of cases, English playwrights face their national disturbances with either a grin or outright laughter; Americans mix indignation with compassion. We find this, for example, in one of our angriest young men, David Rabe. His *Streamers* is a savage play but there is sorrow in it. *The Basic Training of Pavlo Hummel*, Rabe's first play, now being revived with Al Pacino, dealt with the horror of the Vietnam War: in it ferocity is tempered by pity.

The latest manifestation of the tendency to expose the most appalling lesions of our civilization has devolved to the unequivocally horrifying. Now a bill of two one-act plays by new writers is advertised under the title *Monsters*. The first of these is called *Side Show* by William Dews. Its monsters are Siamese twins. They are objects of shame to their family till the day the parents find

that their sons can be a source of income through public display. This so humiliates the twins that they murder their parents and then commit suicide.

The play is obviously symbolic, and its somewhat stylized dialogue and presentation relieve its unpleasantness. Still it alienated a good many in the audience, while some find it nerve-frayingly funny. It is evident that William Dews means his play to evoke commiserations through terror.

The second "monster" of the program is an immensely fat youth whose parents regard him more with shivers of distaste than sadness. The play is called *The Transfiguration of Benno Blimpie*. Its author, Albert Innaurato, is represented at another off-Broadway theatre by a full-length play, *Gemini*. Though *Gemini* is less startling and more conventional in form than *Blimpie*, I prefer *Gemini*.

Both plays are fundamentally realistic and both reflect the same attitude: a fellow feeling for the insulted and the injured. The anguish of *Blimpie*'s subject matter is mitigated by a degree of stylization. Benno, called Blimpie because of his bulk, is placed on a platform situated above the level of the stage floor. Seated in that position, he speaks often in the third person of his early boyhood, while on both sides of the stage scenes take place in the parental home and in the streets outside it. The environment is that of a largely Italian ghetto—as it is in *Gemini*—where no one shows the least sign of kindness. Besides the unfortunate personal reasons for his being mistreated, Benno witnesses nothing but sordidness and violence everywhere around him. He himself is a boy of marked sensibility and artistic inclination. Though his parents, simple Italians of the working class, are incompetent in adjusting to the existence of their ill-favored son, they are not at all bad people. The mother, admirably played by Rosemary deAngelis, especially is depicted with sympathetic humor.

In self-destructive reaction to the suffering inflicted upon him because of his physical unsightliness, Benno is determined to make himself even more hideously obese by eating himself to death. He finally kills himself most brutally. Playing this difficult role, James Coco achieves eloquence.

Gemini is a collective picture of habitants in a scrubby South Philadelphia neighborhood. There is little plot, but the characters are depicted with a salty tenderness. The writing is sound, the observation truthful even when sentimental, and the play imparts a special sense of fun. For though there is raucousness in the air, as in most ghettos, and very few of its people can be considered "happy," a vein of fraternal closeness binds them and soothes the hurts which affect them. We rejoice at our ability to share in the humanity of the least among them.

Gemini too has been cast with actors who bring blood and body to their roles—more varied in this play than in the earlier one.

I also look forward to a new musical called *Annie.* It is reported to be reminiscent of the old-fashioned or homespun sweetness of a more cheerful time. We need that too.

—*WEST*, Apr. '77

THE BASIC TRAINING OF PAVLO HUMMEL
HAPPY END

The Basic Training of Pavlo Hummel, originally produced at Joseph Papp's Public Theatre in 1971, is the first of David Rabe's angrily talented plays. I liked *Sticks and Bones* even better, and *Streamers* the best. The three constitute a kind of triptych; though they do not all have the same theme, there is, along with the ferocity, a vein of moral hurt and compassion in all of them.

Pavlo Hummel is not an anti-war play in the conventional sense, nor for that matter are the others. It shows an ignorant, unhappy, guileless youth with no harm or malice in him slowly becoming degraded and brutalized by the "basic training" of an environment—in this case the Army—even before he serves in Vietnam. Environment might have had some of the same ugly consequences if he had remained at home with such a family as the one depicted in *Sticks and Bones*.

For those who have not seen the play, it is worth seeing now. For those who did see the earlier production, the chief interest in the revival by the Theatre Company of Boston will be the presence in the cast of Al Pacino as Pavlo (Longacre Theatre). It is not news that Pacino is an excellent actor of strongly arresting personality. A store of hot feeling burns within him, stemming from experiences urging him to their half-articulate expression. The personal stress and its only partially understood source most often makes for a feral anger that is all the more frightening because of its semi-suppression. The effect is strikingly theatrical. But there is a limitation in this, for while anger is what existence today most frequently provokes, it prevents the development of more fruitful emotions. Pacino senses this and has tried in private study and in the choice of certain atypical roles to broaden his scope. Up to a point, Pavlo provides him with an opportunity to do so.

Pavlo is an innocent, so much so that his fellow trainees regard him as a freak. As such, Pacino is both amusing and touching. He plays the role with exemplary ease; his street speech is unemphatically enunciated; there is complete naturalness of tone. But the change in Pavlo from the gutter Parsifal of the first act (we hear that he was a virgin at the time of his Army enlistment) to the later soiled and nasty Pavlo is not sufficiently marked. Thus there is a slight monotony in the performance, so that the final scenes, which should be even more bruising than the preceding ones, fall a little flat.

Bertolt Brecht, author of the lyrics for *Happy End*, and Kurt Weill as composer of the music, plagiarized or made a pastiche of the Brecht-Weill *The Threepenny Opera* (Martin Beck Theatre).

Their plagiarism is on the whole gratifying. The original German play, a failure when first produced in the Berlin of 1929 is credited to "Dorothy Lane." But no such person existed; Dorothy Lane was Elizabeth Hauptmann, the woman long associated with Brecht, who suggested that he write a musical play based on John Gay's *The Beggar's Opera*. In the present production of *Happy End* the book and lyrics have been well adapted by Michael Feingold.

The play's "story" resembles that of *Guys and Dolls*. A Salvation Army lass undertakes to reform a gang of criminals in a mythical 1915 Chicago. The girl, Hallelujah Lil a name typical of Brecht in his "American" mode, becomes enamored of the toughest member of the gang, Bill Cracker; he in turn falls for her. But along with the burlesque wickedness by which Brecht and Weill aped the lurid glamour of Berlin in the late 1920's, there is also a touch of their social "propaganda": salvation is possible for the poor by supporting their need with good intentions—along with some of the steely realism gangsters possess. All this is, of course, tongue-in-cheek and tartly carefree entertainment.

There is deliberate as well as accidental crudity in the piece as here produced, yet its sly spirit is infectious. One does not hear all the lyrics distinctly enough, in part because the cast has not learned that for Brecht-Weill emphasis should be placed on *speaking* the words of the songs rather than on singing—very much as Walter Huston did for Weill's "September Song" in Maxwell Anderson's *Knickerbocker Holiday*. Nobody ever rendered it better than Huston who had no "voice" and barely tried to sing. Yet the songs in *Happy End* with their (German) jazz inspiration still evoke a mood of the peculiar gaiety, a combination of venom and friendly mockery, that are the earmarks of the era of which Brecht and Weill were the *minnesingers*.

After numerous mishaps, Robert Kalfin has whipped this odd frolic into shape. Robert U. Taylor's settings have the right look of sleazy cheerfulness, Meryl Streep is a most fetching Lil, Grayson Hall is "Fly," the malefic leader of the reformable gang. Prudence Holmes is a shrilly

virtuous member of the Army, as Alexandra Borrie is a gently comely and mellifluous one. Among the men, Joe Grifasi is a vulnerable Salvationist given to multiple swoons, and Bob Gunton as Bill Cracker, substituting at the last moment for Christopher Lloyd, who was hurt at a preview performance, has a good voice and does his job creditably.

Happy End is disarming.

—*NAT*, 14 May '77

THE THREE SISTERS

The Three Sisters is the most beautiful of Chekhov's plays. I have seen it innumerable times in several languages and, though not by nature lachrymose, I have hardly ever seen it without shedding tears. This happened again at Frank Dunlop's production at the Brooklyn Academy of Music.

It is not in the ordinary sense a sad or tragic play. I rarely cry at *The Seagull*, which ends with the suicide of the young man who, along with his beloved Nina, is the center of the play. And though Tusenbach, one of the most likable of the personages in *The Three Sisters*, is killed in a duel, it is not his death that induces my weeping. What moves me is a strain of feeling that is present throughout. It is the purity and tenderness with which Chekhov endows every moment, his sense of the absurdity of life, together with that element in his people which forever keeps them hoping to make life better no matter how bitterly disappointing it may prove at every turn. It is that special idealism and goodness which, without alleviation or consolation, constitutes the peculiar stamp of Chekhov's vision and artistry. This sentiment— neither optimism nor pessimism—makes Chekhov's plays truer to life than any others written, to say the least, in our time.

For this reason the question of whether his plays are funny or sad, comedies or tragedies is irrelevant. They are both at once. That is why the new cliché, which insists that comedy must be emphasized in Chekhov productions, strikes me as part of an evasive superficiality characteristic of much contemporary thinking. The muddle is largely based on the well-advertised dispute between Chekhov and Stanislavsky: Chekhov thought that Stanislavsky had made his characters into "cry-babies," that his plays had been made too somber and tearful.

To begin with, we should be reminded that such dramatist-director disagreements are inevitable and constant in the theatre—very often on matters of details, nuances. The fact is that, whatever the differences that may have arisen between Chekhov and Stanislavsky, Chekhov urged Gorky and others to write plays for the Moscow Art Theatre. It is clear, too, that if the Moscow Art Theatre had not produced Chekhov's plays, they might never have become known to us today, or even have been written.

I do not say this in defense of Stanislavsky. Chekhov's plays may be produced in different modes, according to historical circumstances—that is, according to the specific audiences whom they are to serve. If one proposes to make a travesty of them it is quite possible to do so. This was accomplished in the Soviet Union itself. In one such production the three sisters were ridiculed as frivolous and silly. It did not succeed theatrically with the Soviet audiences because the play became an arty exercise in directorial conceit and "revolutionary" distortion.

For myself, I am heartily sick and tired of hearing that Chekhov is "funny." Of course he is funny, even at moments when at the same time we cannot restrain our tears. One does not have to equate this with the elimination of Chekhov's humanity, which by virtue of his complete view of the human condition renders his plays both laugh-provoking and heartbreaking.

Very few of the people who now proclaim Chekhov side-splitting, as if they were making an extraordinary discovery, ever saw the original Stanislavsky productions. And I would like to set it down unequivocally that the Moscow Art Theatre's *The Cherry Orchard*, which I saw in Paris in 1922, was actually funnier for the most part than Andrei Serban's Lincoln Center production.

And anyone who takes the trouble to read the chapter in Stanislavsky's *My Life in Art* devoted to *The Three Sisters* will learn that after long weeks of rehearsal he realized that he was on the wrong track: the characters were not conscious of the tragedy of their lives, as he had at first thought them to be, he altered his interpretation accordingly. The now fashionable approach to Chekhov, which would make him a sort of highbrow Neil Simon, betrays not only a juvenile mentality, an inability to face existence with lucid courage or fortitude of spirit but a misunderstanding of the nature of comedy. We mistake it for a string of gags adding up to a "laugh show."

Dunlop is a gifted, skillful and intelligent director and his production of *The Three Sisters* is a careful attempt to deal with the Chekhov "problem." The pace is rapid and crisp, the scenes race along, speech is bright, the tone exuberant. Dunlop wishes to make it evident that the characters are not congenitally gloomy but rather life-and-fun-loving people caught in a social environment fatal to their basically healthy impulses. Everyone speaks loudly, too loudly (this may also be due to a general uneasiness about the perhaps faulty acoustics of the theatre auditorium), and they laugh a lot. On the whole, Dunlop avoids the farcical.

His treatment eschews dark introspection and thus loses something of the relaxation and much of the shadowiness of a backwoods Russian town where the play takes place, and from which the characters' irrepressible yearning for a fullness of experience mounts like a mist to imbue the atmosphere with lyric beauty. Still, Chekhov is not traduced; the play remains moving, because many of the details are understood and well projected.

The players, none bad or altogether "wrong," are uneven. Crudities occur from time to time, partly because in his effort to establish a permanent company with only a limited number of actors at his disposal, Dunlop has had to choose players not entirely suitable as to "type."

Nevertheless, all the actors have their "moments." Denholm Elliott is especially good in the painful embarrassment and ache of his farewell to Masha. Rosemary Harris's Olga is particularly right in her reproach to and defeat by the aggressive Natalia, as well as in her brave acceptance of the cloudy future. Holly Villiare rather overdoes Natalia, who should not be made a ludicrous vixen as she is here, though she is shown as properly strong when she asserts her dominance over Olga. Barnard Hughes's Doctor is touching in scenes of affection and sorrow, but his cynicism is abrasive and brash rather than the consequence of hopeless bewilderment in a crushed being.

Compliments might also be addressed to Stephen Collins's Andrey and to Ralph Clanton's Ferapont. (It might be remarked, however, that Russian octogenarian servants are much more feeble than they are made out to be in this production.) René Auberjonois's Solvony is effective, though he has been directed to a characterization halfway between burlesque and menacing melodrama. The essence of Lolyony's person is hurt: he is shy, lonely, feels himself misunderstood, and is horribly jealous. He hides himself in a mask of abusiveness. Auberjonois, like almost everyone in the cast, would do well if he were permitted to heed Stanislavsky's instruction, "Cut 90 percent!"

The most sustained and winning performances are those of Austin Pendleton as Tusenbach, which is pitched to the nice ease and sweetness of the role, and Tovah Feldshuh, whose aspiring and lovely Irina is shaped to a most believable veracity of expression.

Certain jarring notes in the production may have arisen from a mistrust of the audience. Vershinin and Masha touch each other with an amatory intent contrary to the special reticence that is perhaps the outstanding feature common to the Chekhovian gentlefolk. We know that these married people love each other without needing to have the point made in overt "business." Rex Robbins, because he is himself a large man with a powerful bass voice, should have been required to subdue his playing of Kulygin so we could see that, while the man is certainly something of a fool, he is not an oaf. Kulygin is one of Chekhov's *pure* fools, a soul of kindness with a comprehension deeper than intelligence. Such men and women appear in several other plays and in the stories; they have Chekhov's blessing. There is also some "smartening" of the dialogue in Stark Young's (and other translations). Masha is supposed to offer, "Here's to life. What the hell," as a toast. She means she salutes life despite its difficulties. In the Dunlop production Ellen Burstyn as Masha says, "Here's to life. To hell with it!" which means something quite different. The audience laughs and applauds!

An ending is attached to the play in which Kulygin comes out after the gloriously soul-stirring coda when Olga, speaking also for her two sisters, says: "If we could only know, if we could only know!" (why they suffer). He plays the clown to make them cheer up, a scene both clever and damaging. It is the key to the merit and defect of the production.

—*NAT*, 21 May '77

VIEUX CARRÉ

In a curious way Tennessee Williams's *Vieux Carré* strikes me as still another revival (St. James Theatre). A mood and a matter are repeated which have been dramatized in several of Williams's earlier plays.

The milieu is that of a run-down boarding house in the Vieux Carré or French Quarter of New Orleans. The goings-on are narrated by a young and indigent homosexual, who is remembering them and recording them in both a past and present time scale. His next-room neighbor is a homosexual painter who ekes out a living by making portraits of tourists. He drinks and is ridden by tuberculosis. On the same landing opposite these men are a couple: a handsome man who works as a barker and hustler at a local dive; with him is a young woman of good breeding and looks, sick with a fatal blood disease. She is magnetized by the pull of the fellow's superb physique. The landlady of the resort is an indomitable, hard-bitten, crusty harridan who allows two half-crazed old women derelicts to live alongside her kitchen rent-free. Except for those no longer capable of sex, they all ride on the streetcar named desire.

Sylvia Sidney as the landlady is excellent, even in her Southern accent; she brings a gritty humor and a fund of spiteful understanding which lend sympathy to the role. Tom Aldredge makes the moribund painter credible and pitiful without making him mawkish. The heterosexual lovers, at times semi-nude or entirely so, acted by Diane Kagan and Reb Brownell, also elicit belief in their situation.

The dialogue has some of the usual felicities of Williams's writing, though they are signs of a weakening in precision. There is a certain wretched honesty and boldness in several of the scenes but they also seem tired: the tune has too often been replayed.

—*NAT*, 28 May '77

CURRENT THEATRE

The autobiography of that handsome French actor, Jean-Pierre Aumont, has just been published. It is called *Sun and Shadow*. If I had to name my notes on the productions I have seen during the past month, I would borrow that title in reverse. There were rays of sunshine in the plays and certain shadows in the musicals.

This year's Pulitzer Prize was awarded to a play named *The Shadow Box*. It is about three people—two men and one old woman—who are dying of cancer. Yet the play is by no means dismal: it avoids pain. One might say that this evasion typifies the American approach to the

reality of death. To the American theatregoer the subject if more shocking than anything related to sex: indeed it is practically taboo on our stage. We are still a young and successful country. We are all go-ahead; we shun thoughts which suggest any impediment to our cheerful progress.

Michael Cristofer who wrote *The Shadow Box* is the actor who played the student Trofimov in Andrei Serban's *The Cherry Orchard* at Lincoln Center; he has a canny theatrical knack. He carries out the trick of making the death theme not only bearable but almost light-hearted. He is reasonable about it without being naturalistic or clinical. He is sentimental without being soppy. He is humorous without being coarse. The play is facile yet entirely sympathetic.

Now to the bright illumination of musical entertainments. Outstanding among these is *Side by Side by Sondheim*, and as its title indicates it is a song cycle, of which all the lyrics and most of the music are from Stephen Sondheim's hits: *Gypsy, Company, Follies*, to mention only a few.

The show originated in London and its three performers, two women and a gentleman, as well as its director and witty master of ceremonies are English. For all its simplicity, the presentation is cunningly staged, and the three main participants—Millicent Martin, Julia McKenzie, David Kernan—are wonderfully suited to their assignment. They are sexily good looking, with an aura of stylishness which admirably embellishes the debonair, crackling cynicism which is the essence of Sondheim's talent. Though I use the harsh word, there is no real malice in it. Only if one persists in a close examination of the implications expressed in the clever lines does one perceive there is some shadow in the sunniness. But excessive thought is not required for the occasion. It is a dandy show, appropriately located in the Music Box Theatre.

Most of New York's reviewers raved about *I Love My Wife*: book and lyrics by Michael Stewart, music by Cy Coleman. Its "story" concerns two married couples who attempt an exchange of mates as an experiment to stimulate their sexual appetites for one another. But as the shy one of the lot—charmingly played by Lenny Baker—says or sings "I love my wife," so though the four enter a single bed—not at all conveniently undressed—no damage is done and presumably no offense is given.

The show exploits an area of erotic titillation for purposes of comic relief (relief from what, I wonder) and as such may be considered thoroughly innocuous. I cannot say it aroused any special enthusiasm in me—except for some funny stage business invented by the director Gene Saks, a raffishly amusing quartet of rock players, a few jokes, and an agreeable tunefulness. But mine is probably a minority reaction.

Annie, produced by Mike Nichols, who must have lent a helping hand to achieve its overall dispatch will no doubt pack the Alvin Theatre for many a day to come. This musical, based on the perennial cartoon "Little Orphan Annie" was written by Thomas Meehan, with music by Charles Strouse and lyrics by Martin Charnin. Its assets are a group of lively, talented, winning kids, a smart dog, a very funny and probably prize-winning performance by Dorothy Loudon, some handsomely designed scenery by David Mitchell, and a generally likable cast. The songs are sufficiently pleasant to have warranted special notice from most of my colleagues in the press.

The show is deliberately corny and, therefore, absolves us of the need to deliver ourselves of any ponderous opinion. It radiates good will. It reminds us of how we overcame the bad old days of the Great Depression of the '30s, it pokes affectionate fun at F.D.R., it presents a benevolent billionaire and laughs at its own sentimentality. No shadow here, following a season in which many disturbances, wounds, and sorrows have been displayed. Here at last is a stage parade that excels Macy's.

—*WEST*, June '77

JACOB BEN–AMI
ALFRED LUNT

"Then a new king ascended the throne of Egypt, one who knew nothing of Joseph." This line which opens the Old Testament book of Exodus is one of the earliest recorded observations of the "generation gap." All literate Englishmen are aware of Edmund Kean's reputation (1787-1823); the same is true of Frenchmen in regard to that regal tigress, Rachel (1821-58), as educated Germans are of Josef Kainz (1851-1910). Our Edwin Booth is probably remembered chiefly because his brother, John Wilkes, shot Lincoln.

Teaching a graduate class in theatre at Hunter College, I was shocked to learn that more than half the students had never heard of Alfred Lunt. Lunt was born in 1893 and died early in August, as did another outstanding but less celebrated actor of the same period, Jacob Ben-Ami. Now in this uneventful moment between seasons, I find it owing history to write of them both for the benefit of those who have forgotten or who are unfamiliar with their signal merit.

To speak first of the less eminent, I am reminded that Stark Young, the most perceptive critic of acting in the 1920s, spoke of Ben-Ami in *Samson and Delilah* (produced in 1920) in the highest praise. (Earlier it had been done here on the Yiddish stage where the actor was "discovered" by Arthur Hopkins.) And Lee Strasberg, keen judge of acting that he is, told me some years later that he regarded Ben-Ami's performance in that play the most poignant model of realistic acting he had ever seen.

Samson and Delilah, a translation from the Swedish, had nothing to do with the Biblical story. It was a play about a dramatist's relation to the world of the stage—actors and audience—and his betrayal by both. In 1923 the Theatre Guild presented H.R. Lenormand's *The Failures* in which Ben-Ami was cast as another dramatist, driven to suicide by the wretchedness of a road tour in the French provinces. He played still another writer in Eugene O'Neill's *Welded* and a composer in a German play about Johannes Kreisler.

Most of these parts provide a clue to the nature of Ben-Ami's talent. If he was not an "intellectual" (he directed many productions: one of them with Alfred Lunt in Franz Werfel's *Goat Song*) he was one of the few actors who was convincing as a man of mind and profound intuition. Though he was brilliant in the comedy of eecentric personality, he was essentially a tragic actor. He embodied the tragedy of disability in contradistinction to the tragedy of strength, of which the Greeks and the Elizabethans offer the best examples. It is significant that tragedy of the latter sort ever since 1917 has been beyond the scope of most American actors.

We too often speak of "great" actors. There have actually been only a few at any time. What does being "great" in regard to acting really mean? It means the ability to express something more than proficiency in verisimilitude, the bare projection of the material at hand. Thus, in a scene I shall never forget, Ben-Ami as the playwright in *Samson and Delilah* explains the plot of the play of that name which he has written. His narrative was quiet, unemphatic and entirely without sentiment dity or pretentiousness; but we sensed, as Ben-Ami spoke the rather colorless lines, the hurt of the artist who feels that the true import of what he is saying is not understood by the person whom he is addressing. The suffering of loneliness, of estrangement from his colleagues and audience became the aura and "music" of the scene, a meaning beyond the commonplace meaning.

Ben-Ami's effectiveness was limited by his accent (neither particularly Jewish nor Russian), the lack in our theatre structure of permanent companies and, above all, the fact that when he was not genuinely inspired his acting tended to become opaque; we could not discern what he was about. At his best, however, his performance gave rise to what Stark Young called "the flower in drama," true glamor.

Alfred Lunt was universally acclaimed the finest American actor in the generation which followed John Barrymore. He was delightful in comedy (in *The Guardsman*, for instance) and subtly affecting in serious roles. Rather than attaining the heights or depths of tragedy, except perhaps in Dürrenmatt's *The Visit*, he excelled in pathos. There was a special vulnerability in almost all his playing, an almost feminine, though tearless, touch. This, even more than his instinctive stage sense (Lynn Fontanne, his wife, was the more calculating technician), gave each of his performances its peculiar appeal.

One of his most telling characterizations was in S.N. Behrman's *The Second Man*. It dealt with an urbane and rather flashily successful writer who was all affability and grace in whom there lurked a little demon of sophisticated malice, an ineradicable skepticism not unlike cafe-society spite. Unconsciously, Lunt reversed the picture. The facile wit contained in Behrman's dialogue became the mask; the wounded and tender being beneath was the authentic man. Indeed it was the tenderness in Lunt which made him so beloved an actor. His limitation was that he never assayed the truly great roles as most English stars have done. But, wonder of wonders, Lunt seemed to recognize his limitations. At one of the last rehearsals of *The Seagull* in which he played Trigorin, he was heard to say, "Perhaps we're not good enough for this play."

As Dimitri in Jacques Copeau's dramatization of *The Brothers Karamazov*, he had the character's hysteria but little of the tempestuous masculine drive. At rehearsal, Copeau, who directed, whispered to me, "C'est un gosse": he's a kid. But it was just the kid in him, a mode of innocence and purity, which rendered Lunt's acting enchanting. The difficulty Lunt and Copeau had in understanding each other lay, perhaps, in the actor's being so thoroughly American.

The wholly red-white-and-blue Lunt was charming in European comedy, especially of the Hungarian and Viennese variety. (There was in his speech an odd shade of Scandinavian accent, probably a faint echo of some of his Midwestern neighbors of Norse extraction.) Olivier and Richardson among many other British actors revered him particularly for the ready flow of his emotion, at all times generous, unpremeditated, natural.

—*NAT*, 10 Sept. '77

TARTUFFE
THE GIN GAME
REUNION
THE GHOST SONATA
LANDSCAPE OF THE BODY

Tartuffe, at the Circle-in-the-Square, is a good show. It may seem frivolous to designate this world-famous masterpiece by such a term. In its day (1664) the play was a dangerous thing to write. It was not only controversial but censurable. It was suppressed for several years. Its performances were resumed after Moliere wrote a trick ending to appease the religious coterie in Louis XIV's court.

A black comedy, *Tartuffe* was an attack on bigotry rather than a laugh show. To poke fun on strict religious observance in a dominantly Catholic country such as France in the seventeenth century was no joke. The play was then and is still occasionally acted in France in a manner verging on somber drama.

Some critics therefore object to its farcical treatment at the Circle in the Square. But such treatment is right, I believe, for our day and place. Stringent religious behavior is rare among us; indeed, it strikes most of us as peculiar. Moliere thought it false and did not consider it blasphemous to mock it.

The new production goes all out for yaks. As such it is entirely successful. As a character

Tartuffe is as exemplary as Don Quixote. He is more than a person: he is a universal type, the embodiment of hypocrisy. John Wood's Tartuffe has menace in it (his very look suggests a certain fiendishness) but for the most part he and Stephen Porter's direction are wholly comic. As the object of Tartuffe's lust, Tammy Grimes, clipped in speech, archly dry in attitude, is also in key with the present interpretation, as is most of the cast including Patricia Elliott as the household maid who is the first to see through Tartuffe's mask. The setting and costumes are attractive, the translation by Richard Wilbur brilliant.

Another good show—on an entirely different level—is *The Gin Game* by a new playwright, D.L. Coburn (John Golden Theatre). There has been a tendency in certain quarters (notably in *The New York Times*) to take it too seriously. But plays need not be masterpieces to please us. Masterpieces, the poet W.H. Auden has said, are for high holidays. They are also, it should be remembered, a most infrequent phenomenon.

The Gin Game is nicely written, its humor benevolent, its heart in the right place. A two-character comedy, it is about elderly people who meet in a rather drab home for the aged. They are cut off from their children and relatives and more lonely than they care to admit.

The man is a crotchety, no-nonsense person; the woman a stoically proper lady. The man's chief occupation and pastime at the "home" is cards. He prefers gin to solitaire. So he asks the woman, a new guest, to join him in the game. The source of fun is his ire at her constant winning; he considers himself an expert and she hardly more than a beginner.

As his irritation grows, the play begins to sound a few deeper tones than the surface humors of the situation. A kind of senseless competitiveness, in all its irrationality, becomes clamorously evident. It is symptomatic of the difficulty any two people have in getting along together, and more particularly of the basic isolation of the individual person.

This is revealed without stress or moralizing. Yet for all its sober implications the play remains slight. What gives it body and special entertainment value are the charmingly deft performances of Jessica Tandy and Hume Cronyn under Mike Nichols's knowing direction.

David Mamet, a playwright who at the moment may be set down as the most promising among our younger ones (he is twenty-nine) is now represented by a one-hour play *Reunion* at Yale Repertory Theatre in New Haven and by *A Life in the Theatre* at the off-Broadway Theatre de Lys.

Both plays were written before *American Buffalo* which won the N.Y. Drama Critics Circle Award for the best play. Both *Reunion* and *A Life in the Theatre* were first produced at a small theatre in Chicago. Of the two, I much prefer *Reunion*. I must advise my *Westchester Magazine* readers that in this and other opinions I oppose those of my colleagues of the daily press.

The reunion of Mamet's play is that of a meeting after many years of a father (a reformed alcoholic) and his daughter, long estranged because of his vice and his divorce. A marked tenderness imbues the play.

The second play's attraction for some people (most of the reviewers) is the silliness involved in theatre life, exemplified by an older and rather pompous actor who constantly patronizes a younger one.

Reunion is touching through its understanding of the common man and his need of human support. His more sophisticated daughter, troubled in her marriage, also craves such support, in this case from a father, even though he is a humble and to some degree a flawed person. The play is plainly written with a refreshing sensibility in a vernacular which gives evidence of Mamet's ear for ordinary American speech. It is admirably acted by Michael Higgins and Lindsay Crouse.

A Life in the Theatre is a trifling spoof of stage life. I wouldn't object to it as such if it were not received as something more than that. Its comedy consists of rather commonplace gags: actors forgetting their lines or embarrassed by finding their flies open while on stage, with examples of their ludicrous conceit.

I hardly believed a word of it—even for purposes of fun. One may be amused at show folk antics, but even a cartoon must have a firmer basis in reality. I barely smiled at what some others have said they "laughed till it hurts." The latter reaction is only possible for those only casually acquainted with life in the theatre.

In the "morning" of the season, plays pour onto the stage more profusely than one person can fully review in a single article. I must therefore speak of several other offerings more briefly than they deserve.

This is certainly true of *The Ghost Sonata* at Yale. One of the last plays (1907) of that titanic genius (and madman) August Strindberg, it is considered by many who are familiar with such earlier of his writings as *The Father* and *Miss Julie* as one of his most important works. It is not an easy play; some may find it puzzling, but its meaning is unmistakable.

It is a lament over the total corruption of society and the hardship of living. Its plot is difficult to unravel but its course is expressionistically fascinating, its overall tone lyrical. I do not share its spiritual attitude, but for those who wish to have a more extensive knowledge of modern drama than ordinary theatregoing provides it is something to be seen. The production under the direction of Andrei Serban, who staged *The Cherry Orchard* and *Agamemnon*, is interesting and attractive, though I believe it might have been done in a more shadowy or "spooky" style.

John Guare's *Landscape of the Body* at the Public Theatre is in its material an account of a crime too frequently reported in the newspapers, but its message is one which recurs in several recent plays (*Feedlot* at the Circle Repertory Theatre, for example).

It tells us that in our vale of tears recognition of our sinfulness—mutual forbearance and understanding—will make life more bearable. We cannot wholly cope, the author implies, with the painfully unfathomable enigma of evil in the world. Several of the play's passages are written so that what might appear sordid is rendered in a wryly satirical vein. But the play as a whole does not quite work because its plotting is defective (at moments absurd), and its moral conclusion does not convincingly follow from its story line.

—WEST, Nov. '77

THE YIDDISH THEATRE

If it did not sound forbidding I might declare Lulla Rosenfeld's *Bright Star of Exile* a "monumental" work. For while its historical scope is extremely wide, its tone and flavor possess a quality of warm intimacy which lends its factual data a special glamour; we are *inside* the world and the personalities with which the book deals.

Its concrete material centers on the development of the Yiddish theatre from its inception in the 1870's to its decline of recent times, together with a biography of its most effulgent hero, Jacob Adler. There are many reasons why this subject matter should be of unusual interest to Americans—Jew or Gentile, with or without knowledge of Yiddish, theatre buff or only occasional playgoer. *Bright Star of Exile*, beside and beyond its immediate focus on the Yiddish theatre, is in an important way Russian history, English history, and finally New York and American history.

Most of us have a vague mental picture of Russia under Tsarist rule, or of London in the late nineteenth century. But isn't it true that we have an equally superficial or indifferent view of our own country's past? We may have some notion of the general progress of our civilization, remember signal dates or the names of leading figures in finance, politics, and the arts, but we have little personal feeling of connection with them. We cancel our native experience. What, for instance, were New York, Chicago, or Philadelphia like in the early years of this century? What were their sounds, smells, looks, pleasures, and entertainments like? In almost every one of its pages, *Bright Star of Exile* communicates vivid impressions of these aspects of social life. Lulla Rosenfeld writes the history of the Yiddish theatre from its beginnings in Eastern Europe to its culminating years in America as history should be written—with excitement and passionate personal involvement.

Through their struggle to create a theatre, we come to understand pre-revolutionary Russia, nineteenth-century London, as these Yiddish actors must have known them. Through their experience in the new world of America, we grow acquainted with a broader spectrum, the land of our forbears in all its dramatic particularity.

We all suppose we know about New York's Lower East Side of yesteryear. But do we? We have heard of its squalor, its conglomeration of underprivileged minorities: Jewish, Irish, Italian, Polish. We have seen photos of its pushcarts and peddlers, its toughs and its strays, its crowded tenements and raucous streets. But we know less about its aspirations, its idealism, its boundless resources of talent. From this rich soil with its inner lyricism, amid or beneath what to the naked eye might seem only coarseness and brutality, have come some of the most popularly representative figures of American lore. Irving Berlin, George Gershwin, Paul Muni, Eddie Cantor, the Marx Brothers, Jimmy Cagney, not to speak of eminent men in politics, education, the law, did not simply "emerge" from the massive heaps of New York's ghetto, but were fructified by them.

In the evolution through which the immigrants and their native-born sons and daughters joined to become part of the red, white, and blue mainstream, the Yiddish theatre played a vital part, a part which not only influenced its own audiences but affected people in broad areas beyond its own sphere. Hutchins Hapgood, that Victorian "heir to the saints of Massachusetts Bay" and Lincoln Steffens' journalistic collaborator, once said of the Yiddish theatre in its heyday (1900-1920) that it was "about the best in New York at that time both in stuff and in acting." As I pointed out in my book *The Fervent Years*, the "stuff" was frequently Shakespeare, Tolstoy, Gorky, Andreyev, or charming folk operettas and plays modeled after original works by Sudermann, Hauptmann, and other contemporary Europeans.

In his seminal book *The Spirit of the Ghetto*, illustrated by Jacob Epstein (first published in 1902 and reissued by the Harvard University Press in 1967), Hapgood included a long chapter about the Yiddish stage. He wrote: "In the midst of the frivolous Bowery...the theatres of the chosen people alone present the serious as well as the trivial interests of the entire community. Into these three buildings [the Yiddish theatres on the Bowery] crowd all the Jews of all the ghetto classes—the sweatshop woman with her baby, the day laborer, the small Hester Street shopkeeper, the Russian-Jewish anarchist and socialist, the ghetto rabbi and the scholar, the poet, the journalist."

And because it was only in the theatre that this varied populace could find a common meeting place—the more sophisticated rarely mingled with the Orthodox in synagogues—the Yiddish theatre was in every sense a *people's* or a *community* theatre, that is to say, a *true* theatre, the like of which was rarely if ever to be achieved again in our country. That is one reason why Hapgood was able to say that for him, "The Bowery and Canal Street had more significance for American life than did Broadway and Fifth Avenue."

As I have already suggested, the Yiddish theatre was based in an environment greater in ethnic composition than that of its Jewish population. It was immersed in that seething cauldron over which such Tammany bosses as the notorious William Marcy Tweed and later the wily and redoubtable Charles Murphy reigned. In this

compost of raw conflict and harsh ambition, the Yiddish theatre served as a beacon light, a symbol of striving toward spirituality and human meaning.

Bright Star of Exile brings all this alive for us. We feel as if we were witnesses, as if we had been there. To some extent, I was. For though I began my career in the theatre in 1924, I ascribe my appetite for the stage to the days when my father, who practiced medicine in Manhattan's East Side, took me to see Jacob Adler act when I was seven years old. (I never saw him in private life.) From that early age I became an avid playgoer and saw many of the actors whose fantastic course Lulla Rosenfeld's book traces. She, Jacob Adler's granddaughter, was too young to have seen most of them. But I did.

Before I set down my own impression of some of them, I must cite the opinion of Jed Harris, the brilliant producer-director of the 1920's. To the question, "Whom do you consider the best actor you have ever seen?" he unhesitatingly answered, "David Kessler!"—one of the players who occupies an imposing position in the book you are about to read.

In his earthy emotionalism, David Kessler was indeed an actor of volcanic power, just as Siegmund Mogulesko, another in the Yiddish theatre galaxy, was a character comedian whose insidious shrewdness provided deep delight. Then there was Sara Adler, Jacob Adler's third wife, who bred a bevy of versatile actors: Frances, Stella, Luther, Julia, and Jack. Indomitably female, sturdily knowing and realistic, she was in the school of what may be called romantic realism, unquestionably one of the great talents I have seen on any stage.

But there is no doubt in my mind that the brightest luminary of them all was Jacob Adler. He was extraordinary in every way. His height and bodily strength, his hair, snow white even in his youth, his large eyes and penetrating gaze, his reverberant voice and regal stance were themselves sufficient to rivet one's attention to the point of fascination, and he evoked in his audience something akin to worship. Everything about him breathed a masculine fullness which commanded the admiration of both sexes. With this there dwelled within him a sensibility which one might (even today!) call "feminine." One felt him capable of cruelty abated by an overwhelming sensual tenderness. He had the air of a prophet with a touch of humorous cynicism and not without a remainder of naïveté! His skeptical smile was infectious, reflecting an understanding of the treacherous weaknesses which beset humankind. This gave rise to a forbearance due to a sense of his own sinful vulnerability.

His mode of living was lavish, and there was something larger than life in all his behavior. This gave the roles he played, for all their verisimilitude, a romantic aura that we often term "theatricality." His charm was captivating, his dignity awesome, his wrath terrifying. When he towered as the vengeful patriarch Shylock, or as Uriel Acosta raised the torch of free thought in epic loftiness, or teased as the shrewdly humorous ragpicker of *The Beggar of Odessa*, I was transported and a little frightened by him. The man's *size*—I do not refer to his physique—imposed a sense of peril. Grandeur always inspires a certain shudder at life's immeasurable might and mystery. When Jacob Adler died, two hundred thousand people came to his funeral. The image he created has never been forgotten. It has remained in the consciousness of a people, emblem of the stature of a human being, the overwhelming meaning of what it is to be a man.

—Introduction, *The Bright Star of Exile*, by Lulla Rosenfeld, '77

ST. JOAN
SAMUEL BECKETT

If you have never seen Shaw's *St. Joan*, see it now (Circle-in-the-Square). I say that despite the many faults of this production, for the play is noble in spirit, admirable, in thought, superb in speech. If it is not an absolutely great play, that is because it does not quite attain the intensity or elevation of expression of poetry: it does not always take wing, the rational weighs it down. My disappointment with its present production may stem in part not only from the fact that I have seen several much better ones—notably the original London production in 1924 and another in the late 1940's at the Chamber Theatre in Israel—but from defects which almost anyone theatrically aware can readily recognize.

Comparisons are said to be odious, yet I cannot refrain from observing that Shaw's choice for the role was Sybil Thorndike, a (Fabian) Socialist of heroic disposition, and that Orna Porat, the Israeli Joan, was a woman of gentile German origin who had fought in what there was of underground resistance to the Nazis. I note these adventitious details only to suggest the kind of person Shaw's Joan is.

She is not a sweet girl—a "maid." She is not even a woman, she says. She is a warrior, a headlong idealist of enormous vital force. Though formally uneducated, she is no more simpleminded or innocent than the author who created her. She is pure, but that is not at all the same thing as being childlike. She is endowed with common sense, a keen mind and indomitable will. She can no more be silenced than Shaw could be: she is a rebel, a puritan, a "protest-ant."

Lynn Redgrave, the present Joan, is a beautiful and gifted actress, utterly honest in everything she does, but her performance in this instance is marred by a misconception. The simplicity she brings to the part is almost that of a baby. It is not an heroic simplicity, the simplicity of a deeply inspired conviction, the ineradicable certainty of being right. Joan possesses a projectile-like energy which demolishes every obstacle. The "peasant" in her (her father, it is pointed out, is a "bourgeois") manifests itself chiefly in her shrewdness, her unconscious humor; at the base of all her action is the strength of the embattled leader, which accounts for her success as a commander of soldiers. As such she is something of a "pest," never counting the cost of her determination. Like all saints she is a constant irritant. (That is why they are so often martyred.) When she weeps she does not shed the tears of a hurt kid but of exalted indignation, an outcry against injustice.

In the play's first act when Joan speaks of her voices, she is asked "How do you mean? Voices?" She says, "I hear them telling me what to do. They come from God." She is corrected, "they come from your imagination." To which Joan retorts, "Of course. That is how the messages of God come to us." It is not the reply of someone naive or unknowing.

To reconcile the various alternations of mood of Joan (the stalwart fighter and the abused girl), Ms. Redgrave is obliged to make a too-conscious use of her voice. This sort of vocal gymnastics is even more pronounced in several other members of the cast—sometimes ludicrously so. But differences in vocal key are right only when they are spontaneous, that is, organic to the actor's thought and feeling; they should never be "applied" with deliberate elocutionary intention.

"Joan's judges were as straightforward as Joan herself," Shaw said in his program note to the London production. That directness is the clue to the play's essential tone. It is an unadorned or ascetic style: everyone, except a few fanatics, speaks reasonably, with a basic steadiness even in moments of severity or anger. This note is almost entirely missed in the current production.

There are solecisms of staging: for example, Joan's long address to her antagonists is spoken with her back to them. But most disturbing to me is the lack of an imposing quality in the personality of Joan's opponents. All of them, whatever their human limitations, must be *big men*. The nature of the play demands them.

Paul Shyre as Cauchon speaks well (he has an ear for language), but in the trial scene he looks like a boy outfitted in sumptuous vestments. Nicholas Hormann as Brother Martin has a fine moment when he describes Joan's final agony,

ending with the prophecy "This is not the end for her, but the beginning." The most complete or convincing performance is that of Roy Cooper in two small roles: as Robert de Baudricourt, the captain who sends Joan on her way to the Dauphin, and as the English soldier who in the epilogue reports on the atmosphere and denizens of Hell. Others in the cast are so-so or deplorable.

And yet, and yet, there is always Shaw's towering text.

If Shaw is the most loquacious of Irish dramatists, Samuel Beckett is the most reticent. His gift of speech moves toward a silence which in his later plays is like a death. Shaw, for all his misgivings, is basically cheerful; Beckett, with a grim smile and saturnine humor, dramatizes a quasi-Augustinian rejection of the world (the African saint wrote "Nothing is better than nothing"). Shaw's abiding confidence is "old-fashioned"; Beckett speaks tartly for our contemporary skepticism. Shaw is expansive, Beckett cramped. He is "an old man in a dry month." When an Italian literary critic, Paolo Milano, asked him why, if he felt as he did, he did not commit suicide, Beckett, after a long pause, said, "Doing so would show too much confidence in life."

Beckett is an exigent writer, a signal artist, an extraordinarily original dramatist who has found the right stage metaphors for his mood. In a sense, he is an exemplary, a "classic" writer of our time. He conveys the inner desolation under the noise and bustle of our present day. Three of his short pieces, *Play*, which was first seen in New York at the Theatre de Lys in 1963 (the staging has been improved since then) and two more recent ones, *That Time* and *Footfalls*, are now being given at the Manhattan Theatre Club under Alan Schneider's scrupulous direction. The whole "bill" lasts not much longer than an hour.

Play has three figures, husband, wife and mistress. We hear of the adulterous mess the husband's affair has caused as each of the three recites its details out of the funerary urns above their graves. There had been tumult and heartbreak, but now that it is all past, the man finds that it was a trivial event, just "play." (So, it is implied, are all our emotional crises.) The personages speak almost simultaneously in very rapid whispers, so that their voices sound like the rustling of autumn leaves.

That Time might be thought of as a replay of *Krapp's Last Tape*. It is the memory of an existence lived in acute and perpetual discomfort. We see no more than the head of a gray-haired old man, apparently asleep, high above the stage floor. He recalls various moments of his youth. There was "that time" he went back to look at a ruin, another time spent in a library, still another at a museum, and perhaps most importantly, "that time" he lay beside a girl on a stone not touching but loving her. These memories are spoken in the dark by three different voices which are all his own. From time to time his eyes open as if awakened from sleep; then shut again. At the end his eyes open and he smiles a smile which may be considered pleasure at his memories, or at their unimportance, or relief that, awake, he is free of them. As for love, it was harder and harder to believe "you ever told anyone you loved them or anyone you tell just one of those things you kept up to keep the void out." The void is life itself, all "dust."

Footfalls, the most ambiguous of the three pieces, has a woman of 40, disheveled and gray-haired, pacing from right to left and back again in audible rhythmic tread, speaking to her unseen 90-year-old moribund mother, and apparently wasting away from the burden of caring for her. This may be a symbol of an older generation eroding another. "Will you never have done revolving it all?" the mother's voice asks. The daughter queries "It?" The voice: "It all. (Pause) In your poor mind. (Pause) It all." "It" is life itself.

The daughter insists that she must scrape her feet as she paces. "I must hear the feet, however faint they fall." The mother: "The motion alone is not enough?" The daughter: "No, mother, the motion alone is not enough." In some way, life must give some reverberant evidence of being real,

for the mere living of it would only be an emptiness, a void.

Ionesco spoke of writing "anti-theatre," but, except as a catch phrase, that was nonsense. These Beckett plays—especially the last two—would seem to be anti-theatre. But they are still indisputably theatre, though reduced to a minimum in sound and sight. Though it is difficult to hear distinctly in the dark, there is a spectacular incisiveness in the total impression produced.

Of Beckett's mastery and modern typicality there can be no question. He has found the form for *his* truth or sentiment which many of us share at disheartened intervals. But *is* it the truth, the deepest truth as some would have it? For myself, I reject it because it is a futile truth. It is not a truth by which anyone—except possibly an anchorite—lives. There is another sort of "mysticism": it is the embrace of life.

The performances by Donald Davis, Sloane Shelton, Suzanne Costallos are just what they should be.

—*NAT*, 14 Jan. '78

THE DYBBUK
A TOUCH OF THE POET
COLD STORAGE

Ever since it was first produced in Warsaw in 1920, in Yiddish, S. Ansky's *The Dybbuk* has been a success. It has been presented in Polish, Swedish, Bulgarian, French and Japanese before fascinated audiences. The Neighborhood Playhouse did it in New York in 1925 in a replica of the most memorable of all its productions, staged in Moscow by a non-Jew, Eugene Vachtangov, Stanislavsky's great disciple with the Hebrew-speaking Habima company. I saw that production in New York while it was on its world tour in 1926 and several times since. It was one of the great theatre experiences of my entire career as a playgoer.

The Dybbuk is now being given in still another version developed by Mira Rafalowicz under the guidance of Joseph Chaikin who has staged it (Public Theatre). It can hardly fail to "work" because the play's basic material possesses universal appeal: the wonder and mystery of a fable or "legend" essential to all that is enduring in the theatre.

Its story deals with the deathlessness of love in a manner rare in any Western drama. For the lover, Chanon, a student of the cabala who has exchanged no more than a few hesitant words with his beloved Leah, dies on hearing that she has been betrothed by her father to a youth she has never seen. But at the moment of the wedding Leah speaks in the voice of the dead Chanon: she has become possessed by his spirit, the "dybbuk." A rabbinical exorcism is attempted and the girl dies. In the original text "She leaves her black cape and all in white goes to Chanon to the strains of the wedding march. She stands in his place and her figure blends with his." Those who truly love each other cannot be separated.

Two other strands are interwoven in the play's fabric. One of them is a condemnation of greed: Leah's father, a wealthy merchant, sought a rich bridegroom for his daughter. Above and beyond this there is the particularly Jewish conviction that what is humanly just (the love of two pure souls) is also godly. "Blessed be the true Judge."

Together with the mystic atmosphere of the story, the Vachtangov production emphasized its social aspect. The play was viewed as a kind of phantasmagoria of a past civilization, a world beautiful in its depth of feeling but condemned for its practical organization. All the props (furniture, etc.) stood askew, the characters' faces were strangely masklike as though they were phantoms of a bygone age, while the beggarly poor—crippled, hunchbacked, blind and stunted—danced at the wedding with hate-filled grotesquerie. Leah, as I remember it, did not join the "ghost" of her beloved; the exorcism killed her, for she could not live without her love.

In the Chaikin version the play (except for one added and unnecessary scene) is considerably abbreviated. What is left has been fragmented into "moments," a kind of collage. One of the moments—a woman who comes to the synagogue to pray for her dying child—is touching, while the ending—following the original text—with Leah merging with Chanon in the other world is tenderly effective.

The Vachtangov production was steeped in a chant of "far away" sound, like an echo from another sphere; in the new version most of the music is Jewish singsong, imitative of routine prayer and, when instrumental, rather banal. In the Vachtangov version we did not see the person of the dead Chanon: the dybbuk was present only through the girl's transformed voice. At the Public Theatre Chanon appears each time Leah is seized by his spirit and they speak in concert.

With all the set pieces of raw wood scenery now used to indicate different places and the generally straight or "realistic" performances, the whole Chaikin production seems much less real than Vachtangov's highly stylized and dreamlike rendition of the play. Chaikin's production is more curious than gripping. The assembled parts do not constitute a whole: they are directorial indications without organic focus. There is no moment (except the last) which matches the magic of the Tree of Knowledge in Chaikin's *The Serpent* or the Cain and Abel death struggle in that creation.

Still the play, as I have said, holds a special attraction through its original idea and even more so for those unacquainted with the scenic modes of the European (mostly Russian) theatre of the 1920's. The acting is generally good. I was especially impressed by Shami Chaikin as the heartbroken mother begging God's intervention on behalf of her ailing child; by Marcia Jean Kurtz, the bride deprived of her destined lover; by Bruce Myers as Chanon, with gestures as a kind of manual dance suggesting the twisting and turning of cabalistic lore; by Jamil Zakkai as the bride's bourgeois father. (In the Vachtangov production the image evoked by him was that of a well-heated samovar!) Also telling is Richard Bauer's vocally authoritative Rabbi and Mark Nelson is charming as the stripling terrified at the prospect of a marriage to a "stranger." In short, though I found the production as a whole emotionally meager, Ansky's dybbuk may enchant you through its penetration of Chaikin.

The very qualities which made Jason Robards so strikingly right in *The Iceman Cometh*, as Jamie in *Long Day's Journey into Night* and in *A Moon for the Misbegotten* make him inadequate (except for the final moments) in the role of Con Melody in *A Touch of the Poet* (Helen Hayes Theatre). What Robards cannot convincingly achieve is personal grandeur.

I am not sure that José Quintero as director has wholly understood the play. For while Melody is something of a fool in his Byronic swagger, his aspiration to and feeling for nobility are real. He is dreamer, not a faker; his whole being yearns for what was sound and forever worthy in the old aristocratic ideal of the English gentry, an ideal O'Neill held in high esteem. When Con Melody, an Irishman who had risen to the position of officer in Wellington's Army, comes a cropper in his tavern near Boston in 1828, he breaks down and abandons the image of himself as a nobleman. It is this fall from inner grace which makes him cry out "It's to hell with honor if you want to rise in the world," only to reduce himself to the state of the grubby drifters who hang around his *shebeen* cadging drinks. His American-born daughter Sara, who had previously scorned him for his haughty pretenses, now mourns the grand person he had been and weeps for him. She wants him to be as he was: "deep down that's been my pride too—that I was your daughter." The Melody without his sense of glory "wasn't anyone I ever knew or want to know."

Melody's downfall at the hands of the wealthy New England "tradesmen" is pathetic and meaningful to the play only if we discern the idealistic truth hidden beneath his boastful postures and lordly behavior. There can be no real pathos in the crackup of a pipsqueak or a phony.

To be a sound, complete person, O'Neill (like Whitman) intimates, the American must not forsake his heritage of faith in gallant (moral and spiritual) action for mere moneymaking. *A Touch of the Poet* was to be the "prologue" to the nine-play cycle which O'Neill proposed to name *A Tale of Possessors Self-Possessed*. He once said of its that he "was going on the theory that the United States instead of being the most successful country, is the greatest failure. It's the greatest failure because it was given everything, more than any other country...It's main idea is that everlasting game of trying to possess your own soul by the possession of something outside of it...We are the clearest example of 'For what shall it profit a man if he gain the whole world and lose his own soul.'" If we do not see that Melody is degrading himself into the ordinary common citizen we see only the surface—the "television special"—aspect of the play, which vitiates its real value, its genuine power.

Yet the written play somehow still triumphs despite its turbid presentation. In structure, in writing (though it badly needs cutting), in the lyric characterization of Melody's wife, in the complex characterization of his daughter, *A Touch of the Poet* is one of O'Neill's most realized dramas, than which nothing better has been achieved in this country.

It is quite a trick to make a play about the fatally ill painless. That is what happens in Ronald Ribman's aptly named *Cold Storage* (Lyceum Theatre). Two men are seen sitting on a fashionable hospital's roof garden. One of them, Joseph Parmigian, a successful Armenian in the fruit and vegetable business, in cheerful resignation acknowledges that he is dying of cancer. The other, Richard Landau, a Jewish dealer in objets d'art resists the suspicion that he may be in the same case.

They do nothing but talk. Parmigian is flippant, given to oddball jokes, Landau reveals, besides worry over his present condition, a lasting wound relating to the destruction of his parental family by the Nazis. The play might be termed a "philosophic dialogue," though its persistent levity of tone disguises even that.

Its "message" is based on three propositions: (a) the great "point" of life is that it has no point, (b) that we must have the courage to die and (c) that life is "interesting," even funny. On that combined basis we can live with equanimity day by day.

Put that way, I can raise no objection. Such conclusions stated in a play without actual dramatic context are nothing but blather, the stuff one might hear at a bar or at a coffee klatch. Meaning in a play is not achieved by blank statements, however amusingly phrased but through a construct of situations, images and characters.

The quip which sets Landau laughing for the first time in the play is Parmigian's speaking of a nun who resembles a penguin! (No one else in the house found it funny.) *Cold Storage* is little but palaver sustained by the good nature of Martin Balsam's beefy Armenian and Len Cariou's well-suggested anguish as Landau. But the play exists in a vacuum and that it has been taken by some (reviewers among them) as a serious comedy is the only grave thing about it.

—*NAT*, 21 Jan. '78

CHAPTER TWO

Neil Simon is our champion in the writing of funny lines for the theatre. Even when he essays a play of presumably serious intention we are affected by very little of its subject matter or characters: we only remember that we have laughed. And because the characters and the situation chiefly serve as a scaffold for the jokes we forget the very jokes themselves.

In his latest play *Chapter Two* (Imperial Theatre), Simon deals with supposedly autobiographical material of grave nature. A successful writer, George Schneider, after twelve years of marriage has lost his wife whom he had dearly loved. He is heartbroken, and he repeatedly resists his brother Leo's suggestion that he date some new girl.

We know that if George persists in keeping himself celibate there would be no play—not at any rate a Neil Simon play. He does meet Jennie, recently divorced, still young and charming. They marry. A brief crisis follows their honeymoon: the memory of his first wife hangs over what should be his present bliss like a shadow. He leaves Jennie for the length of time it takes to get to Los Angeles and back. On his return he has overcome his disquiet. We knew all along he would.

Since there is no real obstacle between George and Jennie, there is in effect no play. In the second act, Simon is obliged to pad his story by introducing the issue of an abortive affair between Leo and one of Jennie's married friends. The play's theme—the heavy burden a first happy marriage can place on the success of a second—is evaded. As a substitute for drama we are regaled by an unending flow of one liners, only one of which I could recall when I left the theatre. George describes his writing block by saying, "I just finished three hundred pages of my new novel and I haven't thought of a story yet." That might be applied to the play itself.

The evening's best element is the cast: Judd Hirsch as George, Clifford Gorman as his brother, Anita Gillette as Jennie, and Ann Wedgeworth as her friend. They provide the smoothly simple "realistic" acting which is the forte of our popular stage.

—*WEST*, Jan. '78

A SECOND THOUGHT

"No one becomes a critic out of modesty," the critic Stanley Kauffmann once said. True, but neither does any responsible critic believe himself infallible. With time and further thought—when a subject is worth it—the critic feels obliged to "correct" himself. It is important that his reader should also know this, so that he may allow himself freedom to follow his own bent. I repeat what I have also emphasized: a critic's value is not in his summary opinion but in the quality of his insights and in his capacity to stimulate the possibility of further speculation.

A classic example of what I'm speaking about is Shaw's original (1895) review of *The Importance of Being Earnest*. It was—is—a brilliant piece though as opinion it is wrong. It is brilliant because it is in effect an essay in comedy as distinct from something which is only clever and witty. But the review missed the play's tonality, keyed to fanciful satire of the English Victorian temper and manner. Shaw was wrong, too, in preferring the same author's *An Ideal Husband* which he had reviewed a few months earlier. *An Ideal Husband* is now all but forgotten; *The Importance of Being Earnest* endures. Years later Shaw acknowledged his "mistake," not simply from the evidence of time but by further reflection. To make *his* point he had failed to see Wilde's.

These remarks are preparatory to a few revisions of some of my own recent observations here, which I note not because they have been challenged but because even the three or four days' consideration permitted to me as a reviewer for a weekly instead of the hour or two allowed a reviewer for a daily does not always suffice. The limited time may be altogether adequate for a wretched or nondescript performance, but for a play of genuine merit a longer period of gestation is required if a mature view is to emerge. It is this that makes journalistic reviewing "tricky." When asked immediately after the final curtain falls on opening night, "What did you think of the show?" I am always inclined to reply "I don't know till I've read *The Nation*. But sometimes the joke is on me!

In writing here about *Fefu and Her Friends* (American Place Theatre) on February 11, I said "There is constant talk—to the point of obses-

sion—about women and sexuality." That statement has a note of irritation in it. The fact is that women and sexuality constitute the play's very subject matter and theme. The phrasing of my original statement does not appreciably alter my reaction to the play as a whole but it was misleading as to the play's essence and to my attitude toward it.

In my review of Beckett's *Footfalls* (*The Nation*: January 7-14) in an evening of three of his plays, I quoted a passage in which a mother who hears the sound of her daughter's constant pacing asks, "Will you never have done? Will you never have done—revolving it all?" The daughter answers her mother's further question as to the girl's restlessness: "Mother, this is not enough." The mother: "Not enough...not enough...what can you possibly mean...not enough." The daughter: "I mean, mother, that I must hear the feet, however faint they fall." The mother queries, "The motion alone is not enough?" The answer is, "No, mother, the motion alone is not enough."

This exchange is crucial to the play. My explanation was that for the daughter "life must give reverberant evidence of being real, for the mere living of it would be an emptiness, a void." But it now occurs to me that I should have been more explicit. What Beckett implies is that the world's motion or our daily action, whatever it may be, is not enough for him. Its reality is only a faint footfall, a bleak awareness of his presence or existence. But he yearns, indeed *needs*, more than this to lend substance to his being. He wants its confirmation through that mystery of faith for which the vagrants in *Godot* are waiting. In their consciousness of its harrowing absence lies their superiority. They know they are waiting. Beckett will not say it—he is too modern for that—he in fact refuses to identify "Godot," but it is clear that the core of Beckett's spirit is that he is writing about a world from which God, however conceived, has all but disappeared. His entire work keeps "revolving" about the abyss: his plays and novels are his "footfalls."

In my recently published book *Ibsen* I state in the body of the text, "I find the first-act exposition (of *The Wild Duck*)...somewhat stiff and awkward," but I appended in a last-minute footnote, "I now believe I am wrong about this." My change of mind came about because it suddenly struck me that it was the usual staging of *The Wild Duck* opening scene which made it seem "stiff and awkward" and that another staging would transform it so that if would not only be acceptable but graceful.

These reconsiderations are not meant as apology or avowals of "sin" but are calculated to remind readers of the facts of the critical function and responsibility; even more especially, they are meant to emphasize that, as in music, painting, poetry or any presumed work of art, a play that is not at once recognizably negligible demands a "double think."

Even in his intellectual independence, a critic is wrong to be entirely indifferent to audience reaction. And though it behooves him to be as objective as he possibly can be (total objectivity is impossible), he must be particularly objective about his subjectivity! A critic ought to be aware and frank about his blind spots and prejudices. Stark Young had no taste for musical comedy—and knew it. At one time Kenneth Tynan declared himself averse to any play of marked religious stamp. Shaw proclaimed nearly all the Elizabethan dramatists "duffers"; he deliberately downgraded Henry Irving and blinded himself to what was splendid in Sarah Bernhardt. Max Beerbohm was obtuse about Gorky's *Lower Depths* and failed to recognize Duse's genius.

I have often enough declared my rejection of certain aspects of such masters as Strindberg, Pirandello and Beckett, just as I have shown a predisposition to be generous toward our better American playwrights, though they are barely worthy of mention in the same breath with the former. Let us proceed....

—*NAT*, 4 Mar. '78

RUNAWAYS

Runaways, written, composed and directed by Elizabeth Swados, is an entertainment of benevolent intention (Public Theatre). It purports through song and dance to convey the plight of adolescents who, because of the poverty, brutal ugliness and despair in their parental homes, abandon them. There are thousands of such children in the numerous ghettos of our cities.

Though the show offers a number of attractive features, only a few of them are actually congruent with its theme. There is first of all a large cast of youngsters ranging from 10 to 17, nearly all of them bright-eyed, eager, healthy—well fed! To see them march toward us in a sort of smiling militancy and jovial complaint is a tonic experience—lacking all pathos. As juvenile performers they are to be applauded—certainly not pitied.

There are furthermore, a few charming numbers: one of them is called "Enterprise," derisive of our national fetish. Another is called "Where Are the People Who Did 'Hair'?" It implies that the protest which animated that show managed only to make its participants successful and rich and no longer on the social battle line. But the barb fails to hit its mark because we are inclined to guess that the evening's "runaways" will in the future also be absorbed by show biz. And, by the way, was *Hair* really such strong stuff?

The staging throughout is well managed. The Douglas W. Schmidt and Wodds Mackintosh settings are admirably devised, resembling the rundown gymnasiums of certain city high schools and playgrounds in seedy neighborhoods. The Swados music is utilitarian rather than lyrically or dramatically expressive—it is employed, as in the Japanese and Chinese theatres, as sound to call attention to signal moments.

This brief listing of credits (and debits) hardly goes to the heart of the matter. Even if I had liked more of the numbers than I did, I would still have thought while watching them "too much show!" That was not my reaction to Swados' *Nightclub Cantata*, given at the Top of the Gate on Bleecker Street in January 1977. It was somewhat in the same vein as *Runaways*, but had much greater impact. To begin with, the *Cantata* was based on the writing of such poets as Pablo Neruda, Sylvia Plath, Frank O'Hara, Delmore Schwartz, Muriel Rukeyser, none of it designed to provide clever revue numbers. As I said here at the time, *Nightclub Cantata* was "gritty, brave, somber, and exhilarating withal." The introduction of comic turns did not dissipate its powerful meaning. The evening included a chant written by a former captive of a Nazi concentration camp which ended with "You don't die of anything but death. Suffering is nothing, it doesn't kill you—only death." The effect was sobering and stirring.

Physically bare, *Nightclub Cantata* was crowded onto a tiny café stage with no light effects, no tricky props. It evoked a feeling of stoic courage and joy in a sense of communion among the injured, the oppressed and the indignant.

My attitude toward *Runaways*, it is only fair to say, is undoubtedly a minority one. It should prove popular and might be transferred to Broadway. My reason for going on with this discussion, rather than simply registering a summary opinion, rests on something more than the immediate case.

Runaways has to do, I repeat, with the dreadful condition children find themselves in—homes dogged by the wretchedness of alcoholism and violence, children often poisoned by drugs, driven to prostitution and to armed crime. The subject is real, important. But despite a resolve to avoid the "cutesy," little more is revealed—even by such tellingly titled numbers as "Let Me Be a Kid, Find Me a Hero"—than a talent for entertainment. That is what I mean by "too much show!" There is no pain, bite, nothing in it in the least stinging. It is little more than a jocose condemnation of evil.

Runaways aroused in me some of the same dissatisfaction I felt on seeing the much more brilliant and sensational *West Side Story*, the work of those outstanding artists Leonard Bernstein and Jerome Robbins. The audience heartily approves the liberal sentiments that motivate the authors of such spectacles, admires their craftsmanship and "daring"—and has a damned good time. I do not believe the theatre on any of its levels is for suffering, but when grave subjects are broached the effect ought to be penetrating, challenging, moving us to deeper understanding and to the possibility of foreseeable action.

Exhibits like *West Side Story* and *Runaways* expose the superficiality and basic indifference of the mass of our people in the areas of social issues and politics. We talk about them, we are even excited, but though we do not altogether forget certain scandals, very little is altered. What happened to the rebellion of our youth after Vietnam? Almost the very same people who acquiesced or remained silent in the blacklisting of Hollywood "subversives" gathered some years later to roar their adulation (at "Oscar" celebrations, for instance) of former victims of their ignorance or pusillanimity.

In West European countries major stage performances that pushed against the grain of majority thinking were for a long time rare, precisely because their audiences possessed more social and political awareness: such performances were considered a threat. The slyly ironic *Threepenny Opera* caused riots in the Germany of 1928 just before World War II; Shakespeare's *Coriolanus* divided the audience at the *Comédie Française* into actively hostile camps, as did Genet's *The Screens* at Jean-Louis Barrault's state-subsidized theatre during the Algerian struggle.

At a 1935 performance on Broadway of *Waiting for Lefty* a gentleman in an orchestra seat asked me "Do they mean it?" It was O.K. if it was merely an ebullient pastime. We call a presentation like *Runaways* touching and poignant, and consider ourselves not only radically progressive but noble to think so, and thus relieve ourselves of any responsibility.

It was innocent of those critics who thought *Macbird*, which absurdly hinted at an LBJ role in the assassination of President Kennedy, might be closed by the police. The audience received it for what it was: a sort of spunky college fraternity show. For most of us, politics is a sport or a spectacle. Watergate did not really shock the great public: it was a dandy melodrama. Perhaps this is so because we still feel safe; Europeans have for some time now realized that they aren't. We are an immensely gifted and good-natured people; we are not yet a serious one.

—*NAT*, 1 Apr. '78

ON THE TWENTIETH CENTURY
SCENES FROM SOUTH AFRICA

The "big machine" on Broadway today is the musical comedy by Betty Comden and Adolph Green with music by Cy Coleman, *On the Twentieth Century* (St. James Theatre).

The original 1932 play of cognate title by Ben Hecht, Charles McArthur, and Bruce Milholland was a quizzical farce which poked fun at show biz nuttiness. The musical is much more extravagant, "wild." Robin Wagner's settings are splendid with additional cute scenic gimmicks: airplanes over the tracks, a miniature train to suggest the larger one as it might be seen from a distance at night.

The acting, like everything else in the production, is ebullient—which almost amounts to a style. John Cullum who sings remarkably well for a musical comedy star plays Oscar Jaffe, the cracker-jack and crackpot producer as if he aimed to outdo John Barrymore in the play's movie version. Cullum has neither Barrymore's devilishness nor his teasing wit but his own muscular energy fits the pushiness of the entire show. Madeline Kahn as the screen star Lily Garland (born Mildred Plotka of the Bronx), whom Jaffe discovered and is trying to lure back to the stage, displays her diverse talents in singing, mimicry, and movement with remark-

able aplomb. She dispenses with sentiment and softness in the role, which makes her a little less fetching than she might be. But that is part of the evening's atmosphere.

A handsome young actor, Kevin Kline is quite funny as Lily Garland's temporary Hollywood bred boyfriend. Credit for some of Kline's amusing antics must also be given to Harold Prince's comically inventive direction. Imogene Coca also lends a bit of restful as well as zestful playfulness to the evening.

I judge the show to be a deserved hit. My only quibble, as indicated above, is that its drive precludes charm.

For the rest, all my playgoing (with the trivial exception of Ira Levin's *Deathtrap*, starring John Wood) has been in the peripheral areas of our town where, as I have repeatedly maintained, so much that is interesting in the theatre occurs.

Of these journeys away from the Broadway center I should mention first of all two one-act pieces at the Manhattan Theatre Club which is nearly always worth visiting. I refer in this instance to Athol Fugard's *Statements After An Arrest Under The Morality Act* and *Scenes from Soweto* by Steve Wilmer. Both deal with the unspeakable apartheid rule in South Africa.

Fugard is a white South African who has written a number of excellent plays (*Boesman and Lena*, *Sizwe Banzi Is Dead*) about the South African situation. Wilmer is an American resident in London. Fugard's play, therefore, is marked by a sense of intimate knowledge and subjective feeling; Wilmer's has the heat of indignation; it is stirring propaganda and as such makes for "good theatre" which well articulated and well acted propaganda frequently does.

Fugard's play is based on the South African Immorality Act that makes cohabitation between blacks and whites a crime. In the *Statements* a lonely woman, a librarian past her first youth, has an affair with an impoverished black. He is married to a woman he no longer loves but whom he will not divorce because of family loyalty and compassion for his two children. The librarian and the unfortunate man who are truly in love are discovered together by the police and will undoubtedly be severely punished for infringement of the Morality Act.

We see them bare, literally and psychologically. The woman, being white, is the more staunch of the two. She has not lived a life of fear; she is proud in her love. The black man feels that his existence, forever deprived of dignity, wracked by poverty, garroted by apartheid law, has slowly reduced him to a non-person. The play is movingly acted by Veronica Castang and Robert Christian.

Scenes from Soweto (Soweto is a ghetto outside Johannesburg) deals with a black Oxford University graduate in mathematics and engineering who prefers to return to his people rather than enjoy the favorable prospects held out to him in England. He is as nonpolitical as it is possible to be in the circumstances. Back home he is comparatively safe at his important job in an Anglo-African industrial firm. But the ferocity of governmental repression of his fellow blacks finally turns him into an active rebel, a saboteur. We last see him being tortured by the police who demand that he reveal the names of his co-conspirators. He will not talk except to cry out that thousands will carry on the struggle against oppression. The papers announce his death "under investigation." The play, soberly performed, is shattering in its effect.

In New Rochelle, Robert Lewis who directed William Saroyan's first play, *My Hearts in the Highlands* for the Group Theatre in 1939, and later such commercial productions as *Brigadoon* and *The Teahouse of the August Moon* has opened a season of three plays. The first, John Ford Noonan's *The Club Champion's Widow*, is a madcap comedy with a sound element of good sense to it. Maureen Stapleton, one of our theatre's best actresses, shone in it.

I mention this performance now to call attention to the Robert Lewis Company, which I have reason to believe will be of continuing interest and a fruitful addition to the various groups near but

not of the city. Camus's *Caligula* has been announced as the next production and will probably be on the boards when this report appears.

The Long Wharf Theatre in New Haven recently produced a play by Stewart Parker called *Spokesong*. The odd title refers to the lyrical mood of the play—there are winning songs woven into its story—and to the fact that it is situated in a bicycle shop in Belfast (the author is a native of that troubled area). The bicycle itself is used as a symbol of old-fashioned good will and friendliness in a place where now terror rages. But in the play, delightfully acted and well staged, the nostalgia and good humor wash away the reminder of the wounds.

The Yale Repertory Theatre in New Haven is also a playhouse where the entertainment is nearly always of superior quality. Among the more recent bills I have seen there were Andrei Serban's robust staging of three short Molière farces and a colorfully directed *Man Is Man* by Bertolt Brecht. The Molière program is innocent and shrewd fun; Brecht's play treats social philosophy and anti-war sentiment with wise gaiety, all of which is most commendable.

—*WEST*, Apr. '78

THE LIFE OF GALILEO
THE 5TH OF JULY

Bertolt Brecht's *The Life of Galileo*, written in 1938-39, is a brilliant and beautiful play, surely one of the best of our time. Those who were fortunate enough to see it performed in the physics laboratory at Columbia University last month by a new unit, The New York Actors' Theatre, had a rattling good time.

The text for this production, translated by Wolfgang Sauerlander and Ralph Manheim, was based on Brecht's third version of the play. The second version, acted and translated by Charles Laughton with Brecht's help, was presented in

New York in 1947. The various changes—cuts, corrections and amplifications—were made not simply from a desire for greater dramatic effectiveness but because of an uncertainty as to the play's essential theme, the point or message Brecht wanted to impress on the audience. To begin with, he wanted to dramatize the struggle of the pure scientist, as a champion of Reason, against the authority of church and state which insisted on the Aristotelian or Ptolemaic cosmology as a basis for Faith. The "event" at Hiroshima altered Brecht's focus, giving the play not so much a new meaning as a new emphasis and thrust. At the end of a proposed prologue to the American production (never, I believe, spoken in any of the productions) Brecht in 1947 wrote

> *If you won't learn from Galileo's*
> *experience*
> *The Bomb will put in a personal*
> *appearance.*

This consideration led to still another thought. Galileo, in dread of the torture threatened by the Inquisition if he did not abjure the Copernican thesis that the earth revolved around the sun—a view supposedly inimical to early 17th-century Christian doctrine—recanted. When Andrea Sarti, Galileo's favorite disciple, bitter at his master's cowardly betrayal of the truth, learns that during his "house arrest" Galileo has secretly gone on with his research and written a book recording his findings (the *Discourses*), which he gives to Andrea to be carried out of Italy for publication abroad, the young man discerns a certain wisdom in Galileo's recantation. After all, scientific fact can be suppressed only momentarily: it does not depend on the word or deed of a single individual. But, and here is Brecht's new conviction, Galileo sold out and cannot therefore forgive himself.

"To my mind," Galileo asserts, "the only purpose of science is to lighten the toil of human existence. If scientists, browbeaten by selfish rulers, confine themselves to the accumulation of knowledge for the sake of knowledge, science will be crippled and your new machine will only mean new hardships. Given time, you may well discover everything there is to discover, but your progress will be a progression away from humanity...the response to your exultation about some new achievement will be a universal outcry of horror...If I had held out, scientists might have developed something like the physicians' Hippocratic oath, the vow to use their knowledge only for the good of mankind. As things stand now, the best we can hope for is a generation of inventive dwarfs, who can be hired for any purpose...."

As done at Columbia, the play ends with Galileo speaking the lines that Brecht intended as a filmed epigraph to precede the evening's last scene:

> *May you now guard science's light*
> *Keep it up and use it right*
> *Lest it be a flame to fall*
> *One day to consume us all.*

The generally young audience fervently applauded. There are others who do not readily assent to Brecht's "final" conclusion (I put final in quotes because Brecht was still revising the play at the end of his life in 1956). There is in itself an irrefragable value, some maintain, in the pure pursuit of truth, regardless of consequences which are the concern of other forces. This is certainly a matter for profound argument. What excited me on the occasion was that Brecht's play, witty, colorful, concise in scenic metaphor, makes genuine drama and theatre out of such philosophical-social material.

Considering the extremely restricted confines of the available stage space at Havemeyer Hall the production was admirable. There were some innovative devices: between episodes, for example, instead of songs or printed signs in which the idea or place of the ensuing scene is indicated in Brecht's productions, a young man appeared and very rapidly and handsomely drew in colored crayons emblems required to denote the information. This was one way to achieve the theatrical "distancing" called for in the Brechtian dramaturgy.

Besides Laurence Luckinbill as Galileo, there were good performances by Mary Carver as Andrea Sarti's mother and Galileo's honest and simple-minded caretaker, and Richard Zavaglia as Galileo's shrewd friend, Sagredo, who warns him of the Establishment's inevitable enmity. Luckinbill was more vehement and vociferously passionate than either the Berliner Ensemble's Galileo or Charles Laughton. But Luckinbill is American and his Galileo in this respect is very American and perhaps properly so. In any case, his interpretation possessed the forcefulness as well as the intelligence demanded by the production's circumstances.

Galileo's scene with the Little Monk who fears the despair that Galileo's ideas will cause among his peasant parents and others like them was, oddly enough, much more dryly didactic than in either the German or the Laughton productions. The Carnival, which ordinarily lends itself to a splendidly ironic and musical spectacle was reduced to an unintelligible "number." Also the Pope's transformation with the donning of his vestments from humanist to august and fearsome Defender of the Faith here proved rather ineffective. Still, this New York Actors' Theatre's initial effort was animated by bright skillfulness, energy, a vital rhythm and unmistakable dedication.

If I were challenged to give a strictly accurate account of the plot in Lanford Wilson's *The 5th of July* I am not sure I could do it (Circle Repertory Company). That may be because the play possesses so little of what we ordinarily call "plot." In any case, plot is here not the point. More dismaying, I was not always clear about the inter-relationships among the characters. This latter difficulty may have been my fault; some in the audience around me were able to explain what in this respect I had failed to grasp. But neither of these shortcomings, for which I believe the author must share the responsibility, prevented me from liking his overextended play!

It may be said to occupy a place in a particular tradition of our stage and literature: the description of certain of our native insanities. When we read of them in so signal a novelist as Faulkner we speak of "madness"; in their lighter manifestations we dub the phenomenon as "wackiness". Jane Bowles's *In a Summer House*, Saroyan's *The Time of Your Life* in a whimsical or sentimental key and Wilson's *The Hot'l Baltimore* all treat in one fashion or another with our home-grown oddballs.

The 5th of July is somewhat different from the softer examples in this category in that the people dealt with are for the most part on the "sick" side, and in the style of their depiction very much of today. I am sure that Wilson does not think of them in this way; he might even say they are the people who live next door—in Lebanon, MO., where the play takes place and where he was born. There is no malice in his portraiture; he does not conde-scend to or patronize the group who "sat" for him and carry on for us. His attitude is entirely friendly, even compassionate.

He cannot object to Kenneth Talley, the more or less homosexual and crippled Vietnam veteran (William Hurt) who is trying to live a useful life as a teacher of the socially or physically handicapped. There is also dignity in Jed, his aide and lover (Jeff Daniels) who is a botanist. To the large farm-house—the Talley Place—in which the injured man lives with his sister, June (Joyce Reehling) and Shirley, her daughter (Amy Wright) come two friends on a visit that also has a "practical" purpose. One is John (Jonathan Hogan) who has attached himself to Gwen (Nancy Snyder) a West Coast millionaire's daughter, who is always on the point of freaking out. Both John and Gwen prime themselves with various brands of happy-making drugs. They are devotees of latter-day popular musical styles, and they propose to buy the Talley Place and build a studio on it for their musical recordings. On their way to Nashville, where they hope to sell one of their compositions, they have brought along with them a charming though near-cretinous guitarist (Danton Stone) who finds most of the company at the Talley Place "far out."

Ken's sister, once a "marcher" in the protests of the 1960s, is somewhat embittered but generally sensible. "Under the rose" in the "old days" she bore John the aforementioned Shirley, now 15, who envisions herself as someone who will become "the greatest artist in the world"—of a still undetermined kind. (Up to now, she asserts, the greatest star produced in Missouri was Betty Grable.) Then too there is the Talleys' 67-year-old Aunt Sally (Helen Stenborg) who unaccountably married a nice Jew whose ashes she has removed from their urn, poured into several candy boxes and finally dumped into the river.

Wilson does not treat these people "in depth." In extremely rapid strokes he traces their lineaments in the oddities and obscenities of their behavior and speech. But we observe, if we take pains to think about it, that all of them are romantics, even to a pathetic extent idealists, with no roots to nourish them, no environment to inspire—only sophisticated notions and half-assimilated information. No wonder they are nuts.

The writing is wittily deft throughout, the general tone hilariously batty; and, though the insights are swiftly passed over, we have frequent intimations of their presence. The play is utterly unpretentious; Wilson appears to want merely to amuse us, but something more than simple entertainment is achieved. Wilson *sees*: his sight is cockeyed but on target.

A most important contribution to the fun is the excellent cast. Marshall Mason, very knowing and humane in the direction of actors, has created out of the crazy quilt of the play's jiggling pattern a coherent and memorable "picture." To mention the particular qualities of the individual players would make this review longer than perhaps necessary. I need only say that when the play was over I wanted to marry them all!

—*NAT*, 13 May '78

AIN'T MISBEHAVIN'

"The joint is jumpin' on Broadway," is how an ad for *Ain't Misbehavin'*, the Fats Waller musical show at the Longacre Theatre, reads. It is one of the very few examples of entirely accurate publicity. There is more animation in the occasion than in anything ever devised by the producers of our film cartoons. And a lot more vitality.

Not all the numbers were written by Fats Waller, but all were recorded by him. The dates of composition extend from 1929 to 1943. Whether the tunes or lyrics were the work of black or white authors, they all unanimously share in joyousness of spirit.

Bright or "blue," they are informed by a zest that arises from an embrace of existence on all levels, high and low! Whatever their musicological derivation, their effect is spiritual; they affirm life. Their energy or kinetic power is not mechanical but soulful.

I never knew many of the thirty songs listed on the program. I may therefore be mistaken in the detail of their verbal or musical quality. The fact is I could not make out all the words. The intrinsic value of the music may be a matter of dispute; the vocalization may at times contravene classically accepted canons. No matter: we are carried away, caught in a warmly festive whirl. The occasion is more than exhilarating, it is endearing: it causes a kind of exultation rare even in "legitimate" entertainments.

The medium is above all *theatre*. For good as the songs may be, they would not affect us as they do if it were not for the five actors who deliver them—and the man at the piano and musical supervisor, Luther Henderson. They and Arthur Faria, who staged the numbers, and the director, Richard Maltby, Jr. (who conceived the show in collaboration with Murray Horwitz), make a more integrated ensemble than anything now on a New York stage.

The wonderful interrelation among the players is not a matter of excellence in stage craftsmanship or thoroughgoing rehearsal but the product of blood and environmental kinship. For they appear to be of one body, a single impulse unifies them in absolute coordination. Each actor, while distinctly individual, functions as a limb of one organism. The "beat" is the throb of a common center, one heart! That is what I mean when I speak of the show as essentially theatre. All the show's elements become a whole through performance, through acting.

If the words had been in a foreign language unknown to me my reaction would have been pretty much the same. One sees, hears, senses the significance of the total phenomenon. In such a presentation I hesitate to single out the various participants. Yet I must do so because each "part" possesses his or her own look, sound, personality.

A wicked raciness is everywhere present, and with it purity: a total lack of apology for exuberance gives everything done or implied—naughty or nice—an unimpeachable human validity, a basic health. In Nell Carter we find the most sophisticated knowingness about the "sins" of our urban life, white and black. It is there in her half-closed, shaded eyes, the piercing kazoo-toned voice with a register no single instrument can achieve, the unabashed supercynical swagger proclaims or insinuates the whole "story" underlying the numbers. André De Shields is the protean showman, delightful rascal, constant kidder, devil-may-care playboy. Armelia McQueen is the roly-poly "vamp" and full-bodied tease, a delicately mirthful come-on to pleasures everywhere prized. Ken Page, a pillar of strength, promises sense and stability and his projection of *I Hate You 'Cause Your Feet's Too Big* is a masterpiece of jocular scorn. For awhile I took the newcomer in the cast Charlaine Woodard to be a creature drawn by Walt Disney, a kind of superdoll on jiggling wires in which every feature shines as if illuminated from within by a battery of a thousand-watt force; but then she sang several subdued lyrics with a special tenderness.

I saw *Ain't Misbehavin'* when it was initiated at the "cabaret" section of the Manhattan Theatre Club, when the tiny playing area restricted the possibilities of free movement and broad effects. I was afraid that the show might lose its good-pal intimacy in the two-balcony house on Broadway. But though more lines are lost at the Longacre, the show has gained through John Lee Beatty's adept stage arrangement, the just-right gaiety of Randy Barcelo's costumes and the fitting colors of Pat Collin's lighting, in addition to the very helpful services of a small and expert band.

—*NAT*, 27 May '78

THE PULITZER PRIZE & THE ALSO RANS

The theatre always tells us something about the society from which it emerges, and, conversely, the social climate shapes the kind of theatre which one might expect from it. This thought, by no means new or original, recurred to me with the announcement of *The Gin Game* as this year's winner of the Pulitzer Prize.

The Gin Game is an altogether pleasant piece very nicely acted by Hume Cronyn and Jessica Tandy. It is well written, sympathetic, and comfortably intelligent. It is also very slight, which is not to be taken as an adverse comment, but as description.

But compare this year's choice with such earlier Pulitzer winners as *A Streetcar Named Desire*, *Death of a Salesman*, *Cat on a Hot Tin Roof*, *Long Day's Journey Into Night*, *A Delicate Balance*, some of them also recipients of the critics' awards to which one might add *A Raisin in the Sun*, *Toys in the Attic*, *The Night of the Iguana*, *Who's Afraid of Virginia Woolf?*, *The Homecoming*, *Rosencrantz and Guildenstern Are Dead*, *Borstal Boy*. I do not allude only to differences in merit, but to differences in nature, scope, weight, intent.

If we go back to the twenties, America's coming-of-age in the theatre, we find together with the lush splendor and delight of the musicals (by Gershwin, Rodgers, the Ziegfeld Follies, etc.) and the popular spoofing of George Kaufman's comedies, an atmosphere of challenge in the work of O'Neill, George Kelly, Paul Green, Maxwell Anderson, S.N. Behrman, Sidney Howard, Elmer Rice, Philip Barry. The thirties carried the movement on in a new vein of both fervent protest and hope in the plays of Clifford Odets and others. The early forties emphasized democracy and the struggle against Fascism with a gradual turning inward to the disquiet of the individual soul *vis-à-vis* Tennessee Williams. The fifties sounded notes of discontent with the "normalcy" and conformism of the Eisenhower era (as in Arthur Miller) and manifested itself in eruption on and off stage in the sixties. Not all these playwrights or their plays may have possessed permanent value (except as "history") but they generally faced the world with a sense of conscientious inquiry, a criticism of our existence both as separate beings and as citizens of our State. We are now at a moment of social conservatism amounting to lethargy. We do not wish to rock the boat, for we do not know where we're going, we have no easy remedies or noble ambitions. We play it safe or act "crazy"—just for fun.

Of course I exaggerate for the sake of some clarity in this very brief summary. But see what Broadway now offers us.

There is Bob Fosse's *Dancin'*, all motor power, physically astonishing, expert as machine energy with no "book," no fresh music, no dramatic point, no genuine emotion. It's a hit.

There is *The Best Little Whorehouse in Texas* at the theatre on Second Avenue and Twelfth St., where *Oh, Calcutta* began its sensational run. The new musical by Larry King and Peter Masterson has some catchy dance numbers by Tommy Tune, music and one touching lyric by Carol Hall, passages of rib-tickling roughtalk, pretty and lively girls, a rather good cast. But its tunes lack distinction, its setting is flashy without special invention, and its basic notion, if we take it the least bit seriously, is a rehash of "anti-puritanism." The whorehouse is viewed neutrally or affectionately, the whole without "heart" at its center. Its quality, apart from the exceptions noted, is synthetic.

The most interesting of the "legitimate" plays I have recently seen are *Catsplay* by a leading Hungarian dramatist, Istvan Orkeny, and *The Mighty Gents* by Richard Wesley. *Catsplay*, first staged on its home grounds in 1971, opened at the Manhattan Theatre Club (one of the best of the off-Broadway institutions) may not be on the boards when this article appears, for unlike the glossier shows which do reach the Main Stem, its appeal and meaning are not wholly obvious.

It is a comedy—some of it, in fact, hilarious—about the superiority of a life lived with romantic, so to speak "Bohemian," bravery in the shabby circumstances of Budapest today over a staid or wholly correct and affluent existence elsewhere. The well-acted play skirts the borders of farce but also sounds notes of pathos. It does not glamorize the life endured by the "little people" in Hungary; it simply proclaims the persistence of the will to enjoy even under difficult conditions. There is a kind of Magyar or gypsy savor and charm in the play with an admixture of rueful thoughtfulness.

The Mighty Gents came tardily to Broadway (again from the Manhattan Club) and died there. Eloquently acted by the entire company, it is both a naturalistic and poetic evocation of hopes and sorrows among blacks whose youthful dreams of a bright future are wrecked in adulthood. But Broadway, with its high costs and prices, is not a suitable home for so vibrantly real a play as this, even when it is favored by an appreciative press reception. Such plays upset those who demand nothing but entertainment.

An amiable and well-packaged banality sets the tone of the day. But go to the theatre anyway; on the fringes of the town you will discover certain treasures and pleasures. The "eccentric" is now the center!

—*WEST*, May '78

ON GOLDEN POND

The subject of Ernest Thompson's play *On Golden Pond* is love (Hudson Guild Theatre). Norman Thayer, Jr. is 80; his wife, Ethel, is 69. They have been married forty-five years. Their daughter Chelsea, 42, has been divorced and is about to marry a Los Angeles dentist who has a son of 14. There are slight abrasions in the relationships, with love as a constant.

That is all: no "story." Aristotle said that drama hangs on plot, but he had no predecessor of similar authority to dispute him. Many less distinguished people do so today, and plays like *On Golden Pond* make us incline to their side. It is all character and ingratiating conversation. The new playwright (he is 29) writes with abundant good humor and homely ease. He manages to sustain his five scenes without losing our pleased attention.

Thayer is a crusty and crotchety citizen with a tongue-in-cheek leaning toward deviltry. He employs insult to keep himself going and others at a distance. He abandons these tactics only when his thrusts provoke worthy responses. His wife tells him, "You are the sweetest man in the world and I am the only one who knows it." His daughter speaks of him as narrow and bigoted and his wife agrees. He is suspicious of foreigners and doesn't favor Jews.

A resident of Maryland and retired (we never learn what he did), he regards the rest of the country as alien territory. His daughter complains—most gently—that he never made any close contact with her and she suffered neglect from her mother; her parents were too absorbed in each other. The only one to whom Mr. Thayer shows genuine affection is his future step-grandson when his daughter brings him and her prospective husband to Golden Pond, VT., the Thayers' summer place. As for the rest, Thayer evinces only a roughly amused tolerance. He is a dogged individualist who keeps most folk at arm's length, less from malice than from concern for his privacy. He

thinks a lot and jokes about death.

The play is delightfully sentimental; in which respect it is like *Da*, another of the Hudson Guild Theatre productions. The experience is like dropping in, unexpected and probably reluctant guests, among folk one expects will prove boring or irritating, and finding oneself astonishingly charmed and cheered. The playwright has the saving touch.

Thompson is also extremely fortunate in his cast. Frances Sternhagen has always been an excellent actress. As Ethel Thayer she is at her best. She is the wife of healthy mind and spirit, honest and sensible in all things, a fit match for her impossible husband. Ms. Sternhagen's acting possesses feeling (without pressure), wit (without parade), irony (without bitterness), and utter naturalness (without slackness). Above all, her presence conveys a certain moral freshness.

Tom Aldredge also excels in his perhaps more difficult role of Mr. Thayer. The puckered mouth, the faint grin, the dry playfulness, the desiccated and near-nasal tone, the strident querulousness and the shrewdly observant eye—all are finely drawn. We never lose sight that the man is capable of affection and, with a nudge or a shove, of fair-mindedness.

As director, Craig Anderson helps the entire company and all its members seem true enough to the circumstance to make us feel nicely at home with them.

—*NAT*, 7 Oct. '78

THE CURRENT THEATRE

If you are a sufficiently seasoned theatregoer, you may remember *Shuffle Along*, *Blackbirds of 1930*, or the song "I'm Just Wild About Harry." The tunes for these shows and a great number of others of similar nature were written by the ninety-five-year-old Eubie Blake during the twenties and thirties. They are sung and danced by a splendid company of versatile players in a show which bears Mr. Blake's first name, *Eubie* (Ambassador Theatre).

Gogol's *The Inspector General* (first produced in St. Petersburg in 1836) is a masterpiece. You might call it a Russian "Watergate" story. It is about government corruption: the mayor of a provincial town and his henchmen are petty crooks, though their thefts are as wide as they are long. Their fear of exposure by the visit of a St. Petersburg official only emphasizes the extent of their cupidity, stupidity, and absurdity. The play is a comedy, a comedy which may be projected as a bitingly grotesque satire or as a "Dickensian" group portrait. The characters are quaint creatures out of a strange past, yet very much like the politicans of our day.

There are loads of tricks in the production of the Romanian Liviu Ciulei at the Circle-In-The-Square Theatre (West 50 Street). Some of them are funny, more are heavy handed and repetitious. The result is neither satire nor farce, but burlesque. We are beaten about the head and ears with brickbat blows, a sense of the whole, relevant to its author, is lost.

The Crucifer of Blood, written and directed by Paul Giovanni, is the latest and, I trust, the last of stage entertainments based on Sherlock Holmes (Helen Hayes Theatre). This sour statement need not put you off—the opening night audience loved the show and I predict a smash hit.

If you cared for *Dracula*, you will probably like *The Crucifer of Blood* as much, or more. It mixes the expected melodramatic thrills—abetted by spectacular scenic effects—and has a number of smooth and amusing witticisms. The acting on the whole is good—especially that of Paxton Whitehead as a snobbishly aloof Holmes, Glenn Close, luscious in a beautifully designed gown from Ann Roth's hand, and Edward Zang in a deft caricature of a dumb British detective.

Why then did I remain more or less indifferent? I read the Conan Doyle stories when I was sixteen and saw innumerable plays like them. They piqued my curiosity, but I never was crazy about them. Let us put my captiousness down to personal idiosyncrasy. I was not then and am even less now

such a child. My innocence is of another kind, and my appetite for simple pastimes is requited by a different diet.

—WEST, Nov. '78

CHEKHOV AS HUMANIST

Between 1898 and 1904, the Moscow Art Theatre, under Constantin Stanislavsky's direction produced four of Chekhov's plays: *The Seagull, Uncle Vanya, The Three Sisters, The Cherry Orchard* in that order. Chekhov, up to the time of his first success as a dramatist at the Moscow Art Theatre was chiefly known as the author of short sketches, tales and novellas. Both these and his plays are among the great achievements of literature. Bernard Shaw confirmed that when he read Chekhov's plays he felt like destroying all of his own! Chekhov was only forty-four when he died.

It is an old story; but Chekhov is ever new. Today the plays and the proper mode for their presentation on the stage are the subject of controversy. The dispute on the matter began with the earliest productions. Stanislavsky viewed the plays as tragedies; Chekhov insisted they were comedies. Both were right. Life, it has been said, is a tragedy for those who feel, a comedy to those who think. In a letter he wrote in 1888, Chekhov himself declared, "I look upon tags and labels as prejudices."

The fact is the Moscow Art Theatre production of *The Cherry Orchard* with its original cast which I saw in 1922 (I am one of the very few of those now engaged in the argument who did) had more humor and was funnier than most of the subsequent stagings which stressed its comedy.

There is something futile in the perpetual argument. Take *Uncle Vanya*, for instance. It is difficult to see it without shedding tears, yet the climax of the third act is very close to farce. Chekhov depicts the painful disappointments of his people, but also recognizes their absurdities. He is always compassionate. His least sympathetic, indeed ridiculous characters like the selfish Serebriakof are also pathetic figures. The son of a peasant sexton, he has educated himself to the estate of a professor of literature, a writer of many erudite books, and finds himself a failure and the object of general disdain. His egotism renders him irritatingly and laughingly stupid.

Then there is the pock-marked Telyegin ("Waffles") who says, "You know that the one who deceives his wife or husband is of course an unfaithful person and may very well betray his own country" and follows this bit of wisdom with, "My own wife betrayed me with another man on the day after our marriage, just because of my own unattractive appearance. But I did not forsake my duties. I still love her and I am faithful to her. I help her as much as I can and have given her my possessions for the education of the children she had by the other man..." We are bound to guffaw at the fool and yet we cannot help but find a touching sweetness in him.

There are comic contradictions in nearly all of Chekhov's people: they proclaim convictions and do the very opposite. Vanya himself, a man who wouldn't hurt a fly, a man who has sacrificed his life to support a brother-in-law he believed a genius only to find him a mediocrity, attempts to shoot him and is ashamed of himself for missing, is both pitiable and a joke. Very few of Chekhov's men and women are adequate to the situations in which they find themselves—very much like most of us.

As Chekhov has a peasant say in one of his short stories, "A bird is given not four wings, but two, because it is able to fly with two; and a man is not permitted to know everything but only a half or a quarter. As much as he needs in order to live." That is the cream of the jest—or of tragedy.

The attitude is essentially humanistic. What often summons tears in Chekhov's plays—even as they provoke smiles or chuckles—is the fundamental *goodness* that emanates from their every movement: the quality of his perception and art. Chekhov was neither a facile optimist nor a dour

pessimist. He embraces life because there is no other choice and he sees it whole. In *The Three Sisters*, the tender and doomed Tusenbach believes there can be no solution to the universal ache, while the henpecked Colonel Vershinin like the perpetual student Trofimov in *The Cherry Orchard* looks forward hopefully to a future—even if it be a hundred to two hundred years—when humankind will have emerged from its dark ages. In the meantime we must endure. "He who desires nothing," Chekhov wrote, "hopes for nothing, is afraid of nothing, cannot be an artist."

I call Chekhov "humanist" by which I mean simply *humane*. He was not denominationally a believer. But a close look reveals in him what we associate with the religious spirit. There is no dogma in Chekhov, no strict or absolute "message." It is the least sophisticated of his characters—so simple-minded that we may regard them as utter innocents—who voice sentiments which sound "mystic."

The old nurse Marina in *Uncle Vanya* very gently answers Dr. Astrov, a man both cynical and lofty, who has asked her, "I wondered if the people who live one or two hundred years from now, the ones we're paving the way for now would remember us with a kind word" by saying, "The people won't remember, but God will." To which Astrov rejoins (reflecting Chekhov) "Thank you for that. That was well said."

It is Marina in response to the "no-account" Telyegin, expressing his hurt because he has been called "a sponge," who says, "Don't pay any notice, my dear. We're all sponges on God." Marina never fusses. She consoles and is kind to everyone. She takes the family ructions around her—even the attempted murder—as the quacking of geese. For life must proceed on its normal course. "In the morning we'll have tea at eight, lunch at one, we'll sit down to supper in the evening, everything in order, like in other people's homes...Christian-life." Chekhov's humanism is in the deepest sense Christian in which respect he is very much like most of the great Russian writers.

Conventional and misleading criticism has grown like a fungus around Chekhov's work. His plays, it has been repeatedly asserted, have no action or story. This isn't so. Chekhov's method of building his plays is different from that of his predecessors—Ibsen, for example—or from most other playwrights to the very present. His dramatic narrative does not move in a straight, presumably logical, plot line to an expected or foreseeable high point. It interrupts itself, shifts, eddies so that if we are not sufficiently attentive we do not immediately perceive its pattern. His technique is sometimes spoken of as "impressionism," but it more closely resembles the motion of everyday occurrence and behavior than the traditional modern play does; it is, if you will, more life-like, more truly realistic.

The most fatal mistake is to regard Chekhov's plays as all "downbeat." Tragedy is never that for it is rounded on the struggle to overcome cosmic obstacles which we may call the nobility of tragedy. Chekhov's plays are centered in a basic principle: "We must live." Vanya ends by forgiving his enemy and, in his depression, continues with his thankless job of heeding his niece Sonya's resolve "We shall live." It is the recurrent note stated or implied in all of Chekhov's work. In the final scene of *The Three Sisters*, Irina, the youngest of them who has more cause for despair than the others cries out, "A day will come when the world will know...why all this suffering; there will be no more mysteries...but life must go on...While we wait, we must try to live...we must work, only work." It is the faith that moves mountains. It is the faith of the young in *The Cherry Orchard* who, while their elders weep over the passing of the old establishment, greet a new life that's beginning.

In the short span of his life, Chekhov not only practiced medicine, composed a huge body of writing, helped institute prison reforms, supported libraries, set up a clinic, encouraged other artists and above all, strove to liberate the Russia of his day from its backwardness from which stemmed so much of its people's frustration and misery. "There is something wrong in this house," the beautiful and broken Yelena says. (Shaw, in his own time, called it a "heartbreak house.") But if the play has a central action and its characters a prime wish, it is not alone to complain of life but to make it better, to find a way to be happy. Nearly all seek or yearn for that "light in the distance" of which Astrov speaks—a goal and a grace.

Chekhov hardly ever preaches; he bids us understand. What he understood about his own time and place is, to this very moment, still left for us to realize. In the same letter in which he denounced "tags and labels" he added, "My holy of holies is the human body, health, intelligence, talent, inspiration, love and the most absolute freedom imaginable, freedom from violence and lies, no matter what form the latter two take."

—*STGB*, '78

MAN AND SUPERMAN

*M*an and Superman remains fresh (Circle-in-the-Square). There is nothing more foolish than regarding it as old-fashioned or "dated." (It was written between 1901 and 1903.) It matters little whether some of the ideas are now familiar (as much may be said of most masterpieces); the point is that we hear them expressed in a manner which delights and exhilarates, even if we are inclined to dispute some of them.

Shaw, everyone knows, was Ibsen's herald in the English theatre. But his plays (except possibly the first) were not in the least "Ibsenite." In his preface to *Heartbreak House*, he spoke with utmost enthusiasm of Chekhov, but that play is certainly not Chekhovian. (An artist, Malraux once said, tells us what he would like to do, but does what he can.) As I watched the performance of *Man and Superman* the other evening, it struck me that if I were to name a forebear of the Shavian manner, I would choose Molière.

Molière too had his didactic side. He was often unequivocally "preachy" in *The Misanthrope, Tartuffe* and obliquely so in *The School for Wives, The Imaginary Invalid, The Blue Stockings* (*Les Femmes Savantes*), *Le Bourgeois Gentilhomme* and even in his farces: *Scapin* et al. It is the "preachment" which nowadays "turns off" the younger French. But what engages most of us is the scenic ebullience, the theatre-wise gaiety, the unexpected turns, the swirl of wit, the frolic and the fun.

So too with Shaw. His dialogue—even in its prolixity—has a springiness, an athleticism which sweeps us along in its exuberance. The man is right, we feel, because he is healthy. This fan of the boxing ring always catches us unawares by a sudden swipe, a feint, and the blow lands to our amazed gratification. Our intellectual cavils hardly matter; Shaw disarms us by provoking us to laughter even when we are determined to resist him. Shaw, known and for the most part praised or deprecated as a sort of philosopher, was above all a supreme showman.

His plays are not realism. They are harlequinades, juggling acts in which the props are thoughts and speculations. He wanted actors who could deliver his dialogue like arias; his writing combines music and dance. He made intelligence festive. Let others discuss the validity or platitude of his message—the life force, etc. For my part, I find most of his insights still stimulating and appropriate to the moment and those who, with bargain-basement sophistication, loftily dismiss him as dreary, I hold to be obtuse. Shaw was very much in earnest, but his art is that of the jester, infectious, brave, life embracing and life-enhancing.

Stephen Porter has directed the production with a nice sense of the play's possibilities. One might wish for more personal quality, flash, bravura or charm in the acting but on the whole the cast brings precise intention to every scene. George Grizzard as the playful revolutionary and reluctant suitor John Tanner, a role that will ever remain a challenge to the most accomplished and

dazzling player, requires attributes rarely to be found in any one person. Ann Sachs, Mark Lamos, Laurie Kennedy are among the others who do particularly well.

I should also add that for the first time the production made me accept the inclusion of the *Don Juan in Hell* ("dream") sequence, which I had previously considered an intrusion on the flow of what is essentially, for all its ideational material, a most superior "light comedy."

—*NAT*, 6-13 Jan. '79

THE ELEPHANT MAN
A LOVELY SUNDAY FOR CREVE COEUR

Something like a "documentary" in its linear construction, *The Elephant Man* (Theater of St. Peter's Church, Citicorp Building, Lexington Avenue at 54th Street) is a play of substance. The play is taken from the annals of medical history. John Merrick, who was born an elephant-like "monster," was seen one day in 1886 at a tupenny freak show by the distinguished physician Frederick Treves. Apparently abandoned by his parents, Merrick was being exhibited by a rascally man at sundry fairs in England and Brussels. Treves, professionally curious about the phenomenon, brought him for observation and care to the London Hospital, Whitechapel, where he was a consultant surgeon. Money was raised through private sources so that Merrick might stay at the institution for the rest of his life.

In the play, and in the true story, Treves finds the unfortunate youth sensitive, intelligent and gifted. (Merrick occupies himself by designing and constructing a model for a church.) The good doctor tries to make his patient as much as possible a normal person. He wishes to engage someone who will spend time with Merrick, converse with him, read to him and carry on a friendly relationship with him. The applicants for the task are so horrified by photographs of Merrick that they decline the assignment. But Mrs. Kendal, an actress—an invented character—pretty, witty, endowed with delicacy of feeling, agrees to serve as Merrick's companion.

Merrick develops: he asks questions about religion, he is absorbed by literature, he brings his architectural design to completion. Celebrated people visit him and each of them finds something of him/herself in him. He has never seen a naked woman, and he asks Mrs. Kendal to disrobe for him. She does so discreetly enough, but when Treves enters at this moment he asks her to leave the hospital for good. As a proper Victorian, he considers her behavior unconscionable. Four years later, in 1890, Merrick, whose heart cannot bear the strain of his great weight, dies.

The play is much more than a case history. In a sense, the central character is Treves. Nineteenth-century rationalist that he is, he is deeply troubled by the disparity between Merrick's hideous exterior and the fineness of his inner being. Treves has a dream of himself as Merrick's patient in which his own respectability and correct posture take on the same offensive qualities as Merrick's deformities. What is man? What is normal? Treves is pathetically at a loss to find answers in reason and science. He cannot respond to the metaphysical questions with which Merrick indirectly and directly confronts him. Merrick at least has faith in something which transcends the security of sensible assumptions: he believes in heaven and in God.

The play is modest in its implications. Its suggestions are thought-provoking. Bernard Pomerance, the playwright, makes no special pleas, nor even a bid for tears of human charity. This rather underwritten, spare statement of a play carries a due measure of weight.

It is well acted and produced. When I read the script, I wondered how the terrible sight of the "elephant man," as projected on the screen, could be made bearable on the stage. The solution is simple: we see him as a slightly crippled but otherwise handsome youth, and the device works. Philip Anglim plays the role well. This, along with the free staging—actors recognizably impersonating various characters, moving furniture, props, etc., in full view of the audience—demonstrates that stage illusion does not depend on naturalistic verisimilitude. Audiences will accept any convention provided what they see is intrinsically interesting.

The objectivity of Jack Hofsiss's direction is in accord with the script; Kevin Conway is creditable as Treves, and Carole Shelley turns in a piquant and appealing performance as Mrs. Kendal. I'd like to hear more from the (to us) new author.

Tennessee Williams's *A Lovely Sunday for Creve Coeur* (Hudson Guild Theatre) contains most of the essential ingredients of his dramatic work: the irrepressible need and yearning for love, the compassion for the neglected and the injured, a mortal sense of loneliness and loss. The social or semi-political dimension to be found in *Sweet Bird of Youth*, for example, is absent in the new play.

I refer to the play as "new," for I hope it is. Since *The Night of the Iguana* (1961), I have not cared much for Williams's plays, though all of them bear the marks of his splendid gifts. What pleases me most in *Creve Coeur* is its freedom from bathos.

Williams is one of the very few American playwrights who has a true feeling for women. They are his most touching characters. Nearly all of them are bruised, victims of their own unprotected vulnerability or of masculine misunderstanding or brutality. Williams' women are independent or strong only when they are maniacal or absurd.

The central character in *Creve Coeur* (set in 1935) is Dorothea, a civics teacher at a St. Louis high school. She is a Southern belle with little money and very little brains, but she is nonetheless lovable in her longing for "romance" and in her natural sensuality and un-self-conscious delicacy. Her colleague, Helena, is a selfish, snobbish fool who teaches art history. But Williams draws her with such tart wit that we almost forgive her her faults. The third figure is Bodey, an earthy woman of German heritage, spunky and wise. A lesser character, another German woman, Miss Gluck, is half-demented, laughable in her disarray, pitiable in her isolation.

The men in the play are left off-stage—a good thing too, for one is a philandering high school principal with no conscience; the other, Bodey's obese brother who is addicted to smelly cigars, and who may marry, his dear sister hopes, the beauteous blonde Dorothea.

If I have any complaint in regard to this felicitously written, slight, unproblematic play, it is that I have no complaint about it. But that relieves me from noting the kind of discomfort I have experienced with the steamy sexual obsession of several of Williams's previous plays. In sum, *A Lovely Sunday for Creve Coeur* (Creve Coeur is a suburb of St. Louis where, in the 1930s, an amusement park was situated) is a thoroughly engaging play.

It is well directed by Keith Hack and admirably acted. Shirley Knight is perfect in looks, touch, sound (with perhaps a little too much Dixie accent) as the ineffable Dorothea. Peg Murray is compact with sturdy integrity and good will as Bodey, the woman with whom Dorothea shares a funny apartment, designed for that effect by John Conklin. And Jane Lowry is excellent as the dotty and bereft upstairs neighbor, though her German is faulty and best when indistinct.

—*NAT*, 10 Feb. '79

WINGS

Two intelligent people who accompanied me to see Arthur Kopit's *Wings*, first at the Public Theater and now at the Lyceum, found it boring. I on the other hand was fascinated.

The reason for this discrepancy of reaction—apart from the fact that such contradictions are always to be expected—is that the play is in a sense a monodrama, and it is always a "tricky" matter to maintain interest in a play almost wholly centered on a single individual. But the more

crucial hazard in the project is that it undertakes a visualization of a cerebral stroke, its symptoms, its treatment and the possibilities of its healing.

In the production directed by John Madden (originally under the auspices of the Yale Repertory Theater) the problem of staging such material is handled with considerable ingenuity. Still, the workings of the mind, particularly the disturbed mind, are next to impossible to convey through the all too concrete medium of the theatre. It might be more successfully done in a novel, a poem, or perhaps even in a film.

If *Wings* is viewed simply as a sort of medical documentary, it may be considered informative but it cannot be genuinely evocating or moving in an artistic sense. Screen doors which asymmetrically open and close and through which we glimpse doctors and other attendants, serve both as a means to see into the halls of the hospital and at the same time as emblems of the dark corridors and caves of the patient's struggling consciousness. Booming, crashing, crackling sounds further indicate the mind's pain and turmoil. All this is theatrically inventive and to a degree arresting, but all too material, too specific, too recognizable as stage effects. The mind's "interior," in all its complexity, can hardly be communicated in this way.

But Kopit's play is more than a description of a diseased condition. It is a metaphor, indeed a multi-metaphor. The patient and central figure is a middle-aged woman of some cultivation and sensibility who had been in her youth an amateur aviatrix. While we watch her tormented effort to emerge from her breakdown, we are made aware of the puzzle and miracle of the human soul which science can detail but not explain. That is what *Wings* accomplishes and what gives it its special value.

The woman—Emily Stilson—at first forgets her name, cannot grasp the meaning of the simplest words, and when she does, suffers hardship in pronouncing them. Thus, language itself is perceived here as a wonder, a divine gift which in our heedlessness we take for granted. It is part of the nominal paradox of life itself.

We also hear that Mrs. Stilson, one stormy night, apparently lost because of a defect in her plane, stepped out with unaccountable bravery and stood upright on its wings. She did it for no "reason"—and survived. Her recognition of the madness of the action brought on a kind of euphoria—"wings!" It inspired a surge of spiritual elation. What Kopit implies or suggests is that living itself is something willy-nilly for which we must give thanks. It is a nonrational affirmation of the joy in existence. There is little that is "mystic" in this: whether we realize it or not, it constitutes the very essence of our common experience.

Constance Cummings' performance as Mrs. Stilson is a triumph of clarity, grace and dignity. In the small part of an "executive" nurse, Mary-Joan Negro is most winning in her concentration on every nuance of her patient's agony, in her solicitude and heartfelt pleasure at her progress. The rest of the cast too is just fine.

—*NAT*, 17 Feb. '79

A HARD TIME FOR ACTORS

This is a particularly hard time for actors. In the 1920s and for a good part of the 1930s, the Broadway stage offered them roles in the work of the leading European dramatists as well as in plays by O'Neill, Maxwell Anderson, Sidney Howard, Philip Barry, George Kelly, S.N. Behrman, George S. Kaufman. Managers could suffer three flops in four tries without going broke if there was one success. There was freedom and some boldness in the choice of scripts, even some "experimentation" and many more productions of ample scale. New York had some sixty playhouses suitable for modest as well as large needs.

With the shrinkage all along the line during the 1930s and in the ensuing years, most of our big stars—the Barrymores, Spencer Tracy, Fredric March, et al.—abandoned the theatre for films. Such wonderful artists as Laurette Taylor and Pauline Lord died in the 1940s and the tremendously talented Marlon Brando went west, as did more recent luminaries: Dustin Hoffman, Al Pacino, Paul Newman. An overall impoverishment of our main theatrical arteries became increasingly evident.

Today our better plays are produced in regional theatres, for limited runs off or off-off-Broadway. They reach the main market only if they give promise of wide success. The shortage of New York playing space in advantageous facilities results in an impasse: a good number of meritorious plays are refused entry if theatre owners do not consider them sure-fire box-office ventures.

This gives rise to an artistic paradox. In the 1930s, the young stalwarts of the theatre complained that the stage interpretation of plays was not up to the measure or quality of the scripts. We probably exaggerated the case, but due in large part to the people whose theatrical perceptions were sharpened by the study of European models—especially Stanislavsky—and to the spate of instruction in schools, university theatre departments and private courses with eminent teachers, the general level of acting has grown more sophisticated, and possibly "deeper." We do not now have as many actors on our stage of great scope, impressive emotional power or brilliant skill but we do have an ever increasing number of new players whose seriousness and ability are most encouraging. But where are they to play (remuneratively) with any degree of continuity in a variety of parts in worthy plays?

There now exist among us a considerable number of promising dramatists, but very few are mature craftsmen. They have interesting ideas or notions but they rarely develop them into satisfactory entities. They flash and sputter and too often become extinct. They betray a nervous haste in an atmosphere of overall insecurity and lack of balanced criticism. Because they *are* talented they frequently grow both clamorous and self-indulgent. If they have attained a modicum of success (a "name") or write for film or TV, they teach playwriting.

These generalizations require further examination of the social and psychological temper of our day. I am stirred to make them now because I have recently seen various performances which made me feel especially sorry for actors. Their gifts heartened me, their dedication touched me, and their professional situation caused me something close to anguish.

In some off-off-Broadway circles, I saw actors undertake mighty roles in formidable dramas which exceeded their present abilities. Still, it was consoling (though a little pathetic) to observe that they were closely followed by a devoted audience. The appetite for the theatre has not diminished, though the price of tickets curtails its satisfaction.

—*NAT*, 17 Mar. '79

G.R. POINT
WHOSE LIFE IS IT ANYWAY?

Michael Moriarty is the finest young actor now on our stage. No acting since the appearance of Marlon Brando in the late 1940s has so touched me by its unaffected sensitivity and natural beauty. His spiritual force and his constant responsiveness to every shade of thought and feeling without pressuring himself to "theatricalize," inspire wonder. Watching him, we read a human soul in action. My pleasure in seeing him in David Berry's *G.R. Point* (Playhouse Theatre) very nearly led me to overlook the merits of the text itself.

The subject is the pain and horror of men in war—in this instance the one in Vietnam. There have been other such plays: I generally harbor some resistance to them because it is almost impossible to convey convincingly on stage the direct physical contact of warfare. But *G.R. Point*, besides revealing both the degradation inherent in the experience of war and the virtues war sometimes elicits, also contains an unemphatic but nevertheless cogent portrait of a certain American type—the man of puritan mold.

Micah (played by Moriarty) is a well-reared and educated youth from Maine. His contact with his fellow soldiers and the brute facts of killing bring out all the contradictions of his character: its strength, limitations, capacity for growth—as well as its propensity to decay. He wishes to be "democratically" open and yet shuns or fears personal intimacy, repelling any intrusion into his private being. He unconsciously betrays a sense of superiority in which there is the sin of pride. Moralistic about, and yet coarsened by, the realities of service, he enjoys alarming relief from his "righteousness" but at the same time is assailed by a severe sense of guilt at not finding himself truly superior to the coarsest of his companions.

All this is so adroitly suggested by the script (and by the keen delicacy of the performance) that in the midst of the usual and more violent attributes of the play (the gross language, the rough vernacular humor, the sound and terror of battle) one may lose sight of what is original in it.

Whose Life Is It Anyway?, a London success by Brian Clark, comes to us with its leading London player, Tom Conti (Trafalgar Theatre—the old Billy Rose Theatre—West 41st Street). It is an intelligent, well-crafted and altogether neat piece of work. There is something in its very nicety which strikes me as peculiarly British.

Its theme is strong. On "recovery" from a terrible auto accident, Ken Harrison, a sculptor, learns that due to an irreversible injury to his spine he will never again be able to walk or to use his hands. Under British law, he is entitled to free care and hospitalization for the rest of his life. He pleads for release from such protection, though medical authorities assure him that without it he will die within six days. But he does not wish to live as a perpetual invalid and his plea is in effect a request to commit suicide, which the doctors refuse to grant. Who is in the "right" in such a case? The play follows the process and consequence of this crucial argument.

There is little sentimentality in the telling, no unseemly stress or plumbing of depths. Common sense, reasonableness, kindly discipline and respectability dominate. The matter is presented with crisp decorum, effortless dramatization, verbal clarity, upright sanity.

I certainly do not disparage any of this. But I do ask more than this from the theatre, though it may be said that our stage today rarely provides as much. Certainly one is "given to think": the play is written in civilized discourse resembling much of modern English fiction, comparable to the lesser Maugham.

The acting is just right, that is, in consonance with the mood and style established by the script and the direction. In this vein, Tom Conti is first-rate. One wishes, however, to see him in more ambitious roles. I very much liked Kenneth Welsh as an amiable lawyer, Beverly May as the head nurse Sister Anderson, and Jean Marsh (expressively muted) as an understanding doctor. The setting by Alan Tagg is discreetly artful and perfect for the overall tone and intent of the play, as is Tharon Musser's lighting.

—*NAT*, 12 May '79

THE WOODS

First produced last year in Chicago, David Mamet's *The Woods* can now be seen in a new staging at the Public Theater. One reviewer has maintained that it was beautiful in its earlier presentation but that, chiefly on account of faulty direction, it is at the moment disappointing. Such a thing is possible, but in this case I am inclined to doubt it. There is a crucial defect in the text.

In several of his plays, most notably in *American Buffalo*, Mamet has demonstrated genuine dramatic gifts. He possesses a tender sensibility and a keen sense of the stage. His plays shift in focus and in aim, as if they were meant not so much to interest or entertain us as to discover who he is: Mamet appears to be seeking his theme, his artistic identity. It is a quest which inspires sympathy. If we judge him piece by piece we shall

find the path somewhat bumpy; if we try to "place" him—it is really too early to do so—we are likely to fall into innocent error. It might be more helpful to describe critically the particular nature of each of his "steps" than simply to judge them in relation to our pleasure.

The Woods is about a young man and woman who are in love. They have repaired to a quiet place in the country where the young man, Nick, spent a good part of his boyhood years with his now deceased parents. In their isolation and in the pauses between their bouts of lovemaking, Nick's character and that of Ruth, his companion, emerge. She is healthy, eager for experience, and far more intelligent or, at least, balanced than he. He is inarticulately troubled; he cannot locate the cause of his inner disturbances. His disaffection probably has to do with his childhood, but everything, it would seem, has to do with one's childhood. The easiest tag to apply to him is "neurotic," but what exactly does that mean?

He is abusive and apologetic—how tiresome his constant "I'm sorrys." He wants to be alone, he wants her to go away, he wants her to stay. His lovemaking is a kind of nervous impatience with himself. He requires solace from the nameless and wracking upset of his spirit. His confusion is disruptive of the relationship which he nevertheless pleads to preserve. Ruth, always more lucid, wants to break with him, but she recognizes in him a lost child adrift, and yields to her pity for him.

It is all literally "true to life"—which is exactly what troubles me. Innumerable love affairs everywhere may be similarly graphed, even to the point of the nervously inconsequential fragments of speech with which the lovers communicate. The play implies that, especially in the matter of love, we are all in the "woods." The phenomena of nature itself surround and wrap us in an impenetrable dark mystery, unresponsive to reasoned explanation.

This sentiment in itself may be banal, but that does not preclude its serving as material, even the essence, of sound drama. How many vital truths about life are there anyway? But the "realism" here dispels the larger dimension sought for. In language and behavior the characters are too concrete and superficially recognizable to take wing. We fail to learn anything beyond their immediate and unexceptional situation. They are not transfigured by any special insight, psychological or intuitive. The obvious symbolism—the maze of the lonely wooded landscape in which we find them—evokes nothing, and the realism is so commonplace that it makes the symbolism appear terribly "young."

John Lee Beatty's setting, though striking as a construction, aims to synthesize both aspects of the text—the locale itself and its suprasensible meaning—but like it, fulfills neither function. Christine Lahti and Chris Sarandon's acting, as well as Ulu Grosbard's direction, all of it intelligently straightforward, might have been informed by a desire for emotional poetry, but can hardly ignite the bald and rough specificity of what we see and hear.

—*NAT*, 19 May '79

ZOOT SUIT
BEDROOM FARCE

The audience is always the real star in the theatre: it makes or breaks a show. This becomes evident when a play is a hit in one place (or at a particular time) and, with the same cast and production, a failure in another.

An example of this I often cite is John van Druten's 1943 comedy *The Voice of the Turtle* with Margaret Sullivan which on Broadway achieved a run of 1,557 performances. The play, transferred to London after the war with the original company, not only flopped but was positively resented. The English who had suffered the blitz were unable to appreciate the spectacle of New York hanky-panky and frivolity during that period.

I am reminded of this by the general press reception given Luis Valdez's *Zoot Suit* at the Winter Garden. It was and still is an enormous success in Los Angeles, but with few exceptions our New York reviewers severely panned it.

The discrepancy may be explained in two ways. First: *Zoot Suit* is based on the infamous 1942-43 murder trial in Los Angeles, incriminating a group of seventeen so-called "Pachuco" Chicanos (youths of Mexican origin). The trial embroiled the entire community in either rabid racial prejudice or in staunch (and finally triumphant) defense. In other words, citizens of Los Angeles now experience the shock of recognition at the play; New Yorkers, or at any rate those who tend to echo reviewer opinion, think of it as a "local" California episode with little interest to them.

Second: the play as a piece of writing is certainly crude. But the play possesses meaning. What it dramatizes is emblematic not only of still existent prejudice against a particular people, but of all such sentiments wherever they occur in relation to all "strangers" of whatever color or creed—especially if they are poor.

On the basis of this theme Luis Valdez, himself a Californian of Mexican heritage, together with a generally splendid cast (handsome Daniel Valdez and picturesque Edward James Olmos in the leading roles) have fashioned a rousingly colorful, zestful, raunchily humorous show. Instead of being depressing or heavily propagandistic it enhances the spirit as large scale folk theatre often does. We come to like the emotionally self-assertive and defiant "Pachuco" style with its odd guying grace, its splash and flare. There is bitterness and anger in it but also a virile pride. It stirs optimism in us about the resilience of humankind.

The proceedings offer music and dancing by no means distinguished in themselves, which nevertheless add spice to the occasion. What I liked best of all is the element of festivity: our theatre nowadays is all too tame. *Zoot Suit* is celebrant like a bang-up block party where one anticipates only despair and breakdown.

Bedroom Farce (at the Brooks Atkinson) is the work of Alan Ayckbourn, probably the most popular playwright of the English stage. His specialty is kidding his country's middle class. There are many who regard him as a sharp satirist but I find him more affectionate than astringent. This is not a fault, but a difference. *Bedroom Farce* is a thoroughly amiable play.

We see four couples in three tiny bedrooms. There is a typically elderly and old-fashioned couple—superbly acted by Joan Hickson and Michael Gough—an "average" couple who get along smoothly enough with unromantic routine gratification. Still another is a whacky pair in which the wife (impersonated by the beautifully statuesque Delia Lindsay) is an hysteric and the husband inarticulate and ungainly to the point of goofiness; and last, but not least, two who are happy because the man is a bully thick-headed good fellow whose wife is innocent, dumb, and most adorably genuine in the person of Susan Littler. In fact, all of them are perfectly cast.

Ayckbourn is a crack craftsman. What he manages to accomplish with the interlocking shenanigans of his play is to illustrate the capacity of the British to accommodate themselves with a sort of dogged patience to the dull mediocrity of their present day existence. They "carry on" more or less equably or, as we say, with "no sweat," through all the doldrums of their domestic lives.

This dismays most other English playwrights and gets some of them sore (even as they make jokes) but not Ayckbourn: he turns everything into farce. His *Bedroom* is very funny and only a little tiresome in its second half because the drollery repeats itself.

It remains to be seen whether, after ten weeks when the English cast is replaced by an American cast, the play proves as successful as it is now, acted by the original company from the British National Theatre.

—*WEST*, May '79

THE LITTLE ELEPHANT IS DEAD

As the 1978-79 season nears its end, I am faced with a critical paradox. I have appreciated a number of things, but very little has truly and deeply affected me. There is a compassionate chord in *The Elephant Man* that touched me, and Sam Shepard's *Buried Child*, though obscure in its symbolism, sought a significance for a darkly perceived yet genuinely felt America which stirred me. *Eubie's* dancers and several of its performers—particularly among the women—as well as its popular tunefulness, tickled me. I was warmed by the good will and humor of *Talley's Folly*, and Joseph Buloff's acting in Arthur Miller's *The Price* delighted me.

But still, can I wholeheartedly say that I was actually "carried away"—as the Comden-Green song has it—by anything I saw during the past eight months? Certainly this can only happen once in a long while and one should be satisfied with modest pleasures. Only the daily reviewers are obliged to rave—for reasons of publicity.

Most theatre events aim at clarity of meaning, but too often the meaning is banal or trivial. Of the many productions I have seen this season, only two have thoroughly engaged me—and herein lies the paradox: these two had no "meaning" that I could readily define or explicate. Both were presentations at the La Mama complex on scruffy East 4th Street, and both were produced by foreign companies on visits so brief that my recommendations of them could exercise no practical effect. I speak of *The Dead Class*, a macabre Polish political cabaret performance which transcended politics, and, most recently, Kobo Abe's almost wordless Studio piece, *The Little Elephant Is Dead*.

The latter is "an exhibition of images" which the renowned Japanese novelist Kobo Abe has written, composed and directed with the indispensable aid of his wife, Machi Abe, in settings, costumes and props, and with the hardly less valuable contribution of Tatsuo Kono in lighting. (Without these elements the scenario would not constitute theatre.) In any explicit sense, this spectacle is "meaningless," though with a little work one might plausibly decipher certain social allusions (especially in regard to war and atomic devastation). But there would be more intellectual game than substance in such decoding. The truth is that I was absorbed and captivated by the constant play of colorful imagery, the tantalizing excitement of sound, the physical bounce of the participants, the quirky humor, the scenic inventiveness which somehow remained simple and unmechanical, the flow of exuberant movement, the attractiveness of the youthfully handsome Japanese team, the fancifulness and, for all the undoubted exertion of everyone involved, the ease of it all. Here was mystery and wonder—consummate craftsmanship that did not obtrude itself as such but served the exhilarating totality.

On leaving the theatre I tried to find the perfect epithet for the experience, such as "dreamlike," but this does not fit the concreteness of the means employed; at another moment I thought to compare it with Abstract Expressionism or with Surrealism, but neither of these labels applies. All I could honestly say was that I was entranced, the child as much as the man in me gratified.

It also struck me that the effortless enjoyment provided by Kobo Abe's relatively short "improvisations" must be the result of an extraordinary expenditure of hard work. I asked him how much actual rehearsal time had been devoted to it. "Three years," he answered. No wonder, then, that so much of what passes for experimental theatre among us nearly always seems amateurish. For to attain the completeness we witness in this Japanese instance with all its thought, imagination and skill, support through large subsidy must be available. For great achievements of this kind, great risks must be taken in dedication, time and money.

—*NAT*, 16 Jun. '79

I REMEMBER MAMA

I Remember Mama, a musical with a score by Richard Rodgers, lyrics by Martin Charnin and Raymond Jessel and book by Thomas Meehan, based on John Van Druten's play of the same name, is a placid show which would hardly be noteworthy were it not for the presence of Liv Ullman. Her warm womanliness and simple truthfulness in the character of Mama represent her best work on the New York stage to date. I could not help thinking as I watched her that she is one of the very few real *women* among present-day actresses. There are hardly more than three or four now on the distaff side of the stature of Ethel Barrymore, Laurette Taylor and Pauline Lord whom—quite apart from sheer acting talent—I could designate "true women."

—*NAT*, 14-21 July '79

EVITA
PETER PAN

In London last June, I saw *Evita*, the musical by Tim Rice and Andrew Lloyd Webber (authors of *Jesus Christ, Superstar*), and I wondered what made the show so enormous a hit there. It had been running for two or three seasons (it still is); scalpers were selling admissions outside the theatre and the house was packed.

One reason easily adduced is that English musicals are rarely as razzle-dazzle as Harold Prince, the American director who staged *Evita*, has made it. The show fairly jumps with display. More important, the play centers on a working-class girl, a nightclub performer (like Eva Peron) of little moral stability who becomes the consort of the leader and herself virtually the prime mover of a great country. Her ambition and guile impress;

her sexiness intrigues; her eventual power aston-ishes, and her early death softens the tale. There is, too, something of the tart-with-a-heart-of-gold syndrome back of it all. (The gold, it has been remarked, is deposited in a Swiss bank.)

The piece has no social meaning at all. The audience has very little knowledge of or genuine interest in Peron: Argentina in its mind is connected more with tangos than with politics. To make sure that we understand that Peron and Eva are not beneficent characters, the "symbolic" figure of Che Guevara (never present in Argentina at the time) serves as a Chorus representing the democratic resistance to the Peron dictatorship.

Seeing the show again (at the Broadway Theatre), I was able to judge it on its own terms without worrying about the motives of the public reaction. (It should be noted, however, that due to *Evita*'s immense popularity in London, the advance sale in New York is reported to be close to $2 million and there is a chance that despite a lackluster press reception it may do well here also.) The opening night audience cheered, but opening nights are deceptive: they are crowded with people who have every inducement to wish the enterprise well. The show itself, under its splendiferous cover, is basically threadbare.

The main and oft-repeated musical number, "Don't Cry for Me, Argentina" (nobody does), consists of a pleasantly melancholic and vaguely Hispanic phrase; the rest of the score is nonde-script. The lyrics (when you can hear them) are marked by a philistine "sophistication." There is little "book" or spoken dialogue. What holds the attention is the "scenography." I do not mean just the settings or the lighting but the busyness, the noise, the capering about and the horsing around. Hardly anything is sung by the principals without something extra on the side (a hot couple dancing and swirling), so if one is not amused by the singing, an added gimmick may help out. Off-stage choruses envelop the singers. Twelve army officers in blue-green, red and white stomp around rhythmically (great effect!). True choreog-raphy is either nonexistent or the dancing is banal

in the extreme. Flags are dropped, colors abound, newsreels are projected. (They were about the only thing that interested me, because they showed the "real" Eva Peron being received by Church officials in Rome and by Franco in Spain.)

I liked an attractive young woman, listed as "Peron's mistress," played by Jane Ohringer. Peron turns her out of bed for the new mistress and wife-to-be, Evita. (I wouldn't have done so.) Not that Patti LuPone is without quality: she is in fact an able actress (her death scene is good) and her performance is a brave one, but nothing she is given to do and nothing in the way she does it possesses the glamour which might explain her husband's or the populace's infatuation. She is chiefly asked to be snippy. Mandy Patinkin's Che Guevara looks right, and he has a sound voice which is strained to the point of breathlessness. Bob Gunton looks a bit like Peron—and a little foolish. The chorus belts and belts and belts. Gaudy raucousness, a semblance of historical fact, and a "bad girl" turned powerful who dies at 33 may (with the aid of sweeping publicity) still sell a lot of tickets.

How can I breathe the least word to hurt that perennial winner *Peter Pan* (Lunt-Fontanne Theatre)? *Peter Pan* is *Peter Pan* is *Peter Pan*. This holds true even in its musical version—much less dainty and wry than James Barrie's play. No matter how it is produced, there is something endearing in the material. For it is about a little boy who never wanted to grow up—and most theatre audiences also achieve that goal.

Barrie's play was an expression of sly rebel-lion through fantasy against the stuffiness of the Victorian era, an escape from decorum accom-plished without offense to any of the period's properties. That is why it has never disappeared in England. For us today, the play needs a little prop-ping up, which is done through Carolyn Leigh's lyrics and Mark Charlap's music with the further and very agile aid of lyrics by Comden and Green and music by Jule Styne.

924

Peter's first flying entrance is always exhilarating (I wish I were unable to see the wires), and even more so are the children, twisting merrily along in the air with him. One of the show's major assets is certainly Sandy Duncan's modest performance: she doesn't "star" herself; she has exactly the right body for the part, and she avoids cute embellishments.

As for the rest, some might complain that certain moments of Jerome Robbins's choreography as now adapted by Rob Iscove are too "Broadway"—that is, slightly vulgar—and that Peter Wolf's settings look somewhat tatty. But who, I repeat, can cry "nay" to dear little Peter? I forbear.

—*NAT*, 20 Oct. '79

NIGHT AND DAY
CLASS ENEMY

Diverse elements have gone into the making of Tom Stoppard's *Night and Day* (ANTA Theatre) but they do not give it real coherence.

Its "novelty" is that it is the first example in its author's work of more or less traditionally plotted drama. There still remain characteristic passages of improvisational playfulness and fancy. In this case they relate to Ruth Carson's (the "leading lady's") inner monologue and daydreams. For example, she imagines a consummated flirtation with a youth she has almost just met, attracted to him by his good looks and idealism. Married to a man who owns a mine guarded by the dictator of an African country and threatened by a leftist rebellion, Ruth Carson is given the opportunity to say many amusing things (often only in her mind) about herself, this central situation and the various personages involved in it.

She despises the popular press and the reporters who feed it too often indiscriminately with trivia and grave news. They do so not because they are genuinely concerned with either but out a display of vanity in hunting down headline-making stories. This is one of the play's points, the rebuttal to which, delivered by a cockney news photographer, is that the information provided by the press, despite all the skullduggery which may be involved in unearthing it, is invaluable to a democracy: "It brings light." That, if anything, is the play's thesis. In itself, it may be valid, but it is not dramatized; it is merely stated.

In the same way, Ruth Carson, though she serves as a critic of the press—which is, by the way, rarely "free," because it is usually in the possession of millionaires who protect their own interests in economic, political and social confrontations—is more a decorative and entertaining adjunct to the play than crucial to it.

Much of the play's argument revolves around the news gatherers, a seasoned and cynical reporter and a younger one, who is committed to honest principles of journalism, government and social justice. In addition to these, we are given a portrait of the African dictator, who is financed by certain British capitalists and thus protects Mr. Carson's mine, which would be confiscated by the rebels, were they successful.

These various strands are patched together rather than made integral to a dramatically convincing whole. What keeps the play going is Stoppard's elegantly fluent and sometimes sparkling writing. This is especially true because Mrs. Carson is played by Maggie Smith, the most skillful actress in all English-speaking comedy. Easy and always on target, she is above all endowed with a capacity to *think* funny. The most casual lines she utters, the least gesture she makes take on humorous content. She is the body of wit. A slight nasality of delivery adds to a tone of subtle derision which creates a "distance" between herself and those she addresses. She has had much better roles (in this play, I repeat, her character stands somewhat apart from the whole) but she is always a delight to see and listen to.

She is supported by and is a support to a generally good cast: Peter Evans, Paul Hecht, Dwight Schultz, Clarence Williams and others, ably directed by Peter Wood.

I take note of Nigel Williams's *Class Enemy* (Players Theatre: 115 MacDougal Street) because it is an example of the vehement vituperation which an important segment of British playwrights levels against their society. The angry young men of the late 1950s were mostly middle-class dissidents, but the lower and largely unemployed working-class characters in many British plays of more recent date are far angrier than the former "angries": they are in fact rabid.

In *Class Enemy*, a group of adolescents in a "state comprehensive (high) school" in one of the poorest parts of South London waits for a teacher to arrive. But there is no teacher and we assume that most of the other classrooms are equally deprived. It is unclear (though it may be clear to an English audience) why no teacher is available, though we do see a "master." But such factual considerations do not prevent our understanding the play.

What is communicated with shocking effect is the sense of abandonment that the youngsters suffer, their bewilderment and despair, and finally the all-encompassing hatred which is expressed by the cleverest of them. The constant foul epithets aimed by the boys not only at their environment at large but also at one another are the outward sign of their self-humiliation and the degradation they have succumbed to, and in the venting of which they find a wretched relief. The potential for a decent humanity peeps through at climactic moments, but the overall impression, even when comic, is frightening.

But it is neither to praise the play for its merits nor to censure it for its faults that I speak of it here. It is representative of what English audiences, at least in such institutions as the state-subsidized Royal Court Theatre, respond to—from a sense of recognition—with dogged, sometimes delighted, approval. The prevailing mood now, in the plays outside the West End (London's Broadway), is sadomasochistic—sadistic among the poor, masochistic among the better off. Such stage fare leaves no doubt that England is not only economi-cally but spiritually in deep trouble. Speaking critically, I have much more to say on this subject, but I shall come back to it on another occasion. What I would emphasize now is that I consider it a good sign that these black moods have for some years been loudly voiced in the English theatre. Very little of any sort of social reaction is nowadays manifested on *our* stage.

There are several good performances in *Class Enemy*—those of Lonny Price, Lance Davis and Bruce Wall in particular. But some of these actors must learn how to achieve relaxation within intensity: physical exertion is not the same as fullness of emotion.

—*NAT*, 15 Dec. '79

926

WITH STELLA ADLER IN GREENWICH VILLAGE

THE
EIGHTIES

WITHOUT CLASSIC TRADITION
MARY STUART

Friedrich von Schiller's *Mary Stuart* is a political play with a human face. Written in 1800 about events that took place in 1587, its universality makes it entirely relevant today. It is a masterpiece.

I am impelled, first of all, to set down certain thoughts in regard to its modest production by the Circle Repertory Theatre under Marshall Mason's direction. I speak of the production as modest though in a sense it is extremely ambitious, as is the Circle production of *Hamlet* with which it alternates. The company is hardly equipped with its limited means and insufficient training to produce the great classics in a manner which befits them. There is a paradox in this, for we are seldom given the opportunity to see them done much better anywhere else; in general they are only produced under the auspices of non-profit organizations—in this instance on a tiny stage in a small house.

It's clear that people are still eager to see such plays—witness the free (or nearly free) performances in Central Park that usually draw huge crowds. So despite the fact that on a sheer theatrical-esthetic level I should be severe with the Circle's revivals, I found myself pleased—especially in the case of *Mary Stuart*—to observe that the audiences follow the plays with genuine interest, and pleased to learn that most of the *Hamlet* performances are sold out.

What is wrong with our theatre is not the lack of an audience but the absence of proper auspices to establish and maintain permanent companies of high professional and artistic standards. What we have in the way of such institutions (and it is not the fault of any individual) are in nearly all cases honorable but makeshift enterprises.

The Circle Repertory has done very well with a number of contemporary plays, especially those of Lanford Wilson (*Talley's Folly* and others), and it is a brave thing for them to undertake Shakespeare and Schiller. (I must confess, however, that I have rarely admired any American production of *Hamlet* or of Shakespeare's other tragedies, and very few of the English.) Grandeur in acting has all but disappeared in the last fifty years, as that quality has from the rest of our society.

There is no such thing, Tyrone Guthrie once remarked, as a "Shakespeare tradition"; what is alarming is that almost *all* sense of tradition today has become anomalous. The British citizen who is unaffected by the majesty of Buckingham palace is still somehow related to the idea and panoply of royalty if for no other cause than that he witnesses ceremonies such as coronations, which have remained largely unchanged for centuries. The anticlerical Italian is still so steeped in the environment of Catholicism that he retains a sense of awe at its rituals. But our actors today are strangers to such influences and can only ape the gestures of traditional faiths and past modes of behavior. They have little historical memory or imagination: it is not in our bones.

Our productions of classic plays (and even foreign plays of more recent date) nearly always have a museum stamp about them, an atmosphere of inauthenticity. They do not stir us as living drama, they are for the most part only exercises in style. We are often unable to understand how people of the past could have behaved and conducted themselves as they did. We diminish them when we conceive of them as just like ourselves.

The Circle's *Mary Stuart* is much more telling than its *Hamlet*. It is not that the acting or direction of the first is superior but that Schiller's language (in translation at any rate) is easier to speak and to act. Also, it is less familiar than Shakespeare's, whose significance has become dimmed by routine repetition and banal explication.

Mary Stuart is not like most of our so-called political plays—an exposé or propaganda for a cause. In it Schiller dramatizes both the workings of statecraft—the pressures, machinations, subterfuges and ruses of statesmen in all their complexity—and also their human motivations and effects. Queen Elizabeth and Mary Stuart are depicted with incisive psychological understanding. Both were complex people; neither their virtues nor villainies were trivial. As we follow the conflicts, the dirty tricks, the rationalizations of Schiller's personages, we willy-nilly think of parallels with the politics and politicians of our own day. But the difference is immense, because those old rulers and their ministers were great individuals—or so at least they seem as the master poet-dramatists portray them. They are lofty in thought, big in passion, in daring, in appetite and in eloquence—in that *grandeur* which is so difficult for artists of our epoch, particularly in the theatre—to recapture and make convincing.

The political insights in *Mary Stuart* are traced on the largest scale, and made vital and real. The fiber and pulse of political issues are rendered more illuminatingly and cogently in Schiller's play than they are in all of the news reporting on events that have made headlines and weighted the air and wires for the past twenty-five years.

David Jenkins has constructed a unit setting which, in view of the constricted space and low budget, works well for both *Mary Stuart* and *Hamlet*. Laura Crow has designed some eye-catching costumes, especially those worn by the two central figures of the Schiller play. It is probably unfair in the circumstances to single out individual performances, but the company as a whole shows to greater advantage in the nineteenth-century work. A special note of praise is nevertheless due for Tanya Berezin as Queen Elizabeth, particularly in the moments of her steely calculations, dark resentments and self-determined and regal loneliness.

—*NAT*, 19 Jan. '80

BETRAYAL

Though completely lucid in narrative line, Harold Pinter's *Betrayal* remains a puzzling play (Trafalgar Theatre). Spare in writing, succinct in statement, it hides as much as it reveals. It calls for a do-it-yourself interpretation.

We meet Jerry and Emma in a London pub in 1977, sometime after their affair has ended. They are coolly cordial, slightly benumbed by their present indifference to the heat of their former relationship. On Jerry's part, however, there is still a twitch of jealously in his suspicion that Emma is now engaged in a liaison with a writer (whom we never see) named Casey, though Jerry himself has several such adventures.

From this scene we go backward in time through eight others to the point of Jerry and Emma's embraces in 1968 where the play ends. The embrace occurs at a party where Jerry is the guest of his friend Robert. Robert and Jerry are publishers. Jerry himself, a married man and father of two children, was Robert's best man at Robert's wedding to Emma. Robert and Emma are also the parents of two children.

The Emma and Jerry affair consists of assignations in a rented flat in an unfashionable section of London. When Emma begins to tire of the duplicity involved in her illicit relationship, she tells her husband Robert that Jerry is her lover. Robert is shocked but admits that he has been aware of the fact for a long time.

The revelation causes no break between the two men. Indeed, when Emma confesses her relationship with Jerry, Robert wonders whether he doesn't like Jerry more than he does her, and somewhat banteringly says that perhaps he should have married him. Emma feels, despite Jerry's assurance to the contrary, that their connection was only a matter of lovemaking (she uses a cruder word), and since Jerry will not abandon his wife and children, their connection winds down. After the dissolution of the triangle, Emma decides to leave Robert, who has also been unfaithful; as we have learned in the play's first scene, she is now Casey's mistress.

Pinter does many things with this plot structure. On the simplest level he indulges in tight-lipped irony about English upper-middle-class manners—for instance, in the routine banality of exchanges apropos the playing of squash and the publishing of books. But the absurdities of such palaver, Pinter implies, are a cover-up for rarely expressed emotions. How genuine or profound these emotions may be is hard to say. They may have withered for lack of manifestation: correct social ritual has replaced reality of feeling.

Everyone betrays the other or betrays him or herself. But since there appears to be so little love or passion here, we can hardly speak of betrayal. Or is their betrayal only the absence of true feeling? No one recalls his or her experience with any vividness. Memories fade and past events which we might assume momentous become as something merely dreamed or invented. Life itself becomes a bleak reverie without substance. If all is not vanity, still all vanishes in a haze. Is there no love? Is there no indelible experience? Is life itself a betrayal? We should remark in passing that the subject or object at issue here is a woman, the most neutralized and thus most betrayed creature of all, as are the two wives who never visibly enter the picture.

Is *Betrayal* a paradigm of the spiritual state of contemporary society or has it a much wider reference? Most of what I have suggested here is never declared. Pinter's medium is ambiguity. He diagrammatically traces a pattern of happenings which are shrouded in a veil of questions, questions he refuses to answer because he is not sure that he is in possession of an answer or even that there is one. Hovering over the pleasantries of the play—which is amusing betimes—there is a kind of horror, the horror and perhaps pathos of emptiness, of nullity.

In this respect, *Betrayal* is part of the overall

Pinter creation. In craftsmanship there is great and meticulousness skill, but in this case the method has become on the whole self-defeating. We are not as mystified as we may have been with *The Birthday Party*, *The Caretaker* or *The Homecoming*, but the new play does not impinge as much on our imagination or senses; it will not haunt us as the others have.

If anything, we understand *Betrayal* too readily and even if we believe in what it seems to imply we remain indifferent to it, for we cannot penetrate to the heart of its shadows. For all the concreteness of its specific environment, all has been rendered fleshless and abstract. And yet it is, after all, more interesting than any of the new plays presented this season!

There are several respects in which the New York production of *Betrayal*, staged by its original director, Peter Hall, differs from the one at the British National Theatre. The London cast was, naturally, more authentic and at ease in the play. The Americans evince more personal feeling. Thus, while Roy Scheider as Robert is constrained (through direction) to be as English as possible, his scene at lunch with Jerry, after he has been told that Jerry is his wife's lover, has a hurt and bitterness that brings dramatic vivacity and poignancy to the moment which was absent when I saw the play in London. Raul Julia brings the sauce and charm of his Latinity to the role of Jerry, extraordinary in the circumstances but helpful to our enjoyment. Blythe Danner in the rather unrewarding role of Emma is remarkably right in the confession scene where her inner resentment of the long deception gives way to relief during her calm self-exposure.

The one unmistakable triumph of the evening is John Bury's set. It is the visual equivalent of the play's style with its blank abbreviation of realistic elements, including the scaling down of the scene in the pub to a miniature bar and one table.

—*NAT*, 26 Jan. '80

WHAT WAS BROADWAY'S ALL-TIME BEST SEASON?

Critics and historians agree: the 1920's marked the coming-of-age of the American theatre. I am hard put to select the "best" of those bygone seasons. To set down anything as best may be a pleasant pastime, but it is often misleading. Still, as veteran playgoer the present writer is prepared, in a sportive spirit, to rise to the challenge. A reasonable choice would be the 1919-1920 season, for it was on Feb. 2, 1920, that Eugene O'Neill's first full-length play, *Beyond the Horizon*, opened at the Morosco Theatre. I was present at that historic occasion.

I might just as readily award the honor to the season of 1927-1928, not only for the high quality of its offering but because a record number of plays—264—were then produced. In this connection, it is worth mentioning that at the time there was no such designation as "off Broadway." The Greenwich Village Theater on Sheridan Square and the Provincetown Playhouse on Macdougal Street were considered integral with the overall theatrical scene. It was simply that we expected to see the more adventurous or "experimental" things in the presumably less accessible parts of town.

Arbitrarily, or perhaps only subjectively motivated (I entered the profession then), my choice of a favorite Broadway season goes to that of 1924-1925. For the purposes of this "history" I shall concentrate on it with cross-references to others as a conspectus of the entire decade.

Here, then, is a reduced list of what, for me, were some of the main events. Among the 228 shows presented were O'Neill's *Desire Under the Elms*, with the still little-known Walter Huston; Sidney Howard's *They Knew What They Wanted*, with Pauline Lord; Maxwell Anderson's and Laurence Stalling's *What Price Glory?*; *The Youngest* by Philip Barry, and George S. Kaufman's and Marc Connelly's *Beggar on Horseback*.

Alfred Lunt and Lynn Fontanne, in their second time on Broadway together, appeared in Molnar's *The Guardsman*. (Lunt had attracted Broadway's special attention in 1919 in Booth Tarkington's *Clarence*.) Among the musicals, the Rodgers and Hart collaboration came into focus with the *Garrick Gaieties*, Fred and Adele Astaire graced *Lady, Be Good* by George and Ira Gershwin, and Cole Porter contributed to the *Greenwich Village Follies*.

There were other wonders that shining season of 1924-1925, such as the first production of O'Neill's one-act sea-plays collected under the title *S.S. Glencairn*. Jeanne Engels' luster shone on in *Rain*. And the charismatic Katharine Cornell lent a particular aura to Shaw's *Candida*. For my own special delectation, I also recall John Howard Lawson's *Processional*, a "jazz symphony" or semi-Expressionist play about labor troubles and the Ku Klux Klan, which annoyed some and exhilarated others. George Abbott played the leading role.

No bare listing of ancient miracles can suffice to give the present-day theater-goer a sense of what was new and fresh on our stage in the 20's. Today such a play as *Beyond the Horizon* might be held too gloomy for most commercial managements. Even in 1920, its producer hesitated a long while before he risked putting it on. American plays with unhappy endings were virtually anathema on Broadway before the 20's.

What is peculiar in all this is that while the decade, as mentioned, was one of exuberant optimism, the reaction to *Beyond the Horizon*, in which all the characters come to a sorry end, was one of elation. The play "humanized" us. We were learning to confront tragedy in the theatre and to give sober thought to our own life experience. We were growing up: reality was at last permitted free entry onto our stage.

O'Neill's *Desire Under the Elms* made us look to our national past with new eyes. Certain city officials dubbed it "obscene" and tried to ban it. Others made too much of its Freudian insights. But at its very core were the contrast and conflict of a pre-Civil War generation that had grown tough in the building of the country and the generations that followed, bent on amassing ever greater profit and power from their inheritance only to discover—too late—the blessing of love. Thus the possessors became dispossessed. This was a theme which O'Neill was to develop much more fully in his later work.

What Price Glory? which, as a war play, seems mild stuff today, was important in 1924 because it had a vernacular raciness, a gusto in characterization at a time when American soldiers were always depicted antiseptically as emblems of honor and virtue rather than as they actually behaved amid the muck, horror and chaos of combat.

They Knew What They Wanted dramatized the ruefully honest treatment of compromise we are all constrained to make with the facts of life, in contrast to the evasions that characterized the all but obligatory "happy endings" of Broadway plays before the 20's. Similarly, I mention Philip Barry's early play *The Youngest* because it was one of the first examples of comedy in which good manners, sophisticated speech and serious purpose in social or psychological interpretation was introduced to our theatre. S.N. Behrman, in his *The Second Man* of 1927, a comedy of the same nature, also added much to the gaiety and intelligence of our stage.

Beggar on Horseback by Kaufman and Connelly was an exceptional item in the work of that team, for while it had its source in a German play, it toyed with and teased America's worship of fame and fortune which reached its peak during the Harding-Coolidge administrations. It was characteristic of the day that this potentially satiric material was sweetened by fantasy, injected with music and pantomime and aimed above all to be funny rather than biting. The "bite" that was first felt in the novels of the period—Sinclair Lewis's *Babbitt* and Dreiser's *An American Tragedy*, among others—marked such plays as O'Neill's *Marco Millions*. It was to turn angrier and rebel-

lious after the 1929 Wall Street crash, which put an end to the "fun." A melancholy neon replaced the sparkle of electricity.

Literary merit alone does not encompass the theatre's pleasure. The 20's were also the time our most prestigious actors still were to be seen on the stage. To name only a few: there were Ethel, Lionel and John Barrymore, Laurette Taylor, Pauline Lord, Eva Le Gallienne, Ina Claire, Alfred Lunt, Lynn Fontanne, Noel Coward, Barbara Stanwyck, Walter Huston, Clark Gable, James Cagney, Spencer Tracy, Edward G. Robinson and Paul Muni. Then there were the many stars who made our musicals such joyous occasions: Eddie Cantor, W.C. Fields, Fanny Brice, Will Rogers, Marilyn Miller, Bob Hope, the Marx Brothers, Gertrude Lawrence, Beatrice Lillie.

John Barrymore and Lionel, too, were actors of grand style, eloquence and—John especially— passionate poetic power. An extreme sensibility, verging on the neurotic, coupled with unmistakable virility, beauty of person and thrilling vocal endowment made John Barrymore (who before 1916 had been chiefly thought as gentleman comedian) the supreme figure among our players.

Lionel Barrymore, before he began to parody himself in films, possessed a grandeur and a dramatic thrust unequaled among his peers. Those who in 1919 saw John and Lionel in *The Jest* will never forget the occasion. John's *Richard III* in 1920 (with settings by that pristine pioneer of stage designers Robert Edmond Jones) was one of the truly signal events in American theatre annals. Ethel Barrymore in *Déclassée* in 1919 (she played a good many other plays in the next 10 years) was regal beyond the dream of most royal families, with a fund of inescapable womanly dignity, emotion and command.

Two among the women who most profoundly moved me were Laurette Taylor and Pauline Lord. Miss Taylor is best remembered nowadays for her Amanda in *The Glass Menagerie*, but long before that she had risen to heights of histrionic achievement in a whole series of charming tidbits beginning with *Peg O' My Heart* in 1912. She possessed a wistful as well as a gay humor and a quality of staunchness within vulnerability, a tenderness and a hurt that were rarely expressed in tearfulness but lay buried in her bosom as if they had to be kept secret.

Pauline Lord lifted *They Knew What They Wanted* to the realm of art. Those who have seen this play only as a film or as a musical (*The Most Happy Fella*) can hardly imagine the sense of battered womanhood with which this extraordinary actress imbued her role. There was a shyness within sexual susceptibility in her Amy, and nobody ever portrayed fear at the threat of a gun with so original and truthful a flutter of gesture, startled eye and pallor of feature.

I first saw Lynn Fontanne in 1917 in a "recruiting" play called *Out There* in which Laurette Taylor starred. Miss Fontanne was then already an accomplished comedienne and, in my view, comedy always remained her forte. By the time she appeared in *The Guardsman* she had become a technician of superb presence fortified by immense will and the ambition to achieve mastery in every phase of her profession. No one on our stage had greater proficiency in feminine makeup and no one aimed at greater versatility.

The outstanding actor of the post-Barrymore generation was Alfred Lunt. He was all fluid feeling, intuitive understanding, a certain softness together with quirky humor. He had a light touch but was never superficial or given to mere drawing-room glibness. The span between his comedy performance in *The Guardsman* and the agony he conveyed in *The Visit* describes the breadth of his talent.

When Walter Huston appeared as Ephraim Cabot in *Desire Under the Elms* he was a much younger man than the role called for. There was an intensity of concentration, an unwavering grip which might almost serve as a model for the American Puritan character—a quality which in its more gentlemanly aspect informed his acting in *Dodsworth* and in *Knickerbocker Holiday*. I saw *Desire Under the Elms* three times and his Cabot took on added stature and inner dimension at each performance.

To be especially remarked from these bare sketches of the actors remembered from the 20's is that none of them were "types" as we commonly use the term today. Laurette Taylor was a waif in one play and a grand lady in another. John Barrymore was a weakling in *The Jest* and the maniacal monster of *Richard III*. Lionel was the fighting bully in *The Jest* and the long-suffering Union man hunted as a Confederate spy in *The Copperhead* in 1918. Ethel Barrymore in 1923 played a German peasant girl in Hauptmann's *Rose Bernd* and in 1928 a Spanish nun in *The Kingdom of God* by Martinez Sierra.

The same might be true of the young actors who were prominent in the 30's, 40' and 50's, but a great number of them, because of the shrinkage of production in those years, took themselves to Hollywood, where, with few exceptions, they were obliged to repeat themselves by playing what appeared to be a single part over and over again. It is possible there is no less talent today than in the past, but there are fewer opportunities for growth. O'Neill may have exaggerated, but there is much to ponder in his observation that, while the actors of his father's generation could act the great works of dramatic literature though they did not understand them, the latter-day actors understood them better but could not act them!

These reminiscences, however, are not intended as an exercise in nostalgia with "read 'em and weep" overtones. True despite the recent rise in theatre attendance the count of new productions during the 1977-78 Broadway season came to hardly more than 42, but this does not tell the whole story of the present state of American stage. The public interest in "live theatre" has not diminished to any great extent. The proliferation of "regional" theatres around the country, the ever-increasing establishment of off-off Broadway organizations in New York, indicate a continuing eagerness for dramatic art, as do the hundreds of university theatres, along with college courses in theatre and the plethora of private instruction in acting, directing, etc.

Stringent economic conditions are largely responsible for Broadway's anemia. It requires no special perspicacity to observe that the shows which nowadays reach the "main stem" are (a) musicals, (b) London hits and (c) Neil Simon's output. Most of the notable Broadway productions of the 1970's were first presented in regional theatres or in off and off-off Broadway theatres. Broadway by itself can no longer be deemed the heart of the American theatre, although it still is the lodestar or the point of aspiration for most theatre folk.

Material circumstances have esthetic consequences. Talented young actors—and there are still many—have shifted over to films or TV. Many of our most heralded stage actors at present are still, relatively speaking, neophytes or shooting stars: here today and gone tomorrow. Our playwrights since Edward Albee's emergence are of a different disposition than those who were highly esteemed in the 20's. They are, in too many instances, permanently "promising."

This is not solely a matter of natural gifts. The earlier playwrights still felt themselves at home in a society of more or less stable values, and if their plays reflect a growing distrust of these values, it was in their name that they protested. Our new playwrights have come to be uncertain, impatient or despairing of traditional attitudes and as much as possible eschew established techniques. Convictions, if they exist, are nearly always obliquely disclosed. One must guess at them. They manifest doubts as to the future—their own and the world's. They stand on shifting ground.

They have no time! This induces a hastiness in composition. There is too often a lack of careful craftsmanship. There is more lunging for novelty than penetration or substance. They proceed from clever or even brilliant notions which rarely eventuate in sustained development. Their plays give the impression of sketches, elongated one-acters. A burst of originality alone is taken for accomplishment. Yet the existence of creative ore is frequently perceptible.

The general level of acting today is, I repeat, reassuring, though few actors attain the heights. In earlier generations the leading figures were giants in individuality or in skill, but the teamwork, the ensemble playing, was not as consistent as it is now. There are some who maintain that the mechanically conformist efficiency of contemporary civilization whittles most of us down to standard size and is not conducive to the formation of "big people"—or of towering actors.

Our actors now receive better instruction; actors of former days benefited from more practice, not only on Broadway but on road tours and in stock companies. Still, there can be no doubt that the majority of our younger actors are serious about their work. The trouble is that they do not find enough. The increase of new channels—in regional and university theatres, studios and Off Broadway institutions—augurs well for renewed vigor.

The theatre dies from time to time, but never expires. In one shape or another it always revives and regains its health. The theatre's vitality springs not from trade but from nature; it lies deep in human need. Bland, unvarying, automatic optimism, however, is deleterious to its progress, as is the expectation of and insistence upon a continuous stream of great hits and deathless masterpieces. The theatre requires generous nurture, an unwavering attention—true love—to help it bloom.

—*NYT*, 9 Mar. '80

MAJOR BARBARA

I was not a good critic in 1921! Like many others, I held than that Bernard Shaw was more pamphleteer than dramatist, that his characters were his mouthpieces, that his plays were closer to journalism than to art. I should have asked myself how many plays written in English during Shaw's years as a dramatist (1893-1950) which aspire to the distinction of art (or entertainment) would endure as long as his "journalism."

Shaw insisted that his plays were indeed journalism and that he had slight regard for any play that was not "journalistic," that is, something that did not relate to its time and place. For all works of art, no matter how abstract, are to some degree an expression of immediate living experience and products of their times, just as they are all—whether landscape painting or pure music—autobiographical.

I have come to recognize, as Eric Bentley has taken pains to demonstrate, that Shaw as playwright was primarily an artist. Seeing *Major Barbara* (Circle in the Square Theatre), one of his most forensic plays, has once again impressed me with Shaw's artistic vitality. It is witty, wise and, above all, packed with an enormous theatrical energy that springs from his joy in life.

His craftsmanship is superb. The opening scene is a masterpiece of exposition. The background and argument of the plays are set forth with utmost dispatch while it bubbles with sparkling good humor and rapid strokes of comic characterization.

For all the frequency of long speeches (they are like arias), Shaw's dialogue dances with the verve of Molière or of most Italian comedy with all its merry pranks. There is an inspired and irrepressible clown in Shaw, as shrewd as he is bright. The verbal plenitude not only makes for eloquence but also adds a bounce and fleetness that sweep us along in a happy swirl of jokes both pithy and provocative. We become spectators at a circus of the mind.

I cite some of the quips which lead directly to the play's major issues. When Andrew Undershaft, its miscreant protagonist, is asked his religion, he answers, "Well, my dear, I am a Millionaire. That is my religion." An impoverished workingman challenges Undershaft with "I wouldn't have your conscience, not for all your income," to which Undershaft retorts "I wouldn't have your income, for all your conscience." The big yak for our audience bursts forth when Undershaft, in an attempt to recommend a profession for his son, says, "He knows nothing and he thinks he knows everything.

That points clearly to a political career." A rather silly young man submits this: "The more destructive war becomes, the sooner it would be abolished, eh?" To which Undershaft replies, "The more destructive it becomes, the more fascinating we find it."

We should remember that *Major Barbara* was first produced in London in 1905, a year before the formation of the British Labor Party. It was the time when England was the richest country on earth, when the catch phrase "as solid as the Bank of England" was common among us, and England stood at the peak of world capitalism. That was the moment that Shaw chose to engage in theatre propaganda for socialism—his special brand of socialism. The play is in fact a most daring and adroit piece of propaganda: it might serve as a lesson in how to deal with such material. What made it palatable to the English audience then was that it was funny and tricky, theatrically as well as ideologically. Shaw is never pat or ponderous.

I call Undershaft a "miscreant." One of Shaw's "tricks" was to reverse the audiences' expectation in regard to his personae. The pagan Androcles (in *Androcles and the Lion*) is a gentle creature; the Christian is a belligerent. In *The Devil's Disciple* (about the American Revolution) the redcoat General Burgoyne is urbane, rather cynical about the British cause, almost a pacifist; the New England minister is militant.

In *Major Barbara*, Undershaft, the munitions man, points out that much valuable progress has been made through war, but still challenges the humanist, Cusins, to "make war on war." (Shaw at two crucial moments did.) Cusins, a charming Greek scholar, calls Undershaft "Machiavelli," though he joins Undershaft as prospective partner in the making of cannon and other instruments of war. Undershaft, who considers poverty the greatest of crimes because it is the source of most of civilization's blights, would abolish it. At the same time, Undershaft, as a capitalist, approves of the Salvation Army because it makes the poor docile.

That poverty is a crime is indeed the play's thesis, and for all its frothy clowning, it remains a play of revolutionary sentiment.

The triple-thinking Undershaft, great capitalist that he is, asserts "with a touch of brutality":

The government of your country! I am the government of your country....Do you suppose that you [his son] and half a dozen amateurs like you sitting in a row in that gabbleshop [Parliament] can govern Undershaft?...No, my friend, you will do what pays us. You will make war when it suits us, and keep peace when it doesn't. You will find out that trade requires certain measures when we have decided on those measures. When I want anything to keep my dividends up, you will discover that my want is a natural need. When other people want something to keep my dividends down, you will call out the police and military. And in return you shall have the support and applause of my newspapers....

And what a whopper this declaration by Undershaft must have been: "All religious organizations exist by selling themselves to the rich." Think too of the implications of Cusins's saying "Now the power that is made here (in the arms factory) can be wielded by all men."

The play is not conclusive. Nor does Shaw mean it to be. He has his stupid and even reactionary people say quite intelligent things. He knows that the tides of history or, more simply, the volatile, complex and often mad impulses of humankind produce unpredictable alterations of destiny. His dissent says "Yea" to the forces of life: he is a eupeptic puritan of fundamentally religious bent and, what is very rare in such personalities, a quizzical reveler in the world's comedy.

Stephen Porter, as director, has achieved one most commendable thing: he has made his amiable company speak loud and clear so that everything is as intelligible to the ear as it is to the eye. I might quibble about some of the acting and certain matters of style but I prefer for the sake of the whole to recommend that you see the play: you will seldom see anything so good on Broadway.

When in 1915 *Major Barbara* was first produced here, Shaw was asked if he believed it would prove a success. He replied, "The play certainly will; the question is whether the audience will be." I ask myself the same question.

—*NAT*, 22 Mar. '80

THE FUTURE OF THEATRE

The productions at the Brooklyn Academy of Music (BAM), whatever their individual merit, interest me less as subjects for review than as a new attempt to establish "a resident classical repertory company...a lasting and vigorous institution."

One of the first such efforts was the valiant but ill-conceived New Theatre, established in 1909 at the enormous new Century Theatre. It was situated on Central Park West and 63rd Street, at that time too far uptown for the average playgoer. Though many of its participants were distinguished theatre people, the project was doomed by the incongruity of its theatre's physical size, its location and the weakness of its repertory in relation to the climate of the period.

More viable was Eva Le Gallienne's Civic Repertory Theatre, established in 1926 on West 14th Street, where the company produced thirty-six plays for 1,581 performances at a top price of $1.50. The Wall Street crash of 1929 robbed the venture of its subsidy—and a subsidy, it should be emphasized, is indispensable at all times and everywhere for theatres that aim at continuity of production.

Le Gallienne's Repertory Theatre was not composed of a particularly brilliant roster of actors—though there were a few excellent ones among them—but its productions were intelligent and faithful to the literal intention of plays of Ibsen and Chekhov and other nineteenth-century

European playwrights—the mainstays of the repertory—and thus important at the time.

Without drawing up a complete list of the movements which made permanent theatre companies their goal, one must not fail to recall the pleasant Neighborhood Playhouse on Grand Street in the 1920s, supported by Irene and Aline Lewesohn.

Then, too, out of the early strivings of the Provincetown Players, which first introduced Eugene O'Neill, grew both the Macdougal Street Provincetown Playhouse and the Greenwich Village Theatre at Sheridan Square. They too sought to maintain a permanent company. But when O'Neill was taken up by the commercial managements there was little life or hope left for the Village pioneers.

The Theatre Guild was certainly the most successful and prestigious of the attempts to form a permanent theatre of distinction. It concentrated at first on challenging contemporary European plays, employing some of the best American actors—Lunt, Fontanne, Dudley Digges—and later, it produced a number of O'Neill's plays, such as *Strange Interlude* and *The Iceman Cometh*. The Guild virtually ended its career with *Oklahoma!*

The history of the Group Theatre is too well known to be repeated here. Perhaps its most remarkable achievement is that, without any subsidy at all, it maintained most of its company throughout its career and became in a very real sense the emblematic organization (apart from the Federal Theatre Project) of the 1930s.

The point of this sad sketch is that we must come to understand why our sincere efforts to establish a repertory company have ended, with hardly any exceptions, in disappointment. The reason is not simply an absence of such a tradition in our country. The fact is we still do not know what *theatre* is, how it comes into being, what it is meant to accomplish and consequently how it is to be generated.

A *theatre* is not a shop. It is not just a well-administered assortment of talented actors, directors and worthy scripts. A *theatre* is the projection of a spirit, a style, a technique embodying a specific cultural attitude, a social direction and meaning, a "face" which corresponds or responds to some deeply rooted hope, hunger, anxiety or preoccupation of a sizable part of the community within which it functions. Its very idea of craft, its methods and its manner of organization are calculated to voice its human aim.

The choice of a company is not a matter of collecting able performers but of educating and inspiring men and women of talent who possess a similar moral disposition. It takes time. This is especially true in such a heterogeneous civilization as ours. Unabashedly, I would declare that for a theatre to exist as such—rather than as a market for commodities or entertainment—it must partake to a considerable degree of the nature of a cult.

There are a good number of able and experienced actors in the BAM company. The plays chosen by its artistic director, David Jones, who comes to us from the Royal Shakespeare Theatre, contain parts which show the actors to advantage. Most of their performances are at the very least adequate and at times much better. But they rarely seem to be connected with one another: each appears to be giving a separate performance, as if they belonged to different worlds or to no world at all. There is no genuine style and the word "classic," as it has been applied to the BAM company, has no meaning—except that they perform Shakespeare.

Their *Winter's Tale*, a play I have thus far found, despite its occasional beauties, of little attraction or excitement, was scattered and "square." The second of the season's entries, *Johnny-on-a-Spot*, by Charles MacArthur, is a farcical sequel to the author's collaboration with Ben Hecht on *The Front Page*. *Johnny-on-a-Spot*, written in 1942, is about dirty tricks in the elections of a governor in an unnamed Southern state. Its contrivances and twists are so numerous and so complicated that they strain credulity and diminish their satiric value. Even farce demands some basis in reality. None of the acting was bad; I especially liked Jerome Dempsey as a zany medical officer who is made a reluctant candidate for governor. But there was little unifying rhythm or quality except for what our audiences most appreciate— speed.

Barbarians is for me the most interesting of the three opening productions of the season's program. (Rachel Crothers's *He and She* will come later.) *Barbarians* is not one of Gorky's best plays but everything Gorky wrote had an authenticity of character in which his understanding of place and people is unmistakable. Written in 1905, *Barbarians* is extremely loose in structure: a great number and variety of characters wander in and out of scenes and there is hardly any concentrated plot.

Yet such is the force of Gorky's bitterness and pungent humor that we cannot help but be arrested by the truthfulness of the picture and see in it something still relevant to our own day. The crazy vagaries of most of the characters, their heavy drinking, their failure of purpose and stamina (except among the young and potentially revolu-tionary), the overall brutality arising from a lack of moral and social aim, the latent idealism and the hankering for love are all still with us though in a different and disguised fashion. At the very least, Gorky's eye for the eccentricity of human behav-ior, for the madness which springs from an ideo-logical vacuity, creates a special picture of behavior that is peculiarly absorbing.

Despite the director's inability to achieve true artistic harmony from the actors, there are still a few sharply etched characterizations. Brian Murray, for example, is more convincing here as a woebegone, maritally crushed, deeply wounded minor official than in any of the straight roles I have seen him do. I liked the helter-skelter protest-ing energy of Christine Estabrook, material for the character's rebellious future. And Avril Gentles plays a lady of property with dignity and fortitude.

Though much in this report may sound nega-tive, I hope BAM's program is renewed next season. The present experience and more time for consideration of all its problems (including a better choice of plays to be produced) may lead to a clearer expression of artistic intent. For a theatre to grow, *continuity* of activity is indispensable.

—*NAT*, 17 May '80

Afterword

A Conversation With

Kenneth Tynan

A CONVERSATION WITH
KENNETH TYNAN

I came to New York in the fifties as an English critic. The newspapers used to send me there. He was a critic there and I was a critic and inevitably one met Harold. I met him in the critics' circle, first nights, and things like that. I also used to go to his classes. He had a very good acting class then. And I was immediately astonished! You see, I was brought up in a very gentile English theatrical tradition whereby no director ever raised his voice. The English directors would never do more than lift a warning finger. That's about all. When you wanted a director to raise his voice, you imported a continental director, a Russian director or a French director. I mean, to go to Harold's class...you would hear him a block away almost! An extraordinary combination of intricacies, allusions, howls of derision, howls of ecstasy, and anguish. This was really what I'd been taught to believe a director ought to behave like. But I'd never seen anything like it in my life.

Our best English theatre director, Peter Brook, has never been known to raise his voice above a whisper. He speaks very quietly and often will take an actor into a corner and talk to him for half an hour and that actor will come out of that corner with his life changed. But Harold's classes, I mean, they were more like revivalist meetings. And his voice would suddenly climb into falsetto regions as his temper rose or his excitement increased. I was hypnotized by it. And behind all this rhetoric and his exclamatory style, he was always cutting right through to the practical heart of the scene he was talking about. He was never the sort of director who would just vaguely exhort an actor to intensify an emotion. He was always precise to the exact concrete point of the scene.

I remember his working on an actor who was doing a monologue by Clifford Odets; it was about a man on his way to the subway. A middle-aged bourgeois who is intercepted by a beggar who wants to get money out of him. The well-to-do bourgeois is made to feel guiltier and guiltier and becomes more and more hysterical as this guy, this panhandler, begs. It's a pure play of the depression, about how this guy is made to feel suicidal because of his own guilt. He has the cash and the other guy's starving.

Now the actor playing the bourgeois was playing it in a very tragic way. As if he were being crucified. As if he were Joan of Arc, as it were, being burned at the stake. He got nobler and nobler in his anguish. And Harold began one of his tirades.

"Why the hell are you getting so worked up? What the hell are you trying to do? What's the subtext of this scene? What's your objective?"

And the guy said:"My objective is to tear my heart out and to bring out into the open all the economic guilts I've been feeling over these years."

And Harold said:"Right. Act economic guilt for me. Come on. Let's see some economic guilt. Come on."

The actor said:"Well, that's a little hard to act. It's too abstract."

Harold said:"Exactly. So that's not your objective. You can't have an abstract objective." And he finally refined it down. He said, "The reason you're getting so worked up is because it's raining and you want to get to the subway. Your objective is to *get to the subway* and this guy is stopping you! Everything else is irrelevant, or will not become relevant until you've got the main point."

And the actor, he was transformed. All the smoke screen was gone, all the waffle, all the self-deception. He knew now the basics of the scene. The essentials of the scene. Now that sounds oversimplified, but I was immediately impressed that Harold could cut through so much that was irrelevant and get to the spine of the scene. Quite often with devastating candor. Because he is a good critic as well as a director he would use phrases that would probably burn themselves into the actor's mind. And whenever he was rude to an actor, he would always turn it into a joke against himself. So that was how I first encountered him in action.

But I'd always admired him as critic since I'd read *The Fervent Years* which I still think is about the best study of the 20th century American theatre at one of its most important crises. That one book taught me more about the American theatre before I came to America than anything else.

Another thing about Harold which differentiated him really sharply from most of his contemporaries, both as critic and director, is that he wasn't parochial. Harold is an international man. He's a cosmopolitan man. Harold is probably more at home walking down a boulevard in Paris where he always wears his Legion of Honor, and a broad brimmed velour hat, and he has a little cane with a silver top. He looks exactly like a character out of a Feydeau play. Somebody out of *La Belle Époque*. Harold sauntering down the boulevard in the sunshine or having coffee at one of the cafes fits into the French scene perfectly. He's equally at home in Berlin or Moscow. And that in the American theatre of that period is very rare indeed.

There were very few American critics at that time—I think only Eric Bentley, who had an extensive knowledge of world theatre outside of Times Square. Even a man like Brooks Atkinson—so far as Brooks Atkinson was concerned, the theatre began at 41st Street and ended at 52nd Street. That was it. He was an excellent critic, but within geographical limits. Whereas Harold's horizons were always much much larger. If he were to compare your performance it would not only be with the show at the Music Box or at the Longacre or the Golden Theatre, he would be comparing it with a performance in London, one in Paris, Stockholm. And he also spoke more than one language. Very rare. Very rare in the American theatre.

American playwrights too tended at the time to be very in-growing and not to have many standards of comparison outside their own state. Playwrights like Arthur Miller and Tennessee Williams who were the best American playwrights of the fifties without any question, they were not men who had traveled outside their own country.

And even critics like Walter Kerr knew very little at first hand about the European theatre.

I think it's a great shame myself that Harold wasn't given the job of organizing a truly American National Theatre, at the time that he was at his prime as a director. He had the right background for it. The energy. And because of his directing work in the thirties and forties, he had the respect. I think if in the fifties there had been a really strong movement for an American National Theatre, as there was in England to establish an English National Theatre, Harold would have been the ideal man to run it. Not necessarily to do all the productions, but to be the planner, the chairman, the driving force, the philosopher behind it, as it were. Because later on when Lincoln Center went up, first they tried running it with Whitehead and Kazan and that didn't work out. Then it was Herb Blau and Jules Irving, and that didn't work out. I mean, if it had been launched in the fifties, the early fifties, Harold was just right for it. But unfortunately, the opportunity and the man just didn't coincide.

Harold's review of *A Streetcar Named Desire* I feel is a permanent classic of drama criticism. And perhaps only a director could have written it. At the time when everyone was raving about the play and the production as if they were inseparable, Harold could see a split in this production, and what was wrong was the genius of Marlon Brando. Harold said Brando makes this play but the character was meant to be an ape and representative of all the forces that drag humanity down. Yet, he plays it with such poetic charm that you find yourself on his side, hating the affectations of Blanche who is meant to represent everything that's civilized about human beings. I agree with that completely. Brando turned the whole emphasis around so that instead of being a plea for the preservation for people like Blanche DuBois, the play seemed to be saying they are useless butterflies. Crush them. Get them out of the way. Let only the fittest survive. And Brando was the fittest. In the play, and I also think it was true in the film, Brando gave a performance of such delicacy and sexiness and charm that he overbalanced the entire play. And only Harold saw that! Because only Harold could distinguish between the performance and the text. Now, to do that you have to probably be either a damn good critic or a man whose had a great deal of experience working with actors. Without question, I think that is probably his best single review.

You know, when you first meet him you think—this is Harold Clurman? This is *the* Harold Clurman? He's a charming man. He's a thoroughly charming guy. No doubt about that. He's a little like the great movie comic Hugh Herbert, you think! And then when he gets really carried away with an argument about a play, he's really an inspiring talker. When I sat in, he could really rouse an audience to the sort of enthusiasm, and as his voice goes higher and higher up the scale until it's sometimes audible only to bats and dogs, you go with him. He really takes off, in a sense.

Now he's got his limitations. I'd be hard put to describe them. At times he can't resist puncturing things, beating them over the head with a balloon. He tends to do this sometimes when he feels he's in the presence of something pretentious; he tends to deflate it rather crudely, but that's a fault on the right side.

But I don't think he's ever failed to recognize a new talent. Whether actor or playwright or director. And he's never made the mistake of overpraising a talent. He was not deceived by the charming but slight talent of a man like Christopher Fry. While many other critics were deceived into thinking that Christopher Fry was a sort of Shakespeare, or that T. S. Eliot's play was going to save the theatre. I can't think of many occasions when I've really hotly disagreed with him (laughs) which of course means that he must be right.

Yet Harold's a very good person to have a controversy with because he never gets malicious in an argument. He's totally without malice. I enjoy arguing with him! He's one of the very few people you can shout at and be quite sure that it will be water off a duck's back to them. Because he's one of the great shouters himself. And he's a world figure rather than a product of Broadway. That's what's so rare about him. And he's respected world-wide.

You know, there are so many American directors who, when you see them in the European theatre, look totally lost. As if it's a totally alien world.

I think I remember when I first saw him! He was walking down Fifth Avenue with Stella Adler. He was married to her at the time. The person I was with said,

"That's Harold Clurman and Stella Adler."

I said, "Nonsense. That's Mata Hari and Charlie Chan."

Another thing about Harold. He's never made a strict distinction between what you might call the "art" theatre and the so-called "popular" theatre. You could take Harold to a burlesque show and he would take his whole mind to it. He wouldn't regard it just as something to entertain you after dinner. He would regard it as a form of theatre with its own laws and he'd be trying to discover what those laws were. He would bring his whole sensibility to bear on it. When he went to write about it he would go about the job with the same passionate curiosity as he would a performance of Shakespeare at Stratford. He's never been a theatrical snob which a great many less talented men are.

You see, that's where he differs from the more academic critics like Bentley. They have this absolute criterion that anything that's a hit on Broadway must be bad. Harold has never been concerned whether or not there was a line outside the box office. When he goes to review a play, he's always going as if it's none of his business whether it's a hit or not. Whereas you feel that the other sort of academic critic goes to a hit with his lip already curled in contempt. Harold never goes to a play that way. Harold sneers less then any critic I've ever known.

When he dislikes you, he comes out fighting rather than knocking you or damning you with derision. He's not at all derisive. And you know a lot of directors get locked into actors of their own age and can't handle anybody young. Harold's very good with young people. Terrific with them.

I've often wondered at the time Atkinson retired, whether it wouldn't have been a better thing for the American theatre if Clurman had taken over. They would probably have insisted that he curtail his directing activities. I don't even know if he would have wanted the job, or if he was ever approached. But I do think that it's a pity somebody of his stature didn't take over the job then. A guy called Howard Taubman took over for a while and somebody called Stanley Kauffmann. Then Clive Barnes. But these are not men of weight in the theatre.

If he had been a German he would have been given control of the state theatre and he would have run it. He'd have formulated a policy when it was very young and would have guided that theatre's destiny for 20 years or so. In Europe where you don't have those pressures, where there is public subsidy, there's not that enormous competition from the film industry to take your actors away. You can build an ensemble, which you can't in England and you can't here because actors are doing TV and films. But in the fifties it was possible. And in the sixties.

It was always Harold's dream to build a permanent company. He could have done it marvelously. Now, I'm not saying it would always be an easy ride working with Harold. He's extremely volatile and mercurial and excitable and all those things. But he bears no grudges. He's very open-minded, open hearted, and certainly, I worked with Olivier who is also extremely volatile, much more turbulent and in many ways a more violent man than Harold Clurman. And if it were possible for him to work within the confines of a State Theatre, it certainly would have been possible for Harold. In a strange way, I felt the same way about Orson Welles in the thirties. They were very different completely! Believe me, I'm not comparing them. But, if there had been the possibility of a permanent State subsidized theatre in this country in the forties after the Federal Theatre project folded, Orson would have been the man to run it. But there was no such organization. So he became a free-lance vagrant really which he's remained ever since. Eventually, if you have no permanent power base *like* a nationally subsidized theatre, you become a laborer and let yourself be hired out to whomever will pay the price. For most serious talents, this is not a good thing.

He is the kind of guy you wouldn't only go to for advice on acting problems. If you're going to run a theatre, you've got to be the sort of person that if your marriage is breaking up or if you want to maybe get a loan, you can go and talk to him. You'd go to him. It has to be someone who you don't only bring your artistic but also your personal problems to. And Harold would have been very good at that. Olivier was too. He had that father quality at the National Theatre during the sixties. You've got to have that.

He was enormously hospitable and helpful. He'd introduce you to people. Give advice on when to see him and when to avoid him. And one knew that his standards were not alien to him because he was an internationally cultured man. The American Theatre is in its popular sense, the creation of Jewish talent. Harold had that. A very strongly Jewish strain. Plus a very strongly international, European "Man of the Theatre" strain. He was a little of both. That was almost a unique combination in the thirties and forties in this country.

The English theatre has always had a discretely veiled anti-Semitism about it. There have never been any great, serious actors who were Jewish in the English theatre. Now nobody in the

English theatre will admit this, but Jewish talent has always gone to...there's a ghetto for it, and that is where Jewish talent belongs. There have never been any great classic actors who were Jewish people. No open anti-Semitism, but if you were Jewish, you would just never get asked to play. So we never had that...that juice of Jewish talent. The sheer exuberance of it. That's why we've never really had a musical theatre. And *that's* what I found in Harold that I didn't find in any English director, or anybody in the English theatre, for that matter.

As soon as you say that, that something's Jewish, it sounds like a racist remark. I would mean it to be that, but in the best sense that there is something about the combination of exuberance and cynicism, of worldly wisdom and childish enthusiasm, that you find in a person like Zero Mostel. And you also find it in Harold Clurman. So when Harold visited Europe, it was like a blood transfusion, really. I found the same was clearly true in Germany after the War for obvious reasons because there were no Jews working. And the French theatre. So it was like a blood transfusion because his reactions to plays were always that much more intense, excitable, volatile. Harold would always rather write a passionate paragraph than an elegant one, you know. It tends to be the opposite in England and Europe.

Boris Aronson is one of his greatest friends too. Going all the way back to The Group. One of his favorite stories is about Aronson. I'm sure this is in one of his books. He's applied it to quite a few plays that he's reviewed. It's about how he went to a play by Odets with Aronson.

"What do you think of it?"

Aronson said, "It's interesting. It's kind of foggy."

After the second act, he asked Boris, "How do you like it now?"

And Aronson said, "Not so good. It's clearing up."

He's written very well about Olivier; he has many reservations. He writes almost a sort of diagnostic, a doctor's report more or less year by year. Like a fever chart. I think he finds Olivier can do anything except make him cry. And to Harold, this is very important. To be able to move him. He claims he has never really been moved by the man. I have. Maybe this is because I belong to an English tradition and by contrast to the English tradition, Olivier is a volcano. By contrast, maybe, with the kind of Jewish actors Harold is talking about on Second Avenue, Olivier might seem like a drawing room, tea drinking sort of actor. But it's perfectly true; that sense of grandeur and that sense of the theatre being a world-wide evolving tradition is again something that is virtually unique in the American theatre. You don't get much of that.

I saw very few of his productions because I, as a critic, would come to the States for about a month every year. Unless one of his shows happened to be on, then I'd miss them. I did see *The Flowering Peach*, an Odets play about Noah, which he directed very well indeed. But I didn't see any of the things that he was famous for because I didn't become a critic until the fifties and most of his best known work had already happened by then. So it was really through his classes that I got the flavor of the man in action. He respected Strasberg, but he always felt that Strasberg concentrated on the wrong Stanislavsky. I mean, he always felt that Strasberg had invented a Stanislavsky of his own, that the real Stanislavsky would not have made. Harold was always trying to rectify the balance by pointing out that the real Stanislavsky was just as concerned with the artifice and with the musical theatre and with the formal aspects of the theatre as he was concerned with affective memory and the subtext. Not only what went on beneath the surface but with the surface itself. That was *very* valuable at a time when everybody was looking to Strasberg as the ultimate authority. Harold, you see, was caught between two fires, so to speak. The Stanislavsky purists regarded him as a vulgarian who worked on Broadway, and the really popular Broadway directors regarded him as sort of an academic, sort of an intellectual. So on one side, the hit manufacturers regarded him as "that intellectual who writes for *The Nation*," whereas people like Bentley and the other critics regarded him as a "Broadway sell-out." He did direct one film that wasn't much of a success, but he never had Hollywood to fall back on, as it were, as people like Kazan did.

A most un-chic man, let us say. One word you'd never call Harold is fashionable. But, of all the directors working in the American theatre since I've been going to it, he was, although I say, I haven't seen many of his productions, I would certainly put him the top half-dozen, the top handful.

He mapped out the whole territory. Not only for me, but for a whole lot of Europeans. He said, "This is what American Theatre ought to be about, this is what to look for. This is what we're good at." And he could say it with authority because he knew what he could compare it to in other countries. And he is, as I say, an inspiration. Somebody to go to to have your vision of the theatre replenished. If you're losing faith, you can go talk to Harold.

—Kenneth Tynan's home in Santa Monica;
Summer, '77

REMINISCENSES

An Oral History

REMINISCENCES: AN ORAL HISTORY

This edited and abridged text is the result of tape-recorded interviews conducted by Louis Sheaffer for the Columbia University Oral History Research Office with Mr. Harold Clurman in New York City on May 25, September 11, September 19, and in Brooklyn Heights on September 24, 1979. The primary emphasis of Mr. Sheaffer's interviews was to explore areas of Clurman's life not fully discussed in his autobiography, All People Are Famous.

Q: Your father had some fairly serious, good books when he was in Russia. Did he read them in Russian?

Clurman: Yes, my father read them in Russian. His father, my grandfather—who was extremely orthodox, was very much opposed to his son's reading any books in Russian. He considered it a heathen language. As a matter of fact, once when he found him with a book in the Russian language, he threw it into the fire.

Q: Your grandfather was a fanatic.

Clurman: Yes, he was an extremely bigoted orthodox Jew. And my father was in rebellion. So he must have read those books on the sly.

Q: Of course your folks were quite poor. The grandparents were quite poor, weren't they?

Clurman: No they were not. They were quite well-off. My grandfather (whom I never met; I never saw any of my grandparents) was supported by the community, quite well supported by the community (and my father would have been, until the coming of the Bolsheviks); I suppose, because he was so learned in Hebrew law and religion that

he was considered brighter than the highest rabbi. In other words, he was an intellectual in that particular sphere.

Q: So your father was close to an intellectual Jewish—

Clurman: That's right. He was prompted by his curiousity, I suppose, to extend his learning and then was able to read these very serious books. He was a critic himself. He wrote the first review in Yiddish of *The Kreutzer Sonata* by Tolstoy; and when he was a young man he wrote in Yiddish about Mark Twain and many other literary subjects, and he wrote some dramatic criticism. Later he wrote a whole series of articles in a paper called *The Jewish Day* on popularizing medical information. So he was actually a writer. My father was a great influence on me because he brought me these very good books. He brought me Thomas Hardy when I was pretty young.

Q: You weren't as close to your mother as to your father.

Clurman: No, partly because my father paid much more attention to me than he had to any other sons because I was youngest. He was a doctor and he didn't have to struggle anymore to earn a living by the time I came along, so he could pay more attention to me. He spent a lot of time with me. He used to take me to his cases and let me drive the car when I was fourteen. Very often he took me upstairs to his office and had me sit and wait for him. I used to wander around his office even when he was dealing with patients.

My father read history; he read Marx; he read Schopenhauer—whereas my mother would read the good novels and all the things that would interest a woman of the time. I remember once telling her about Isadora Duncan's biography or autobiography, and she read that with great interest, too—so there was that.

In other words, she was capable of thought. She had curiosity, but she didn't have the opportunities to exercise it intellectually. As a matter of fact, she used to say—and I was very affected by that—that later in her life she hadn't appreciated the fact that she hadn't enough education; and if she had realized (it was like pre-woman's liberation) what she could have done with an education and how much cleverer she might have been than her husband (and in certain practical ways she might have been). He was a very impractical man and very timid in relationship with the big world. Not intellectually timid, but....

Q: You talk about his being timid. I've wondered. You've talked about you being very shy.

Clurman: I was.

Q: What do you think could have been the causes? You had a supportive, protective, loving father and mother. What do you think...?

Clurman: I have a feeling that one of the things that made me shy was that my parents didn't manifest tenderness to me overtly till quite late—but more especially, my parents quarreled a bit, quite a bit, and that scared me; horrified me. Since then I've read child psychologists who said it's a terrible mistake for parents to quarrel in front of their children. I know it had a terrible effect on me. I remember once lying in bed and hearing them quarrel—I must have been about eight or nine years old—and putting a pillow over my ears not to hear them.

And that, of course, is terrifying—and it took me a long time to get over it. I could be comfortable with a close friend like Aaron Copland, with him I could express myself fully. He himself, whenever he gets up to speak about me, always says the same thing over and over again. He says, "I can't understand what happened to Harold. Because how a shy boy could..." When we were in Paris, he knew French better than I did—he says I "would not speak and only let me speak. I don't know what happened." Well, of course, I know what happened, but yet with him I was always

fully articulate. But with the rest of the world, unless I knew a person very well, I would retreat.

One of the funniest stories I'm told about myself (I don't remember it—my brother told me)—that one day I was taken to be enrolled in a primary school, grade school. The principal said, "You're Dr. Clurman's little boy," and I said, "Yes," and she said, "You mustn't say yes," meaning I should have said, "Yes, ma'am." So I said, "No." I was very obedient. If I wasn't supposed to say "Yes," I said, "No."

Q: You talk about your early addiction to the theater. Your father took you to the theater at the age of six. But you don't say anything about going to the movies.

Clurman: I didn't go to the movies as frequently as the theater nor was I as avid about movies...even at that time. I went to see them. I remember Fatty Arbuckle, John Bunny; I remember Maurice Costello; I remember Wild...what is his name? Bronco Bill.

Q: He was Jewish.

Clurman: I didn't know that. It's very amusing. By the way, Douglas Fairbanks, Sr. was half Jewish. I didn't know that until the other day I read a book about Max Reinhardt.

I used to see movies. I saw Theda Bara. I went to see them. And I enjoyed them. I enjoyed the pretty women. But it never had the same fascination as the theater.

Q: You talk about putting on neighborhood shows when you moved to the Bronx from ages of about 12 to 16. What kind of plays were they?

Clurman: Oh, they were melodramas, sort of melodramas. I do remember writing a play, which I didn't act in or put on—I must have been about 17 at that time—which I read to my father. He liked it. It was a play about hypocrisy really. It was a one-act play about a small town where a man came in to a small town newspaper which was always advertising a drug that was supposed to be a cure-all but actually was deleterious to health. He wanted this exposed. And he tries to convince the editor to run his exposé—he's a chemist—and it finally comes out that the man who owns the paper is the man who also manufactures the medicine. The chemist is enraged and he says he's going to expose the paper and they tell him, "That's silly because we own the paper." But, they add, "However, we'll tell you what we're going to do. We'll give you a column you can write and employ you as a medical/pharmaceutical columnist." And he accepts. In other words, he sells out.

Q: It sounds like *An Enemy of the People*.

Clurman: Exactly. As I recognized years later, it was an unconscious plagiarism of *An Enemy of the People*. But it's interesting how that should have happened. It means that I read *An Enemy of the People* about the age of 16 or 17; and second, that the reason I could transform it as I did is that my father was a doctor, and he used to tell me that there are medicines that are no good. I remember one line of the play—because my father noticed it: "Even your sincerity is insincere." My father liked that because he also took a dim view of what was going on in the world, especially as he thought, in America. But after I got to be 18 or 19 I realized that was a plagiarism.

So I gave up the idea of writing plays. But I was reading books like Archer's *Playmaking* at that time. In other words, I was interested in the technique of playwriting. Up to the age of about 18, 19, I used to take plays by Pinero or Ibsen and study their structure, which stood me in good stead later on when I began to work in the theatre.

Q: You said you were hooked on the theatre from the age of six, the first time your father took you, and then you put on these plays from the ages of about 12 to 16. And then when you went to the Sorbonne you wrote your thesis on a theatrical subject. And yet it wasn't until the age of 23 that you decided to make the theatre your career. Which strikes me as a little bit...

Clurman: Yes, it is strange, but I explain it this way: that my feeling for theatre was an appetite. But I had never thought of anything in my life professionally. My father was basically a great idealist, and a very impractical man. He didn't know much about money; he didn't know much about Wall Street. He didn't know anything except literature and medicine, of course; so that talk about money was very rare in my house except for my older brothers, but I didn't join in the conversations.

Q: Yes, but you would think about your life's work.

Clurman: No, I didn't think about a life's work. My life's work was just to have fun, to be— to live. It was almost a shock when I told my mother once in Vienna when I was about 22 that "it's time for me to earn a living." She thought my saying such a thing was almost an impropriety.

Q: Well, that is so unusual among Jewish families.

Clurman: We were atypical in that respect. When people asked my father, "What is he going to be?" he'd say, "I think maybe a teacher." He was more or less right, because I've done a lot of teaching in my life even in the theatre. They never felt they had to urge me toward my career. When I got a job as an actor, they didn't say, "Well, how much can you make that way?" There was a basic confidence my father had that somehow or other I would eventually find my role, and eventually I would be what he would call "a nice, decent man."

Q: What gave you the idea to go to Paris?

Clurman: What gave me the idea? I really didn't like formal education at all. I was very poor in mathematics, and I was always getting in great trouble about it. And in most of the sciences I was very poor except for biology—I was good at that. The things I was good at were English, philosophy and history.

Then one day I saw a sign in one of the Columbia buildings that listed the University of Paris and other of the French universities. I was very interested in France because my father—like most people who were born in Russia and who had an intellectual education—looked to France as the great cultural center. So I said, "I'd like to go to Paris to study." And he said, "If that's what you want, you can go." It wasn't expensive. And there were these courses which cost almost nothing, and I matriculated there and I stayed there two years until I got a diploma. By the way, I don't know where that diploma is. It was lost. I very rarely accumulate stuff, you see.

Q: You roomed with Aaron Copland, so that helped expenses, too.

Clurman: Yes, that helped expenses, but you could live very cheaply, more cheaply than we did because we ate in not the best restaurants but at fairly good ones; we went to a lot of concerts. I got a great musical education that way. And we went to the theatre a lot. I took him to the theater; he took me to the concerts.

Q: You got a well-rounded...

Clurman: Yes. I learned a great deal about painting because we also knew painters. People used to say, "How can you review books about painting and even shows?" At one point when I was writing for a magazine called *Tomorrow*, I used to review all the arts: painting, music, the theatre and motion pictures. I made some discoveries before the regular art critics did, partly because of that early education in Paris. I owe more to Paris than just the things I learned in classes, which was mostly literature and history. I learned a great deal about the arts due to various people that I met.

Q: You admired Jacques Copeau very much I know, and you had quite a bit of contact with him.

Clurman: Yes. First of all, I used to go to see his productions, the full meaning of which (that is, historical and theatrical and technical meanings) didn't strike me at the time. Sometimes I thought his productions were a little too ascetic. But I really didn't appreciate exactly how they fit into the whole picture of French theatre. But he was impressive when he spoke; he read beautifully. He was highly admired among the avant-garde in Paris at the time because he was against the Boulevard theatre—the conventional theatre. He avoided the kind of ostentation or old-fashioned colorfulness of the regular stage.

Q: Would he be opposed to Sacha Guitry's work?

Clurman: Oh, yes, completely.

Q: Did you meet Sacha Guitry?

Clurman: No, I saw him in many plays. I saw his father whom I admired, but Copeau was against practically all the rest of the French theater. That was the time of rebellion against the theatre of Henri Bernstein and all those writers of the French theatre whom they brought to New York. Even Feydeau was not at that particular period as popular as he later became. Copeau was against the whole Boulevard theatre. He was originally the editor of the *Nouvelle Revue Française*, which was the prestigious magazine up to the war and part of the publishing house which published Gide and Proust.

He was an intellectual who became an actor, quite a good actor, a director associated with Jouvet and all those people who later broke away from him. He first came to the United States during the First World War and directed a season of French plays, a new French play every week at the Barrick theatre downtown. I didn't attend them—I was too young. He delivered a series of talks at the American Laboratory Theatre, where I had attended classes and a course in direction with Boleslavsky. I took a course in directing there. (That's where I first saw Stella Adler, whom I later married.) But Copeau was asked to give a series of talks and readings at the Lab—which I followed and then grew more and more impressed with.

One time he asked "Does anybody here know French?" and I said, "I do"—and I got up and translated for him. He understood English, but he couldn't easily translate what he had to say into English. At the same time I volunteered to help him translate some of his more abstruse ideas to the cast of the *Brothers Karamazov*, which he was directing at the Guild Theatre. And he availed himself of the opportunity. He liked me. He didn't know me in Paris. I knew him because I followed his classes and his courses, I followed his lectures particularly: wherever he was announced to appear I came to listen.

I had acted and been a stage manager for the Guild so they allowed me to attend his *Karamazov* rehearsals; and they also wanted somebody who knew something about him, and I volunteered to write a piece about him, which I think was published in the *New York Post*, he was shown the piece; and he must have liked it a lot because he exclaimed, "My God, this man knows what I'm all about. And he's followed my career", because I'd even read his dramatic criticism. So he was very pleased to have me sit with him. I sat with him: one day he turned to me and said to me, "Learn from my mistakes. Watch me and learn from my mistakes." That's how I learned. I couldn't discern many mistakes. But he said to me one time about Lunt: "He's a kid." (c'est un gosse, which is French for "He's a kid.")

Q: He said that about Lunt.

Clurman: Yes. The one actor in the company he thought was a real actor at that time was Dudley Digges (Copeau was mistaken about Lunt who was a wonderful actor; I don't think he thought he was

a bad actor, but he thought there was a certain immaturity about him he thought childlike, I suppose; I didn't ask him, "What do you mean he's a kid?" except there was a certain kind of innocence in Lunt very good for his acting). I don't think he understood Lunt as well as he might have. After all, Copeau only saw him in that one part. It wasn't a typical Lunt part.

I also saw Copeau play a trick on Lynn Fontanne, which I thought was amusing. He sat in the back of the house, and all of a sudden in rehearsal she started complaining about the pillow or mattress that she had to lie on in one scene, and she started complaining, and he decided he didn't want to call off the rehearsal on that account. He thought that the inconveniences that she was complaining about could be handled by the property man or the stage manager, but she seemed to not want to go on until they were fixed, and she started calling out "Monsieur Copeau..." He wouldn't answer. He pretended to be absent. She couldn't see him. He was way back in the rear of the orchestra floor, and I was sitting with him; and then I realized what he was doing. He was making himself seem absent so that she would continue and after a few more shouts, she did continue; That's exactly what he wanted her to do. So I learned about director's tricks with actors under certain circumstances.

Q: Nadia Boulanger—you met her?

Clurman: Oh, yes, I met her many many times.

Q: You met her through Copland.

Clurman: Yes. She always gave weekly teas and sometimes dinners. Since Aaron said he was living with a young man who was interested in the theatre and was intelligent and liked music too, she said, "Bring him around." And so I used to go to many of these teas and dinners and got to know her fairly well.

Q: Was she part Russian?

Clurman: She was half Russian. Her mother was Russian. She was a wonderful, large, you might say Czarist, or pre-Bolshevik lady—old-fashioned, the kind you might meet in Chekhov, very aristocratic and yet very plain and down-to-earth in speech.

I remember a big argument. I remember one thing I said about Chaliapin. I said, "You know, when Chaliapin sings, you don't think he's singing. You think it's just his natural speech." And she said, "Well, that's really singing."

Then I remember other arguments when I said that the theatre wasn't just a matter of the words of the play—and I still believe that. The theatre was something that you saw, and what you saw were actors, and therefore the artistic value of the whole might be greater through the actors than through the words, especially as most play are rather mediocre. Occasionally a great actor has made a work of art of something which if you read as literature is very trivial. Boulanger couldn't understand that. I almost shouted, but she still wasn't convinced.

The more I tried to convince her, the louder I shouted. And then Aaron Copland sort of broke it up by saying, "Well, you know, when he's convinced as all that, there must be something to it—but maybe he doesn't express himself well enough. She laughed. Today I think I could do a much better job of persuasion.

I also remember that she thought that Roy Harris would become a more famous composer in America than Copland. I think there was a little tinge of anti-Semitism in that. What was implied was that Jews very rarely accomplished the greatest things in the Arts. Aaron was talented, but he wasn't going to be great. Well, Harris was certainly very talented and a good composer (in fact, he went to study with Boulanger because Aaron recommend that he do so). I always remembered that as a sign that even with an enlightened woman of that kind there still might be a hangover of prejudice.

It wasn't a virulent kind of prejudice because she knew Aaron, and I remember her predicting that Aaron would be a success because he was very "diplomatic"—he never gave offense; he was very tactful—which was very perceptive on her part because Aaron is one of the most balanced persons I know; the most tactful, knowing exactly what to say to each person. He wouldn't yield to anything that he didn't want to do. He wouldn't declare anything he didn't mean. But he is never aggressive in any way, and he always knows exactly the right thing to say in the right circumstances. It has helped him not just as a composer but as a man of the world. The United States could send him abroad with full confidence that he would represent it well because he has an extraordinary sense of justness. He had it when he was young and he has it still. Boulanger recognized this immediately.

She never married, and one of the reasons possibly that she never married is that it is said there was a certain French pianist by the name of Pugno whom she was in love with. This was never corroborated, but I saw a picture of the gentleman, that pianist. She was young when he died and she determined never to marry at all. She clung to tradition very very strongly, although she was very open to new influences. Still she didn't like Schoenberg's music because he seemed to her part of a very Germanic tradition; and when certain Frenchmen like Leibowitz who was a conductor and composer and one of the first to preach the gospel of Schoenberg in France (he was a Polish Jew who had become a Frenchman)—when these people began to teach or preach the techniques of Schoenberg, she didn't approve. She thought the Schoenberg "school" was "unFrench". She was very nationalistic, yet she was always a great champion of Stravinsky.

Q: How did she feel about "The Six?"

Clurman: Oh, she was very friendly towards them. I heard a great many concerts of "The Six." I remember those very vividly. She was friendly toward them. Stravinsky always used to say when people came to study with him, "If you want to study music, anything I can teach you would be taught better by Boulanger." Of course, she had a great number, starting with Copland and Virgil Thomson, a great number of American students. She trained a whole generation of American composers; and I imagine that to this day she has many American students, although she's virtually blind now.

She always dressed in long dresses. She was very correct in everything. She didn't smoke. A very proper lady of an olden time. But she was a modernist in a musical sense. One day Aaron heard her give examples of interesting music from Moussorgsky's *Boris Godunov*, and Aaron thought that was unusual because at that time in France, Moussorgsky, was never considered a model for students to study.

Q: Did you meet Ezra Pound?

Clurman: I never actually met Ezra Pound, but I saw him a good deal and watched him because I knew his importance. He was tall, handsome, with a thick shock of red hair. And the two things I remember best relate to George Antheil. Pound was a great champion of this new, young composer. After the first great splash of Antheil's reputation in Paris, later on it turned out that most of his stuff though very musical was not all that original. But Pound chose to be his champion. At one concert there was a piece by George Antheil, being played, in which six to eight pianos were used—(to go Stravinsky, one better). And the audience began to laugh and hiss, and I remember Ezra Pound screaming, "Taisez-vous, imbeciles," which means, "Shut up, you dopes" or "imbeciles." That was very characteristic of his bravado.

Aaron Copland set one of Pound's early poems to music and I read a lot of his writing, at that time in the *Paris Tribune*. It had very good writers. Ford Maddox Ford used to write for it, and I used to read him all the time. Ford Maddox Ford said of Ezra Pound that his prose was a national

calamity. I was pleased by that. Later on and to this day I can't overcome my prejudice against Pound because of his anti-Semitism and his attitude during the war.

He was always around Sylvia Beach's bookshop where I also saw Joyce quite often. He sat there for hours. One of the things that most impressed me about Joyce was that he would sit for hours with his back toward the street so that the light wouldn't bother his eyes. He could sit for hours without saying a word. And when he spoke, he spoke in monosyllables.

I'll never forget when he asked Sylvia Beach, "Who's Ibanez?" Ibanez was the author of the *Four Horsemen of the Apocalypse*, which was made into a movie, and was a best seller in the United States. Everybody was reading it—I mean everybody who read best sellers—"Oh, he's a Spanish novelist," she said. "Any good?" he asked. And that was the end of the conversation. He never spoke much. I saw him once at the theatre laugh uproariously at a line from Shaw's *Androcles and the Lion*. The line in French (it probably exists in English, too, but it was being done in French) when Androcles addresses Caesar as, "Mr. Caesar, Mr. Caesar..." The actor, by the way, who played Caesar was the famous Michel Simon. To which Simon as Caesar responded, "Mr. Caesar, Mr. Caesar, you'll be calling me Jules next." This elicited an enormous laugh from Joyce.

I also saw him at night drinking at the Cafe Rotonde. He seemed to become much more animated at night. Aaron and I lived across the street. And I'd see Joyce sitting there drinking but even then he was generally silent. The French called him "the sad Jesus."

The first time I heard anything of *Ulysses* was in French in a translation which was being made of *Ulysses*. It was a reading of the Molly Bloom soliloquy. Joyce was there. Amid a very select group. The entrance fee was costly, but Aaron and I thought it worth attending the occasion to go, just as we thought it was worthwhile to buy *Ulysses* in its first edition. Joyce listened to the reading by the translator, Valéry Larbaud, but he listened with his back to the audience. He wanted to avoid the light or a recognition by the audience.

Q: When you came back to this country, the first job you got was with the Provincetown Players.

Clurman: Yes, in Stark Young's play.

Q: *The Saint*.

Clurman: Yes, and then years later on, I followed Stark Young as the theatre critic for *The New Republic*.

Q: How did you get the job with *The Saint*? This was as an extra, wasn't it?

Clurman: Yes, I was an extra. It is a funny story. I found it difficult to get a job in the theater. One day, I heard that the management of the Greenwich Village Theatre—McGowan, Jones and O'Neill—were looking for extras and a number of people volunteered. By the way, I think Donald Oenslager, the scenic designer, was among them. We were sitting in the house at the Greenwich Village Theatre, (which no longer exists) on Sheridan Square. He addressed the group of the people who had come to get jobs and said, "We're going to use a certain number of extras in this play. Now, how many people are willing to work for nothing?" And some people put their hands up. "How many people are willing to work for five dollars a week?" I put my hand up for five dollars a week, (I thought I at least ought to have a little money for a lunch or something, so I put my hand up.) "How many people will only work for ten dollars a week?" Later on I got a call, and when I got the job as an extra they gave me ten dollars a week instead of the five I asked for.

The play was a flop, but it was very useful to me. First of all, I observed Richard Boleslavsky's direction. Robert Edmond Jones was supposed to have directed the play, but apparently Stark Young didn't think he was quite good enough to direct at

the time, and they called in Boleslavsky. Boleslavsky I think had done something on Broadway, a musical or something. They called in Boleslavsky, and Boleslavsky directed the play. Leo Carillo was in the play, and so mas Maria Ouspenskaya. She may have recommended Boleslavsky. It was her first part in English. She had followed him to America and remained here with him . (He was Polish, by the way). She was in love with him all her life.

They started the American Laboratory Theatre. So it was at the rehearsal of *The Saint* where I met him for the first time, and I was much impressed with him. I was only there for those two weeks before they closed.

I did work again as a property man in the Provincetown Theatre. The McGowan-Jones-O'Neill management ran two theatres—the Greenwich Village Theatre and the Provincetown. They used the Provincetown for the small productions, and the Greenwich Village Theatre for the large productions. They weren't really large; they were still small—like *Desire Under the Elms* and all the others.

I was present for the first night of *Desire Under the Elms*, which in 1954 I directed on Broadway.

Anyhow I was a property man, a very bad property man. They were doing a thing called *Beyond* by Hasenclever, a German expressionist. Helen Gahagan was in it and Walter Abel; and they made me a property man. They paid me 50 cents an hour or so, and I was very poor at the job because I am very unmechanical, very awkward with my hands, inept at anything mechanical.

The most invaluable thing to me on that job was that I watched Robert Edmond Jones light a very small scene with only one prop on it, a couch in front of a cyclorama, and he stayed hours and hours and hours on it till four in the morning lighting this simple scene; and the difference between one shade of light or another was almost imperceptible, at least to me. There was a scrupulousness in his lighting which was deeply impressive to me.

Q: How was Jones personally?

Clurman: Very shy, very reticent. When we employed him in the Group Theatre to design Maxwell Anderson's *Night Over Taos*, I once said to him, "I think the set's beautiful." It was all white stucco, "But don't you think you ought to have more color there or contrast in the set. Everybody looked at me and as if to say, "How dare you?" I wasn't even the director. I was the director of the theatre, the Group; but I wasn't the director of the play. I think my years looking at paintings had helped me make a suggestion of that kind. It wasn't a criticism—it was a suggestion. And everybody stared and some whispered, "How dare you tell this great designer what he ought to put on the set?" And before I could start apologizing, he said (I don't know if he called me Mr. Clurman or Harold), "I think you're right. I know exactly what should be there." And he placed a very large crucifix at the center of the back wall. And I notice that in his book of collected sets, that picture with the great cross is there.

The second thing I noticed was that he was easily shocked by bad language. I'm sure that in the theatre he must have heard a certain amount of bad language—four-letter words, though they weren't as commonly used as they are today—and I once said in a fit of anger something about: "What is the stagehand doing back there?" He had been late in getting something done—I can't remember exactly what. "Is he masturbating?" Jones absolutely blanched. He almost fell off his seat with shock.

His own use of language always had something quasi-mystical about it. It had a kind of exalted tone and vocabulary which I found inappropriate to the people he was addressing and to specific things he wished to accomplish. It was very touching. When I said something to that effect in *The Fervent Years*—that he didn't speak to actors the way actors might understand (or that might effect them)—he thought I intended to mock him. I didn't at all...I had enormous admiration for him. Lee Strasberg once said during a rehearsal he was directing in the Group Theatre, "When Jones talks about the theatre, it sounds as if it was something in heaven. When Harold talks about the theatre, it sounds like bread." He meant that I am more earthy, more direct. In the theatre when you talk to actors, you have to make what you say pertinent to the way they live and the way they are.

Lee Strasberg and I were once looking for a job and we stopped in to see if we could get a job at the Greenwich Village Theatre and we heard Jones speaking to his cast after the first reading of *The Great God Brown* on the Greenwich Village Theatre stage; and we listened for a moment, so we didn't know exactly what he was referring to, but I was struck by the way he spoke: how the play unveiled itself clearly at moments and then a certain mist descended upon it and obscured it and it was like clouds, etc. I thought to myself: "Well, that's not very specific. That's a strange way of talking about a play." When you deal with actors you've got to tell them: "This is the kind of play it is, and this is the kind of way we'll do it." In other words, I would want to make it artistically and technically more concrete.

Arthur Miller once said that he heard me talk to a cast and while he didn't understand what I was saying to them, they understood and were mesmerized. But in Jones' case I was sure that the actors didn't understand nor would I have understood him except by way of—hyperbole.

The only times Jones was specific—and then he was very specific—was when he dealt with lights or fabrics, design. Composition or colors. Then he knew exactly what he wanted. But the minute had had to talk in more general terms about acting, which is not easily translatable into specifics, although there is a way of doing it, he became vague. So I never thought he was a great director.

Q: It was his religion.

Clurman: Oh, yes, theatre was his religion.

Q: It is yours, too, but...

Clurman: In a different way because I always say, "Art is my religion only insofar as it serves my greater religion, which is the respect for life, the respect for creation, the respect for human beings and for the totality of existence, which some people might call God."

Q: You worked for Jed Harris for a short time.

Clurman: Yes. It took a long time for me to get the job because they were holding out. Mr. Streger, who was Harris' casting director, kept on saying, "Come back next week. Come back next week."

Q: What were they casting for?

Clurman: A play called *Spread Eagle*, which was one of Harris' first flops. It was directed by George Abbott and it ran about ten weeks. It was about American oil interests in Mexico. And I don't remember the play very well except that I played a Mexican; and, by the way, I got the job by lying. I kept on coming back, and Streger got absolutely furious—but he also became impressed at my doggedness, which is one of my salient qualities. I remember the first one who noticed it was Copland. He said, "You're very dogged." "When you want something, nothing is going to stop you. You'll bang your head against a stone wall, but you'll get through somehow." This happened with my first job at the Guild, too—I kept on coming back and coming back. Well, anyhow I kept coming back to the Harris office so often that they were probably saying to Streger, "Well, why don't you send the man down for that part?"

Then it turned out to be a part all in Spanish and finally he said to me when I came in : "Do you speak Spanish?" I said, "Yes." But I did not speak a word of it. He sent me down and there I was and they put this script in my hand, with my lines in Spanish and along with the translation;

and I immediately realized I couldn't pronounce Spanish correctly. But I noticed a lot of Spaniards, Mexicans, Puerto Ricans around, so I ran up to one of them and said, "How do you say these words?" He pronounced them for me. I remember the first one in English was: "Maybe there'll be a war." And when I came on the stage I was able to pronounce it. Anyhow I couldn't tell whether it was well or badly pronounced.

One day all the people who were playing Spanish parts were asked to come to Harris' office, and I said to myself, "Here's where I get fired because all these Spanish-speaking people are here and I don't know Spanish. And Harris had Sophie Treadwell, the author of *Machinal,* with him; she had lived a long time in Mexico. He said, "I have Miss Treadwell here who knows all about Mexico and Mexicans, and she says you extras are not speaking as Mexicans do. "Again I thought, "Here's where I lose my job." He said, "start your lines." And we all spoke our lines. Then she said, "There's only one person who's saying them right," and she pointed at me. And I realized that what she was talking about was not the pronunciation of Spanish but the manner. That is, I had a timid manner—an intimidated manner—which she thought was typical of the illiterate Mexican, and she like my acting, whereas the others were Spanish-speaking but had no feeling for the stage whereas I had a feeling for the character and I knew something about drama.

But what I noticed about Jed Harris at the time was that his criticisms were excellent. George Abbott was the director, and he didn't like to have the producer (Harris) give critical orders. This was before he began to direct himself. But what I noticed about Jed Harris' remarks was that they were extraordinarily keen, very apt; and he was very talented. He still is, but he isn't active anymore in the theatre.

I had other experiences with him because later on when the Group Theatre was flourishing he kept trying to woo Odets away from the Group. Once, while he was rather mocking my production of one of Odets' plays, Odets put me on the other line. He said, "Get on the phone. Jed is trying to get me to give him my next play. Listen to what he's saying." Harris had no idea that I was listening. He said scornful things about me and the Group. But he didn't succeed in getting any of Odets' plays.

Many years after I had written a review of his *Uncle Vanya* for some magazine in which I made some slightly critical remarks about the production, he remembered it nearly verbatim. It was very characteristic of him. However, he liked my articles in the magazine called *Tomorrow*. I came to get a ticket one day for one of his shows, and he said, "Anybody who writes such intelligent articles when the play is selling out can have a free ticket any day." Incidentally, I was critical of that production, too. I think I was over-critical in those days, partly from lack of experience and partly because I expected every play and every production to be a master work.

Q: It was also to make a reputation, too, by being critical. Like Mary McCarthy, when she was a drama critic, was very tough.

Clurman: No, there's a difference. The difference is that Mary McCarthy expects and wants to review everything from the standpoint of the greatest things. She thinks that the greatest things are not only the greatest things of the theatre, but the greatest things ever written as literature. In other words, everything has to be on the level of Chekhov or of Ibsen or whomever she admires. And I was that way, too. When you actually are in the theatre for any length of time, you realize that that's going to be a very rare occasion. One has to balance oneself between the highest ideal and what you are likely to see. You become a little more lenient, a little more realistic.

Q: You get more of a perspective.

Clurman: Exactly. And I still have that quarrel with people like Brustein and Gilman who always are carping at playwrights like Arthur Miller because they aren't on the level of Ibsen, Strindberg, Pirandello and others of similar rank. I think that's nonsense. I think they have to ask them: "What are the possibilities in American theatre?"

In our theatre, Miller is a superior talent and one has to recognize it. He's important for our theatre and for the life of our country. When Piscator, the German director said something disparaging about *Awake and Sing!* He said, "We had that kind of play long ago in Germany." I said, "But right now you have Hitler and we have Roosevelt." We have a different history, and you have to think of the theater in terms of history, not of absolutes which you establish by your history."

Q: You didn't find Harris the tough bastard that some people did.

Clurman: He never had occasion to do that with me, at least not face to face. I was young; I was beginning...

Q: You were no threat to his dominance, no competition.

Clurman: No, but he would mistreat people like Thornton Wilder and refuse him royalties each week—not that he was going to cheat him but just to hold him back a little bit so as to make him plead or argue. As a matter of fact, he was rather sweet with Odets, but finally when Odets seemed to be succumbing to his charm—and he had a lot of charm, with women and with men, too; he said something to Odets which made Odets threaten to hit him.

Harris would do that with a lot of people and torture them. On the other hand, he could be charming and persuasive. He was very friendly with one of Jacob Adler's sons. He became a friend of the Adler family (he was a bright young man and they liked him). They revered Jacob Adler. (He wasn't just the father to his children—he was a king; he was God; he was a very imposing and handsome man, and all his children were in love with him, the boys and the girls, all were deeply in love with him, incestuously in love with him). Then one day Harris just to show that he wasn't going to be part of this worship put his foot up on the table in front of the old man. At which point one of the oldest Adler sons came over, took him by the scruff of the neck and threw him out, and he never was allowed back, he never was allowed back nor would they ever speak to him. He was always very down on the Adlers after that. And they remembered his saying to them: "By the time I'm 26 I'm going to be a millionaire." And by the time he was 26 he was a millionaire, and he once stopped the man who had thrown him out, (he was Jacob Adler's son and business manager) on the street. And all Harris said was: "You remember I told you I'd be a millionaire by 26? Well, I am." It was true. He had three plays on Broadway at the time. That was true. That was all he said. He never got to be friends with him again.

Then finally Harris lost all his money on the stock market, which began his decline. He couldn't take it. He was extraordinarily successful. He had *The Front Page, Broadway*, which was an excellent production. It was George Abbott who directed it. But I'm sure Harris had something to do with its success because he was a very talented theatre person. I think one of the things he introduced was a certain kind of jazzy rhythm into American direction that was partly Abbott but also had a lot to do with his own nervous 1920s temperament. He was enormously perceptive, enormously gifted in terms of memory. If he had a better character—just like a lot of people with talent—if he'd had a nicer character, been a more compassionate person, he'd have....

Q: But if he'd had that, he wouldn't have had this nervous...

Clurman: Perhaps that's true, perhaps it was a defect of his virtue, but it really did him in, because after a while no one wanted to deal with him. He was a kind of ugly character. Hecht wrote a book based on Jed Harris, and people said it was an anti-Semitic book because it was about Harris and he happened to be Jewish. The Big Bad Wolf, by the way, has the face of Jed Harris—that kind of perpetual, fascinating leer.

Q: Which Big Bad Wolf?

Clurman: Disney's Big Bad Wolf. That's Harris' face. I mean made into an animal. There are a number of people whose talent might flower into something more valuable than mere "talent" and be more respected if their character were better. There was venom in the man.

My original *Fervent Years* script, which has somehow been destroyed—I don't know how—was twice the length of what the book was in publication. It had much information. It was twice as long, but it was written during the war. It was published right after the war, but it was submitted during the last years of the war, and there was a need to cut down on paper and publishers limited the length of books. They said, "We can only use 125,000 words," and I sent them in. I wrote 250—and I sent in 190—, and they insisted that I cut it down to a specified number of words. It had been a much more complete work.

Q: You worked for John Golden.

Clurman: John Golden? Yes, I worked for John Golden. He didn't like me much as an actor; he thought I overacted terribly. He was strictly commercial in his tastes, but, you see, he was half Jewish and half Irish, which made him a perfect New Yorker and a good politician of the period, and there was a certain kind of Dutch uncle quality about him. That is to say, he had a certain kind of charitable benevolence. I think he was active in John Golden Prizes and so forth. He was personally a do gooder. Also, he had his own barber at the barber shop on 44th Street next to the St. James—the barber would go up every day and shave Mr. Golden and get paid a dollar. At that time a shave must have been a quarter, and Golden paid a dollar. He was very much of a gentleman, an old-fashioned gentleman, a glad-hander, but without hypocrisy I think.

Q: You just acted for him. Is that all?

Clurman: Yes, not in New York. He brought the play to New York with Paul Muni (he was then called Muni Weisenfreund), *Four Walls*, and in it were Lee Strasberg in the cast and I think Sanford Meisner. They were chosen to play in the New York production of *Four Walls*, but I was not because Golden felt I overacted. And the funny thing is that Strasberg and I played two criminals. One of them was a dope fiend—that was myself. I thought I had the right to overact a little bit if I was a dope fiend. And I remember one line which always broke us up, both of us. Strasberg had to say about me: "Louie has been hitting the pipe again." And that always broke us up because we were friends. It was in those days that we were thinking those thoughts which created the Group Theatre. But I played in Atlantic City in the tryout and I got to know Paul Muni very well.

Q: What was Muni like in those days? Very serious I'm sure.

Clurman: Muni? Very serious. He liked to tell funny stories. Temperamental, but...George Abbott would say to him very quietly, "Don't be temperamental with me—it doesn't work." Abbott directed *Four Walls*. The author's name was Dana Burnet.

Abbott always had great respect for me. Right from the beginning he seemed to think, "Well, this fellow is an intelligent man." He could tell that I had more education than the average actor, which I had. Abbott never raised his voice; I don't think he ever raised his voice in rehearsal, but he was very, very definite; and if he said something, he had that Yankee kind of...very strict control. I remember his saying, "Don't do that." But he didn't get angry when Muni threw a little fit. He said, "Don't do that. I won't take it." Almost as quietly as I'm

speaking now, but you knew that there was steel there, that he wouldn't tolerate any "temperament" because he didn't think any actor indispensable, and certainly at that time Muni was no star.

On the other hand, Abbott was very appreciative of fine work because I remember one day on the first reading of a new scene given to the cast to read and Muni read it beautifully Abbott said, "That's really very fine. I must say that's very fine. I've nothing to add." He was a very fair director, very fair to his co-workers.

Q: How did he get this famous Abbott tempo? What did that consist of?

Clurman: That period, the 20's, had a nervous tempo. That was the tone of the time. What he said about tempo, which made an impression on me was: "You don't get tempo, as a lot of people still think, by going fast. Tempo is a matter of contrast. And if you have something slower, then if another thing is a little faster, it seems very fast. Variety creates the feeling of tempo. He was a very knowledgeable director. I learned a great many things from him. For example, I remember during a scene about the East Side streets there was a line an actress who was playing a Jewish mother had to say, (*Four Walls* is about a Jewish gangster) and offstage music was playing—an off-stage handorgan was playing—"Ah, and the streets give off music." Abbott said, "Cut that line. We'll hear the music. It'll tell us its own story and make its own comment." Very perceptive, very astute. He had been an actor and in one play a very good actor. In *Processional*. That was a play by John Howard Lawson, one of the first experimental plays of the period—1925—which had a scene about the Ku Klux Klan in it. He was excellent in it. He played a miner. And he used a word which was then still explosive on stage, "Those Puritan sons of bitches." That word had only been used once before on the American stage, in O'Neill's...or "bastard" was used in O'Neill's *The Hairy Ape*, I think, and also "son of a bitch" was used in *What Price Glory?* It was said offstage. And then later on it was used with great effect in *The Front Page*, the last line of *The Front Page*: "The son of a bitch stole my watch."

I saw all those plays. About a year or two ago they had a little ceremony at the Morosco Theatre, because that was where *Beyond the Horizon* had its premiere. Anyhow I said "The only one here who was present at that first performance of *Beyond the Horizon* is myself." They were astonished, and I think a little incredulous. They didn't know my age.

Q: That was first performed in February, 1920.

Clurman: Yes. That's right. And they put a plaque in the theatre and they had me make a little speech in front of a building where he was supposed to have been born, but of course he was born a block away. What most impressed the Gelbs, was my making a three-minute speech which seemed to cover the essence of his contribution insofar as anybody could do so in three minutes. After the speech Barbara Gelb said, "What were you doing at the time?—that enabled you to come to a special matinee? And why did you come down to the special matinee? How old were you?" I said, "I was about nineteen." "What were you doing?" I said I was going to Columbia. "Why weren't you in class?" I said, "I cut the class to go."

Q: To see the first performance?

Clurman: Yes, the first performance ever. So I said, "I cut the class." She said, "Why did you do that?" I said, "Because even then I knew it was an important event."

Q: Had you seen any of his things at the Provincetown Theatre? *The Emperor Jones*....

Clurman: I think I saw that and *The Hairy Ape* later on Broadway. But what made me know that O'Neill was important—I don't have a distinct memory—is that I read his plays in *The Smart*

Set—*Ile* and some other plays. I immediately noticed that he was writing a different kind of a play and that already attracted me because, as I say, I was already an experienced playgoer at 19, since I began seeing plays at the age of six. And I remember Kenneth McGowan, who was then the critic of *The Globe*, said a little later: "The most important moment in the history of the American theatre is *Richard III* with John Barrymore." I told a friend of mine at Columbia: "I don't agree with that. I think the most important moment in the American theatre was the first performance of *Beyond the Horizon* because that was the first real attempt, successful attempt to write an American tragedy." It was the first tragedy written by an American, and representative of America. As a matter of fact, my book on O'Neill would be based on the idea that his plays are not simply a record of his own life and his own tortures, which is true enough, but are a response of an Irish Catholic of the first generation to the American scene and to the failure of America to live up to its ideals.

Q: How did you first get a job with the Guild? That's another case where you kept on persisting.

Clurman: Yes, I kept on persisting. Philip Loeb was the casting director. On meeting him I told him I had been with Copeau. I had studied with Copeau. But actually I had only listened to his lectures, which you couldn't call study, but it was a form of study. I went to all his lectures in Paris. I had seen his productions. Theresa Helburn was very interested because that was very prestigious. And I'd been at the Sorbonne, which meant that I had some education, and she wanted to give me the job as assistant stage manager on *The Guardsman*. Philip Loeb who acted in it and was the stage manager and the casting director, said, "No, I don't want to give him the job." She said, "Why not?" He said, "He's too shy. He trembles when he talks." In those days I was shy. "He can't utter words, and he'll irritate me." But I kept coming back and coming back. He said, "Come back two weeks later." He didn't dislike me. He just thought,

"Why is this boy so inordinately shy? That doesn't work in the theatre, when you're that shy." But I kept coming back and kept coming back and finally he was very impressed and so he accepted me—that was after *The Guardsman*—for a small part in *Caesar and Cleopatra*, in which Helen Hayes acted. And I opened the Guild Theatre in the sense that I was in the cast.

Q: How did you find H.H. at the time?

Clurman: She was very cute, charming. She wasn't very good in that part, but nobody else was because none got any real direction. She was very charming when she played in *Dear Brutus* with William Gillette, which I saw in 1917. (I have an extraordinary memory for performances—you know, way back. People say, "He must be lying. I don't know how he remembers that.") But I didn't have much contact with her. I was an extra and she was the leading lady. Later on I got to direct her in *A Touch of the Poet*. Later on I became the play reader at the Theatre Guild....

Q: We'll come to that. Lionel Atwill had quite an actor's ego, I understand.

Clurman: Yes, I remember him bawling out an actor for upstaging him. I remember the other actor upstaging him, but he was of the old school in which actors sometimes upstaged one another. So Atwell said, "Don't you upstage me". I don't think he was a pleasant character. For some reason Mr. Belasco, who introduced him to this country, I believe, gave him leading parts in plays like *Deburau* by Sacha Guitry. I can't remember—I think—yes, I first saw Atwell in the Ibsen season around 1918 with Nazimova, which Arthur Hopkins put on in the Plymouth Theatre. Atwell was in it. He was quite good playing foolish characters. He was very good as George Tesman and he was rather good as Helmer in *A Doll's House*, but I don't think he ever had star stature, but apparently Mr. Belasco did. He used him in several productions.

Q: What was your first meeting with the Lunts? On *Brothers Karamazov*?

Clurman: Actually the first meeting was earlier than that. I was in *Goat Song*. That was with Lunt. She wasn't in it. Clare Eames was in it. I was playing a poor peon. I was very dark—you know, black hair—and I was playing a poor peon, and Maximilian, who was played by Lunt, comes along; Maximilian, who is rather compassionate, sees this poor peon soldier in his army eating something very foul and he asks, "What are you eating, my good man?" "God knows," and the director said, "No, no, don't say, 'God knows,' say 'Who knows?'." The first two or three performances I said, "Who knows?" nothing happened. One evening Lunt bent over to me and asked, "What are you eating, my good man?" and I answered "God knows," and the whole audience burst out laughing and Lunt came close and winked as if to say, "Ah, pretty smart boy. He knows how to get a laugh."

But I had a lot of other little parts in *Goat Song*. One was as a scribe—I had to play a very old man, a scribe—so Lunt got to know me a little bit that way.

But I didn't get to know Lynn Fontanne, except superficially, until I assisted Copeau. Then she knew me as a boy who translated for him and also later on as the Guild play reader. I liked him better. She was rather a cold person compared to him. He was more outgoing. She couldn't bear anybody watching her. She was so aware of anybody outside the cast that I remember once when I was a play reader I had access to the balcony—it was dark in the balcony—and she suddenly turned around and said, "Please don't watch me," and she didn't even know who it was watching her. Whether it was a stranger or somebody working for the Guild. I immediately walked out. She was so aware of everything that was going on. They were constantly working together by themselves on every little movement of these scenes.

Q: You don't talk in your book, *All People Are Famous*, really personally about the Guild brass—about Langner, Helburn....

Clurman: Well, I have impressions of them, but I don't want to go into them except...Obviously, Miss Helburn was a very efficient woman, a very good manager in her ability to handle those people because they were crazy together. They fought like mad. They were intimate enough with each other to be able to fight.

I don't think that Lee Simonson liked them much. He was an artist. He felt that they weren't cultivated artists. He thought they were as I thought of them: business people or dilettantes. He used to say, especially when they got rid of him because as a scene designer he was too expensive and too arrogant in their view—he charged them high rates, and he was with Jo the leading designer in America. He had a great influence on Jo Mielziner. But he was a man with a bad temper. He looked green. He was dark, but he looked green. He looked like an angry Arab. But he had great respect for me. He used to read my reports, and he liked the way they were written.

Helburn cheated me once in a way that was quite normal for her to do. I don't think I should hold it against her. But when, after the experimental matinees of the *Garrick Gaieties*, of which I was the first stage manager, and they decided to go in for a longer run, there were only two salaries—$35 and $75—obviously, I as stage manager should have gotten the $75 because I was working almost harder than anybody in the show. But she saw that I was naïve. She offered me 35, and I didn't have the gumption to say, "I won't do it." They would have been helpless. I accepted it. I was living with my folks, who supported me, but I realized even then that I was being cheated. I was too shy, as I've already explained, to protest.

Q: How about Langner?

Clurman: Langner was a shrewd man, very forgetful, absentminded. Sometimes he even

seemed foolish. But he did have a feeling for the theatre. He had a practical value for the Guild. He knew when a show was not working. You see, they were all what I would call more or less enlightened theatre goers. The only one I thought was a real craftsman was Lee Simonson. But they all had some value, including Maurice Wertheim, who was their financial genius, and who represented the same kind of idealism, too. He spent his money on good things. He bought *The Nation* long before I had anything to do with it. They were all Ethical Culture people. I don't know if they all went to Ethical Culture—they weren't all Jewish—and of course Ethical Culture is not denominational, but there's a strong Jewish element there. And they were all what I call Ethical Culture people. They were German Jewish largely. Helburn was not Jewish. Westley, of course, was not Jewish. But the others were, and they were that part of the German Jewish (group), more educated than the Russian Jews, with a few exceptions, tended to be in the early years of the 20th century. And they had a certain kind of savoir faire, a certain kind of Americanism that was not common among the Russian Jews of my generation.

Q: The German Jews at home were very snobbish toward the Russian Jews.

Clurman Oh, they were terrible. I remember the Guggenheim family and Stella Adler's half-brother who was one of the first people to practice dietary medicine to people who must get thin and so forth. He married one of the Guggenheims. Stella and I were invited to one of their dinners. This half-brother thought that we were sufficiently cultivated to be trusted with the wealthy Guggenheims, and I remember the kind of aloofness they had, which was aggravated by Stella being deliberately (I didn't realize it at the time) mean to them, because "you Jews don't want to recognize your Jewishness or acknowledge it as a part of your patrimony. You see what you're suffering now in Germany?" She was deliberately turning the knife on them and acting like a spoiled actress, almost putting it on a little bit, as if to say, "I don't give a damn about you."

Q: You talk in your book, *All People*, about Larry Hart's pain and unhappiness because of his homosexuality. Was that known at the time?

Clurman: No, I didn't know it myself. He never let on. I remember there were discussions among us about homosexuality at times, but he never uttered a word that would lead one to believe that he was one, nor as far as I was concerned could I see any manifestations of his being homosexual. That's why the suffering. I think maybe that if it were today, he probably might have been more open about it, although I think it wasn't his public reputation that he was concerned with but his family reputation. He probably thought that if his mother found out that he was homosexual, it would break her heart; and he was very attached to his mother.

Q: I was interested that his idol was Heine.

Clurman: That's right. Well, Heine was Jewish, although a convert. He was a Jewish German who was both lyric and satiric, and that's the way Larry felt himself to be and I didn't know that at that time he knew German quite well— Larry did—so he was able to read Heine in the original, which is the only way you can really get a real sense of him as a poet. He was sort of a model to Larry, as if to say: "If I could be really an important poet, I'd be as Heine was or I'd be one in the same vein as Heine."

Q: Edward G. Robinson. The thing that intrigues me about him is that in the Theatre Guild he was this fine character actor who played so many different kinds of parts and then he went to Hollywood and was typecast. Did you ever talk to him about this? Did you meet him in Hollywood?

Clurman: I knew him fairly well. He was a very sweet man really, very sincere in his work,

very devoted. He was a real craftsman in the sense that he played any kind of a part. Before the Guild I saw him in a play called *The Deluge* by Hjalmar Bergman, which was a Danish play which took place along the Mississippi. Arthur Hopkins produced it. Robinson also played Japanese roles, Filipinos, Norwegians. He was always playing some foreign character, and he always did it with a great deal of feeling: that it didn't matter what he played—he was an actor and he was acting. He had a kind of openness toward the acting profession. In other words, that was his job and he did it, and he always did it with a great deal of skill, aplomb. He was not an actor you needed to direct much. He seemed always to know what to do without much guidance. He had a certain natural flair. He was very honest in his acting.

I remember he invested a lot of money on Wall St. in later years, in the '20s boom period, when we were in a play together called *Juarez and Maximillian*—that was around 1927. He was losing a lot of money at that time, and was very worried about it. I think that's one of the things that precipitated his move to Hollywood. He would have gone anyhow because for a character actor of that kind at that time, the amount of money you could make on the stage was not very great. It was not as if he was a leading man like Lunt. So it was natural for Robinson, especially after 1929, when the theatre began to shrink, to go to Hollywood.

He was extremely facile. In one film he had an enormous speech where he played a detective. He was either a detective or a man in an insurance company who had to find out whether the claims against the company were honest ones. There was a murder case where he was trying to discover a suspected person (Fred MacMurray), about the manner of somebody's death; and he had an enormously long speech about the kinds of suicide that were possible. This man was supposed to have fallen off the back of a train. The man had died. He'd never heard of suicide in that style before. He listed a long, long, long list of more common ways that people had been murdered or committed suicide, and he had never hard of that method of suicide. It was a speech that must have been a typewritten page or more. We all thought: This is going to take all day to do, because there were so many possibilities of slips, and it had to be spoken very rapidly, as if the speech came right off his fingertips. Robinson did it in one take. Studio hands applauded because they'd never witnessed such facility. Somehow or other there was some noise outside in the studio that had interfered with his speech, so they said he'd have to do it again. And he did it with the same facility and they applauded even more, because generally in those cases the actor is so disturbed that he begins to hesitate where he once was free-flowing.

Q: He was a professional.

Clurman: Yes. And he was a good-hearted man. He would help people if he could. He had a very close friend, Sam Jaffe. Sam Jaffe's wife died and Jaffe was extraordinarily broken up about it (He's a rather fragile man, Sam Jaffe—delicate, highly sensitive). He asked him to come and live with him, and I think Jaffe did live with Robinson for a long time.

Q: Although the Group began in 1931, it wasn't until *Awake and Sing!* in 1935, '36, that you first directed a play.

Clurman: At that time I didn't feel confident that I could direct because I had little experience. My experience was mostly literary, and my interests were literary—that is to say, an interest in scripts—whereas Mr. Strasberg had done some work in a settlement house in what today we would call Off-Off Broadway. He had done some work, so I made him our director, but ideologically...I have a telegram that Strasberg sent to me at the occasion of the recent Tribute tendered me in which he said, "You were the ideological heart of the Group Theatre. If you hadn't been there, there never would have been a Group Theatre" So in that sense I was the spark plug. First of all, I was the one who addressed most of the meetings and

collected the people and did most of the propaganda.

Q: It was your passion...

Clurman: Yes, my passion was the idea for such a theatre, my speeches covered everything about the theatre and what it should be that had started the Group. But I was a little timid about actually directing until I felt I had seen enough direction. I'd been around enough, I'd been criticizing enough, to undertake such a thing. I also had a feeling for Mr. Odets' work which really started me going.

Q: But in time didn't a kind of rivalry develop (I've heard) between you and Strasberg over who would be the dominant figure of the Group?

Clurman: Yes. It was not an overt rivalry. It was subcutaneous. Because I never wanted that rivalry or friction between us to emerge as an unsettling factor.

Q: Well, he's quite competitive, isn't he?

Clurman: Oh, he's extremely so and much more so now than he was then. As a matter of fact, now he'd like to wipe everybody else—every teacher, every director—off the map. I used to think that when he became successful—and he began to be even in those days—that he would become a little more, how shall I say, retiring: not retiring in the sense of...but he wouldn't have to blow so hard because his success was acknowledged. But on the contrary, it got worse. So that now I'm shocked sometimes by the fact that he will say disparaging things publicly about various of his colleagues—for example an actress who worked for him and actors who worked with him and other teachers. As to myself I heard he said in an interview, "Clurman's book *On Directing* isn't about direction, it's about how he directs." Well, that amused me because the first line of my book says: "This is not a how-to book—it's a book about how I direct." So he's criticizing me for saying what I had already said in the very first line. But as I say, we never got to the point of an open quarrel.

One day I said to him when I became the managing director...There were two stages: when we were all equal and then later I said, "I have to be the managing director and guide the organization." He said, "That's good. Fine." He agreed. But then he was very dissatisfied with the way I was managing things, and he probably was right. I mean there were many things that today, looking back, I could criticize myself for. There were personal reasons for that. I saw he was very restive, and I said, "I tell you what to do: you write me a letter and tell me what your complaints are against me, and I will read it and I will know and it will be clear. You're not expressing yourself, so get it on paper. I won't hear the vehemence in your voice—I'll only see what's on paper." Then I also said: "And when you have written this, I will write one about you." And he said, "No, no, that I can't take." It was very honest. "I cannot take that." So I said, "I'll take it." And he wrote the letter. It was a sharp letter—it was an honest letter, since I allowed him to be. But the fact that he said he couldn't take it was very characteristic.

Recently I spoke to his biographer—a woman named Cindy Adams has written a biography of him, which is coming out in six to eight months. She doesn't know anything about the theater so she wrote down everything he told her. And one thing she told me privately—I don't know if she has this in the book (the book goes on to say how everybody thinks he's the greatest man in the world and so forth and so on)—that his greatest fault, as far as she could make out (she doesn't know anything about him theatrically: she wasn't around), was, she said, "He never made a mistake. He never had a fault. He was always right." So much so that there are a few instances where he pointed out that I made a mistake but he had corrected me. Well, the instance he gives is a very bad one because (a) it was written in *The Fervent Years* that it was Cheryl Crawford that corrected me, and not he,

and (b) it took place at a time when he wasn't even present. So I said to the author: "You can't decide because you don't judge between my veracity and his, but you go to Cheryl Crawford, and she will be the witness." I don't know if she ever did it.

There were also things he said that he didn't want to have known he said. In other words, he had to wash the slate clean. He had to be beyond reproach. And that's very characteristic.

Now, of course, Lee's made a legend of himself, which a lot of people know to be false. I mean there are things about him which are very good, very complimentary. In other words, there's certainly enough value in the man for him not to need to apologize for his faults. O'Neill had a lot of faults, but he was a very fine playwright, so one doesn't have to apologize for O'Neill.

He's an important figure, and now that he's politely questioned by quite a number of teachers, he always takes an opportunity to belittle them. He has his enthusiasts and his champions, and I think quite rightly so because he has helped a lot of actors, and he's had a lot of distinguished students, and he has made a valuable contribution. But some of that contribution has been challenged by other teachers. I never got into that controversy, partly because I have never tried to teach in the sense that the other teachers do. I've never tried to teach in terms of starting a person on his career, giving him or her a technique. The classes I've had for actors were mostly for professional actors and mostly to teach them something about interpretation, more like a director with an actor than a teacher with a student. But Strasberg has taken to saying very disparaging things, partly because he knows he's being criticized, partly because Sanford Meisner and Stella Adler have become extraordinarily important teachers and Robert Lewis and a great many people who oppose some of his methods.

We have different kinds of reputations. I think my reputation is as a sort of general force in the theater—criticism, lecturer and so forth—and his is mostly as a teacher. But I don't feel any sense of competition with him or with anybody else. First of all, I say each of us has made a contribution. If you like Ibsen, you don't have to dislike Strindberg—not that I'm comparing us to them. But the idea that you have to be partisan in all these matters is childish.

There's also a book coming out on Odets by Margaret Gibson, the playwright William Gibson's wife. There were disparaging things said about me by members of the Group Theater, and she said, "Do you object to them?" I said, "No." She said, "Why?" I said, "Because they were said, and it doesn't bother me and at the moment of pique or of genuine criticism, they may have been true. I'm not a pure character."

Q: We're all fallible.

Clurman: Of course, and I'm perfectly willing to acknowledge the validity of the criticism because I think that on the positive side there's enough to overbalance the negative side.

Q: You don't say much about your Hollywood career. I know that you only made one movie, which was *Deadline at Dawn* at RKO.

Clurman: Yes, I really didn't belong in Hollywood at all. I was grateful to be there because it got me out of a great financial difficulty.

Q: The Forties were a bad period about ten years after the Group Theater.

Clurman: 1941 after the Group Theater folded was a very bad time for me financially, apart from my being unhappy about the Group Theater's folding. So Hollywood was very useful to me. But I didn't really belong there. I'm a completely un-Hollywood character.

Q: You first went to work for Columbia. Is that right?

Clurman: No, I had a whole series of jobs. First I was with Walter Wanger. That was during the interregnum, so to speak, if you want to call it that. Then I went out there when the Group actually folded, and I think the first job I got was with Fox. First of all, they made me a producer, and I wanted to be a director, and I read film scripts and made reports, but I wasn't kept there more than six months.

I worked mostly with Darryl Zanuck insofar as I worked with anyone at all. That is, I went to his conferences. I didn't actually confer with him, but he wanted me to listen to his conferences with other producers (Kenneth Macgowan was one) so that I'd get the hang of things. He also asked me to write reports on actors. So I watched him work. One of the things I noticed about Darryl Zanuck which was very funny was the way the associate producers always remained quite silent as if the king were speaking and they dare not utter a word. I remember Macgowan was absolutely quiet and listened to everything that Zanuck said. When what they called an associate producer, like Macgowan (there were others, too), or a screen writer said something, Zanuck wouldn't pay any attention, but about five minutes later he would exclaim, "I have an idea," and he would repeat almost *verbatim* what had just been said to him. I don't know if it was a trick or if he really forgot that somebody had said this or he was so self-deluded that he adopted the thing and it became his, so that he wasn't receiving it, he was giving. But no one dared say: "But Darryl, that's what I just said." They were rather pleased—I mean if they knew what they were doing.

There's a wonderful story that Kenneth Macgowan told me about Zanuck. Somebody corrected Zanuck; one of the producers or writers said, "You mistook the word 'millstone' for 'milestone'." When he left the room, Zanuck said, "Fire that guy." Macgowan tried to defend the poor fellow. He said, "Well, he was just—it was just a slip. It wasn't serious. He didn't mean to be contrary." Zanuck said, "I don't want him here. He thinks words are important."

Like all producers, he was pretty forward with girls. I think you never knew when you came in for a interview about a part whether you were going to get a part or a part of him. He could be both gracious and brutal, but he was a dynamo. I mean one could understand why he was successful. Louis Milestone said he would pull the chain...when he was an underling he would pull the chain for people—men of influence, who had power—in the toilet. The man was bound to get ahead—enormously energetic, enormously energetic.

Q: Did he swing his polo mallet at these conferences?

Clurman: I never saw him do that. I know he carried it around a lot, and he used to go swimming in iced water in his private pool. If he saw you with a girl, if he saw me walking on the—I was going to say "campus" but—the grounds with a girl, he'd pay very strict attention to that. He didn't like that. I don't think he liked to see any of his producers walking around with a girl. I guess all the girls in town were supposed to belong to him.

Q: Well, after Zanuck who did you work for?

Clurman: I worked for Harry Cohn, the head of Columbia.

Q: He was monstrous, I believe.

Clurman: Yes, he was monstrous. I think it was six months at Columbia and six months at Paramount and six months at RKO. But at RKO I finally decided, "I must do a picture, and the way I'll get to do a picture is to accept anything that comes in before I even read it," especially if the company had paid very little money for it. And that's how it happened. I said, "You bought a story for $10,000? I'll do it." Well, they were very anxious to find a use for a picture that generally didn't get made. The thought was: "Well, let's just put it on the shelf for a while and see what happens." And I made this picture.

It was shown not long ago at the Museum of Modern Art, and the audience partly liked it, partly didn't. I made a joke about it. I told them how it was made—that is, the fact that I'd gotten so fed up with not making any pictures that I thought, "Before I go home I've got to show that I did something at the studio." So I made this picture. I said, "You know, the man who wrote it for me, Clifford Odets, was a good writer, and the man who did the music was Hanns Eisler, who was a good composer, and the man who assisted me choosing the setups was a good designer by the name of William Cameron Menzies, and I think I'm a pretty good director. And the picture proves that all these talented people together can make a lousy picture." Which disarmed the audience. It may be some of them liked it.

But I didn't fit in—my way of thinking, my appetites, my tastes are all anti-Hollywood or if not anti-Hollywood, un-Hollywood.

At Paramount, I think there was a man on the board who heard that I had been the head of a left-wing—what they used to call a left-wing theater—and therefore I was suspect, not because they had anything on me, in a legal sense or any other sense. But since I was the head of the Group Theater, which was known to be left-wing, especially through Odets, someone in the New York office said, "Get rid of that guy." That was before the McCarthy scare, but that was the beginning or prologue.

Q: You've written often about John Barrymore....

Clurman: I saw him on the stage all the time. I'm one of the few people around nowadays, except for Atkinson I guess, who actually saw Barrymore on the stage. Every time I speak about him I say that I think he was the most talented American actor I ever saw. So they talk about his drunkenness and that sort of thing. And I say, "You're talking about his last days in Hollywood."

I'm thinking about when he played *The Jest* or when he played *Redemption*. I think he was the most talented man, all-around gifted man, all-around beautifully equipped actor, that we ever had—just as I think Laurette Taylor was the best actress we ever had at that time.

Barrymore really was filled with contempt for himself at the end of his life and for movies and for the theater, for everything. He was really an interesting character. He got up to make a speech as part of a picture I saw him working in. He stood in a box for he had to say something very dignified as a producer, and the audience was applauding him. And there was this houseful of extras because the scene was set in a theater. Barrymore started his speech and then he got lost and he said, "You can kiss my ass." Of course they all bust out laughing, the whole audience—that is, the fake audience of extras. He couldn't remember his lines, so he just said, "You can kiss my ass." But the remark wasn't just a joke. He was pouring out his complete contempt. He looked like a wrecked man at the time.

Q: Did you ever meet Garbo or Salka Viertel?

Clurman: Oh, Salka Viertel I knew very well. I never met Garbo. Salka Viertel I knew extremely well, a wonderful woman, very educated, spoke German, French, Polish, Russian. She had the best salon—it wasn't called that—in Hollywood till she began to be suspected of being subversive. I mean she was about as subversive as my foot. Few people continued to visit her. But all the best people in Hollywood—I mean the best writers like Heinrich Mann and Thomas Mann and Brecht and all the best people, both American and German, whatever...French...came to her house every week, and later on they faded away when they found that she was under a cloud. She finally retired, got to be very poor and had great difficulty.

Q: In your memoir, *All People Are Famous*, you talk a little about Franchot Tone and Joan Crawford. Did you get the feeling that her adopted daughter gives....

Clurman: She didn't have any adopted daughters when I knew her. I knew her before that. She was later angry with me because I hadn't invited her to join the Group Theater—not that she would have accepted such an invitation. But when I said to Franchot, "Would you come back to the theater to act with the Group?" and I didn't mention her coming back too...It never occurred to me to make such a statement. That's why I'm really un-Hollywood. If I was Hollywood, I would have said, "You too." But it never occurred to me that she would be interested, and she wouldn't have been interested. But she wanted me to ask her. After that, she wouldn't come to our Sunday dinners. Franchot would be there and he'd gives some excuse for her not being there, but she wouldn't come; she was furious with me.

I don't know if I told this story. One day I met Joan Crawford many years after at Sardi's and she came over to me and said, "I'm Joan Crawford," as if I would not know her. She had the feeling that she was passé and that I wouldn't pay any attention to her. I said, "Yes, of course, I know who you are." Then she asked me if I had any influence at the Actor's Studio, so that her daughter (whom I didn't know at that time was an adopted daughter) could be admitted.

Q: The first time you met Marlon Brando, was that when you were casting for *Truckline Cafe* or did you meet him when he was going with Stella Adler's....

Clurman: Daughter. I met him one day at Stella Adler's house—well, it was my house, too; we were married—and I looked at him and I said, "Stella, can he play a part of So-and-So?"—a returned soldier. She said he looked a little too young. Then I called him in to read the part and he read very badly, but he looked so interesting to me that I cast him anyhow—I and Kazan who was my partner in that production.

Q: Well, how was he in the part?

Clurman: Great. I don't think he ever did anything better. He didn't get the notices that he deserved. Possibly because it wasn't the leading part. The critics didn't like the play, and the audience applauded for a minute after his big scene. A minute on the stage is a long, long time. They kept on applauding and applauding and applauding and applauding. I'd never seen anything like that. And most of the critics hadn't remarked on it.

Q: Have you seen him in recent years?

Clurman: No, not recently, no. He always asks for me. He still calls up my daughter and always talks of me as a noble person. That's the word he uses. One day he said to her, "Why don't you marry someone noble? You should marry a real noble person. You shouldn't just marry a nice fellow but a noble person." She said, "Who's a noble person?" He said, "Harold's a noble person." "Well," she said, "I can't marry Harold!"

I find it so difficult to get to him. I'd like to see him but he keeps himself so secluded. First of all, he goes away a great deal. He goes to Tahiti. My daughter has seen him. I think she saw him about a year or so ago. He invites her out once in a while and they always quarrel. She says that he only sees a very limited number of people, and generally they're people he knew when he was a kid...very unprominent people. He keep's the prominent people at arm's length—that is, people who are in pictures with him or producers or directors and so forth.

I think the last time I saw him was when he was making a picture for Charlie Chaplin in England, *A Countess from Hong Kong*. And he said to me that Chaplin knew exactly what he wanted but had no idea how to get it from any actor except by acting for them. Marlon said Chaplin acted very well but he acted as only Chaplin could act but nobody else could. So the results were ineffective.

Q: There was some conflict there.

Clurman: Well, you know, because Chaplin was a man who really was inarticulate except through gesture and pantomime. That was not the way Marlon could work because Marlon is entirely an "internal" actor—which is antithetical to film technique, especially the kind of film and the kind of pantomimic acting which is essentially Chaplin's way of acting.

Chaplin said a great thing, you know. He said, "I don't like Shakespeare." And I asked, "Why?" And he said, "You can't act him—too many words."

Q: Oona was sort of a buffer against him and...You saw quite a bit of Oona, didn't you?

Clurman: Yes, Oona is a very wonderful woman, I think. She knew exactly how to handle him—not in I think a bad sense, but through love: she understood him. I thought an entirely admirable woman.

Q: I find her, too—a great woman.

Clurman: And God, oh...when I first met them, they were not married; they were going to be married. She was just about nineteen at that time, and she was one of the most beautiful women I have ever seen—a very distinguished beauty. Of course O'Neill, as you know very well, was a handsome man; and she had almost all of his features. She was extraordinarily beautiful. And I remember sitting with them in the El Morocco. We were having dinner. And I looked at her arms— beautiful arms—and I said, "Your arms are like soft marble." He was absolutely delighted with that. He thought the phrase was as nice as the compliment.

Q: Yes, that was a great marriage.

Clurman: It's interesting, isn't it? Ironic, to you as the biographer of O'Neill, that he was very contemptuous, opposed to that marriage, and Oona was the one person in the whole family who turned out quite well?

Q: He really cut himself off from someone who would have been a great comfort to him if he had allowed it.

Clurman: He did his children irreparable harm. Wasn't Carlotta a little bit to blame for his being so cut off from them? Oona told a story about her coming to visit him and Carlotta said, "You can't come in. You can't come in. He doesn't want to see you." I mean she just shut the door on her.

Q: It was complicated....*All My Sons*, which you co-produced with Kazan and Walter Fried—weren't you supposed to direct that originally?

Clurman: No, I wasn't supposed to direct it. I read the play and liked it, thought it was an interesting play, and was going to produce it—when Kazan came to me and suggested we make a partnership. And I said, "Fine, and I have a play that we can produce and you can direct it." I had a feeling that Kazan's ambition was of such a nature that if I had said, "I'll direct it," he wouldn't have been very interested in a partnership. I wanted to show him that I was not trying to push myself as a director.

And of course it was a big success. After that he resigned from the partnership.

Q: That was the same year that *The Iceman Cometh* was done.

Clurman: And George Jean Nathan was furious that it hadn't won the New York Drama Critics Prize.

Q: Did you really feel that *All My Sons* deserved it over *The Iceman*?

Clurman: I didn't feel it deserved it over anything. I mean I had no feeling about what plays are the best. I never liked *Iceman* as much as

everybody else did. It's something that troubles me, and when I write the book, I'll have to enter into why—it still does trouble me: *Iceman*.

Q: You see, I think it's one of his great ones.

Clurman: I know. Everybody does. And I'm not opposing the opinion because I'm certainly in the minority, and I directed it, and there's something about it that I don't accept.

By the way, there's something in your book which I think is very fine, and it never occurred to me, and no one has ever mentioned it—that *All God's Chillun* is partly about himself and his wife. It's not simply about black people.

Q: Of course.

Clurman: But it never occurred to me. I never saw anybody express that except you. it's a very subtle perception.

Q: In the 1949 season you directed *The Young and the Fair* with Julie Harris. What was your impression of her? Did she come to auditions?

Clurman: No, I had seen her in *Sundown Beach*. It was a play which ran a week—it was an Actor's Studio production under Kazan. And I liked her. And when they suggested doing *The Young and the Fair* it was immediately agreed that she should play in it. She made a terrific impression on the audience and also got a terrific hand, but most of the critics didn't mention her because she wasn't playing the leading part. Later on when my producer said, "We're going to have Julie Harris play *The Member of the Wedding*," which I directed...

Q: That established her reputation and yours also.

Clurman: That's true. That's my second reputation. I have two reputations—one for *Golden Boy* and *Awake and Sing!* (Of course everybody forgets everything. I suppose if I directed a play now and it was well liked, they'd say "Gee, there's a newcomer on Broadway." Because one of the things that's very noticeable about Broadway is that nobody remembers anything. And even now when I say, "I directed *The Member of the Wedding*," they say, "Oh? You directed *The Member of the Wedding*." I mean they forget.) But Harris is one of the best people I've ever directed—not only in her acting but in her attitude, her discipline.

Q: There have been rumors that Tennessee Williams, who became very friendly with Carson McCullers, polished up *The Member of the Wedding*.

Clurman: No, he wrote two scenes, which were later discarded. He encouraged her. He said, "I'll help you." After the first version of the play, which I never read, just threw her into a fit of distress (which some people said brought on a stroke—I don't believe it). She just gave up, "No, it will still make a good play," said Tennessee. He said, "I know how you should write this play. You just put down what ever you choose from the book. After all, you've got the scenario there, and I'll help you." Then she said, "I don't know how to handle that scene in the saloon," where two soldiers pick her up. Well, those two scenes he wrote for her, but we discarded them—so it's all hers. I don't think he intended to write any of it. He just said, "I'll help you." He didn't want to write it. He knew it was her work.

Q: But there was nobody else ever considered for the part of Frankie except Julie Harris.

Clurman: That's right. When I came on the scene, they said, "We've got Julie Harris," and I said, "That's great," because I'd already worked with her. They already had Ethel Waters and Julie Harris.

Q: You had a bit of trouble with Ethel Waters, I gather.

Clurman: Not at the beginning. We had trouble, but it wasn't that she made trouble. She had a great deal of difficulty in remembering lines, and when she remembered lines, she forgot the business. When she remembered the business, she forgot the lines. And even in Philadelphia, where she made such a great success, she was being cued in the dressing room through the first night, and she did go up a few times her first night. She had a great deal of trouble getting it all together. But when she got it all together, she was wonderful.

But when she got on the road, she began to "improve" it; and then she got to be very naughty, and she acted as if she had really created everything—she was the light, she was the thing. And she began to say naughty (things). She said wonderful things about me right after the opening: "This is a great man—this wonderful angel" and so on. The minute I said, "Ethel, don't do this" or "don't do that because you don't have to do that," she got a little edgy and began to do things which really threw the thing out of whack to the point where when I saw her in New Haven—I went up to see it, and I was absolutely in distress. I said, "I feel like taking my name off the show." And I told her this, but I was very gentle—I said: "You don't need these improvements—you're giving a wonderful performance." Well, she added more—until she went to another out-of-town engagement and a critic said, "This isn't the performance she gave in New York." In other words, she wouldn't listen to the director, but when an out-of-town critic said the same thing, she would. So in that sense she was troublesome. And she began to make slurs against Whitehead and myself. It was as if to say: "I want all the credit. To hell with those bums." But I never had any words with her. I just felt: "What can you do with this strange woman?" I rarely have words with anybody.

Q: You went right from directing *Member of the Wedding* to directing Arthur Laurents' *The Bird Cage*. That must have been a busy time in your life.

Clurman: Well, I had a way of going from one show to another. In fact, *The Member of the Wedding* opened on Thursday. I went away opening night. And I started rehearsing *The Bird Cage* on Monday.... In the meantime, by the way, I wrote a review.... I was writing criticism for a magazine called *Tomorrow*, and that weekend I wrote a review which included *The Member of the Wedding*. On that weekend I also prepared *The Bird Cage*, which I started on Monday. And I didn't know till I got back that *The Member* was a big hit. I was so scared of a failure.

Now, people said to me *The Bird Cage* was an inferior play. "Why did you do that after you had such a big success?" There were two reasons. One was that I promised to do it after I finished with *The Member of the Wedding*. And once I promised, I didn't say, "Well, I have a big hit. I can't afford to take a show that I'm rather skeptical about." I thought that would be cowardly. And secondly I didn't know what was going to be a hit or wasn't, because I didn't even think *The Member of the Wedding* would be a hit. I did it because I liked it. And I said, "I don't want to decide these things." But when I said I was going to do *The Bird Cage*, it was a time when I desperately needed a play to do because it was my livelihood. I wasn't a critic and I wasn't a lecturer then. So I did it. So when people said: "You shouldn't have done *The Bird Cage*. You could have gone from hit to hit." I said, "I never thought in those terms." I never have and never will.

Q: The next season you did *The Autumn Garden* with Lillian Hellman. About all you said about Lillian was that she was like a "Sabra"— tough on the outside and sweet on the inside. Some people say she's tough on the inside also.

Clurman: Yes, she's tough on the inside also. She's a very strange woman. There's a certain rigidity about her, a certain self-protective element. Also, I don't think she really understands the theatre very well. That's true of a lot of good playwrights. That is to say: they know how to write plays. In that sense they understand the theatre very well, but they don't understand the process of work in the theatre. For example, she began giving me notes the second day or third day. It's as if I gave a playwright—if I went to Mr. O'Neill and said, "You know, I read that first four pages of that script—the play's no good." I mean he'd kill me. Any playwright would. He'd probably say, "Hey, I don't know what I'm writing yet." Well, she did that. She'd take notes and she'd whisper most audibly at rehearsals. I said, "Don't do that. It's disturbing me and it's disturbing the actors. They hear whispering going on when they've hardly begun working." "This is not a school," she answered. So she didn't understand that the actor is also a sensitive being just as she is. She was a very hard person to work with.

On the other hand, she knew that she was difficult. There's a great deal of fairness in the woman, and yet superficially she's very tough. No, she really is tough, but it's hard to match her sense of honesty and fairness with...

Q: She has a strict sense of justice.

Clurman: Yes, that's what I mean. She has probity. I warned her that the last lines of *The Autumn Garden* weren't right and she rewrote it and rewrote it and rewrote it and each time it wasn't right. Finally I said, "Now it's right," and she said, "Dashiell Hammett wrote those lines." She was very honest. When I told her that *The Autumn Garden* was a good play in a Chekhovian way but in Chekhov all those foolish people came to be lovable while in her play one doesn't love them, she said, "But Chekhov's a much better writer than I am." That endeared her to me, despite the fact she irritated me a great deal during rehearsal.

I'll tell you another story. This I don't think I ever told. She would sit with me and an actor would read a line and she'd say, "He's an utter shit." And I'd say, "Kent, in that moment will you please not plead but command?" Okay. Then a few lines later she would say what an idiot that other actor was. And I'd say, "Jane, in that moment will you not show that you're troubled but hide it?" And then she'd say about the third actor, "God, how stupid that person is! What an idiot!" And I would say, "Colin, don't cry on that line." The she said, "Harold, you must be the most diplomatic person in the world." And I said, "Lillian, if I said any of the things you're saying to the actors, in about half an hour you wouldn't have a cast." But she called it diplomacy, not understanding that I was translating what she was dissatisfied with into actor's terms so that an actor could do something about her criticism. It's a technical matter.

In that sense she didn't know anything about the theatre. All she knew was that she was dissatisfied but she didn't know exactly what it was that she was dissatisfied with or how to correct the actor. If you tell an actor, "That's no good," he looks at you blankly and says, "What's no good and how do I improve it?"

But I did admire what I felt was her probity, but I found it very difficult to work with her.

Q: Did she continue this throughout the rehearsals?

Clurman: Yes, almost always. But on the other hand, she was very funny in a way. When she went away, while *Autumn Garden* was being prepared for the road she came back the last day before we were about to leave town for the road tour. By the way, in one of her books, she wrote that, "Somehow or other the second company was better than the first." The second company was not better than the first. The first company was better. But she didn't realize that her absence had helped in the improvement because the way she behaved during rehearsals for the first New York engagement discouraged the actors, deprived them of a

fullness of emotion. She had dehydrated the atmosphere.

But on that last day she said, "Okay, Harold, I have notes for you." She did not appear to realize that I had been working all day long, after four weeks of work. I said to her, "Yes, I'll take your notes. I'll take your notes, Lillian, after I've had dinner." She said, "I want to give them to you right now." I said, "I'm going home for dinner. My wife has prepared a dinner, and my family has dinner, and you can give me the notes after that." And she said, "I want to give them to you." I said, "I will not take them now." She began to cry like a little girl. And I didn't know whether it was just a way of softening me up by tears...

Q: That surprises me.

Clurman: Yes, you're surprised at this tough woman. She cried like a little...like a child who's told: "You can't go to the movies." And I did not take the notes then, but I did after dinner. She gave me the notes—they were simple notes—and there was no reason why she couldn't postpone them. Most of them I agreed to. Many of them were trivial. But she cried.

She wanted to rule. For example, when we were doing *The Autumn Garden*, one day she agreed that there should be cuts. We agreed that I would cut the play and she would cut the play separately. And then we would compare the cuts, and those that she didn't agree with that I had made, would not be made in the script, and those that I had not made which she put in, I would cut. We agreed. She said, "I will come tomorrow at ten o'clock and I'll give the cuts to the company."

Next morning at ten-thirty—no Hellman, and the same at quarter to eleven. I had many things to do. So I said, "I'll give you the cuts. They're all cuts agreed upon by Lillian Hellman." In other words, I added nothing, changing nothing except what had been agreed upon. About eleven-thirty she came in. She was furious because I was giving the cuts. So I said, "But, Lillian, I explained to them that they weren't my cuts. They were cuts jointly made, jointly agreed upon." She said, "This is my script, and you have no right to cut." I said, "I haven't cut it." "No, I have to do the cutting. The script belongs to me." When I reviewed her book for the L.A. *Times* called *An Unfinished Woman*, in which I called her "an unfinished woman," I quoted her. She said, "I have no talent for collaboration." And I wrote, "A person who has no talent for collaboration, should not be in the theatre," because the theatre consists entirely of collaboration. There's not one aspect of the theatre which is not collaborative.

Q: You cut *The Autumn Garden* in tandem with her. Were there any other scripts that you directed which you changed?

Clurman: Oh, in the Odets I even added characters. I suggested whole...

Q: Which plays would that have been?

Clurman: Well, in *Golden Boy*, for example, there was a character who was the brother of "Golden Boy," or Joe Bonaparte, who sold score cards, at the Polo Grounds. I told Odets "That's not a good character. What you need is a character...a strong person, a person who sticks to his guns. And since it's in the '30s, let's make him a labor organizer; a person to whom Joe Bonaparte says, 'You don't know anything about my problems because you have an easy life. I want to fight.' His brother—the labor organizer says, 'I fight but I fight for others not just for myself.'" And that was a suggestion of a different kind of person to show what was wrong with Joe.

Originally the boy Joe Bonaparte, who wants to be a fighter but who's a trained musician—his father was a violinist in the Philharmonic... I said, "That's no good. It's very natural for such a man to be interested in music. Joe's father should be a simple Italian man, who sells vegetables or watermelons or whatever on a pushcart; if such a man has a feeling that 'I want my son to be a violinist because it's noble,' you get a type of an immigrant which was

very prevalent among the Jews, who often says, 'My son is going to be a lawyer or doctor.'"

I gave Odets the whole idea of the last act. Finally Joe's won the big fight and he goes out and gets killed, and his racketeer manager/partners come. They begin to fight over who owns most of the property. (Joe Bonaparte's, that is.) In other words, they begin to treat Joe like a property, which is the whole point of the play—that he becomes a commodity. Odets wanted to change the ending in some strange way, and I said, "Nothing doing. You'll do it my way." And he did. And there were many many motivations I suggested and long, long discussions about them. In other words, I practically did enough to call myself the collaborator of *Golden Boy*, but I never thought of it. And in all the plays I suggested an enormous number of cuts, because Odets never could quite discipline himself completely. He had difficulty writing almost all his plays. He always needed somebody to help him.

Q: It was mostly with Odets that you worked in this way. Miller's very firm about any changes.

Clurman: Yes, but sometimes he's not firm enough. I know of cases—not with me but with other people—where he should have been firmer.

Q: Is that Kazan?

Clurman: I don't know whether it was Kazan who urged him or somebody else to make changes in *Death of a Salesman*. When they came to discuss these changes, Walter Fried told me: "Now that the play is changed, it's clearer but it's less interesting." So they went back to the original, so the play advanced more or less as it was originally written.

Miller's plays that I did, either as a producer or as a director, were all solid scripts to begin with. He was very careful. He didn't turn in such solid scripts with some of his later plays. One I resigned from.

Q: *The Creation of the World and Other Business*.

Clurman: Yes, I resigned from that for a number of reasons. But after I resigned, he changed it and changed it and changed it for five weeks. It was a hopeless case. He wouldn't admit it, but it was a hopeless case.

Then there was another play that I read called *The Archbishop's Ceiling*. It never came to New York. I read it and didn't think it would work, but still I thought it was interesting. And then I heard he tried to fix it, and when he fixed it, it was much worse. But I didn't direct that play. I told his producer, Robert Whitehead: "This is much worse than the original script."

Miller was a very careful craftsman. So is Lillian, a very careful craftswoman.

But there were many plays for which I've suggested new scenes, speeches, lines.

Q: In 1951 and '52 you directed *Desire Under the Elms*, the revival at ANTA. Did you have any contact with Carlotta at that time?

Clurman: The only contact was that I suggested Patricia Neal for Abbie who wanted to do it, and she said, "You can have anybody but Patricia Neal." I didn't talk to Carlotta because I heard she was difficult, and I thought that a better impression on her would be made by Bob Whitehead, who is much more suave, a WASP, and very good-looking. So he did make the contact. I never talked to her at all. I met her once, but that's all. We later on found out that O'Neill had liked Patricia Neal and that Carlotta was jealous. And although he wasn't around—he couldn't have been around—that rankled in her even after his death. So we had to choose somebody else. And the girl we picked, Carol Stone, was nowhere near as good an actress as Pat Neal.

Q: You said that you'd met Carlotta once. Was that about your cuts on *Touch of the Poet*?

Clurman: I just said, "Hello," and sat down far away from her in the theatre because I thought my scalp would come off, that she'd recognize the cuts and say, "How dare you do this?" She didn't recognize any cuts. They were all trembling. They said, "My God, he's going to get killed or we'll get killed and Bob Whitehead will get killed." I cut three-quarters of it and she didn't recognize any of the cuts.

Q: In 1952-'53 you directed *The Time of the Cuckoo* by Arthur Laurents. I've heard that Shirley Booth insisted that he soften the character which she played.

Clurman: I don't think Arthur did any softening of the character, but she feared an identification between herself and the character, and she always had a resistance to the play and to me and to everything—not an overt resistance—because she was very insecure about it. But it was mostly due to the fact that she was afraid that the woman she played, who was afraid of sex and afraid of taking a lover, was too close to what people might think she (Shirley Booth) was like. That disturbed her, but she wouldn't ever admit it. It was never made clear, and the author didn't wish to make it clear, whether that woman really had an affair with the Italian she met in Venice. And Arthur said he thought she did, but he never insisted on it. And she said, "No, no, she didn't." I sort of solved the difficulty by saying, "It's not really important for the play either way."

Q: What was Julie Harris like personally? I mean what illustrates her approach as an actress?

Clurman: Well, once she did an Actors' Fund benefit with about 102 fever. She was in great pain. She had a very sore throat. But she gave a completely normal, effective or better-than-normal performance—because it was an audience of professionals, and she wanted to appear at her best. And she came off the stage sobbing with pain, and she went right through the thing.

Q: Which play was that?

Clurman: *The Member of the Wedding*. And one day one of the actors who played with her in that play was slightly drunk and wasn't really up to scratch, and she got very very angry at him for coming on stage drunk; and the next night he thought he'd make up with her by bringing her some flowers, and she threw the bouquet of flowers in his face. She said, "It's not forgivable under any circumstances—flowers or no flowers—for him to have been drunk at a performance."

Q: Was she a quick study?

Clurman: A very quick study. Although I didn't encourage learning the lines of a part before rehearsals began, I had a feeling that she had. And in her case it didn't hurt at all because she kept herself so very flexible. She was very inventive in her creation, extraordinary—altogether a delight to work with.

Q: Can you think of any personal stories away from the theatre about her personal life?

Clurman: I can think of one story that's very amusing to me on a psychological level. One day when she hadn't seen me for a long time she said, "I heard you got married again"—the second marriage. I said, "Yes." She said, "Why didn't you marry me?" She said it perfectly seriously. I had never indicated any great passion for her. I had a great fondness and regard for her, but she had never showed that she would welcome any advances on my part. And what it signified to me is what she demanded from her husband was a protectiveness, a taking care of her career, keeping the world—the obtrusive world—away from her. She regarded me as a kind of father figure. And therefore the idea that I should be a husband was not so much "Oh, you're a great lover" or "I find you very attractive," but "I think you're a very fatherly person, and therefore you should have

married me to take care of me in my career and my person."

Q: She's been married three times, hasn't she?

Clurman: I believe so.

Q: Anything else you can add about her?

Clurman: I always felt that nothing really existed for her very much except the theatre. There was a friend I had who was a wonderful critic and man of culture, Waldo Frank, who lived in Truro. When she went to Truro, I said, "You ought to meet him. He's a very erudite, cultured person." She said, "Well, first of all, I'm shy. And secondly, I don't have much intellectual capacity." She's very modest about herself. All that she was and thought went into her acting.

When I spoke of "Frankie" in *A Member of the Wedding*, I described what it was to be young—a 12-year-old kid—and the process of growing up, she said, "When you talk about that character you make me cry." I asked, "Why so?" She said, "I don't think I'll be able to achieve all that you're talking about." She had a great modesty. I reassured her, "You don't have to achieve it in the terms in which I speak of it. You have to achieve it in your own acting terms."

Q: You had quite a bit of contact with Maxwell Anderson since you directed the *Truckline Cafe* of his, which was 1945 and '46. And then later you did *The Day the Money Stopped*.

Clurman: He was a very gentle person. He was capable of anger, indignation; but he was basically a very gentle person. It was very interesting—all his sweetness and his very nice sense of humor—in that very big man. He was like a kid. He was about 6'2 or 3. He must have weighed 250 pounds. He was enormously tall, and extraordinarily gentle. There was a kind of innocence and vulnerability about him. He was easily hurt. He was, of course, very susceptible to women. He liked very tiny women, by the way. This big man liked tiny women, and I think they all treated him as if he were a child, although they were always of child-like size and he was a massive person. He was sentimental about women and about love. Our greatest disputes (but they were never acrimonious, never acrimonious at all—we got along quite well, because he was, as I say, a gentle person with very little hostility) arose from the fact that I kept on insisting it was a mistake for him to write plays in verse. I thought that he did his best work in prose, that his prose was much more vigorous and more effective in the theatre than his verse. But he never agreed with me, because he felt that all the great plays in the past were plays that were in verse.

Q: You turned down *Winterset*.

Clurman: Yes, I turned it down, and I never thought highly of the play then or now as the dramatic critics did (Joseph Wood Krutch thought it the best American play up to that time), but I think I made a mistake in turning it down (in fact, I'm pretty sure I made a mistake) because, while I'm still not convinced of its value or its great stature, it was a play that, given the fact that there weren't very many scripts and given the fact that we did a few scripts in the Group Theater that were inferior to his, I should have been more receptive. But I think that I was misled in a certain sense or misguided in my misjudgment by the fact that the actors to whom the play was read were also indifferent to it.

I made two great mistakes in relation to plays. One of them I realized immediately after making it, but it was too late. That was my turning down of *The Time of Your Life*. The day after turning it down, I called Saroyan and said, "I've changed my mind," but it was too late. No one had to point the mistake out to me. I admitted that it was a foolish thing to have rejected the play.

Q: At the same time you directed *The Emperor's Clothes*, Jed Harris was directing Arthur Miller's *The Crucible*, and you seem to be a much more logical person...

Clurman: Well, Arthur Miller was a funny man and still is to some extent. He's always looking for some great director, and he's always inclined to take a new director. Maybe the next play will be saved by a director. And if a play fails, for example, or doesn't go over well, he then becomes sour on the director. So he liked *Incident at Vichy*, and he wanted me to direct his future plays. But I did direct his next play called *The Creation of the World and Other Business*, which didn't succeed; I didn't even finish the job. I resigned. That's the only time that I ever resigned my directing of a play. For five weeks another director took it over, a good director, and it still failed. He still associates that failure with me. When it came time to choose a director for another play (it so happened that the other play was also a failure out of town), he didn't agree to my directing it, because the cloud of *The Creation* hung over me.

Or he would get enthusiastic. Ulu Grosbard did a good job apparently with a play called *A View from the Bridge*... He insisted that the next play, *The Price*, be directed by Ulu Grosbard. Mr. Whitehead said, "Why don't you let Clurman do it? He'd be a good man for the new play." "No, no, I want Ulu Grosbard." And then Ulu Grosbard, while he got official credit, was forced to resign by the cast. They didn't like him very much—for whatever reason, I don't know. Arthur took it over. Later on when they were going to London, Miller said, "All right, let Harold direct it in London," and I said, "No. Since I didn't direct the original production, I have no desire to direct it in London." I think Miller's warmer now and more relaxed.

I think a number of things have happened. He realizes, for example, how harsh Broadway is, how severe a test it is to have success nowadays on Broadway. And so he was very glad to have *The Price* revived at this little Harold Clurman Theater. And it turned out to be successful. He got better notices than he got to begin with. The play has moved. And now he tells me he's writing another play. I said, "Where do you intend to have it done?" He said, "At the Harold Clurman Theater." Which means: "I'd rather succeed there—or fail there even...."

Of course he doesn't want to fail anywhere. It isn't such a big issue when you put on a production in a small theatre with smaller costs. It doesn't get to be such a life and death matter. "And also if I fail in a theatre with this small number of seats, there's a possibility I can rewrite the play, I can rethink the play, and then do it again." He's had a number of failures. And he began to realize that his plays are no longer automatically going to be successful and that everyone's not automatically going to be nice to him. There's a tendency of certain people to be—how shall I say?—kind of chary with praise. Miller is no longer in vogue. Many now turn to people who write more harshly.

Q: What is it about our American playwrights? They're hundred-yard dash men, but they're not long distance runners. O'Neill is the only one.

Clurman: And Williams, too. He keeps on writing. He doesn't give up. He sticks to his last; whether the last is a little worn out is another matter, but he does keep on writing. He doesn't get discouraged. He doesn't say, "The hell with it. I'm going to write movies" or "I'm now going to write for television." He told me yesterday—I saw him yesterday—that he's got a little experimental play now going into some tiny theatre somewhere, and he's got a play about Zelda Fitzgerald that's coming out.

I like Tennessee Williams. I think he's one of the best playwrights, if not the best—I'm not sure—since O'Neill. But my feeling about Miller, which makes me defend him all the time, is that the range of his interests is wider than Williams'. Williams is so hooked on the sexual. There's more to Williams than the sex theme, but his plays seem always to center around the vulnerability of certain disturbed people, the neurotic people. I have no objection to that, but the scope is narrow at the center. Whereas Miller, although he doesn't write with that great sensitivity has a greater social consciousness.

Q: In 1953-'54 you directed *The Ladies of the Corridor* by Dorothy Parker and Arnaud d'Usseau. What was Dorothy Parker like?

Clurman: Well, she was one of the most sentimental women I'd ever met, and that's funny—curious, not funny—because she's known for her biting humor; her epigrams; and she's associated with the gay life, so to speak, of the Algonquin set in the Twenties. But actually she was terribly sentimental, very easily hurt. When she was hurt, she could be very nasty; but basically the nastiness, when it occurred, stemmed from an extraordinary vulnerability.

Q: Why do you say she was sentimental? What were the indications?

Clurman: Oh, she would cry. She was always ready to weep. If she talked about the sufferings of people on strike when she was in her radical phase, she would begin to cry at the thought of unemployment or the sufferings of the under-privileged. Of course, one is always aware of people's pain, and one should be. In her case the sentiment became overpowering so she wasn't very lucid in her political thinking, if you want to call it that at all.

Q: Well, this is a new image of her, which I have never heard.

Clurman: No one ever mentions that, and I had cause to see it at various meetings and discussions—also at rehearsals. The first day of rehearsal, when we actually put the play on the stage, and it was working out very nicely, she began to cry because there it was coming to life.

Q: Did that require much rewriting?

Clurman: No. What was terribly crucial in that

play was a suicide which everybody objected to. "You'll have a hit if you cut that suicide." One of the characters, played by Betty Field, is so tortured by her situation that she throws herself out of a window of the hotel. I got letters and letters saying, "Look, you've got to have a hit." Because the first part of the play was unquestionably a hit.

Q: Letters from whom? From Dorothy?

Clurman: No, to Dórothy and to me, saying, "Cut that suicide scene out and the unhappy ending."

Q: Letters from whom?

Clurman: Letters from the audience, from the public, after Philadelphia, where there was a chance to do something about it. I kept on saying, "Look, I'm not urging you to cut the thing if you don't wish to, because I respect authors. But I'm telling you: you're getting a lot of this flak and we've got to take it into account." But she wouldn't. The same thing happened opening night. The play was going along beautifully. The first act was full of laughs and the audience was absolutely entranced. They loved the production—even Atkinson, who didn't like the play, partly because he didn't like pessimistic plays; they wounded him. He thought it was a beautiful production, with marvelous acting, but he didn't like the play. I have the feeling that if we had cut that suicide, he would have written a very different review. But Parker insisted on it. And I kept on repeating. I said, "Look, I don't feel offended by the unhappy ending, because it's part of the pattern, part of what you have to say. But the audience must be considered." If it only came from one or two or five people.... And George Jean Nathan, who liked the play a lot, said the only mistake in the play—and he liked the production and he voted it the best play of the season—the only thing he objected to was that suicide scene, which he said was not necessary and not valuable.

Q: How about the actors? How did they feel?

Clurman: Well, of course, Betty Field, who had nothing to do with it in a sense—I suppose if I had taken that scene out, she would have resigned from the part. But that was not a consideration. We never asked her, "What do you think?" Obviously, she's not going to cut herself out of the play. But, no, it was only I who didn't urge Parker to cut it.... In fact, some people blamed me, said, "You should have done what Kazan did with Williams on *Cat on a Hot Tin Roof*." When Williams cut out Big Daddy after the second act and didn't have him reappear in the third act, Kazan said, "Well, if you do that, I don't think you're going to have a hit." So Williams changed it and put Big Daddy back in the third act. When Williams was criticized on this account, he said, "Well, Kazan asked me to do it." Then he published both endings.

Q: I remember that.

Clurman: And I always was a little annoyed with Mr. Williams, because I said, "After all, you have the last word, but you're afraid of a failure."

Q: Did you know that Dorothy Parker left her money to Martin Luther King, Jr.?

Clurman: I didn't know that.

Q: Whom she had never met.

Clurman: I didn't know that. It's very interesting. I wouldn't say it's entirely sentimental, but she was a bleeding heart.

Q: During the McCarthy period. Were you ever named?

Clurman: I was never named, but I was questioned a number of times in Washington, privately, not publicly. The reason I was questioned privately was because they knew I'd never been a member of the Communist Party. They knew that because so many people had told them so. However, they said, "This man was a leader of the Group Theater, and the Group Theater had many people in it who were of Left orientation and some who were confessed, admitted Communists. Therefore, he must have had some influence in this matter." So they tried to scare me into some kind of denunciation of various people or self-denunciation without getting me to say that I was a member of the Communist Party because I wasn't and they knew I wasn't. But they were very eager to see if they could extract information from me.

Q: Did you ever meet McCarthy?

Clurman: No, I was never in any hearing of either of the committees because again they had nothing on me. You see, when they had this or they had a definite denunciation from someone, then they could frighten the wits out of a man. But they knew that wasn't true of me. So the only thing they could do was suggest that I was being watched carefully and I was under suspicion, and therefore if I wanted to clear myself—they didn't say that since I wasn't guilty of anything—but they did question me. I think a member of the FBI or an investigator for them questioned me in a Washington hotel. But they never pressed the point.

Q: There was a lot of bitter feelings against Kazan for naming names.

Clurman: Yes, there was for a long time, and he suffered acutely because of it because a lot of people wouldn't speak to him anymore. Some people still don't speak to him.

Q: Do you recall meeting him the first time after he had named names?

Clurman: No, I don't recall meeting him, but he assumed or he was told that I felt bitterly about his behavior and that I would never work with him. Somebody told him that I said I'd never work with

him again, I'd never talk to him again; and so he gave me a wide berth. And many years later, his wife or the woman who became his wife, Barbara Loden, asked me about this, and I said, "I think Kazan thinks that I'm anti-Kazan," and I told somebody that I was sad that he was in that situation; I was rather sad that he had named names but that I wasn't going to sit in judgment on him. I couldn't sit in judgment on him. I couldn't sit in judgment on anybody. I wasn't neutral but I certainly wasn't up to a judgmental position or condemnation. I certainly have never felt that I was in a position to condemn anybody, because I don't know how under certain pressure I would behave. I would have to face it, because I knew in several cases, like that of Odets, where I felt they wanted to behave one way and then behaved another way it was because they were so terrified of being unpopular and having their careers damaged. So I didn't know how I would behave if I were to face the music myself—I wasn't in a position to say, "You are a bad man—you've done something wrong." When Kazan realized this, he became much more cordial, but for a long time he was very annoyed with me or suspicious of me.

Q: Now, you had a big hit—*Bus Stop*. That was the first Inge play that you directed. Wasn't that in good shape when you got it or did that require much rewriting?

Clurman: There was one moment—the end of the second act, which had a kind of filthy joke (not sexually filthy but an unpleasant joke); it referred to vomiting. It made the audience laugh. I said, "That must be changed because that joke has nothing to do with the essence of the play." And for days Inge couldn't think of a new ending, and I said, "You must think of it because that one line— you have to have a funny line there to end the act, but you have to have a funny line which relates to the story of the play. This has nothing to do with the story of the play. It's just an unpleasant joke which the audience will think funny, and I insist that you change it." He finally did change it.

Q: How was Inge to work with?

Clurman: He was a very easily disturbed person—a very nice man really, very gentle. He submitted his next play to me because he liked the job I had done on *Bus Stop. The Dark at the Top of the Stairs*. When I read it, I wasn't absolutely prepared to say yes because I was going abroad. When I want to go abroad, I don't like to think too much about what I'm going to do next season. And I said, "I'd like to wait and talk to you when I come back." I felt it needed changes, but I hadn't read it carefully enough to suggest changes. When I came back, I found Inge had shown the play to Kazan and Kazan said, "I must do this play." And Kazan got it. Inge kept asking, "When is Harold coming back?" I told him that I was coming back, and he could have waited, but he gave it to Kazan because Kazan was so eager to do it. Inge was terrified when I returned that I would never speak to him again. And he kept on saying, "I love Harold, and I hope he doesn't hold this against me." But I didn't. When I reviewed it, I reviewed it rather cordially; and he was very grateful for that. He thought I would pan the devil out of it. And the changes that Mr. Kazan made were good changes and were probably the ones that I might have asked for if I had studied the play. But I had held it in abeyance, and because of my indecision he turned the play over to Kazan, which was a kind of weakness on his part, since he could have waited for me the two weeks or so to have my yes or no. But I didn't hold what he did against him. I understand that there are very few people of strong principle in the theatre.

Q: He was also very insecure.

Clurman: Oh, terribly insecure. He was insecure to the point of pathology.

Q: His homosexuality was...

Clurman: Yes, he didn't approve of his homosexuality. Men like Tennessee Williams and others, are very open about it, especially nowadays, although there's one speech in a play called *Small Craft Warnings*, which is a diatribe against homosexuality and homosexuals, which I thought rather shameful.

There was one trait which betrayed Inge's neurosis. When he went to the theatre—and this was at the height of his success when he was comparatively secure—he always wanted to sit in the last row. For one of my productions, I gave him a good seat in the first or second row, but he changed it to the last row, which meant he had a form of claustrophobia, to the point that he refused to sit anywhere except near the exit. And then again he had had an alcoholic problem. He had overcome that alcoholic problem, but he was always going back to the analyst to be reaffirmed. Several times he spoke to me about homosexuality disparagingly. He just couldn't accept it. Probably some analyst or somebody else had gotten the idea into his head that it was a form of evasion of responsibility. I think that's a mistaken idea. The last play he did, which I directed, he has a homosexual man protecting the young man encourage him to go out and face life as a married man.

Q: What was the name of that play?

Clurman: *Where's Daddy?*—which got two very good notices, but Mr. Kerr and Mr. Kauffmann disliked it intensely. And so the play, which had been very successful with the audience during two weeks of previews, failed because of the two critics. Watts and several others liked it very much. It really broke Inge's heart.

Q: Do you have any anecdotes about him?

Clurman: He left a lot of short plays. Some of them were very powerful, very powerful—very unpleasant, very painful plays, but very powerful. They were really unjustly neglected. At the present time they'd probably be produced off-Broadway. They might have been successful. In fact, I saw one or two of them off-off-Broadway. Well, one play is about a novelist or a playwright—I can't remember which—who commits suicide by an overdose of pills because he's been so badly treated by the press, neglected after being very successful. In this play the writer calls up two people—one is his mother, whom he has some grudge against and I think fears that whatever is wrong with him is his mother's fault (he's not homosexual)—and then he calls up a critic and says, "I despise you. I hate you, I despise you, not because you didn't like my play, but the way in which you talked about me. After all, I am a writer—I am a playwright—I've written good things. I'm not a bum. And the manner in which you write is so despicable, and in a certain sense my death I lay in part at your door." This was written some time before Inge himself committed suicide. I heard that he had actually called Walter Kerr at one time to say something to this same effect. Inge was a very neurotic person, but under severe control. As a matter of fact, if William Gibson, who confessed to having made a mistake (about Inge)... Margaret Gibson, William's wife, is a psychoanalyst at that Riggs Institute.

Inge called her and said, "I want to come to see you desperately." And he called Gibson— Gibson tells the story himself; he wrote about it— Gibson said, "You better wait a while because we have no place to put you. Riggs is full and my house is full, and if you can wait a while...." Gibson didn't know what the consequences might be—that Inge was so desperate that he would commit suicide. I don't blame him. He was taking on some of the responsibility, which he needn't have done. If he had said, "All right, you can sleep on the floor" or "we'll get some friend to put you up if you're that desperate." But he didn't think of that. He must have thought, "Well, Inge will wait for two weeks or three." But Inge couldn't wait. It was a terrible thing.

After a while they were turning down, turning him down as a writer, you know what Hollywood is like. If you haven't had a success.... All this was terribly depressing to him.

He was so vulnerable. One day he called me up and said, "Harold, I'm giving up my subscription to *The Nation*. I said, "What did I do?" He said, "No, no, no, you're a fine critic and I love you and I respect you. But Hatch wrote a review of that picture [*Splendor in the Grass*] and he said I was writing for the box office just to make money. Now, I don't mind his not liking the movie, but why should he ascribe such motives. I'm giving up my subscription." I said, "Well, you're doing me harm because I'd like you to read me." And he said, "Well, I'll still read you and other people in *The Nation*, but I'm not subscribing...."

Q: Kind of childlike.

Clurman: Of course. He didn't have to read that critic anymore because he liked me and he liked the paper in general, but it would always remind him forever of Hatch's bad notice. I mean if you can't take criticism at all, you've got to quit because no matter what you do and who you are, you're going to find somebody who dislikes you or dislikes one of your works.

Q: Then you had a nice hit: *Tiger at the Gates*. How did that happen to come your way?

Clurman: Robert Joseph, who is an intelligent producer, and who admired me, came to me one day and said to me: "There's a play called in French the equivalent in the English translation: *The Trojan War Shall Not Take Place*. I would like to produce that, and I would like you to direct it." I said, "That's a very difficult play to put over in New York unless you have a very fine actor."

Q: You had read this play?

Clurman: Yes. I'd read it in French. And I had read a translation—a rather poor one, I thought— in English, but I said, "It's a very hard play to put over." It takes place in Greece, legendary Greece and Troy, etc., etc. It's very difficult. However, I would do it if I could find an actor. But there are very few actors I know who could do this play.

American actors don't speak well enough. Maybe Freddie March among the Americans, and in England I think Redgrave could do it and certainly Laurence Olivier. But Joseph said, "Well, suppose I can find an English actor for you?—or one of the men you name?" I said, "Then I would do it."

One day I get a letter from Redgrave that said, "Mr. Clurman [I don't know how he came to think of me; perhaps he had a great admiration for the Group Theater, had seen the Group Theater work in England in *Golden Boy*], have you ever thought of directing *The Trojan War Shall Not Take Place*?"

I thought, "My God, that's wonderful!" I said to Bob Joseph, "This is really a fortunate coincidence. Why don't you go over and see if you can sign him?" Then I said, "There's another thing you can do. You have to get a new translation and I think the man to do it is Christopher Fry. I know Christopher Fry's agent. He's a friend of mine. See if you can persuade the agent to persuade Christopher Fry to do it."

Bob Joseph went over and lo and behold he got Fry and he got Redgrave. And I went over to England to speak to Redgrave and to cast the other very important part in the play: Helen of Troy. I met Kenneth Tynan and described the part as I saw it, and he suggested an actress who was not yet well known: Diane Cilento. I read her and gave her the part. She was absolutely perfect for it, and she made a great success in it, especially in the United States.

Q: Is this the first time that you directed in London?

Clurman: The first time I had initiated a production. In *Golden Boy* I brought over my company and had made a reputation with it. The Group Theater was almost a legend in England. The English were very cordial to the idea of my directing *Tiger* because they admired my work.

A very funny thing happened. One day Redgrave had lunch with me. He said, "Listen, what about this business of The Method? I hear that you're a champion of The Method. Are you going to have a lot of pauses?" Why he associated The Method with pauses, I don't... I do know, but I don't associate The Method with pauses or anything of that sort. "That's just a misunderstanding," I said, "But, Michael, the pauses are antithetical to the whole style of the play." "That's all I wanted to know—that you realize that—and I'll be happy to work with you." And he has been a great friend of mine ever since.

Q: You directed the national companies of both *Streetcar* and *Salesman*. How did this happen to come about?

Clurman: Mr. Kazan didn't like to direct second companies because after he was through directing a production he was sick and tired of the plays, so Mr. Bloomgarden said: "Let Harold do them." Those plays were both very successful. In the case of *Streetcar*, Kazan said, "I don't want Harold Clurman's name on the production." I needed a job badly at the time, and so I said I'd go along with the arrangement. After all, they didn't want me to change the staging—they just wanted me to work with the new cast—Uta Hagen, Tony Quinn. When the play was produced in Chicago, Claudia Cassidy said, "What a great director Kazan is! This production is even better than the one in New York." Which offended Kazan. I hadn't said anything about it, and she didn't know anything about it.

Eric Bentley said later on: "I didn't understand why, but it seemed much better in Chicago." Then somebody told him, "Clurman directed the new cast." I didn't change the staging, but I did change the interpretation through the actors.

Q: Wasn't your name in the program?

Clurman: I was just getting money. So the next time it was suggested: "What about Harold's doing *Death of a Salesman* on the road?" he said, "Yes, but this time he can put his own name on it, because I don't want that to happen again."

Kazan tried to do *Streetcar* again with Uta Hagen, and Uta Hagen complained to Irene Selznick. Uta said, "I don't feel I've been directed in this. Mr. Kazan hasn't really directed me. He has no interest in directing the play anymore. I can understand that but it isn't good for me. His problem is his problem, but what about my problem? I deserve a good director." "Well, who would you like?" I had directed her once before. She said, "I'd like Harold Clurman." So they called me in, and that's how I came to direct her in *Streetcar*.

Q: In 1955-'56 you directed your first musical, *Pipe Dream* by Rodgers and Hammerstein. How did that happen?

Clurman: Well, Rodgers and Hammerstein liked my work in general. And they found working with various stage directors who weren't associated with musicals had turned out rather well in certain cases, and they asked me if I wanted to direct one. I repeated "You know, I don't know anything about musicals. I mean I know about musicals, but I'm not a director of musicals." And Hammerstein said, "It's not really difficult, because you have a choreographer and other assistants, and we'd like you to direct *Pipe Dream*." And I did. It wasn't a very successful musical. I made a lot of money on it. I don't think I was the right director.

Later on somebody asked me to direct *1776*, and I said, "I don't think I should direct this play. I don't think I'm a good director for musicals. I've had one experience." Also, I had trouble in the casting of *Pipe Dream*. Rodgers didn't want the cast that I wanted. I wanted Julie Harris to play the leading part. He said, "She hasn't got a good enough voice." I suggested Tammy Grimes. "She hasn't got a good enough voice." So I said, "Look, Gertrude Lawrence didn't have a good enough voice for *The King and I*, but she was marvelous." "Well," he said, "I don't want anybody like that. I want real voices."

What happened was that Traubel was cast for the show because she had had a great voice, but she

no longer had it. But Rodgers and Hammerstein didn't know that. And then they chose a girl who was a night club singer, and she had a good voice but it was a belting voice. It was not very sympathetic. So the show was not at all what it should have been. I don't use that as an excuse. I don't think that I did particularly well. They were satisfied—Rodgers and Hammerstein were—but I don't think I was the best person for the job.

I have a way of saying, "Look, there are better directors for this particular play." I know what I can direct well. In those cases I'm very proud, even arrogant. I would say, "I'm the best director for this play, better than anybody else you might find." I would still say that about certain plays today. On the other hand there are occasions when I say, "This is going to be a hit, but I don't want to do it, and I don't think I'm the best director for it." I remember telling the original producer of *1776*: "I don't think I'm the right director for this." He said, "We don't agree with you." I said, "You can't tell me about myself. If I say I'm not the best director, please believe me."

Q: Well, that's very unusual.

Clurman: That's because I have a much better critical eye than most directors; they don't really know themselves. I remember the opening night of *Pipe Dream* when there wasn't the full applause Rodgers was accustomed to after each number, he whispered, "This is murder."

Q: How did you find Hammerstein to work with?

Clurman: Very nice, very nice—a very nice man. He was a less sentimental man in a way than Rodgers; Rodgers could be tougher. Rodgers seemed to be brusque and could be impolite and could be angry, but he was very sentimental. While Hammerstein was very polite but tougher.

Q: That's curious, because his lyrics can be so sentimental.

Clurman: Yes. His art was a sentimental art, but his nature was tough; and he also was tough on himself: that famous time when everybody congratulated him on the enormous success of *Oklahoma!*, and he took an ad in *Variety* in which he listed ten flops that he'd done in the last ten years and said, "I did it once—I can do it again. I have a right to flop." That's a real artistic point of view: "I have a right to flop." Which is exactly the opposite of the Broadway attitude.

Q: In 1957-'57 you had another one of your big hits, *The Waltz of the Toreadors*.

Clurman: Yes, that was only damaged by the fact that Richardson developed a bad throat and couldn't go on with it, but it was a big hit; and it was a hit again with Melvyn Douglas on the road. It got wonderful notices. I developed a great friendship with Ralph Richardson. On the road, by the way, Melvyn Douglas was very good, too, but the management shouldn't have brought the play back to New York because people said it was an old show and they'd seen Ralph Richardson.

Q: I meant to ask you before about Redgrave. Did you ever meet his daughter Vanessa?

Clurman: Oh, sure, she came to all my rehearsals of *Tiger at the Gates*. She told her father that she learned more—she was about seventeen then—watching my rehearsals than she'd ever learned in her drama school.

Q: What was she like personally?

Clurman: Very pretty. She had more flesh than she has now. She had a little puppy fat still, but she was very attractive.

Q: In '56-'57 you directed *Orpheus Descending*.

Clurman: Just before it opened Mr. Williams said to me: "This is the best interpretation of any of my plays—the truest and the best." When he got mixed notices he was no longer sure, and he began to blame me, even though every place he saw it, it was a failure. But he had to blame somebody. That's typical of most playwrights.

I saw *Orpheus* in London. I was there opening night. In fact, I reviewed it, and I gave it a fairly good notice—the play that is. But a very strange thing happened with that play. When I first read the play I found certain weaknesses that could not be remedied. However, I was told that it was going to be acted by Brando and Anna Magnani. I said, "With such a cast I must direct it." So I did.

Well, I was later told, "Magnani isn't going to do it. so I said, "That doesn't bother me because I don't think it should be done by an Italian. The woman is an American woman of Italian parentage, which makes her American. I'll get somebody else: Maureen Stapleton. But Brando is essential."

Well, at the last minute Brando decided not to do it. So at the last minute I didn't have the two actors on the basis of which I had chosen to do the play. But I never mentioned that to Williams. Nor did I ever tell him that I thought there was a crucial weakness in the play, although I thought it a very worthy play: very interesting from many standpoints—which I still believe.

But it was very stupidly received. Williams thought the failure was my fault. Because all the people began to persuade him that "Harold didn't do a good job." And playwrights in such circumstances are anxious to believe that somebody didn't do a good job—an actor or a scene designer or somebody. They can't admit, "My play has a weakness." Which shows that they are really not strong egos. I have an enormous ego. If I do a play and it's a failure, I say, "I think I did a good job" or "I did a bad job." So what? I have a right to do that, too. My ego is strong. It's not going to be destroyed because of a bad notice. But I always tell playwrights who have to find someone to blame for a flop: "You've got a weak ego. You aren't able to accept any setback. You aren't able to say: 'I did a bad job—I was weak—I made a mistake.'"

Q: Do you remember any personal stories about Williams that illustrate?

Clurman: Well, the fact that he said to me, "This is the best production of any play" two days before it opened.

Q: Did he ever talk about his family, his mother?

Clurman: No, I very rarely try to enter into people's personal lives unless they offer to speak about it. I never inquire.

Q: No, I didn't expect you to, but I meant...

Clurman: No, he never did. The only time...two times...three times he revealed himself he probably did so in order for me to make no mistake that he was homosexual. I had no doubt about it.

One day I saw him accompanying a woman to buy her a dress in a Parisian shop, an Englishwoman—he's still a friend of hers. He told me: "She's the only woman I ever was in love with when I was a young boy." Which meant he hadn't been in love with any women since then.

There was an expression in *Orpheus*, "going juking," in which a girl describes how she goes juking, playing juke boxes and then drinking and finally going to bed with a fellow. That's where the expression came from. One day after a performance of *Orpheus* in Philadelphia I said to him just kidding: "Tennessee, do you want to go juking with me?" not to tease him but just to see what his response would be. He said, "Harold, you and I don't go the same way." Which was his way of saying "You know I'm a homosexual."

On one occasion I touched on the really crucial fault in *Orpheus*. He has a fellow who falls in love (rather ambivalently) with the lady of the house after she has given him a job. She falls in love with him, and he apparently has an affair with her. I asked Williams at an early rehearsal: "Tennessee, does this boy really love this woman?" And he gave me a wise look and said, "He's very fond of her." Here lay the play's main weakness: the audience couldn't believe that he was in love with her. Not that there was anything suggested of the homosexual in the boy. As a matter of fact, the boy had been a naughty boy like the fellow in *Sweet Bird of Youth*. He'd been a sort of a hustler. But Williams really evaded the matter. The ambiguity came through in the play though the audience was not conscious of it, but I knew that it was not convincing.

For example, in *Streetcar Named Desire* there's no doubt about the complete heterosexuality of Stanley Kowalski, but in *Orpheus* there was quite a bit of doubt of the character's exact nature.

Q: Tell me about your O'Neill book.

Clurman: I sent out a word that I would like to do a biography of O'Neill, in which I said that although I was never an unqualified admirer of O'Neill (I didn't like some of his plays) I still thought he was the most important American playwright...

Q: This was before *Long Day's Journey*.

Clurman: Oh, yes, this was long before it. This was 1950, a little earlier. It was a little bit after my *Desire Under the Elms* revival. Anyhow I put my project for an O'Neill book in an agent's hands; you know what the response was from publishers? Who the hell cares nowadays about O'Neill? That's so typically American, because he hadn't written any new plays for some time.

O'Neill wasn't dated! *Desire Under the Elms* isn't a sex play; it's about America. That's one of my theses. If you read my book, *On Directing*, you'll find an analysis of *Desire* in which I say, "The play's crucial line is, 'It's a mighty dandy farm. I wish I owned it.'" What is the farm? It's America.

Finally Oliver Rea through Harper & Row (I think it was) said that he would publish the book. Finally I realized that I couldn't do a book because it required so much research, and I wasn't free to do research. You have to give all your time to it, and I was directing plays. I returned the advance.

Q: S.N. Behrman?

Clurman: One day he said something about how practical he was. I said, "You're not practical at all. Look, for example, right now you're wearing one black shoe and one yellow shoe." He was very hurt. He was so absent-minded. I didn't intend what I had said as an insult. I might do a thing like that myself. I'm absent-minded, too. But he took it as an affront. And for a while he said, "I'm not sure I can work with this Clurman."

Q: This was when you were directing *The Cold Wind and the Warm*?

Clurman: Yes, and I thought what I had said, though true, was a joke. I meant, "Look, I'm not such a practical man. I bumble about. I'm always getting wrong numbers because I dial wrong numbers." One day I said, "Where do you get your suits?" He answered, "From Knize," a very expensive place. At that time the cheapest suit at Knize was $500. The most expensive suits were selling for $300 elsewhere. He then took out a Havana cigar, I said, "You would be wearing all those things and smoking that kind of cigar." And he said, "You son of a bitch," knowing very well that what I was talking about was... These very poor boys when they get rich want the very best, the very best. Now, I was never a poor boy except in the Group Theater days, but I wasn't brought up poorly—I was brought up by a father who was a doctor. I never felt that I needed the best of everything. I thought I would just be well clothed in the normal way. If you were terribly poor and later on you get money, it's impossible to keep you down. You've got to be super-rich."

Q: That's like Moss Hart, the same thing.

Clurman: The same thing, yes. Moss Hart once said to my wife, and I quoted it in a review:

"Happiness is when you can shop at Bergdorf-Goodman. You can't be unhappy as long as you can shop at Bergdorf-Goodman." Well, I put that in as an explanation of the fact that he became so optimistic and genial, as contrasted with George Kaufman, who was always dour. Well, Mrs. Moss Hart, whom I liked very much, Kitty Carlisle, thought I was trying to insult her husband and said, "I'll never speak to him again." And I went, "Oh, if I had known you took this as an insult—or anybody took it as an insult..." I said, "Look, we all say silly things that... Why are you so offended? I'm aware of a lot of my faults or things people say against me. They're included in books, and when people say, 'Do you object to this?' I say, 'No, I don't object. They have been said against me, and who am I not to have anything said against me. Why should I be so far above the crowd that nobody may say anything bad about me?'"

Q: You did *Heartbreak House* with many English actors.

Clurman: Pamela Brown didn't think I was a very good director because I directed differently from the way the English are used to being directed. Some of the English actors thought I fumbled. They were used to more technical directors, they're not used to the direction of acting— they're used to technical directing: "You stand here"—"The lights are here"—the movements and all that sort of thing about which I am much more casual and experimental. Pamela didn't think me a good director, and she told Tynan so. I don't know what Tynan's response was, but later on when he saw it he told her, "You're crazy. It's a beautiful production. What's the matter with you?" She wanted to leave before the end of the play, which she did; and I came in and I begged her to stay and she burst into laughter. The reason she busted into laughter was I knew, and she didn't know I knew, that here I was saying how wonderful she was and she'd said bad things about me. I was going to say, "I know what you think of me as a director, but I don't give a damn what you think of me as a direc-

995

tor. I care that you're a good actress."

Richardson once said to me, "You're a man who would go out naked on the roof on a cold day for the sake of the production, and that's what I love about you. You don't set your ego in front of the play. You put the play ahead of your ego." I said, "Of course, because my ego's in the play. I mean I'm involved, and therefore the success of the play is my success to some extent."

Then one day somebody suggested some pieces of business to Maurice Evans while I was away, and the producer, Robert Josephs, was indignant. He said, "Don't accept them, don't accept them." I said, "Let me see them." And when they showed them to me, I said, "I accept three out of the four." And of course Evans was delighted, and he conceived a great respect for me because I wouldn't say, "What do you mean by altering my direction?" I said, "I don't give a damn if the janitor gives me a suggestion. I'll take it from anybody if I think it's right."

I'm not interested in my name. Nobody gives a damn who directed. Only the professionals talk about directors, and they don't know much about it either, especially the producers, and neither do playwrights. If it's a hit, the director is good. If it flops, he's not a good director.

Q: In '72 you did your final Miller play, *The Creation of the World and Other Business*, which you left. How did this strike you when you first read it?

Clurman: I liked the first act very much. By the way, it's going to be done soon I think as a musical play with fewer characters. I liked the first act very much, and it was very funny and altogether successful. I liked the second act 50/50. I didn't like the third act, and I told the author and producer it would never work. But there were many other troubles. I don't blame it on the play, although I think the play could never work as it stood.

The proof of it was they took it on the road for five weeks with a good director, Gerald Freedman;

they got the cast they wanted. Many left the cast: Barbara Harris left the cast before I did. Hal Holbrook left after Freedman took over for me.

So there was a lot of trouble. Then Miller rewrote the third act. I told him many many times it would never work. Eve's part which was originally very much longer—was cut down when they had the actress they wanted. My choice, Barbara Harris, was right, but she was a very difficult actress to handle. I never was able to do what I wanted to do—everyone was too impatient. The play needed a lot more time for work. The company was very difficult. They had all become stars. They all were trying to tell me how to direct, so there was a lot of trouble.

Before the out-of-town opening night I announced my resignation, not to the company but to Mr. Miller and Mr. Whitehead.

Opening night out of town did fairly well with the audience, and the critics gave me good notices. I laughed. I said if I had been a critic I would have panned hell out of my direction, because I didn't direct it much.

Q: Who took over—Miller?

Clurman: Only for a few days. Then Gerald Freedman did. And he said, "I don't want to hurt Harold Clurman. I have great respect for him." They said, "Harold Clurman's delighted for you to take over. He wants his name off the show, and he thinks well of you, and he resigned with the hope that somebody else could do what he wasn't able to do."

Q: Did you leave on good terms?

Clurman: Oh, sure, I didn't fight with anybody. I never fight with anybody.

Q: Well, it wasn't that you would fight, but I thought Miller might be hurt or...

Clurman: He was hurt. He was hurt, and he was angry, understandably so. He didn't want to hear about me for a long time because I had shot an arrow into his heart. He tried to direct for a while. I said, "You take over. Do anything you want," even while I was there. He took over and couldn't succeed either. I mean he had a difficult company, and they weren't satisfied with his play, his direction. They weren't satisfied with mine, which had gotten less and less, because after three days, right at the beginning of rehearsals, I met Michael Kahn at a restaurant, and he said, "You look so worried. You've got a great cast." I said, "I'm not worried about the cast. I'm worried about me." And the reason was I felt I could not control that cast because everyone was a genius: Hal Holbrook, who had been very very pliable in *Incident at Vichy*; I was dissatisfied with Mr. Whitehead, although he didn't know it. When I would try something, they would say, "It's no good." So I'd change it. I shouldn't have. I should have said, "Shut up and let me do my work." No, they wouldn't let me do it. Dishy also thought he was a great...

Q: Who?

Clurman: Bob Dishy, who was playing Adam. The third day Barbara Harris said to me, "If you tell me what to do—" and I wasn't telling her what to do. I was trying to tell her, something I always try to do, how I envisioned the play. All she said was, "If you tell me what to do, I won't do it."

Q: If you tell her what to do, she won't do it?

Clurman: Yes, and I wasn't telling her yet what to do. And I'm not a person to tell people exactly what to do unless they're receptive, and even so, I hope that they'll do things. So all this disarmed me, castrated me; but the trouble was in the play.

Q: I saw it.

Clurman: It was in the play.

HAROLD IN HIS PARIS APARTMENT 1921

APPENDICES

THE TWENTIES

•

DAILY WORKER ESSAYS (AS HAROLD EDGAR)

•

UNPUBLISHED PAPERS

APPENDIX A
THE TWENTIES

A STUDY OF ANDRÉ GIDE
(PAPER FOR A COLLEGE ASSIGNMENT)

That André Gide, the moral artistic mentor of one of the most considerable literary groups in France today, should be almost entirely unknown in our country might be considered a disheartening attestation of our intellectual insularity, if he were more generally acclaimed and appreciated in his own. André Gide has never succeeded in winning the eager and intelligent attention of a large public, and it may be doubted whether his growing prestige or notoriety, though it will permit historians to determine his proper position in contemporary French literature, will help make him, in any sense, a popular author.

No moment could be more favorable for the examination of the work of André Gide than the present, when the question in the air, the central preoccupation of all artistic discussion seems to be the question implied in the opposition of the terms romanticism and classicism. For, perhaps the most striking, surely one of the most disconcerting aspects of André Gide's work consists in its being at once both intensely romantic and consummately classic. But, though the stuff of Gide's art is derived from a romantic source and the manner in which this stuff has been fashioned—his art—is properly classic, there is no evidence of strife, of inner dissension in his work. So perfectly indeed have matter and manner been brought into harmony that to appreciate the excellence of the latter would be impossible without a familiarity with the contexture of the former.

Gide's novels and plays then are the histories of strange people who seek, each in their own way, to leave the open prairies of the known for some unexplored moral wilderness, there to meet with doom or, perhaps, with a superior mystic bliss. Gide's criticism, contained in the volumes of *Pretexts* and *New Pretexts* (works that take their place beside the finest literary criticism in French literature) may likewise be considered the record of the success or failure of literary men in setting out on this adventure.

Habit is the dead-weight which keeps us imprisoned in our homes, our ideas, our beliefs. In *Marshes* (*Paludes*) which is a sort of ironic preface to Earthly nurture, Gide has satirized, with a kind of grimacing humor peculiar to him, the unbeautiful moral congealment in which the complacent "normal" person lives. Gide mocks your "average" man who comes to take pleasure in his confinement, enjoys his indolence and makes a virtue of his mediocre satisfaction or resignation. In *Marshes* we hear Gide's cry of despair and revolt, "Ah, we are terribly confined." The book is Gide's *invitation au voyage*: "Perception begins where there is a change in sensation. Hence the necessity of travel." And the travel he recommends is intellectual and moral (as his admirable lecture on literary influences in *Pretexts* indicates) even more than literally geographical travel. In all phases of life, we should seek foreign landscapes.

Memory is mother to convention: we remember every act we performed with pleasure and the remembrance of that pleasure induces us to imitate it by repetition. Thus convention, the dogma of habit, is born. But, voices Gide with humorous exaggeration, "I prefer to walk on my hands today, rather than walk on my feet—like yesterday."

It is not surprising therefore to find that what interests Gide in a particular man is his special, his extraordinary vice or virtue. The protagonists of Gide's plays and novels are people who have overstepped the bounds of the conventional and have entered upon the road of the abnormally vicious or of a not less abnormal saintliness.

At the very core of Gide's individualism is the idea of renunciation. Thus the attentive reader must be struck with the constant recurrence of the precept of Christ which Gide has charged with the highest moral and aesthetic significance: "For whoever would save his life shall lose it; but whosoever shall lose his life, the same shall save it" (or, more literally, "make it truly living," says Gide.) The individual's salvation, both in art and in morals, lies in the renunciation of his individuality. Just as Christ taught that he who would enter the Kingdom of God must renounce his material possessions so a man before he can realize his true self must cast off his conventional habits of thought, the accretion of his opinions and prejudices, which he comes to regard as peculiarly his own, although they are the legacy of his environment or his education and must therefore ever remain external to him. In Gide, Nietzsche and Christ join hands.

Gide, profoundly "individualistic" though he be, would not make a "superman" of every mediocrity (even if this were possible).

Gide makes it fully evident that he recognizes the difficulty, not to say, impossibility for people to escape the well-tried and the habitual in their conduct of life. "Well, sir," says the author's interlocutor in *Marshes*, "you reproach people for living as they do, on the other hand you deny that they can live in any other way and then you reproach them for being happy in living as they do, but if it pleases them to live as they do, well sir, well-well—." And as a reply Gide cries out in mock despair, "But what I am complaining about is that no one complains!"

Morally, it has been Gide's function to remind us that the territory for discovery is infinite, that the land that lies beyond the last clearing-ground is equally fertile, equally capable of producing fine fruit. With one hand, he points to the undiscovered country before him, with the other he beckons for a companion to follow or advance him.

The supreme Christian precept—"For whoever would save his life shall lose it, but whosoever shall lose his life, the same shall save it"—serves Gide as the directive principle of his aesthetique, for "the laws of art and morals are the same." But whereas this dictum in Gide's morals takes on a dangerously romantic significance, in his aesthetique it becomes the motto of the sanest classicism.

What is the artist's "life" and what must he renounce to "save" it? Every artist is possessed of an Idea—an individual angle of vision, an individual sense of the comic and the tragic—an Idea for which he must find the proper symbols, the proper style. But in expressing his Idea, the artist often becomes enamored of his symbol, he begins to admire his means of expression for its own sake and the result is empty literary artifice and mannerism. The artist who creates a living work will have nothing but his Idea in view and he will seek to express it in the commonest terms possible. In other words (Gourmont's words) "Style means no more than a way of feeling, seeing, thinking."

Gide knows that "a new personality can only express itself in a new form." He knows that "the demands of sincerity always cause a certain difficulty and recalcitrance of style and of technique which, at first, must necessarily seem like preciosity, willful peculiarity, even artificiality, simply because it does not conform with the conventional." The truly original artist endeavors to employ the most general, most common terms and ends by achieving a genuinely individual style.

There is a peculiar reserve in Gide, his words seem to contain only part of his whole meaning and enigmatically to insinuate the rest. His sentences vibrate with an almost imperceptible nervous tremor; they escape us by their elusive fluidity even when their pitch is steadiest, their course most direct. Sentences that move swiftly seem to hesitate and draw back. Frequently lyrical in the earlier books, his style reveals the subdued and modest lyricism of the contemplative mind, and even in his most ecstatic outbursts there is a certain constraint which adds to rather than detracts from its intensity, so that at no time does Gide's lyricism ring hollow and "worked up." There are subtly nuanced fluctuations here, delicate lambencies that show "under the surface."

It is a musical rather than a pictorial style but its music is not made by sonorous, strange-sounding words but rather by the peculiar flow of the melodic line. It is, to continue this musical analogy, a chamber-music rather than an orchestral style. It has no great surge, no powerful impetuous movement, it persuades delicately. Though shunning cacophony at all times, Gide never seeks to be obviously ingratiating. He knows the secret of being to the point without becoming audibly intense, significant without becoming prophetically turgid. Gide writes beautifully, but in reading him one is never oppressed by the obligation of having to clasp one's hand in admiration over every fine effect. Beside the assertiveness and downrightness of most contemporary authors, the discretion of Gide's style almost takes on the aspect of a peculiar sort of preciosity. In some people, Gide's extreme moderation provokes irritation as if it were an excess!

Gide's art is an art of reticent and subtle suggestion. (In this respect, the sway of Stephen Mallarmé's genius and the example of the Gospels might be suggested as Gide's immediate influences.) An ineffable veil, which prevents us from immediately penetrating all their meaning, seems to hang over the simple words that make Gide's books. A sense of mystery pervades all his works. But there is nothing of the theatrically oracular, nothing of the picturesque mystic, nothing of the sibilantly intense in this mysteriousness. Mystery is not the synonym here of obscurity but, on the contrary, seems to arise from the fact that what is complex, hidden and unsettled is presented with too great a simplicity, too luminously and serenely.

Gide is an author for the few not because he is "difficult"—a good part of the reading public today is curiously attracted by "difficult" authors—but because, instead of making the

obvious sound "deep," he tells us profound things simply. That is why many readers go through Gide's novels, for instance, with almost too great a facility, only to experience a baffling sense of unsatisfaction at the end, a sense of having allowed something to escape them, all the more troubling since it cannot be ascribed to any well marked impediment to perfect comprehension. The secret of Gide's elusiveness is that he refuses to underline his "points," he avoids undue emphasis, he sets down everything he has to say with the same perfect equanimity, the same evenness of tone. "He insists so little."

Gide's art in his more mature works is an art in which reason or more precisely the critical faculty dominates, corrects and holds in check the inchoate romanticism which seethes in the amorphous pages of *Early Nurture*. In the hands of another, so perfectly designed, finely tempered a work as the *Immoralist* might have resolved itself into a verbose, violent and incoherent book.

It is interesting to study how these qualities manifest themselves in Gide's most characteristic novels: the *Immoralist* and *Strait is the Gate*. Both books are, so to speak, unilinear in construction. They contain but a single line of action without any digressions or underplots: they are stripped of everything but essentials. Few events are recorded, yet this very rigorous exclusion of all but the significant points of the action, though it helps create a certain atmosphere of morose colorlessness, which Gide's detractors mistake for dullness, directs our attention to the essential drama, the scene of which is in the protagonists' souls. These books would hardly gain in real significance or conviction by being more elaborately developed on the dramatic plane.

"Psychological novels" then? Certainly, these novels are of interest only as revelations of the moral, intellectual and, perhaps, physical motives which impel his characters to act, but there is a curious difference between a Gide novel and the "psychological novel" in its usual form. The difference is that Gide never "psychologizes," he never explains his characters. Gide's psychology is not discursive, it is dramatized, it is a psychology in action. And this may prove disconcerting to the reader who always wants to be sure he understands the character of a book at every step, since the acts that are recorded in these novels are of an exceedingly unconventional, strange, sometimes even monstrous nature!

Gide chooses the simplest methods to make himself appear entirely "absent" from his work. In the *Immoralist*, one of Michel's friends records the story as he heard Michel tell it to a group of friends. In *Strait is the Gate* the method is more roundabout. Jerome, the main agent of the external drama of the book tells us what happened to him in his relations with the girl he loved (Alissa). He tells us the actual facts of the story, the part he played in the drama of which however Alissa is really the central figure. When all the facts are recorded, the significance of the story still remains obscure, the reader is perplexed for the characters are seen only by the light of external events. But Alissa dies and leaves her diary to Jerome who publishes it as an appendix to his own record. This diary provides an indirect revelation which shows the events of the story to be the effect rather than the cause of Alissa's strange character.

Yet these characters (Michel, Jerome, Alissa) offer no explanation of themselves—at least not conscious, not complete explanations. They rarely explain their own mental reactions and when they do, the reader more frequently treats these explanations as additional factors in the character's spiritual make-up than as a key to its comprehension. These characters tell us what they have done, what they have been, what they think, but they never give a final explanation of themselves, they do not tell us why they have done a particular act, why a particular thought occurred to them. And they offer no explanation because they can not know the manifold motives for their actions.

In a certain sense, it may be said, Gide voluntarily places his characters beyond his control. If he does not submit a direct explanation of his char-

acters it is because he feels that there may be even a greater number of interpretations than even he can possibly conjecture. By directly offering his interpretation he would be limiting their fascinatingly human enigmatic quality. Gide wants the reader to see these characters very much as he would in real life, if he could see only the significant events in their development. Gide's novels are strewn with countless suggestions and half-explanations of the subtlest nature that are part of the story and which might nevertheless be completely overlooked or forgotten if these novels were not stripped of everything unessential.

Even these half-explanations, let it be repeated, are not formulated and applied by the characters themselves because they are unconscious of them, nor are they formulated and applied by the author because he does not wish to simplify and mechanize them overmuch. Thus, in *Strait is the Gate*, we learn that Alissa as a child had seen her mother in the arms of her lover. The incident is never mentioned again; the author draws no conclusion, makes no comment. The reader must make his own "diagnosis", formulate his own theory—the reader must be his own "psychologist."

No more eloquent proof of Gide's complete aloofness or objectivity in his character portrayal can be found than in the fact that various critics have offered entirely opposed interpretations of Gide's characters. Some critics, for instance, consider Alissa as the victim of her Huguenot environment and *Strait is the Gate* as a satire of Protestantism, whereas others will discern in Alissa, a typical Gidean heroine sacrificing the ordinary joys of possession for some greater, less accessible joy in the subtler satisfaction of ecstatic renunciation.

What cannot be doubted, in any case, is the artistic reality of Gide's characters. And though Gide offers no "key" to the solution of the problem which their strange behavior presents, they not only impress us with their reality but, like the characters of Dostoyevsky, they actually become comprehensible. But whereas we arrive at a comprehension of Dostoevsky's characters almost instinctively, Gide's characters can only be fathomed by an act of the intelligence.

"The artists work to be perfectly satisfying," Gide has said, "must show a direct relationship with the exterior world as well as an intimate relationship with the author's personality itself." Gide's work cannot, perhaps, be entirely satisfactory (how many authors' can?) because it realizes more thoroughly the second of these conditions than the first. Gide's work does not sufficiently reflect the superficial, the physical world with its treasure of sights and sounds, the amazing chimera of facts and faces. Gide's eye is perpetually engaged in examining his inner world; he is more interested in the emotion evoked by a landscape, than in communicating that emotion by making us see the landscape itself. Gide, in a word, is too interested in the subjectively psychological to satisfy our hunger for the material: his work betrays a dearth of things and of people, a lack of movement and action.

The lack of variety in Gide's work might perhaps be added as a corollary to this criticism. Gide, for all the dissimilarity in form of his various works, has hardly even treated more than one theme: he seems to have but a single preoccupation, a single "message." Each one of his books strikes me a as separate chapter within the covers of a single volume. All Gide's books seem to be elaborations on themes indicated in the Note-books of André Walter.

These defects which are even part of his qualities must be noted not so much for the sake of preserving "critical balance," as to point out that the fusion of matter and manner in Gide's work has been so perfect that all his artistic shortcomings may be ascribed to moral or temperamental shortcomings. To insist on these shortcomings however would be to succumb to one of the most ridiculous vanities of which contemporary criticism is constantly guilty: the absurd procédé of blaming an artist for what he is not: Jane Austen is not as muscular as Fielding, Fielding is not as

subtle as Stone, Stone is not as direct as Swift, Swift is not—etc., etc. This is unintelligent begging of the question. No artist—none!—completely satisfies all our needs. All the genuine artist can do is to offer his own greater or lesser contribution to create a synthesis which is always in the process of being completed. If the artist were what he is not (what the critics complain of his not being) he could not be what he is!

—Columbia University, '21

AMERICAN NIGHT AT THE SWEDISH BALLET
(LETTER FROM ABROAD)

Before its departure for New York the Swedish Ballet gave three performances at the Théâtre des Champs-Elysées of two more or less American ballets. *Within the Quota* a ballet-sketch by Gerald Murphy with music by one Cole Porter, orchestrated by Charles Koechlin, and *La Création du Monde* by Blaise Cendraars, with music by the inexhaustably prolific Darius Milhaud were the works performed.

But to fully appreciate the savour of these evenings at the Théâtre des Champs-Elysées, now one of the most interesting theatres in Paris, the mere record or even a criticism of these works and the manner of their performance would hardly suffice. The theatre is perhaps above all things a show-house, and here as elsewhere, not the least interesting spectacle is provided by the public itself. Indeed I am not sure in this instance that the spectacle provided by the public was not superior to the one presented on the stage. Physically, the public that attended the farewell performances of the Swedish ballet looked for all the world like the living models for the photographs and portraits in the *Vanity Fair* magazine! And it is no self-intoxicating exaggeration to add that intellectually it represented the most interesting, the most fascinating element in cosmopolitan Parisian society. Just as in America the most faithful reading public is that portion of the public which hopes eventually to be read, so here there were no ordinary theatre-goers. The audience was made up almost entirely of people directly interested in the arts: musicians, composers, painters, music and art students, critics and expensive women in still more expensive gowns, who "go in for the moderns."

Like the naïve French, who protest that it is unfair to judge them by the Parisian boulevards and their cafés, the Folies Bergères and the yellow-back novels published for foreign exportation, certain Americans believe that our movies together with extravagant newspaper reports, American "dancings" etc., have given Europeans an entirely superficial and caricatural conception of American manners and morals. The present ballet by Messrs. Murphy and Porter is supposedly a satire on this excessively simplified conception of the American scene, though without the preliminary warbling furnished by the program one would be hard put to it to tell precisely whether the satire was directed at the European view of America or whether it was intended as a satire on Americans for the amuse-ment of Europeans.

The stage is thoroughly bare save for the back-drop, an only slightly exaggerated replica of the front page of a typical American newspaper, presenting the usual phantasmagoria of amazing financial coups, stale divorce scandal, blatant monstrosities, baseball returns, lurid advertise-ments, all announced in the common jargon of busi-ness lyricisms. The Immigrant (orange complexion, sky-blue suit, light brown derby, handbag and tag on jacket) appears and turns in amazement at the view of the extraordinary horizon. Duly flabber-gasted, the Immigrant visions all the familiar and yet somewhat exotically piquant figures of the American wonderland: the Billionaire, the sepul-chral forbidding Puritan, the decorative Colored Gentleman, the Cowboy, the Jazz-Baby, the Prohibitionist and finally the Queen of all Hearts, a cross between Mary Pickford and Lillian Gish.

The authors of this ballet, it seems to me, have achieved a tour de force in rendering so dull and lifeless figures which even the movies, in its mock-serious fashion, can make amusing and almost appealing. We should have been gratified to find an American satire that wasn't more boring, more stupid than the thing it satirized, though we ought to remind ourselves that it is time Americans gave up satirizing themselves like embarrassed college boys. (It is true that in this case the satire is proba-bly directed at foreigners but, at bottom, the process is identical.) Satire is not the supreme art-form that many young intellectuals endowed with a sense of humor seem to believe. I will even venture to say that there is something narrowing and debilitating in satire. Morally, we need the cathartic of the fresh, robust lyricism of genuine comedy more than satire.

The music written for the occasion by Cole Porter was a fit accompaniment to the ballet. Betraying hardly a glimmer of an idea, entirely destitute of originality, it might have been simply boring had not Charles Koechlin's intricate, stri-dent orchestration made its poverty exasperating. Being a respectable musician, Koechlin tried to stifle and drown the music with sound. Alas! One heard it all the more. If unadulterated American lowbrow melodies in their frequently delicious vulgarity had been used as the accompaniment for this ballet, how moved the Americans present would have been, how delighted the French. Folk song has an irresistible appeal; it breaks down all resistances. And jazz is the true American folk song. It is the chant of the spoiled children of the big cities and America is a country of big cities. Our tiniest "one-horse town" is a would-be New York.

Milhaud's *Création du Monde* is, strictly speaking, not a ballet. It is a composition for orchestra. The costumes and décor by Fernand Léger, though diverting enough, are thoroughly irrelevant. The music does not appreciably paint the emotion of the ballet, nor does the ballet illus-trate the music.

On first hearing, this work, which indicates that jazz is destined to exercise an even more considerable influence on the younger European composers than on American, impresses one as less unified in style than the same composer's *L'Homme et Son Désir*. However this impression may be illusory. An American finds it difficult to admit jazz in any but its raw, primitive form, which he has come to love in spite of himself. He refuses to admit that jazz rhythms may be employed like any other, that they do not necessarily go with barber shop tunes, that they are not necessarily and inextricably bound up with the noisy vulgarity of dance halls and variety shows. The jazz rhythm has infinite possibilities. Because it has been applied only to particular kinds of melodies in a very limited manner is no sound reason why a genuine musician shouldn't use it in an altogether new manner, applied to any kind of melody and to a new effect. It is not a question of "catching the spirit of jazz", it is a question of adding a new procédé in musical technique.

Our surprise on hearing frank jazz rhythms in Milhaud's score, beside melodies of a solemn, almost tragic character, prevented us from detecting whether his use of them was merely a trimming up of jazz rhythms or whether these rhythms were given an individual Milhaudian quality. However there is little doubt of the profound earnestness of this as of all Milhaud's best works. One was also compelled to admire the mastery by which a small orchestra is made to sound as rich as a full sized one. Moreover, in spite of its superficially chaotic character and the seething abundance of its material, the work is dominated by that fine glow, that suave harmony which all really finished works achieve.

A word about the Swedish ballet itself. It is an organization that prospers without dancing. The music and the decors of the ballets performed are always the chief sources of interest. Not only is this true of snob ballets as *La Création du Monde* and *L'Homme et Son Désir* which are nothing more than orchestral scores with animated illustrations, but even of the more conventional ballets where one would expect to find the art of dancing practiced for its own sake. In "aesthetic and interpretive dancing" only superlative performances are

tolerable. The dancing of the Swedish ballet is always mediocre, lacking grace, brilliance, vigor— neither beautiful as art, nor stimulating as acrobatics. Yet, it has encouraged many young and interesting composers to write works that without it might never have won the benefit of public performance. That is why, with all its faults, it is a valuable organization.

—Nov. '22

MODERN MUSIC IN SALZBURG

In Salzburg, Mozart's birthplace, everybody makes music. The least ludicrous of European and American tourists come here to spend a cool week, climbing hills, wandering through woods, reading at the café about the comic-tragic diplomatic tug-of-war, as if it were history, (for how is one to take war or rumors of war seriously in this lovely valley?) and sending picture post-cards to their less favored friends. But in the "higher sense", music seems to be Salzburg's veritable raison d'être. You hear the young at their pianos, beating out the accords of a Beethoven sonata; in the Kurgarten a many-voiced orchestra plays Wiener waltzes as well as the Classics; the peasant yodels and yells, makes strange music on quaint instruments. At the hotel, you overhear guests explaining almost apologetically to their newly made acquaintances that though they are not quite musicians, they are, at least, ardent music-friends.

Here the International Society for Contemporary Music gave its first chamber-music festival—a series of six concerts with programs chosen from the works of some thirty composers out of fourteen different countries.

The three finest works of the series were unquestionably Maurice Ravel's *Sonata* for violin and violin-cello, Stravinsky's *Concertino* (one of the few works that have had the distinction of being hissed at a N.Y. performance) and Arnold Schönberg's song cycle, *Die Hängenden Gärten*, all of them, it must be noted, admirably given— which was to be expected where the level of excellence in performance was almost uniformly high.

Stravinsky's and, even more, Ravel's positions in modern music are firmly established. They are, each in his own manner, classics (as Sainte-Beuve understands the word) and it will probably be as quaint in a few years to object to Stravinsky as a musical iconoclast or to Ravel as a weaver of intricate but essentially trivial musical embroideries as it would be to cry out against the painfully dissonant Wagner trilogy.

The "shocking" element in Stravinsky's music, the element which is his most individual feature, his rhythm, causes his somewhat upset listeners to overlook the almost naked simplicity of his music.

His detractors, however, would have it that this simplicity betrays a fundamental poverty. For us, the variety and eloquence of Stravinsky's rhythms lend his work the greatness of primitive art, with a difference. This primitive is of our day; his music in so far as music may be said to express anything but itself, is the expression of a certain force in the life of our time.

In the *Concertino* for string quartet, this great Russian composer succeeds in adapting his genius to a form which might have seemed inimicable to it. It is a short succinct work based on two themes, the one violently sharp, the other, a pitiful popular lament the two forming a truly organic whole. Like most of Stravinsky's supposedly cacophonous compositions, the Concertino really sounds well. It is true, some modern theorists notwithstanding, that there are works that will sound as unpleasantly in the future (if they are played!) as they do at the date of their composition. *Le Sacre du Printemps* and the present Concertino are by no means in this class. As for *Petrouschka*, even the most "sensitive" listener must agree that it is a positive delight—even if only considered as pure sound.

It is no longer necessary to expatiate on the perfection of Ravel's art. Today the good Parisian bourgeois in the gallery of hideous Châtelet shouts an ecstatic "bis" whenever the Colonne orchestra plays Ravel—about once every week. Ravel's music is so essentially French, his grace, his skill, his wit, his delicate sensuality spring so directly from the "esprit français" that he may well be considered, with Gabriel Fauré, the first of the "established" musicians of France today.

The *Sonata* for violin and violin-cello, his most recent work, is not only another triumph, another masterpiece to place beside *Le Tombeau de Couperin* and *Ma Mère L'Oye* but marks a step forward in Ravel's art—and development is always a sign of vitality. The Sonata has all the usual qualities of Ravel's production with perhaps an even greater melodic opulence; suggestions of asperity, a certain rude power emerge from the hitherto always amiably facile grace of this "eighteenth-century-tempered" charmer. There is a trace of the Stravinskian here, though certainly no imitation—conscious or otherwise.

This Ravel *Sonata* is not an "easy" work; it does not immediately yield its secret. I had heard it twice before in Paris without appreciating all its loveliness, its amazing technical brilliance, its manifold variety. Yet all who hear it will agree that even today—and "today," in music, is always so hopelessly decadent, perverse, wrong-headed!— works of genuine beauty, really absolute music is being composed.

To return to the third of the really important works of the series, Schönberg's *Hanging Gardens*. Like *Pierrot Lunaire*, which is its logical development, this earlier song-cycle for voice and piano is, in its limited way, an extraordinary work, classic in the perfect adaptation of matter to means, in its simplicity and restraint.

It may or may not please us to hear the cries of Schönberg's tortured innards, his moral writhings and fevers, his bleak, painfully thin complaints, just as not all of us feel ourselves quite comfortable in Debussy's sensuous, iridescent shadowland (except in *Pélléas*) but he is, like Debussy, a master, and in much the same way.

Four other interesting, if not wholly satisfying, compositions were performed that are worthy of special note, the Hungarian Béla Bartók's second *Sonata* for violin and piano, the Czech Alois Haba's second string quartet, the third string quartet of Ernest Krenek and the clarinet quintet of Paul Hindemith, both Germans.

Béla Bartók is, with Schönberg, probably one of the most important figures in contemporary music. His earlier violin and piano sonata has been called one of the most important compositions for violin that has been written in the last two decades. In the second sonata, as in the earlier, Bartók has achieved the technical feat of having written the first work, in this form, in which the piano plays a completely independent part, never taking the same theme as the violin.

The work is unequal—the first movement far less successful than the second. This latter is typically Bartók, rude almost to savageness, vigorous Hungarian folk songs put to a marked brutal rhythm, with a touch of both the bitter and the tragic.

In Alois Haba's string quartet, also the second of its kind, the composer experiments with the quarter tone. Experiments are always interesting but unless the thing experimented with is assimilated, unless it becomes indistinguishable from the very content of the music and given aesthetic significance, the experiment remains mechanical and unimportant. The use of the quarter tone in the first movement of the Haba work does not, save for a few rare moments, make it a whit more interesting than it might have otherwise been. The quarter tone, like dissonance, becomes artistically significant only when it is inevitable. In the second movement the composer forgets his quarter tones for music.

The Krenek and the Hindemith compositions—the work of men generally considered the most important of the younger German composers—do not permit the passing of any judgment, on first hearing, beyond the observation that

they seem to be significant works. The first movement of the Krenek quartet struck one as ugly with an ugliness that was planned, *voulu*. "The work is logical," we seem to hear the composer say, "the themes are exposed according to the traditional rules of form and if the combination of notes sound badly—well, they won't when people have become accustomed to them. In the meanwhile, I don't care what they sound like."

This is the answer most frequently made to the usual reproach addressed to the modernists for their supposed "culte de l'informe." Though it may all be very true, this answer is based on an aesthetic fallacy. Classicism is not achieved by simply imitating the methods and technique of the classics. The point is to adapt your music to the classic technique or to create a new form and achieve a really personal classic utterance.

"Modern" music, finally, is no better than it ought to be. Critics would perform a great service to musicians and their public if they refrained from writing art-holy diatribes against "modern" music or, on the other hand, from intoning ecstatic hymns in its praise. There is no new musical aesthetic; there are only technical, formal novelties, neologisms in the musical vocabulary, that are born with the coming of new personalities, with their individual idiom. If the "new art" offers a superficially uniform aspect, it is because the artist uses the common vocabulary of his time. Alone the genesis, the purpose and the effect of art, of music in particular, has never changed.

To protest, as some of our well meaning critics have been doing, that it is impossible to distinguish the good from the bad in "modern" music, the genuine from the spurious, is pathetically ludicrous. One would think that there is a "trick" in judging the new music! There is no more a way of proving Brahms superior to Bruckner than there is a way of proving Irving Berlin the most talented writer of American popular songs.

You will hear only when you have renounced the habit of listening for the already-heard. Come to each new work fresh and free, listen with a naif (an unprejudiced) ear, unlearn everything but the essentials—imagination and sensibility. In the words of André Gide, "Chaque nouveauté doit nous trouver toujours tout entiers disponibles." — You may be temperamentally incapable of loving the new work but that is a new complaint entirely—and probably irremediable.

—'23

LETTER FROM ABROAD: A PORTRAIT OF A PARISIAN CRITIC

SIRS: The theatre always has the criticism it deserves. How true this is may be judged by considering the situation in France today where dramatic criticism is as completely conventional, limited and stale as the French theatre itself has been for the last two decades. But every rule engenders its exception. The exception to this rule is M. Maurice Boissard. Boissard has been signing the *chroniques dramatiques* in the most eminent French periodicals, notably the *Mercure de France*, and, since the war, in the *Nouvelle Revue Française*, and in the weekly, *Les Nouvelles Litéraires*.

Yet one hesitates to speak of him as a dramatic critic. For though one finds in his discursive and highly amusing feuilletons many valid opinions of the plays reviewed, one is constantly struck with the fact that drama interests Boissard only incidentally, that art is not his chief concern. Moreover, the reader never seeks in Boissard's chronicle to know what its author thinks of the latest theatrical success, he is never deeply impressed by the soundness of Boissard's judgments nor is he very much shocked by Boissard's unfair thrusts. In all of Boissard's writing, one seeks the man, not the man in the literary sense but in the most literal sense. Boissard is interesting as a personality.

His literary efforts include dramatic reviews (soon to be collected in a volume), a novel, *Le Petit Ami*, published under the pseudonym Paul

Léautaud, and (with the collaboration of Adrien van Bever) an anthology of modern French poetry, published under the same pseudonym. Yet in spite of this record Boissard is essentially not a literary artist. His novel hardly differs either in form or in content with his dramatic reviews, and some of the latter might very easily have served as a chapter of his novel. Boissard is essentially a *causeur*; talk is the mainspring of all his literary work. Everything he has written has the air of an apropos. His talk, however, has little in common with the brilliant verbal fencing of the *salons* where conversation is practiced as a fine art. Boissard's talk is rumination *à haute voix*; it is very much like what a man might say to himself in a bathtub soliloquy.

But good talk is free improvisation and admits with difficulty the restrictions of form. Boissard has no care for composition. "When I write," he says, "I have only to find my first sentence. After that I pay no attention to the sentences at all. I write with my idea in view, putting down whatever comes to mind." With such a temperament as his, what form of literature would most conveniently answer his needs? His ideal, he has confessed, would have been "to write something like Letters or Memoirs, the only writing that count." Unfortunately, only the dead or dying achieve literary success by publishing Letters or Memoirs.

Boissard chose dramatic criticism as the proper medium for his purpose, since, after a few words of acrid depreciation or tepid praise, sufficient for most plays, he might freely pursue the vagrancies of his quizzical humor, but the theatre itself appealed irresistibly to his lazy, slightly sensuous temperament. The theatre attracted him, as it does many of us, not merely because of the plays he would see there but because of the show it provides, the make-believe and the mask. "The theatre," he says, "is pleasure, laughter, imagination, lively repartee, the unexpected turn, the swift and penetrating dart; it is both the unreal and the true, self-amused observation revealing itself in comic flashes; it is movement, farce and even horseplay."

If Boissard's *bavardage* is his most striking characteristic as a writer, indolence is the essential quality of his personal character. This moral, physical and intellectual indolence undoubtedly colors all his views on life and literature. "I always prefer doing anything rather than what I am supposed to do, and what I must neglect always has more charm for me than the thing I am occupied with," he says in a manner which makes one wonder whether he thinks he is confessing a weakness or indicating a superior trait. Even his love of literature is an indolent, irresolute love:

Certainly, I enjoy writing. I even believe that it is the only thing in the world I really love—together with the pleasure of idling, dreaming alone in silence, in a comfortable armchair. But no matter how pleased I am with what I have written, when I have done fifteen pages, you must ask no more of me, whether I have finished or not. My enthusiasm is gone; I have already begun to think of something else. I am no longer interested and rather than continue I finish haphazardly.

This artistic indolence explains, in part, his impatience with purely artistic activity, his contempt for all preoccupation with form. Boissard might have defined form as "a way of saying brilliantly what might have just as well been left unsaid." "In the books I love," he tells us, "there is no fine writing; there are even many imperfections, but their author [probably Stendahl, who is Boissard's greatest admiration] is worth all the Flauberts in the world."

Boissard's mediocre sensuality, too, is marked by the same quality of lassitude and indolence. His preferred milieu is the brilliantly vulgar, somewhat stale, smoke-scented, liqueur-laden atmosphere of the popular music-halls. He is happiest with the girls who haunt the foyers of the Folies-Bergères and the Casino de Paris. "I was pleased," he says in his novel, where in his familiar, rambling style he tells of his childhood and youth, "not to return

to my books. What was there for me at home? Literature? I was more at ease with these women, and at the bottom I resembled them so much! Aren't they tired before they've begun their work, don't they cultivate desire without experiencing it, and don't they mimic the gestures of love just as I, for the most part, perform only the cerebral movements of literature?"

Not only will Boissard allow no thought of the beyond to torment him, but he betrays an old-modish contempt for religion and the "soul." He mocks patriotism. "I am interested in all peoples and in none, not even my own." Heroics of all kinds annoy him. Hence Corneille, who celebrated human will, becomes "that odious Corneille, whose declamation, emphasis and heroism are so unpleasant, flat and false. I once wrote 'stupid as a Corneille hero' and that is a good definition of stupidity." Boissard is contemptuous of the crowd, and he defines the public as "several hundred asses made the more asinine for having been assembled."

Yet for all this there is a decided strain of wry wistfulness in all Boissard's work, a kind of sentimentality without which no Parisian seems to be complete. He talks of his childhood in Monmartre with characteristically disenchanted tenderness; he speaks with amused gentleness of the streetwalkers of the Place de Clichy, who according to his account played so large a part in his development. But the creatures he loves most and upon whom he lavishes his warmest affection are his cats and dogs, not such as would find favor with the ordinary abandoned little cats and dogs taken up from the gutters. Here is the story of the dog Span:

I met him one day on the Rue de Vaugirard, scared, skeleton-like, baffled, running in all directions. I followed him without being able to pick him up. Finally I succeeded in taking him in my hands, although, in his terror and distrust, he tried to bite me. I bought him a good portion of food at a restaurant. Then, seated on a bench, I fed him. I shall always remember how this dog, who had been almost ferocious a quarter of an hour before, laid his head on my knees and looked at me with reassured and grateful eyes. I lost him in 1913, and his grave is in my garden, along with many others.

Boissard knows that both the mediocre play and the critic who declares it to be such will be forgotten. Thus the part of his reviews devoted to the passing of judgments is short, concise, cruel. However, his ferocity is never blatant or pretentious; it is a rather nonchalant ferocity. His prejudices, of course, are violent, but amid the faint murmurs of his fellow-critics Boissard's sweeping overstatements ring fresh and true. In what esteem does he hold the contemporary French theatre?

For the last fifty years our theatre has been stifled by stupidity, like our age. When we consider that the boring and mediocre Alexandre Dumas fils, together with glum and glacial Henri Lavedan, who make plays out of the works of science they have just read, and Porto-Riche, who refines upon what is already artificial, are still considered masters, we have an excellent idea of the state of hebetude to which we have fallen. Silliness, pretension, talkiness, grave stupidity, obscure preciosity—that is, in its ensemble, our theatre for the last fifty years. It is no longer the theatre; it is a pulpit. It is no longer art; it is pedagogy. The only thing that really is funny is the grandiloquent Guignol provided by the dramatic works of Victor Hugo. On the one hand, we have authors so delighted with having learned something that they burn with the desire to communicate their knowledge; on the other hand, we find a dull public desirous to look as if they were escaping the bogwater of their ignorance and to learn something.

Boissard is hardly more edulcorated in his comments on actors and actresses. "The performance is killingly funny," he says in a review of a very dignified play in verse at the Comedie Française. "What made Mademoiselle Ventura go on the stage? She is ugly, small, ill-formed; she has a nasal voice and ridiculously affected mannerisms. I can more easily imagine her as a saleslady in a department store than as an actress on any stage. It is not true that ridicule kills. If this were so M. Le Bargy [one of the 'glories' of the French stage] would be buried today." It is Boissard too who defined the Comedie Française as "The French Academy of the boulevard theatres," a remarkably apt characterization.

On the positive side, Boissard is hardly so expansive. For, as he himself explains, "admiration makes me timid, fills me with scruples, I doubt whether I am capable of giving adequate praise and so often prefer to remain silent. How often I have felt how much more easy it is to attack a bad play than to prove the merits of an excellent one." Yet Boissard has encouraged most of the really interesting French dramatists of today—Crommelynck, Vildrac, Mazaud. He has praise for Jacques Nathanson, the brilliant boulevard Marivaux, and he admires Sacha Guitry "the Molière of our day!" Boissard may be read with pleasure; he can not be imitated.

I am, etc.,

H.E. Clurman

—*FREE*, 23 Jan. '24

OUR THEATRE: A Monologue with Interruptions

The Outsider: If you will omit the evangelical tone, you may talk to me about the theatre.

The Theatre-Man: Fanaticism is not only inevitable with us, it is almost indispensable. Craig, Jones, Copeau, Stanislavsky, all are possessed by it. We have difficulty enough in making cultivated people outside the theatre take more than a casual interest in our art, but what is worse, we have to establish order within the theatre itself. Because life is not only its subject but its material, the theatre always verges on dissolution; its integrity is constantly endangered by those who should preserve it. To maintain values in such an art one needs a quixotic earnestness.

The Outsider: You betray yourself with your first words. You speak of degradation of values, of the indifference of the cultivated outsider. You speak as if you treasured some secret. I like the theatre, my friends like the theatre. We know that distinguished talent is rare, that very few performances are inspired, that good plays are infrequent. But why this outcry? The theatre is not the victim of a special conspiracy. It suffers as do all arts in our day.

The Theatre-Man: There are other arts, there is no theatre.

The Outsider: I don't understand that. There are...

The Theatre-Man: There are hundreds of theatrical productions, yes, but they do not make a theatre. You mention the dearth of talents. That should not even enter this discussion. If you think my complaint lies in that direction, you prove the seriousness of our misunderstanding. But that misunderstanding is universal. That is what makes the situation seem hopeless.

The Outsider: Well then, bring light to bear! Why have we no theatre?

The Theatre-Man: We lack a coherent conception of the theatre. We welter in a sea of little notions about plays and producers, actors and directors, prices and the public. But none of this is integrated in an all-embracing synthesis. We need—I know the word will not frighten you—a

complete theory. The theory I speak of is not a poetic estheticism but an honest consideration of fundamentals. Without such a leading principle we can have no adequate technique, and all our strictures and remedies must go wide of the mark.

The Outsider: There is something disconcerting to me in your emphasis on theory. I have heard you say yourself that theories of art always follow rather than precede the creation of art-works. Yet here you insist on the necessity of a conscious approach. However, since everything depends, according to you, on formulating a theory, I wish you would get to it at once.

The Theatre-Man: It is a delicate matter. But the main lines may be traced.

The Outsider: I am all attention.

The Theatre-Man: The first thing to recognize in considering the theatre is that what gives it its special character among the arts is the presence of the actor. The theatre begins with the actor and achieves expression through him. The theatre begins with the actor, that is, he is its first and essential element but he is not by himself the theatre.

The Outside: As a melody is not a symphony.

The Theatre-Man: Yes. But, of course, a single actor may be able to create a complete work of art, if the thing he wishes to express can be fully realized by himself alone. However, some things cannot be expressed by one person; they represent a group experience. To express them a number of persons must unite their efforts. It is absolutely essential, however, that all be related to the central experience.

The Outsider: I am not sure I follow you.

The Theatre-Man: Imagine a group of savages in celebration. Their festivities include the representation of some major event in their lives, such as the hunt. Only those who share this experience can become part of the play. They may share it in two ways: either they have actual knowledge of the hunt or they know it imaginatively—they have been made to feel all the emotions that hunting arouses. This group of experience is the generating element of the play. But to transform this experience into art, a leader must emerge from amongst the actors.

The Outsider: Are you talking about the director or the playwright?

The Theatre-Man: They are really one. The leader is a sort of high priest of the play. He takes the material of the common experience and creates from it the scheme of a performance of actors. If words are necessary they come to the actors as spontaneously as do their gestures, though the leader in designing the form of the performance may give them words as he gives them actions to carry out. Or there may be another actor in the group with a gift for speech who will suggest the words to be used.

The Outsider: But I don't see who writes the play.

The Theatre-Man: The play can never be written! Only the words of the play may be. The play is the sum of the activities of the group under the leadership of one of its actors.

The Outsider: Have you now all the main elements of your theatre?

The Theatre-Man: Not quite. The group of actors I have been talking about springs from a larger group—the tribe. By the same process of specialization that produced a leader from amongst the actors, the tribe develops a body of performing actors and another of passive actors or spectators. And the spectators, being actors, share in the experience of the others. The spectators share the expe-

rience not only because they themselves may have known the joy and terror of the hunt but because they are anxious for those who do participate in it or because they know that its result may affect their own lives or simply because they love the movement and struggle visioned in the performance. Should the same play be presented before the spectators of another tribe, where conditions are so different that it could no longer be appreciated, you would no longer have the elements for a complete theatre. In short, there can be a theatre only where there is a community of desire, interest and understanding on all sides.

The Outsider: That would be an ideal state anywhere!

The Theatre-Man: With the development of the theatre, the process of specialization continued beyond the breaking point. The play-leader first ceased to be an actor—although this does not prevent him from being one in spirit; the creator of the play-form and the writer of the play's words isolated their functions. And we have the stage-director and the modern playwright. This was not necessarily a calamity so long as the latter remained a member of the theatre-unit. But the playwright began to dote on his words. He withdrew from the theatre; he became an independent literary artist. He no longer believed that his words were written for the theatre, it was the theatre which was made for his words. Literature which had come into the theatre as an element of the play began to dominate it. The theatre suffered from this, but it did not die. Only its energies scattered. And complete chaos set in. The serious public was won over to a literary conception of the theatre, while the simpler, unlettered public remained faithful to the more complete theatre, which, because of its audience, was devoted exclusively to the lighter aspects of life.

The Outsider: Well, how do you relate all this to our own American theatre?

The Theatre-Man: It provides the horrible example of this last phase. You know, I suppose, something of the organization of our theatre. A producer buys a play—that is, a play in the ordinary sense, a book of dialogues with more or less valuable suggestions for theatre use. After the play is bought, the producer begins to think of a director, actors and a scene-designer. He collects these anywhere and everywhere. When all these separate universes are gathered and temporarily tricked into a sham harmony, they are placed before the public. The production is then hawked around like any other merchandise. That is show-business.

The Outsider: You speak as if there had never been a...well...a reform, a new movement.

The Theatre-Man: It is precisely this theatre of the new movement which disheartens me. For some years now I have followed it with the greatest sympathy. In the beginning, I was as enthusiastic as anyone; I watched its playwrights, its producers, its scene-designers with the keenest interest. But I've come to realize that its progress was a superficial one.

The Outsider: Be concrete. It is time for specific instances.

The Theatre-Man: Let us see what the new movement has accomplished. It systematically produced good plays. That was its first noteworthy contribution. Its second was the recruiting of a public for such plays. Its third was the adoption of the permanent company idea. The movement introduced intelligence to the American theatre. It made taste a paying proposition. It revealed a number of very interesting artists. But the only striking difference between the new theatre and the old is that the former sells better stuff.

The Outsider: These are considerable gains, it seems to me.

The Theatre-Man: But hardly any of them go to the root of the matter. I said a theatre arose with a group of actors sharing a common experience and a common aim. These theatres always begin with a play. Actors are chosen for the plays, instead of plays for the actors. What is meant by choosing an actor for a play? It means, practically speaking, choosing an actor for a part. If your part calls for a fat, sluggish boor, choose an actor as like such a man as possible. Or you will find a group of playwrights with radical social ideas, who believe in the necessity of a worker's theatre. They hire young actors, whose chief ambition it is to become sufficiently well known to be engaged by Broadway managers, and set about producing their plays. There is no careful selection of the people who are to work with them, no preliminary attempt to weld them into a unified body. If these playwrights understood the theatre, they would see that the result of each production would not be one play but almost as many different plays as there are actors in the cast. A hundred tunes but no music. Engaging permanent companies will not solve the problem. For unless there is unity of outlook in a company, this system only fosters permanent discord.

The Outsider: I have permitted you to proceed without interruption, so that you might present a connected statement of your views. But you have delivered yourself of some appalling assertions. Not begin with plays, you say. I have never heard of beginning any other way.

The Theatre-Man: The Moscow Art Theatre is generally acknowledged the leading theatre in the world. It achieved its greatest success in the plays of Chekhov, but it did not originate with Chekhov. If it had merely produced Chekhov as tomorrow the Shuberts may produce Shakespeare, it would hardly be any more important as a theatre than had it produced the works of very inferior authors. The group of actors of the Moscow Art Theatre had for a long time been trained under their two directors, and were chosen by them not only for their ability, but because they all had a like feeling for their art and formed a more or less homogeneous unit. They were prepared to express in terms of the theatre that experience of Russian life that had inspired Chekhov to write his plays. Had an inferior author brought them the same kind of material, it would still have been a great theatre. Had it begun simply as a collection of talented actors and set about to do all the fine plays of the world, it would not only not have been a great theatre, but, in my sense, it would not have been a theatre at all.

The Outsider: Protest as you may, you cannot shake my conviction that our stage has shown some fine productions.

The Theatre-Man: Perhaps. But you still fail to see the difference between a production and a theatre. A production is a single piece of theatre-art, while a theatre is a cultural unit.

The Outsider: That has a grandiose ring. I prefer more matter-of-factness. Nevertheless, it is true, a certain degree of importance has been attached to the activities of our more ambitious theatres. Yet you hardly rank them above the ordinary Broadway producing firms.

The Theatre-Man: I have already mentioned their first error, from which, perhaps, all others derive. Their theory, in so far as they have any, assumes that good scripts plus a capable company to act them constitute a theatre. But perhaps you are not yet ready to regard this as an error. Let us therefore follow a line closer to your way of thinking. Begin with the axiom: the theatre is an art. Like every other art it expresses something and from this the technique of that art is developed. The play, you will agree, is what the theatre expresses. And the plays of our advanced theatres, we admitted, are superior to those of the commercial theatres. Now in what way has the technique of the new theatres been modified by its new themes? The only positive development has been in scenic design. We are no longer invited to look at a poetic play in a dull realistic set. But the direction in our new theatre is what it was in the old, though rarely so competent or thorough. Its method consists in hiding tricks borrowed from Broadway, under the distinguished craftsmanship of the scene-designer. Unlike the avant-garde *régisseurs* of Russia and Germany, our directors express their new subjects with an old technique, which amounts to not expressing them at all. The failure of these directors is most apparent in the acting of their productions. What plays are most convincingly acted in our "art-theatres"? Precisely those which are most akin to the commercial theatre. To these plays the actors really respond. But the producing organizations will ask them to do a French poetic-rhetorical drama, a modern German tragedy in the classic manner or something equally foreign to them. Thus, false impressions are given of many fine plays by actors unprepared to cope with them.

The Outsider: Will you allow me a somewhat rhetorical question? Is it really so essential for the actors to understand the plays they are doing?

The Theatre-Man: For a play to live in the theatre, the word of the playwright must become flesh in the actor. Unless this happens we cannot speak of any theatre-art.

The Outsider: I am afraid your theatre would soon be transformed into a laboratory. Actors are supposed to have mastered the rudiments of their art before they appear on the stage.

The Theatre-Man: The theatre need not be a school, but work in a theatre should constitute a schooling. Theatre-artists must perfect their craft as do other artists. But other artists are rarely called on to produce their work to a regulation time. Why are theatre-workers forced to do so? Commercialism, you say. Yes, to a great extent, but I suspect there is a truer reason. The theatre does not occupy the status of an art even in the minds of its friends. Theatre people are constantly egged on to performance, as if there were no period of creative gestation in the theatre as in all other arts. It has not yet been recognized that the laws of the theatre are the laws of all arts, and that a theatre-work—though collective—must be judged as if it were the work of a single artist.

The Outsider: I see now what you mean by a theatre being a cultural unit. It is not a picture gallery in which each work of art preserves its value independent of the others or with little relation to the personality of the exhibiting agent. The theatre is a collaboration of artists to express a single vision. Unless that vision is common to all there will be no complete expression. In such a collaboration the lone artist must wither from inanition. But should the impossible happen, should a group of artists merge their wills to one purpose, then the theatre would become a truly representative body as there can hardly exist in any other art. But is it possible for a theatre to enjoy such a blessed state?

The Theatre-Man: In the theatres of the day before yesterday, in the theatre of Molière, of Shakespeare, of the Italian comedians, the theatre as a cultural unit was almost an automatic fact. From the beginnings actors and playwrights were one with each other and with their public, and they could express all their experience of past and present in a common language. To have unity they did not need to come to the theatre with a theory, they were, so to speak, born with it. But today, with our inheritance of the theatrical forms of many cultures, with the estrangement of all our artists, we need a conscious approach. For as the experience of the last fifteen years has taught us, we can have good plays, good actors, good directors and not have a real theatre. The theory of a theatre must act as its starting point.

The Outsider: It must form the basis of its unity.

The Theatre-Man: But for this we need leaders, men who are at once students, workers and craftsmen, men of ability and passion. They will not succeed if they attempt to force their theory on unyielding material. They must gather together people predisposed to accept it, they must communicate its spirit to the humblest member of their group. The artistic will of one must then become the artistic will of all. We shall not have a theatre until this is realized.

The Outsider: It is not easy.

The Theatre-Man: It is not easy. Shall it therefore not be done?

—'29

APPENDIX B
DAILY WORKER ARTICLES

MURDER AT THE VANITIES

No matter how you look at it Earl Carroll's *Murder at the Vanities* is not an important show. The daily reviewers found it dull, the audience whose appetites it is intended to satisfy will not enjoy it, and before long everyone will have forgotten its run at the New Amsterdam Theatre.

Shows like this are produced all the time. By hook or crook, a sum of money of no less than $50,000 is collected from various sources—the movies, dizzied bankers, prosaic sugar-daddies, eccentric racketeers—and the results of their corporate business acumen, tastes and hopes make up the greater part of the theatre of Broadway. In this instance, Mr. Carroll, who has produced huge successes to the tune of staggering deficits, guessed wrong and his losses will be heavier than usual. But just as the characteristics of health may be deduced from the symptoms of a sick person, so *Murder at the Vanities*, by its crude simpleness reveals the anatomy of show business in all its phases.

The theatre program runs the usual series of advertisement credits—this, of course, as a means of lowering costs on the items for which credit is given. "Laces used in this production exclusively by Gehring, Solomon and Birnbaum, Inc. Lingerie in 'Novelty Scene' designed by Werther Friedman. Dogs by Toy Department, Gimbel Bros. Miss Baclanova's trimmed suit and wrap by Russeks, Fifth Ave. Blue panels used in second act are manufactured by Westinghouse," etc., etc.

This combination of art and trade is reproduced in subtler forms in the text and staging of the show. To begin with, the idea on which it is based is the old two-for-a-nickel, extra-pair-of-pants bargain bait of combining the thrills of such a mystery melodrama as *The Spider*—in which a crime is committed in a theatre during performance—with the allurement of Mr. Carroll's most beautiful girls in the world. The suspicion that the more seductive the girls the less exciting the mystery might become seems not to have disturbed the producer's faith in his idea. So the odd combinations multiply.

There are references in the dialogue to Roseland—advertisement for the benefit of the gallery—to the Essex House—advertisement for the benefit of those who buy their tickets at a premium—to the taste that makes Chesterfields better—advertisement for the whole house which is further reminded of this fortunate cigarette by a full page on the program cover. The entertainment further includes a rather pleasant roller-skate artist, a prima-donna from the Moscow Art Theatre, a character actress from the Yiddish Art Theatre, a romantic villain from the Hungarian National Theatre, a handsome lead from the higher-brow dramatics of Katherine Cornell, an ingénue from nowhere, whose experience begins under Mr. Carroll. The only performance which is not perfunctory is that of a comedian from vaudeville and musical comedy.

These sundry attractions assembled at high expense from everywhere give "class" to a show. Here we see them displayed together—not as lavishly as Mr. Carroll is accustomed since even he has learned to "economize"—like dummies in a show-window. They move dispiritedly because they do not belong together, because they certainly do not realize what has brought them there.

What has brought them to this chaos and collapse of art and of business, whether they like it or not, is that they are simply commodities which a decaying system permits blundering privateers to sell to a public no longer interested in buying. These actors—some of them talented—are working hard and getting little either in terms of money or human recompense, because in the last analysis they do not know the theatre—the world to which it belongs, its inner mechanism, its economic foundations, what part they play in it, how it can be changed and how they can help change it.

In fact, they are not part of the theatre at all, for a theatre, as a Soviet Theatre director recently defined it, is an "ideologically cemented collective," and the Broadway theatre is at best nothing more than a bazaar, a haphazard assortment of wares thrown together to be auctioned to idlers on the market place. These actors are all victims of a more bloody murder than Mr. Carroll's, with his spectacular imagination can show at $3.30 a seat. Across the street from the New Amsterdam, a more realistic entrepreneur advertises *Slaughter at Minsky's*. Take your choice.

—*DW*, 20 Sept. '33

BROADWAY AND THE SOVIET THEATRE

The present writer has not as yet visited the Soviet Union and has seen only the work of the Moscow Art Theatre whose productions outside Russia were not representative of its latest tendencies, the Moscow Kamerny Theatre which, during its first foreign tour also presented only the efforts of its pre-revolutionary days and *The Dybbuk* as produced by the Habima Theatre.

This is hardly sufficient by itself to permit one an opinion of the Soviet Theatre. But there are other ways of becoming acquainted with the Soviet Theatre though, to be sure, less satisfactory ones than the actual witnessing of performances. There are profusely illustrated monographs in Russian, German, French and English. There are magazines (notably the *International Theatre*, organ of the International movement of worker theatre.) And it is a sign of the enormous vitality of the Soviet Theatre that even an acquaintance with it through such indirect sources can be of real value to the American

theatre worker, both as inspiration for a feeling about the theatre and as a guide in actual theatrical technique.

That the Worker's Theatre movement has everything to learn from the example of the Soviet Theatre must be clear to everyone close to that movement, but that the Soviet Theatre is a mine of theatrical instruction even for the professional bourgeois theatre, is something that hardly any of the American theatre workers who have visited the Soviet Union and become enthusiastic over its theatre seem to have grasped. The Soviet Theatre—and it is a theatre-worker of the professional bourgeois stage who says this—is the greatest school of theatrical craftsmanship that the world possesses today. That so many workers of the bourgeois theatre without having learned some of its countless lessons, without having understood that they as theatre-people could profit in their own work by what they have seen, is simply an indication that the American bourgeois theatre is mostly dead or non-existent. The living elements in the theatre all over the world must be galvanized and reshaped by the actual organization and procedure of the Soviet Theatre.

True, it seems nearly impossible to build a culturally organic theatre within the orbit of the professional bourgeois stage in America, and much of what has been accomplished by the Soviet Theatre has been made possible by the revolution; but by courage, integrity, intelligence and hard work some progress may be effected even here and now. The point is that no individual and no theatre in Western Europe or in America—and I am not forgetting Gordon Craig whose suggestive writings and drawings were undoubtedly an important influence in the theatre before 1917—can make us visualize the goal, teach us the necessary steps to be taken toward it, and serve as a universal theatrical school better than the theatre of the U.S.S.R.

—*DW*, 25 Sept. '33

BROADWAY AND AN ALIVE THEATRE

Double Door at the Ritz Theatre is about a woman who lords it over one of those sedately monied mansions which were once considered to give grace and dignity to Fifth Ave. Her sense of family, which is a sense of class and a sense of property, drives her to maniacal lengths of maliciousness, avarice and crime. With this material we might expect a melodrama, a character study or a piece of social investigation. But as melodrama *Double Door* lacks action, as a character study it lacks background and subtlety, as a social investigation it lacks ideas. It is played with that studied accuracy which is adequate for the communication of the trivial and obvious points needed to make the plot intelligible. It is technically above the average of early season shows which means that it is a fairly smooth mechanism with a content that could not possibly entertain any adult intelligence.

Such is the state of the Broadway theatre, however, that this production was greeted by a cordial press. The acting, which is stock-company realism, was highly praised, and the direction which is careful over little nothings was likewise treated with serious approval. What does this mean except that the Broadway audience satisfies itself with banalities when they are camouflaged with surface authenticity: good-looking period costumes, oak-finish paneling, suave lighting or, in other instances, the latest model serving table, real refrigerators, genuine lobster aspic! The aim of such productions apparently is to add a simple story interest to a commercial exposition.

This is the very death of the theatre. To realize completely what is wrong with it we must turn to a theatre which is alive. The livest theatre today—and since the collapse of the German theatre through Hitler perhaps the only one alive—is the Soviet Theatre. If the Soviet Theatre teaches

nothing else, it teaches that the theatre must use every element at its command to create action that is vibrant with emotion, movement, color, music—all in the service of some specific and unified ideas.

To get away from the actor's sterile imitation which is Broadway's method of "registering points," the Soviet Theatre uses the Stanislavsky system for the summoning of the actor's true feeling, or the Meyerhold method for a more definitive communication of ideas through bodily movement or the Vacktangov synthesis which teaches the use of true feeling for the arriving at forms of expression more complete and symbolical than those of realism. When the play is a melodrama, every human reaction, every sound, every scenic effect is called into play—as in the Moscow Art production of *The Armored Train*. When the play is a study of social manners every rhythm, characteristic manifestation of folk-life is studied and given a theatrical elaboration—as in Tairov's production of O'Neill plays. If the play is a fantasy every form of make-believe, joyous improvisation, theatrical invention is released for the delight of an audience that does not take its function passively—as in Vacktangov's *Princess Turandot*. If the play is a musical comedy, the musical setting, the dances, the comic by-play, the use of the chorus is original and different in every case, depending on the nature of the material—as in Danchenko's and Tairov's productions.

The point is that in every production there is the presentation of a whole gamut of human emotion, action, and general stage life that is new and particular to each play—so that the theatre always remains theatre and not a form of limited movie. The theatre preserves its own thrill, not to be replaced by any other art or entertainment.

Bourgeois critics like to emphasize the "propaganda" elements in the Soviet Theatre—elements which they can slight because they do not believe in them; what they fail to point out is that this theatre so committed to "propaganda" is the most theatrical of all theatres—the gayest, the most exciting, the most colorful. And, of course, they never ask themselves what relation there is between the "propaganda" which they shy from and the theatrical craft which they are forced to admire.

—*DW*, 27 Sept. '33

THE GROUP THEATRE

The Group Theatre is an important unit for two reasons: it is the only professional theatre in New York organized as a collective, that is, as a theatre in the complete sense of the word; and, like many activities of the lower middle-class intellectual world today, it manifests a recognizable movement toward the "left."

The most significant and conclusive aspect of the Group Theatre's work at present is the technical one. From its theatrical method, which applies to the American actor the basic precepts of the Stanislavsky system especially as developed and enriched by the Moscow Art Theatre Studios under Vachtangov, all who are interested in true theatre—and particularly in a revolutionary theatre—have much to learn.

It is necessary to stress, however, that this assimilation of the doctrines of the great Russian theatre is not merely a question of pedagogy. Other organizations, notably the American Laboratory Theatre, have taught the principles of the Stanislavsky system. They were neither able to survive, nor to impress any audience with the advantages of their methods. The Group Theatre has a company of actors talented enough to engage any audience, intelligent enough to understand the value of real work, honest enough to want to develop not only their commodity-personalities but their intrinsic abilities, courageous enough to maintain periods of discouragement and indifferent results. The Group Theatre has directors of substantial theatrical experience. It has the aim of saying something in the theatre, and the will to learn a technique whereby what it has to say may be said in appropriately effective theatrical terms. Finally, it believes that the best theory is practice,

and the most eloquent program in the theatre is what the audience can be led to see, feel and understand from the action on the stage. The result of its two years effort, despite retards and setbacks, is that it is embarking upon its most ambitious season immediately after a good many funeral services had been performed over it.

The content of the Group Theatre's ideological tendencies is not a subject for abstract argument. Its list of plays, which in the past included Claire and Paul Sifton's *1931—*, the first unemployment play to reach Broadway, and which promises new plays by John Lawson, John Dos Passos, Melvin Levy, and Keene Wallis' adaptation of Hauptmann's *Weavers* for the future, must be taken as the final test of the progress or its lapse in this respect. Each play must be especially examined and criticized from this viewpoint. Such criticism should be comparative in relation to now-existing conditions both of society and of the theatre, and absolute in relation to the ultimate goal of a fine drama, the drama of a classless society, which, in terms of the present, must be a revolutionary drama.

The Group Theatre's present production, *Men in White*, at the Broadhurst Theatre is chiefly noteworthy for the fact that it is the first which has brought the Group's collective technique prominently and successfully to public notice. Other Group productions—particularly *The House of Connelly* and *1931*—have been remarkable for their ensemble or "teamwork," but these were considered special plays. *Men in White* reveals this technique—which is not a trick that can be applied indiscriminately and at will whenever desired, but an accumulative theatrical discipline for the organization and the individual within it—in a play of a more popular nature. The result is what the reviewers call a good show.

Men in White, which deals with doctors and the life of a hospital, is thematically based on the conflict in a young intern between personal happiness and the scientific pursuit of medicine. Despite this the play is not distinguished by any particular social comment or definite intellectual value. And whatever its emotional quality may be, it derives mainly from its vivid subject-matter and unusual milieu as seen through the simple intelligence and devotion to the task with which the Group actors perform their various duties.

The production simply marks the first box-office success of a sound theatrical technique achieved through the most valid principles of collective work in the theatre. We hope that the Group Theatre, having found a modicum of recognition for its methods, advances toward an increasingly important employment of them.

—*DW*, 3 Oct. '33

BROADWAY COMEDY

Despite the anarchy of the Broadway theatre, it seems to have its laws. One of the most indisputable of them permits a writer to treat almost any theme if he can make it funny. The first prominent anti-war play was a comedy, *What Price Glory?*; the first racket play was another comedy, *Broadway*; the first play to examine the movies was still another comedy, *Once in a Lifetime*; the most successful political play was a musical-comedy, *Of Thee I Sing*.

One might suppose from this that we were a nation of humorists, a jolly people. But Broadway comedy is a very special thing with a character all its own. True comedy uses the materials of experiences as frankly, as boldly, as completely as any tragedy. *Don Quixote* is comedy, so are the plays of Molière, the novels and plays of Gogol. All of them are close to life, increase our understanding of it, and are just as concerned with truth as are the great tragedies. But Broadway comedy eliminates the truth of every subject, in fact it removes the subject altogether. So that the audience which applauds the comic anti-war play is composed of the same people who were "patriotic" during the war, and will be again; the audience which howls with glee over *Of Thee I Sing* are Democrats

whose laughter would turn sour if a really revolutionary idea were suggested to them by the show. And the audience which proved its superiority by laughing over the absurdity of the movie industry in *Once In a Lifetime* is the audience which supports Hollywood.

Crack a joke, pull a gag, do a tap, turn a somersault apropos of any subject; everyone will laugh and the subject will not have been touched, and what is more important, the audience will not have been touched by the subject. The fun is never built upon the truths of these themes—which is a legitimate and mature process—but is always beside it—a juvenile means of escape. The comedy of these plays is the equivalent of that of the wise-cracker who can break up any conversation by a remark entirely irrelevant to it. Thought, experience, knowledge, understanding, are unnecessary for the appreciation of these plays. They substitute slapstick high-jinks, puns, acrobatic stunts.

This is the cream of traveling salesman comedy, a comedy which contains no element of contact between the comedian who cracks the joke and the object about which the joke is cracked, and no real contact either between the person who hears the joke and the one who makes it. Most representative of this type of comedy at its best are the Marx Brothers who begin and end their fun-making without a subject, and reduce everything to sheer nonsense. They symbolize the big-city middleman always glibly selling something he has no respect for to someone who has no need of it. The sum total of such comedy in human content is zero.

Two plays produced recently exemplify this tendency of Broadway comedy in different ways; *Kultur*, at the Mansfield Theatre, and *Sailor, Beware!*, at the Lyceum. *Kultur* has been called a "propaganda play" by some of the dailies, but it is advertised as "the most amusing play in town." Here is a play that is presumably a satire on the anti-Semitic aspect of Hitlerism and the whole affair is brought down to a few sentimental jokes about the chancellor's life being saved by a Teuton giant of purest Aryan blood who turns out to be a converted Jew. The whole agony of the situation is set aside, its social and human connotations never enter into the question at all, and a few foolish laughs are the end of the whole matter.

But this play is so primitive and guileless in writing and production that it becomes fairly harmless. But plays like *Sailor, Beware!* which get good notices, make money, and are finally distributed through the movies, are more injurious than they seem.

The play is supposed to be a "Rabelaisian comedy" about the occupations of U. S. Navy sailors in peace time, in other words, about the sex exploits of the gobs. Rabelaisian indeed! Rabelais was a great writer, a man of learning, a true satirist, a rebel. *Sailor, Beware!* is a collection of cigar-store jokes, only less obscene and less funny than those one might hear in a cigar-store; its figures are not comic characters but simply "stooges" for each others comebacks; its atmosphere removed from any reality whatsoever. Its rowdiness has no virility in it, its lustiness has no sex, its bawdiness is just "nice clean dirt." (Otherwise it might offend the customers!) And finally it has less to do with the U. S. Navy than a barber shop. Every ingredient of the play is a sham; so that a rough comedy about sailors is nothing more than a frolic of undeveloped high-school boys, dangerously innocent and unbelievably ignorant. Can an audience that relishes such stuff as comedy know anything at all about the world in which it lives? Can it ever grow mature? A theatre such as this seems to have no other purpose but to perpetuate imbecility.

—*DW*, 6 Oct. '33

EUGENE O'NEILL

The quality and merits of Eugene O'Neill's latest play, *Ah, Wilderness!* at the Guild Theatre, are easy to recognize. The play is a very slight comedy of middle-class life in the earlier part of this century. It deals with the first loves and adolescent experiences of a senior high-school boy, the more reputable and ordinary problems of tender parents, the mild sex frustrations of so-called average Americans. It is the kind of comedy at its best that is rather infrequent on our stage, although quite usual in continental plays of pre-war years, the comedy of simple home-life, of uneventful days in a bourgeois household, of small tempests in a teapot. As such it has its value—particularly in the purely domestic scenes—since American comedy tends too much to strain itself toward big scenes and belly laughter.

Aside from these gentle passages of reminiscent observation, which take up about three-quarters of an hour of a rather longish evening, the writing and the content of the play are hardly superior, though perhaps a little more robust, than the milkiest of the Booth Tarkington novels. Indeed, O'Neill's picture of a seventeen-year-old boy is entirely conventional, banal, false. One observes with no little irritation that the playwright, who is supposed to have broken away from stereotype stage figures, can remember nothing more about his youth than that there were fellows who rebelled against their environment through Swinburne, Wilde, Ibsen and Shaw, and mouthed callow Socialist phrases, while there were others who made dates with fast girls in the back of barrooms, and that both were fundamentally genial good Americans!

We wonder whether this play, harmless and inconsequential in itself, is not a clue to much of O'Neill's later work, and a sign of what we may expect from him in the future. As a youth, O'Neill was surely not like the young hero of his latest play. He must have been passionate, intense, emotionally uncontrolled, impatient with the dead forms of life and of art around him, obstinate and questioning. He broke loose, he met real people, he went where life was raw, difficult, painful. And the result was the early plays, which, for all their shortcomings, had the beat of life in them, the savor of the soil, the sea, sweat, struggle, misery.

During this period, O'Neill, immersed in the confusion and darkness of the life he saw, tended toward a romantic pessimism, intellectually immature but creative nonetheless because it was close to reality. Then as the leisure afforded him by success permitted him to do some reading he probably dipped into Freud and Nietzsche. Freud furnished him with a sort of scientific chart to individual behavior; Nietzsche, a lyrical way out of chaos, through the exaltation of tragic experience as an end in itself. The result was a kind of half-baked optimistic pessimism! It was half-baked in the sense that O'Neill had ceased to experience life except through chateaux in France, Park Avenue apartments, Georgia country homes, the Theatre Guild and a very limited library. It was a thin pessimism since it was based on a conception of life, no longer on any contacts with it; it was an unconvincing optimism since it could not be translated into terms of human action. In this spirit O'Neill wrote his academic plays, beginning with *Marco Millions* down to the present. These plays were successful, for the most part, because together with an always tangible dramatic talent, their pessimism seemed profound, their optimism reassuring. But they were mainly dead, demanding no dynamic response from the audience, no positive point of view. For all his sincerity and vehemence O'Neill was a safe dramatist.

Today a choice must be made. Either one sinks into a suicidal despair or one goes forward toward the revolution as envisaged by Marx and Lenin. But there are people who are afraid, and there are people who are protected. In one way or another, they go backward to thoughts of a happy yesterday—to the happy yesterday which in O'Neill's case was not happy at all—to the times when the struggle of life was less acute, when there were not so many disturbing depressions, inflations, strikes, and omens of war. They write "comedies of recollection" not with an alive feeling of today but with a nostalgia for a past that never was. That is why juvenile idylls like *One Sunday Afternoon* are rapturously taken to the bourgeois bosom, and that is why Eugene O'Neill can't remember the real young man he was.

We do not wish to accuse O'Neill of political fascism—he would no doubt scorn or shudder at the idea—but the state of mind which his latest play betrays is a reflection of one aspect of the spirit which makes for fascism. And it is instructive to note, from a cultural standpoint, that the period which led to this newly found bliss, in which O'Neill sings the beauty of autumn and winter while he pats the memory of an unreal youth, produced such puerile "problem plays" as *Dynamo*, such pompous melodrama as *Mourning Becomes Electra*. They are not the plays of the young O'Neill; they are the plays of the now empty O'Neill, whose symbolic image we see in the boy of *Ah, Wilderness!* What will this distorted boy—the bastard creation of a young man grown old without having grown up—bring forth in the future? We fear further and more pernicious forms of intellectual fascism.

—*DW*, 10 Oct. '33

NEW LIFE

The literature of the Workers' theatre in this country has the opportunity at the present moment of making really original and valuable contributions to our general literature of the theatre. Writing about the theatre on Broadway is almost exclusively limited to the hit-and-run reviews of the journalistic chain-gang. The reviewers, honest enough fellows for the most part, are familiar with all the minute gossip of show-business, but are woefully lacking in the most elementary information about the real theatre. The critics of the liberal weeklies write more expansively and are somewhat more "sensitive," but they remain strictly within the confines of a Bachelor of Arts conception of the theatre. And such a monthly as "Theatre Arts," though it has performed a valuable function in its time, is so anxious to please everybody, to avoid polemics, and to escape the dogmatic that is lacks all substantial character.

The Workers' Theatre publications are not bound by the many fears of the bourgeois press and therefore they are in a position to strike out boldly and make new discoveries for themselves. An analysis of acting on the Broadway stage from the revolutionary point of view, for example, though a difficult thing to do, might prove extremely illuminating; a study of the work of men like Robert Edmond Jones or Lee Simonson, not in the sugar-water style in which most articles on such subjects are written, but done with a trenchant Marxian objectivity, would be genuinely instructive; articles on the Stanislavsky system of acting, on the relation of theatre organization to theatre art, on the technique of Soviet playwriting, on the history of the proletarian elements in American dramaturgy, on revolutionary dramatists through the ages—all of these subjects and many more would provide excellent material for renewed investigation.

The first issue of "New Theatre" (formerly known as "Workers' Theatre") begins promisingly with answers to a questionnaire on the prospects for the American theatre by various well-known theatre people and writers including Sidney Howard, Barrett H. Clark, Michael Gold, Albert Maltz, Paul Peters. The questions themselves tend to oversimplification in the answer-yes-or-no tradition, and the replies suffer as a result. Nevertheless, the idea of such a questionnaire is a good one, and when all the answers have been published we shall have an interesting document to examine. Mordecai Gorelik's article on scenery is also very much in the right direction. Gorelik is one of the most important scene designers in the American theatre and his writing is strongest where it refers to actual matters of craft. The more workmanlike it becomes the more useful it is.

In general, however, "New Theatre" gives evidence of one serious error, an error shared by many who enter the field of revolutionary culture. On the one hand it proves the need for a workers' theatre and the inevitability of its rise by pointing to the collapse of the bourgeois theatre; on the other hand it stands somewhat in awe of bourgeois technique. What is wrong with this is that it unwittingly robs the workers' theatre movement of its own organic and independent basis. The revolutionary theatre must develop not because the bourgeois theatre is at its last gasp—the present season thus far has been exceedingly prosperous on Broadway—but because it alone has the seeds of life in it, it alone is significant for the future, it alone proceeds from the creative soil of reality with the aim of reacting on life, enriching it, changing it. Actors, playwrights, scene designers must come to the revolutionary theatre not because they will go hungry on Broadway—with the least sign of "recovery," such as the number of hits now running, this argument loses some of its validity—but because the whole set-up of the Broadway theatre leads inevitably to artistic sterility and death.

More important still, the proletariat creates its own needs, its own life force, its own objectives which the bourgeois theatre, even if its work were better, could not satisfy. Finally, the Broadway theatre, like many of the overnight wonders of capitalist society, is a fully grown fruit which gives very little nourishment to its bourgeois audience, or, to put it more accurately, the American theatre is weak even from any sound standards of bourgeois art. That is why, though certain things can be learnt from it—it has its talented craftsmen—its technique should not be taken as final in any sense. The Moscow Art Theatre before the revolution was a bourgeois theatre, so were the theatres of Meyerhold, Tairov and others, but many of our successful theatres reveal a stagecraft that, aside from sheer mechanics, is childish from any legitimate artistic standards. Much of the direction of O'Neill's *Ah, Wilderness!*, for example, is amateurish, and there is hardly a moment of genuine acting from one end of *Sailor, Beware!* to another.

This means then that the workers' theatre, by keeping its own true ends clear to itself, can, without succumbing either to an abstract disregard of the bourgeois theatre or of an equally blind envy of its technical competence, lay the foundations of a really healthy, mature, complete theatrical art in America. This is the arduous, thrilling, essential task that the various workers' theatres, and "New Theatre" as their organ, should set for themselves. In the meantime, we welcome it again as a sign of new life.

—*DW*, 16 Oct. '33

NOTHING AND LESS

The period of Eugene O'Neill's *Ah, Wilderness!* is 1800; the period of *One Sunday Afternoon* and the musical show *Hold Your Horses* is about 1900; the period of Clare Kummer's *Amourette* at the Henry Miller Theatre is 1840; and *The Pursuit of Happiness* at the Avon Theatre take us back to 1777. Mae West's movie *She Done Him Wrong* turned to the Nineties, the operetta *Music in the Air* harked back to a Tyrolese past, and announcements are made of an adaptation of Molière's *School for Husbands* and Johann Strauss' *Fledermaus*—"Anywhere but of this world!" cried the French poet Baudelaire, and here we have the theatre train to forgetfulness, the $2.50 road to nowhere.

No matter how strenuously an artist resists his times, no matter how fervently he wraps himself in mists of the past, he always remains strictly contemporary. His quest of a bygone day must be interpreted as either an effort to understand his own time—in which case his use of history is valid—or as an attempt to run away from it—in which case he is merely drowning his sorrows. In the instance of our present plays, however, we have nothing as serious as either of these processes. It is largely a case of exhaustion. The entertainers—playwrights and producers—have taken up almost every conceivable subject, and the number of possible novelties seems to be dwindling. Of course this does not mean that any of the subjects that have been used have actually been given artistic treatment, but there have been plays about journalism, prize-fights, night-clubs, radio, rackets, politics, movies, doctors, lawyers, Indians, thieves, marriage, divorce, homosexuality and what not. Broadway shuns labor plays, and the more direct aspects of the class struggle are taboo. There seems so little left to be cynical about; there is certainly nothing to be enthusiastic about, and to be profound or thorough about anything takes time

and hard work, which is very doubtful business. So the newest novelty is the past. The past, moreover, is safe; whether one is cynical or sentimental about it comes to the same thing—it need not affect what one is doing or thinking today. It is a kind of colorful void.

So our costume plays are really 1933 after all, a delicate symptom of capitalism's arrested development. Only *The Pursuit of Happiness*, the newest pleasantry to please the boys uptown, derives its inspiration a little from the heyday of Greenwich Village. Time was, when the refugees from middle-western drabness, New England Methodism and Ethical Cultura or Riverside Drive Judaism, congregated below Fourteenth St. and wrote skits, playlets and even dramas to rout American puritanism. Some of them composed semi-Freudian tragedies of sex repression, but most of them dabbled in antique motifs: pseudo-Greek, pseudo-Renaissance, pseudo-Romantic and generally pseudo. The point of these plays was that their authors were "free," that the audiences that applauded them were "free," and ain't we got fun! Some of these pranks were not without talent, they brought a new tone into the American theatre, and the shrewder and more energetic of these talents moved uptown and established formidable institutions.

Their chief artistic characteristic was their eclecticism. These plays had a cute minimum of everything: a touch of history, a bit of Shaw, a whiff of continentalism, a dose of naughtiness. It was all very sweet really and quite harmless as the subsequent development of this tendency proved. What didn't become the Theatre Guild became the Little Theatre. At heart, it was a spoiled child, given to unorganized reading and an independent income. The child goes to many literary parties and travels abroad. But despite the advance of years it fits in perfectly with the Broadway Theatre of 1933.

Even in the diluted form of *The Pursuit of Happiness* it has its tickled audiences. They do not notice that the laugh lines are borrowed from everywhere including old A. H. Woods bedroom farces, they do not mind that the production is acted like a prep-school show, they do not think that the old bugaboo of Puritanism in its Greenwich Village form has long been forgotten. What they like is the novel—that is the 1777—setting, the suggestion of set so quaint and innocent that it might be the Three Little Pigs, the feeling that though it is quite up-to-date it is all as trifling as any musical comedy plot. They like it because one can hardly remember what it is all about even while it is happening, because it does not interfere with the light-headed cheeriness of these N. R. A. days. They like it because it is nothing.

If this is nothing, *Her Man of Wax* at the Shubert Theatre is less. It would hardly be worth mentioning at all were it not for the fact that it illustrates what the Broadway theatre can accomplish in reducing talent to shame. The comedy Walter Hasenclever wrote, *Napoleon Greifft Ein* (Napoleon Takes Hold), was a better than average example of European political vaudeville, slightly reactionary in effect, but with certain theatrical possibilities. Broadway turns it into a vehicle for a hot-cha artist, Miss Lenore Ulric. In this transformation, an actress once full of promise and genuinely attractive as well as gifted, masquerades vulgarity like an empty-headed Bronx stenographer imitating Miss Lenore Ulric. Everything is cheapened, degraded, robbed of every last vestige of intelligence, invention, humor or charm. It is a fair example of Broadway commodity-production.

—*DW*, 18 Oct. '33

WORKERS THEATRE NIGHT

Last Sunday at the City College Auditorium, the newly formed Theatre Club of the Workers' Laboratory Theatre presented a program of short scenes representing the activities of various organizations which are either part of the Workers Theatre Movement or sympathetic to it. A large audience attended.

Bob Lewis of the Group Theatre gave the "to be or not to be" soliloquy from *Hamlet* in terms of a revolutionary agitator haranguing a crowd. This is quite an imaginative effort of theatrical interpretation and should be very suggestive to actors and directors in all branches of the Workers' Theatre. Lewis based his attitudes and poses on drawings from the New Masses—some of them representing an agitator in moments of sincere passion, others representing him as caricaturing his class foes— and these poses are alternated with moments in which the speaker makes his own comments. The relation of the parts—the poses and the straight comments—are not altogether unified so that the number remains incomplete as an artistic whole, and makes the impression, for all its merit and excellent showmanship, of a studio exercise. Lewis, at the request of the audience, added satiric impersonations of the dancers Mary Wigman and Shan-kar. They are entertaining tidbits in a more conventional manner.

The Theatre Collective gave the flop-house scene from Claire and Paul Sifton's *1931—*. This was the most ambitious part of the program. The scene is decidedly effective, but it seemed badly prepared Sunday night. It was far too deliberate in tempo, the religionist's speech was much too obviously pointed—it had an almost recitation class quality—and altogether it lacked freedom, flow and unity. This scene was better played at the first Theatre Collective performance last spring, and therefore no one could think of calling the Collective severely to account for its deficient production on this occasion.

Yet, we believe there is something to be learned here. It is simply this: that the more highly organized forms of theatre—long plays, ballets, etc.—to be interesting artistically and so valuable as propaganda, need the most careful, the most highly developed, the most skilled preparation possible. The wholly untrained workers from the Bronx did admirably with their recitation, the Theatre of Action managed, despite handicaps, to put over their humorous turns, but the Theatre Collective, with better actors, could not do justice to their material since they had not rehearsed enough under the proper auspices. The Theatre Collective would do well to consider, in making their seasonal plans, that one production thoroughly prepared is worth three hasty productions which satisfy no one and belie the material they employ. In the doing of full length plays such as the Theatre Collective announced, a strictly professional competence and a better than Broadway technique must be insisted upon. Only in this way can such a theatre be of real service to the revolutionary movement.

—*DW*, 23 Oct. '33

THE ARTEF AND OTHERS

The Artef—the only Jewish workers' theatre in America—is presenting Saturday and Sunday nights at the Hecksher Foundation (Fifth Ave. and 104th St.) a translation by Molssaye J. Olgin of *The Third Parade*, a drama of the Bonus March, by Charles Walker and Paul Peters.

As the Artef has produced a greater number of plays than any other workers' organization in New York, and has built up a permanent company and something of a permanent audience, its work should be seen by every one interested in the development of a revolutionary theatre. Their productions always have an inner simplicity and conviction and even a kind of maturity that communicate themselves to the audience despite many serious obstacles. One feels that the roots of this organization are set deeper than those of almost any other similar group, and that whatever may come to disturb the progress of their movement, the Artef will nevertheless survive.

For this reason it is important to discuss the shortcomings as well as the qualities of this group, for they will be the shortcomings of other groups who propose to present full length revolutionary plays for workers' audiences.

The present production suffers somewhat from being a translation of a play typically American in its idiom and in its characters. It is true, of course, that the conditions of the class struggle are virtually the same for workers everywhere, and that since the Bonus March is as familiar to the audience of the Artef as to any other, this play is a proper vehicle for production by them.

But such a rational argument does not hold in the logic of the theatre. To be exciting and convincing in the theatre, the audience must feel that the workers represented are not ideological abstractions, but men and women whom they know well, people whose rhythm of thought and habits of life are akin to their own. In such a play as *The Third Parade* the workers are the laconic, hard-boiled, open-road type of American born of the pioneer industrialism of the West. This type of worker is difficult for any but an equivalent type of actor to suggest, and the pale-faced actors of the Artef, more characteristic of shop-workers than of the heavy industry workers the authors had in mind, bring to the play an element so foreign as to create a sense of unreality.

More serious than this, however, is the matter of direction. The sense of authenticity that we got from the Artef productions comes entirely from the actors: it is they who have within them those qualities of simplicity and maturity we have mentioned. Theirs is the chief reality of the plays they present. But these qualities tend to be hidden rather than released by the kind of direction imposed upon them. Not that this direction is unskillful, but the more skillful it is the more damage is done to the actors.

It is the kind of direction that emphasizes stage-business, numerous details of individual action, theatre effects, tricky outward characterizations. Such directions might be very useful in a Second Ave. theatre or on Broadway, but for actors comparatively new to the stage, and moreover for actors whose natural qualities are much fresher than those of most professional actors, this direction only creates self-consciousness and an actory posiness entirely alien to the spirit of a revolutionary theatre.

In other words, the direction of the Artef endeavors to make its actors appear experienced and stage-wise in the manner of a Yiddish Art Theatre actor, which militates against the Artef actor's spontaneity and injects an element of false and incompatible theatricality into the play. What is needed is a direction that will preserve the actor's natural endowment and allow him the freedom to be himself in a way that is both unforced and yet interesting on the stage.

This is a problem that faces all stationary workers' theatres. To make the actors of a workers' theatre proficient in the Broadway manner is impossible, except with actors of Broadway experience, and it is undesirable in any case. To make them theatrically alive in their own right—as young actors of a revolutionary theatre—takes time, hard work, and a properly trained director. But there will be no truly satisfying workers' theatre without this.

—DW, 25 Oct. '33

TWO MUSICAL COMEDIES

There can be no doubt that by comparative standards, *Of Thee I Sing*, and even the sequel *Let 'Em Eat Cake* are superior musical comedies. But to say this is not enough for most of the uptown critics. *Of Thee I Sing* was no ordinary show with funny lines, pleasant tunes, good tricks and pretty girls. It was a real satire, a "contribution" to American drama, yes, a work of art! And some of our comrades, who should have known better, joined in the chorus.

There is a certain type of showman in the moneymaking "theatre" who is shrewd enough to know the temper of his customers to the extent of always being able to guess how far he may exceed the bounds of their conventions in regard to subject matter without in the least disturbing their fundamental, and still conventional, point of view. Thus, when the customers are beginning to tire of conventional triangle plays, he writes or produces a homosexual play which is basically the old triangle play with a new turn. Or he realizes that the

mother as an object of sweet sentiment is beginning to bore his audiences, so he brings forth a mother as conventionally perverse as the old mother was conventionally Christian. On another occasion he guesses that star-spangled patriotism in relation to war might make an audience uncomfortable, so he writes a pathetic or humorous war play proving that soldiers are only human after all. He understands that the best way to please the customer is by a daring novelty; daring because some other manager hasn't tried it yet; novel because though it presents an attitude quite acceptable to the theatregoer in his home, it has not yet found expression on the stage. In short, such a showman will sell the bourgeoisie anything including dynamite, and the bourgeoisie, as it decays, prefers to buy dynamite if it is guaranteed to smell and act like talcum powder.

This is the nature of the satire in *Of Thee I Sing*. For all its jibes at the existing order it never once betrays a point of view different from the average American—that means the good Democrat or Republican—when he complains about politics and graft. There is no hint at any moment that the madness of our political life has its tragic side or that its folly might become sense if our whole economic structure were altered. The cleverness that marks *Of Thee I Sing* is greater in degree but not different in kind from the usual Broadway hocus-pocus, here-today gone-tomorrow that delights radio audiences. It is the kind of cleverness that leads nowhere and has no other intention than to provoke a momentary guffaw.

The proof of this is the kind of audience it attracts, the kind of praise it wins, and the Pulitzer Prize. But another and more conclusive proof may be found in *Let 'Em Eat Cake*, now playing at the Imperial Theatre.

Let 'Em Eat Cake carries its satire of American politics from the crisis of one presidential administration to the "revolution" of the next. *Let 'Em Eat Cake* is a musical comedy about revolution! And in this amazing finale of revolution we get the final measure of the whole enterprise.

The reviewers were disappointed in *Let 'Em Eat Cake*. They found its second act soggy and tiring. They are right, but they do not analyze the cause for this sudden drop into the doldrums. The cast is the same as before; the expertness of the authors has not diminished and the appetite for their brand of fun has not lessened. The reason for the dullness of *Let 'Em Eat Cake* in its second part is that the authors haven't the slightest knowledge or feeling about the things they are kidding.

In order to make an effective wisecrack you and your audience must know something about the subject of the crack. This audience and these authors are familiar with the presidential campaigns (though we may doubt whether they really know anything about them!), they are familiar with the existence of vague vice-presidents, they are familiar with gabble and gossip about war debts. So their jokes about them in *Of Thee I Sing*, based on that disregard of politics common to most Americans and so emblematic of the general ignorance which their once unquestioned security bred, were successful jokes. But in *Let 'Em Eat Cake* the cracks are about dictatorship, international politics, revolution, and for these things the authors and their audience have not even a common background of familiar jokes—so the latter part of their show is a dud.

—*DW*, 2 Nov.'33

A GOOD THING

The German dance group directed by Kurt Jooss, now appearing at the Forrest Theatre, is something new in the way of ballet. Its most successful subjects are contemporary, and its tendency is toward the left. Above all, its collective technique is not merely a matter of mechanized ballet discipline characteristic of most professional dance groups, but derives from an actual unity of spirit, a real connection of mind and heart, background and desire. This ballet is not a collection of individuals hammered by a virtuoso dance director into an arbitrary form, it is a real organism whose parts naturally belong together.

The Jooss Ballet is petit-bourgeois rather than proletarian in its make-up, and it manifests the qualities of nearly all such German groups as well as the shortcomings which are part of these qualities. They have tendencies, humor, a sprightly energy, an almost milky youthfulness, and a certain good-heartedness, which appears to be a combination of the charming behavior of well-brought-up children, and the shyness that comes from a life-time of lower middle-class worry. These elements taken together create a very appealing impression, particularly as they go with a quiet intelligence and sincerity, but they also explain why the total effect of their work rarely gives one the sense of strength, of militancy, of potential revolutionary power. They explain too why the actual dance numbers are a little less striking, a little less sharp than the dancers imagine them to be.

The most original number, of course, is "The Green Table", the anti-war ballet which has given this group renown in Europe. The first and last episodes of this piece, showing the diplomats at their futile debates, constitute a little masterpiece of dance design. The movement is fresh, the observation delightful, the caricature sound. And much of the war episodes that follow, showing the marching of young troops, the greedy enthusiasm of the profiteer, the growth of protest, the development of hysterical cynicism and debauchery, and with it all, Death—sweeping everything and everyone away with him, is fascinating and exciting to watch. Yet the idea of introducing Death as a personified figure carrying each character away in a dance isn't altogether consonant with the modern idiom of the whole, and though there is something of a tragic vision in the final effect, one feels the lack of a truly transforming conception of war, a new hate or a real fire of revolutionary understanding and will.

It is not enough to show silly diplomats, and a vulgar roly-poly profiteer, and a woman crying out against it all; there must also be a ruthless clarity, a harsh candor which will give lightning evidence of their proper relation and connection. To put it badly, there is not enough class-consciousness in "The Green Table" to make it transcend the realm of the now useful propaganda piece which says no more in the final analysis than that war is sad and bad. This middle-class type of well-wishing pacifism, though it finds an unusually talented and sympathetic expression in this ballet, still remains its integral artistic fault.

For all these reservations, the Jooss Ballet is decidedly a step in the right direction—almost unique of its kind. Without having attained the final degree of technical perfection, it still is free not only of the musty and insipid prettiness of the old ballet organizations, but also of that studio vigor and twilight sensitivity which are the mark of nearly all modern dancers.

—*DW*, 17 Nov.'33

A NEED FOR CONTROVERSY

The reason for the absence of controversy on Broadway is not far to seek. Business knows lawsuits, competition, various brands of sabotage, but controversy in the theoretic sense has no practical value for it. And the theatre of Broadway, despite all its sincere and talented craftsmen, is primarily a business. To analyze the elements of a popular success in a way that might be interpreted as derogatory is to damage its commercial chances, to point out the new reactionary tendencies of a playwright like O'Neill, or to suggest that an actress like Katherine Cornell has something to learn about her art, is to lack respect for honored institutions; to debate the program of a new theatre is to interfere with its possible success.

The reviewers will frown on a current show (when it is the product of an influential writer or manager, however, they tend to express themselves very mildly) but very rarely indeed will a freelance article be permitted to appear on the candied falseness of a play like *Green Pastures* or on the cheap magazine-fiction quality of a play like *Grand Hotel*. Let the reviewers "razz" a play—e. e. cummings' *him* (a play meriting severe criticism, but still far more significant than shows like *Animal Kingdom*)—and no article or letter will be published in the same pages to show that the reviewers have missed the point. Let the reviewers agree that Jed Harris is an extraordinary man of the theatre and you will see no word commenting on the paltry standards by which such judgments are passed. After all, *Green Pastures*, *Grand Hotel*, and *Animal Kingdom* were money-makers, while cummings' *him* only drew a small audience of intellectuals down in Greenwich Village. To question these values would be to fly in the face of all American business tactics.

On October 8th, *The New York Times* published an unusually long article by Elmer Rice, purporting to be a Plan for a Theatre of the People. This article was compact with good intentions, high hopes, liberal dreams and a whole tissue of theatrical errors. Its intrinsic vagueness was attested by its failure to compare and contrast the new project with the attempts of already existing organizations moving in the same general direction. But we do not mean to discuss Mr. Rice's article here, only to point out that part of its vagueness was due to Mr. Rice's fear of criticizing anybody else—for then he might himself be criticized—and that this article, controversial in essence, met with no response either from the public or from any of the reviewers throughout the town.

The value of controversy is not that it provides occasion for a fight, but the opposition of opinions forces upon each side the obligations of greater definiteness, clarity, firmness. In short, from a policy of intelligent argument a concrete, healthy point of view may be arrived at. The Russian Theatre has always thrived on continuous and massive controversies. And from the controversies of the early years of the theatre in the Soviet Union, the synthesis of a clear and balanced program of activity may be read in all accounts of the recent Soviet Theatre.

The latest number of *The International Theatre* (Organ of the International Union of Revolutionary Theatres) gives evidence of this synthesis. The magazine itself has improved greatly since its first appearance, and now it may be said without exaggeration that it not only is the finest publication devoted to the revolutionary theatre, but one of the best theatre magazines of any kind. Its leading articles, such as Lunarcharsky's paper on "Problems of Style in Socialist Art," are meaty and important—the only articles of this kind to be read anywhere in English. Reports of the Jewish Theatre in the U.S.S.R., The Moscow Region Trade Union's Conmell Theatre, are all extremely instructive and should be studied by everyone engaged in the building of revolutionary theatre groups in this country.

—*DW*, 23 Nov. '33

ANALYSIS OF A SUCCESS

No fair judgment can be passed on Maxwell Anderson's play, *Mary of Scotland*, until it appears in published form. The production that may be seen at the Alvin Theatre makes what appears to be a very attractive show for the theatre-going bourgeoisie, but obscures and practically betrays Mr. Anderson's script. Because this production represents the combined efforts of the Theatre Guild, the most firmly established American theatre; Robert Edmond Jones, in some respects the "dean" of American scene-designers, and an unusual number of high-salaried actors, it is important to examine in as much detail as space will allow the result of their collaboration.

We must sacrifice for the moment a general discussion of Maxwell Anderson's work. He is one of the few American playwrights who merit serious consideration. He is a sincere romantic and he brings to the theatre a feeling for the heroic—for the broad gesture, the full word, the fearless action and a longing for a wind-swept, unfettered

existence. It is this spirit and an original and invigorating sense of the English language, born of this spirit, that may be set down without dispute as notable contributions to the American stage.

In the thrice-told tale of *Mary of Scotland*, moreover, Mr. Anderson has found material not only for a colorful story, but for a theme that is central to his thought. Briefly, it is Mr. Anderson's intention to contrast the ruler who would govern on a basis of humanitarian tolerance and sensitivity with the ruler whose tactics are shaped by considerations of reason and interest. The first ruler, Mr. Anderson says in effect, is doomed, and although his sympathies follow her (she is Mary Stuart in this case) he recognizes the impractibility of her principles as the basis of a political method. Whatever our opinion of this thesis, we will concern ourselves today only with an analysis of how it is expressed in terms of its 52nd Street production.

Helen Hayes, who is ordinarily an actress of simple charm, gives a rigidly conventional performance. To mask the impression of queenliness she holds herself with tense uprightness—chin in the air, eyes in the skies—and speaks in the most naïve tradition of declamatory acting. Her unnatural carriage and elocutionary articulation of the lines, added to her small body, create the effect of a clever high-school girl imitating an actress of the old school. With these attributes, it is impossible to believe in her womanliness, her passion or her pride. Thus the love scenes are not only ineffective as such (being devoid of true emotion), but do not convey the author's purpose, which is to show the conflict between her personal feelings and her political ideals. Lacking the quality of maturity, moreover, the contrast between Mary's sensibility and Elizabeth's logic fails to be anything more than a matter of the author's lines. This failure becomes a catastrophe when Mary's antagonist is the Elizabeth of Helen Menken, who plays the part like a gilded witch, and reduces Mr. Anderson's theme to nothing better than an academically melodramatic struggle between a sweet little noblewoman and a big bad ogress.

At this point we must turn to Mr. Jones's costumes and sets. He has clothed Miss Hayes in materials so rich and hues so bright that her unregal size is emphasized rather than counteracted, and in the last scene Miss Hayes in black is made to look like Priscilla beside Elizabeth who in opulent gold looks like a glorified wanton. This is a striking effect—precisely opposite to the need of the play. And, in the castle scene, Mary is made to look quite comfortable in paneled oak surroundings, whereas one might suppose this an excellent opportunity to contrast visually Mary's sensuous Southern nature with a forbiddingly gloomy Northern environment. Mr. Jones's sets and costumes may be considered handsome, but they actually militate against the meaning of the play.

For the rest, Mr. Merivale, who looks and speaks well, is emotionally wooden, and the rest of the expensive cast are merely passable types, not actors adding color and complexity of characterization so important to the background of a romantic play.

Communist critics are often accused of demanding a revolutionary viewpoint from bourgeois artists, but what is to be noted here is that in the production of an "orthodox" historical play the directors of the leading middle-class theatre in America are unaware that in casting, acting and setting their production belies and nullifies every serious value the play contains. This show, from any but a "*Sailor Beware!-Double Door*" standard of the theatre, is a thoroughly adolescent, pitifully hollow job of play-production. If it displays a certain technical proficiency it also betrays a fundamental ignorance of what it means to translate an author's idea into terms of the theatre.

—*DW*, 21 Dec. '33

GORKY AT THE ARTEF

We should be very grateful for the opportunity given us by the Artef (the Jewish Workers Theatre) to see Maxim Gorky's latest play, *Yegor Bulitchev and Others*. It is something that no one person interested in the revolutionary cultural movement should miss. For despite reservations that might be made, it is the most stimulating play that this season has brought forth on any stage.

In fact, this play might be taken as an object lesson to every one in the theatre. Critics can learn from it that a play may be meager as a literary work and still be highly significant as well as moving on the stage, that characters may be simply and almost schematically drawn and still be suggestive and rich in their affect on an audience. Playwrights can learn how an ideologically correct play may be written without the use of stock slogans, without situations that remind one of the radical classroom. Even conservatives, who are generally mystified by the idea that a character may be presented from a Marxian viewpoint and at the same time satisfy the demands of objectivity, can see in the play proof that this seeming contradiction does not exist.

Of course, audiences who go to see *Bulitchev* need not, and probably will not, concern themselves with anything but the actual drama itself, with all its savage humor and strange force. Yet we pause to emphasize these general considerations because so much of our talk about revolutionary plays is abstract, based on rule-of-thumb notions rather than on concrete examples. *Bulitchev* at the Artef permits us to see a good revolutionary play in the flesh. It permits us to compare a dramatic reality with our dramatic theories, it permits us to study a worthy model.

There is something of a miracle in the make-up of this play. For what could be simpler than the story of a merchant who is dying of a cancer and the conspiracy of various people of this household to assure themselves of his fortune. Bulitchev wants to live, and though he knows he is condemned to die, he seeks some spark of hope or solace from priests, soothsayers and charlatans of all kinds. The corruption of his family—part of which he himself is responsible for—and the impending revolution (the period is 1916-17) lead him to see in a dim but inescapable way how both these facts, the social upheaval outside and the domestic debacle inside, are interrelated and leave him no possibility of salvation. Bulitchev is an individual and yet the unmistakable symbol of his class. He is shown as a man of passion, endowed with rude intelligence, a slowly awakening consciousness and a certain kind of wry honesty. In other words he is drawn sympathetically, yet without a touch of sentimentality, for he is the emblem of that bourgeois which is blind, despite all its power, spiritually helpless despite all its pride.

How has Gorky succeeded in making such a limited plot gripping and big? By the strength of his conviction, by a real knowledge of his character, and by an extraordinary instinct for theatrical symbolization. It is this latter quality, the ability to translate an idea into a simple, striking, meaningful dramatic image, that is the source of this play's superiority, the touchstone of its theatrical vitality. One example will suffice: the second act curtain in which a town faker who calls himself "Gabriel" offers to play the trombone to cure Bulitchev's sickness. Bulitchev asks him to say whether he is a fool or a scoundrel. "Gabriel" replies that he is no fool, but that many people ask to be fooled. The sick man pays 25 rubles for his answer, and "Gabriel" goes on to remark, "Still, it helps," and, encouraged by Bulitchev, he proceeds to blow his trombone. We have rarely seen a more arresting symbol of the bourgeois artist whose art is supposed to heal all ailments, but who knows if he is honest that his "playing" is only a forlorn trumpeting of a false cure!

By all means go to see their production, which is given at the Heckscher Theatre, Fifth Ave. and 104th St., on Saturday and Sunday nights.

—*DW*, 10 Jan. '34

TOBACCO ROAD

To most of the yellow press *Tobacco Road* at the Masque Theatre is a dirty, disagreeable play with an outstanding performance by Henry Hull. To the liberal opposition *Tobacco Road* is a racy folk study that contains the pathos and humor of everyday life amongst the outcast poor white of the South. Neither of these views is acceptable to us.

The merit of *Tobacco Road* is its subject matter. The countryside not only in the South, but all over the U. S., is peopled with such derelicts—the heirs of completely broken-down farmers or farm laborers—as we see depicted in *Tobacco Road*. They live in conditions of indescribable misery which no one could properly call human. In the midst of sunshine and rich lands, they inhabit shacks without light, air or comfort. Whole families sleep, eat and perform all their natural functions in one room. They live without interests or hope off the little patches of soil that surround their dwellings; they beg, borrow or steal. Many of them are inevitably born stunted or diseased.

Since the American theatre is almost entirely given over to unimaginative adventures in unreality, to put such characters as these on our stage is in itself something so unconventional as to earn our interest and to a certain extent our applause. We prefer by far the bare naturalism of *Tobacco Road* to the high-school naughtiness of *Sailor, Beware!*

Nevertheless, *Tobacco Road* remains, for all its details, a fragmentary picture and, what is more disappointing, a casual one. The reason for this may be the author's attempt to be "objective" and unsentimental. But there is the objectivity of the artist who maintains a detached approach in order to see and render the truth more clearly, and there is the detachment of the reporter who is essentially unconcerned about his material and looks at it as an outsider making clever notations of strange phenomena.

The authors of *Tobacco Road* (it is a dramatization by Jack Kirkland of a novel by Erskine Caldwell) do not reveal the emotion that comes from a true connection with their material, a real understanding or sympathy. It lacks a point of view and seems to address itself to nobody in particular. Thus it arouses neither sorrow, pity or anger. It leaves one coldly amused, and when one realizes that one is laughing at unfortunate human beings one leaves the theatre with a lowered sense of one's own humanity or a suspicion that the authors have not told the whole story, have in fact cheated us with half-truths.

In only one scene—where the banker comes to put these wretched "creatures who once were men" out of their decayed shanty—is there any suggestion of the social forces that produce these distorted lives. And this scene is presented in the same accidental manner as the rest. It seems nothing but an incident of the plot, whereas we should see in it the real causes of the whole situation. And just as these social forces are only vaguely suggested, so the individual characters, too, suffer from a lack of background in their portrayal.

They are striking as such characters must be, but they are thin. One feels in them little more than what one sees, which does not make them anything better than superior caricatures. In a way that the authors surely did not intend, their play contributes to the cynicism and indifference of a bourgeois audience to whom the play's characters are little more than a strange breed of animal that a tourist might observe, watch for a moment, and forget.

The performance, like the play, ranges from the curious and almost touching to the downright crude. It mixes the casual and pointless with occasional shrewd theatricality, trickiness. It, too, has a broken, undecided, unorganized manner and never creates a completely unified impression. Henry Hull's performance is the living embodiment of the whole show's virtues and shortcomings. It is sincere and partly genuine, convincing, by a certain disinterested naturalness, but it is a little "blind" and disconnected.

The most encouraging thing about *Tobacco Road* as a whole is that it was produced at all on Broadway, and that having been produced, it survives the typically superficial reception of half-baked "razz" reviews.

—*DW*, 15 Jan. '34

O'NEILL'S LATEST

Practically every one has agreed that Eugene O'Neill's latest play, *Days Without End*, at the Henry Miller Theatre, is a bad play. There would be little point therefore, in repeating this bare fact. The play is bad because its writing is dry, its characters conventional, its plot amateurish.

Yet the most important aspect of this play is not its badness—most plays are bad and many are the work of good authors—but the cause and nature of its badness. It is amazing that reviewers, in attacking the play fail to remark that in this, O'Neill's poorest play, he still holds one's attention because the play is about something, whereas most plays that the reviewers praise are admittedly nothing; and it is even more amazing that all of them fail to talk about that something with which the play deals. In failing to discuss the play's theme, they actually fail to discuss the play itself, for how can one judge a dramatist's artistry unless one compares his subject matter with the treatment he has given it.

Let us, for the moment, be "liberal" with O'Neill, and say that *Days Without End* does not necessarily signify that he has confessed himself a sinner, repented and formally returned to the Catholic Church. Let us say that when the hero of his play kneels before the cross, alongside a priest who gives thanks for his soul and cries out "Life laughs with love," that O'Neill simply means to take the crucifix as a symbol of suffering humanity, and the expression of faith expressed in the play's last line means only that O'Neill wishes to voice his belief that life is worth living, and that despite all the pain, a man should be willing to struggle, hope and look forward to its continuance. Here is a statement and belief that we can share. Yet when we ask ourselves what such a statement leads to, we realize that it directs us to combat the forces in our world that are destructive of life on all its levels—biological, social, cultural—it leads to a fight to the death with capitalism.

O'Neill's credo realistically viewed must become a summons to action which in turn means the education of the workers, farmers, intellectuals and indeed every one who truly wants to eradicate the blight of capitalism—and live.

But precisely this struggle for life is what O'Neill tells us is Evil! His hero frees himself from his ancient heresies of "atheism, Socialism, Nietzscheanism, Confucianism and mechanism!" And ends in what? In a belief so abstractly stated that it means exactly nothing in terms of everyday humanity, but which may mean a good many very real things when once translated into terms of life. The choice is clear: on the one hand, an abstraction which is as static as death, on the other hand the road to conflict, a conflict with the capitalist civilization of today for the sake of a life which will be freed of capitalism's devastating contradictions. O'Neill hugs his cold, empty abstraction.

Yet the Church is no abstraction. If O'Neill's affirmation is to mean anything it must mean the church. And the reality of the church is an organization as concrete and as practical for its own ends as any other. Let O'Neill try to find out what these ends are, and what means the Church uses to achieve them. He will find them to represent a practice that systematically turns people's eyes away from reality, that leads them into a mystic darkness where there is no pain because there is no life. If Mr. O'Neill were in contact with the world and looked at it, he would see that it is the Church today which is "the spirit that denies."

And the proof of this is the play itself. Just as its fleshless ideology is in the last analysis obscure and rigid, the creation it leads to, makes for characters without life or movement, scenes that are drawn mechanically out of the dramatic dustbin and peter out into melodramatic tableaux. When O'Neill was a "heretic" he was hardly a better thinker than he is today, but he wrote plays like *Beyond the Horizon*, *The Hairy Ape* and *Desire Under the Elms* which, faulty though they may have been, had in them the breath of life, a sense of struggle that meant growth, a passion that showed a living connection with the world around him.

Today his religious "optimism" doesn't cheer, his new-found "clarity" doesn't reveal, his "rebirth" doesn't create. O'Neill's church is a mausoleum. One more such play as *Days Without End* and we shall pronounce him dead.

The Theatre Guild's production is smooth, careful, cold, unrelated to life. It fits the play.

—*DW*, 22 Jan. '34

TAMIRIS

Theatre is a dancer in need of radicalization. This might be said of all artists who have not yet associated themselves in some direct way with the proletarian revolutionary movement, but it is especially true that radicalization in our direction would be of immediate value to Tamiris and to our cultural front. This observation is based on the evidence of her own work at her latest recital in the Booth Theatre.

Tamiris' dance, more than any other American dancer's, has a vigor, a sturdiness and an enthusiasm that derive from popular sources. One feels in her a lyricism of big city streets, of modern life not in the studio sense but in the sense of actual contact with everyday things—shops, bus-rides, parks, department stores, corner flirtations, Coney Island, hitchhikes. There is nothing sickly in her work, nothing pretty-pretty. There is animal spirits, there is hope and youth, and there is little vulgarity or cheapness. Yet all these qualities so much closer to workers than to the arty audience of Broadway dance recitals, lack a focus. The forms Tamiris chooses to express herself in are largely foreign to her. They are abstract and cold. (Even when they are supposedly based on Whitman poems.) In relation to what Tamiris is, and to what we sense in her handsome, energetic body, her subjects seem pretentious and forced. They seem borrowed.

If Tamiris would give herself concrete subjects (specific dramatic themes) strong definite working class lines with a clear revolutionary ideology, her forms would become much her own, her art would become organic and her capacity for hard work, her ambitiousness, her beauty would take on meaning, would count for something. Tamiris' gifts should not be wasted in the frigid realms of modern "neo-classic" dancing but should be put at the service of people whose lives are rooted in the most inescapable realities of our day, people whose lives are a constant struggle, people in whose hands lies the destiny of the world—workers! These people—their hopes, fears, defeats and triumphs—can enrich her and complete her, and she in turn can bring joy to them, a healthy pleasure for which they would be truly grateful as only workers can be. Her body now beating itself a little futilely against the vacuum of 57th Street art, could become a symbol of workers' splendor and workers' wholesomeness.

—*DW*, 2 Feb. '34

THE INFLUENCE OF THE CRISIS ON BROADWAY:
Emphasis in the Bourgeois Theatre Clearly Toward Reaction, Says "Daily" Critic

The Communist prediction that with the sharpening of the capitalist crisis, intellectuals would show definite tendencies either toward a revolutionary or a reactionary position is being amply borne out by recent theatrical developments. Even Broadway, traditionally immune to social currents, bears witness to the inexorable logic of the social-economic situation. Naturally on Broadway the emphasis is toward reaction. While plays like the Siftons' *1931—*, Rice's *We, the People* and some of the forthcoming work of John Howard Lawson, Melvin Levy and John Dos Passos prove that an awakening revolutionary consciousness may be anticipated among certain sections of the middle-class intelligentsia, the burden of Broadway production is given over to plays devoted to pleas for the past and apologies for escape.

The unusual number of costume plays this season is the less conscious form of this reactionary trend. Not that a costume play must necessarily be reactionary: the interpretation of the past in the light of present revolutionary understanding is one of the most interesting and fertile methods available to the artist. But Broadway costume plays are not of this kind: they generally aspire toward the glossy picture post-card version of the past. Thus the *School for Husbands* instead of being the psychological farce-comedy of Molière's original is transformed into a Little Theatre decoration. *Champaign Sec* becomes a futile pseudo-satire without style or fun, *The Pursuit of Happiness* is a bit of Greenwich Village naughtiness for old maids, and even the more serious *Mary of Scotland* is an elaborate evasion. To finish the picture, Alardyce Nicoll, the English scholar who now heads the Yale School of the Theatre, writes in *The New York Times* that the new drama is turning away from realism, but he neither attempts to explain this phenomenon nor does he point out that the reaction against "realism" on Broadway is at the same time an abandonment of reality.

This drift away from reality (after all, many Soviet plays are non-realistic but they are always close to life and the immediate problems of the day) is just as clearly discernible in such "realistic" comedies as O'Neill's *Ah, Wilderness*. The whole method of the latter play—and there will be more like it—is to give one the impression that the past was simpler, more cheerful and generally saner than the present. This is done by giving the audience not a portrait of the past as it was sensed and lived by the author when the "past" was present for him, but by writing about the ideals and hopes of the "old days" without any of the impulses and passions out of which those ideals and hopes sprang. The result consequently is a sentimental chroma without life. But it pleases the harassed bourgeoisie to indulge themselves in such memories because it relieves them of the need of facing the facts of today. This is the psychology of the old man who wants to live out his remaining time on earth with as little disturbance as possible.

And now, one step further along the path of reaction, come the Catholic plays, O'Neill's *Days Without End* and Philip Barry's *The Joyous Season*. The fact that these playwrights rather than two unknowns should have begun this progression backward is significant. Just because they are earnest people and sincere they were amongst the first to feel obliged to choose. But their choice is the negative one towards "mother church"—back to the beginning and the protective womb! What is more significant still, however, is that for men such as O'Neill and Barry this chain cannot be made without the atrophy of their creative capacities, a falling off of their early strength. O'Neill was never a "thinker" but he had passion and a sense of teeming life; his growth urged him to question his environment, to probe beneath the surfaces of our superficially placid rural life and all our taken-for-granted industrial activity. Barry's gifts were never much more than slight: his plays always had in them the quality of sweetbreads for frail intellectuals of the semi-Bostonian type but they had a wit and a sensitivity of the finger-tips which made him aware of a little more than many of his fellow playwrights. But now that they have surrendered their positive seeking sides everything which distinguished them has disappeared.

In the days of Catholicism's maturity, leading philosophers and artists came out of the Church (Thomas Aquinas, Dante); but in this country when an artist attempts to relate his own problems and living impulses to the Church, he finds himself in a complete vacuum. The Church as a creative force has never existed in this country—certainly not since the Civil War—and artists who want to find sustenance in it are either forced to behave like foreign tourists in ancient places (Thornton Wilder) or revert to a faith so simple that it is silly; like O'Neill whose religion as voiced in *Days Without End* is that of the most ignorant parish priest, or like Barry in *The Joyous Season* whose Catholicism is a vague, sugary, timid acquiescence to anything mama says! There is very little in either of these plays to indicate that their authors once were promising. Their reactionary faith has laid them low.

This, however, is not yet the final stage of reaction though it leads to it. The final stage is the point at which the artist comes out directly and unequivocally in defense of the existing society as against a new order emerging from a revolution of the working class. If the O'Neills and Barrys who write these naïve religious plays were to realize that this is the course they will have to follow in the future, would they flinch or would they face it? If they could answer the question, they would know a little more of what they are talking about today.

—*DW*, 9 Feb. '34

U.S.S.R. PROVIDES MOST ORIGINAL MATERIAL AT THE THEATRE ARTS EXHIBIT AT THE MODERN MUSEUM

The significance of this exhibit is least of all technical. For sheer information and for a sense of the aliveness of the modern theatre the exhibit held in 1927 under the auspices of the Theatre Arts Monthly was far superior, and certain European exhibits of a similar nature have also been more stimulating than the present one. What is significant then about the current show is the social environment in which it comes to us.

The Modern Museum is a curious Institution. It is endowed and supported chiefly by Mrs. John D. Rockefeller, Jr. For some reason this lady is interested in putting art over in a big way. With each exhibit she borrows the best examples of various modern painters from wealthy friends who are glad to help the "cause" and proud to be known as the possessors of fine modern paintings—which incidentally, become more valuable every year. Exhibit after exhibit is run off with a sense of an ever new surprise, a sensation, a knock-out. An opening at the Modern Museum takes on some of the auspiciousness of a premiere at Radio City! Rivera is the Clark Gable of the gallery, Matisse is its Marlene Dietrich, and a general show of French moderns is like a de luxe Lubitsch production.

From these exhibits, many of which have been very brilliant indeed, we learn who owns modern painting and for whom, in turn, the successful modern painters must produce. And so, despite the real artistry of many of the individual paintings, one comes away from them with the growing suspicion that the paintings shown are merely commodities of class snobbery, that the people who own them have very little relation to them in terms of feeling or emotional need (have we not seen in one of the patronesses' homes an Oroszco painting of impoverished peons side by side with the extravagances of an ivory tower super-realist?) Our suspicion becomes certitude; we realize that modern painting, because of the aristocratic hothouse atmosphere in which it is shown and because of the unconsciously mercenary spirit which permeates their presentation, is rapidly losing whatever general value it might have had, is becoming the specialty of the rich, not a symbol of life and of joyous humanity but rather a symbol of wealth and phony refinement.

In this setting the Theatre Art exhibit was opened. This opening was a greater social occasion than any other. Not only was the "cream" of the intelligentsia there and the "cultured" money—people of every description, but such great students of the theatre as Mary Pickford and Charles Lindbergh! To give the show true "distinction," furthermore, it was written up not by the theatre reviewers—they lack "class"—but by the art-critics. And this despite the fact that Lee Simonson who is in charge of the exhibit, has repeatedly stated that scene designs are not to be considered as separate artistic entities but as parts of the theatre for which they were intended. No matter. Catalogues are sold at $1.50 a copy, and delicate ladies go about the galleries "lorgnetting" the designs as they would the Cézannes and Picassos of previous exhibits. The whole atmosphere of the show is fashionable, bewildered, listless. People looking for the "beauty" of painting can't rhapsodize over these designs; people who care about the theatre are a little puzzled about the relation of these "pictures" to the art they love.

Technically, one is given very little idea as to how the designs are actually used in the productions for which they were made. Except for certain classics, we get no idea of the plays they are meant for, no sense of the acting that is supposed to go with them. (This relation could be made clear by pages of text from the play, or by reviews of the play in production or by figurines of the costumed actors placed on the models.) Historically, the relation of the various designs is merely chronological: we cannot trace the development of forms from one period to another because everything is presented in a museum sequence not in the order of influences in the actual life of the theatre.

—*DW*, 16 Feb. '34

THEY SHALL NOT DIE DRAMATIZES SCOTTSBORO

One cannot hem and haw before the naked directness of John Wexley's *They Shall Not Die*. It calls for a response as simple and unmistakably clear as the play itself. It is not a play of "ifs," "maybes," "perhapses": it demands a Yes or No. Our response is emphatically Yes: it is a play to be seen, to be applauded, even to be cheered.

They Shall Not Die is unusual amongst American plays of its type because while it almost entirely omits dramatic subtleties it still manages to convey a sense of substantial reality. Most of our social dramas either tend to lose themselves somewhat in the playwright's personal reactions to his subject, so that the audience's emotions always bear a little more on the playwright than on his theme, or they blurt out the facts of the case so bluntly that they give the impression of a crude distortion. Wexley's play falls into neither of these categories. His play is documentary: he has taken all the outstanding points of the Scottsboro case and with a few transparent minor changes has set them before us in excellently organized scenes. He uses many of the actual statements of all the people concerned—the Negro boy with his "I wasn't tried in Scottsville (Scottsboro) I was framed there," the Southern attorney with his references to "Jew money from New York,"—and his dramatic licenses are employed mainly to create an intelligible, gripping continuity. Yet the documentation is so wisely selected and so expertly arranged that one is both satisfied as to the authenticity of the facts and moved by their import. The characters become not only credible, but real, despite the fact that there is no "character portrayal" here in the ordinary sense of the word: It is their placement in the pattern of events that gives them form, makes living people of them.

The author does not strain for plausibility: he does not trouble to show that he is "impartial" and "fair." He tells his story—or lets it seem to tell itself—and we see that it is true. It is impossible to sit before this narrative and skeptically murmur "melodrama": it is too utterly straightforward, it is equally difficult to sniff the air and whisper "propaganda": it is too forcefully factual. *They Shall Not Die* is dramatic reporting of the best type.

This does not mean that it is flawless. The "love-story" of Lucy Wells (Ruby Bates), though dramatically useful, is fairly feeble, and much of the first act is sketchy and unconvincing. The first weakness is incidental; the second vital. Wexley knows and tells us in the course of the play that the victimization of the Negro boys falsely accused of rape is no horrible accident or miscarriage of justice, but an outgrowth of that economic fear on the part of the southern ruling class in the face of its vast population of Negro workers. But precisely this connection, though inevitably implied all through the trial scene and directly stated in other places, is very lamely and vaguely contrived in the beginning of the play. Wexley's knowledge is still only conceptual, that is, something he realizes with his head, but which he does not yet see clearly as it works itself out in terms of everyday life, and is therefore unable to give it a truly concrete and interesting dramatic embodiment.

The other shortcoming of *They Shall Not Die* is its audience! A large part of Theatre Guild subscribers and the so-called "general public" which makes up Broadway "houses," are simply miscast in relation to this play: they will not act as an audience should at such an event. They try as hard as possible not to be "taken in": their whole idea of "art" is something that "moves" you without disturbing you, something that permits you to shed a consoling tear and which one "raves" about and forgets after one has seen the next big hit. If they take sides, if they should forget too completely that what they are seeing on the stage is truly an image of life and involves a responsibility on their part, their "artistic" pleasure might be spoiled. They do not want to be involved: they prefer to sit contemplatively in their seats and regard the spectacle solely as a "show." Such an attitude, of course, has practically nothing to do with art—it is closer to the dead-letter office of the post-office and the dust of forgotten museums—and it can kill even so stirring a play as this.

However, this is a weakness that can be remedied. Readers of the *Daily Worker* can become part of the audience for *They Shall Not Die*, remake it, revitalize it and transform it into the thrilling theatre it essentially is. By a different kind of echo, and a new kind of answer they can add to and complete the play's significance. They can teach the Theatre Guild's usual audience and the dramatic reporters that the world of the theatre is not bounded by Eugene O'Neill on the north and by romantic masquerades on the south. They can teach them that the world of the theatre is not a world of make-believe but part of the whole thunderous, passionate, struggling world in which ecstasies over George M. Cohan and Helen Hayes play a very tiny role indeed.

—*DW*, 23 Feb. '34

PLAY OF NEW ORLEANS NEGRO LONGSHOREMEN SEETHES WITH STRUGGLE: *Stevedor* Ranks High in Revolutionary Drama; Outstanding Negro Cast

There are too many important aspects to the production of *Stevedore* the play by Paul Peters and George Sklar which the Theatre Union opened on Wednesday night to deal with adequately in a first review. Let it suffice for the moment to say that it is an intensely exciting, thoroughly rousing, and in every respect provocative play. Argue about it as one may, pick flaws here and there, it has a steadily mounting dramatic line that reaches a climax to which no one can remain indifferent. To put it mildly, it gets you.

The special merit, moreover, of this play is that for almost the first time in the recent history of our social drama, we are presented with the image of successful revolt in immediately effective, plausible American terms. The spectacle of temporary defeat from which one may derive a bitter determination to carry on the struggle is, of course, the natural and realistic ending to most plays which set out to describe the beginnings of any revolutionary movement. But there comes a time when an audience in the theatre demands the even more inspiring picture of the struggle at the moment of high hope, direct action and concrete advancement: the moment which symbolizes for them in the most inescapably graphic terms the possibility of achievement, the break from suppressed discontent to the flame of combat and triumph. The final scenes of *Stevedore* and the whole spirit of the acts which precede them have a forward rhythm, a forceful movement toward what, one feels, cannot but be a decisive confrontation of issues with the sense of victory in the very act of that confrontation. The spirit of *Stevedore* is young, aggressive, almost gay. It laughs with the confidence of fresh power. It

shows the proletarian movement (and incidentally the new theatre) moving onward with the assurance of undeniable strength. This is *Stevedore*'s first contribution.

Its second is its expert treatment of the Negro problem as part of the vaster problem of the working class. Its purpose, one might say, is the embodiment of Earl Browder's statement, "The cause of the emancipation of the Negro from their special oppression is inextricably bound up with the cause of the emancipation of the working class from the oppression of capitalism." No play that we remember has so clearly dramatized this connection between Negro persecution and the economic causes for that persecution.

First one sees a white girl beaten by her lover, and in fear that her husband might discover her infidelity, takes refuge in the safest lie that she can think of: a Negro attacked her! We then see the brutal, wholly illegal methods by which the police try to fasten the imaginary crime of "rape" onto almost any Negro whom they can possibly brand with it. Finally, we are introduced to the Negroes' place of work—the New Orleans docks—and we are shown the utterly slave-like condition in which the white bosses resolutely keep them. All sorts of Negro workers are presented: the "good" Negro whose refuge and gospel is the bent back and the cringing acceptance of every humiliation the white employers impose; the playful Negroes who are content to laugh and sing everything off in the way certain white dilettantes most enjoy to picture them; the slow-thinking Negroes whose minds are still unformed but in whose arms and hearts there resides great power and heroic deeds—and the increasing minority who are aroused to consciousness by militant union organizers as well as by the stirrings of their own pride and understanding. The native humanity and decency of this seething group of people is outraged by the savage "manhunt" that follows the barbaric cry of "Rape," and the inevitable pressure of events acts as a lever to hoist them to the level of defiance and resistance, led by the class-conscious Negro and sided by their comrade "dock-wallopers" from the union.

If *Stevedore* has no other scene in it but the one in which we first meet the colored workers during their lunch hour on the wharf, it would still be a distinctive addition to American drama. The whole of the Negro situation is lucidly, entertainingly, unforgettably drawn there. It contains the most creative work in the play and easily ranks as one of the leading pieces of dramatic writing in our steadily growing revolutionary literature.

The cast is good; some of it—we hate to mention names in a fundamentally collective effort—magnificent. And the audience on the opening night with its prolonged cheers and eager enthusiasm must have been a "liberal education" to the "critical gang" from uptown! Altogether a very encouraging occasion in the history of the American revolutionary theatre.

—*DW*, 20 Apr. '34

APPENDIX C
UNPUBLISHED PAPERS

PLANS FOR A FIRST STUDIO

It is a common practice of the American theatre to say that "theory is one thing and practice another." But a "theory" that is divorced from practice is mere vaporizing and a theatrical practice that is not grounded in any general conception is simply a mechanical functioning along lines laid out by people with no connection with the theatre at all. So that whatever we may say in the exposition of our aims though it may at first appear to have the bug-a-boo aspect of "theory" is, in point of fact, a statement of technical procedure. Let there be no misapprehension on this point; we can translate every one of our generalizations into its practical equivalent.

Up till now work on the American stage has been based on the assumption that the combination of sound theatrical elements will produce a correspondingly sound theatre or, at least, a good show. In other words, take what everybody will agree in calling a good play, a company of good actors, a good director, a good scene-designer and the result will inevitably be a good production. Make this arrangement permanent, introduce a repertory system, insure yourself of an audience by the subscription plan and you will have surely founded a real theatre.

It is hardly necessary at the moment to enter into the aesthetic error of this assumption; we know as a matter of record that good plays have been produced by good directors with good actors which have not only been disappointing but, at times, downright bad. The essential weakness of these productions does not lie in the elements that compose them but in their relation. They are no more alive than a man would be who was put together by joining Mr. A's good head, Mr. B's good heart, Mr. C's good stomach and Mr. D's good legs.

If the image of a man's body may serve as a definition of a true organism we may take the individual artist—poet, painter or composer—as a symbol of the kind of unity which, in the final analysis, a theatre, to be a Theatre, must also possess. When we utter the names of Bach, Beethoven, Wagner, Giotto, Cezanne or Picasso we do not simply refer to separate men as we do when we say John Smith or Sam Cohen, but to great bodies of experience that have become real to us through works which for all the variety of their forms have not only a recognizable identity of personality but a singleness of direction, meaning and, one might say, faith. If the theatre is an art, if it has any value beyond that of decorating the emptiness of our existence, it too, collective art though it be, must have an analogous singleness of meaning and direction. It too must say something, it too must create from the chaos which is the common experience of its members an expression that will have, like that of the individual artist, an identity and a significance with which people, sharing the common experience, may sense their kinship and to which they can attach themselves.

Now, how does the individual artist perform the miracle of transmuting his millions of impressions, memories, fears and aspirations into the separate manifestations of his art and finally into a complete body of work with a single message? Quite simply by being himself, by being one. Just so no body of theatre workers, however talented, can constitute a Theatre unless they are fundamentally one. For the elements of a theatrical production to be shaped into a true artistic organism it is not sufficient for them merely to be "good," they must be homogeneous, they must belong together, they must form an organic body.

These are not abstractions. The first thing that happens in any group that evolves as a Theatre is that certain people, with a sense of their common interests, common tastes and a common direction—all of which are created by their mutual recognition of a common experience and a common interpretation of that experience—unite to devise ways and means whereby they may give their group feeling an adequate theatrical expression. They seek out people who, for all the superficial differences of their temperament, fundamentally share the same feeling. They seek them amongst directors, actors, playwrights, scene-designers—confident all the time that the thing that binds them together must be a reflection of a sentiment that animates many people in the world about them. But they are not content with finding just talent: what they are looking for is a particular kind of talent the whole nature of which has its roots and takes its color from this common feeling and which shall be representative of it. When they have found each other in sufficient numbers they can function together as a Theatre with the sure knowledge that the forms they make in the way of separate productions will be a true expression of the thing they all want to say.

This is an exact description of what has occurred amongst us. Early in 1928 Lee Strasberg and I were able to recruit actors whom we knew, through our association with the Guild and other organizations to be in sympathy with our aims. These actors—all of them professional, including several who have since established themselves as very desirable players—worked with us in actual rehearsal for over seventeen weeks and are to this day eager to continue the work we then began. Later we found Cheryl Crawford, who had started from another point, in full accord with our point of view and methods. And when we came to the conclusion that the time was ripe for such a Theatre as we visioned to become a concrete fact, we set out to do two things: first, to find the people who desired such a Theatre; second, to make clear exactly how we proposed working, what ends we

had in view and, more essentially, what means we proposed taking to accomplish these ends.

Today, as Cheryl's list will show, we can point to a group of theatre people more experienced in the profession than perhaps any other body of people at the inception of such a theatre has ever before possessed. These people are not merely willing to be "employed" by us; their attitude is not one simply of perfunctory acquiescence or tame approval. On the contrary, they are literally clamoring for the opportunity to work with us (many of them at the sacrifice of more remunerative engagements) because they feel that only in such a Theatre as we are projecting will their talents as actors and their value as people achieve their fullest expression.

If the artist's career is significant only insofar as his progress represents a development of his inner experience or a constant effort in perfecting the forms that are to express this experience, so too the progress of a Theatre is not a matter of extension but of intensification, or organic growth. Here, from a practical point of view, is one of the outstanding features which differentiates us from what has gone before in the American theatre-world. Take a group of the most talented Broadway actors, put them in a permanent company and give them all the greatest variety of parts to play. Their work will hardly show any real development; they simply add one performance to another and play one part in much the same way as they did the preceding one. They remain "type actors" even though they may not be cast according to the type system. Why? First, because there is no existing theatre which is either truly interested in or understands the problem of the actor's development in any validly creative way; and second, because most actors, spoiled by lack of standards, slogans of easy success and the deep indifference of American show-business, have none of the true artist's will-to-perfection, none of that driving honesty which might make him question himself and his work even when he is being drugged with ignorant praise. No theatre today, I repeat, commands the means to undertake the development of actors (I refer to experienced actors as much as to beginners) and no theatre has collected a company which has the necessary personal qualities to accept and follow the kind of work which such a program entails. But we—Cheryl Crawford, Lee Strasberg and I—have not only selected our actors with an eye to this all-important problem, but we are now prepared to come forward without any vain modesty and say that we feel equipped to face it.

I have chosen to speak of the actors because they represent the theatre's most essential element. But the problem I have brought up really affects everybody in the theatre. Just as a Theatre must not only engage actors but develop them (the Theatre's very life being dependent on this development) so it must adopt analogous methods with the playwright. It should not confine itself to doctoring his plays, but criticize them, not simply criticize them but come to grips with him on fundamentals—in other words, actually collaborate with him. It must change the playwright's present status as an isolated purveyor of literary goods who is interesting only when he has sold a particular play to the theatre but make him as much as possible an integral part of the theatre. This point is worth particular emphasis because it predicates the kind of people that this theatre demands in order to preserve its true nature. The kind of humility that actors, playwrights, directors must be endowed with to give themselves to the group discipline which our method implies is a moral quality that might perhaps serve as a touchstone to the whole character of our effort, and what we sometimes call, for want of a better word, our Idea.

Actors who have attended our meetings this winter have been mystified and even troubled (as others will be) by our constant reference to this Idea. Everything depends on this, and yet we have not set down any dogmas or commandments to represent it. Our reply to the plea for a black and white statement is this: "You know Cheryl Crawford, Lee Strasberg and me. You have heard what we think about the theatre; you have listened to our interpretation of plays, you know how we are attacking this project for a new theatre. In other words, you see us in action. If you are in sympathy with what we say and do, if your response is one of spontaneous affirmation then you probably share our Idea. You have the first qualification for work in our theatre."

If such a reply seems evasive it is not because we are vague as to what we want but because words are so inadequate for the definition of essences and because a lack of a common vocabulary creates so many harmful barriers in the minds of those that hear them. But for those who desire some assurance that no magic key to universal understanding is being withheld from them and for those who fear lest some new hocus-pocus be concealed in our schemes, I believe I can at least put down a few basic propositions.

We are not interested in simply doing "amusing" things in the theatre, not in contriving technical innovations or tricks of stage-craft, nor in foisting upon the public a new "style" or *ism*. Whatever novelty our work may show will inevitably derive from our message. We are passionately devoted to the theatre because only through it can we most successfully say the things we have to say.

Skepticism, not as a means but as an end, was the fashion with many of our seniors; we are no skeptics. We believe that there are supremely desirable ends in life, but that they do not happen to be the ends of power and comfort that the practical tradition of the day dictates. We believe that the deepest need of man today, as always, is self-realization, but that the current and all-prevailing shibboleths of Success stand in the way of any such realization and even blind us as to its meaning. We believe that men must fashion a life in their own image—not merely dream it or wish for it. We believe that men cannot live without giving themselves completely to some force outside themselves and that this must have the concrete object and form which can absorb the activities of men in their daily lives.

The generations before us seemed to have been strenuously individualistic without believing very steadily in any particular good for their individuals. We, on the contrary, feel that the individualism of self-assertion which made of the ego the sole and final reality of life is self-destructive and we believe that the individual can realize himself only by seeking his spiritual kindred and by making of their common aspirations and problems the object of his active devotion. We believe that the individual can achieve his fullest stature only through identification of his own good with the good of his group, a group which he himself must help to create. The old individualists possessed nothing but their own egos and were forced in the end to knuckle under to the very forces of standardization from which they tried to preserve themselves and became in the last count both the instruments and the victims of these forces. Willy-nilly these self-asserters savagely bent on self-expression became part of the machine that was destroying them. Hence their despair. A kind of cocky pessimism was the result, a despair with a flourish—a flourish of smartness, cynicism, negativism. This mood of despair is abhorrent to us— abhorrent and ridiculous. But we are not the Pollyannas of a new day, nor its Messiahs. We are perhaps certain of nothing except our own strength and our will-to-find. We believe that life is essentially tragic but the movement of our muscles is sufficient warrant for our belief that it is also "worth-while." We do not know, we believe. We have not found, we are seeking. But we are seeking not in the texts of ancient creeds or in those of the up-to-the-minute intellectual academies but in the maze of our own lives, in the lives of those closest to us, in the ordinary routine of our work and our pleasures. We know that the task we have appointed ourselves is not simple and we expect our period of discovery to take a long time, so that our efforts will be the record of a continuous growth. What we find our work will show. We are sure at least that we are not alone in anxious interest over the results of our quest—there is an audience waiting.

This, of course, is not what we tell our actors nor do we propose to address our potential public in these terms, since this is, as I have said, merely a verbalization in somewhat abstract form of the mood we hope our work will engender and promote. We know as well as the hardened showman that it is not very important to talk of the emotional and psychological effects which our work should generate. For art cannot lie—it always reveals the spirit that gave it birth. But we also know what apparently the showman does not realize or care about: that for the theatre to exercise any positive, dynamic influence—for it to really mean anything—its work must issue from an integrated body with a single purpose and direction. This, to a great extent we already have, this we shall continue to foster.

But, what more need be said at present than that a group of people, after having served their apprenticeship and proved their competence in the existing theatre are now ready—even impatient— to begin work in what they feel is a truly productive, valuable and new effort. These people you know. If you have faith in their intelligence, character, talent (and their presence and position amongst you is a sign of such faith) it is now within your means to help them in the important experiment which they most eagerly desire to undertake. The Theatre Guild made history by being first to prove that intelligence has an audience in this country; it is now in the position to continue and enrich its tradition by providing new opportunity for further growth.

It should be noted, moreover, that in this aiding the foundation of a new (and, we have every reason to believe, important) group, the Guild would hardly incur upon itself a much larger expense than it does with some of its larger productions. Also, it should be added—nor can it be too often repeated—the more complete the Guild's faith, the greater the chances for the success of the new venture; the more freedom the younger group is given the more distinctive and significant will its contribution be. Without a bona fide "bill of independence" our group can hardly achieve its true stature or reflect much honor on the Guild.

POST-SCRIPTUM

To illustrate the above remarks with specific examples would probably entail the writing of a whole volume. I have been trying to give such illustration in weekly talks which have been going on since last April, and I have not yet exhausted my material. Nevertheless, there are a few points so crucial to the understanding of our Idea that to omit all mention of them would be to lead ourselves into a dangerous impasse. They concern actors, plays and directors.

We have said enough about actors—Cheryl and I—to make clear that we are looking for something more than just effective talent. That is not to say, however, that we are putting all our emphasis on either any generalized idealism or enthusiastic youth. There may be more than a few older, seasoned actors who could be acceptable to us—though, of course too great a disparity in age would militate against perfect group homogeneity. The chief thing to be kept in mind in the choice of actors is that unless the actor is a certain kind of person even his acting talent, howsoever genuine, would not prove of any great theatrical value to us. The actor who is primarily moved by exhibitionistic tendencies always reveals his exhibitionism in performance; the actor who is primarily a neurotic, seeking in the theatre a solution for his maladjustment nearly always makes an audience quite aware of his maladjustment. And though qualities of exhibitionism and neuroticism may be valuable for actors in some theatres, they would be altogether out of place in ours.

The actor must not only possess certain qualities as a person so that he may be capable of exemplifying the group's content, but he must be a person, whatever his age or experience, still capable of development. We may be glad to take in actors "with names"—if they are our sort of actors—but we are not at all interested in actors who have reached the final point of their development—"finished actors." Two further technical

factors must be kept in mind; first, that since our actors are not to be engaged as a "stock company" but as a group they will be required—no matter how imposing their Broadway position—to play small parts as well as big; second, they will probably have to play in a style that may be different from anything for which their former training and experience has prepared them. If the actor in short, is not endowed by nature with a certain spiritual adaptability or capacity for growth, he is not for us—regardless of his other qualifications.

"Experimentation" is not the goal of art, and I hope we have said enough to make it plain that ours is not to be an "experimental theatre." We simply wish to say the things we feel urged to say, and to say those things as clearly, cogently and aptly as possible. Our policy in plays therefore is not guided by any program of novelty but by appositeness of content. "What scripts," we shall ask ourselves, "will best permit this group to manifest itself in the theatre?" But it is possible that many playwrights whose spirit is akin to ours may not yet have achieved a thoroughly adequate technique for their message. Such playwrights, however, are of more value to us than the slick craftsmen the content of whose work is alien. If a playwright is moving in our direction and has produced what may at least be considered a workable script, we shall take him on in the faith that we can aid him to a more perfect expression of his content.

In short, our policy in plays is related to our policy in actors: we want them both to be of a kind, and if that kind may be found amongst the so-called established actors or playwrights—well and good, but it must be remembered that a younger and less expert actor or playwright will always be more important to us than the deftest of actors and playwrights of another kind. For what we are seeking is the most complete articulation of our Idea that the theatre can give it. To accomplish this end, conscious development of our material must be our watchword and ambition.

If what we have said about our spirit does not mean anything to you in terms of plays and playwrights, perhaps a few examples will help clarify our statement. In feeling, we prefer the robust tragedy of a Gorky in *Lower Depths* to the slightly ornamental (romantic) ache of an Andreyev; we prefer the frank Rabelaisianism of such people as E. P. Conkle to the mincing cosmopolitan naughtiness of Noel Coward, we prefer the O'Neill of the last of *The Straw* to the O'Neill of *Diff'rent*. In form, we prefer *The Hairy Ape* to *Beyond the Horizon* (though the latter may be considered a more finished piece of work) and *Dynamo* (though it is certainly a bad play) point more in the direction that we wish to take than plays like *Welded*.

To put it more generally, we seek plays that have a life-affirming rather than a life-negating, a yea-saying rather than a nay-saying, spirit, while in method, we prefer plays that stress the immediately universal, social aspect of events rather than their particular and personal aspect. Our ideal would be a play that presented the most urgent modern problems in a form that for purity, directness, intensity, simple imaginativeness and high moral purpose was akin to Greek drama while remaining thoroughly contemporary in its terms, a kind of modern legend play—tragedy, comedy, farce or burlesque. We want to do plays which—whether they be contemporary or classics—have something to do with *us*—something recognizably related to our own actual needs.

But the value of our proposed theatre is not to be judged merely on the basis of the independent, literary merit of the scripts it chooses. We look upon the script as an organic part of the theatre product, but it is only a part—it does not by itself constitute the Play. In other words, such things as *The Front Page* or *Once in a Lifetime* in our hands would acquire a very different significance from that of their Broadway productions—would in fact be different plays. What would constitute the difference is more than a matter of "production-ideas"; it is a matter of the Idea behind all our "production-ideas."

Various foreign directors have been recommended to us because of their talent, their avant-garde sympathies, their novel methods. When such recommendations are made we realize that our conception of the theatre has not been truly understood. The excellence of a director, insofar as it affects the aesthetic worth of the production actually seen, depends on his relation to the group with whom he works. Just as certain Moscow Art actors prove themselves fairly mediocre apart from the context of their theatre, so a Danchenko or a Stanislavsky directing Broadway actors could not create the equivalent of their Russian productions. A Meyerhold production of a negro play like *Potters Field* done for an American audience would probably be much less important than *Blackbirds*. The theatre is a group art, and we cannot speak of a group homogeneity unless the director who is the group leader is part of the group, that is, unless he naturally shares and embodies the group's will and aspiration, unless he speaks its language. If the director, howsoever distinguished his talent, is in any sense an "outsider," he and the group inevitably become obstacles to one another and really sound work is made impossible.

If Cheryl Crawford, Lee Strasberg and I feel that we are at present the only possible directors for our group, it is not from any mere egotistic assertion of our personal ambitions but because we know that only through our technique of direction will the group be able to say what it has to say. Other directors might be able to turn out "good shows" with it—but only through us who have formed it, can it become a Theatre.

This is not to say that we shall forever and forever insist on doing all the directing ourselves but that new directors must either arise from within the group itself or must work with us till they have trained themselves in the group's methods and have indeed become group directors....

—Drawn up for presentation to the Board
of the Theatre Guild, Apr. '31

WHAT THE GROUP THEATRE WANTS

A theatre to us is a Theatre only when all its members are integrated by a common ideal of what they wish to say and a common understanding and employment of the methods by which these things may best be said. This common ideal however can only be effective for the group if all its members form a potentially homogeneous body sharing, to begin with, a certain common feeling not only about the theatre but about life, a certain spiritual kinship and mutual recognition of problems that are real to all of them.

Let us see if we can translate this abstract credo into the detailed points of a general theatrical policy.

(1) A good play for us is not one which measures up to some literary standard of "art" or "beauty" but one which is the image or symbol of the living problems of our time. These problems today are chiefly moral and social, and our feeling is that they must be faced with an essentially affirmative attitude that is, in the belief that to all of them there may be some answer, an answer that should be considered operative for at least the humanity of our time and place. Such plays may be tragedy, comedy, fantasy or farce; they may be identified with any aesthetic category; but they must be directly relevant to the audience for which they are presented.

(2) To give complete theatrical expression to such plays the actors of a company must be the kind of people who spontaneously share our author's spirit, and they must be technically equipped to use their personal endowments of experience and character for the creation of various parts in the play. For this reason the company must be permanent; and definite steps must be taken toward the continuous, conscious development of its individual actors. As a group, the actors must grow ever more intelligently aware of the signifi-

cance of their theatres' purpose; as individuals, the actors must bend their efforts to an ever more concrete mastery of their craft.

(3) All workers in the theatre must be as completely an integral part of it as possible and must be trained for their work in essentially the same way. A play should have no extras and no stars. Actors are chosen to play certain parts according to the needs of the play, not according to their "position."

(4) The theatre must create and develop playwrights, actors, scene-designers. The repertory system does not by itself effect this but it permits a theatre greater freedom to do so. It is our aim to establish a repertory system. In the end, however, the development of playwrights, actors, repertory and the rest are important only as they lead to the creation of a tradition of common values, an active consciousness of a common way of looking at and dealing with life. A theatre in our country today should aim to create an audience. Where an audience feels that it is really at one with the theatre; where audience and theatre-people can feel that they are both the answer to one another and that both may act as leaders to one another, there we have the theatre in its truest form. To create such a theatre is our real purpose.

—Program Notes, Mansfield Theatre, Dec. '31

TRIBUTE TO MAX REINHARDT

It may appear strange to our European friends if before paying tribute to Max Reinhardt I pause to identify him. Max Reinhardt—the real Reinhardt so familiar and beloved in his homeland before the advent of the Hitlerite terror—was almost an unknown figure to American theatregoers of the past fifteen or twenty years. The reason for this, I hasten to explain, is to be found in the nature or our theatrical commentary.

Nearly all writing on the theatre in this country is publicity: it retails countless bits of bright information that end by obscuring rather than furthering our understanding of its subject. Thus Reinhardt was a "great name" in the New York Sunday papers when his production of *The Miracle* opened at the Century Theatre in the early twenties, or when his own company came over to play some seven productions in 1927, and still later when he arrived in Hollywood to direct for Warners; he was a "great name," I say, but an unknown artist. For with us a "great name" is, as you know, someone to gape at, envy, slander and forget.

The proof of this is that the reputation that had finally been fabricated for Reinhardt in show-business was that of an aesthetic Barnum, a purveyor of big packages of educated entertainment. *The Miracle, The Eternal Road,* even *Midsummer Night's Dream* had come to represent for us "colossal" shows that could be produced only through the benevolence of gentlemen willing to drain their surplus funds in imperial theatrical enterprises. In recent years whenever a Reinhardt production was broached to a potential manager his hands would rise as if in fear of a cultural stick-up.

When *The Miracle* was first presented in New York, one of our more venturesome reviewers wrote an article in which he praised Reinhardt to the top of his bent. Reinhardt, he said, was the greatest stage director of our time. And the mark of Reinhardt's superiority, the gentleman affirmed, was his versatility, that is, Reinhardt had no special "style," he could do every type of play equally well. Such recommendation might more appropriately come from an agent than from a critic. The man who has no style, the man who can do everything equally well, may belong in some super jazz band: he does not belong in the realm of art.

Reinhardt's contribution to the modern theatre was that he brought back to it the fullness of its means. As a reaction both to the merely literary theatre in which reading or elocution are the main vehicles of communication, and to the naturalistic theatre in which psychology and truth-to-life were

emphasized with an almost burdensome sobriety, Reinhardt brought playfulness, movement, color, music, once more to the theatre. In Reinhardt's productions, as distinguished from those of his immediate predecessors in Western Europe (around 1903), the play did not live simply in terms of the Thought and the Word, the play became the sum of all the theatre's possibilities in terms of mimetics, improvisation, make-up, costume and a fluent dance-like interrelation of parts.

The play in Reinhardt's hands became a noble game in which sound and sight, a vivid atmosphere, a fond sense of the audience, a relish in all the graces of the theatre's body were used to express the poet's dream. By his example, Reinhardt saved the theatre of his day, which had taken up the gospel of Ibsen, Hauptmann and the realists generally, from the danger it ran of becoming severe, solemn, and stuffy.

Reinhardt's was thus a festive theatre. The words game, play, frolic, and pageant, all come to mind in defining Reinhardt's art. His work was basically joyous. His was a gay science. It was rich, sensuous, enamored of the good things, the creature comforts of life. Reinhardt's art was calculated to give pleasure, to provide fun. But when we say "fun" we usually mean to indicate something fragile, cute, springy—with little virility or scope. In Reinhardt's art the whole gamut of man's experience became the subject for a spectacle of utmost delectability, both suave and attractively vital. In Reinhardt's theatre life's comedy and tragedy were served as at a sumptuous banquet at which all of us might sit down and enjoy the fare with easy dignity, light decorum and good appetite. Reinhardt's world was the world in which the joys of the mind were not meant to dilute but rather to heighten the savor of wine, woman, and song!

Reinhardt looked to the plays of the past for subtler colors, bolder plots, broader canvasses, more elaborate rhetoric and action than contemporary taste allows; his treatment of modern repertory was shrewd, ironic, tolerantly wise. But in all things he was ever the Epicurean of the theatre, a hedonist with conscience, and enlightened prince pouring a prodigious bounty of the world's treasure over all the stages of Europe.

What relation, you may ask, have these qualities to the "big shows" and religious themes with which Reinhardt's name in America is still associated? It is very simple. Huge proportions are dramatic and conducive to that will to believe which is at the root of theatrical glamor; religion offers elements of mystery, complexity, wonder and the awe of ancient legend. All these provide fertile sources for theatrical inspiration. But it is to be noted, no extravaganza was ever more lavish in color than Reinhardt's *Miracle*, no ballet more insidiously alluring than his *Everyman*. Behind every Reinhardt production, no matter how serious its subject, lurked the canny magician of the theatre's vast instrumentation, the spirit of play with its myriad inventions.

The Reinhardt I prefer, however, was the intimate, puckish weaver of spells, the Reinhardt who hypnotized us into jolly dalliance. The examples of this talent in his extensive repertoire far exceed his "big" productions. One of the most delightful samples of this aspect of his art—its essential aspect I believe—was his production of the eighteenth century Italian farce, *The Servant of Two Masters*. It was a play about nothing—or if you must have a story—a play about the plight of a servant too enmeshed in his master's intrigues to sit down to a square meal. Out of this trifle, this something less than a notion, Reinhardt wrought an enticing tapestry of mad entertainment in which the climax revealed the famished hero making indecent passes at the curves of a plum pudding, and abandoning himself in sinful ecstasy to a cascading downpour of spaghetti.

You may have heard tell of Reinhardt's ingenuity, and of the dazzling effects in scenery, lighting, costume and architecture that marked many of his productions. By themselves they were of little moment. The core of Reinhardt's productions was always the actor. Through Reinhardt's multiple imaginative resources the actor flourished in Reinhardt's theatre. Almost every eminent German actor of the past generation—Rudolf Schildkraut, Albert Basserman, Max Pallenberg, Alexander Moissi—to mention only a few, owed much of his development to the stimulus of Reinhardt's genius. To be directed by Reinhardt was to come in contact with the very well springs of histrionic creativeness.

From all I have said it will be readily understood that Reinhardt was the product of a stable society. The warmth and laughter that characterize Reinhardt's art, the ease, glow and comfort of it, its moderation within the framework of luxury, its universal indulgence and benign air could only spring from an atmosphere of security and well-being. For this reason Americans of my generation—those who came to maturity during the thirties—often regarded Reinhardt as a fine relic of a remote past. Ours was a more strenuous time; our needs more attune to moral, social, even political factors. We were a noisier, hungrier, angrier, more ascetic generation. Beside his largesse and charm, his facility and trained knowledge, we may as well confess ourselves primitive and uncouth. But in the light of the barbarism that drove Reinhardt from his natural environment and seeks now to engulf the world, we Americans today may well learn to appreciate and to pay tribute to the sound spirit and healthy humanity of our cultural past. For they are the norms of the good life for all time.

Those who in one way or another participate in the fight to perpetuate these norms should be the first to keep artists like Reinhardt sacred in their memory. From their example comes nurture and instruction for the future.

—Speech delivered at Reinhardt Memorial
Meeting, Hollywood, 28 Nov. '43

LETTER TO CLIFFORD ODETS

Dear Cliff,

Now that I have expressed structural and practical aspects of my thought on the playwright play let me give you a critical and spiritual inkling of my relation to it.

It seems to me that just as *Lefty* and *Awake and Sing!* and *Paradise Lost* got the essence of the lower middle class of the thirties so *The Tides of Fundy* seems to contain in it the essence of the forties. What is that essence? It is a fear of the consequences of creativity. To create is to exceed oneself and thus to court danger. It is much safer to accommodate oneself to the goods that exist. But since life always moves on one cannot simply stand still, one is obliged to keep on fighting. Only this fight under the new conditions becomes a fight against creation. So the more creative a person is the greater degree of his destructiveness when he has begun to fear the going forward into the unknown of the future which is demanded by the creative act. In effect your play is saying: he who does not create must destroy.

The reason why this is important—apart from any G.D. playwright—is that my aphorism now applies to practically everything and everyone on every level including the political. The role that our beloved U.S.A. is now playing is to stop any movement toward the unknown future. The result is that we are clamoring about a free economy and a free enterprise which doesn't even describe the nature of our status quo. Because of this unreality we are not even able to enjoy this status quo in a good decadent fashion. We are becoming hysterical not as we were in the twenties but with a kind of sluggish fear that makes all our behavior reactionary without charm or grace. (I was reading Fitzgerald last night and I realized that the twenties with its ideal of pleasure and fun were really a lyrical period because when you adopt pleasure as a kind of ideal it has in it an element of protest and of fervor.

Nowadays people aren't even seeking pleasure, they are trying to hide themselves away in a protective hot-house, cautiously nursing their comfort and sneakishly accumulating security. Obviously there is no glamor in that, obviously it isn't even fun. Obviously the only positive action that can come from such an attitude must be criminal and destructive. It would seem that in such an atmosphere the only solution is dissolution. I found France the most hopeful of European decadent countries because they realize there that a smash-up might at least serve to break the impasse—so that those with guts and luck enough to survive would live in a more honest world.)

All this is terribly abstract when it is abstractly stated, but your play states this theme with great concreteness and on a basic human level. The sex angle in your play contains a terrible truth—which is that in the atmosphere I have described love cannot exist except in terms of conquest—which means in destructive terms. You once told me that you felt surprised that I had a whole philosophical nightmare in Paris about this statement. What I realized was that to will takes courage: the courage to believe that the object of one's will is worth the trouble of willing. Now the desire one has for a woman is only important in so far as one believes the woman and what she represents is worth struggling to get and to preserve. This means ultimately that one has to accept the world which follows as a consequence of winning a woman.

But since no one really believes in the world as an object worth fighting for except as a cushioned, airless, sluggish entity, the woman is always taken nowadays with no real desire or will. In other words the woman is a commodity to be added to the other comforts of our safety or, what amounts to the same thing, an escape and a diversion from the pain and boredom which living in such an atmosphere entails. An emotional syllogism follows: we have lost our will because to will the status quo is to will nothing at all and in a sense to desire nothing—an unnatural state which must end in madness for stupid people and in cruelty for energetic people.

Now all this would not be worth saying in a play if its author was wholly the kind of man who exemplified the state I am describing. But you are, as so few of our writers are today, a lyric, passionate and a moral person and if you combine these qualities with the correct dramatic analysis of your play's concrete situations you can create a very powerful and moving statement of truly revolutionary force. It can be a play without preachment and without any of the labels that I have attempted to define in this letter. It could reach the conscience of the people even in our Broadway theatre. Because dear Cliff, despite the bitterness that I feel about the state of the world today I believe in the creative possibilities of the American human being. I see on every side of me the eagerness, the hunger, the will to life which make for a real world. I see it mostly in young people. They go on believing, dreaming, hoping and struggling with true faith, even in the midst of the present corruption. Most of it is knocked on the head by what they meet in the theatres, in literature, in politics and in human relationships. Whenever I reach such people in classrooms, lectures and personal conversations, their eyes light up, they are full of love and gratitude and they re-awaken in me the desire to help them.

They are the people who still remember you Odets and still believe in you. You have included these people in your play in the lyric form of the girl and the savage and comic form of the young boy. And though in your play you intend to show how the older generation destroys them, the play itself written by you out of the turmoil of your heart will act as a protest and a denunciation against those forces which are trying to create darkness for the new youth. This play written apparently from a negative impulse will foster a positive and creative energy. The inchoate rage that you speak of will form itself in this play into a generative power. That rage will be the gasoline which will make the motor run, and your mind will guide it to its proper objective, its healthy destination.

I have always believed that the artist must be sincere and that when he is, even his cruelest, most destructive impulses will emerge as health. In other words, you do not have to write a pleasant play, a hip-hip-hooray poster in order to write a play as significant, as true, as vitally salutary as *Awake and Sing!* or *Lefty*. You have only to harness your own emotion and understand your own confusion. No matter how violently negative you may think you feel you have only to analyze this feeling to resume your path as one of the healthfully revolutionary forces in the American arts. Your "blackness" is not merely subjective it is the reflection in the mirror of your nature of the image of our times. But as an artist and as a thinking person you can do what the mirror cannot. You can show how this "blackness" is part of the light that dwells within you and dwells within all of us. By your saying this man David Storm is a monster because he is a frustrated angel we shall understand what it is to be an angel—what it is to be possessed of creative light. Put these things back on the stage and we shall once more see something that has all but disappeared in all phases of our life during the past five years.

Love,
Harold

—1 Aug. '47

THE OPENING OF THE HAROLD CLURMAN THEATRE
With Aaron Copland and two actresses from the company

INDEX